Reformations

Reformations

The Early Modern World, 1450–1650

Carlos M. N. Eire

Yale UNIVERSITY PRESS   NEW HAVEN AND LONDON

Published with assistance from the Kingsley Trust Association Publication Fund established by the Scroll and Key Society of Yale College, from the Ronald and Betty Miller Turner Publication Fund, from the Frederick W. Hilles Publication Fund of Yale University, and from the foundation established in memory of Oliver Baty Cunningham of the Class of 1917, Yale College.

Yale University Press books may be purchased in quantity for educational, business, or promotional use. For information, please e-mail sales.press@yale.edu (U.S. office) or sales@yaleup.co.uk (U.K. office).

Set in Adobe Garamond by Newgen.
Printed in the United States of America.

Library of Congress Control Number: 2016933635
ISBN: 978-0-300-11192-7 (hardcover : alk. paper)

A catalogue record for this book is available from the British Library.

This paper meets the requirements of ANSI/NISO Z39.48-1992 (Permanence of Paper).

10 9 8 7 6 5 4 3 2

Contents

Preface

Sometimes, the course of history can change instantly, in the blink of an eye, and everyone notices. Sometimes, however, change is imperceptible. Either way, it is always left up to historians to argue about how, when, and why things changed, how much change took place, how long its effects lasted, what to call that span of time, and what significance should be attached to it. Despite much wrangling, most historians have agreed for five centuries about when and where one such epochal shift took place. The time was late October 1517. The place was the University of Wittenberg in Saxony, a new and undistinguished school. The man involved was an obscure monk named Martin Luther. The event was a simple act of defiance: Luther's public questioning of widely accepted teachings concerning the forgiveness of sins. The era supposedly initiated then and there was called the Reformation.

Should so much change be ascribed to one person and one event?

Like many such turning points in history, the controversy sparked by this monk was long in coming. In fact, the way had been prepared for Martin Luther over several generations, by countless individuals and impersonal forces, and he was as much a product of change as an agent of it. What he did—so to speak—was spark a colossal explosion with a powder keg not of his own making. The volatile elements were there already, everywhere, in plain view. Only an obtuse observer could have failed to notice their presence, for discontent and cries for reform were endemic. What no one could tell at the time, not even Luther, was how much of a punch those explosive elements really packed.

Luther's outburst in late October 1517 was couched in scholarly terms and ostensibly addressed to a learned audience. It should have caused only a few ripples, but instead it set off a chain reaction, much to everyone's surprise, and the end result was a conflagration of epic proportions. History does not always follow a predictable path, especially when religion is involved. Nor are deviations in history's path easy to sum up. To say that Luther changed his world single-handedly or that 1517 was the absolute beginning of a new epoch would be wrong, but to say that nothing was ever the same after Luther's act of defiance is to settle for understatement. What he set in motion in 1517 not only changed the world as it was then; it still continues to shape our world today and to define who we are in the West.

What drove and defined this great transformation was religion. No doubt about it. But to assert this is also to acknowledge that religion played a different role in Western civilization back then than it does now. Religion was so deeply intertwined with all social, political, economic, and cultural structures as to be inseparable from nearly every aspect of daily life. Religious defiance, then, was much more than what we might call "religious" in our own day: it was, in fact, the most potent sort of defiance, for to redefine religion was to redefine the world.

This book deals with an epochal change, and with the role played in that change by religion. It is above all a narrative, a retelling of a story that has been told many times before, but that takes into account the latest findings of those who study this segment of the past, with an eye firmly fixed on present-day concerns. It also analyzes what occurred, and its significance for us five centuries later. One of its chief assumptions is that no Westerner can ever hope to know him- or herself, or the world he or she lives in, without first understanding this crucial turning point in history. And the same goes for any non-Westerner who wants to understand Western civilization. Naturally, this book also assumes that the ancient Greek aphorism "know thyself" is still valid, and a key to survival and continual progress in our increasingly amnesiac global village. Given that those who are ignorant of the past can be more easily fooled and controlled in the present by power-hungry ideologues, or by their own worst impulses, this book has been written with a sense of urgency.

This book also assumes that to understand this crucial period in Western history, one must take religion seriously as a real factor in human events, as something that gave shape to that age and to our own in ways that we now find difficult to imagine or comprehend. This is not to say that religion was some monolithic, isolated sphere of human activity back then, or that it could ever be the sole concern for any individual or society. Much less is it to say that religion is the most significant sphere of human activity, or that theology and beliefs are the sole lens through which to view this epochal shift. What is assumed in this book is something that nearly all experts on this period agree on: that religion permeated all of life, even though not everyone was equally religious or pious.

Religion was a language of sorts at the turn of the sixteenth century, a way of conceiving and of expressing, and a way of interacting with one's neighbors, near and far. It was also the very marrow of all social, economic, political, and cultural exchanges. Even the minutest details of daily life could be inseparable from religion, shaped by it to some extent, in various ways. Some sociologists and anthropologists speak of religion as a "social glue," a cultural reality that binds society together. Religion was more than a social glue back then: because it linked everyone in every village and kingdom, it also allowed them to transcend seemingly insurmountable social, political, cultural, linguistic, and ethnic boundaries. From Portugal in the southwest to Lithuania in the northeast, and from Sicily in the far south to Scandinavia in the extreme north, a common set of myths, rituals, symbols, and ethical norms linked all Westerners, and so did one ancient and complex institution that mediated this religion: the Catholic Church, led by the pope in Rome. To break with this church was to turn it from an adhesive into an explosive, to change it into social dynamite.

The name for this transitional moment in history has changed over the years. In the English-speaking world, as in several other European cultures, this era came to be known as the Reformation. Implicit in this designation is the judgment that something corrupt had been reformed or improved. More than that, the singular capitalized name given to this historical period implied that this event was the ultimate, definitive step in the right direction: it was not a reformation, but *the* Reformation. Such a perspective on the past stemmed from certain religious convictions and from the fact that English culture itself was shaped by a break with the Catholic Church. In other words, English culture was Protestant, the name by which all who broke with the Roman Catholic Church came to be known. In England and all of its colonies, as in all other Protestant cultures, the only true Reformation—with a capital *R*—was that brought about by Protestants. All narratives shaped by this Protestant consciousness shared an unquestioned assumption and a common plot line: some time after the fourth century, the true Christian Church founded by Christ and his apostles fell into gross corruption for a thousand years, a defilement so deep and thorough that the only way to restore the genuine Christian faith on this earth was to reject the church led by the pope in Rome and to replace it with one that had nothing to do with "Romishness" or "popery." This plot line made it necessary for the history of the Reformation to be approached in terms of a pathology, that is, as a diagnosis of what ailed the post-fourth-century church, and a description of the cure that saved it and brought it back to health in the sixteenth century.

Oddly, even though Protestants were not always of one mind and actually created a number of distinct competing Reformations and churches, each of which claimed to be the genuine article, they nonetheless took to speaking of the Reformation in the singular rather than the plural, and to assigning it capital letters. The term stuck, despite its obvious inadequacy, because Protestants were willing and eager to accept the notion that their break with Rome defined all of Christian history. As Protestant historians saw it, that break put all of their competing, bickering churches on the same side of a titanic struggle and on the right side of history, over and against the corrupt and "false" Catholic Church. As a result, this simple duality that distinguished only two camps—Protestant and Catholic—made the singular capitalized noun *Reformation* seem perfectly appropriate.

Catholics never agreed with any of this. Even back then, in the sixteenth century, they mocked the presumption behind the term *Reformed*. In France, for instance, Catholics referred to their Protestant countrymen as "heretics" and to their faith as "the so-called reformed religion" (*la religion prétendue réformée*). Moreover, as the number of competing Protestant churches increased, Catholics grew ever fonder of pointing out that this splintering in the camp of the "heretics" proved the falsehood of all Protestant claims, and that it was illogical to speak of *the Reformation* as long as so much disagreement continued to divide them. To Catholics, genuine reform meant only one thing: improving the Catholic Church while remaining faithful to it. As Catholics saw it, Protestants were not Reformers with a capital *R*, but rebels, and their so-called Reformation nothing more than a misguided revolt.

Up until the late nineteenth century, then, the term *Reformation* remained strictly Protestant. Catholics used the words *reform* and *reformation* more broadly, without a capital *R*, when referring to the many reforming movements throughout the history of their church, including those of the sixteenth and seventeenth centuries, which tended to be called Tridentine reforms, in reference to the Council of Trent (1545–1563) and all of the many changes and improvements it had set in motion. In contrast, on the Protestant side, whatever Catholics reshuffled within their religion as a response to Protestantism tended not to be considered a reform per se, but rather a reactionary turn. This perspective led Leopold von Ranke, one of the most influential nineteenth-century German historians, to refer to the inner renewal of Catholicism in the sixteenth and seventeenth centuries as a Counter-Reformation (*Gegenreformation*). That term stuck, too. So, for nearly a century, up until the 1970s, historians tended to think of two distinct and opposing Reformations, with the Protestant one being the Reformation and the Catholic one being the Counter-Reformation.

In the meantime, as social history began to eclipse intellectual, cultural, and religious history, the very concept of a Reformation began to be questioned. And so did that of a Renaissance, or rebirth of classical culture. These period concepts, which for generations had served as the twin pillars of the portal between the medieval and modern epochs, became hazier to scholars, less and less revered after the 1970s. A new name for the period formerly identified as the Renaissance and the Reformation quickly gained acceptance: *early modern*, a period concept as vague as it is free of associations with religion or with any particular approach to history.

The growing acceptance of *early modern* notwithstanding, those who continued to focus on the religious dimension of the age hung on to the more traditional nomenclature, with a new twist. Over the past few decades, a growing number of historians have abandoned stark dichotomies between Protestant and Catholic, proposing instead that it is far more accurate to think of the changes that took place in the sixteenth and seventeenth centuries as Reformations, in the plural, rather than as the Reformation or the Counter-Reformation. This perspective emerged principally from historians who ceased focusing on theology and the institutional history of churches and turned their attention instead to social, cultural, economic, and political issues. It also emerged from historians who began to transcend confessional concerns, that is, from historians who no longer sought to prove that a particular church or tradition was in sole possession of the Truth, with a capital *T*. This shift in focus brought into much sharper relief patterns that had been overlooked before, and which made evident the fact that all of the churches that emerged from the fragmentation begun in 1517 had similar pragmatic goals in mind—despite all the obvious differences in theology and ritual.

This book accepts the concept of multiple Reformations wholeheartedly, and also seeks to deepen that concept, paying equal attention to all of the different movements and churches that emerged in the sixteenth and seventeenth centuries, stressing their interrelatedness. One of its central assumptions is that no individual reform movement in this era can be fully understood in isolation from all the others. Namely, it is taken for granted here that from 1517 on, and especially during the next century and a half, all changes in religion were shaped as much in reaction or opposition to the others as they were by any internal logic. Protestant self-definition relied on identifying what was wrong or false in Catholicism. And vice versa, Catholic self-definition strained to be the polar opposite of all things Protestant. Moreover, within Protestantism this same process played itself out in two directions, for it was just as important for each of the various Protestant churches to distinguish what was wrong or false within all the other opponents of the pope, as it was to prove that the Catholic Church was totally wrong. This constant process of defining what was true and right in opposition to what was false and wrong became inescapable, even for reforming groups that sought to live in isolation from the rest of the world. Exclusion is as important in religion as inclusion, and this is especially true of the Christian religion, which has always cared immensely about determining and clearly defining what makes the true different from the false, the genuinely faithful different from all that is deviant, the communion of saints different from all others.

Viewing all of the disparate movements as interlocking Reformations and viewing religion as the key feature of an entire age are two central defining characteristics of this book. While there is no denying that other perspectives could be taken and that this time period could be analyzed differently—with less of a focus on religion, or no focus on it at all—there is also no denying that such perspectives would be somewhat lacking in their capacity to survey the entire landscape of this period. In fact, it could be argued that the significance of religion to this age is still evident in a very concrete, physical way all over Europe: in its churches. In the same way that no serious tour guide could ignore the churches that dot the map of Europe, nor should any survey history of the early modern period or the Reformations neglect religion. Of course, it is also true that focusing on the churches alone or just on religion would be a grave error. The fortresses, guildhalls, customhouses, dungeons, palaces, and theaters should never be neglected either. Balance is the key.

This book makes no reductionist claims. While it does view religion—broadly understood—as the efficient cause of a unique transformation of the West during the sixteenth and seventeenth centuries, it never assumes that religion is some isolated dimension of human experience. Religion is here understood as a means of interpreting the world and of interacting with it. And the focus here is always on interaction, on the constant two-way exchange through which religion is shaped by its environment and that environment is shaped by religion. There is no chicken-and-egg question here, no asking which came first, religion or environment. In this period, more so than in our own, this constant exchange had no beginning or end. Their symbiosis was a given, and inescapable. And much like the biosphere, it had an infinity of overlapping and interdependent components, each of which can never be fully understood in total isolation from the others.

Writing a survey history of an entire era is a perilous venture, even for a specialist in that era. Every discipline has its rules, and those rules themselves are bound to a specific time and a particular culture. History is no exception. We historians observe lots of rules, and we judge one another's work according to whichever rules we hold in the highest esteem. Disagreement is not only common, but actually is the very lifeblood of the historical enterprise. Questioning and challenging previous understandings of the past along with those that are new is what drives the discipline forward (a process very similar to the one that spawned the Reformations). But no matter what the disagreements are among historians, each age has its core list of characteristics, and this list is passed on from master to disciple, from generation to generation, even as some items are scratched off and others are added, sometimes gradually, sometimes suddenly. In purely practical terms, this list ends up serving as a research guide, an index of the most important subjects that deserve attention. At this particular point in time, the index of important subjects for the early modern era is in flux. The challenge, then, is to acknowledge shifts in focus and to balance the new and the old assumptions.

This book is not written for a learned audience, though savants of all sorts have been on my mind constantly, giving shape to the narrative through all of the potential objections and expert appraisals that I could imagine issuing from them. In many ways, much of this text is a dialogue with colleagues, especially those who are at opposite ends of the spectrum of opinion: on the one end, those on whom I have relied heavily and with whom I agree; and on the other end, those with whom I disagree. Many an imagined glare or disapproving book review has given shape to sentences, paragraphs, and pages. Many a hoped-for nod of agreement or approval has done the same, too. No matter how intense their presence throughout the book, however, these lurking savants are not those being directly addressed in this book.

This is a narrative for beginners and nonspecialists. It is an introduction and a survey. Condensing vast amounts of information, generalizing, summing up, dispensing at times with the fine details, this survey aims not so much to prove any approach definitive as to make the past come alive. It seeks to provide basic knowledge about the Reformations and to call attention to their significance. It also seeks to make the reader thirst for more, principally through narrative. Firmly convinced of the power of verbal imagery, the author has relied extensively on it, often counting on a single example or even on a single detail to convey the full complexity of history as no list of facts ever could. Footnotes have been kept to a bare minimum and restricted mostly to quotations from fifteenth-, sixteenth-, and seventeenth-century texts, not out of indolence or disregard for proper scholarly form, but rather out of concern for the novices who are the intended audience, who do not need to be overwhelmed with minutiae of the sort that bring some experts—myself included—close to ecstasy. References to scholarly debates have also been avoided as much as possible. For those who wish to delve more deeply into any subject—or for those who are curious about which books I have consulted, a chapter-by-chapter list of suggestions for further reading can be found in the back pages of this book.

This book covers two centuries, more or less: roughly from 1450 to 1650. Those dates are flexible estimates. Sometimes the narrative reaches back to before 1450; sometimes it goes beyond 1650. But there is nothing arbitrary about these chronological boundaries. These two hundred years do have an intrinsic unity to them. They contain very clear signs of a beginning and an end, though both are far from absolute. By poetic coincidence, the period covered here is the same stretch of time it took to build the new St. Peter's Basilica in Rome, the very project that set Martin Luther to fuming in 1517 and, as a consequence, changed the world. The different phases in the construction of this immense church between 1450 and 1667 neatly parallel the way this book is arranged.

At the starting point, sometime around 1450, Pope Nicholas V conceived the grandiose project of demolishing the fourth-century basilica of St. Peter in Rome and replacing it with a new one. At the same time, in Mainz, Germany, Johannes Gutenberg and some associates invented movable-type printing. This technological quantum leap is as precise a turning point as one can find in history. Before Gutenberg, information flowed very slowly, and all knowledge had to be painstakingly preserved and transmitted by scribes through handwritten documents. After Gutenberg, the Western world was transformed. Passing on knowledge and information becomes much easier, faster, and cheaper. Thanks to the printing press, an argumentative monk in Saxony could gain an international audience overnight and change the world. No printing press, no Reformations. It is that simple, at the most basic level. But there was also much more going on in 1450: trends flowing gradually and steadily on various levels, which make that date seem as definite a transition point as the Panama Canal. These were large-scale trends that brought change gradually, but at a faster pace than in earlier generations. Among these fluid, momentum-driven trends, the most significant were a renewed interest in classical culture, known as the Renaissance; the emergence of centralized states; the growth of the Western European economy; the rise of a literate bourgeoisie; and an increased awareness among many clerics and lay people of the enormous gap between the world they lived in and the ideals of their religion.

At the other end, 1648 marks the end of the Thirty Years' War—a long and bloody conflict that many experts consider the ultimate outcome of the Reformations. The two years tacked on to the endpoint of the span covered here—making it 1650 rather than 1648—are a rounding off, added for the sake of symmetry. The endpoint remains somewhat fuzzier than the invention of the printing press, for the dates in this case are emblematic rather than absolute, guideposts rather than portals. For instance, in 1650 the new basilica of St. Peter, then two centuries in the making, was not yet complete. And it would take another seventeen years for Gian Lorenzo Bernini to erect the piazza and colonnade that finally brought all of the work to an end. Of course, in the case of 1650, as in that of 1450, there were other large-scale trends developing that signaled an epochal shift. Among these, the most significant were the emergence of skepticism, rationalism, and religious tolerance; the birth of empirical science; the waning of witch hunts and of the Inquisition; and the imperialistic expansion of European civilization to other continents.

The Reformations used to be contained strictly within the sixteenth century. There were cogent reasons for doing that previously, when the prime motivation for writing about the Reformation was to uphold the success of the Protestant break with Rome. But now that such a motivation is no longer dominant, there are compelling reasons for ignoring the older chronology, especially because of the advances that have been made in our understanding of the Reformations. One of the most significant of these advances is the realization that the Reformations of the early modern era were more of a process than an event, and that limiting their beginning and end to the sixteenth century is neither wise nor appropriate. In many ways, today the Reformations look a lot more like the Renaissance once did: as an era with no fixed starting date and no clear ending. Nowadays, it matters little that we can pinpoint the beginning of Luther's Reformation—31 October 1517—with great accuracy. That event can no longer be approached or understood in isolation from what preceded it or followed it. This change in perspective stems principally from two major changes that took place in the 1960s and 1970s, in both European and North American scholarship.

First, some scholars began to reassess the continuities between medieval Catholicism and Protestantism and to downplay the discontinuities. Among secular historians, this shift in focus was driven largely by the spirit of the age, which questioned every venerable assumption and favored social over intellectual history. Among church historians, this new effort stemmed largely from the growth of the ecumenical movement, a good-hearted attempt to foster greater unity among all Christian churches—Protestant, Catholic, and Orthodox. This "rediscovery" of the common ground that linked Catholics and Protestants led historians to take a medieval perspective and to stretch the era of the Reformations back in time, into the fifteenth century, or even earlier. Searching for roots in all directions, some historians strained to trace not just theological or spiritual continuities, but also those changes in the social, political, economic, and cultural fabric of Western Christendom that made possible the great Protestant eruption of the sixteenth century. In addition, as the history of reform in the late medieval Catholic Church began to be reassessed, it became even clearer to many experts that there was indeed a much stronger unbroken continuity to be taken into account.

As these perspectives gained acceptance, that precise beginning date of 1517 began to look less and less accurate or convincing. By the late 1980s, the redefinition was complete: to study the era of the Reformations properly, it was necessary to begin with its roots, and the soil in which they formed, and the conditions that allowed for growth, as well as all of the furious branching that ensued. The beginning had become much fuzzier and much earlier. Without a fixed starting date—and with no desire on the part of any expert to find one—all survey histories of the Reformations must now begin in the late Middle Ages.

Second, some scholars began to also reassess the endpoint and outcome of the Reformations. Several key questions drove this research. Where did all the furious proliferation of competing churches and religious claims lead? What fruit did this branching produce? How long did the process of reforming continue? What did all of this turmoil have to do with the transition from the Middle Ages to modernity? The concerns of most of these scholars were far less theological and ecumenical than the concerns of those who focused on medieval perspectives. Much of the early work carried out at this latter end of the Reformations focused on social, political, economic, and cultural issues. The net result was a symmetrical extension of the Reformations forward in time, into the seventeenth century. So, now, in the same way that the Reformations have to be placed in a medieval context at one end, they also have to be fully integrated into the transition to modernity at the other. Some of the pioneers of this boundary stretching spoke of this later period as "the second Reformation" or "the long Reformation." Naturally, because they referred to *the* Reformation, these experts tended to focus on Protestants. But their colleagues who focused on the Catholic side of things also quickly began to assume a similar perspective, especially as more attention began to be paid to the legacy of the Council of Trent, and to its reforms, which did not begin to be enforced until the late sixteenth century and reached their apogee in the seventeenth.

Though this longer timeline gives us a more accurate perspective on the Reformations, it also makes it more challenging to summarize the era and to keep the narrative reasonably compact and manageable. In this book, form follows function. Since this work is intended as an introduction, the material is sorted into self-contained units that allow readers to make progress gradually, and to grasp complex bundles of information bit by bit, building on what they have already learned.

This book contains four distinct parts, each dealing with a distinct phase of the history of the Reformations: first, the late medieval period; second, the emergence of Protestantism; third, the reform of Catholicism; and fourth, the outcome of all of the various Reformations in the seventeenth century. Each of these parts could be approached as a separate volume—and in years past, they might have been published that way. But the object here is to keep these four distinct phases as interlinked as possible, and to make evident the unity of the whole.

The first part focuses on the late medieval period, more specifically on the fifteenth century, an era that Protestant historiography has referred to wistfully as the pre-Reformation period, and that cultural historians have preferred to call the Renaissance. The chapters in this part explore the many developments and factors that led up to the explosion of discontent in 1517 that undid medieval Christendom. Many histories of this period written from the Protestant perspective tended to place a heavy emphasis on the pathology of this age, that is, on the corruption and abuses that made the Catholic Church an object of loathing and disdain. These very same histories also emphasized the emergence of dissenters who were "precursors" or "forerunners" of the Protestant Reformation, such as the Waldensians of the Alpine regions, the Lollards of England, and the Hussites of Bohemia. Cultural histories tended to focus on the renewal of classical culture best known as the Renaissance. Traditional Catholic narratives took a different tack, naturally. Catholics who wrote about this period emphasized efforts at reform more than the corruption or abuses that were the object of reform. In other words, although Catholic historians admitted that there was much to fix in the late medieval church, they tended to argue that reform was well under way. In this book, these various approaches have all been modified and interwoven into a single narrative, placing reformers, heretics, forerunners, Renaissance humanists, corrupt churchmen, and simple lay folk side by side, much as they were in real life five to six centuries ago. One distinguishing feature of this part is its inclusion of early Catholic attempts at reform. Traditional Reformation histories tend to include this material in some later chapter that covers all of Catholic reform in one fell swoop, with a much greater focus on the Catholic reaction to Protestantism.

The second part consists of what formerly passed for a complete history of the Reformation. In other words, it is a history of the churches that broke openly with the pope in Rome. This section focuses on the genesis of each of the various competing Protestant traditions: Lutheran, Swiss Reformed, Radical, Calvinist, and Anglican. The chapters on these traditions have no common endpoint, but they tend to go no further than the mid- to late sixteenth century, which is where many traditional Reformation histories come to an end. A conscious effort has been made to pay equal attention to each of these traditions, and to the subtraditions within them.

The third part deals with the reforms undertaken in the Catholic Church after the advent of Protestantism. In traditional twentieth-century Reformation histories this subject tended to be a single chapter that emphasized Catholic reforming as a Counter-Reformation. Though there is no denying the fact that Catholics responded directly to the Protestant challenge, and that the chapters in this part do sometimes focus on this counter-Protestant dimension of Catholic reform, the central aim of this part is to explore the full complexity of early modern Catholicism. Having multiple chapters on the Catholic Reformation—including some on its overseas missions—has never been common in surveys of this sort. Traditionally, the detailed coverage given here to early modern Catholicism has been found hitherto only in books dedicated solely to the Catholic Reformation.

The fourth and final part deals with the immediate outcome of all of the Reformations, and with the various ways in which the radically fragmented civilization once known as Christendom (*Christianitas*) evolved into the one we now call modern Europe. In this part, all the various traditions and churches previously covered one by one will be examined together, side by side, all the way to the mid-seventeenth century, and sometimes even further. Traditional histories of the Reformation have seldom included this slice of time in their narrative, or tried to examine the impact of the religious divisions of the sixteenth century on the following three or four succeeding generations. In a very concrete way, this part expands on and modifies the concept of a long Reformation or second Reformation in two ways, by doing away with the notion that there was ever a single Reformation and by refusing to accept these later developments as a "second" or separate phase. This section is about outcomes, and the continuation of plural Reformations. Its implicit argument is that what began in the sixteenth century took a long time to sort itself out, and that the transition to modernity was far from quick or neat.

This book has been a long time in the making, and its present form is far different from the one first conceived. In great measure, this discrepancy between the initial goal and the final execution is directly related to the exponential increase in studies of this particular era. Keeping up with what has been published in the past fifteen years has been a challenge. And this challenge has led to many new and unexpected insights, and a fair number of surprises—even to changes of opinion, some subtle, some extreme. Teaching this subject to very bright students has also had an impact on the development of this book, especially because of those totally unexpected questions raised in class that force professors to reexamine some of their assumptions.

Three features of this book have remained constant, however, and have given shape to every sentence, paragraph, and chapter. The first of these is the conviction that religion is a real factor in history, and that beliefs and ideas do play a significant role in human events, especially in epochal shifts such as that of the early modern era. The second one is the conviction that there were multiple Reformations and that none of them can be fully understood in isolation. The third is the conviction that we cannot begin to comprehend who we are now as Westerners without first understanding the changes wrought by the Reformations of the early modern era. This third conviction, it could be said, is the chief overarching assumption of the entire book.

This book does not argue that the West became "modern" as a result of the Reformations; nor does it attempt to pinpoint the birth of modernity. Determining the birth of modernity with precision or defining its essence has become something of an obsession for scholars lately, and also a fierce competition. Not surprisingly, as conflicting claims for a definitive assessment of modernity continue to proliferate, the usefulness of the concept diminishes. What this book does concern itself with is transformations and transitions, and with their effects on the Western world. It also seeks to analyze the two-way relationship between those transitions and religion. As understood here, modernity is a horizon, a set of conditions, even a state of mind, rather than a concrete reality that can be identified with scientific precision. Modernity is also understood here as a socio-political cultural environment that developed gradually, haltingly, always piecemeal, and never as the result of a single factor or set of events. The Reformations were part of the gradual and painful transition to modernity, undeniably, but assessing their role in the development of something as vague and contested as modernity serves no good purpose in a survey history such as this.

At a certain point in a historian's career—certainly after more than thirty years of research and writing and teaching, and of reading hypercritical book reviews that could make even the most hardened of demons cringe—it becomes obvious that no book is ever flawless or definitive, and that the best one can hope for is to sum up the past in a way that makes sense for one's own time with a unique voice and in a convincing way. Writing history is a peculiar way to teach, or even to converse, for the author can only imagine the readers or guess what their questions might be. In addition, anyone who writes a survey history such as this one also has to imagine how other experts might assess it. To summarize on a grand scale is to invite criticism and dissent, for what is left out can seem a greater offense to some experts than what is included. Reconciling oneself to the limitations of any book one writes, especially one long in the making, is part and parcel of the historian's lot. It is also an essential part of the historian's craft. In the end, the author surrenders control of the narrative he or she has crafted, and every reader assumes the role of judge.

A sardonic Winston Churchill, very secure in his own achievements and of his place in history, summed up in 1949 what many authors since ancient times have felt, but have not had equal nerve to joke about. "Writing a book is an adventure," he said. "To begin with it is a toy, then an amusement. Then it becomes a mistress, and then it becomes a master, and then it becomes a tyrant and, in the last stage, just as you are about to be reconciled to your servitude, you kill the monster and fling him to the public." Churchill's mordant jest has a real bite to it. One can only assume that the words were not chosen lightly by this man who had just led his people in a costly war against real tyrants and monsters, arguably among the very worst ever to walk the earth. Wry humor was as much a trademark of Churchill as his cigars. Like all sensitive writers, he loved his metaphorical mistresses, masters, and tyrants—and he always flung his beloved metaphorical monsters to the public with no small measure of optimism, hoping that they would help his readers keep the real ones at bay.

Similarly, I hope that my own metaphorical monster, now in your hands, does the same.

Reformations

Out with the old. This drawing by Maarten van Heemskerck gives us a view of the old Basilica of St. Peter's and the Apostolic Palace as it looked before construction of the new basilica became visible from the front approach across the Tiber River.

PART ONE

On the Edge

Prelude: Rome, 1450

A
s he begins to rebuild the roads, aqueducts, and walls of the crumbling
city of Rome, Pope Nicholas V proclaims a jubilee in 1450. Anyone
who makes a pilgrimage to Rome that year and follows certain prescribed rites can receive a plenary indulgence, that is, full forgiveness
for all of the sins he or she has ever committed. Rome is flooded with
pilgrims, and the pope's coffers fill up. These pilgrims return home with no memories of
gleaming churches—there are none to be seen in Rome, where the ancient Forum is now
a cow pasture and the Capitoline Hill is full of goats—but many are duly moved by the
sacred power of the city's crumbling sanctuaries and by the spiritual benefits guaranteed
by the pope. Many of these pilgrims fail to notice that Nicholas V has moved the papal
residence from the palace and Basilica of St. John Lateran to the Vatican Hill and its
palace and Basilica of St. Peter. The papal residence of St. John Lateran, built in the fourth
century, and home to more than a hundred popes over the previous millennium, is in
ruins. St. Peter's, where the apostle Peter is buried, is also in very poor shape, since it also
dates from the fourth century.

What the pilgrims of 1450 do not know as they trek from sacred site to sacred
site in Rome, or even as they enter St. Peter's, is that Pope Nicholas V has decided to tear
down that ancient church and to replace it with "a temple so glorious and beautiful" that
it will seem "rather a divine than a human creation."[1] They also have no way of knowing
that Pope Nicholas intends for all future popes to reside at the Vatican, and for St. Peter's
to become symbolically linked to the papal office, or that he intends to strip marble
from the ancient Colosseum for the construction of his new St. Peter's, and that more than
two thousand cartloads of stone will eventually be hauled away. At the very same time,
Pope Nicholas has no way of knowing that he will be dead within five years and that his
grandiose plans will lie dormant for five more decades. And no one at all has any clue that
a method of book production just invented in the German city of Mainz—movable-type

printing—is about to change the world, or that the eventual revival of Pope Nicholas V's plans for St. Peter's in 1505 will lead to the undoing of Western Christendom.

No one alive in 1450 can fully realize that they are living on the edge of a new era or envision the transitions that hover on the horizon. Some may be very aware of the changes that are taking place, and of the differences between their age and that of their immediate forebears. But no one can really imagine the magnitude of the changes that their progeny will live through.

Change was much harder to imagine in the fifteenth century, and especially so in Rome, with all its thousand-year-old churches, feuding nobles, and legions of clerics.

CHAPTER ONE

An Age of Breakthroughs

On 10 November 1483, in the Saxon town of Eisleben, a mining entrepreneur named Hans Luther and his wife, Hanna Lindemann, welcomed a son into the world whom they christened Martin. Seven weeks later, on 1 January 1484, about 330 miles away, in the Swiss village of Wildhaus, in the high Alpine valley of Toggenburg, another couple rejoiced at the birth of a son. They were Ulrich Zwingli and Margaret Meili, prosperous peasants, and they named the boy Ulrich, after his father, who was an *Amtman*, or village administrator. Both boys would eventually become priests: Ulrich Zwingli in 1506, at the age of twenty-two; Martin Luther in 1507, at the age of twenty-three. When they reached their midthirties, both of them would rebel against their own Catholic Church and establish new rival churches. Ulrich Zwingli would be killed in battle, at Kappel in 1531, at the age of forty-seven, fighting against fellow Swiss confederates over questions of faith. Martin Luther would die in bed in his native Eisleben, in 1546, at the age of sixty-three, beset by illnesses. Though they came to distrust one another and became bitter foes, there is no denying that they led a common assault on centuries of tradition, and that by the time each of them died, the world was a much different place thanks to them.

One has to ask: What was it that allowed these two priests from families of relatively modest means to challenge the pope and the emperor and to undo their world? What allowed them to succeed where so many others had failed before? What was it about their world and their culture that turned them into Reformers and made their Reformations possible? In what ways was their world ripe for change?

A clue is immediately offered by their birthdates, for the first leaders of the Protestant Reformation were all born after 1480. Another clue is offered by their profession, for nearly all of them were ordained as priests in the Catholic Church before turning into Reformers (an asterisk in the list indicates a clergyman):

1480	Andreas Bodenstein von Karlstadt*
1482	Johann Oecolampadius*
1483	Martin Luther*
1484	Ulrich Zwingli*
1485	Johann Bugenhagen*
1485	Balthasar Hubmaier*
1487	Bernardino Ochino*
1488	Oswald Myconius*
1489	Guillaume Farel
1490	Thomas Müntzer*
1490	Michael Sattler*
1490	Friedrich Myconius*
1490	Hans Hut
1491	Martin Bucer*
1492	Ambrosius Blaurer*
1492	George Blaurock*
1493	Justus Jonas*
1494/95	Caspar Hedio*
1495	Melchior Hoffman
1496	Menno Simons*
1497	Philip Melanchthon*
1498	Conrad Grebel
1498	Andreas Osiander*
1499	Johannes Brenz
1499	Justus Menius
1499	Sebastian Franck*
1500	Ludwig Hätzer*
1500	Jacob Hutter

While it is easy enough to explain why the leaders of a religious revolution should have been clerics, and trained in theology, it is perhaps not as easy to figure out the age factor. Why was it that none of them was over the age of thirty-seven when that movement began? Of the great Protestant Reformers, only two were older than Luther and Zwingli (and barely so). Why?

One way to approach the age question is to consider what was going on in Europe between 1480 and 1500, when these men were born.

Trade and Exploration, 1480–1500

In 1480 the world was much the same as it had ever been for Europeans, as far as maps were concerned. Ptolemy's *Geography*, which had been written in the second century, was still the reigning authority concerning the earth. Although a few islands had been discovered out in the Atlantic Ocean, beyond the northern coast of Africa, no one in Europe knew how far south the African landmass reached, much less what lay hidden in its interior. Asia was still a very distant place, and hard to reach. Whatever lay on the other side of the Atlantic Ocean remained a mystery. To many, the earth was still flat and full of marvels such as giant sea serpents, unicorns, and wild, freakish humanoids. By 1492, all of this would change radically. Thanks to an increase in trade and the expansion of their economy, Europeans would encounter lands and peoples previously unknown to them, and they would begin a long process of commercial and cultural exchange with them—a process that in many cases included establishing overseas colonies and launching religious missions.

Commercial ties with Asia had grown over the previous century, and they continued to flourish, mostly in the hands of Italian merchants. Spices made up the bulk of the merchandise from the so-called Far East: exotic commodities such as ginger, nutmeg, cinnamon, cloves, and pepper, which were then cultivated only in Asia. Europeans craved these rare substances that livened up their otherwise bland cuisine. At the higher end, silk and jewels normally made for nice profits too. But this trade involved traveling great distances, at great expense, and it also meant dealing with many middlemen. There was no direct sea route linking Europe and Asia. The Mediterranean was but a narrow Italian funnel, and a relatively short leg on a very long journey over land and sea. Trading with India and China also meant having to deal with Muslims in the eastern Mediterranean, in either Egypt or the Levant, and having to contend with the vast Ottoman Empire, an ever-warring, ever-expanding Muslim state larger than any single Christian kingdom. In Europe itself, all of Greece and much of the Balkan Peninsula was already theirs by the time Bayezid II came to the Ottoman throne in 1481. The fall of the ancient imperial capital of Constantinople to the Turks in 1453 was still within living memory for some Europeans but already receding into a distant past. Constantinople, the "second" Rome founded by the emperor Constantine in the fourth century and the onetime seat of the Byzantine Empire, was now called Istanbul, and its grandiose church of Hagia Sophia, built in the sixth century by the emperor Justinian, was now a mosque, where Muslims worshiped Allah. Egypt and the entire Near East were not yet part of the Ottoman Empire, but the Ottomans overshadowed the entire eastern end of the Mediterranean, producing an instability that tended to drive up prices steadily.

The Ottomans were much more than a nuisance for traders. They were a very real enemy with perilous designs. Under Sultan Mehmed II (1451–1481), the Ottoman Empire had nearly doubled in size, mainly by conquests in the Balkan Peninsula of southeastern Europe. Under Sultan Bayezid II (1481–1512), the Ottomans made further gains in the Balkans, taking Herzegovina in 1483. To the northeast, Bayezid II also made conquests north of the Danube River in 1484, along the Black Sea coast, giving the Ottomans control of the mouths of two major European rivers, the Danube and the Dniester. And despite peace treaties, such as the one made with the king of Hungary in 1484, the

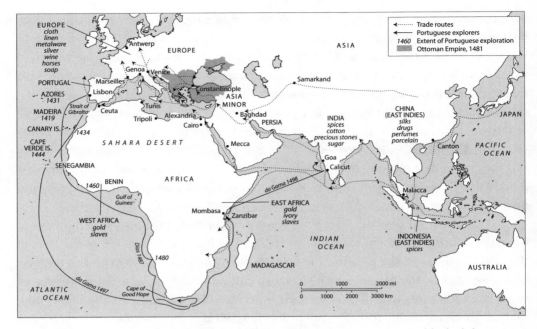

Searching for a sea route to the Orient. The fact that the Ottoman Empire blocked the major overland trade routes between Europe and Asia forced Europeans to seek a sea route instead around the African continent and into the Indian Ocean. Portugal was the first nation to explore and develop this alternative.

Ottoman advance into Europe continued to be a very real threat. By 1499 the Ottomans were once again at war, this time with Venice, and the menace was enormous. With a well-trained army that outnumbered that of any individual European monarch, and a growing navy that easily controlled much of the eastern Mediterranean, the Ottoman Turks stood poised to march even deeper into Europe and to subject more Christians to Muslim rule. By 1500, the threat posed by the Ottomans had reached apocalyptic dimensions, literally, for many Christians came to believe that "the Turks" were a scourge of God that presaged the end of the world. And this threat would intensify under the next two sultans, Selim I (1512–1520) and Suleyman I, the Magnificent (1520–1566).

In the 1480s, then, finding a direct sea route to Asia seemed a great idea, especially for anyone with direct access to the Atlantic Ocean. But it was a costly and risky enterprise. Portugal, a kingdom on the Atlantic and close to Africa, took a lead in searching for such a route at the same time it searched for gold. Sub-Saharan West Africa was rich in gold then, and the gold trade had long been in the hands of Muslim traders who crossed the Sahara Desert back and forth and sold it to Europeans at port cities on the Barbary Coast of the Mediterranean, such as Algiers and Tunis. Under the direction of Prince Henry the Navigator (1394–1460), Portuguese traders began to sail south along the West African coast, in waters previously unknown to Europeans, with the hopes of getting to the source of this gold directly. As they made their way along the unfamiliar coastline, exploring, the Portuguese set up trading posts. Eventually, they would find their way to Guinea and the Ivory Coast, and there they would seize the bulk of the gold trade away from Muslim traders. They would also establish sugar plantations and set up a lucrative trade in ivory, ebony, and slaves. But all that success did not in any way slacken their craving for Asian spices or curtail their search for a direct sea route to the Far East. So they kept trading and exploring, sailing farther south, little by little, even past the equator, which many Europeans believed was a lethal boundary beyond which no one could cross.

In the mid-1480s, around the time that Luther and Zwingli were born, Christopher Columbus was still a struggling mariner, sailing with the Portuguese, trading along the Guinea coast and the Gold Coast of tropical West Africa while he formulated his daring plan to sail westward across the Atlantic Ocean to reach Asia. But when he sought funding for such a trip in 1484 from King John II of Portugal, he was turned down.

King John II had good reason not to fund Columbus. In 1481 he had ordered new voyages down the Atlantic coast of Africa, with the specific goal of finding a way to the Indian Ocean and the riches of Asia. As with previous Portuguese exploits, these ventures were part exploration, part commerce, and part empire building. King John II gave his navigators stone pillars with which they dotted the West African coast, staking claims for the Portuguese crown farther south every year. His strategy paid off. In 1488, while Columbus was still searching for a royal patron to fund his westward voyage, Bartolomeu Dias and his crew became the first Europeans to round the Cape of Good Hope, opening a sea route to Asia via the Atlantic and Indian oceans. It would take another decade for the Portuguese to find their way around all of Africa to the Malabar Coast of India. But by the time Vasco da Gama finally made it to the fabled Indian spice markets in 1498, other "Indians" had already entered the picture.

Next door to Portugal, a new nation was in the making that would stumble on the greatest discovery of all. In 1469, Isabella of Castile and Ferdinand II of Aragon had married, joining their realms and giving rise to the political entity that came to be known as Spain. Driven by a common crusading spirit, these two monarchs began a war in 1481 against the last remaining sliver of Muslim dominion in Iberia, the kingdom of Granada. Town by town they reclaimed Granada, slowly and deliberately, until all that was left was the city of Granada itself, with its ethereal palace, the Alhambra. Finally, on 2 January 1492, the Moors of Granada surrendered. Christopher Columbus was there in Granada on that fateful date, eager to pitch his preposterous project to Ferdinand and Isabella, a voyage that was largely based on the thirteen-hundred-year-old miscalculations of Ptolemy. Fortunately for him, the fall of Granada emboldened the Spanish monarchs, who thought not only of gaining trade advantages over the Portuguese but also of continuing their crusade against all Muslims via a westward sea route. This time around, Queen Isabella chose to fund Columbus's expedition.

What happened next is one of the best-known stories in human history. Columbus set sail with three ships on 3 August 1492, hoping to land in China; instead, he stumbled upon the Bahamas some weeks later, on 12 October, and then spent a few more weeks exploring the islands of the Antilles. It took a few more voyages by him and others to finally figure out that the lands at the western end of the Atlantic—which were erroneously named the Indies—were a new world full of previously hidden marvels. Asia remained the goal of many westward-sailing expeditions, but that did not stop the Spanish from reaping the windfall of Columbus's surprising discovery. Very quickly, Spain became the richest and most powerful nation in Europe and the largest empire in the entire world. Portugal and many other European states would do their utmost to compete and catch up with Spain, or to thwart its designs, but there was no stopping the Spanish, at least for another century or so.

The conquest and exploitation of the New World transformed Europe economically, politically, socially, and culturally. It altered commerce and the balance of power not only among European nations but also between Europe and the rest of the world. Religion was affected too. The "discovery" and subjugation of vast numbers of pagans set in motion a process of Christianization on an unprecedented stage, and also brought Europeans face-to-face with a whole range of beliefs and practices that forced some of them to think of their own faith in a different context. The cultural and religious impact of the encounter with the native Americans would be subtle, slow paced, and of long duration, but it would be nonetheless profound.

Suddenly, at the end of the fifteenth century, the world seemed on the threshold of an entirely new age in human experience. Luther and Zwingli were mere boys when Columbus stumbled upon the Bahamas in 1492, proving, quite by accident, that the accumulated wisdom of the past could be seriously flawed. To their generation, it was no longer unthinkable that tradition and accepted authorities could be wrong. In essence, proving that one's wisest elders had erred became commonplace, and as routine as the constant discovery of new lands and cultures. With every passing year, more and more previously unknown things were revealed through exploration. None of the Protestant Reformers ever said or wrote much about the New World, for it had little direct impact on them. But discoveries and novelties were a constant for them since their childhood, or from birth. Luther and Zwingli and their contemporaries were accustomed to change early in their lives and in more ways than we can count.

The Information Revolution

When it came to education and learning, Luther and Zwingli's generation was the first to fully benefit from the invention of the printing press. In the city of Mainz, in 1455, German craftsmen produced a gorgeous Bible by printing each page with a machine: the first printed book in Western history. Johannes Gutenberg (1395–1468) was the man responsible for this invention, though others were involved too, most notably Johann Fust (1400–1465) and Peter Schöffer (1425–1502). A combination of technological breakthroughs made it possible: being able to assemble small, uniform, and durable precut

The old meets the new. The *danse macabre*, or dance of death, became a popular genre in art and literature of the late Middle Ages, largely due to lingering memories of the bubonic plague of 1348–1349, which wiped out about a third of Europe's population. In the dance, skeletons or decaying corpses were depicted in the act of carrying various different social types to the grave. The message was a brutally simple memento mori, or reminder of death: no one is ever spared, and the end can come unexpectedly. In 1499, in the city of Lyons, Matthias Huss brought the dance of death into a print shop for the first time, and in the process he gave the world its first glimpse of the new technology. Huss depicts the key steps of the new publishing business in three well-integrated scenes. From left to right: Death overtakes a compositor as he loads letters into the platen, Death grabs a press man as he reaches for the lever, and Death seizes a bookseller whose shelves are well stocked. The lines of French text that accompany this memento mori reveal one more detail about the new craft: the persistence of errors. Death tells the unlucky threesome that they no longer have any time to correct their mistakes.

blocks with letters on them and being able to ink them repeatedly and keep them fixed in place as page after identical page was printed on paper by means of a press. It also required the right kind of oil-based ink and an ample supply of paper. Printing and engraving on paper with blocks was not exactly new. Movable type and paper had been around for centuries, since their invention in China, but the Latin alphabet used by Europeans allowed for their use in a radically new way. With only twenty-six characters as opposed to thousands in Chinese, European writing made it easier to manufacture a complete set of interchangeable symbols and to assemble precut blocks into text. The revolutionary invention first used at Mainz allowed for entire pages of text to be printed at once. Whereas every book ever produced before 1455 had to be written by hand, now books could be reproduced mechanically and in any numbers one desired, even hundreds or thousands.

The invention from Mainz had an immense impact on European culture. Texts written by hand could never be reproduced quickly or distributed widely, but in the time that it took one scribe to copy a single book, a printing press could churn out a wagonload of copies. And booksellers could distribute the identical books to a wide reading audience at a price far below that of any handwritten copy. Those who witnessed this change were astounded. One Italian said about a printer who had just set up shop in his city: "He prints more in one day than could be copied in a year."[2] Even more, whereas scribes could easily err in transcribing a text, or make unwanted additions or deletions, thus corrupting the original text, the printing press ensured that identical copies of the same text could be reproduced over and over with no errors, or maybe just a few. Now, for the first time in human history, definitive texts could be established and rare texts rescued from oblivion. It also meant that hundreds and thousands of people could read the same text at once and rest assured that it was a "true" unaltered version—texts such as Ptolemy's *Geography*, which Columbus relied upon. And no book could have been more deserving of a "true" version than that which was the first to be produced by a printing press, the Bible, which was believed to be the Word of God.

By the time Luther and Zwingli's generation began their university studies, the printing revolution was already well under way. Printing houses spread relatively quickly and widely throughout Western Europe in the latter part of the fifteenth century, and made a quantum leap after 1500 or so. Italy, Germany, and France led the way. In France, for instance, forty towns had printers by 1501, and in some locations the competition was stiff. In Paris alone there were sixty printers cranking out books, pamphlets, and calendars.

A new sort of erudition was now possible, which could be expected of students all over Christendom, at a level broader and deeper than that reached by any previous generation. Libraries were filling up with printed books, and the books themselves became increasingly more affordable. Students could all read the same text at once, and teachers could change their methods and assignments accordingly. Texts could be consulted and compared, and information exchanged more readily across political borders, even across seas and wide oceans. National identities could become more cohesive now, while at the same time readers in each nation became more aware of the wider world. While Latin would remain the lingua franca of the educated elite for several generations, the vernacular languages of Europe could flourish as never before and begin their evolution into the languages we know today. Last, but not least, authors could gain much larger reading audiences almost instantly.

Along with the larger reading audiences, the printing press also brought into existence the best seller and the widely recognized celebrity author. By 1517, when Luther

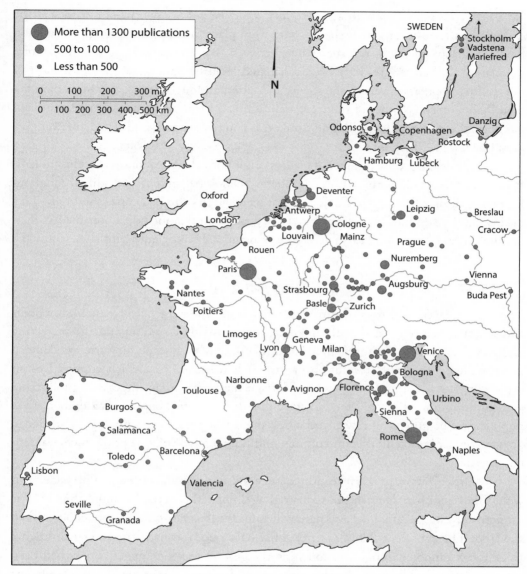

Printing in 1500. By the beginning of the sixteenth century, printing presses could be found throughout most of Europe, but some regions—especially in Germany and Italy—had higher concentrations of printers and produced more texts.

and Zwingli were poised to challenge the status quo, a network was already well set in place for the rapid production and distribution of their writings. An audience was there too, especially among those of their generation who had grown up with printed books and expected consistency and definitive editions, and whose worldview was increasingly shaped by this means of communication. For many in that audience change was not something to be feared, but rather something to be desired and expected.

We do not know with any certainty what the literacy rate was in Europe at the end of the fifteenth century. Estimates vary from place to place, but a rough calculation for all of Europe places the rate somewhere between 10 percent and 15 percent of the total population. Different rates have been calculated for urban and rural areas, for most of the reading population was in the towns and cities, and literacy was also higher among men than women. Neither of these generalizations is surprising, given that peasants did not normally need reading skills and rural areas had few schools, and also that fewer girls than boys attended school.

While the precise number of readers cannot be calculated, one fact seems undeniable: most experts maintain that the number of schools began to rise steadily throughout Europe in the late fifteenth century, and that literacy rates climbed correspondingly. This means that Luther and Zwingli belonged to a generation that included more readers than ever before, and that with every succeeding generation literacy rates kept increasing.

Commerce and Politics

Literacy rates were tied to commerce and urbanization, for the need to establish schools and educate children was directly linked to the changing economy and the increasing complexity of urban environments. The urbanization of Europe, in turn, was due to the so-called commercial revolution of the High Middle Ages, which consisted of an expansion of trade, the development of foreign markets, and an increase in production and consumption. Historians tend to agree that this economic boom led to an increase in population, the growth of towns and cities, the development of technological advances, greater contact between different cultures, and the eventual collapse of the medieval feudal order.

Urbanization in the fifteenth century did not depopulate the countryside, as it would four centuries later in the industrial age, but rather settled it more thickly. The economy of Europe remained agrarian, which meant that vast numbers of people worked the land. The continent that a squirrel could have once traversed end to end through a thick forest canopy without ever touching the ground was long gone. Forests had been cut down, marshes drained. Except for areas with mountainous terrain, the landscape of Europe was transformed by the end of the fifteenth century. With a population of 60 million–70 million people, the continent was a vast network of farms, villages, towns, and walled cities, almost all connected by roads, with some forests dotting the landscape still, thicker in some places than others. Seaports dotted the coastlines, and navigable rivers teemed with traffic. And there were churches everywhere—so many of them, and so close to one another, that no church steeple ever seemed out of sight of another. Some historians think that these economic developments helped to weaken the church's power and influence, yet one of the graphic images often employed by some of them to represent the urbanization of Europe is that of town portraits, cranked out by printers, most of which feature skylines bristling with church steeples.

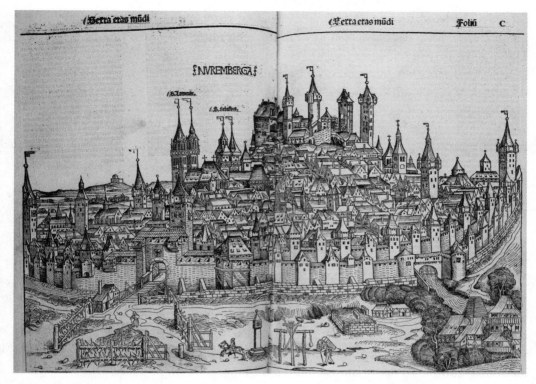

The city of Nuremberg. One of the first encyclopedic texts mass-produced with the invention of the printing press was *Nuremberg Chronicle* (1493). Such texts helped disseminate information to greater numbers of people than ever before in human history. This image of Nuremberg shows how densely packed many cities were, and how thickly dotted with ecclesiastical buildings.

When Luther and Zwingli were born, this booming economy was in full swing and just about to expand and to be transformed by the discovery of the New World and of a new sea route to Asia. The cities, towns, and countryside of Europe had been emptied by the bubonic plague of 1347–1349, which killed an estimated 21 million–27 million people—a third of Europe's total population. For a century or more, as one historian has put it, "Europe had the aspect of a child wearing its parent's clothes."[3] But the horrendous effects of this epidemic, known as the Black Death, were now a dim memory.

The late fifteenth century was a time of intense political change in Western Europe, as medieval feudalism gradually gave way to new power structures and new ways of governing. Historians speak of this transformation as the emergence of the sovereign state; many also identify this process as one of the markers that signal the end of the Middle Ages and the beginning of the early modern age.

Although there is some disagreement about when and where this process of political change began, exactly, most experts agree that it was set in motion around 1300, peaked between 1450 and 1550, and then intensified until 1800 or so. Generalizing about something as gradual and complex as this reordering of power relationships is risky:

exceptions abound, and so do contradictions. But there is no denying that many of the political structures that one sees in place throughout most of Western Europe by the time Luther died in 1546 had not existed a century earlier.

Consolidation and centralization were the defining features of this shift. Power structures in medieval Europe had been somewhat fragmented, having evolved in the crucible of a warring society in which power was shared in varying amounts among the warrior class, who were most often also those who owned the land. The feudal system of Western Europe was based on reciprocal obligations among warriors: monarchs, princes, lords, and knights shared in the responsibilities and the privileges that came with ruler-ship. Within this system, the church and its clergy also played a complex and often contested role. At the very top of the feudal power structure, monarchs were the chief lords, or suzerains, over a hierarchy of vassals; they were not absolute rulers. Kings and emperors may have been anointed and crowned with great pomp, and have lived in the grandest castles, but they still had to share power with the vassals who fought for them and the clergy who consecrated all legitimate authorities. They may have locked horns disdainfully with the pope and his bishops, but their very legitimacy was always contin-gent, for it was subject to the church's approval. The feudal "state" was not reducible to the monarch and his court. Indeed it was hardly a "state" at all: the functions associated with rulership, such as the power to wage war, to tax, and to define and enforce laws, were all shared with the landed aristocracy and the clergy in varying degrees.

Even more, the power wielded by secular authorities was considered a hereditary right and was privately owned by the aristocracy. Feudal kings were relatively weak and ruled their lands in concert with their vassals, always dependent in some way on the ap-proval of the church, which could always threaten to undercut secular authority through its power of excommunication. Feudal states were therefore decentralized networks of power with plenty of overlapping and conflicting claims to authority—networks held to-gether by personal loyalties and mutual obligations. Monarchs may have had more rights and privileges than any of their vassals, and also more responsibilities, but the vassals and the clerics still had rights and privileges of their own, which they guarded jealously.

Sometime around 1300, Western European monarchs began to claim more power and to consolidate their resources. Gradually, they found ways to increase their income. At the very same time, other developments weakened the feudal structure, giving monarchs greater advantages. Cities and towns became powerful corporations of their own, beholden to no lord but the monarch, and their leading citizens began to acquire the kind of power and prestige that had once been reserved solely for nobles. Within the cit-ies, new governing structures arose, along with new conceptions of authority and political identity. Then, with the rise of the universities came an increase in the number of learned laymen, especially jurists, who could turn to ancient Roman law in defense of the power of monarchs. These lay jurists squared off with clerics who defended papal supremacy and clerical superiority. The end result was the invention—or "rediscovery"—of a legal basis for royal sovereignty.

The vanishing feudal order. In this late fifteenth-century image peasants are laboring for their feudal lord. The nobleman's castle—a necessity as well as a prerogative of a decentralized society—was on the verge of becoming obsolete in many parts of Europe, as monarchs increasingly consolidated their authority.

Along with the inflated claims of the jurists came the emergence of bureaucracies, that is, networks of skilled royal officials whose business it was to interpret the laws in the king's favor and to manage his resources. Gradually, many monarchs began to assemble and rule through councils—permanent assemblies handpicked by them that assumed some of the functions previously limited to feudal vassals or representative assemblies. Along with the councils came officers of state, or ministers, whose job it was to do the king's bidding and to ensure that his will be done. And along with the councils and the ministers came officers who represented the monarch at the local level, usually in cities and towns. Whether justices of the peace in England, or *corregidores* in Castile, or *lieutenants de roi* in France, these officials extended the king's authority into realms that had once been the fiefs of other vassals, or of clerics, or of corporations. These royal representatives made the monarch's presence felt on a local level, enabling kings to concentrate more power in their own hands and to lessen its fragmentation among a hierarchy of clerical and secular lords. They also were instruments of royal justice, and as such they extended the jurisdiction of the king to the local level.

Claiming power and exercising it are two very different things, however. No matter how many jurists they hired to defend their claims, or how many ministers and bureaucrats they appointed, monarchs still had to be able to back up their claims with brute force. So along with the centralization of power and finances, and the creation of royal representation at the local level, came the creation of permanent armies. It mattered little that many of these armies were made up of hired mercenaries, some of whom were not the monarch's own subjects. By creating and funding armies of their own, monarchs began to monopolize the means of waging war, which they had previously shared with the nobility. This process did not happen overnight throughout Western Europe, or at the same pace in every place, but rather it occurred over the span of a century or so, roughly between 1450 and 1560. The creation of permanent armies who did the king's bidding not only altered the relation between monarchs and their vassals but also affected international relations.

Warfare changed too. Pitting these new armies against one another required a new way of fighting. Throughout the Middle Ages, the mounted knights who had dominated the battlefield had mostly been the nobles, those vassals of the king who not only funded warfare but also enjoyed a certain degree of autonomy. But in the late fifteenth century heavy cavalry began to be outnumbered by nonnoble foot soldiers who needed much less armor and equipment. Armed with pikes—long, sharp-tipped spears with an axelike weapon at the end—the infantry could skewer charging cavalry and hack them to pieces. In essence, the nobility gradually lost control of warfare: whereas before they served as vassals who offered military assistance to their lord, they now began to assume a different role as subordinates of the monarch, whose chief role was to lead his paid soldiers.

And it was not just this shifting pattern of command that changed warfare. Gunpowder played a very significant role too. The foot soldiers were armed not only with pikes, bows, and swords but also with handguns: at first harquebuses, and then muskets. Though these primitive firearms were cumbersome to load and shoot, they nonetheless made soldiers much more vulnerable. No longer could any fighting man depend on armor or a shield to protect himself from his opponents. Metal shot turned knights in shining armor into relics. And artillery made mincemeat out of them. Though also crude and cumbersome—and sometimes unreliable—cannon began to be used with more frequency in the late fifteenth century. Technological advances also made it possible for artillery and missiles to increase in size, range, and destructive power.

The impact of these weapons was immense, not just on the battlefield, where they could kill and maim on a scale previously unknown, but also in the art of the siege. The thick high walls that had once fended off whole armies no longer seemed sufficient, for castles and towns could be besieged with greater ferocity. Nothing proved this more decisively than the Turkish siege of Constantinople in 1453, in which more than seventy artillery pieces were used to breach the walls of the once-impregnable seat of the

Byzantine Empire. Fortifications had to be adjusted to this new type of warfare, so defensive walls became ever thicker and more complex in design, and more reliant on defensive artillery. Naval warfare was transformed too as artillery became more commonplace. All of this made warfare increasingly expensive, and as the cost of war climbed, it became an extraordinary enterprise that could be funded only by a centralized state. And as the cost of war increased, so did the sovereign state's need for revenue.

Which brings one full circle and face-to-face with the centralizing cycle of early modern state building, through which rulers consolidated and enhanced their power. The new warfare could not take place without a bureaucracy that could ensure the flow of revenue to the monarch, but that warfare also ensured the success of the state's centralizing ambitions. And as the increasing sovereignty of the Western European rulers ensured greater autonomy for individual states, so did that increased autonomy lead to a greater fragmentation of what had once been called Christendom.

And it needs to be stressed that kings were not alone in consolidating their power in the late fifteenth century. While it is undeniable that the rulers of great kingdoms such as France, England, Castile, and Aragon were able to gain sovereignty and amass power on an impressive scale, it is also undeniable that many smaller states engaged in the same process, some of which, such as the duchies of Burgundy, Milan, and Savoy, could easily hold their own against larger rivals. But there were also many other configurations of power in Western Europe, and various roads to sovereignty. Switzerland, which supplied armies everywhere with paid mercenary soldiers, was a loose confederation of independent city-states and cantons, each of which was ruled democratically by oligarchies. Northern Italy was a jigsaw puzzle of thriving city-states, some ruled autocratically like small kingdoms, others ruled more democratically as republics, and yet others in flux from one type of rulership to another. Venice was ruled by an oligarchy and even had an empire of its own. And, in fact, it can be argued that some of these Italian city-states led the way when it came to the creation of the sovereign state, in many respects, even though they lacked kings. In Central Europe, particularly in what was euphemistically called the Holy Roman Empire, which was headed by an emperor who had little real power, one could find a bewildering array of political entities, ranging from kingdoms, such as those of Bavaria and Hungary, to principalities, such as Saxony and Hesse, to free cities that ruled themselves, such as Augsburg and Ulm—each of which took its own approach to sovereignty.

Different states, different approaches, but similar developments. By gaining a greater degree of sovereignty in the late fifteenth century, Western European states made it possible for changes or for new political, social, economic, and religious arrangements to take hold in isolated spots, and to endure. As sovereignty increased, so did the chances for polarization. Whether as kingdoms or republics, sovereign states were gaining the capacity to claim their own identity, steer their own course, and resist outside interference, even from the pope in Rome. And this is precisely what made it possible for Christendom to disintegrate. By 1515 Western Europe was no longer an assemblage of various peoples linked by a common religion and a common feudal sociopolitical structure. Europe was a collection of states, each capable of going its own way, and each capable of fighting for itself and its traditions, and capable of creating its own churches, in defiance of Rome.

In summary, by 1515 conditions were ripe for a perfect storm.

CHAPTER TWO

Religion in Late Medieval Christendom

An Age of Faith?

The celebration of the Mass had just begun in the parish church of Yébenes, a small town near Toledo, in Spain. It was the penitential season of Lent, when everyone was supposed to abstain from food, drink, and sex, and to amend their sinful behavior. Suddenly, two women began shouting at each other very loudly, drowning out the Latin prayers of the priest at the altar. One of the women, María Fernández, struck the other woman on the head with a wooden plank, gashing her head. The injured woman, Ana Díaz, lunged at María, shrieking. As the priest stood silent and motionless at the altar, some in the congregation rushed to stop the fight; soon enough the women were restrained, and the Mass resumed. Days later, when Ana and María were hauled into court, they admitted that they had fought over a seat in church. Court records tell us that the two women formally pardoned each other, and that they were fined and admonished to keep the peace.[1]

Two women fighting over a seat in church, drawing blood in the presence of the sacred during Lent, apparently for reasons of status and privilege: What does this event tell us about religion in early modern Europe? Or about what preceded it in medieval times? What does it tell us about the place of religion in any culture? What does it reveal about the Europe that was once united in a common faith and could call itself Christendom?

These are leading questions, and to some extent also unsound. Faith is difficult to measure, even impossible. Seemingly divergent or even contradictory values can coexist in any culture. Faith and religious values are hard to assess in any culture at any point in history, but even more so in the premodern world, when religion was interwoven into nearly all facets of daily life.

To say that premodern Western European culture was deeply religious or that all Western Europeans once lived in "an age of faith" is not to say that Europeans were necessarily pious, or that they lived up to their ideals, or that they believed in the doctrines professed by their church. In many ways, religion functioned as a means of communication, not just with the invisible divine realm, but also among all Western Christians. Religion made all human interaction intelligible according to certain set values—it helped people to make sense of life and to impose order on the world. Above all, religion was simply there. It was inescapable. Everyone had to be baptized into the same church, and to observe its laws. The only exception to this rule was the Jews, who were always a small minority. Some kingdoms, such as France and England, did not even have any Jews at all after expelling them en masse. In parts of medieval Spain and the Balkans one could find some Muslims, too, but in general, their existence was an anomaly within Christendom. King and pauper alike defined their place in society and their daily experience according to the teachings and rituals of a common faith and a common institution—the church.

Compulsory Christianity.
Membership in the Catholic Church began at baptism, a rite performed on all infants. Other rites of passage, or sacraments, ensured continual engagement with religion throughout life, as well as an unavoidable need for the clergy who performed the essential rituals. By 1215, the Catholic Church had identified seven sacraments as necessary for salvation. This altarpiece painting by Roger van der Weyden (1445–1450) depicts three of them. From left to right: baptism, received once in infancy; confirmation, received once in late childhood; and penance, or the confessing of one's sins to a priest, which was required at least once a year throughout one's adult life. The other two panels of the altarpiece depicted the remaining four: the Eucharist, a daily rite that offered communion with the body and blood of Christ; marriage, which was expected of most adults; holy orders, which consecrated as priests those men who received it; and extreme unction, administered to all who were at death's door.

Because it was always there, touching all aspects of life through myth, symbol, ritual, and ethics, religion could always be ignored or twisted to meet one's own needs. And because religion was everywhere, encompassing all aspects of life, the profane and the sacred intermingled, sometimes to the point at which boundaries dissolved.

The two feuding women just mentioned reveal to us that the sacred and the profane were two sides of the same coin. In the very presence of the holy, within the sacred precincts of a church, while attempting to engage in the practice of their religion, women could fight over a seat. They were not supposed to act that way according to their religion, but they did. Extend this seemingly contradictory pattern of behavior to society at large, and we can come closer to understanding the place of religion in late medieval and early modern Europe. Premodern Europeans lived in a world full of para-doxes and contradictions. The ultimate values offered to them were derived largely from the Christian religion, through a single church, but values and behavior could often be at odds, since each individual could embrace values differently.

Such is the natural order of religion and everything touched by it. Religious values are abstract and concrete, absolute and relative, static and fluid, powerful and impotent, priceless and worthless, everything and nothing. Religious values are paradoxi-cal, like religion itself. They strain to transcend the constraints of earthly life, but they are directly embedded in these limitations, and embodied in the irascible wills of human beings, who often bend values or redefine them to suit their needs. Religious values are a coincidence of opposites, a representation of what is unseen, a mingling of the human and the divine, the natural and the supernatural, flesh and spirit. Religious values, like promises, are pure wishes; like ritual, they speak in the subjunctive mood and tell of what should be.

And in late medieval Europe, the central values were all religious—or at least they were supposed to be.

Religion in the Late Middle Ages

Experts on late medieval European religion tend to agree that there was a definite upsurge in piety and that nonclerics became more active than ever in shaping and living out their religion. But this is where agreement ends. Some historians see this increased lay fervor as hollow and anxious, and ripe for reform;[2] others see it as robust and satisfying.[3] Some perceive the clergy and their flocks as sharing a common piety;[4] others detect a great gulf between them.[5] Where some discern genuine Christian fervor, others find far too many surviving pre-Christian elements.[6] Some have gone as far as to argue that much of late medieval religion was "magical,"[7] while others propose that Europe was not truly "Christianized" until the sixteenth century.[8]

These different points of view can be seen as reflections of ideological differences, some of which date back to the sixteenth century, some of which are more recent. All of these interpretations have something to do with larger questions about the meaning of history, and about the relation between religion and culture. Reconciling them is impossible, and also unnecessary. When it comes to understanding the great religious upheaval of the sixteenth century, all we need to keep in mind is the inescapable fact that religion was as symbiotically linked to politics, social structures, culture, the economy, and even the climate as all these other factors were to another. It was a symbiosis as intense and complex as that found among components of an ecosystem: all changes and developments were somehow related to one another. Whether religious life was sincere or hollow, vibrant or anxious, nearly pagan or truly Christian is beside the point. All experts seem to agree: at the turn of the fifteenth century religion was an integral part of life into which Western Europeans were investing much of their time, energy, and resources.

But what was this religion like? Outlining its beliefs may not be the best way to provide a thumbnail description, for beliefs take us into the private realm of the heart and mind: they are shared unevenly and cannot be precisely described or measured. Rather, let us approach religion from a more practical angle. Piety—the living out of religion—was shared in common by all Europeans, at least in public, and can be fathomed more readily.

The religion shared officially by all Western European Christians sought to establish links between earth and heaven, body and soul, the human and the divine, the living and the dead, and also between neighbors. Religion was more practical than theoretical: though informed by the theology of the church, it was not focused as much on thinking about beliefs, or on myth, as on rituals, symbols, and ethics. Behavior was the stuff of religion, along with the search for protection and deliverance from mundane ills. In addition, the body and its five senses were strongly involved in the central Christian promise of redemption. The world was continually in the process of being sacralized, that is, of being brought into contact with the divine. This sacralization took place in multiple interlocking spheres of behavior, all of which were seamlessly woven into the fabric of daily life.

The Social Structure

Though there were many local variants, all of late medieval Western Christendom shared some basic traits in regard to social structure. One way of understanding medieval society views it as divided into three basic classes: those who fought (the nobility), those who labored (farmers, artisans, and merchants), and those who prayed (the clergy).[9] An even more basic division, as far as religion is concerned, sees it as composed of two classes: the clergy and the laity.

From its earliest days, the Christian religion distinguished between those who held religious authority, in a direct line of succession from Jesus and his apostles, and those who did not. In Western Christendom those with religious authority came to be known as clerics, or collectively as the clergy.[10] Everyone who was not a cleric came to be known as a *lay* person, and collectively, as the laity, a term that reveals its utter simplicity in its Greek origin, *laos*, or *laikos*, "the people."

The distinction between clerical and lay, though somewhat blurry and controversial at times, dominated much of religious life, in theory as well as in practice. Whether they performed key rituals deemed necessary for salvation, or defined and guarded beliefs, or simply prayed for society at large, the clergy were supposedly in charge of "the people," leading them to salvation. In the practice of religion, the clergy were not just the gatekeepers to heaven, they were those who made religion their profession—a truism confirmed by the fact that clerics were known as *religiosi*, that is, "the religious." But this distinction was not as simple as it seems, for "the people," or laity, defined the very existence and purpose of the clergy. Because the laity and clergy were intrinsically linked, and shared the same myths, rituals, and symbols, the religious life of the laity was never distinct from or totally independent of the clergy, or vice versa. In late medieval and early modern Europe, lay Christians could take the lead in the observance of religion, although the clergy were always somehow involved, directly or indirectly. Any religious practice that excluded the clergy ran the risk of being judged by them as wrong, or, as in the case of witchcraft, even demonic.

This binary division between clerical and lay, or clergy and people, extended to all of society, and also to the relation between the authority of the church and that of civil rulers. Although all Christians belonged to the church together, it was the clergy who embodied the church most concretely in everyone's mind, so much so that in common parlance, even to this day, some continue to speak of the clergy as "the church." In one way, this conflation made sense, for the clergy ran the church. They were the interpreters of its beliefs, the ministers of its rituals, the guardians of its symbols, the custodians of its ethics. Their job was to stand in the place of Christ and make salvation possible. Poised between heaven and earth, they ostensibly held everyone's eternal fate in their hands.

The fact that he clergy ostensibly dealt with the realm of the spiritual and eternal gave them an otherworldly status, above the laity. In theory, they were *in* the world, but not *of* the world. By the twelfth century the terms *temporal* and *secular* had already come to denote anything related to the world beyond the church, that is, anything that was not spiritual, or sacred, or anything that concerned earthly time rather than eternity. This distinction was applied most directly to questions of power and privilege, especially in regard to the political authority held by civil rulers.

As much as the clergy tried to distinguish between the sacred and the secular, or to claim power or privilege in the name of God, the line between the two realms could never be drawn very clearly, which often led to conflicts between "the church" and "the world," that is, between the clergy and lay rulers. But in all such conflicts, no matter how exalted the claims of the clerics, or how precise their distinction between sacred and secular, a tangible difference often held sway: the secular realm could employ brute force, and the clerics could not. Unlike the secular powers, the clergy did not normally have armies or weapons; when physically abused by soldiers with real swords, the clergy could employ only a spiritual weapon: the threat of damnation. And even then, the clergy were at a disadvantage, for their exalted claims stemmed from lofty responsibilities, and one of their principal functions was to forgive those who repented. While being hacked to pieces, the clergy were supposed to pray for their enemies. Even worse, if their adversaries sought forgiveness, they had to pardon them.

Beyond the basic distinction between clergy and laity, the structure of the clerical class itself was immensely complex, perhaps even more so than that of the laity. The clergy were arranged according to rank—a hierarchy ostensibly devised by Jesus himself. At the very apex of the clerical hierarchy stood the pope (Latin: *papa*, "father"), who claimed to be the direct successor of the apostle Simon Peter, to whom Jesus had given supreme authority in Matthew's gospel, with the words that are inscribed in gigantic gold letters inside the dome of St. Peter's Basilica in Rome: "You are Peter, and upon this rock I shall build my church, and the powers of death shall not prevail against it. I will give you the keys of the kingdom of heaven, and whatever you bind on earth shall be bound in heaven, and whatever you loose on earth shall be loosed in heaven."[11] Directly under the pope, the role of the other eleven apostles was continued by *bishops*, a title derived from the Greek *episkopos*, "overseer," which is found in the New Testament, in the letters of St. Paul. Below the bishops (collectively known as the *episcopate*), priests fulfilled the role of the *presbyters* or *elders*, also mentioned in the New Testament.

Though the pope, the bishops, and the priests all shared in the same ministry, presiding over the rituals of the church, only the pope claimed supreme authority, and only the bishops could consecrate new priests. Each bishop had jurisdiction over a specific territory, known as a *diocese*, which in turn was subdivided into smaller units known as *parishes*, which were administered by priests. The pope, too, was a bishop. Ancient tradition had it that St. Peter had been the first bishop of Rome, and that he was martyred and buried on the Vatican Hill. Consequently, the bishops of Rome claimed to be his successors, and gradually expanded the claims they made for the seat of Peter, or the apostolic *see* (Latin: *sedes*). The early medieval popes referred to themselves as "vicars of Peter," but by the twelfth century, they began to use the title "vicar of Christ." By the fifteenth century, despite many setbacks and dismal shortcomings, the pope at Rome could claim universal jurisdiction over all of Christendom, even over the whole world. When Spain and Portugal needed to agree on how to share all of the "new" lands they were beginning to discover, it was none other than Pope Alexander VI—a Spaniard from Valencia—who rendered a decision, by drawing a vertical line of demarcation from pole to pole down the middle of the Atlantic Ocean, and granting Spain dominion to the west and Portugal to the east of the line. Thus, through what came to be known as the Treaty of Tordesillas (1494), a pope made himself the arbiter of who would own the world. It matters little that Alexander VI neglected to draw a corresponding line down the middle of the Pacific Ocean, and that other European nation states ignored the pope's claims. Popes had a long history of claiming more authority than they could ever exercise in "the world."

The clerical class was much more complex than the trifold division of pope, bishops, and priests might suggest. The episcopate consisted not only of bishops, but also of archbishops and cardinals, who stood higher up in the hierarchy. Originally, the cardinals were Roman clergy who assisted the popes, but by the tenth century they had risen in stature and expanded beyond Rome, turning into an elite corps within the episcopate, appointed directly by the pope, and enjoying exclusive privileges. When a pope died, it was the College of Cardinals who elected a new pope, usually from their own ranks. In addition to parochial churches and parish priests, there were also collegiate churches and priests known as canons, who could be independent of episcopal jurisdiction or, in many cases, enjoyed a privileged relationship with their bishop, and minor clergy, such as deacons, porters, lectors, and crucifers, who were often men on their way to becoming priests.

As if this were not bewildering enough, the clergy were divided into two very distinct groups: *secular* and *regular*. The secular clergy, whose name seems to be an oxymoron or a contradiction, were those who lived in "the world," among the laity to whom they ministered. The secular clergy were directly under episcopal jurisdiction, in the parish churches, as the historical descendants of the ancient presbyters. The regular clergy were the monastics, the descendants of the ancient Christians who had fled into the desert and established isolated communities. The original monks had little to do with "the world." In fact, the very first monks had been hermits, and the origin of the term *monk* is the Greek word for one who is alone, *monos*. But by the fourth century, monks began to gather into communities, and that way of life became normative. These men came to be known as "regular" clergy because they followed a written *rule* (Latin: *regula*). Originally, the regular clergy were all monks, that is, men who took vows of poverty, celibacy, and obedience; devoted their lives to prayer; and lived behind the walls in a cloister, under the authority of an abbot (Hebrew: *abba*, "father") rather than a bishop. As the centuries wore on, however, variations on the monastic lifestyle developed, and some monastics began to minister to the laity in "the world." Many, but not all, of these monastics with a public ministry were known as *friars* (French: *frère*, "brother"). By the thirteenth century, regular clergy were preaching, teaching, and taking care of the sick and poor throughout Christendom. Many had churches in the towns and cities, often cheek by jowl with the parish churches of the secular clergy. Since monastics were usually exempt from episcopal authority, jurisdictional problems could easily arise between bishops and the regular clergy within their dioceses.

Throughout the Middle Ages, monastics bound by a common rule developed into *orders*, that is, communities with their own distinctive dress, way of life, and authority structure. Orders functioned very much like present-day business franchises, making available on a local level a standardized, universal set of behaviors and services. Just as one knows what to expect nowadays when one walks into a McDonald's restaurant anywhere on earth, one would have known what to expect when one entered a Benedictine, Carthusian, Cistercian, or Franciscan house anywhere in Christendom. By the fifteenth century, the number of orders had proliferated wildly, dotting the landscape with a wide variety of monastic communities, each of which had its own rule and authority structure.

And that is not all. Though monastics were part of the clerical class, not all monastics were priests, for becoming a priest was not universally required. And there were also female monastics, known in English as "nuns," who existed in a liminal state, poised somewhere between lay and clerical status. Since women could not become priests or receive any of the "minor" orders that would grant them clerical status—such as that of deacon—their identity and their roles remained distinct from those of the male regular clergy. This is not to say that the liminal status of the nuns left them powerless in relation to the male clergy or the world at large. Female monastics often exercised moral authority and engaged in charismatic leadership beyond their cloister walls, especially if they were perceived as holy. One of the best examples is St. Catherine of Siena (1347–1388), a very young Dominican nun who settled disputes, negotiated peace treaties, and corresponded with bishops and the pope directly, giving advice, and even scolding when she deemed it necessary. In a world in which men held tight to the reins of power, entering the liminal state of the female *religious* could often be the only way a woman could claim authority and a measure of autonomy.

In sum, although it is certainly appropriate to speak of "the church" as a single entity within medieval Christendom, and also to speak of "the clergy," the fact remains that this church was no monolithic institution, but rather a dizzying assemblage of units managed by clerics with overlapping and sometimes conflicting authority. Popes may have claimed supreme power, but they were in fact often hemmed in or stymied by

Mystical authority. Though nuns were not part of the Catholic Church's hierarchy, holy women such as St. Catherine of Siena could exert substantial authority, even reprimand popes. In this fifteenth-century depiction of St. Catherine by Giovanni di Paulo, she is in direct contact with the divine, dictating to a subservient male monk.

secular rulers or their own clergy when they attempted to exert their authority. Cardinals, bishops, abbots, priors, canons, vicars, curates, monks, and friars each exercised their authority to varying degrees, and often with no small amount of conflict or negotiation—either among themselves or with the laity. Thinking of all the clergy as an elite is not entirely wrong, insofar as they claimed a higher status than the laity, and insofar as a good number of the canons, abbots, and bishops came from the higher ranks of lay society. But their claims, no matter how exalted, could not undo economic and political realities. Status and power varied wildly among the clergy themselves, and, further, in relation to the social hierarchy of "the world." An illiterate or barely literate curate of a poor rural parish could hardly be considered one of the "elite" when compared to a titled noble, or a rich merchant, or even a successful brewer.

In the long run, given the somewhat bewildering organization of the church—the result of fifteen centuries of tradition and haphazard development—it can be argued that Christendom was bound together more by the piety of the church than through its authority structure. Naturally, institutional structure, clergy, and piety were tightly intertwined, but piety was a more constant part of life for the laity, and arguably their most personal engagement with religion, regardless of fervor or faith. Let us now turn to religion as it was lived, keeping in mind that every universal custom or pattern had its local variations.

Late Medieval Piety
Sacred Rites

The rites of the church known as sacraments, which were conducted by its priests, were the basic structure of piety and the framework for devotion. Though early medieval theologians did not always agree on which rites should be considered sacraments, by the thirteenth century, the Catholic Church had defined the sacraments clearly and set their number at seven. In 1439, these seven sacraments were definitively proclaimed: baptism, confirmation, penance, the Eucharist, marriage, ordination as a cleric, and extreme unction (also known as the last rites). These rites served specific functions for each individual and the community as a whole: initiation (baptism), purification and sanctification (penance), transitions in life (confirmation, marriage, ordination, extreme unction), and communion with the divine (the Eucharist).

Sacraments that were rites of initiation and transition were received once in a lifetime—or just a few times, in special cases regarding marriage (for widows and widowers) and extreme unction (for those who recovered from a close brush with death). Women were barred from receiving the sacrament of orders, since ordination to the priesthood was restricted to males. Penance and the Eucharist were constantly celebrated. The rite of penance, which offered forgiveness of sins, entailed confessing all one's misdeeds to a priest. Though the church taught that this sacrament should be received at least once every year, most lay people went to confession very few times, and preferred to make one final confession at the time of death. This is not to say that the sacrament of confession was not taken seriously. On the contrary, it has been argued that this sacrament weighed heavily upon the laity, inspiring more fear than solace.

The Eucharist was the most densely encoded Catholic ritual and the centerpiece of all piety. The celebration of this sacrament took place within the ritual, or liturgy, commonly called "the Mass," during which, according to the teaching of the church, the sacrifice of Christ on the cross was made present again and the bread and wine consecrated by the priest were miraculously transformed into the body and blood of Christ, and offered for consumption by the faithful. Though the laity attended Mass regularly, especially on Sundays and feast days, to pray and witness the consecration of the bread and wine, very few people actually partook of the physical communion with God offered to them in this sacrament. In addition, while the priests partook of both bread and wine, the laity were allowed to receive only the bread, in the form of unleavened wafers that were referred to as "hosts" (from the Latin *hostia*, or "sacrificial victim").

Though lay communion was rare, the Mass still played a pivotal role in piety. As the most frequently celebrated rite, the Mass brought communities together for prayer, instruction, and celebration more often than any other ritual. As an enactment of the deepest mysteries of the faith, expressed symbolically, the Mass allowed the laity to experience repeatedly a synthesis of the ultimate Christian values they ostensibly shared. As the ultimate ritual in which the divine was addressed and made present, the liturgy of the Mass also acquired a therapeutic value. Masses known as "votive" could be offered to ward off or correct as many ills as can befall the human race: to protect crops from hail, to be spared by plagues, to prevent evil thoughts or lust, and even to help find lost objects.

The Mass also loomed large for yet another reason. Because every Mass was believed to transcend time and space, and to link all Christians, past and present, to Christ's sacrifice on the cross, this liturgy also assumed a practical spiritual and social function connecting the living and the dead. Theologically, masses for the dead lessened the time spent in purgatory by the souls of the deceased; practically, these masses functioned on various levels to cement relations among kin and neighbors. By the fifteenth century, masses for the dead had become a key element of piety throughout Europe.

Within and beyond the ritual of the Mass, the consecrated bread also became a focus of devotion. Because the church taught that Christ was made physically present in the eucharistic bread and wine, the Mass itself, and the consecrated bread, especially, became the supreme *locus divinitatis*, the ultimate materialization of the divine. If each consecrated host was indeed God, then devotion to this sacred object seemed right and just. Consecrated hosts were displayed for adoration in a special vessel known as a monstrance, which could be set up inside the church, or taken out for processions. Hosts were believed to work wonders, especially when denigrated by skeptics, heretics, and infidels. Reports of eucharistic miracles sharply increased in the fifteenth century, as did the number of shrines built to revere hosts that reportedly bled, levitated, or impaired their would-be assailants. It was also during the fifteenth century that the yearly feast devoted to the

The Eucharist as a constant miracle. Every celebration of the Mass was believed to make Christ physically present. One of the most popular themes of late medieval art was that of the Mass of St. Gregory, which depicted a seventh-century miracle in which Pope Gregory the Great saw the bleeding body of Christ at the altar, along with his cross and all the implements employed in his crucifixion.

Eucharist, Corpus Christi, or Domini, which had been established in 1264, assumed an especially privileged place on the Christian calendar. This summer feast was observed in towns and cities with pageants, mystery plays, and grand processions that sought to include the whole community, and especially its elites. On Corpus Christi day, the focus of devotion was the consecrated host that processed through the streets, sacralizing the world outside the churches.

Piety was significantly affected by the fact that throughout Western Europe, all of this sacramental ritual was conducted in Latin. This uniformity in the language of ritual made the church more universal and bound together a vast array of disparate cultures. Though Latin was an alien tongue for most of the laity, especially in Central, Northern, and Eastern Europe, this language barrier did not necessarily make the ritual incomprehensible; rather, it made it intelligible in a different manner, surrounding it with an aura of mystery and holiness. Latin was also the language of the theologians, the clergy, and the church hierarchy, who ultimately supported their claims to authority with texts from sacred scripture in Latin. The Bible itself was available only in St. Jerome's fifth-century Latin translation, known as the Vulgate, which was considered a holy text, divinely inspired and error-free. Latin assumed a sacred and mystical quality—an attribute that constantly made manifest the different identities of the clergy and the laity.

Sacred Space

Though the sacred and profane were deeply intertwined in late medieval religion, the world itself was not seen as an indistinct plane where all space was equally numinous. On the contrary, one of the most salient traits of medieval piety was the keen fixation on specific earthly points that were believed to be closer to heaven. Because it was generally assumed that the divine manifested itself more fully in certain places, people, and objects, space itself assumed a hierarchical order in Catholic piety. Consequently, much of religious life revolved around the processes of identifying, confirming, approaching, and venerating those special junctures between heaven and earth, and of seeking to tap the supernatural power that was believed to reside in specific loci, with the hopes of obtaining specific favors. In brief, piety was strongly inclined to localize the divine, make it tangible, and harness its power.

The most basic spatial distinction was that between sacred and mundane space. Churches were the most obvious, and most numerous, sacred sites. Every church was the house of God, and a nexus between heaven and earth, principally because God made himself present in all his houses through the celebration of the Eucharist (the Mass). But not all churches were equally prominent on the spiritual map. Divine power was believed to reside more strongly in churches where certain saints and martyrs were buried, or where divine apparitions and visions had taken place, or in churches that housed certain sacred objects. These special churches, known as shrines, could draw worshipers from near and far. More often than not, shrines were places where miracles were expected and sought out. The promise of healings—more often physical rather than spiritual—filled the map of Europe with tens of thousands of urban and rural shrines.

The sacred spaces of churches and shrines were themselves differentiated. The altars where Mass was celebrated and the tabernacles where consecrated hosts were kept were especially holy. Large church buildings that had several side chapels and altars had many such foci, but they also had a main altar, which was the central visual focus and usually also the sacred axis. Saints' graves and their relics were also singularly sacred and powerful. Relics were the physical traces of human beings who had died and gone to heaven; as such, they localized the divine. Devotion to relics had been part of the Christian religion since its earliest days, when the remains of martyrs began to be enshrined and venerated. By the fifteenth century, the cult of relics was deeply woven into the fabric of piety, and thriving. But for every genuine relic, there seemed to be many of doubtful origin. Remnants of the true cross of Christ could be found nearly everywhere; the head of John the Baptist was revered in at least seven different shrines; fragments and entire bodies of the apostles were claimed simultaneously in unlikely places. Geneva, for instance, boasted of having the brain of St. Peter, whose body was entombed in Rome. Some among the clergy and laity apparently resolved these conflicting claims by believing that God miraculously multiplied relics for the benefit of humankind. By the fifteenth century, however, some of the more educated were no longer willing to accept such reasoning.

In addition to relics, churches also contained sacred paintings and statues, and piety was intensely focused on these objects. Sacred images were visual representations of the holy: like relics, they localized and made present the divine. Images were not just the *libri pauperum*, or books of the poor and illiterate, as some of the clergy taught; they were also the focus of veneration. Though the official theology of the church distinguished between worship offered to God alone (*latria*) and reverence (*dulia*) shown to images, this distinction was ambiguously understood and observed in piety. People knelt and bowed as they prayed before images, burned candles and incense, or offered flowers to them. Images also extended sacred space beyond the church, for they could be set up and venerated in public spaces or within the home. More significant, images stamped on wax or metal could be worn on one's body, not just in remembrance, but for personal protection, as private points of contact with heaven.

Because the laity often commissioned sacred art, it has long been considered an index of popular devotion: the subjects represented in art and the quantity of commissions reveal much about the content and intensity of religious fervor. Sacred art was funded in various ways. Often, it was the clergy themselves who commissioned the artists. Kings and nobles made a heavy investment in sacred art too. By the fifteenth century, much of the religious art produced throughout Christendom came from the laity, and not just from rich and powerful families. Communal associations such as trade guilds, chantries, and confraternities pooled their resources to commission art. As the European economy recovered from the devastation of the Black Death (1348–1349), more and more money began to be invested in the creation of sacred art. By all accounts, the fifteenth century

Localizing the divine. Pilgrimage was an essential part of medieval Catholic ritual, and it served multiple functions: as an expression of devotion, a means of doing penance, a way of bargaining with God and the saints ("If you grant my petitions, I will visit your shrine"), and as a way of seeking cures for physical, mental, and spiritual ailments. Here we see pilgrims at the shrine of the Schöne Maria (Beautiful Mary) in Regensburg on the eve of the Protestant Reformation. This was a relatively new and somewhat slapdash shrine, built on the site of a destroyed Jewish synagogue. The shrine gained immense popularity quickly when healing miracles were reported in the early part of the sixteenth century. This 1519 engraving by Michael Ostendorfer depicts a frenzied mob displaying extreme gestures that some reform-minded intellectuals considered improper. The edifice depicted here would eventually be replaced with one much more grandiose.

stands out as a time of unparalleled growth for religious painting and sculpture. And there is plenty of evidence pointing to an even more astonishing investment in the early sixteenth century, even in the most unlikely places. To cite but one example: in the city of Zurich, which would ban religious art and destroy all of it in 1524, the commissioning of sacred art works had increased a hundredfold between 1500 and 1518.

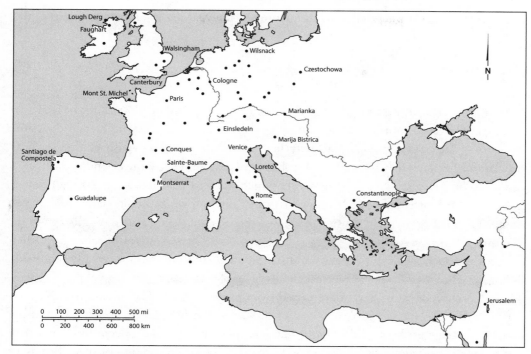

Major pilgrimage sites. Some shrines were local, some regional, and some truly international. This map shows the location of some of the most significant pilgrimage sites in medieval Christendom. Those identified by name drew high numbers of pilgrims.

Ritual had a place outdoors too, and so did symbols. Pilgrimages were a way of sanctifying space through movement. The very process of traveling to a holy site was both a means of devotion and a sacralizing gesture. Pilgrimages could cover short distances, to a local shrine, or require incredibly long journeys to a distant holy place, such as Jerusalem, Rome, or Santiago de Compostela. These trips were undertaken for all sorts of reasons, and especially as a means of fulfilling vows or atoning for sins, but as anyone who has read *The Canterbury Tales* knows, pilgrims were not necessarily devout, and pilgrimages could be anything but an act of genuine penance.

The most common type of outdoor ritual was the procession, especially in those parts of Christendom with temperate climates. Processions usually took place during feast days or on special occasions. These parades sought to sanctify mundane space temporarily as carefully structured group journeys that emerged from churches and shrines and made a circuit within definite boundaries, filling the streets and squares through which they moved with prayers and sacred music. Some processions were broken up with pauses, others were continuous; some were brief, others long. Most processions involved the conveying of sacred objects. Some were held to celebrate fixed feasts, others to deal with crises such as plagues or drought. Pilgrimages and processions were a means of appealing for divine favors or forgiveness. On a social level, they were a means of forging group identity, as well as of confirming or establishing the rank and status of the participants.

Sacred Time

Space was not the only grid upon which sacred locations could be plotted, for heaven and earth were believed to intersect differently at specific times, sanctifying certain days and seasons on the calendar. Medieval piety had a rhythmic quality—with endless cyclical oscillations between feasting and fasting that were determined by the calendar.

The shortest cycle was the week, which marked off Sunday as a sacred day, a holy time when attendance at Mass was required, and all work should cease. Feasts that marked certain events in salvation history were observed universally by all the faithful. Among these were Epiphany, Good Friday, Easter, Pentecost, and Christmas. Other major feasts such as Corpus Christi and All Saints' Day were also universally observed. Saints were honored on the anniversary of their deaths, according to the church calendar. The celebration of saints' feast days varied from place to place. The midsummer feast of John the Baptist, for instance, was one of the more widely observed. Each community and even each parish or guild would have its own special feasts, according to which saints were considered patrons. Feasts were marked by the celebration of special masses, processions, and public celebrations. Evidence suggests that religious feasts could often turn into riotous occasions in which lines dissolved between the sacred and profane.

In addition to Sundays and feast days, the calendar also marked off certain seasons. The Christmas season, which celebrated the birth of Jesus, and the Easter season, which celebrated his resurrection, were both marked by joyous celebrations. But feasting was always preceded by fasting. Each of these two major feasts came at the end of long periods in which fasting was required: the four weeks of Advent in December and the forty days of Lent in late winter and early spring. Fasting was a penitential exercise that aimed to tame the sinful instincts of the flesh, to atone for sins, and to soften God's wrath in times of plague, war, and famine.

Feasting and fasting were a perpetual rhythm of piety, often well balanced, but sometimes discordant and prone to extreme swings. Within this dialectic, religion and irreligion could become thoroughly mixed. Throughout much of Europe, for instance, the penitential season of Lent was preceded by days or weeks of feasting, a time known as Carnival, which was not officially on the church calendar. Carnival was a celebration of indulgence in food, drink, and sex: it was the total inversion of Lent, and a paradoxical constant in piety.

Sacred Bonds

Social relations, too, were sacralized to a considerable extent, and in myriad ways. Nearly every aspect of communal life involved some sort of ritual, nearly every relation, bond, and association required sanctification. Dealings with one's king, magistrate, and neighbor were framed, at least formally, in religious terms. For instance, monarchs and other civil rulers were installed in their offices and granted authority through religious ceremonies, which usually involved consecration at the hands of the clergy and the swearing of oaths. Some monarchs, such as the kings of France and England, claimed that their consecration imbued them with sacredness and even gave them healing powers; before the thirteenth century, some theologians even thought of the consecration of rulers as a sacrament. Initiating craftsmen into guilds, closing contracts, signing pacts and treaties, writing last wills and testaments, and testifying in court were all routine social interactions that required some ritual act, though not necessarily the presence of the clergy. In such a sacralized society, outward conformity to Christian piety could be required as a matter of routine, with or without sincerity. Needless to say, the frequency and ubiquity of such formalized ritual in human relations during this period poses problems for anyone who is trying to assess devotion or discern religious values.

Beyond what was required, however, laity and clergy alike participated in relationships that further enhanced the religious bonds of community, and even transcended time and space. Being a member of the Catholic Church meant belonging to a community that extended way beyond one's locality and even one's nation; it also meant belonging to a community composed of both the living and the dead. The same bond that linked Christians over vast distances and across frontiers also linked them across time itself. Consequently, a distinctive feature of late medieval piety was the commerce between those on earth and those in the afterlife: the saints in heaven were sought out as patrons and intercessors, and the souls in purgatory were showered with attention. Bonds and obligations linked heaven, earth, and purgatory: the dead could intercede for the living, the living for the dead. The time and money spent in this commerce by the laity could be substantial.

Relations with the saints could assume a contractual and legal nature. Since heaven was conceived of as a court, and God as a king and judge, patrons were deemed essential. As in an earthly court, the supreme throne was not to be approached directly, but rather through intermediaries and advocates. Communities and individuals established client-patron relationships with the saints, and their association could take on a distinctively transactional quality. The laity routinely sought favors from patrons by means of pledges, or vows, which usually involved the performing of some act of reverence if the favor was granted. Many local celebrations of saints' feasts were, in fact, established through such vows.

In the fifteenth century the cult of the saints expanded in various ways: with the creation of chapels and shrines, the donation of images, and, after 1455, the printing of hagiographies (lives of the saints), miracle accounts, and prayer books. As the cult expanded, so did the patronage system whereby saints were assigned special spheres of influence over particular social groups and specific needs. The most popular saint of all—and the one believed to be the most effective advocate—was the Virgin Mary,

Mother of God and Queen of Heaven. Paradoxically, Mary was the most universal saint, revered everywhere, but also the most local, for she was often assigned a regional persona, especially at shrines where miraculous images were venerated, where she was known as "Our Lady of such-and-such a place . . ." as at Montserrat in Catalonia, or Chartres in France, or Walsingham in England.

Among the living, the bonds of Christian fellowship were further enhanced through baptism, which required that every infant have godparents, who were not necessarily blood relations. The social ties established through being godparents created a wider kinship, and a more intricate network of relations in every community, for by the Late Middle Ages godparents came to be considered legal relatives.

Bonds were also strengthened by the formation of smaller, special-interest societies known as confraternities (also called brotherhoods, guilds, or sodalities). Confraternities could include both men and women, and sometimes children. Membership was voluntary, and each confraternity usually devoted itself to a narrow range of devotional activities. Their objectives varied widely but always involved the fulfillment of both spiritual and physical needs. On the spiritual side, fellowship and communal prayer were a large part of confraternity life, as were processions. Confraternities established and perpetuated certain types of devotion, or set up chapels and shrines. They often guaranteed that none of their members would ever die alone, for attendance was required at the deathbed and funeral of every member. Confraternities could also take on an intercessory function by performing acts of expiation, to purify and protect the larger community. The most common penitential practice among confraternities was the flagellant procession, in which the members would march together along a prescribed route whipping themselves. The services of flagellant or other penitents were considered especially useful when God was perceived to be angry over a community's sins, such as in times of plague or famine. During the devastation wrought by the Black Death, for instance, flagellant processions attracted thousands of penitents in some places.

On the physical side, most confraternities were involved in charitable work. Confraternities could specialize in caring for the sick, meeting the needs of the poor and homeless, or burying the dead. Confraternities were not only the living conscience of Christian Europe, but also its sturdiest social safety net. Until the sixteenth century, in much of Europe, the poor, ill, and needy were most often assisted by confraternities rather than by the clergy or civil authorities. Membership in a confraternity ensured one of fellowship and assistance, as well as of the spiritual merits earned by acts of charity and devotion. In a clerically dominated society, it may have also offered the laity an opportunity to take the initiative, and to express a relative degree of spiritual independence. Each confraternity drew up its own set of ordinances, or rules, written by lay people for lay people who wanted to take charge of their life of devotion. It stands to reason, then, that much of the scholarship on lay piety has focused on confraternity life. At one extreme, some have argued that confraternal ordinances had a greater influence on the shaping of the Christian conscience of Europe than sermons, and that they should be considered a genuine expression of lay piety. At the other extreme, there are plenty of studies that take a functionalist approach, viewing confraternities as clubs that chiefly met mundane social needs related to identity and status. Disagreements aside, however, it remains beyond dispute that confraternities could meet both spiritual and temporal needs.

Sacred Behavior

Religion meant much more than attendance at public rituals, or the profession of certain beliefs: it involved *undertaking* certain kinds of behavior and *avoiding* others in two spheres: private devotion and ethics.

Private devotion consisted primarily of the recitation of prayers and of pious reading. The illiterate had access to texts only when they were read out loud to them. The prayer life of the laity consisted mainly of the repetition of short orations that were memorized in childhood, especially the Pater Noster (Our Father, or Lord's Prayer), the Ave Maria (Hail Mary), the Gloria (Glory Be), and the Credo (I Believe, or Creed).

On the whole, then, prayers tended to be fixed formulae, repeatedly recited over an entire lifetime. Number and repetition were key. One of the more popular devotions among the laity was the rosary: a ring of beads arranged as numerical sets that marked a specific number of Ave Marias, Pater Nosters, and Glorias. Extemporaneous prayer was possible but uncommon among the laity. The literate laity had access to a wider range of prayers in books known as primers or *horae* (books of hours); some of them even had access to breviaries, books intended for the clergy that contained the biblical readings, psalms, hymns, and prayers that were to be recited or sung at specific times each day of the year. These books did not encourage improvisation in prayer; on the contrary, the fixed texts of the prayers themselves were held to have a power of their own, and their efficacy depended on a literal recitation and on frequent repetition.

The invention of the printing press and the expansion of literacy increased devotional reading among the laity considerably after 1455. In addition to *horae*, presses turned out devotional treatises and lives of the saints in Latin and in vernacular languages. Devotional texts could be practical manuals, such as the *Ars moriendi*, or *Art of Dying*, which helped the laity prepare for a good death, and *The Imitation of Christ*, by Thomas à Kempis, an immensely popular fifteenth-century text, which introduced self-denying models of behavior and meditation to the laity. Two other texts that helped shape the lives of many lay people were *The Life of Christ*, by Ludolph of Saxony, written in the fourteenth century, which offered models for Christ-like behavior; and the *Legenda aurea*, or *Golden Legend*, written by Jacobo de Voragine in the thirteenth century, a collection of edifying stories from the lives of the saints. After the invention of printing, more and more hagiographies began to appear in vernacular languages, and the genre increased in popularity among the laity. In the early part of the sixteenth century, mystical literature written by monks and nuns—previously unavailable to the laity—began to appear in vernacular editions as well, and this, too, proved an immensely favored genre.

The art of dying well. Since the Catholic Church taught that one's eternal destiny was determined by the state of one's soul at the moment of death (*salus hominis in fine consistet*), preparing for that awful moment became a great concern for many in the late Middle Ages. Instruction books in the art of dying well (*ars moriendi*) were the ultimate self-help best sellers, often lavishly illustrated with depictions of the worst temptations one needed to overcome at the final hour. This fifteenth-century image shows a dying man surrounded by the demons of despair while all his heavenly helpers hover nearby, encouraging him to resist temptation.

Ethics, or morality, was another essential component of piety, for salvation itself hinged on one's behavior. In fact, much of religion had a legalistic focus, and involved actions rather than thoughts or beliefs. Avoiding sin and practicing virtue were crucial, for sins made one deserve punishment, both in this life and in the next; virtue was the key to eternal bliss. Much of life was carefully codified, and much of religion revolved around what one should or should not do, what was permissible or forbidden. Long and precise lists distinguished sins from virtues and assigned corresponding values to each specific human act.

Sermons and devotional literature tended to promote the imitation of self-denying role models as the surest road to salvation. Asceticism, or self-denial, was not reserved for monks and nuns alone: fasting, sexual abstinence, and other forms of self-control were required of the laity too, though on a lesser scale. Moreover, clerical elites tended to promote their state as the highest Christian vocation, and the lay life as a compromise of sorts. Lay responses to this message varied widely. At one extreme, some lay people tried to adopt a semi-monastic existence, either as individuals or in groups such as the Beghards and Beguines, which developed their own style of devotion. One of these lay associations, the Brothers and Sisters of the Common Life, had a profound impact beyond their own circle, spreading their inwardly focused piety, known as the "modern devotion," or *devotio moderna*, through their schools and their writings, especially the popular *Imitation of Christ*. Sometimes whole communities could be gripped by reformist ascetical tendencies, too, as in the case of Florence in 1494–1495, under the leadership of the friar Girolamo Savonarola, when bonfires were lit to consume "lewd" books, "ostentatious" clothing, "inappropriate" art, and other such "vanities" of the people. At the other extreme, many clerics reported lay indifference and resentment not just to ascetic ideals, but even to the most basic ethical teachings of the church. There is still substantial disagreement among scholars as to how to interpret lay responses to clerical moral direction, but there is little disagreement concerning the kind of behavior that was universally recognized as necessary for salvation.

Sacred Contention: Distinguishing Truth from Error

Though lay piety was symbiotically related to the theology, worship, and ethics of the church, and even shaped them to some extent, it also often tested or crossed the boundaries of what was deemed proper by the clergy. As a rule, the further that lay piety sought to distance itself from the clergy, the more likely it was that it would be condemned.

One area of constant tension between the clergy and the laity was the interpretation of ritual and its adaptation to purposes that could be deemed "magical" or "superstitious," such as scattering consecrated hosts on the ground to ensure a good harvest or insisting that certain votive masses be celebrated with a specific number of candles. Clergy and laity could also clash over attitudes toward symbols and rituals, such as believing that an image of St. Christopher could protect one from accidents or that those who recovered their health after receiving extreme unction should remain celibate and barefoot thereafter. Contention over such issues was not inevitable in all cases, however, since the clergy themselves could also share the laity's attitudes and behavior, and even promote them, as in the case of priests who performed the rites of exorcism on swarms of locusts, seeking to drive away the demons that supposedly possessed the insects.

Exorcisms and other rites aimed against the devil were an integral part of piety because both the clergy and the laity believed that evil was personified in spiritual entities who had some degree of control over the material world, and who could wreak all sorts of spiritual and material havoc. Demons lurked everywhere, causing harm and constantly tempting humans to sin; even worse, demons attracted veneration in exchange for magical or miraculous favors. Such beliefs were as old as Christianity itself, and solidly grounded in the New Testament, but official Christian teachings and pre-Christian beliefs in evil forces had become so closely intertwined in the Middle Ages as to make the boundary between the sacred and the demonic one of the most highly charged in medieval piety, especially when it came to the clergy's take on many ancestral folk customs, which they could easily deem to be "demonic." Drawing lines between God's camp and that of the devil was necessary, but not always easy. Magic and witchcraft lurked dreadfully close to the surface, as close as the demons themselves. In such a world, the laity could turn in either direction: toward the rites of the church that warded off demons or toward occult rites that tapped demonic powers for various ends. And for many, ignorance of the line drawn by the church between God and the devil was all too common.

Moreover, concern over the demonic began to intensify in the fifteenth century. We know this not only because of the sharp increase in witchcraft trials in the fifteenth century, but also because of the high number of witchcraft treatises written at the time. A key development in the codification and prosecution of witchcraft was the invention of the printing press, which made it possible for information to be disseminated more widely and rapidly, and helped civil and church authorities throughout Europe to discern—or invent—a common enemy and attack it with vigorous efficiency. No witch-hunting manual was more influential than the *Malleus maleficarum* (*The Hammer of Witches*), first published in 1486, which had gone through nineteen editions by 1520. Authored by Heinrich Institoris and Jacob Sprenger, two Dominican friars who had served as inquisitors at scores of witch trials in Constance, the *Malleus* emphasized two points that laid the foundation for all subsequent witch hunting. First, the *Malleus* argued that the greatest danger posed by witches was their ability to inflict physical harm on others (*maleficium*). This made witchcraft a civil crime and gave secular authorities the right to prosecute witches. Second, the *Malleus* insisted that the devil was at the heart of all witchcraft, and that each and every Christian who practiced rites not sanctioned by the church entered into a pact with Satan, no matter what. This position turned all sorcery and many ancestral customs, even the most seemingly benign, into a denial of the Christian faith. As the crime of apostasy, then, witchcraft also remained squarely under the jurisdiction of the church. This linkage of church and state in the prosecution of witches would have a tremendous impact on post-medieval Europe, especially in the seventeenth century, long after Christendom had been torn asunder by religious differences. It may well be one of the most enduring continuities linking medieval and early modern Europe.

In medieval piety the spiritual world was full not just of demons, but also of good spirits who sometimes communicated with the human race. Apparitions of Christ, Mary, the angels, and saints were frequently reported by monks and nuns, and also by lay people. These extraordinary religious experiences on the part of the laity helped give shape to piety, but they could also sometimes gave rise to friction with the clergy. If they had the clergy's endorsement, lay visions could give rise to cults and shrines, as could visions reported by clerics. All such claims came under scrutiny in the Late Middle Ages. Winning approval could be a difficult and divisive process, principally because distinguishing between the demonic and the divine was not always easy, as witnessed most clearly by the case of the peasant visionary Joan of Arc. Though she was burnt as a witch in 1431, with the backing of the bishop of Beauvais and the University of Paris, Joan was declared innocent by Pope Calixtus III in 1456, and eventually canonized as a saint in 1920.

Beyond the confines of Christian ritual, lay people and even clerics could engage in many practices that can be considered of pre-Christian origin, and that the higher clergy judged heathenish or demonic. Magic, necromancy, and witchcraft abounded in Europe well into the early modern period, always impinging upon and even becoming the focus of piety at all levels of society. Medieval piety was so fluid, and so prone to admixture with elements that could be deemed non-Christian, that, to this day, scholars are still debating the issue of how "Christian" or "un-Christian" piety might have been in the Middle Ages. In some ways, those who argue for the "un-Christian" nature of medieval piety are echoing the charges made by Protestants in the sixteenth century, who rejected much of medieval piety as nothing more than pagan idolatry.

Conclusion

The rejection of medieval piety by Protestants would not exactly come as a bolt out of the blue, but the same was not true about extent of their success, which seems to have taken many by surprise. Others had clamored for change before, but they had often failed or been contained within circumscribed or remote corners of the map. Protestants would succeed where many others had failed and forever undo Christendom.

The changes that were to take place in the sixteenth century would be enormous. If one tries to think of them in the context of historical periodization, they call to mind a fault line on the surface of the earth, or any other landmark that indicates a great rift. Before it was all swept away by the flood of the Protestant Reformation, one can speak comfortably in the singular of *medieval* piety and of *the* church. After the deluge, one must rely on the plural, use other terms and speak differently of what medieval called *Christianitas*, or Christendom.

The change was so profound that it is hard to miss. For instance, take what the Protestant Reformer John Calvin had to say about the religion of his childhood, which he rejected and fought against. Calvin was born in 1509, in northern France, when Western Europe was still wholly Catholic. He would never reveal much about himself or his past, though his writings fill fifty-nine hefty volumes. But once, while ridiculing the veneration of relics, he slipped in a personal anecdote, probably because of his own revulsion at having once partaken of a piety that he came to view as abject evil. "I remember what I saw them do to images in our parish when I was a small boy," he testified, wagging a rhetorical finger. What he saw was this: on feast days, the ignorant folk of his native Noyon would decorate all of the images, bedecking them with flowers and lighting candles beneath them. Their devotion was so blind, and so wrong, said Calvin, that they even did this to figures of the devil.[12] As Calvin saw it, medieval Catholicism was nothing but an "abominable sacrilege and Babylonish pollution."[13] And he went as far as to argue that his fellow Frenchmen should flee from their native land and shake the dust from their feet, for, as he put it, "any country where the worship of God is abolished and his religion is annihilated well deserves to be regarded as foreign and profane."[14]

If one compares what Calvin has to say about medieval Catholic piety with what the Spanish conquistadores said at just about the same time about Aztec piety, especially about the Aztecs' grisly fondness for human sacrifice, it is not difficult to spot many similarities.[15] In both cases, the religion of "the other" is viewed with utter revulsion, as demonic and dehumanizing. In and of itself, this similarity may not seem very remarkable, since it is common enough for one culture to demonize another. But one must pause and consider that in Calvin's case "the other" were his own people, his kin, his parents, his own past self, and that the sacrifice that made him recoil in horror was that of the Mass, not that in which bloodstained priests tore out the beating hearts of their victims.

How could this happen? How was it that a European baptized into the Catholic Church as an infant and reared in a totally Catholic culture could come to see his own religion as that of "the other," and as an absolute evil? That is the question that needs to be answered in the next few chapters.

CHAPTER THREE

Reform and Dissent
in the Late Middle Ages

To reform is to renew and improve, that is, to do away with imperfections and to lessen the gap between ideals and the status quo. Reformers, then, are idealists, whether they admit it or not. Reformers are also pathologists of sorts, or diagnosticians, who identify the ills that plague society and prescribe the best cure. In religious terms, reform is a call to repentance and renewal, often accompanied by dire warnings of impending doom. The preacher Girolamo Savonarola warned his fellow Florentines in 1495: "O Italy, O princes of Italy, O prelates of the Church, the wrath of God is over you, and you will not have any cure unless you mend your ways! . . . O noblemen, O powerful ones, O common people. . . . Do penance while the sword is not out of its sheath and while it is not stained with blood!"[1]

Savonarola was not alone in thinking this way. In the fifteenth century, Western Europe seemed full of reformers and would-be reformers who perceived a wide gap between Christian ideals and the behavior of their fellow Christians, or saw Christendom as perched on the edge of an abyss. Talk of reform was in the air. Buzzwords such as *reformatio, renovatio, restauratio, reparatio,* and *instauratio* were frequently used by ever-growing numbers of the elite, and all of the terms had a similar meaning: "improvement." Rulers, clerics, and intellectuals alike seemed to share in a common sense of purpose, with optimism about the possibility for change. Egidio da Viterbo, vicar-general of the Augustinian order and a future cardinal, summed up the reforming mind-set of his era in the opening address to the Fifth Lateran Council in 1512, which had been convened by the worldly Pope Julius II. Warning that the church needed to turn back to its old purity, its ancient brilliance, its original splendor, and its own sources, Viterbo added that "celestial and human things . . . crave renewal."[2]

The idea of reform was not at all new, however; in fact, it was already an ancient tradition in the Catholic Church and European society. Paradoxically, the church itself bred corruption and reform simultaneously, in an ongoing dialectic, as old as Christianity itself, which was driven by an intensely bipolar idealism: on the one hand, the church taught that all humans are bound to sin, while on the other hand, it encouraged all to obey Jesus's command "be ye perfect as your heavenly Father is perfect" (Matthew 5:48). Most often, the clerics themselves strove to bridge the gap and bring church and society closer to perfection. And as many of these reform-minded clerics saw it, the only way out of this dilemma was for the clergy to purify the church. One should not think of these idealists simply as "religious" reformers. Since religion was so intricately woven into nearly every aspect of life in medieval Europe, all religious reformers were also social, cultural, and political reformers. But the phrase often used toward the end of the Middle Ages, *reformation in head and limbs* (*reformatio in capite et in membris*), which relied on a bodily metaphor and on medical theory, figuratively summed up the assumption that all reforms had to begin with the head, that is, at the apex of society, among the pope and his clerics.

But reforming the church was easier said than done, even for a pope or an emperor. By the beginning of the sixteenth century, despite all the cries for reform, the Catholic Church was as rife with problems as the world itself. The situation was not necessarily worse than it had been for centuries—on the contrary, in some ways the church and religious life were more vibrant than ever. Experts speak of this period as being more "churchly-minded and devout,"[3] or as marked by an "immense appetite for the divine,"[4] and "an enormous unfolding of religion in daily life."[5] The difference between this and preceding ages was one of perception, not necessarily of increased corruption: during the course of the fifteenth century the abuses and failings of the church became more conspicuous, more openly discussed, and more deeply resented by a wider spectrum of people. Also, after 1450, the invention of the printing press not only allowed for the wider dissemination of information and reforming ideas, but also speeded up the process of consciousness-raising among both the clergy and the laity.

Clerical Corruption

What, specifically, did reformers find objectionable about the late medieval Catholic Church? In what ways did they find the church and its clergy corrupt? Which failures and abuses were singled out most often?

At the very top, in Rome, the papacy itself seemed the epitome of corruption, an office controlled by worldly men who seemed to embody sin rather than redemption from it. A popular Latin pun played on the meaning of the city's name, *Roma*, by suggesting that it was an acronym for the proverb *radix omnium malorum avaritia*: "avarice is the root of all evil."

Beyond Rome, scattered throughout the map of Christendom, the bishops who were ostensibly in charge of the dioceses were a mixed lot in terms of their commitment to their vocation, but overall, it was relatively easy to find fault with many of them. One of the worst problems at the episcopal level was absenteeism, that is, bishops who did not

Nepotism reified. In 1519, the great Renaissance painter Raphael captured the very essence of elite privilege and papal corruption in this portrait of Pope Leo X (Giovanni di Lorenzo de' Medici), and two of his nephews, the cardinals Luigi de' Rossi (son of Leonetto de' Rossi and Maria de' Medici), and Giulio de' Medici (who would become Pope Clement VII). The wealthy Medicis, a Florentine banking family, were among the most powerful clans in Italy. A patron of art and learning, Leo X did not shrink back from bestowing the highest posts in the church to his young relatives. Yet despite his wealth and power, Pope Leo was unable to stop the onset of the Protestant Reformation, a crisis that reached the point of no return as he sat for this portrait.

live within their dioceses, or even visit them. Another problem was pluralism, that is, the holding of two or more church offices at once by some of the high clergy. Nepotism and simony also proved persistent problems in the episcopate. Nepotism (from Latin, *nepos*, "nephew") is the practice of bestowing offices on one's relatives. Though church offices could never be made hereditary, there were no laws forbidding the appointment of relatives, and certain offices sometimes remained in the hands of the same families for generations. Simony is the practice of selling church offices (named after Simon Magus, who tried to buy influence from St. Peter in Acts of the Apostles 8:18–24). Though simony was forbidden outright by the church de jure, it was very much in place de facto, thanks to dispensations and to some inventive loopholes in canon law.

Lower on the hierarchy, similar problems and abuses could be found nearly everywhere among the secular clergy. Preaching at a convocation of priests in 1512, the English humanist John Colet (1466–1519) complained about the lifestyle of many clerics:

> They give themselves to feasting and banqueting; spend themselves in vain babbling, take part in sports and plays, devote themselves to hunting and hawking; are drowned in the delights of this world; patronize those who cater for their pleasure . . . mixed up and confused with the laity, they lead, under a priestly exterior, the mere life of a layman.

Colet was no detached observer. As dean of St. Paul's Cathedral in London, he had to deal with the failings of the clergy on a daily basis. He added, "Who is there who does not see this? Who that sees it does not grieve over it?"[6]

Down the ecclesiastical ladder, one step below the episcopate, the cathedral clergy and the collegiate clergy were also usually drawn from the various tiers of the upper class. These canons or collegiate clerics, who normally drew a larger income than parish clergy and claimed special rights and exemptions, would prove to be among the most difficult to reform, given their privileged position in society. Further down the ladder, most of the secular clergy were very poorly educated, or not educated at all, and many parish priests lived lives that were barely distinguishable from those of their flocks, tilling the earth, minding the livestock, and drinking and brawling. In a list of complaints presented to Emperor Charles V in 1521, the lower clergy of Germany are described in very unflattering terms:

> The majority of parish priests and other secular clerics mingle with the common people at inns and taverns. They frequent public dances and walk about the streets in lay garments, brandishing long knives. They engage in quarrels and arguments, which usually lead to blows, whereupon they fall upon poor folk, wound or even kill them, and then excommunicate them unless the injured parties agree to offer money for a settlement with the offending priest.[7]

The state of the monastics—the regular clergy—varied tremendously from place to place and house to house, but overall, monasteries were not at all immune from the shortcomings that seemed to plague the secular clergy. Tales of mischief among monks and nuns

Monks behaving badly. Tales of wayward monks and nuns competed for attention with lives of the saints in the late Middle Ages. This manuscript image from the fourteenth century shows the tragic result of monastic misbehavior: a woman seduced by a monk ends up killing their illicit child by tossing it into a latrine.

abounded in the late Middle Ages. Often their failings were ridiculed in literature, as in Geoffrey Chaucer's *The Canterbury Tales* (1390s), reinforcing the myth that gluttony, drunkenness, greed, deceit, and lechery were as much a part of their lives as the habits they wore. It was a cheap shot, commonly taken. Yet paradoxically, these signs of contradiction pointed to an expected solution, for inasmuch as they were a cause for scandal, monks and nuns were also potential agents for change. It is no accident that the man who sparked the Protestant Reformation was an Augustinian monk, and that so many of the leading reformers of the Catholic Church also belonged to the regular clergy.

To be a successful reformer, however, one had to discern the line between reform and rebellion, criticism and disobedience, dissent and heresy. It was a fine line at times, wrongly drawn by some who chose to cross it. Consequently, while some reformers would be recognized as saints, others could end up condemned as heretics. And there was certainly no shortage of either saints or heretics in the Middle Ages.

Medieval Dissent

Calls for reform were endemic in the Middle Ages, as were confrontations over the supremacy of the pope and his clerics. Some of the greatest challenges faced by the medieval church were those posed by the Cathars and Waldensians, sects who set up rival churches, principally in the south of France and northern Italy. Both of these movements made much of corruption in the established church and of the need for reform.

The Cathars, also known as Albigensians, were the most extreme of all medieval dissenters, for they believed that the material world was the creation of an evil deity, and that the pope's church was not only corrupt, but also false and evil. Led by clerics known as "the Perfect," who observed celibacy, total poverty, and extreme fasting, the Cathars also believed in reincarnation and rejected the sacraments, prayers for the dead, and the veneration of images and relics. The church's response to this challenge was as brutal as it was successful: Pope Innocent III called on the Catholic nobles in the north of France to wipe out the heretics. The resulting crusade (1209–1229), which was marked by numerous massacres, crushed the Cathars. A few survivors hung on in isolated spots for another century or so, but they were gradually wiped out by a new institution established expressly to root them out: the Inquisition.

Doing away with the Cathars did little to silence dissent or opposition to corruption in the church. At the very same time that the Cathars were suppressed, in roughly the same areas, a less extreme reform movement took root: the Waldenses, or Pauperes ("the poor"). Established by Peter Waldo, a layman from Lyons, these reformers were committed to a principle of radical poverty and to public preaching. Obviously influenced by the Cathars insofar as their organization was concerned, the Pauperes were led by itinerant preachers who crisscrossed the map in pairs, criticizing corruption and calling for reform. Though Waldo sought approval from Pope Alexander III in 1179, he and his followers began to distance themselves a bit too much from the corruption they condemned, and by 1184 Pope Lucius III proclaimed them to be heretical. His response was unavoidable, for by that date Waldo and his followers had begun to argue that the ultimate supreme authority was the Bible, not the pope. In addition, much like the Cathars, the Waldenses questioned the validity of the church's sacraments and rejected prayers for the dead and the veneration of images and relics. Although their

The war on medieval heresy. In the thirteenth century Cathars and Waldensians challenged the Catholic Church in many areas, but the church fought back. The Order of Preachers, founded by Dominic de Guzmán to stem the tide of heresy, would become heavily involved in the work of the Inquisition, a new institution also established at that same time to wipe out error. This late fifteenth-century painting by Pedro de Berrugete depicts St. Dominic throwing the heretics' books into a fire. While the books containing their errors burn, an orthodox book taken from them levitates miraculously above the flames, unharmed. The zeal of the Order of Preachers—better known as the Dominicans, after their founder—earned them the nickname "Domini canes"—or "hounds of God."

theology was radically different from that of the Cathars (who believed in two deities and in reincarnation), the Waldenses' rejection of the pope's authority and of the church's symbols and rituals made them heretics all the same, and subject to persecution. Slowly but steadily these unorthodox reformers were violently suppressed, until only a few remained in remote regions of the Alps, one of the very few Western heretical movements to survive total extinction. These mountain folk would eventually join the Protestant Reformation in the 1530s, at which time they came to be seen "forerunners," or spiritual ancestors of sorts, a sure sign of the fact that the "true" church was never totally extinguished by Rome.

A very similar preoccupation with poverty led to very different results in the case of St. Francis of Assisi (1182–1226), the founder of the Friars Minor, better known as the Franciscan order. The son of a wealthy cloth merchant, Francis committed himself to a life of poverty after undergoing a conversion experience. Waldensian and Cathar influence is not only probable, but also highly likely, since both heretical groups were present in his area. However, unlike Waldo's *poor men*, who condemned the established church and insisted on a thoroughgoing reordering of all of society, Francis had a very different sort of reform in mind. Following what was already an ancient pattern in his day, Francis focused on creating a religious order. But he did so with a new twist, placing a heavy emphasis on radical poverty and preaching. As Francis envisioned his new order, he and his followers were to own nothing at all, not even a place in which to live, and they were to subsist solely by begging. The vow of poverty was as ancient as monasticism itself, but the emphasis on mingling with the world and preaching to the laity was not. Up until that time, monasticism had been all about leaving the world behind and praying for it, not ministering to it directly. The success of the Cathar and Waldensian preachers, however, had made it necessary to redefine the role of those who were most intensely committed to a denial of power and wealth, especially in a cultural matrix in which the church's wealth and corruption had become burning issues.

Francis of Assisi's commitment to radical poverty was highly impractical, and it would later cause all sorts of problems for his followers, but at the very beginning of his public ministry, it was his extremism that propelled his movement forward, especially in the context of the Cathar and Waldensian challenge. The attractiveness of the Franciscans to church authorities is easy to understand: here, at last, the pope had a virtuous man with virtuous followers who did not condemn the church for its failings, but rather sought to obey and reform from within, by example rather than by force. Two legends that became an integral part of Franciscan lore shed light on this aspect of Francis's work as an inside reformer. The first tells how soon after Francis's conversion, Jesus spoke to him from a crucifix: "See to the repair of my church, which has fallen to ruin." The second tells how Pope Innocent III—the very same pope who launched the crusade against the Cathars—had a prophetic dream in which he saw a ragged beggar prevent the collapse of the papal basilica of St. John Lateran in Rome, and how that dream convinced him to approve St. Francis's new order despite his misgivings. Both of these legends highlight and support a vision of reform quite different from that of the Cathars and Waldensians, one that did not require the rejection of the status quo.

Nonetheless, while Francis and his early followers escaped censure, some of his later followers would not. And the issue, again, would be that of poverty, or more specifically, that of the church's relation to property and wealth. The problem surfaced in Francis's own lifetime, as ever-increasing numbers of men and women joined the order, and it became obvious to everyone that Franciscans could not effectively train new recruits or minister to the laity if they observed their rule literally, without "anything of their own," including places in which to live. The sheer impracticality of the original Franciscan rule seemed to call for a compromise: perhaps one could still be faithful to radical poverty while assuming control of some property, just to ensure the survival of the order itself? Eventually, the Franciscans split on this issue: one branch, the Conventuals, chose to interpret the Franciscan rule more loosely; the other branch, the Observants (also known as Spirituals), dug in their heels on the property issue. Eventually, this controversy led to conflicts with the papacy, which tended to insist on "inner" rather than external poverty. Some among the Observant Franciscans became more radical in outlook, even apocalyptic, expecting a new phase of human history to be on the horizon, one in which the entire human race would live in a communist utopia without private property. Between 1311 and 1329 a series of papal bulls asserted that the strict Observant position was wrong: private property was an inherent human right, established by God before the fall of Adam and Eve, not a symptom of original sin.

The papacy's reluctance to accept the extreme position of the Observant Franciscans is understandable, and very revealing. At issue here was the question of the church's relation to the world and its commitment to apostolic or evangelical principles, that is, its fidelity to the life of Jesus and his apostles as portrayed in the gospels. The Observants claimed for themselves a calling higher than that of the other clergy in the church, including the pope himself: in essence, they were arguing that only those who embraced radical poverty were totally faithful to the gospel. Implicitly, the Observant Franciscans' attitude toward property made the church as a whole less close to perfection than the Observants themselves. Taken to its logical conclusion, their reform agenda raised them above the pope not only in terms of virtue, but also perhaps in terms of moral authority. At another level, their position also implied that property ownership was tainted with sin, and that they alone in all of Christendom were therefore on the right track.

One of the more remarkable achievements of St. Francis was his ability to tap into Cathar and Waldensian dissent and still be considered one of the greatest saints who ever lived, canonized in record time, a mere two years after his death. Even more remarkable was his ability to adapt Cathar and Waldensian lifestyles and organizational structures to Catholic tradition. When all is said and done, however, Franciscan reform could be acceptable only when it conformed to the status quo. What the Spiritual Franciscans proved, as did the Cathars and Waldensians, was that although the line between reform and rebellion was thin, it was very clear: to be a reformer rather than a rebel, one always had to remain submissive to the church's hierarchy and show respect for its teachings, symbols, and rituals. In other words, one had to accept that the church had never been perfect and never could be. To be a reformer one had to focus on one's immediate environment, not the entire church, and to compromise on many issues and tolerate all sorts of corruption, no matter how pervasive. In the eyes of the church hierarchy, a genuine reformer required a healthy dose of two of the seven virtues: patience and fortitude.

Not everyone agreed. The impatient dissent manifested by the Cathars, Waldensians, and Observant Franciscans did not simply evaporate with their condemnation and persecution. In some places, it continued to manifest itself vigorously, with remarkably similar features.

One of these places was England, where an Oxford professor named John Wycliffe (1330–1384) stirred up dissent that spilled out, far beyond the classroom. Trained as a scholastic philosopher and theologian, Wycliffe expressed some of the very same reforming ideas as the Waldensians with greater clarity and precision than ever before, especially in two treatises, *On Divine Lordship* (1375) and *On Civil Lordship* (1376). For Wycliffe, the genuine head of the church was Christ, not the pope, and the supreme guide for all doctrine, ritual, and ethics was the Bible. Anything that did not square with Holy Writ, therefore, was to be rejected. This position led Wycliffe to condemn many essential teachings and practices of the medieval church as false: clerical celibacy, monasticism, the sacrament of ordination, the intercession of the saints, the veneration of images and relics, pilgrimages, belief in transubstantiation (that the substance of the bread and wine in the Eucharist are transformed into the flesh and blood of Christ), and belief in papal authority, to name but a few. In addition to criticizing corruption in the church, Wycliffe also took aim at the church's vast wealth and its immersion in worldly dominion, which he condemned as contrary to the gospels. To top it all off, Wycliffe's teachings on authority were as clearly articulated as they were revolutionary. According to Wycliffe, every position of authority on earth "both civil and ecclesiastic" comes straight from God and is never inherently the possession of its holders. All lordship, then, was contingent on performance: God granted it on the condition that it be properly administered. This meant that anyone who failed to live up to the duties of his office should be removed from it, including the pope. It also meant that the property of unworthy clerics and civil officials could be taken away from them.

Even though he was excommunicated in 1377 by Pope Gregory XI, and soon after removed from his teaching post, Wycliffe continued to preach and write freely until he died of natural causes in 1384, mainly because he had attracted such a large following in England across a broad social spectrum, including merchants, artisans, gentry, clerics, and even some nobility and members of Parliament. Wycliffe's followers—who were called Lollards by their enemies (an insult with several possible derivations)—multiplied rapidly throughout the 1380s and 1390s. Not even Wycliffe's death could slow their growth, or their boldness. In some areas where the Lollards gained sufficient clout they did more than grumble and read the Bible in a new English translation: sometimes they even destroyed sacred images and relics. One account reveals the extent of Lollard hostility toward images and the impunity with which they could act. On taking an image of St. Catherine from a chapel, one Lollard said to another:

> Aha . . . my dear chap, now God has sent us fuel to cook our cabbage and appease our hunger. This holy image will make a holy bonfire for us. By axe and fire she will undergo a new martyrdom, and perhaps through the cruelty of those new torments she will come at last to the kingdom of heaven.[8]

Unwilling to brook any such irreverence or further challenges to the status quo, King Henry IV finally began to persecute the Lollards in 1399, and within two years some of them were being burned at the stake. But Lollard resistance was strong. It was not until 1414 that the movement was decisively crushed, when a Lollard uprising led by Sir John Oldcastle failed and its surviving leaders were hunted down. Vanquished, but not extinguished, the Lollard movement was forced underground, so to speak, where it survived for several generations, principally among tradespeople, merchants, and artisans. Eventually, as was the case with the Waldensians, the Lollards would rise out of their relative obscurity and join the Protestant Reformation in the 1520s and 1530s.

Wycliffe's influence also reached far beyond England. Thanks to the marriage of King Richard II to Anne of Bohemia in 1381, which initiated a student exchange program between the universities of Oxford and Prague, Wycliffe's teachings would make their way into the hands of another academic, Jan Hus (1370–1415). By 1403, at the very same time that the persecution of the Lollards increased in England, Hus was teaching and preaching in the vein of Wycliffe in Bohemia, and attracting a large following. Hus did not agree with Wycliffe on all points, but their teachings were nonetheless very similar. Convinced that the Bible was the ultimate authority and that the church needed to be brought back in line with Holy Scripture, Hus challenged tradition and the church hierarchy along Lollard lines. He was also especially outspoken in his critique of clerical corruption, insisting even more intensely than Wycliffe on the idea that sinful clergy could have no real authority and should be removed from office and have their property taken away from them. At a university where there was constant friction between a dominant German faculty bent on conservatism and the native Czechs, and in a land where the clerical class owned nearly half of the real estate and collected heavy taxes on it, Hus's critique rapidly acquired a populist and nationalistic character. Hus was condemned by church authorities and banned from preaching and teaching, but it made little difference. Ever the scholar, Hus would eventually pen a very learned exposition of his teachings, *On the Church* (1413), but by that time Hussite dissent had already acquired a life of its own and swept through Bohemia like wildfire. As in the case of Wycliffe, condemnation proved hollow, and Hus was able to find plenty of powerful protectors who helped him avoid capture.

Hus was also aided immensely by the fact that at this point in history the Roman Catholic Church was in nearly total disarray, with three rival popes claiming legitimacy: one in Rome, one in Avignon, and one in Pisa. This crisis, known as the Great Schism, had also played a role in Wycliffe's initial success, and it needs to be taken into account at this point.

The schism had begun in 1378, but its roots stretched farther back in time, to 1309, when Clement V relocated the papal court from Rome to Avignon in the south of France. This move was intended as a temporary escape from the diseases and political turmoil that plagued Rome, but as it turned out, the refuge would assume a feeling of permanency. Between 1309 and 1378, a string of seven French popes kept their court in Avignon, turning the papal see and the curia into a French monopoly (111 of the 134 cardinals created by the Avignon popes were French). To many outside of France this seemed wrong, not just because the legitimacy of the pope's authority was physically bound to the see of Peter in Rome, but because it seemed that the pope had become a vassal of the French crown. The effects of this dislocation, which came to be known as the "Babylonian Captivity," cannot be underestimated, especially in regard to papal authority, and also to popular sentiment. When the Black Death wiped out a third of the population in Europe in 1348–1349, many interpreted the disaster as divine retribution for the pope's absence from Rome and the sins of the papal court in Avignon. Even worse was the ultimate outcome of the move: the Great Schism of 1378–1415.

When Pope Gregory XI finally moved the court back to Rome in 1377, he unwittingly created a crisis of succession when he died shortly afterward. As crowds demanded an Italian pope who would stay in Rome, the largely French conclave of cardinals (eleven out of sixteen) caved in and elected the bishop of Bari, who assumed the papal throne as Urban VI. A mere four months after the election, however, after Pope Urban had made clear his plans to curb the power of the French cardinals, the eleven French cardinals who had elected him declared their vote null and void, charging that they had been coerced by the unruly Roman mob. Then they took the fateful step of deposing Urban and electing a cousin of the French king to replace him: Cardinal Robert of Geneva, archbishop of Cambrai, who took the papal name Clement VII and immediately set up his court back in Avignon.

Now there were two popes: one in Rome and another in Avignon, each elected by the same eleven cardinals who made up the majority of the electoral conclave. And there were two rival colleges of cardinals too, one at Rome and another at Avignon, each with newly minted members as well as some veterans of the original disputed election. Naturally, each pope excommunicated the other and all of his followers, bringing every soul in Europe into the fray. Such a crisis was not new: popes and antipopes had made rival claims to the papal throne previously, numerous times. What was new in this case were the circumstances, which prevented a quick resolution of the dispute. Now, unlike in previous cases, there was no single dominant figure or power block that could force one of the claimants to step down. Europe was evenly divided in its allegiances with France and its allies supporting the Avignon pope (this camp included Castile, Aragon, Naples, and Scotland), and England and its allies backing the Roman pope (this camp included Portugal, Hungary, Bohemia, Scandinavia, Poland, and the Holy Roman Empire). A few of these allegiances would shift, especially in Central Europe, but without any impact on the whole. Even some individuals who were regarded as living saints were divided along national lines too, with Catherine of Siena in the Roman camp and the great preacher Vincent Ferrer in that of Avignon.

The impasse could not be broken. Months turned into years and years into decades without a solution. Not even the deaths of the Roman pope Urban VI (1389) and the Avignon pope Clement VII (1394) solved the problem. As soon as they died, successors were duly elected by the rival cardinals: Urban would be succeeded by three other

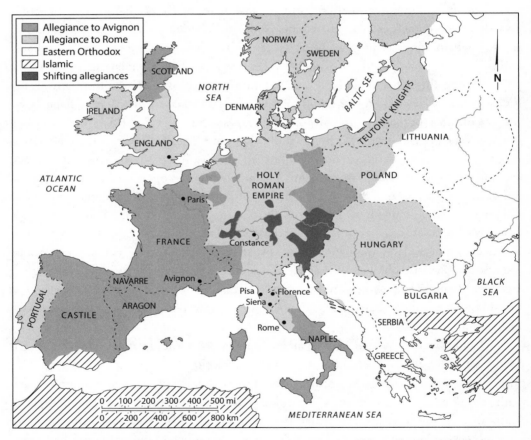

The Great Schism, 1378–1415. For thirty-seven years Western Christendom was divided in its allegiance to rival claimants to the papal throne, with one at Rome and the other at Avignon. In the early fifteenth century, a third rival was created by the Council of Pisa. As this map shows, the balance of political support for each of the rivals remained so evenly distributed that the deadlock was hard to break.

popes at Rome, and Clement by one pope at Avignon. And in the meantime heretics such as Wycliffe and Hus could elude the flames and point to the crisis in the papacy as the surest sign anyone could ask for of the falsehood of its claims. Convening a universal church council to settle the schism seemed like an obvious solution—and scholars pressed this point vigorously—but practical questions stood in the way. First, under whose authority could such a council be convened? Second, even if any such gathering of bishops and cardinals could be brought about, how could the evenly divided factions ever be persuaded to agree on anything? Third, and most important, what power would any council have over a pope?

Convinced that a council was the only solution, many eminent scholars scrambled to answer such questions. The net result of their searching was the gradual development of conciliarism, a range of theories that argued for the ultimate supremacy of councils over popes, especially in times of crisis. One of the most eminent of these conciliarists, Jean Gerson, chancellor of the University of Paris, summed up the conciliarist view by arguing: "The pope can be removed by a general council celebrated without his consent and against his will." As in grammar and in morals, Gerson reasoned, all general rules have exceptions, even rules that govern the relation of popes and councils.[9]

Tragically, when a council was finally assembled at Pisa in 1409, conciliarist theory failed to trump political realities. Composed of a large number of prelates from both camps who decided to take matters into their own hands, the council convened itself without papal approval. The list of those in attendance was impressive, and indicative of the urgency of the business at hand: twenty-two cardinals and eighty bishops, along with the representatives of one hundred bishops who could not attend in person, eighty-seven abbots and their proxies, forty-one priors and generals of religious orders, three hundred doctors of theology or canon law, and ambassadors from all of the Christian courts of Europe. At the very same time, however, each of the rival popes assembled much smaller and less impressive countercouncils of their own at other locations, packed with their most ardent supporters.

Confident in their own authority, the prelates at Pisa deposed both rival popes and chose a new one to take their place: Cardinal Peter Philarghi, who was immediately installed as Alexander V. To all present, it seemed as if conciliarism had won the day, but this perception was an illusion. Benedict XIII at Avignon and Gregory XII at Rome refused to step down, arguing that the council at Pisa had no legitimate authority, and both of them mustered enough secular political support to keep themselves in office. All that had been accomplished at Pisa, then, was the election of a third claimant to the papacy and a deepening of the Great Schism. Not even the sudden death of the pope elected at Pisa made a difference. Immediately upon Alexander V's demise in 1410, he was succeeded by one of the leading figures of the Pisan council, Cardinal Baldassare Cossa, who ruled as Pope John XXIII from his see in Bologna.[10] Under pressure from the Holy Roman Emperor Sigismund, in the autumn of 1414 John XXIII convoked another council, this time at the free imperial city of Constance. So, as the Lollards mounted their great uprising against the crown in England, and as Hussites openly defied all three popes and their local prelates, yet another attempt was made to end the schism through a council. After a very rocky start, which seemed to doom it to failure, the council managed to gain sufficient momentum and to successfully depose all three popes.

John XXIII, the Pisa pope, was the first to fall. Seeing that things were not going well for him, he fled from Constance, hoping that his departure would strip the council of its legitimacy. But his flight had the opposite effect. Emboldened by Emperor Sigismund's support, the council continued its work, issuing a decree, *Sacrosancta*, which affirmed the power of general councils over the pope and thus sealed the validity of its decisions. Shortly afterward, John XXIII was captured and forced to step down.

The two other popes proved harder to dislodge from their thrones. Benedict XIII at Avignon refused to recognize the council's validity. Gregory XII at Rome was more realistic, and shrewder than the council itself: he agreed to abdicate on the seemingly small condition that he be allowed to convene the council retroactively, in place of John XXIII. As soon as the council agreed, he formally convoked it, and only then abdicated. This procedure was a small and seemingly illogical technicality, but a significant one, for it undercut all of the authoritative claims that John XXIII or Emperor Sigismund or the Council of Constance could make, and thus confirmed the legitimacy of the Roman line of popes all the way back to the beginning of the schism. This move also made it impossible for any future council to claim that it had the authority to convene itself—as the conciliarists at Constance claimed—or that councils possessed an authority higher than the pope's. In essence, what Gregory XII secured with this tiny footnote was nothing less than the death of conciliarism, though none present at Constance seemed to sense it.

With Rome's Gregory XII out of the way, in July 1417 the council formally deposed Avignon's Benedict XIII, who soon after lost the support of all of the secular rulers who had previously backed him, save for the king of Scotland and the count of Armagnac in France. Unrepentant and seemingly unable to cope with the harsh reality of his demotion, he insisted until his dying day that he was the only legitimate pope. At his family's castle near Valencia, "Pope" Benedict established a papal court in exile, which he compared to Noah's Ark, where he created his own cardinals and peevishly continued the Great Schism in relative obscurity for a few more years, spawning after his death a couple of powerless antipopes who eventually gave up all claims to legitimacy.

In its darkest hour, when the church was on the verge of disintegration, the Council of Constance had saved the day. In November 1417 the council elected as pope a vigorous forty-one-year-old cardinal who had taken part in the ill-fated Council of Pisa: Oddone Colonna, who assumed office as Martin V. Many throughout Christendom greeted the news with great relief, save for all malcontents, including the Lollards and Hussites.

The Hussites, especially, had plenty of reason to grieve, for the council was as intent on wiping them out as on solving the schism. In fact, one of the first items of business for the council was to pass judgment on Wycliffe and Hus. Here again conciliarist theory was put to work, with the council assuming a role normally played by the pope. Jan Hus himself was summoned by the council and guaranteed safe passage by Emperor Sigismund. Placing his trust in the emperor's promise and on his own ability to convince others of the truth, Hus traveled to Constance in October 1414. Although he had already been excommunicated, he expected a fair hearing and a chance to defend his views. Instead, he was charged with heresy and arrested. Although he did get the chance to address the council and to defend his own views and those of Wycliffe, Hus managed only to make things worse for himself. Having drawn up a list of thirty errors found in Hus's *On the Church*, the council sentenced Hus to death. As he awaited his punishment, Hus railed against the council's duplicity and its inconsistencies. His description of the fate of John XXIII seethes with anger:

> These spiritual men, who declare themselves to be the holy church and the council thrice holy and infallible . . . after adoring John XXIII on the knees and kissing his feet and calling him most holy, condemned him as a dissolute murderer, sodomite, simoniac, and heretic. They have therefore cut off the church's head, torn out its heart.[11]

On 6 July 1415, Jan Hus was burned alive at the stake, at the orders of the Council of Constance, despite the emperor's guaranteed protection. A few months later, the council also burned his colleague Jerome of Prague.

Constance may have disposed of two arch-heretics—and turned them into martyrs for their cause—but it could do nothing about their followers back home in Bohemia, where all hell broke loose. Unwilling to cave in, the Hussites engaged in nearly constant battle with their persecutors, tearing Bohemia apart. Pope Martin V did his utmost to wipe out the Hussites, calling two crusades against them in 1420 and 1431, neither of which was very successful.

Ultimately, neither pope nor emperor, nor the kings of Bohemia and their vassals could do much to stem the tide of heresy. The Hussites themselves split into different factions, the main two being the Utraquists and the Taborites. The Utraquists, who were the more numerous, derived their name from one of their distinctive practices: taking communion under both species (Latin: *utraque*, "both and"), that is, receiving both the bread and the wine. This practice—which challenged the ancient tradition of denying the wine to the laity—also earned them the name Calixtines, in reference to their drinking the communion wine from a chalice (Latin: *calix*). On the whole, the Utraquists were not at all opposed to a peaceful solution, even if they were willing to defend themselves by force. The Taborites, in contrast, were militant radicals with an apocalyptic bent. Having established a stronghold south of Prague that they named Tabor (after the biblical mountain from which the Israelites waged war on the Canaanites), these Hussites dedicated themselves to bringing about the kingdom of God on earth through warfare.

In their struggle for survival, the Utraquist Hussites summed up their position in the *Four Articles of Prague* (1419), in which they insisted on having the freedom to preach, partaking of both bread and wine at communion, barring the clergy from owning

Hussite dissent. The unvanquished Hussites developed apocalyptic tendencies. This image from the Hussite book *The Antithesis of Christ and Antichrist* depicts the pope and the Catholic Church hierarchy embraced by the seven-headed beast of the Apocalypse.

property or exercising secular authority, and allowing civil courts to punish sinful clerics. The Taborites insisted on much more, convinced as they were of their apocalyptic role. In addition to believing in the supreme authority of the Bible, they used Czech in their liturgies rather than Latin, allowed their clergy to marry, and reduced the sacraments from seven to the only two mentioned in the New Testament: baptism and the Eucharist.

The history of Hussite survival in the fifteenth century is exceedingly complex, given the differences between the Taborites and Utraquists and repeated attempts at reconciliation between the Utraquists and the Catholic Church. The appearance of a third Hussite movement in the mid-fifteenth century, the Unitas Fratrum (Unity of Brethren), complicates matters even more. In 1431 the Utraquists turned against the Taborites and gained some major concessions from the Catholic authorities as a reward. In 1436 they were allowed to have their own independent church, with communion in both kinds, and they won the right to expropriate property from the Catholic clergy. The Taborites put up a very fierce fight until 1452, when their stronghold was captured. But they never gave up the ghost. Much like their distant spiritual cousins the Waldensians and their native brethren the Unitas Fratrum, they survived on the fringe, in relatively small numbers.

Hussites proved to be very successful dissenters, relatively speaking. A full century after the burning of Jan Hus, Bohemia was uniquely diverse. Nowhere else could one find a livelier resistance to Catholic hegemony, or a tolerant compromise such as that reached with the Utraquists. Eventually, when the Protestant Reformation broke out in 1517 in nearby Saxony, the affinities between these old dissenters and the new ones were apparent to all concerned. So apparent, in fact, that many thought of the relation in terms of a family tree. Among the many strategies adopted by the Catholic Church against Martin Luther when he first challenged the status quo, one of the most prevalent—and most effective—was to link him to Jan Hus.

And this linkage was not restricted to Hussites. As the Protestant Reformation expanded and matured, and histories began to be written, most of these medieval dissenters would be folded into the history of Protestantism, both by Catholics and by Protestants themselves. The reasons for making these connections were as obvious at that time as they are today. When compared side by side, three medieval heresies seemed very similar to Protestantism: the Waldenses, the Lollards, and the Hussites. All of them upheld the Bible as the ultimate authority, and all of them rejected papal authority and many customs, rituals, and symbols, including pilgrimages; prayers for the dead; the veneration of saints, images, and relics; clerical celibacy; monasticism; and some of the sacraments.

Catholics had another reason for lumping all heretics together: ever since the time of the earliest church fathers, it had been common to think of all errors as linked to one another and to a common source. What St. Polycarp said of the heresiarch Marcion in the second century—that he was "the firstborn of Satan"—applied to all heretics. So, if the devil was the ultimate source of error, there had to be a certain seamlessness to heresy, a consistency that mirrored that of orthodoxy, in reverse, and placed all heretics, including

Protestants, on the same road to hell. Protestants had their own reasons for claiming the medieval dissenters as their spiritual forebears. First, by identifying "forerunners" to their Reformation, Protestants could deny the charge that they were inventing a whole new religion. Second, by finding a continuity of witnesses to a biblically centered "truth" in the midst of corruption, they could also claim that genuine Christianity was never fully snuffed out by the "false" church during the so-called Dark Ages. In other words, finding spiritual forebears in the past was a way of proving that Protestantism was the original and true form of the Christian faith, which God had never allowed to disappear altogether. Moreover, the linkage of so many dissenters over time allowed Protestants to portray the Catholic Church as a common enemy and an abomination.

One of the traits shared by all those who were branded as heretics was their belief that the Catholic Church could not reform itself, or was corrupt beyond hope. At the opposite end of the spectrum, among those optimists who had plenty of confidence in the church, some of the most earnest were the conciliarists. Pinning their hopes on an ancient institution, and on collegiality rather than autocracy, conciliarists aimed to keep the church in a constant state of renewal. They had reason to be optimistic in 1419, after the resounding success of the Council of Constance, which had not only solved the schism and prosecuted the top two Hussite heretics, but also drawn up an impressive reform plan and set it in motion through two decrees. The first of these was the aforementioned *Sacrosancta*, which declared the ultimate superiority of councils over popes, especially in times of crisis, and had made it possible for the council fathers to knock three popes off their thrones. Its language was crystal clear, and so was its focus on reform:

> This holy synod of Constance . . . , legitimately assembled in the Holy Ghost . . . declares that it has its power immediately from Christ, and every one, whatever his state or position, even if it be the Papal dignity itself, is bound to obey it in all those things which pertain to the faith and the healing of the said schism, and to the general reformation of the Church of God, in head and members.[12]

Equally significant was the decree *Frequens*, issued after the election of Martin V in 1417, which demanded that councils be convened on a regular basis, every ten years. In essence, *Frequens* was an attempt to make councils an integral part of church governance and to put into effect the power invoked in *Sacrosancta*. By ordering regularly scheduled councils, *Frequens* also set up the Council of Constance as the authority that would convoke all future councils, stripping the pope of that power, or at least making him subservient to its commands.

Beautiful as such a plan may have seemed to its framers, it proved a failure. Paradoxically, the ultimate success of conciliarism at Constance was also the beginning of its demise, for by restoring the papacy and installing a vigorous young man on the papal throne, Constance weakened conciliar authority. Martin V did not dismiss the decrees of Constance, but he did what he could to diminish their effect on his rule.

The first council convoked in Pope Martin's reign met at Pavia in 1423. It accomplished little or next to nothing, other than moving to Siena when plague struck Pavia, and then dissolving in March 1424. The second council was more significant, but utterly disastrous for the conciliarists. Following the dictates of *Frequens*, Martin V convoked a council at Basel, in Switzerland, in July 1431, but died almost immediately. His successor, Eugenius IV, locked horns with conciliarists at every turn. And he had reason to worry: over the following six years, the council relentlessly sought to whittle away his power and his privileges. Among other things, it curtailed appeals to Rome, set limits on the number of Italian cardinals, and reduced the revenues the pope received from abroad by more than half. Adding insult to injury, the council also met with Hussite representatives in 1434 and granted them liberal concessions.

Though it seemed as if the conciliarists were transforming the pope into a mere figurehead, Pope Eugenius found a way to thwart their plans. Announcing that a rare opportunity had arisen for reunifying the Catholic and Eastern Orthodox churches—which had excommunicated one another in 1054—Eugenius adjourned the council and ordered that it move to Ferrara, a location where he could join the council fathers and meet with the Greek delegation. Although this situation was a legitimate reason for moving the council, it was also a golden opportunity for Eugenius to regain control, as many of the conciliarists at Basel sensed. Most of the council fathers obeyed, and moved on to Ferrara, but some of the diehard conciliarists refused to leave Basel. Flushed with confidence, these renegade bishops proclaimed themselves the legitimate continuation of the council convoked in 1431, suspended Eugenius, and denounced his council at Ferrara as invalid. Eugenius had no choice but to excommunicate them all. And they had no choice but to depose Eugenius and elect a "legitimate" successor: Duke Amadeus VIII of Savoy, a layman, who was crowned as Pope Felix V. So, in June 1439, once again, there were rival claimants to the papal throne.

Frightening as the prospect of another Great Schism seemed, Pope Eugenius paid little attention to the rump council at Basel. Instead, he focused his energies on reuniting the Greek and Latin churches and on reclaiming his authority. The Council of Ferrara opened with much fanfare in January 1438, and an impressive delegation of seven hundred Greeks, which included a score of bishops, the patriarch of Constantinople Joseph II, and the Byzantine emperor John VIII Palaeologus. Forced to move from Ferrara to Florence by plague, the council finally managed to iron out all significant differences with the Orthodox Church and to issue a bull in July 1439, *Laetentur coeli*, which proclaimed the reunion of the two ancient churches. In the end, desperate for Western aid against the advancing Turks, it was the Greeks who made all the great concessions, accepting points of Catholic doctrine they had rejected for centuries, including the long-disputed *filioque* clause in the Nicene Creed, and certain controversial definitions regarding purgatory, the Eucharist, and the primacy of the pope. As much of a victory as this reunion was on paper for the pope, the council, and the Greek delegation, it proved to be an abject failure on the streets of Constantinople, which was by then the sole sad remnant of the Byzantine Empire, under siege by the Turks. Repudiated as a betrayal and a compromise with heresy, *Laetentur coeli* was consigned to oblivion by the Orthodox, along with the "traitors" who had agreed to it.

Pope Eugenius fared much better in his scuffle with the conciliarists at Basel, who dug their own grave by choosing to separate themselves from the majority. Far removed from the momentous business of reunion with the Orthodox, presided over by a puppet antipope who seemed content as a mere figurehead, the Basel diehards continued shouting that they were superior to the pope, but to no avail. No one was there to listen to them, save for a few minor secular rulers who liked the idea of a church with no papal strings attached, and some other ecclesiastics who shared their viewpoint and also turned a blind eye to reality. Eventually, the conciliarists ran out of options and admitted defeat, somewhat gracefully. When Pope Eugenius died in 1447, the renegade Council of Basel, which had moved to Lausanne, agreed to accept the election of his successor, Nicholas V. Some months later, they even convinced their own antipope Felix to abdicate, thus ending their little schism.

Conciliarism had flared up, suddenly, in a glorious display, much like a firework shot into the night sky. But it fizzled out just as quickly too, and along with it vanished its plan for ongoing reform. Pope Pius II wrote its obituary in his bull *Execrabilis*, which condemned all appeals to conciliar authority as "pestiferous poison . . . erroneous and detestable."[13]

With the death of conciliarism, all hope for reform devolved on individuals, be they popes, bishops, abbots, nuns, mystics, or laymen and laywomen. The need for reform was still there, and so was the craving for it, and the dissent, but corporate responsibility for renewing church and society seemed to have evaporated. Into the breach between the ideal and the real many brave souls would venture as the Middle Ages waned, ready to bridge the gap. The story of reform was by no means over, but the narrative would be very different.

Conclusion

Dissent is constant in history, and inevitable, for disagreement is as much a part of human experience as breathing. Religion is not exempt from this rule; in fact, one can argue—as some social scientists have—that religion is eminently susceptible to dissent, and also fertile ground for it. Religion speaks in the subjunctive mood, fusing the imagined and the real into a unified vision. It seeks to impose order on a seemingly chaotic universe, offering a glimpse of what should be, or could be, holding up ideals of the ultimate and optimal. Religion is a means of transcending and redeeming mundane reality as well as a process of social interaction and control.[14] Religion, then, has an ambivalent potential, highly charged: it can be all about idolizing the status quo and bowing and scraping to the powers that be, and it can also be all about casting down idols and remaking the world;

its very essence is not only to venerate what is ultimately true, but also to expose what is false and to wage war against it.

Dissent comes in various guises: it is a broad spectrum rather than something with a definite outline, with shadows to cast. At one extreme, dissent is passive and silent; at the other, fierce and deafening. Somewhere in between these extremes there is a boundary line in this spectrum, sometimes imperceptible, as thin as patience when tried to the utmost, and as scalding as red-hot lava. This is the line that marks the difference between rebel and reformer, fiend and martyr, heretic and saint. By the end of the fifteenth century many a would-be reformer had tested that boundary line or crossed it while pushing for reform, and many, perhaps in greater numbers, had refrained from doing so. Any way one looks at this point in the history of Western Europe, there is no denying that reforming and dissenting were closely intertwined, and that both were intensifying. As the sixteenth century dawned, many knew that a change for the better was inevitable, but few, if any, had any inkling of how intense, painful, and messy that change would be.

CHAPTER FOUR

Italian Humanism

It is at the very sources that one extracts pure doctrine.

—Erasmus of Rotterdam[1]

I n 1485, on the ancient Appian Way, just outside of Rome, three marble tombs were unearthed. One of these contained a great surprise: the intact body of a young Roman maiden who might have been a contemporary of Jesus and St. Peter, perhaps even older than them. Suddenly, in a city where many were gripped by the desire to recover the classical past, an ancient Roman had nearly come back to life.

The uproar caused by this unique find was unlike any other caused by the ancient ruins, statues, and artifacts that were being constantly dug up in and around Rome at that time. We know this because the event is one of the best documented of all in the history of fifteenth-century Rome, detailed in at least twelve surviving eyewitness accounts. "The whole of Rome, men and women, to the number of twenty thousand visited the marvel that day," said one of the eyewitnesses, Daniele da San Sebastiano, a cleric. Having described the corpse as "a young girl, intact in all her members, covered from head to foot with a coating of aromatic paste, one inch thick," Da San Sebastiano then went on to dwell on fine details, just as many medieval clerics had done when describing the uncorrupted bodies of Christian saints:

> On the removal of this coating . . . a face appeared, so lovely, so pleasing, so attractive, that, although the girl had certainly been dead fifteen hundred years, she appeared to have been laid to rest that very day. The thick masses of hair, collected on the top of the head in the old style, seemed to have been combed then and there. The eyelids could be opened and shut. . . . By pressing the flesh of the cheeks the color would disappear as in a living body. The tongue could be seen through the pink lips; the articulations of the hands and feet still retained their elasticity. . . . I am sure that if you had had the privilege of beholding that lovely young face, the pleasure would have equaled your astonishment.

Pleasure and astonishment, indeed, and all at once: mixed emotions that teetered on the edge of necrophilia, but frankly expressed so much about Rome and Italy at that point in history. For many of the thousands who saw the girl, or heard about her, she became as much of a metaphor as a marvel and a cause for joy. The girl seemed to bear silent yet eloquent witness to the reigning cultural paradigm of the day, that of bringing back to life the grandeur of ancient Rome. To many, she seemed to embody all of the good things that their Christian culture had undervalued for centuries, blindly preferring spirit over matter. The cleric Da San Sebastiano must have sensed this too, for he added: "I hasten to inform you of this event, because I want you to understand how the ancients took care to prepare not only their souls, but also their bodies for immortality."[2]

To the Past, and Forward

It mattered little that the Roman girl from the Appian Way began to decompose soon after she was found. Through her the past had lived again, even if fleetingly. At once an image from a lost world and a mirror, she had allowed Romans to see one of their own distant ancestors and to imagine themselves reflected in her. At that time, for many, nothing seemed more important than that kind of live encounter with the past.

Few slogans have captured the essence of an era so perfectly as "Ad fontes!" or, "Return to the sources!" These words were much more than a trendy slogan in the fifteenth and sixteenth century: they were also a battle cry, a paradigm for genuine reform. *Ad fontes* became a mentality, a way of thinking beyond questioning: ancient languages, ancient wisdom, ancient arts, ancient piety—all became undisputed models to follow, blueprints for a brighter future.

As counterintuitive as such a paradigm may seem in the twenty-first century, such was the predominant mindset of the European elite in the late fifteenth and early sixteenth centuries. In that age, nearly every reformer privileged the past in one way or another. Erasmus of Rotterdam (1469–1536), a Dutch scholar with strong reformist impulses and an incredibly wide reading audience was so convinced of this truism that he never questioned it. Take, for instance, what he had to say about the original text of the New Testament and the writings of the ancient Greek fathers:

> For we have in Latin only a few small streams and muddy puddles, while they have pure springs and rivers flowing in gold. I see that it is utter madness even to touch with the little finger that branch of theology which deals chiefly with the divine mysteries unless one is also provided with the equipment of Greek.[3]

What led Erasmus and many others of his generation to say things like this was the fact that their education had emphasized the superiority of the distant past, thanks to a cultural shift that had been gathering momentum for about a century and a half. Erasmus was one of the most brilliant scholars of his day, the ultimate exemplar of the eloquence, learning, and wit—and change in attitudes—favored by those who had taught him. And he was certainly not alone in thinking as he did about the days of the ancient Greeks and Romans and the early Christians. With the classical and primitive Christian past looming large in their minds and hearts, a whole generation had been trained to favor ancient paradigms. In France, another great scholar, Jacques Lefèvre d'Étaples, who had Latinized his name to Faber Stapulensis, turned this outlook into a metaphysical claim, saying, "The closer a thing is to its origin, the more purely it retains its own nature."[4] Chances are that he was paraphrasing some ancient Greek or Roman author, too.

But to get to Faber Stapulensis and Erasmus, one must first turn to Italy in the fourteenth and fifteenth centuries, where the process of privileging the classical past had begun. It was in Italy that urban life and commerce first began to break through the limits imposed by the feudal order, creating an economic and cultural climate in which the luxury of studying the past could become attractive and affordable. It was in Italy, too, that antiquity lay closest at hand, almost at every turn. Whether in Rome, full of half-buried ruins among which cattle and sheep grazed—and under which perfectly preserved corpses could be buried—or in Fiesole, near Florence, where the barbarian Lombards had planted their crude Stone Age–like tombs right next to a vastly older but infinitely more refined Roman amphitheater, or elsewhere, everyone in Italy could literally bump into remnants of the classical past and be awed by its superiority. Consequently, just as Italy had once been the birthplace of the ancient Roman Empire, so too would it be the cradle of the movement that sought to resurrect its long-dead glory.

Rebirth and Renewal

Conceiving of a long-gone past as an ideal age was the essence of the era that historians have dubbed the Renaissance (French: "rebirth"). Coined in the early nineteenth century, *Renaissance* is a vague and elastic term that is now viewed with some measure of suspicion, particularly because it applies to high culture and the elites of Europe rather than to the vast majority of those who lived during this time. Whether or not it is a viable concept is beside the point, however. Even those who dislike the concept of the Renaissance as a distinct era have to admit that many fifteenth-century European intellectuals and artists realized that something made their time *different* from the preceding millennium, and that they rapidly accepted the very concept of medieval, that is, of a *middle age*, or even a *dark age*, that stood between them and the glory days of the Greeks, Romans, and early Christians.

Whether one uses the term *early modern age* or *Renaissance* does not alter the fact that something changed drastically in European culture between the fifteenth and sixteenth centuries, and that the changes hinged on new paradigms. No one can easily overlook the fact that a consciousness of rebirth and reform was as much a part of early modern life, even for nonelites, as were all of the political, social, technological, and economic changes. *Renovation, renewal,* and *reformation* were closely related terms, perhaps one and the same, and so were *restoration* and *rebirth*. These concepts were in the air and hard to ignore or escape. Addressing a large crowd in Florence, the preacher Savonarola

Idolizing classical antiquity. Raphael's *The School of Athens* reifies the essential goal of the
Renaissance: returning *ad fontes*, and emulating ancient Greek and Roman paradigms in art,
philosophy, and science. This fresco painted in 1512 for the palace of Pope Julius II depicts the
greatest mathematicians, philosophers, and scientists from classical antiquity. The central figures
are Aristotle and Plato, two pagan philosophers who had considerable influence on Christianity.
Granting a place of honor to all of these non-Christian figures in the room where the most
important papal documents were signed is an indication of the triumph of Renaissance ideals at the
church's highest levels, and especially of the desire to find inspiration in the continuities between
Greco-Roman and Christian teachings.

took this awareness of change for granted, telling his listeners, "If you are a Christian, you
have to believe that the Church must be renewed."[5]

Savonarola also took it for granted that his congregation had a certain view of
history, for to believe that change was necessary and inevitable was to admit that the
immediate past was an age of decline. In other words, it required believing that a very
large slice of history was inferior to what had preceded it, and that the time was ripe to
return to the original, pure models of a golden past. Understanding the Renaissance
as this change of historical perspective allows one to better understand what made the
Reformations of the sixteenth century possible, at least on a conceptual level. This is to
say not that the Renaissance caused the Reformation, but rather that the Renaissance
helped make the Reformation possible.

The Essence of Humanism

"One can state this pointedly: No humanism, no Reformation"—thus argued the
historian Bernd Moeller years ago.[6] He might as well have said, "No Renaissance, no

Reformation," for humanism was, in essence, the defining intellectual characteristic of the Renaissance.

The term *humanista* was used in late fifteenth-century Italy to characterize those who followed the curriculum at the heart of the Renaissance, the *studia humanitatis*, that is, the study of grammar, rhetoric, poetry, history and ethics, or as one *humanista* himself defined it, "the pursuit of activities proper to mankind . . . . learning and training in virtue."[7] Derived from Greek ideals of *paedeia* (culture or education), this curriculum sought to revive ancient erudition and eloquence. It also sought to dethrone theology as the queen of the sciences. There were other names for this curriculum: *artes liberales*, *bonae artes*, *humanae artes*, all of which were highly charged with meaning. It was a curriculum devised in a world in which learning was no longer dominated by clerics, the world of the rising merchant class and the sovereign state; at once ancient and new, it exalted the classical past and downgraded the scholastic learning of the medieval universities very self-consciously.

Focusing on the emphasis that Renaissance learning placed on "human arts" and their capacity to liberate the human mind and will, German historians coined the term *Humanismus* in the early nineteenth century. At that time, the term had a sharp polemical edge to it, for it suggested a stark contrast between the "dark ages" when God and the clerics ruled supreme and the modern "enlightened" age when the human began to be exalted over the divine. In the nineteenth century, humanism was associated with progress and tended to be seen as the engine that drove the West into modernity. Nowadays, historians accept a much more complex relation between humanism, religion, medieval culture, and the Reformations of the sixteenth century, taking it for granted that humanism was many things at once, and that skepticism and secularism were not necessarily its defining characteristics.

Humanism looked forward as much as it looked back, striving to give birth again to what seemed to be a lost wisdom. It was an outlook and a trend as much as an educational program, bringing together many different disciplines and attitudes, giving rise simultaneously to a new learning and a new piety. Its most immediate effect was the creation of a new, self-propagating class of scholars, many of whom were laymen rather than clerics; its most enduring impact took several generations to become manifest, for humanism shattered the reigning paradigms that had guided Western Christendom for a millennium, inspiring a new confidence in the powers of the human intellect, promoting new kinds of inquiry, giving voice to a critique of the past and the status quo that was at once radical and utterly conservative. Something of that magnitude cannot happen overnight.

Humanism focused above all on the study of ancient languages and texts by both pagan and Christian authors. Greek therefore became an essential part of the humanist curriculum, and eventually Hebrew too. What marked off the early humanists was their unabashed love for pagan antiquity, and especially for the work of ancient historians. Beginning in Italy in the fourteenth century, scholars such as Francesco Petrarca, or Petrarch (1304–1374), and Giovanni Boccaccio (1313–1375) turned to the ancient classics for inspiration.

Petrarch, a poet who had grown up in the rarified atmosphere of the papal court at Avignon, not only pored over classical texts and extolled their value, but also traveled widely, searching for long-lost manuscripts and making contacts with other scholars. Petrarch's reach was very wide, embracing both Christianity and pagan antiquity, and he wrote in the best Ciceronian Latin as well as in the Italian vernacular. Petrarch was as much at home reading Livy and Cicero as St. Augustine, whose *Confessions* he treasured; and he was as gifted in writing poetry to Laura—a woman he loved from afar—as in denouncing the failures of the scholastics. In addition, he was just as intent on exalting the central place of human beings in God's creation as in bemoaning their sinfulness.

Petrarch's disciple and good friend Boccaccio was equally complex. While also deeply committed to the study of the ancients, Boccaccio managed to raise vernacular literature to the level of the classics, especially with his masterpiece, the *Decameron*, a collection of tales written in the fourteenth century as the Black Death devastated Italy. Like Petrarch, Boccaccio did much to promote the classics, collecting lost texts, sponsoring the study of Greek, and writing treatises on antiquity, such as his encyclopedic *De genealogia deorum gentilium* (On the Genealogy of the Pagan Gods) and *De casibus virorum illustrium* (On the Fates of Famous Men).

A New Approach to the Past

Humanism was not simply an antiquarian scholarly obsession, but rather a pragmatic initiative for forging a new society, more learned and more virtuous. Rhetorical skills were highly prized by humanists, not for their own sake, but for the power eloquence can have in moving people to action. Humanism was an educational program well suited for the elite, especially for those laymen gradually claiming their place alongside the clergy. Although humanism did much to enrich culture, it was above all a way of ensuring and maintaining good rulership. And it was a fast-moving tidal wave, which swept through Italy, flourishing in republican city-states and in monarchical royal courts, supported by universities and wealthy patrons alike; eventually, it would cross the Alps and permeate all of Europe.

To study the classics one needed texts and the linguistic skills with which to read them. Much was accomplished on both of these fronts by the man who inherited Petrarch's mantle, Coluccio Salutati (1331–1406), chancellor of Florence for the last twenty-seven years of his life. Under his leadership, humanism flourished, not only because he collected many manuscripts and built up a spectacular library, but also because he actively sponsored classical studies. One of Salutati's most significant accomplishments was to make it possible for the first generation of humanists to dive deeply into Greek texts, and he did so by inviting Manuel Chrysoloras (1353–1415), a Greek scholar, to teach in Florence. Chrysoloras had originally come to Italy in 1394 as an envoy of the Byzantine emperor seeking military aid against the relentless advance of the Ottoman Turks, but he found for himself a fairly comfortable and rewarding niche as teacher and translator in Florence. He would be among the first of many Greek scholars who came to Italy loaded not only with great knowledge to impart, but also with texts that had long been lost or forgotten in the West.

The hard luck of the Byzantines was a godsend for the budding humanist movement: as interest in Greek increased, the Ottomans kept advancing, forcing more and more Greek scholars to seek exile in Italian cities with receptive audiences. With the fall of Constantinople to the Ottomans in 1453, the stream of exile scholars swelled, suddenly flooding Florence and other centers of humanist learning with Greek texts and with teachers who held the keys to their hidden treasures. The gains for the West would be immeasurable, for scholars such as Chrysoloras had a double impact: among learned circles, they were instrumental in creating a revolution of sorts, making accessible for the first time translations of many long-forgotten texts from classical antiquity and the Greek fathers of the church. The fact that this influx of Greek learning coincided with the invention of the printing press made the impact of the exiles even greater.

Focusing on the study of ancient languages and on the rhetorical arts meant looking at history with a pragmatic eye, and imbuing the past with a transforming power. Above all, the past had an ethical dimension. Some humanists, like Pier Paolo Vergerio, would even argue that history was the queen of the liberal arts:

> I accord first place to history, on grounds both of its attractiveness and of its utility, qualities which appeal equally to the scholar and to the statesman. . . . History, then, gives us the examples of the precepts inculcated by philosophy. The one shows what men should do, the other what men have said and done in the past, and what practical lessons we may draw therefrom for the present day.[8]

Focused as they were on the ancient past, humanists could not help but rewrite history. And it was precisely through its historians, all of whom were also superb classicists, that the humanist movement forged its critical apparatus and its agenda. It could be said that the most significant achievement of the Renaissance humanists was not that they turned to the classics—for these had not been entirely abandoned in the Middle Ages—but that they developed a new historical perspective from which to view the classics and all of the past. Among the early pioneers, three historians stand out for their contributions: Leonardo Bruni (1370–1444), Flavio Biondo (1392–1463), and Lorenzo Valla (1406–1457).

Leonardo Bruni, chancellor of Florence from 1427 to 1444, was a master orator, historian, and political theorist, credited with giving birth to so-called civic humanism, that is, a humanism that extolled the virtues of republicanism. Bruni was also highly representative of a new turn in the writing of history—and highly influential in its inception and development. Inspired by ancient historians, Bruni began to write about the past with a new sense of purpose, and a far more critical eye, approaching evidence in a way that we might recognize as "modern" or empirical: carefully weighing the evidence he found in original sources, searching for causal explanations other than the hand of

Divine Providence, delving even into the psychological motivations of historical figures. In addition, Bruni put to work the Greek he had learned from Chrysoloras, translating texts by Plutarch, Xenophon, Plato, and Aristotle into Latin.

Even more impressive was the work of Flavio Biondo, a papal secretary in Rome. Sometimes hailed as the greatest historian of his century, Biondo availed himself of different kinds of sources, including architectural ruins, coins, objects, and inscriptions. Biondo was most keenly interested in reconstructing the ancient Roman past as a means of providing models that could be used in his own day. Two books of his—*Roma instaurata* (1444–1446) and *Roma triumphans* (1459) would have an enormous impact on his contemporaries, not only because they awakened an increased respect for Rome's ancient glory, but also because they helped elevate the humanist predilection for the classical past to new heights.

After traveling throughout Italy and doing what we would today call field research, Biondo also produced *Italia illustrata* (1448–1458), a topographical and historical survey of the entire Italian Peninsula from antiquity down to his own day. This work did much to acquaint its readers with the destructive impact of the barbarian invasions. It was also a great piece of humanist propaganda—perhaps the first self-conscious history of the Renaissance—for Biondo outlined the revival of classical letters that he and his colleagues had embarked upon. This work was followed by the massive *Historiarum ab inclinatione Romanorum Imperii decades* (1439–1453), which focused on the decline and fall of the Roman Empire, and dealt with its aftermath. By attributing the collapse of Rome to the barbarian invasions, and by dealing with the rise of Christian Europe in the succeeding millennium as a continuous event, or a single epoch, Biondo contributed significantly to the conceptualization of the interval between Rome and his own day as a distinct period, or "middle age." It could be said, then, that Biondo might have unintentionally invented not only the Middle Ages, but also the Renaissance.

Lorenzo Valla had a more ambitious reach than Bruni or Biondo, and he was a pioneer on several fronts. Valla turned a critical eye on texts, employing philological and historiographical skills with startling results. In 1440, while working as court secretary and historian for Alfonso of Aragon, who was also king of Naples, he analyzed one of the texts cited most often by the papacy in defense of their rulership of central Italy, the *Donation of Constantine*, a document supposedly dating from the fourth century, in which Emperor Constantine gave Pope Sylvester and all his successors control of Rome and surrounding areas. Since Valla's employer, King Alfonso, was then engaged in a war with Pope Eugenius IV, Valla's scrutiny of the *Donation* was not a purely scholarly exercise. Yet in the process of exposing the Donation as inauthentic, for pragmatic reasons, Valla would nonetheless achieve a remarkable feat in philology and historiography.

Conceiving of the text as necessarily bound to its own time and place, Valla hunted for anachronisms, that is, bits of text that betrayed the real age of the document. By looking closely at the Latin style and vocabulary of the *Donation* and at its content, Valla determined that the document had to be a forgery. His logic was irrefutable: the

Donation's Latin style was out of sync with that of other fourth-century texts. Moreover, the document was full of words and concepts that did not yet exist in the fourth century, such as fief, and it also alluded to later beliefs and customs. For example, the *Donation* threatened anyone who doubted it with hellfire. Knowing that no emperor used such language in Constantine's day, Valla honed in for the kill:

> What shall I censure the more, the stupidity of the ideas, or of the words? . . . This terrible threat is the usual one, not of a secular ruler, but of the earthly priests and flamens, and nowadays, of ecclesiastics. And so this is not the utterance of Constantine, but of some fool of a priest who, stuffed and pudgy, knew neither what to say nor how to say it, and, gorged with eating and heated with wine, belched out these wordy sentences which convey nothing to another, but turn the author against himself.[9]

Anyone who knew the real classical past had to admit Valla was right. Even Flavio Biondo, secretary to Pope Eugenius, had to cease citing the *Donation*.

Valla had unmasked a great fraud by means of textual criticism and historical logic. And in proving that a papal document was nothing more than a tawdry medieval invention, he had reclaimed the genuine past and revealed a whole new level of corruption. The church was corrupt not just because of abuses and clerical misbehavior, but also because it had twisted the truth itself. In sum, Valla proved by clear, cold logic that popes could be deceitful:

> For some centuries now, the popes have either not recognized the Donation of Constantine as an invention or a fake, or have fabricated it themselves, or have later followed the deceitful steps of their predecessors. And although their deceit is clear, they have defended it as the truth and thereby dishonored the glory of the papacy . . . and the Christian religion.

Valla went even further, arguing that this duplicity corrupted the entire church. It was a virtuoso feat of scholarship, with implications far beyond the ivory tower:

> For we see that the ruin of the Italians and of many other nations have flowed from this one source. If the source of the water is bitter, so too is the stream; if the root is impure, so too are the branches; if the yeast is spoiled, so too is all of the dough.[10]

No surprise, then, that Valla's *Falsely Believed and Forged Donation of Constantine* would be printed in Germany in 1517, just as the Protestant Reformation got under way.

Unmasking the *Donation* was just the beginning for Valla. He also exposed the fraudulent identity of Dionysius the Areopagite, one of the most important authorities in medieval theology, proving that this author who called himself Dionysius could not have been the man converted by the apostle Paul in Athens (Acts 17:34), as everyone believed. Dionysius carried an awful lot of weight: only the Bible itself and St. Augustine were cited more often. His texts, which had been translated into Latin in the ninth century, had given the West access to a Christian whose thinking was deeply colored by the late antique pagan school of philosophy known as Neoplatonism. Valla turned his suspicious

Lorenzo Valla (c. 1406–1457). One of the most formidable of Italian humanists, Valla raised the study of Latin and Greek to new heights. Employing his philological skills and keen acumen to unmask the spurious authorship of key documents, Valla also made great methodological strides in historical research. In addition, by comparing St. Jerome's translation of the Bible with the Greek text of the New Testament for the first time, Valla also led the way in critical biblical scholarship.

eye to the original texts, and discovered all sorts of painful anachronisms, heretofore ignored. As in the case of the *Donation*, Valla used contextual evidence to prove that the author of the Dionysian texts had assumed a false identity. Most damning were those slips of the author's tongue that proved he was borrowing from much later authors, such as Proclus, a fourth-century Neoplatonist. The capstone of Valla's argument, however, was a silent and invisible piece of evidence. Why was it, he pointed out, that no one at all prior to the sixth century had ever quoted Dionysius? If Dionysius really was Paul's convert and the first bishop of Athens, he should have been quoted repeatedly alongside other apostolic fathers. How could anyone explain away the puzzling absence from the historical record of such a great figure?

To unmask Dionysius as a fraud was not the same as to call his theology into question, but it was nonetheless an assault on tradition, since Dionysius was not only a crucial source for medieval theology and piety, but also the patron saint of the French monarchs, who preferred to be buried at the Abbey of Saint-Denis, where they wrongly believed Dionysius was interred. Even more momentous, that abbey itself was the birthplace of Gothic architecture, which was self-consciously linked to Dionysian mysticism. So, taking on this giant was a lot like taking on the whole Middle Ages. And Valla seemed to thrive on such challenges.

Valla was also one of the first humanists to submit the Bible to the same rigorous scrutiny as any ancient text, and in doing so he laid the foundations for a revolution in biblical scholarship. Aware as he was of the way in which texts became corrupted by transcription, invention, and translation, Valla sought to obtain as pure a text of the Holy Scriptures as possible. In his *Annotations on the New Testament Collected from Various Codices in Each Language* (1449), Valla collated the original Greek text of the New Testament with the Latin Vulgate translation, submitting both to philological analysis

and questioning the adequacy of the Latin text. Two assumptions implicit in Valla's biblical work would eventually gain wide acceptance, especially among Protestant reformers:
that the Bible texts are authoritative only in their original versions, that is, the Hebrew
of the Old Testament and the Greek of the New Testament, and that good philological
training is therefore absolutely necessary for a full understanding of the Bible. By returning *ad fontes* in such a literal way with the Bible, Valla thus sought to turn every
theologian into a philologist.

As could be expected, Valla was attacked for this suggestion, and it is no surprise
either that his *Annotations* would end up in the Catholic Church's *Index of Forbidden
Books* about a century after his death. His influence on Protestants would be substantial.
Valla's *Annotations* would be published by Erasmus of Rotterdam in 1505 and would
guide Erasmus as he prepared his edition of a Greek New Testament, which, in turn, after
being published in 1516, would become the foundation of the new Protestant Bibles of
the sixteenth century.

Valla was a gadfly with a purpose, and a very wide reach. His aim was to identify
the genuine, and to return to the sources as a means of purifying everything. But he
also seemed to thrive on controversy. The list of "truths" that he challenged is long and
impressive, and not just limited to medieval authorities. Risking the ire of fellow humanists, he dared to critique the Latin of Cicero and to correct Livy's facts, and then he poked
fun at those who challenged him. In some ways, he seemed as much a "forerunner" of the
Protestant Reformation as Hus or Erasmus. He questioned the authorship of the Apostle's
Creed, one of the church's most important prayers, earning himself a brush with the
Inquisition (from which he escaped unpunished). He also accused the monastic clergy
of having usurped too high a place for themselves, and he blasted them for paying too
much attention to vows. What counted most in religion, he said, was "devotion" rather
than the formal observance of rules. As a final act of insolence, late in life, he mercilessly
roasted the great thirteenth-century scholastic theologian Thomas Aquinas at a ceremony
at which he had been invited to sing his praises, and he proposed that the Bible and the
ancient fathers were far superior to Aquinas.

That Valla managed to stir so much controversy in his own day and go unpunished should not be too surprising. His targets were not doctrines or rites, but contemporary mores, factual errors, ancient texts, and the identities of authors. In the fifteenth
century, the Catholic Church could tolerate much more dissent than it would later, and
it often did. Even a pope could see the good to be gleaned from Valla's brilliance, and in
1448, the man who had cast doubt on the *Donation of Constantine* and denounced papal
corruption won himself a post as apostolic secretary to Pope Nicholas V, and was later
appointed a canon of the basilica of St. John Lateran by Pope Calixtus III. In some ways,
Valla was on the cutting edge, perhaps even ahead of his time, but in other ways, he was
also very much a man of his age. It helps to keep in mind that Valla ended his career as a
papal secretary, and that he held numerous benefices while keeping a mistress and siring

three children. Philologists and historians may make good critics and gadflies, but not necessarily good reformers.

Humanist historians and philologists such as Bruni, Biondo, and Valla brought about changes in thinking, but they were never directly engaged in the work of reforming their church or their society. Their accomplishment was nonetheless immense, and without it the great changes of the sixteenth century would have been literally unthinkable.

Conceiving of the millennium circa 400–1400 as a distinct period—and as an age of darkness—was the great imaginative leap of the Renaissance. Inchoate at first, and a mere whisper shared by a few learned men, this reconfiguration of time gradually gained lucidity and acceptance; by the late fifteenth century, it seemed as obvious to all of educated Europe as the sky itself, or as the difference between day and night. Seeing history this way required breaking with much of the past and a privileging of both antiquity and the present. It also required an imaginative leap over Christian conceptions of time and history, and an implicit rejection of the very calendar by which the years were reckoned, with those before Christ, *B.C.*, receding ever backward into the darkness of the expulsion from Eden, and those afterward moving ever forward toward the resurrection and the fulfillment of salvation history, each one brightly christened an *anno Domini*, *A.D.*, or year of the Lord.

It was the monks who had come up with the calendar, as a means not just of keeping track of time, but also of reifying the Christian view of history. Thinking of all the past in terms of ages, or periods, was not new. The ancients had followed this practice, layering their map of time with successive ages. But Christian periodization was much simpler, and purely binary, with one single point in time dividing "before" from "after." For Christian thinkers, the incarnation of God was the only truly decisive change that had ever taken place in the history of the human race, the sole turning point from darkness to light.

The periodization suggested by the Italian scholars not only changed the number of ages, but also reshuffled the light and the darkness. In the humanist scheme, there were three periods: antiquity, the "middle ages," and the present. The advent of Christ or the creation of the church had no place in the value assigned to these ages: darkness did not apply to religious beliefs, but to cultural achievements. Consequently, instead of viewing antiquity as dark simply because it was pagan, the humanists saw it as a golden age. To them, it was the Middle Ages that were dark—that entire millennium from the fall of the Western Roman Empire to the fifteenth century.

In sum, the humanists were right in perceiving their own age as different, and they had no one to thank but themselves: their reinterpretation of history was arguably the most dramatic departure in Western thinking in more than a millennium. Yet for all of their novelty, the humanists still drew on ancient traditions. The very concept of a middle age was already in place, though in a very different form: Christians believed that they lived in an interim of sorts, between the incarnation of God in Jesus and his return at the end of the world. All of Christian time was a "middle age," a twilight zone between realized and delayed eschatology: Jesus Christ was the Alpha and the Omega, the beginning and the end of all things. He had saved the human race through his death and resurrection and had promised to return, to judge the entire human race at the end of time. Awaiting his return, Christians measured time with an apocalyptic horizon in view. The humanists proposed an alternative and much less apocalyptic reading of history— one that relocated the horizon of the Final Judgment much farther away from the present.

Throughout the Middle Ages, many apocalyptic movements had focused on decline and corruption and the imminent return of the Lord. Apocalypticism was widespread in medieval Europe, and nearly always tied to dissent in one way or another, bubbling up from below here and there. By far the most significant apocalyptic ideology was that of Joachim of Fiore (1132–1202), a monk whose periodization of history was somewhat similar to that of the humanists. Joachim divided all of human history into three periods, on Trinitarian terms, and prophesied the coming of a third age, or final millennium. First came the age of the Father, which spanned the time from the creation of Adam and Eve to the birth of Christ. This period was followed by the age of the Son, a "middle" age that spanned the time since the church came into being and was bedeviled by corruption. Next would come the age of the Spirit, the last age before the Final Judgment, when all humans would renounce private property and live as monks. Joachim's apocalyptic prophecies were adopted by various individuals and groups, especially by the Observant Franciscans, some of whom believed that the world would change in the year 1260. Though that apocalypse did not take place as predicted, Joachimite expectations endured for centuries. Some of the first Spanish Franciscan missionaries to set foot in Mexico in the 1530s, for instance, were full of Joachimite fervor.

Now the humanists were claiming a vantage point similar to that of Joachimite prophecy and other sorts of apocalypticism, but with one huge difference: the decline and corruption that presaged the end were certainly there, but the end at hand was not the Final Judgment, but rather a new beginning. So, although the humanists had a quasi-apocalyptic bent, insofar as they debased the recent past at the expense of the pregnant *now* and incipient future, they diverged significantly from medieval apocalypticism in having a frame of reference that was not at all theological, and that, in addition, also privileged the distant pagan past.

Civic Humanism and Political Thought

"Man is a mortal but happy *god* because he combines capacity for virtuous action with rational understanding," said the humanist Leon Battista Alberti (1404–1472), echoing the all-important Cicero. Action and thinking were related for Alberti and his fellow humanists, for one of their chief assumptions was that human beings had a free will, that is, an inborn capacity for choosing between good and evil. Moreover, as Alberti and many other humanists saw it, human agency was often the direct cause of events—rather than fortune or the will of God—and it was therefore up to human beings to choose their own destiny, ultimately.

This godlike happiness was active rather than passive. "Man was born to be useful to man," said Alberti. Being nearly divine in their capacity to know the truth and to act correctly, humans bore a heavy responsibility to do their best, not only for themselves, but also for one another, and especially for their community. For most humanists, the dignity of human nature was above all social.

In the second half of the twentieth century, two interpretations of the Renaissance became widely accepted. Paul Oskar Kristeller argued that humanism was not a specific philosophy, but rather an approach to learning deeply imbued with a high regard for the dignity of human nature.[11] Hans Baron argued that the second generation of Italian humanists were chiefly devoted to "civic humanism," that is, a political philosophy that emphasized human freedom and favored republican ideals over monarchist tendencies.[12] Both of these views of the Renaissance gained favor for the same reason: they called attention to the very practical nature of the historical bent of the Italian humanists and to their great emphasis on the ethical potential of human beings.

Whether or not one accepts the term *civic humanism* as useful, the facts remain that Italian humanists turned to history as a means of renewing the present, and that their work was intensely focused on ethics and politics. Beginning with Petrarch, humanists seized on the notion that humans were above all political creatures, and that the study of the classics should be most intensely concerned with the promotion of virtue. The virtues were fixed points, as unalterable as the very laws of nature, and they were the key to good government. The chief assumption of the early humanists, then, was that there were ethical principles that were universal and unchanging. To deviate from virtue was always to court disaster. No humanist could be totally blind, however, to the cruel misfortunes and twists of fate that bedevil human history. Though humanists tended to place a high value on human agency, they also left room for Divine Providence or for chance, usually dressed up in classical garb as *fortuna*. But the relation between human agency and *fortuna* was not at all lopsided: relying as much on Christian theology as on pagan classical philosophy, humanists tended to argue that the only sure protection against unpredictable chance was virtue, or *virtú*. In the mind of many a humanist, fortune was ultimately powerless against the truly virtuous.

So, starting with Petrarch, humanists counseled rulers to love their subjects, and to govern according to the seven virtues: prudence, temperance, fortitude, justice, faith, hope, and love. For years, humanists ransacked the pagan classics and Christian texts for historical examples of rulers who had overcome *fortuna* with *virtú*. This lesson, above all else, was *the* point of doing history, and of focusing on the past. But in the late fifteenth century, as the political situation became more unstable in Italy, changes began to take place in humanist ethical and political thinking. Wracked by nearly constant wars between city-states, most of which were waged by mercenary armies led by *condottieri*, or hired military leaders, some of whom were foreign, Italy itself seemed a denial of all of the values touted by civic humanists. Instead of proving a beacon to the world, or living proof of the power of virtue, Italy had fallen prey to marauding armies, and to plunder, murder, and extortion. What was said about one of the foreign *condottiere*, the Englishman Sir John Hawkwood, seemed to summarize the situation succinctly: "un inglese italianato e un diavolo incarnato" (an Italianized Englishman is a devil incarnate). In other words, Italian values had sunk so low that they debased rather than elevated those who adopted them.

Two historians who lived through this period did much to realign humanist ethical and political thought with the harsh new realities: Francesco Guicciardini (1483–1540), and Niccolò Machiavelli (1469–1527). Relying on the new critical tools bequeathed to them by earlier Italian humanists, Guicciardini and Machiavelli further divorced humanist historiography and political philosophy from theology. Men of the Renaissance, both of these writers did much to transcend it, and to prove that its legacy was far from homogenous, or liberal.

A Florentine patrician, Francesco Guicciardini distinguished himself as historian, diplomat, warrior, and statesman. After receiving a humanist education at Ferrara, Padua, and his native Florence, Guicciardini served as ambassador at the Spanish court (1511–1514), and then as a governor of various territories of the Papal States (1514–1540). Though his accomplishments as a statesman were significant, it was as a historian that Guicciardini distinguished himself, particularly in his *History of Italy*, written during the last years of his life and published posthumously.

Guicciardini's most radical proposition was also his most enduring. Combining his own experiences in the courts and battlefields of Italy with a keen skepticism for reigning paradigms, Guicciardini proposed that history had no clear lessons to teach, much less any proof to offer that virtue could always prevail over fortune. Going against the very grain of the early humanist program, he argued that history was not to be seen as a set of fixed of examples, or of models to follow, for the circumstances of each historical event are unique. For Guicciardini, history therefore never repeated itself exactly, and he warned that the past and the present needed to be viewed with critical distance as not necessarily related to one another. To Guicciardini, the best that one could do with the past was to use it cautiously in assessments about the present.

Another Florentine, Niccolò Machiavelli, mounted an even greater assault on reigning paradigms. Reared in a noble family of modest means, Machiavelli was never able to fully immerse himself in the study of Greek or classical letters, but he was nonetheless exposed to a humanistic education. Self-taught to some degree, never totally committed to humanist assumptions, Machiavelli proved himself a most original thinker while displaying the eloquence and intellectual rigor that humanists so loved.

Like Guicciardini, Machiavelli was no ivory-tower historian. Deeply involved in the political life of Florence and of Italy, Machiavelli took part in many of the turbulent events that shook his homeland in the late fifteenth and early sixteenth centuries. Imprisoned and tortured in 1512 as a result of his political allegiances, Machiavelli was

Niccolò Machiavelli (1469–1527). By laying aside Christian ethics and redefining the meaning of "virtue" in real-world politics, this Florentine made his name synonymous with political deviousness. Portrait by Antonio Maria Crespi.

forced to live in poverty on a small estate outside of Florence for many years. It was while he lived under such conditions that he wrote his two most famous works, *Discourses on the First Ten Books of Livy*, a historically grounded analysis of republican government, and *The Prince*, a manual for rulers.

Machiavelli's *The Prince*, his greatest achievement, was the fruit of humanistic learning and the very epitome of its constantly evolving nature. It was also an outright rejection of any conceptions of virtue held dear by humanists or Christian moralists. In it, Machiavelli boldly argued that the only genuine virtue in rulership is the ability to gain and maintain power. Gone are many of the chief assumptions of so-called civic humanism, such as an unquestioning belief in the seven virtues, or in the necessity of modeling one's behavior on fixed principles that favor love of one's neighbor, justice, magnanimity, or faith in anything other than raw power.

Indebted as much to the Christian notion of original sin as to his own observations, Machiavelli argued that human beings were driven by selfishness and greed, and deeply prone to violence; consequently, ignorance of human nature seemed worse to him than ignorance of history. It was not through the arts of rhetoric and observance of the seven virtues that one could attain and maintain power, he argued, but rather through the exercise of power, and even through cruelty, if necessary. According to Machiavelli, people did not respond as well to a fine speech or a magnanimous gesture as they did to plain fear. "Is it better for a ruler to be loved or feared?" he asked. His answer was as dispassionate as all of his advice, and every bit as calculating: fear is the better tool, he said, perhaps even a mix of love and fear, for love alone will never prevail over human wickedness.

Machiavelli thus stood the humanist concept of virtue on its head, deliberately playing on the multiple meanings of the Italian term *virtú*, which meant not just "virtue" but also "ability" and "manliness" or "virility." Being a ruler required strength and the ability to judge every situation individually, free of any concern for fixed values. Employing historical examples, Machiavelli went on to show how the classical and Christian virtues could be seen as vices in some cases: temperance could turn into inefficiency, generosity into bankruptcy, and charity into vulnerability and collapse. Conversely, cruelty, judiciously applied could turn into a virtue higher than any other. In his own words, the successful ruler should discover that "something which seems to be a virtue, if pursued, will result in his ruin; while some other thing which seems to be a vice, if pursued, will secure his safety and his well-being."[13]

Machiavelli was an unflinching realist who used the best Renaissance rhetoric and historiography to demolish some of the dearest assumptions of humanism. In arguing that the role of the good prince was to maintain his government by all means possible, even by ignoring the classical and Christian virtues, Machiavelli denied the assumption that government should seek to conform to ideal values. To succeed, he argued, a ruler needs to seize the moment rather than to imitate great leaders of the past or anything found in books. His advice was utterly antithetical to reigning paradigms, and as brutal as the world itself: "The man who adapts his method of procedure to the nature of the times will prosper, and, likewise, the man who establishes his procedures out of tune with the times will come to grief."[14]

Published posthumously in 1532, *The Prince* went on to elicit a wide range of responses, from emulation at one end to fear and loathing at the other. Though thoroughly condemned by Catholics and Protestants alike, Machiavelli's book would never disappear from view, a constant reminder of the gulf that existed between the real and the ideal, or the best and the worst in human nature. It is not at all surprising that his name was turned into an adjective that described devious, unscrupulous behavior (*Machiavellian*), and that few other names, save for that of the Borgias, so readily conjure up images of villainy in this age. After all, Cesare Borgia, one of the most ruthless of Renaissance warriors, was greatly admired by Machiavelli, and served as a model example in *The Prince* itself. It helps to keep in mind that Cesare Borgia was the illegitimate son of Pope Alexander VI (Rodrigo Borgia), himself the embodiment of all the corruption the so-called civic humanists sought to wipe off the face of the earth. And his great-uncle was Pope Calixtus III (Alonso Borgia), patron of Lorenzo Valla. Like Valla, that other fearless pioneer who seemed ahead of his time, Machiavelli remained deeply enmeshed in the paradoxes of his era.

If Machiavelli proved anything at all besides the fact that humanist idealism had become but a dream by the 1530s, it was that humanism itself was a complex movement that could produce a bewildering array of disciples and points of view, including some that exploded the central assumptions of the earlier humanists. It is with this in mind that we must now turn to the other end of the humanist spectrum, to those who initiated a unique philosophical and theological revival with a deeply spiritual dimension.

Reviving Plato

Diametrically opposed to the skeptical and secularizing Machiavelli stood a number of scholars who sought to revive Platonism, one of the most spiritual and idealistic of all of the ancient schools of thought. Although the ancient Greek philosopher Plato (427–347 B.C.) and his later disciples had never entirely disappeared from view in the Middle Ages, especially because of the influence of St. Augustine, Dionysius the Areopagite, and other ancient Christian fathers who were Platonists, there was no denying that Aristotle had reigned supreme among the learned for several centuries.

Enumerating the differences between Aristotle and Plato is unnecessary at this point. Suffice it to say that Aristotle had reigned supreme among scholastic theologians since the thirteenth century, when many of his previously lost works were translated into Latin, and that displacing Aristotle and recovering Plato meant returning to a way of thinking that stressed the superiority of spirit over matter, and of ideals over mundane realities. The key difference lay in metaphysical issues, that is, in the way Plato conceived of reality. The metaphysical outlook of Platonism was based on a dualistic interpretation of reality. Platonists spoke of a higher realm in various ways, in terms of either pure ideas or spirit, but the bottom line for all Platonists was basically the one Plato had drawn in his dialogues *Phaedo* and *The Republic*: the material world was an inferior, shadowy reflection of higher realities; the body was a prison for the soul, which had somehow ended up trapped in it; and the true goal of human life was to rise above and beyond the material world, back to that higher realm. Aristotle's metaphysics, in contrast, rejected this dualism and emphasized the integral connection between matter and form, or the body and the soul.

In many ways, Christianity had always been profoundly influenced by Platonic metaphysics, especially in its conception of the world and the flesh as inferior to spirit and always in constant tension with it. In fact, all clerical claims to power were at bottom Platonic, for they appealed to the clergy's expertise with the "higher" eternal and spiritual realm. Monasticism itself was deeply grounded in Platonic conceptions of the relation between spirit and matter, and, by natural extension, so too was much of Christian piety. Even as eminent an Aristotelian as St. Thomas Aquinas had relied on Platonism to some extent. It could be said, then, that Plato was not so much rediscovered as acknowledged and revived by humanism, for he had never been completely lost. But there is also no denying that the renewed interest in Platonism gave rise to intellectual and spiritual movements that were quite novel, not just in their zeal to recover ancient pagan wisdom, but also in their interpretation of the relation between Platonism and "genuine" Christianity.

The Platonic revival began in earnest in Florence, under the patronage of its ruler Cosimo de' Medici (1389–1464), who—according to tradition—founded an academy in 1462 solely dedicated to the study of Plato and his disciples. Marsilio Ficino (1433–1499), a medical student turned priest and classicist, was the leading light of this academy, and also its heart and soul. A man of profoundly mystical inclinations, Ficino was wholly

Reviving Plato. Marsilio Ficino's Latin translations of Plato made the works of
this ancient philosopher more accessible than ever, thanks largely to the printing press.
As if to belabor the obvious, one of Ficino's publishers acknowledged the intimate bond between
new learning and new technology by placing an image of a print shop on the title page of his
edition of Ficino's work.

devoted to reconciling Platonism and Christianity, and to spreading the Platonic revival
as widely as possible. His influence was enormous, not so much in light of the number
of people affected by the Platonic revival—which was always a tiny fraction of European
society—but in terms of the scholars he reached, directly and indirectly, many of whom
were highly placed in the church, in government, and in the universities. In part, his

success, like that of many of his scholarly peers, was due to the new invention of the printing press, which made his treatises and translations available all over the continent.

Ficino promoted a synthesis of Christianity and Neoplatonism, most notably in his *Theologia platonica* (1472) and *De religione christiana* (1474) as well as in his commentaries on Plato and Plotinus and in his correspondence. In addition, Ficino produced the first full translation into Latin of all of Plato's dialogues, and a fresh translation of the works of Dionysius the Areopagite (whose influence had not been diminished by Valla's unmasking). He also made accessible the writings of the chief so-called Neoplatonists of late antiquity, translating works by Plotinus (205–270), Porphyry (232–303), and Proclus (410–485), disciples of Plato who although pagan had many affinities with their Christian contemporaries. Venturing beyond Neoplatonism, Ficino also translated some of the so-called *Hermetica*, a collection of texts from the third century that were ascribed to the Egyptian god Thoth, known in Greek as Hermes Trismegistos, or Hermes the Thrice-Greatest. The Hermetic books were an odd blend of ancient occult religion, gnostic secrets, astrology, medicine, alchemy, magic, and late-antique pagan philosophy, including traces of Neoplatonism.

Ficino's horizons were broad indeed, and his aim quite lofty. Love was the prime moving force of the universe, he argued, and its very purpose. Humans were microcosms of the whole universe, and gifted with unlimited potential. "It is indeed necessary to remember that the universe, which is the end of the soul, is entirely infinite," wrote Ficino. The human soul therefore necessarily shared in infinity, and its destiny was cosmic: "The soul in its own way will become the whole universe," he boasted.[15]

With such mystical goals in mind, the humanist impulse to return *ad fontes* took a giant leap at the Platonic Academy, at once literal and metaphorical. Returning to the ancient sources in Ficino's way meant blurring many of the boundaries that the church had drawn between Christian and pagan, or even between creature and creator. Gone in Ficino is the sense of taboo one finds in Augustine, who, though deeply indebted to the Neoplatonists, had warned Christians to "separate themselves in spirit from the miserable fellowship of these men."[16]

All the leading tendencies of Renaissance humanism became manifest in one of the younger disciples of Ficino at the Platonic Academy, the precocious Giovanni Pico della Mirandola (1463–1494). Unwilling to limit himself to any single set of sources, or to Latin and Greek alone, Pico became fluent in Hebrew and Arabic as well. Most remarkable of all was Pico's interest in the Kabbalah, a collection of secretive Jewish mystical texts that claimed to reveal the inner structure of reality through the Hebrew language. Pico's life was cut short at the age of thirty-one, but while he blazed his way through the Platonic Academy, always brushing uncomfortably close to charges of heresy, he was able to expand the meaning of the return *ad fontes*, and to draw others to the study of Hebrew and of esoteric doctrines from ancient non-Christian sources. His hope, as he put it, was that "all rational souls not only shall come into harmony in the one mind which is above all minds but shall in some ineffable way become altogether one."[17]

In 1486, Pico invited scholars from all of Europe to Rome for a public debate on nine hundred theses that he had drawn from Greek, Hebrew, Arabic, and Latin writers, in which he sought to reconcile a bewildering array of traditions and opinions. Though Pope Innocent VIII barred everyone from attending, and declared thirteen of Pico's theses heretical, Pico remained undaunted in his search for a wisdom that crossed all cultural and religious boundaries. His *Oration on the Dignity of Man*, which he wrote as an introduction to the nine hundred theses, has long been considered one of the most the most remarkable summations of humanist attitudes toward ancient wisdom and an eloquent defense of human potential.

Drawing from many sources, Pico argued in his *Oration* that human beings were capable of using their free will to rise to the greatest heights or sink to the lowest depths. "Thou shalt have the power to degenerate into the lower forms of life, which are brutish. Thou shalt have the power, out of thy soul's judgment, to be reborn into the higher forms, which are divine." Pico hoped to offer his audience hope in the limitless spiritual and intellectual potential of humanity. "Let a certain holy ambition invade our souls," he advised, "so that, not content with the mediocre, we shall pant after the highest and toil with all our strength to obtain it, since we may if we wish."[18] At the very core of his thinking, however, there was an overpowering Neoplatonic sense of the inferiority of the material world and of embodied existence, a metaphysics of suspicion toward matter that would be passed on to numerous younger disciples throughout Europe, especially to those who embraced what historians would later call Christian humanism.

Even more significant, at the heart of this Neoplatonic revival and so-called Christian humanism lay a profound sense that the medieval millennium had discarded what was best in late antiquity and in the early church. As Erasmus, the most famous of all of the northern humanists would say in his *Enchiridion*, by ignoring "the divine Plato," medieval scholars had "strangled" the beauty of the gospels. This assumption, a religious adaptation of the Renaissance paradigm, would make many a young humanist willing to believe that the Catholic Church had to be discarded along with the "middle ages."

Conclusion

In traditional Reformation historiography, Renaissance humanists have long been seen as forerunners of the Protestant Reformation, or at least as trailblazers who showed others the way. The attribution of Protestantism to humanism began in the sixteenth century itself, as the religious unity of Europe was shattered: it was a truism forged in the heat of battle, as it became evident that many Protestant teachings bore a close resemblance to humanist ideals and that many fine humanists had a habit of turning Protestant, especially if they lived north of the Alps. Humanists who turned Protestant readily acknowledged the connection; humanists who remained Catholic would bemoan it, and implicitly own up to it. Renaissance humanism did not inevitably lead to Protestantism, but it did lay the groundwork for much of its conceptual structure, especially its central historical paradigm, which privileged the early Christian era and viewed the medieval heritage as corrupt.

Beyond Italy, the principles of humanism would be embraced by many reform-minded young scholars and clerics, and its ultimate impact would be much different, as shall be seen in the following chapter. But a cultural movement such as the Renaissance should not be thought of as an ideology, much less as a unified anti-Catholic juggernaut. At heart, Renaissance humanism was ideologically and theologically neutral, in the sense that it did not *necessarily* lead to a single logical conclusion. In the same way that it would inspire some to turn away from the Catholic Church, Renaissance humanism would also influence the reforming efforts of many who chose to remain Catholic and to defend their ancestral religion.

CHAPTER FIVE

Humanism Beyond Italy

The Christian religion has utterly extinguished all traces of barbarism in
Germany.

—Franz Friedlieb, *Germaniae exegeseos volumina duodecim*[1]

By the early 1500s, humanism had already established itself among elites throughout Europe, thanks largely to the invention of the printing press and the expansion of European commerce, and signs of its diffusion could be found nearly everywhere. In Germany, for instance, the spread of humanistic concerns and pretensions is conspicuously evident in the very name of the twenty-three-year-old man who wrote the passage quoted above in the epigraph to this chapter. Born in 1495, Franz Friedlieb had stopped using his German name by 1518. Instead, he was publishing under the name Franciscus Irenicus, employing the Latin form of his first name and the Greek form of his surname (*Friedlieb*, "peace, love," *Irenicus*). He was not alone. Many learned young men had taken up the fashion of classicizing their names, and of addressing one another by them. One of these young men went by the name of Beatus Rhenanus, a classical echo of his German surname of Rhinower. Like Irenicus, Beatus Rhenanus strove to prove that Germans were no longer uncouth barbarians, so he wrote treatises that not only displayed the erudition and rhetorical flair favored by Italian humanists, but also reinterpreted the history of the German-speaking peoples by means of the methodological advances pioneered by Italian historians.

Classicizing one's name had become a fashion among the intellectual elites of Northern Europe. It was a very intimate way of returning *ad fontes*, of vanquishing the barbaric medieval past, and of broadcasting one's love for all things classical. Scholars great and small bought into this trend. In France, Jacques Lefèvre d'Étaples had become Faber Stapulensis. In Germany, Johann Reuchlin had toyed with becoming Capnio Phorcensis, in reference to his birthplace of Pforzheim. The less well-known humanist

Johann Königsberg (King's mountain) became Johannes Regiomontanus. The significance of this fad should not be underestimated, for it reveals much about the heritage of the Renaissance and its connection to religious reform in the sixteenth century. The adoption of a new Latin or Greek form of one's name signaled very clearly a break with the immediate medieval past and a willingness to reform the present according to models from a distant, more acceptable epoch. On many levels, it was the very embodiment of the chief paradigm of the Renaissance, which would also be one of the chief assumptions of the Protestant Reformation. It is no accident that many of the leading Protestant theologians of the sixteenth century used literal translations of their German family names. Among the best known of these would be Philip Melanchthon (Schwarzerde, or "black earth")—a former schoolmate of Friedlieb—who not only adopted a Greek version of his surname, but also became Luther's closest associate at Wittenberg, and Johann Oecolampadius (Huszgen, or "house lamp"), the leader of the Protestant Reformation in Basel. Others would simply Latinize their surnames, as did Joachim Vadianus (von Watt), at St. Gall, and John Calvin (Cauvin), at Geneva.[2] The new names reflected an audacious attitude toward established authority, and a wholesale commitment to renewal.

All of these men changed their names to proclaim their identity as members of a learned guild that scorned the immediate past and were ready and willing to change the world. Irenicus and Rhenanus had an additional axe to grind, for they felt compelled to prove that they were as civilized as the Italians, and perhaps even better Christians. And these two men were not alone in feeling and acting this way.

One of the earmarks of humanism outside of Italy was this decidedly religious bent, a penchant for returning to the past to reclaim not just long lost pagan treasures, but also those of the early Christian era, so that Christendom itself could be renewed: *Christianismus renascens*—Christianity born anew, a Christian renaissance—this was a key aim of many humanists outside of Italy, and one of their most distinctive traits.

Crossing the Alps

Humanism acquired an international following through various means. The first to export humanism were Italian scholars who spent considerable time abroad: Poggio Bracciolini in England, Pier Paolo Vergerio in Hungary, Aeneas Sylvius Piccolomini at the imperial court in Vienna. Then there were those scholars who went to study in Italy and brought their humanistic training back home: Antonio de Nebrija to Spain, Jacques Lefèvre d'Étaples to France, John Colet to England, Christoph Scheurl to Germany.

As personal and professional connections increased between scholars everywhere, letter writing became one of the most important means by which humanism established itself throughout Europe. This development was made possible largely by merchants and bankers, who in the fifteenth century established better means of ferrying letters from one place to another. This increase in traffic and communication helped turn correspondence into an art form among the humanists, and as a result, the highly polished Latin epistle served to imbue scholars from different nationalities with a common sense of identity and purpose. All of this letter writing, in turn, made humanism truly international.

Travel and correspondence were just the start. With the advent of the printing press, the process of cultural transmission gained speed and intensity all at once. This boom was especially evident in the schools run by humanists, where a new generation of students began to be taught with printed books in Latin and Greek, and where everyone could read exactly the same definitive texts. It was also increasingly evident in many universities, where humanist philology and historiography began to make their way into the curriculum, along with the resurrected texts from antiquity.

Conrad Celtis. The German "Erzhumanist," or arch-humanist, wearing his poet laureate's crown.

By the early 1500s humanism was so deeply entrenched throughout Western Europe that it was no longer necessary pick up humanistic learning in Italy. The case of Conrad Celtis (1459–1508), the great German scholar—known as the *Erzhumanist*, or archhumanist—is proof positive of this change. Celtis studied first in Cologne, Heidelberg, Rostock, and Leipzig, and he was well versed in the classics before he ever set foot in Italy. After a sojourn in Venice, Padua, Bologna, Florence, and Rome, where he honed his humanistic skills, he went on to the Jagellonian University in Krakow, Poland, to round out his education in mathematics and astronomy. He ended up teaching at Vienna, training a whole new generation of German humanists, some of whom became Protestant Reformers.

Even more significant, by the 1510s, it was becoming increasingly fashionable for the elites of Europe to send their children to schools where the curriculum was shaped by humanistic learning. This was the ultimate triumph of the humanists throughout Europe: the establishment of schools where successive generations of children would be educated in the *studia humanitatis*, the liberal arts, not necessarily as scholars-to-be, and much less as churchmen, but as literate, well-rounded laymen who could engage in any profession or follow any calling. It was also in these schools that the ruling class of the emerging nation-states of Europe were to be trained: the sons—and at times the daughters—of the nobility and the rising bourgeoisie, the free, civilized, useful citizens who would assume significant roles in society, empowered and ennobled by their training in history, ethics, and rhetoric, bound to one another in class identity through their exposure to a curriculum and a worldview that gave them a common frame of reference.

Gone were the days when literacy and erudition were reserved for the clergy. Though embraced by many clerics, humanist education was above all a lay phenomenon that affected the children of the rising merchant class and the old nobility, those two segments of the population that formed the new European elite as the old feudal order began to wane. For those who wanted to remain in the ruling class, an education was increasingly necessary. Noble lineage steadily lost out to sheer ability as the modern nation-state emerged and the bureaucrat became as indispensable as the knight. Within the space of a few generations, then, the humanists gradually turned a liberal arts education into a prerequisite for privilege. And the old aristocracy knew it was a sink-or-swim situation. Jean de Lannoy, a Flemish noble who had not learned his Latin, put it this way to his son:

> No day passes that I do not regret this [lacking a good education], and especially when I find myself in the council of the king or of the Duke of Burgundy, and I know not nor dare to speak my opinion after the learned, eloquent legists and scholars who have spoken before me.[3]

A Christian Renaissance

In many ways, the work of Renaissance humanists of Italy had a religious dimension from the very start, and the evolution of what came to be called Christian humanism began quite early. In a culture as profoundly religious as that of late medieval Italy, the battle cry *ad fontes* could not avoid encompassing the earliest sources of the Christian faith along with those of the pagan past. So, it was in Italy that the early Greek Church fathers were rediscovered, and that many of their crucial texts, long lost to the West, were assembled and translated into Latin. It was also in Italy that Lorenzo Valla began to study Bible texts critically, with his *Annotations on the New Testament*. It was also Valla who moved church history into a whole new dimension with his work on Dionysius the Areopagite and the *Donation of Constantine*. Other Italian humanists such as Giannozzo Manetti continued working on the text of the Bible, moving beyond the Greek New Testament into the Hebrew scriptures. Then, finally, it was also in Italy that Marsilio Ficino and Pico della Mirandola began to broaden religious horizons and to inspire a whole new generation of humanists, such as Erasmus of Rotterdam, to reexamine the faith.

As part of the effort to identify and typologize different sorts of humanism—a preoccupation that dominated Renaissance scholarship for decades—and especially as a means of distinguishing the spiritualizing dimensions of the Renaissance from its secularizing tendencies, twentieth-century historians began to speak of Christian humanism as a distinct movement, particularly in reference to the religiously centered concerns of a group of scholars outside of Italy. The term became especially useful to historians who wanted to highlight the undeniable link that exists between the Renaissance and the Protestant Reformation. As in the case of "civic humanism" there are good reasons for using the term, but there are also good reasons to exercise caution. While it is true that there were a good number of humanists who saw themselves as deeply involved in religious reform, it is also true that there were significant differences among these scholars, that they never formally referred to themselves as Christian humanists, and that many of them could also be called civic humanists.

Whether or not one uses the term *Christian humanist*, the fact remains that many non-Italian humanists began to give a distinctly religious turn to the principle *ad fontes*, seeking to recover an "original" or "pure" Christianity that had existed in antiquity but had somehow been corrupted. Guided by the central paradigm of the Renaissance—the assumption that there was a "dark age" to overcome—these so-called Christian humanists applied themselves to the study of ancient languages and history as a means of finding what had been lost and of bringing it back to life. Naturally, these humanists tended to focus more intensely on the Bible and on the writings of the early Church fathers than on pagan authors. As was the case with all humanists, they expressed great disdain for scholastic theology and philosophy, whether their education had exposed them to it or not. They also had a tendency to stress piety and ethics over doctrine. Though there are some exceptions, these Christian humanists fell into two distinct generations: those born before 1475, who tended not to break with the Roman Catholic Church, no matter how much they criticized it, and those born after 1475, who could either remain Catholic or turn Protestant. This chapter is concerned mostly with the older generation, and with their relation to the changes that would occur in the sixteenth century.

The so-called Christian humanists can easily be sorted out geographically and linguistically into four groups—German, Spanish, English, and French—even if in doing so one runs the risk of de-emphasizing the truly international nature of their movement. In addition, there is also the towering figure of Erasmus of Rotterdam, the Dutchman who seemed to be everywhere, transcending frontiers and influencing all nations.

The Germanic Lands

Renaissance humanism made its way to German-speaking regions in the late fifteenth century, and it took root quickly. Among the great pioneers, a place of honor has always been reserved for Rudolf Agricola (ca. 1442–1485), who, in true humanist fashion, latinized his family name of Huysman. Agricola's training in the classics is proof positive of the speed with which humanism spread to Northern Europe. Enthralled by Latin literature at the University of Louvain, Agricola went on to earn a master's degree in Paris, where he deepened his acquaintance with antiquity, and from there he moved to Italy for seven years, where he joined humanist circles in Rome and Ferrara and honed his skills among experts. Upon returning to Germany, Agricola embarked on a personal campaign to promote humanistic learning. In 1482 he began teaching at the University of Heidelberg, where he turned to the study of Hebrew and published a translation of the psalms.

Though he died young and did not publish much, Agricola exerted a profound influence on many of his contemporaries, imparting to his students and to other young scholars a deep love for the sources of Christian and German culture. In his last years, he also began to study theology and to promote a piety centered on renewal—the sort of piety that would lie at the heart of Christian humanism. His devotional treatise *De nativitate Christi* (On the Birth of Christ) is not only erudite, but also a heartfelt meditation that in typically humanist fashion is aimed at lay readers rather than a monastic audience.

Another great pioneer—already mentioned—was Conrad Celtis, founder of the College of Poets and Mathematicians at Vienna. Born as Conrad Pickel in 1459, just a few years after the invention of the printing press, Celtis became the first German ever to be crowned by the Holy Roman Emperor as poet laureate. As a professor at the University of Ingolstadt, and later at the University of Vienna, Celtis did much to promote the superiority of ancient texts—*ad fontes*—and the renewal of Christianity, not only through his teaching, but also by establishing learned societies or circles. The *Sodalitas danubiana* in Vienna would exert an enormous influence on a whole generation of humanists, including many who became Protestant reformers, among whom were none other than the two Swiss Protestant reformers Ulrich Zwingli and Joachim Vadianus. Since his intense love of classical culture was matched by his passion for German culture, Celtis also did much to impart to his students and followers a sense of national pride and patriotism, laying a solid foundation for the articulation of anti-Roman Protestant sentiments at a later date.

By far the most controversial of the pioneering Germanic humanists was Johann Reuchlin (1455–1522). After studying at Freiburg im Breisgau and Basel, where he specialized in Greek literature, Reuchlin trained as a lawyer at Orléans and Poitiers, and served as imperial judge for the Swabian confederation for ten years (1502–1512). A master of Latin and Greek, Reuchlin published a Latin dictionary in 1478 and also devoted himself to translating numerous classical Greek texts. Though he was convinced of the importance of Hebrew for biblical studies, Reuchlin's interest in learning that ancient language remained latent until he traveled to Italy in the 1480s, and Pico della Mirandola introduced him to the study of Jewish Kabbalistic texts.

Smitten by the mystical lure of the Kabbalah, and its truth claims about the links between the Hebrew language and all the secrets of the universe, Reuchlin learned Hebrew and began to devote his attention to these medieval Jewish texts. His research led to the publication of a book, *De verbo mirifico* (The Miraculous Word), in which he sang the praises of the Kabbalah and its hidden divine powers. To make the language of the Jews, the Old Testament, and the Kabbalah more accessible to Christians, in 1506 Reuchlin published a Hebrew grammar and lexicon entitled *De rudimentis hebraicis* (On the Fundamentals of Hebrew). Then, suddenly, he found himself under attack, even accused of heresy. For the first time ever the humanists' battle cry of *ad fontes* was directly challenged within the Catholic Church. The Renaissance itself was under siege.

The attack on Reuchlin was led by the Dominican friars of Cologne, and especially by Jakob Hochstraten, their inquisitor. Another tenacious adversary was Johannes Pfefferkorn, a convert from Judaism who saw Reuchlin's love for the Hebrew language and the Kabbalah as no more than the ancient heresy of "Judaizing." As is often the case with converts to any religion, Pfefferkorn had embraced his new faith with a vengeance, proclaiming that all Hebrew books were hostile to Christianity. Fearful of Reuchlin's agenda, Pfefferkorn and Hochstraten and the Cologne Dominicans called on Emperor Maximilian in 1509 to order the destruction of Hebrew books. Faced with a charge of heresy, and also with the prospect of seeing much of his life's work obliterated, Reuchlin appealed to Pope Leo X in Rome.

Thus began the first culture war of the modern era, a long and heated controversy that, while intense and immensely significant, never involved very many players and went largely unnoticed by the vast majority of the populace. Though it seems clear that the Cologne Dominicans and Pfefferkorn seemed motivated much more by anti-Jewish prejudices than by fear of humanism and ancient non-Christian sources, most of those who had any appreciation for humanistic studies could not help but see the attack on Reuchlin and Hebrew studies as an obscurantist assault on learning. Many scholars came to Reuchlin's defense, including a most unlikely ally, the German knight and humanist Ulrich von Hutten, who contributed to the publication of a satirical pamphlet titled *Epistolae obscurorum virorum* (Letters of the Obscure Men) in 1515, which lampooned scholasticism and the Dominicans with an acid tongue and did much to fan anticlerical sentiment among the European intelligentsia. Thanks to the printing press, and thanks to the fact that throughout Europe there was now a substantial audience that could read Latin, what would have otherwise remained an unnoticeable local dispute had become an international affair.

The Reuchlin case became a cause célèbre and a call to arms for those who viewed themselves as humanists. As Reuchlin's supporters saw it, the forces of darkness had gathered against the light of learning and laid siege to civilization itself. As the days, weeks, and months passed, the polarization intensified. Finally, in 1516, Reuchlin was declared free of heresy by a papal commission. The following year, when a young monk named Martin Luther seemed to be in a fix similar to Reuchlin's, there was an instant audience ready to hear what he had to say, even eager to take up his cause. A network had been set in place, and more important, the printing press now provided a means of expanding the audience for any noteworthy spat.

At first, Reuchlin would joke about the parallels between Luther and himself, saying, "God be praised that now the monks have found someone else who will give them more to do than I."[4] But soon enough, when serious comparisons began to be made, he would be appalled. In the eyes of some, the linkage seemed to make sense because a nephew of Reuchlin's was Luther's closest friend and associate at Wittenberg: a brilliant young scholar named Philip Schwarzerde, who preferred to be known as Melanchthon, with typical humanist affectation. Though many of those who loved Reuchlin and benefited

Victory over ignorance. This 1518 illustration from the *Triumphus Capnionis*, attributed to Ulrich Von Hutten, celebrates the victory of the pro-Reuchlin humanists over the Dominicans of Cologne, who sought to condemn him. Capnio was the name Reuchlin had assumed, in the fashion of German humanists. It was the Greek word for "smoke" (*kapnos*, or *rauch*). Reuchlin rides a triumphal chariot while crowds cheer and his opponent Pfefferkorn is dragged along the ground, bound hand and foot.

from his labors ended up leaving the Roman Catholic Church—such as the brilliant Hebraist Konrad Pellikan (1478–1556)—Reuchlin would reject Luther, his own nephew Philip, and several former students as heretics. Blood was certainly not thicker than water in this case, and neither was humanism some sort of virus that made everyone reject the Catholic faith. Like other notable Germanic humanists, such as Willibald Pirckheimer (1470–1528), Conrad Peutinger (1465–1547), Johannes Trithemius (1462–1516), and Conrad Mutianus Rufus (1471–1526), Melanchthon's uncle would remain within the Catholic fold.

Spain

The Reuchlin affair—which became a pitched battle between traditionalists and proponents of the new learning and would later be cited by Protestants as proof positive of the backwardness and intolerance of the Catholic Church—was a highly localized German aberration. The papacy and the Catholic hierarchy as a whole were not necessarily opposed to the new learning or to the renewed interest in the Bible that seemed to be cropping up nearly everywhere. Anyone who doubts the positive reception of the new biblical studies within church circles needs only look to the Iberian kingdoms collectively known as Spain, where the study of Hebrew and the retrieval of biblical texts in their original languages became one of the highest priorities of the leadership of the church.

For centuries, Spanish humanism tended to be seen as a withered branch on the Renaissance family tree, especially by historians outside of Hispanic culture. This opinion originated with Protestant historiography in the sixteenth century itself, when Spain proved itself unfertile ground for Protestantism. Accustomed as Protestant historians were to seeing their own religion as a natural outgrowth of humanism, most of them concluded that Spain must have had very few humanists because it produced so few Protestants. Two facts helped make this a widely held opinion, even long after confessional rivalries had died down: one was Spain's steep decline in the seventeenth century, which made all of the glamour of its Golden Age seem hollow at the core; the other was Spain's reputation for intolerance, thanks to its Inquisition, which made it seem a benighted land to modern eyes.

Because humanist scholarship was always limited to an elite few, it is not exactly correct to say that the Renaissance took Spain by storm. But it is certainly safe to say that the new learning found very fertile ground among academics and ecclesiastics in Castile and Aragon, the two Iberian kingdoms that had recently united into a single nation, and that many of these elites reformed Spanish education in such a way as to have a profound impact on all of society. In part, the rapid growth of the new learning in Spain was aided by the fact that the study of one of the ancient sacred languages, Hebrew, had never been lost there.

Throughout the Middle Ages, the Iberian Peninsula had been home to two sizable religious and ethnic minorities. In the south, especially in Valencia and Andalusia, large numbers of Muslims could be found, many of whom were Arab-speaking Berbers from North Africa. Spain was also home to the largest Jewish community in all of Europe. Nearly everywhere, Jews lived in towns and cities, facing an increasingly hostile environment, but holding fast to their scholarship and their traditions. Persecution and forced conversions in the late fourteenth century had created a new class of people in Castile, the conversos, that is, Jews who had converted to Christianity but were suspected of still practicing the religion of their forebears and their unconverted Jewish neighbors. In 1492, intolerance would lead to the forced conversion or expulsion of all Jews from Castile and Aragon. Though tens of thousands fled, tens of thousands also chose to convert and remain. Their presence would make Iberia unique, providing it with large numbers of well-educated Jews and Jewish converts who not only knew Hebrew, but also were deeply engaged with ancient texts and scholarly and philological traditions.

It is not at all surprising then, that the revival of Hebrew studies would thrive in Spain. One of the men most directly responsible for the renewal of biblical scholarship in Spain was an unlikely candidate, a cardinal named Francisco Jiménez de Cisneros (1436–1517), head of the Spanish Inquisition. Jiménez was probably exposed to the new learning in Rome, where he had served as an advocate at the consistorial courts for a few years in the 1460s. Back in Spain, he took it upon himself to learn Hebrew and Aramaic from a local Jew in the 1470s, a decade before Reuchlin. At the same time he renewed his theological studies and became ever more convinced of the need for an *ad fontes* return to the Holy Scriptures. Though he would never dedicate himself entirely to scholarship, Jiménez would eventually rise to the highest ecclesiastical and civil positions in Spain, as confessor to Queen Isabella, Grand Inquisitor, regent of Castile, and cardinal archbishop of Toledo, and he would use his income and his influence to become an energetic and successful patron of the new learning.

Wholly committed to reforming the church in Castile, and especially taken with the idea of improving the education of the clergy through humanistic studies and a return to the Bible, in 1508 Jiménez, as archbishop of Toledo, established a university at Alcalá de Henares, near Madrid. This new university was instituted primarily to train an elite corps of reforming clergy who would be exposed to the new humanistic learning alongside scholastic theology and medieval spirituality. In addition to gathering some of the best philologists available and establishing professorships in the ancient languages of Greek and Hebrew, Jiménez also collected an impressive number of ancient manuscripts of the Holy Scriptures and commissioned a group of scholars to embark on the most ambitious biblical project of all time: the production of a definitive Bible that would contain not only the original Hebrew and Septuagint Greek Old Testament texts, but also the Greek New Testament, the entire Vulgate Latin translation of both Testaments, the Aramaic version of the Hebrew Pentateuch (the first five books of the Old Testament), known as the Targum of Onkelos, and the Latin translation of that text, along with annotations on textual variations and other scholarly apparatus, including a Hebrew and Aramaic lexicon, a Hebrew grammar, and a Greek dictionary. The prologue to this Bible, in which

Cardinal Jiménez spelled out for the pope why such a vast project was sorely needed, was a perfect summation of humanist reforming principles:

> Words have their own unique character, and no translation of them, however complete, can entirely express their full meaning. This is especially the case in that language through which the Lord Himself spoke. . . . Moreover, wherever there is diversity in the Latin manuscripts or the suspicion of a corrupted reading (we know how frequently this occurs because of the ignorance and negligence of the copyists), it is necessary to go back to the original source of Scripture, as St. Jerome and St. Augustine and other ecclesiastical writers advise us to do, to examine the authenticity of the books of the Old Testament in the light of the correctness of the Hebrew text and of the New Testament in the light of the Greek copies. And so that every student of Holy Scripture might have at hand the original texts themselves and be able to quench his thirst at the very fountainhead of the water that flows unto life everlasting, and not have to content himself with rivulets alone, we ordered the original languages of Holy Scripture with their translations adjoined to be printed. . . . We employed men the most outstanding for their knowledge of languages, and we had the most accurate and the oldest manuscripts for our base texts. . . . May your Holiness receive, therefore, with a joyful heart this humble gift which we offer unto the Lord so that the hitherto dormant study of Holy Scripture may now at last begin to revive.[5]

This Bible came to be known as the Complutensian Polyglot because of its multiple tongues (Greek: *poly*, "many"; *glotta*, "tongue") and the humanist conceit of using the ancient Roman name for the town of Alcalá (Complutum). Though it took several years to complete, the Complutensian was produced relatively quickly—given the immensity of the task: the New Testament being finished in 1514 and the Old Testament in 1517, shortly before the death of Cardinal Jiménez. The results were stunning, both as a triumph of humanistic scholarship and a masterpiece of the new art of printing. It was also a relative bargain, selling at only six and a half ducats.

The impact of the Complutensian Polyglot never matched its quality, however, for various reasons. The print run was rather small, somewhere around a mere six hundred copies. It was also massive and somewhat unwieldy, filling up six huge volumes. Even worse, its publication was held up for four years after it had been completed. The reasons for this delay were complex. First, although the New Testament was printed and ready for distribution in 1514, it was not immediately released, for Jiménez de Cisneros wanted the whole Bible was to be sold as a complete set. Then, by the time the entire project was finished three years later, politics and scholarly competition stood in its way. In the interval between 1514 and 1517, Erasmus of Rotterdam (with whom we shall deal presently), had hurried to produce his own edition of the Greek New Testament in 1516, and had obtained an exclusive four-year publishing privilege from Pope Leo X and Emperor Maximilian. Finally, in 1521, when the pope gave permission for the Complutensian Bible to be sold, Erasmus's New Testament—which also included his own new Latin translation of the Greek text—was already well established as definitive. To top it off,

The Complutensian Polyglot Bible is a masterpiece of humanist scholarship as well as of the nascent art of printing.

since two editions of the Hebrew Bible published by Jews already existed, and another appeared in 1518, the Complutensian Old Testament had much of its thunder stolen.

Although its impact was limited, the Complutensian Bible was nonetheless a remarkable achievement and a testimony to the triumph of humanistic learning in Spain. Its place in the development of biblical studies was as undeniably significant as the impact that it had on the University of Alcalá and on the future of the new learning in Spain. The project itself, and the scholars who gathered there, gave an indelible humanistic stamp to the University of Alcalá. An entire generation of humanistically trained reformers would flow out of this new university, ready to change the world on both sides of the Atlantic Ocean. Many of them would play a key role in the reform of the Spanish church, and later, in the reform of the entire Catholic Church, convinced that medieval traditions and humanistic learning were not antithetically opposed to one another, but rather totally compatible.

Although there is no doubt that the University of Alcalá played a leading role in the spread of humanistically inspired reforms, its legacy remains a matter of debate. For centuries, Protestant historiography portrayed Alcalá as an anomaly, a brief burst of light that was quickly snuffed by a hostile Catholic Church. Catholic historians viewed Alcalá differently, as the wellspring of the reforms that the church would institute in the late sixteenth century. At issue between Catholic and Protestant histories was the fate of humanism in Spain, which some indices seemed to suggest had been suppressed along with Protestantism after the late 1520s, and especially after the works of Erasmus had been censured at a public debate in Valladolid in 1527. Since the 1930s, the most widely accepted assessment was that of historian Marcel Bataillon, who argued that all the humanistic progressives in Spain became followers of Erasmus and were quickly silenced or driven away by conservative forces, and especially by the Inquisition.[6] Bataillon's stark dichotomies went unquestioned for decades, but are now being challenged by a more nuanced approach that views the legacy of the Spanish Renaissance as a complex interplay of various traditions, refusing to identify anyone as a pure "Erasmian" or to pigeonhole Spanish scholars and ecclesiastics into a mere two categories, as either "progressives" or "conservatives."[7] We will return to the story of the fate of humanism in Spain in a later chapter, when we take up the subject of the Catholic response to Protestantism.

Any list of humanist luminaries in Spain must include the scholars most directly responsible for the success of the Complutensian Bible project. At the top of every such list, one usually finds Antonio de Nebrija (1444–1522) and his much younger colleague Juan de Vergara (1492–1557). Antonio de Nebrija—full name Antonio Martínez de Cala y Jarana—was one of those humanists who preferred to be known by a Latin version of his place of birth, which in his case was the city of Lebrija, in the south of Spain, known as Nebrissa in Roman times. Nebrija was as much of a pioneer in Spain as Lorenzo Valla was in Italy. A graduate of Spain's venerable University of Salamanca, Nebrija picked up his love of ancient classical learning in Italy, where he continued his education for ten years. Returning to Spain in 1473, he was among the very first to promote humanistic learning, first at Salamanca, where he taught rhetoric and grammar, and later at Alcalá. In 1492, just as Columbus was about to stumble on the New World, Nebrija published the first grammar of any European vernacular language, *Gramática sobre la lengua castellana*, a systematic analysis of the Castilian dialect, which was at that time quickly becoming known as "Spanish," the official language of the emerging nation-state of "Spain." Summoned to Alcalá by Cardinal Jiménez, Nebrija worked on the Greek and Latin texts of the Complutensian Bible until he ran into a disagreement with Cardinal Jiménez over the Latin Vulgate text. Like Valla, Nebrija, wanted to point out where the Vulgate translation was flawed, but this did not sit well with Cardinal Jiménez, who considered the Vulgate text sacred. Though he was a patron of humanism, Jiménez revealed his lack of understanding for Nebrija and advanced humanist philology by insisting that the Vulgate be placed in the middle column in the Old Testament, "as the cross of Christ stood between those of two thieves,"[8] and as the Roman Catholic Church stood between the unbelieving Jews on one side and the schismatic Greek Orthodox on the other.

Juan de Vergara, a product of the new University of Alcalá, and a descendant of Jewish conversos, proved such an able student of Greek that he was asked to join the

Polyglot project, along with much older scholars such as Nebrija. Placed in charge of the Wisdom books of the Septuagint Greek Old Testament, the young Vergara went on to acquire a reputation as one of the finest philologists in Europe. Secretary to the archbishops of Toledo and chaplain for Emperor Charles V, he would strike up a friendship with the great humanist Erasmus, but later, in the 1530s, he ran afoul of the Inquisition. Though he was cleared of all charges of heresy, he was nonetheless punished for minor procedural infractions, and lived the rest of his life in relative obscurity. His unfortunate brush with the Inquisition has long been cited as proof of the crushing of humanism in Spain by "conservative" forces.

Another converso alumnus of the University of Alcalá who is representative of the complex legacy of Spanish humanism is Pedro Ciruelo (1470–1548), mathematician, philologist, and theologian. Ciruelo, who learned Hebrew at Alcalá, and may have worked on the Complutensian Bible, went on to publish several Latin translations of the Hebrew Scriptures, always with an eye toward vindicating Jerome's Vulgate text. He also wrote treatises on logic, mathematics, philosophy, religion, and popular beliefs. Among his many contributions, it is his *Treatise Reproving All Superstitions and Forms of Sorcery* (1530) that most clearly displays his humanist training and reforming zeal, cataloging, analyzing, and censuring a wide range of devotional practices as un-Christian.[9] A thorough defense of medieval demonology, *Treatise* is also a consummate scholarly critique of popular religion. Daring to tackle common practices such as necromancy and witchcraft, which Erasmus and other humanist critics never dared to mention, Ciruelo would prove influential in the development of early modern elite attitudes toward folk religion, and also in the formulation of the Catholic Church's attack on all suspected remnants of pagan religion. In many ways, Ciruelo is precisely the kind of humanist that Protestant historians would find typical of Catholic Spain up until the late twentieth century: deferential to medieval traditions and to the authority of the Vulgate Bible text. In other ways, however, he is also everything they would never think could be found in Catholic Spain: a great Hebraist, deeply convinced of the value of reading Holy Scripture in the original languages, and a stern critic of pagan holdovers in popular religion.

The legacy of humanism in Spain will be a topic of debate for years to come. Of this there is little doubt. What remains totally beyond dispute, however, is the fact that humanism had a profound impact on Spain, helping to make it a hotbed of reform in the first decades of the sixteenth century, even in ways that outstripped the rest of Europe. And there is also no denying that humanistically trained Spaniards would lead the way to reform within the Catholic Church later in the sixteenth century, especially at the Council of Trent (1545–1563).

England

Humanist learning came to England through London, and the universities at Oxford and Cambridge. As early as the 1430s, Italian scholars such as Poggio Bracciolini began to visit

England, bringing with them the new learning. Before long, a few Italians were teaching at Cambridge and Oxford. English students trekked to Italy too, and returned home well versed in the classics and the ancient languages, eager to revolutionize learning at home.

Three such students were William Grocyn (1446–1519), William Latimer (1467–1545), and Thomas Linacre (1460–1524). Grocyn returned to teach Greek at Oxford and also lectured on Dionysius the Areopagite in London. Latimer would become tutor to a young man who eventually presided over the reforming Council of Trent, nearly became pope, and served briefly as archbishop of Canterbury: the future cardinal Reginald Pole. Linacre, the best known of this trio, would not only become the personal physician of King Henry VIII and founder of the Royal College of Surgeons, but also a leading expert in Greek, author of a grammar and numerous translations. In his later years, Linacre turned his attention to the original Greek text of the New Testament. What he found there shocked him. "Either this is not the gospel or we are not Christians,"[10] said Linacre after returning *ad fontes*, summing up the astonishment of his generation over the differences that could be perceived between the late medieval church and the teachings of Jesus.

And it was precisely that gap, that glaring difference, which struck young humanists most intensely. Another English youth who studied in Italy and sought to recover the original Christian spirit was John Colet (1467–1519), son of the mayor of London. Colet devoted himself to the new learning, and especially to the study of the New Testament. Above all, he was most interested in interpreting the biblical text within its original grammatical and historical context. After lecturing on the letters of St. Paul at Oxford, Colet was named dean of St. Paul's Cathedral in 1505, one of the most prestigious clerical posts in the realm. At St. Paul's, Colet won fame as a preacher who dwelled on the biblical texts and eschewed medieval glosses and commentaries.

Colet also gained renown as a critic of the church's many faults. In one of the few sermons of his that has survived, preached in 1512 to an assembly of the English clergy at St. Paul's, we get a clear glimpse of Colet's biblically inspired reforming rhetoric. Anchoring the entire sermon on the Pauline text "be not conformed to this world" (Romans 12:2), Colet blasted the hundreds of clerics gathered before him, blaming them for all of the church's ills:

> If the priests and bishops, the very lights, run in the dark ways of the world, how dark must the lay people be! . . . What eagerness and hunger after honor and dignity are found in these days among ecclesiastical persons! What a breathless race from benefice to benefice. . . . Who is there who does not see this? Who that sees it does not grieve over it? . . . Let . . . the goods of the Church be spent not in sumptuous buildings, not in magnificence and pomp, not in feasts and banquets, not in luxury and lust, not in enriching kinsfolk or in keeping hounds, but in things useful and needful to the Church.[11]

Colet was not alone in thinking this way. Reform had become the aim of English humanism. A kindred spirit, also highly placed, was Thomas More (1477–1535).

Educated solely in England, More would come to epitomize homegrown English humanism. More was not a scholar, but rather a lawyer and statesman who would eventually
become chancellor of the realm. Although deeply engaged in the affairs of the world,
More never ceased being a man of letters. His most famous work, *Utopia*, published in
1516 and translated into many languages, gained him instant fame throughout Europe.
A reformist manifesto, More's *Utopia* was pure fable and satire rolled into one: an ideal-
ized description of a pagan city-state that resembled a selfless monastic community and
was, in essence, more Christian than any state in Christendom, or perhaps even any
real Christian monastery. Whether or not More's Utopia was attainable was beside the
point: in true humanist fashion, More sought to educate through allegory, using an ideal
community to highlight his own society's faults. The title said it all: *Utopia* was a Greek
pun on *ou-topos* ("no place") and *eu-topos* ("good place").

   Utopia was only one of More's many achievements. Despite his work as a judge
and royal official, his engagement with ancient texts was constant, as was his conviction
that the key to reform lay in a return to the original sources of classical antiquity and
ancient Christianity. Along these lines, one of his most significant contributions was not

FAMILIA THOMÆ MORI ANGL:CANCELL:

Thomas Morus Æ:50. Alicia Thomæ Mori uxor Æ:57. Iohannes Morus pater Æ:76.Iohannes Morus Thomæ filius Æ:19. Anna Grisacria Iohannis Mori Sponsa Æ:15. Margareta Ropera Thomæ Mori filia Æ:22.
Elisabeta Dauncia Thomæ Mori filia Æ:21. Cæcilia Heronia Thomæ Mori filia Æ:20. Margareta Giga Clementis uxor Mori filiabus Condiscipula et cognata Æ:22. Henricus Patensonus Thomæ Mori morio Æ:40.

Humanism at home in England: Thomas More and his family. The great English humanist
and Chancellor of the Realm believed that immersion in ancient languages should not be limited to
the classroom. In his own home, his daughters conversed in Greek and Latin. Sketch by
Hans Holbein the Younger.

a text, but rather the friendship he and Colet struck with the greatest of all northern humanists, Erasmus of Rotterdam. It would be none other than More, along with Colet, Latimer, Grocyn, and Linacre, who would convince the young Dutch scholar to immerse himself in Greek, and especially in the early Church fathers and the New Testament. It could be argued that when Erasmus came to Cambridge as a visiting lecturer in 1503, he was a man of letters, but that when he was done lecturing and meeting with the English humanists, he went back to the Continent as a religious scholar and reformer. More and Erasmus became fast friends and collaborated on several translation projects. They also promoted the same reforming agenda.

More would end up a martyr to his Catholic faith, beheaded for refusing to accept Henry VIII rather than the pope as head of the Church of England. And before getting to that awful point, he would have a hand in the persecution of English Protestants, many of whom were deeply influenced by humanism. We will have to return to these events in a later chapter. For now, what matters most is that More and the English humanists were no different from humanists anywhere else: they revered the Bible and the early Christian fathers and were committed to reforming the church and society through education and a return *ad fontes*. Privileging the ancient past did not necessarily lead them to break their ties with the Catholic Church, but it did make them a force to be reckoned with.

And one of their greatest contributions, it could be argued, was the way they shaped the reforming vision of that young Dutch guest lecturer at Cambridge, Erasmus of Rotterdam, to whom we will turn our attention at the end of this chapter.

France

One of the most salient characteristics of humanism in France was its deep and intimate connection with reform tendencies. Another was the towering presence of the greatest humanist in all of France, Jacques Lefèvre d'Étaples (1455–1536), better known in learned circles as Faber Stapulensis. Lefèvre was a devout Christian humanist, who, much like Colet and Erasmus, was deeply affected by Neoplatonic thought and dedicated his life to renewing learning and piety through a return *ad fontes*. He was not only a conduit for reform ideas in France, but also a very active and influential scholar whose own work on the Bible and active commitment to change helped shape a whole generation of reformers. As early as 1499, in his preface to the works of Dionysius the Areopagite—that arch-Neoplatonist mystic—Lefèvre openly expressed his desire to return to the "pristine" sources of the early church:

> The more nearly a light approximates the intensity of the sun, the more brightly it shines . . . and the closer a thing is to its origin, the more purely it retains its own nature. . . . It follows that of all the writings, the Holy Gospels are recognized as having the greatest dignity, splendor, and authority, as writings which have emanated directly from God and have been infused into ready minds.[12]

Deeply convinced of the need to rely on the gospels as the clearest revelation of truth, but also deeply influenced by the piety of the *devotio moderna*, Lefèvre did not reject all medieval texts wholesale. Having first annotated the works of Aristotle and edited the works of the great Dionysius (seventh century), he turned his attention to publishing the mystical texts of Hildegard of Bingen (twelfth century), Richard of St. Victor (twelfth century), Ramon Llull (thirteenth and fourteenth centuries), Jan van Ruysbroeck (fourteenth century), and Nicholas of Cusa (fifteenth century). In 1509 he began to work almost exclusively on the Bible, issuing his *Psalterium quintuplex*, a landmark edition of five Latin versions of the psalms. This work was followed in 1512 by a commentary on the epistles of St. Paul. Both of these texts had a profound influence on a younger generation of scholars and clerics, including the future reformers Martin Luther and Ulrich Zwingli.

In 1507 one of Lefèvre's former students, the abbot Guillaume Briçonnet (1472–1534), invited him to live at his Parisian monastery of St.-Germain-des-Prés, where a group of young devoted reformers became his disciples and learned to distrust all materially oriented, non-biblically-based piety. As Lefèvre told them and all his readers, following the Bible was essential, for without it "the flame of religion is extinguished, spiritual things are traded for earthly goods, heaven is given up and earth is accepted—the most disastrous transaction conceivable."[13] When Briçonnet was appointed bishop of Meaux in 1516, several of these younger reformers would help him institute reforms in his diocese that were very much in line with Lefèvre's biblically centered critique of medieval piety. In 1520, they would be joined by Lefèvre himself. Guillaume Farel was among this group, and as we will see in a later chapter, so were some of the most important figures who helped define the early French Reformation.

While at St.-Germain-des-Prés and at Meaux, as he labored on several other significant biblical projects, Lefèvre grew increasingly critical of popular piety as that "disastrous transaction" that exchanged heaven for earth. He also became ever more outspoken about the need for a thoroughgoing reform of religion. After his arrival in Meaux in 1520, especially, the scholar Lefèvre turned his attention to the subject of worship, and most intensely to the veneration of saints, images, and relics. By 1521, Lefèvre was advocating a return to biblical purity in ritual that was even more strident than that proposed by Erasmus, affirming a sharp distinction between things of divine origin and those created by human beings:

> The Word of God suffices. This alone is enough to effect life everlasting. This rule is the guide to eternal life. All else, on which the Word of God does not shine, is as unnecessary as it is undoubtedly superfluous.[14]

This antithesis between divine and humanly devised religion would be passed on to the reforming circle at Meaux and become a central tenet of French Protestantism. When coupled with a strong Christocentricism, it would also lead Lefèvre to the brink of condemning the veneration of the saints as pure idolatry:

Let your trust be upon God without solicitude, address him in every prayer and supplication; in returning thanks let your petitions be addressed to God; and the peace of God, which surpasses all understanding, will protect your hearts and minds in Jesus Christ. Anything different from this is a superstitious and human thing, not from the commandment of God.[15]

Lefèvre would eventually run afoul of church authorities, as would most of the reformers at Meaux, and that group dispersed. We will need to return to their story in a later chapter. For now, we must be clear that Lefèvre never broke with the Catholic Church, even though he also never renounced his strong opinions, and after finding refuge at the court of Marguerite de Navarre at Nerac, in the south of France, he eventually translated the Bible into French. Even more of an enigma than Erasmus, whose influence on Protestantism would be acknowledged only as a wrongly hatched egg, Lefèvre made his way into Protestant histories of the Reformation as a genuine forerunner or even a founding member of the Protestant Reformation, and Catholic histories tended to mistrust his legacy well into the twentieth century. Whether or not Lefèvre would be pleased by this assessment of his achievements remains a matter of dispute. After all, he never broke openly with the Catholic Church. What cannot be denied is the fact that Lefèvre, the scholar, was the very embodiment of Bernd Moeller's aphorism "no humanism, no Reformation," and that he gave rise to a kind of reforming in France that could go in different directions.

Lefèvre and his disciples were not the only humanists in France. By the time Lefèvre joined Briçonnet at St.-Germain-des-Prés in 1521, humanism had made deep inroads in French schools and universities. As far as reform was concerned, another significant scholar is Guillaume Budé (1467–1540), adviser to kings Louis XII and Francis I. A product of homegrown humanism, educated in Paris and Orléans, Budé went on to become a true Renaissance man, expert at philology, Greek literature, philosophy, law, medicine, and theology. Budé the polymath is best remembered as an editor and translator of ancient Greek texts, and the driving force behind the renewal of classical studies in France. Like Erasmus and Lefèvre, with whom he corresponded regularly, Budé favored a renewal of religion as much as a renaissance of letters, and helped foster reform through a return to ancient sources.

At a practical level, Budé worked for a reform of education in France and was instrumental in the revamping of the curriculum at the two leading law schools of Bourges and Orléans. Applying the *ad fontes* principle to the study of law, Budé and his supporters overturned centuries of tradition by insisting that medieval commentaries on Roman law should be ignored and that the ancient legal texts be approached directly and interpreted in light of both the classical context and present-day needs. In other words, Budé helped to evict medieval glosses and commentaries from the law curriculum, a bold move that paralleled the humanist desire to rid theology of its scholastic medieval baggage. One law student at Orléans and Bourges who would be deeply affected by this *ad fontes* approach and use it to develop a new kind of systematic theology was John Calvin (1509–1564), future reformer of Geneva.

Budé was also instrumental in the creation of a center of humanist learning in Paris that survives to this day, albeit in much different form. Close to King Francis I, who relied on his sage advice, Budé convinced the crown to fund royal lectureships in classical studies. These lectureships eventually evolved into the Collegium Trilinguae (College of Three Languages), established by Francis I in 1530. Now known as the Collège de France, this institution became one of the premier centers of humanist learning in all of Europe and an engine of educational reform. Its legacy cannot be quantified or illustrated with charts and graphs, but can nonetheless be assessed as one of the crowning achievements of French humanism.

As far as religion is concerned, Budé's legacy is close to that of Erasmus and Lefèvre. Adamant in his belief that Christianity needed to be reformed according to the ancient paradigms found in the Bible and the fathers and ever impatient with devotions that smacked of superstition, in the classrooms of Orléans and Paris, Budé would transmit the *ad fontes* principle to another generation of younger reformers. Some of them, like John Calvin, would reject the Catholic Church; others, like Ignatius Loyola (1491–1556) would use their humanist education to reform the Catholic Church from within. Budé remained faithful to the Catholic Church and wrote against Protestants, but his wife and children would move to Geneva after his death and become followers of John Calvin, the great Protestant Reformer. This fact has heightened the ambivalence of Budé's legacy.

Lefèvre and Budé represent the triumph of humanism in France and also its openended unfolding. Lefèvre and his disciples, especially, prefigure not only the Protestant Reformation, but also a type of Catholic Reformation that seemed quite possible for a brief while, before the backlash against Protestantism made it wholly unacceptable. These reforming French humanists are, in sum, the Catholic Reformation that could have taken place in the 1500s but had to be postponed for four centuries until the convening of the Second Vatican Council in 1963.

Erasmus

One humanist would eventually overshadow all others in Europe: Erasmus of Rotterdam (1469–1536), a man who embodied all the reforming impulses of the new learning and late medieval piety. Ever the consummate scholar and man of letters, Erasmus never tired of critiquing the ethics and religious life of his own culture, often with a healthy dose of humor and no small measure of sarcasm. A philologist, translator, satirist, philosopher, poet, and theologian, Erasmus would become the first literary superstar in modern history, thanks to the printing press and his unique talents. He would influence his contemporaries as no writer ever had in all of human history, receiving invitations to teach in nearly every nation from Spain to Poland, and giving rise to an entire generation of young "Erasmians" throughout all of Europe Although he was a pacifist who prized tolerance above all and

Erasmus of Rotterdam. In this 1526 engraving by Albrecht Dürer the great Dutch humanist is portrayed as the consummate scholar.

loathed strife and theological wrangling, Erasmus attracted many followers who were less charitable or accommodating. Much to his chagrin, Erasmus would be blamed for creating a whole generation of rebels, and for destroying the unity of Christendom. Many came to believe, in fact, that Erasmus had laid the egg hatched by Martin Luther.

Erasmus, however, would have a troubled relationship not just with Luther, but with all of the hatchlings ascribed to him. In 1524, he met one of these wayward disciples face to face in Basel, a young French reformer named Guillaume Farel (1489–1565). Their meeting quickly devolved into a heated argument. Farel accused Erasmus of hypocrisy and cowardice. Erasmus called Farel "Phallicus" instead of "Farellus," and added that there was no point arguing with anyone so "ferocious, inflated, bombastic, and virulent." Summing up his disgust with Farel, Erasmus quipped: "He says I am no more of a theologian than a printer's wife. I'd be a great theologian if I called the Pope 'Antichrist,' human constitutions 'heretical' and ceremonies 'abominations.'"[16] Of course, Erasmus was utterly opposed to such extremism. Yet by rejecting Farel, Erasmus was also dismissing a disciple.

When Erasmus was born, no one could have predicted his upward trajectory. The illegitimate son of a priest, Erasmus literally embodied clerical corruption and the grief it caused to everyone. Stigmatized and deprived of a proper inheritance, he nonetheless received an excellent education, first in Gouda and then at Deventer, at a school where humanism had already entered the curriculum and the headmaster was a friend of the great Rudolf Agricola. At Deventer, Erasmus the schoolboy lived a semi-monastic life in a house run by the Brethren of the Common Life, where the discipline was strict and the food was awful, but where a deeply interior piety was emphasized, in the tradition of the *devotio moderna*. Founded in the late fourteenth century, the Brethren were a semi-monastic community devoted to teaching. The so-called modern devotion that they advocated, which Erasmus absorbed and took to heart, was adamantly opposed to the rote observance of prayers and rituals and highly distrustful of all external expressions of faith. In the most famous and influential treatise written from within this tradition, Thomas à Kempis's *The Imitation of Christ*, "flesh" and "spirit" were often contrasted as polar opposites, even to the point of advising, "Strive to withdraw your heart from the love of visible things, and direct your affections to things invisible."[17]

Exposed to both humanism and the modern devotion, Erasmus reached a critical crossroads when both his father and mother died of the plague within a year, leaving him a paltry inheritance. Sent in 1484 to another school, which he considered inferior, the penniless orphan made the best of a bad situation by becoming a monk and joining the Augustinian canons at Steyn. Although later, in 1492, he would be ordained as a priest, after completing his studies at the University of Paris, Erasmus would always claim that his true vocation was not to a monastic life or to the priesthood, but rather to scholarship. Eventually, once he had become the most admired scholar in all Christendom, he would be released from his vows.

By the time of his ordination, Erasmus was already fully committed to the new learning and steeped in the classics. He was also wholeheartedly devoted to the idea of reforming and renewing the Christian faith. The humanist paradigm of returning *ad fontes* guided all of his thinking. "It is at the very sources," he argued, "that one extracts pure doctrine."[18] No reform could take place, therefore, without knowledge of Greek and Hebrew, for no translation could ever convey the real meaning of the biblical text. Comparing the Latin Vulgate translation of the New Testament to the original Greek text, Erasmus would say:

> For we have in Latin only a few small streams and muddy puddles, while they have pure springs and rivers flowing in gold. I see that it is utter madness even to touch with the little finger that branch of theology which deals chiefly with the divine mysteries unless one is also provided with the equipment of Greek.[19]

As Erasmus privileged the original languages, so did he exalt the authority of the early church fathers. For him, Christian antiquity was a paradigmatic age, filled with a "splendid host" of writers and teachers who drank deeply from the purest crystalline source of all, the Holy Scriptures. An admirer of Lorenzo Valla, Erasmus labored with ancient texts throughout his life, as editor and translator, helping to make available the treasures of the past, both pagan and Christian, in all their pristine splendor.

To make the return *ad fontes* possible, Erasmus published definitive texts from the works of Irenaeus, Origen, Athanasius, Cyprian, John Chrysostom, Basil the Great, Jerome, and Augustine, as well as some texts from pagan authors. His greatest contribution to scholarship and piety, which dwarfed his work on the fathers, was his edition of the Greek New Testament, which up until then had been unavailable in print. In addition to collating and annotating various available Greek texts, Erasmus also provided a new Latin translation that differed substantially in some places from the sacred Vulgate text of Jerome. The impact of this New Testament was immense. First published in 1516, and again in 1519, ahead of the New Testament in the Complutensian Bibles that were gathering dust on the publisher's shelves in Alcalá, thanks largely to Erasmus's shrewd scholarly one-upmanship, his Greek New Testament and Latin translation would come to be the single most important text for an entire generation of reformers, both Catholic and Protestant, enabling them to return *ad fontes*, and providing a common text for all who wished to theologize by scripture alone. In turn, it would also become the basis for many a translation into vernacular languages, from Luther's in German (1522) to the King James English version (1611).

The introduction to this New Testament, the *Paraclesis*, also had a tremendous impact on younger reformers. It was in this prefatory exhortation that Erasmus summed up his entire reform program most clearly and succinctly, developing his biblically centered "philosophy of Christ" into a powerful critique of medieval religion and a blueprint for change.

Viewed against the biblical backdrop of the gospels and of the early church, late medieval religion seemed corrupt to Erasmus. Scholastic theology was an abomination, even "utter madness," simply because it devoted itself to the dissection of logical puzzles rather than to piety, relying more on its own methodology than on the Bible. Piety was wholly corrupt too, focused as it was on external symbols and rites. Influenced not only by the *devotio moderna*, but also by Neoplatonism, which he also assimilated deeply, Erasmus employed an unforgiving hermeneutic of suspicion to all rituals and external symbols, and also to any teachings or practices that could not match up exactly to those found in the ancient sources.

Erasmus was especially influenced by the Neoplatonist revival of Pico's Florentine Academy, which had spread so widely by the end of the fifteenth century that he came to encounter it most directly not in Italy, but rather in England, in 1503, through the humanists John Colet and Thomas More. Especially taken by the distinction that Neoplatonist metaphysics made between matter and spirit, which gave an intellectual framework to the piety he had picked up from the *devotio moderna*, Erasmus became an uncompromising critic of popular religion, championing the claim that the spiritual realm is superior to the material, and stressing that genuine piety requires a certain distancing of oneself from rites and symbols.

What mattered most in life, argued Erasmus, was the inner disposition of one's heart and mind. Genuine Christian faith was not to be found in abstract doctrines or in rites such as pilgrimages, processions, fasts, the lighting of candles, and rote prayers, but rather in a total surrender of the self to the divine, and in a total dependence on Christ alone. Rites were necessary, Erasmus argued, but only as entry points into a deeper, purely spiritual connection with God that transcended the visible world and the rites themselves. Never content with the "barren letter," or with anything visible, he encouraged Christians to "pass on to the more profound mysteries."[20]

In 1504, Erasmus published a devotional manual that he titled *The Enchiridion*, or *Manual of the Christian Soldier*, which advocated a highly interiorized sort of piety and was, in essence, a pointed critique of much of late medieval religion. Though it did not attract much attention at first, the *Enchiridion* would rapidly gain popularity and enjoy tremendous success, especially after 1515, undergoing numerous translations and editions and becoming the ultimate manifesto for religious change.

Taking its central cue from a passage in John's gospel (6:63), "The flesh profits nothing, it is the spirit that gives life," Erasmus laid out a very clear path for his readers, distinguishing sharply between matter and spirit, defining true devotion, or *pietas*, with an urgent voice:

> You will find that you can best maintain this piety if, turning away from visible things which are for the most part imperfect or of themselves indifferent, you seek instead the invisible. . . . I feel that the entire spiritual life consists in this: That we gradually turn from those things whose appearance is deceptive to those things that are real . . . to those things that are immutable and everlasting.[21]

Relying heavily on Origen and Dionysius the Areopagite, two of the most Neoplatonic of the early church fathers, Erasmus insisted that God is pure mind and pure spirit, and that everything visible or tangible should be approached allegorically, as a reflection of that highest reality of all.

In true Renaissance fashion, Erasmus backed up his arguments by citing the ancients, and by advising his readers to ignore the scholastic theologians. Erasmus's position, which also takes aesthetics into account, was a naked acknowledgment of his Platonism and of what lay at the very heart of his disdain for everything medieval:

> I find that in comparison with the Fathers of the Church our present-day theologians are a pathetic group. Most of them lack the elegance, the charm of language, and the style of the Fathers. Content with Aristotle, they treat the mysteries of revelation in the tangled fashion of the logician. Excluding the Platonists from their commentaries, they strangle the beauty of Revelation. . . . The great Christian writers of the past were able to treat even the most arid subjects with a beautiful prose. They enriched and adored their sermons and commentaries with the constant use of allegory.[22]

Questions of beauty mattered to Erasmus because, as a Platonist, he was convinced that beauty was inseparable from truth and goodness. This conviction gave Erasmus's allegorical hermeneutics a very pragmatic edge: beautiful allegories were superior because they led more directly and efficiently to goodness and truth. Conversely, immersion in the things of this world merely helped to keep one mired in error. And such formulae gave shape to

Erasmus's distrust of visual and tactile religious symbols, and to his Christ-centered piety, which was intensely *logocentric*, that is, focused on words, or, more specifically, on Christ the Word:

> When you venerate the image of Christ in the paintings and other works of art that portray Him, think how much more you ought to revere that portrait of His mind that the inspiration of the Holy Spirit has placed in Holy Writ. . . . If our Father in heaven finds His perfect reflection in His divine Son, so the words of His Son are the closest image of His divine personality.[23]

The Word, then, was not so much enfleshed as written. Literally, the Word became *text*, or *letters*. In Latin, Erasmus says that it is in the *litteris evangelicis* (letters of the gospels) that one finds Christ.[24] No mention is made at all of the body and blood present in the Eucharist, or of that other body of Christ, the ecclesiastical one, the *corpus christianorum*.

The Christ of the *Enchiridion* is above all an "archetype," or a paradigm to be followed. He is not so much God incarnate, a transformer of the structure of material reality, but rather a spiritual reflection of the Father, temporarily enfleshed, whose primary purpose is to reveal the spiritual realm where the divine dwells. "If the very physical presence of Christ is *useless* to salvation," asked Erasmus, "how can you put your trust in corporeal things?" If Christ's body made any difference at all, Erasmus asked, then why was he crucified? Did not Judas kiss him? Did not the Jews who rejected him also see and touch him? Erasmus went as far as to argue that the reason that Christ had to ascend to heaven was that his flesh was a source of distraction; it "stood in the way" of the apostles ever realizing the true meaning of the incarnation.[25]

The *Enchiridion* boldly insisted that God revealed himself most directly and fully in the Word—literally in the Bible—rather than in the incarnation, or the Eucharist, or the church itself. Given that the sacraments of the church were all rooted in the dogma of the incarnation, that is, on the belief that God had redeemed matter and made it capable of conveying divine grace, Erasmus was de-emphasizing the sacraments. And given that the sacraments were the link between ritual and belief, the very means of redemption and the lifeblood of medieval Christian devotion, Erasmus was challenging much more than "superstition" or aberrant piety. He could easily be accused of challenging the very foundation of the church itself.

The *Enchiridion* was only the first of many such attacks that Erasmus would launch against medieval piety. Everything he wrote was of one piece, ever focused on the superiority of the spiritual over the material, the internal over the external, and the allegorical over the literal. His critique was always consistent too, up until his death in 1536. His collection of proverbs and sayings from ancient pagan authors, the *Adagia*, which he kept enlarging through four editions (1500, 1508, 1515, 1536) became a staple in classrooms all over Europe. This anthology was carefully crafted as yet another weapon to be used against medieval darkness and superstition. His immensely popular *Praise of Folly* (1511) served the same purpose, filled as it was with poignant lampoons of the selfish materialism of his contemporaries. Even the Latin essays he composed for schoolchildren, the *Colloquies*, were replete with caustic references to the spiritual and moral ills caused by faulty materialistically inclined religion.

The *Colloquies*, in fact, contain some of the most sarcastic and most damning indictments of medieval piety that Erasmus ever dared to publish. Even more surprising, these Latin exercises for schoolchildren grew ever more critical of medieval piety as Erasmus aged, and as the religious crisis of the sixteenth century intensified. Erasmus was not one to backpedal. Colloquies such as "The Shipwreck" and "A Pilgrimage for the Sake of Religion" were written in the 1520s, when Erasmus was already on thin ice, having been blamed for spawning the Protestant Reformation.

Take, for instance, the following dialogue from "The Shipwreck," written in 1523, which ridicules the veneration of the saints. In this colloquy, the characters of Adolph and Anthony discuss the attitudes of passengers on a sinking ship. Anthony quizzes Adolph, who survived the shipwreck, about his own reaction:

> ANTHONY: But you called on some saint for help?
> ADOLPH: Not even that.
> ANTHONY: But why?
> ADOLPH: Because heaven is a large place. If I entrust my safety to some saint—St. Peter, for example, who perhaps will be first to hear, since he stands at the gate—I may be dead before he meets God and pleads my case.
> ANTHONY: What did you do, then?
> ADOLPH: Went straight to the Father himself, reciting the Pater Noster. No saint hears sooner than he, or more willingly grants what is asked.[26]

Erasmus makes it clear that the veneration of the saints is essentially useless, even insinuates that it might be wrong. As the dialogue unfolds, the character of Adolph lets it be known that all the passengers who prayed to the saints drowned. Keeping in mind that this work was written for a young lay audience at a time when any critique of tradition could be interpreted as a sign of sympathy with the "Lutheran" heresy, the boldness and consistency of Erasmus's critique stands out in high relief.

One did not have to search very hard to find questionable propositions in Erasmus. The great humanist argued for the superiority of the Bible over tradition, and for the inferiority of the Vulgate translation. He also lampooned the pope, especially in *Julius Excluded from Heaven* (1514), a satirical piece in which St. Peter denies Pope Julius II entrance to heaven. He scolded the clergy for their immorality and their eagerness to abuse the laity, dismissed scholastic theology as insanity, and derided monasticism as too legalistic and overly concerned with external trivialities. He denounced the piety of his day as misguided and as "the worst plague of Christianity"[27] Pilgrimages were not only a waste of time and money, but also occasions for sin and irresponsibility. "Pilgrims are rarely holy," he insisted.[28] Prayers to the saints were "hardly a Christian practice" and "not very different from the superstitions of the ancients," he charged. The sole difference between pagan and Christian heavenly intercessors, he observed, was that "the names have been changed."[29] Vows were an abomination too: crass tit-for-tat exchanges that dealt with God and the saints as if they were merchants at a farmer's market. Religious images were "stupid and dull" figures that represented nothing other than themselves and detracted attention from the sacred.[30] Relics were the very dregs of misdirected piety, not just because many of them were fraudulent objects, but also because they were bits of filthy rags or stinking bones enshrined in gold- and jewel-bedecked reliquaries, tying up valuable resources that should be spent on the needy.[31] Relics also stretched faith to the breaking point, for many were simply "contrived for profit" by greedy clerics.

Erasmus could turn it all into a joke, as he did with the relics of the true cross, which could be found nearly everywhere, even in sizable pieces. "If all the fragments were joined together," he quipped, "they'd seem a full load for a freighter." But Erasmus seldom joked for fun, and most of his humor was deadly serious at heart. Although he never broke openly with the Catholic Church and was never formally condemned, many of his disciples would take his critique further and borrow his jokes for other purposes, overlooking the irony with which they were so generously laced.

When many young scholars and clerics began to break away from the Catholic Church after 1517, Erasmus would be quickly blamed for their rebellion. And not only his opponents saw the connection. Some of the rebellious reformers thanked him directly. Ulrich Zwingli, leader of the Protestant Reformation in Switzerland, would claim it was Erasmus who taught him that praying to the saints was wrong.[32] Heinrich Bullinger, Zwingli's successor at Zurich, would say that Erasmus was "a truly great man, worthy of eternal praise," and would commend him for having spoken "truthfully, piously, wisely and justly" about the superstitious rituals and symbols of medieval Catholicism in the *Enchiridion*, *Praise of Folly*, the *Colloquies*, and many other books.[33]

Erasmus was much more tolerant than many of his disciples, however, and far more willing to accept the paradoxical necessity of external rituals and symbols,

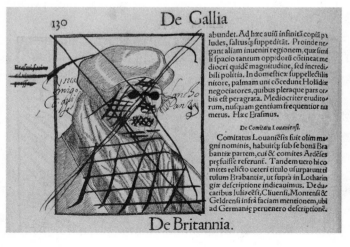

Erasmus defaced. The great humanist's sarcastic critique of medieval piety alienated and offended many traditionalists. In Spain, a bitter opponent of Erasmus displayed his dislike of him by defacing his image in a copy of copy of Sebastian Münster's *Cosmographiae universalis*.

especially for those who were not well educated or very spiritually advanced. Although he formulated the philosophical and theological foundation for the rejection of Catholic piety, stressing the superiority of spirit over matter and of the Bible and the fathers over tradition and the church hierarchy, he simply refused to consider extremes or to break with the Catholic Church. As he so aptly put it, "What I laid was a hen's egg: the bird Luther hatched was altogether different."[34]

Erasmus saw much of medieval theology and piety as flawed, but not as utterly wrong or evil. Moreover, by writing exclusively in Latin and ridiculing the "simple folk," Erasmus circumscribed his own critique, leaving the actual task of reform to a circle of readers over whom he had no direct control. Providing intellectual and spiritual guidelines that were elitist at heart, highly paradoxical, and limited in scope, Erasmus distanced himself as much from tradition as he did from rebellion, and as much from his critics as from his disciples. To the very end, he would remain an enigmatic figure, steadfastly committed to two principles that many of his contemporaries found contradictory: religious reform and Christian unity.

All in all, then, Erasmus proved that humanism could lead in different directions. He embodied the ambiguous legacy of Renaissance humanism more intensely than most of his learned reform-minded colleagues throughout Europe, but as he led the way in the return *ad fontes* and in the promotion of spiritual and intellectual reform, so did he set limits to the transformations he envisioned. He may have attracted a higher number of followers than any of his scholarly peers, but, at the very same time, he also won for himself an uncomfortable distinction: the ability to alienate a broader spectrum of contemporaries than almost any other reformer.

CHAPTER SIX

Forerunners of the Catholic Reformation

F aithful Catholics who wished to reform their church faced a daunting challenge, for the privileges, power, and wealth of the church hierarchy were immense, and inertia and resistance to change were endemic. At the very top, the popes who were in charge of the church in the late fifteenth and early sixteenth centuries offered no solution; they were, in fact, one of the church's greatest liabilities. Scions of powerful families such as the Borgias (Calixtus III and Alexander VI), the Della Roveres (Sixtus IV and Julius II), and the Medicis (Leo X and Clement VII) entangled themselves in complex alliances with secular powers, and did little to thwart dissenters or to reform the church from within. Although many among the clergy and laity still believed that councils could bring about reform and handle dissent, popes generally balked at the suggestion, fearing that their authority might be successfully challenged.

Not much could be expected from bishops either, at least not collectively. Proof of their impotence could be found in the Fifth Lateran Council (1512–1517), which held its last session only a few months before the outbreak of the Protestant Reformation.[1] Other than calling for a new crusade against the Ottoman Turks, establishing norms for pawnshops, and calling for stricter church control over book publishing, this council accomplished little. Its condemnation of many clerical abuses in the bull *Supernae dispositionis arbitrio* (1514) reiterated proscriptions that were already in place, yet flagrantly ignored, but it made no provision for their enforcement. A catalog of what needed to be fixed, rather than a plan for reform, this bull had a hollow ring. Yet when reading the address given by Egidio (Giles) da Viterbo to the Lateran Council in 1512, one cannot help but be struck by its reforming fervor. Egidio, a very popular preacher and general of the Augustinian Order, was certainly not alone in condemning his church and its place in society.[2] His critique itself and his zeal reflect a certain zeitgeist, or spirit of the times. Egidio attracted approval, along with brusque dismissals, simply by playing the prophet. "When has ambition been more unrestrained, greed more burning?" he asked the council fathers:

When has the license to sin been more shameless? When has temerity in speaking, in arguing, in writing against piety been more common or more unafraid? When has there been among the people not only a greater neglect but a greater contempt for the sacred, for the sacraments . . . and for the holy commandments? When have our religion and faith been more open to the derision even of the lowest classes? When, O sorrow, has there been a more disastrous split in the Church? . . . When have the signs, portents, and prodigies both of a threatening heaven and of a terrified earth appeared more numerous or more horrible?[3]

For Egidio, a council was the answer, the very council gathered before him. Putting his oratorical skills to the test, Egidio baited his audience with a challenge that most of them—and the pope himself—were unwilling to accept:

> Hear the divine voices everywhere sounding, everywhere demanding a Council. . . . For what else is a holy Council if not an object of fear for the evil, a hope for the upright, a rejection of errors, a seed-bed and revival of virtues, whereby the deceit of the devil is conquered, the allurements of the senses removed, reason restored to its lost citadel, and justice returned from heaven to earth? Indeed God returns to men . . . [through] the leaders of the Church. If John calls the shepherds of the churches angels [Revelation 1–3], what is there that so great an assembly of angels cannot seek by its petitions or obtain from its prayers from God? . . . Oh, those blessed times that have brought forth Councils! How foolish are the times that have not recognized their importance! How unhappy those that have not allowed them!"[4]

More than a hint of desperation seems embedded in Egidio's rhetoric. His appeals to conciliarism hinted also at a failed and self-fulfilling prophecy, for, as he probably suspected, his audience paid him scant attention. In essence, all that the Fifth Lateran Council seemed to accomplish was to confirm the death of conciliarism and the weakness of the high clergy, leaving nothing in its wake but missed opportunities for reform, along with censure and dissent.

At the end of the Middle Ages, then, Catholic reformers were more or less on their own. This is not to say that reform could not take place, but rather that it was difficult for any reformer to have an impact beyond a local level. Without papal or conciliar support, the best anyone could do was to focus on one's immediate environment. And there was certainly no shortage of heroic figures who dared to take on the challenge. Some of the most prominent of these reformers managed to accomplish a great deal, and not just in their lifetime, for they planted seeds that would bear fruit later. A complete listing of all of these reformers could easily extend to scores of pages. So, for now, let us look at just a few, to gain a better understanding of the range of their activities and of their successes and failures.

Oddly enough, one failed reformer provides us with a good starting point, for his case gives us a glimpse of the eagerness with which reform programs could be embraced, and also of the most significant variables that could determine their success or failure.

Girolamo Savonarola (1452–1498) was an austere and very learned Dominican friar who had a gift for preaching, and for creating genuine popular interest in reform.[5] In 1490, because of his reputation as a holy man and a gifted preacher, he was brought to Florence by its ruler, Lorenzo de' Medici. Within a year, he was elected prior of the convent of San Marco, and by 1493 he not only had reformed that Dominican community along very strict lines, but also had gained a substantial popular following. An electrifying speaker, well versed in the Bible and in humanist learning, Savonarola took aim against every sort of corruption, and he did so not only with eloquence, but also with a heavy dose of apocalypticism and calls for repentance. Florence was on the brink of disaster, he prophesied in 1493, about to be scourged for its many sins by a divine avenger. In 1494, as Savonarola intensified his crusade for repentance, that dire prediction came true in the person of King Charles VIII of France, who invaded Italy, conquered Florence, and drove out the ruling Medici family.

Out of the chaos caused by this invasion, Savonarola emerged as the undisputed leader of Florence. Revered as a genuine prophet, backed by a tidal wave of popular acclaim, Savonarola sought to turn Florence into a Christian republic. And he began to prophesy that the city would lead all of Italy and all of the church into a new era of reform. Now that he could actually root out sin rather than just preach against it, Savonarola also initiated a puritanical campaign the likes of which no one had ever seen. Florence, the New Jerusalem, had no place for the ungodly; gamblers, prostitutes, homosexuals, adulterers, drunkards, unworthy clerics, and libertines of all stripes were all to convert, or be driven out. Zealous young followers, based at San Marco, enforced the new rules through intimidation. Sermons, frequent processions, and public prayer replaced all feasting. And from the pulpit, Savonarola thundered against all corruption, and especially against those at the very top:

> When you see God permitting the heads of the Church to overflow with wickedness and simony, say that the scourge of the people draws near. . . . I saw through the power of the imagination, a black cross above Babylonian Rome, on which was written: *Ira Domini*, the wrath of God: and upon it there rained swords, knives, lances, and every kind of weapon. . . . O Italy, and princes of Italy, and prelates of the Church, the wrath of God is upon you, and you have no remedy but to be converted! . . . Do penance while the sword is not yet out of its sheath and while it is not yet bloodied.[6]

For three long years Savonarola held on to power, as opposition mounted at home and at the papal court. But for Savonarola there was no backing down. In 1497, as the penitential season of Lent approached, he intensified his prophetic mission by calling on all Florentines to rid themselves of their "vanities," that is, anything that smacked of sin. On Shrove Tuesday, instead of celebrating carnival, Florence sealed its ongoing purification with a giant bonfire of the vanities, into which were consigned wigs, masks, costumes, playing cards, cosmetics, musical instruments, suggestive or costly clothing, books, paintings, and anything deemed immoral. Among those who took part, gleefully,

Reforming from the pulpit. Girolamo Savonarola's fiery sermons against vice and corruption attracted a large following in Florence at the end of the fifteenth century, but also won him some powerful enemies, including Pope Alexander VI. Savonarola was excommunicated and executed in 1498.

was none other than the great artist Sandro Botticelli, a devout follower of Savonarola, who tossed some of his own paintings into the flames.

As this crusade against corruption reached fever pitch, so did the ire of the pope, and that of Savonarola's enemies in and around Florence. Having refused a summons to Rome by Pope Alexander VI, as well as a papal order to stop preaching, Savonarola was excommunicated and the entire city of Florence threatened with an interdict (a papal decree that cancels all sacraments in a specified location). By the spring of 1498, support for the prophet had waned. Captured by a mob of his opponents within the city, Savonarola was tortured, tried, and forced to confess that he was a false prophet and that he had conspired with foreign powers against Florence. On 23 May 1498, he was executed, along with two of his closest associates. Then their corpses were incinerated in a bonfire— ironically enough—and their cinders dumped into the Arno River from the Ponte Vecchio (Old Bridge), so there would be no relics left to collect. An eyewitness account tells of people who tried to gather the ashes that floated downstream, adding: "Those who did so, however, acted in secret and with fear. No one could either mention what had happened or speak about it without risking his life, as Savonarola's enemies wanted to extinguish all memory of the friar."[7] Stripped of Savonarola's presence, Florence returned to its corrupt old ways.

Savonarola's "reign of virtue" had come to a sudden and violent end for several reasons, chiefly political. First and foremost, his very success posed a threat to many powerful figures, both inside Florence and elsewhere. Chief among those he alienated was

Pope Alexander VI, who could not abide being disobeyed by a mere friar, and especially by one who constantly wagged an accusing finger at him, prophesying doom for Rome. Savonarola also made other enemies closer to home: the Medici family, their supporters, and all in the Florentine oligarchy who had been displaced or forced into virtuous living. Also, by allying himself with foreign powers, especially the French invaders, he had made himself the enemy of all those who resented France's foray into Italy. Ultimately, however, it was the very nature of his reform program that led to his downfall. Reform by coercion and intimidation is usually hollow and short lived. And this is especially true of any reform guided by apocalyptic or utopian enthusiasm, for those who seek to make saints out of everyone by force usually only succeed at making enemies for themselves.

So, what does it take to be an effective reformer? A very different sort of friar provides us with some answers: Francisco Jiménez de Cisneros (1436–1517)—already mentioned in connection with the Complutensian Polyglot Bible—a remarkable man whose ability to amass power and privilege was matched by his talent for putting it to use effectively.[8] The son of a Spanish tax collector, Jiménez began his ecclesiastical career humbly enough, as a beneficed cleric who spent six years in prison (1473–1479) for disagreeing with the archbishop of Toledo over an appointment to a certain post. Disheartened by his experiences among the secular clergy—despite an appointment to high office after his release from prison—Jiménez retreated from "the world" and became a Franciscan friar in 1482.

At the time, no one could have predicted his trajectory, but by 1492, Jiménez had acquired such a reputation for holiness that he was appointed as personal confessor to Queen Isabella of Castile, and by 1495, he had won for himself the highest ecclesiastical post of all in Iberia, that of archbishop of Toledo. Austere, industrious, and bent on

Multitasking reformer. Cardinal Francisco Jiménez de Cisneros, a Franciscan friar who became archbishop of Toledo, held multiple offices and carried out many reforms simultaneously. As a patron of humanist learning and of clerical education, he founded a new university at Alcalá de Henares and sponsored the production of the Complutensian Polyglot Bible. He also reformed his own Franciscan order in Spain and funded the translation and publication of many devotional texts. In addition, he served as inquisitor general and regent of Castile, and led a crusade to North Africa.

reform *in capite et in membris*, the friar-turned-archbishop dedicated himself tirelessly to the cause of improving his immediate environment. Convoking his bishops to synods at Alcalá (1497) and Talavera (1498), Jiménez enacted a number of significant reforms, such as forcing all clerics to reside in their parishes, placing harsh penalties on clerics who broke their vow of celibacy or lived with common-law wives, and ordering all clerics to preach every Sunday and to go to confession regularly. And this was only the beginning. Turning his attention to the regular clergy, he first cleaned up his own Franciscan order, expelling hundreds of lax friars and forcing all Franciscan communities to observe their rule more strictly. Then he began a similar crackdown on other monastic orders. Despite strong resistance, which included all sorts of appeals to Queen Isabella by well-connected monks from elite families, Jiménez won that battle too, even to the point of driving more than four hundred monks and their "wives" out of Spain.

Convinced that the health of the church and the kingdom depended on having good, holy clerics, and virtuous lay people, Jiménez also embarked on two other ventures that would eventually have an enormous impact in Spain and abroad. First, he sponsored the translation and publication of devotional texts, flooding the bookstalls of Castile with works that upheld the faith and inspired the pursuit of holiness. Many of these texts, which had previously been found only in monasteries, opened up all sorts of spiritual horizons to a much wider readership, among both the clergy and the laity. A good number of these books were in the Castilian vernacular rather than Latin, and many also hailed from the Rhineland, where a mystical tradition had developed that emphasized the presence of God in the human soul. Later in the sixteenth century, Spain would experience a religious revival in its monasteries and convents, thanks largely to this mystical tradition, producing scores of visionaries who would, in turn, transform Catholic spirituality: St. Teresa of Ávila, St. Peter of Alcántara, St. John of the Cross, to name some of the best known. The earlier texts promoted by Jiménez, along with those written by this second generation of mystics, would also have an impact on the laity and would help turn Spain into a formidable bastion of Catholicism, unlike any other in the world.

It needs to be said, however, that Jiménez was no innovator in this respect: he was picking up wider currents of reform and on trends found elsewhere in Europe, where the printing press was quickly changing culture, making all sorts of texts available to a broad reading public. In an age when theology was still the queen of the sciences and piety was often indistinguishable from ethics and good manners, it was inevitable that religious texts should make for best sellers, and that those who had access to religious manuscripts would devote themselves to editing and translating them. One place where this was done most intensely was the Rhineland, especially the German city of Cologne, where Carthusian monks translated and published many devotional and mystical texts, either from German into Latin or from Latin into German, opening up the chain of translation and the distribution across national and linguistic borders of previously esoteric texts. Many of the German and Dutch texts published in Castilian under the sponsorship of Jiménez had first been translated into Latin by the Cologne Carthusians. It could be said, then, that the localized success of Jiménez's publishing campaign was not so local after all, but rather linked to a much larger and very lively network of renewal.

The same could be said about Jiménez's greatest achievement: the establishment of the University of Alcalá. Convinced that reform could best be brought about by a well-educated clergy, Jiménez used part of his vast income to create a new school in which the traditional approaches of the Middle Ages would be cultivated along with the new learning of the Renaissance humanists. Established a few miles east of Madrid, at Alcalá de Henares, this new university opened its doors in 1508, with the goal of producing the best-educated and most well-rounded clergy in the world. In addition to having professorships in all of the major philosophical and theological schools, Alcalá also boasted of its wide range of specialists in ancient languages, and especially in Greek and Hebrew, and of its commitment to the Renaissance goal of returning *ad fontes*. Even the name acquired by the university reflected humanist pretentions: reaching back into the Roman past, when Alcalá was named Complutum, the school and everything associated with it became *Complutensian*. Its impact was immediate and enormous: attracting the best and the brightest, and those most interested in the new learning, the University of Alcalá became a hotbed of reformist fervor, producing scholars and clerics who would make their mark on the world.

Part and parcel of Alcalá's innovative thrust was that great project funded by Jiménez that we encountered in the previous chapter: the Complutensian Polyglot Bible. In the long run, however, his Complutensian Polyglot would be as much a symbol of his accomplishments as of his limitations, for Rome would not grant permission for the publication of this Bible until 1522, and then only in very small numbers.

Cardinal Jiménez de Cisneros is a complex transitional figure, part reformer, part zealot, very modern in some respects, but still steeped in traditional ideals. He was a Franciscan who wore a hair shirt under his cardinal's garb, something of a mystic, with an ascetic bent, with little tolerance for corruption. Yet he also served as Grand Inquisitor, and as such, he persecuted Jews and Muslims, hoping to convert them all by force. He was a cleric through and through who slipped easily into the secular realm, serving as regent of Castile and securing the throne for Ferdinand and Isabella's grandson, Charles of Ghent (the future Holy Roman Emperor Charles V). To top it all off, this patron of learning also donned armor and led a crusade into North Africa. Reforming a church or a nation has never been easy or simple, but in Spain, under Jiménez's direction, reform was as visible as it was complex. No one doubts or downplays the fact that the church in Spain was more thoroughly reformed or more vibrant than any other when the Protestant Reformation broke out in 1517. When the Catholic Church finally got around to assembling another council, at Trent in 1543, Spanish clerics would play a leading role, thanks in large measure to Cardinal Jiménez and to scores of younger men trained at his Complutensian University.

Reformers who accomplished as much as Jiménez de Cisneros were rare, but if one does not measure success in terms of scale, it is easy enough to find other men and women who worked to reform church and society, and succeeded. Often, one finds these reformers in unlikely places, displaying heroic virtue in nearly imperceptible ways, preparing the way for larger-scale reforms by subsequent generations. For instance, many monasteries and convents throughout Europe underwent reforms in the late fifteenth and early sixteenth centuries. These reforms often achieved changes on a local level similar to those that Cardinal Jiménez de Cisneros achieved throughout Spain. The relatively small scale of such reforms can easily make them seem limited in scope and of small consequence, but when we take into account their collective impact on the creation of a new generation of potential leaders who could defend tradition, push for further reforms, and resist Protestant advances, their significance is far from negligible. Most of these reformers were clerics, as one might expect, but some were lay people, both male and female. And they came from all walks of life. A few examples will enable us to gain some sense of the various ways in which the Catholic Church went about the task of reforming itself along lines that were at once novel and traditional.

A prime example of lay reform is provided by the case of Caterina Fieschi Adorno (1447–1510), better known as St. Catherine of Genoa, whose life is intertwined with those of other small-scale reformers. Born into a prominent family and subjected at an early age to an arranged marriage, Catherine underwent a religious conversion in 1473 and thereafter took it upon herself to minister to the poor and sick at the Great Hospital of Genoa, assuming the most distasteful tasks while she put up with an abusive and philandering husband at home. Given to mystical ecstasies, and stricken with a constant fever and a mysterious darkening of her skin, Catherine gained charge of the hospital and attracted other religious seekers to her side. Eventually, she also managed to convert her husband, Giulano, who abandoned his adulterous relationships for a life of service at the hospital, alongside his wife. Inspired by Catherine, a layman named Ettore Vernazza

B. Catharina Genuensis ex Patre Flisca, ex viro Adurna, annorum triginta, ex visione cordis Jesu Crucifixi, instar Solis tripliciter excurentis, adeo excarsit, ut facta sit Seraphim in amore, et Cherubim in sapientia, unde ceteris quoque clamabat, Sic Amantem diligite.vit.c 2.29 G. Piola del.ᵗ G. Tasniere sculp. Taurini

Reform by the laity. Caterina Fieschi Adorno (1447–1510), better known as St. Catherine of Genoa, was a married woman when she embarked on a life of service to the sick. Her selfless dedication to the needy and her mystical piety inspired others to join her, and led to the establishment of other charitable enterprises.

established a confraternity in 1497 that was dedicated to prayer and a life of service to the needy. This Oratory of Divine Love, as the confraternity was named, would in turn spur the creation of other similar confraternities, all of which saw holiness as rooted in works of charity. Before long, clergy were drawn in, and from these pious circles would arise many notable reformers.

Confraternities were nothing new. Throughout the Middle Ages these lay associations had served multiple social, political, economic, and religious purposes. Most notably, as we have already seen, they had assumed two large roles, which were often intertwined: that of maintaining and promoting popular piety—observing certain feasts or practicing other sorts of devotions—and that of dispensing aid to the poor and the sick through almsgiving and the establishment and management of hospitals, orphanages, asylums, and such. But the Oratory of Divine Love was different: it attracted people bent on reform and served as an incubator for change.

Out of the Oratory of Divine Love, for instance, sprang two formidable churchmen: Gian Pietro Carafa (1476–1559) and Gaetano da Thiene (1480–1547). Committed to the work of the Oratory, Carafa and da Thiene set their sights on establishing hospitals, and on promoting moral reform among clergy and laity. Along with two other confreres, they established a religious order, the Theatines, which was approved by Pope Clement VII in 1524. Named after the see of Theate, where Caraffa had been bishop (Chieti, in Italian), the Theatines dedicated themselves to a life of service among the laity and to increasing the devotion and moral rigor of diocesan clergy. In essence, they were innovative urban missionaries—a monastic order that was not confined to a monastery, which quickly spread to several cities, mainly in Italy, and which established very active centers for piety and charity. Above all, the priests of the Theatines provided an example through their lives of virtue. In a day and age when many of the clergy were indistinguishable from impious laymen, their comportment was no small achievement.

No matter how virtuous or how dedicated they were, however, the Theatines never became a large order, or a very powerful one. Their significance rests more on the relatively high number of reforming bishops that they would end up producing than on any large-scale reforms. The trajectories of two of their founders are indicative of their legacy. Gaetano Da Thiene would eventually be recognized as a saint. Beatified by Urban VIII in 1629 and canonized by Pope Clement X in 1671, he not only exemplified the virtues of the Theatine order, but also testified to its continued influence. After all, in the seventeenth century, as in our own, no one is ever canonized without the help of powerful patrons. In 1555 Gian Pietro Carafa became Pope Paul IV, at the age of seventy-nine, and he spent the final four years of his life in constant turmoil, acquiring a reputation for austerity and tactlessness. Ironically, the old reformer did his utmost to keep the Council of Trent from meeting during his four years on the papal throne, even as he sought to clean up Rome and his court. Unlike his confrere St. Gaetano, Pope Paul IV would never be canonized or even held in high esteem, proving that character and approach often determine the difference between a crank and a saint or between a despot and a reformer.

Another highborn reformer who made his way to the papal court—though not to the papacy itself—was Gasparo Contarini (1483–1542), a Venetian noble. Learned and pious, torn between a monastic calling and political life, Contarini spent much of his adult life in the service of Venice, including stints as ambassador at the courts of Emperor Charles V (1521–1525) and Pope Clement VII (1528–1530). Painfully aware of the failings of the church, and convinced that genuine reform had to be initiated at the top, this layman penned a treatise in 1516 that outlined how bishops should conduct themselves: *On the Episcopal Office*. One of the most remarkable aspects of this treatise, written only a year before Luther's incendiary ninety-five theses, is its unflinching assessment of clerical failures, which is coupled with a resolute conviction of the clergy's unique potential for reforming church and society. "A far greater perfection of soul is required of the bishop than the prince," argued the young Contarini, for bishops stand "between the divine spirits and mankind." As he saw it, bishops were more than mere human beings, for the ideal bishop "must share in a certain sense both in the angelic nature and in human nature."[9] *On the Episcopal Office* is as much an indictment of the higher clergy as it is a blueprint for reform. Anyone searching for evidence of lay discontent on the eve of the Protestant Reformation need look no further. But along with that discontent, there is also a deep reverence for tradition and hierarchy, a reverence that refuses to countenance any kind of redefinition of the nature of the church. Contarini moved in pious reform-minded circles while serving in government.

Eventually, Contarini linked up with Carafa and the Theatines in Venice, and got the chance to put theory into practice when Pope Paul III made him a cardinal and brought him to Rome in 1535. His presence made an immediate difference, even though he was not ordained a priest until 1537: Contarini not only curbed some of the most

Cardinal Gasparo Contarini (1483–1542). Contarini was a Venetian diplomat and cleric who pushed for reform within the Catholic Church. His *Consilium de emendanda ecclesia* (1537), a summary report on what needed fixing, commissioned by Pope Paul III, was not too well received by other highly placed churchmen in his own lifetime, but many of his proposals for change eventually prevailed.

flagrant abuses at the papal court, but also set about finding like-minded reformers for the College of Cardinals. Placed in charge of a commission to reform the high clergy, which had a list of members that reads like a who's who of reformers, Contarini delivered a blistering manifesto titled *On the Mending of the Church* (1537), which called for nothing less than a total overhaul of the clerical state. Its assessment of the clergy as a whole is representative of its overall tone and content:

> The first abuse in this respect is the ordination of clerics and especially of priests, in which no care is taken, no diligence employed, so that indiscriminately the most unskilled, men of the vilest stock and of evil morals, adolescents, are admitted to Holy Orders and to the priesthood. . . . From this has come innumerable scandals and a contempt for the ecclesiastical order, and reverence for divine worship has not only been diminished but has almost by now been destroyed.[10]

By the time Contarini's commission delivered its unflattering report, reformers of his ilk were no longer an oddity at Rome, or elsewhere. Four of its members were cardinals with exemplary reputations: Gian Pietro Carafa, Jacopo Sadoleto, Gian Matteo Giberti, and the Englishman Reginald Pole. Two were archbishops who had begun to reform their dioceses: Federigo Fregoso, of Salerno, and Girolamo Aleandro, of Brindisi. One of its members, Cardinal Gian Matteo Giberti, bishop of Verona (1495–1543) had perhaps the most impressive reform record of all.

Giberti began his clerical career at the papal court in Rome, serving first under Pope Leo X, and then as secretary to Leo's cousin, Cardinal Giulio de' Medici, the future pope Clement VII. Needless to say, Giberti was as familiar with the worst faults of the higher clergy as anyone could be, having been awarded multiple benefices and curial offices. Under Pope Clement VII, he would increase his income and his power substantially in the post of datary, that is, as head of the curial office that handled marital dispensations and all benefices reserved to the pope. In addition, he was appointed bishop of Verona in 1524, a post he could hardly fulfill from Rome.

Unlikely as it seemed, however, Giberti earned a reputation as an austere and incorruptible man who gravitated toward reform-minded clerics. It was none other than Giberti, for instance, who gave the Theatines their house in Rome. And even as an absentee bishop he took steps to reform the clergy in Verona through his vicar. But the great turning point in Giberti's life came in 1527, when the imperial troops of Charles V sacked Rome, took him hostage, and nearly killed him. This event was not so much a conversion experience as a moment of reckoning, after which he turned his back on the papal court and politics and gave himself totally to serving his diocese of Verona. Beginning in 1528 and continuing until his death fifteen years later, Giberti dedicated himself tirelessly to pastoral duties and to reform—a plan he carefully outlined in ordinances for his diocese published in 1542 under the title of *Constitutions*.

Giberti dismissed unworthy clerics who lived openly in sin or were ignorant of doctrine, and he began educating a new generation of disciplined, virtuous diocesan priests. To those who claimed to be exempt from his authority, such as the cathedral canons and several religious orders, Giberti showed no leniency. Relying on his connections in Rome, he acquired special power as a papal legate, and cleaned house with impunity. In addition to making constant visitations of parishes, monasteries, and convents, and instituting ways of correcting whatever abuses were discovered, Giberti also set up schools and even a printing press that published devotional and scholarly texts, including everything from catechisms for children to exquisite editions of St. Paul's epistles and the writings of some of the Greek church fathers. Giberti combined pastoral zeal with love of learning: he confronted corrupt priests in person, handled marriage disputes himself, funded an academy for humanists, and established charitable societies in every parish for the care of the poor. In sum, Giberti became a model bishop. His idea of reform, like that of so many clerics of his generation, was based on the assumption that without virtuous priests, church and society could never improve. For Giberti, it was the duty of every priest to be a saint:

> It is fitting that all of us exert every effort to recognize, in view of the fact that we are in the place of the saints, that, mindful of our name and profession, we have the need to live well and have not gained a license to do wrong. We must do this lest we give laymen any pretext to sin or cause them rightly to have a low opinion of the clergy and derive therefrom an excuse to persevere in their faults. Therefore, we must make a special effort to do the works of the saints and to make our deeds shine in the presence of men, and to be watchful and solicitous of that evangelical salt in our ministry, planting, weeding, scattering, and with the greatest zeal building up what makes for holiness.[11]

It stands to reason, then, that when a younger generation of reformers came of age, many turned to Giberti and his work at Verona for guidance and inspiration, not because they were naive enough to believe that every priest could be a saint, but because Giberti had provided the church with ample proof that high expectations alone could make a world of difference.

Another reformer of Giberti's age who had a profound influence on the following generation was merely a priest, rather than a bishop: St. John of Ávila (1499–1569). John could be considered a beneficiary of the earliest wave of reform as much as one of its shining lights, since he was deeply affected by the reforms of Jiménez de Cisneros and the writings of Erasmus of Rotterdam. Although he first attended the University of Salamanca, John finished his studies at Alcalá, where the writings of Erasmus had attracted a very large following. Like many of the Erasmians at the Complutensian University, John blamed the clergy for the decline of Christian faith and morals. He also thought that the priesthood had been corrupted by insincere, uneducated men of privilege who collected benefices without any intention of ministering to their flocks. Ordained a priest in 1526, John sold his entire inheritance and distributed the proceeds to the poor. He quickly became a very popular preacher in Andalusia, in the south of Spain, where he focused attention on the needs of the poor, and on the lack of adequate clergy, and where he often railed against

St. John of Ávila (1499–1569). St. John was a Spanish reformer, preacher, theologian, and mystic. Known as the "Apostle of Andalusia," he pressed for the establishment of seminaries, schools, and colleges, and for better religious education among the laity. His efforts, as well as his writings, strengthened the Spanish church and inspired many later Catholic reformers.

the chaplaincies that the rich established for their clerical relatives. "In many places," he charged, "there is a sufficient number of masses and extreme want among the poor."[12]

In 1531, John was accused of heresy by some of those wealthy Andalusian families that he criticized in his sermons. Brought before the Inquisition, John was acquitted two years later despite the power and influence of his accusers. Vindicated by this ordeal, John dedicated himself to the improvement of clerical education, establishing numerous schools and seminaries throughout Spain. A prolific writer of devotional literature, John also authored some very practical treatises on clerical reform and the nature of the priesthood that would later have a profound influence on the reforms devised at the Council of Trent (1545–1563). His reform ideals and his spirituality—especially his focus on mental prayer and inward piety (*recogimiento*), that is, on a way of addressing God quietly and intimately rather than through the mere vocal repetition of set prayers—would play a key role in the life and work of several other major reformers, including Ignatius Loyola, the founder of the Jesuits, and Teresa of Ávila, leader of the Discalced Carmelite reform (see chapter 16). The young men educated in the schools established by John would provide Spain and the Catholic Church as a whole with a new breed of clerics who paved the way for even greater reforms.

Reformers could also be found in monasteries, and sometimes their efforts to renew the church from within cloister walls could have a significant impact on the world outside. Of the many such men and women who could be mentioned, three provide us with a particularly clear glimpse of the reforming spirit that was at work in the Catholic Church before the Council of Trent. The first two of these exemplars, Marie de Bretagne and Renée de Bourbon, labored to reform the French monastic order of Fontevraud, and, in the process, not only breathed a spirit of renewal among the regular clergy in France, but also raised their own order to new levels of political power. The third exemplar, Francois-Louis de Blois, better known as Blosius (1506–1566), not only reformed his Benedictine community at Liessies, but also became a popular devotional writer.

The order of Fontevraud, founded in the twelfth century, had fallen into disarray by 1450, largely because of the devastation wrought by the Hundred Years' War between the English and the French. An order of male and female monastics, led from the motherhouse at Fontevraud, it had lost many of its priories and their revenues during the war. Even worse, in those houses that remained standing, monastic discipline was very lax and in dire need of reform. Bringing the order out of its nadir began under Marie de Bretagne, who recovered and repopulated many of the lost cloisters in the years 1459 to 1491 while insisting on stricter enforcement of a common rule among its male and female members. This work was continued by Renée de Bourbon from 1491 to 1534. A member of one of the leading noble families of France, Renée was instrumental in bringing all members of the order under her authority as abbess of the motherhouse at Fontevraud, giving rise to a most unusual monastic reform, in which males were placed under obedience to a female. In addition, Renée and her two immediate successors Louise and Eléonore—also members of the Bourbon family—vested the order with an uncommon degree of financial and political influence during the sixteenth century, a time of extreme turbulence in France, proving beyond a shadow of a doubt that women were as capable as—or more capable than—men in achieving great things.

The accomplishments of Blosius were less dramatic, but no less significant. In 1530, Blosius, a former page at the court of Emperor Charles V, became abbot of the Benedictine monastery of Liessies, in Flanders. Eager to conform his monastery more closely to the Rule of Benedict, but unable to force his wayward monks to change their ways, Blosius ended up being followed by only three members of his community. Eventually, however, he attracted new followers, and by 1545, the abbey at Liessies was officially confirmed as fully reformed by a bull of Pope Paul III.

Offered the abbacy of Tournai and the archbishopric of Cambrai by his old friend Charles V, Blosius refused both appointments just so he could complete his reforming work at Liessies. A scholar and a contemplative, very much a disciple of the Rhineland mystical tradition and the spirituality of the Brethren of the Common Life, Blosius also had a profound influence beyond Liessies through his numerous devotional writings, many of which were translated and widely distributed after his death in 1556. The truest measure of his stature, perhaps, is the fact that of all the devotional texts available to him, King Philip II of Spain chose Blosius to be read to him in 1598 as he was dying.

Conclusion

Blosius, Marie de Bretagne, Renée de Bourbon, John of Ávila, Giberti, Contarini, Carafa, St. Gaetano (Cajetan), St. Catherine, and Jiménez de Cisneros: one could keep adding names to this list of forerunners of the Catholic Reformation, such as John Colet

(1467–1519), dean of St. Paul's cathedral in London, and Guillaume Briçonnet (1472–1534), bishop of Meaux, both mentioned in the previous chapter, or the self-effacing Carthusian monks of Cologne, who lived exemplary lives out of sight behind their cloister walls and dedicated themselves to translating and publishing devotional literature, or the monks and nuns of the Congregation of San Benito in Castile, and the monks of Montserrat in Catalonia, who reformed themselves through a stricter interpretation of the Rule of Benedict. And on and on. All these reformers, in turn, influenced or gave rise to other reforms. It was a slow process, often limited to specific locations, but it nonetheless gained momentum over two generations and eventually yielded significant results. Listing all of the reformers who dedicated themselves to mending church and society at the turn of the sixteenth century is not only impossible, but also unnecessary. Alongside these well-known cases just mentioned, many others struggled to do their part in narrowing the gap between the ideal and the actual. Most labored in obscurity, and their impact was felt in their immediate environment.

Catholic reform can be best understood as a collective effort that had been simmering throughout the Middle Ages, and began to gather strength in the late fifteenth century from the ground up, so to speak, thanks to the efforts of determined individuals, very few of whom wielded great power. It was a movement that certainly had its share of leaders but was never centrally coordinated or controlled by any single individual, much less by any pope. Reform resonated with the laity, even if most of the reformers were clerical. As the extreme case of Savonarola reveals, lay people were often hungry for reform and ready to embrace it.

A handful of tiny pearls in a stinking sewer, Protestants would say. What is the use of focusing on such isolated cases? Do they really prove that the Catholic Church was beginning to reform itself before all hell broke loose in 1517? Up until recently, the answer to such questions depended on the confessional allegiance of the responding historian: Protestants would say no and Catholics, yes; the confessionally uncommitted tended not to care about such questions or simply followed the predominant disposition of their culture. Since the 1970s, when confessionally driven history began to wane, the general trend has been toward the yes, with all sorts of qualifications. Yes, there was reform in the air and also on the ground, but it was all piecemeal. Better to speak of early modern Catholicism than of a Catholic Reformation.[13]

When all is said and done, asking whether these reforms were genuine or of any consequence is like asking whether a rare, invasive species of plant matters much. The answer to the question depends on environmental circumstances. If the species is contained within its original restricted area, it remains exotic, a mere curiosity. But place just one tiny specimen of that rare plant in the right environment, and it will take over the entire landscape. Bring one aggressive intruder into the right biosphere, and unlucky native species can become endangered or extinct, regardless of how long or deep their entrenchment has been. End of story.

This is precisely what happened with Catholic reform in the early sixteenth century. In the right environment, some reformers began to exert their influence and to flourish, and their efforts would eventually lead to the expansion of reforms on a wider scale. It was a slow start, at first nearly imperceptible, but the reformers would eventually prevail. Yet all of their efforts, admirable and important as they were, paled in comparison to those that would be spurred by the greatest shock of all: the lightning-quick rise of the Protestant "heresy" and the broad appeal of its critique of Catholicism. Having to meet that challenge forced the Catholic Church to approach reform in a whole new way and to reinvent itself.

And the time has now come for us to examine that formidable challenge.

Sacred mess. If it had been possible for Martin Luther to visit Rome in 1546, the year of his death, he would have seen this untidy heap of structures at the construction site of the new St. Peter's Basilica. The fresco by Giorgio Vasari celebrates the role of Pope Paul III in directing the project. By the time this memorial was painted the Catholic Church had lost much ground to the rival churches known as Protestant.

PART TWO

Protestants
Prelude: Rome, 1510

A young Augustinian monk from Germany arrives in Rome in the fall of 1510, sent there on a business errand by his order. He eagerly visits all of the holy sites, trying to rack up indulgences for himself and his loved ones. One of these sites is St. Peter's Basilica. What he sees there is unlike anything else in Rome or anything he has ever seen: a partially demolished ancient church without a roof over the main altar, and two massive newly built pillars rising behind it, 90 feet tall, 30 feet thick, and 232 feet in circumference. He cares little, if at all, that Pope Julius II has resurrected the plans of Pope Nicholas V, begun the demolition of the ancient St. Peter's, and commissioned the architect Donato Bramante to build a new basilica that is supposed to surpass all other churches of the world in proportions and splendor. That colossal dome planned for the new St. Peter's, which the incongruous pillars he has just seen are designed to support, matters much less to him than other sacred sites, such as the twenty-eight steps of the Sancta Scala, or holy staircase, from the court of Pontius Pilate, which was supposedly brought to Rome from Jerusalem in the fourth century by St. Helena, mother of Emperor Constantine.

Irritated by the superficial piety of Romans and their disdain for Germans, the young monk is not in the least concerned with how Pope Julius intends to pay for his epic building program. He also has no clue that just a few years later, in 1517, the funding scheme recently devised by Julius will cause him to defy the papacy and to destroy the Catholic Church in much of Northern Europe. Pope Julius II, in the meantime, is very confident of the eventual success of his plan, which is quite simple: to offer a full remission of time to be spent in purgatory—that is, a plenary indulgence—to anyone who contributes to the building of the new St. Peter's Basilica. Pope Julius does not know, however, that he will die within three years and that his successor, Leo X, will push this fund drive and the building program very aggressively. Neither the young monk nor the pope can foresee in 1510 that in seven years' time a representative of this fund drive will reach Saxony, where this young monk lives, and that this representative and the pope's building scheme will be challenged by the young monk on theological grounds. No one alive then, in 1517, will have any inkling of the revolution about to be set in motion by this German monk. Nor will anyone be able to foresee how the construction project in Rome will parallel the disintegration of Catholic hegemony and the creation of new rival churches throughout much of Europe.

And the monk, whose name is Martin Luther, will have no way of knowing in 1517 that when he is finally overtaken by death in 1546, the massive pillars he had seen in 1510 and those erected by 1513, which he never saw, will still be awaiting a dome to support, with all of that patience that comes so naturally to anything made of stone or to any institution that is 1,500 years old and claims eternity as its fiefdom.

CHAPTER SEVEN

Luther

From Student to Monk

I t was the peak of summer, the second day of July 1505, when a twenty-one-year-old student found himself overtaken by a storm outside the Saxon village of Stotternheim. As he feared, the heavens unleashed their worst fury; lightning flashed all around, and a blinding bolt struck so close to him that he was blown off his feet. Shaken to the core, he did what he had been taught to do: he bargained with heaven, crying out, "Help, St. Anne, I will become a monk!"

The student was Martin Luther, who had recently earned a master of arts degree at the University of Erfurt and was aiming to become a lawyer. He had already bought the books he needed for his legal studies, including an expensive student edition of the law code of the sixth-century Roman emperor Justinian. His father Hans, who had paid for the books, was quite eager to have a lawyer for a son. But the lightning bolt changed it all. Two weeks after making his vow in the thunderstorm, Martin Luther entered the monastery of the Augustinian Hermits at Erfurt, despite his father's stern objections. Some of Martin's friends bid farewell forever at the cloister door. Like all who became monks, Martin would be leaving the world behind. Or so everyone thought.

What if Luther had become a lawyer instead of a monk, or what if he had been struck and killed by lightning in 1505?

Ironically, the young man who became a monk after making a vow to a saint would eventually renounce vows, monasticism, and the cult of the saints. He would also attack the Catholic Church as the seat of the Antichrist and bring it to ruin in many places. Martin Luther was not wholly responsible for ending the hegemony of the Catholic Church in Western Europe. He was but one of many reformers in his generation, some of whom pressed for more radical changes than he was willing to accept. And he was far from the first to challenge the medieval status quo. But he has earned a special place in history and casts a longer shadow than other reformers of his age for many reasons. In his day, he was the one who lit the fuse, so to speak: the first whose cries against corruption reached far and wide and struck deep chords among all sorts of people, the first to exploit the medium of printing in new ways, the first to obtain a large following at home and abroad, the first to secure firm political support, the first to make himself an untouchable archenemy of the Roman Catholic Church, and the first to capture the imagination and the hearts of vast multitudes.

Granted, much of what he accomplished came as a surprise to him and much of what was ascribed to him was not truly his to claim, but that does not diminish his significance. By the sheer force of his personality, and by sheer luck too, Luther was the first to succeed where many others had failed. He challenged the supremacy of the pope and the legitimacy of the Roman Catholic Church, he redefined religious authority and church-state relations, and he changed the focus of Christian piety and ethics. He managed to prevail against the pope and the Catholic Church on a scale previously unknown, in spite of brutal opposition. And he died in bed at the age of sixty-two, a victim of nature alone rather than sword, scaffold, or flames.

But how does a monk become a reformer, or how does he turn into a heretic in the eyes of his church? In the case of Luther, one must retrace his steps and first follow him into the monastery, for it was his vow and all it entailed that led to a profound crisis in his life—an inner struggle and a search for truth that eventually transcended his person and led to the unraveling of Western Christendom. Indeed, this may be one of the most peculiar aspects of the Protestant Reformation: that it should have been set in motion by one monk's spiritual odyssey.[1]

Yet, no great mystery lies hidden in this turn of events. Luther's titanic role in history was shaped by the intense symbiosis that existed in his day between religion and the civic order, an interdependence so thorough that a challenge to any one aspect of religion, no matter how seemingly trivial or narrow, could have an immense impact on the whole of the social fabric. Hence, a commonplace theological disagreement between two clerics—a "mere squabble of envious monks," as Pope Leo X allegedly called Luther's initial challenge—could quickly ignite a revolution and change the world.

From Monk to Scholar

Martin Luther was born on 10 November 1483 in Eisleben, a mining town in Saxony. The printing press had been in existence for thirty years already, and literacy was on the rise. Martin the schoolboy grew up with printed texts at hand as he attended schools in Mansfeld, Magdeburg, and Eisenach. At the University of Erfurt (1501–1505) young Martin gained a liberal arts education that exposed him not only to the ancient classics, the church fathers, and the traditional medieval scholastics, but also to the *via moderna*, a relatively new philosophical tradition that would give shape to much of his thinking. In brief, though Martin was aiming at a career in law, he had unintentionally prepared himself to be a religious reformer: his master's degree at Erfurt prepared him for his later work as a theologian and polemicist, and his entire education had exposed him to the new means of communication made available by printed literature.

But along came the fateful thunderstorm and the vow. If one lingers over this pivotal moment in his life, much can be learned about who Martin was and what he would later reject.

First, the structure of the vow itself needs to be explained. By striking a bargain with heaven—"Help, St. Anne, I will become a monk!"—Martin followed the norms of late medieval piety. Praying for favors from heaven most often involved two steps: invoking the right patron and promising some sort of exchange.

Why did Luther need a patron, and why did he call on St. Anne? Heaven was viewed as a royal court, much like any on earth, and prayer itself was tailored to fit that image. Everyone in Luther's day knew that to obtain favors from any earthly ruler, patrons and intercessors had to do the bidding on behalf of clients. Consequently, it was commonly assumed that just as no one would dare implore the king directly, no one should go straight to God. This conception of heaven and of prayer that Erasmus had vigorously lampooned was obviously part and parcel of the worldview of the Luther family. St. Anne had long been a patron invoked by miners, and Luther's father was in the mining business. What better patron could he hope to find?

What about the vow itself? Why would such a promise be deemed necessary in prayer? As in the case of patron saints, the history of this practice was ancient, older than Christianity itself. But its existence was reinforced not just by the weight of tradition: it too was suggested by commonsense observation of the way in which earthly courts and patrons worked. In the ancient world and in medieval Christendom alike, all client-patron relations demanded an exchange of goods, services, or homage: the fulfillment of vows was crucial and utterly unavoidable. In brief, reciprocity was essential: one always had to *do* something in exchange for favors rendered. Erasmus also poked fun at this conception of heaven and prayer, not only because it seemed to ignore the intercessory power of Jesus Christ, but also because it seemed to lessen the majesty and generosity of God and the saints. As Erasmus saw it, all this bargaining made heaven far too much like earth and God as small minded as any greedy merchant. But Luther was unaffected by Erasmus in 1505, and he did the only thing he thought would help him survive the storm: he struck a bargain.

But why vow to spend a lifetime in a monastery, where he would have to fulfill three more vows, those of poverty, chastity, and obedience? Obviously, such a decision requires having some preconceptions about monasticism, as well as its value in the economy of salvation. And Luther surely knew what he was doing. When faced with death and utter terror, Luther, like all of his contemporaries, would most likely think of what it took to earn God's favor on Earth and eternal life in heaven. At that awful moment of death, or near death, with one's eternal fate about to be decided, one had better be prepared to go to the right place, even to make the ultimate sacrifice of surrendering one's life totally to God. Death was the doorway to three other worlds, according to the teachings of the church: hell, purgatory, and heaven. And this cosmic geography seems to have been as real to Luther as the lightning bolt that knocked him off his feet. In other words, Luther's vow was inextricably linked to his conception of the afterlife.

Hell was a place to avoid, but it nonetheless exerted a strong pull on the whole human race, including baptized Christians. It was the place to which all temptations led, the potential outcome of each and every sin. It was the abode of Satan, devils, and humans who had died unrepentant with the stain of mortal sin on their souls. The road to hell was easy enough to find and follow, for it was imprinted in the base and unavoidable instincts of the human race: the church had a very long list of sins that counted as "mortal," and some of them were very difficult to avoid, such as lying or getting drunk or coveting one's neighbor's wife, or even having sexual intercourse with one's own spouse on a Sunday. The seven deadly sins were especially hard to avoid, for they involved attitudes as much as actions, and they could not easily be extinguished: pride, envy, greed, anger, lust, gluttony, sloth. Hell therefore lurked close for everyone, especially in an age with relatively short life spans and a high mortality rate. Those who died unprepared were most likely headed straight for the flames of hell, which theologians believed was under the earth's core. God's justice demanded such a punishment.

But justice was not the sole attribute of God. He was also merciful, ostensibly, and eager to save humans. Hence the existence of purgatory. Purgatory was believed to be located directly above hell, heated by its fires, and to be the temporary abode of the vast majority of Christian souls, who needed to pass through purgatory and be purified before being admitted into heaven. This painful cleansing was necessary not only because moral and spiritual perfection was rare and venial sins common (that is, lesser sins that do not merit hell), but also because it was believed that all sins committed in one's lifetime, whether small or large, required a commensurate penance or penalty. In other words, even when a sin had been forgiven, it still had a penalty attached to it: sins had to be paid for either in this life or the next. It was also believed that sins made one impure and thus incapable of facing God directly. The length of time required for one's purification varied according to the severity of one's sins and also to the rituals performed through the church on earth on one's behalf, but by Luther's day an otherworldly reckoning of time had become widely accepted that measured suffering in purgatory by thousands of years. The most widely recognized formula proposed that one day's suffering on Earth equaled a thousand years of suffering in purgatory. Three theological assumptions upheld the reality of purgatory for Catholics in Luther's day: first, most Christians led less-than-exemplary lives; second, a lifetime on Earth was not sufficient to cleanse one from the stain of sin or to pay the penalties owed to God; and third, God could not require absolute moral perfection from the fallen human race. God's mercy demanded that here *had* to be some chance beyond this life to make up for one's failings.

Heaven was the best place of all, of course. Heaven was the abode of God, the good angels, and the saints. Only those whose souls were pure could get there, that is, only those whose souls were free of the stain of sin. In Luther's day, it was a foregone conclusion that hardly anyone entered heaven upon dying, since the entrance requirements called for a degree of virtuous living unattainable by most men and women. The formula was rigorously simple: heaven is gained only through the very best behavior.

Fearsome justice. Depictions of the Last Judgment were difficult to ignore in medieval Europe, especially for town and city dwellers, since many churches had at least one such image. Martin Luther claimed that this scene terrified him when he was a monk, for it reminded him of his sinfulness and of the fate that he deserved. This 1505 woodcut by Hans Baldung Grien is true to form: we see Jesus the divine judge sitting on a rainbow, separating the just from the damned on the last day. The just rise from the dead to eternal bliss, while demons drag the damned to hell for eternity. On one side of Jesus's head is a lily, which symbolizes his mercy, on the other is a sword, which symbolizes his justice. Brother Martin, who focused on the sword, and on his own inescapable sinfulness, could not bring himself to look at the Last Judgment scene in his monastery's refectory.

Heaven required not only the avoidance of sin, but also the performance of many good works and a full possession of the seven virtues: faith, hope, charity, fortitude, justice, temperance, and prudence. This was an unquestioned assumption, so deeply woven into Luther's culture that even the rudest of peasants were made aware of it, in myriad ways. In brief, Luther was not at all alone in believing that hardly anyone ever breezed through the gates of heaven at the moment of death.

Ultimately, salvation hinged on one's behavior and one's attitude toward one's behavior. This assumption is perhaps the most basic theology grasped by all Catholic Christians of Luther's day. The church's theology of salvation—its soteriology—was more complex than this simple proposition, and it was the subject of many scholarly debates. Yet, even in its most sophisticated and erudite formulations, Catholic theology taught that the salvation effected by Jesus Christ through his church on Earth ultimately hinged on what one *did* or *did not do* in this life. Christ saved one from sin and damnation, yes, but one's behavior determined whether or not one would gain heaven, or how long it might take to get to heaven from purgatory. Theologians had many ways of speaking about this process and many elaborate approaches and fine distinctions, some clear and others blurry, and there were points on which they could not agree, but the bottom line was simple enough to understand: God is eager to save you, and he does offer you help through the sacraments, but it is ultimately up to *you* to cooperate with him, to *do* the right thing, and to *earn* your salvation.

Brother Martin accepted all of this in the same way that any educated person in our century accepts the unquestionable fact that the universe is made up of atomic and subatomic particles and that the earth orbits the sun, and that this sun is a relatively small star that will flare out in a mere five billion years. And in similar fashion, Luther also accepted the fact that the surest way to heaven was the monastic life.

Monasticism was a way of life that was already more than a thousand years old in Luther's day. It had come into existence very early in Christian history, and formed an integral part of the whole in the Catholic and Orthodox traditions. Christian monasticism is a way of life that seeks to provide a straight and narrow path to spiritual and moral perfection. The path followed by monastics is one of self-denial, of constant warfare against "the world, the flesh and the devil," as monastic writings would put it. The aim of the monastic life was to grow in holiness, to train oneself in making right choices, to become ever more like God and thus to ready one's soul for heaven. The path to holiness, however, was narrow, steep, long, and filled with innumerable pitfalls. The closer one drew to God and the holier one became, the more one would be assailed by soul-wracking temptations and torments at the hands of demons.

No one should underestimate the presence of the devil in monastic culture: the Great Fiend, the Evil One, the Tempter, the Father of Lies was no metaphor. Monks and nuns and many other people in the Middle Ages—including Luther's family—seemed utterly convinced of the devil's presence in their midst. Take, for instance, the following narrative from Julian of Norwich, a fourteenth-century English hermit who claimed to be in close touch with God:

> The devil returned with his heat and his stench, and kept me very busy. The stench was vile and painful, and the physical heat was fearful and oppressive; and I could also hear in my ears chattering and talking. . . . And so they occupied me all that night and into the morning, until it was a little after sunrise; and then all at once they had all gone and disappeared, leaving nothing but their stench, and that persisted for a little while.[2]

Luther would have similar tales to tell later, even after he was no longer a monk.

Temptation and struggle were only one face of the coin, however. Something infinitely better awaited those who persevered, and monastic culture codified this progress in three overlapping stages. First came purgation, or cleansing, much like that undergone

Devils and the holy man. Monastic culture stressed the omnipresence of the devil and the constant torment of his temptations. Genuine holiness, it was commonly believed, involved struggling with demons. In this image from the late fifteenth century, Martin Schongauer depicted a an account from the fourth-century *Life of St. Antony*, by St. Athanasius, which details how the great father of Christian monasticism was physically abused by a horde of demons. Martin Luther would have been familiar with this and other such narratives, and with visual representations of them.

by souls in purgatory. It was a basic step, and an ongoing process, never fully left behind. Purgation would be accompanied by an overlapping second stage, illumination, in which one gradually began to see more clearly and directly the true nature of things and to experience the love and presence of God directly. If one continued on the right path, a third stage could also be ultimately reached: union, that is, an intense bonding of the human soul with God, a state of total bliss, a foretaste of life in heaven.

In theory, monasticism was supposed to breed mystics, that is, men and women who would experience God's presence directly, or even join their souls with God in an ineffable embrace. As expressed by the great scholastic theologian St. Thomas Aquinas, "The contemplation of divine truth . . . is the goal of the whole of human life," and such a goal could best be achieved through the renunciation of the world and the embrace of the cloistered life.[3] It mattered little that monasteries often fell short of their goals, or that the number of acclaimed mystics who reached the zenith remained relatively small: these lofty goals remained fixed, as if in stone, in the *Rules* every monastery was supposed to follow, *Rules* that constantly reaffirmed the promises of the monastic life. A twelfth-century monastic text long attributed to St. Bernard of Clairvaux summarized the potential benefits of the monk's life: "Is not that a holy state in which one lives purely, walks more cautiously, falls more rarely, rises more speedily, is consoled more frequently, dies more confidently, is purified more quickly and rewarded more abundantly?"[4] Luther's culture tended to assume that men or women who embarked on the monastic path could actually become *holy*, that is more God-like than other humans, less prone to sin, more capable of genuine love of God and neighbor, perhaps even able to converse with God or perform miracles. In other words, they could *perfect* themselves and become saints.

And when he joined the Augustinians at Erfurt, Luther settled for no goal other than the very summit, or at least he claimed so when years later he boasted, sarcastically:

> I was a good monk, and kept the rule of my order so strictly that I may say that if ever a monk got to heaven by his monkishness it was I. All of my brothers in the monastery who knew me will bear me out. If I had kept on any longer, I would have killed myself with vigils, prayers, reading, and other work.[5]

So it was that Brother Martin set off on the path to holiness and love of God. He tells us that during his first few years, the devil left him alone, and he was able to make progress. After taking his vows, he was ordained a priest and said his first Mass in May 1507. But soon enough he was overcome with doubt and temptation, overwhelmed by his own sinfulness, and his fear of God's wrath. Such painful introspection was part and parcel of the monk's quest for God, an essential component of purgation and illumination. In fact, much of monastic life was focused on awakening such an intense awareness of sin: it was only by scrutinizing one's behavior that one slowly inched towards heaven. But in Luther's case, by his own admission, the only illumination he found was an ever-clearer vision of his own failings and of the infinite distance between him and God. "I was a very pious monk," he would say years later, in 1533, "but I was sad because I thought God was not gracious to me."[6]

Luther's demons wormed their way into his mind, reminding him of his short-comings, filling him with doubt, despair, and anger. Satan spoke to him directly: "God doesn't want to forgive you." Relentlessly, the demons needled Luther: "Behold, you're weak. How do you know, then, that God is gracious to you?" Luther would reply out loud: "I have been baptized, and by the sacrament I have been incorporated in Christ." But the demons had a way of twisting things around for him, and even of using Holy Scripture itself to sink him further into despair, saying: "That's nothing, for many are called, but few are chosen [Matthew 22:14]."[7]

Luther's demons were inseparably linked to his understanding of God. This was his ultimate torment, to see his own sins as God must see them, to hear his own conscience damning him, to feel the divine wrath he deserved. It was an unbearable, unending dark night of the soul in which every attempt to please and love God led away from him. A wise confessor upbraided Luther: "You are a fool. . . . God is not angry with you, but you are angry with God."[8] These words apparently struck home. Years later, shortly before he died, Luther would say:

> Though I lived as a monk without reproach, I felt that I was a sinner before God with an extremely disturbed conscience. I could not believe that he was placated by my satisfactions. I did not love, yes, I hated the righteous God who punishes sinners, and secretly, if not blasphemously, certainly murmuring greatly, I was angry with God. . . . I raged with a fierce and troubled conscience.[9]

This "fierce and troubled conscience" (*saeva et perturbata conscientia*) brought Luther to the brink of madness, through awful bouts of despair, or *Anfechtung*, a German word that has no English equivalent. For Luther, *Anfechtung* was an affliction inseparable from temptation, yet even worse: it was doubt, panic, despair, desolation, and rage all rolled into one abysmal experience, a downward spiral leading into hell itself, which made Luther think that God had abandoned him forever and that God's promises were false. "In our hearts He begins to become a liar," said Luther, admitting that the anguish made him wish for annihilation.[10] Worst of all, he was living a life wholly dedicated to this awful God, who would some day judge him. Images of Christ terrified him, and especially those that depicted the Final Judgment. So did the consecrated host, and Corpus Christi processions. Unable to withstand the thought of Christ as judge, rather than as redeemer, Luther could find no solace in the Mass, or in the iconography that surrounded him.[11]

Monasteries had ways of handling cases such as Luther's. Overactive consciences, obsessive-compulsive scrupulosity, and feelings of despair were as old as monasticism itself, and a necessary experience for all monks, to varying degrees. Since the days of the desert fathers, the greatest safeguard against wrong turns with such introspection was the assigning of older and more experienced monks as spiritual directors to novices and

AETHERNA IPSE SVAE MENTIS SIMVLACHRA LVTHERVS
EXPRIMIT·AT VVLTVS CERA LVCAE OCCIDVOS
·M·D·X·X·

Brother Martin. Luther the Augustinian monk, gaunt and tonsured, as sketched by Lucas Cranach the Elder in 1520.

young monks. When Brother Martin was transferred in 1511 from Erfurt to the new university town of Wittenberg, where the Augustinians had established a cloister, he was lucky enough to find a highly placed and well-skilled adviser, Johann von Staupitz (1469–1524). Luther would later say of this dean of the faculty and vicar-general of the Augustinians, "If it had not been for Dr. Staupitz, I would have sunk into hell."[12] Once, at table with his family and students, Luther would go further: "I got nothing from Erasmus. Everything I have came from Staupitz."[13]

Since Brother Martin was so troubled by sin and his unworthiness, Staupitz first advised that he seek forgiveness in the sacrament of penance. Going to confession helped Luther, but only to a point. Luther began to confess his sins frequently, often on a daily basis, and sometimes in great detail. He analyzed every sin, every motive, every circumstance, scrupulously. His fellow priests grew tired of hearing his obsessive confessions. Some even began to avoid him on purpose. Johann von Staupitz, a very patient man, exploded one day: "Look here," he said to Luther, "if you expect Christ to forgive you, come in with something to forgive—parricide, blasphemy, adultery—instead of all these small faults."[14] But this advice was useless to Luther. His anxiety was not over the magnitude of his sins, or their sheer number, but over whether they had been correctly confessed. What about unrecognized sins? Or forgotten sins? What about his motives, especially? After all, a good act committed for the wrong motive could count as a sin—for example, performing an act of charity out of vainglory. Motives were so hard to discern correctly. And confession was no cure for Brother Martin.

But Staupitz was not stumped. The intensity of Luther's despair may have been unusual, but it fit into a well-understood pattern in monastic culture. Staupitz knew that Brother Martin needed to busy himself with tasks other than self-scrutiny, so he ordered him to obtain a doctorate in biblical studies. Luther complained that he was much too fragile and unstable for such work, but Staupitz would not back down and Luther had no choice but to fulfill his vow of obedience. And he fulfilled it with a vengeance, becoming one of the best-known interpreters of the Bible in all of Christian history.

In October 1512, at the age of twenty-eight, Luther was awarded his doctorate, and he soon began teaching at the University of Wittenberg, where he lectured on the book of Psalms, analyzing and interpreting it as any good biblical scholar of his day would, to discern the various levels of meaning in the text, aided by all prior interpreters in the Christian tradition. Studying the Bible was a complex and demanding undertaking, and also an ancient task, full of tradition. Luther the expositor of the Holy Scriptures did not just have to engage with the text of the Word of God: he also had to familiarize himself with the way in which that Word had been read by the great fathers of the church and medieval scholastics over the previous fifteen centuries. In true Renaissance fashion, Luther also adopted the approach that was very much in vogue in scholarly circles: the desire to return *ad fontes*, to the pure sources, and to allow the text in the original language speak for itself.

As Luther began teaching at Wittenberg, he was not some Renaissance purist, convinced that he had to scrape away from the original text all of the glosses of earlier generations like barnacles off a ship's hull—and especially those of the medieval scholastics—nor had he yet reached any revolutionary conviction about discarding such traditions altogether, but he had definitely picked up on the humanists' assumption that it was infinitely better to engage with the Bible directly than to always read it through its interpreters. Moreover, as a monk who taught other monks and clerics, Professor Luther was not just a scholar engaging with an ancient text on a purely intellectual level: he was a servant of God who was trying to engage with God's Word existentially, to bring himself and others to eternal salvation. Everything was riding on each and every one of those words he analyzed in God's book, literally as well as figuratively.

It stands to reason, then, that as he worked his way through certain books of the Latin Vulgate Bible, Luther began to find a solution to his spiritual crisis. We cannot pinpoint exactly when Luther achieved his breakthrough, or, as his monastic brethren might have said, his transition from purgation to illumination. According to Luther himself, a gradual awakening took place in his early teaching years, as he lectured on the psalms (1513–1515), and St. Paul's letter to the Romans (1515–1516) and letter to the Galatians (1516–1517). Although Luther's principal focus was the interpretation of these biblical texts, his exegesis was influenced not only by his learning, but also by his spiritual training. Luther himself never denied that dimension of his engagement with the Bible. In fact, it is thanks to the books he left behind, with his notes in the margins, that we know what he read during this critical period, and that we are able to see how he drew on these other sources for his interpretation of the Bible. We know that he first read broadly and deeply in the works of St. Augustine in 1509–1510 and those of the Augustinian nominalist theologian Gregory of Rimini, and that he used Jacques Lefèvre d'Étaples's *Psalterium quincuplex* while teaching the psalms in 1513. We also know that in addition to consulting many patristic and medieval Bible commentaries, he pored over the sermons of the fourteenth-century German mystic Johannes Tauler in 1515–1516, and the works of the fifteenth-century scholastic theologian Gabriel Biel in 1517. In addition, he edited an anonymous fifteenth-century mystical treatise known as the *Theologia germanica* in 1516, which he would later publish and promote as a foreshadowing of his own "Wittenberg theology." From his friend and associate Philip Melanchthon we learn that he was so influenced by another nominalist theologian, Pierre D'Ailly, that he memorized some of his texts.[15] D'Ailly (1351–1420) was not just a nominalist, but also a conciliarist, that is, a proponent of the theory that supreme authority belongs to church councils rather than to popes.

In sum, then, we know that during this critical period Luther was heavily influenced by five major traditions: (1) the theology of St. Augustine, which stresses the total corruption of human nature by original sin, and proposes that it is only through God's grace that we are saved; (2) the scholarly tradition of Renaissance humanism, with its stress on returning to the Bible as the chief authority and its commitment to the study of texts in their original language; (3) the Rhineland mystical tradition, which stressed the paradoxical concept of *Gelassenheit*, or letting go, a radical abandonment of the self to God in which one passively allows the divine to redeem the human self; (4) the late scholastic *via moderna*, or modern way, also known as nominalism, which stressed the radical otherness and total freedom of God and the absolute necessity of accepting all propositions about God and salvation by faith rather than by reason; and (5) the conciliarist movement, which denied that popes were the ultimate authority in the church.

It was while lecturing on the psalms, those ancient, emotionally charged Hebrew prayers, that light first dawned for Luther. All it took was one brief passage: the first verse of Psalm 22, "My God, my God, why have you forsaken me?" In a blinding flash of insight, it dawned on Luther that this anguished question bridged the Old and New Testaments, for those were the very same words spoken by a desolate Jesus on his cross (Matthew 27:46; Mark 15:34). If Jesus was divine and sinless, Luther asked, why would he have to suffer and die on the cross? Why would he have to cry out in anguish? Could God feel forsaken, as Luther himself did? Could God Almighty suffer *Anfechtung* too, that all-consuming despondency that seemed worse than death itself? Since the answer was obviously yes, it meant that Luther's despondency—his feeling of being forsaken by God—had been taken on by Jesus Christ, by God himself. So, the paradox was the solution: by becoming human in Jesus Christ, God had had taken on not just all sin, but also all of the alienation that flowed from it. This fact meant for Luther that *Anfechtung* was necessary for salvation, that it had to be felt because it was shared by Christ, the savior. "They are damned who flee damnation," Luther would say, "for Christ was of all the saints the most damned and forsaken."[16] Ultimately, then, he who hung on the cross feeling totally deserted was also he who would pass sentence at the Final Judgment: Jesus, the terrifying Divine Judge who could justly send everyone to hell was not stern and wrathful after all, but rather a compassionate savior. Somehow, all of humankind's inescapable sins were made null and void by Christ's suffering, and especially by his feeling forsaken and alienated.

Luther had made a breakthrough, for he could now trust God's promise of salvation: God who willingly suffers the ultimate pain of being human could not be a liar, or an exacting judge. But Luther had yet to figure out the "somehow" in this redemptive formula. How is one saved, precisely? He was still especially troubled by the fact that genuine righteousness was impossible. "For many days and nights" he meditated on what St. Paul meant by *justitia Dei*, which in English can be translated as "God's justice" or "righteousness." How can a just God overlook sin? How can any sinful human be made righteous, or just, when sin is unavoidable? His greatest breakthrough came as he was wrestling with the Latin text of Romans 1:17: *iustus autem ex fide vivit*, "Moreover, the righteous shall live through faith." Suddenly, in the library of his cloister at Wittenberg, up in a tower, he had found the key to the mystery of salvation:

> Then I began to understand that the righteousness of God [*justitia Dei*] is that by which the righteous live by a gift of God, that is, by faith, and that the Gospel reveals that a merciful God justifies us by faith with a passive righteousness, as it is written, "The righteous shall live through faith." This made me feel as if I had been born again and passed through open doors into paradise itself. All of Scripture appeared different to me now . . . and I then began to love that term I used to hate, "the righteousness of God" [*justitia Dei*], as the sweetest of all. Thus, Paul truly became my gateway to paradise.[17]

Luther would quietly absorb the effects of this so-called tower experience for several months, incorporating its insights into his teaching and his spiritual life. Gradually, throughout 1516 and much of 1517, he began to develop a new hermeneutic, that is, a new way of interpreting the Bible, and also a new soteriology, or theology of salvation. Convinced that all of theology should rest on the Holy Scriptures and that the key to the entire Bible could be found in the apostle Paul's epistles, and especially in his letters to the Romans, Galatians, and Ephesians, Luther began to formulate a theology in which salvation became a question of pure faith rather than specific behavior, turning constantly to Paul's texts, and especially to those that contrast the damning power of God's law with the saving grace of the gospel.

From Scholar to Rebel

Had Luther been limited to teaching other monks, his transformation might have had little effect on others outside the cloister. But Luther was much more than a monk. He was a busy priest who not only taught university students at Wittenberg, but also preached and ministered to a rural congregation in a nearby village. Being involved in pastoral work, he had to apply his theology to everyday life in the messy, sinful world of his flock. Luther simmered, his anger rising against a whole range of church practices that seemed wrong to him, or even abusive. What upset him most of all, across the board, was the way the church focused on punishments, or penances, as the means for the ultimate forgiveness of sins. Such theology ran counter to his newly found insights about the saving power of faith, and more than once, Luther's critiques began to surface in his sermons. By the fall of 1517, the thirty-four-year-old Luther was a rumbling volcano, ready to erupt. And all it took to make him explode was one traveling preacher, his awful sermons, and one issue that conjoined the church's theology of salvation with its ritual. The preacher was a fifty-two-year-old Dominican friar named Johann Tetzel. The issue was indulgences, and the rites that supposedly alleviated the suffering of the souls of the dead in purgatory. Concerned about the potential harm embedded in Tetzel's message, Luther decided to challenge him, and in so doing he took a most fateful step.

Johann Tetzel's preaching and all the circumstances surrounding it summed up much of what was ailing the late medieval church. It is no mere accident, then, that when an obscure monk named Luther attacked a relatively insignificant preacher named Tetzel over a seemingly minor theological issue, pandemonium ensued so quickly. When the layers of corruption surrounding Tetzel and his sermons are peeled back, one by one, the dynamic of the unexpected crisis becomes readily apparent.

Tetzel, an undistinguished Dominican, had been assigned to distribute indulgences throughout Germany by Archbishop Albrecht of Mainz (1490–1545) and Pope Leo X. Bishop Albrecht was a member of one of the most powerful noble families in the Holy Roman Empire, the Hohenzollerns, and was the son of the margrave of Brandenburg, one of the seven imperial electors. Albrecht had acquired the archbishopric of Mainz—the primatial see of Germany—by wheeling and dealing. Like many of the

The high cost of simony. Cardinal Albrecht of Mainz and Brandenburg, sketched by Albrecht Dürer in 1519. The debt incurred by Cardinal Albrecht in the purchasing of high church offices unintentionally sparked the Protestant Reformation. This question has long been asked: if Cardinal Albrecht had not promoted indulgences in Saxony to pay off his debts, would Martin Luther have ever emerged to challenge the religious status quo?

younger sons of powerful families, Albrecht had been pushed into a clerical career at a very early age, and in 1513 he had been named bishop of two sees simultaneously, Halberstadt and Magdeburg, even though he was much younger than the age of thirty required by church law. When the see of Mainz became available the following year, he was determined to add it to his collection, and he literally bought the office by offering to pay an installation fee of ten thousand ducats out of his own pocket. Since the diocesan treasury of Mainz was low on funds at that time, and no other candidate had offered to pay as much as Albrecht, the bishopric was gladly handed to him.

But Albrecht had two obstacles to overcome before his installation as archbishop of Mainz: first he had to borrow the ten thousand ducats; then he had to obtain permission from Pope Leo X to hold three bishoprics simultaneously, something that was contrary to church law. To ensure that the pope would grant him this favor, Albrecht offered to pay another ten thousand ducats to Pope Leo X, to help him complete the building of the new basilica of St. Peter in Rome, the very expensive project that had been launched by his predecessor, Pope Julius II. Asked to make his contribution up front but unable to come up with the cash, Albrecht borrowed the funds from the House of Fugger, the pope's exclusive banking agents in Germany. It was the Fuggers who had negotiated the amount of the contribution in the first place, so they were more than happy also to arrange for the loan, at high interest, at a sum total of twenty-six thousand ducats. And Pope Leo X was also more than happy to allow Albrecht to pay off his loans by granting him the right to dispense plenary indulgences in his lands for a period of eight years. It was a very sweet deal through which everyone profited at every level, even in the afterlife. One half of the amount collected would go to Pope Leo X—in addition to the thousands of ducats already collected from Albrecht—for the building of St. Peter's Basilica; the other half would go directly to the Fuggers, to pay off Albrecht's massive debt. Leo would get funds for his building project; the House of Fugger would collect its loan; Albrecht would get to hold three bishoprics, with all their income, and gain the imperial elector's seat that came with the see of Mainz; the faithful would be given the chance to obtain a full and perfect remission of all penalties for sins, either for themselves or for their dearly departed relatives in purgatory.

The Fugger loan was, understandably, not to be mentioned when the indulgences were offered. Technically, by the letter of the law, the indulgences were granted solely in exchange for contributions to the building of the new St. Peter's Basilica in Rome. Indulgences were never bought and sold, even when money exchanged hands; rather they were ostensibly offered in exchange for acts of piety, charity, and penance. Since that was the case, the donations to be collected in Germany were carefully stratified according to class and status, under the assumption that all should be able to afford this wondrous opportunity: at the top of the social hierarchy, monarchs, princes, and bishops were expected to contribute twenty-five florins; higher clergy and nobility, twenty florins; lower clerics and nobles, six florins; merchants, artisans, and burghers, three florins; everyone else near the bottom of the heap, one florin, or even a half or a quarter florin; at the very bottom, the poor could ostensibly obtain their indulgences by praying and fasting.[18]

The indulgences offered through Albrecht were extraordinary, and rare to come by, for they were plenary, or full, indulgences, which meant that they canceled out all of one's sinful debts. Partial indulgences, which remitted only a certain fixed amount of suffering in this life and the hereafter, were routinely available through a variety of means, such as pilgrimages, acts of charity and devotion, almsgiving, and prayers and fasts. By the late Middle Ages, certain acts and rites had been assigned a very specific value in terms of years to be shaved off one's sentence in purgatory, according to that formula that one day's suffering on Earth equaled ten thousand years in purgatory. These meticulously calculated partial indulgences were readily available everywhere. In Wittenberg, for instance, where Luther lived and worked, the Saxon prince Frederick the Wise, the founder of the university, had amassed a relic collection in his chapel that surpassed all others in Germany for its indulgence potential. His chapel, which contained more than nineteen thousand relics—including bones from great saints such as Jerome, Augustine, and Bernard, and treasures such as some the Virgin Mary's hair, the swaddling clothes of baby Jesus, a thorn from the crown of thorns, and a twig from the burning bush of Moses—was a spiritual treasure trove. Proper reverence shown to these relics on those days specially marked for such purposes by papal decree could reduce one's stay in purgatory by an amazingly precise 1,902,202 years and 270 days.[19]

Johann Tetzel was an experienced indulgence peddler, well known by the papacy and the House of Fugger, and he seemed the perfect man for the job. Though barred from preaching in Wittenberg by Prince Frederick the Wise, who would never allow any competing indulgences near his relic collection, Tetzel circled the area, sometimes so closely as to draw some of Luther's parishioners. Luther not only got to see the indulgences they proudly showed him, but also heard them describe what they had seen and heard. What his parishioners told Luther enraged him. Tetzel followed the same routine as he made his way from town to town, preaching the same sermon, more or less. He would always make a grand entrance, accompanied by the right officials, and stage a solemn procession to the best open square, holding high the papal coat of arms on a cross, prominently displaying the pope's bull of indulgence on an ornately trimmed velvet cushion. Then, as soon as a large enough crowd had assembled, he would launch into his sermon.

Exposing a yawning abyss between official theology and popular piety, and dredging up nearly every guilt-inducing, pocket-picking pitch through which he could hawk indulgences to an anxious laity, Johann Tetzel earned Luther's wrath by preaching these words to many a Saxon crowd in 1517, on behalf of Pope Leo X and Archbishop Albrecht of Mainz:

> All of you, run for the salvation of your souls. . . . Listen now, God and St. Peter call *you*. Consider the salvation of *your* souls and those of *your loved ones* departed. . . . Listen to the voices of *your dead relatives* and friends, beseeching *you* and saying, "Pity

us, pity us. We are in dire torment from which *you* can redeem us for a pittance." Do *you* not wish to? Open *your* ears. . . . Remember *you* are able to release them, for *as soon as the coin in the coffer rings, the soul from purgatory springs*. Will *you* not then for a quarter of a florin receive these letters of indulgence through which *you* are able to lead a divine and immortal soul into the fatherland of paradise?[20]

In late autumn 1517, as All Saints' Day approached, Professor Luther sprang into action. Since that feast, 1 November, was one of the few days out of the whole year when indulgences were granted in return for the veneration of Frederick's relic collection, Luther chose 31 October—All Hallows' Eve—as the day on which he would publically challenge Tetzel. Wittenberg would be mobbed with indulgence seekers. What better time to challenge the itinerant indulgence hawker to a debate on indulgences? To spark controversy, Luther did what every academic was trained to do: he drew up his theses for debate, all ninety-five of them, in Latin. Old legends tell of Luther nailing his theses to

Fateful indulgences. Johann Tetzel and his sermon are featured in this crude woodcut by an unknown artist. Tetzel holds the papal bull of indulgence in his right hand, its margins ringed by wax seals that confirm its authenticity. Lay people eagerly deposit their coins in the indulgence chest he has brought along. The text includes Tetzel's most infamous pitch: "As soon as the Gulden in the coffer rings, the soul from Purgatory springs."

the door of the castle church, but historians have cast serious doubt on this iconic story. What Luther did for certain was to send letters—and the theses—to his Augustinian superiors and to other church authorities. Whether Luther "posted" the theses by nailing or by mailing makes little difference, in the long run. What matters most is the furor ignited by them.

In all likelihood, Luther had the ninety-five theses printed up so they could be distributed widely, since he knew that Tetzel could not set foot in Wittenberg. Sending copies to his superiors and to Archbishop Albrecht and other bishops and notables was the best way to attract attention and begin a debate in the public sphere. We have no surviving copies of a first print run, but there are copies of many other editions, printed immediately afterward in both Latin and German, produced by presses in locations as widely scattered as Leipzig, Magdeburg, Nuremberg, and Basel. This quick proliferation of Luther's theses is highly significant, for it shows clearly how instrumental the new technology of printing was to the spread of his message. From the very start, Luther availed himself of the printing press as means of addressing the German people directly, and the printers rushed to meet the reading public's demand for Luther as a best-selling author. It was a perfect symbiosis, the kind all authors and publishers still dream of.

Luther proved himself not only savvy about the potential of the printing press, but also very daring. Sending a copy of his ninety-five theses to Archbishop Albrecht took nerve. So did telling the bishop how to do his job. "The first and only duty of the bishops . . . is to see that the people learn the gospel and the love of Christ," wrote Luther. "On no occasion has Christ ordered that indulgences should be preached. . . . What a horror, what a danger for a bishop to permit the loud noise of indulgences among his people, while the gospel is silenced, and to be more concerned with the sale of indulgences than with the gospel!" It mattered little that he spoke of himself in this letter to Albrecht as "a grain of dust" or "the least of all men." Even his self-debasement was brash and laced with threats. "I beg Your Most Illustrious Grace to accept this faithful service of my humble self," said Luther. "I, too, am one of your sheep." Were he to ignore his advice, added Luther, Archbishop Albrecht would suffer "the greatest disgrace."[21] Albrecht did what any bishop would have done under the circumstances: he sent a copy of Luther's ninety-five theses to Rome. Pope Leo X did nothing in response. According to tradition, the pope supposedly dismissed Luther as a "German drunkard," and brushed off the whole controversy as a "monkish squabble."[22] In the meantime, as the leaders of the church went about their daily routines, unconcerned about yet another intraclerical spat far from Rome, Luther's fame and popularity kept growing in Germany and beyond, especially with lay people.

That Luther should have caused an uproar among the laity with something as dull and academic as ninety-five theological propositions shows that he had hit a raw nerve. The theses themselves touched on those fine points that scholastic theologians excelled at debating, but embedded in the text were all sorts of questions and complaints that any lay person could understand. In fact, in some of the theses Luther goes so far as to quote the laity. Many of the theses assumed a clever rhetorical stance that was superficially deferential to the pope, but really laid the blame for the corruption of Christendom directly on the papal office. For example, take thesis number 50: "Christians are to be taught that if the pope knew the exactions of the indulgence preachers, he would rather that the basilica of St. Peter were burned to ashes than built up with the skin, flesh, and bones of his sheep."[23] Or take the series from number 81 to 91, in which Luther cleverly assigns all the blame for abuses on bad clergy rather than the pope, yet points out that the laity hold the pope responsible and uses their voice to question both indulgences and papal authority. The first two of these bombshells pack quite a punch:

81. This unbridled preaching of indulgences makes it difficult even for learned men to rescue the reverence which is due the pope from slander or from the shrewd questions of the laity,
82. Such as: "Why does not the pope empty purgatory for the sake of holy love and the dire need of the souls that are there if he redeems an infinite number of souls for the sake of miserable money with which to build a church? The former reasons would be most just; the latter is most trivial."[24]

Luther appealed to the laity on three levels. First, he agreed with some of their complaints, implicitly and explicitly, giving them voice within the theses. Second, he spoke of indulgences as a form of clerical abuse, and he raised questions about the price the laity was asked to pay for their salvation, arguing that "the treasures of indulgences are nets with which one now fishes for the wealth of men" (thesis 66). More specifically, Luther let the laity speak directly in thesis 86 against the pope's new basilica in Rome, citing their complaint: "Why does not the pope, whose wealth is today greater than the riches of the richest, build just this one church of St. Peter with his own money, rather than with the money of poor believers?"

Third, Luther questioned the intercessory role of the papacy and the clergy, or even boldly proclaimed a more direct relationship between each person and God, saying that "every true Christian, whether living or dead, has part in all the blessings of Christ and the Church" (thesis 37). In some of the theses, Luther went as far as to hint that the clergy abused the laity by making them pay for God's forgiveness, something that came directly from God himself and was already theirs. In thesis 28, for instance, he said, "It is certain that when the penny jingles into the money-box, gain and avarice can be increased, but the result of the intercession of the Church is in the power of God alone." In thesis 52, he was even bolder: "The assurance of salvation by letters of pardon is vain, even though . . . the pope himself, were to stake his soul upon it, this is granted him by God, even without letters of pardon."

Siding with the laity and giving voice to their complaints, Luther turned himself overnight into a reforming leader and a German national hero. A cleric himself, he lashed out against corrupt clergy and the abuse of power, arguing that salvation was to be found not in the indulgences they constantly peddled, but rather in God himself, directly. Still very much a pastor at heart, Luther also complained that indulgences made salvation seem cheap and easy to come by, therefore leading the laity astray and causing them to stay mired in their sins. The ultimate danger of indulgences, Luther argued, was their power to lull Christians into a false sense of confidence: "They will be condemned eternally, together with their teachers, who believe themselves sure of their salvation because they have letters of pardon" (thesis 32).

Pastoral concerns and theological arguments of this sort were the centerpiece of the ninety-five theses, but there was much more to Luther's challenge than mere theology. This first salvo from Luther addressed some of the most intense concerns of the laity and even gave voice to them directly. It would prove to be an embryonic manifesto of Luther's reforming agenda and a testament to his popular appeal. It would also prove to be a prophetic warning. "To repress these arguments and scruples of the laity by force alone, and not to resolve them by giving reasons," Luther argued, "is to expose the Church and the pope to the ridicule of their enemies, and to make Christians unhappy" (thesis 90). Without fully realizing it, perhaps, Luther was letting Leo X know that his enemies were there already, among those unhappy German Christians, and that he, Professor Luther, would be more than willing to lead them.[25]

Within less than a year of the publication of the ninety-five theses, Luther would no longer be an obscure monk or professor, or even a gadfly in Pope Leo's eyes. Instead, he was a dangerous opponent, possibly among the most formidable of all the enemies that any pope had ever faced from within the church itself. The speed at which this change took place was a surprise to everyone.

Johann Tetzel had little to do with the events that followed the posting of the ninety-five theses, even though his fellow Dominicans awarded him a doctorate so he could take on Luther as an equal in rank. All he could do was to threaten: "Within three weeks I shall have the heretic thrown into the fire."[26] Undaunted, Luther kept up the battle against indulgences by writing directly to Archbishop Albrecht and by preparing a simplified version of his views in German, for the common folk. Thanks to the printers, *Luther* soon became a household word throughout Germany, although what kind of word depended on the household. While some hailed him, others cursed.

From the very start, Luther was able to carry on this work with the support of his fellow Augustinians and his prince, Frederick the Wise, whose delight in relic collecting was suddenly eclipsed by the presence of a superstar on the Wittenberg University faculty. In 1518, at a chapter meeting of the Augustinians in Heidelberg, Luther was warmly received as a celebrity not just by his brethren, but the Count Palatine, who proudly showed off his chapel and castle and invited Luther to dine with him. At Wittenberg, Prince Frederick likewise ignored all cries of heresy and carefully guarded his prize professor, promising him constant protection and ensuring that no one would drag him to Rome, under any circumstances. Luther's students, as one might expect, also rallied around him. When the newly minted *Doktor* Tetzel published his own countertheses against

Powerful patron. Elector Frederick the Wise of Saxony (1463–1525) was Luther's sponsor and protector. Without Frederick's support, Martin Luther would have never survived unscathed, much less launched a successful revolt against the papacy.

Doktor Luther, students at Wittenberg got their hands on about eight hundred copies and gleefully tossed them into a bonfire.

Encouraged by this support, Luther pressed on with his critique of indulgences, and with new assertions that distanced him further from orthodoxy. Step by step, very rapidly, he began to question other key teachings in 1518, such as the supremacy of the pope and the infallibility of the Vulgate Latin text of the Bible. One did not have to read much of what Luther was publishing to catch his drift. Holy Roman Emperor Maximilian was so horrified by some sermon excerpts he read that he immediately asked Pope Leo X "to stop the most dangerous attack of Martin Luther on indulgences, lest not only the people but even the princes be seduced."[27] It did not take long for Luther to be summoned to Rome, on suspicion of heresy. Once more, the protection offered to Luther by Frederick the Wise saved his life, for thanks to the prince's efforts, Luther's case was transferred from the papal court to Germany. In October 1518, one year after he had posted his ninety-five theses, Luther had his first formal confrontation with church authorities, at Augsburg, when he faced the papal legate to Germany, Cardinal Tommaso de Vio (1469–1534), better known by his religious name of Gaetano, or Cajetan.

Rome had sent one of its biggest guns against Luther: Cardinal Cajetan was master general of the Dominican order and one of the leading theologians of the day. A reform-minded ecclesiastic and top authority on the work of St. Thomas Aquinas, Cardinal Cajetan also had firsthand experience in dealing with heresy, for he had previously investigated the case of the controversial Italian friar Girolamo Savonarola (1452–1498). Luther's three meetings with the cardinal were painfully strained. At their very first encounter, Cajetan immediately asked Luther to recant what he had been saying about indulgences, and Luther refused. Instead he lectured the cardinal, quoting the Bible in support of his belief that one is saved by faith in Christ's redemptive sacrifice, not by the purchase of indulgences. When Cajetan pointed out to Luther that his rejection of indulgences went against church doctrine, as spelled out in the papal decree *Unigenitus* of 1343, Luther refused to accept the cardinal's judgment and appealed to be heard instead by the theological faculties of Basel, Freiburg, Louvain, or Paris. Cajetan responded by pressing Luther further on the issue of papal authority, focusing on the decree *Unigenitus*. Luther responded by rejecting the authority of the pope, arguing that Bible was the supreme authority, not papal decrees. When Cajetan pointed out to Luther that the pope was the chief interpreter of scripture, above councils, and above everyone else in the church, and that all papal decrees were therefore to be accepted as scripturally based doctrine, Luther rejected that proposition, arguing that the pope blatantly abused biblical texts and denying that the pope's authority trumped that of the Bible. Cajetan, the expert on heresy, knew that it was useless to continue, and he ended the interviews. "I am not going to talk to him again," Cajetan said to Luther's spiritual adviser, Johann von Staupitz, who was also present: "His eyes are as deep as a lake, and there are amazing speculations in his head."[28] Knowing that the worst was yet to come, Staupitz released Luther from his vow of obedience to the Augustinian order. It was not quite an excommunication—not yet. But Staupitz knew excommunication was inevitable, and he felt compelled to protect his order from the stigma of producing and harboring a heretic.

Luther left Augsburg knowing he had reached the point of no return. Until his meeting with Cajetan he had always excused the pope from responsibility for the church's ills. Whether or not that had been a rhetorical ploy did not matter any longer. From October 1518 on, Luther became convinced that the papacy was an unscriptural human invention, and that it was because of the popes themselves that the church had become thoroughly depraved. Undaunted by all the threats that began to reach Wittenberg, and buoyed by the enthusiastic support of many colleagues and of thousands of readers all over Germany, Luther pushed his challenge even further, writing openly against the papacy. By March 1519, Luther had begun to associate the pope with ultimate evil, saying: "I do not know whether the pope is the Antichrist or his apostle, so does he corrupt and crucify Christ, the truth, in his decretals."[29] As Luther's thinking became ever more radical, Prince Frederick continued to protect him, fending off all potential threats, appealing to Rome for yet another hearing in Germany. Writing directly to Pope Leo X, Frederick pleaded: "Luther's offer to debate and submit to the judgment of the universities should be considered, and he should be shown in what respect he is a heretic instead of being condemned in advance."[30]

Unable to obtain the kind of debate he wanted, Luther accepted the challenge of a neighboring theologian. Johann Eck (1486–1543), professor at the University of

Ingolstadt, had been writing against Luther since the posting of the ninety-five theses, even though the two men had once been friends. Unlike Cajetan, who was Italian and older, Eck was a fellow German of the same generation as Luther. Eck's challenges had been a thorn in Luther's side from the start. Safely ensconced at Wittenberg, where he had the support and admiration of many colleagues and students, and where he constantly received reports of how well his writings were selling, Luther had come to believe in his challenge of the papacy as a very German and very *young* reform movement. Two of his colleagues at Wittenberg confirmed this for him: one was a professor of Greek, Philip Melanchthon (1497–1560), a nephew of the brilliant and controversial humanist Johann Reuchlin; the other was Andreas Bodenstein von Karlstadt (1486–1541), professor of theology and chancellor of the university. Melanchthon, a gifted scholar and a very popular lecturer, had quickly become Luther's closest friend and associate, and his staunchest supporter. Karlstadt was Luther's senior colleague, though he was slightly younger. He had joined the Wittenberg faculty in 1511, while Luther was still a student, and as chancellor, he had actually awarded Luther his doctorate. Karlstadt had also been an outspoken critic of church abuses for many years, and he instantly recognized Luther as a kindred spirit. Given the close friendship that he developed with these two young colleagues, and how openly they supported him, Luther could not help but think of Eck as a traitor of sorts—the potential friend and colleague who had turned against him on his own turf—and as someone whose authority needed to be challenged.

Johann Eck was eager to take on Luther in person. He had already attacked him in print, and had grappled with Karlstadt too, after Karlstadt published his own attack on indulgences. In the spring of 1519, then, Eck baited Luther by arranging for a debate with Karlstadt at the University of Leipzig. Eck's ploy worked. In July 1519, Luther, Karlstadt, Melanchthon, several other professors, and two hundred axe-wielding students set out from Wittenberg. At Leipzig, the town council had assigned seventy-six armed guards to Eck. The potential significance of this contest pleased the sponsor and moderator of the debate, Duke George of Ducal Saxony, a relative and constant rival of Luther's Prince Frederick.

Karlstadt was prepared for what he considered *his* debate, but on the road to Leipzig, he was injured in an accident, and as was common in his day, he was subjected to a bloodletting—the cure for all ills, including sprains. Weakened by the loss of blood, Karlstadt proved weak against Eck, stumbling in his arguments, straining his memory, constantly flipping through the books he had brought in search of supporting texts, and reading from them at length, causing many in the audience to fall asleep. Eck was pleased by Karlstadt's fumbling, but he really itched to take on Luther himself, and when he finally got his chance, the sparks began to fly. Luther was quick and articulate, and able to cite texts by chapter and verse straight from memory. The opening topic—whether the papacy had been established by God or man—could not have been more controversial.

Luther began by arguing that the papacy was a humanly devised institution that had evolved over the centuries. Skilled at proving the errors of his opponents, Eck immediately accused Luther of agreeing with the teachings of John Wycliffe (1320–1384) and Jan Hus (1369–1415), both of whom had been condemned by the church. Bringing Hus into the debate was a winning move on Eck's part, not just because there were still rebellious Hussites in nearby Bohemia, but also because Hus had been declared a heretic by the Council of Constance rather than by a pope. Luther denied the charge of "Bohemianism," but also lost no time in arguing that the Council of Constance had made an awful mistake in burning Hus at the stake in 1415. Many of Hus's teachings were "plainly Christian and evangelical," argued Luther, adding that Hus was especially right in denying the authority of the papacy and in defending the supremacy of scripture. Switching from Latin to German, so he could be understood by everyone in the audience, Luther boldly burned yet another bridge behind himself:

> No believing Christian can be coerced beyond holy writ. By divine law we are forbidden to believe anything which is not established by divine Scripture or manifest revelation. . . . I assert that a council has sometimes erred and may sometimes err. Nor has a council authority to establish new articles of faith. . . . A simple layman armed with Scripture is to be believed above a pope or a council without it.[31]

Eck had forced Luther to admit that he was in league with a known heretic. Even more important, he had also made Luther admit that he rejected the authority of councils. Could anyone now doubt that Luther was a heretic? How could anyone remain a faithful member of the Roman Catholic Church and believe that Bible-clutching simple laymen had more authority than popes and councils? Luther had sealed his fate, but the debate dragged on; until Duke George called it off at the end of the eighteenth day, Eck mined Luther for heretical nuggets relentlessly, pressing him on a variety of points, forcing him to grapple with his own statements and come up with definite conclusions. Luther rose to the challenge and followed his logic to startling ends, and he defended himself tenaciously, as if he were arguing with the Antichrist or the devil himself. Before it was all over, Eck had extracted a treasure trove of heretical statements from Luther. Aside from denying the authority of popes and councils, Luther had also redefined the one remaining authority he respected, the Bible, rejecting the scriptural authenticity of certain books of the Vulgate Old Testament, those so-called deuterocanonical or apocryphal texts from the Hellenistic age that had been written in Greek rather than Hebrew. Among the texts Luther would no longer consider part of the Bible were the two books of Maccabees (ca. 100 B.C.), the sole place in the Vulgate Latin Bible where mention is made of prayers for the dead, and the ultimate biblical proof text for the doctrine of purgatory. Finally, Eck kept hammering away at Luther with several versions of the same question, which happened to be something that Luther had already asked himself many times: "Are you the only one that knows anything? Except for you is all the Church in error?" Luther's swaggering reply to that question could be taken as his definitive epiphany and the moment he willingly abandoned the Catholic fold:

I am a Christian theologian; and I am bound, not only to assert, but to defend the truth with my blood and death. I want to believe freely and be a slave to the authority of no one, whether council, university, or pope. I will confidently confess what appears to me to be true, whether it has been asserted by a Catholic or a heretic, whether it has been approved or reproved by a council.[32]

After his debate with Eck, Luther knew exactly where he stood, and it was not at all a comfortable place to be. Luther was aware that in the eyes of the church he kept attacking, he had become a rebel and a heretic. As if sent by Divine Providence, letters from Bohemia arrived at Wittenberg after Luther's return from Leipzig, and along with them a copy of Jan Hus's magnum opus, *De ecclesia* (*On the Church*). "I agree now with more articles of Hus than I did at Leipzig," Luther would say, after reading Hus's book. Divine Providence and good spying had also seen to it that copies of the Bohemian correspondence ended up in Eck's hands. In these letters, Hussite leaders encouraged Luther to stand firm. It was redundant proof. Eck already knew that Luther was a worse threat than Jan Hus, and that is precisely what he told the pope.

Everyone now prepared for the inevitable bull of excommunication from Pope Leo X, the flames, and the stench of Luther's roasting flesh.

CHAPTER EIGHT

Luther

From Rebel to Heretic

That Luther was never burnt at the stake had as much to do with his strong personality as with the political circumstances that kept him out of the hands of his enemies. Despite spells of introspection and *Anfechtung*, which continued to assail him until his dying day, Luther had more than the requisite backbone for defying pope and emperor. Take, for instance, his words in 1521 to Hieronymus Emser, an opponent he addressed as "the goat of Leipzig":

> I am and, God willing, shall remain a stable, proud and fearless spirit in my defiance of you, Eck, the pope, and your mob, even the devil. With God's help I shall defy and despise you as senseless and blind minds and poisonous liars. . . . But I refuse to debate very much about whether I am a proud man, since this concerns not my teaching but my own person. I have said more than once that anyone may attack my person in any way he pleases. I do not pretend to be an angel. But I let no one attack my teaching without a counterattack, since I know that it is not mine, but God's.[1]

Yet as indispensable as this prophetic bluster was to his survival, and as important as his message was for his success, there is no denying that Luther would owe both his survival and success to a unique set of social conditions and political circumstances. Before continuing with the narrative of Luther's rise to prominence, then, we must pause to examine the landscape he inhabited as a German, literally and figuratively.

Luther's Germany

Luther's Germany was one of the most politically complex places on earth. For starters, there was no nation called *Deutschland* or "Germany" even though millions of people shared an identity as "Germans" and spoke versions of a language that could be identified as *Deutsch*, or "German." Luther, like Jan Hus before him, lived within the highly paradoxical political entity known as the Holy Roman Empire, which, as all wags knew, was neither holy nor Roman, nor an empire. Nor was it wholly German. Though composed mainly of German-speaking states, this empire also included a wide array of peoples with other identities and languages, including Alsatians, Bohemians, Slovaks, Slovenians, Hungarians, Moravians, Poles, Croatians, Jews, Gypsies, and others yet. In existence since Charlemagne was crowned Imperator Romanorum by Pope Leo III in 800, the *Reich*, or empire, was an extremely loose confederation of very different states, cities, and towns, all ostensibly ruled by Charlemagne's successors, who took the titles of king of the Germans and Kaiser, or Caesar, and were normally chosen by seven electors, each of whom ruled his own territory. In Luther's day, the seven electors, known as *Kurfürsten* (electing dukes) were the count palatine of the Rhine, the king of Bohemia, the duke of Saxony, the margrave of Brandenburg, and the archbishops of Cologne, Mainz, and Trier. The existence of three ecclesiastical electors who were also civil rulers pointed to one of the most salient characteristics of the empire: its constituent principles derived as much from Christianity as from ancient Germanic customs. It was the *Heiliges Reich*, or "Holy Empire," after all. Needless to say, the boundaries between church and state were often neither easily discerned not readily agreed on, and constant jurisdictional conflict was also one of the empire's chief characteristics.

A bewildering array of overlapping and often conflicting authorities made political life in the empire somewhat chaotic at times, but also allowed for a great deal of local independence. The emperor was no mere figurehead, since all of the entities in the empire owed him allegiance, but his power as Kaiser was severely limited, not only by local entities, but also by the Imperial Diet, or parliament, a heterogeneous assembly that met irregularly whenever and wherever the Emperor convened it. Although the office of emperor was not hereditary, during the empire's long history some families such as the Hohenstaufens (1138–1208, 1212–1254) had occupied the imperial throne as dynasties. At the time of Luther's birth in 1484, one Austrian family, the Hapsburgs, was in fact on its way to becoming one of the longest-lived dynasties in the history of the empire, but at that time their hold on the throne still seemed precarious. As a child, Luther lived under the rulership of Frederick III (r. 1452–1493), the last emperor ever to be crowned in Rome. As a young man, Luther was a subject of Frederick III's son, Maximilian I, who ruled from 1493 to 1519. As a hunted heretic and reformer, he would be a constant thorn in the side of Charles V, Maximilian's grandson and successor.

The constituent states of the empire ranged as widely in size as they did in in political structures, and their ever-shifting and often noncontiguous boundaries could be maddeningly illogical. Nonetheless, it was an orderly sort of chaos. Though there were numerous variations and exceptions to their governance—all of which lead experts on the empire to quibble over classifications—most of the states within the empire could be classified under three basic types: territories ruled by the nobility, territories ruled by the clergy, and imperial free cities.

Territories governed by titled nobles, such as princes, dukes, counts, landgraves, margraves, and in some cases kings, tended to be hereditary dynastic states. Because of

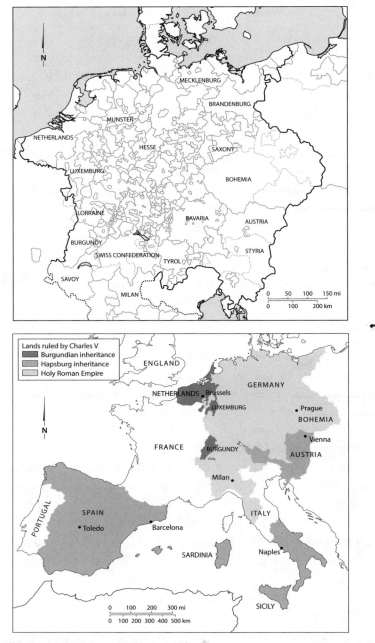

Charles V and his European empire. No European ruler since Charlemagne in the ninth century had ruled as vast an empire as that of Charles V. Adding the lands he also claimed in the New World, his empire rivaled that of ancient Rome. But the authority wielded by Charles V differed from place to place, and was weakest in the Holy Roman Empire, that impossibly complex assemblage of principalities, duchies, prince-bishoprics, and free cities. Charles was constantly engaged in conflicts with neighboring rulers too. His nearly total encirclement of the kingdom of France helped make King Francis I his bitterest and most constant foe for decades. The aggressive northward advance of the Ottoman Turks from the Balkans toward Austria was another of his major preoccupations.

the endogamous marriage code of the higher nobility, these lands always remained in the hands of the same circle of families, even though the boundaries and dynasties of these states were ever in a state of flux from one generation to the next. Sometimes, territories might be subdivided among different branches of the same family. The University of Wittenberg was in one such territory, Ernestine Saxony, which was the seat of one of the seven electors, and was ruled by one branch of the House of Wettin, known as the Ernestine line. Luther's prince, Frederick the Wise, was one of the most powerful nobles in the empire, but being a lifelong bachelor, he had no direct heir and therefore no firm territorial claim to the electorship, which was coveted by his Wettin relatives. Next door to Ernestine Saxony lay Albertine Saxony, which was ruled by the another branch of the Wettins, known as the Albertine line.[2] When Luther arrived in Wittenberg, that "other" Saxony next door was in the hands of Prince Frederick's cousin, Duke George (1471–1539), the sponsor of the 1519 Leipzig debate between Eck and Luther. Relations between the two Saxonies, which had always been strained, would become much worse after 1519, given religious differences between the cousins Frederick and George.

The second type of territories, those ruled by bishops, could not be hereditary, since the clergy's vow of celibacy prevented them from having wives or legitimate children. But the higher clergy were drawn almost exclusively from the noble class, and ecclesiastical offices and territories therefore often cycled and recycled through the hands of the same families that ruled the other states as titled nobles. In Luther's day, abuses were common when it came to episcopal succession in such highly prized territories. A typical example is provided by none other than Archbishop Albrecht of Mainz, of indulgence fame. A scion of the Hohenzollern family—the margraves and electors of Brandenburg—Albrecht was the consummate office and title collector, who managed to win a second electorship for his family by purchasing the see of Mainz. While all the higher clergy were considered princes of the church, only the *Reich* had prince-bishops such as Albrecht, who held secular and ecclesiastical powers and ran both church and state with a single office. To further complicate matters, the two jurisdictions of every *Fürstbischof,* or prince-bishop, such as Albrecht, did not necessarily coincide on the map, for a bishop's diocese was often much larger than his secular territory, and his secular office might not include the very city in which his cathedral was located. Such was the case in Cologne, for instance, where the prince-bishops had no temporal jurisdiction and resided in nearby Bonn. This discontinuity of jurisdiction explains why Frederick the Wise could turn away Johann Tetzel from Wittenberg, even though Archbishop Albrecht had sent him to preach all over his diocese. The most prominent prince-bishops of all were the three electors: of Mainz, Cologne, and Trier, near the empire's western boundaries, in that thin sliver of German soil that had once been colonized by Rome.

Cologne, just mentioned, was representative of the third type of territories, the imperial free cities, each of which had its own government and was subject to no lord other than the emperor. Because of the peculiar history of the empire, many such cities dotted the map, especially in southern Germany. Imperial cities had originated in the Middle

Ages, especially from the eleventh century on, as various emperors granted independence to urban areas that had been part of their personal estates. From an original handful, the number of imperial cities continued to grow throughout the later Middle Ages. Some were simply granted their status; others purchased it or fought for it, or simply seized it in chaotic times. Given that conflict and warfare were endemic in the empire, imperial cities might also lose their status too, either when they were absorbed by territorial lords, or when they willingly placed themselves under some lord's protection. To be free and remain free, a city had to be prosperous, for running a small urban state was an expensive proposition, especially in times of war, plague, or famine, which could always be expected. Strictly speaking, the term *freie Reichsstadt*, or imperial free city, applied only to seven cities that had won independence from their ecclesiastical lords—Basel, Strasbourg, Speyer, Worms, Mainz, Cologne, and Regensburg—but it was used interchangeably with the original, simple *Reichstadt*. In 1521, at the Diet of Worms, eighty-five such city-states were listed as "Free *and* Imperial Cities (*Frei- und Reichsstätt*).[3] Such usage of the term made sense, for all imperial cities were really autonomous and politically independent from the states that surrounded them on all sides: they were like small islands of representative government scattered over a large sea of autocratic rule. A popular refrain summed up this complex situation, *Stadtluft macht frei*: "city air makes you free." Though each city had its own constitution, most of them had very similar governmental structures. All imperial cities were ruled by a town council or by a collection of councils. Each council, or *Rat*, was composed of elected representatives who served terms of specific length; those who could vote were usually male property owners. All imperial cities were oligarchies, their councils composed of a few patrician families and of representatives from the city's merchant class and trade guilds.

No two imperial cities were alike in terms of structure, or wealth, or power and influence. Some had more political privileges or a greater ability to stave off outside interference; some had a richer cultural life or higher literacy rates. Some had more churches and monasteries, or bigger churches and monasteries. Wealthy cities such as Lübeck, Nuremberg, and Augsburg could rival much larger states, commanding armies and waging war—with either well-paid mercenaries or their own homegrown citizen soldiery. But a small state can accomplish only so much, no matter how affluent it is. Imperial cities thus made alliances with one another, to protect their rights and privileges collectively, and these leagues, or *Bünde*, could carry a lot of weight in times of crisis. In 1489, when Luther was a small child, the political clout of the imperial cities was formally recognized at the Diet of Frankfurt (one of those occasional parliamentary gatherings called by the emperor), where their right to be represented in the Diet was formally recognized. In the last decade of the fifteenth century, when Luther was still a student, the representatives of the imperial cities gathered even more strength and formed their own voting block at the Diet, which then split into two benches, or chambers: the Rhenish and the Swabian.

Another salient characteristic of the imperial cities was their intense religiosity, which derived from the high concentration and close proximity of churches, monasteries, charitable institutions, and confraternities within their walls. Urban environments provided greater access to formalized religion than rural settings, simply by virtue of the fact that cities were crammed with clerics, ecclesiastical institutions, and lay religious associations. City air did not just make people free; it could also make them more devout, or at the very least, more aware of the presence of the sacred. Conformity in religious behavior was a necessary and routine part of everyday social life. One German historian has gone as far as to argue that the imperial cities can be characterized as "sacred societies" in which the boundaries between the sacred and the secular were so porous and evanescent that the average burgher, or town dweller, found it hard to distinguish between material welfare and eternal salvation. "In such towns," Bernd Moeller has argued, "the civil community was confused with the religious. In principle, we should not even consider them separately, for they coincide."[4] Given this intertwining of the spiritual and temporal, and the many ills that plagued the church in the early sixteenth century, it stands to reason that imperial free cities would prove a fertile ground for religious reform movements.

If the political structure of Luther's Germany was difficult to manage or comprehend, so were relations between the temporal and spiritual authorities. Conflicts between church and state were endemic everywhere in Europe, but in the empire the tension and confusion was heightened by the political complexity of the civil state. To a considerable extent, church and state had a greater chance of butting heads in Germany for two reasons: because the secular powers had so much relative autonomy, and because the church was so tightly integrated into the political structure. Whether a locale was ruled by a duke or a city's *Rat* made little difference, insofar as relations between the temporal and the ecclesiastical realms were concerned: within the empire every political authority needed to deal with the clergy on the local level in much the same way as the monarchs of much larger centralized nation-states like France, Spain, or England. In other words, the contact between every secular authority and the clergy in its domain could be very direct and intense, and the possibility of the secular power extending its power over the clergy even greater. That it was relatively easier for smaller states to gain greater control of their clergy is proved by the imperial cities, which had already begun to take over the distribution of church offices by the end of the fifteenth century, and were pressing hard to make their clerics full citizens who paid taxes and could be tried in civil courts.[5] Given that the great monarchs of the centralized states were all busy trying to gain control of *their* national churches at this time, it stands to reason that the lesser rulers would also follow this model and perhaps be more successful at turning "the" church into "my" church or "our" church. The existence of prince-bishops further complicated matters in myriad ways in the empire, chiefly because they had dual identities, blurred the line between church and state, and already exercised the kind of control over the church that most secular rulers craved.

Luther's Emperor

In addition to living in a highly fragmented place with an intricately complicated political landscape, Martin Luther also happened to live in a time of great political turmoil, when the empire was ruled by a dynasty with vast ambitions and more territories and challenges than any single ruler could handle adroitly. To understand how the Protestant Reformation began in Germany in 1517, one must take all of this complexity into account.

At the turn of the sixteenth century, when Luther was still a student, the political landscape of Europe had begun to change at a very fast pace. As has already been discussed in chapter 1, the most significant change of all was the rise of the early modern nation-state and the gradual eclipse of the medieval feudal order. Another significant development that immediately changed the balance of power in Europe was the expansion of some of its states to other continents, most notably into Asia and the Americas. In Europe itself, maps were being redrawn quickly and dramatically, for different reasons.

Looking out from Germany, at Europe's other states, Luther might not have noticed any of these developments, but they nonetheless affected him. To the far southwest, Portugal and Spain were leading the expansion of Europe at an incredibly fast pace. "Spain," that collection of kingdoms that had been recently united by King Ferdinand of Aragon and Isabella of Castile, was leading the way on many fronts—as detailed earlier in chapters 1, 5, and 6—including the centralization of authority, the development of state bureaucracies, and the reform of the church. Spain was also colonizing other worlds and about to become the wealthiest of all European states thanks to silver and gold from the Americas.

Directly to the west, France was quickly centralizing under the direction of the Valois dynasty while it also engaged in wars of conquest in Italy, which it had invaded in 1498. Italy itself was under siege, and reeling from the turmoil of war, especially in the regions north of the Papal States. Although Italy was still the unquestioned cultural leader of all of Europe, and the epicenter of the church, many of its very wealthy and ever-feuding city-states had fallen on hard times. Venice remained the "serene republic," *la serenissima*, fabulously rich and largely unaffected by this turmoil, but nonetheless constantly challenged throughout the eastern Mediterranean by the Ottoman Turks.

Between Germany and Italy lay the Swiss Confederation, a fiercely independent mountainous enclave of prosperous urban and rural states that seemed to be the antithesis of the emerging centralized nations and could best be described as a smaller-scale Holy Roman Empire without an emperor. Between France and Germany lay smaller territories that were among the most prosperous in Europe: the Netherlands, Luxembourg, and Burgundy, all of them under dynastic rule.

Across the English Channel, in the British Isles, England was still recovering from civil war, but the Tudor dynasty's hold on the throne remained firm. As ever, England and France remained bitter rivals. To the north, in Scandinavia, and to the east, in the Slavic lands, the pace of change was slower. But to the south and southeast change was alarmingly constant and fast paced, for the expanding empire of the Ottoman Turks kept creeping northward up into the Balkan Peninsula, toward Austria, Hungary, and Germany, an awful, seemingly unstoppable menace.

No dynasty in all of Europe was directly connected to more of these developments than the House of Hapsburg, the rulers of Luther's Germany. Relatively quickly, within three generations (1452–1515), this dynasty had managed to acquire more territories through marriage than anyone would have thought possible, or desirable. In brief, the Hapsburgs excelled at expanding their reach in Europe through a shrewd nuptial strategy that mixed their blood with that of some of the most powerful ruling families on the continent, thus allowing them to stake claims to many thrones. This shrewd process of linking Germany to nearly all of Western Europe through marriage was already well under way when Luther was born in 1484. By the time Luther got to Wittenberg in 1512, one young Hapsburg—the grandson of Emperor Maximilian I and the Catholic Monarchs of Spain, Ferdinand and Isabella—stood poised to become the most powerful ruler in all of Europe, perhaps even in the whole world. A matter of statecraft rather than romance, dynastic marriage alliances had always been part of life for Europe's ruling class: quite often these attempts to entangle bloodlines were complex deals that involved treaties, alliances, and mergers between ruling houses. Given the close identification between ruler and state in feudal Europe, dynastic alliances were one of the surest ways to link destinies, secure peace, improve commerce, and expand the power and influence of the families and states involved in the deal. Sometimes, dynastic marriages could create new hybrid states, as happened when Ferdinand of Aragon (1452–1516) married Isabella of Castile (1451–1504) and their kingdoms were joined to form "Spain." The Hapsburgs excelled at this kind of deal making. How they managed to acquire more thrones than any other dynasty in a relatively short time was no mystery, but it was certainly dazzling.

It began in 1452, with the marriage of Frederick III (1415–1493) to Eleanor of Portugal, and it continued with the marriage of their son Emperor Maximilian I (1459–1519) to Marie of Burgundy (1457–1482), which linked all the possessions of the sprawling Duchy of Burgundy to the personal lands of the Hapsburgs in Austria. Then their son Philip the Bold (1478–1506) married Juana (1479–1555), one of the daughters of Ferdinand of Aragon and Isabella of Castile and better known as Juana la Loca, or Juana the Insane, for she became totally unhinged when her husband died. Though the handsome Philip died young, he and Juana had managed to have six children, who included two boys, Charles (1500–1558) and Ferdinand (1503–1564), who stood in line as heirs to an astonishing array of thrones and titles. Who would inherit what, and when, was never set in stone. A lot depended on circumstances at the time that each of the potential thrones became vacant. Ironically, his mother's madness—a wild card of the worst sort—allowed all the pieces to fall into place for Charles. When his maternal grandfather, King Ferdinand, died in 1516, while Luther was lecturing on Paul's letter to the Romans at Wittenberg, young Charles found himself ruler of more territory than any monarch since Charlemagne.

Combining his father's Burgundian possessions with his grandparents' Spanish lands, Charles had inherited the Netherlands, Burgundy, Alsace, Castile, Aragon, Naples, Sicily, Sardinia, the Balearic Isles, the Canary Islands, and all of the rapidly growing territory claimed by Spain in the Americas. As a direct descendant of Eleanor of Portugal, he was also related to the Avis dynasty of that kingdom. As if all this were not enough, in January 1519 on the death of his paternal grandfather, Emperor Maximilian and as Luther began to deny papal authority, Charles also acquired all of the vast Hapsburg possessions in Austria and Central Europe and instantly became the prime candidate for the throne of the Holy Roman Empire. Charles was poised to rule over more territory than anyone in all of human history up to that point, at least nominally, if Spain's overseas possessions were taken into account.

Charles of Burgundy, as he was known in Castile, was ill prepared to become King Charles I of Spain, not only because "Spain" had been recently invented by his grandparents, but also because he was an inexperienced sixteen-year-old who knew none of the languages spoken there. Charles had been reared at the Burgundian court and in Flanders by his paternal aunt Margaret of Austria, regent of the Netherlands, and knew only French well, his mother tongue. Though he had received a fairly good education and was as expert in chivalry and Burgundian court life, his Latin and Flemish were very poor, and he knew next to nothing about cultures other than his own. When Charles arrived in Spain to assume the throne in 1516, an awkward teenager with a prominent jaw, he immediately raised hackles with his ineptitude and his insensitivity to Spanish customs. Relying almost exclusively on Flemish and Burgundian courtiers, Charles alienated the Spanish nobility and could not help but make one mistake after another.

Charles was equally unprepared to become Holy Roman Emperor, for he knew little about the empire's complexities and spoke none of its tongues, not even German. Moreover, given how much territory he already governed, Charles was too powerful and too thinly spread out. The addition of the imperial crown to his collection was a risky step. In a hotly contested election, many power brokers, both within and without the empire, looked for an alternative to Charles. In Spain, many nobles opposed Charles's candidacy, fearing they would end up with a negligent foreign ruler. At Rome, Pope Leo X was adamantly opposed to Charles, knowing very well that powerful emperors always mean trouble for the papacy, in one way or another. The strongest opposition of all came from the French king, Francis I (1494–1547), who did not want to see his realm hemmed in on all sides by Charles. Within the empire, opposition to Charles was also strong for many reasons, ranging from internal power politics to the fears similar to those expressed by the papacy, the French, and the Spanish. Two electors whose lives intersected with Luther's initially opposed Charles: Archbishop Albrecht of Mainz and Frederick the Wise of Saxony. Frederick, in fact, was a himself a contender for the imperial crown, encouraged by the pope; Pope Leo X would, however, eventually throw his support behind Francis I.

Although a French king was a most unlikely candidate for the position of Holy Roman Emperor, Francis I quickly seized the opportunity to compete with Charles for the crown. With the pope's backing, Francis and his supporters lobbied the electors aggressively, painting Charles in the worst possible light as the bungling son of a madwoman who was already overwhelmed by his responsibilities in far-off Spain. Charles counterattacked by portraying Francis as a power-hungry tyrant who would ride roughshod over traditional German liberties. And while the imperial throne stood vacant and all of the empire's high nobility focused their attention on the election for seven months, between January and July 1519, none of the empire's elites seemed to give a second thought to Martin Luther, or to the outrageous things he was saying and publishing, or to the pamphlets that were already streaming forth in great numbers from Germany's many presses in support of him.

Thanks largely to the lobbying efforts of contender Elector Frederick the Wise, who expected a marriage deal with the Hapsburgs between Charles's sister Catherine and his nephew, Crown Prince John Frederick, the seven electors voted unanimously for Charles on 28 June 1519, just a few days before the Leipzig debate between Johann Eck and the Wittenberg theologians Karlstadt and Luther. So it was that Rey Carlos I, king of Spain and all its overseas possessions and ruler of the Netherlands, Burgundy, and Austria became also Kaiser Karl V, Holy Roman Emperor and ostensibly the most powerful man on earth. As Holy Roman Emperor, Charles would also be blessed—or cursed—with the ultimate responsibility for silencing a troublesome monk and professor from Wittenberg who seemed hell bent on destroying the unity of the Catholic Apostolic Church.

On 23 October 1520, almost three years to the day since Luther had posted his ninety-five theses, Charles was crowned in Charlemagne's sublime eighth-century Palatine Chapel at Aachen by two of his electors, the archbishop of Trier and the archbishop of Mainz. Crowning was a sacred ritual carried out by the church, which confirmed the divine origin of a monarch's power and sealed the intertwining of church and state. It was such a key ritual that some early medieval theologians had actually counted it as a sacrament. Having two bishop-electors seal this link between the spiritual and temporal realms made the crowning of Charles even more powerfully symbolic. Given the lofty ideals represented at that ceremony, it was doubly ironic that the archbishop of Mainz at that time was Albrecht, the very same elector who had opposed Charles and the very same pluralist bishop who had commissioned Johann Tetzel to preach and distribute indulgences in Saxony so he could pay off the loans with which he had bought his office. Albrecht was now even higher in the church hierarchy, having been raised to cardinal by Pope Leo X the previous year. Cardinal Albrecht was thus now a member of the Roman Curia; in addition to electing Holy Roman Emperors and crowning them, he could also elect popes. Short of becoming pope or emperor, one could rise no higher in sixteenth-century society. Short of pure satire, neither could history have been more ironic.

Emperor Charles V was typical of many rulers of his day: pious yet overtly pragmatic all at once. At first unable to address most of his subjects in their own tongues, the practical Charles gradually learned several languages—at least to some degree—and made it possible for some historians to believe that a quote attributed to him was genuine:

The young emperor. Charles V, around the time when he became Holy Roman Emperor. This portrait by the Flemish School was given to King Henry VIII of England and remains in the Royal Collection. The artist has made no attempt to hide Charles's prominent jaw, a characteristic trait of the Hapsburgs, which many of his descendants would also inherit.

"I speak Spanish to God, Italian to women, French to men, and German to my horse."[6] Although he would have several extramarital affairs and sire two illegitimate children, wage many wars of conquest and also oppose the pope himself on several issues, and even bear the ultimate responsibility for the sack of Rome in 1527, Charles was also a man of faith who held deep religious convictions. He had been brought up to be a faithful Catholic Christian who believed that the "one holy Catholic and Apostolic Church" mentioned in the essential prayer known as the Creed was the church led by the pope at Rome, and that it had never, ever ceased to be the very church founded by Christ himself. He was a "modern" man too, trained in the life of the spirit by the theologian Adrian of Utrecht (later Pope Adrian VI), a disciple of the *devotio moderna*, that broad-minded mystical movement in which Erasmus of Rotterdam had also been steeped. Charles V, the emperor who would one day resign all his titles and retire to a monastery, committed himself wholeheartedly and at great expense to maintaining the unity of Christendom both as an ideal and as a matter of imperial policy. But something huge stood in the way of Charles's ultimate goal: the revolt begun by Martin Luther, that irksome monk who would be the bane of his existence.

From Rebel to Heretic

While all the nobility of the empire were distracted with the issue of the German emperor's succession, Pope Leo X was busy preparing his bull of excommunication against Martin

Luther. "Arise o Lord [*Exsurge Domine*], and judge thy cause," read the first line of this bull, "the wild boar from the forest seeks to destroy your vineyard." Issued at Rome on 15 June 1520, this document listed forty-one "ancient" errors that Luther had revived in Germany, like some "restless evil, full of deadly poison." This wording was standard procedure against all heretics, for the accepted thinking on theological error was that it had but one source, the devil, and was also of one piece, linking all heretics together. Luther and his followers were interpreting the Holy Scriptures "just like heretics have done since ancient times," charged Leo, "inspired only by their own sense of ambition, and for the sake of popular acclaim." The bull roared against Luther and anyone who agreed with him:

> We condemn, reprobate, and reject completely the books and all the writings and sermons of the said Martin Luther, whether in Latin or any other language . . . and we forbid each and every one of the faithful of either sex . . . to read, assert, preach, praise, print, publish, or defend them. . . . Indeed immediately after the publication of this letter these works, wherever they may be, shall be sought out carefully . . . and burned publicly and solemnly in the presence of the clerics and people. As far as Martin himself is concerned. . . .We can, without any further citation or delay, proceed against him to his condemnation and damnation as one whose faith is notoriously suspect and in fact a true heretic with full severity.[7]

Getting this document up to Saxony took three months. Since Luther received news of the bull long before it ever reached him, and he was given sixty days to recant upon receiving it, he knew for several months that he had a sword hanging over his head. In a separate letter, Pope Leo also issued clear instructions to Prince Frederick the Wise. "We can no longer allow the disease-ridden sheep to infect the whole flock," said Leo. "We exhort you to persuade him to return to sanity, swallow his stubborn pride, and receive our clemency, along with God's. . . . But if he persists in his madness, put your authority and power to work, and take him prisoner."[8]

Seizing Luther would not be easy, and Frederick knew this. The church itself had no power to lay hands on heretics, and no means of doing it; their capture was the responsibility of secular authorities. By now Luther had won a great following at all levels of German society, and he had many noble friends besides Frederick. He had become a German hero, a champion of German liberties in the eyes of many. This was part of his appeal: it was not just Luther's theology that excited his followers, but also his firm stance as a German against the "Romanists." Luther had the support of many powerful nobles who pledged to fight for him, such as Ulrich von Hutten and Franz von Sickingen. While the threat of capture and execution enveloped Luther, the knight Ulrich von Hutten, wrote to him:

> Long live freedom! . . . I hear that you have been excommunicated. If this is true, how great a man you are! . . . Stand firm. Do not waver. . . . You will have me by your side, no matter what comes our way. Let us defend our common freedom. Let us liberate our oppressed fatherland. We have God on our side.[9]

And it was not just nobles who had been won over by Luther. Burghers in the cities and students had also joined his camp. Those carrying the bull *Exsurge Domine* to Saxony were supposed to publish it in every city and town where they stopped and to see to it that Luther's texts were burned. The two men chosen for this task, Girolamo Aleandro, former rector of the University of Paris, and Johann Eck, Luther's debating nemesis, encountered stiff resistance nearly everywhere in Germany, especially from students, who rioted and threatened them with physical violence, or burned anti-Lutheran works rather than those of Luther. With the people and his many noble supporters at his side, Luther stood firm during this tense time, writing and publishing a series of explosive texts that marked a complete break with Rome. As the clock ticked on his deadline to recant, Luther blasted away with lightning speed, laying out his call for reform in three hastily written but eloquent treatises.

The first of these salvos, *An Address to the Christian Nobility of the German Nation*, appeared in August 1520. Its argument was an echo of the voices of Wycliffe and Hus and

Luther, saint, and prophet. Despite Luther's theological emphasis on the sinfulness of all human beings, and despite all his efforts to portray himself as no less wretched than anyone else, Luther's followers did not hesitate to depict him as a saint, especially as his Catholic opponents stepped up their attacks against him. These two images invest Luther with the iconographical symbols of sanctity. On the left, a woodcut by Hans Baldung Grien (1521) depicts Luther the monk, with a halo and a nimbus, and, in case anyone should think this insufficient, the Holy Spirit (as dove) is suspended over his head. This was one of the most popular, best-selling images of the young Luther. On the right, Daniel Hopfer copied Lucas Cranach's portrait of Luther in his doctor's cap, aglow in holiness and divine inspiration, indicated by the nimbus around his head (1523).

as simple as it was revolutionary: whenever the church cannot reform itself because of the corruption of the clergy, it becomes the responsibility of the secular authorities to clean house. To suggest that the church should be subject to the state was a radical departure. Throughout the Middle Ages, in all its conflicts with secular rulers, the church had developed a very sophisticated theology that defended the supremacy of the papacy and the superiority of the spiritual over the temporal. Stressing the point that this theology was unscriptural, and therefore wrong, Luther struck at the root of all claims for clerical superiority and papal supremacy. Advocating a total leveling of authority, and granting the secular rulers the power to cleanse the church, Luther redefined the dynamic of church-state relations:

> All this is nothing but mere ordinance of human invention. It follows, then, that between laymen and priests, princes and bishops, or, as they call it, between spiritual and temporal sons, the only real difference is one of office and function, and not of estate. . . . Therefore I say, forasmuch as the temporal power has been ordained by God for the punishment of the bad and the protection of the good, we must let it do its duty throughout the whole Christian body, without respect of persons, whether it strike popes, bishops, priests, monks, nuns, or whoever it may be.[10]

In addition to theologizing, Luther also made specific recommendations, urging the German nobles to take over the German churches. In a very long list filled with scores of specific proposals, Luther asked for a total revamping of the church and of popular piety. Some of these changes were immense. Six proposals, in particular, pointed toward the creation of a very different church and a new kind of piety. First, Luther urged the creation of a German national church, proposing that all clerical appointments, including those of bishops, be taken away from Rome, and that the pope be stripped of the right to interfere in German church affairs. Second, he suggested that the clergy be allowed to marry, on the grounds that all vows, including that of celibacy, were wrong and marriage was a natural right of every man and woman. "The pope has as little power to command this," argued Luther, "as he has to forbid eating, drinking, the natural movement of the bowels or growing fat."[11] Third, he called for the abolition of masses for the dead. Fourth, he asked for the calendar to be stripped of all feast days, proposing instead that the only proper celebration should be the Sunday Eucharist. Fifth, he called for the destruction of all rural shrines and places of pilgrimage and the abolition of the cult of the saints. Sixth, he asked for a reform of the universities in which the study of the Bible would be central and scholastic theology would be driven out. In addition, Luther also called upon the princes to reform society, offering some specific suggestions such as putting an end to begging and prostitution, and banning extravagant dress and excessive eating and drinking, which, as he put it, "gives us Germans a bad reputation in foreign lands, as though it were our special vice."[12] In sum, Luther spelled out his vision for a renewed and reformed Germany, and also made it very clear that it was up to the nobles to effect the changes that were so sorely needed: "the Christian nobility should set itself against the pope as

Luther's message simplified. This woodcut from the early 1520s depicts the leaders of the Roman
Catholic clergy as wolves who are raiding Christ's sheepfold. The wolf with prey in his mouth
wears the papal tiara, and the other wolf a cardinal's hat. The apostles Peter and Paul stand watch
on the hilltop. A very Lutheran St. Peter holds a Bible, rather than the keys to heaven, in his hand.
Immediately to the right of St. Peter are some goats, who represent the damned, a visual reference
to the Last Judgment, when Christ will separate the sheep from the goats—that is, the saved from
the damned. Luther stands courageously in the lower right-hand corner, preaching to the sheep,
saving them from their ravenous clerics. In the text below, Luther exclaims: "Beware, you sheep,
run not away from him who hangs on the cross. Let this wolf run his course, he will sell a kingdom
in hell. He has eaten many a sheep, and is to be accounted as equal to Satan. The shepherds have
become wolves. . . . The flock that they should shepherd is scattered, strangled by false doctrine.
This greatly saddens my heart, as I see the great harm visited upon Christendom by pope, cardinal
and bishop. . . . Thus I preach and teach and write, even at the cost of my life."

against a common enemy and destroyer of Christendom, and should do this for the salvation of the poor souls who must go to ruin through his tyranny."[13] Moreover, throughout
this treatise Luther constantly referred to his opponents as "Romanists," underscoring the
nationalistic dimension of his proposal and denying outright the universalist claims of
the Catholic Church with a single pejorative noun. And he wrote in German, and saw to
it that it would be printed and widely distributed.

Two months later, in October 1520, Luther fired off an even stronger round
against the so-called Romanists, in a treatise provocatively entitled *On the Babylonian
Captivity of the Church*, in which he took on the subject of the sacraments and explored

the place of ritual in the church and society. As he had done with his *Address to the German Nobility*, Luther used this tract to point out what he thought was wrong among the Romanists and to outline his vision for a reform of church and society that was fully "evangelical," that is, in full conformity with Jesus's teachings in the gospels. The premise of the treatise is boldly expressed in the title: Rome was the new Babylon, the tyrannical power that prevented God's people from living and worshiping as they should. In the same way that the ancient chosen people had to endure exile in Babylon, so now did Christians have to endure the despotism of a heathenish false church. The true church, argued Luther, was no longer visible: all one could see was a corrupt church that suffocated Christians with far too many unnecessary burdens. To prove his point, Luther turned to the sacraments, those key rituals that defined Christian life in medieval Europe. As always, Luther minced no words:

> To begin with, I must deny that there are seven sacraments, and for the time being maintain that there are only three: baptism, penance, and the Eucharist. All three have been subjected to a miserable captivity by the Roman curia, and the church has been robbed of all her freedom.[14]

In one fell swoop, Luther thus wrote off four sacraments as unbiblical: confirmation, marriage, ordination, and extreme unction. Not much later, he would add penance to the list, reducing the sacraments to two: baptism and the Eucharist. Luther was too good a theologian to overlook the connection between faith and worship: he thoroughly understood the Latin adage *lex orandi, lex credenda*, which sums up the fact that the way one prays determines what one believes, and vice versa. He was also too good a theologian not to know that by tossing out four sacraments he had crossed yet another line, denying a sacred dogma that had been confirmed in 1215 by the Fourth Lateran Council.

A month later, in November 1520, Luther penned and published what many think is his ultimate manifesto and the clearest formulation of his theological vision, a compact treatise titled *On Christian Freedom*. This text was written expressly for a large lay audience, in German, and it left no doubt about where Luther was headed. Part polemics, part devotional text, part theological disquisition, Luther's *Christian Freedom* tackles the central subject of redemption, seeking to answer the question that drove him to the edge of insanity in the cloister and prompted his attack on Tetzel: how one is saved, or, as Luther rephrases it, how one becomes acceptable in the eyes of God. Luther's answer is very complex and full of paradoxes, but it is such a rhetorical masterpiece that its effect was immense. Luther begins with two paradoxical statements: "A Christian is a perfectly free lord of all, subject to none. A Christian is a perfectly dutiful servant of all, subject to all."[15] As he unpacks this conundrum, Luther relies at every turn on his most basic hermeneutical principle: that Christians should be guided by Holy Scripture alone, *sola scriptura*, the term that had already become the chief battle cry of his war against the Romanists. Then, relying very heavily on Paul's letters to the Galatians and Romans, he articulates a second key principle: that one is saved by faith alone, *sola fide*.

The two principles alone do not explain the whole of Luther's theology, but it is impossible to understand Luther and the whole Protestant Reformation without them. The *sola scriptura* principle led Luther to scrutinize all theology and piety according to his interpretation of the Bible, and to reject anything he judged as nonbiblical. The *sola fide* principle, which Luther claimed was the true, biblically centered way of understanding how Christ saves from sin and death, was paradoxical, but reduced to its simplest elements it boiled down to this: salvation is never earned; it is simply and freely granted by God to those who have faith in the saving sacrifice of Jesus Christ. "It is faith alone which worthily and sufficiently justifies and saves the person," Luther thundered. "A Christian has no need of any work or law in order to be saved since through faith he is free from every law and does everything out of pure liberty and freely."[16]

As Luther saw it, largely through his interpretation of St. Paul's theology in the New Testament, one is saved not by one's own good works, or by penances, but by Christ's sacrifice on the cross, through which God chose to overlook the sins of the human race. One is saved by faith alone, not works, and there is nothing one can do to obtain faith. Faith is purely and simply a gift of God. This meant that the Catholic Church was dead wrong in asserting that no one could go to heaven until their souls were spotless, for sinlessness was impossible to attain, and no one could ever hope to make satisfaction to God for their sins. Salvation was paradoxical: every Christian who had faith was at once righteous and sinful, *simul justus et peccator*. Standing accepted theology on its head, Luther redefined the meanings of *goodness* and *holiness*:

> The Christian who is consecrated by his faith does good works, but the works do not make him holier or more Christian, for that is the work of faith alone. And if a man were not first a believer and a Christian, all his works would amount to nothing and would be truly wicked.[17]

It would take Luther several more years to fully articulate this paradoxical theology and turn it into a consistent ethic, but he did understand most of its implications very clearly. Above all, Luther grasped how this theology necessarily redefined the role of the church and its clergy. If one was saved by faith alone, *sola fide*, then one was one saved by grace alone, *sola gratia*. Salvation came directly from God to each believer on a one-to-one basis, not through any intermediary. All Christians were therefore equal, and the clergy could not claim a special status for themselves:

> Lo, this is the inestimable power and liberty of Christians. Not only are we the freest of kings, we are also priests forever. . . . Thus Christ has made it possible for us, provided we believe in him, to be not only his brethren, co-heirs, and fellow-kings, but also his fellow-priests. . . . Injustice is done to those words *priest, cleric, spiritual, ecclesiastic,* when they are transferred from all Christians to those few who are now by a mischievous usage called *ecclesiastics*.[18]

Luther was quick to point out that although all Christians were equally priests, not everyone could "publicly minister and teach." This qualification did not make his theology of the priesthood any less radical, however. Luther had stripped the clerical state of the special ontological status it claimed, and even gone as far as to redefine its proper name. True clerics were not "priests" who dispensed grace, forgave sins, or offered the Eucharist as a *sacrifice*. Christ had offered the ultimate sacrifice, once and for all, and he had also made all Christians share in his priesthood. Clergy were *ministers, servants, and stewards* of the Word, pure and simple. It was only for the sake of order in the community that some Christians took on the role of "serving others and teaching them the faith of Christ and the freedom of believers."[19]

This talk of freedom and equality was heady stuff, printed in German for all to read. That Luther was still in the process of articulating his highly paradoxical theology mattered little to his readers. It also mattered little that the text was focused on seemingly recondite theological issues, for the social and political dimensions of the theology were easy enough to grasp. "A Christian is a perfectly free, lord of all, subject to none," said Luther. Taken literally, this statement was downright dangerous. Equally dangerous was its inversion: "A Christian is a perfectly dutiful servant of all, subject to all." Both statements were a challenge to all hierarchies, civil and ecclesiastic. In sum, the text of *Christian Freedom* was unlike anything anyone alive at that time could have ever read. Provocative to the core, its subversive tone was hard to miss and easy to misinterpret.

In November 1520, when Luther's sixty days expired, he was formally excommunicated. But since it was up to the civil authorities to arrest Luther, and Frederick the Wise was squarely behind Luther, fending off all potential enemies, Luther's life was spared, at least for the time being. In August, Luther had already appealed to Emperor Charles V for a hearing. As he waited for a reply to his request, he penned his response to Pope Leo, in two versions, in Latin and German. The Latin text was provocatively entitled *Against the Execrable Bull of the Antichrist*. The German text, which differs substantially from the Latin, removed the *execrable* from the title, but contained just as much antipapal vitriol. In it, Luther fumed against "the Roman Antichrist and Doctor Eck, his apostle," heaping scorn on the bull of excommunication, mocking his foes, and exposing the pope as "God's enemy, Christ's persecutor, the destroyer of Christianity, and the true Antichrist."[20] The Latin version, too, brimmed over with rage and a stark dualistic imagery:

> I consider whoever wrote this bull to be the Antichrist, and it is therefore against the Antichrist that I respond. . . . Whether authored by Eck or by the pope, this bull is jam-packed with of the worst of the worst: impiety, blasphemy, ignorance, impudence, hypocrisy, lying—in sum, it is Satan himself and his Antichrist. . . . You, then, Leo X, you lord cardinals of Rome, and the rest of you there at Rome . . . I call upon you to renounce your diabolical blasphemy and brazen impiety, and, if you will not, I and all who worship Christ shall all hold your seat as possessed and oppressed by Satan himself, and as the damned seat of the Antichrist.[21]

To underscore his defiance, and to demonstrate the strength of his following, Luther and his students at Wittenberg made a bonfire into which they threw the bull of excommunication and the *Corpus juris canonici*, the text of the church's canon law.

Since Luther's prince refused to lay a finger on him, and no other authorities seemed willing to challenge Frederick the Wise, it was up to the new and very young emperor to take care of Luther. Aware of the urgency of this matter, and eager to avert a war among his princes over Luther, Charles V called for a meeting of the Imperial Diet at the city of Worms, and summoned Luther to attend. When the time came, in April 1521, Luther had every reason to fear for his life, despite Frederick's military escort and promises of protection. Not only the emperor himself would be at Worms, but also most of the temporal rulers and highest ecclesiastics of Germany. All in all, the danger was undeniable, no matter how much support there might be for Luther. When Charles and his retinue arrived at Worms they were quite surprised to find that the city seemed overwhelmingly in favor of Luther: placards defending him were everywhere, and the book stalls overflowing not only with his texts, all recently printed, but also with images of Luther, poems in his honor, and other tracts and pamphlets critical of the Romanists. Pope Leo X had sent two legates to Worms (and both would later be elevated to cardinals): the humanist scholar Girolamo Aleandro, who held the official post of papal nuncio, and Marino Caracciolo (1468–1538). Aleandro wrote to Leo: "Nine tenths of the people here are shouting 'Luther!,' and the rest of them shout 'death to the papal court!'"[22] When Luther entered Worms, after being received as a hero in town after town along the way from Wittenberg, more than two thousand people clogged the streets and squares merely to get a glimpse of him.

Charles V knew what he had to do. He had not summoned Luther to discuss the merits of the bull *Exsurge Domine*. The pope had already spoken. According to the oath he had sworn when crowned emperor, Charles was obligated to serve as the court of last appeal for his subjects. Luther deserved his final chance to be heard, but not much else. "That man will not make a heretic out of me," vowed Charles. Luther expected much more than another chance to recant, but he was in for a rude disappointment. Instead of being asked about specific points of doctrine or being allowed to debate openly, when Luther finally stood before the emperor, he was simply shown a stack of twenty-five of his books, and after each of their titles had been read out loud, he was asked whether he was ready to renounce them all. Luther stalled, and begged for a recess.

On the following day, 18 April 1521, Luther faced the emperor and the Diet again, in a hall so tightly packed with people that no one but Charles V had room enough to sit down. Luther did his best to distinguish between the different types of texts he had authored, but at one point, when he made mention of how the "papists" had corrupted the church, Charles V—according to one account—impatiently grumbled that Luther should simply shut up and state whether or not he would recant.[23] Undaunted, Luther continued elaborating on the "evil and tyranny" with which Rome oppressed the German people, playing his nationalism card in a room brimming over with German princes. "I cannot escape my duty to my Germans," he said, refusing to recant and revealing a possessive attitude toward the whole of his own "poor miserable people," and an exalted sense of prophetic mission that put him on a par with the emperor himself. Believing he was there to speak for all Germans, Luther addressed the princes and the emperor as equals. A double-barreled final question was put to him: did he really think that he was the only one who understood the Bible correctly, and was he really willing to assume that his knowledge and judgment surpassed that of all of the famous theologians and churchmen he rejected? Given one last chance to repudiate all of his books without exception, and to repent for his attacks against "our holy Church, and against the councils, decretals, laws, and rites that our forefathers upheld and we still adhere to today,"[24] Luther refused. His reply was as brief as it was bold:

> Since then Your Majesty and your lordships desire a simple reply, I will answer. . . .
> Unless I am convicted by Scripture and plain reason—I do not accept the authority of
> popes and councils, for they have contradicted each other—my conscience is captive to
> the Word of God. I cannot and I will not recant anything, for to go against conscience
> is neither right nor safe. God help me, Amen.[25]

Some accounts printed right after the Diet of Worms added the phrase: "Here I stand; I cannot do otherwise" at the end, even though these words do not appear in any of the official transcripts. Whether it was uttered or not makes little difference: the phrase would forever be linked with Luther, as the ultimate summation of his appeal to his individual conscience.

After adjourning that day's meeting, Charles gathered with six of his seven electors and several princes, and told them exactly what he thought, in French:

> A lone friar whose opinions contradict the past thousand years of the Christian reli-
> gion, down to our own day must surely be wrong. Therefore I am totally determined
> to commit all of my resources against him: my lands, my friends, my body, my blood,
> my life, and my soul. For not only I, but you of this noble German nation . . . who are
> preeminent defenders of the Catholic faith . . . would be forever disgraced, along with
> our successors, if by our negligence not only heresy but the mere suspicion of heresy
> were to survive.[26]

Charles V agreed not to arrest Luther then and there, but rather to honor the promise he had been made of safe conduct back to Wittenberg. That said, however, he also set out to make Luther an outlaw of the empire, and in the Edict of Worms he proclaimed Luther fair game for anyone who wanted to hunt him down. Luther's safe conduct undermined, he was now literally outside the protection of the law. Then, at the eleventh hour, Frederick the Wise, who had refused to sign the edict, decided to take matters into his own hands: he arranged for Luther to be "kidnapped" and spirited away in such a manner that no one would know for sure whether he was dead or alive. While Luther was on his way back to Wittenberg, protected by the emperor's safe conduct promise, a gang of armed knights nabbed him with a show of force and took him to one of Frederick's castles, the Wartburg, near Eisenach. Frederick was cunning enough to instruct the kidnappers not to tell him where Luther had been taken, so he would not have to lie about his knowledge of Luther's whereabouts. Charles V fumed, but he could do nothing. Someone had apparently taken it upon himself to either kill or shelter Luther, but no one could finger the culprit. Safely hidden behind the Wartburg's ramparts, Martin Luther shed his religious habit, grew his hair and beard, and assumed a knight's identity under the name *George*. It was a total transformation, and a successful ruse. Given the labyrinthine complexities of the Holy Roman Empire, the emperor could be easily hoodwinked and thwarted, no matter how much he wanted punish a heretic.

Luther was gone from the scene, but the momentum that had built under his leadership could not be easily stopped. So, while Luther spent time in hiding as an outlaw under an assumed identity, other forces quickly filled the vacuum he had left behind. One man's campaign against perceived corruption, waged largely through the printing press, became a much broader and much more extreme rebellion against the status quo. With Luther in hiding, momentous changes began to take place. The Protestant Reformation as we know it began in earnest, as what had been theretofore limited to the printed page began spilling out into the churches, palaces, guild halls, households, streets, and battlefields of a civilization no longer bound by a common faith.

Beyond the Hiding Place

Charles V and all who opposed Luther knew all too well that his condemnation at the Diet of Worms might have come a bit too late, for they could not help but notice that Luther seemed to be everywhere, embodied in his followers, his voice amplified and echoed in hundreds of texts and pamphlets, as well as in sermons, and conversations in taverns and public squares.

The link between the printing press and the sudden expansion of open dissent against the Roman Catholic Church was hard to miss, for it was not just texts by Luther that were cranked out, but also hundreds authored by others, many written not just by learned clerics, but by laymen from different walks of life, with concerns specific to their class or profession. The production of pamphlets (*Flugschriften*) and broadsheets (*Flugblätter*) spiked in tandem with Luther's growing disdain for all things papal and Roman. Many of these publications, cheaply produced and very affordable, not only echoed Luther's defiance, and that of other dissenting clerics, but also put a more practical spin on it, digesting his radical rejection of the status quo, popularizing it, giving it the accent of the common man and woman. As the layman Lazarus Spengler confessed in a 1519 pamphlet: "To my mind, and as I think any rational man will easily see, Luther has removed such scruples and errors [abstaining from meat on Friday] with sound Christian evidence of holy, divine Scripture; and for this we owe him well-earned praise and thanks." Spengler's pamphlet precluded subtlety and any mincing of words. It was—as its subtitle openly boasted, "a beautiful, true, and gallant confirmation of Martin Luther's teaching."[27]

Luther and his close associates had no control over this literature, so, strictly speaking, whatever is found in this flood of pamphlets cannot always be identified as

"Lutheran," even though it extended Luther's reach and presence. Nor can it be attributed to any single region or specific social class. But it can certainly be called anti-Romish and "evangelical," that is, fiercely committed to the promotion of a biblically centered religion, to the dismantling of the Roman Catholic Church, and to a program of change that had social and political issues very much in mind. Most of this literature was not theological, though it touched on theological issues. Its sharpest edge was always practical and its tone sarcastic.

German pamphlet literature was devoted to exposing the corruption, error, and abusive power of the Roman Catholic clergy and to contrasting it with the liberating ethos of the new evangelical message. Whether written in rhymed verse—for easier memorization—or in plain prose, the evangelical pamphlet aimed to reach the laity, first and foremost.

Simplification was the chief objective of pamphlet literature, and polarization its preferred idiom. Tirades against the pope, "fat monks," and "horned bishops" often assumed center stage. Identifying the pope as the Antichrist and the Catholic Church as the devil's abode was the genre's most vital simplification. As one preacher put it in 1522: "Christ has his church and the Antichrist also has his church . . . and in that church the devil is worshiped, and the laws of the Antichrist are held in higher esteem than God's laws."[28] Liberation was the key promise of the evangelical message. One pamphlet prayed: "O Christ, redeem us from the darkness of the Antichrist at Rome who instead of caring for his flock rather trammels it with his tyrannical laws."[29] Jörg Vögeli, a layman from Constance, stressed the uselessness of these nondivine laws:

> How much divine favor can you expect to gain from mumbling the canonical hours, endowing great benefices and churches, ringing many bells . . . or by smearing the fore-head with oil, which is called confirmation, and other such human inventions, when speaking with all tongues, chastising the body even unto death, giving away all earthly goods, and having faith strong enough to remove mountains cannot make one pleasing to God in terms of the sure faith and love of God and man which are required?[30]

Taken as a whole, early evangelical pamphlets contrasted the "unnecessary" burdens of the pope's church with the liberating power of the gospel, and did so with a specific set of changes in mind. The most significant issues were these: the promotion of biblically based preaching; the abolition of confession and fasting, and of clerical celibacy and monasticism; the abolition of masses for the dead; the reduction of clerical privileges, coupled with increased lay control over the clergy; the dismantling of existing episcopal bureaucracies; the redistribution of the church's wealth; and the creation of new social welfare programs. Nationalistic grievances against Rome and Italian clerics also figured prominently.

And the attack on Rome was not limited to words: the evangelicals invented the satirical cartoon. Never before in history had images been put to such use, as a medium of dissent. Images could be found in texts, as illustrations. They could also be reproduced

Luther's Catholic opponents

individually, as broadsheets. Some of these contained brief texts; others relied exclusively on the image to carry the message. In the sixteenth century, as in our own day, messages were astutely and very effectively delivered through images, and especially through caricatures. In a time and place with much higher illiteracy rates, the images might have been even more instrumental in winning hearts and minds than any text.

Images of Luther abounded. Many portrayed the rebellious monk as a saint and prophet, replete with halo and nimbus, or with the holy spirit hovering overhead. Luther's Roman opponents could be belittled, mocked, even dehumanized. One cartoon turned his chief opponents into animal characters worthy of the Disney studios.

One broadsheet depicts Luther's Catholic opponents as beasts, and the text associates each of these figures with the attributes of the corresponding species. From left to right, we see Thomas Murner (the cat), Hieronymus Emser (the goat), Pope Leo X (the lion), Johann Eck (the pig), and Jacob Lemp (the dog). Thomas Murner, who challenged Luther head on, is depicted as a cat because *murr* was a German equivalent of the English *meow*, the sound made by a cat. Luther took to calling him "Murr-narr," or "Meow-fool." Emser is a goat because his family coat of arms displayed a leaping goat. Luther opened one of his responses to Emser with the phrase: "Dear Goat, do not butt me!" The text corresponding to Emser attributes randiness to him, and it reads, in part, "Ah, virgin goat, you stink so awfully of chastity in your long beard." Pope Leo X, who is also labeled as the Antichrist, is naturally associated with a lion because of his name, and is typified as cruel and ferocious. Johann Eck, one of Luther's earliest and most formidable opponents, is lowered to the pigsty and is ascribed swinish habits. Jacob Lemp, the least of these

Paſſional Chriſti

Die Wucherer Chriſtus austreibt vom Tempel ſein —

Und er fand im Tempel ſitzen, die da Ochſen, Schafe und Tauben feil hatten, und die Wechsler. Und er machte eine Geißel aus Stricken und trieb ſie alle zum Tempel hinaus, ſammt den Schafen und Ochſen, und verſchüttete den Wechslern das Geld und ſtieß die Tiſche um; und ſprach zu denen, die die Tauben feil hatten: Traget das von dannen und machet nicht meines Vaters Haus zum Kaufhauſe. Joh. 2, 14—16. Umſonſt habt ihrs empfangen, umſonſt gebet es auch. Matth. 10, 8. Petrus ſprach zu ihm: Daß du verdammet werdeſt mit deinem Gelde, daß du meineſt, Gottes Gabe werde durch Geld erlanget. Apoſt. 8, 20.

34

und Antichriſti.

Mit Bullen, Bannbriefen zwingt ſie der Pabſt wiedr — hinein.

Hier ſitzt der Antichriſt im Tempel Gottes und erzeigt ſich als Gott, wie Paulus vorherverkündigt 2 Theſſ. 2, 4., verändert alle göttliche Ordnungen, wie Daniel ſagt Dan. 11, 36—38., und unterdrückt die heilige Schrift, verkauft Dispenſation, Ablaß, Pallia (Biſchofsmäntel), Bisthümer, Leben, erhebt (das heißt, er fordert ein) die Schätze der Erde, löſ't auf die Ehe, beſchwert die Gewiſſen mit ſeinen Geſetzen, macht Recht und um Geld zerreißt er das. Erhebt Heilige, benedeit und vermaledeit bis ins vierte Geſchlecht, und gebietet, ſeine Stimme zu hören, gleich wie Gottes Stimme, c. Sic omnes. Dist. 19. (I, p. 56.), und niemand ſoll ihm einreden. c. 17. q. 4. c. Nemini. (I, p. 716.)

35

Contrasting Christ and Antichrist

opponents, was more involved with the Swiss Reformation than with Luther, and had lost out to Zwingli in the 1523 Zurich disputation. He is portrayed as a snarling dog more than willing to fight for the bone he is holding. Image and text combine here to ridicule these Catholic churchmen and theologians, bringing them to a subhuman level. Theology is beside the point here.

One extremely popular pamphlet, *The Passion of Christ and the Antichrist* (1521), with illustrations by Lucas Cranach and text by Philip Melanchthon, reduced the evangelical message to thirteen pairs of woodcuts that contrasted Christ and the pope.

In the twelfth panel of the woodcuts Christ expels the money changers from the temple. On the opposite page, the pope/Antichrist usurps God's throne in the temple. Instead of cleansing the temple, he pollutes it, greedily collecting money in exchange for indulgences, dispensations, church offices, and other favors. Although Melanchthon's text spells out the lesson to be learned, carefully and precisely, his words are rendered unnecessary by Cranach's images. The thirteenth and final panel depicts the ultimate contrast: while Christ ascends to heaven, the pope/Antichrist descends to hell.

Antipapal and anticlerical sentiments could be depicted in even more graphic terms, with offensive imagery. Linking the devil to the pope and all Roman Catholic

Passional Christi
Christus uffsteigt uß dieser Welt —

Und da er solches gesagt, ward er aufgehaben zusehens, und eine Wolke nahm ihn auf vor ihren Augen weg. Dieser JEsus, welcher von euch ist aufgenommen gen Himmel, wird kommen, wie ihr ihn gesehen habt gen Himmel fahren. Apost. 1, 9. 11. Seines Königreichs wird kein Ende sein. Luc. 1, 33. Wer mir dienen will, der folge mir nach; und wo ich bin, da soll mein Diener auch sein. Joh. 12, 26.

36

und Antichristi.
In Abgrund der Pabst fällt.

Und das Thier ward ergriffen und mit ihm der falsche Prophet, der die Zeichen that vor ihm, durch welche er verführete, die das Malzeichen des Thiers nahmen, und die das Bild des Thiers anbeteten; lebendig wurden diese beide in den feurigen Pfuhl geworfen, der mit Schwefel brannte. Und die andern wurden erwürget mit dem Schwert deß, der auf dem Pferde saß, das aus seinem Munde ging. Offenb. 19, 20. 21. Und alsdann wird der Boshaftige offenbaret werden, welchen der HErr umbringen wird mit dem Geist seines Mundes, und wird sein ein Ende machen durch die Erscheinung seiner Zukunft. 2 Theß. 2, 8.

37

Contrasting Christ and Antichrist

The origin of monks

Jobannes Cochleus: Des Heiligen Bebstlichen stuels geborner
Apostel: Prophet: Merterer vnd Jungfraw.

Cochlaeus and demons

clergy was a common theme. In another image, *On the Origin of Monks and the Antichrist*, a devil in a latrine gives birth to monks, and the monks are then thrown into a boiling cauldron, stirred, stewed, and turned into the pope/Antichrist (a homunculus easily identified by his triple crown).

Despite its religious context, visual anti-"Romish" propaganda could convey messages crassly, linking scatology and eschatology, all for the sake of simple folk. For instance, *Johann Cochlaeus, the Natural-Born Apostle, Prophet, Killer, and Virgin of the Holy Papal Stool*, one of the most obscenely outrageous of all Reformation images—the very epitome of smear tactics—reduces the work of Johann Cochlaeus to fecal matter. In this image, the devil defecates into Cochlaeus's mouth, and Cochlaeus, in turn, excretes books out of his rear end. As devils gleefully dance in celebration of this process, a monk and a prince pick up the books, and a crowd of bystanders—some covering their noses— look on in disgust. The image speaks for itself: the text, aside from identifying the central figure, brings the Reformation to the lowest possible level.

With images like this, and texts that were equally unrestrained in their simplistic reduction of theological fine points and in their portrayal of demonic and divine antitheses, the evangelical Reformation message reached a wide audience, as no message had ever done before: compared to what had been possible with Wycliffe and Hus, for instance—which amounted to furtive whispering, or to lobbing small homemade incendiary devices—this was saturation carpet bombing. To a great extent, the medium became the message, but in the process, that message was also simplified, made less theological and more down-to-earth, and, as some have argued, more focused on release from perceived oppression than on salvation by faith alone.

Luther himself was not responsible for all that was printed, or even a fraction of it, but he was inextricably connected to it, and he benefited from it. That connection, however, also had the distinct disadvantage of being unmanageable.

CHAPTER NINE

Luther

The Reactionary

W hile Luther was in hiding at the Wartburg, Frederick the Wise's castle, from April 1521 to March 1522, all hell seemed to break loose, as if a demonic trinity had encircled him. On one front, Luther saw the devil working through the pope, who was the Antichrist himself, and through all of the pope's clergy. On another front, the pope's secular minions ranged against him, from the emperor on high to Duke George of Albertine Saxony, right next door. George was the Elector Frederick's cousin and a virulent foe who would have loved nothing more than to rid the earth of Luther and his followers. On a third front, Luther saw the devil struggling against him through zealots who quickly stepped in to usurp his rightful place and hijack his Reformation. As if this were not enough, at the Wartburg itself, in the still of the night and in the full light of day, the devil was also inescapable. Luther admitted that when he was "imprisoned" at Frederick's castle, he was often tormented by the devil.[1] And these were not purely spiritual attacks. For instance, Luther once found a strange dog in his tower room and quickly flung the beast out of the window, convinced that it was a shape-shifting demon.[2] Of course, by the time he got to the Wartburg castle, Luther would not have fended off the devil with holy water, as monks had done for centuries, because he had already rejected such a practice as an unbiblical human tradition rather than a legitimate Christian ritual. Luther was not defenseless, however. He had other ways of warding off the demons:

> Almost every night when I wake up the devil is there, itching to argue with me. I have come to this conclusion: when the argument that the Christian is without the law and above the law doesn't help, I chase him away with a fart.[3]

Interweaving eschatology and scatology, soteriology and flatulence, Luther had found a solution to one of his most pressing problems. But Luther did more than fart at demons. Legend has it that during one of these demonic assaults at the Wartburg, Luther hurled his inkwell at the devil. For centuries, visitors to Luther's room at the Wartburg would be shown an ink stain on the wall as proof of that encounter. How the legend of the inkwell and the stain on the wall began, no one knows. As in the legend of Luther nailing the ninety-five theses to the castle church door, the hero himself makes no mention of it. Chances are that it arose from Luther's having said that he had fought the devil with ink, meaning that whatever he opposed in his many texts was of demonic origin. So, while the inkwell never really missed its mark, and the stain shown to thousands of tourists and pilgrims was a pious fraud—quite similar in nature to many of the relics once collected by Elector Frederick—the thought behind the contrived stain was definitely on target. The devil was very real for Luther, and certain as he was that his many opponents were all on the devil's side, his battles were never waged against a figurative enemy, and they were usually very messy.

Although Luther's followers have often tried to clean up or hide his foul language, which appears most frequently in the notes that his students and colleagues took at the dinner table, no one has been able to remove the devil from his speech. Nor has anyone denied that demons were as real to Luther as the pope in Rome or the stones in his kidneys.[4] Luther's demons were very much out in the world, guiding the Catholic clergy and the emperor's vassals and soldiers, blinding those other reformers who did not agree with him, stirring up radicals, troubling consciences, performing annoying pranks, making pacts with witches; when driven away from the houses they haunted, they found new homes in heretics, fanatics, usurers, and such.[5] Occasionally they also possessed some people, just as they did in the time of Jesus and the Apostles.[6] The devil was always there, tempting and taunting Luther, eager to annihilate him. If one takes Luther at his word, one must accept that these evil spirits hardly gave him a moment's peace—at least as *he* saw it. One might even grant that at a very basic level, Luther needed his demons as much as his society did. No matter what, however, Luther always fought demons on their terms, with shocking language, insults, and crude behavior:

> The devil seeks me out when I am at home in bed, and I always have one or two devils waiting to pounce on me. They are smart devils. If they can't overwhelm my heart, they grab my head and plague me there, and when that proves useless, I show them my ass, for that's where they belong.[7]

Where Luther saw demons, modern historians see human nature, politics, and economics at work. That Luther should have trouble at his right and his left was to be expected, especially after his abduction. Luther's disappearance from the public eye could not stem the tide of religious unrest that he had helped to stir up. Having challenged the status quo without changing anything in terms of the church's structure, symbols, or rituals, Luther had left behind an unfinished reform agenda that was now too much a part of public discourse to be ignored. Moreover, Luther had never been alone to begin with: the very reason that he had risen to prominence so quickly was that he embodied something much larger than himself and articulated most eloquently the disappointments and aspirations of so many others. But the mere fact that many found him appealing did not necessarily mean that they would see eye to eye with him on any or all points. Conflict with other reformers was as inevitable as conflict with Rome, for the German-speaking world was teeming with other visions of reform and other potential leaders, especially in the years 1517–1525. At that time, the collapse of the Catholic Church in parts of Germany was due to an enormously complex and diverse movement in which Luther played a key symbolic role that did not at all grant him exclusive leadership rights. Swirling all around the Wittenberg professor were forces that sprang from the same discontent that he had tapped but had more democratic and egalitarian aspirations and a greater longing for liturgical and theological change than he could ever tolerate. Consequently, distinguishing between collaborators and competitors was often difficult in those earliest years.

There are two ways of looking at Luther's position. One is to see Luther as borne aloft by a rising tide of discontent and reformist impulses that sprang up from below, so to speak, which he tapped but could not always control. This upswell, which has been dubbed "the communal Reformation" (*gemeinde Reformation*) tended to represent ideals that were more egalitarian and liberal than Luther's and also favored a more active role for the laity in the running of the church. In this binary model, Luther represents the "ruler's Reformation" at one pole, that is, a conservative state-run church that tends to be autocratic; at the other pole, the more liberal communal Reformation makes Luther's success possible but at the same time creates tension and inevitable conflict. In this view a certain sameness and cohesion is assumed for the communal Reformation, which is seen as incompatible with Luther's "ruler's Reformation," and as a lost cause of sorts that ends up being overpowered by the Lutheran state church.

A second way of interpreting the dynamics of the early Reformation is not to assume that the so-called communal Reformation was a monolithic whole, and to approach Luther's opponents exactly as he did, on a one-to-one basis. All in all, Luther would end up facing three major sets of interrelated and sometimes overlapping opponents in his own antipapal camp: those he branded as "fanatics," who pressed for more change than he could stand and are now known collectively as the Radical Reformers; those who were more moderate than these Radicals but disagreed with him on questions of theology and ritual and are now known as Reformed Protestants; and those who interpreted Christian freedom literally and rose up in armed revolt against their feudal lords in an uprising known as the Peasants' War, or the Revolution of the Common Man. The Reformed Protestants were close to Luther theologically and far from Wittenberg geographically, and therefore they did not trouble Luther as deeply or as immediately as did the Radicals and the peasants. Consequently, like Luther, we shall first turn out attention to the Radicals and the peasants. The Reformed Protestants will have to wait their turn.

Luther the Exile

Luther was not completely sealed off from the world at the Wartburg, but it was nonetheless an exile that removed him from center stage. Luther corresponded with several close friends and associates, including Philip Melanchthon and the humanist Georg Spalatin (1484–1545), who kept him well informed of events out in the world or asked him for advice. Much of what would happen at Wittenberg while Luther was in hiding would be tacitly approved by him, but certain things would slip from his grasp altogether. The hunted outlaw Luther issued messages that let the world know that he was alive without revealing his hiding place. In December 1521, he even wrote directly to Cardinal Albrecht of Mainz to upbraid him once again about the sale of indulgences, saying, "You need not think Luther is dead. . . . I will show you the difference between a bishop and a wolf."[8] That same month he would also made a brief furtive visit to Wittenberg, to stabilize the process of change there as much as he could and to inquire about the publication of some treatises he had written. Luther kept busy in exile, promoting his Reformation the only way he could under the circumstances, by writing obsessively. His output at the Wartburg was astonishing: he not only translated the New Testament into German, but also penned a slew of letters, commentaries, treatises, and other translations.

Being invisible or taken for dead is not the most effective way to lead, however. Like nature, reformations and revolutions abhor a vacuum. Early on, when it seemed Luther might be dead, some called on Erasmus to step in and fill Luther's shoes, much to the humanist's dismay. The artist Albrecht Dürer, for instance, wrote in 1521:

> O, God, if Luther is dead, who will now explain the gospel to us so clearly? . . . Erasmus of Rotterdam, where are you? Look at what the unjust tyranny of worldly power and the forces of darkness are doing. Hear, knight of Christ, ride forth with the Lord Christ, defend the truth, earn the martyr's crown. . . . O, Erasmus, stay on this side, that God may take pride in you.[9]

Erasmus did his utmost to distance himself from such pleas, but he did not have to try very hard, for others jumped at the chance of finishing Luther's work, especially in Wittenberg and the surrounding area. Wittenberg already had two other shining lights who had accompanied Luther to his debate with Johann Eck at Leipzig in 1519: Andreas Bodenstein von Karlstadt and Philip Melanchthon. A third colleague, the Augustinian monk Gabriel Zwilling, was also very eager for change and willing to bring it about. Immediately after Luther's disappearance Melanchthon and Zwilling picked up the slack, but it was Karlstadt, Luther's senior colleague and the university's rector, who was best poised to assume the reformer's mantle. Karlstadt had already made a name for himself, not just at the Leipzig debate, but also through his writing, which complemented Luther's and touched on some issues that had not caught Luther's attention, principally concerning symbols and rituals.

In 1520 Karlstadt had published *On Holy Water and Sacred Salt*, a treatise that reinterpreted the meaning of symbols and rituals. In this text Karlstadt argued that matter and spirit were so radically different from each other as to be incompatible. Material symbols could never convey spiritual benefits, he argued: they were mere signs that pointed to a higher unseen reality, much like a road sign that points to a certain destination. Holy

Radical Reformer. Andreas Bodenstein von Karlstadt assumed leadership at Wittenberg in 1521, bringing about greater changes than Luther had ever dared to embrace.

water and sacred salt—the church's weapons against demons—were really no more than mere natural elements. Since they were ineffective in and of themselves, and incapable of accomplishing what can be gained only by faith, Karlstadt argued, the time had come for Christians to stop acting like brute beasts and to let go of such trifling nonsense.[10] Karlstadt had also published a treatise in June 1521 titled *Instruction Concerning Vows*, in which he blasted away not just at clerical celibacy and monastic vows, as Luther had done, but also at the cult of the saints and their images, arguing that traditional piety was mired in idolatry.[11] This assault was followed with an attack on the Catholic theology of the Eucharist titled *On Both Forms of the Holy Mass*, in which Karlstadt not only denied the sacrificial dimension of that sacrament, but also proposed a more spiritualized understanding of Christ's presence in the bread and wine.[12] Karlstadt's views on this subject differed greatly from Luther's.

With Luther gone, Karlstadt and Zwilling stepped up their calls for reform and began to press for changes in Wittenberg that would keep pace with the new "evangelical" theology. Melanchthon was swept along too, as he and Luther exchanged letters. Monks and nuns began to leave their cloisters, forsaking their vows. Some of them got married. And some married each other. Priests also began to marry. Karlstadt surprised everyone by taking a sixteen-year-old bride. In secret, some of the laity began receiving the communion wine. Karlstadt and Zwilling preached against religious images, the Elector Frederick's relics, and endowed private masses—which were said for the dead, usually without a congregation—and pressed for further reforms in ritual. Some priests agreed and stopped performing such masses, which had usually funded their income. Fasts were deliberately ignored, and meat was consumed on Fridays. In December 1521 the dam gave way. At the beginning of that month, after Karlstadt had fired off several iconoclastic sermons, students began to destroy images, pull down altars, and intimidate clerics as they celebrated Mass. Formal demands were made to the Wittenberg magistrates for the abolition of the Catholic Mass and the institution of a more biblically based celebration of the Last Supper. On Christmas Eve students rioted, destroying more images and interrupting Mass at the castle church. The following day, Christmas 1521, Karlstadt took matters into his own hands. Unsanctioned by any civil or ecclesiastical authority, Karlstadt conducted a radically new evangelical communion service for an overflow crowd at the castle church in place of the traditional Mass. Wearing a plain cloak instead of liturgical vestments, facing the congregation instead of having his back turned to it, omitting certain prayers, speaking the words of consecration in German instead of Latin, and making no mention of sacrifice in a simplified eucharistic prayer, Karlstadt distributed the bread directly into the congregation's hands, instead of placing in on their tongues, and passed around the communion cup so they could all drink of the wine directly, as Hussites did. Then, to top it off, he invited the entire congregation to partake of the bread and wine without first confessing their sins to any priest, saying they were all worthy of receiving communion. It was a daring application of Luther's theology, realized during Luther's very noticeable absence:

> Even though you have not gone to confession you should still go joyfully in good confidence, hope, and faith, and receive this sacrament. . . . You should not be afraid because of sin. . . . Stand freely and boldly in your faith. Fear no deed or misdeed. God gives to all who call on him in faith, and reproaches no one for his wickedness. . . . God is gracious, kind, merciful, forbearing, and forgives evils. He remembers them no more.[13]

Frederick the Wise did nothing to stop Karlstadt; instead, he deferred to his stellar Wittenberg theologians. In the meantime, on 27 December, proof positive arrived in town that Luther and the Wittenbergers were definitely not the only ones engaged in reform. Three wandering preachers came to Wittenberg from the town of Zwickau, which was near the Bohemian border, to the south. The Zwickau Prophets, as they came to be known, were all laymen: Nicholas Storch, a weaver; Thomas Stübner, a former student at Wittenberg; and Thomas Dreschel, a blacksmith. These self-proclaimed prophets had been driven out from Zwickau for their extreme views eight months after the expulsion of their pastor and mentor, Thomas Müntzer (1489/90–1525), a firebrand who would eventually become one of Luther's greatest enemies. Claiming to be under the direct inspiration of the Holy Spirit, Storch and his two companions began to preach in Wittenberg, announcing that the end of the world was near, calling for the establishment of Christ's kingdom on earth here and now, and advocating the abolition of infant baptism, the Mass, confession, images, relics, and all forms of oath taking. Although they were pacifists who advocated the total separation of the church from the state, their goal was to establish the rule of the spiritually elect over the world. Led by Storch, they preached against social hierarchies, insisting on the equality of all human beings and on the necessity of sharing all goods in common, as the earliest Christians had done. In sum, their message was an odd and fiery mix of apocalyptic fervor, biblical literalism, charismatic pretensions, and revolutionary ideology of an egalitarian and communistic bent.

As Storch, Stübner, and Dreschel whipped up apocalyptic expectations, claiming that God favored them with dreams and visions, Karlstadt and Zwilling continued to preach aggressively against the status quo, not as prophets who received messages from God, but as biblical interpreters. Within a month of Karlstadt's Christmas liturgy, on 24 January 1522, the Wittenberg magistracy enacted the very first evangelical reformation ordinance, sanctioning Karlstadt's previously illegal service and banning all private masses. More significantly, they also called for an orderly removal of all religious images from Wittenberg's churches. The Reformation with a capital R had begun in earnest, with Luther nowhere in sight, and it had been made possible by bold acts of civil disobedience.

A precedent had been set, and Karlstadt had to make it known to the world. Within a few days Karlstadt published an enormously influential pamphlet, *On the Abolition of Images, and That There Should Be No Beggars Among Christians*, in which he defended his iconoclastic theology and laid out a program for rapid social change. In this revolutionary text, which was far more incendiary than anything Luther had published to date, Karlstadt warned all civil authorities that they would incur the wrath of God if they failed to take action against idolatry. Linking the reformation of ritual to a redistribution of the church's wealth, Karlstadt proposed an uncompromising interpretation of the Ten Commandments. Whereas Christian theologians had been arguing since the third century that the prohibition of images contained in the second commandment was made null and void by Christ's New Covenant, along with circumcision, dietary restrictions, and other Jewish rituals, Karlstadt proposed that making such a distinction was a gross error:

> Certain image-kissers say: "The Old Law forbids images; the New does not. And we follow the New, not the Old Law." Dear brothers, may God protect you from this heretical statement and prevent you from ever saying it. . . . Why do you not also say: "We want to permit adultery, theft, murder, and so on in churches because those crimes are forbidden in the Old Law?" . . . I say to you that God has forbidden images to no lesser degree and no less expressly than murder, theft, plundering, adultery and the like.[14]

No matter how much Karlstadt agreed with Luther on his *sola fide* and *sola scriptura* principles, this interpretation of the second commandment as still binding on Christians would prove to be an insurmountable difference between the two reformers. At bottom, Karlstadt and Luther were guided by different interpretative or hermeneutical principles. Whereas Luther tended to interpret all of the Bible through the theology of Paul's letters, focusing first and foremost on the *sola fide* principle, Karlstadt approached biblical texts more literally, at face value, guided by a hermeneutic of transcendence that emphasized God's otherness and the chasm between matter and spirit. Karlstadt's God might have been as forgiving as Luther's, but he was much more demanding about the kind of worship he expected. Karlstadt's God hated idolatry because it reversed the cosmic order, placing matter at the same level as spirit and creation at the same level as the creator. "All who truly worship God, worship him in the spirit," argued Karlstadt, "and all who worship God in images, worship in untruth."[15]

Karlstadt's biblical interpretation was also guided by pragmatic social concerns, and a sense of the kingdom of God more utopian than Luther's. One can see this in his argument against religious imagery, which was much more than an attack on the metaphysical error of mixing matter and spirit in worship. Karlstadt hated religious imagery and railed against it because he also saw images as tools of oppression, and as one of the key means through which the clergy kept the laity ignorant. Whereas the church had been claiming since the time of Gregory the Great in the sixth century that images were the *libri pauperum*, or books of the poor—a means to teach the illiterate—Karlstadt argued that the very distinction between poor and rich, literate and illiterate had to be abolished, along with the images that kept such distinctions in place. In principle as well as in practice, then, Karlstadt had a more literal and more pragmatic or socially conscious take on Luther's theology of the priesthood of all believers. Images should be abolished not just because they were against the second commandment, he argued, but also because they were a denial of Christian equality and an obstacle to the laity's access to the Word.

Junker Jorg. While sequestered at Wartburg Castle, Luther had assumed a false identity as the knight George, shedding his clerical garb and growing a full beard. Lucas Cranach the Elder depicts Luther as he appeared when he returned to Wittenberg in 1522, unshaven, to drive out Karlstadt and his followers.

In early February 1522, with Luther still at the Wartburg, the Wittenberg magistracy announced a date on which all images were to be removed from the churches. But Karlstadt and Zwilling preached that the common people had the right to take matters into their own hands when magistrates refused to act against idolatry, and before the order of the magistracy could be put into effect, a mob of Wittenbergers who were upset by the delay stormed the churches and destroyed many images. An aggressive revolutionary precedent was being established by Karlstadt and his followers, and Elector Frederick ordered a halt to all changes. The mayhem frightened and angered Luther enough to force him out of hiding. On 6 March 1522, a bearded Luther showed up in Wittenberg again, dressed as a knight, to reclaim his Reformation. Instantly, all the old rituals and symbols Karlstadt had abolished were made legitimate again. The ruined images could not be replaced or restored as easily as the rituals, but the remaining icons were protected from further harm. Luther did his best to undo Karlstadt's reformation as thoroughly and quickly as possible, reprimanding him in a series of fiery sermons that ultimately stripped Karlstadt of all authority and dignity and forced him to leave town in disgrace, along with Storch, Stübner, and Dreschel, the so-called Zwickau Prophets.

Luther and the Unheavenly Prophets

Outwardly, the fundamental disagreement between Karlstadt and Luther seemed to be over issues of policy rather than theology, but inwardly their disagreement also stemmed from profound theological differences. Luther's first objection focused on policy and tactics: Karlstadt's reform program was disorderly, and it moved too far too quickly, giving offense to those who were weaker in the faith. But Luther hardly spent any time at all in his sermons dealing with this concern. His second objection and the bulk of his attack on Karlstadt is theological, and it is framed in terms of the subject that was at the very center of all of Luther's thinking: that salvation is gained by faith rather than by works. "Faith must not be chained and imprisoned," Luther charged, "nor bound by any ordinance to any work."[16] Focusing on external things and obedience to the Law and insisting that certain actions must be taken was nothing more than a return to legalism of the worst sort. Arguing from this central vantage point, Luther thus lumped Karlstadt and all iconoclasts together with the "Romanists," as proponents of works-righteousness. In so doing, Luther completely ignored Karlstadt's metaphysical concerns about the nature of worship and its place in the Christian life, and in the process, he also claimed to trump Karlstadt's interpretation of the Bible. All of Luther's attacks on Karlstadt from this point forward would be centered on this theological argument. But there was one more dimension to the disagreement: the personal one. At a very basic level, Luther resented Karlstadt for usurping his place. "If you were going to begin something and make me responsible for it . . . you could have consulted me," Luther thundered from the pulpit. "I was not so far away that you could not reach me with a letter, whereas not the slightest communication was sent to me."[17]

Luther would interpret what Karlstadt had attempted as a betrayal, and as the work of the devil, and he would spend many years wrangling with his former colleague, speaking ill of him to anyone who might listen. "Doctor Andreas Karlstadt has deserted us, and on top of that has become our worst enemy," Luther would say. Warning others to stay away from him, he would add:

> Dr. Karlstadt and his spirits replace the highest with the lowest, the best with the least, the first with the last. Yet he would be considered the greatest spirit of all, he who has devoured the Holy Spirit feathers and all.[18]

More than that, Luther would forever associate Karlstadt and the Zwickau Prophets with the devil and brand them all as *Schwärmer*, a German word that served as his shorthand for *fanatic, fiend, maniac, enthusiast, zealot, demoniac,* and *madman* all at once. It was the perfect highly charged name for all those false brethren like Karlstadt who agreed with Luther about scripture being the sole authority over all Christians, but disagreed with him about how to use it as a guide for reform. In 1525, Luther would take on all the *Schwärmer* in a very long treatise titled *Against the Heavenly Prophets in the Matter of Images and the Sacraments*, in which he would deal with them with utter contempt, as he had with the devil himself, whom he believed they represented. By then he would have many worse spirits than Karlstadt to exorcize from the earth, but he would still demonize Karlstadt and his followers and address them with the same scatological disdain he reserved for the devil:

> They boast of possessing the Spirit, more than the apostles, and yet for more than three years now have secretly prowled about and flung around their shit. . . . He [Karlstadt] is a treacherous, secret devil who sneaks around in corners until he has done his damage and spread his poison.[19]

A significant rift had opened up among the opponents of the Romanists. Though Luther had chased a rival out of Wittenberg, he could no more silence Karlstadt than could the pope, for the circumstances that gave Luther his freedom also gave Karlstadt his. Squeezed out of Wittenberg, Karlstadt became pastor of Orlamünde in 1523, a town in Thuringia, about one hundred miles southwest of Wittenberg, and there he established a model community that welcomed all his reforms, including a democratic church constitution and a system of poor relief. Expelled from Orlamünde at Luther's instigation, Karlstadt spent the remainder of his life moving from place to place, becoming ever more steeped in the teachings of the medieval Rhineland mystics, those disciples of Meister Eckhart (1260–1327) who believed that at the deepest core of their souls, all humans possess a divine spark that can be reached only through a process of self-abandonment, or *Gelassenheit*. For a brief while Karlstadt even lived as a peasant and small-time merchant, practicing the total abandonment to God that he preached, asking everyone to call him "Brother Andrew." Luther would mock him mercilessly for trying to reinvent monasticism.

What think you now? Is it not a fine new spiritual humility? Wearing a felt hat and a gray garb, not wanting to be called Doctor, but Brother Andrew and dear neighbor, as another peasant, subject to the magistrate of Orlamünde and obedient as an ordinary citizen. Thus with self-chosen humility and servility, which God does not command, he wants to be seen and praised as a remarkable Christian, as though Christian behavior consisted of such external hocus pocus.[20]

But Karlstadt never became a recluse or vanished from view, no matter how marginalized or mystical he became. Eventually he returned to university teaching among those who inherited part of his legacy, the Swiss Reformed Protestants of Zurich and Basel. Author of ninety texts, printed and reprinted in 213 editions, Karlstadt never ceased writing and publishing after his expulsion from Wittenberg, even though his output decreased. His peak period of influence was definitely between 1518 and 1525, when he was the second most popular evangelical author, surpassed only by Luther when it came to numbers of German titles and editions. But in Karlstadt's case, as in many others, quality would matter a lot more than quantity.

One of Karlstadt's post-Wittenberg texts topped all others in terms of influence: *Whether One Ought to Behave Peacefully and Spare the Feelings of the Simple in Matters That Concern God's Will*. Published in Basel in 1524, this impassioned counterblast against Luther was an eloquent exposition of revolutionary iconoclastic theory in which the responsibility for outward change was placed directly in the hands of the laity. Karlstadt's argument was as simple as it was extreme: no community can afford to delay in conforming to God's commands, and neither can any individual. Whereas Luther had argued that reforms must always be moderate and tempered to the spiritual development of the weaker members of a community, Karlstadt argued the reverse. Those weak in faith threatened the entire community if their lack of conformity with God's commands prevented a full reformation of faith and morals: "I ask whether one should not stop coveting another's goods until the others follow? May one steal until the thieves stop stealing?"[21] Focusing on the question of images, Karlstadt argued that every believer and every community had to act on its own against idolatry. Defending the right of his fellow Orlamünders to smash images and abolish the Mass, Karlstadt asserted that they could not afford to wait for the "guzzlers at Wittenberg" to agree with them. As he put it, everyone, regardless of their social station, "is obliged, if he loves God and his neighbor, to take from the foolish their dreadful and offensive things irrespective of the fact that they therefore become angry, howl, and curse."[22] Allowing idols to be worshiped was no different from allowing an infant to play with a sharp knife, he suggested. Those who know the danger of idols need to spring into action, no matter what, and save the simpler folk from peril. If these simpler folk cry and throw a tantrum when they lose their rotten idols, so be it. "The time will come," he added, "when they who now curse and damn us will thank us."[23]

Karlstadt had conceived of a fully revolutionary defense for iconoclasm in particular and for religious and social change in general: God's law was above any human law and above neighborliness, so magistrates or neighbors who opposed change had to be ignored. Revolution was not just the right of every Christian, but also his or her duty. "Where Christians rule," he argued, "there they should consider no government, but rather freely on their own hew down and throw down what is contrary to God, even without preaching."[24] Karlstadt has yet to receive the credit he truly deserves for being the first to articulate this very modern concept and for giving rise, directly and indirectly, to innumerable acts of defiance, both great and small. When King Charles I of England mounted the scaffold on 30 January 1649, to be beheaded by Puritan revolutionaries, he probably did not know that the spirit of Karlstadt guided his executioner's hand. But if history were as fair and wise as most historians think that they themselves are, Karlstadt ought to have been on the deposed king's mind at that awful moment, as someone who deserved to be cursed or forgiven—or maybe both.

In the long run, Karlstadt's abortive reformation would bear fruit elsewhere, among both the Radical and the Reformed Protestant traditions, and his legacy would eventually be a touchstone for rebellions in Germany, Switzerland, France, the Netherlands, Scotland, England and far-off North America. Karlstadt would also leave a lasting impact on Luther and help determine the shape of his reformation. As is often the case, one's enemies have as much of a role in forging one's identity as one's allies and friends. Enemies make drastic and unpleasant choices necessary. Karlstadt and the Zwickau Prophets had forced Luther, a rebel and heretic in the eyes of the Romanists, to become a reactionary in the eyes of some of his admirers and followers. And in 1522 the worst was yet to come as Luther stared down the *Schwärmer*. The most treacherous enemy of all on his left flank, the arch-zealot or *Überschwärmer* Thomas Müntzer had yet to join forces with rebellious peasants in the name of Christian freedom and the kingdom of God and give all Luther biographers a most painful chapter to write.

Thomas Müntzer, mentor to the Zwickau prophets, was slightly younger than Luther. He was ordained a priest around 1514, and spent some time at Wittenberg in 1517–1519, where he came to know Luther, Melanchthon, and Karlstadt. Profoundly influenced by his reading of John Tauler (1300–1361), one of those Rhineland mystics that Karlstadt also loved, Müntzer developed a very intense conviction of his own divine inspiration and prophetic mission, which he interpreted in apocalyptic terms. In May 1520, Müntzer obtained a preaching post at Zwickau, which he accepted with an ominous flourish, signing his contract as *Tomas Munczer qui pro veritate militat in mundo*, or "he who fights for truth in the world."[25] At Zwickau, he quickly gained a following and alienated the town authorities with his extreme claims. Expelled from Zwickau, Müntzer went to Bohemia, where he made contact with Hussites and became even more extreme in his apocalyptic views. By the end of 1521, he was openly proclaiming his role as prophet of the End Times in Prague and insisting that direct revelations from the Holy Spirit were a necessary supplement to biblical authority. "All true pastors must have revelations," he argued.[26]

Müntzer's rhetoric was unrestrained, and filled with invective. Convinced that God spoke through prophets who, like himself, had been tried in the mystical furnace of spiritual self-abandonment, he mocked the "donkey fart doctors of theology" and "whoremongering," "scrotum-like doctors of theology" and "diarrhea-makers" who led the world astray with their "inexperienced Bible" and the "mere words of scripture." Raging against the blind "straw doctors" and their "twaddle," Müntzer proclaimed his own mystical calling:

> The clergy have never been able to discover, nor will they ever, the beneficial tribulations and useful abyss which the providential spirit meets as it empties itself. . . . In brief, each person must receive the holy spirit in a sevenfold way, otherwise he neither hears nor understands the living God.[27]

Even more extreme was his distinction between "the elect" and "the godless." For Müntzer, all spirit-inspired, suffering mystics were "the elect," and they could be found only among the poor and downtrodden. All who lived comfortably and defended the status quo were "the damned," or "the godless," and their punishment was near. Müntzer minced no words when speaking about the apocalyptic dimensions of this distinction and of his role in the unfolding of divine history:

> The elect must clash with the damned, and the power of the damned must yield before that of the elect. . . . Oh how ripe are the rotten apples, . . . the time of the harvest is at hand! Thus God himself has appointed me for his harvest. I have made my sickle sharp.[28]

Müntzer returned to Germany in early 1522, as Luther was regaining control. He paid a brief visit to Wittenberg and wandered about the area until March 1523, teaching and preaching, stirring up unrest, and worrying Luther. Somehow, Müntzer managed to become pastor of a church in the town of Allstedt, about eighty miles west of Wittenberg, without the Elector Frederick's approval. Immediately, the prophet reformed the town's worship, instituting the very first fully vernacular liturgy of the Protestant Reformation (Karlstadt's eucharistic prayer had retained some of the Latin). Very quickly, Müntzer's new worship service became immensely popular, obviously fulfilling some great need. Allstedt's *Deutsche Messe*, or German Mass began to attract worshipers from near and far, and the town rapidly became an anti-Romanist and anti-Wittenbergian pilgrimage site of sorts. True to form, Müntzer also began to turn Allstedt into a hotbed of apocalyptic fervor. In June 1524, Luther published *An Open Letter to the Princes of Saxony Concerning the Rebellious Spirit*, in which he blasted away at Müntzer's prophetic claims and called upon the civil authorities to drive him away, reminding the princes that it was their "obligation and duty to maintain order . . . and to prevent rebellion."[29] The conflict between Luther and Müntzer now escalated into a tragic confrontation.

Müntzer's relations with secular rulers were equally strained, and became even worse after some of his followers set fire to a nearby pilgrimage chapel, at Mallerbach,

Apocalyptic avenger. Thomas Müntzer, revolutionary prophet of the end of the world, bitter foe of Martin Luther, idolized by the communist regime of the former East Germany on its currency.

in March 1524. To defend himself and his disciples, Müntzer preached a sermon on 13 July in the presence of Duke John of Saxony and his son John Frederick, the heirs of Elector Frederick the Wise, that could easily be ranked as one of the most inappropriate and impolitic homilies of all time. Interpreting passages from the apocalyptic book of Daniel, Müntzer told the princes that he had been appointed by God as their prophet, and urged them to join his cause and to wield their swords against the godless. Focusing on the approaching apocalypse, Müntzer called on the princes to slay the ungodly, for, as he put it to them twice, "the godless have no right to life except that which the elect decide to grant them."[30] Then he issued a stern prophetic warning: if the princes would not fight on God's side, their swords would be taken from them. "Rejoice, you true friends of God," said Müntzer, "that the enemies of the cross have crapped their courage into their pants."[31]

It did not take very long for Müntzer to be chased out of Allstedt by his princes. Luther's *Open Letter*, coupled with the sermon they had heard with their own ears and news of an armed league being created by Müntzer among his followers, convinced them that the prophet had to go. Müntzer's parting shot, as he fled Allstedt and once again took to the road, was an incandescently angry response to Luther's charges, published at Nuremberg in November 1524, *A Highly Provoked Defense and Answer to the Spiritless, Soft-Living Flesh at Wittenberg, Who Has Most Lamentably Befouled Pitiable Christianity in a Perverted Way by His Theft of Holy Scripture.* The long title captured the gist of Müntzer's disagreement with Luther succinctly, but it could not contain all of his anger, which seemed boundless. Convinced of his own prophetic office, positive that the Final Judgment was around the corner, and pushed to the brink of madness—or perhaps over it—by what he perceived to be his own society's great sins and failures, Müntzer pounced on Luther with all the ferocity he could muster, and in the process, he surpassed Luther in the forging of insults. Ablaze with rage, Müntzer found it hard to mention Luther's name, so hard, in fact, that all he could do is spew forth a torrent of crass epithets against him:

Doctor Liar . . . Doctor Mockery . . . Brother Soft-Life . . . the godless flesh at Wittenberg . . . Malicious black raven . . . Father pussyfoot . . . poor flatterer . . . godless one . . . overlearned scoundrel . . . arch-scoundrel . . . new pope . . . hellhound . . . clever snake . . . sly fox . . . arch-heathen . . . arch-devil . . . crook . . . rabid, burning fox . . . ambassador of the devil.

For Müntzer, the mystic and prophet who had placed himself in league with the suffering poor of the world, Luther seemed worthy of total contempt simply for siding with the rich and powerful. "Your flesh is like that of an ass, and you would have to be cooked slowly," he told Luther. "You would make a tough dish for your milk-sop friends."[32] Luther was "totally incapable of shame,"[33] and also incapable of embracing genuine suffering. "It astonishes one how this shameless monk can claim to be terribly persecuted, there [at Wittenberg] with his good Malvasian wine and his whores' banquets."[34] Moreover, Luther was theologically wrong, and a hypocrite, especially in regard to sin: "You want to make God responsible for the fact that you are a poor sinner and a venomous little worm with your shitty humility."[35] Worst of all, Müntzer concluded, Luther was wrong about the Bible and about the role that divine inspiration and the prophetic office have to play in its interpretation:

> Luther makes a mockery and an utterly useless babble out of the divine word. . . . The godless one [Luther] drags Paul around with such an idiotic comprehension that even to a child it becomes as ridiculous as a puppet show. Nevertheless Luther wants to be the cleverest fellow on earth and he boasts that he has no equal.[36]

Müntzer knew that Luther was so powerful by now that to go against him was dangerous. In fact, that power of Luther's was the very focus of his anger. He was also keenly aware of Luther's tactics, and especially of the way in which Luther was most like him, always quick to demonize his opponents. "With your pen you have slandered and shamed me before many honest people," complained Müntzer. "With your vicious mouth you have publicly called me a devil. Indeed you do the same to all your opponents."[37] But the wandering prophet chased out of Allstedt was too fired up to let anyone stop him, or to allow the last word to Luther and his "donkey fart doctors of theology" at Wittenberg.[38] A prophecy was embedded in the long rambling text of Müntzer's *Highly Provoked Defense*, and it was a warning everyone should have heeded: "I warn you that the peasants may soon strike out."[39] As it turned out, that would be the only prophecy of Müntzer's ever to come true.

Luther and the Peasants

When the peasants rose up in 1524, Luther predictably said, "It is the devil's work that they are at."[40] Many in Germany, however, blamed Luther himself for putting the devils in control of the peasants. The question of Luther's responsibility has been a matter of debate since Luther's day, principally because the participants in this struggle invoked

Luther's name in one way or another. Given that Luther had led a rebellion against the pope and his church, it was inevitable that all rebellions would be linked to him, especially by his opponents. But that the rebel-turned-Reformer was shaped as much by his loathing of mayhem as by his rejection of Rome is key for understanding Luther and his Reformation.

The German Peasants' War of 1524–1525 was one of the most significant events of the early modern period and the largest mass uprisings in the history of Europe before the French Revolution in 1789. It is also an event that is still being reinterpreted. We now know that the traditional name for this rebellion, German Peasants' War, which was used for centuries, is as misleading as the term *Holy Roman Empire*, for several reasons. First, although the uprising occurred mostly in German-speaking lands, it also spilled over into other areas such as Alsace, Franche-Comté, South Tyrol, Carniola, and East Prussia, areas where German was not spoken. Second, although it is true that many of the rebels were peasants, the uprising was not limited to rural areas or devoted simply to agrarian concerns; this uprising also swept through towns, cities, and mining areas. Third, it is called a war because the armies of the landlords fought with bands of rebels, but this uprising was more than mere skirmishes and massacres; it could easily be considered a social revolution that sputtered and failed.[41] Given, then, that the term *Bauernkrieg*, or "Peasants' War," is so misleading, historians have begun to call it the Revolution of the Common Man, or the Revolution of 1525. In the communist world, behind the so-called iron curtain, Marxist historians preferred to speak of the Early Bourgeois Revolution, or *frühburgerliche Revolution*, and to interpret this uprising as the first great manifestation of the class struggle in modern history. For Marxist historians, in fact, the *real* Reformation was not the religious upheaval initiated by Luther, but rather the Early Bourgeois Revolution. In their interpretation, Luther and all the other clerics who worked with the status quo simply articulated yet another way for the elite to exploit the workers, for all that clerics can do is supply a different strain of opium for the masses. Consequently, for Marxists, the great figure of this time was not Luther, the landlords' lackey, but Thomas Müntzer, the communist visionary.[42]

The prominent role played by religion in this uprising cannot be attributed solely to the upheaval sparked by Luther, but by the same token, religion cannot be totally disassociated from it. Peasant uprisings were nothing new: they were part and parcel of medieval history, and some of them, such as the one that shook England in 1381, were similarly large in scope. That peasant insurgencies should touch upon religion was nothing new either. Because religion was closely interwoven with all aspects of daily life and clerics were often prominent landlords, it was inevitable that uprisings could appeal to religion or take issue with corruption in the church or perceived clerical abuses. Nonetheless, the most prominent feature of such previous uprisings was their focus on social, political, and economic questions.

Agrarian discontent had been brewing in Germany for a full century before Luther came on the scene, and small-scale peasant insurgencies had plagued some regions, especially southern Germany. Between 1493 and 1517, the Bundschuh movement had already articulated many of the demands that would surface again in 1524. The Bundschuh uprisings were all loosely linked and highly localized insurgencies in southwestern Germany that rallied under the symbol of the peasant's heavy rustic shoe. Under this banner, agrarian and urban rebels fought for social and political reforms, seeking to rid themselves of high taxes, political oppression, seemingly arbitrary courts, serfdom, restrictions on hunting and fishing, and other such temporal problems. Yet clerical corruption was also a target of protest, and many a Bundschuh flag also included some religious imagery. Uprisings took place at Niklashausen in 1476, Alsace in 1493, Bruchsal and Untergrombach in 1502, Breisgau in 1513, and along the Upper Rhine in 1517, on the eve of Luther's appearance. All of these rebellions were quickly crushed, and their leaders executed.

The vast majority of the peasants' grievances stemmed from changes that had come about gradually in the fifteenth century, as the old feudal system began to give way to the consolidation of power and centralization of the early modern state, and as hard currency replaced exchange in kind in an ever-expanding economy. By 1515, in varying degrees, some of these changes came to be viewed as oppressive by those at the bottom of German society. Growing bureaucracies were financed largely through increased levies on the land, and the new taxes usually ended up being borne by the peasants and other laborers. In addition, ancient German laws and local customs, which created a legal patchwork that paralleled the intricately confusing map of the empire, were being universally replaced with Roman law. It was a painful process, which could easily seem arbitrary or unjust to those who were caught up in it. Roman law favored private property over common rights. Consequently, other ancient freedoms were also quickly disappearing, such as the right to hunt or fish anywhere, or to collect firewood in any forest, or to graze one's herds on common meadows. The change in law also affected serfs adversely, for Roman law dealt only with slaves and free men, and therefore invested serfs with a status closer to slavery than to freedom. Whereas the feudal system had been based on reciprocity and mutual agreements between lord and tenant, the new Romanizing landlords tended to be more autocratic, setting terms without their tenants' consent. Increasingly, landlords had begun to claiming ownership of the serfs on their lands, as fixed possessions not much different from livestock, rocks, trees, and streams. Arguing that the ability to restrict movement and marriages was their due, feudal lords had seriously curtailed the rights of serfs throughout Germany; serfs up until then had been able to migrate and choose their landlord, and to marry outside of their lords' territory. To make things worse, economic changes had driven those who worked the land further into servitude. Cash poor in a cash-based economy, restricted largely or exclusively to their crops and livestock for income in an economy where those who tilled the soil never set the prices, and mindful that their parents and grandparents had not been so dependent on cash, the peasants could easily imagine the past as a much better age.

The German uprising of 1524–1525 was not a well-coordinated war or revolution, but rather a series of localized struggles, many of which were spontaneous. The rebels were not necessarily poor peasants, and those who articulated the grievances were often prosperous landholders themselves, or city dwellers. All in all, their demands encompassed every sphere of life, but they tended to focus on gaining greater influence in society and on closing the gaps that they perceived between their real economic power and their downgraded social and political status. The so-called Peasants' War began in the Black Forest in southern Germany on 30 May 1524, when tenants of the abbey of St. Blasien rose up against their clerical landlord. From this area close to the Swiss border, the tumult began to spread to Swabia and Allgäu, where literate leaders formulated very specific demands and formed alliances among themselves, such as the Christian Union of Upper Swabia. From the very start, in many of the lists of grievances, appeals were made directly to the Word of God and to Christian freedom. Explicit demands were also made for the reshaping of all of society according to "divine law" and other very Lutheran-sounding gospel principles. The Swabian rebels who drafted a constitution for their Christian Union, for instance, displayed their Lutheran sympathies quite openly, appealing expressly "to the holy gospel and the divine word," asking for reforms such as the following:

> Pastors and vicars should be requested in a friendly way to preach only the holy gospel. And the ones who want to do this should be given what is needed to live in moderation. But those who do not do this ought to be replaced with others.[43]

As if to make their religious allegiance as clear as possible, the authors added a list of the theologians they deemed competent to determine the substance of divine law—a list that could serve as a who's who of leading anti-Romanist Reformers, with Luther at the very top. The Memmingen Constitution was but one of many local lists of grievances crafted by the rebels. The lists are very similar in scope, and all reveal an overwhelming preoccupation with "worldly" concerns—as Luther would see it—rather than with religion. Nonetheless, an obviously Lutheran bent can be easily detected. The most widely circulated of these petitions—and the one that provided the template for most of the uprisings of 1525—was the one drawn up by another group of Upper Swabian peasants in Memmingen, which was originally titled *Just and Fundamental Articles of All the Peasantry and Tenants of Spiritual and Temporal Powers, by Whom They Think Themselves Oppressed*. This manifesto, which is better known as *The Twelve Articles*, was a clear summation of the frustrations of the "common man" and of the rebellion's aims. Authored by Sebastian Lotzer, a furrier, and Christoph Schappeler, a Lutheran minister, *The Twelve Articles* poured forth from printing presses all over the empire in the early spring of 1525—in twenty-five different editions totaling more than twenty-five thousand copies—spelling out for everyone how the rebels hoped to bring an end to oppression and restore their traditional political and economic rights. Conscious of the fact that many of their opponents were associating "the new gospel" with lawlessness and violence, the authors of *The Twelve Articles* argued that it was the landlords who were the real cause of all the turmoil, because they had departed from divine law. The uprising was not being caused by the gospel, then, but by those who failed to live up to the gospel. The rebels appealed to the Bible as the highest authority of all, demanding the following improvements:

1. The right of every community to appoint and remove their own clergy. This request had an additional Lutheran-sounding proviso: "This elected pastor should preach the gospel to us purely and clearly, without any additional human doctrine or commandments."

2. Abolishing or readjusting certain tithes, especially on cattle (a tithe being a 10 percent tax imposed by church or state), arguing that God created cattle freely for all humans, according to Genesis 1:30, the rebels argued, "We regard it as an improper tithe which has been contrived by people."

3. The abolition of serfdom. Arguing that Christ had redeemed all humans equally, the rebels demanded: "As true and just Christians, you will also gladly release us from serfdom, or show us from the gospel that we should be serfs."

4. Freedom to fish and hunt on landlords' estates. The rebels aimed to return to ancient German custom by way of the Bible, arguing that such restrictions were selfish and "not compatible with the word of God."

5. Freedom to gather firewood in landlords' forests. Once again, ancient Germanic rights were reclaimed in Christian terms, according to "our knowledge of brotherly love and holy scripture."

6. A reevaluation of all services due to feudal lords. Arguing that their forefathers served their lords only "according to the Word of God," the rebels asked to be shown "gracious understanding" concerning their feudal duties.

7. A stricter observance of all agreements between landlord and tenants. Demanding the abolition of arbitrary demands and a return to the mutuality of feudal arrangements, the rebels argued: "Lords should not force or compel their peasants, seeking to get more services or other dues from them, without payment."

8. An equitable and just restructuring of rent assessments. Citing Matthew 10, the rebels argued that "every laborer is worth his wage."

9. A return to customary (German) law: "Burdened by the great outrage that new laws are constantly being made . . . it is our conviction that we should be punished according to ancient written law."

10. The return of previously common fields seized by landlords. Arguing that land that had once been held in common by the community could never become private property, the rebels asked for a "benevolent and brotherly agreement" between lords and tenants on this issue.

11. Abolition of the death tax: "We will never accept that the property of widows and orphans should be taken from them so shamelessly, contrary to God and honor."

12. That the legality of all of these requests be judged according to the Bible alone, and that any or all be rejected if found to be against scripture. Convinced that all their demands were "contained in God's Word," and that their interpretation of the Bible was beyond questioning, the rebels naively offered up this very Lutheran *sola scriptura* article as their trump card.

Without a doubt, the most revolutionary of these articles were the ones that demanded the abolition of serfdom and a thorough reform of tithing. In many areas like Upper Swabia, serfdom was an essential component of the social, political, and economic structure—so essential, in fact, that one could reduce the situation to a simple formula: no serfdom, no lordship. Doing away with the small tithe on cattle and restructuring the distribution of the large tithe was just as threatening to the status quo. In the area of Swabia, tithes provided landlords and urban welfare institutions with one-third to one-half of their income. Any change in tithing could easily lead to a disastrous financial crisis. The other demands were not as revolutionary, but they could be seen as equally threatening, and as derived strictly from religion. Although the "secular" or "worldly" nature of most of these demands is prominent, and in keeping with late medieval grievance

Faksimile des Titelblattes einer Flugschrift von 1525, enthaltend die zwölf Artikel der Bauern.

The revolution of the common man. Title page of the Twelve Articles of the Upper Swabian peasants. Armed with crude weapons, the rebels caused mayhem but had little real chance of success.

lists, what makes them momentous is their constant appeal to the Bible and divine law. Prior peasant uprisings had touched on similar grievances, appealing to ancient custom or law or even natural law or reason. Now, in the wake of Luther's *sola scriptura* revolt against Rome, the peasants and artisans were appealing not only to Germanic customs, but also to the Bible, and asking for changes that they thought were a return to ancient Christian practices, such as the power to appoint and remove clergy. Much to Luther's chagrin, the peasants had explicitly involved him in their insurgency, dragging in the Bible too. Also much to his horror, the peasant uprising hit home all too soon.

In the spring of 1525 rebellions sprang up in other parts of Germany, most notably in Franconia, the Rhine Palatinate, Alsace, Austria, Thuringia, and Saxony. Along the Lower Rhine, the movement became increasingly urban, involving townsmen and artisans. Calls for reform in the towns included demands for greater participation in the town councils, less restrictive membership in the guilds, and the subjection of the clergy to civil authorities. In Thuringia and Saxony, Luther's home turf, none other than Thomas Müntzer assumed a leading role, adding his apocalyptic fervor to the movement. And among those who also joined the peasants in Thuringia was another of the *Schwärmer* expelled from Wittenberg, Nicholas Storch, leader of the Zwickau Prophets. The presence of Müntzer and Storch confirmed the obvious for Luther: hell had emptied out, and all of the demons were now inside the German peasants, guiding their every move. Even worse, Luther saw himself as the chief target of this great upheaval:

> I see well that the devil, who has not been able to destroy me through the pope, now seeks to exterminate me and swallow me up by means of the bloodthirsty prophets of murder and spirits of rebellion that are among you [the peasants].[44]

The Revolution of the Common Man may have not been very well organized, but it was bloody and costly. Pillaging, burning, and slaughtering were as much a part of the uprisings as the drafting of grievances. Given that the brute force available to the landlords far exceeded anything the rebels could muster, the war turned out to be a one-sided conflict for the most part: heavy artillery and disciplined soldiers could always make mincemeat of hordes of peasants armed with relatively few firearms and the crudest of weapons. But the ragtag armies of the common man did manage to get their licks in here and there, inciting their opponents to counterattack without restraint. Monasteries, castles, manor houses, and anyone who defended them were targets for the rebels, and many suffered greatly at their hands. The rebels themselves were the prime targets for the landlords and their armies, and they were mowed down by the thousands. Caught right in the middle of the fray was Luther himself, the most aggrieved party of all, who had no weapon to wield other than his pen.

Luther's first response to the crisis came in April 1525, in a treatise titled *Admonition to Peace: A Reply to the Twelve Articles of the Peasants in Swabia*. Seeking to hold the highest possible moral ground, Luther reprimanded both the landlords and the rebels: "Because both of you are wrong and both of you would avenge and defend yourselves, both of you will destroy yourselves and God will use one knave to flog another."[45] Blaming both parties was a risky move on Luther's part, but by now he was used to all sorts of risks. Upbraiding the powerful with rhetoric that was fully laced with anti-Romanist strains, he charged:

> We have no one on earth to thank for this mischievous rebellion except you princes and lords, and especially you blind bishops and mad priests and monks, whose hearts are hardened, even to the present day, and who do not cease to rage and rave against the holy Gospel, although you know that it is true, and that you cannot refute it. Besides, in your temporal governments, you do nothing but flay and rob your subjects, in order that you may lead a life of splendor and pride, until the poor common people can bear it no longer. The sword is at your throats, but you think yourselves so firm in the saddle that no one can unhorse you.[46]

Luther had equally harsh words for the rebels, whom he accused of misinterpreting the gospel and the relationship between the flesh and the spirit. Christian freedom was not at all something "carnal" or "fleshly," Luther argued, but rather a purely spiritual principle. Stressing this dualism of flesh and spirit, Luther accused the rebels of focusing too much on their bodies and their property, and of seeking to cover their selfish enterprise under a pious veneer when, in fact, their aims were purely materialistic. Focusing most intensely on the third article, which called for the abolition of serfdom, Luther undercut all of the rebels' demands by means of a dualistic rhetoric of the most extreme sort. Christian freedom, he charged, was not at all some democratic or egalitarian principle, but a purely spiritual one that posed no challenge to the social and political status quo. Calling for the abolition of serfdom was wrong because any such demand was based on a "carnal" reading of the Holy Scriptures. The Bible did not advocate political or social equality. "The gospel does not become involved in the affairs of this world, " he huffed, "but speaks of our life in the world in terms of suffering, injustice, the cross, patience, and contempt for this life and temporal wealth."[47] Luther asked: did not Abraham and other patriarchs and prophets have slaves? His final word on the anti-serfdom article was brutally clear and unabashedly elitist:

> This article is dead against the gospel. It is a piece of robbery, by which every man takes from his lord the body which has become his lord's property. . . . This article would make all men equal, and turn the spiritual kingdom of Christ into a worldly external kingdom.[48]

Few other passages in Luther's works spell out as clearly his dualistic thinking and his conservatism and authoritarianism, and here, during the Peasants' War, we see his political theology and applied ethics at work in the toughest of circumstances. Luther's logic was as paradoxical as his theology and his behavior. Guided in his thinking by stark dualities and the coincidence of opposites, Luther accepted violence not just as inevitable, but also as sometimes necessary and even as good. By 1525, he had given definitive shape

Robbing and murdering hordes. Peasants sack a monastery in Weissenau. Luther denounced the rebellious peasants as "mad dogs" and called for their extermination.

to a dualistic understanding of Christians' place in the world, which was rooted in the theology of St. Augustine, especially in his magnum opus, *The City of God*. As Augustine distinguished between humans who belonged to the city of God, whose lives were given over to love of God and neighbor, and those who belonged to the city of man, who wallowed in self-love, Luther distinguished between the kingdom of God and the kingdom of the world. As Luther saw it, Christians inhabited two realms simultaneously. Just as they were *simul justus et peccator*, that is, redeemed from their sins but never fully sinless, Christians were never fully freed from entanglement in the nasty business of their fallen world. This meant that Christians sometimes had to bloody their hands because love of neighbor demanded it.

This enigmatic perspective on Christian ethics guided Luther during the uprisings of 1524–1525, and helps explain his response to it, from start to finish, as he made clear in his *Admonition*:

> There are two kingdoms, one the kingdom of God, the other the kingdom of the world. . . . Anyone who knows how to distinguish rightly between these two kingdoms will certainly not be offended by my little book [*Against the Robbing and Murdering Hordes of Peasants*]. . . . God's kingdom is a kingdom of grace and mercy, not of wrath and punishment. In it there is only forgiveness, consideration for one another, love,

service, the doing of good, peace, joy, etc. But the kingdom of the world is a kingdom of wrath and severity. In it there is only punishment, repression, judgment, and condemnation to restrain the wicked and protect the good.[49]

The bulk of Luther's *Admonition* is devoted to scolding the rebels rather than the landlords, and to pointing out that secular authority ought not be challenged. Luther was succinct: "The fact that the rulers are wicked and unjust does not excuse tumult and rebellion," he charged. "For to punish wickedness does not belong to everybody, but to the worldly rulers who bear the sword." The peasant rebels were actually doing "much more wrong" than their abusive masters by trying to usurp their lords' God-given authority. Luther's ultimate admonition to the rebels was as monastic and mystical as it was politically conservative:

> Suffering, suffering; cross, cross! This, and nothing else, is the Christian law! . . . O worthless Christians! . . . No matter how right you are, it is not for a Christian to appeal to law, or to fight, but rather to suffer wrong and endure evil; there is no other way.

Forget about social and political change, argued the champion of Christian freedom, "a worldly kingdom cannot stand unless there is in it an inequality of persons."[50] Luther was not necessarily inconsistent at this point, given the central place of paradox in his thinking, but it does seem as if his theology had certainly proved itself too highly paradoxical for the mind of the so-called common man.

Luther's *Admonition* could not stop the violence from spiraling out of control. In May 1525, as uprisings spread all over Germany and the violence came ever closer to Wittenberg—along with Müntzer's unwanted presence—Luther penned and published the most controversial text of his entire life, *Against the Robbing and Murdering Hordes of Peasants*, a very brief but exceedingly blunt text that flew off printers' and booksellers' shelves in twenty-one different editions. Müntzer casts a long shadow over this pamphlet. Two months earlier, on 22 February 1525, Müntzer had returned to nearby Mühlhausen and led a revolt that established a communistic utopia. In addition, Müntzer had also created the revolutionary Eternal League of God to help the uprising spread throughout the area. At Allstedt, his former pastorate, he preached a fiery sermon at the end of April that gives us a glimpse, centuries later, of what Luther so feared and despised:

> The time has come, the evil-doers are running like scared dogs! Alert the brothers. . . . Go to it, go to it, go to it! Show no pity. . . . Pay no attention to the cries of the godless. They will entreat you ever so warmly, they will whimper and wheedle like children. Show no pity, as God has commanded. . . . Go to it, go to it, while the fire is hot! Don't let your sword grow cold, don't let it hang down limply! Hammer away ding-dong on the anvil of Nimrod, cast down their tower to the ground![51]

Lashing out against such rhetoric and "the work of the archdevil who rules at Mülhausen, and does nothing else than stir up robbery, murder, and bloodshed," Luther unleashed all of his pent-up frustration on the rebels.[52] Arguing that rebellion was a much worse crime than murder, because it is always "like a great fire which attacks and lays waste a whole land," Luther proposed that all rebels were "outside of the law of God and Empire." The only right thing to do with a rebel, said Luther, is to slay him. To make sure no one missed his point, Luther issued a chilling call to arms that was ironically similar to those that had once been issued to crusaders, with promises of spiritual rewards:

> Let everyone who can smite, slay, and stab, secretly and openly, remembering that nothing can be more poisonous, hurtful, or devilish than a rebel. It is just as when one must kill a mad dog: if you do not strike him, he will strike you, and a whole land with you. . . . Stab, smite, slay, whoever can. If you die in doing it, well for you! A more blessed death can never be yours, for you die in obeying the divine Word and commandment in Romans 13, and in loving service of your neighbor, whom you are rescuing from the bonds of hell and of the devil.[53]

By the time this tirade against the rebels appeared in print, the lords had already begun to massacre the rebels, and the bad timing made it seem as if Luther was simply adding fuel to the fire. Whether or not Luther's harsh words emboldened the landlords to be more brutal than they would have otherwise been remains an open question. What we do know for certain is that the landlords did precisely as Luther suggested, stabbing, smiting, and slaying about seventy thousand to one hundred thousand rebels, most of them peasants. Precise figures are unavailable, but descriptions of the slaughter abound. In Thuringia, at the battle of Frankenhausen, more than five thousand peasants were killed in a single day by the armies of George of Saxony, Henry of Brunswick, and Philip of Hesse. Among those captured alive after that battle was none other than Thomas Müntzer, who had led his army of "elect" rebels into the fray after proclaiming that a rainbow that had appeared in the sky was a sign of God's favor. Müntzer was tortured and beheaded. Luther did not exactly rejoice at his death, but saw it as a fitting end, and something of a blessing.

Luther considered all the rebel deaths justifiable, and he made no apologies. As he saw it, he had helped save Germany from ruin, and from the devil. "From the start I had two fears," Luther admitted: "If the peasants became lords, the devil would become abbot; if these tyrants became lords, the devil's mother would become abbess."[54] Luther harbored no illusions about the lords: they, too, were blameworthy. But the important distinction he made was this: the rebels were the devil himself, whereas the lords were the mother who held back the devil. The rebels deserved no pity, as Luther saw it, even if his critics howled. As the fighting subsided and the rotting carrion was cleared from the battlefields, Luther acknowledged in yet another treatise on the rebels that his previous "little book" had given rise to "many complaints and questions, as though it were un-Christian and too hard." Calling his critics hypocrites who never shed a tear for the rebels while they posed a real threat, Luther made no excuses:

> If they think this answer is too harsh, and that this is talking violence and only shutting men's mouths, I reply, "That is right." A rebel is not worth rational arguments, for he does not accept them. You have to answer people like that with a fist.[55]

And Luther made no apologies for the lords who were still scouring their lands for trouble-makers, seeking vengeance. Reports of atrocities reached Luther. He was horrified to learn that Müntzer's wife had been raped after his capture and execution, and that the margrave Casimir of Brandenburg-Ansbach—a Lutheran lord—had gouged out the eyes of sixty of his subjects who had not looked at him with the proper measure of respect.[56] Such atrocities made Luther think that the devil had jumped out of the peasants and straight into their lords. He lashed out against the victors as "furious, raving, senseless tyrants, who, even after the battle, cannot get their fill of blood. . . . Scoundrels and hogs . . . it is all one whether they slay the guilty or the innocent, whether it please God or the devil."[57]

Nonetheless, as Luther saw it, divine justice still prevailed, no matter how much damage the devil inflicted on earth. The peasants had been unwilling to listen, he said, "and now they had their reward"; in the same way, "the lords too will not hear, and they shall have their reward also. . . . Hell-fire, trembling, and gnashing of teeth in hell will be their reward eternally, unless they repent."[58]

All in all, the Revolution of the Common Man had tested everyone's faith as well as their mettle, and few outside the blood-soaked battlefields were tested as much as Luther. Years later, he would sum up his role in this tragedy at the dinner table as only a prophet could:

> It was I, Martin Luther, who slew all the peasants during the rising, for I commanded them to be slaughtered. All their blood is on my head. But I throw the responsibility on our Lord God, who instructed me to give this order.[59]

His conflict with the peasant armies marked a turning point in Luther's Reformation. Though he may not have been haunted by his own command to "smite, slay, and stab," those three words would forever cast a pall over his image. Many contemporaries who had admired Luther up to that point became sorely disillusioned; others who had mistrusted or loathed him now found proof positive of his duplicity and of the ultimate consequences of his heresy. Even in far-off East Prussia, a Lutheran pastor at Königsberg spoke of the "swift, intolerant cry everywhere against Luther."[60] The peasants and townspeople who had rebelled could not help but feel alienated from Luther's Reformation. By siding with the landlords rather than with the "common man," Luther made himself and his reforms less attractive among a large segment of the population, especially in rural areas. Ironically, given the fact that in Germany it was the rulers who decided whether or not a region would turn Lutheran, the peasants normally had little or no say in religious matters, so those who ended up in the Lutheran Church did so because the lords who had crushed their uprising had made that choice for them.

Critics of Luther have long argued that his response to the rebels made the German peasantry and a large segment of the German population apathetic to religion and politics. Others have even argued that Luther's response to the uprising of 1525 made Germany as a whole more prone to insensitivity and despotism.[61] Luther's invocation of Romans 13 in his *Against the Hordes* was carefully placed. Having come perilously close

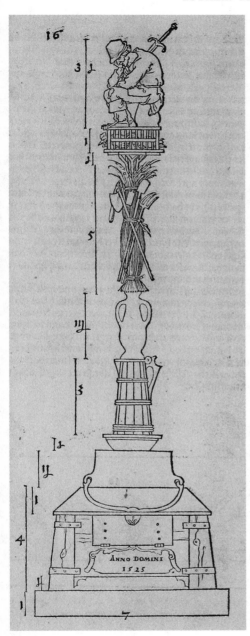

Ambivalent victory. In 1527 the great pro-Lutheran artist Albrecht Dürer completed this design for a monument in remembrance of the defeat of the peasant rebels. The memorial column, which was never erected, shows a peasant seated atop the tools and fruits of his labor, slumped over, with a sword sticking out of his back. This representation of the uprising of 1524–1525 has been interpreted in various ways, as sympathetic to the peasants or to the landed aristocracy who slew them, but it ultimately represents the tragic nature of the conflict, and the unease many felt toward the brutality with which it was quelled.

to preaching what he would have called works-righteousness, insisting that the slaying of the rebels was not only necessary (as Karlstadt had argued that iconoclasm was necessary), but also worthy of merit in God's eyes (as Catholic theologians argued that some acts pleased God more than others), Luther turned to the one Pauline text that made civil obedience necessary, the key biblical passage that would dominate all discourse in early modern political theology:

> Let every person be subject to the governing authorities, for there is no authority except from God, and those authorities that exist have been instituted by God. Therefore whoever resists authority resists what God has appointed, and those who resist will incur judgment. (Romans 13:1–2)

Catholics would naturally ignore Luther's attempts to defend his position through biblical proof texts and blame him for the whole mess, finding his fingerprints on every inch of the crime scene. From the language of the grievance lists, to the high number of Lutheran pastors who participated in the uprising, Luther's influence seemed visible everywhere. Among his Catholic critics, few summed up the charges against Luther more succinctly than Johannes Findling, former commissioner general of indulgences and author of a very popular pamphlet titled *Luther Speaks with Forked Tongue; or, How Luther Led the Peasants Astray with One Hand and Condemned Them with the Other*. Arguing that Luther had opened a Pandora's box with his highly inflammatory anti-Romanist rhetoric, and that he also had a knack for inciting others to radical behavior and then attacking them for taking his teachings to their logical conclusion—as in the case of Karlstadt— Findling painted the darkest possible portrait of the arch-heretic at Wittenberg, as a shrewd and duplicitous self-promoter who never shrank back from using others to further his own political ends. Luther's cunning knew no bounds, charged Findling. What better evidence of his deviousness, he asked, than Luther's *Admonition to Peace*, which served no other purpose than to inflame the rebels further with its unrestrained criticism of the lords and princes?[62] More than three centuries later, German Catholic historians such as Johannes Janssen were still echoing Findling's argument, pointing to the slippery slope upon which Luther knowingly perched his nation:

> When once it had become a settled fact that for centuries past the nation had been purposely misled and preyed upon by its spiritual rulers, it was but a slight step further to discovering that the whole fabric of secular government also, closely bound as it was with spiritual rule, was contrived for the sole purpose of fleecing the lower orders, and that Divine justice demanded its complete overthrow.[63]

Finding a cause for the disasters of 1525 is only half of the historian's task, however. The other half entails assessing the damage and dissecting the corpse, so to speak. Nowadays, Janssen's very unecumenical assessment is not taken very seriously. But, oddly enough, part of his argument is very much in line with some current thinking, for some historians continue to argue that the Revolution of 1525 took the German Reformation out of the hands of the common people and handed it over to the state, and that from that point forward religion became a means of control and a tool for state formation and social disciplining.[64] As one historian has put it: "Not only were the peasant revolts lost, but also the entire Reformation as a joint enterprise of laymen and clergy."[65] In such an assessment, whether or not the lords and rulers caved in on any of the material demands of the so-called common man is immaterial. What seems to matter most is the fact that elites who ran the state and the church monopolized the religious life of the so-called common man. Not everyone agrees on this point, as one would expect. At the other end of the spectrum are historians who look upon the "Reformation of the princes" in a very positive light, arguing that the Protestant Reformation would have failed utterly without the support of the civil authorities.[66] Other historians have argued that Luther's stance against the peasants saved the Reformation, for if he had followed the path of Karlstadt or Müntzer he would have been snuffed out very quickly.[67] Then, there are also historians who argue that the governing elites never managed to control the religion of the people, and that the peasant uprisings of 1524–1525 therefore did not effect much of a change in religious life or popular piety.

The validity of all such assessments is something we will have to take up later, as we move on to examine the ways in which the Protestant Reformation spread far and wide. For now we will leave Luther behind, as the Reformation he sparked expands and his role diminishes. We will have to leave him poised not just between God and the Devil, or Karlstadt and Müntzer, or the pope and the peasants, but also between his past and his future. The year 1525 was a momentous one for Luther in many ways, and a time of great changes when he caught up with his own Reformation and came to terms with its limitations. Three great transformations took place that year, and one more in 1526.

First, as the lords were busy fighting the ragtag armies of the common man, Elector Frederick III, "the Wise," died, on 5 May. He was succeeded by his brother John (1468–1532), who came to be known as "the Steadfast," for his continued support of Luther. It would be John of Saxony's responsibility to oversee the establishment in 1527 of the state church in Saxony, which became the model for all Lutheran churches, with the civil lord in control—the model church that sealed the end of the communal Reformation in much of Germany. Up until that point, the church in Luther's Saxony had been re-formed ad hoc, its structure and governance sustained de facto more than de jure by the Saxon lords. Now, by law, a church was established in which secular authorities took on the administration of the church, appointing and removing clergy and supervising visitations (inspections) of all of the clerics and churches in their territory. To John would also fall the task of protecting Luther from pope and emperor during a time of great crisis.

About the time that Frederick died, a great step was taken at Wittenberg with the very first evangelical ordination service, at which new clergy were installed in their offices through a revised ritual. Another very important bridge to Rome was burned on that day, that of apostolic succession. The Catholic Mass had just been abolished, in January 1525; now the Catholic priesthood was gone too. The Latin liturgy that Luther had been clinging to was on its way out.

Two months after Frederick's death, in July, as the lords were busy mopping up what was left of the rebels, Luther finally caught up with Karlstadt, Müntzer, and many other former priests and monks, by marrying Katherine von Bora, a former nun sixteen years his junior. Luther had helped Katherine escape from a Cistercian convent in 1523, along with eleven other nuns, and after months of trying to find her a husband, he decided to wed her. In early June 1526, almost a year after their wedding, the ex-monk and ex-nun welcomed into the world the first of their six children, a boy, Johannes. The Elector John bestowed on Luther the former Augustinian cloister where he had once resided as a monk, and he and Katherine made it their home, rearing all of their children there, taking in some orphans, and sharing the space with students.

Finally, in 1526, Luther brought his church almost full circle, back to where Karlstadt had taken it on Christmas 1521 (and where Müntzer had taken Allstedt in 1524), by instituting a new liturgy that was entirely in German. Although Luther's liturgy was not as plain and simple as the liturgies of Karlstadt or Müntzer, the innovation was nonetheless momentous, and perhaps also a reluctant nod toward some of those who had been chased away for insisting on greater changes at a faster pace.

All of these changes were made possible by a combination of factors, but chief among these factors was the support of Frederick the Wise and John the Steadfast. Without them, Luther might have ended up like Hus, burned alive at the stake. Luther knew it, and adjusted his thinking and his policies to that cold, hard fact. The pope knew it too, and fumed. Toward the very end of Frederick's life, Pope Adrian VI, former tutor to the Emperor Charles V, admonished Frederick, making him personally responsible for Luther and his Reformation: "We have you to thank that the churches are without people, the people without priests, the priests without honor, and Christians without Christ."[68]

The pope was both wrong and right. Frederick was indeed responsible for keeping Luther alive, but he was not solely responsible for the changes that were sweeping over Western Christendom. Luther was not solely responsible either. The movement that came to be known as the Protestant Reformation could not be pinned on any individual. But all of those involved would have been quick to pin it either on God or on the devil.

It would prove to be a very costly difference of opinion.

An Uncertain Future

Surviving the papal bull *Exsurge Domine*, the Edict of Worms, and the Revolution of the Common Man was difficult enough, and truly amazing, but Luther's fate remained uncertain for quite some time after 1525. A sword hung over his neck constantly. And it was not metaphorical: Emperor Charles V had sworn to wipe Luther off the face of the earth, along with all his followers, and Charles was the most powerful ruler on earth.

If he could ever concentrate his energy and resources against Luther, stopping Charles V would be next to impossible.

Fortunately, for Luther, Charles V had many unwanted distractions, and far too many unexpected emergencies. But the possibility that he might be able to focus on the Lutheran "heresy" was very real, and the survival of Luther and his Reformation remained in peril. Charles V's main distraction was his war with France, which was being waged mainly in Italy. This war seemed to have been won by Charles at the Battle of Pavia, in February 1525, when Francis was captured by Charles's forces, along with

King Francis I, by Jean Clouet. Nearly constant conflict with this French king prevented Charles V from devoting full attention to the religious crisis in Germany. The situation made it relatively easier for Lutheran princes and free cities to break away from the Catholic Church without any immediate reprisals from their emperor. In due time, however, King Francis would have to deal with his own native "Lutherans" in France, and his response to them would be harsh.

several high-ranking nobles. Francis was imprisoned in Madrid, Spain, which was then a backwater town with a third-rate royal castle that seldom housed the monarch and his court. Charles could demand almost anything, so the humiliating terms imposed on Francis in the Treaty of Madrid in January 1526 included a permanent nonaggression agreement on the part of the French, and the exchange of King Francis for his two sons as hostages.

Charles then seemed free to focus on the Lutherans, but Francis was too clever and too unprincipled a foe. Claiming that the Treaty of Madrid had been signed under duress and was therefore not valid, Francis reneged on all his promises as soon as he was back in France and renewed his war against Charles. This time around, Francis formed an alliance known as the League of Cognac with the Republic of Venice, the Kingdom of England, the Duchy of Milan, the Republic of Florence, and none other than Pope Clement VII. Ironically, then, the ruler most committed to wiping Luther off the face of the earth found himself at war not just with a host of other Catholics, but with the pope himself. The War of the League of Cognac, from 1526 to 1530, along with the alarmingly rapid advance of the Ottoman Turks into Central Europe, would deflect Charles's attention away from the Lutherans in Germany. But his eyes never strayed far from those lands where heretics ran amok, and this meant that the fate of Luther and his followers remained all too uncertain.

The tenuous hold that Lutherans had on their survival seemed to become slightly more secure at the Diet of Speyer in 1526, which Charles V was not able to attend.

Presided over by Charles's brother Ferdinand, who was not too experienced, the Diet was commandeered by princes and cities that supported Luther. Its ultimate decision was to call for a council that would settle the religious question and for an immediate suspension of the Edict of Worms (which had pronounced Luther an outlaw). The Diet stipulated that in the interim, while such a council was in the process of being convened, "every state shall so live, rule, and believe as it may hope and trust to answer before God and his imperial Majesty."[69] In other words, all secular governments, including those of free imperial cities, were temporarily free to chart their own course when it came to religion.

Unbeknownst to anyone at the time, the Diet of Speyer had set in place the rules that would henceforth govern religious choice in Germany. But no matter how liberating, these rules were, and no matter how much the anti-Romanists profited from them, their contingent and ephemeral nature seemed all too real to those alive at that time, as seemed to be convincingly proved at the following meeting of the Imperial Diet, which reconvened again at Speyer in 1529.

This Second Diet of Speyer, which was also presided by Charles's brother Ferdinand, but was attended by a higher number of Catholic representatives, reversed the decisions of the earlier Diet by reaffirming the Edict of Worms and its condemnation of Luther. Even more disturbing to Luther's followers, it rescinded the right of secular authorities to decide the religious question and called for a reinstatement of the Catholic Church in those areas where it had been abolished and dismantled.

The outlook could not have seemed grimmer to Luther's followers, as well as to all others who had broken with Rome (which by this time included a large array of individuals, cities, and states who disagreed with Luther on many issues). On 19 April 1529, six princes and fourteen imperial cities who represented the religious minority at the Diet issued a "Protestation" against its decision, in which they called for the right of every state to choose its religion, and the right of all opponents of Roman Catholicism to advance their cause.

Although they had no way of knowing it at the time, this legal procedure undertaken by the dissenters—who preferred to call themselves "evangelicals," or followers of the gospel—would forever be linked with their movement and brand them as "Protestants." These dissenters were not in the least worried about names, however. Their main concern at the time was mere survival.

Luck was on their side, though they had no way of knowing it at that time. Charles V would go on to win another Pyrrhic victory over the French and the League of Cognac in 1529, but neither the French nor the ever-advancing Turks would give him the break that he needed to crush the "Protestant" heretics.

In 1529, with a triumphant Charles riding high and a reversal of fortune at the Second Diet of Speyer, prospects seemed grim for Luther and his followers: terribly dark and most uncertain, blacker perhaps than any of Luther's bouts of *Anfechtung*.

And it was not just Luther's followers who felt threatened. By 1529 there were many opponents of the pope at Rome who disagreed with Luther, far more entrenched than Karlstadt or Müntzer or any Schwärmer had ever been, and far better poised to steal Luther's thunder, but just as vulnerable as the arch-heretic at Wittenberg and his brood.

The most formidable of these "false brethren," as Luther preferred to call anti-Romanists who disagreed with him, were to his south, in Switzerland. And it is to them we must now turn our attention.

CHAPTER TEN

The Swiss Reformation

L uther might have sparked the Protestant Reformation, much to everyone's surprise, but he was far from alone, and not even the first in his generation to challenge Rome.

The Swiss city of Zurich is 468 miles southwest of Wittenberg. There, in Zurich, before Luther took on Johann Tetzel, another young cleric had been challenging the whole of the Catholic tradition for a few years. In some ways, he was far ahead of Luther when it came to envisioning a thorough reform of the Christian religion. His vision was more systematically consistent and less paradoxical, and focused on a different set of theological issues. Most significantly, his reforming vision involved symbols and rituals at its very center, and linked this concern to a conception of church/state relations very different from Luther's.

This Reformation tends to get second billing, largely because of chronology and of its initial impact. The Reformation led by this Swiss cleric, Ulrich Zwingli, progressed more slowly and cautiously on a smaller stage, almost as if hidden from view by the towering Alps. It seemed to lack the same sense of drama and edge-of-the-cliff suspense: its leader never confronted the Holy Roman Emperor face-to-face at the Imperial Diet, never vanished mysteriously, never gained international notoriety and celebrity, never attracted as wide a reading audience, and never managed to survive to a ripe old age.

But being the first to bolt from the starting gate, or having the larger, splashier stage setting, or the wide readership, or the longer life does not necessarily mean all that much in terms of the eventual unfolding of history. The Swiss Reformation proves this to be true, several times over, for when all is said and done, this Reformation would end up affecting a greater array of countries and a larger number of people than Luther's ever did.

Wild Growth

Andreas Bodenstein von Karlstadt, Thomas Müntzer, the Zwickau Prophets, and the Revolution of the Common Man proved beyond a shadow of a doubt that Martin Luther's leadership was questionable. More than forty years ago, the German historian Franz Lau tried to put this insight into perspective by speaking of the "wild growth of Reformation ideas" that took place in the early 1520s. As Lau saw it, focusing too much on Luther could be a mistake, for if one looked beyond Wittenberg—and even if one looked at Wittenberg itself—it was easy to see that there were more ideas in play than those of Luther's, and that reform was not necessarily driven by theological concerns or even by the historical dynamic imagined by Luther's followers.[1]

Lau's contention was perceptive, but hardly novel. Even in Luther's own day, there were those who saw him as only one of many characters on a crowded stage. To some Catholics, for instance, Luther was but one among a horde of heretics, merely a single branch on an old tree that suddenly sprouted exuberant new growth in 1517, an evil tree with roots as deep and ancient as those of the church itself and branches as numerous as all the devils in hell. For those who did not follow Luther's lead but also sought to break with the past, the image of wild growth was definitely perceptible, but with a different twist: for them, Luther's role in the wild growth was ambiguous, or negative. Luther perceived the wild growth too, but he saw all others who challenged him in any way as branches that needed to be cut off.

The images of furiously branching trees or invasive brambles that are evoked by the concept of the wild growth of the early Reformation are apt, for it was indeed an abrupt burst of religious energy that expanded very rapidly and in many directions, and in diverse places, all at once, and not to everyone's delight. Much like fractals, those complex repeating patterns in nature such as trees, leaves, river systems, and blood vessels that mathematicians can turn into equations, the history of the Protestant Reformation can be systematically comprehended only through multiple narratives that parallel each other in time and even mirror each other, but sometimes interlace or branch out. And when it comes to the earliest branching, none was more significant than that which took place in the Swiss Confederation.

In 1516, a young priest named Ulrich Zwingli was already preaching straight from the Bible in Glarus, Switzerland, calling into question many of the teachings and practices of the Catholic Church. After Luther made his dramatic appearance in late 1517 and became the chief lightning rod for all religious turmoil, this young priest Zwingli— like all other reformers of his day—found himself constantly compared to Luther, or even mistakenly placed in his camp. In 1523, as Zwingli was in the midst of reforming the city of Zurich, he would defend his originality:

> "You must be a Lutheran," you say to me, "for you preach exactly the same way as Luther writes." My reply is this: I preach exactly the same way as Paul wrote; why don't you call me a "Paulist," then? Yes, I preach the word of Christ; why, then, don't you call me a "Christian"?[2]

Zwingli's irritation was justifiable, for he and Luther disagreed on many issues. Naturally, the door swung both ways. Luther took umbrage whenever anyone suggested Zwingli was his disciple. Such was the spirit of the times.

Ulrich Zwingli was born six weeks after Luther, on New Year's Day in 1484, in the small village of Wildhaus in the county of Toggenburg, in the northeastern corner of the Swiss confederacy. Like most of their neighbors, the Zwinglis were a prosperous peasant family deeply committed to the local and regional independence of their mountainous land, and also to its democratic tendencies. Self-reliant, militaristic, and fiercely opposed to great lords, the peasant communes of the Swiss cantons had won de facto independence from the Holy Roman Empire in the fourteenth century, even though the emperors refused to recognize their status de jure. Experts at warfare, and ever eager to supplement their income and assert their independence by fighting for the highest bidder, the Swiss had also become Europe's most formidable mercenaries.

Ironically, the man who would come to embody the urban Reformation most intensely, and who would also be credited with creating a godly city, grew up close to the land, in a rural setting where autonomy was highly prized. Zwingli would never tire of employing rustic metaphors in his writings and sermons. His distinctive regional accent would also brand him, as all accents do, and lead prejudiced northern Germans to question his erudition and urbanity, and perhaps also his ability to think clearly. Luther, for one, was horrified by Zwingli's parochial argot, which he would describe as "a shaggy, tangled German, which makes you sweat before you understand it."[3]

As accents within the same language family reveal cultural variations, so do they signal political differences. What Luther perceived as alien in Zwingli's diction was a reflection of the relative isolation of the Swiss and of their independent character.

Erasmian Reformer. Ulrich Zwingli (1484–1531) not only broke with Roman Catholicism, but also called for a thorough reform of worship and church-state relations in the Swiss city of Zurich. He also insisted that he had been influenced by Erasmus, but not Luther.

Zwingli's Switzerland was a unique political entity, and the unfolding of the Protestant Reformation—even its very theology—would be deeply affected by this distinction. After all, theology is inseparable not only from piety (*lex orandi, lex credendi*), but also from daily life and the norms of specific social, cultural, and political environments (*lex vivendi, lex credendi*). Ulrich Zwingli's thought, like Martin Luther's, was shaped as much by his political and social environment as it was by all of the universal Christian principles and particular theological and philosophical traditions he had picked up in his schooling. In sum, Zwingli was as Swiss as Luther was Saxon, and the difference between the two Reformations these men led was as much a matter of social and political factors as of personal quirks or predilections. To understand Zwingli and the Swiss Reformation, then, one must first grasp the uniqueness of the Swiss Confederation.

Zwingli's Switzerland

The territory that called itself the Swiss Confederation was a political anomaly without a common language. Although German was spoken by about 70 percent of its people, mostly in the north and east, French was spoken in the Pays de Vaud to the west, and Italian in the south. In addition, a small number of confederates spoke an isolated Latin dialect known as Romansch. Originally composed of eight states, or cantons, the confederacy expanded to thirteen in the early sixteenth century, during Zwingli's childhood. Each canton enjoyed a remarkable amount of independence, though some areas had relatively less sovereignty or self-rule as "common lordships" that were administered by the eight original states. Although still nominally part of the Holy Roman Empire, the confederation had been governing its own affairs since the fourteenth century without a permanent parliament or a central authority. Local autonomy was supreme. The cantons could call for a meeting of a diet, or common legislative assembly, when foreign affairs seemed to demand it, but no state was obliged to send a representative to the Diet, nor were there any means of enforcing the decisions of this legislative body throughout the confederation. Although there were plenty of differences and disagreements among the confederates—most often between the highly urbanized areas and the rural districts—the Swiss tended to be fairly unified when it came to foreign affairs.

At the regional and local level, Switzerland was governed by elected representative assemblies. Each canton had several councils for the regulation of its internal affairs, and cities and towns also had their own councils, or a series of overlapping legislative assemblies. As could be expected in such a patchwork of polities, the political and legal systems of the states varied tremendously, as did the distribution of power among their citizenry. Though most officials and representatives were elected, voting was far from a universal right. In Zwingli's day, it is estimated, about 30 percent of the total population formed an oligarchic power block with greater rights and privileges than the remaining 70 percent, who ended up being second-class citizens. In summary, the Swiss Confederation was somewhat democratic, but idiosyncratic.

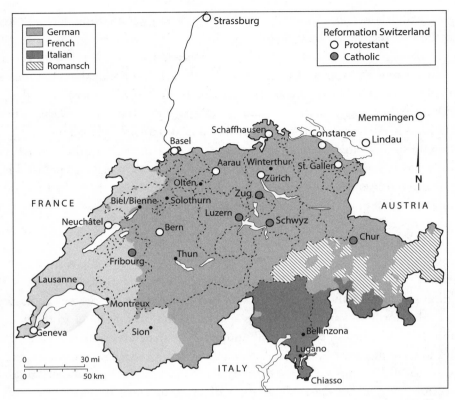

Complexity. In addition to sharing no common language, the Swiss Confederation ended up divided into Catholic and Protestant regions.

As the Swiss prided themselves on having no emperor, kings, princes, dukes, or titled nobility, so did they boast of their independence from the pope. The same urban and cantonal councils that oversaw civic affairs also held considerable power over the church, supervising the activities of the clergy, taxing church property, and even binding the higher clergy to civil law courts. So, whereas in most of Europe at the dawn of the sixteenth century all significant power tended to rest in the hands of those at the top of the social hierarchy, among the Swiss power tended to be communally shared; and whereas in most of Europe the clergy and the church claimed to be above and beyond the reach of secular rulers and courts, among the Swiss they were more closely subjected to local civil authorities. With greater participation in government and greater control of the church, the Swiss naturally approached religious reform differently from those Germans who lived in autocratic principalities such as Luther's Saxony, or even from those Germans who lived in free imperial cities, ostensibly under the emperor's remote authority.

The Making of a Reformer

Ulrich Zwingli's father, after whom he was named, embodied the political, social, and economic self-sufficiency of the Swiss peasantry, having served as *Amtman*, or head administrator of the village of Wildhaus. The Zwinglis were involved not only in local and regional politics, as was customary, but also in the church, and they seem to have been as devout as they were civic minded. Out of their eleven children, three boys would be destined for the priesthood and two girls would become nuns. The children also had a maternal uncle who was an abbot and a paternal uncle, Bartholomew, who was a priest. Uncle Bartholomew would help considerably with young Ulrich's education and his clerical career.

At almost every turn, Zwingli's biography reads very differently than Luther's. Unlike Martin Luther, who became a monk and a priest against his father's wishes, Zwingli seems not only to have been groomed for the priesthood, but also to have eased his way into a clerical career without a spiritual crisis. At the age of five he was sent to Wesen, where his uncle Bartholomew gave him a basic education. Five years later, in 1494, the ten-year-old was sent to Basel, where he learned Latin, and three years later, then an adolescent, he moved on to Bern, where he briefly came in contact with the well-known humanist Heinrich Wölfflin. In 1498 Ulrich began his studies at the University of Vienna, where he was exposed to traditional scholastic theology—the *via antiqua* of Aquinas rather than the *via moderna* of John Duns Scotus or William of Ockham—and where he was also introduced to Renaissance humanism by the greatest of all German humanists, Conrad Celtis (1459–1508), the *Erzhumanist*, or arch-humanist. Four years later, Zwingli went to the University of Basel, where he earned a bachelor's degree in 1504 and a master's in 1506. At Basel, a center of humanistic learning, Zwingli was mentored by Thomas Wyttenbach (1472–1526), who further encouraged him to return *ad fontes*, to the Greek text of the New Testament, and also to loathe the theology and philosophy of the *via moderna*. At Basel, Zwingli struck up close friendships with a circle of young humanists, and was introduced to Florentine Neoplatonism, that dialectically inclined philosophical strain that tended to stress the superiority of the spiritual over the material, which would eventually guide much of his thinking.

Ordained a priest in 1506, Zwingli immediately became pastor of the town of Glarus, where he apparently had ample time to pursue his humanistic interests, immersing himself in the classics and the church fathers, learning Greek and Hebrew, as Thomas Wyttenbach had counseled him to do, and corresponding with prominent young humanists of his generation, such as Vadianus (Joachim von Watt, b. 1484), a physician and poet laureate, Beatus Rhenanus (Rhinower, b. 1485), a close friend of Erasmus, expert editor of ancient texts and advocate of reform, and Glareanus (Heinrich Loris, b. 1488), yet another poet laureate. In addition, he also founded a school for the children of Glarus and taught there. More significant yet, at Glarus Zwingli fell under the spell of Erasmus of Rotterdam, purchasing and devouring as many of his texts as he could get his hands on, becoming ever more enthralled by the Dutch humanist's biblicist and Christocentric reforming agenda. Some time between 1514 and 1516, during that most critical of periods when Luther was undergoing a spiritual transformation, Zwingli would travel to Basel to meet Erasmus. It was a pilgrimage of sorts, the kind disciples often make to venerate their masters, the only kind of pilgrimage Erasmus would approve of. By this point, toward the end of his ministry at Glarus, Zwingli had undergone a conversion of his own, but it was far different from the one Luther was experiencing at roughly the same time. Zwingli's was an Erasmian conversion.

We know from Zwingli's own testimony that no one else shaped his piety and his thinking as much as Erasmus. The influence was so direct and so strong, in fact, that those who charged Erasmus with laying the egg that Luther hatched were totally mistaken. Zwingli truly hatched Erasmus's reforming egg; Luther would merely scramble it. While Luther's conversion began with the biblical texts of the Psalms and of Romans, and focused solely on the issue of justification, Zwingli's began with a poem of Erasmus, with a focus on ritual and piety and on the question of proper worship. These two different starting points would remain firmly fixed at the center of each reformer's hermeneutics, and prevent them from ever agreeing with each other on the meaning of symbols and rituals or on the larger goals of the Reformation.

Zwingli gave no exact date for his Erasmian conversion, but he admitted it took place some time between 1514 and 1515, while he was still at Glarus. The brief life-altering poem in question was titled "The Complaint of Jesus," which lampooned the cult of the saints and popular attitudes toward prayer. Speaking in the first person, Jesus bemoans that he has nothing to do in heaven because no one ever prays to him. Bored and restless, he complains that everyone prays to the saints instead, and especially to his mother, the Virgin Mary. Zwingli's own description of his response to this poem, written several years later, in 1523, lays out in explicit detail the nature of his conversion, and of the reforming vision that would guide all his work from that point forward:

> I shall not keep from you, most beloved brethren in Christ, how I arrived at the opinion and the firm belief that we need no mediator other than Christ, and also that no one other than Christ alone can mediate between God and us. Eight or nine years ago, I read a consoling poem about the Lord Jesus by the most learned Erasmus of Rotterdam, in which Jesus complains, in a most beautiful way, that men did not seek all good in Him in order that He might be a wellspring of goodness for them, a redeemer, comforter, and treasure of the soul. And then and there I was convinced that this was true indeed. Why, then, should we seek help from any creature?[4]

Good Erasmian that he had become, Zwingli turned directly to the Bible, which he had already accepted as the supreme authority, and also to the church fathers of the second through fifth centuries, whom he accepted as the best interpreters of Holy Scripture, "in order to find in them evidence for the intercession of the saints." Finding no mention of the cult of the saints in the Bible, and very little in the fathers, Zwingli turned away from medieval Catholic piety and down the path toward a total break with the past. At this point, then, Zwingli was already convinced of the primacy of the Bible, something akin to Luther's *sola scriptura*, and of the need to scrutinize all piety by scriptural guidelines. In this respect, he had arrived at a very similar conclusion regarding scriptural authority by means of a very different route. But the differences are as manifest as the similarities: Zwingli was more intensely focused on the issue of worship and intercession, and on the need to return to a strict Christocentric piety, than on the soteriological questions that so consumed Luther's attention. His burning preoccupation became how to best approach God and relate to him, not how to find forgiveness.

Around the same time as this conversion experience, in 1515 Zwingli underwent yet another transformation. Accompanying five hundred mercenary soldiers from the Glarus area as their chaplain, Zwingli got to witness the bloody reality of war at the battle of Marignano, where the Swiss mercenaries were mowed down by French forces and thousands of men lost their lives. Although he had been criticizing Swiss mercenary activities since 1510, warning his fellow Swiss that these entanglements with foreigners might eventually cost them their independence, the slaughter of the Swiss soldiers at the battle of Marignano drove Zwingli to become even more outspoken about the questionable ethics and the political risks of mercenary warfare, particularly in a poem he published in 1516 titled "The Labyrinth." This was no Erasmian pacifist plea, but rather a clearheaded rejection of foreign entanglements by a Swiss patriot. As could be expected for a place where many depended on mercenary service for income and a sense of identity,

The Battle of Marignano, 1515. The artist Urs Graf depicted the fury of battle in the background and highlights its grim aftermath in the foreground. Witnessing this battle gave the army chaplain Zwingli firsthand experience in the horrors of war and soured him on Swiss mercenary adventures, but did not prevent him from waging war to defend his Reformation.

Zwingli's views were not very well received at Glarus. Somewhat uncomfortable and restless, he requested a transfer from his post and was quickly reassigned to Einsiedeln, a nearby town, in April 1516.

Einsiedeln would prove to be a challenging assignment for a young Erasmian such as Zwingli, for the town was home to a Benedictine abbey that housed a miracle-working image of the Virgin Mary that had been attracting hordes of pilgrims from near and far for five centuries, and had turned dark from the soot of their thousands of candles. Appointed as "people's priest" (*Leutpriester*), Zwingli immediately began to preach against the belief that pilgrimages were a way of doing penance and gaining pardon, against the intercession of the saints, and against the very notion that divine grace could be localized at a pilgrimage site. "Christ alone saves," taught Zwingli from his pulpit, "and he saves everywhere." Strange words for a preacher at one of Europe's top pilgrimage sites, but not at all strange for an Erasmian. At Einsiedeln Zwingli continued his study of the Bible, becoming fully proficient in Greek and Hebrew, going as far in his attempt to imbibe the Scriptures as to copy by hand, in Greek, all of Paul's epistles from Erasmus's New Testament. Already an expert on the work of St. Jerome (340–420) and St. Augustine (354–430), he deepened his study of them and also turned to the work of St. Ambrose (340–397) and St. Cyprian (200–258), and also of St. John Chrysostom (347–407), the "golden-mouthed," arguably the most famous preacher among all of the church fathers.

Early in 1518, a few months after Luther took on Tetzel and his indulgence peddling, Zwingli launched a campaign of his own against another coin-in-the-coffer indulgence peddler, Bernard Sanson, who showed up at Einsiedeln. From the pulpit, Zwingli denied the value of Sanson's indulgences and urged his congregation to stay away from him and to rely instead on the saving merits of Christ. Unlike the case at Wittenberg, which was already a red-hot controversy, Zwingli's stance caused no stir. As it turned out, the bishop of Constance backed Zwingli, and so did the Confederate Diet, both of whom condemned Sanson's tactics. The differences between Luther's and Zwingli's challenges, then, seem as startling as the similarities. Zwingli's protest at Einsiedeln is ample proof that the late medieval church was far from a monolithic institution ever ready to stifle reform or crush dissent and that indulgences were questionable for many, even in the church hierarchy. It also demonstrates that Luther's dissent did not have to lead ineluctably to conflict, and that he was far from alone on the front lines pressing for change.

For nearly five centuries now, a question has lingered: to what extent was Zwingli influenced by Luther in 1518? Zwingli denied that he ever followed Luther's lead in any way and never gave Luther any credit, saying that long before Luther was known in Switzerland, he himself had already begun to preach the pure gospel, and that he had learned about the "fraud" of indulgences from his mentor Wyttenbach in Basel. Whether or not Luther influenced Zwingli matters little in the long run, for it is quite obvious that Zwingli did indeed experience a significant conversion before Luther became well known, and that the two men disagreed on several key points and came to distrust each other. What remains unclear is how Zwingli's progress as a reformer was influenced by the Lutheran texts that he undeniably read or by the tide of events and expectations that Luther set in motion, for much of what Zwingli and the Swiss did on their own would not only be linked to what was happening in Germany, but also always be encircled by the Lutheran story as its unavoidable background. Conversely, Luther would always have the Swiss in view, as yet another set of false brethren.

Zwingli's startling sermons obviously found a welcoming audience. Instead of being censured, Zwingli was invited to apply for a more prestigious position as "people's priest," at the most important church in Zurich, the Grossmünster, where his main duty would be to preach. But before he could land the post he had to compete for it, and in the process some of his past sins caught up with him. Sponsored by the young humanist Oswald Myconius (Geisshüssler, 1488–1522), who was a friend of Erasmus, Zwingli soon hit a roadblock, created not by his theology, but by his personal life. When rumors emerged that Zwingli had broken his vow of celibacy at Glarus, he frankly admitted that he had been seduced by a barber's daughter and vowed that nothing of the sort would happen again. Fittingly, the sins of the whole church came into play, for the other candidate for this post was a priest who had six illegitimate children and a concubine, or common-law wife, as was customary for many priests. Much to his delight, Zwingli won the post, and he assumed his duties on New Year's Day of 1519, his thirty-fifth birthday.

War Against the Idols

From the very start, Zwingli acted as a reformer in Zurich, preaching straight from the Bible, without the aid of the commentaries he was expected to use. He also decided not to follow the texts prescribed by the church for each day, preaching instead on the gospel of Matthew bit by bit, focusing exclusively on the life of Christ. An electrifying preacher, Zwingli quickly attracted a very large following, and as that first year progressed, his sermons became increasingly critical of all aspects of devotion that he deemed unscriptural, such as prayers to the saints, the doctrine of purgatory, and the observance of fasting. After nearly dying from the plague during his first few months in office, Zwingli seems to have devoted himself even more energetically to the cause of reform. And the larger a following he attracted, the more commonplace it became for Zurichers to accept Zwingli's central point, that the Bible should be the ultimate measure of all church reform.

For three years, as Luther made his way from the Leipzig debate to his exile at the Wartburg castle, Zwingli preached and taught in Zurich, gaining many disciples but changing nothing at all. During that time, as Zwingli's attacks on "un-biblical" practices intensified, his thinking began to resemble Karlstadt's more than Luther's. Finally, at the beginning of Lent in 1522, about two months or so after Karlstadt began reforming the liturgy and smashing the religious images at Wittenberg, change came to Zurich. And in a way that would become highly typical for Switzerland, it came from the people themselves, rather than from Zwingli or any other cleric, as a direct challenge to the civil statutes that upheld Roman Catholic observances. On the first Friday of Lent, 1522—when abstinence from meat was required—a group of laymen met at the home of the great printer Christopher Froschauer to eat sausages with great fanfare. Zwingli, who was present, declined to partake of the forbidden food. As soon as news of this incident reached city authorities, Froschauer and the sausage eaters were arrested, and Zwingli came to their defense immediately, challenging the very legality of the church's fasting rules strictly on the basis of biblical authority. Their prosecution was precisely what the sausage eaters wanted. By breaking the law, they sought to challenge its legitimacy in court.

So, as Luther returned to Wittenberg to rein in Karlstadt's reforms, Zwingli's supporters initiated the Protestant Reformation in Zurich by eating sausages. This contrast speaks volumes about the differences between the two reformers and the movements they led. Zwingli may have refrained from breaking the law himself, but he pushed for immediate practical changes nonetheless, and most important of all, he allowed the laity to act on their own while pressing for all laws to be judged by Scripture alone. As the magistrates deliberated during Lent, more and more Zurichers began to violate the abstinence and fasting laws flagrantly, as a blatant challenge and a counterritual. Pressing the legal point that Lenten fasting laws were unscriptural, Zwingli's party won. The councilors gave in, acquitting all of the sausage eaters and setting a very significant legal precedent: the civil authorities had ruled on a religious question on the basis of the *sola scriptura* principle.

A wedge had been driven between civil and ecclesiastical law. Although the councilors had declared Lenten fasting rules illegal, Bishop Hugo of Constance, who was in charge of the church in Zurich, most definitely had not. Hugo condemned Zwingli and his sausage eaters, arguing more or less along the same line as Luther did against Karlstadt, that all reforms had to take into account those who were less spiritually advanced. Zwingli's reaction to Hugo paralleled that of Karlstadt to Luther. "What harm is going to happen if the whole rubbish heap of ceremonies be cleared away," he asked, "since God declares that he is worshiped in vain by these things?"[5]

Emboldened by their success, early that summer the very same group that had staged the Lenten sausage eating began heckling the sermons of some of Zurich's monastic preachers, targeting especially those who defended the intercession of Mary and the saints. Led by Conrad Grebel, future leader of the Anabaptists, these laymen further tested the law by asking the city council to prohibit any preaching in Zurich that did not focus squarely on the Bible. Zwingli, too, joined in, disrupting a sermon by an itinerant mendicant preacher from Avignon. In mid-July 1522, a momentous legal precedent was set when a committee of some of Zurich's councilors were given the authority to determine what could be preached from the pulpit by means of a public debate between the heckled monastic preachers and the protesters. Judging that Zwingli and his followers had won the debate, this committee ordered that all monastics in Zurich were henceforth to preach straight from the Bible, without any references to scholastic theologians. Although this decision had been made by one committee rather than the city council, and although it applied to monastic clergy only, the triumph of the Protestant Reformation had been sealed in Zurich, on legal grounds, at the local level, and principally through acts of civil disobedience.

The next step was to challenge church ordinances on biblical grounds at the confederate level. Undaunted by the fact that Bishop Hugo had already condemned them, in June 1522 Zwingli and several other clerics from an area wider than Zurich itself chose to test the church's authority further by publicly asking Bishop Hugo to abolish priestly celibacy and nonscriptural preaching. Appealing to the Bible as the sole authority, the petition argued that marriage was a perfectly natural right that the church should not deny to its clergy. This appeal to Bishop Hugo was a hollow one, for the petitioners were really seeking not his permission, but rather a wider audience for their claims. Though first sent as a private letter, this trouble-seeking missive was published two weeks later under the title *A Friendly Petition and Admonition to the Confederates*. The Zurichers and their neighbors were asking the civil authorities in Switzerland not only to supplant papal and episcopal authority, as Luther had asked the princes in his *Address to the Christian Nobility*, but also to protect the Swiss clergy from their bishops. Moreover, whether or not clergy could marry was a moot question by this point, for Zwingli had secretly married a widow named Anna Reinhart a few months before. Other clerics had married too. Bishop Hugo responded as one might expect, by ordering the civil authorities in Zurich to restore order and defend the church's status quo in their city. Zwingli countered as one might expect too, by declaring Bishop Hugo's authority null and void, in a treatise titled *The First and Last Word (Apologeticus Acheteles)*.

Having crossed this last line toward open heresy and schism, Zwingli and his clerical associates in Zurich stepped up their attack on "non-biblical" religion, and especially against images and the Mass. By late 1522, a definite gap between theology and practice was clearly evident: although many clergy and laity in Zurich were opposed to images and to the celebration of the Mass, the ritual and the symbols stood firmly in place, as did recalcitrant clergy who supported them. No amount of theorizing or preaching seemed to dislodge the ancient idols and their defenders, but another precedent-setting legal decision would soon begin eroding their legitimacy. In January 1523, the Zurich government called for a public disputation on religious reform, insisting that the Bible alone be used as the sole authority for all questions. That premise alone was a great victory that guaranteed a sound trouncing of all Catholic appeals to tradition. At the disputation itself, the Catholics challenged that assumption, but to no avail. Appealing constantly to tradition, Bishop Hugo's vicar summed up his frustration with what he considered a rigged, unfair contest in which the very premise upon which all debate was grounded was the biggest error of all:

> I see very well that the game is going beyond me. . . . They undertake to drive us from old customs, which have endured and stood in honor these seven hundred years, planning to overturn and upset all things. For first they went at the pope, cardinals, and bishops, then they turned all cloisters topsy-turvy, after that they fell upon purgatory. And when they had left the earth they at last ascended to heaven and went at the saints and great servants of God. Saint Peter with his keys, indeed our dear lady, the mother of God, could not escape their disgraceful attacks.[6]

Zwingli deflected all such criticism by doggedly conflating the Bible and all of his teachings, insisting that he was simply citing the only authority that mattered in a direct, unmediated way, without engaging in any kind of interpretation. In other words, he argued he was speaking for God himself: "I am confident and indeed I know, that my sermons and doctrine are nothing else than the holy, true, pure gospel, which God desired me to speak by the intuition and inspiration of His Spirit."[7] In addition, as Zwingli pointed out to his opponents, the Bible spoke so clearly that it made those who followed it infallible. Turning the tables on his opponents, Zwingli claimed for himself and his followers the ultimate authority:

> There is another Church which the popes do not wish to recognize; this one is no other than all right Christians, collected in the name of the Holy Ghost and by the will of God, which have placed a firm belief and an unhesitating hope in God, her spouse. That church does not reign according to the flesh . . . but depends and rests only upon the word and will of God. . . . That Church cannot err.[8]

Given that this basic premise was the a priori basis for all discussion, it was no surprise that those who assembled to judge the disputation deemed that the sixty-seven conclusions drawn up by Zwingli were "proven" and that they ordered all of the clergy of Zurich to preach and teach according to the Bible alone from that day forward.

The First Zurich Disputation, as this event came to be known, marked a legal break with the Roman Catholic Church and a point of no return. Nonetheless, change was slow in coming, for despite all of the biblical teaching and preaching, the "idols" despised by Zwingli and his followers remained firmly ensconced Attacks on images and the Mass intensified in the sermons of Zwingli and his associate Leo Jud, and also in some of the literature that made its way to Zurich, especially in one pamphlet that proved very popular, *A Judgment of God Our Spouse Concerning How One Should Regard All Idols and Images*, by Ludwig Haetzer, a follower of Karlstadt. Haetzer's *Judgment* not only summarized why religious images were forbidden by God in the Bible, but also encouraged the destruction of all "idols" as a praiseworthy act. As Haetzer's pamphlet began to circulate, and as sermons against idolatry increased in the late summer and early fall of 1523, some of the laity began to take matters into their own hands, as they had done with sausages at Lent. Sporadic attacks on sacred art and other material objects of devotion began to take place in and around Zurich, at the hands of both individuals and groups of men, forcing the Zurich authorities to call for a another disputation, to deal specifically with images and the Mass. As before, the rules for the dispute predetermined its outcome, for all arguments were to be defended solely on scriptural grounds.

The Second Zurich Disputation, which took place in late October 1523 was a resounding victory for the iconoclasts, and the penultimate step toward the establishment of a fully reformed church. Calling for an end to idolatry and bringing idolatry to an end were two very different things, however. Despite the outcome of the disputation, and despite intense agitation by those who wanted to remove the "idols," the city authorities could not bring themselves to act against the old religion. Iconoclasm had its fervent supporters, but there were still faithful Catholics in Zurich who firmly opposed the removal of images and the abolition of the Mass. As opposition to the decrees of the disputation mounted, the city council stalled, calling for more debate. But the debating led nowhere. The Third Zurich Disputation ended with a call for more debate; and the resulting Fourth Disputation ended in January 1524 once again with a decision against images and the Mass, to no avail. The Zurich city council continued to stall in the face of resistance from staunch Catholics in the city and beyond. Such was the nature of urban politics in Zurich, where repercussions had to be carefully weighed, and where the balance of power ensured no easy victory for any one party. Two issues in particular gave the authorities pause. One question had to do with external relations, for despite its autonomy and sovereignty, the city of Zurich would have to answer to all those other members of the confederacy who were opposed to such profound changes. War clouds hung low over its decision. Confederates had waged war against one another in the past, and they could easily do so again over the question of religious change. Another question dealt with internal relations in the city itself, where some citizens still wanted to cling to tradition: what would be the cost of such profound changes, literally and figuratively? Religious art was expensive to produce, and many donors who had invested in such art had legal claims on its value. Sacred art also touched people deeply in an emotional way, either positively or negatively, as objects of devotion or as despised "idols." The same was true of the ritual of the Mass. On the one hand, the authorities had to ponder whether the social fabric of Zurich would be able to withstand something as divisive as the abolition of the old religion. On the other hand, they had to weigh whether or not their community could continue to survive the polarization that every delay caused. Waging war on the "idols" was risky business in such a highly charged atmosphere.

Eventually, after the sudden death of a councilor who was adamantly Catholic, the council stopped stalling. On 15 June 1524, as sporadic acts of iconoclasm intensified, the city council called for an orderly removal of all of the sacred art in Zurich, and for the dismantling of all its pipe organs. The city's three people's priests—Ulrich Zwingli, Leo Jud, and Heinrich Engelhard—were placed in charge of the project. Craftsmen were selected from the relevant guilds, and they went to work immediately, obliterating with stunning speed all of the artistic treasures that Zurich's churches had amassed through the centuries. One by one, Zurich's churches were closed as workmen carefully dislodged and demolished each and sacred images and ritual objects, including crucifixes, holy water fonts, communion vessels, votive lamps, vestments, organs, and carved choir stalls. Though some items were returned to donors, everything else was consigned to oblivion, in a very orderly way. Objects made of wood or cloth went up in smoke, consumed by flames. Precious metals were melted down for the city's treasury; iron and bronze for other uses. Gold vessels and jewels were carefully recycled too. Objects made of stone, glass, or plaster were smashed to bits, along with the bones of the saints. Murals were scraped away, and the walls whitewashed. At the end of two weeks, not a single "idol" remained in place. Zurich was now a godly city, and its Reformation a stark reality. Zwingli could exult, as Luther never would: "In Zurich the churches truly gleam; the walls are so beautifully white!"[9]

By April 1525, the Mass was gone too, banished for good along with all the sacred music. Gone were the priests who mediated salvation and forgave sins, replaced by ministers of the Word who preached the gospel alone; gone were the altars, replaced by simple tables; gone were the jewel-encrusted chalices, replaced by plain wooden cups; gone were the costly, ornate vestments, replaced by plain gowns; gone was all talk of sacrifice or real presence, and gone were the consecrated hosts, replaced by a simple memorial meal during which *mere* bread and wine were consumed rather than the fully present body and blood of the Savior. The Word alone and the words of the minister and the congregation reverberated in the vast, whitewashed, ritually clean spaces, echoing the pure gospel. Zwingli's austere zeal had captured the hearts and minds of the people of Zurich, or at least taken the city by force. And this was just the beginning of a Reformation that would one day—unlike Luther's—seek to transform the world.

Defining the True Religion

Although Zwingli formulated much of his theology as he waged war on "false" religion in the years 1522–1524, his most complete treatment of the subject did not appear until all the battles had been won, in his *Commentary on the True and False Religion* and in another work, *An Answer to Valentin Compar*. Like Luther, Zwingli would never condense all of his theology into one systematic tome, but these two texts from 1525 contained a full enough summary of his thought to create an agreed-on foundation for the religious tradition that came to be known as "Reformed." These texts were also a potent summary of Zwingli's reforming vision and would provide other reformers in Switzerland and south Germany with blueprints, so to speak, which they could follow in their own communities.

Zwingli's main objective as a theologian and reformer was to discriminate between true and false religion, and to discern the ultimate object of Christian belief and behavior. Influenced as he was by humanism, and especially by Neoplatonism and Erasmus, Zwingli conceived of religion as more than mere theology: religion was a way of life to him, a total integration of the individual and the community with a higher reality, in the here and now. Zwingli's religion was above all a practical, problem-solving endeavor to align oneself and one's world as much as possible with the divine will. His concept of the divine was very different from Luther's, and so was his conception of the proper relationship between the created world and its Creator. Zwingli's God was a transcendent Other who dwelt in the realm of the spirit and demanded to be worshiped as such, without material mediation. Largely because of the influence of Florentine Neoplatonism and Erasmus, Zwingli was keenly focused on metaphysics, and especially on the distinction between spirit and matter, which he considered two distinct realms. In this, Zwingli differed greatly from Luther, for whom matter and spirit were not polar opposites. Zwingli's matter-spirit dialectic and his sense of God's utter transcendence stand at the very center of his thought, and also at the heart of his most pragmatic reforms. Distrustful of mediation, Zwingli insisted that the true object of Christian belief and behavior is to have this transcendent God as the ultimate focus of faith and worship. Right worship, that is, worship as commanded by God, was most important of all. Sharp distinctions were the marrow of Zwingli's religion. As Zwingli saw it, anyone who failed to worship God alone was in error:

> They are not believers who go to anyone else for help other than to the one true God. For thus are the believers differentiated from the unbelievers in that the believers, or those who are trusting, go to God alone; but the unbelievers go to the created.[10]

Zwingli was adamant that true religion could not admit any meditation through matter. "They, then, who trust in any created thing whatsoever are not truly pious," he argued.[11] Going even further, Zwingli turned this principle into something resembling a mathematical equation: *quantum sensum tribueris, tantum spiritui detraxeris*, which loosely translated means "whatever binds the senses diminishes the spirit."[12]

This principle shaped Zwingli's interpretation of rituals and symbols, and especially of the sacrament of the Eucharist, which for him could never be understood literally

Zwingli's battle gear. Ulrich Zwingli believed so deeply in his Reformation that he died fighting for it in 1531. The helmet he wore into combat and the sword he wielded against neighboring Swiss Catholics are stark reminders of the violence that accompanied religious change in his day and age.

as a "real" communion with the body and blood of Christ. In his eyes, the Catholic doctrine of transubstantiation was wrong not only because it was unbiblical, but also because it was the greatest of all affronts to God's transcendence. The Mass, therefore, was itself the worst idol of all, and adoration of the consecrated host the grossest insult to God.

Some have argued that whereas Luther's Reformation sprang from a purely theological question, Zwingli's starting point was the social and political distress of his people.[13] Such an assessment not only assumes a very narrow definition of theology, but also overlooks what was most obvious to Zwingli himself: that theology, piety, and social and political concerns were inseparable. All of Zwingli's theology hangs together: from the most abstract points to the most practical, Zwingli bases all his thinking on the basic dialectic between matter and spirit and on the need to worship God correctly. For Zwingli, obedience to God's commandments—which includes the reordering of social and political structures—hinges on faith, and faith itself hinges on correct worship. "Faithfulness" for Zwingli is much more than Luther's *sola fide*. Faithfulness is action as much as it is belief, and is most fully manifest in correct behavior, in obeying both the first table of the Mosaic Law (the first four of the ten commandments), which demands correct worship, and the second table (the fifth through tenth commandments), which demands correct relations with other human beings. Faithfulness demands goodness, and goodness is impossible without true worship:

> Faithfulness demands, first, that we learn from God in what way we can please Him, in what manner serve Him. Next, it demands that we shall add nothing to what we have learned from him, or take away anything. . . . True religion, or piety, is that which clings to the one and only God.[14]

For Zwingli, then, there is much more to religion than finding forgiveness, or placating God and keeping his wrath at bay; for him, the most pressing issue is that of faithfulness, for without faith—which includes the right kind of behavior—nothing good can happen. Since it is impossible to be faithful without right worship, the social fabric cannot be correctly ordered or sustained in the midst of idolatry. Moreover, Zwingli was convinced that the presence of images in churches always necessarily led to a decrease in faith because human beings are naturally drawn to worship then. For this reason, he thought religious images were inherently dangerous and should be abolished.

Zwingli's activism, which makes him so different from Luther, derives precisely from this notion of faithfulness. Serving God correctly is the goal of Christian life, both personally and communally. Whereas Luther's principal dialectic is that between "Law and Gospel," Zwingli's is that between faithfulness and faithlessness, or true religion and false religion, or obedience and disobedience. All three dialectical pairs are one and the same for Zwingli. Unlike Luther, who could only conceive of a paradoxical synthesis between "Law and Gospel," and of an ethics in which the constant breaking of the divine law is inevitable—summed up in his *simul justus et peccator* formula—Zwingli believed that "the law is a Gospel for the man who honors God." The commandments, therefore, were "the constant will of God," working upon the world.[15] Unlike Luther, for whom works-righteousness was an offensively wrong concept, Zwingli devoutly believed in the regenerative power of faith and in a measure of reward for effort. Faithfulness, in fact, is the same as effort for Zwingli, for whom life was a constant battle that could be won not just in the hereafter, but also in the here and now. The life of a Christian, he said, was "a battle so sharp and full of danger that effort can nowhere be relaxed without loss. . . . [I]t is also a lasting victory, for he who fights it wins, if only he remains loyal to Christ the head."[16] Remaining loyal, of course, entailed both right worship and right behavior.

If Zwingli retains any sense of paradox in his theology, it is in his conception of divine providence. Convinced as he was that human effort played a role in redemption, Zwingli also believed that God ultimately controlled everything, including who would be the faithful. Although he never dwelt on predestination, or elaborated on the concept systematically, Zwingli spoke of election and sometimes even used the term *predestination*, as when he said "predestination is born of providence, nay is providence."[17] Far from a fatalist, Zwingli believed in a predestination that turned the elect into energetic agents of the divine will. The fact that God chose his own did not mean that one had no choice. In fact, it was precisely because the divine act of choosing was a mystery that one was commanded to be active, for predestination was not about one's merits but about God displaying his power and mercy through human agency.

Armed with such a dynamic theology in which worship and ethics were one and the same and in which every errand was a mission from God, Zwingli's associates and followers set out to transform their confederation. Later, after his death, some of his disciples would seek the transformation of the whole world.

Beyond Zurich

Iconoclasm had sealed the triumph of the Reformation in Zurich, and confirmed the city's leading role in the process of religious change within the Swiss Confederacy and in parts of southern Germany. Although Zwingli could never be credited with having caused the Swiss Reformation single-handedly, it is as difficult today as it was back in his day to deny that his leadership was crucial for its success during these early years. At Zurich, he had many like-minded colleagues, most notably Leo Jud (1482–1542), Oswald Myconius (1488–1552), and Heinrich Bullinger (1504–1575). Elsewhere, other associates encouraged him, keeping track of what happened in Zurich and drawing inspiration from it. By 1525, when Zurich was fully transformed, change was already sweeping through many other places. Leaders who were very close friends with Zwingli could be found throughout the northern cantons: Joachim Vadianus (1484–1551) at St. Gall, Ambrosius Blarer (1492–1564), and Johannes Zwick (1496–1542) at Constance, Sebastian Meyer (1465–1545) at Schaffhausen, Johann Oecolampadius (1482–1531) at Basel, Berthold Haller (1492–1536), Franz Kolb (1465–1535), and Caspar Hedio (1494–1552) at Bern.

Beyond the boundaries of the confederation, Zwingli also formed strong ties with Martin Bucer (1491–1551) at Strassburg, in Alsace. As we shall see more clearly in the next chapter, these leaders were important, but only part of a much larger movement. Throughout northern Switzerland and southern Germany—especially in the cities—the new message of gospel-based reform won popular support among vast numbers of people who then took it upon themselves, in one way or another, to make change possible. Nonetheless, throughout this entire area there were also great numbers of people who resisted change, which made conflict inevitable. The history of the early years of the Swiss Reformation is marked by conflict, and so too is it defined to a large extent by a pattern very similar to that of Zurich, in which iconoclasm plays a central role.

The progress of the Reformation in Switzerland can be traced most efficiently and revealingly by following the trail of iconoclastic ruin. From Zurich, iconoclasm spread in waves to smaller communities under its jurisdiction, and, in turn, to other major cities and their territories. Bern and St. Gall would follow suit in 1528; Constance, Basel, and Schaffhausen in 1529; Neuchâtel in 1530; and Geneva in 1535. In addition, under the jurisdiction of these larger cities, there were numerous smaller communities where the old religion was attacked and dismantled. Older histories of the Swiss Reformation have a keen awareness of the significance of iconoclasm. Contemporary chroniclers such as Johannes Stumpf and Jeanne de Jussie, for instance, structured their narratives around the attack on traditional symbols and rituals.[18] It made no difference that Pastor Stumpf was Protestant and Sister Jeanne a Catholic: back then both parties knew that the Reformation was all about hand-to-hand combat over symbols and rituals. Three centuries later, major historians of the Reformation such as J. H. Merle D'Aubigné were still aware of the significance of this pattern. D'Aubigné depended on iconoclasm for his narrative structure, and also wisely used it as an interpretative lens, observing that "in the times of the Reformation, the doctors attacked the pope and the people the images."[19]

The pattern of reform in Switzerland is laid bare by iconoclasm for a very simple reason: the war against the "idols" always brought the conflict with the old status quo to a head, since it questioned the legal status of the images and the Mass. Wherever the Catholic Church was still legally ensconced, iconoclasts always had to be tried for their crimes, and the trials had a unique potential for bringing the religious conflict to some sort of resolution, whether by public debate, popular vote, or magisterial decision. The pattern set in Zurich was followed nearly everywhere else in Switzerland: first, the old symbols and rituals would be challenged through iconoclastic acts, then the legality of these acts would be openly debated in a disputation where the iconoclastic Reformers hoped to "prove" that the Bible was the sole authority and that it demanded the abolition of images and the Mass. As in Zurich, it would be the civil powers—the lay oligarchy that ruled the city—that would approve the Reformation. And with the abolition of the old religion, a whole new church and a new society would be established, with a very different relationship between church and state.

Fallen idols. The destruction of sacred images became commonplace throughout the northern cantons of the Swiss Confederacy between 1525 and 1536.

Bern was the first major city to follow the example of Zurich. In Bern, Berthold Haller and Franz Kolb, two friends of Zwingli, had been actively preaching and teaching against traditional religion since the early 1520s, even though an overwhelming majority of the city's magistrates opposed them at first. By 1527, however, their efforts had paid off. Six of the city guilds had abolished the Mass in their chapels, and seven others were sharply divided on the issue. As tensions mounted in the city between those who were demanding an end to "idolatry" and those who did not think of their faith as "idolatrous," the Bernese magistrates agreed to hold a public disputation à la Zurich on the legitimacy of the established religion.

Berthold Haller drew up ten theses for discussion, which Ulrich Zwingli revised and tightened, with the aim of bringing down the "idols" and the old status quo they embodied. The Bern disputation began on the feast of Epiphany, 6 January 1528, and dragged on for twenty days, with Zwingli leading the iconoclastic party. When the debate ended, the city council declared the iconoclasts the winners, and ordered that all images and altars be carefully removed over the space of a week, as had been done in Zurich.

The effect of this proclamation was quite different in Bern, however. On 27 and 28 January, mobs stormed the city's churches and destroyed all of the art and the ritual objects. As the churches were being sacked, children sang in the streets, "We have been saved from a baked god"—meaning that the "idol" of the consecrated host had been destroyed—revealing how deeply the new theology had sunk in. On the second day of the rioting, Zwingli proclaimed the triumph of the Reformation in a sermon at the cathedral. "Victory has declared for the truth," he exclaimed, pointing to the rubble that encircled the congregation:

> There you have the altars and idols of the temple! . . . Now there is no more debating whether we should have these idols or not. Let us clear out this filth and rubbish! Henceforth, let us devote to other men, the living images of God, all the unimaginable wealth which was once spent on these foolish idols. There are still many weak and quarrelsome people who complain about the removal of the idols, even though it is clearly evident that there is nothing holy about them, and that they break and crack like any other piece of wood or stone. Here lies one without its head! Here another without its arms! If this abuse had done any harm to the saints who are near God, and if they had the power which is ascribed to them, do you think you would have been able to behead and cripple them as you did?

The powerless "idols" had been overthrown. Their very annihilation was proof enough of their falsehood, and the wealth lavished on them was now to be given to the poor. Moreover, Zwingli also spoke of a kind of freedom that was the inverse of Luther's: not freedom from works-righteousness, but rather freedom through action, and righteousness through the work of iconoclasm: "Now, then, recognize the freedom which Christ has given you, stand fast in it, and, as Paul says in Galatians [8:1], 'be not entangled again with the yoke of bondage.'"[20] In citing a passage from Galatians that was key to Luther's arguments against Karlstadt, Zwingli boldly proclaimed the difference between his Reformation and Luther's. The Bernese were now free from the yoke of "false" religion, rather than from bondage to works-righteousness, and they had themselves to thank for that freedom. Zwingli's sermon laid bare the spirit of the Swiss Reformation.

Reformed Bern, in turn, ensured that all of the communities under its jurisdiction rid themselves of "idolatry." Eventually, the Bernese would be largely responsible for spreading their Reformation into French-speaking Lausanne in 1530 and Geneva in 1535, but the most immediate effect of their iconoclastic riot was to spark similar outbursts in other towns within their canton. Mobs invaded the churches in Auberg, Zofingen, Brugg, Arau, and Buren, and wreaked havoc. Other cantons soon followed suit, and the first of these was St. Gall, where less than a month after Bern's iconoclastic riot, the magistrates ordered the removal of all "idols" from the city. Under the leadership of Vadianus, mobs stormed the cathedral and all the churches in town, and did what iconoclasts are wont to do. From the cathedral alone forty-six wagons full of rubble were carted away and burned. As at Zurich and Bern, gold and silver items were melted down, jewels carefully saved, and some of the wealth distributed among the poor or deposited in the town treasury.

Soon, much of northern Switzerland was ablaze with burning "idols." In Zwingli's native Toggenburg, young men destroyed all the altars and images without anyone's approval. In Wesen, where Zwingli had lived as a child for five years with his uncle Bartholomew, another group of youths removed all the images from the churches and piled them up outdoors, where they mocked them and encouraged them to flee before setting them on fire. In Schaffhausen, where iconoclasts had always heretofore been swiftly punished, in 1529 the city council finally caved in to pressure from Zurich and Bern and called for an orderly destruction of all of its sacred art and ritual objects. In Constance, which Bishop Hugo had already fled in 1527, pressure from Zurich ensured the demise of the images and the Mass in 1529.

For every town and city that did away with traditional religion, however, there were others that dug in their heels, and tensions began to mount within the Swiss Confederacy. In Schwanden and other many towns, iconoclasts fell victim to violence at the hands of traditionalists. As the Reformed cities sent out missionaries and printed texts, hoping to bring others to their side, resistance and resentment soon surfaced, in other cities and cantons, including Lucerne, where Zwingli's associates lost a public disputation against Johann Eck, Luther's old foe, and especially the less urbanized cantons to the south, such as Uri, Schwyz, and Unterwalden, and some of the French-speaking cities in the Pays de Vaud, such as Fribourg. Rumors of civil war began to surface on both sides as religious differences tore away at the social and political fabric of the Swiss Confederation.

This tension could also be highly visible. By 1528, Basel, home to Erasmus of Rotterdam and other learned humanists, was a powder keg of religious and political tension, ready to explode. Johann Oecolampadius and some associates had been preaching against "idolatry" since 1523 and had even managed to gain control of some churches and to reform their rituals according to Zwinglian principles. But the all of the churches, including those seized by Oecolampadius's followers, remained full of "idols" and the city as a whole remained full of committed Catholics who still venerated images and of churches where the Mass was celebrated. The city's oligarchy and its guilds were bitterly divided, and at an impasse. The city council tried to "sit on two stools," as Oecolampadius put it, allowing for religious pluralism in the city and refusing to decide in favor of either side while maintaining that the removal of religious images was against the law. Erasmus, who was also often accused of sitting on two stools, or three or more, watched nervously, with more than his usual measure of tolerant despair.

Shortly after New Year's Day in 1529, the magistrates called for a disputation and insisted that the Catholic Mass could continue to be celebrated at the cathedral and two other churches until that time. As the sharply divided magistrates argued, armed gangs roamed the streets of Basel for a month. Finally, on 8 February, a large mob stormed the town hall and demanded that the city council expel twelve of its most devoted Catholic members, change the city's constitution to expand the role of the guilds, and abolish idolatry. Since the Catholic core in the inner council consisted of high officers in the four merchant guilds of Basel, this revolt can be seen as directed not only against the old religion, but also against the guild structure and the Basel magistracy. "Idolatry" thus served as the focus of wide-ranging discontent: in clamoring for the removal of the images, the citizens of Basel were also demanding the transformation of the oligarchy that had stubbornly defended their legitimacy.

On 9 February, Ash Wednesday, as the council deliberated and armed men from both parties rambled through the streets, hundreds of men stormed the cathedral, unleashing the anger that had been pent up for so long, "to commit frightful ravages," as Erasmus put it.[21] Some magistrates hurried to the cathedral to stop the iconoclasts, only to be met by defiant rioters who huffed: "All that you have failed to effect in three years of deliberation we have accomplished within this hour."[22] Tons of rubble from the cathedral fueled huge bonfires in the surrounding squares, while the rioting spread to the other remaining Catholic churches of Basel. To complete their revolt, the iconoclasts demanded that the magistrates finally consent to what had taken place. Overcome by the smoke from the bonfires and the angry mobs, the council had no choice but to accede to their demands. The twelve Catholic magistrates were deposed, concessions were made to the guilds concerning their future role in the city's governance, and the images and the Mass were legally abolished. As Oecolampadius saw it, a "hard knot" had been split in Basel by "the wedge of the Lord," that is, by the rebellious iconoclasts.

The riot also chased away Basel's most famous resident idol, the great humanist Erasmus. Troubled by the violence of the iconoclasts and unable to cope with the total abolition of the old faith, he packed his bags and moved to Freiburg im Breisgau, outside of the Swiss Confederation, bidding farewell to Oecolampadius and the other young reforming humanists he had so inspired. For a man who loathed extremes and prized the arts, the puritan spirit of the new Basel—which he had unwittingly helped to create—seemed too much to bear, too much like having to live with a wayward child.

Reformed Protestantism: Cities and their reformers

City and year	Reformers
Zurich, 1524	Ulrich Zwingli
	Heinrich Bullinger
Strassburg, 1524–1525	Martin Bucer
St. Gall, 1528	Joachim von Watt (Vadianus)
Bern, 1528	Berthold Haller
	Franz Kolb
	Caspar Hedio
Constance, 1529	Ambrosius Blarer
	Johannes Zwick
Schaffhausen, 1529	Sebastian Meyer
Basel, 1529	Johann Oecolampadius
Neuchâtel, 1530	Guillaume Farel
Geneva, 1535	Guillaume Farel
	Pierre Viret
	John Calvin
Lausanne, 1536	Pierre Viret
	Guillaume Farel

Erasmus would return to Basel six years later and die there in 1536, even though he was still a Catholic and the city had outlawed his faith. Whether or not he was able to receive the last rites from any Catholic cleric is unknown. What this reveals about Erasmus is open to interpretation, but the ultimate outcome of his critique of traditional religion is beyond dispute.

The Great Rift

By the time Basel had done away with images and the Mass, it had become very clear to all opponents of Roman Catholicism that there were major differences among them, and that the Swiss and German Reformations were progressing on two separate tracks.

By 1529, especially after the Second Diet of Worms had renewed the Edict of Worms, it had also become clear that Emperor Charles V might finally be able to assemble an army large and powerful enough to crush all "heretical" Reformations, everywhere. Meeting the challenge posed by Charles V and ensuring their survival would not be easy, but many of the evangelical Reformers and their secular authorities realized that their cause would stand a better chance of success if they were joined by a common bond, perhaps even by means of a single unified anti-"Romish" church.

One secular ruler who rose to meet this challenge in Germany was Philip I, Landgrave of Hesse, known as "the Magnanimous" (1504–1567). Philip had been very favorably impressed by Luther at the Diet of Worms in 1521, and three years later, after meeting with Melanchthon, he fully embraced Luther's cause. He also played a significant role in crushing the peasant uprisings of 1524–1525, and could boast of defeating the forces led by Thomas Müntzer at the Battle of Frankenhausen. Although popular support for Luther was not very strong in Hesse, Philip abolished Catholicism and imposed a Lutheran church order on all of his subjects. In 1527 he also opened a new university in Marburg, for the education of Lutheran clergy.

Convinced that the Catholic princes of Germany—including his father-in-law Duke George of Saxony—were forging a military alliance against him and other evangelicals, Philip of Hesse resolved to form a counteralliance among all those who opposed the Roman Catholic Church, including the Swiss and those southern German cities that followed the Swiss Reformation.

Philip's efforts bore fruit most dramatically at the Second Diet of Speyer in 1529, where, after the majority of representatives in this parliament voted to impose severe restrictions on evangelicals and reverse the spread of their "heresy," six evangelical princes and fourteen imperial free cities banded together and issued a dissenting "Protestation." Philip, who played a key role in galvanizing the evangelicals at the Diet, soon emerged as the leading "Protestant," as the dissenters came to be known.

Fearing an imminent attack from Catholic princes, Philip stepped up his efforts to further unify the Protestant camp. The most successful of his endeavors was the creation in 1531 of the Schmalkaldic League, a Protestant military coalition. This league—which took its name from the Thuringian town of Schmalkalden, where it was created—would play a key role in defending the Protestant cause, especially in 1546–1547. The success of the league, however, obscures the fact that it was less powerful than Philip wanted it to be, and that its creation involved one of Philip's worst failures: his attempt to reconcile all Protestants. And this is where the Swiss come into the picture.

Hoping to create a military alliance that included the Swiss, Philip invited the top leaders of the Protestant Reformation to meet in Hesse, at his Marburg Castle, in early October 1529. This meeting included not just the leading lights of the Lutheran and Swiss Reformations, but also of the South German lands (who differed from the Swiss and the Lutherans in theology and ritual). Though lopsided in favor of the Lutherans, the list of participants is a veritable who's who of the early Protestant Reformation: the Lutheran camp was represented by Luther himself, as well as by Philip Melanchthon, Justus Jonas, Caspar Cruciger, Oswald Myconius, Johannes Brenz, Veit Dietrich, Johannes Agricola, and Andreas Osiander; the Swiss by Ulrich Zwingli, Heinrich Bullinger, and Johann Oecolampadius; and the South Germans by Martin Bucer, Caspar Hedio, Wolfgang Capito, and Jakob Sturm.

Luther and Zwingli did most of the talking, or, more accurately, most of the arguing. Although everyone in the room agreed on fourteen points of doctrine—including fundamental issues such as infant baptism, justification by faith, and belief in the Trinity—agreement proved impossible on a fifteenth point: the sacrament of the Eucharist.

The sticking point was this: How should the bread and wine be interpreted? Was the sacrament a real communion with Christ, or merely a symbolic remembrance? While the Lutherans believed that Christ was physically present in both elements, the Swiss argued that such a belief was irrational and unnecessary. The South Germans tended to be comfortable with no precise assertions, and they contributed relatively little to the debate. Luther insisted on a literal interpretation of the words uttered by Christ at the Last Supper: "Take this and eat, this *is* my body; drink this cup, for this *is* my blood." For Luther and his followers, then, the word *is* did not at all mean anything other than "*really* is." Zwingli and the Swiss, in contrast, argued that the word *is* should be understood metaphorically as "signifies" or "symbolizes."

Zwingli and the Swiss had a rational approach with no tolerance for paradox: if Christ had a fully human body, they argued, and that body ascended to heaven, how could it be present in the eucharistic elements? Human bodies are finite and can be present in only one place at a time, so claiming that Christ could be in heaven and the Eucharist at the same time was not only illogical, but also a denial of his real humanity. Luther accused the Swiss of being "too mathematical" and of misunderstanding the omnipotence of God.[23] Yes, retorted Luther, Christ had a human body, but Christ was also divine, and God is not only omnipotent, but also omnipresent: God can do anything and can be present everywhere simultaneously.

Parting of the ways. The Marburg Colloquy failed to unify the Lutheran and Reformed traditions, chiefly because of profound disagreements over the meaning of the Eucharist, especially of Christ's reference to the bread and wine as "my body" and "my blood." In this contemporary image, Philip of Hesse is surrounded by the major Protestant leaders who attended his conference, with Ulrich Zwingli and the Swiss at his right and Martin Luther and the Germans at his left.

"I do not ask how Christ can be God and man and how these natures could be united," said Luther, "for God is able to do more than anything we can imagine."[24] He continued, "Who am I to measure the power of God? The driving force of the universe is not in one place."[25]

Zwingli and Oecolampadius denied this basic premise of Luther's, pushing hard on the core metaphysical issue that defined their approach to rituals and symbols: spirit is far superior to matter, even incompatible with it. So while Luther focused on the biblical texts in which Christ said "this is my body" and "this is my blood," and on what *is* must mean, Zwingli and the Swiss focused on texts that supported their core metaphysical assumptions and their metaphorical interpretation of the eucharistic ritual, especially on Christ's statement, "It is the Spirit that gives life; the flesh is useless" (John 6:60).

Sparks began to fly as both Luther and Zwingli grew angry with each other's unwillingness to budge. According to one eyewitness account, "there was much shouting."[26]

LUTHER (TO ZWINGLI): "Your logic is very poor; it is the kind of logic for which a schoolboy is caned and sent to the corner."

ZWINGLI: "This passage (John 6:60) is going to break your neck."

LUTHER: "Don't boast too much. Necks do not break that easily here. You are in
Hesse, not Switzerland."[27]

Useless as it seemed to continue, the colloquy dragged on, and after two full days of
rancorous debate, no agreement could be reached. Philip of Hesse's dream of a unified
Protestant front had fizzled, right before his eyes, for the animosity between the Lutherans
and the Swiss intensified in that room at Marburg Castle as they each dug deeper and
deeper trenches around their positions and lobbed insults at one another. According to
Caspar Hedio's notes, the colloquy ended on a very sour note:

> Zwingli asks Luther to pardon his harshness, and says that he has always deeply desired
> his friendship and seeks it even now. Then he added, almost weeping: There are no
> men, neither in Italy nor in France, who he would rather see.
> Luther says: Pray God that you may come to a right understanding of this matter.
> Oecolampadius answers: You, too, should pray for this, for you have the same need.[28]

After Marburg, the Lutheran and Reformed traditions went their separate ways,
fully aware of the differences between them, and resolutely determined to consider the
"other" in error, despite all the beliefs they shared in common. It was an epochal parting
of the ways, a great rupture that no one could ignore. And the rift itself not only defined
each tradition henceforward, but also made it impossible for all Protestants to unite in the
face of Charles V's ominous threats.

But no matter how central the theological quagmire of the Eucharist was to their
differences, it was far from the only issue that made the Swiss Reformed tradition very
different from Lutheranism.

Godly Cities

Turning all citizens into good Christians was the principal aim of the Swiss Reformers,
and another key difference between them and the Lutherans up north. Whereas Luther
deepened his paradoxical *simul justus et peccator* approach to "good works" and to his
equally paradoxical two-kingdom political theology after 1525, Zwingli and his associates
in Switzerland and southern Germany became wholly committed to building communities in which good works and obedience to the Ten Commandments were expected, and
in which church and state worked hand in hand to ensure "faithfulness," pure worship,
and good behavior.

Consequently, although the Swiss and the Lutherans shared the same soteriology, believing in salvation by faith alone, the Swiss took a less paradoxical approach
to the pervasiveness of sin in the individual and society. While Lutherans stressed the
inevitability of sin in the individual and the community, and the dissonance between
faith and behavior, the Swiss emphasized the transforming power of faith, especially of
faith under the aegis of the state. In other words, whereas Luther stressed the forgiveness

of sins and the enduring corruption of the world, the Swiss insisted on the avoidance of sin and the perfectibility of the community. Whereas Luther taught that everyone was a constant sinner, that a Christian prince was a rare bird, and that the kingdom of Christ was simply a promise for some postapocalyptic future, the Swiss insisted that sin could be controlled and that the state itself had a duty to suppress it and build the kingdom of Christ on earth, here and now. To put it in practical terms: a Reformed Swiss community had no place at all for anyone who sinned boldly, as Luther advised his followers to do. It also had no place for rulers who were not good Christians. In sum, sin could be tolerated no more than idolatry, because both were avoidable, immensely displeasing to God and dangerous to the collective welfare of the community.

Some historians used to speak of the community created by Zwingli as a theocracy, that is, a state in which ultimate authority is held by those who represent God, but this term is no longer accepted as valid or useful in this case, for in Zurich and the other Swiss states that followed its lead, the government was never in the hands of the clergy, directly or indirectly. Instead, church and state cooperated with each other and corrected each other, without either one claiming supremacy. In such a community, all civil laws were ostensibly in accordance with the Bible, and the civil authorities had the power to enforce all discipline. The clergy had a role to play too, beyond their ritual functions, but, in essence, they were as much under the authority of the civil rulers as any other resident of the godly city.

Several institutions developed in Zurich helped ensure that the city would remain a godly one, and these institutions, in one way or another, would become distinctive traits of all the communities that followed Zurich's lead or drew from Zwingli's theology.

The most distinctive innovation was the marriage court (*Ehegericht*), created in 1525 to replace the court formerly run by the bishop of Constance. Originally designed to handle all questions that dealt with sex, marriage, and family—including cases of adultery and fornication—the marriage court quickly became the magistracy's chief tool for overseeing and enforcing Christian discipline. By 1530, the *Ehegericht* had broadened its jurisdiction considerably and become a total fusing of church and state. It was composed of four laymen—two members of the city's Large Council and two from the Small Council—and two clerics. The clerics were the experts in theology, naturally, but their authority was in no way greater than that of the laymen.

Another distinctive Zurich institution that ensured a godly community was the synod, which was created by the city's magistrates in 1528 to oversee the clergy. The synod, which met twice a year, was directly under the magistrate's supervision. Its main role was to examine the behavior of all the clergy and, if necessary, to discipline them. In addition, it also provided the clergy with a forum for discussing their duties with one another and addressing any problems they encountered in their ministries. In 1532, the magistrates extended their control of the clergy by creating the office of church deacons, who would visit the parishes and evaluate the performance of the ministers. Through the synod and the diaconate, then, the civil authorities exercised a balance of power and ensured that the church would be free of abuses and that the clergy would never place themselves above the law.

A third institution was the *Prophezei*, a new type of continuing education program, designed by Zwingli as he reorganized the schools in Zurich, that gathered ministers and students five times a week to read and discuss biblical texts in Latin, Greek, and Hebrew, and to hear lectures. These assemblies were intended not only to maintain a knowledgeable clergy, but also to help in the training of new clerics and in increasing knowledge of the Bible among the laity.

Another innovation that could be called an institution, even though it had no name, was the centralization of all the city's charity under the supervision of the civil authorities. Care of the poor and needy had always been a high priority for Zwingli, and an essential component of his iconoclastic theology. Like Karlstadt, who linked the destruction of images with the abolition of begging, Zwingli argued that a Christian community had a duty to manage its collective wealth carefully and effectively, to alleviate or eliminate poverty and sloth. Christian charity, Zwingli argued, was too important and too complex a task to leave in the hands of individuals, or guilds, or confraternities. Consequently, as the monasteries and convents were confiscated by the city authorities, the endowments for masses and chapels seized, and the church plate melted down, the revenue was funneled into the town treasury and much of it earmarked for charitable purposes. Some monasteries and nunneries became hospitals, administered by the city. Laws were passed against begging that distinguished between the "deserving" poor, that is, those who had genuine need, and the undeserving poor, who were too lazy to work. Begging was outlawed, and a badge system created whereby only those who had been designated as "deserving" of charity would receive alms. This system of identifying and funding the "deserving" poor was handled at the parish level, but its uniformity was ostensibly guaranteed by the city's laws.

And so Zurich was turned into a Christian city, where "faithfulness," godly behavior, and efficient charity were to be the norm rather than the exception. The idea of establishing such a sacral community wholly dedicated to Christian principles was not new; in theory at least, this had been the goal of all medieval communities. Now, however, that theory had been put into practice in such a way that the civil authorities were granted much of the power that the clergy formerly reserved for themselves. This puritanical reforming impulse would become the ethos of the Swiss Reformation, evident in all the cities and cantons that abolished images and the Mass. It would also reach beyond the Swiss Confederation, to cities such as Strassburg, Ulm, and Geneva, and take root in France, the Netherlands, Scotland, England, and the North American colonies. This distinctive collusion of church and state and this sense of building a purified "faithful" Christian republic, which were inseparable from a theology of election, would become the most recognizable features of the Reformed Protestant tradition. When John Winthrop admonished the New England–bound *Mayflower* Puritans, "We must consider that we shall be as a City upon a Hill, the eyes of all people are upon us," Zwingli's Zurich was his paradigm, whether he knew it or not.

Christian Soldiers

For Zwingli and his followers, as for their spiritual progeny, the English Puritans, the sacred and the secular were of one piece. Waging war on the idols required waging war on sin and the seven vices, and taking on the devil himself. Zwingli would die on the battlefield in 1531, sword in hand, like many a Swiss soldier. When Zurich decided in its own democratic way to wage war on those other cantons to the south that were unreceptive to its missionaries, he fulfilled his duty, which was at once civic and religious. That he would don armor and charge the enemy—he, a minister of the Word of God—says it all. That the enemy should have been his fellow confederates who considered him an arch-heretic and a threat to their way of life speaks volumes about the complexity of the religious crisis of the sixteenth century, and about its human toll. The Battle of Kappel, at which Zwingli lost his life, marked the beginning of a long truce among the Confederates, a very Swiss agreement to leave each other alone. Bereft of Zwingli, Zurich would rely on Heinrich Bullinger for leadership. Bereft of a mission field within the Swiss Confederacy, the Reformed communities of the north redirected their energies and found other more fertile fields to sow. Zwingli's Reformation not only survived his death, but also grew by leaps and bounds.

In what is surely one of the most extreme ironies in all of world history, Zwingli's enemies burned his corpse and scattered his ashes to deprive the Zurichers of their martyr's relics. Anyone who doubts that men can kill each other over things they do not understand need look no further than this event. In a further ironic twist, rumors began to circulate that Zwingli's heart had miraculously survived the flames and was enshrined somewhere in Zurich.[29] Catholic polemicists believed the rumor, accepting it as proof that Zwingli's relics were being worshiped idolatrously by his followers in Zurich. As comic as it is tragic, this misunderstanding stemmed in part from the belief that Zwingli's spirit somehow lived on and in part from sheer ignorance and gullibility. If there is any poetic justice at all in such an anecdote, it is that in a figurative sense Zwingli's heart did continue to animate his followers, all of whom were iconoclasts down to their marrow.

CHAPTER ELEVEN

The Radical Reformation

Lutherans may have irritated Zwingli and Catholics may have killed him, but these were not his only opponents. Close at hand, in Zurich, Zwingli had to contend with dissent from some of his closest supporters. And he dealt with them as he had with the idols he so despised.

A few days after Zwingli's forty-third birthday, on 5 January 1527, a young man named Felix Mantz (b. 1498) was led to the fish market in Zurich, forced into a boat, and rowed out to the deepest part of the Limmat River, his hands and feet bound to a sturdy pole. At the appointed moment, Mantz, the illegitimate son of one of Zurich's canons and a constant thorn in the side of Zwingli and the city authorities, was thrown into the icy blue water, and drowned.

Mantz, a reformer, thus earned himself the sad distinction of being the first Protestant to be martyred by other Protestants. His crime was that of rebaptizing. According to a law passed by the Zurich authorities in March 1526, such an offense carried the highly ironic penalty of death by "rebaptism," that is, by drowning. This law invoked the ancient Roman law codes of Emperors Theodosius II and Justinian I rather than the gospel or local Swiss custom, due to the simple fact that rebaptism had not been a problem for Christians since the days of the Donatist heresy, back in the fifth and sixth centuries.

Writing about this unprecedented event, Heinrich Bullinger, Zwingli's successor as leader of the church in Zurich would later say:

> His mother and brother came to him, and exhorted him to be steadfast; and he perse-
> vered in his folly, even to the end. When he was bound upon the pole and was about to
> be thrown into the river by the executioner, he sang with a loud voice, "Into thy hands,
> O Lord, I commend my spirit."[1]

That Mantz's final words should have been the same as those uttered by Jesus on the cross, and that Bullinger could find them the epitome of foolishness, points to a

Protestants killing Protestants. The execution of Anabaptist martyr Felix Mantz in January 1527, as depicted in Heinrich Bullinger's *Reformation Chronicle.*

major cultural rift and an epistemological meltdown. This dissonance offers us a glimpse not only into Mantz's faith and his desire to emulate the New Testament in every way, but also into the chaotic religious climate of the 1520s, the wild growth of dissent, and the inability of the Zurich authorities to come to terms with a dissenting interpretation of the *sola scriptura* principle from within their own fold—an interpretation they saw as heretical and a dangerous threat to the stability of church and state, so dangerous, in fact, that the authorities had to reach back to ancient Roman law to deal with it.

Mantz and his brethren were deemed heretics for insisting that the church in Zurich conform in every way to that described in the New Testament, especially in the Acts of the Apostles and of Paul's epistles, a church that, as they saw it, was composed strictly of believing adults. The danger as perceived by Zwingli, Bullinger, and others in authority was that if such a church should be reestablished, church membership in Zurich would be strictly voluntary, and the ancient symbiosis between church and state would disappear, along with all reforming theocratic ideals. In other words, it would make a thorough Reformation of society absolutely impossible.

But Felix Mantz was no outsider. He had for a while shared the same vision as Zwingli, even pushed him to come to terms with the gap between his preaching and his actions. He and his two closest associates, Conrad Grebel (c. 1498–1526) and George Blaurock (c. 1491–1529), had been among the most active participants in the overthrow of Catholicism in Zurich. Unlike the Zwickau prophets, who came to Wittenberg from elsewhere, the "rebaptizers" in Zurich were not only homegrown; they were from the inner circle of the Reformation, close to Zwingli himself, and had been among the first to put into practice what Zwingli preached, like eating sausages during Lent or destroying religious imagery.

Mantz and those others who practiced rebaptism came to be known as Anabaptists (Greek: *ana*, "again," and *baptizo*, "to baptize") or rebaptizers. Some opponents even took to calling them catabaptists (Greek: *kata*, "down, away") or antibaptists. These opponents of the Roman Catholic Church did not believe themselves "rebaptizers" in the strict meaning of the term, since they considered infant baptism null and void. As they saw it, genuine baptism could be conferred only on believing adults, and they were therefore merely baptizing people for the first time. Their vision of the true church as an intimate association of genuine believers—rather than an institution coextensive with all of society—bespoke a fervent desire to follow biblical models much more closely than Zwingli or Luther, and to revive a church that had ceased to exist more than a thousand years before. They were restitutionists; that is, they believed that the true church of Christ had disappeared from the earth and that they were called to restore it, in all its apostolic, biblical purity. In many ways, their literal interpretation of the Bible, and especially the New Testament, followed the reforming principle of *sola scriptura* to logical conclusions that neither Zwingli nor Luther was willing to accept.

These Anabaptists in Zurich were not alone. They were but one local expression of a much larger and very diffuse wave of dissent, with many branches and regional variations. This, the third major branch of Protestantism (alongside the Lutheran and Reformed), has come to be known as the Radical Reformation, because of its collective desire to return to the very roots of the Christian faith (Latin: *radix*, "root"), and because it called for more aggressive and extensive changes in the social fabric. This name seems to have stuck, after much debate, but its wide acceptance does not mean that all experts agree about its usage, let alone about whom to include in this category, or why. A bewildering array of communities and individuals falls into this category, which is much more than a simple catchall "other" or "none of the above." In essence, what allows historians to use the term with confidence, albeit with all sorts of caveats, is that an essential set of features distinguishes all those who are lumped under the category of "Radical":

1. Belief in the church as having fallen and disappeared at some point in early Christian history
2. Belief in an essential, unbridgeable chasm between Christians and "the world"
3. Belief in strictly voluntary Christianity, and in a church composed only of believers
4. Rejection of infant baptism as an earmark of the compulsory, fallen, territorial churches
5. Belief in the freedom of the human will, and in the role of human effort toward salvation

Believing in these five points also entails dismissing the reforms led by Luther, Zwingli, and their colleagues, which were rejected as incomplete and insufficient. At bottom, then, one could argue that a single belief unites all those listed as "Radicals": their rejection of any church that mixed with "the world," that is, any church that relied on civil power and insisted on including everyone in the community. As the Anabaptists' Schleitheim Articles stated in the starkest possible terms:

> A separation should take place from the evil which the devil has planted in the world. We simply will not have fellowship with evil people, nor associate with them, nor participate with them in their abominations.[2]

The flip side of the Radical Reformation—what all radicals rejected—has come to be known as the Magisterial Reformation, for that Reformation depended for its existence on magistrates or princes and other civil rulers, and employed magisters (university-trained masters or teachers) and civil law to enforce its teachings and ritual among all who lived within particular jurisdictional boundaries.

Focusing on the Radicals' rejection of the Magisterial Reformation as their most distinctive common thread brings to light their boldest characteristics: their grievances and their nonconformity, as well as their organizing principle stemmed from ethical concerns. As Radicals saw it, the major defect of the Magisterial Reformation was a moral one, for it had not transformed Christian behavior, leaving the Lutheran or the Reformed churches indistinguishable from the Catholic. As different as some of the Radicals could be from one another, they could agree on this: being a Christian required the total transformation of an individual's life, for a sinner had no place in the true church of Christ. Ulrich Zwingli, for one, detected that this was their defining trait, and their worst mistake:

> As long as we are in the flesh, we are never without sin. For the flesh and the spirit are contrary the one to the other. . . . But the Anabaptists do hold that they live without sin. . . . They are committed absolutely to the view that they can and do without sin. . . . In so doing they make God a liar and bring back the hypocrisy of legal righteousness. . . . Is not that the height of presumption?[3]

This very basic difference of opinion, which all parties in the sixteenth century acknowledged, suggests that another name for the Radical Reformation, perhaps a more appropriate one could be that of *alternative* Reformation or alternative Protestantism. After all, what linked all Radicals most intensely was their conviction that personal transformation could be achieved only through a path other than those offered by Catholics, Lutherans, and the Reformed.

Naming this thing, this *other* kind of Reformation, has been a problem for far too long.

Interpreting the Nonconformists

Trying to distill or define the essence of a phenomenon as complex and variegated as the Radical—or *alternative*—Reformation entails imposing a certain degree of order, making distinctions and classifying. In fact, this is so unavoidable that ever since the Reformation itself, the devising of typologies for religious nonconformists has been a defining characteristic of Reformation historiography. The first of all typologies was a simple and binary. Luther lumped all evangelical dissenters together as *Schwärmer*, dangerous fanatics possessed by the devil rather than the Holy Spirit, as they claimed. Müntzer, Karlstadt, the Zwickau prophets, the Swiss Anabaptists—all of them were kindred spirits. It mattered little that they disagreed among themselves on many issues; the mere fact that they disagreed with Luther put them all in the same evil camp, as "false brethren." Zwingli and the Reformed tradition had a very similar opinion of dissenters, and called for their suppression. Thanks largely to the fact that they were very effectively suppressed, and to the fact that they shunned "the world," the Radicals themselves remained small in number and uninterested in broadcasting their interpretation of events.

So it was that the grand narrative of the Protestant Reformation came to be written by historians within the Magisterial Reformation itself, and that this binary typology stood unchallenged until the nineteenth century, when secularizing trends took the writing of Reformation history beyond confessional rivalries. Thanks largely to the work of Max Weber (1864–1920) and Ernst Troeltsch (1865–1923), founders of modern sociology, a new narrative emerged in which the dissenters were no longer on the margins, but rather at the cutting edge of the Reformation. Drawing on Weber's work, Troeltsch devised a distinction between religious communities he called "churches," which sought hegemony over entire societies and included even the wicked or spiritually indifferent in their number, and those he called "sects," which were nonconformist, and separatist, and tended to gather in a select few, voluntarily. In addition, Troeltsch also identified a third type of religious community, which could exist within or outside of the churches and sects: the spiritualizing or mystical fellowship, or spiritual *ecclesiola*. Eventually, in the mid-twentieth century, these typologies would be applied to the Protestant Reformation as a whole, and to the dissenters specifically.

But Troeltsch did more than devise typologies. He also passed judgment on the Reformation and put forward as a scholarly argument what the dissenters had been saying all along: that the "sects" and the "Spiritualists" of the Reformation were more logically consistent than the Magisterial Reformers. Troeltsch went even further, proclaiming these nonconformists to be "progressives" who were closer in spirit to the Renaissance humanists, praising them for establishing the first truly "modern" churches that were totally voluntary, divorced from the state, committed to egalitarianism and toleration, and adamantly opposed to the coercive "patriarchialism" of the Magisterial Reformers.[4] So, in tracing the arc of progress and modernity, which Troeltsch associated with liberalism and the separation of church and state, the Radicals became daring leaders and enlightened forerunners rather than dangerous fanatics.

The link between progressive or liberal ideology—then considered "leftist" in some circles—was best promoted by Roland Bainton, one of the leading historians of the Reformation in the mid-twentieth century. Arguing that the sectarians and Spiritualists should be known as the "left wing of the Reformation," Bainton, a Quaker who identified closely with the Radicals and their liberal political correctness, switched the typologizing to the political rather than the theological or sociological sphere, arguing that the so-called left wing

> anticipated all other religious bodies in the proclamation and exemplification of three principles, which, on the North American continent, are among those truths which we hold to be self-evident: the voluntary church, the separation of church and state, and religious liberty.[5]

About the same time that Bainton was promoting this interpretation, Franklin Littell put forward a different but complementary thesis, arguing that the nonconformists were all linked by one common trait: the belief in the restitution of the apostolic church. This belief, argued Littell, made them all "restitutionists" rather than Reformers, since they found all existing churches to be corrupt beyond redemption. It also turned them into a sect, in Troeltschian terms, and worthy of the name of "sectarian Protestants."[6]

As it turned out, however, neither Bainton's "left wing" nor Littell's "sectarian Protestantism" would gain universal acceptance. Both terms were quickly eclipsed by "Radical Reformation," principally because of the work of George Hunston Williams, whose massive survey of the subject proved definitive.[7] The term *radical* seemed perfect, not just because it had acquired a new depth of meaning in the politically turbulent 1960s, but also because Williams coupled his painstakingly thorough research with a persuasive argument and an attractive typology. Arguing that the nonconformists were not simply a more extreme version of the Protestantism of the Magisterial Reformers, either as "left wingers" or as "sectarians," but rather a wholly original collection of independent dissenters, Williams set them apart and gave them a common identity, despite all of their seemingly incompatible differences, or, as he put it, their disparate, "far-flung" actions were all linked by "a coherent, gripping, and dramatic unity."[8] Williams also devised a classification system for the Radicals that still stands largely unchallenged after half a century.

Following Troeltsch closely, especially when it came to distinguishing "spiritualism" as a distinct sociological category, and in identifying "rationalist" precursors of the Enlightenment, Williams proposed that there were three types of radicals: Anabaptists, Spiritualists, and Evangelical Rationalists (Anti-Trinitarians). Williams subdivided each of these three types into various subcategories, and he did so with consummate skill and a passion for symmetry, managing to convince most scholars and readers, for instance, that the violent revolutionaries who took over the town of Münster really belong among the Anabaptists, in the same category as the meek, pacifist, communistic Hutterites, and the highly individualistic and mystical southern German Anabaptists led by Hans Denck. We shall examine Williams's typology and suggest some modifications a few pages from now.

Another great change that has taken place in the study of this branch of the Reformation is the contribution made by Anabaptist historians, especially in North

The Radical Reformation according to George Hunston Williams

I.   Anabaptists
   1. Mainstream-evangelical
      New Testament model, pacifist: Swiss Brethren, Hutterites, Mennonites
   2. Contemplative-mystical
      Individualistic, influenced by medieval mystics: Hans Denck
   3. Revolutionaries
      Violent, apocalyptic: Münster
II. Spiritualists
   1. Mainstream-evangelical
      Spiritual perfection: Manifest later in Pietism
   2. Contemplative-mystical
      Individualistic, influenced by medieval mystics: Frank, Weigel
   3. Revolutionaries
      Violent, apocalyptic: Zwickau Prophets, Andreas Karlstadt, Thomas Müntzer
III. Evangelical Rationalists and Anti-Trinitarians
   1. Erasmians, Libertines, and Nicodemites
   2. Skeptics and Rationalists
   3. Anti-Trinitarians

America, since the second half of the twentieth century. Turning their attention to their own history, Anabaptist scholars—many of them from the Mennonite tradition—not only have collected and published hundreds of previously hard-to-find texts and documents, but also have contributed through their research to a deeper, more finely nuanced understanding of their tradition.

Among the various subjects highlighted by these Anabaptists scholars, such as pacifism, martyrdom, and communitarian life, one of the liveliest has been that of Anabaptist origins, which raises many questions about typologies and classifications. The main question addressed is a large one: did Anabaptism begin in one place (monogenesis), or did it begin in several places simultaneously (polygenesis)? This question branches out into others. Are the early Saxon Radicals Karlstadt, Müntzer, and Storch the founders of Anabaptism or widely different sources of inspiration for other Anabaptists? Were the earliest Anabaptists really separatist nonconformists, or did they turn to that option only after the Magisterial Reformers tried to suppress them? To this day, the issue of Anabaptist origins—and that of classification—remains a lively one, and not just among historians within the Anabaptist tradition.[9] And it is precisely this question of origins, and its conjoined twin, the question of typologies and classification that we have to turn to now, to survey this subject, which is the most complex and potentially confusing chapter of Reformation history.

With some modifications, this chapter follows the overall structure of Williams's typologies, breaking down the radicals into three broad categories: Anabaptists, Spiritualists, and Evangelical Rationalists (Anti-Trinitarians). The first category, that of

A modification of Williams's typology

I. Anabaptists
    1. Pacifists
        Model: New Testament Church
        Distinguishing traits: Segregation, persecution
        Adherents: Swiss Brethren, Tyrolese Brethren, Dutch Brethren, Mennonites
    2. Apocalyptic Activists
        Model: Old Testament prophecy and New Testament apocalypticism (New Israel/
            New Jerusalem)
        Distinguishing traits: Prophecy, apocalypticism, openness to violence
        Adherents: Thomas Müntzer, Hans Hut, Melchior Hoffman, Münsterites
    3. Moderates
        Model: New Testament Church
        Distinguishing traits: Willingness to avoid extremes
        Adherents: Andreas Karlstadt, Moravian Brethren, Pilgram Marpeck
II. Spiritualists
        Model: Jesus in the desert; Jesus alone in prayer; the apostles at Pentecost
        Common traits: Individualism, interiorization, inspiration through the Holy Spirit, distrust
            or rejection of the visible church and its sacraments
        Adherents: John Denck, Sebastian Franck, Sebastian Castellio, Caspar Schwenckfeld, Dirk
            Coornherts
III. Evangelical Rationalists
        Model: Jesus as the supreme paradigm for human existence
        Common traits: Denial of orthodox Christology and/or Trinity; emphasis on ethics as the
            key to salvation; appeal to reason and common sense
        Adherents: Michael Servetus, Giorgio Biandrata, Fausto and Lelio Sozzini, Socinians,
            Unitarians

Anabaptists, will be modified most intensely; the second and third—Spiritualists and Rationalists—only moderately. One of the drawbacks of Williams's typology has always been its highly detailed and nearly obsessive parsing of small theological distinctions among groups and individuals, who end up in different categories despite the fact that they share many traits. Another drawback has been Williams's insistence on symmetry and his penchant for matching sets of characteristics in subcategories, which sometimes leads to questionable distinctions. The outline followed here aims to reshuffle Williams's typology a bit, especially in the case of the Anabaptists, to shift attention to larger patterns that he tends to overlook.

The Earliest Radicals

Experts cannot yet agree on how to classify the earliest Radicals and nonconformists of the Protestant Reformation, or on how they may or may not be linked to others of their ilk, but everyone seems to agree on who the first such dissenters were: the Zwickau prophets, Andreas Bodenstein von Karlstadt, Thomas Müntzer, and those who gathered around them, whether at Allstedt, Orlamünde, or Mülhausen, or some other places. These were the first of many who would challenge the authority of Magisterial Reformers along with that of the pope, proposing changes that were more sweeping. Strictly speaking, none of them can be called Anabaptists, since they did not necessarily practice rebaptism, but their thinking, their actions, and their legacy place them squarely within the radical camp. Among these earliest dissenters one can already see the emergence of certain patterns and the evolution of two distinct radical traditions that could be called Anabaptist, one violent, socially concerned, and very mystically inclined, and the other pacifist and socially concerned, and moderately influenced by mysticism.

Among the Zwickau prophets and Thomas Müntzer, one can clearly discern the origins of the apocalyptic activist tradition, with its three distinctive traits full blown: intense eschatological expectations, coupled with belief in prophetic inspiration and the need for immediate action. Thomas Müntzer would become the prototype of the mystical Spirit-filled prophet and radical apocalyptic activist, ever eager to hasten the arrival of Doomsday and the establishment on Earth of the New Jerusalem through violence. After his death in the Peasants' Revolt of 1525, Müntzer would prove influential, for the path he blazed would be clearly visible to others who followed in his footsteps, driven by the same obsessions: prophecy, apocalypticism, and revolution. It matters little whether or not these later radicals quoted Müntzer. Their actions would speak for themselves, recall his legacy, and lead them to the same tragic end. Some historians argue, nonetheless, that Müntzer's real legacy was overwhelmingly negative, for his failure and that of the revolution he championed soured the lower classes to radical Protestantism, leaving them indifferent to religion and excessively submissive to their secular and ecclesiastical overlords.

In Karlstadt, one sees traces of pacifist communitarian Anabaptism, evinced by a commitment to egalitarianism and even a rejection of infant baptism. Karlstadt had his violent streak too, which expressed itself in iconoclasm, but he was not at all given over to prophecy or revolution. His influence on later radicals is widely recognized, especially in regard to social issues and certain theological questions concerning the sacraments and the freedom of the will. In some ways, Karlstadt could be seen as a prototype of the pacifist Anabaptists, but not entirely. Though he did abolish infant baptism at Orlamünde in 1524, dress as a peasant, and express his disdain for hierarchies and titles by calling himself "Brother Andrew," Karlstadt never established or joined a fully voluntary Anabaptist believers' church. Instead, he fled to Switzerland, befriended the Reformed clergy in various towns, and ended up as a professor of Old Testament at Basel in 1534. The older Karlstadt proved himself more of a stodgy academic than a radical, even demanding that all of the Reformed clergy attend university and earn doctoral degrees. When all is said and done, then, Karlstadt was a moderate radical who seemed to grow somewhat comfortable with compromise as he aged and as he realized that his own complex ambivalence had stranded him on the margins of a major revolution.

The Anabaptists

The dissenting movement known as Anabaptism began in Zurich, among some of Zwingli's most ardent followers. To some extent, then, it is fair to say that the Reformed and Radical traditions emerged at the same time, in the same place, from a common reforming matrix, and that the Radicals can trace their roots directly to Zwingli, perhaps even more so than to Karlstadt and Müntzer.

Two men who were in the vanguard of this movement, Conrad Grebel and Felix Mantz, were university trained and inclined toward humanistic studies. Both of them belonged to a reading group run by Zwingli in which they studied Erasmus's Greek New Testament and improved upon their proficiency in Greek and Hebrew. Both Grebel and Mantz were fourteen years younger than Zwingli, and both came from prominent families. Grebel was brother-in-law to the eminent humanist scholar Joachim Watt (Vadianus), the future Reformer of St. Gall; Mantz was the illegitimate son of a cleric, like Erasmus. Faithful disciples of Zwingli, their teacher and mentor, these two men rapidly assumed important positions on the cutting edge of the Zurich Reformation. In 1522, they took part in the Lenten sausage-eating protest that tested the legal status of Catholic observances. A few months later, Grebel took the lead in heckling mendicant friars who had come to preach in Zurich, and also successfully lobbied the city council to prevent any further "nonbiblical" preaching. At the same time, Grebel and Mantz became two of the most fervent opponents of religious images, the Mass and the cult of the saints, all of which they sought to abolish. In 1523, Grebel assumed a leading role for the iconoclastic party in the public disputations that were held in Zurich, even though he was still nothing but a youth in his midtwenties.

It was at these debates that a rift began to grow between Zwingli and his eager disciples. Grebel, especially, began to express doubts about Zwingli's leadership and the course of his reform program. What irked Grebel the most was the slow pace of reform, and the way Zwingli seemed way too patient, always eager to submit the Reformation to public debates, ever careful about obtaining legal approval for all of the changes that were needed. This disagreement with Zwingli became public at the October disputation of 1523, when Grebel called for the immediate suspension of the Mass, without the approval of the city council. As the cautious and future theocrat Zwingli saw it, the abolition of "idolatry" could wait until the city was ready for it; but as Grebel saw it, any delay was an affront to God. So he disputed with Zwingli, arguing that the Word of God called for the immediate "purification" of the city, regardless of its civil laws.

From that moment forward, Grebel and Mantz and others who had been on the vanguard of the Zurich Reformation began to press for more immediate and more profound changes, appealing with increasing frequency to biblical norms, calling for the reestablishment in the city of the first-century church described in the New Testament, growing ever more estranged from Zwingli. Grebel also began to correspond with Müntzer and Karlstadt, praising them for their work, sharing theological questions, and seeking counsel.

Throughout 1524, as Zurich finally rid itself of the "idolatry" so despised by Grebel and his circle, the issue of infant baptism came to the fore in all discussions between the two estranged reforming camps. The same issue also surfaced in the correspondence with Müntzer and Karlstadt. Intent as they were on re-creating the New Testament church, Grebel and his like-minded companions came to the realization that such a church would have to consist of only genuine believers. Measuring all theology and ritual against New Testament paradigms, they quickly seized on adult baptism as the key to genuine reform, insisting that Jesus never intended this sacrament to be administered to infants. As they came to see it, the foundation of a true church rested precisely on this point: it was a church for believers only, not for everyone, pell-mell.

In September 1524, Grebel wrote to Müntzer: "Your writing against false faith and baptism . . . pleases us greatly and we would like further information from you." He added, "We would also like to be informed whether you and Karlstadt are of one mind. We hope so, and believe it to be the case." Grebel thus reached out to kindred spirits for confirmation of the beliefs he and his party held true. It was not so much a request for advice as a carefully worded profession of faith:

> We maintain that children are saved without faith and that they do not have faith, basing ourselves on the aforesaid biblical texts, and we conclude from the description of baptism and from the historical accounts, according to which no child was baptized . . . that the baptism of children is a senseless, idolatrous abomination, contrary to all Scripture.[10]

Given the fearlessness that Grebel and his group had displayed to this point, it did not take long for them to act upon their convictions. As children were born to these relatively young parents—many of the women being their prime childbearing years—they refused to baptize them, and as the tension mounted, Grebel and his group continued to huddle together, meeting as a church within a church, supporting one another in their defiance, spreading their vision of reform to other towns, whenever possible, where similar radical conventicles began to form. By now, some learned young priests from nearby towns and villages were lending their theological weight to the radical cause: Ludwig Hätzer (c. 1500–1529), one of the leading iconoclastic theorists, who had been influenced by Karlstadt; Wilhelm Reublin (c. 1484–c. 1539) and Johannes Brötli (1494–1529), preachers at Wytikon and Zollikon; Simon Stumpf (dates unknown), pastor at Höngg; Balthasar Hubmaier (1481–1528), pastor at Waldshut; and George Blaurock (1491–1529), a newcomer to Zurich.

As had happened with images and the Mass, since the civil law was being flagrantly disobeyed, the Zurich authorities had no choice but to call for a public disputation on the issue of infant baptism, to be held on 17 January 1525. Grebel and Mantz squared off against Zwingli, Leo Jud, and the established clergy of Zurich. The outcome of the disputation was a crushing blow to the dissenters. Zwingli and the established clergy of Zurich argued that assent and conviction were not required for baptism, and that it served a sign of God's covenant and an initiation rite for infants, much as circumcision had done among the Jews. The city council pronounced in favor of Zwingli's position, affirming that infant baptism could be defended on biblical grounds, even though the New Testament made no explicit mention of it. The fact that the scriptures spoke of entire households being baptized at once (Acts 16:15), they argued, meant that children must have been included, and that all infants in Zurich must be baptized, "as soon as they are born." All parents who had not yet baptized their children were ordered to comply within one week, on pain of banishment. The following day, a city ordinance was enacted that prohibited all meetings of Grebel and his dissenting conventicle.

Forced into a corner, the dissenters responded by defying the authorities. On 21 January 1525, at the home of Felix Mantz, in a simple yet solemn ceremony, the first Anabaptist church was established. Conrad Grebel baptized the newcomer George Blaurock, who, in turn, baptized Grebel. In unison, these two then baptized all who had gathered there. An early Anabaptist chronicle reads: "They gave themselves to the name of the Lord together . . . and they began to teach and keep the faith. Therewith began the separation from the world and its evil works."[11]

The dissenters had broken the law, but as they saw it, they had also restored the true church. Like the earliest followers of Christ, all of whom were persecuted, the Zurich Anabaptists steeled themselves for the ordeal to follow, buoyed by the self-fulfilling premise that their inevitable persecution was but one more indication that their church fit the New Testament paradigm perfectly. Emboldened by their great act of faith, yet wary of the Zurich authorities, these Anabaptists, who called themselves, "the Brethren," or simply "Christians," fanned out beyond their city and began a vigorous missionary campaign, baptizing thirty-five adults in the nearby village of Zollikon in a single week during that fateful January. But it did not take Zurich long to rally against these law-breakers. Having declared rebaptism a capital offense, the Zurich authorities swooped down on them over the following two months. Grebel, Mantz, Blaurock, and several other leaders of the Anabaptists were tried and sent to prison, to subsist on mere bread and water until death, chained and shackled. Freed from this fate by a daring jailbreak, Grebel and his companions scattered, as did many of their followers in Zurich, spreading out across northern Switzerland and surrounding areas, preaching, teaching, and making new converts. Though they made inroads in the cities and large towns, they soon discovered that they were welcomed much more warmly in villages and rural areas, and that they could gain many converts among the peasantry. But wherever they went, no matter how remote the area, persecution tended to dog them.

Felix Mantz was the first to be captured and executed, after a few months of vigorous missionary activity. Many others would follow. Grebel fell victim to the plague in May 1526, after having won over many souls to Anabaptism in St. Gall, Schaffhausen, and other Swiss towns, and was thus spared his inevitable martyrdom. Blaurock headed east into the Tyrol region in Austria and gained a large following before being burned at the stake in 1529. And it was not only the Anabaptist leaders who became martyrs. Many of the rank-and-file members—most of whom tended to be humbler folk of modest means with relatively little learning—also fell victim to all sorts of horrific tortures and brutally inventive means of execution at the hands of both Catholics and Protestants. Yet, as had been the case with the earliest Christians, whom they sought to emulate, the blood of their martyrs became the seed of their church, which spread quickly and widely, not only throughout Switzerland and surrounding areas, but also throughout Western, Central, and Eastern Europe, and eventually also to places colonized by Europeans. Though their numbers always remained relatively small, their geographical reach became immense, far out of proportion with their influence on the surrounding cultures.

The Spread of Pacifist Anabaptism

The spiritual heirs of the Zurich Anabaptists have come to be known as the Swiss Brethren, an imprecise, catchall term that includes many disparate communities, many of which migrated or took root outside of the Swiss Confederacy. Some of their direct descendants are also known by other names, such as the Moravian or Tyrolese Brethren, or the Hutterites. As they crossed paths with other Anabaptists with different approaches to the restoration of the true church, the Brethren sorted themselves out as best they could, linked by a common disdain for hierarchies and professional theologians, and a fervent desire to separate themselves from "the world" and its violent ways.

One of the Anabaptist leaders who gave the clearest voice to the core beliefs of the Brethren was Michael Sattler (c. 1490–1527), a former Benedictine monk. Rebaptized in 1525, around the time that peasant rebels attacked his abbey, Sattler engaged in missionary work throughout southwestern Germany, Alsace, and Switzerland, and he died a martyr's death after briefly ministering to the Anabaptist community of Würtemberg. Sattler would also be very influential in securing a fair amount of toleration for Anabaptists in the uniquely open city of Strassburg, where he befriended the Magisterial Reformers Martin Bucer and Wolfgang Capito.

In February 1527, Sattler penned the earliest and most thorough Anabaptist confession of faith, a text known as the Schleitheim Articles, or Schleitheim Confession. Written for a group of Anabaptists that met in Schleitheim, a town north of Zurich, this document would have an immense effect on the subsequent development of pacifist Anabaptism. It circulated widely not only among Anabaptists, but also among the Magisterial Reformers, some of whom wrote against it, point for point.[12] This very brief text was not a systematic confession of faith or a theological treatise, but rather a succinct summary of the seven major principles that the Brethren agreed on, and which made them seem like a formidable menace to social and political stability:

1. Baptism and church membership are strictly for believing adults only.
2. Discipline is to be maintained solely through "the ban," or excommunication.

3. The Eucharist is the ultimate sign of exclusion, reserved for those who do not sin, for Christians "cannot at the same time partake and drink of the cup of the Lord and the cup of devils."

4. There is to be no mingling with "the evil that the devil planted in the world," and this applies not only to all sinful behavior, but also all "diabolical weapons of violence—such as sword, armor, and the like."

5. Pastors are to be elected by their congregations, and also removed by them when necessary.

6. Christians are never to hold any civil offices, for all earthly governments rely on violence for discipline, and "the sword is ordained of God outside the perfection of Christ."

7. Christians are never to swear oaths.[13]

All of these seven points rejected the interweaving of church and state and defied established authority in one way or another, disparaging civil offices, law courts, and the established church, granting ultimate power to the congregation rather than the clergy or the magistrates. Calling for adult baptism and a wholly voluntary church meant nothing short of the total undoing of Christian society. Moreover, this ethic called for much more than the creation of a segregated social class, as had been the case with monks who withdrew from "the world" into their own communities: it demanded the toleration of a sect with no regard for hierarchies or allegiance to the civil order, almost as a state within the state. Nothing drove home the potential threat posed by Anabaptists better than the sixth and seventh points: How could one hope to hold society together without

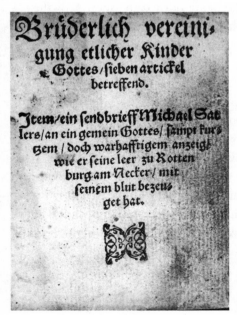

Breaking away. Title page of the *Schleitheim Confession* (1527), a seminal statement of Anabaptist beliefs, which called for adult baptism, pacifism, and a strict separation from "the world."

magistrates, executioners, and soldiers, or the oaths that bound people to one another, not just as Christians, but as citizens? What kind of citizen could an Anabaptist be?

Those who persecuted the Anabaptists thought that these dissenters were inherently evil and interpreted their behavior—no matter how exemplary—as anything but a threat to society. The Anabaptist Brethren called for nothing short of moral perfection, and for a rejection of wealth and power and all worldly values, as monks, friars, and nuns had been doing for centuries. And it seems that many of them managed to lead remarkably holy lives. Ironically, the testimony of their worst enemies is filled with oblique praise for their virtues. "If you investigate their life and conduct, it seems at first contact irreproachable, pious, unassuming, attractive, yea, above this world. Even those who are inclined to be critical will say their lives are excellent," said Zwingli.[14] Bullinger echoed him, noting that they denounced covetousness, pride, profanity, lewd conversation, immorality, drinking, and gluttony. But Zwingli and Bullinger were intent on proving that all Anabaptists were lying hypocrites, for, as everyone knew, heresy could never lead to virtue. One Catholic observer summed up this peculiar logic: "No lying, deception, swearing, strife, harsh language, no intemperate eating and drinking, no outward personal display is found among them, but rather humility, patience, uprightness, meekness, honesty, temperance, straightforwardness, in such measure that one would suppose they had the Holy Spirit of God."[15]

None of their persecutors was willing to grant that the Anabaptists had the Holy Spirit of God. Instead, they were linked with the devil and persecuted. Dialogue was out of the question, as the court clerk said to Michael Sattler during his trial: "The hangman will instruct you; he will dispute with you, arch-heretic." Sattler had his tongue cut out and his skin ripped off with red-hot pincers before being burned to ashes; his wife was drowned a few days later. To the bitter end, Sattler and his wife appealed to the Bible, convinced they alone lived up to its message. "We say that we who live and believe are the saints," Sattler said boldly.[16]

Neither fire nor sword could prevent the growth and expansion of the pacifist Brethren. Although thousands were martyred between 1527 and 1590, the worst years of persecution, no one was able to stop them from multiplying. Having executed 350 Anabaptists, one of their German persecutors said in desperation: "What shall I do? The more I kill the greater becomes their number!"[17] This ethic of steadfastness and martyrdom, coupled with that of meekness, proved one of the Anabaptists' most remarkable—and most appealing—features. Anabaptist missionaries held up this trait as proof of the fact that they were indeed re-creating the ancient Christian church anew, and it seems to have been an effective tactic. Eventually, in mid-seventeenth century, narratives of these martyrdoms would be published as *The Martyr's Mirror*, and the text would become an integral part of Anabaptist devotion, and a favored gift at Mennonite and Amish weddings.[18]

As the Brethren scattered in all directions, the ethic of the Schleitheim Articles began to cross borders. In southern and central Germany, the Brethren's growth seems to have been very rapid. The same was true in Alsace, especially in Strassburg. Some went south across the Alps into Italy, where their legacy would mingle with other dissenting religious currents. Others followed the Rhine downstream, bringing their message to very receptive communities in northern Germany and the Netherlands, where the Dutch Brethren would become a major branch of the tradition, and where, without a strong charismatic leader, they would continually have to contend with other radicals who were not pacifists. Ironically, up to 1536, their own history would be shaped most intensely by these other radicals and the turmoil they caused. After 1536, it would be a very different story, when a strong leader named Menno Simons finally rose to the challenge of leading them, and of shaping their identity. We will return to the Dutch developments later. Eastward, the Brethren poured into the Tyrol and Carinthia in Austria, and eventually into Moravia in present-day Czech Republic. Though most of these lands were nominally under the rule of the archduke of Austria, Emperor Charles V's brother Ferdinand, who outlawed Anabaptism and called for its extermination, local control was left in the hands of nobles who tended to be tolerant, or at least not too consistent in following their lord's commands.

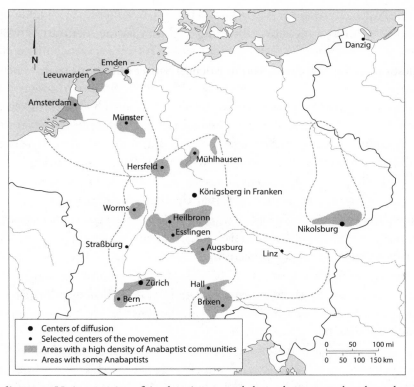

Radical diaspora. Various strains of Anabaptism spread throughout central and northern Europe in the sixteenth century. Though dispersed, and often persecuted, these radicals managed to survive and even thrive in some areas.

One of the most significant Anabaptist communities in this vast region, the Tyrolese Brethren, was founded by George Blaurock and Wilhelm Reublin, onetime dissenters at Zurich. After Blaurock's capture and execution in 1529, leadership of these Brethren was assumed by Jacob Hutter (1500–1536), a hatmaker by trade. Having deemed the situation in the Tyrol to be too dangerous, Hutter and his elders sought refuge in Moravia, farther east and north, where they prospered and eventually developed into one of the most distinctive Anabaptist communities. In contrast, those who remained behind in the Tyrol fell victim to persecution eventually, as Emperor Ferdinand—the successor to Charles V—sought to rid his lands of Anabaptists.

In Moravia, the Brethren began to share all of their belongings in common, following an ancient Christian practice described in the New Testament (Acts 2:44–46; 4:32–37; 5:1–12). In essence, this form of communism was not much different from that practiced by Catholic monastic communities, which held all property in common, but it was quite a departure from the monastic norm to apply such an economic structure to an entire community of families with children. In other words, the Moravian Brethren had transposed the monastic economy onto a lay setting in which marriage and procreation were not only allowed, but encouraged, and where the ancient Benedictine motto *ora et labora* (pray and work) took on a whole new meaning.

The Moravian Brethren had begun to practice this sharing of goods and property as an emergency survival measure, when they fled persecution in a hurry and settled in a new land, but it did not take very long for them to turn this practice into a permanent institution, under Hutter's charismatic leadership. This way of life had been espoused in principle by other radicals, especially some, though not all, of those who were involved in the Revolution of 1525. Many leaders of the revolt, including Thomas Müntzer, clamored for the community of goods, and certain Swiss Brethren with links to the revolt, such as Wilhelm Reublin and Johannes Brötli, favored the idea, as did two Brethren connected to the founding of the Moravian experiment, Wenceslaus Rinck and Balthasar Hubmaier. The intersection of peasant discontent and Anabaptist reform shows through very clearly in this case, lending weight to the claim that the rejection of private personal property found among the Brethren was a logical extension of the social gospel message of the early Protestant Reformation, and that the revolt and Anabaptism sprang from the same egalitarian matrix, with shared goals concerning social, political, and economic inequalities. But theology alone is not the sum total of any reformation, and especially a "Radical" Reformation. As a leading expert on Anabaptism has said, "Although Anabaptism is not important for understanding the Peasants' War, the Peasants' War is very important for understanding the Radical Reformation."[19]

Despite waves of persecution, the loss of Hutter to martyrdom in 1536, and continual pressures to relocate, these communities survived and became known as Hutterites. In 1542, their leader Pieter Riedemann (1506–1566) made their communitarian arrangement part of their confession of faith, sealing its place alongside the other principles they accepted from the Schleitheim Articles. Successful farmers and artisans,

Hutterite family. The Hutterites practiced a form of communism very similar to that of Catholic monastics, with one significant difference: rather than living as celibate men and women, Hutterites married and placed a very high value on family life. This image from 1589 highlights the centrality of the family within Hutterite communal life.

the Hutterites continued to grow and prosper, never wavering from their quasi-monastic ideals and lifestyle, engaging in some commerce with "the world" that surrounded them, but never blending in. War, persecution, and modernization drove them eventually to Slovakia, Transylvania, and Ukraine. In the nineteenth century, some would establish themselves in North America, where they now number more than thirty-five thousand.

Magisterial Anabaptism

The tenets expressed in the Schleitheim Articles were not accepted by all Anabaptists. Some were willing to engage more directly with the world and sought to transform it rather than to withdraw from it. Two such moderate Anabaptists who won substantial followings were Pilgram Marpeck (c. 1495–1556) and Balthasar Hubmaier (c. 1480–1528). Because they and their followers believed in believers' baptism and in the necessity of engaging with the established civil order, they are sometimes called "Magisterial" Anabaptists, to distinguish them from the separatists.

Pilgram Marpeck was a magistrate with many talents who joined the Anabaptists some time around 1527, in Rattenberg, Austria, and in 1528 moved to Strassburg, where he was soon imprisoned. Freed in 1530, he published two texts in which he devised one of the very first typologies of the Radical Reformation, classifying distinct groups of Anabaptists and outlining their differences. Expelled from Strassburg in 1532 after a debate with Martin Bucer, Marpeck fled to Switzerland and traveled widely throughout south Germany, Alsace, the Tirol, and Moravia, gaining followers. In 1544 he moved to Augsburg, where he continued his mission as an Anabaptist leader while working as a forester and engineer. Among the beliefs he passed on to his followers—who were spread out over a wide area—the most distinctive one was a deep concern for society as a whole, and a desire to undo economic injustices. Unlike those Anabaptists who upheld the Schleitheim Articles, Marpeck and his followers saw nothing wrong in the taking of oaths, obedience to established governments, or participation in civil politics. Marpeck, however, drew the line at the issue of deadly force, which he condemned. Scattered as they were, and moderate as they were, Marpeck and his followers had a subtle and somewhat invisible influence on Anabaptism as a whole, and, curiously, may have had more of an influence on twentieth-century Mennonites, who embraced his rediscovered works as quintessentially Anabaptist. Unlike many other Anabaptist leaders, Marpeck never faced martyrdom, and he died peacefully in Augsburg in 1556.

A different sort of moderation was advocated by Balthasar Hubmaier, leader of the first influx of Anabaptist Brethren into Moravia. Refusing to embrace pacifism wholly, Hubmaier and his Brethren claimed a middle ground of sorts, arguing that Christians did not have to abstain from civil life and that violence was sometimes necessary for self-defense. Moreover, their vision of a believers' church did not exclude the possibility of a Christian commonwealth, or theocracy, much along the lines of Zurich. Consequently, these Brethren are sometimes referred to as *schwertler* (sword carriers), in contrast to the pacifist Brethren, who are called *stäbler* (staff bearers).

Balthasar Hubmaier was one of the oldest Anabaptists, a member of Zwingli's generation rather than Grebel's. Born sometime between 1480 and 1485, he may have even been a few years or months older than Zwingli. He also had a more impressive academic résumé than Zwingli or any other Radical. A student of the eminent Johann Eck, Luther's Catholic nemesis, Hubmaier had a doctoral degree in theology. An ordained priest, he served from 1516 to 1521 as cathedral preacher at Regensburg, where he became immensely popular and where he also embodied many of the values and beliefs he would later condemn. In 1519, as Luther was already jousting with Eck and the pope, Hubmaier had caused the expulsion of the Jews from Regensburg and the destruction of their synagogue, in retaliation for their alleged disrespect of the Virgin Mary. The synagogue was replaced with a church, the shrine of Schöne Maria (Beautiful or Blessed Mary), where Hubmaier became chaplain, and where miraculous cures instantly began to attract crowds of pilgrims. For two years, Hubmaier preached with great enthusiasm to the tens of thousands who flocked to the shrine. Then, in early 1521 he left this post for that of preacher at Waldshut, a quiet town on the Rhine, not far from the Swiss border.

While in Waldshut, Hubmaier gradually parted company with the Catholic Church and began to lead all of his flock in the same direction. In 1524, as peasant unrest first surfaced nearby, Hubmaier became involved with the rebels, began to read Karlstadt, and may have met with Thomas Müntzer. In addition, he made contact with radicals from Zurich and was drawn into their camp. His conversion to Anabaptism took place in 1525, when Wilhelm Reublin arrived in Waldshut after being driven out of Zurich. In

April, Reublin baptized Hubmaier and sixty others. Hubmaier, in turn, baptized about three hundred more. In July of that same year, Hubmaier published a treatise, *On the Christian Baptism of Believers*, which many still consider the ablest theological defense of the Anabaptist position. Some scholars have proposed that but for Hubmaier's association with the peasant rebels—which made the civil authorities wary—his theology of believer's baptism might have won much greater acceptance throughout urban and rural Switzerland. In Waldshut, Hubmaier had tried to put this theology into practice, seeking to prove that a believer's church need not be a small sect, but could rather be a transforming power and the controlling force in a community.

But Hubmaier never got the chance to prove his case in Waldshut. Instead, he was driven away by the Austrian authorities in December 1525. After stints in Constance, Augsburg, and Zurich, where Zwingli treated him very roughly, Hubmaier gravitated to Nikolsburg, in Moravia, where Count Leonhard von Liechtenstein, the local ruler, granted toleration to religious dissenters. An ethnically mixed area, Moravia was also home to many Czech Hussites and open to Lutheran and Swiss Reformed influences. It was there at Nikolsburg, in 1526, that Hubmaier tried to take charge of an Anabaptist community numbering around ten thousand, but with only limited success. Though he managed to convert and rebaptize Count Leonhard, his patron's tolerance made it difficult for Hubmaier to gain full control. Nikolsburg filled up with religious refugees of various stripes, including Hutter and his followers and others who espoused different versions of Anabaptism, some quite extreme. Religious tension ran high, naturally, especially among the competing Anabaptists. Quite by accident, it was Hubmaier who gave rise indirectly to the communism of the Anabaptists who came be known as Hutterites. Unable to abide their pacifist separatism, and eager to prevent any slippage among his followers, Hubmaier managed to force them out of Nikolsburg to another location in Moravia. And, as fate or Divine Providence would decree, it was during their arduous exodus to Austerlitz, when they were forced by sheer necessity to pool their resources, that those Anabaptists stumbled upon their communism, and discovered it could actually work very well.

After writing another influential treatise, *On the Sword*, in which he defended the idea of a "Magisterial" Anabaptism, Hubmaier was overtaken by events beyond his control as Moravia passed from Louis II, king of Hungary—who was killed by the Turks at the epic Battle of Mohács—into the hands of Ferdinand, archduke of Austria, overlord of Waldshut. Within a few months of Ferdinand's accession, Hubmaier was extradited to Vienna and handed over to the new king's authorities. Hubmaier's fate was sealed: found guilty of aiding the peasant rebels at Waldshut, he was burned alive in March 1528. His wife was drowned in the Danube a few days later. Count Leonhard of Lichtenstein continued to tolerate the Anabaptists on his lands, among them Hubmaier's followers, but their moderate, halfway pacifism would not outlive them. Instead, it would be the strict pacifism and communalism of the Hutterites that would endure.

To some extent, Hubmaier's undoing was caused by more radical Anabaptists who stirred up trouble in Moravia and raised questions in Count Leonhard's mind about the thousands of refugees who had flocked to his lands. Complex as this may seem, it is only part of a larger whole. There were other offshoots of Anabaptism in Moravia, and all over Europe. It is to another of those branches that we must now turn, that which was most feared, and with good reason.

The Apocalyptic Activists

Though some may quibble and object to "hairsplitting" distinctions, Thomas Müntzer can rightly be considered the first of the radical apocalyptic activists. Müntzer's obsession with the imminent end of the world and with the violent role that the "elect" would play in it marks him off very clearly as the first of a long line of radical Protestants who combined *sola scriptura* biblicism with elements of medieval mysticism and millennialism, and added on top of that a highly charged critique of social, political, and economic inequalities. Müntzer's execution in 1525 might have been a serious blow to the peasant armies he led, but it was not at all the end of the story, for Müntzer had many followers. Some were direct intellectual and spiritual disciples, and some were not. All of them spelled trouble for the authorities.

One such disciple was Hans Hut (c. 1490–1527), a merchant who had joined the peasant uprising and fought alongside Müntzer at the battle of Frankenhausen. A native of Haina in central Germany, Hut became a very active Anabaptist missionary after the defeat of the peasants, broadcasting apocalyptic prophecies about the imminent end of the world, which he predicted would take place in the summer of 1528. Like Müntzer, Hut viewed the coming apocalypse as a social revolution that would wipe out economic and class distinctions and allow the elect to judge the godless. And also like Müntzer, Hut tended to identify the elites as the godless and the downtrodden as the elect. But Hut differed from Müntzer in two respects. First, he did not think it was necessary for the elect to wage war, for Christ himself was about to return and dispose of sinners and their hierarchies. Second, he took biblicism a step further, finding a place for himself in the sacred text. Convinced that he was the avenger mentioned in Ezekiel 9:1–4, Hut became the first of several Anabaptist leaders to identify himself as the incarnation of some biblical figure, preaching the End Times with divine authority, blurring the boundary between himself and the Word of God, the prophet and his prophecies, and the past, the present, and the future.[20]

Though Hut did not assemble or join an apocalyptic army, he stirred the waters through his Doomsday message, which included a strong dose of revolutionary rhetoric. Always on the run, Hut nonetheless made many disciples in Germany before going to Moravia in 1526, where he tried to win over Hubmaier's flock, and where he also alienated the elites, including the all-important Count Leonhard von Liechtenstein. After a brief stay in Moravia, Hut went on to preach in Austria and Bavaria. In August 1527, Hut attended a synod in Augsburg at which sixty Anabaptist leaders from different communities had assembled to iron out their differences and attempt an accord. This meeting, which came to be known as the Martyrs' Synod, provided the authorities with a perfect opportunity to track and seize Anabaptists. Hut was arrested, along with most of the others, thrown into prison, tortured, and sentenced to death. Before the sentence could be carried out, however, Hut died from smoke inhalation, in December 1527. It is believed he may have started the fire that killed him as part of an escape attempt. The following day his corpse was burned.

Hut never lived to see his prophecy fail. But he left behind many convinced followers who expected Christ to return to earth presently. Hut also left behind some influential texts, most of a highly spiritual and mystical nature rather than apocalyptic. Though he was not trained as a theologian, Hut was fairly skilled at weaving together the personal and communal dimensions of salvation, linking the need for individual regeneration with apocalyptic expectations. Influenced by the Rhineland mystics, Hut focused on Christ's suffering as the bond that linked believers to God and to each other in a mystical embrace:

> Christ, the crucified, has many members in this body . . . [and] every member bears the work, or suffers, or consents to suffer under the model of the head [Christ]. Without this remedy no one knows Christ; and in another way no one is known by Christ. This is the power of the father, which makes us pleasing to him.[21]

Not exactly what one might expect from an apocalyptic firebrand, but just what one should expect from an immensely complex religious tradition that is often forced into tidy, rigid categories by those who study it. Hut played a very important role in the transmission of apocalypticism among Anabaptists, but could also be classified in that other category of "spiritualist," like his mentor and friend John Denck, who baptized him in Augsburg in 1526. Much can be learned from Hut's case, but perhaps most important of all is the lesson that the lenses we historians fashion are not always as useful as we think they are. Some of the most important details of Anabaptist history, especially their multiple influences and identities, do not deny the value of our categories, but they certainly transcend them.

Soon after Hut's death, another charismatic leader emerged to take his place: Melchior Hoffman, a furrier turned preacher who began his ministry in the Baltic region in 1523, making converts to the Lutheran cause in Lithuania, Sweden, and northern Germany. Given over to apocalypticism and to theological positions that differed from Luther's—especially concerning the Eucharist and the nature of Christ—Hoffman drifted to Strassburg in 1526, where he found kindred spirits among the Anabaptists. Some time around 1530, Hoffman fell under the influence of three apocalyptic prophets, Lienhard Jost, Ursula Jost, and Barbara Rebstock, who convinced him not only that the end was at hand, but also that he, Hoffman, was the reincarnation of the prophet Elijah, as predicted in Revelation 11:3. Once more, as also in the case of Hut, the Bible became incarnate and prophesied through a recycled soul. Secure in his newly revealed identity, Hoffman soon surpassed Rebstock and the Josts, and even Hut, and began to

Apocalypse now. Melchior Hoffman gained many followers by predicting the imminent end of the world and the establishment of the New Jerusalem. Although none of his predictions came true, apocalyptic "Melchiorites" caused alarm wherever they surfaced.

proclaim that Strassburg would be the epicenter of the apocalypse to come, the New Jerusalem from which Christ would send out 144,000 preachers to the whole world. Not surprisingly, this scenario also involved the destruction of the godless and their selfish, sinful, hierarchical society. Driven away from Strassburg in 1530, Hoffman headed to Frisia, on the coast of the North Sea, where he made many converts, rebaptizing more than three hundred in a single ceremony at the cathedral in the city of Emden. Hoffman also gained many converts nearby in the Netherlands, where, thanks to him, Anabaptism began to spread rapidly. Two of his disciples would play pivotal roles in very different communities: Obbe Phillips among pacifist Dutch Anabaptists, and Jan Mathys among revolutionaries in the nearby city of Münster.

Strassburg called to Hoffman, however. He had to be there, no matter how many converts he was making up north. What else could the reincarnated Elijah do when Strassburg was the promised New Jerusalem? Traveling back and forth between his northern mission field and Strassburg, where he faced arrest, Hoffman grew bolder in his prophetic role. Having announced that Christ would return in 1533, the new Elijah encouraged all of his followers to prepare. As the civil and ecclesiastical elites in Strassburg grew ever more fearful of Hoffman and his followers, Hoffman himself grew more fearless about his presence in the city, almost as if provoking the authorities. Arrested and cast into prison, Hoffman announced that the end was very, very near, but soon afterward he reversed himself and announced a delay. In the meantime, the Strassburg authorities outlawed Anabaptism and expelled many of its leaders. As a result, one of the liveliest and most influential Anabaptist communities suddenly vanished.

Prison did nothing to dampen Hoffman's spirits at first, for he viewed his lot as a clear sign of Christ's impending return. His followers, who came to be known as

Melchiorites, continued to be gripped by apocalyptic expectations. For some, the waiting became intolerable, especially after Hoffman prophesied that Christ would return by November, at the latest. Christ, however, failed to conform to Hoffman's timetable, or to free him. As the fateful year passed, Hoffman's prophecies—like all failed predictions—had to be amended or reinterpreted. And before too long, other prophets stepped in too, some of whom were not as passive as Hoffman. Much to everyone's surprise, the long-expected end of history—the Eschaton or Parousia, as the theologians call it—soon erupted in a most peculiar location, in a way not foreseen by Hoffman.

The much-awaited Anabaptist apocalypse began in the northwestern German city of Münster, near the Dutch border, one of the places where Hoffman's disciples had multiplied. Münster was ostensibly ruled by its bishop, but, like most German cities, it was also governed by elected councils and magistrates. The city had been steadily turning Lutheran since 1532, under the leadership of a former Catholic priest, Bernard Rothman (c. 1495–1535), but Anabaptism made inroads quickly. In the summer of 1533, Rothman—who disagreed with Luther on the Eucharist—allowed some radical Melchiorite preachers into town. Their fervent work soon gained them converts and also drew other Melchiorites from the surrounding area. Among these visitors was the firebrand Jan Bockleson, also known as John of Leiden (1509–1536), a young tailor who would play a key role in Münster.

By November, many in Münster had become Melchiorite Anabaptists, including Rothman. On 5 January 1534, as the Melchiorites adjusted the date of Christ's return, Rothman was rebaptized by the leader of the Amsterdam Anabaptists, Jan Matthijs, a former baker from Harlem who claimed to be the prophet Enoch and successor to Elijah (Hubmaier). A week later, when 1,400 adults were baptized, the Melchiorites began to gain the upper hand. Among those who flocked to join the swell of expectation was John of Leiden, who, together with Matthijs, began to eclipse Rothman, and after only a few weeks, gained control of the city. On 8 February Matthijs announced that Hoffman had been mistaken: Münster was to be the New Jerusalem, not Strassburg, and the date of Christ's return would be Easter 1534. All true believers were urged to flock to Münster as soon as possible, and to arm themselves. In desperation, the prince-bishop, Count Franz von Waldeck, called for a siege of the city, which began on 23 February, the very same day that a new, heavily Melchiorite city council was elected. Realizing that the long-expected final battle had begun, Matthijs called for the immediate creation of the New Jerusalem, and the newly installed government complied by expelling from the city all who refused baptism. About 2,000 Münsterites, many of them male, went into exile; at the same time about 2,500 eager Melchiorites poured into the city, to take their place. By early March 1534, Münster had become a New Jerusalem indeed, the very first city on earth ever to be composed entirely of baptized believers, or as they preferred to call themselves, saints.

Very quickly, every fear that had been voiced by Catholics and Magisterial Reformers came true in Münster. First came the economic reforms. Private property was abolished, titles and contracts destroyed, and all funds confiscated. Money would no longer be needed in Münster. All would share and share alike, as true Christians did in apostolic times. "One thing shall be held in common as well as the other," the Münsterites were told. "It belongs to all of us. It is mine as well as yours, and yours as well as mine."[22] To remind everyone of their common ownership, a law required all doors to be kept open continuously, even at night. Seven deacons were appointed to ensure the fair distribution of all goods and services. All food was to be shared, and meals were to be eaten as a community, in the city's squares. Artisans were encouraged to produce everything the city needed for its survival, but forbidden to ask for compensation. The community would provide all the necessary materials; their labor would belong to the community as a whole. Then came the ideological reform. Except for the Bible, all books and documents were burned. Then the churches were stripped of all idolatrous remnants, their steeples demolished, the flattened towers filled with artillery. The cathedral was renamed "the Great Stone Pit" and the cathedral square "Mount Zion." Münster became "Israel" and its citizens "Israelites." Legal reforms established a new autocratic oligarchy, and a new way of life. Bernhard Knipperdolling, the burgomaster, became "sword-bearer," or chief executioner. Sins quickly became capital crimes, punishable by death. It was a daunting list that included blasphemy, seditious language, disrespect to parents, disobedience to superiors, adultery, lewdness, slandering, cursing, complaining. John of Leiden summed it all up thus: "If we are sons of God and have been baptized in Christ, then all evil must disappear from our midst. . . . If, however, you do evil, then beware! The authorities wield the sword not in vain; they are God's servants, his avengers to punish the evildoer."[23]

Münster also became an armed camp under siege, with able-bodied males conscripted into military service. In some ways, the strict laws put into place were needed as much for military discipline within the city as for eschatological correctness. The siege was fierce, and tight. Not surprisingly, the besieging forces were uniquely ecumenical, drawn from surrounding cities and principalities, both Catholic and Lutheran.

Things went from bad to worse on 4 April 1535, when Jan Matthijs was killed during a skirmish. Matthijs had predicted Christ's return on 5 April and apparently believed that no harm could come to him at such an auspicious time. While leading a sortie, he was pierced by a pike and hacked to bits. And after strewing his mutilated remains over the battlefield, the besiegers hoisted his severed head high on a pole for all of Münster to see. The battle for Münster was far from over, however. As soon as he emerged from a three-day trance, John of Leiden assumed the top slot vacated by Matthijs, dissolved the council that had been elected just a few months earlier, and set up twelve elders in its place, to assist him in ruling the New Jerusalem. Rapidly, John of Leiden and the elders tightened their association with Old Testament paradigms. In July, polygamy was introduced. Since Münster was about 70 percent female, this unprecedented return to the ethic of the ancient Hebrew patriarchs made sense to the elders. How else could God's commandment to be fruitful and multiply be obeyed? Twenty-six-year-old John of Leiden ended up collecting sixteen wives, including Jan Matthijs's widow, Divara, whom

Executioner of the end of times. Bernhard Knipperdolling, "sword-bearer" of the Anabaptist kingdom of Münster, oversaw the confiscation of property as well as all executions, and his daughter became one of "King" John of Leiden's many wives. Lutherans and Catholics joined forces to besiege and conquer this apocalyptic dystopia, where polygamy had become the norm and where private property had been abolished.

he would crown as queen. Forty-year-old Bernard Rothman had to settle for only nine wives. And all of these wives had to call each other "sisters" and their husband "lord."

Opposition to John of Leiden began to mount within the city walls, but after the torture and mass execution of forty-eight dissenters in July, who were found guilty of plotting a coup, only a handful of brave souls dared to resist. In early September, John of Leiden had himself crowned as "king of righteousness over all" and "king of the people of God in the New Temple," and took to associating himself with King David, as precursor to Christ. He also conflated his reincarnations, alluding to himself as a new King Solomon. Once again, that odd radical faith in biblical reincarnation surfaced among Melchiorites, with a vengeance. The new David ruled with an iron fist and a secret police, and enjoyed a lavish lifestyle and a Burgundian-style court, à la Charles V, replete with courtiers, armed guards, thrones, royal robes, orbs, scepters, ritual displays, banquets, enviable jewelry, and the best dwellings in town. A sardonic contemporary account sums it up this way:

> The Anabaptists in Münster, especially the leaders, such as Jan van Leiden and the twelve elders, were planning it well. They had done away with money, gold, and silver, and had driven everyone from his property. They sat in the houses, held the property, and also wanted to have ten or twelve wives. I presume they call this the "right baptism."[24]

Within Münster, these extreme changes were justified on strictly biblical grounds, and also on charismatic claims of direct divine inspiration. Bernard Rothman, chief theologian and spokesman for the ruling elite, made their claim very clear:

> The Kingdom of Christ has begun in Münster . . . God has again restored the Scripture through us; He has abundantly made his will known to us. And as we earnestly put into practice what we understand, God teaches us further every day.[25]

Speaking for God and carrying out his will, John of Leiden and the elders thus became divine agents on earth. Their role, and that of the entire Münster community, was neatly summarized by Rothman:

> Now God has risen in his wrath against his enemies. Whoever wishes to be God's servant must arm himself in the same way and manner. . . . The day of wrath has begun meaningfully in our midst, and will spread over the entire world. . . . Thus we, who are covenanted with the Lord, must be His instruments to root out the godless on the day which the Lord has prepared. . . . God has awakened the promised David, armed together with his people, for revenge and punishment on Babylon.[26]

Although the prophets of Münster saw themselves as engaged in a cosmic struggle rather than a local insurrection and tried to attract other Anabaptists to their New Jerusalem, help never arrived and their population never came remotely close to the biblically requisite 144,000. Münsterite influence on Anabaptists elsewhere remained ineffective. Only in Amsterdam did their flame flicker briefly, in early 1535, when some Anabaptists made a futile attempt to storm the city hall and seven men and women pronounced the "naked truth of God" by running naked through the streets, in imitation of the prophet Isaiah (Isaiah 20:2).

As the siege of Münster wore on, conditions deteriorated even further inside the city walls. Food ran scarce and before long every animal within the city had been cooked and eaten. Rumors of cannibalism began to spread, too. Given the other excesses at Münster, and the constant executions, the rumor seemed credible. Escaping was difficult, for those who fled risked death on either side of the city walls. Finally, on 25 June 1535, thanks to information provided by defectors, a well-coordinated assault by Lutheran and Catholic armies managed to breach the walls, defeat the Münsterites, and take control of the city. Though many inside the city were slaughtered, King John of Leiden and his sword-bearer Bernhard Knipperdolling were spared, along with some other leaders. Rothman simply vanished without a trace, and rumors of his survival, like those of cannibalism, could never be put to rest.

Imprisoned and questioned for six months, John of Leiden met his end on 22 January 1536, in the Münster marketplace alongside Knipperdolling and Bernd Krechting, a leading preacher. After having their skin burned off with red-hot pincers and their tongues torn out, the three men were stabbed to death before a large crowd; their remains were then placed in three cages that were hoisted up the tower of St. Lambert's church for everyone to see. There they rotted and turned to dust, and there the cages still hang today, empty. It matters little whether the cages are replicas or not. They are a focal point for Münster's tourist guides and a grim reminder of religion gone mad.

His authority in Münster restored, Bishop Franz von Waldeck set about returning his city and diocese fully into the Catholic fold. It would not be an easy task, but gradually he and his successors managed to make a Catholic stronghold out of the former New Jerusalem. Ironically, it took an Anabaptist revolution and a siege that involved

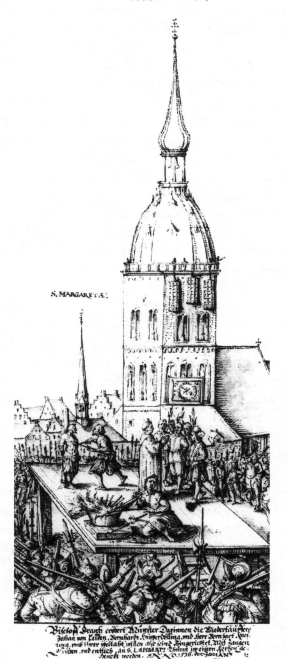

The end of the New Jerusalem. John of Leiden and his two top henchmen, Bernhard Krechting and Bernhard Knipperdolling, were tortured and executed before a large crowd in January 1536. The three cages hanging from the steeple of St. Lambert's church, which held their disintegrating remains for fifty years, can still be seen there to this day, a haunting reminder of the consequences of religion gone mad.

Lutheran armies to rid Münster of the Protestantism that had crept into it. In many ways, then, the undoing of the Münster experiment can be counted as the first major victory of the Catholic Counter-Reformation in Germany, and perhaps also its most exceptional.

Though confined to one mere city in Westphalia, the events at Münster had an enormous impact throughout Europe. Authorities everywhere, Catholic and Protestant, found proof in Münster of all of the dangers posed by Anabaptism. This disaster, therefore, fanned the flames of persecution. Among Anabaptists, Münster had a sobering effect. Though Melchiorites of various stripes survived and tried to regain ground, Münster was the end of the line for Anabaptist apocalyptic activism. After Münster, the Anabaptists in northern Germany and the Netherlands regrouped under the guidance of Menno Simons (c. 1496–1561), a former Catholic priest who stressed pacifism and espoused beliefs more in keeping with the Schleitheim Articles.

A gifted leader in every respect, Menno Simons marginalized those Anabaptists who were at either extreme, such as those who sought to continue what had begun at Münster or those who held external ceremonies in low regard, like David Joris (c. 1501–1556). Working together with other leaders in the Netherlands, such as Dirk Phillips (1504–1568) and Lenaert Bouwens (1515–1582), Simons brought greater theological rigor and stricter ethical codes to a community in disarray. His emphasis on ritual and on the necessity of maintaining a separation from "the world" gave his followers not only a firmer sense of community, but also cohesion and a distinctive identity, traits sorely needed by a persecuted minority. His pacifist stance also worked wonders in terms of public relations, especially for a separatist minority, helping Anabaptists regain the trust of their neighbors after the spectacle of Münster. And it was their behavior, not just their thinking, that made Mennonites seem acceptable.

Emphasizing the transforming power of Christ, Menno Simons taught that divine grace enabled Christians to lead a life of obedience. His was a theology of deeds and sanctification, rather than of salvation by faith alone. This tended to make Mennonites very virtuous, rather than troublesome neighbors. In Simons we see again the impulse toward moral rigor and perfection that had been part of the Anabaptist movement since the earliest days, which Zwingli and Luther had detected and condemned. In Simons, and in his followers, one finds a summation of the core beliefs of mainstream Anabaptism, and especially of the Anabaptist emphasis on improving and transforming the behavior of believers. Mennonites were thus utterly distinct, as different from the Magisterial Reformation as from the Catholic Church.

One Mennonite belief in particular made them unique. Menno Simons had passed on to his disciples a distinctive Melchiorite trait—belief in the "celestial" flesh of Christ," that is, that Jesus Christ could not have a body with common human flesh derived from his mother Mary. To Catholics and Magisterial Reformers, this seemed an awkward return to the ancient heresies of Docetisim, Nestorianism, and Monophysitism, condemned by the early church. Other Anabaptists also rejected this teaching, and the possibility of entering into communion with anyone who professed it.

Despite various internal divisions, the followers of Menno Simons managed to retain a common identity. Like the Hutterites, some communities would migrate eastward, especially to Ukraine and Russia, and also west, to the Americas. Simons towers over Anabaptist history. No better proof of his defining influence can be found than the fact that, eventually, most of the Dutch, German, and Swiss Anabaptists whose spiritual and physical descendants survive to this day would end up being known as "Mennonites."

The Spiritualists

David Joris, the Anabaptist teacher rejected by Menno Simons, belonged to another branch of the Anabaptist family tree, a very loosely connected assemblage of individuals and communities that George Williams has identified as "Spiritualists." Even more so in the case of the spiritualists than in that of the mainstream Anabaptists, boundaries and distinctions can often prove permeable or arbitrary. Could it be any other way with people who did not hold boundaries sacred or actually spurned them? The very essence of a "spiritualist," after all, is a disdain for theological precision, external symbols and rituals, institutions, and any religious classification other than "Christian." In some cases, spiritualists would even redefine the name "Christian." Immediately, then, it is easy to see why those identified as spiritualists by Williams can tax the patience of everyone who studies them: they tend to be highly individualistic and idiosyncratic. They also tend to keep to themselves, with few exceptions, and are nearly impossible to count. A true spiritualist, by definition, does not need to make himself or herself known, or even break openly with any established church. Only those few who dare to speak out and those who claim to follow them can ever be truly counted. But these few are so disproportionately significant, and so often labeled "ahead of their time" or "precursors" of modernity, that they cannot be ignored.

Despite the fact that these so-called spiritualists were all highly individualistic, all of them are linked by one characteristic, and this link is so strong that it is the very source of their idiosyncratic inspirations. The common thread that binds them all is their mystical bent, that trait identified by Troeltsch as the spiritualizing or mystical fellowship, or spiritual *ecclesiola*. All of the Radical spiritualists were convinced that personal encounters with the divine were all that mattered in religion. In one way or another, all of them were deeply influenced by medieval mystical texts, even if they only received them through other spiritualists. The most influential were those texts written by the so-called Rhineland mystics: Meister Eckhart, John Tauler, Heinrich Suso, Jan Ruysbroeck, and their many followers and disciples, including the anonymous author of the *Theologia germanica*. The Rhineland tradition, which was also a major influence on the *devotio moderna*, and therefore on Erasmus, stressed the presence of the divine within each human being, and proposed that this presence is not only the core of the human self, but also something that can be realized by a process of self-emptying and detachment. This emphasis on an indwelling divine presence that can be experienced and on separation from the world leads all who follow the tradition to accept a basic dichotomy between inner and outer, spiritual and material, soul and body, in which the inner, the spiritual, and the soul are considered superior, or even as all that matters.

Although it may seem odd that a tradition deeply rooted in monasticism and the Catholic tradition would have an influence on Bible-centered Protestants who believed that the Roman Catholic Church was the seat of the Antichrist, one must keep in mind that the core dichotomy proposed by this tradition—the inner-outer distinction—is exactly what allowed Protestant Radicals to embrace it, for the distinction nullified the question of provenance or church affiliation. In fact, this inner-outer binary becomes the very structure of their thinking, and the source of their most distinctive trait: their affirmation that the individual's direct relationship with the indwelling divine is not only far superior to any relationship that any church and its rituals can offer, but also actually all that matters in life.

Hans Denck (1495–1527) was one of the first Anabaptists to propose that the ultimate religious authority resided in the inward seed or image of God implanted in every human soul. Deeply influenced by the medieval mystic Johann Tauler (1300–1361), as well as by Karlstadt and Müntzer, Denck was expelled from Nuremberg in 1525 because of his unorthodox beliefs. A wanderer committed to pacifism and nonresistance, Denck lived for a while in Augsburg, Strassburg, and Worms, where he crossed paths with several early leaders of Anabaptism, including Hut, whom he inspired. His influence cannot be measured in numbers of converts or in institutions established, for his disdain of dogma and all outward expressions of religious belief did not lead him to gather followers around himself. Nonetheless, Denck did convince others, and he is often viewed as a pioneer in the spiritualist tradition and a key mediator of the Rhineland mystical tradition to other Radicals. Denck's wanderings ceased in 1527, when he died of the plague.

Another pioneer spiritualist was Kaspar Schwenckfeld von Ossig (1489–1561), a nobleman from Silesia, one of the easternmost outposts of German culture. Like Denck, Schwenckfeld privileged personal encounters with the divine, and he claimed many life-altering mystical experiences, which he called "visitations." Schwenckfeld was attracted to Luther's camp as early as 1519, but he broke with it gradually, as he grew increasingly convinced that Luther focused too much on externals. Expelled from his native Silesia in 1529, Schwenckfeld went to Strassburg, the ultimate crossroads of religious dissent, where he influenced many Anabaptists and alienated the Magisterial Reformers Bucer and Capito. In 1534 he felt compelled to leave for Ulm, but two years later Bucer convinced the Ulm authorities to expel him. Schwenckfeld spent the remainder of his long life moving from one place to another in Germany, including even a brief stint in a Franciscan convent under an alias.

Unlike Denck, Schwenckfeld attracted many disciples throughout Germany, and especially in his native Silesia. He also left behind an astonishing number of writings, so many, in fact, that Philip Melanchthon called him "Stenkfeldius, the hundred-handed."[27] Because of his conviction that all genuine religion was inward and that Christ worked directly in the soul rather than through outward signs, Schwenckfeld became one of the earliest and most eloquent champions of religious freedom, arguing that belief should never be compelled and that all state-supported churches were a betrayal of true Christian principles. His scorn for externals was very consistent, and extended to all churches equally, even to the Anabaptists, who, as he saw it, placed way too much faith in the external ritual of baptism. His consistency also led him to call for a total suspension of eucharistic celebrations, for he saw no point in practicing a rite that caused so much theological wrangling. Paradoxically, the man who placed little faith in externals left behind a large enough following in Silesia to give birth to the Schwenckfelder Church, which still survives in the United States, but vanished from Silesia in the nineteenth century. Schwenckfeld's legacy also lived on in later movements, especially among the German Pietists and the English and American Quakers.

Few spiritualists can rival Sebastian Franck (c. 1499–1542) when it comes to being considered "ahead of their time" or harbingers of enlightenment. A former Catholic priest and Lutheran who ended up as a printer, Franck was one of the most extreme critics of established religion in his day. In many ways, the fact that he was able to live and write without being martyred says as much about the relative freedom one could find in certain parts of Germany as it does about his talent for avoiding confrontations. Franck had met Luther in 1518, at the Heidelberg Disputation, and joined his camp early. But after serving as a Lutheran pastor in Nuremberg, from 1525 to 1529, Franck gave up not only his position, but also his beliefs, and he fled to Strassburg, that very special haven for dissenters.

At Strassburg, where he met and befriended Schwenckfeld, Franck began to develop a theology that rejected all outward religion. Boasting that he did not want to be a Catholic, Lutheran, Zwinglian, or Anabaptist, Franck gave voice to a skepticism that was at once irreverent and highly mystical, Christian and universalist. At bottom, like Denck and his soul mate Schwenckfeld, Franck preached an inner faith, and a one-to-one, unmediated connection between every human and God. For him, Christianity was but one of many roads to the divine. The events described in the Bible, which he took to calling "the paper pope," were only timeless symbols and metaphors of God's relationship with the human race. Eternal truth, Franck argued, must always express itself in historical form, dressed in specific cultural garb, but the form it takes is not to be mistaken for the truth itself, which is always inward, and eternal. "The histories of Adam and Christ are not Adam and Christ," he proposed, taking the inner-outer dichotomy several steps beyond any contemporary. "The external Adam and Christ are but the expression of the inward, indwelling Adam and Christ."[28]

Franck's convictions, based as they were on the unquestionable presence of the divine within every human, are not skeptical in the same vein as those of the Enlightenment philosophes would be in the eighteenth century. But they were nonetheless similar enough to give pause to Troeltsch and others who have seen in the spiritualists the very first awakening of the modern consciousness. Take, for instance, Franck's critique of Christian rituals, which was based not only on spiritualist dichotomies of spirit and matter, but also on an evolutionary theory of culture and religion:

> Nowadays everyone imagines that God has need of our work and service and takes a special pleasure in these things, like children with their playthings. . . . God permitted, indeed, gave the outward signs to the church in its infancy, just like a doll to a child. . . . I ask what is the need or why should God wish to restore the outworn sacraments . . . contrary to his own nature, which is Spirit and inwards, and yield to weak material elements . . . taking refuge again in the sick elements of the world and reestablishing the besmirched holy days and sacraments of both Testaments?[29]

Franck's contempt for ritual was still solidly enmeshed in a theological matrix and in mystical language, but the critique itself aimed at a solution for Europe's religious crisis that hardly anyone wished to contemplate: the complete abolition of churches, creeds, and sacraments. At bottom, Franck was the ultimate iconoclast and ultimate heretic rolled into one, a daring missionary for universalism who used Christian discourse to undo Christianity:

> Consider as thy brothers all Turks and heathens wherever they be, who fear God and work righteously, instructed by God and inwardly drawn by him, even though they have never heard of baptism, indeed of Christ himself, neither of his story or Scripture, but only of his power through the inner Word perceived within and made fruitful. . . . There are many Christians who have never heard of Christ's name.[30]

Such explosive language had a distinctively Anabaptist accent, for Franck stressed above all, as did the Anabaptists, the absolute centrality of behavior and ethical transformation. But Franck was as dismissive of the Anabaptists as he was of Catholics and Magisterial Reformers. And, paradoxically, he was as deeply indebted to the Catholic Rhineland mystics as he was to Luther, Zwingli, Bucer, and the Anabaptists.

Franck was expelled from Strassburg in 1532 and fled to Ulm, which had just become Protestant the year before. Despite pressure from Ulm's pastors, the civil authorities granted Franck citizenship, and it was there that he was able to write most of his works while eking out a living as a printer. The fact that he never tried to make a disciple out of anyone helped him to survive, and not to be expelled like his friend Schwenckfeld, but that alone does not explain how he managed to avoid being killed in a highly charged and often intolerant religious maelstrom of his day. His survival seems to suggest that he may not have been too far ahead of his time, after all, and that exceptions may have actually been the rule in many places in the sixteenth century, including Ulm.

One way spiritualists ensured their survival was by hiding behind a mask, that is, by denying their own convictions in public. We have no idea how many such spiritualists there might have been, but one notable example alone, that of David Joris (c. 1501–1556), reveals how relatively easy it could be to hide. His success also suggests that there may have been many others like him. David Joris was a stained-glass painter from Delft who mixed prophetic apocalypticism with spiritualism. In 1536, shortly after the defeat of the Münsterites, Joris proclaimed himself "the third David" and a precursor to Christ's return. Stressing the superiority of direct divine inspiration over external rites and established religion, Joris attracted many followers, who came to be known as Davidists. Joris dispensed with boundaries between true religion—which was always inward and spiritual—and whatever might be deemed false worship, and he advised his followers to dissemble, arguing that it was perfectly acceptable for any truly spiritual person to feign his or her religious convictions in order to escape persecution. After locking horns with Menno Simons, Joris took his own advice and moved to Basel in 1544, where he lived under the alias Johann van Brugge, pretending to be a faithful Reformed Protestant while he penned spiritualist texts. Joris, like Franck, is usually praised for being precociously "modern." Aside from championing religious liberty and disparaging the value of external ceremonies, including baptism and marriage, Joris was among the first to deny the existence of the devil, whom he reduced to a metaphor for the evil inclinations within human beings. But such "modern" ideas were not well received in sixteenth-century Basel, or in most of Europe. Joris knew this, and the fate of his corpse proved he had been wise to dissemble. When the Basel authorities discovered his true identity in 1559, three years after his death, they dug up his remains and burned them.

Proof that Franck and Joris may not have lacked company is the fact that there were other prominent spiritualists who gathered a following, such as Johann Bünderlin (c. 1498–1533), one of the few spiritualists to have been executed; Obbe Phillips (c. 1500–1568), who spent the last twenty-eight years of his life in obscurity; Dirk Coornhert (1522–1590), who further refined Joris's dissembling theology; and Valentin Weigel (1533–1588), who lived as an exemplary Lutheran pastor, but harbored radical ideas that later had an enormous influence, after his hidden texts were published posthumously.

Ultimately, the spiritualists appealed to mystical rhetoric or personal experience, but this is not to say that their proposals lacked an appeal to reason. Taken together, these individuals and their unnumbered followers represent one of the most imposing challenges to the reigning epistemology of their day. Even though they were making truth claims of their own about the link between the divine and every human, the spiritualists refused to accept the idea that the truth could be codified, or ritualized, or forced upon people. And all of them pointed to the violent disagreements of their age as conclusive proof that they were right, and thus refused to engage in any sort of struggle for dominance. What they argued, in essence, boiled down to a simple formula: ultimate truth claims are beyond human reason. Sebastian Franck expressed this point of view eloquently:

> Anyone can be pious all by himself, wherever he may be. He is not to run hither and yonder, seeking to establish a special sect, baptism, church, or group of followers. . . . This we can neither tell anybody nor write nor read it, but everyone will in himself experience it. Therefore, one can neither say, read, nor write what is God, God's Word and truth. The Holy Spirit does not allow itself to be regulated, nor suffers truth to

be put into letters nor speak God's word. It is only picture and shadow what one can speak, rule, write, or read, conceived as from afar.[31]

Mystical as it was in essence, the spiritualist argument was also an eminently rational appeal for a new sort of epistemology, one that denied the possibility of precision in theology and admitted that the human intellect is incapable of grasping, expressing, or ritualizing the ultimate truth. It was also an eloquent plea for toleration and the right of every individual to worship as he or she saw fit. A slightly different version of this argument—one without mysticism—would resurface again with a vengeance in the Enlightenment of the eighteenth century, and would culminate with Immanuel Kant's (1724–1804) anti-metaphysical philosophy, which came to affect skeptics and mainstream Protestants immensely. But even before then, various other versions of this rationalist tendency had surfaced, within the third major branch of the Radical family.

The Evangelical Rationalists

The Radicals who tend to be listed as Evangelical Rationalists do share some traits in common, but their independent perspectives naturally gave rise to differences of opinion. The two common threads that bind them most tightly and distinguish them from the spiritualists are their indifference to mystical claims and their tendency to dismiss some paradoxical central dogmas in Christian theology as irrational and unnecessary. Two other traits that bind them to the Radical tradition are their intense concern for ethics and moral transformation, and their tendency to reject infant baptism. The history of these so-called Evangelical Rationalists is not always tidy, full as it is of connections to humanism, Magisterial Protestantism, and Anabaptism, as well as cross-fertilizations of many sorts from all directions, including individuals who expressed rationalistic tendencies, but were unwilling or unable to break totally with established dogmas.

Erasmus always tends to be the starting point for all histories of rational evangelicalism. George Williams attributes a key influence to him, and to humanistic learning in general, and he identifies many personal links among evangelical rationalists in reformist Erasmian circles. But Erasmus is usually left off the list, because he remained nominally Catholic and also espoused a somewhat mystical spirituality. Oddly enough, for reasons still largely unexplored, Erasmus's rationalistic progeny come not from Northern Europe, but rather from the two areas least affected by Protestantism: Spain and Italy.

Most surveys of this branch of the Radical Reformation begin with Erasmians in Spain, and especially with Alfonso de Valdés (c. 1500–1531) and his brother Juan (c. 1505–1541). Alfonso, secretary to Emperor Charles V and a Protestant sympathizer, is given credit for the rationalist tendencies expressed in his *Dialogue Between Mercury and Charon* (1528). Juan is cited for having created a circle of rationalist-leaning Evangelicals in Naples, and especially for his book, *The Christian Alphabet* (1536). Since some of this group in Naples remained Catholic, others turned Protestant, and others yet ended up as

Radicals with openly rational tendencies, the jury is still out on the nature and extent of his influence.

Bernardino Ochino (1487–1564) is also often classified as a rationalist. A former Franciscan friar and vicar-general of the Capuchin Order, Ochino converted to Protestantism in 1545, married, and spent the rest of his life migrating from one place to another: Augsburg, England, Zurich, Poland, and Moravia. Ochino defies classification. His rational tendencies tended to offend all Magisterial Reformers and most Anabaptists, especially his thinking on the Trinity.

The first full-blown rationalist on nearly every list is Michael Servetus (c. 1511–1553), a Spanish physician, scientist, geographer, astrologer, and amateur theologian who denied the full divinity of Jesus Christ and also the Christian dogma of the Trinity. Arguing that the concept of the Trinity was illogical and a form of polytheism, Servetus sought to return to the ancient heresy of Modalism, teaching that God is one, but merely accommodates to humans in three different ways. A brilliant scientific researcher, the first ever to discover the circulation of the blood through the lungs, Servetus published three books on the Trinity that greatly offended Catholics and Protestants alike. Denying the divinity of Jesus Christ made matters worse. After living in France for years under an assumed name, pretending to be a faithful Catholic, Servetus was unmasked and thrown into prison. He managed to escape, but ended up in Geneva, where the authorities arrested him, tried him for heresy, and burned him alive in 1553. Authorities in France and Geneva were also able to seize and burn nearly all copies of his last book, *The Restitution of Christianity*, which is now among the rarest of all early printed books, with only one full surviving copy. We will return to Servetus in the following chapter, when we deal with Geneva and its Reformer, John Calvin.

Servetus, in turn, influenced others. Among those who picked up where he had left off, Camillo Renato (c. 1500–1575), a former Franciscan friar from Sicily known as Paulo Ricci before he renamed himself, is one of the hardest to classify: part Reformed, part Anabaptist, part rationalist, Renato (which means "the reborn") was hounded by both the Roman Inquisition and the Magisterial Reformers for his idiosyncratic views and his denial of the Trinity. He would eventually influence Lelio Sozzini, a later anti-Trinitarian leader whom we will return to shortly. By far the most important of Servetus's disciples was Giorgio Biandrata (1516–1588), a physician who became Protestant and moved to Geneva three years after Servetus's execution. A Piedmontese from northern Italy, Biandrata soon began to dispute with John Calvin and the pastor of Geneva's Italian refugee congregation, mostly over the issue of Christ's divinity. Seeking a home more open to his ideas, he tried several other Swiss cities before heading east to Poland, and then south to Transylvania, where he was welcomed at the royal court. Well protected by his Eastern European patrons, Biandrata published *On the True and False Knowledge of the One God* in 1568, in which he argued that the dogmas of the Trinity and of the full divinity of Christ were a betrayal of early Christian monotheism. Among those he thanked for bringing him to this realization were Erasmus, Ochino, and Servetus. Having established a non-Trinitarian church in Transylvania, Biandrata soon fell into conflict with one of his own disciples, a former Calvinist pastor, Francis David, who had helped him write *On the True and False Knowledge*. Following Biandrata's own logic, David had concluded that it was incorrect to worship Jesus, who was just a man. After much wrangling, Biandrata caused David to be imprisoned for life, and also forced all of his followers to reject David's theology.

Servetus, Biandrata, and David all rejected as illogical the two central paradoxes affirmed by the councils of Nicaea (325), Ephesus (431), and Chalcedon (451): that there is only one God, but that he is three distinct persons—Father, Son, and Holy Spirit— and that the Son, Jesus, the Christ, is both fully divine and fully human. Each of these rationalists had their own way of arguing against the Trinity and the full divinity of Jesus Christ, and this meant that their followers also disagreed with one another about how to disagree with Trinitarian and Christological orthodoxy. The work of consolidating anti-Trinitarian belief and the churches that sprang up around it, which later came to be known as Unitarian, fell to two younger Italians, Lelio Sozzini (1525–1562) and his nephew Fausto (1539–1604).

Lelio Sozzini was educated in Italy, Vienna, and Switzerland, and he traveled widely before settling in Zurich. Well acquainted with Heinrich Bullinger, John Calvin, and Philip Melanchthon, he constantly posed logical questions to them, raising more doubts than any of them could tolerate. After signing a confession of faith in 1555 that was worded carefully enough to please the Reformed clergy, Lelio escaped banishment or imprisonment, but kept doubting anyway. In 1559, less than three years before his death, Lelio wrote a book, *Brief Explanation on the First Chapter of John*, in which he laid out well-reasoned denials of the Trinity and Christ's divinity. Both Giorgio Biandrata and Francis David were heavily influenced by this work, and even included the text in their own *On the True and False Knowledge*, without mentioning the author's name.

Another young rationalist deeply influenced by Lelio was his nephew Fausto, who was converted to anti-Trinitarianism when he retrieved Lelio's manuscripts from Zurich and read them. After living in Switzerland for some years, where he wrote in secret, Fausto moved to Poland in 1579 and assumed leadership of the existing Minor Reformed Church—also known as the Polish Brethren—and gradually converted it to his way of thinking, also adding "Socinian" to the list of names by which it came to be known. Under the protection of Polish nobles, the Socinian anti-Trinitarian Brethren flourished, growing to three hundred congregations in the seventeenth century, and even establishing a Socinian publishing house and a university at Raków. Fausto continued writing and publishing, unhindered, giving shape to his Unitarian theology. In 1605, it was this press that published the *Racovian Catechism*, the definitive formulation of Socinian anti-Trinitarian beliefs. As had happened with the early Anabaptists, persecution eventually dispersed this church and spread its influence. When ordered to convert to Roman Catholicism in 1658, most Socinians fled to more tolerant lands, such as

Transylvania, the Netherlands, Germany, and England, and some of these communities survived until the nineteenth century. In England, John Biddle (1615–1622), the founder of English Unitarianism, was influenced by the Socinians, as were the first Unitarians in eighteenth- and nineteenth- century New England.

The Radical Legacy

If historians were to pay attention only to movements that involve large numbers of people, the spiritualists and the entire Radical Reformation could easily be overlooked. In the case of the spiritualists, as with all other Radical groups or individuals, the number of adherents was always relatively small and so undetectable that any estimates are, in fact, mere guesses. But Radicals are significant beyond their numbers for three reasons. First, they offered an alternative sort of religion in which communal bonds were redefined, and in doing so they shaped not only their own identity, but also that of their opponents, who had to come to terms with them. Second, they were the first Western Christians to break completely from the medieval symbiosis of church and state and to insist that church membership should never be compulsory. Third, save for the Münsterites and other apocalyptic activists, the Radicals tended to champion toleration and the right of every individual to choose his or her faith. These three contributions to Western culture, one might argue, are among the most significant made by anyone in the sixteenth century. In many ways the Radicals were indeed ahead of their time. Even opposite ends of their spectrum seem eerily modern: whether one looks at the Münsterites, with their totalitarian nightmare, or the spiritualists, with their solitary quest for truth within themselves, it is fairly easy to see more than a dim reflection of our own day and age.

CHAPTER TWELVE

Calvin and Calvinism

In February 1545, Philip Melanchthon received two letters from Geneva, in the same envelope. One letter was for him, the other for the ailing Martin Luther, who, at that point, had only one year left to live.

The letters were from John Calvin (1509–1564), leader of the Protestant Reformation in the independent city-state of Geneva. Calvin merely sought to ask Luther a single question, but he felt it would be best to approach him through Melanchthon, given Luther's animosity to all missives from the Alpine regions. As he said in his cover letter, Calvin hoped that Melanchthon could use his "dexterity" and not do anything "rash" that might lead to "unhappy results." Calvin knew that Luther had little patience for anyone who disagreed with him on anything, and that he had just published a "savage" blast against all Reformed theologians entitled *A Short Confession on the Lord's Supper.* Theological wrangling separated the Reformed and Lutheran camps, but Calvin desperately hoped that Luther would read his letter anyway. Addressing him as "my most respected father," and expressing a desire to speak with him at length in person some day, Calvin begged Luther to give his opinion on a burning question: was it permissible for Evangelical Christians to escape persecution by attending Roman Catholic rituals and pretending that they were Catholic?[1]

Luther never read Calvin's letter. "I have not shown him your letter," replied Melanchthon. "For, truly, he interprets many things suspiciously, and does not want his replies to the kind of question you proposed to him being passed around."[2] Melanchthon covered politely for his superior, adding that all letters from Switzerland made Luther explode. Calvin was not terribly disappointed, however, for Melanchthon gave the answer Calvin was fishing for. Speaking for all Lutherans, Melanchthon said: no, a true Christian should never pretend to be a Roman Catholic.

Although Melanchthon seems to have grasped the seriousness of the issue raised by Calvin, neither he nor Luther could really fathom its full significance, not just because persecution was a rare problem for Lutherans in Germany and Scandinavia, but also because the two churches did not share a common vision concerning ritual. Calvin was touching on worship, the point that divided Lutheran from Reformed most sharply. And in addressing worship, he was also touching on one of the points that gave him a distinctive voice and allowed him to shape the Reformed tradition into an international cause. Melanchthon had no way of knowing that this young Frenchman whose letter he had kept from Luther would soon surpass Luther in terms of influence and authority, and that he would help convert countless thousands to Reformed Protestantism, not just in his native France, but also in the Netherlands, England, Scotland, Germany, Hungary, and Poland, giving rise to an international cluster of churches that would rival Lutheranism and make the Reformed faith a formidable agent of change.

Utterly convinced that he had a special calling from God to fulfill, Calvin was very successful at nearly everything, save overcoming a reputation for coldness. But that, in and of itself, was oblique praise—perhaps even grudging admiration—for his resolve and his passion for order. And, as with all reputations, the grain of truth embedded within can seem larger than it really is. Calvin was indeed a most successful reformer, but he paid a high price, personally, for his life was filled with constant frustration and no small amount of worry. He would die in his prime, wracked with constant pain, beset by

Icon of an iconoclast. This portrait of John Calvin at age fifty-three, two years before his death, features the two key words from his signature motto: "cor meum tibi offero domine *prompte et sincere*" (my heart I offer to you Lord, *promptly* and *sincerely*).

more illnesses than he could count. But he worked tirelessly until the bitter end, keeping several notaries busy at his deathbed, dictating until he could speak no more. When asked to take it easy by his friend and colleague Theodore de Bèze, the dying Calvin knew just what to say: "What? Would you have God find me idle?"[3] Fitting words for the man Max Weber identified as the father of the Protestant work ethic. Fitting words too for a man whose name is still associated with stoic rigor, determination, and clear thinking.

Calvin may have agreed with Luther on many points, but the differences between the two men and the churches they helped create are substantial. Most of the key differences are not the result of disagreements on basic issues, but rather questions of emphasis. Luther was most keenly interested in defending theological concepts; Calvin tended to focus on both theology *and* ritual. Luther spun most of his theology from the central concepts of *sola fide*, *sola gratia*, and *sola scriptura*; Calvin embraced not only these ideas, but also the concepts of election and predestination as their logical conclusions. Moreover, Calvin also added another *solus* (alone): *soli Deo gloria*, "to God alone be the glory."

Calvin's Early Years

Jean Cauvin, as he was then known, was only eight years old when Luther posted his ninety-five theses in 1517. Needless to say, his generation experienced the breakdown of medieval Catholicism in a different way from Luther's. Born in Noyon, in Picardy, about sixty miles northeast of Paris, on 10 July 1509, the young Cauvin represented—even embodied—the twilight of the ecclesiastical corruption that the Protestant and Catholic Reformations struggled against. His father, Gerard Cauvin, was a lay administrator for the bishop and cathedral chapter of Noyon. When his son was only twelve years old, Gerard obtained for him a chaplaincy at the cathedral of Noyon. Although Jean Cauvin was not ordained and was not yet studying for the priesthood, he collected the income from this post, pocketing the lion's share, and using the remainder to pay a priest to perform his duties. Six years later, his father Gerard was able to trade this benefice for a more lucrative one, and eighteen-year-old Jean Cauvin became the unordained absentee curate of Marteville, a village near Noyon. Poetic justice, some might say: the handsome income from these two posts funded all of Jean's education, and without that education he would not have become a Protestant Reformer. Whether his parishioners ever set eyes on him or not, and whether Jean the student gave them any thought, is irrelevant. This was a common practice, widely accepted as scholarship aid, and it would not be until May 1534, after he had already turned Protestant, that Jean Calvin—as he renamed himself, following humanist fashion—would let go of these posts and their income. By then, his education had provided him with all the tools he would need to redefine the Protestant Reformation.

Calvin was very tight-lipped about his own life, so we know relatively little about his early years. What, if anything, he may have heard of Luther or Zwingli or Erasmus remains a mystery. All we know is that his mother was a pious woman who exposed him to Catholic devotion. Years later, writing as a Protestant Reformer who despised his own past, he could not speak about Catholic piety with detachment. In one of his most popular treatises, *The Inventory of Relics*, he made the following observation about Catholic piety in his native Noyon when he was a child:

> I remember what I saw them do to idols [*marmousets*] in our parish when I was a small boy. On the eve of the feast of St. Stephen, they would adorn all the images with garlands and necklaces, those of the murderers who stoned him to death (or "tyrants" as they were commonly known), in the same fashion as the martyr. When the poor women saw the murderers decked out in this way, they mistook them for Stephen's companions, and offered each of them his own candle. Even worse, they did the same with the devil who struggled against St. Michael."[4]

It was precisely this kind of observation of Catholics as the "other"—as primitives of sorts vastly different from himself—that would allow Calvin to formulate a theory of the origins of "false" religion and of the difference between such falsehood and the "true" religion he believed he was defending. And it was this detachment, this ability to think of Catholics as others that made Calvin an inveterate enemy of "idolatry" and of those who practiced it. This posture also made him an accidental anthropologist, or, as has been argued, one of "the first armchair ethnographers of the Western world."[5]

In 1523, at the age of fourteen, Calvin went to the University of Paris to train for the priesthood, and he resided first at the Collège de la Marche, briefly, and then at the Collège de Montaigu, one of the finest theological colleges, where Erasmus had also lived, and where conditions were so unpleasant that the students took to calling it "the cleft between the buttocks of Mother Theology." Montaigu may have been a dismal experience for many, but it was a cradle of sorts for visionary reformers. It counted not only Erasmus and Calvin as alumni, but also the Catholic reformer Ignatius Loyola, founder of the Jesuit order, who went there immediately after Calvin's departure. Needless to say, harsh Montaigu did not breed like-minded ideologues.

Gerard Cauvin had a church career in mind for his bright son, but in 1527, after he became embroiled in a dispute with the Noyon cathedral chapter, which led to his excommunication, he abruptly asked Jean to switch careers and become a lawyer. Unlike Luther, who had broken his father's heart by becoming a monk instead of a lawyer, this obedient son did as his father asked, and took up study of the law between 1528 and 1531, first at Orléans, under the brilliant jurist Pierre L'Étoile, and then at Bourges. In May 1531, when his father Gerard died, the young Calvin, now his own master, returned to Paris, to study Greek and Hebrew and train as a humanist scholar.

Back in Paris, Calvin enrolled in the prestigious Collège Royal, newly established by King Francis I, where he began using the name Calvinus. Immersing himself in classical studies, and especially in Latin, Greek, and Hebrew, Calvin was also exposed to the work of Erasmus and Jacques Lefèvre d'Étaples. By now he had already befriended disciples of Lefèvre's and Briçonnet's reforming circle, including the cleric Gerard Roussel (1500–1550), who had worked at Meaux, taken refuge at Strassburg briefly in 1525, and corresponded with Martin Bucer and Johann Oecolampadius. Roussel was highly placed too, as preacher to Princess Marguerite d'Angoulême (1492–1549), the king's sister and future queen of Navarre. When, exactly, Calvin became Protestant remains a mystery, for he never pinpointed the date. But it had to be during this period, in Paris, through contacts with Roussel and others, like Nicholas Cop (1501–1540), a physician and Protestant sympathizer who was appointed rector of the University of Paris. His own testimony tells us it was a "sudden" conversion, but that can be interpreted loosely. We do know that by 1533 Calvin feared persecution for his beliefs because he fled hastily from Paris in December 1533, after Cop gave a sermon so thoroughly laced with Protestants sentiments that it alarmed King Francis I and caused the authorities to drive Cop away, along with his associates.

Calvin hid for the next few months in the home of his friend Louis du Tillet, a canon of Angoulême, but surfaced again in May, in his native Noyon, where he renounced the benefice that had funded his education. Then, in October 1534, when the first large-scale persecution of Protestants was launched by King Francis I, Calvin had to flee France once again. The persecution had been sparked by the so-called Affair of the Placards. On Sunday morning, 18 October 1534, residents of Paris, Blois, Rouen, Tours, and Orléans had awakened to find posters plastered throughout their cities that ridiculed Catholic rituals as idolatrous superstition and condemned "the gross, horrible, and unsupportable doctrine of the Popish Mass." The placard also denounced the Catholic Church as a whole, and anyone who supported it:

> The Pope and all his vermin of cardinals, bishops, and priests, monks and other sanctimonious Mass-sayers and all those who agree with them are false prophets, damned cheats, apostates, wolves, false pastors, idolaters, seducers, liars and wretched blasphemers, killers of souls, renouncers of Christ, of His death and passion, perjurers, traitors, thieves, rapers of God's honor and more detestable than devils.[6]

Astonished to discover that the "Lutherans" in his realm were now very well organized and bold enough to tack up one of these posters inside his bedchamber at Amboise while he slept, King Francis called for the immediate punishment of those guilty of such sacrilege. Scores of Protestants were rounded up and burned alive. As a prelude to this mass execution, Paris itself was purified through one of the most impressive rituals in the city's long history: processions carrying the consecrated host were launched simultaneously from every church in Paris, and all of them wound their way to the cathedral of Notre Dame, where High Mass was celebrated with the king in attendance.

Calvin the Reformer

The Affair of the Placards marked a turning point not just for all of France, which began to descend into violent chaos from that day forward, but also for Calvin, who fled from

France to the Swiss city of Basel, fearing the worst, not knowing that the exile that awaited him would turn him into one of the most significant figures in Western history.

Welcomed at Basel, where the aged Erasmus had returned, Calvin set about writing the first version of his greatest masterpiece, *The Institutes of the Christian Religion*, a summary of the Reformed Protestant faith intended for the education of the Protestant faithful and also as an apologia, or defense, of their cause. Calvin would revise and expand this book three more times between 1536 and 1559, increasing its size fourfold, amplifying, clarifying, touching on new subjects, but never changing the essence of its teachings. And he would write each of these three later editions in both Latin and French, making the text accessible to the learned throughout Europe and the faithful in France. Immediately after its publication at Basel in early 1536, Calvin's *Institutes* began to attract attention and win him acclaim among Protestants, and for good reason. The first edition of the *Institutes* immediately impressed its readers as the most orderly and systematic presentation of Reformed Protestant theology available. It was clearly and elegantly written, blessed with a lawyer's penchant for precision and a humanist's love for poetic expression and rhetorical flourishes. Most important for a people bent on following the Holy Scriptures alone, the *Institutes* aimed to complement rather than supplant the Bible. Calvin's goal, in his own words, was precisely to prepare readers for their encounter with the divine Word,

> in order that they may be able both to have easy access to it and to advance in it without stumbling. For I believe I have so embraced the sum of religion in all its parts, and have

Magnum opus. Calvin would update and expand his great theological summary, *The Institutes of the Christian Religion*, four times in the course of his life. First published in Latin in 1536, this magisterial text would be translated into many other languages and would become the cornerstone of Calvinism. This 1562 English translation of Calvin's fourth and final edition by Thomas Norton would make an essential contribution to the development of Puritanism and shape English and American culture for generations to come.

arranged it in such an order, that if anyone rightly grasps it, it will not be difficult for him to determine what he ought especially to seek in Scripture, and to what end he ought to relate its contents.[7]

In offering a thorough and masterful, systematic digest of biblically based theology that was also a practical manual for Christian living, Calvin had surpassed his distinguished predecessors. The *Institutes* was as much a how-to manual and devotional text as it was a systematic compendium of Reformed Protestant belief. The work also provided Calvin and all Reformed clergy with a brilliant means of controlling biblical exegesis among the faithful and of defending the *sola scriptura* principle at the same time. Calvin had an advantage over Zwingli, Luther, Bullinger, Bucer, and Oecolampadius, in that he was writing two whole decades after their Reformation had begun, and long after heated disputes among Protestants had forced each camp to be theologically precise about its beliefs and its approach to biblical exegesis. In keeping with the old scholastic saying, Calvin could stand on the shoulders of giants and see much further.

The Marrow of Calvin's Theology

The 1536 *Institutes* included a preface to King Francis I in which Calvin distilled the very essence of his political theology. Calvin spoke to the monarch directly, ostensibly to convince him that the "Lutherans" he was persecuting were actually the best subjects he could hope for, not at all a seditious cabal, but rather "an example of chastity, generosity, mercy, continence, patience, modesty, and all other virtues."[8] But this preface was not merely a brief for the defense, or even directly aimed at the king. Putting his legal and rhetorical skills to work, Calvin addressed King Francis in such a manner as to lay out for all readers a very sharply edged attack on the Roman Catholic Church and its "butchery of souls," accompanied by all sorts of warnings about the divine wrath that could descend on France and its king if the falsehood and idolatry of the Catholic Church were not removed from the land.

Employing all the deference one might expect in a letter to monarch, but subverting that deference, Calvin assumed the role of prophet, preacher, and teacher, not just to the king, but also to all of France. With consummate skill, he laid out precisely what was at stake and issued a direct, yet subtly veiled threat to the king:

> Your mind is now indeed turned away and estranged from us, even inflamed, I may add, against us; but we trust that we can regain your favor, if in a quiet, composed mood you will once read this our confession. . . . Suppose, however . . . that . . . you . . . rage against us, with imprisonings, scourgings, rackings, maimings, and burnings. Then we will be reduced to the last extremity even as sheep destined for the slaughter. Yet this will so happen that we . . . may await the strong hand of the Lord, which will surely appear in due season, coming forth armed to deliver the poor from their affliction and also to punish their despisers, who now exult with such great assurance.[9]

The preface could be read in at least three ways: first, as an ultimatum to the king, challenging him to change course and listen to Calvin, who spoke for God; second, as a liberating manifesto to all subjects of an idolatrous monarch, whether in France or elsewhere, spelling out for them why their religious dissent was not really seditious or disobedient, explaining that their rulers were actually "brigands" and enemies of God who did not have to be obeyed; and third, as a compact lesson on the core message of the Reformed Protestant cause, giving all readers a sound dose of the truth, as Calvin saw it. The message of the Reformed Protestant cause was distilled into a tightly packed sentence:

> It will then be for you, most serene King, not to close your ears on your mind to such just defense, especially when a very great question is at stake: how God's glory may be kept safe on earth, how God's truth may retain its place of honor, how Christ's Kingdom may be kept in good repair among us.[10]

Here, in a nutshell, we find the very essence of what came to be known as Calvinism: a theologically based political ideology that would brook no compromise with "idolatry" and false religion. Distilled into the maxim *soli Deo gloria* "glory to God alone," this would become the battle cry of Calvin and his followers. Calvin's concept of the glory of God and of the honor due to him is very similar to Zwingli's. But even more so than Zwingli, Calvin developed a political theology that encouraged active resistance to "false" religion and "idolatry," promoting the idea that Christians owe their ultimate allegiance to God, and not to any earthly ruler who sullies God's glory. That resistance would define Calvinism everywhere, and especially wherever Calvinists were a minority.

In many ways, Calvin adheres closely to Old Testament conceptions of God, and of his relation to his elect. Reward and punishment are an essential part of this relationship. Calvin's God abhors false worship and demands his proper glory; those who obey are rewarded, but those who do not are punished. This conception of divine punishments and rewards led Calvinists to seek the total transformation of society into the kingdom of Christ, and to insist that the civil sphere exclude "false" religion and be kept "in good repair": religious impurity infected the entire society and provoked God's wrath. So, while trying to convince Francis that the evangelicals were obedient, virtuous model citizens, Calvin delivered a mixed message that contained a serious challenge to any ruler's authority:

> That king who in ruling over his realm does not serve God's glory exercises not kingly rule but brigandage. Furthermore, he is deceived who looks for enduring prosperity in his kingdom when it is not ruled by God's scepter, that is, his Holy Word.[11]

The closing line of the preface was a cheeky and priceless rhetorical gem, a prophetic warning, tightly packed with deference, prayer, and condescension all at once: "May the Lord, the King of Kings, establish your throne in righteousness, and your dominion in equity, most illustrious King."

The 1536 *Institutes* also laid out two other key distinguishing features of Calvin's theology and of Calvinism in general: belief in the thorough corruption of human nature by original sin, and belief in election and predestination.

On human corruption, Calvin laid out very clearly an anthropology deeply steeped in the work of St. Augustine of Hippo (354–430), stressing that all human beings are deeply affected by the curse of original sin—as St. Augustine did—and that they are powerless to overcome their evil inclinations without the aid of God's grace. As in St. Augustine's formulation: after the Fall of Adam and Eve in Eden, it became impossible for humans *not* to sin: *non posse non peccare*. This corruption made all humans inherently sinful, disorderly, and worthy of eternal punishment. It also made strict social controls and a church an absolute necessity, for sins and crimes such as theft, murder, drunkenness, fornication, and adultery were an ever-present likelihood in all human communities, and churches were the only conduit to divine grace. Human corruption was also the source of all false religion. Espousing a binary concept of religion, as either true or false, Calvin argued that false religion was a mere human invention, an extension of the fallen natural world, always focused on the flesh and the material world. True religion, in contrast, was derived straight from God, and therefore divine or genuinely spiritual and supernatural. Calvin's binary understanding might have been very traditional, and in keeping with Erasmian spirituality and the central message of the Protestant Reformation, but his conception of false religion was strikingly modern. Whereas most of the ancient and medieval theologians and even other Reformers had ascribed the origin of false religion to the devil, and to demonic deception, Calvin shifted the blame directly to human beings. False religion was not demonic, therefore, but pure fiction—a twisted projection of human hopes and fears. Idolatry was the ultimate sign of human corruption: an attempt by humans to worship their own image and likeness in fantasies that were mistaken for divine realities.

False religion, then, as Calvin saw it, was embedded in the flesh itself and an ever-present instinct. This congenital defect meant that human nature, unaided by grace, was always prone to idolatry, and that false religion was a constant temptation. In other words, human beings could not remain uncontaminated by false worship whenever they encountered it. This inevitable slippage is why Calvin believed that idolatry had to be avoided at all costs, under all circumstances. This conception of human nature and of the origins of religion is strikingly modern. By objectifying false religion (Catholicism) as a purely natural, socially constructed figment of the human imagination, Calvin began to divorce ritual from the supernatural, and to cast doubt on the possibility that religion, per se, always connects human beings to some numinous dimension. Banning the devil from the scene heightened human responsibility, too, and made religion seem even more illusory and less connected to the world of spirit, even a mere figment of the darkest recesses of the human mind and heart. Further steps would have to be taken to dismiss all religion as some false figment or delusion, along with the very idea of God, but it could be argued that Calvin was something of a pioneer on that steep trail of doubt. Two centuries later, thinkers such as Giambattista Vico, David Hume, the Baron d'Holbach, and Julien Offray de la Mettrie would follow that same route to the summit and dispense with God altogether.[12]

On predestination, Calvin was equally bold. Luther and Zwingli had led the way toward this belief that God alone determines who will be saved or damned with their "faith alone" principle and their persistent affirmation of salvation as a gift from God that cannot be obtained by human effort. In essence, belief in salvation through faith and grace alone—*sola fide, sola gratia*—necessarily implies some sort of election, for if salvation is entirely up to God's will alone and humans can do nothing to be saved, it means that God chooses to dispense his saving grace to some, but not to all. Luther and Zwingli had dealt with this implicit election openly, but never very thoroughly or systematically, and neither Reformer had incorporated the notion of election fully into the theological traditions he founded. Luther had argued against Erasmus that the human will is always in bondage to sin, always dependent on God's grace for salvation: it was like a beast of burden, an ass that was ridden either by God or by Satan. Zwingli was not so blunt, but nevertheless he insisted that salvation was entirely in God's hands. How one received the gift of faith, however, remained somewhat hazy in the theologies of Zwingli and Luther.

John Calvin, in contrast, embraced the logical conclusion of *sola fide, sola gratia*, and he made God's overwhelming agency the very fabric of his systematic theology, passing on to his disciples a firm, strident belief in election and predestination. This theological principle, already elucidated in the 1536 edition of the *Institutes*, would be refined by Calvin many times, but never altered. By 1559, in the final edition of this work, Calvin would assert, unequivocally:

> No one who wishes to be thought religious dares simply deny predestination, by which God adopts some to hope of life, and sentences others to eternal death. . . . We call predestination God's eternal decree, by which he determined with himself what he willed to become for each man. For all are not created in an equal condition; rather eternal life is fore-ordained for some, eternal damnation for others.[13]

Far from leading to fatalism, this Calvinist doctrine helped create an international community of very driven individuals who thought of themselves as God's elect.

Calvin's take on predestination was overwhelmingly positive. Stressing that every single event, no matter how small, was expressly willed by God, Calvin offered his followers the hope of believing that anything that came their way, no matter how unpleasant, must be God's will, and therefore good. This belief gave Calvinists immense resolve, especially in the face of adversity:

> Yet when that light of divine providence has once shone upon a godly man, he is then relieved and set free not only from the extreme anxiety and fear that were pressing him before, but from every care. . . . His solace, I say, is to know that his Heavenly Father so holds all things in his power, so rules by his authority and will, so governs by his wisdom, that nothing can befall except he determine it. Moreover, it comforts him to

know that he has been received into God's safekeeping and entrusted to the care of his angels, and that neither water, nor fire, nor iron can harm him, except insofar as it pleases God as governor to give them the occasion.[14]

And that was not all. Calvin also spoke and wrote directly to his audience as if they were indeed the elect. Presuming that all who cared about their salvation or all who agreed with him were already graced, Calvin tried at every turn to make his congregation and his readers think of him as God's agent and of themselves as God's elect. Moreover, Calvin also spoke of the elect as those who did God's bidding and made his will effective on earth. Election was no passive state, no blinding flash, no bolt out of the blue direct from God to each individual: it was a social process, carried out through the agency of the elect and their church, for the only way that God could reach his elect on earth was through his chosen ones, as individuals and communities. In other words, God did not reach his elect directly from heaven, mystically, but only through other human beings on earth: through the preaching of the Word, through teaching, through the sacraments, and through the establishment of godly communities. The way Calvin saw it, the elect could have no clearer sign of their election than the fact that they were busy trying to build Christ's kingdom on earth. It was simple: if one busied oneself with God's work, then one was among the elect, thus bringing the elect to the realization of his election— and the reprobate to an acknowledgment of his damnation. Predestination, as Calvin saw it, was not an anxiety-ridden teaching that paralyzed people or made them indifferent; but rather, it was a great "comfort." And that comfort made a world of difference. It could even make believers do that which they hated the most.

Calvin and Geneva

Calvin's own life story is one of the best examples of the way in which a predestinarian mentality could work. Having published his *Institutes* in 1536, Calvin briefly spent some time in northern Italy at the court of Duchess Renée of Ferrara (1510–1575), who surrounded herself with Protestant refugees from France and elsewhere. Then he resolved to move to Strassburg, where he thought he could lead a scholar's life in peace, furthering the establishment of Christ's kingdom by studying and writing. In the most revealing autobiographical statement he ever made, Calvin explained his situation thus:

> I, who was by nature a man of the country and a lover of shade and leisure, wished to find for myself a quiet hiding place—a wish which has never yet been granted me; for every retreat I found became a public lecture room. When the one thing I craved was obscurity and leisure, God fastened upon me so many cords of various kinds that he never allowed me to remain quiet, and in spite of my reluctance dragged me into the limelight. . . . I desired no fame for myself from it [The Institutes]. . . . No one knew that I was the writer. For I had kept my authorship secret and intended to continue to do so.[15]

As it turned out, however, Calvin had to take a life-altering detour that would also affect the course of Western history. Warfare blocked the road to Strassburg, forcing Calvin to travel through Geneva, which had only recently declared its independence from the Dukes of Savoy and turned Protestant after an iconoclastic riot. At the helm in Geneva, directing this nascent Reformation, was none other than Guillaume Farel, that French disciple of Lefèvre and Briçonnet who had become a Protestant missionary in French-speaking Switzerland (see chapter 5). When Farel learned that the author of the *Institutes* was staying overnight in Geneva, he barged into Calvin's inn, and demanded that he remain there and become his assistant. Calvin resisted, in total shock, but Farel would not take no for an answer. Placing his hand on Calvin's shoulder, he spoke for God, revealing his will to Calvin. Twenty-one years later Calvin would recall that fateful moment thus:

> Farel, who was working with incredible zeal to promote the gospel, bent all his efforts to keep me in the city. And when he realized that I was determined to study in privacy in some obscure place and saw that he gained nothing by entreaty, he descended to cursing, and said that God would surely curse my peace if I held back from giving help at a time of such great need. Terrified by his words, and conscious of my own timidity and cowardice, I gave up my journey.[16]

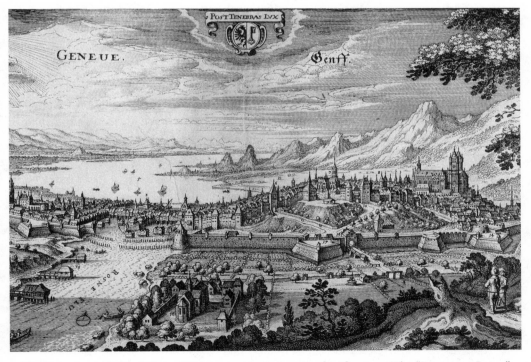

The Protestant Rome. View of Geneva and its impressive fortifications. The "Protestant Rome" was relatively small, and well aware of its precarious position as an independent city-state, perched beyond the westernmost edge of the Swiss Confederation, surrounded by Catholic France and Savoy.

Duly terrified, Calvin stayed in Geneva and transformed it into the Protestant Rome, a model experiment in civic godliness, and the epicenter of an international world-shaking enterprise. But Calvin was never happy about being there; in fact, he complained loudly about the role God had assigned him while giving it his all. Reforming Geneva was his calling, revealed to him by Farel, and the fact that it was a difficult task was the clearest possible indication that it was what God had willed for him, and what he must do. Predestination may have been a godly person's greatest comfort, but one's calling in this life was not necessarily trouble-free. In fact, trouble was an essential part of the deal.

Calvin's work in Geneva began very modestly, as a lecturer on the Bible. A year into his stay, he was appointed preacher. Working closely with Farel, he struggled to bring his vision of Christ's kingdom to fruition in Geneva, but the Genevans seemed to resist at every turn. The worst conflict was a power struggle between the clergy and the city council over the right of excommunication, which the ministers wanted to control, against the wishes of the magistrates. Having just rid themselves of what they viewed as an oppressive church, the elites of Geneva were not eager to see another one take its place. Unwilling to compromise, insisting on the clergy's right to excommunicate, Calvin and Farel were expelled from Geneva in May 1538. Relieved to discover that God had apparently willed an end to his stay in Geneva, Calvin gladly shook the dust off his feet and headed straight for Strassburg, where he had wanted to be all along. And he was even more pleased to discover that God had willed he should be welcomed there.

By his own account, the years Calvin spent at Strassburg, from 1538 to 1541, were the happiest of his life. Freed from having to shepherd an unruly city whose residents always viewed him as a foreigner, Calvin gladly took on the task of ministering to the French refugees in Strassburg, and he quickly learned to distinguish what made Strassburg's Reformation unique and so successful an experiment in civic godliness. Having battled Anabaptists in Geneva, he was glad to see they had been vanquished in Strassburg, and immensely pleased to marry a former member of their flock, a widow named Idelette de Bure, who apparently met his exacting criteria: "I am none of those insane lovers who . . . are smitten at first sight with a fine figure," he had confessed to Farel. "This is the only beauty that allures me, if she is chaste, if not too fastidious, if economical, if patient, if there is hope that she will be interested in my health."[17]

Calvin also learned much from his colleague Martin Bucer. On the eucharist, Calvin adopted a position about halfway between the Lutheran and Swiss Reformed, something Bucer had long advocated: he refused to accept the real presence of Christ in the bread and wine, which Lutherans defended, but at the same time affirmed that a real communion with Christ took place, spiritually—a communion that other Reformed leaders in the Zwinglian tradition found hard to accept. This one issue would create many tensions between Geneva and its Swiss brethren, especially those at nearby Bern. On the question of how to reform society to create a Christian commonwealth, Calvin also owed more to Bucer than to Luther or Zwingli, though he was certainly closer to Zwingli. Years after Calvin's stay in Strassburg, when Bucer penned *De regno Christi* ("On the Kingdom

of Christ"), his ultimate treatise on Christian political theology, written expressly for the
child king Edward VI of England, the principles espoused in that text were very similar
to the principles Calvin had attempted to put into practice at Geneva upon his return
in 1541.

For return to Geneva he did. Invited back after an election changed the composition of the city councils, Calvin agreed to return on his own terms, "compelled, against
my own will," as he put it. God had willed it, and he could not refuse, even if he hated to
return. "With how much grief, with how many tears, and in how great anxiety I went,"
he groaned.[18] But, convinced as he was of God's calling, Calvin knew exactly what to
demand. The contract drawn up, *The Ecclesiastical Ordinances* of 1541, gave Calvin a
greater degree of control over the city than he had enjoyed before, and placed the clergy
in a privileged position, as coadministrators of the city, "to instruct, admonish, exhort
and censure, both in public and in private, to administer the sacraments, and to enjoin
brotherly corrections along with the elders and colleagues."[19]

The agreement Calvin sealed gave Geneva a unique political and ecclesiastical
structure that would become the pattern eventually followed by hundreds of other communities. Asserting that this structure was "taken from the Gospel of Jesus Christ," the
Ecclesiastical Ordinances established four offices in the Genevan church: pastors, elders,
doctors, and deacons. The pastors were in charge of preaching the gospel, and of enforcing
all discipline, and they selected all candidates for that office, subject to the city council's
approval. The doctors, or teachers, instructed the faithful "in true doctrine in order that
the purity of the Gospel be not corrupted either by ignorance or by evil opinions."[20] They
were to be trained in a *collège*, established in the city for that sole purpose. The elders, or
presbyters, were men whose office was "to watch over the life of each person," to admonish all those who were leading "disorderly" lives, and to report all such delinquents to the
pastors. These elders were to be drawn from the various city councils, God-fearing men
"without reproach and beyond suspicion," representing all quarters of Geneva, "to keep
an eye on everybody," and "to have oversight of the life of everyone."[21] The deacons were
given charge of the poor and the sick in Geneva, to ensure that charity be fairly administered. The city's hospital, which had been established before Calvin's arrival—was to be
entrusted to these deacons, and medical care would be dispensed there to all those who
needed it, free of charge if necessary. In addition, begging would be forbidden, and the
poor carefully screened, to ensure that only the truly deserving would receive aid directly
from the deacons. In other words, the distribution of all charity was to be centralized, and
carefully regulated by the deacons.

The church in Geneva, a city of ten thousand, was thoroughly redesigned. First,
the number of churches was reduced to three parishes, served by ten pastors. This was a
97.5 percent reduction in the clerical class: before 1536, Geneva had around four hundred
clerics, including monastics. But the lower numbers did not tell the whole story. These
ten pastors would be given more authority over the people of Geneva than their predecessors ever enjoyed. And they would have to work much harder too. Throughout the

week, the three parishes were to offer seventeen sermons, not only on Sunday, but also on Monday, Wednesday, and Friday. The eucharist was celebrated four times a year—at Easter (spring), Pentecost (summer), mid-September (autumn), and Christmas (winter), and all excommunications strictly enforced. (Calvin had requested a monthly celebration in the *Ecclesiastical Ordinances*, but ended up compromising on this issue). On Sunday at noon, all children had to be brought to their parishes for religious instruction. Attendance at sermons was required of everyone, and so were punctuality, and attentiveness. Arriving late, leaving early, being noisy, or falling asleep was not allowed. In 1547, for instance, a parishioner was imprisoned not just for leaving during the sermon, but for not doing so quietly. From 1545, home visits by the clergy were mandated, on a regular semiannual basis, so that every family's morals could be checked.

In addition, Calvin established a disciplinary committee named the consistory, which would oversee the behavior of all Genevans, define godliness, and impose binding penalties on offenders. Its purpose was to control morals in Geneva and ensure its Christian purity. The consistory was composed of the pastors and twelve lay elders elected once a year from the city's municipal councils, one of whom was always one of the city's four syndics and charged with presiding over its sessions. As part of the city's civil structure, its power was backed by law, and it quickly became a formidable and very intrusive institution. Like the Inquisition in Spain and Italy, the consistory relied on informants, and encouraged everyone to report scandalous behavior. It also kept very detailed records of its cases, leaving behind a treasure trove of information for historians to examine. Meeting once a week, nearly always with Calvin present, the consistory handled a wide variety of moral lapses, such as blasphemy, foul language, adultery, fornication, lewdness, quarreling, gossiping, slandering, showing disrespect for civil and church authorities, not going to church, practicing witchcraft, taking part in idolatrous or superstitious rites, and spreading heresy.

Once established, the consistory quickly set very high standards, showing little tolerance for misbehavior, and micromanaging the personal lives of Genevans. Quite often, the consistory was lenient with first-time offenders, and took to admonishing, teaching, and counseling rather than to punishing. This was especially true in cases of marital problems, ranging from loud quarreling to flagrant adultery. In some cases, the consistory actually advised incompatible couples to divorce. Repeat offenders, however, could expect little leniency. Fines and imprisonment were common punishments. Banishment from Geneva was reserved for the utterly incorrigible; execution for those convicted of witchcraft, and, at times, also for those who spread heresy. But—as was also the case with the Catholic Inquisition—the consistory had no power to impose these two extreme penalties. That power belonged to the civil authorities, namely to the magistrates of the city's Small Council. The numbers speak for themselves, revealing some restraint with the harshest sentences: between 1541 and 1564, when Calvin served as leader of Geneva's Reformation, fifty-eight people were put to death and seventy-six were banished. This boils down to an average of roughly three executions and four expulsions per year in a city of ten thousand.

The consistory had no intention of turning Geneva into another Münster, composed entirely of saints (see chapter 11). Rather, it worked on the assumption that it could be the instrument of God's election, reproving sinners, forcing them to find Christ's forgiveness and to mend their ways. Calvin and the consistory never assumed that the entire population of Geneva consisted of the elect, but they acted on the assumption that one could never know with certainty who was and who was not. Habitual sinners could be among the elect too, they presumed, for Christ had come to save all sinners, no matter how hardened. Conversions were possible, they thought, and the consistory might be the instrument through which God would make them happen. But Calvin and the consistory also worked on the assumption that the reprobate would always be part of the community, and that no amount of preaching, teaching, or admonishing would turn their lives around. After all, it was God himself who ordained that part of the human race would end up in hell. When it came to the reprobate, however, Calvin and the consistory assumed a prophylactic role, preventing the contamination of the city as a whole by their sinful behavior and the scandals caused by it. Keeping in mind that God dealt with his elect as a community—as revealed in the model of the ancient Israelites in the Old Testament—Calvin and the consistory sought to ensure that Geneva remained as pleasing to God as possible, so the elect could keep their covenant with God and fulfill their proper role as God's agents on earth.

Working in tandem, Calvin, the city magistrates, the pastors, and the consistory tried hard to turn Geneva into a godly community. But it was not easy. Throughout the 1540s and up until 1555, Calvin and his godly elites faced stiff opposition from many in Geneva who did not see things their way and resented the imposition of new laws on their city. Many of the leaders of this opposition were members of old, privileged Genevan families. Among them, the Perrin family was the most prominent. Ironically, Amy Perrin, one of their patriarchs, had been instrumental in bringing Protestantism to Geneva, and was therefore largely responsible for creating the church that now found him and his family lacking in Christian virtue. Calvin took to calling his local opponents "Libertines," linking their desire to cling to old Genevan customs with unbridled license. Resistance was both passive and active. Court records provide us with evidence of disputes, riots, and all sorts of challenges. In a city with elections, the opposition retained a majority in the various councils for many years and made their voice count, until 1555.

But Calvin, the pastors, and the consistory plowed ahead with their Reformation, and wrestled with these so-called Libertines at every turn. Being outnumbered did not matter to the elect. Austerity, sobriety, and devotion were expected of every Genevan. The Libertines—even when they had political clout—were often frustrated. Because some laws enacted by the magistrates could reflect the puritanical goals of the clergy, who acted in unison as the Company of Pastors, Geneva became an uncomfortable place for anyone who was less than godly. Before long, clothing was carefully regulated: all were to dress modestly, without extravagance, shunning loud and expensive fabrics or ornamental frills, including velvet and certain kinds of bows, buttons, and lace. Lewd, revealing fashions were strictly forbidden, such as codpieces for men or low-cut dresses for women. Women were also forbidden to wear shoes that revealed any part of their toes. Certain hairstyles were declared un-Christian, and so were any banquets or parties with over twenty guests and an "excessive" number of dishes.

Names were carefully regulated too, especially after 1545. Genevans were encouraged to give biblical names to their children and forbidden to use "idolatrous" names linked with revered Catholic saints formerly popular in Geneva, such as Claude and Martin, who had nearby shrines, or names of saints whose existence was unlikely, like Gaspar, Melchior, and Balthazar (the three Wise Men), or "silly" names such as Dedet, Ayme, Mama, Pentecost, or Christian and Christine (since everyone in Geneva was Christian anyway). Even naming one's pet incorrectly could lead to trouble, as one man who called his dog "Calvin" found out. His was a double offense, one must assume: using the wrong name and showing disrespect for authority.

Enforcement of this law was up to the pastors, who could accept or reject names at the time of baptism. Often enough, parents and sponsors found themselves corrected, as pastors rejected a name and imposed another on the infant being baptized. In August 1542, for instance, as the law was first being put into effect, a pastor refused to baptize a child as Claude and instead named him Abraham on the spot. The name Claude was especially troublesome, not only because of a nearby shrine to St. Claude, but also because it was a very popular name in Geneva, passed from one generation to another. Getting Genevans to break so completely with their past would not be easy. In the case of the child named Abraham, the parents flew into a rage and refused to accept the baptism as legitimate. Snatching the child from the baptismal font, they took him home and baptized him themselves as Claude. The following day, the dispute was brought to the city's Small Council, where the magistrates sided with the pastor and banned the name Claude as idolatrous. But that case did not settle matters. Confrontations between parents and pastors continued for quite some time. As late as 1552, ten years later, Calvin reported that a riot had broken out in church when he rejected the name chosen for a child by its parents.[22]

The imposition of Christian values on the city was relentless, despite opposition. In 1546 a new law required every inn and tavern to have a French Bible at hand, and to encourage religious conversation and Bible discussions. It seemed like a great idea to the pastors, but, as often happens, the ideals of the clergy proved a bit too lofty for their flock. Admitting that the discussion sessions turned out poorly, the authorities had to call them off after only three months. But they would not let go of the entire plan: inns and taverns were still required to have a French Bible on hand, for their godly customers. Rules were also designed to prevent contagion from the outside world, and innkeepers were placed on the front lines, assigned to policing all customers. The regulations they were asked to enforce clearly display an obsessive concern with maintaining the city's purity. Take, for instance, these few samples:

- If anyone blasphemes the name of the God . . . or gives himself to the devil or uses . . . execrable imprecations, he shall be punished.
- If anyone insults anyone else the innkeeper shall deliver him up to justice.
- The innkeeper shall be obliged to report . . . any insolent or dissolute behavior committed by the guests.
- The innkeeper shall not allow any dissoluteness like dancing, dice, or cards, nor receive anyone suspected of debauchery.
- The Innkeeper shall not allow indecent songs.
- No one shall be allowed to sit up after nine o'clock at night, except informers.[23]

Though not exactly under siege, Geneva assumed a siege mentality. Censorship was routine, and it applied not just to printed texts, but also to private correspondence. Those who traveled outside Geneva were closely watched, as were those who came in contact with Geneva's many neighboring Catholics. With the city surrounded on nearly all sides by Catholic territories, and therefore also with Catholic churches and shrines, dissenting Genevans could be constantly tempted into idolatry. Consequently, all exchanges with the outside world were carefully monitored, and Genevans were encouraged to report all cases of Catholic backsliding to the consistory. During the first fifteen years after Calvin's return, the consistory handled numerous such cases: visits to shrines, attendance at Mass, the use of rosaries and Catholic prayers, the invocation of saints, and even one case of a visitor to the city with a suitcase full of "idols" for people to venerate in the privacy of their homes.

Beyond Geneva

Calvin's battles with the Libertines and his struggle to gain full control of Geneva were only part of his work. While taking part in the day-to-day business of Geneva, Calvin continued to write and dictate ceaselessly: theological and polemical treatises, biblical commentaries, sermons, and letters—enough to fill fifty-nine large folio volumes in the modern critical edition. He also kept a close eye on developments in his native France and became deeply involved with its underground network of Protestants, who continued to grow in numbers. The two most serious problems that Calvin handled among his fellow French Protestants were that of persecution and a response to it that came to be known as Nicodemism.

Nicodemites were Protestants or sympathizers who pretended to be good Catholics to escape persecution, and who argued that their outward behavior was not a sin or a betrayal of their principles as long as their inner faith was pure. It was a survival tactic that relied on a sharp dichotomy between spirit-matter and inner-outer, claiming that what really mattered was inward and spiritual. No one knows with certainty where, how, or when the name arose, but its meaning has always been clear: Nicodemites were dissemblers who found inspiration in the person of Nicodemus, the righteous Pharisee mentioned in John's gospel, who followed Jesus and believed in him, but came to see him only at night, in secret (John 3:1–9, 7:50, 19:39). Some scholars have argued that the Nicodemites were an international network of elite spiritualists who shared a common theory of dissimulation (see chapter 11), but evidence of such a cabal remains unconvincing.[24] While it is true that many spiritualists espoused and practiced dissimulation, the fact remains that dissembling behavior had been prevalent among French evangelicals since the 1520s, and therefore among reformers who were not spiritualists. Many of the Meaux group, including Calvin's friend Gerard Roussel, were Nicodemites (see chapter 5). Calvin had most definitely rubbed shoulders with Nicodemites, and may have possibly been one for a while, which would explain his intense revulsion toward the practice. From 1537 to 1562, a period that spans his entire public career, Calvin never tired of writing against the subject, in letters, sermons, and treatises. His stance was utterly uncompromising: dissembling was always a sin, and an affront to God's honor, because outward behavior always matters to God, especially when it comes to worship. Participation in idolatrous rites is always an offense to God, he argued, no matter what. "The Christian," said Calvin, "ought to honor God, not only within his heart, and with spiritual affection, but also with external testimony."[25] In 1536, Calvin addressed a long, angry letter to his friend Roussel—whose dissembling was extreme. It was published a year later under the title *On Fleeing the Illicit Rites of the Ungodly*. Calvin's judgment was as harsh as it was unequivocal:

> You deceive yourself if you think you have a place among the people of God, when, in fact, you are a soldier in the army of the Antichrist. You deceive yourself if you hope to partake in the Kingdom of Heaven with the Son of God, when, in fact, you keep company with wretched brigands and take part in their robberies and depredations. . . . Think what you want about yourself: I, at the very least, will never consider you a Christian, or a good man. Farewell.[26]

Though solidly rooted in theological principles, Calvin's opposition to Nicodemism was eminently practical. And its impact should not be underestimated. By telling his fellow evangelicals in France that they could not mingle with Catholics, or camouflage their faith, Calvin was forcing them to become a distinct people, a visible dissenting minority. He was also forcing them to create their own church in hostile territory or to flee into exile. Calvin received many anguished letters from France asking for his advice about dissembling. His response was always the same: stay and bear witness to your faith, even to the point of martyrdom, or go somewhere where you can practice your religion openly, in peace. Many found his position harsh and unacceptable. In 1543, a friend who was a member of the Paris Parlement, wrote to Calvin:

> A number of people think your assertions are thoroughly wretched. They accuse you of being heartless and very severe toward those who are distressed; and they say that it

is easy for you to preach and threaten over there [in Geneva], but that if you were here you would perhaps feel differently.[27]

Others were even more blunt, complaining that Calvin would consider as Christians only those who came to Geneva and had their ears blasted with his sermons.[28]

Calvin denied that he shrewdly aimed to fill Geneva with refugees, saying he esteemed those who stood their ground in France "a hundred times more, point for point than we, who enjoy freedom and peace."[29] Nonetheless, in 1550, he proudly boasted to Philip Melanchthon, "many, in order to avoid idolatry, are fleeing France and coming here to us in voluntary exile."[30] The exiles came, indeed, flooding Geneva and altering its social and political structure. But many remained behind in France, too, and stood their ground, establishing Protestant communities, one by one, in many places. Eventually, these Protestants would come to be known as Huguenots. The origin and meaning of the term is uncertain—some have proposed that it is derived from the Swiss term *Eidgenossen*, or "federated"—but the cohesiveness of these communities was always beyond question. They were tightly knit, disciplined, and as fixed on Geneva as a compass on one of the earth's magnetic poles. Calvin's opinion held sway, and the advice he had been dispensing since 1536 became inseparable from the gospel for them:

> Consider it always forbidden to let anyone see you communicating in the sacrilege of the Mass, or uncovering your head before an image, or observing any kind of superstition . . . through which the glory of God is obscured, His religion profaned, and His truth corrupted.[31]

By opposing Nicodemism and rejecting any sort of compromise, Calvin made necessary the establishment of Reformed churches throughout France and Europe. Moreover, Calvin also drew a blueprint for social and political conflict. To call for a choice between "true religion" and "idolatry" in the sixteenth century, when religion was inextricably woven into the social and political fabric, was to call for revolution. In 1561, the Venetian ambassador to France was able to perceive the inherent threat posed by Calvinism. "Religious affairs will soon be in an evil case in France," he wrote home. Throughout much of France, he continued, the followers of Calvin met "without any respect for the ministers of the king or the commandments of the king himself." Having penetrated every province and "every class of persons," and having gained total control of many areas, he continued, the Huguenots were shunning the Mass as if it were the plague, turning their back on king and church. The ambassador could see only two possible outcomes, both deadly: either France would split into two separate societies, or civil war would ensue. And he laid the blame for this crisis directly on Calvin:

> Your Serenity will hardly believe the influence and the great power which the principal minister of Geneva, by name Calvin, a Frenchman, and a native of Picardy, possesses in this kingdom; he is a man of extraordinary authority, who by his mode of life, his doctrines, and his writings rises superior to all the rest; and it is almost impossible to

believe the enormous sums of money which are secretly sent to him from France to maintain his power.[32]

The Venetian ambassador was very perceptive. Calvin's uncompromising stance against Nicodemism led inevitably to civic unrest, or at least helped to legitimize it, especially in France, where the monarch insisted on "one king, one law, one faith" (*un roi, une loi, une foi*). The same can be said about Calvinist-inspired strife in England, Scotland, and the Netherlands.

In his own day, Catholics saw Calvin as a "grand master" of sedition, and his uncompromising stance as the linchpin of his grand strategy.[33] Even Lutherans could agree. Duke Christoph von Württenberg (1515–1568), was blunt: "Calvinism, as is proved by many examples, is seditious in spirit, and wherever it enters it is determined to usurp dominion, even over magistrates."[34] Whether or not Calvin's intransigence led to the creation of the French Reformed Church or caused the French Wars of Religion is

The circle of faith. French Calvinists (Huguenots) preferred to call their houses of worship temples rather than churches, and they built many of them throughout France, since they could not always take over existing Catholic churches. This circular temple in Lyon reifies the Calvinist attitude toward sacred space as a theater of God's word, devoid of images and altars, where preaching is absolutely central. In this interior view, men and women are segregated, and everyone listens attentively to the preacher, even the children and the dog near the pulpit.

debatable, but one point seems beyond question: Calvin's theology was far from disengaged with daily life. Speaking of his political motivations and theology as distinct from one another, or as mutually exclusive, is not only pointless, but also foolish. Calvin's vision of the proper order of things was always shaped by the harsh realities of politics, so it is highly unlikely that he failed to see the consequences of his attack on Nicodemism and compromise. Opposition to idolatry can very easily evolve into resistance to an idolatrous ruler. Calvin would never go that far, but some of his followers did. Calvin would have shuddered at the thought, but those Frenchmen who said in 1577 that "the Gospel is the seed of rebellion"[35] probably had him in mind, and with good reason.

As refugees poured into Geneva in the early 1550s, the conflict between Calvin and his opponents intensified, especially because some native Genevans felt that foreigners had taken over their city. The Libertines, led by Amy Perrin, tried to thwart the growing power of Calvin, the consistory, and the Company of Pastors—many of whom were French exiles—but to no avail. Tensions led to a riot in 1555, and to the defeat of the Libertines. Gaining control of the city government, Calvin's supporters charged the Perrin faction with treason; some were executed, and many expelled. Amy Perrin and his family not only were forced to leave Geneva, but also had their property seized. So it was that the city of Geneva, haven of exiles, turned many of its leading citizens into refugees, and in the process handed itself over to Calvin and his fellow French pastors.

Unhindered by local opposition, Calvin intensified Geneva's international role. Property taken from the Perrin family was funneled into the creation of the Geneva Academy, a school that opened its doors in 1559. The academy was both a preparatory school for local Genevan youths and a seminary for the training of pastors. Its first rector, the French émigré Théodore de Bèze (1519–1605)—whose surname is sometimes spelled *Beza* in English-language texts—was Calvin's right-hand man and anointed successor. Under his direction, the academy quickly became a veritable factory of Reformed clerics, and especially of hundreds of French natives, who returned to their kingdom immediately. Full of zeal and well educated in Reformed theology, these missionaries trained at Calvin's academy brought home with them the Genevan model, and set about creating throughout France a tight, growing network of Huguenot churches. In the sixteenth and seventeenth centuries, Geneva would thus play a role in French history more significant than any other French city, save Paris.

Geneva would also figure prominently in the history of many other nations. In the 1550s, especially, Geneva became a truly international center of religious fervor, earning itself that title of the Protestant Rome: Italians, Spaniards, Germans, Scots, Englishmen, Netherlanders, Poles, Hungarians, Moravians, and others took up residence, or passed through. Those who returned home, like the French clergy trained in the academy, brought with them Calvin's theology and his Genevan blueprints for reform. In 1556, the Scottish refugee John Knox described the city in ecstatic terms as "the most perfect school of Christ that ever was in the earth since the days of the Apostles. In other places I confess Christ to be truly preached; but manners and religion to be so seriously reformed,

I have not yet seen in any other place besides."[36] John Bale, an English refugee, concurred: "Geneva seemeth to me to be the wonderful miracle of the whole world; so many from all countries come thither, as it were into a sanctuary, not to gather riches, but to live in poverty, not to be satisfied, but to be hungry . . . not to save their goods, but to leeve them . . . [to] . . . dwell together like a spiritual Christian congregation."[37]

The growing renown of Geneva made Calvin all the more influential, for it seemed to prove that his theology—unlike that of the Münsterites—could really help create a nonapocalyptic New Jerusalem of sorts, or at least an approximate copy of the church of the apostles. Calvin's and Geneva's success became a myth larger than history, an avatar of the *sola scriptura* principle, and as Calvin's fame grew along with Geneva's, the myth became a paradigm. Five decades after Calvin's death, John Winthrop, an English disciple of Calvin, would have Geneva in mind as he prepared to sail across the Atlantic to establish a Puritan outpost in the New World. "We must consider that we shall be as a city upon a hill. The eyes of all people are upon us," he told his congregation.[38] The city he spoke about was not just a figure of speech in a gospel passage (Matthew 5:14), but a real place, on the earth. So it was that Calvin's spirit sailed to America, long after he was dead, along with Zwingli's, upon whose blueprints Calvin had elaborated; and so it was that Geneva became embedded in the American consciousness.

What made Calvin's Geneva appealing to his followers, however, was also exactly what could make it seem appalling to others. Calvin and his adopted city acquired a reputation for coldness, intolerance, and cruelty. *Dour, gloomy,* and *puritanical* soon became the adjectives most commonly used by non-Calvinists to describe Calvinists. And nothing seemed to exemplify the dark character of Calvin's Geneva more vividly than the 1553 trial and execution of Michael Servetus, the Spanish spiritualist and anti-Trinitarian. To this day, no one knows for sure why Servetus went to Geneva. He knew very well that Calvin abhorred his work, for he had been sending Calvin copies of his writings for years, and Calvin had consistently condemned them all. Servetus had also just escaped from a Catholic prison in Lyons and knew he must keep a low profile. Yet up the Rhone River he went, straight into the lion's den. Some have speculated that he might have been invited by the Libertines, to bait Calvin and cause further trouble, or that he might have thought it possible to join in their fight against Calvin. Perhaps he sought to confront Calvin on his own. Whatever his reasons, Servetus made a fatal mistake. In August 1553, someone spotted him in town, and he was immediately arrested and tried for heresy. Calvin took charge of his prosecution and pressed successfully for the death sentence. On 27 October 1553, Servetus was burned alive. Calvin wanted to see him beheaded instead, but the civil authorities took no pity on the heresiarch and forced him to undergo a slow and painful death. Later, Calvin would report that Servetus had "cried like a Spaniard: Mercy! Mercy!"[39]

Servetus's execution sparked no great uproar. The burning of heretics had become all too common by 1553. But his case did attract the attention of Calvin's enemies. Catholics saw the incident as proof positive of Calvin's cruelty and megalomania, as well as his hypocrisy. How dare a heretic burn anyone else for heresy? Lutherans expressed dismay, over both Servetus and Calvin. Anabaptists and Spiritualists, as one might expect, shed the most tears. One former colleague of Calvin's at Strassburg, Sebastian Castellio, a well-respected humanist, cried the loudest, and with the most resolute sense of purpose. In 1554 Castellio—who had broken with Calvin years before—published a book in which he decried the killing of Servetus and the persecution of heretics in general, pleading for religious freedom and toleration among all Christians. "The true fear of God and charity are fallen and grown cold," he argued:

> Our life is spent in contention and in every manner of sin. We dispute, not as to the way by which we may come to Christ, which is to correct our lives, but rather as to . . . the Trinity, predestination, free will . . . and other like things which do not need to be known for salvation by faith. . . . Although opinions are almost as numerous as men, nevertheless there is hardly any sect that does not condemn all others and desire to reign alone. Hence arise banishments, chains, imprisonments, stakes, and gallows and this miserable rage to visit daily penalties on those who differ from the mighty about things hitherto unknown, for so many centuries disputed, and not yet cleared up.[40]

In retrospect, from the vantage point of an age and culture in which toleration is highly prized, Castellio's protest can seem much more significant than it was in its own day. The sad truth is that hardly anyone paid attention to Castellio, least of all in Geneva, where he was instantly branded an enemy and a traitor to the Reformed cause. Castellio continued to press for toleration, nonetheless, from Basel, where he was tolerated, but not well liked. In 1562, he would publish one of the most impassioned defenses ever written for religious toleration, titled *Advice for a Desolate France*, in which he begged the French to stop killing one another over religious differences. By then, however, few in blood-soaked France cared to pay attention to his arguments, which rested on the assumption that it is illogical to kill anyone over beliefs that cannot be proved or denied. Castellio was too much of a rationalist and religious skeptic for his day, and, like all such thinkers who were ostensibly "ahead of their time," he won many more hearts and minds after his death than during his life. His last book, *On the Art of Doubting*, which he never finished, spoke directly to following centuries rather than his own, and to people who were not Calvinists.

International Calvinism

One of the most remarkable aspects of Calvinism is the way one man's influence eventually reached far beyond the walls of a cramped city-state at the foot of the Alps. Its spread did not happen overnight, but we can certainly pinpoint when something that can be called "Calvinism" became an international movement.

One trait above all distinguished Calvinists: their conviction. Doubt may have been part of their mind-set, since faith is conjoined to doubt, but Calvinists tended to suppress their incertitude and to stifle their own questions. Doubt was a temptation— inescapable, but definitely surmountable with the aid of God's grace, which was showered upon the elect. And God certainly seemed to favor Geneva, lavishing the city with men from elsewhere who would try to duplicate Calvin's feats in other lands. The English exiles who came there in the 1550s, fleeing the wrath of their Catholic queen Mary, would return to their native land full of Reformed Calvinist fervor, ready to purify England and rid it once and for all of its traces of popery. The same was true of the Scots, and especially of John Knox, who would turn an entire nation Reformed Protestant in 1559. And the same could be said for the less-well-known exiles, such as Kaspar Olevianus from the Palatinate (Pfalz), in Germany, or Philip and John Marnix Saint Aldegonde, brothers from the Netherlands, and others like them from Poland, Hungary, and Moravia.

Wherever Reformed Protestant Calvinists surfaced, established authorities cringed. The most significant question Calvinists raised everywhere was whether or not a ruler immersed in "false worship" or "idolatry" had any legal right to force his subjects to dishonor God. Since Calvin offered his followers in "idolatrous" lands two drastic choices—stay and suffer the consequences of never compromising with the ruler's religion, or flee to some other place where they could worship God correctly—those who took the first option and stayed put had one more choice to make: should they be slaughtered like sheep, or should they defend themselves? Calvin had said very little about the possibility of resistance. Whenever he wrote about idolatrous rulers or tyrants, Calvin was careful to point out that private citizens had no right to resist, for the apostle Paul had made it clear in chapter 13 of his epistle to the Romans that all earthly governments were established by God, and therefore could not be overturned under any circumstances. The best an average Christian could hope to do in an idolatrous land was to abstain from false worship and resist passively, Calvin said, even to the point of martyrdom. His 1559 *Institutes*, which appeared at a critical time in French history, had but one brief paragraph on the subject, and an equivocal one at that. All Calvin said was that under certain conditions, according to some local or national laws, some lower magistrates might have legitimate power to resist an idolatrous ruler. The only examples he provided were from ancient Sparta and Rome.

Others who followed in his footsteps would disagree and use Calvin's own theology to reach an opposite conclusion. One of the first to do so was John Knox, who argued that subjects not only are justified in resisting an idolatrous ruler, but actually are duty bound to do so, by God's commandments. In his "Exhortation to the Commonality of Scotland," Knox reminded his fellow Scots that idolatry was everyone's business, for it polluted the whole land, and that not just the monarch and other elites were responsible for its removal, but also the people as a whole. "I say all men are equal," thundered Knox, "and that God requires no less of the subject, be he ever so poor, than of the prince and rich man, in matters of religion." His argument was downright revolutionary:

> It will not excuse you, dear brethren, in the presence of God, neither yet will it avail you in the day of his visitation, to say, "We were but simple subjects; we could not redress the faults and crimes of our rulers, bishops, and clergy; we called for reformation, and

wished for the same. . . . These vain excuses, I say, will nothing avail you in the presence of God, who requires no less of the subjects than of their rulers.[41]

Reversing a metaphor earlier employed by Andreas Karlstadt—who had compared idolatry to a knife in the hands of an infant that had to be taken away by its father—Knox compared idolatry to a sword wielded by a deranged father, which had to be snatched away by his own children (see chapter 9). So, now, for Knox, it was not the idols themselves that needed to be removed, but the governments that supported them. This action, the final step in the war against idolatry, was also eagerly embraced by other Calvinists.

Among the most significant Calvinists who formulated theories of resistance, two were close friends of Calvin. One of the first to speak unequivocally on this subject was Pierre Viret (1511–1571), who ran the Reformed church in nearby Lausanne from 1536 to 1559 and published several influential treatises on idolatry and resistance aimed at Huguenots in France. Viret was also joined by Calvin's successor, Théodore de Bèze, who argued in his *Rights of Magistrates* (1574) that God alone was to be obeyed "without exception," and that all "irreligious and iniquitous" commands issued by earthly rulers were null and void to Christians. Both Viret and Bèze were somewhat cautious, nonetheless, defending only the rights of lower magistrates to resist, rather than granting that right to all believers, as Knox had. But others who came after them were less guarded. The very same year Bèze published his treatise, Philippe du Plessis-Mornay (1549–1623), argued in his *Vindiciae contra tyrannos* that all rulers and magistrates who support false religion forfeit their right to rule. Mornay echoed Knox arguing not only that it was lawful for Christians "to resist a king who overturns the Law and the Church of God," but also that not to do so made them "guilty of the same crime and subject to the same penalty" as the idolatrous king.[42]

The French Calvinist theorists, however, lagged behind their English and Scottish counterparts. Knox already had his fully revolutionary theory formulated as he traveled

Religion and politics. The Reformation memorial in Geneva, erected in 1909–1917, at the base of the old city walls, honors four Reformed theologians who were deeply involved in the politics of their age, and contributed to the development of theories of resistance and revolution. From left to right: Guillaume Farel, John Calvin, Theodore de Bèze, and John Knox. A fifth figure who deserved to be included in this monument to aggressive reforming was Pierre Viret.

through Switzerland in 1558. So did the Englishman Christopher Goodman, whose treatise on the subject spelled out his argument clearly in its title, *How Superior Powers Ought to be Obeyed by Their Subjects: And Wherein They May Lawfully by God's Word Be Disobeyed and Resisted* (1558), and John Ponet, whose *Short Treatise on Politicke Power* (1559) would eventually influence John Locke and some of the leaders of the American Revolution.

Calvinists did not just theorize; they were also eager to overthrow false religion and any ruler who defended it. And it was not a simple cause-and-effect relation between the resistance theories and their behavior that turned them into activists, but rather a more complex interweaving of their theology as a whole with social and political realities. Beyond Geneva, in France, Germany, the Netherlands, England, Scotland, and Central and Eastern Europe, Calvin's followers tended to be a minority of the population, and they were often subjected to harassment or persecution. Calvin's theology and his uncompromising take on idolatry and Nicodemism forced these minorities to take a stand against the established religion of the majority.

The Calvinist strain of Reformed Protestantism became a force to be reckoned with internationally, far beyond Geneva. Unlike Lutheranism, which after an initial burst of popular fervor and proselytizing in the 1520s remained confined to areas in Germany and Scandinavia that had turned Lutheran largely because of the initiative of temporal authorities, Calvinism spread across the map of Europe through the missionary efforts of its faithful adherents despite the opposition offered to it by secular rulers. In other words, the geographical expansion of Calvinism was generated from within: it came from below rather than from above, relied on the zeal and initiative of its advocates, and challenged whatever resistance it met from established authorities. Calvinists tended to be aggressive, impatient, and bent on continual growth. And wherever they surfaced, their activism would kick into high gear. Consequently, in many places, conflict ensued.

Scotland was the first nation to deal with the Calvinist tidal wave, in 1559, when Calvinists seized enough power to abolish the Catholic Church. England was not far behind, thanks to exiles who had imbibed Calvinism on the Continent and returned full of reforming zeal after Queen Mary's death in late 1558. These English Calvinists, who came to be known as Puritans, would gradually steer their nation toward crisis and civil war in the mid-seventeenth century. France, which received the greatest number of missionaries produced by Geneva and had a sizable Calvinist population, would be plunged into long cycle of religious violence, from 1562 to 1598. And the religious tension would not abate for another century. The Netherlands, too, became a hotbed for Calvinist activity, and would have to contend with nearly continuous warfare against its Spanish Catholic rulers from 1566 to 1648.

The spread of Calvinism in other lands led to far less violence, but not to any diminution in Calvinist zeal. On the whole, this expansion took place in Central and Eastern Europe, in areas that were politically fragmented or lacked strong centralizing monarchies. The circumstances led to the creation of Calvinist islands, so to speak, within which local rulers or aristocrats could sponsor and protect their local Calvinist churches. Though often intermingled with or surrounded by hostile Lutherans and Catholics, persecution of these Calvinists was less likely and therefore so, too, were instances of armed resistance or religious warfare. Because local independence was a key factor in many of these areas, regional variations flourished.

In Germany, Calvinism made inroads in some of the borderlands with Switzerland, France, and the Netherlands, and it gained a foothold in territories farther inside the Empire, such as Anhalt, Hesse, and the Upper Palatinate. Among these territories, the Palatinate (Pfalz, in German) rose to prominence after 1561, not just because of its size and power, but also because of a series of rulers in the Wittelsbach dynasty who were committed to the Calvinist cause and the creation of a godly society. The chief contributions of this area to international Calvinism were its intake of refugees and the swift rise in prominence of the University of Heidelberg, which, along with the University of Leiden in the Netherlands, came to rival and eclipse the Geneva Academy as a center for Reformed theological study. This region also contributed the Heidelberg Catechism, which was composed by a team of ministers in 1563, some of whom had spent time in Geneva. Its summary of Reformed Calvinist faith and doctrine would prove immensely influential beyond the Palatinate, and it would help give shape to international Calvinism for centuries to come. German Calvinism evolved in its own way due to its environment, adapting to local circumstances in the bewildering patchwork quilt of the Empire.

In Hapsburg-ruled Hungary, which then included Moravia and Transylvania, Calvinism took root in various pockets, always in competition with Catholics and other Protestants, and always under two large shadows: that of Hapsburg efforts to promote Catholic hegemony and that of the ever-pressing Ottoman Turkish threat. In Hungary, where the Reformed faith was first introduced from Basel and Zurich rather than Geneva, tensions with the existing Lutheran presence often ran high, but as Genevan Calvinism made serious inroads, internal pressure points within the Reformed camp also formed. Despite quarrels among themselves and with Lutherans and Anabaptists, and despite persecution, Hungarian Calvinists managed to survive and to play an important role in the development of Hungarian nationalism. Always proud of its independence, the Reformed Church in Hungary would be one of the very few to adopt an episcopal structure.

In Poland and Lithuania, which had a very weak monarchs and a powerful nobility, Calvinism found very fertile ground around the mid-sixteenth century and spread quickly among its nobles, many of whom lived in the Grand Duchy of Lithuania and belonged to the Russian Orthodox Church. At that time, the Polish-Lithuanian commonwealth established in 1569 was one of the most religiously diverse states in Europe: it had not only a very large Orthodox population, but also many Jews and a wide assortment of other Christians, including Lutherans, Anabaptists, Bohemian Brethren, Armenian Monophysites, Unitarian Socinians, and freethinking spiritualists. Religious toleration was not only observed, but also made the law of the land, in 1573. For a while in the late sixteenth century, it looked as if Calvinists had the upper hand, with a majority of the seats in the Lower Parliament and nearly half the seats in the Upper Parliament, and most of the parishes in some areas. This success was relatively short-lived, however; mostly because the Calvinist faith remained a thin veneer among the aristocracy.

At its peak, Calvinism claimed about 45 percent of the nobles, but less than 20 percent of the total population. Among the peasantry, the percentage was much smaller. Poland's upper crust Calvinists could not withstand a very aggressive campaign launched against them by the monarchy in the late sixteenth century, with the aid of Jesuit missionaries (a Catholic religious order that achieved great gains worldwide by establishing superior schools; see chapter 18). Faced with many restrictions imposed by the crown on the one hand, and with the opportunity of sending their children to great Jesuit schools on the other, most of the Calvinist nobility became Catholic. Attrition was further intensified in 1668, when an edict made it a capital crime for Catholics to abandon their faith. From that point forward, winning new converts became virtually impossible for Calvinists. By then, however, it was way too late to hope for new blood: Calvinism in Poland-Lithuania had been reduced to a nearly ghostly presence, with very few churches.

Given such diversity, is it proper to speak of "Calvinism" at all, as if it were a monolithic tradition? Yes, certainly, but with caution. Calvinism was above all a very adaptable religion, or, if one prefers to think of it more broadly, a flexible ideology that adjusted to its environments. Yet when push came to shove, Calvinists always adapted without conforming: they held on to core principles and a certain worldview regardless of local circumstances, whether their churches were run by presbyteries or synods, and whether or not they had consistories. Their uncompromising zeal was the most essential component of their identity and what linked them to Calvin and to one another. This is not to say that Calvinists were all of one mind. Disagreements were as numerous and as heated among them as in any other religious tradition, and as divisive as those that vexed Calvin in his own day. Of all of the disagreements that shook Calvinist unity, the most intense had to do with the subject of the human will and its relation to God's grace. Adapting predestination to daily life was always a big challenge to Calvinists, and for some, especially New England puritans, a source of anxiety. Am I one of the elect or not? Can I play any role in my salvation? These were burning questions. Some Calvinists would tinker with this aspect of Calvin's theology, offering milder interpretations of predestination that gave the human will some role to play, and these propositions would lead to major disagreements and schisms. These developments will be dealt with in a later chapter.

Calvin's Legacy

Calvin spent the last years of his life dealing with Geneva's religious life, teaching, preaching, writing controversial works against his many enemies, and refining the theology of the *Institutes*. Calvin also immersed himself in the growing crisis in his native France, and in the missionary enterprise at the Geneva Academy. He worked ceaselessly until his dying day, 27 May 1564, when Bèze took his place at the helm. Calvin was only fifty-five at the time of his death, but a sketch drawn by a student in his later years depicts someone who looks much older, and very frail. A small man with a wiry build, Calvin was plagued by illness. Ulcers, hemorrhoids, migraine headaches, and kidney stones tormented him persistently, as did other ailments. Yet he never stopped working, and he accomplished so much that his name came to be attached to one of the most influential traditions in modern Western history: Calvinism.

Among his enemies, Calvin acquired a reputation as a misanthrope, a tyrant, and a small-minded puritan who fashioned a God much like himself. By the eighteenth century, the only portrait that the "enlightened" could draw of Calvin was one that emphasized the grossest features of this caricature. Take, for instance, what Thomas Jefferson, a Deist and the third president of the United States, had to say in a letter to John Adams, his predecessor in office:

> I can never join Calvin in addressing his god. He was indeed an Atheist, which I can never be; or rather his religion was Daemonism. If ever man worshiped a false god, he did. The being described in his five points is not the God whom you and I acknowledge and adore, the Creator and benevolent governor of the world; but a daemon of malignant spirit. It would be more pardonable to believe in no god at all, than to blaspheme him by the atrocious attributes of Calvin.[43]

To his many followers, however, Calvin remained a sage, a prophet, and a holy man, a model of genuine devotion and Christian sobriety. His emphasis on purity, austerity, restraint, moderation, and hard uncomplaining work as quintessential Christian virtues made his followers a force to be reckoned with. In 1905, the sociologist Max Weber would argue in *The Protestant Ethic and the Spirit of Capitalism* that modern Western society owed more to Calvin than to almost anyone else. According to Weber, Calvin not only "disenchanted" the West by ridding it of its attachment to miracles, superstition, and magic, but also made possible the upward ascent of reason over faith itself. As if this were not enough, Weber also argued that Calvinist theology and ethics enabled the West to develop its unique capitalist economy and to achieve dominance over the rest of the world. Large claims, indeed, to lay at the feet of a frail and pious workaholic, so large, in fact, that they still spark debate a century later. Their brazen political incorrectness makes them a lightning rod of sorts, and an unavoidable subject—as unavoidable as Calvin himself, or Calvinism.

Given the place Calvin has assumed in Western history, it is easy to forget that he was a religious man, above all, and that his particular genius was the ability to link religion to every aspect of life in a logically consistent way. The Calvin who appears in books such as this one is not necessarily the Calvin who has inspired thousands to unseat tyrants and establish godly societies. Calvin, the man of faith, is easy to miss, so easy, in fact, that some leading scholars have argued that he was not a theologian at all, but rather a shrewd politician.[44] It helps to keep in mind, then, that among Calvin's most enduring legacies, one project is often overlooked: the reform of ritual in Geneva. The significance of ritual should not be underestimated, for ritual speaks to the whole person, heart and mind. As is the case with most religions, the core messages of Calvinism were communicated and accepted most intensely through ritual, both individual and communal.

One of the first reforms instituted by Calvin upon his return to Geneva in 1542 was the creation of a Psalter, a hymnal composed entirely of psalms from the Bible. Subsequent editions added more psalms to the original Geneva version, culminating with the 1562 edition, which contained all 150 psalms in French, the language of the people, set to simple, singer-friendly tunes in poetic meter. The Genevan Psalter was a collaborative effort, but chiefly the work of the musician Louis Bourgeois, the poet Clément Marot, and the churchman Théodore de Bèze. Eventually reprinted hundreds of times and translated into many other languages, the Geneva Psalter would come to have an enormous influence on Calvinists everywhere, as the psalms became both a way to pray to God and a way to listen to God. It helps to keep in mind, however, that while this psalter sought to make a biblical text the heart and soul of the liturgy—to ritualize the *sola scriptura* principle—it was not at all a Protestant invention, but rather a continuation of monastic piety.

In many ways, Genevans lived up to the imperative ideal of St. Benedict's monastic rule: *ora et labora* (Pray and work)! Ironically, Calvinists ended up worshiping in a way similar to that of the medieval monks they so despised, singing the Psalter on a regular basis as a community. They also sanctified work itself, as a holy calling, and they practiced discipline and exclusion. Geneva, like a well-run monastery, was no welcoming refuge for sinners or slackers. But the parallels end there. Calvinists were committed to transforming the world by living in it, not by setting themselves apart, and there is a world of difference between these two ways of life. Calvinists saw themselves as a continuation not of monasticism, but rather of Israel, as God's chosen people. And within this self-conception one very important difference distinguished Calvinists from the ancient Israelites: the Promised Land of the Calvinists was the whole world, not just some tiny patch of arid land wedged between the Jordan River and the Mediterranean Sea.

In the preface to his commentary on the psalms, written toward the end of his life, Calvin complained that when he first arrived at Geneva in 1536, there was no church, and that Farel and his congregation were interested only in the smashing of idols. Aware that iconoclasm can never be the sum of any religion, no matter how central it may be to its theology, Calvin dedicated his life to establishing a disciplined community and guiding it. And that community became a model to be followed. Genevans, like all Calvinists, were taught to see themselves as the spiritual children of Abraham, as the elect. The covenant, the pact, and the law therefore ruled in Geneva and any spot on earth where Calvinists pitched their tent. Like the psalmist, Calvin and his followers found great comfort in their election and in the hymns that ratified their convictions, such as Psalm 119:1–3: "Happy those whose way is blameless, who walk by the teaching of the Lord. Happy those who observe God's decrees, who seek the Lord with all their heart. They do no wrong; they walk in God's ways." As everyone knows, those who think they can do no wrong tend to be among those who influence history the most. Especially if they also happen to be believe that they are on a mission from God.

Calvinists may have disagreed with one another, sometimes vehemently, but they tended to adhere to Calvin's guiding principle of *soli Deo gloria* (Glory to God alone). It can be argued that this precept more than any other shaped Calvinism's distinctive ethic, or spirit. Ever since Weber proposed that Protestants—and Calvinists above all— brought on "the disenchantment of the world" (*Entzauberung der Welt*), his thesis has stirred debate. At issue in this ongoing discussion is the very definition of religion, and how it differs from "magic" (*Zauber*). Also at issue is the question of the secularization of the West, and of the role played by Protestantism, and especially Calvinism, in engender- ing the separation of religion and culture. But if we think of "disenchantment" in non- Weberian terms—that is, not as the eclipse of "magic," but rather as a drastic redefinition of the metaphysical and epistemological paradigms governing Western thinking—we encounter what was most distinctive about Calvinism and its legacy: its redefinition of the boundaries between the human and the divine, the world and the church, the natural and supernatural, matter and spirit. It was a new worldview, a major paradigm shift in the definition of reality.

This Calvinist redefinition of the sacred was revolutionary on two fronts. First, it was a theological and epistemic upheaval, a cognitive iconoclastic crusade against the me- dieval worldview, and against the paradigm of mystical union with God that church and society had promoted for centuries as the ultimate human goal. John Calvin recoiled in horror at the thought that humans might claim any sort of divinization or gain intimacy with the divine, for his God was "entirely other" and "as different from flesh as fire is from water."[45] Calvin had no place in his theology for raptures, trances, visions, or miracles, either. But his elect were God's agents on earth. Calvinists, as a whole, embraced this worldview of Calvin's, bringing about a desacralization of the world, a "disenchantment" which made the earth itself less charged with the otherworldly and supernatural, but at the same time lent an aura of divinity to those who were God's elect. This desacralization of the world, which went hand in hand with the near divinization of the elect, redefined the relationship not only between humans and God, but also between church and state, rulers and subjects. When all is said and done, this momentous realignment of the axis between heaven and earth is why Calvinists can be seen as reformers of the Reformation and avatars of modernity.

CHAPTER THIRTEEN

England, Wales, Ireland, and Scotland, 1521–1603

The English Reformation

Of all the Reformations that took place in the sixteenth century, none was more drawn out than England's. And none had as many twists and turns or generated so many scholarly disagreements. Everywhere one looks, whether in primary sources or academic texts, conflicting images and opinions abound when it comes to the English Reformation, and the categorizations employed in the study of Continental Protestantism often prove woefully inadequate.

Take, for instance, the case of King Henry VIII (1491–1547), the monarch who broke with the papacy and assumed control of the Church of England as its "supreme head." His case is not the most complex or bewildering, or most representative of the whole of the English Reformation, but it is nonetheless instructive. King Henry cannot be called a Protestant or a Catholic. His ambiguous and ironic place in Reformation history is most clearly reflected in a title he passed on to all English monarchs, down to the present, that of *Defensor fidei*, or "Defender of the Faith." The title was originally awarded to Henry in October 1521 by Pope Leo X, in recognition of Henry's repudiation of Martin Luther. Earlier that year, in *Assertio septem sacramentorum* (Defense of the Seven Sacraments), Henry had written against Luther, and more specifically against Luther's sacramental theology, arguing in favor of the sacramental nature of marriage and the supremacy of the pope. What King Henry had to say about Luther in 1521 would later seem highly ironic and hypocritical to Catholics in his realm and elsewhere:

> For what avails it to dispute against one who disagrees with everyone, even with himself? Who affirms in one place what he denies in another, denying what he presently affirms? Who, if you object faith, combats by reason; if you touch him with reason, pretends faith? If you allege philosophers, he flies to Scripture; if you propound Scripture, he trifles with sophistry. Who is ashamed of nothing, fears none, and thinks himself under

no law. Who contemns the ancient Doctors of the church, and derides the new ones in the highest degree; loads with reproaches the Chief Bishop of the church. Finally, he so undervalues customs, doctrine, manners, laws, decrees and faith of the church (yea, the whole church itself) that he almost denies there is any such thing as a church, except perhaps such a one as himself makes up of two or three heretics, of whom himself is chief.[1]

Henry had good reason to joust with Luther, other than to court favor with Pope Leo X and Emperor Charles V. Henry was also addressing trouble at home, for by 1521 Luther's supporters were making inroads to his own realm. At Cambridge, for instance, a dedicated group of Lutheran sympathizers had been gathering regularly at the White Horse Inn, and their affinity with Luther was so well known that the locals had taken to calling their pub "Little Germany." No one could count heads, but other individuals and groups with similar leanings had also begun to surface in various places. In addition, rumors flew about pockets of surviving Lollard dissenters who were drawn to Luther, especially in the southeast of England. Entranced by the *sola scriptura* principle, and by *sola fide* soteriology, the new heretics and the old ones (if in fact they still did exist) posed a threat to the stability of Henry's England, and also to his authority.

One of the prime distinguishing features of the English Reformation is the fact that it occurred at various levels simultaneously, with no single trajectory. Unevenly pursued over the reigns of several monarchs, and resisted in places, the anti-Roman Reformation imposed at once from above, as act of state, based principally on appeals to monarchical authority, always had to contend with an anti-Roman Reformation that bubbled up from below, based on appeals to biblical authority. Sometimes the two merged, but more often than not they ran on parallel tracks, or even clashed with each other while contending with Catholic resistance. And after 1553, when Henry VIII's staunchly Catholic daughter Mary inherited the throne, much of the opposition to the state-run Reformation was linked to Geneva, in one way or another, thanks to the English dissenters who sought refuge there and in other cities where Calvinism reigned supreme. In addition, both of these anti-Roman Reformations had to contend with Catholic resistance, for in addition to those who were zealously reformist and anti-Roman, and those who were indifferent, England also had a fair number of people who wished to remain faithful to Rome and their ancestral religion.

Debate still rages about the nature of the English Reformation. Did it take hold quickly or slowly? Was it welcomed or resisted? Did it displace a vibrant faith or a moribund one? Did it secularize England or make it more religious? Was it more Catholic than Protestant, or the other way around? Did England become Protestant under Henry VIII or under his son, Edward VI? Or under his daughter Elizabeth I? Is it possible to generalize about all of England? Is it possible even to speak of an English Reformation?

Though there are many differences of opinion, the historiography tends to sift itself into two camps: the traditionalists and the revisionists. The traditionalists prefer to see the English Reformation as a positive change—largely welcomed by the people—and as a positive cleansing of a corrupt church and its hollow, unsatisfying piety.[2] This traditional view, which has been in place for centuries, has been challenged by many revisionists, who offer evidence that the Reformation imposed from above was resisted by the English people, and that it deprived them of a piety they found lively and satisfying.[3] The list of questions being debated could be much longer, but, at this point, the shorter we keep it, the better. Suffice to say that there is no end in sight for the scholarly wrangling. As long as either-or reductionism guides the research, disagreement is inevitable, for evidence can be marshaled to support either side of every question posed. The evidence speaks for itself and it speaks equivocally: the English Reformation—if one dares to speak of it as a single event—was many things at once, and very different from any of the Reformations that took place on the European Continent, or even that which took place in neighboring Scotland.

The Reformation from Below

As in the case of Bohemia, with its Hussites, England had a recent history of religious dissent, and of underground nonconformist communities. The disciples of John Wycliffe, known as Lollards, had never been totally wiped out. Even after the defeat of their final uprising in 1414 and under the weight of sustained persecution, the Lollard movement survived clandestinely, chiefly among artisans and tradespeople, and perhaps some clerics. We cannot know how many of these secret Lollards could be found in England on the eve of the Protestant Reformation, or how consistent or cogent their Lollard beliefs might have been, but evidence from episcopal courts points to a Lollard revival of sorts around 1500, or at least to increased persecution of suspected Lollards, especially in London, Coventry, Leicester, and the southeast of England. Profoundly antipapal and anticlerical, biblically centered, and iconoclastic, these surviving Lollards—dissemblers whom Calvin would have called "Nicodemites"—may have provided England with fertile ground in which Lutheranism could quickly take root and flourish. Given the relatively small number of Lollard trials on the eve of the Reformation, however, the extent of their contribution remains in question.

What is unquestionable is their later role in Protestant historiography, in which they would always be cited as precursors of the Reformation and proof positive that Protestantism was not a recent invention at all—as Catholics loved to charge—but rather a return to the original apostolic message and to the true church revived by Wycliffe and his followers. John Foxe would claim in his *Acts and Monuments*, the definitive Protestant history of the English Reformation, that "before the name of Luther was heard of in these countries among the people," the Lollards of Lincolnshire had already rejected "the Church of Rome, in pilgrimage, in adoration of the saints, in reading Scripture-books in English, and in the carnal presence of Christ's body in the sacrament."[4]

In England, as nearly everywhere in western Europe, reforming sentiment could be found most intensely among the educated, both clergy and laity. As explained in chapter 5, the humanist reforming circle led by John Colet and Thomas More had quite an influence on none other than the ultimate ur-Reformer, Erasmus of Rotterdam. It was during his stay in England, after all, that Erasmus embraced the study of Greek and Neoplatonism, so it could be argued that it was English humanism that fertilized the egg laid by Erasmus, which was later hatched or scrambled by Luther, depending on which viewpoint one takes. Colet and More remained faithful to the Roman Catholic Church, but others influenced by humanistic learning would not. As in France, Germany, and Switzerland, some younger humanists immediately gravitated toward Luther and his message, while the those who were older shrank back from that message or denounced Luther. At the very center of this brewing storm was the Bible, and the *sola scriptura* challenge to the status quo. Dissenting groups, such as the one at Cambridge, focused intensely on the Bible as the ultimate authority. They also discussed Luther's texts. Many of those who met at the White Horse Inn would later become leaders of the Protestant cause in England, or would even die as martyrs. The list is impressive: Robert Barnes (1495–1540), an Augustinian friar, who involved many other Augustinians; Miles Coverdale (1488–1569), future translator of the Bible into English; Nicholas Ridley (1500–1555), future bishop of Rochester and London; Hugh Latimer (1487–1555), future bishop of Worcester and fiery preacher; Thomas Cranmer (1489–1556), future archbishop of Canterbury and master architect of the Protestant shift of the Church of England.

But in the early 1520s few of these young men had yet made a full leap to Protestantism, and many went on to hold church positions in which they functioned faithfully as Roman Catholic clerics. England was still resolutely Catholic then, and Luther remained a distant voice. Moreover, this group of reform-minded men was not made up entirely of future Protestants and martyrs. It also included individuals who would never break with Rome, such as Stephen Gardiner (1483–1555), the future bishop of Winchester and Lord Chancellor for Queen Mary (1553–1558), the Catholic monarch who made martyrs out of Protestant Cranmer, Ridley, and Latimer.

The Cambridge proto-Protestants were not alone. Throughout King Henry's realm, others sided with Luther more openly or took bolder reforming steps. Among these early leaders of the Protestant cause, William Tyndale (1494–1536) stands out. Educated at Oxford, Tyndale translated Erasmus's *Enchiridion* into English and became a very popular preacher. Tyndale petitioned Cuthbert Tunstall (1474–1559), the humanist bishop of London, for permission to translate the Bible into English. When Tunstall refused, Tyndale fled straight to Wittenberg, where, at Luther's own university, he translated the New Testament into English. In 1525, Tyndale published his translation at Worms, in Germany, and copies began to make their way to England, where the translation was condemned by church authorities. Hiding successfully among the English cloth merchants of Antwerp, Tyndale wrote and published a number of influential tracts defending basic Protestant principles over the following few years, all of which were smuggled into England. In addition, Tyndale began translating the Old Testament, and he managed to publish its first five books before he was betrayed and thrown into prison at Brussels in 1536.

Though outlawed in England, Tyndale's English New Testament would have a profound effect, not just in terms of its religious impact, but also linguistically. All subsequent Bible translations into English would be influenced by Tyndale's, including the King James Version (1611). Captured and tried for heresy by Catholic authorities, Tyndale was burned alive near Brussels. Ironically, although he defended the authority of the king over the pope, it is highly likely that if Tyndale had stayed in England, he would have met the same martyr's fate, but even earlier. King Henry and the majority of the English church hierarchy had no tolerance for the likes of Tyndale, or for English-language Bibles, and by the time he died in Brussels in 1536, several of his spiritual brethren had already been put to death in England, on the king's orders.

Some of these kindred spirits of Tyndale's who were executed had been carefully examined by Lord Chancellor Thomas More (1477–1535), the court official Henry VIII placed in charge of weeding out the "Lutherans." A prominent humanist and close friend of Erasmus, and the author of the idealist political text *Utopia*, More seemed an unlikely choice for the job of grand inquisitor. Nonetheless, he performed the role with apparent enthusiasm, writing numerous treatises against "Lutheranism," and prosecuting thieves, murderers, and heretics with equal severity. Ironically, the continued spread of Protestant influence was made possible by changes instituted by king and parliament. In May 1532, More resigned his post in utter frustration, feeling that the policies of his government were undermining the very fabric of the Catholic Church in England. Despite Henry's jabs at Luther and his followers, king and parliament had begun to implement religious changes so tremendous that they would have seemed unimaginable a mere decade earlier. The Reformation from above had arrived.

Reformation as an Act of State

The religious ferment that King Henry VIII tried to suppress never disappeared, but rather flourished, both at home and in exile abroad. But all changes in religion rested in the king's hands, not those of dissenters. Ultimately, the English Reformation would be dominated by the crown, through a succession of monarchs who gained total control of the Church of England and directed the pace of religious change. This makes England unique in Reformation history. Only Lutheran states in Germany and Scandinavia had similar Reformations, imposed on the people by a ruler, but those Reformations remained solidly Lutheran, with few major reversals, shifts, or variations. Moreover, the English monarchs transformed the English Church to fit their personal convictions and political needs much more directly than most other rulers on the continent. The English

Reformation, therefore, can feel like the wildest roller-coaster ride in any survey history of the Reformation.

Because the English Reformation was directed by the monarch—in conjunction with Parliament—its history has a dynastic structure in which marriages, sexual relations, births, and deaths figure prominently. The best way to approach it, then, is through narratives that detail the reigns of four Tudor monarchs: Henry VIII (1509–1547), Edward VI (1547–1553), Mary I (1553–1558), and Elizabeth I (1558–1603). And that will only be about half of the story.

Henry VIII

The Reformation that King Henry VIII forced on his subjects was sparked not by reformist ideals, but rather by a domestic problem with enormous political ramifications: Henry's desire for a male heir. Initially, at least, what drove Henry VIII away from the pope was his unhappy marriage to Catherine of Aragon (1485–1536), whom he had wed in 1509. Catherine had been married previously to Arthur, Henry's older brother and heir to the throne, but when Arthur suddenly died in 1502, the dynastic marriage between the crown of England and the crown of Castile-Aragon was passed on to Henry. Although canon law prohibited marriage to a sibling's widow or widower, the royal families involved had petitioned Rome and been granted a dispensation, with the pope's blessing. As with all royal marriages, the prime aim was for the couple to produce suitable dynastic heirs, but Henry felt extra pressure to ensure a smooth succession because his family, the Tudors, had only recently acquired the throne of England, after a long and costly civil war (the Wars of the Roses, from 1455 to 1485). Because England had never had a female monarch, Henry and Catherine were expected to produce at least one boy, preferably more. Replacements were a necessity in an age with high child mortality rates.

Between 1510 and 1518 Catherine gave birth to six children, including two sons, but the only one of these offspring who survived was a girl, Mary. Henry became convinced that the string of miscarriages and deaths was divine retribution for having married his brother's widow, as spelled out in the biblical curse of Leviticus 20:21: "if a man shall take his brother's wife, it is an unclean thing . . . [and] they shall be childless." Desperate for a male heir, Henry petitioned Rome in 1527 for an annulment of his marriage to Catherine, on the grounds that their papal dispensation of 1502 was invalid, as their childlessness proved. Pope Clement VII found himself backed into an uncomfortable corner, with a no-win proposition: if he were to grant the annulment, he would be canceling a prior papal decision and casting doubt on his own authority, but if he were to withhold the annulment, he would risk alienating one of his staunchest anti-Lutheran monarchs. To make matters worse, Catherine of Aragon was the aunt of Emperor Charles V, the same ruler whose troops had just sacked Rome and were still encamped all around his city. Clement VII could not afford to earn the wrath of the emperor who had turned him into a virtual prisoner.

Clement did his utmost to stall the petitions brought forward by Cardinal Thomas Wolsey, Henry's Lord Chancellor, but this delay infuriated Henry. As he fumed, King Henry stripped Wolsey of his titles in 1529, and had him imprisoned on charges of treason. Wolsey was then replaced by Thomas More. In the meantime, Henry fell in love with one of the ladies at court, Anne Boleyn (1507–1536), the sister of one of his former mistresses. Like many monarchs and aristocrats of his day, Henry was prone to marital infidelity, but his bond with Anne Boleyn was no mere affair; it became an all-consuming obsession. Determined to be rid of Catherine and to replace her with Anne Boleyn, Henry searched for a solution and found it right at home, thanks to the advice of two courtiers with similar names, Thomas Cromwell (1485–1540) and Thomas Cranmer (1489–1556), a former member of the Lutheran circle at Cambridge.

Following Cromwell's advice, King Henry decided to detach the English Church from obedience to the pope and transform it into a branch of the government, with himself, the monarch, as the ultimate church authority in England. The first fateful steps were taken in 1531, when all English clergy were asked to submit to the king as the "sole protector and supreme head" of their church. The following year, the break with Rome widened, with Parliament's issuance of the Act in Restraint of Appeals, which made the King of England—rather than the pope—the final legal authority in all disputes. With Henry as the new head of the English Church, the annulment of his marriage became a purely English matter, for English courts to handle. Henry married the already-pregnant Anne Boleyn secretly in January 1533, and was granted his annulment in May by Thomas Cranmer, the archbishop of Canterbury. In September, much to Henry's dismay, the new

Defender of the faith. Although Henry VIII had written against Luther and earned the title "Defender of the Faith" from the pope, he broke away from the Roman Catholic Church and made himself supreme head of the independent Church of England. Portrait by Hans Holbein.

queen gave birth to a girl, Elizabeth, rather than to a male heir. Henry's first marriage having been annulled, Queen Catherine was stripped of her title, and their daughter Mary pronounced a bastard. Parliament ratified this arrangement in March 1534, in the Act of Succession. To prevent any sort of international conspiracy, both mother and daughter were forced to remain in England, under humiliating circumstances.

To formalize Henry's takeover, Parliament passed in 1534 the Act of Uniformity, which granted the crown complete control of the Church of England, including "the title and style thereof, as all honors, dignities, preeminences, jurisdictions, privileges, authorities, immunities, profits, and commodities."[5] The king would henceforth have the power to appoint all bishops in his realm and to prosecute all heretics, and he would become the sole owner of all church property and the manager of all church revenues. Moreover, the Act of Uniformity made any challenge to the king's ultimate authority over the church an act of treason, and therefore a capital crime. Fusing together the church and the monarchy, the Act of Supremacy thus placed all English Catholics in a situation nearly identical to that of the French Huguenots, forcing them to choose between allegiance to their church and obedience to their monarch, with their lives in the balance. After 1534, then, all faithful Catholics who rejected the Act of Supremacy became traitors deserving of death.

Among the first to lose his head for dissenting was none other than Erasmus's friend the former Lord Chancellor, Sir Thomas More, who was imprisoned in the Tower of London for several months, found guilty of treason and beheaded on 6 July 1535. "Pluck up thy spirits, man, and be not afraid to do thine office," said More to his executioner. "My neck is very short."[6] More's execution had been preceded by that of John Fisher (1469–1535), bishop of Rochester, former chancellor of Cambridge University, and former chaplain to King Henry VIII's mother. A well-known humanist and church reformer, Fisher remained as steadfast as More. After his execution on 22 June 1535, his head was stuck on a pole outside the Tower of London for one day and then thrown into the river Thames, its place taken by Thomas More's a few days later. In addition, a number of clerics, mostly monastics, were rounded up and executed for refusing to accept the Act of Uniformity. At the trial of five of these men, John Houghton, Richard Reynolds, Augustine Webster, John Hale, and Robert Laurence, in May 1535, the jury at first found them innocent of treason, but the next day Thomas Cromwell pressed for a guilty verdict, successfully. All of the monks were disemboweled while fully conscious, one by one, in front of one another, and then hanged. Having been tried as commoners, they could not receive the more merciful penalty of beheading handed to the nobles Fisher and More. All of these early victims of King Henry's wrath would be revered as Catholic martyrs, but they were not canonized as saints until the twentieth century.

While King Henry had broken with the Roman Catholic Church—and had been duly excommunicated—nothing at all had changed yet in the Church of England. Its theology, rituals, and ethics remained exactly as before. Among the Protestant sympathizers who hoped to bring about change, the most highly placed were none other than the new queen, Anne Boleyn, and the archbishop of Canterbury himself, Thomas Cranmer. In addition, Anne Boleyn surrounded herself with chaplains deeply affected by evangelical ideas, one of whom, Matthew Parker (1504–1575), would become archbishop of Canterbury during her daughter Elizabeth's reign. But none of Anne's efforts mattered much to Henry. In a fit of jealous rage, the king accused her of adultery, and, after being tried and found guilty, Anne Boleyn was beheaded on 19 May 1536, two days after Thomas Cranmer had annulled her marriage to Henry. Still searching for a male heir, Henry VIII married for a third time two weeks later. The bride this time was Jane Seymour, a former lady-in-waiting to the recently executed Anne Boleyn. And this time, Henry VIII finally got the male heir that he needed. In September 1536, four months into her marriage, Jane Seymour gave birth to a frail boy, Edward, but she died as a result of complications during the birth. Henry VIII had an heir to the throne, at last, but he was a widower once again.

In the midst of this domestic turmoil, King Henry plowed ahead with more drastic ecclesiastical changes. In February 1536, Parliament met to enact a law that dissolved all monasteries with a yearly income of less than two hundred pounds and handed over all of their property to the crown to be dealt with "at its pleasure, to the honour of God and the wealth of the realm." Moral grounds were advanced for this momentous upheaval: after a visitation of the monasteries by agents of the king, it was deemed that these smaller communities were sinkholes of vice and corruption. Yet despite their alleged immorality, the heads of these monasteries were given pensions, and the monks allowed to seek places for themselves at the larger and ostensibly more observant communities, or to become secular priests. Beginning in April 1536, more than three hundred monasteries were closed and stripped entirely of their belongings, their wealth funneled into the royal treasury by the newly established Augmentation Office. Some fifty or so houses were offered the chance to be rechartered by the crown, for a steep price, only to be confiscated again, after payment had been made. English monasticism was not yet at an end, but a large step had been taken in that direction. The dissolution of the smaller monasteries went hand in hand with a publicity campaign set in motion by Thomas Cromwell in which itinerant preachers went through the realm, visiting local churches; railing against the monks as hypocrites, sorcerers, sexual deviants, and idle drones who made the land unprofitable; and promising that once the monasteries were gone, the king would never need to collect taxes again.

Such drastic changes met with resistance. In the north of England, in October 1536, a popular uprising that came to be known as "the Pilgrimage of Grace" challenged the king's policies. Although scholars disagree on how to sort out the causes of this rebellion—political, social, economic, geographic, or religious—there is no denying that the focus of discontent was the dissolution of the monasteries and the rumor of even greater religious changes on the horizon. Led by Robert Aske (1500–1537), a lawyer, this uprising spread quickly over much of Lincolnshire and Yorkshire and the north of

England in the fall and early winter of 1536–1537. Though the rebels won some concessions from the king and even managed for a while to reinstate some monastic communities in their recently seized properties, the uprising was brutally suppressed through massacres and executions. This event is often cited to prove two points: first, that not everyone in England welcomed the Reformation willingly; and second, that there were distinct regional preferences concerning religion in the sixteenth century. However it is interpreted, the Pilgrimage of Grace was a serious outpouring of dissent that was quelled through brute force. Some historians have argued that this uprising gave King Henry pause, and caused him to hold back from further reforms that would have brought the Church of England closer to Protestantism.

The dissolution of the lesser monasteries was only the prelude to a full assault. In 1539, the crown seized all remaining monastic institutions, wiping out monasticism. The vast wealth and properties that fell into the hands of the monarchy turned Henry VIII into a great patron who could shower his supporters among the nobility with gifts of land or bargain purchases. Important for its redistribution of land and income, and in terms of relations between the crown and the nobility, the suppression of the monasteries was also a huge step in the direction of Protestantism, not just because an entire clerical class had been wiped out, but also because the physical spaces formerly sacralized by the monks and nuns now became purely profane. Even more significant, on the symbolic level that underlies all religion, the sacred buildings themselves were pillaged and intentionally destroyed. Many were left standing in ruins, monuments that resembled bleached bones or fossils, as a stark reminder of the destruction of the medieval status quo. Shakespeare's "bare ruined choirs, where of late the sweet birds sang" were very new ruins in his day, relatively speaking, and for that very reason particularly powerful symbols of the suppression of Catholic piety.

King Henry VIII was no Protestant Reformer, however. Those around him who favored Protestantism, such as Cromwell and Cranmer, pushed for greater changes, but could not override the king's conservatism. Even the most dramatic changes effected during Henry's reign were tinged with ambivalence, or even reversed. Take, for instance, the issue of images. Although the crown called for the removal of "idolatrous" sacred art and relics, no firm guidelines were established for determining which devotions fell into this category. Iconoclasm under Henry VIII was therefore far from thorough. At the very summit of popular devotion, the shrine of St. Thomas à Becket in Canterbury was dismantled, and the saint's bones discarded, but no concerted attack was mounted on shrines or images throughout the realm. The same hesitancy applied to the Bible. Even though an English translation by Miles Coverdale was published and in 1538 all churches were required to have at least one copy, in 1543 restrictions would be placed on who could read that sacred text. As far as ritual was concerned, King Henry's Anglican Church could have easily been mistaken for Roman Catholic, for Latin continued to be used, and for the most part, church furnishings remained untouched. Moreover, King Henry VIII actively blocked Protestant influence through legislation. The Act of Six Articles, issued in 1539 as the great monasteries were being seized, was nothing less than a wholesale rejection of Protestant Reformation ideals. Quickly dubbed "the bloody whip with six strings" by those who favored Protestantism, the act reaffirmed key Catholic teachings and practices, such as clerical celibacy, private masses, vows, suffrages for the dead, auricular confession, and belief in transubstantiation, making it a capital crime to deny their validity. Persecution of religious dissenters was stepped up, too, and the number of martyrs continued to grow on both sides of the religious spectrum: on one end, those who defended the papacy and the old order, and on the other end, those who challenged the king's conservatism. Among those who were painfully silenced at the stake were Anabaptists, many of whom were foreigners. But even some at the very top ended up on the chopping block, including Thomas Cromwell, Henry's vice-regent and close confidant, who was arrested on charges of heresy and treason, ostensibly for siding with Reformed Protestants on the Eucharist. Court intrigues had more to do with Cromwell's arrest than with theology, but Henry's antiheresy legislation allowed him to prosecute Cromwell, and to execute him without a trial in July 1540. Since Cromwell had managed the dissolution of the monasteries and pushed hardest for the publication of an English Bible, his death was a serious blow to the Protestant cause during the remainder of Henry's reign.

Such policies were a decisive rejection of Lutheranism. Whatever warm relations had existed between Wittenberg and highly placed Englishmen such as Cranmer and the ill-fated Cromwell evaporated, and Henry's subalterns bowed to his will without complaint. Unintentionally, Henry VIII's conservatism managed to bring England closer to the Reformed Protestant camp, for most of the religious refugees he created through the Act of Six Articles did not end up in Wittenberg or other Lutheran cities on the continent, but in Reformed communities, where they imbibed Zwinglian and Calvinist ideology. Upon returning to England after Henry's death, these refugees would help reshape the Church of England along Reformed rather than Lutheran lines.

Marriages and the issue of succession continued to hover over Henry's reign like a dark cloud, given that Prince Edward was a very frail and sickly heir, and his two sisters had been legally barred from inheriting the throne. Henry married three more times after the death of Jane Seymour, but none of those marriages produced an heir. His fourth wife, Anne of Cleves, was a German princess who gave Henry a direct link to Lutheran military alliances, which vice-regent Cromwell was trying to establish as added protection against Emperor Charles V and Francis I of France. Henry had agreed to marry her, sight unseen, after viewing a flattering portrait of her by Hans Holbein. When he finally laid eyes on Anne in 1540, however, he was as displeased with her as he was with Cromwell for having arranged the marriage. An ungainly woman unsuited to English court life, Anne was shunned by Henry, and rumors flew that he spoke of her as a "Flanders Mare." Weighing his political options, and also his recent infatuation with another young lady at court, Catherine Howard (1521–1542)—who was first cousin to his second wife, Anne Boleyn—Henry asked for an annulment, which was granted by the archbishop of Canterbury, Thomas Cranmer, in July 1540, after Anne of Cleves testified that the marriage had never been consummated. Sixteen days later, he married his fifth wife, nineteen-year-old Catherine Howard. But Catherine proved too fond of flirting with young men at court, and within a mere eighteen months she was beheaded for adultery and treason. The aging Henry, who could barely walk because of his enormous weight and a leg wound that would not heal, married again in 1543, within a few months of Catherine Howard's execution. Henry's sixth wife, Catherine Parr (1512–1548), managed to survive his unpredictable wrath. Even though she was accused of Protestant leanings in 1546—a capital crime—she convinced Henry of her innocence and nursed him through his final year, transacting much court business in his stead. She also devoted herself to reconciling the irascible Henry with his two daughters, the future queens Mary and Elizabeth.

Edward VI

When Henry VIII died on 28 January 1547, the crown passed to Prince Edward, who was only nine years old. For resolute Protestants and Catholics alike, the prince's religious leanings were of the utmost importance. Thanks to King Henry's break with Rome, religion nominally had fallen into the hands of a boy king. Real control of the kingdom passed to the regency council, and the man they designated Protector of the Realm, Edward Seymour (1500–1552), Duke of Somerset, brother of the late queen Jane and uncle to his namesake, Edward VI.

Under the leadership of Archbishop Thomas Cranmer, who was no longer held back by a conservative monarch, greater changes began to take place. First came the repeal of Henry VIII's Act of Six Articles, and of heresy legislation and restrictions on Bible reading. Then came the promotion of preaching in the Reformed vein, and the arrival in England of leading continental Reformers who were awarded professorships at Oxford and Cambridge, including Martin Bucer and Peter Martyr Vermigli (1500–1562). In 1549, all ritual for the Church of England was revised through the issuance of the first Book of Common Prayer, which a new Act of Uniformity compelled all churches to use. Gone was the use of Latin, replaced by English. Gone were many of the ancient prayers, litanies, and rubrics, but still in place were prayers for the dead, talk of the real presence of Christ in the Eucharist, and traditional vestments. The 1549 Book of Common Prayer held on to some traditions, but it contained innovations that redefined the roles of the laity and clergy. Communion in both kinds was now allowed, and so was clerical marriage. In addition, the Ordinal of 1550—the book of rules to be observed in the ordination of clerics and the consecration of bishops—made very clear that the clergy were ministers of the Word rather than intercessory priests. Images and relics came under attack as idolatrous remnants of "popery," and in many churches throughout England, iconoclasm became the order of the day.

Turning Swiss. When Henry VIII's young son Edward ascended to the throne, the break with Rome initiated by his father was intensified by highly placed advisers to the boy king who were partial to the Swiss Reformed tradition. This depiction of King Henry's transference of power to Edward highlights the men who sought to turn England wholly Protestant. Directly below Edward we see the pope and his clergy linked to the vanquishing of "idolatry" and "superstition." To Edward's left, above his key advisers on the Privy Council—including Protector Somerset and Archbishop Thomas Cranmer—we see iconoclasts destroying religious imagery.

Protector of the Realm Edward Seymour was somewhat cautious about change, despite his preference for Reformed theology and ritual. His impact on policy was limited, however, more because of fate than his restraint. As the result of intrigues led by John Dudley, onetime Earl of Warwick and Duke of Northumberland, and Seymour's chief rival on the regency council, in late 1551, Seymour was removed from office, imprisoned, tried, and executed for treason. This palace coup resulted in the emergence of a more solidly Reformed Protestant leadership. By 1552, thanks to the efforts of the self-appointed Lord Protector Dudley (1504–1553), and of Thomas Cranmer and two of his old White Horse Inn colleagues, Hugh Latimer (1487–1555), former bishop of Worcester turned popular preacher, and Nicholas Ridley (1500–1555), the bishop of London, England was well on its way to becoming fully Protestant.

First, Dudley seized more church property in the name of the crown. Then, a new Act of Uniformity required acceptance of a revised Book of Common Prayer that was decidedly Protestant in tone and content. The 1552 Book of Common Prayer did away with prayers for the dead, talk of sacrifice or real presence in the Eucharist, the use of traditional vestments, and even altars, which were replaced with communion "tables." Then, as all of England was forced to accept these changes, Archbishop Cranmer insisted the clergy subscribe to a very Protestant formulary, the Forty-Two Articles. Though some clerics resigned, most complied, tending to their flocks as best they could in the midst of such rapid change.

The burning question that continues to obsess historians of the English Reformation is whether the English people accepted all of these changes willingly, indifferently, or with hostility. Plenty of evidence can be marshaled in support of each of these options: all three attitudes can be found side by side, sometimes even in the same parish. Edward VI's reforms were accepted silently and obediently by most of the clergy and many of his subjects. How the majority felt about all these changes remains a matter of debate. As had been the case with Henry VIII's reforms, there were pockets of resistance. In the summer of 1549, faithful Catholics in the southwestern corner of England rose in rebellion. At issue was the wholesale redefinition of belief and ritual embodied in the Book of Common Prayer, which now had to be purchased and used by every church in the realm. The so-called Prayer Book Rebellion was a failure, and a fairly insignificant event, at least in relation to the whole of England, which seemed to slide rather quietly into Protestantism. In most surveys of the English Reformation, it attracts little or no attention.

The rebels of 1549 did not fare well. If they had not been massacred on the battlefield, they fled, either to return home disappointed or to be captured and executed. Father Robert Welshe, the vicar of St. Thomas's Church in Exbridge embodied the defeat, and its agony: he was hung from his church tower by a chain around his waist and left to die, "in his popyshe apparrell and having a holye water buket, a sprincle, a sacringe bell, a payre of beddes and such other lyke popyshe trash hangued about him." For several days he hung there, suffering an excruciatingly slow death in silence, resigned to his martyrdom and all it represented. An eyewitness later said that Father Welshe "made a verie smale or no confession but verie patientlie toke his dethe."[7]

There was much more to this rebellion than rebel priests such as Father Welshe, left dangling as a warning to all potential dissenters. Gruesome punishments were the order of the day for rebels. It was Welshe's vestments, aspergillum, sacring bell, and his rosaries—his "popyshe trash"—that were at the heart of the rebellion. They were part of a religion that was so deeply embedded in every aspect of daily life that to some they seemed as important as life itself, or even more important. On one side stood those who revered such a religion and defended it; on the other, those who despised it and sought to annihilate it, and somewhere in between were countless others who seemed not to care at all.

Given what happened next, it seems that indifference or passive acceptance ruled the day. In July 1553, as England was well on its way to becoming a fully Reformed

Protestant nation, the ever-frail King Edward died, with no direct male heir to the throne to succeed him. The most likely successor was Mary, eldest daughter of Henry VIII, whom Henry VIII had named in his 1547 will his default heir in the event of Edward's death. Although Mary had remained resolutely Catholic, her succession enjoyed substantial support from Parliament and the power elite. Nonetheless, shortly before Edward VI's death, John Dudley, Duke of Northumberland, who thought he had the reins of power firmly in hand, forged a scheme to keep the crown in Protestant hands and within his family circle. Having arranged for his son Guilford Dudley to marry one of Edward's resolutely Protestant cousins, Lady Jane Grey (1537–1554), Northumberland then convinced the dying King Edward to bequeath the monarchy to Jane and her male heirs. Upon the king's death, Northumberland quickly proclaimed the fifteen-year-old Jane Grey queen of England. But he had seriously underestimated Mary's supporters. Within nine days, on 20 July 1553, he, his son, and his daughter-in-law "Queen" Jane were forced to surrender to Mary Tudor, the very Catholic daughter of Henry VIII and his first wife, Catherine of Aragon. Mary was crowned queen—the first female ruler of England. Northumberland, his son Guilford Dudley, and Jane Grey were tried for treason and executed. Overnight, England became Roman Catholic again, and with a vengeance.

Mary I, Bloody Mary

As quickly as she could, Queen Mary abolished the changes made under her father and brother, repealing the Act of Supremacy, replacing the Book of Common Prayer with the traditional Latin ritual, outlawing Protestantism and clerical marriage, and replacing all bishops who opposed her, including Thomas Cranmer and Nicholas Ridley. At the very top of the church hierarchy, she appointed her exiled relative Cardinal Reginald Pole (1500–1558) as archbishop of Canterbury. She also restored bishops who had been deprived of their offices under Edward VI, such as Edmund Bonner (1500–1569) in London, and Stephen Gardiner (1483–1555) in Winchester. Gardiner, who had spent five years imprisoned in the Tower of London for rejecting Cranmer's reforms, was named Lord Chancellor by Queen Mary, and he wasted no time in turning the tables on his persecutors.

But Mary and her bishops faced a monumental task. The changes wrought in the past two decades had been profound, and the English people had been exposed to new ways of thinking, believing, and worshiping: priests had married; the churches had been stripped clean; religious gilds and confraternities had disbanded; and the monasteries were empty ruins, their monks and nuns dispersed to the four winds. Restoring the monasteries was a daunting challenge, because the nobles who owned the lands and wealth confiscated by Henry VIII were keen on keeping their windfall, and Mary could not afford to alienate them all.

But Mary was Henry VIII's daughter, after all, every bit as headstrong, and not afraid of alienating anyone. To realign England with Rome, Mary embarked

"Bloody Mary." When Henry VIII's daughter from his marriage to Catherine of Aragon assumed the throne in 1553, she sought to return England to the fold of the Catholic faith. In the process, Queen Mary executed more than two hundred Protestants, including the most prominent among them, such as John Hooper, Nicholas Ridley, and Thomas Cranmer. This illustration from John Foxe's very popular *Book of Martyrs* depicts the burning of Cranmer.

on two courses that made her very unpopular. First, she decided to wed her cousin Philip II, king of Spain, the most ardent of Catholic monarchs. Second, she began to hunt down and execute Protestants. The marriage to Philip was disastrous, in a personal as well as a political sense. The persecution of heretics was an even costlier mistake, which not only alienated many of her subjects, but also earned her the infamous title of "Bloody Mary."

Mary and Philip were married at Winchester Cathedral on 25 July 1554, despite protests on all sides. Gardiner, her own chancellor, opposed this union openly, as did the House of Commons, which begged her to marry an Englishman instead. English fears of a Spanish and Hapsburg dynastic alliance were not necessarily xenophobic or religious. For many of Mary's contemporaries, Philip posed a grave threat to English independence, since he was poised to inherit much of Europe and of all of the New World from his father, Charles V. Philip could not only tap resources that were inconceivable in England, but also drag it into endless conflict. To make matters worse—compounding the uncertainty that surrounded the absolute novelty of a female monarch—the terms of this dynastic marriage gave the impression that England was being given away to the Hapsburgs. Philip acquired not only the title of king of England, but also the right to have his name on all official documents and legislation, and all summons to Parliament. The symbolic impact would be even greater, as Philip's likeness was to appear on coinage, jointly with Mary's.

Mary's marriage plans were so unpopular that they led to insurrections, the most significant of which was led by Thomas Wyatt in Kent. Wyatt and his three thousand rebels marched all the way to London in February 1554—five months before the proposed wedding—but were defeated. Among those charged with conspiracy in this uprising were Lady Jane Grey's father, the Duke of Suffolk, and Queen Mary's sister Elizabeth. Suffolk was executed, along with Wyatt; Elizabeth was imprisoned in the Tower for two months, and afterward subjected to house arrest. Immediately, dissenters began to revere Wyatt and his coconspirators as heroes and martyrs.

Dynastic marriages are founded on the hope that children will be born who can inherit the titles and power of the married couple. For Mary, who was thirty-eight years old, the stakes were particularly high. Philip spent a restless fourteen months in England trying to sire an heir, with no results except for two heartbreaking false pregnancies. Philip had a vast empire to inherit, and England was a most inconvenient place from which to do so, especially in the company of an unattractive wife who was eleven years his senior and seemed to be infertile and too susceptible to imaginary pregnancies. In September 1555 he returned to Spain. Mary, childless and despondent, waited until March 1557 for Philip to return, her biological clock ticking away. Philip's visit was brief. Having inherited the crown of Spain, Philip was the world's most powerful ruler, and also the busiest, a compulsive micromanager who spent most of his days buried in paperwork. In July 1557, he left Mary alone again, to deal with yet another false pregnancy all by herself. Though he would never again set foot on English soil, Philip would continue to use the "king of England" title for the rest of his life.

With the specter of Spanish Hapsburg Catholic oppression hanging over her reign, Mary also took the fateful step of joining Spain in a war against France—a poorly run venture that became highly unpopular and led to more agitation against her and Philip. The crowning blow to this flawed endeavor came in January 1558, when the English lost Calais, their last outpost on French soil. Calais was a mere speck on the map and something of a financial burden for England, but the loss had a tremendous symbolic significance, not just for Mary herself, but for England as a whole. Coming after a wave of persecution at home, the fall of Calais seemed to cap off a disastrous time for England.

No grief could compare, however, with that caused by Mary's crusade against Protestants. Soon after she ascended to the throne, Mary had the leaders of King Edward's Reformation rounded up and tried for heresy, including Cranmer, Latimer, Hooper, and Ridley. Some of them were imprisoned and badgered for months, or years. Others were quickly tried and executed. Cranmer's case was especially tragic. Convinced that his life would be spared if he denied his Protestant beliefs, Cranmer signed a long a detailed recantation that was published and widely circulated. But when he discovered that he would be executed anyway, he renounced his denials, and steeled himself for martyrdom. At his execution, before the flames had touched his body, Cranmer professed his faith and held the hand with which he had signed the recantation over the flames unflinchingly, until it was totally burned, frequently exclaiming, "This unworthy right hand!" And then, as he was engulfed in flames, Cranmer died intoning the same remorseful refrain, over and over: "This unworthy right hand, this unworthy right hand . . ."

In all, about three hundred Protestants were executed during Mary's reign, most of them tradesmen and artisans, but the impact of these deaths extended beyond mere figures in a print culture where information could be easily disseminated. Reports of the constant roasting of heretics circulated so rapidly and thoroughly that the busiest burning field of all, at Smithfield, London, became as well known in England as any local spot. The relentless burnings may have pleased some Catholics, but they ended up having a negative effect too, giving rise to feelings of revulsion among many of Mary's subjects—feelings strong enough to convince previously indifferent or undecided folk of the errors of Catholicism, rather than of its merits.

Thanks largely to the work of one chronicler, John Foxe (1516–1587), the details of Mary's persecution were preserved and popularized after her reign, and the accounts themselves became an integral part of English Protestant identity. Foxe's *Actes and Monuments of These Latter and Perillous Dayes* was first published in March 1563, and became better known by its popular title *The Book of Martyrs*. Its success was immediate. An expanded edition appeared in 1570, a third in 1576, and a fourth in 1583. Foxe's text was a very detailed account of the persecution of Christians from apostolic times down to his own day, including those proto-Protestant medieval Christians, the Lollards, and Hussites. The bulk of the book, however, was dedicated to Mary's reign, and to the torments endured by those who were martyred for their Protestant faith. While Foxe's partisan work does not conform to the standards of scholarship now followed by historians, it was nonetheless a painstakingly researched collection of narratives and documents, unlike any published before. Foxe was a brilliant propagandist who instinctively grasped the polemical potential of graphic details, and especially of gruesome ones. Fully aware of Tertullian's ancient formula, "the blood of the martyrs is the seed of the church," Foxe inventoried every drop of blood that could be counted, and every scrap of testimony left behind by participants and eyewitnesses. Foxe's description of John Hooper's martyrdom is representative of the tone and content of his execution narratives:

> In this fire he prayed with a loud voice, "Lord Jesus, have mercy upon me! Lord Jesus receive my spirit!" And these were the last words he was heard to utter. But when he was black in the mouth, and his tongue so swollen that he could not speak, yet his lips went

until they were shrunk to the gums: and he knocked his breast with his hands until one of his arms fell off, and then knocked still with the other, while the fat, water, and blood dropped out at his fingers' ends, until by renewing the fire, his strength was gone, and his hand clave fast in knocking to the iron upon his breast. Then immediately bowing forwards, he yielded up his spirit.[8]

Foxe's *Book of Martyrs* would become the second most important book after the Bible among English Protestants, especially those of a Calvinist persuasion. It would help create an image of Queen Mary, Cardinal Pole, and Bishop Gardiner as bloodthirsty monsters, and of the Roman Catholic Church as a demonic institution. Its descriptions of the Spanish Inquisition helped intensify anti-Spanish sentiment in England and contributed significantly to the development of the so-called Black Legend, that is, the English tendency to portray all things Spanish as consummately dark and evil.

As Mary unwittingly helped the Protestant cause by creating three hundred martyrs, more or less, so did she also shape its character by causing about eight hundred refugees to flee across the English Channel to Reformed communities, especially in Emden, Strassburg, Wesel, Aarau, Frankfurt, Heidelberg, Basel, Zurich, and Geneva. These exiles were a mixed lot, including a high number of clerics, theological students, and gentry, and some merchants and artisans. Many leaders or future leaders of the Protestant cause could be found among them—activists who would return to England filled with Reformed fervor: John Aylmer, Miles Coverdale, Richard Cox, John Ponet, John Scory, John Bale, John Jewel, James Pilkington, Thomas Bentham, Edwin Sandys (future archbishop of York), and Edmund Grindal (future archbishop of York and Canterbury). While abroad, the vast majority of the exiles were influenced by Reformed Protestantism rather than by Lutheranism, which reinforced the trend that had begun in Henry VIII's day and permanently affected the character of English Protestantism. The dispersed exiles did not always agree with one another, or with the communities that took them in, often reflecting the differences among their host cities. The disputes that erupted over church organization, discipline, and ritual would spill over onto their native soil once they returned, giving shape to the religious politics of the late sixteenth and early seventeenth century.

Ever since the end of Mary's reign, when her Catholic revival died out, historians of the English Reformation have tended to portray Mary as a tragic failure, and her every move as an ironic victory for her opponents. Given that England steered away from Rome after Mary, such an assessment seems sensible, though laced with traces of Protestant triumphalism. In her own day, however, among those subjects who were adamant about their Catholic faith or leaned toward it, Mary's reign did not look like a dismal failure at all. Those who search for proof that England was not ready to become Protestant overnight find Mary's reign especially rich in evidence. Above all, historians can point to the relative ease with which Catholic symbols and rituals made a comeback: how all of the "popyshe trash" that was supposedly abandoned or destroyed surfaced again from the cellars and nooks and crannies where such things had been hidden, and how readily the Book of Common Prayer was replaced by the missal and breviary. Historians can also point to the fact that a five-year reign is relatively short, and that there is no way to know what might have become of England if Mary had reigned for longer or left behind a Catholic heir to the throne. Taking into account that much of the infrastructure of Catholicism had been very efficiently dismantled by Henry VIII and Edward VI, the rebuilding Mary attempted during a brief and turbulent reign can seem one of the more successful chapters of the Catholic Reformation, perhaps even a glimpse of an alternative Counter-Reformation. Ultimately, however, positive assessments of Mary verge on counterfactual history, on trying to figure out what might have been rather than what actually happened. Asking "what if?" questions can be an immensely helpful analytical exercise, especially in the case of Mary, but only as long as one keeps an eye firmly fixed on the fact that when Mary breathed her last, England ceased being a Catholic nation.

Elizabeth, the Virgin Queen

Mary died of natural causes on 17 November 1558, at the young age of forty-two. To those who despised Mary and her Catholicism, her death must have seemed like proof of God's divine intervention, for within hours of her premature exit, Reginald Pole, archbishop of Canterbury, also passed away. With one stroke, it seemed, God had removed the two chief agents of the pope in England.

England's first regnant queen had proved that a woman could wear the crown as securely as any man. When her half sister, Elizabeth, ascended to the throne, she faced no serious opposition. Instead, she was greeted by jubilant crowds, blazing bonfires, and ringing bells. We can assume, however, that Catholics did not take part in these celebrations, for it was well known that Elizabeth had Protestant leanings.

Queen Elizabeth quickly reversed Mary's religious policies. Early in 1559, three complementary pieces of legislation sealed a clean break with the immediate past. First, a new Act of Supremacy again cut off the Church of England from Rome's jurisdiction, enjoining every cleric in the realm to obey the monarch as "the only Supreme Governor . . . in all spiritual or ecclesiastical things or causes."[9] In addition, Elizabeth also issued a third Act of Uniformity that did away with all traditional Latin rituals and required every church in the realm to worship according to the 1552 Book of Common Prayer, which was reissued with some minor changes that intentionally avoided theological precision on contentious issues, folding contrary points of view into one another in vague language. On the most troublesome of all topics, the Eucharist, and, more specifically, on the question of Christ's presence in the bread and wine (is it physical, spiritual, or simply metaphorical?), the Elizabethan version spoke with intentional fuzziness of the ritual as a memorial and communion, both physical and spiritual. Distributing the bread into the hands of the faithful, as they knelt, the minister would say: "The bodie of our lord Jesus Christ, which was geven for thee, preserve thy body and soule into everlasting

The Virgin Queen. When she ascended to the throne in 1558 after the death of Mary, her Catholic half-sister, Elizabeth immediately broke with Rome once again, reestablishing the independent Church of England. Elizabeth's refusal to align herself with Lutherans or Calvinists led historians to describe her religious reforms as a *via media*, or middle way, between Protestantism and Catholicism. Her refusal to marry any of her many suitors—which allowed her to keep England free of myriad political entanglements—led to her becoming known as the Virgin Queen and to the naming of the first English colony in North America as Virginia.

life: and Take and eate this in remembraunce that Christ died for thee, feede on him in thine heart by faith, with thankesgevynge." Distributing the wine in a cup shared by all, the words remained equally ambivalent: "The bloude of our lorde Jesus Christ, which was shedd for thee, preserve thy body and soule into everlasting life: and drinke this in remembraunce that Christes bloude was shedde for thee, and be thankeful."[10]

All of these changes were mandatory, not merely an option, and the entire process of embracing the new liturgy was closely monitored and strictly enforced. To ensure that the required changes in ritual would take place, the crown sent visitors to every parish within that first year of Elizabeth's reign to collect the Latin missals, administer the oath to pastors, and make sure there were copies in every church of the Book of Common Prayer and the English Bible.

The 1559 Acts of Supremacy and Uniformity were accompanied by a list of fifty-two directives that came to be known as the Elizabethan Injunctions, which spelled out the break with traditional Catholicism very clearly. The injunctions not only rejected the pope's authority, but also allowed clerical marriage and called on the clergy to "purely and sincerely declare the Word of God" in sermons, and to encourage their flocks to read the Bible Employing language that was at once Erasmian and Calvinist, the injunctions denounced all "works devised by human fantasies" and called upon the clergy to forbid all sorts of devotions, such as "wandering to pilgrimages, offering of money, candles or tapers to relics, or images, or kissing and licking of the same, praying upon beads, or such like superstition," and to remind their congregations that such rituals had "not only no promise of reward in Scripture, for doing of them, but contrariwise, great threats and maledictions of God, for that they be things tending to idolatry and superstition."[11]

Despite such decidedly anti-Catholic policies, disappointment quickly surged through the ranks of those who had hoped for a thoroughgoing reformation of the Church of England. The deliberate theological ambivalence of the 1559 Book of Common Prayer was accompanied by an equally calculated attempt to retain much of the outward display of Catholic ritual: liturgical vestments, candles, bells, the gesture of kneeling, and so on— precisely the kind of "popyshe trash" that Reformed Protestants despised as idolatrous trappings. Though closer to Protestantism than Catholicism, Elizabeth's Reformation came to be seen as a *via media*, or middle way, between Catholicism and Protestantism. The Elizabethan Settlement, as it came to be known, was sui generis—truly unique, in a class of its own. First and foremost, while all of the other churches sought precision in theology, the Church of England avoided it. Focusing intensely on ritual rather than dogma, and seeking to retain many of the external forms of traditional worship that were not explicitly in conflict with the Bible, Elizabeth's church forged a new path while giving the impression that extremes had been avoided. Although it rejected scholastic terms such as *transubstantiation*, along with the doctrine itself, the Elizabethan church managed to pull off some sort of transubstantiation of its own: keeping the visible outward features unchanged, but transforming the invisible substance within.

Elizabeth's Grand Strategy

Finding a relatively safe path through the minefield of religion was only one facet of Elizabeth's strategies for England, and for herself as queen. Surrounded by potential enemies both at home and abroad, Elizabeth quickly proved herself a genius at keeping her options open, and at keeping everyone guessing about her motives and her plans. Overall, her main objectives were all closely bound to one another: to stave off religious conflict at home, to avoid costly involvements in Continental affairs; and to defend England's sovereignty in all respects: political, economic, and religious. Addressing Parliament in 1601, Elizabeth summed up her legacy by saying: "I was never so much enticed with the glorious name of a king, or royal authority of queen, as delighted that God hath made me His instrument to maintain his truth and glory and to defend this kingdom from peril, dishonour, tyranny and oppression."[12]

On the domestic front, the religious issue was the most sensitive and volatile. To some she could seem a consummate Machiavellian, faithless and interested only in whatever policy might keep her in power; to others she could seem a crypto-papist; and to others yet, a Protestant zealot. "I have no wish to open windows into men's souls," she said, revealing her policy but not necessarily her own beliefs, which she kept to herself. Stressing outward conformity to a church that avoided all extremes, Elizabeth saved England from the kind of violence that consumed France in the sixteenth century. But her compromises may have only delayed the inevitable, for in the seventeenth century, England, too, would be plunged into chaos, chiefly because of religious differences (see chapter 21).

Another burning issue at home was that of marriage and the succession. Still unmarried when she came to the throne at the age of twenty-five, Elizabeth was constantly showered with advice and marriage proposals. Everyone around her assumed she would marry and provide England with an heir to the throne. But Elizabeth refused to be rushed into marriage, fully aware that her control of the throne might become more tenuous if she had to share it with a husband, be he an English nobleman or a foreign monarch. Marrying a fellow Englishman had its risks, most notably that of being drawn into factional politics; but marrying a foreigner involved greater complications. England in the 1560s and 1570s was not yet a great military or commercial power, and was still very dependent on the alliances that dynastic marriages could offer. But an alliance could also plunge England into some other nation's wars. Dynastic marriages were therefore always a gamble, and Elizabeth found a way to make ambivalence and uncertainty work in her favor. Elizabeth did her best while she was of marriageable age to keep all suitors pending, milking the uncertainty for all it was worth. For instance, she kept Philip II hanging for some time and while he waited, thinking that Elizabeth might perhaps become his wife and therefore also a Catholic, Philip did his best to keep the papacy off Elizabeth's back. Similar maneuvering went into play with other foreign rulers who proposed marriage, such as Charles, Archduke of Austria, and François Hercule, Duke of Anjou, both Catholics, and Eric XIV of Sweden, a Lutheran. Diplomatic negotiations kept everyone in suspense, both at home and abroad, allowing Elizabeth to remain in control, with many more diplomatic options than she would have otherwise had.

Aside from being asked to fulfill the traditional role of wife, Elizabeth was also pressed to become a mother, for if she were to die childless, the Tudor line would be extinguished. The next in line was her cousin Mary, Queen of Scots, a granddaughter of Henry VIII's sister Margaret. But Mary was a Catholic and a closely bound to troubled France, where she had been reared. Fears that Elizabeth's childlessness might lead to instability, or, worse, to a Catholic resurgence were not unwarranted, but, in the end, they proved unnecessary, for as it turned out, Elizabeth would be succeeded by Mary's son, James, who was reared as a Protestant.

In a society in which queens seldom held the reins of power—and in which women were considered weak and indecisive—commanding the respect of men was no easy task. Yet Elizabeth won more than respect from those men who ran her administration; she won most of their hearts and minds too, along with those of many of her subjects. As savvy about her own image as she was about politics and religion, Elizabeth openly courted her subjects' adulation by touring her realm frequently in regional visits known as "progresses," riding on horseback, greeting her subjects face-to-face. Elizabeth's reign would come to be viewed as triumphant, even in her own day. It was during her long forty-five-year reign that England began to outstrip its rivals, not only defeating the Great Armada sent to conquer England by Philip II in 1588, but also harassing the Spanish treasure fleet on the high seas, sending explorers to chart the North Atlantic, and making its first claims on the New World. It was also during Elizabeth's reign that the East India Company was established, opening doors in Asia. Last but not least, hers was also a golden age for the arts, literature, and theater: the queen herself attended the premiere of William Shakespeare's *A Midsummer Night's Dream*. The aging spinster queen spoke of England as her spouse, and she came to be called "Gloriana," "Good Queen Bess," and "The Virgin Queen," esteemed as a selfless woman who always placed her nation first, above her personal happiness. In 1601, near the end of her reign, she said to Parliament, as she might have said to some of the suitors she kept in suspense: "There is no jewel, be it of never so high a price, which I set before this jewel; I mean your love. . . . I do not so much rejoice that God hath made me to be a Queen, as to be a Queen over so thankful a people."[13] But there is perhaps no better summation of her grand strategy than the words she once spoke in a moment of anger to Robert Dudley, Earl of Leicester, who was rumored to be her lover: "I will have here but one mistress and no master."

Protestant Nonconformists

Avoiding open religious conflict may have been Elizabeth's greatest success, but the very thing that made the Elizabethan Settlement acceptable for most of England—its mixing of Catholic traditions and Protestant spirit—also caused the greatest friction. At both extremes of the religious spectrum, no one was pleased by these compromises. Catholics viewed the traditional elements retained by the Church of England as nothing more than a transparent veneer over schism and heresy, while Protestants of a Reformed or Calvinist bent objected to all the compromises that stained "that unperfect book" (the 1559 prayer book), which, as they saw it, had been "culled and picked out of that popish dungehill, the Mass book full of all abominations."[14] Given the presence of these two extremes, to insist on uniformity was also to exclude, and to create dissenting minorities.

On the Protestant side, the issue that caused the greatest stir right from the start might seem trivial, but as is often the case with symbols and rituals in religion, what might seem most insignificant to outsiders, or most irrational, can be of the utmost importance for the faithful. It all began with vestments, and more specifically, with one piece of liturgical garb that Elizabeth's Act of Uniformity required all clerics to wear during church services: the surplice (a white wide-sleeved gown). Reformed Protestants made an issue out of this requirement not just because surplices were unbiblical "popish" remnants, but because they were an indifferent item, that is, totally unnecessary and unrelated to salvation. The Greek theological term for such indifferent things was *adiaphora*, and the concept itself was biblical, raised by the apostle Paul in 1 Corinthians 8, in regard to whether Christians could eat meat from pagan animal sacrifices. Opponents of the surplice objected most strenuously to the way in which consciences were being forced, for requiring any Christian to observe some trivial ordinance was tantamount to raising human laws over divine commands. It was akin to asking that one deny the absolute, unconditional subjection that every Christian owed to God's will.

Surplices were not a big issue in and of themselves, but they stood for everything that Reformed Protestants detested about the Elizabethan settlement, and thus they became avatars of the unholy and impure, negative symbols as heinous as any heathen idol. So it was that one mere vestment came to stand for error in the eyes of the Reformed, and that the conflict it created came to be known as the "vestiarian" controversy, a term that must be interpreted very loosely. The vestiarian controversy was about much more than vestments for the Reformed: it was about all "traces of popery" that still polluted the Church of England: all the trivial adiaphora forced upon English Christians, such as the wearing of certain caps by ministers, kneeling at communion, making the sign of the cross at baptism, bowing at the name "Jesus," ringing church bells, or using wedding rings in marriage services. Reformed Protestants objected to many different "Romish" remnants, but this one issue first polarized the anti-Romanists into two camps, forcing some to become nonconformists. And their adamant will to rid the Church of England of all its impurities, in turn, soon earned them the name of "Puritans"—an identity constructed not by the nonconformists themselves, but by their opponents, for polemical purposes.

The tension built gradually, as enforcement of conformity was somewhat spotty at first. In 1566, however, Matthew Parker, archbishop of Canterbury, grew impatient with reports of nonconformist clergy, and at the queen's urging, he issued directives that called for strict conformity to every detail of "ornaments" rubric in the Act of Uniformity, including surplices. The first fierce storm broke over London, where thirty-seven ministers refused to comply, and were suspended from their duties. Although most of these ministers eventually caved in grudgingly, a few would not, and were summarily dismissed from their posts and imprisoned. Pamphlets and counter-pamphlets flew, as was common in England, and before long the controversy grew into something larger, with ominous rumblings. One of the distinctive characteristics of the Church of England was its episcopal polity, that is, its governance by bishops. The Reformed had never been too keen on this arrangement, since the Genevan and Swiss churches had a less hierarchical structure that some considered more faithful to New Testament models. Now, as the vestiarian conflict heated up, the Reformed had yet another reason to question the episcopal polity of the English Church, for it was the bishops who were enforcing conformity, persecuting good Christians, and preventing genuine reform. By the 1570s, a good number of those puritan nonconformists would be including the episcopacy itself in their list of impurities to be cleansed. And in place of an episcopal polity, they proposed a nonhierarchical presbyterian church, in which elders (presbyters) and clergy shared authority.

Elizabeth's response to the puritan challenge was a firm assertion of the *via media*. Her steady convictions can be seen most clearly in the Thirty-Nine Articles, first issued in 1563 and revised and ratified in 1571. Elizabeth's articles sought to update the Forty-Two Articles that Thomas Cranmer had issued in 1553, and Queen Mary had repealed in 1558. The document is a list of the core beliefs that all English people were to hold, and a carefully worded expression of the *via media*. On the whole, the articles defend key Protestant principles, such as *sola scriptura*, *sola fide*, predestination, and clerical marriage. But all affirmations tend to be qualified in such a way as to dilute their precision. Take, for instance, article 12, on the relation between faith and works:

> Albeit that good works, which are the fruits of faith and follow after justification, cannot put away our sins and endure the severity of God's judgment, yet are they pleasing and acceptable to God in Christ and do spring necessarily out of a true and lively faith, in so much that by them a lively faith may be evidently known as a tree discerned by the fruit.[15]

Objecting to such a "mingle-mangle," nonconformists began to pull away from the state church, not as a unified group with their own list of beliefs, but rather as individuals and communities that shared a common vision despite numerous disagreements among themselves. In 1572, a coalition of these puritans published a manifesto that came to be known as the *Admonition to Parliament*, in which they demanded that Elizabeth rid the Church of England of all "Romish" traces and restore it to the "purity" of the New Testament. The *Admonition* also called for the abolition of the episcopacy and the creation of a presbyterian polity, such as that of Geneva, in which elders and ministers ruled in close cooperation. A second *Admonition* appeared soon thereafter, authored by Thomas Cartwright, leader of the presbyterian cause. Elizabeth responded by imprisoning the authors of the first *Admonition* and chasing the author of the second into exile. Queen Elizabeth shrank back from outright persecution of the puritans. Instead, she chose to undermine them from within. Taking advantage of the vacancy created in the see of Canterbury by Matthew Parker's death in 1576, Elizabeth appointed Edmund Grindal (1519–1583), a nonconformist, as Parker's successor. Grindal, a bishop who had once refused to wear the surplice, was a moderate puritan who opposed the presbyterian cause. Grindal's appointment was a gamble that Elizabeth would come to rue.

With some of their number fleeing England—as had happened under Bloody Mary—the puritans continued to press for reform at home with renewed vigor and a more radicalized point of view. In the 1570s, a new generation of leaders entered the fray. These young puritans had close ties to Cambridge University and a nucleus at London. They also more closely followed the theology spun at Geneva by Calvin's successor Théodore de Bèze, and tended to view themselves as persecuted by the episcopacy. One means of reform adopted by some of these puritans was the creation of "prophesyings": public debates attended by the laity at which clerics examined specific biblical texts through sermons and discussion. A practice borrowed from Protestant brethren on the continent, these prophesyings quickly developed a following all over England, becoming a flash point for conflict with the bishops and the crown. Fearing the spread of puritan sentiment through these gatherings, and seeking to defend her own authority and that of the bishops, in 1576, Elizabeth ordered her newly appointed archbishop of Canterbury, Edmund Grindal, to stop all prophesyings. But Grindal, an anti-surplice nonconformist, flatly refused. Even worse, he penned a remonstrance to the queen in which he scolded her for meddling in church affairs and trying to usurp the power of the bishops. Elizabeth responded swiftly, throwing Grindal in prison and suspending him from office. Had she been able to eject Grindal outright, Elizabeth might have done so, but the legal and practical repercussions were risks that she preferred not to take. The primal see of Canterbury therefore remained vacant, for all practical purposes, until Grindal's death in 1583. In the meantime, Elizabeth managed to push some bishops into suppressing the prophesyings in their dioceses, but these meetings continued to grow in popularity, especially in the north of England. And puritanism continued to spread, wider and deeper.

As soon as Grindal died, Elizabeth appointed a staunch anti-puritan to the see of Canterbury, John Whitgift (1530–1604), who tried to crush nonconformity by deposing hundreds of clerics who refused to comply with his orders. From 1583 on, then, the crown and the episcopacy entered into an open confrontation with the puritans, employing a constant harassment that verged on outright persecution. Whitgift's strict measures worked for the most part, and most of the clergy ended up complying; but he also drove the staunchest of the nonconformists right out of the Church of England. The Elizabethan settlement was thus rescued at a high price: the creation of breakaway dissenters who saw themselves in the same light as those persecuted and exiled by Queen Mary, as the only true Christians.

Among the dissenters, disagreement was the rule rather than the exception. At one end of their broad spectrum of opinion, moderate puritans of various stripes clung to the dream of reforming the entire Church of England from within. At the other extreme, there arose various separatist factions that abandoned that dream and chose to create their own independent, purified churches, much along the same lines as the Anabaptists, basing their ecclesiology on predestination rather than on belief in free will. Eventually, a branch of this puritan family would take up adult baptism and evolve into the English Baptist Church, offering proof positive that theological propositions do not work like mathematical or chemical formulas, with precise, consistent results. Somehow, in that crucible where exegesis, theology, and political life are fused into a singular matrix, these English Calvinists managed to arrive at many of the same logical conclusions as the Anabaptists Calvin had despised, and they did so by employing Calvin's own theology.

One of the first to lead the separatist charge was Robert Browne (1550–1633), who established an independent congregation at Norwich in 1580, even before Archbishop Whitgift began his crackdown on dissenters. Browne and his followers advocated a "free church" with a congregational polity rather than a presbyterian or episcopal church. Relying on covenant theology—the belief that God enters into covenants, or contracts, with his elect—Browne argued that God established a one-on-one relationship with individual communities of the elect rather than with whole nations. As he saw it, this meant that elect communities should be totally free and independent from any earthly authority and therefore not subject to state control. Exiled in 1582, Browne would return to England and be imprisoned a total of 32 times. His book *A Treatise of Reformation Without Tarying for Anie* (1582) was very influential not just among his followers, who came to be known as Brownists, but also among many other puritan separatists, including those who stayed in England and those who fled. Seeking exile first in the Netherlands, and later in America, one branch of this separatist tradition, the Pilgrims, would play a leading role in the establishment of English colonies across the Atlantic Ocean.

The puritan challenge to the Elizabethan settlement strengthened in the last two decades of Elizabeth's reign. Puritan dissent would be the largest problem inherited by her successor, James I, and his son, Charles I. Eventually, it would lead to civil war and the undoing of the nation.

Catholic Recusants

Unlike the puritans, who gradually recognized their exclusion from Elizabeth's Reformation, steadfast English Catholics knew from the very start of Elizabeth's reign that there would be no place for them in the state church. Ironically, what distressed the puritans the most about Elizabeth's compromise—all those "shells and chippings of popery"—also angered the Catholics, who saw nothing but error within those trivial fragments of their traditional faith.

It was their disdain for those hollow scraps offered to them by the *via media* that led Catholics to coin the sarcastic name of *puritan* for their enemies at the other end of the religious spectrum, as a symmetrical counterpart to *papist*. The most pressing question faced by Catholics was a practical one: what were they to do about church services? They had no priests or churches. Even worse, refusal to take part in the rites of the state church as demanded by law was a crime termed *recusancy* (Latin: *recusare*, "to refuse"), from which was derived the name they were given: *recusants*. The Act of Uniformity required Catholics to participate in the rites of the Church of England, the Act of Supremacy demanded they place their queen above the pope, and the Thirty-Nine Articles forced them to deny the core beliefs of the Catholic Church. Much like the Huguenots in France, the Catholics of England had few choices: dissembling, exile, martyrdom, or resistance. None of these options was satisfactory, or easy.

During the first years of her reign, Elizabeth tended to leave the Catholics alone, even turning a blind eye to their recusancy. We have no accurate figures for the number of Catholics, but it seems that all of England was dotted with them, and that Catholicism may have remained the majority religion in certain locales, especially in rural Lancashire and Cumbria, in the north. The *via media* placed all of England's eight thousand parish clergy in a tough spot. Most were poorly trained and poorly paid. Under the new Act of Uniformity they faced stiff penalties for recusancy. Failure to use the Book of Common Prayer could result in a fine of a year's income and six months in prison. A second offense meant dismissal from their post and a year in prison. A third offense could earn a lifetime in prison. Given such stiff penalties, it stands to reason that only about three hundred clergy, less than 4 percent of the total, refused to conform. Nonetheless, despite such strictures, England teemed with rumors of priests who continued celebrate the Catholic Mass in secret.

At Oxford, Catholic resistance was strong, and several recusant heads of colleges were dismissed. Among Catholics, it was rumored that only 5 percent of Oxford men had taken the Oath of Supremacy during those first years of Elizabeth's reign. The bishop of Salisbury, John Jewel, warned that Oxford was a perilous place for any young Protestant. But even in heavily Catholic places, it was difficult for Catholics to communicate openly or to link together through printed texts. Some writers and printers went abroad, then, especially to Flanders, and more specifically to Louvain, where Catholic scholars from Oxford and Cambridge began to publish pamphlets and books that could be smuggled into England. And it was not just books that could be produced overseas. From the very start of Elizabeth's reign, English Catholics determined that an entirely new generation of priests could be trained abroad. And so it was that English Catholics began to embrace exile as a means of turning their native land into a mission field and their young men into missionaries.

William Allen (1532–1594) proved to be one of the most important of these Oxford émigrés. Principal and proctor of St. Mary's Hall, Oxford, Allen resigned shortly after the accession of Elizabeth, so he could avoid taking the Oath of Supremacy. He fled to Louvain in 1561, but soon returned to England, to spend two and a half years crisscrossing the Oxford countryside, drumming up support for the Catholic cause. Ordained a priest in 1568, after he had returned to Flanders, Allen then helped to create an English college across the Channel at Douai, for the explicit purpose of training Catholic missionaries who would be sent to England. This English college would play a significant role not just by producing missionaries, but also as a Catholic center of learning. In 1582, as the college moved temporarily to nearby Rheims, William Allen was instrumental in publishing an English translation of the New Testament, aimed specifically at English Catholics, giving them a version that was ostensibly free of all the "errors" found in Tyndale's and Coverdale's translations, along with notes that defended and explained the text in a Catholic vein, against Protestant points of view.

Translated by a group of Oxford scholars directly from the Latin Vulgate text that the Council of Trent had just approved as authoritative, the Douai New Testament flew off the Flemish presses and across the Channel into English hands The Old Testament would be published in 1609–1610. This Douai-Rheims Bible, as it came to be known, would be used by English-speaking Catholics until the twentieth century. Its creation and use speak volumes about the flexibility within sixteenth- and seventeenth-century Catholicism, and about the character of the underground English Catholic community. According to the canons and decrees of the Council of Trent, published in 1563, Catholics were forbidden to read the Bible in the vernacular on their own. But the Douai-Rheims translation was never condemned, principally because authorities of the Catholic Church understood that the English recusant minority was being constantly exposed to "incorrect" translations anyway. The Douai-Rheims Bible was supposed to immunize English Catholics as much as it was supposed to educate and inspire them. So, rather than becoming a bone of contention with Rome, the translation became a major feature in the identities of Catholics everywhere in the English-speaking world.

The early years of Elizabeth's reign, up to 1570, were relatively quiet for English Catholics. Enforcement of uniformity was far from consistent, or even possible. Many Catholics were able to remain in high offices simply because of a shortage of properly qualified non-Catholics to replace them. This situation seemed to be especially common for lawyers, since many of the landed gentry tended to be Catholics, and these nobles had been trained as lawyers. At the London Inns of Court, the Middle Temple was rumored to be "pestered with papists." Avoiding the oath became a Catholic art, as did dissembling. Feigned illnesses or travel could easily keep one from swearing the Oath on the appointed day. Some argued that swearing the oath on a Protestant Bible made the oath invalid for a Catholic. Some also argued—just like the Nicodemites—that it was no sin to dissemble or participate in the rituals of Elizabeth's state church, and many of the Catholics who continued to follow their traditional faith in private also regularly attended services in the Church of England as a way of escaping the penalties that nonattendance would bring. Quickly, these Catholics acquired the name of "church papists"—the English equivalent of *Nicodemite*. Focusing on the letter of the law rather than its spirit and finding ways of deceiving without actually lying became essential survival skills that would serve Catholics well in England.

The vast majority of the clergy seem to have slipped into their new roles rather quietly, baptizing infants, burying the dead, and presiding at marriages as before. But they no longer heard confessions, and they could not conduct worship in Latin. Most, like Christopher Trychay of the small village of Morebath, in Devonshire, simply carried on after they surrendered their vestments, missals, votive lamps, and images, leaving behind nary a word about their own feelings or those of their congregation. Father Trychay, an excellent record keeper, did not ever say whether his flock's faith was shaken or enhanced by all of the changes they experienced, or whether families were divided by the choices foisted upon them. He merely kept the books, doing whatever he was told to do by the crown as vicar of Morebath.[16] We have to assume he was not among those who said Mass and heard confessions clandestinely, and that he represents the vast majority of the clergy.

Everything changed quickly for English Catholics in 1570, when the pope issued the bull *Regnans in excelsis*, which excommunicated Queen Elizabeth and all her followers, denouncing her as a "Servant of Wickedness" and a "heretic and an abetter of heretics." Worst of all, Pope Pius V deprived her of "her pretended Title" as queen and absolved all her subjects "perpetually" from "any oath of allegiance and from any type of duty in relation to lordship, fidelity, and obedience," reminding all of England that any Catholic who obeyed Elizabeth would be automatically excommunicated. One phrase in particular turned every English Catholic into a potential traitor and rebel, instantly: "We command and forbid all and sundry among the lords, subjects, peoples, and others aforesaid that they have not to obey her or her admonitions, orders, or laws."[17] As if this were not enough, authorities in Rome reminded English Catholics—as Calvin constantly reminded the Huguenots—that they were not supposed to mix with the ungodly. The message was clear: attending services in the Church of England was a mortal sin, that is, an offense against God that merited eternal punishment in hell.

This papal decision was not a move that Catholics necessarily favored. Some, in fact, dreaded it. Even the most Catholic Philip II, who still held on to the title "king of England," and had been courting Elizabeth, thought Pius V had gone too far. Philip had been counseling the pope not to take this step, fearing that such a drastic move would "embitter feelings in England and drive the Queen and her friends more to oppress and persecute the few good Catholics still remaining in England."[18] Philip was right. The excommunication produced a flurry of anti-Catholic legislation: one law made it treasonable to call the queen a heretic; another prohibited anyone from bringing papal bulls into England, or any Catholic devotional objects, such as rosaries; yet another prohibited Catholics from leaving the country or from being trained for the priesthood. Those who had already left England were given six months to return and repent, on pain of losing all their possessions and incomes.

Elizabeth and her ministers had every reason to worry, for the papal excommunication was directly linked to a failed uprising in the north of England known as the Revolt of the Northern Earls, or the Rising of the North, which sought to depose Elizabeth, install Mary Stuart, Queen of Scots, on the English throne, and return

Catholic martyrdom. When Pope Pius V excommunicated Queen Elizabeth in 1570 and absolved her Catholic subjects from obeying her, all Catholics in England became subject to the charge of high treason and to the most extreme form of execution: hanging, drawing, and quartering, which involved dragging the condemned man by horse to the place of execution, hanging him almost to the point of death, reviving him, then cutting off his genitals, disemboweling him, and finally beheading and chopping his corpse into four pieces. Afterward, the traitor's remains were displayed in prominent places. This image from 1584 depicts the martyrdom of the Jesuit priest Edmund Campion, who suffered such a fate. The executioners are depicted as ancient Roman soldiers to link Campion to the martyrs of the early church. Queen Elizabeth executed hundreds of Catholics during her long reign, but because her religious policies prevailed, she avoided going down in history as "Bloody Elizabeth."

England to Catholicism. Led by Charles Neville, sixth Earl of Westmorland (1542–1601) and Thomas Percy, seventh Earl of Northumberland (1528–1572), the uprising began in Durham on 14 November 1569, when men under the command of the two earls stormed the cathedral, cleared out the protestant communion table and reinstated the Latin Mass, not just in the cathedral, but also in eight other churches. These northern rebels who fought under the banner of the Five Wounds of Christ were as doomed as those who had launched the Pilgrimage of Grace against Henry VIII in 1536.

Elizabeth quickly dispatched other nobles and their armies up north. Outnumbered and unable to attract help from abroad or to turn their rebellion into a mass uprising, the rebellious earls fled into Scotland after gaining only a few Pyrrhic victories. Within less than two months, the uprising had been crushed: 400 rebels were executed, and 350 had their death sentences set aside. In 1572, the Earl of Northumberland fell into Elizabeth's hands, and he was executed. Speculation still surrounds the timing of Pope Pius V's bull of excommunication, which arrived in England after the rebels had been crushed. Elizabeth, however, did not need conclusive proof that the two events were linked. The uprising and the excommunication, in and of themselves, were proof positive that Catholics were enemies of the crown.

Further evidence arrived in 1575, when priests trained at Douai began sneaking into England. It is estimated that within seven years about one hundred such priests made it across the English Channel undetected. And along with them came a flood of Catholic texts printed in Douai and elsewhere on the Continent. In addition, at Rome, the new order of the Society of Jesus, better known as the Jesuits, agreed to send some of their priests to England. The first two of these secret agents proved to be among the most formidable: Edmund Campion and Robert Parsons, two Oxford graduates. Traveling in disguise, Campion and Parsons snuck into England in the summer of 1580. Early in July, the two organized a secret meeting with London's leading Catholics that came to be known as the Synod of Southwark. Outlining their mission and discussing questions of Catholic discipline, they reiterated Rome's position on mingling with heretics, reminding all present that it was a mortal sin to be a "church papist." After this meeting, the two Jesuits went each their own way to minister to England's Catholics.

In the eyes of the English authorities these missionaries were nothing more than traitors and subversive foreign agents, given that the pope had absolved all Catholics from allegiance to the queen. Their presence in England known, a law was passed that made it an act of treason to convert anyone to Catholicism, or to be converted. In addition, hiding a priest became illegal, and fines and penalties were increased for those found guilty of participating in Catholic rituals or failing to attend the Church of England. The fines were so steep, only the wealthiest could afford to pay them. For instance, the fine for refusing to attend church rose to twenty pounds a month, a princely sum at the time. And those absent from their parish church for a year were now required to pay at least two hundred pounds.

Undaunted by such measures, the missionaries set up a printing press in the attic of an estate at Stonor, in Oxfordshire, which was run by Catholic printers disguised as gentry. By late June 1581, the secret press was cranking out copies of a book by Edmund Campion entitled *Ten Reasons Proposed to His Adversaries for Disputation in the Name of the Faith and Presented to the Illustrious Members of Our Universities.* More than four hundred copies were smuggled into Oxford, where they were dropped at strategic places, such as the university church of St. Mary. The net effect of this subversive act was similar to that of the French affair of the placards in 1534: it made the authorities realize that their enemies were not only everywhere, but also very well organized. But the Oxford incident was only a first step. In 1582, nearly five thousand copies of the Catholic translation of the New Testament published by William Allen at Douai and Rheims began to make their way into the hands of English Catholics, who eagerly welcomed them, probably unaware that they were the only Catholics in the world who were being encouraged by Catholic priests to read the scriptures in their mother tongue.

By the time the New Testament arrived, however, Campion had been caught by one of the many spies that the authorities had sent to infiltrate the Catholic network. Arrested with two other priests and taken to the Tower of London in July 1581, Campion was subjected to extreme torture, and pressed in vain to deny his faith. Four months later, he was found guilty of plotting to overthrow the queen, hanged, drawn, and quartered. Campion was one of the first of these clandestine priests to be executed during Elizabeth's reign, but he would prove to be only one of many. Between 1582 and 1591 alone, sixty-seven priests from Douai met the same fate. And other seminaries on the Continent were also sending a steady stream of priests to England. After Campion's arrest, his Jesuit associate Parsons snuck out of England and returned to the Continent, where he was placed in charge of directing the Jesuit mission to England. In 1588 he went to Spain, and spent nine years setting up seminaries for English priests at Valladolid, Seville, and Madrid, all of which, in due time, sent their clandestine missionaries. By the end of Elizabeth's reign, about eight hundred priests had made their way to England, and about three hundred remained active, underground.

In 1585, as the priests continued to sneak into England, more laws were passed to stem the flow, including one that assigned the death penalty to anyone who "willingly and wittingly" sheltered a priest, another that called for the confiscation of all goods and property from anyone who sent money to English seminaries on the Continent, and yet another that leveled heavy fines on parents who sent a child abroad without the proper license. Failing to report the whereabouts of a priest was also made a crime subject to heavy fines and imprisonment.

By the late 1580s English Catholics were involved in a life and death struggle with the Elizabethan authorities. Then, in 1588, one of the worst possible blunders in Western history made life even more intolerable for the underground Catholics in England: the arrival of the Spanish Armada off the shores of England. Convinced that an invasion of England by his troops would spark a massive Catholic rebellion against Elizabeth—thanks, in part, to mistaken advice from William Allen and Robert Parsons—King Philip II of Spain sent a fleet of 130 ships and nineteen thousand soldiers to pick up an additional thirty thousand Spanish troops in the Netherlands and ferry them across the channel to England. Outmaneuvered by smaller and swifter English vessels and shot to pieces by them, Philip's invincible armada was soundly defeated in a three-day battle in early August. As the victors rejoiced, Catholics in England prepared for the worst. Nothing seemed to prove their treasonous intentions more convincingly than Philip's failed invasion. Some Catholics had offered to fight against the Spanish, but to no avail. Prominent Catholics throughout the realm were imprisoned or put under house arrest, and the hunt for priests and secret Catholic conventicles went into high gear.

During this period the building of "priest-holes," or secret hiding places for priests, intensified in Catholic households, particularly those of the gentry. This architectural oddity has become emblematic of recusancy. The "holes" and all of the deception seemed to work, at least for a while, for during the remainder of Elizabeth's reign Catholicism could never be wiped out completely. For every priest captured and executed, two more would show up. For every lay person imprisoned or fined, or even executed, others joined the underground movement. And the recusant books kept pouring in from the Continent. Ironically, the same kinds of horrors witnessed by crowds and described by Protestant martyrologists during Mary's reign again became commonplace, though with lesser frequency. And as could be expected, the Catholics came up with their own martyrologies, which served the same purpose among them as John Foxe's *Acts and Monuments* among the Protestants. The violence expressed against Catholic "traitors" could be intense. In July 1589, for instance, four priests were hanged, decapitated, disemboweled, and drawn and quartered in Oxford. Their heads were displayed on the wall of Oxford Castle, where Protestant extremists hacked away at them. What was left of their butchered bodies ended up on display at the town gates. As Catholics shared this story, they seldom hesitated to add that the right arm of George Nichols, one of the slain priests, swiveled ominously as it hung on the gate, pointing an accusing finger at Oxford.

Yet despite the bloodshed, the penalties, and the need for priest-holes, the recusants among the gentry refused to fade away. By 1592 so many fines were being collected from the gentry for recusancy that a special department was established by the Exchequer to handle them. But the restrictions placed on recusants would also increase. By the mid-1590s recusants were forbidden to move about freely, and they were forced to report at regular intervals to local authorities. Between 1593 and 1597 Recusant Rolls were produced, which listed all known Catholics and the fines paid by them. Since the rolls listed only those who paid fines, they dealt only with the gentry who were wealthy enough to afford their recusancy. But even among these elites, the price for nonconformity could prove too steep, for the rolls show that many of them ended up losing much of what had been theirs.

Catholics were a great threat to Queen Elizabeth and her *via media*, perhaps greater than the puritans, for the Catholics had powerful allies all over the Continent, and especially in Rome, the alleged seat of the Antichrist. Despite her ruthlessness in hunting down their priests and their leaders, Elizabeth was nonetheless restrained by lingering feudal structures that prevented her from denying the gentry their own religion. As one might expect in a rigidly hierarchical society, the gentry had more choices than everyone else, principally because some of them could afford to pay fines and fund a life in exile. For all practical purposes, however, even when one takes into account the relatively few nobles who could thumb their noses at the queen—and pay dearly for it—the Elizabethan settlement was an oppressive, crushing burden to those who wished to remain Catholic.

By the time she died in 1603, Elizabeth's authorities had executed nearly two hundred Catholics—123 priests and more than 60 lay people—most of them during the last twenty years of her reign. Unlike her half sister Mary, who killed Protestants for their religious beliefs, Elizabeth made every effort to identify her victims as traitors rather than heretics. Pope Pius V unwittingly gave her the legal basis for such a claim, and perhaps also the reason for the violence. Catholics tried to defend themselves against the charge of treason, to little avail. In 1584, William Allen published an impassioned apologia on behalf of his fellow Catholics in England titled *A True, Sincere and Modest Defence of English Catholiques That Suffer for Their Faith*, in which he argued that they were not traitors at all, but really the best possible subjects the crown could ask for. His argument rested on the assumption that their chief virtue was their religion, which was true and divinely established, unlike that of the crown, which was heretical. It was a dizzying logical circle, very similar to that drawn by Calvin in his address to King Francis I in 1536 and that of the Protestants who developed resistance theories, like John Knox and John Ponet. It was a vicious circle, made necessary by religious chaos in an age when politics and religion were inseparable.

We will never know how many Catholics still survived in England by the end of Elizabeth's reign. Estimates range from 1.5 percent of the population to 25 percent. The existence of "church papists" of various degrees makes guesswork difficult, if not foolhardy. Then there are also regional differences to take into account, with larger percentages in the north of England and smaller percentages in the southeast. Perhaps exactness is irrelevant. What matters most is the simple fact that anyone who wanted to remain Catholic under Elizabeth had to pay a very high price, and that for that very reason Catholicism was reduced to a shadowy underground existence full of priest-holes and relegated to a place in early modern English history that can be best described as a dead end—which is why Elizabeth is not remembered as Bloody Elizabeth, but rather as Good Queen Bess and the Virgin Queen.

When all is said and done, Elizabeth managed to steer England rather peacefully through a period of tremendous change and religious turmoil. Her successors to the throne, however, would be less adept at managing the religious crisis. And their failures would thus make her achievements seem all the more remarkable.

Wales, Ireland, and Scotland

The history of the English Reformation is inextricably connected to that of the three realms closest to it, both in geographical and in political terms: Wales to the west, Scotland to the north (both part of the same island), and Ireland, a separate island, westward across the Irish Sea. Each of these realms had its own distinct relation to England, and each had its own approach to the religious changes that its more powerful neighbor undertook or tried to impose on them. Ultimately, their destinies proved inseparable.

Wales

Wales was politically integrated with England, but far from similar in culture. Subjected to the crown of England in 1284, the Celtic people of Wales retained their own language, customs, and laws, which they guarded fiercely. In 1536, as he was dissolving the monasteries, Henry VIII began incorporating Wales more fully through the Act of Union, which granted the Welsh the same political status as the English, subjected their courts to the common law of England, and granted Wales representation in parliament. Consequently, all changes to the Church of England also applied to Wales.

Henry VIII's measures did not apply to the Welsh language, however, which remained firmly ensconced in a land where English was a foreign tongue spoken by the colonizing elites. This language barrier would prove a serious obstacle to the acceptance of future reforms, since the English rituals of the Book of Common Prayer, which was imposed on the Welsh by Edward VI, were then even less comprehensible than the traditional Latin rituals they replaced. In all other respects, however, the Reformation imposed from above seems to have been accepted quietly and without much resistance on the part of the clergy or the laity, even though there was more grumbling about change in Wales than in most of England. The fact that most landowners remained very loyal to the crown ensured this grudging acceptance of the new church and that its unintelligible "Saxon" liturgies could never flare into open resistance.

Queen Mary's brief attempt to reinstate Catholicism seems to have been warmly received, for it produced very few Protestant martyrs or exiles, but as in England, Mary's efforts did not lead to a lasting Catholic revival. With the accession of Elizabeth, the Book of Common Prayer was again imposed on Wales. Although the Welsh bishops complained loudly about how difficult it was to wean their flocks from ancient customs, no organized resistance to religious change ever materialized.

Recusants were few in number and no obstacle to the Elizabethan settlement. Elizabeth's policy of appointing a high percentage of Welshmen as bishops seems to have paid off, too, and smoothed the way for uncontested change. By 1567, the native bishops had produced a Welsh New Testament and prayer book. In 1588, an improved translation of the Bible was published by Bishop William Morgan, followed in 1599 by a more successful Welsh prayer book. By then, the Welsh were as immersed in the Elizabethan *via media* and as unconnected to the Catholic past as the English. But they nonetheless remained as foreign to the English as the English were to them: so close, and yet so far away.

Ireland

Much more so than in the case of Wales, native political structures, ancient traditions, language, and resentment toward England often stood in the way of change in Ireland. Superficially colonized by the English and regarded by them as one of the "dark corners of the land," Ireland strongly resisted many of the reforming efforts of the Tudor monarchs, but was nonetheless affected by them. In 1536–1537, when the Dublin Parliament accepted the Act of Supremacy, a rebellion broke out in protest, led by the Irish noble Thomas Fitzgerald, Lord Offaly, but the unsuccessful rebels only succeeded in increasing English control. After their defeat and the execution of Fitzgerald, opposition to Henry VIII weakened. In 1541, Henry was granted the new title of king, as opposed to mere "lord" of Ireland. This change was more than cosmetic, for it was accompanied by a larger administration that tied the Irish more directly to England. In addition, one of the king's first steps was the seizure of monastic lands and the property of Fitzgerald's rebels, which led to the dissolution of about half of Ireland's monasteries.

All Anglo-Irish relations were complicated by the fact that Ireland was sharply divided not only by regional and clan rivalries, but also ethnically and linguistically, among native Celts, older English colonists, known as the Anglo-Irish or Old English, and more recent English arrivals. In the early seventeenth century Scots would be added to the mix in the north, as part of a resettlement plan devised by the English crown. Henry VIII tried to win over the native and Anglo-Irish nobles by offering them new titles and land grants in exchange for their acceptance of the Act of Supremacy. Many nobles caved in and rejected the pope's supremacy, but in the long run, these deals struck by Henry VIII would prove hollow. Under Edward VI, English officials were virtually alone in supporting the Protestantizing changes required by law. Even more so than in the case of Wales, the imposition of English language rituals and an English Bible made little sense to the native majority, or to most of the bishops. Moreover, without an efficient administrative structure to enforce change, all such English reforms were doomed. Resistance to change was also stirred up by Catholic missionaries from the Continent, who began arriving in 1542, three decades earlier than in England. The Church of Ireland—the official state church, with bishops loyal to the crown—thus began its transformation into a colonial branch of the Church of England that ministered only to a small minority of the population.

The brief interim of Mary's reign reversed Edward's policies, but brought little change, since so few in Ireland had complied anyway, both among the Old English and the native Irish. As one might expect, friction increased under Elizabeth. Her Acts of Supremacy and Uniformity, and her *via media* proved unenforceable, not just because they were resisted, but also because of political instability. Three major uprisings challenged Elizabeth's authority and reshuffled the balance of power among the Irish lords: that of Shane O'Neill (1559), that of the Fitzgeralds of Desmond (1568–1583), and, finally, that of Hugh O'Neill and Hugh O'Donnell (1594–1603), also known as the Nine Years' War.

Meanwhile, as the Elizabethan settlement failed to take root and violence swept the land, Ireland was made even less receptive to change, gradually, by the reforming and missionary efforts of the now-reinvigorated Roman Catholic Church on the continent. A blueprint very similar to that drawn for recusants in England was also used for Ireland: seminaries for the training of Irish priests in Catholic Europe began producing a steady stream of well-educated clerics faithful to Rome. The first to open its doors, at the University of Alcalá, near Madrid, in 1590, was followed in 1593 by the Irish College at the University of Salamanca, in Spain, established by King Philip II, and yet another in Lisbon, Portugal. In the seventeenth century, three more Irish seminaries would be established in Spain, along with one in Rome, three in Belgium, and seven in France. By the time the state-run Church of Ireland got around to issuing a Gaelic New Testament in 1603 and a Gaelic prayer book in 1608, it was too late. Ireland was already fully committed to recusancy, and well on its way to becoming one of the few places in Europe where the religion of the established authorities failed to become that of the people.

The only way that Protestantism could take root on Irish soil would be through immigration, and that is precisely what King James I would foster, beginning in 1609, through the resettlement of Lowland Scots into Ulster province, in the north of Ireland. The colonization of Ulster was made possible by the confiscation of the lands of the native Irish nobility in that region, in retaliation for their rebellion in the Nine Years' War. The end result was the creation of a mixed population that developed deep animosities towards each other, the effects of which are still felt to this day.

Scotland

Unlike Wales and Ireland, which were subject to the English monarchy, Scotland was an independent kingdom at the beginning of the sixteenth century. Its relationship with England was as tight as it was complex. Ancient cultural, economic, and political ties were entwined with rivalries, and strained by a long history of conflict. Ethnically and linguistically diverse, Scotland's culture was nonetheless closer to England's than to Wales's or Ireland's. Scots, the language spoken in the southern Lowlands by the majority of its population, was derived from Old English. Like the north of England, which it bordered, Scotland was primarily rural, not too prosperous, and politically decentralized. Its landowning noble class enjoyed relative independence from the monarchy, which its parliament was often willing—and able—to defy. For all of these reasons, the path taken by Scotland in the sixteenth century would be very different from England's, yet full of intersections.

The closest and perhaps most troublesome connection between England and Scotland on the eve of the Reformation was dynastic. In 1502–1503, the Scottish king James IV, Stuart (1488–1513) patched up years of conflict with England by signing a "treaty of perpetual peace" and marrying Margaret, daughter of the English king Henry VII. In 1512, Margaret's brother, newly crowned King Henry VIII, invaded France, England's archrival. Since Scotland had a long history of ties with France, the "perpetual peace" agreed on in 1502 was strained to the breaking point.

Renewing Scotland's "auld alliance" with France, James IV invaded England in 1513. Disaster followed at the Battle of Flodden, where King James and thousands of his troops were slaughtered by the English. James IV was succeeded by James V (1512–1542), his infant son and Henry VIII's nephew. Relations between England and Scotland remained strained for the remainder of Henry VIII's reign.

Caught in a tug-of-war between pro-French and pro-English factions at the Scottish court, the boy king James V served merely as a figurehead. But as James V matured, he gained control and strengthened his ties to the French, even entering into two dynastic marriages to seal his allegiance. His second wife, the French noblewoman Marie de Guise, daughter of the militantly Catholic Duke of Guise, gave birth to two sons and one daughter. The sons would die in infancy, leaving the girl, Mary Stuart, as heir to the Scottish throne.

Resolutely Catholic and opposed to Henry VIII's religious policies, James V resisted Protestant influences, but not very effectively. As early as the 1520s, the Protestant message leaked freely from England, and later through contacts with France, where Protestants were growing in numbers. By the 1540s, Scotland had a thriving Protestant community, strongly supported by an increasing number of nobles, and heavily influenced by Swiss Reformed theology.

Tensions with England over the religious issue mounted as Henry VIII continued to press his nephew James V to break with Rome. Angry over a meeting that James failed to keep at York in 1541, the ailing and rancorous Henry instigated a rash of border clashes and raided Scotland in 1542. In response, James invaded England, with dire results. On 24 November 1542, at the Battle of Solway Moss, the Scots beat a hasty retreat back across the border, leaving 1,200 troops, 3,000 horses, 20 cannon, 120 guns, and 4 cartloads of lances to be captured by the English. Two weeks after watching this humiliating defeat from afar and withdrawing to a castle, James died suddenly, just as his wife, Marie de Guise, gave birth to their daughter Mary. Rumors spread about James having been killed by shame, embarrassment, or even a madness caused by the crushing burden of his many disappointments. He was only thirty years old, and none of his several illegitimate children could inherit the throne.

As the monarchy passed to the newborn half-French Mary Stuart, the nobles of Scotland assumed virtual control of the kingdom. Across the border, Henry VIII offered to exchange his 1,200 Scottish captives for a marriage contract between the infant Mary Queen of Scots and his five-year-old son, Edward, hoping to undermine Scotland's French alliance and its obedience to Rome. The deal was sealed by the Treaties of Greenwich (1543), but it was soon broken by the political instability of Scotland. The infant Mary, much like her child-king father, was a mere figurehead claimed by two factions: a pro-French party that supported traditional Catholicism and a pro-English clique that favored Protestant reforms.

In 1544, the pro-French faction, led by Cardinal David Beaton, archbishop of St. Andrews and a papal legate in Scotland, and Marie de Guise, the queen mother, nullified the marriage contract. Though close to death, Henry VIII refused to accept this setback and launched a war against Scotland—a war that was continued after his death in King Edward's name by Protector Somerset. In 1547, the Scots were trounced at the Battle of Pinkie, where 5,000 men were killed and 1,500 captured. This loss further destabilized Scotland: the child-queen Mary was sent to France to be betrothed to the young future King Francis II, and the English occupied several large parts of the Lowlands and the border areas.

Eventually France came to the rescue and helped the Scots to drive out the English, but at a heavy price. By the time Mary was married to Francis II in 1558, at the age of sixteen, fears of French domination ran high among the nobility, many of whom were now deeply committed to Reformed Protestantism. In 1559 a Protestant firebrand named John Knox (1514–1572) led a religious revolt marked by violent iconoclasm, which effectively wiped out the Roman Catholic Church in Scotland and replaced it with a presbyterian Scottish kirk (church) based on Genevan models. The Protestant victory was secured by the nobles, not by Knox's preaching, but Knox's role in this momentous change was undeniably essential. Knox himself not only led the Protestant cause, but also embodied it, through his personal history and his efforts. Even though some revisionist historians have tried to minimize his significance, his name is likely to remain as inseparable from the Protestant Reformation in the British Isles as Luther's is from Germany, or Calvin's from France.

Little is known about John Knox's family or his early years, except that he hailed from a rural environment and that his father and both of his grandfathers had fought against the armies of Henry VIII. Knox was ordained as a Roman Catholic priest around 1535–1540, probably after studying at the University of St. Andrews and being taught by John Major, a notable theologian who also taught John Calvin at Paris. Though he was unable to find an appointment at first, Knox eventually did serve as a parish priest, before converting to Protestantism. Knox's exposure to Protestantism is a perfect example of the links that bound England to Scotland, for it was a former Cambridge tutor and close associate of Hugh Latimer who was exactly his age, George Wishart (1513–1546), who influenced Knox the most. Wishart was well versed in Lutheran and Reformed Protestant theology, having spent time in Germany and Switzerland. He fled to Scotland

𝕰 𝖛𝖎.   𝕱 𝖎𝖏

𝕹𝖔 𝕼𝖚𝖊𝖊𝖓𝖊 𝖎𝖓 𝖍𝖊𝖗 𝖐𝖎𝖓𝖌𝖉𝖔𝖒𝖊 𝖈𝖆𝖓 𝖔𝖗 𝖔𝖚𝖌𝖍𝖙 𝖙𝖔 𝖘𝖞𝖙 𝖋𝖆𝖘𝖙
𝕴𝖋 𝕶𝖓𝖔𝖐𝖊𝖘 𝖔𝖗 𝕲𝖔𝖔𝖉𝖒𝖆𝖓𝖘 𝖇𝖔𝖔𝖐𝖊𝖘 𝖇𝖑𝖔𝖜𝖊 𝖆𝖓𝖞 𝖙𝖗𝖚𝖊 𝖇𝖑𝖆𝖘𝖙.

Reform as revolution. John Knox spearheaded the forced conversion of Scotland into a Reformed Protestant state, despite the fact that its monarch, Queen Mary, remained steadfastly Catholic. He also promoted the revolutionary teaching that it is the duty of all true Christians to rebel against idolatrous rulers. This woodcut depicts Knox and his English Puritan colleague Christopher Goodman—who also argued for the legitimacy of resistance against "idolatrous" rulers—challenging their respective monarchs. The trumpets refer to Knox's misogynist and revolutionary 1558 treatise "The First Blast of the Trumpet Against the Monstrous Regiment of Women," in which he argued that it was unnatural for women to rule over men.

after being accused of heresy in England, and he embarked on a preaching campaign, fairly unhindered by Catholic authorities. Wishart passed on to Knox and others the full iconoclastic fervor of the Swiss before being betrayed by the Earl of Bothwell and executed by Cardinal Archbishop Beaton in 1546.

Wishart's martyrdom sparked an abortive Protestant revolt at St. Andrews, which began with the murder of Cardinal Beaton and culminated with the takeover of the city's castle. Drawn into this rebellion, Knox rapidly assumed a leadership position, which convinced him he had a divinely appointed role. When French forces stormed the castle and captured the Protestant rebels, Knox was sentenced to serve as a galley slave in the French navy—a punishment that was almost a guaranteed death sentence for any normal man. But Knox was far from average. He not only survived for nineteen months, but after being freed as part of a prisoner exchange between England and France, he returned to the fray angrier than ever about the Church of Rome, absolutely incandescent, ready to turn his world upside down, and employing the adjectives *bloody, beastly, rotten,* and *stinking,* so often in his diatribes against Catholicism that he made them seem essential theological terms.

Since he could not go home to Scotland, Knox went to work in England, where the reforms being implemented in King Edward's name enabled him to spread the Protestant message. Licensed as a preacher by the Church of England, Knox barreled through the north of the kingdom, propagating Edward's Reformation in the strictest Reformed Protestant terms, inveighing against the smallest concessions to "idolatry," such as kneeling at communion. When the bishopric of Rochester was offered to him, Knox turned it down, and pressed on with his zealous wandering ministry until the accession of Mary Tudor drove him into exile in 1553.

Knox the refugee stayed very active, serving first as minister to English refugees at Frankfurt am Main in Germany, and then as pastor to the English exiles in Calvin's Geneva, a city state that captured his heart and mind totally, as the paradigm for all godly reformations. While in exile, Knox began to formulate and espouse a radical political theology that not only defended the right of Protestants to rebel against Catholic rulers, but turned rebellion into a divine command. Knox posed four rhetorical questions to John Calvin. The first asked whether it was necessary to obey a child-monarch (such as Mary Queen of Scots); the second, whether "divine law" allowed women to govern at all; the third and fourth rose in a revolutionary crescendo, asking: "whether it was necessary to obey a magistrate who enforces idolatry and condemns the true religion?" and "to which party ought godly men to adhere if devout men of position resist an idolatrous king by war?"[19] Calvin could not tacitly approve of the arguments that Knox had dressed up as questions—lest he provide the French crown with yet another reason to persecute the Huguenots as subversives—but he nonetheless encouraged him to seek approval from other leading lights of the Reformed cause, knowing they would cautiously support him. Heinrich Bullinger at Zurich, nodded in assent, along with Pierre Viret in Lausanne, who encouraged Knox to be even bolder. In 1558, much to Calvin's chagrin, Knox published at Geneva a controversial treatise, *The First Blast of the Trumpet Against the Monstrous Regiment of Women,* which was at once incendiary and misogynist, in which he argued that "it is more than a monster in nature that a woman shall reign and have empire over man, " and that

> to promote a woman to bear rule, superiority, dominion, or empire above any realm,
> nation, or city is repugnant to nature, contumely to God, and a thing most contrarious

against His revealed will and approved ordinance, and finally it is the subversion of all good order, of all equity and justice.[20]

Knox's *First Blast* was an extension of his resistance theory. Given that Knox's own turf was controlled by a trio of idolatrous women—Mary Stuart (titular queen of Scotland), Marie de Guise (mother of Mary, Queen of Scots, and regent of Scotland), and Mary Tudor in England—*Blast* aimed to undermine their authority by arguing that it was unnatural and against divine law for women to rule over men, and perfectly alright for men to rebel against them. Immediately upon publication, Knox would be caught in a bind as Mary Tudor was replaced by Elizabeth, a woman bent on fostering Protestantism. Queen Elizabeth would forever hold Knox at arm's length because of *Blast*, but her disapproval of him would have little effect on events in Scotland.

Even more incendiary and influential were two other treatises published by Knox in 1558, his *Appellation to the Nobility, Estates, and Commonalty of Scotland* and his *Letter to the Commonalty*. Knox's argument in both of these treatises was fully revolutionary: "The sword of justice is God's, and if princes and rulers fail to use it, others may." At the heart of Knox's theory of resistance lay the claim that any ruler who supports false religion instantly becomes illegitimate, and that God not only allows the subjects of such rulers to rebel, but actually expects them to do so. Not to rebel against an idolatrous ruler, then, is a sin, punishable by God:

> Neither would I that you should esteem the reformation and care of religion less to appertain to you, because you are not kings, rulers, judges, nobles, nor in authority. . . . And if you think that you are innocent, because you are not the chief actors of . . . iniquity, you are utterly deceived; for God not only punishes the chief offenders, but with them he also condemns the consenters to such iniquity. . . . To speak this matter more plainly: As your princes and rulers are criminal, with your bishops, of all idolatry committed, and of all the innocent blood that is shed for the testimony of Christ's truth . . . so are you . . . because you assist and maintain your princes in their blind rage, and give no declaration that their tyranny displeases you.[21]

While Knox was in exile, clandestine Protestant congregations began to form back home, in Dundee, Edinburgh, Perth, St. Andrews, and Brechin. By 1557, their leaders felt ready to take action. In December of that year, a gathering of Scottish nobles that would come to be known as the "Lords of the Congregation" signed a solemn covenant, promising to oppose "the congregation of Satan," and to "set forward and establish the most blessed Word of God and His Congregation."[22] In many ways, this covenant put into practice Knox's idea of "the people assembled together in one body of a Commonwealth, unto whom God has given sufficient force, not only to resist, but also to suppress all kinds of open idolatry."[23]

Knox returned to Scotland in 1559, and launched a preaching campaign against the Catholic Church that led to rioting and attacks against altars, images, and monasteries. That was but the first step. The death of the regent Marie de Guise in June 1560 opened the way for the nobles and the parliament to press their cause and petition for the total abolition of Catholicism in Scotland and the confiscation of all church revenues. Accordingly, a thoroughly Calvinist *Confession of Faith Professed and Believed by the Protestants Within the Realm of Scotland*, more commonly known as *The Confession*, was submitted to the Scottish parliament and ratified in August 1560. Ignoring the crown altogether, parliament then abolished the Mass, papal authority, and all things Catholic, setting itself up as the ruling authority in Scotland, and establishing a new church. This new Reformed church would be run by elders elected annually by the congregations, and these elders were to oversee the morals of their communities. The congregations were to elect their ministers, but all ministers had to be examined and held to strict standards of conduct. Guidelines for the organization and financing of the new church would be summarized in a *Book of Discipline*. A *Book of Common Order* (known as *Knox's Liturgy*) would also be issued, which outlined all of the ritual for the Reformed Scottish Kirk (church). So, with young Queen Mary out of the way—she was in France, married to King Francis II—the Protestant lords replaced the Catholic Church with a church modeled along Genevan lines. And they also contemplated finding a suitable Protestant to replace Queen Mary as monarch.

Assuming that Mary was as good as gone was a mistake, however. In December 1560, as the Scottish Kirk was being transformed, Mary's husband, the sixteen-year-old Francis II, died suddenly from an infection. Bereft of a place in the French court, as well as of a husband, eighteen-year-old Mary returned to Scotland in August 1561 to face the lords who had usurped her place. A teenaged queen who had spent most of her life in France was no match for the lords or for John Knox, who continued to ignore her authority. But Mary did at least succeed in remaining Catholic, and in having the Mass celebrated in her chapel. Any way one looked at this situation, it seemed scandalous to have a monarch who did not share in the religion of her nation. Catholics were scandalized by the way in which their church had been dismantled and their queen tossed aside, through what amounted to a revolution. Protestants were scandalized by the presence of the idolatrous queen herself, and by the fact that her papist rituals polluted the whole land. John Knox, stymied by the laws that kept such an abomination in place, did all he could to make the queen uncomfortable, calling her a "slave of Satan," and reducing her to tears and whimpers in face-to-face encounters and shouting matches.

Other than having Knox tried for treason—only to see him acquitted—Mary did nothing to alter the Reformation set in motion by the Lords. Her lassitude earned her their grudging support, but did not change the fact that while she attended Mass in her chapel, many of her Catholic subjects were rounded up and punished for their commitment to "popery" and "idolatry." Ultimately, this anomaly imploded as a result of the queen's youth and inexperience, and the intrigues that swirled furiously around her. The fact that she was next in line for the English throne raised the stakes on all her choices, especially when it came to marriage. In 1565 Mary wed her younger cousin Henry Stuart, Lord Darnley (1545–1567), in a Catholic ceremony that greatly infuriated the Protestants. Darnley proved a poor choice. Given to fits of jealousy and anger, and to plotting against his real and perceived enemies, he ended up murdered in 1567. But Darnley left behind both a widow and an infant son, James (1566–1625), who would eventually rule as James VI of Scotland and James I of England.

Giving birth to an heir made Mary's hold on the Scottish throne more tenuous than ever, especially because many Protestant lords were ready to unseat her. Now, with James at hand, the lords saw an opportunity: here was an heir to the throne who could possibly be turned away from the Church of Rome. Shortly after Darnley's murder, Mary married James Hepburn, fourth Earl of Bothwell, another troublesome choice. Bothwell was rumored not only to have had an adulterous relationship with the queen prior to Darnley's death, but also to have plotted with the queen to murder Darnley. Though this wedding was a Protestant ceremony, which Mary thought might please her opponents, it only served to infuriate them further, for it seemed an insincere gesture. Having had their fill of idolatrous and scandalous behavior, the Protestant Lords arrested Mary, forced her to abdicate, and immediately installed the infant James as king—Scotland's third child-monarch in a row. Though Knox pressed for Mary's execution, he never got the chance to see it. Mary escaped, fled to England, and begged for asylum from her cousin Queen Elizabeth. Unable to trust Mary, Elizabeth imprisoned her. And Elizabeth had good reason for being wary. Mary would attempt to escape several times, and engage in plots, and give rise to rumors of plots. In 1586, Mary became involved in a reckless plan to murder Queen Elizabeth, set herself up on the thrones of England and Scotland, and return both nations to the Catholic fold. Mary was tried, found guilty of treason, and beheaded in February 1587.

Back in Scotland, the young king James never saw his mother again. Reared as a Calvinist Protestant, under the close watch of Protestant lords, James would ensure the triumph of the Scottish Reformation begun in 1560. Although he formally assumed control of the government at the age of twelve, he continued to be subservient to his seniors for several more years. He, too, was buffeted by rivalries, and drawn into plots and intrigues. In 1582, he was pressed into joining a plot to reinstate his mother Mary, but only managed to get kidnaped by the Protestant Earl of Gowrie, who held him hostage. After escaping from Gowrie's hands, James did his best to free himself from all factions at court. He also set his sights on inheriting the English throne, and worked out an alliance with Queen Elizabeth that stayed in place even after Elizabeth executed his mother. James gradually mastered the art of governing on his own and playing off the Scottish nobles against one another. In 1584, he secured for the crown the headship of the Presbyterian church in Scotland, and the right to appoint all of its bishops.

The Scottish Kirk, like the Church of England, became a state church, serving the majority of the population, presbyterian in structure, but also episcopal—headed by the king, and run by both bishops and elders. As was the case in England, weaning the people away from traditional religion and ancient customs proved to be a messy challenge, as did the job of maintaining strict Calvinist discipline. Consistories *à la Genève* spread throughout Scotland, upholding godliness, admonishing, and rooting out sin, idolatry and superstition. Witchcraft, which was a crime punishable by death, was handled by secular courts.

The Scottish war on witchcraft was not a simple case of binary oppositions, such as high versus low culture, elite versus popular religion, protestant versus Catholic beliefs, or modern versus medieval world views. King James himself, head of the kirk, believed that spells had been cast against him and took an active interest in ferreting out and burning witches, even authoring an influential book on the subject in 1597, entitled *Daemonologie.* As only a royal author could, he also banned one of the books he disagreed with, which denied the existence of witches: Reginald Scot's *Discoverie of Witchcraft* (1584). Scotland would distinguish itself by carrying out one of the most violent witch hunts in all of history.

The ultimate traditionalists, the Catholics, did not slink away quietly, and the authorities had to contend with recusants among both the nobility and the populace. But as was the case in England, their numbers were whittled down considerably through constant persecution and harassment. Scotland produced its share of Catholic martyrs and refugees, as did England. It also had its own Catholic seminaries on the Continent, including one in Rome, founded in 1600, and others in France, Belgium, and Germany. The last few powerful Catholic lords fled Scotland in 1595, taking with them the remaining shreds of political power Catholics had in Scotland. But that was not the bitter end: missionaries continued to be trained overseas and sent back to keep the traditional religion alive.

King James' accession to the English throne in 1603 would have a profound impact on Scotland, and Scotland, in turn would cast a longer shadow on English affairs, especially in regards to religion. With a nominally Calvinist neighbor to the north now under the same crown, the puritan minority in England became bolder. Eventually, the conflict avoided by Elizabeth with her *via media* would descend upon England with a vengeance. And Scotland would have its role to play in that, as shall be seen in later chapters.

Conclusion

Bound to one another by geography and politics, though not necessarily by language or customs, or even by ethnicity, England, Wales, Ireland, and Scotland would grow ever closer in the seventeenth and eighteenth centuries, eventually becoming the patchwork entity known as the United Kingdom of Great Britain in 1707.

By then, their shared history was already greatly shaped by religion, both positively and negatively. By then, also, their Reformations had already crossed the Atlantic

Ocean pell-mell and implanted themselves in a string of settlements along the eastern seaboard of North America. And these outposts would grow and expand, way beyond the expectations of the original settlers. So would the complexity of their approaches to the Reformations of the sixteenth century. Eventually, these colonies would come up with their own distinctive approaches to the complex heritage bequeathed to them by the migrants from four realms with an untidy welter of traditions, all of which paradoxically proclaimed that *a* Reformation had taken place, but there were many Reformations all at once, only one of which could be the "true" one.

One of these colonies, Maryland, was settled by English Catholics. These recusants were no different from the Protestant settlers to their north and south in one respect: they thought that the Reformation being carried out by their church was the only True one.

And it is to that Reformation that we must now turn our attention.

ARFAE ET PALATII PONTIFICII VATICANI TOPOGRAPHIA · PONTIFICISQVE POPVLVM SOLEMNI RITV BENEDICENTIS IMAGO
ACCVRATISSIME DELINEATA

Slow progress. This anonymous engraving from 1567 shows the drum of the new
St. Peter's hulking behind the older structures that had not yet been demolished, including the
steeple of the old basilica. At this time, the reforms of the Council of Trent were not yet being
implemented and much of the life of the Catholic Church reflected the hodge-podge of old and
new that is visible in this image.

PART THREE

Catholics

Prelude: Rome, 1564

A s the Council of Trent draws to a close in the northernmost reaches of Italy and its delegates return to their dioceses, some of them eager to put the council's reforming decrees into effect, the four new pillars behind the ancient Basilica of St. Peter in Rome finally have something to support. But it is not a dome. Not yet. The multitalented Michelangelo Buonarroti has completed the drum, that is, the tall base on which his magnificent dome will rest eventually. The base of the drum is nearly thirteen feet high and thirty feet thick. The drum itself is fifty feet high—a ring of stone and Corinthian columns punctuated by sixteen windows that will flood the main altar with light from above. But Michelangelo has just died, three weeks shy of his eighty-ninth birthday, and this drum is his final achievement.

More than half a century has passed since Pope Julius II laid the first stone for the new St. Peter's. While its construction has progressed in fits and starts, the world and the Catholic Church have been irrevocably changed by the Protestant Reformation. The Council of Trent, which began meeting in 1545, two years before Michelangelo replaced Donato Bramante as chief architect of St. Peter's, has laid out a comprehensive reform plan that defends everything rejected by the Protestants and, at the same time, calls for major improvements within the Catholic Church. Much like the old and partially demolished St. Peter's, which still squats awkwardly beneath the towering unfinished structure of the new St. Peter's, the Catholic Church is in a state of transition. In 1564 everyone involved in the reform of the Catholic Church and in the building of St. Peter's is painfully aware of the magnitude of the obstacles they face, and of how much time it will take to overcome them.

In 1564 no one can foresee that Michelangelo's dome—redesigned by Giacomo della Porta—will not be completed until May 1590, or that the last surviving remains of the ancient St. Peter's will not be totally razed until 1608. And in 1608, as a yet-unfinished new St. Peter's awaits a facade and further embellishments, the Catholic Church will be contending with challenges far greater than those of the Protestant Reformation.

CHAPTER FOURTEEN

Catholic Reform

Facing the Challenge

The Challenge of Reform

Protestant reformers were not alone in risking their lives for change. Catholics, too, faced danger whenever they challenged the status quo. The Catholic Church was a very ancient institution, deeply set in its ways and controlled by a privileged class. To be a Catholic reformer, one needed large doses of every virtue, especially those of courage, temperance, humility, and patience. It also helped to have faith, hope, and charity, along with thick skin and nerves of steel. To reform was to stir up trouble, or invite violent opposition.

Three examples make this situation very clear.

First, consider the reforming archbishop of Milan, St. Carlo (Charles) Borromeo, whose clergy resisted him at nearly every turn. On the night of 26 October 1569, during the liturgy of evening prayer, as he was kneeling at the altar, the bishop was shot in the back by a disgruntled priest from his diocese, Gerolamo Donato, better known as "Il Farina," a member of the order of the Humiliati. Farina had not counted on a miracle, however: the bullet hit its mark, all right, but it could not penetrate all the way through the bishop's thick vestments, leaving him with only a superficial wound. The would-be assassin was executed for this crime (even though Borromeo forgave him and pleaded for clemency), but that did not make the bishop's reforming task any easier. Nor did it cancel out the fact that Borromeo could have died on the spot, or that there were many in his diocese who sided with Farina. As a matter of fact, before he was shot in the back, Borromeo had already escaped another shooting a few months earlier, when he was nearly killed by the canons of the collegiate church of La Scala and a mob of their supporters.[1]

Second, take another bishop: Francesch Robuster y Sala had to flee from his diocese of Vic, in Catalonia, after three shots were fired at him from the city walls in 1609—according to a contemporary account, "as a result of the troubles in that city between the said bishop and his canons." Apparently, most of the clergy supported the

Exemplary leadership. When the archbishop of Milan Carlo Borromeo attempted to reform his diocese in the 1560s and 1570s, he encountered so much opposition from those with entrenched interests that two attempts were made to assassinate him. But Borromeo eventually prevailed, turning his diocese into a model of reform while also ministering to his flock personally. This engraving of Borromeo visiting plague victims celebrates his fearlessness as well as his sanctity and his role as an emblematic Tridentine bishop.

bishop, but the city government supported the canons, who were the bishop's clerics in his own cathedral, and who normally hailed from the wealthiest and most powerful families. The resulting power struggle was as intense and as potentially violent as any civil dispute. An observer had this to say: "Because of this conflict they put armed guards in the bishop's house, and his palace is closed and there are over a hundred armed men guarding it. An interdict has been placed on the city and masses are not said. All the priests and canons go armed with two or three pistols."[2] Even if we keep in mind that those pistols could fire only one shot, the image of clerics loaded down with multiple firearms, ready to kill one another, seems to contradict all notions of religious "reform."

Third, ponder the fate of the mystic St. John of the Cross (Juan de la Cruz), one the best-known saints of the sixteenth century; his story proves that bishops were not the only reformers subjected to violence. John, a Carmelite monk who wrote love poems to God, was imprisoned in late 1577 by his superiors in Toledo for interpreting his order's rule rigorously. For nine months, John endured beatings and floggings, with hardly anything to eat or drink, while enclosed in a dark, cramped cell, six feet wide by ten feet long, with a tiny window, high up in the wall. Had he not escaped in August 1578, in the dark of night, he might not have survived. And this was only the beginning of his struggles with those who ran the Carmelite order. For the remainder of his life,

St. John was hounded, punished, and humiliated by superiors who did not want to accept his reform plan, which was not only backed by the pope but also based on that of another great mystic and reformer, St. Teresa of Ávila, the founder of the Discalced Carmelites.

And these are only three of hundreds of similar stories that could be told of reformers who met violent resistance. "Some reformation," one might be tempted to say.

In chapter 6 we examined the reforming work that took place just before the outbreak of the Protestant Reformation. These reforms were at once a continuation of late medieval movements and instances of a new spirit of change, based on the ideals of the Renaissance. It is enormously difficult to pin down the exact date that separates these earlier attempts at reform, which were not undertaken as a response to Protestantism, from those that were fully conscious of the Protestant challenge after 1517. Where to draw the line depends on place, circumstances, and people involved. But just as there is a seamlessness to the continuity of reform within the Catholic Church, so is there also a noticeable difference in its tone and vigor after the emergence of Protestantism. Polarization always sets in motion a certain dialectic between opposing sides, as they sharpen their identities in contradistinction to one another. In other words, each side seeks to be *unlike* the other. Protestantism, then, did as much to define early modern Catholicism as did the ancient principles and traditions of the Catholic Church. To see this response to the Protestants as a Counter-Reformation, therefore, is not entirely wrong, for the changes wrought in the Catholic Church after the initial success of Protestantism could not help but be informed by the existence of a "false" sort of Christianity that was a very real threat to its hegemony nearly everywhere. Simply by surviving and thriving, Lutherans and Zwinglians and Calvinists and Anabaptists changed everything for Catholics, as they did for one another. And Catholics responded to the challenge, fully conscious of the differences that separated them from these "heretics."

When dealing with Catholic reform, one must take into account that it was a very long process, much more complex and gradual than it can seem when viewed from our perspective, across the span of several centuries. Much like St. Peter's, which has an architectural integrity that belies the fact that it had many different designers and was built piecemeal over a long stretch of time, the Catholic Reformation can easily fool the untrained eye.

Nonetheless, the progress of reform among Catholics can be measured somewhat objectively, even if imprecisely, and it can also be divided into five phases, keeping in mind that all chronological boundaries are permeable and that there were plenty of local variations to the broader developments:

1. From 1378 to 1517, when the challenges tended to be purely internal and heresies were locally contained
2. Between 1517 and 1545, from the rise of Luther to the opening of the Council of Trent, when Catholic responses to a seemingly unstoppable Protestantism were often uncoordinated

3. During the Council of Trent (1545–1563), when Catholic reformers hit their stride and the leaders of the church were forced to devise coherent plans for genuine reform.

4. Between 1563 and 1618, when the reforms of Trent began to be implemented and Catholics started to win back some territories that had become Protestant

5. From 1618 to 1700, when Catholic Baroque culture reached its apogee, and when the proliferation of religious wars, and the rise of skepticism and empirical science all began to erode the church's authority with ever-increasing intensity

In this chapter, we shall deal mostly with the second, third, and fourth phases, with occasional references to the years before 1517 and after 1618.

Though the reforms carried out by Catholics were so numerous and diverse and so intertwined—and sometimes also so slow and imperceptible—as to defy cataloging, they can be sorted out into different areas, each of which pertains to a specific aspect of renewal and change. In this chapter we cover each of these areas one by one, tracing their development from 1517 to the early seventeenth century. And there is no better place to begin than at the flash point of conflict itself: the initial Catholic response to the Protestant challenge.

Reacting to Protestantism: Polemics and Colloquies

The rise of Protestantism caught the Catholic Church by surprise. This is not to say that Catholics lacked resolve or eloquent advocates, but rather that the Catholic leadership as a whole failed to understand the nature and extent of this new "heretical" threat, and therefore also failed to react quickly and effectively.

From the very start, in 1517, when Leo X dismissed Luther's run-in with Johann Tetzel as a "monkish squabble" between a Dominican and an Augustinian, the response from the very top was torpid. By the time Leo got around to excommunicating Luther in 1519, it was too late: Luther had already secured the political support that would enable him to survive and thrive. And at the Diet of Worms in 1521, the imperial battle against the new heretics was already lost before it began: with Elector Frederick the Wise and other princes on his side, Luther could thumb his nose at the young emperor Charles V and get away with it.

No matter how loudly or how eloquently they condemned him, those who opposed Luther on paper or face-to-face were unable to stop him. Cardinal Tomasso de Vio, better known as Cajetan (1469–1534), was the first to grapple with Luther, at the Diet of Augsburg in October 1518, and the first to denounce him with authority. But Cajetan could do nothing to stop the firestorm that was already sweeping through parts of Germany. The eminent cardinal would never give up the fight, but all his attempts were aimed high, at the theological stratosphere rather than the man or woman on the street. Cajetan would compose detailed Latin refutations of Lutheran theology concerning the primacy of the pope (1521), the real presence of Christ in the Eucharist (1525), the sacrificial dimension of the Mass (1531), and the cooperation between the human will and grace (1535), but these learned treatises could not diminish Luther's popularity. Ironically, Cajetan seemed to have a grip on what made Luther popular, and he displayed a flexibility that later polemicists would lack, but at the very same time, he also demonstrated a cluelessness about what it would take to resolve the religious crisis caused by Luther. In 1530, for instance, he suggested to Pope Clement VII that the Lutherans could be brought back into the Catholic fold with merely two concessions: clerical marriage and allowing the laity to receive both the bread and the wine in communion.

Others immediately joined Cajetan on the battlefield, but they, too, kept their aim too high: Johann Eck (1486–1543), Hieronymus Emser (1478–1527), Johann Cochlaeus (1479–1552), and Jacobus Latomus (1475–1544) all locked horns with Luther in print. And as other leaders emerged in the Protestant camp, these Catholic polemicists took them on too. But Luther and his brethren would ridicule their Catholic opponents with impunity, a result of the protection they received from secular authorities, and of their access to printers and publishers. Moreover, when Catholics entered the fray at the personal level, as Cochlaeus did when he wrote a biography of Luther, their focus tended to be on the theological errors of the Protestants they opposed rather than on issues more accessible to the laity. In other words, Catholic apologists sought to undercut the integrity of Protestantism at a high intellectual level, by pointing to its most apparent fundamental flaws: novelty, inconsistency, and plurality. If the leading Protestants contradicted themselves and disagreed with one another, argued the Catholic apologists, how could they possibly lay claim to the truth? And how could these newcomers dismiss centuries of tradition as error? The very novelty of their message proved them to be wrong. Even nontheologians such as King Henry VIII of England and Erasmus of Rotterdam would take the same approach: King Henry would challenge Luther on the issue of the seven sacraments (1521), and Erasmus on the freedom of the will (1525). Henry VIII summed up the gist of the Catholic attack succinctly:

> I am so far from holding any further dispute with him that I almost repent myself of what I have already argued against him. For what avails it to dispute against one who disagrees with everyone, even with himself? Who affirms in one place what he denies in another, denying what he presently affirms? Who, if you object faith, combats by reason; if you touch him with reason, pretends faith? If you allege philosophers, he flies to Scripture; if you propound Scripture, he trifles with sophistry. Who is ashamed of nothing, fears none, and thinks himself under no law. Who contemns the ancient Doctors of the church, and derides the new ones in the highest degree; loads with reproaches the Chief Bishop of the church. Finally, he so undervalues customs, doctrine, manners, laws, decrees and faith of the church (yea, the whole church itself) that he almost denies there is any such thing as a church, except perhaps such a one as himself makes up of two or three heretics, of whom himself is chief.[3]

Turning the tables on Lutherans.
Very few Catholic polemicists employed humor or satire against Luther and his followers, preferring instead to take the high road and to address learned clerics rather than the laity. One of the exceptions was the Franciscan friar Thomas Murner, whose "Great Lutheran Fool" poked fun at Luther and his teachings. The title page of this satire depicts Luther as a fat jester who is having his foolishness extracted out of his mouth by a cat in a Franciscan habit. The cat is none other than Murner himself, who had earlier been dubbed a "meowing fool" by Luther.

Scoring points in a theological debate was not enough, however—not even for a king. The success of Protestantism can be attributed in large measure to its popular appeal, and to the pamphlets and sermons that spread the Protestant message in the vernacular, employing humor, satire, and illustrations. On the whole, early Catholic apologists failed to engage at that level. An exception was Thomas Murner, a Franciscan friar. In 1522, Murner composed the satire in rhyme titled *The Great Lutheran Fool*, which also contained humorous woodcuts. This was no theological treatise, but a sarcastic exposé of Luther's worst shortcomings, and it gave Protestants a taste of their own strong medicine. But even this exception failed to hit its target, for its circulation appears to have been very low in comparison with Lutheran texts.

Convinced of the leading role of the clergy, Catholic polemicists tended to write for a theologically sophisticated audience. Even a book as useful as Johann Eck's *Arguments Against Luther and Other Enemies of the Church* (1525), which had gone through forty-five editions by 1576, focused on arguments that only the learned could fully grasp. Whether it was through exegetical rebuttals of Protestant views, such as Peter Canisius's *Commentaries on the Corruption of the Word* (1585), or accounts such as Pedro de Ribadeneyra's *History of the Schism of the Church of England* (1588–1594), Catholic authors struggled to gain the upper hand with heavy tomes not intended for the laity, many of which were in Latin. Among these, some of the most important were Robert Stapleton's *Principiorum fidei doctrinalium demonstratio* (1579), Roberto Bellarmino's *Disputationes de controversiis Christianae fidei* (1581–1592), and Martin Becan's *Manuale controversarium* (1623) and *De ecclesia Christi* (1633).

This is not to say that the defenders of Catholicism ignored the laity altogether. Some grappled with heresy at the street level, so to speak, as did Jacopo Sadoleto, bishop of Carpentras, and St. Francis de Sales, titular bishop of Geneva. In 1539 Sadoleto wrote a letter to his neighbors in Geneva, which had recently turned Protestant, in which he pointed out the error of their ways. But the results were not exactly what Sadoleto had hoped for. The magistrates of Geneva read the letter carefully and passed it on to John Calvin, who wrote a blistering point-by-point response, which was then published in pamphlet form, along with Sadoleto's letter. Confident of the superiority of Calvin's arguments, then, the Protestants used Sadoleto's letter to "prove" him wrong and make him look like a fool. Much more successful was the approach taken about fifty years later by St. Francis de Sales, who took to writing leaflets against Protestant teachings

Demonizing the enemy. Lutherans repeatedly associated the papacy and the Roman Catholic Church with the devil. Catholics did exactly the same with Luther, but not as frequently. In this woodcut from a 1535 pamphlet, Luther is making a pact with the devil with his right hand while his left rests on a Bible and a demon whispers in his ear.

that were widely distributed in the area around Geneva, sometimes inserted into copies of his sermons or slipped under doors or posted on walls in public places. These tracts, combined with Francis de Sales's sermons and his untiring pastoral visits, were credited with converting around seventy-two thousand Protestants back to the Catholic faith in the Chablais region, south of Geneva. Whether that figure is accurate is immaterial: the point is that Francis de Sales did manage to find a receptive audience. Fifty years after his death, these vernacular tracts were collected and published as a single volume, *Controversies* (1672). By that time, Catholic polemical texts numbered in the thousands, from slim pamphlets to weighty tomes.

Naturally, Catholic polemics against Protestantism also made their way into the pulpit, and it was through that medium, more than through print, that the Catholic clergy carried out the fight against Protestantism. Preaching had been an essential component of earlier heresies: the Cathars, Waldensians, Lollards, and Hussites. The Catholic Church had learned an important lesson and had reinvigorated its own preaching mission in response. But now with the Protestants, the stakes had been raised, for the effect of preaching was expanded by means of the printing press, which could multiply any sermon by the hundreds or thousands, and distribute it far afield. Catholics caught on quickly in this arena. Sermons denouncing Protestantism rang out with frequency, not just in Germany, but nearly everywhere in the Catholic world. Catholic preaching styles also tended to change in the face of Protestant competition, becoming less structured and more focused on key theological issues and biblical exegesis. A parallel change also took place in the printing of sermons, which not only increased, but also employed vernacular languages with increasing frequency.

Another venue for polemics was the public, face-to-face debate. The first and perhaps best known of these disputations is the one held at Leipzig in 1519, at which Johann Eck confronted Martin Luther and Andreas Bodenstein von Karlstadt. Debates of this nature had a lot more riding on them than a rhetorical victory. At Leipzig, for instance, the outcome was Luther's excommunication, for Eck forced him to declare his heterodoxy in no uncertain terms. In cities throughout Germany and Switzerland debates often had a wider impact, for they were repeatedly used to legally define which was the "correct" side that the entire community should embrace. In Switzerland, especially, this type of debate became essential for the progress of Protestantism. The pattern was usually the same: Catholic and Protestant clergy would discuss points of doctrine in public, and the magistrates would then declare the winner. More often than not, Protestants would win, not only because they set the agenda for discussion in terms of *sola scriptura*, closing off all arguments from Catholic tradition, but also because of their high numbers in the city councils that decided who had won the contest. Zurich became Protestant after a series of such debates, in 1524–1525. The same would be the case at Bern in 1528, Geneva in 1534–1535, and Lausanne in 1536. Catholics usually knew that the deck was stacked against them, but some participated in the charade anyway. At Geneva, two Catholic priests took part in a carefully rigged "disputation" that allowed only discussion of the following Protestant propositions:

> Justification is solely from Jesus Christ.
> The Bible is the sole foundation of the Church.
> All worship and adoration should be directed solely to God.
> Jesus Christ is the sole mediator between humans and God.
> The veneration of saints and their images is wrong.
> The Mass does not aid in salvation at all.[4]

At Lausanne, the city council ordered all Catholic clergy to attend the disputation, but only about half of them showed up, and none took part at all, having been ordered by their bishop to remain silent, in protest. But not all Catholic clergy found these debates futile, and not all of them were judged by Protestant-leaning panels. At Baden, Switzerland, in 1526, Johann Eck debated Johann Oecolampadius and was declared the winner.

Confrontation and polemics were not the only road taken. From the very start, there were many on both sides who hoped for a reconciliation and the restoration of Christian unity. Some, including Emperor Charles V, hoped that a general council could accomplish this. But calling a council proved very difficult, for various reasons, chiefly political ones in nature. In the meantime, as the years passed and the divisions between Christians became sharper and more numerous, secular and church authorities negotiated for special conferences, or colloquies, at which representatives of the rival churches could meet and iron out their differences. It was a lofty goal, which in retrospect seems unrealistic, but at that time the prospect of dialogue and reunion had not yet been abandoned. The delegates who attended these colloquies always hoped for some concessions by the other side, but experience proved that no one was willing to concede on what they considered essential points of doctrine and on practical matters. Through failure after failure, these colloquies demonstrated how important theology could be, for the theologians ran the show and could not be forced into agreeing by the princes and magistrates who sponsored these meetings.

The first major attempt at reconciliation took place at Augsburg in 1530. In attendance were a number of German princes, including Luther's patron, Elector John Frederick of Saxony, and teams of theologians. On the Catholic side, the major players were Johann Eck and Johann Cochlaeus; on the Protestant side, Philip Melanchthon and Johannes Brenz. Among the topics that raised the most intense disagreement, as one might expect, were those of justification, the sacraments, and papal supremacy. But practical questions also became sticking points: Should priests be allowed to marry? Should the wine be offered to the laity at communion? What sort of compensation, if any, should be paid for monastic property that had been confiscated? The theologians worked hard, sorting out the trivial from the substantial, hammering out agreements on some points, such as the precise meaning of the term *communion of saints*. No number of concessions to fine distinctions could close the gap between both parties at this colloquy, however, or at any other. Augsburg established a paradigm: some points were nonnegotiable. So, as much as everyone longed for union, it proved impossible. All subsequent attempts to come to an agreement would fail too: Hagenau in 1540, Worms in 1540–1541, Regensburg in 1541, and again in 1546, Worms in 1557, Poissy in 1561, and St. Germain in 1562. What is most surprising about all of these colloquies is the fact that so many were held, despite the obvious record of failure, all with genuine interest in reconciliation and unity, and that it took more than thirty years for Catholics and Protestants to finally admit that compromise and union were impossible. If Protestants could not achieve unity among themselves through their own intra-Protestant colloquies—such as Marburg in 1529, Maulbron in 1564, and Montbeliard in 1586—it should have been most reasonable to assume that all attempts at agreeing with Catholics would fail too. Pursuing an unrealistic goal was quixotic, at best, but at least the colloquies reveal the existence of something that did not surface very often in the sixteenth century: a willingness to discuss religious differences somewhat amicably.

The Council of Trent, 1545–1563

Although the Council of Trent began inauspiciously enough, fraught with uncertainty about its role and with fewer than thirty bishops in attendance, it would turn out to be one of the most significant moments in all of Catholic history. This council, convoked in December 1545 by Pope Paul III in the city of Trent, in the Italian Alps, met in twenty-five sessions over three separate periods over the span of eighteen years (1545–1547, 1551–1552, and 1559–1563), with long gaps in between that caused many to despair of ever seeing it conclude its business. Yet this council reformed the church from top to bottom, setting the course Catholicism would follow for the following four centuries.

The date and location chosen for the council were both odd, and need some explanation. First, why did it take so long to assemble a council? After all, calls for such a gathering went out around 1519, as soon as the seriousness of Luther's challenge became obvious, and never stopped, as the threat posed by Protestantism increased. Among those who never tired of calling for a council was the emperor himself, Charles V, arguably the most powerful ruler in Europe. Yet all such calls proved futile for more than twenty-five years, given politics and inertia. Even the selection of a location was politically charged: Germans tended to object to an Italian council, whereas the popes and the Roman Curia resisted any effort to hold the council far from Rome. Fitting the preferences of the Protestants into the picture made the question of location an even touchier issue.

Politics aside, much of the delay can be blamed directly on the popes and cardinals who objected not only to a non-Italian location, but also to the very idea of a council. Fearful of a resurgence of Constance-style conciliarism, two popes blocked all efforts at holding a council: Leo X (1513–1521) and Clement VII (1523–1534). Pope Clement VII's successor, Paul III, stalled as much as possible, but he was finally pressured into convoking a council during his ninth year in office, by which time the religious division of Western Christendom was irreversible. But why assemble in the Alps rather than in Rome? The highly unlikely location of Trent was chosen as a compromise between Rome and Germany, because it was technically within the boundaries of the Holy Roman Empire but still Italian speaking. In other words, it was far enough from Rome to please the Germans, and close enough to the Papal States to please the pope.

The council's agenda was overwhelming, and the expectations placed on it immense. Those who gathered at Trent were assigned three intertwined objectives. First, they needed to solve the Protestant "problem." Second, the council needed to clarify several points of doctrine and ritual, especially in response to the challenges that Protestants had mounted. Some of those who gathered at the council saw this clarification as its principal task. Others, however, thought the council should focus on its third objective: the herculean task of eliminating the corruption and abuses that had fueled Protestant dissent.

The first objective, that of bringing Protestants back into the fold, was doomed from the start. By 1545 it had become clear that no amount of dialogue would make Protestants relinquish their independence and return to the Catholic Church. At the opening of the council there were some who still harbored hopes for such a reconciliation, but as the years dragged on, this objective was abandoned altogether. The final nail in the coffin was driven in by the Protestants themselves. Invited to attend the second phase of the council in 1551—with high hopes on the part of a few on both sides—Protestant delegates immediately made demands that the council found unacceptable. In addition to demanding a larger role than the council was willing to grant them, the Protestants also insisted a priori on a reaffirmation of *Haec sancta*, the decree from Constance that subjected the papacy to the superior authority of councils. Once this nonnegotiable demand that no pope could accept had been made, all hope of reconciliation was lost.

The other two objectives, institutional reform and theological clarification, were dealt with in tandem, after some wrangling over which should be given priority. This intertwining of objectives proved a wise decision, for it allowed the council to make steady progress on both fronts and never to neglect one in favor of the other. Such a decision also ensured continuity for a deliberative body with a membership that kept changing and meetings that stretched out over many years, with long recesses in between.

The first phase of the council lasted from December 1545 to March 1547, during which time much was accomplished, especially on the doctrinal front. The council turned at once to theology. First, the council issued two decrees on Holy Scripture, both of which were aimed squarely against Protestant claims. The first was a counterblast to the Protestant principle of *sola scriptura*: it affirmed the authority of the church to interpret scripture and the role of tradition in Christian life, and it firmly established the legitimacy of the so-called deuterocanonical Hebrew Old Testament texts that Protestants had excluded from their Bible, such as Tobit and Maccabees.[5] The second decree struck at the heart of Renaissance humanist claims, and especially against the *ad fontes* principle, by pronouncing the Latin Vulgate translation of the Bible to be error-free. The decrees that followed were equally dismissive of Protestant theology and firmly focused on the paradoxical nature of central Catholic doctrines, which tend to affirm the coincidence of opposites. Its decree on original sin, for instance, stressed both the corruption of human nature and its essential goodness. Its decree on justification affirmed salvation by both faith and works, thus rejecting the Protestant principle of *sola fide*:

> If anyone says that the sinner is justified by faith alone, meaning that nothing else is required to cooperate in order to obtain the grace of justification, and that it is not in any way necessary that he be prepared and disposed by the action of his own will, let him be anathema.
>
> If anyone says that men are justified without the justice of Christ, whereby He merited for us, or by that justice are formally just, let him be anathema.[6]

Concerning the troublesome doctrine of predestination, the council also affirmed a paradoxical *both-and* proposition, maintaining that the necessity of human effort did not essentially contradict the reality of predestination. And rather than explaining how this could be, the council merely affirmed the paradox, with a warning to those who might want to ponder the mystery too much, or take too much comfort in it. Taking a swipe at Calvinists, especially, for whom predestination was explicitly a central doctrine, and at Lutherans and Zwinglians, for whom confidence in predestination was implicit, the council said:

> No one, moreover, so long as he lives this mortal life, ought in regard to the sacred mystery of divine predestination, so far presume as to state with absolute certainty that he is among the number of the predestined, as if it were true that the one justified cannot sin any more, or, if he does sin, that he ought to promise himself an assured repentance. For except by special revelation, it cannot be known whom God has chosen to Himself.[7]

The final sessions of this phase of the council focused on the sacraments. And here, too, long-standing traditions were affirmed in such a way as to condemn Protestant teachings. First and foremost, the decree on the sacraments reiterated that there were seven sacraments, not just two, as Protestants believed. It also reconfirmed their objective efficacy *ex opera operato*; that is, the decree insisted that the sacraments were made effective by God himself, and that their power was never nullified if the priest or the recipient was in a state of sin.

The institutional reforms of the first phrase of the council were more modest, but it did manage to issue a decree that set new, stricter rules for the assignment of benefices, and also called for the residence of all bishops in their dioceses and of all clergy at their beneficed posts, thus closing the door, at least in principle, on the rampant pluralism and absenteeism that had plagued the church for centuries.

The second phase of the council lasted barely one year, from May 1551 to April 1552, and it did not accomplish very much on either the doctrinal or the institutional front. Its most important decree was on the Eucharist, and it reaffirmed everything that Protestants had rejected: transubstantiation, reservation and veneration of the consecrated host, withholding of the cup from the laity, and several other points that may seem trivial in our own day but were grave concerns in the sixteenth century, such as bringing the consecrated host out of the church to the sick and dying, and insisting that communicants go to confession first, so they could be totally free of mortal sin.

The third and final phase was delayed by nine years because the new pope elected in 1555, Paul IV (Gianpietro Carafa), steadfastly refused to reconvene the council. A reformer himself but austere and domineering, Paul IV preferred not to have his authority challenged by anyone, especially a council that might revive conciliarism (see chapter 3).

Voting for reform. The Council of Trent handled the most pressing issues facing the Catholic Church in a parliamentary fashion, depending on the work of committees and on the votes of those bishops who attended it. The reforms it set in motion in 1563 would shape and guide the Catholic year for the following four centuries. This 1588 fresco by Pasquale Cati da Iesi, a pupil of Michelangelo, was commissioned for the church of Santa Maria in Trastevere, Rome, by one of the German ecclesiastics who took part in the council, Cardinal Mark Sittich von Hohenems Altemps. At the upper left, the Holy Spirit hovers above the council in a hazy glowing nimbus. In the lower half, an allegorical scene depicts Holy Mother Church crowned with the papal tiara, vanquishing heresy, surrounded by the seven virtues and other feminine allegorical figures. A globe of the earth symbolizes the worldwide reach of the Catholic Church.

It was thus left to his successor, Pius IV (Giovanni Angelo Medici), elected in 1559, to reconvene the council in 1561. This phase was very different from the first two, and arguably the most productive and significant. Although according to the letter of the law Pius IV had only reconvened the council first convoked in 1545, this was a very different assembly, so much so that any inexpert observer might have mistaken it for a new council. Whereas the first phase had attracted fewer than thirty bishops, most of whom were Italian or Spanish, this final phase was attended by nearly two hundred bishops who represented many nations, including France, which had not yet played much of a role. As before, the Spanish presence was significant, not just because of the Spanish bishops in attendance, but also because of the Spanish theologians involved. All in all, a new generation was in charge during these final sessions, a generation reared and educated in a climate of reform and religious conflict, intent on renewing the Catholic Church.

On the doctrinal front, again the council reaffirmed beliefs rejected by the Protestants: the sacramental nature of marriage, the sacrificial dimension of the mass, the existence of purgatory, the value of indulgences, and the veneration of saints, images, and relics. One item, however, came close to tearing the council apart: the issue of episcopal authority. Did bishops derive their authority directly from God or from the pope? This question had been taken up before, but now that a final decision had to be made, fissures widened. The Spanish and the French pressed for direct divine authority, a view that lessened the pope's power and was therefore advantageous to the monarchs of these two nations. The pope and the curia naturally defended papal authority. The final formula was a masterful compromise that managed to defend both positions through vague language, but it still allowed the pope a great measure of control over the bishops.

On the reforming front, this third session issued some of its most important decrees, establishing strict procedures for the appointment of bishops and cardinals, demanding that all bishops make annual visitations of their dioceses (to monitor the behavior of the clergy and religious life of the laity), calling for regularly scheduled diocesan synods and provincial councils, and setting strict penalties for clergy who broke their vow of celibacy or lived as married men with common-law spouses whom the church considered "concubines." The council also called on all bishops to establish schools for the training of the clergy in their dioceses. Astounding as it may seem, the education of the lower clergy had not been regulated until this point. By demanding the creation of seminaries, the Council of Trent ensured that all subsequent generations would have priests who were well trained in theology and pastoral care. And the seminaries also became an important filter that helped ensure that those who were lacking in aptitude or virtue would not be ordained.

In addition to all of these reforms, the council also denied the clergy the right to marry, after substantial discussion of the touchy issue. The final decision was a deliberate rejection of Protestant beliefs concerning sex and self-denial. From the very start, one of the most distinctive traits of the Protestant Reformation—and some would say among the most appealing—was its affirmation of marriage as "natural" and its rejection of celibacy as "unnatural." As Protestants saw it, celibacy had no intrinsic merit not only because it was contrary to human nature, but also because acts of self-denial contributed nothing to one's salvation. Though some at the council favored an end to mandatory clerical celibacy, the majority chose to reaffirm the sexual ethic bequeathed to the Catholic Church by the monastic tradition. This decision was very much in keeping with the overall thrust of the council, which made a concerted effort to underscore the differences between Protestantism and certain Catholic traditions. The repudiation of the "other" is evident in the final decree on marriage: "If anyone says that the married state excels the state of virginity or celibacy, and that it is better and happier to be united in matrimony than to remain in virginity or celibacy, let him be anathema."[8]

To properly assess the Council of Trent, one must distinguish between its doctrinal decrees and those that called for institutional reform, although both would have an equally monumental impact on subsequent generations, all the way down to the twentieth century. When it came to doctrine, many of the council's decrees can be seen as a narrowing of theological options, a process that distinguishes the most important councils in the history of the church. As at Nicaea with the Arians, Ephesus with the Nestorians, Chalcedon with the Monophysites, and Second Nicaea with the iconoclasts, Trent was forced to clarify fine points and close off options that "heretics" had chosen to emphasize. The history of heresy, after all, is but the mirror image of the history of Christian doctrine. On two issues, Trent left the door partially open. The subject of papal authority did not trouble Catholics much until the nineteenth century, when the question of papal infallibility surfaced. The relationship between grace and the human will, by contrast, was a smoldering issue that blazed again within Catholicism in the seventeenth century, with the emergence of the movement known as Jansenism. In this respect, then, one might say that Trent left some significant loose ends dangling. In all other respects, however, Trent drew its doctrinal boundaries very clearly, leaving little room for reconciliation with Protestants.

When it came to practical reform, the impact of the Council of Trent was arguably more profound than that of any previous council in Christian history. Its guidelines for reforming the clergy were not only clear, but also very thorough. And the same can be said for its decrees on ritual, which would become the heart and soul of Catholic identity for the following four centuries.

Nonetheless, to issue decrees is one thing; to enforce them is quite another. The success of the Council of Trent has seemed a predetermined given to many historians, evidenced by the extended life of the adjective *Tridentine*, which many of them commonly applied for a long time to all things Catholic after 1563. But as the council adjourned, some participants might have even thought its failure inevitable, given the obstacles that had to be overcome. Success was not guaranteed. In fact, implementing the reforms demanded by the council depended on many variables, and chiefly on a supportive papacy, a willing episcopate, and cooperative secular authorities. The laity, too, had their role to play.

At the very top, Pope Pius IV ratified all of the council's pronouncements in early 1564, but not all secular rulers were as quick in their approval. In fact, the initial response was not at all encouraging. Among the few places that received the Tridentine decrees with little or no hesitation, Portugal, Venice, and the Catholic cantons of Switzerland stand out—all relatively small spots on the map. In the Holy Roman Empire, the emperor's representatives approved the council's decrees immediately, but the imperial diet never gave its assent, nor did the Hapsburg kingdom of Hungary. Eventually, most of the Catholic cities and principalities in Germany would approve Trent's decrees individually, but in some places only with reservations. In Poland, where many nobles were turning Calvinist, King Sigismund Augustus approved the decrees, but the parliament refused to go along, claiming that the Polish church had not been adequately represented. In France, where the bloodbath of the Wars of Religion had just begun, the situation seemed even more hopeless, for in the midst of utter chaos, the crown and the Estates-General would rebuke the decrees of Trent as opposed to the traditional privileges of the French church. As a result, the French bishops never accepted Trent's disciplinary canons, and they delayed acceptance of its doctrinal decrees until 1615. In Spain, the staunchest and most powerful defender of the Catholic cause, there were substantial misgivings about Trent, especially its affirmation of papal authority. Nonetheless, by 1565, with the crown's support, Spain became one of the first countries to hold synods in order to put Trent's reforms into effect. The reforming momentum was also passed on to Spain's dependencies in Europe, most notably in Italy and the Netherlands, and also to its colonies overseas, making the Tridentine reforms the first truly global initiative in human history.

Gradually, sometimes at a snail's pace, Trent had its desired effect. Its success was due in the long run not to the men who crafted its decrees, but to individuals who took it upon themselves to implement its practical reforms: popes, cardinals, bishops, abbots, monks, priests, nuns, and lay people who struggled to bring about change against entrenched interests, financial obstacles, suspicion of their motives, and hostility toward innovation. A great deal was also accomplished from the top down, from the head to members, precisely as Trent envisioned. Without the support of the church hierarchy and secular rulers, genuine reform would have been impossible. The reforms can be rightly considered the work of a large and ever more centralized institution, but ironically, and even paradoxically, the most effective and significant changes were often brought about at the local level through the efforts of specific individuals. It could be argued, then, that the reform in "head and limbs" was effected in large measure by the limbs themselves, thanks to a healthier head.

Tightening of Censorship and Vigilance

Having defined the contours of Catholic orthodoxy clearly at Trent, the church could turn its attention more intensely to identifying and censoring questionable individuals and texts. The twenty-fifth decree of the Council of Trent dealt with three issues and gave the pope total control of all three of them: the reform of ritual, the creation of a catechism, and the censorship of texts. In the minds of the council fathers, then, controlling heretical expression seemed to be of one piece with ritual reform and catechetical instruction. Such was the essence of the Catholic reform aimed at the laity as summed up in a single Tridentine decree: worship uniformly, instruct thoroughly, police intensely.

The practice of condemning specific texts as heretical was as old as the Christian religion itself, but the principle of canvassing printed texts and issuing a list of dangerous titles that should be off-limits to the faithful was first proposed by the Fifth Lateran Council in 1515, as the printing industry was beginning to change the flow of information. No one at Rome took up this task, however. The first lists of "dangerous" books were local: beginning with the Netherlands (1529), then Venice (1543) and Paris (1551). The Council of Trent reaffirmed the necessity of producing such a list in 1546, but it was not until 1559 that Pope Paul IV issued the first comprehensive *Index of Forbidden Books* (*Index librorum prohibitorum*). This long list, which came to be known as the Pauline Index, banned everything written by about 550 authors, along with a long list of individual titles and all translations of the Bible into the vernacular. Included on the list were all Protestants, naturally, and other likely suspects such as Erasmus of Rotterdam, Niccolò Machiavelli, Girolamo Savonarola, Peter Abelard, Marsilius of Padua, and Lorenzo Valla. In Spain, an even more stringent index was published by the inquisitor general Fernando de Valdés that included authors who had been well received in Catholic circles, such as Francisco de Osuna, Luis de Granada, Juan de Ávila, and Francis Borgia. To many of the devout, the censorship seemed excessive. At the Convent of the Incarnation in Ávila, none other than Teresa de Jesús—the future St. Teresa of Ávila—was forced to give up some of her favorite books. "Frightened people warned me that we were living in rough times," she dared to say in her autobiography.[9]

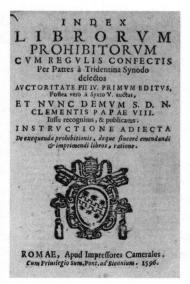

Sacred censorship. The title page of the 1596 *Index of Forbidden Books* prominently claims the Council of Trent and Pope Clement VII as the sources of its authority. The index clearly identified those texts that Catholics should not read, but enforcement of its prohibitions was difficult, especially outside of Spain and Italy, where substantial numbers of non-Catholics could be found.

The Council of Trent took up the issue of censorship in 1562 and created a commission to come up with a list of forbidden books, but the council closed before the work could be completed, so the task was left in the pope's hands. Having listened to many complaints about the harshness of the 1559 index and its blanket condemnations, Pope Pius IV supplanted it with a slightly laxer index in 1564, which allowed for expurgated versions of some authors and titles. Though the changes made were slight, overall, in some cases they made a large difference. When it came to Erasmus, for instance, only six titles were listed as forbidden, rather than all of his works. This new list—which came to be known as the Tridentine Index—also included rules for the reviewing of all texts before publication, the supervision of printers, and the enforcement of censorship. The Tridentine Index was updated in 1596 and revised numerous times afterward, to keep up with the ever-growing number of objectionable texts.

The index had two inseparable objectives: protecting the Catholic faithful from heresy and safeguarding unity within the church itself. It was as concerned with morals as with doctrine, because, as the censors saw it, theological error and moral failure not only were linked, but also led to damnation. Inclusion in the index did not guarantee the disappearance of any title but certainly hampered its circulation, for all books included in that list were ostensibly subject to confiscation and destruction. Suspicion of heresy was enough to land a title on the index, and the lists grew to include an odd assortment of works, not all of which were explicitly heretical. In those places where the Catholic Church was strong, such as Spain and Italy, the censorship was fairly efficient because civil authorities worked hand in hand with the ecclesiastical censors. In lands such as France, Germany, Hungary, and Poland, where substantial numbers of Protestants could be found, and where there was no Inquisition to police the presses and booksellers, the *Index of Forbidden Books* was much harder to enforce. Its list became a matter of conscience rather than law, for printers and distributors could find ways to ignore it.

Which brings us to the Inquisition, that essential agent of control in the Catholic Church. The Inquisition was an extremely complex institution, unevenly spread over the map, never fully centralized. In many ways, it is actually wrong to speak of *the* Inquisition, for it was not a single institution, but rather a scattered and asymmetrical assemblage of tribunals. It had come into existence in the thirteenth century, largely in response to the rise of the Albigensian heresy, and it had always operated at a local level, as a church-run court that depended on the cooperation of the civil powers. Wherever it was set up to deal with heresy, the Inquisition brought with it a merging of the local and universal, for while focused strictly on local affairs, its authority was derived directly from the pope, who appointed its judges and empowered them to carry out their work in his name. It mattered little that the pope was not directly involved, or even aware of specifics. His presence was represented by the inquisitors themselves, and by their judgments.

The largest, most active, and best-known tribunal of the Inquisition was that of Spain, which also extended to its colonies. On the eve of the Protestant Reformation, in November 1478, developments in Spain brought about the creation of a national

Inquisition, under the direction of the monarchs Ferdinand and Isabella. Revamped under papal direction in 1482, this national Inquisition became an instrument of both church and state, run by the Grand Inquisitor, who was appointed by the crown and confirmed by the pope, and who in turn appointed regional inquisitors who were independent of the diocesan church structure and had the power to process anyone, including the highest churchman. (Indeed, in 1559, the Inquisition denounced and imprisoned Bartolomé de Carranza, the archbishop of Toledo, whose case dragged on for seventeen years). As the Spanish crown extended its authority to many other lands over time, the geographical extent of its Inquisition also expanded, with mixed results. In the Netherlands, for instance, it was intensely resented and became a strong incentive for rebellion against Spanish rule; in the New World, despite many obstacles, it proved fairly efficient.

At first, the central aim of the Spanish Inquisition had been to deal with the tens of thousands of Jewish and Muslim converts who continued to practice their former religion in secret. Gradually, however, it expanded its scope, especially as the number of crypto-Jewish and crypto-Muslim cases declined over time. In the 1520s, as Protestantism was making inroads in northern Europe, the Spanish Inquisition turned its attention to Christian heresy, most notably to the so-called Illumined (*Alumbrados*), to Erasmians, and to the handful of Protestants who surfaced here and there. At the same time, it also processed a wide range of cases that included lay people and clerics: blasphemers, false prophets, sexual deviants and predators, sorcerers, and anyone who claimed to have divine visions. The Spanish Inquisition was ever vigilant, and successful in ferreting out deviancy of all sorts. A key to its success was not just the zeal of its inquisitors, and their discipline, but also the fact that withholding information from the Inquisition was itself considered a crime. Relying on agents known as "familiars," and on the populace in general, the Spanish Inquisition had millions of eyes and ears, literally. When small groups of Protestants were discovered in Valladolid and Seville in the late 1550s, they were quickly rounded up and condemned. Grand Inquisitor Valdés boasted to the pope that no place on earth had fewer Protestants than Spain, "thanks to the great care and vigilance of the Holy Office of the Inquisition."[10]

By then, the popes had gotten into the act themselves. In 1542, Pope Paul III established the Sacred Congregation of the Roman and Universal Inquisition (later known as the Holy Office), a tribunal of six cardinals with the pope presiding that was to handle appeals, as well as process cases reserved for none other than the pope himself. In 1588, Pope Sixtus V reorganized the Roman Inquisition, adding more cardinals and turning it into one of his fifteen congregations. When Pope Sixtus established these congregations all at once to handle the church's business more effectively, the Inquisition was ranked first, above all others, giving a clear indication that vigilance and the suppression of error were his highest priorities.

By this time, the Spanish Inquisition had been at work for a century, but it had not yet run out of deviants to hunt down. A good number of its cases did not concern heretics, however, for the Spanish Inquisition had become an arm of clerical reform, an in-house reforming agency of the first rank. Moving in tandem with the implementation of Tridentine decrees, in the late 1560s the Spanish Inquisition began to hunt down corrupt priests accused of "abuse of the confessional," and for the following few decades it waged a dedicated campaign against clerics who sexually harassed their flocks. By the time these abuse cases had dwindled to a very few, two decades later, a new generation of priests was in place, trained in the art of reform and renewal, and in the art of vigilance.

The Inquisition became an important aspect of the Catholic Reformation, especially in Spain and its colonies and the Papal States, and in other places in Mediterranean Europe that set up their own tribunals, such as Portugal and Venice, but its reach was never universal. In light of those geographical limitations, the symbolic value of the Inquisition within Catholicism as a whole was perhaps greater than its actual power. But symbolic value should never be underestimated. For Catholics everywhere, even those outside its jurisdiction, the Inquisition exerted its influence by establishing a paradigm for the suppression of deviance, and by guiding the work of censors who kept the *Index of Forbidden Books* up to date. Among Protestants, the institution assumed a monstrous, menacing character as the embodiment of all that was wrong with the Church of Rome. Save for a relatively few unlucky Protestants devoured by the Inquisition in southern Europe, most Protestants did not have to fear the Inquisition, yet it was an essential component of their own propaganda and historiography. By its mere existence, the Inquisition shaped the Protestants' very identity, for, as they saw it, the Inquisition was evil incarnate, and everything they were *not*. Yet in Protestant polemic little or no attention was paid to the fact that in many Protestant communities, especially those of the Reformed tradition, there were institutions of a similar sort, the main function of which was to keep the community free of heresy, unbelief, blasphemy, deviancy, and immorality. Calvinists had their consistories, for instance, and in Calvin's Geneva, as elsewhere, the records reveal that they pursued wickedness and error with consummate zeal, sometimes more vehemently than their Catholic counterparts did. The consistories were not law courts, de jure, and they were engaged as much in admonishing, teaching, and reconciling as in bringing the wayward to punishment, but they nonetheless served a de facto function, similar to that of the Inquisition.

Most of the research carried out on the Inquisition at the end of the twentieth century has made a significant difference in our understanding of its workings, and of the many ways in which polemicists exaggerated its cruelty while downplaying that of their own similar institutions. The Inquisition, as it turns out, could be patient, even compassionate. But when all is said and done, like its Protestant counterparts, the Inquisition did suppress and punish, as well as stifle free expression. Zero tolerance for freedom of expression was the rule rather than the exception throughout Europe in the sixteenth and seventeenth centuries. The same could be said for cruelty, which all too often trumped compassion. In an age that saw error as contagious and immorality as polluting, medical metaphors were routinely employed to uphold repression and the use of force. Early modern authorities could view their repressive measures as a form of tough compassion, equivalent to a surgeon's scalpel and bone saw or an enforced quarantine. We may wish it had been different, but, unfortunately, wishful thinking is irrelevant in history.

CHAPTER FIFTEEN

Catholic Reform

Healing the Body of Christ

The Church is called the Body of Christ, as may be seen in the epistles of St. Paul to the Ephesians, and Colossians: appellations each of which has considerable influence in exciting the faithful to prove themselves worthy of the boundless clemency and goodness of God, who chose them to be his people.

—*Catechism of the Council of Trent*[1]

Inherent Polarities

Catholic reformers relied intensely on a hierarchical top-down, trickle-down model, embracing the metaphor of the church as the Body of Christ, assuming that a healthy head (the pope and his clergy) would necessarily lead to a healing of the whole body (the laity). This metaphorical trope was not just a figure of speech, but rather a plan of action, a way of bringing about change within an authority structure that never questioned the basic division of Christian society into two distinct classes: clergy and laity. This binary structure determined who could reform as well as how reform would take place, for the clergy were given the lion's share of agency as successors of Christ and his apostles. This is not to say that the laity played no role in reform, or that they were merely passive, always reacting to the guidance of the clergy, but rather to stress that whatever active role they played always hinged on the approval of the clergy.

Understanding the clergy's role is essential for understanding the nature of the Catholic Reformation, and two other binary polarities that guided it: that between the local and the universal, and that between the self and the other, or *us* and *them*. These polarities, it could be argued, were the very structure of the Catholic Reformation.

The polarity between local and universal had always been part and parcel of Christianity, from the very start. As a religion that offered salvation to all humans through the acceptance of a particular historical narrative, and that also claimed that its message had to be preached throughout the entire world, Christianity had to constantly face that tension between the "here" and the "everywhere." The church that called itself *Catholic*, or "universal," also happened to rest upon a very local foundation, not just through its far-flung bishops and particular churches in specific places on the map, but also through the bishop of Rome, the pope, the successor to Peter, from whom all authority flowed. This binary juxtaposition eventually became the church's very identity, reified in the inherently paradoxical name by which it came to be known: the *Roman* Catholic Church—an illogical name that makes as much sense as a square circle or, more appropriately, a circle in which center and circumference are one and the same.

Up until the sixteenth century, the relationship between the local and the universal had been negotiated ad hoc, for the most part, with a haphazard yet cogent composition that made the most of local color within a universal framework, much like the glass shards in any stained-glass window. It is no accident that throughout most of Christendom, the word *church*—be it *ecclesia, iglesia, église,* or *Kirche*—signified a specific building in which locals gathered for worship as well as the entire institution, including every single church building within itself. It is also no accident that in common parlance, the word *church* often also referred to the clergy. And this intertwining of the here and the everywhere was seldom questioned, if ever. In daily life, the accommodation of local and universal could be seamless, as evidenced by the existence of countless shrines to the Virgin Mary that made her present nearly everywhere on the map as a local avatar: Our Lady of Walsingham, Notre Dame de Paris, Nuestra Señora del Pilar, Unsere Liebe Frau von Einsiedeln, and so on.

This polarity proved manageable most of the time, in most places, but some tension was inevitable, as with all paradoxical binary structures. Sometimes tensions led to conflicts, and even to irreparable breaches, as had happened in 1054 when Pope Leo IX and Patriarch Michael Cerularius of Constantinople excommunicated each other and their followers, causing the permanent division of Western and Eastern Christendom—a schism centered precisely on the claims to *universal* authority being made by the bishops of Rome, which were unacceptable to the Byzantines.

The Protestant Reformation could not help but alter the polarity between local and universal within Catholicism, especially since it coincided with the rise of the centralized state and the dissemination of printed texts, two other fast-moving developments that redefined the relation between the here and the everywhere. As printing made texts truly universal and uniform, lessening the significance of each precious local manuscript, and as territorial rulers enlarged the authority of their centers at the expense of subaltern peripheries, imposing a greater homogeneity in governance, the Roman Catholic Church sought to superimpose a tighter universal grid on the local. Facing a welter of competitors who emphasized the local at the expense of the universal, the leaders of the Catholic Church chose a path that was diametrically opposed to such fragmentation, that of centralization and global uniformity. As some of these church elites saw it, this was not just a necessary tactic, but also the very essence of Catholicity. And the tactic ensured a more efficient reform as well as a sharpening of the Catholic polemical edge. Arguing against the Calvinist Huguenots of France, Bishop Francis de Sales highlighted the strictly local reach of Protestantism as the ultimate proof of its illegitimacy. Referring to all Protestants as "pretenders" who claimed to be the true church, he blasted away at their highly circumscribed reach, their lack of uniformity and their need to compete with one another for members:

> You pretenders pass not the Alps on our side, nor the Pyrenees on the side of Spain; Greece knows you not; the other three parts of the world do not know who you are, and have never heard of Christians without sacrifice, without altar, without head, without cross, as you are; in Germany your comrades the Lutherans, Brentians, Anabaptists, Trinitarians eat into your portion; in England the Puritans, in France the Libertines;— how, then can you be so obstinate, and continue thus apart from the rest of the world?[2]

De Sales put his finger on a touchy issue here: Protestants were not only highly localized and fractious; they also lacked the universal traits of the true church, as defined by Catholics. Their ritual was "empty" (without sacrifice or altar), they had no leader (without head), and they shunned even the most traditional symbols (without cross). In other words, they were "others": different from one another and from "the rest of the world."

This polarity brings us to an essential dialectic found in all cultures, that of the self and the other, or *us* and *them*. This dialectic had always been an inherent characteristic of a church bent on converting the world. The "others" were always there, outside the circle of faith. They included not only the heathen, but also those who had lapsed into error, the heretics who perennially sprouted everywhere, like weeds in God's garden. Throughout its long history, the Catholic Church had always been engaged in a constant dialectic with "error," defining its ethics, beliefs, rituals, and symbols in reference to the errors of the heretics. This dialectic was a constant process of identity formation in which formulations of the "true" faith were defined positively—as in the "I believe" of the church's Creed—but always with an implicit negative dimension. What one *affirms* necessarily negates or excludes all other options. Heretics, then, often play a decisive role in the definition of orthodoxy, through a dialectical process in which the "other" forces the self to define its identity more precisely. It is a process as natural and fixed as Newton's law of physics: to every action there is always an equal and opposite reaction.

Catholic reform could not help but be defined by the Protestant Reformation. In many ways, both subtle and overt, Protestants gave shape to the Catholic drive for reform that was already in process before Luther came along. Lutherans, Zwinglians, Calvinists, Anglicans, and Radicals forced Catholics to react to very specific challenges, and an essential part of every Catholic reaction was the need to define Catholic identity more

Avatars of identity. St. Ignatius Loyola stomps on heresy triumphantly, while holding a copy of the rules for the order he founded, the Society of Jesus. The Latin motto of the order—*ad maiorem Dei gloriam* (to the greater glory of God)—is prominently displayed alongside the book's title. A writhing figure that represents error is being pushed over the edge by his foot, along with a heretical book and a snake. This sculpture from St. Peter's Basilica in Rome embodies the ethos of what was once called the Counter-Reformation, as well as the dynamism and bluster of the baroque style. It is as stark a representation as can be found of Catholic convictions regarding Protestants as an enemy who must be vanquished.

precisely in contradistinction, point by contested point. This process applied to all aspects of reform, from the correction of abuses to the most abstract points of theology. So, for instance, in the case of religious imagery, Catholics not only attempted to clean house by attacking the errors and superstitions that plagued the cult of images; they also began to promote the correct veneration of images more aggressively, and to develop their sacred art—and music—under guidelines shaped by anti-Protestant sensibilities.

Catholic reform was as sensual as it was spiritual, for at the core of the Catholic faith lay the claim that all of creation is a gateway to the Creator and that matter and spirit are not antithetically opposed to one another. Exuberance is the hallmark of Catholic art and music from this period. In the nineteenth century, derisive moderns would dismiss this ebullience as *baroque*—a French word meaning "strange" or "bizarre"—but in the seventeenth century especially, lack of restraint became a virtue in Catholic aesthetics and so did the blurring of distinctions between the heavenly and the earthly, and this baroque sensibility became the very essence of the faith. Nowhere could the senses be more overwhelmed than in a baroque church at High Mass, and nowhere else could the stark aesthetics of Protestantism and its *sola scriptura* principle be more thoroughly challenged or denied.

This binary dialectic between self and other is central to Catholic Reform, and the very essence of the Counter-Reformation, a term that definitely has a legitimacy of its own, apart from polemical usage. While it is neither necessary nor useful to think of "Counter-Reformation" as the only label for early modern Catholicism (a term originally conceived by the German Protestant historian Leopold von Ranke in the nineteenth century), it is extremely important indeed to acknowledge that the Catholic Reformation did include a certain amount of deliberate reacting to Protestantism, a process of self-fashioning in which the traits of the "other" were willfully shunned, and countervailing traits were enlivened and given greater definition and prominence.

The epochal changes effected by Catholic reformers and the Council of Trent gave Catholicism a greater uniformity than it had ever enjoyed, a more precise definition of its beliefs and rituals, and a deeper awareness of the boundaries between orthodoxy and heresy, and religion and superstition, as well as between itself and all "others," be they heretics, sorcerers, witches, magicians, or necromancers. And it was an identity shaped largely by three interwoven concerns that involved polarities and necessarily implicated the dialectic between binary structures: between clergy and laity, between the universal and the local, and between the "other" and the self. These concerns were not mere abstractions. On the contrary, they were pragmatic choices made in the gritty process of reform. In other words, reforming required the balancing of these polarities in everyday life.

Reform and Standardization of Ritual

One of the most significant changes brought about by the Council of Trent was its reform of ritual, which gave a firm definition to Catholic identity as nothing else could.

Rituals are a very special window on to the soul of any culture. Anthropologists and ethnographers have known this for a long time, and some historians too. Rituals express and confirm a society's myths through symbolic behavior: they enact, materialize, and realize beliefs, giving participants a chance to attain faith as they portray it. Rituals are perfect circles of sorts, serving both as models of beliefs and models for those beliefs. Moreover, rituals are multidimensional, attempts to bridge dimensions: they seek to impose order on a seemingly disorderly, painful, and indifferent universe, to turn the world as it is into the world as it should be, to fuse together the imagined and the real into a unified vision. As one anthropologist has put it, rituals speak in the subjunctive mood.[3]

What can we learn about the Catholic Reformation from its ritual? First and foremost, we see that all liturgical reforms come from Rome, that a universal template is imposed on the periphery from the center. We also see that universality is a high concern, for the Council of Trent insisted on retaining Latin as the sole language for all Catholic worship, and also supplanted most local liturgies with a new universal ritual code. All these aspects of liturgical reform are a firm rejection of Protestantism, as well as an affirmation of papal and conciliar authority—of the supremacy of the center over the periphery.

The papacy assumed control of liturgical reforms, even though all such reforms are commonly referred to as Tridentine, and even though their implementation was contingent on local circumstances. The Council of Trent did play a role, at least in forming a commission to study the issue and in calling for reforms, but its definitive word on the subject came at the last session of the council, in December 1563, in a brusque decree that left all the details in the pope's hands. Implementing this decree was a difficult challenge and a very lengthy process. The first step was taken by Pope Pius V, who revived the commission from Trent and appointed new members to it. Its goal was not to reinvent ritual, but to return as much as possible *ad fontes*, Renaissance style, to the *pristina patrum norma*, that is, "the original rule of the Fathers."

The Breviary was a central part of the life of the clergy, so it is no mere accident that the reform of ritual began with this important book. The breviary was a compendium or collections of prayers known as the canonical hours or Divine Office, which the clergy were expected to recite every day. It had evolved over centuries, from its monastic origins, and in the course of time a great number of local variations came into existence. This meant that there was no uniformity and that variations were spread all over the Catholic world geographically and among the different religious orders. The reform commission could not review and amend all breviaries, but neither did it wish to condone such lack of uniformity. Using the Roman breviary adopted by Pope Nicholas III in the thirteenth century as its template, Pius V's commission produced a new version in which universality and uniformity were emphasized.

The structure of the breviary was as complex as one might imagine a compendium that had developed gradually and haphazardly over a long period to be: it contained in five different sections the prayers, psalms, homilies, and Bible readings for every day of the year, arranged by liturgical seasons and saints' feast days. All 150 psalms were to be recited every week, parceled out at roughly 20 psalms per day. The commission faced a thorny problem: how to find an equitable balance between the number of saints' feasts (which had readings and prayers that focused on the saints' lives rather than on the psalms and gospels) with the rest of the church calendar (which had biblically oriented readings and prayers that pertained to the spirit of the seasons of Advent, Christmas, Lent, Holy Week, Easter, and Ordinary Time). By the sixteenth century, the number of saints' feast days had increased to the point that they monopolized much of the calendar. The messiness of the breviary was compounded by two other problems: local saints competed for attention with universal saints, and some of the hagiographical readings were filled with legends that could not stand up to even the laxest historical scrutiny.

The solution found by the pope's commission was brutally simple: it pruned the number of saints' feasts, restricting them to only about 160 days of the year and giving preference to saints of universal renown over local saints. That new breviary was first issued in 1568. And it had the papal bull of approval, *Quod a nobis*, for a preface in which

Pius V condemned the use of any other breviary that was less than two hundred years old. Pius V had made it clear that this was to be *the* breviary for the entire Catholic Church. Only the dioceses of Toledo and Milan and religious orders with breviaries that could be traced back to at least 1368—such as the Benedictines and Dominicans—were exempt. The net result of such a radical effacing of local breviaries was precisely what the pope's commission had intended: it universalized how the clergy prayed. As one might expect, there was grumbling and resistance, but there were also plenty of exemptions granted. Ever mindful of the need to maintain some local flexibility, Rome allowed for the celebration of local feast days on a case-by-case basis. But such exemptions themselves—even if liberally granted—made clear the centrality of Rome and the authority of the pope, who had to be petitioned. From 1568 on, the universal trumped the local, even in the granting of exemptions, and in all subsequent revisions, as more saints were minted and their feasts brought into play. Again, one should keep in mind that this was a long process, unevenly implemented: creating a universal breviary and ordering everyone to use it was one thing; replacing the old with the new everywhere was quite another.

Next in line for reform was the central ritual of the Catholic Church: the Mass. As with the breviary, there was no standard text, or missal. Although there was relative uniformity when it came to the basic structure of the ritual, and especially of the consecration of the Eucharist, each diocese usually had its own missal and its own minor variations. With the advent of printing in the late fifteenth century, the publication of missals *secundum usum* (according to the practice) of individual dioceses further intensified local variances. The greatest problem caused by this lack of uniformity was the proliferation of votive masses, that is, of masses specifically offered for some special need, many of which were celebrated on a rigid schedule of multiple-day cycles (such as thirty days in a row, or the first Friday of each month over the space of nine months). The possibilities for variation were as countless as the ills that can plague the human race. There were masses for specific illnesses, for plagues, for rebellious children, for adulterous spouses, for evil thoughts, for lust, even for lost or stolen items, and for those who had lost their voices. Many Mass cycles focused on the dead and on their speedy release from purgatory. These cycles—many of which had supposedly been revealed to saints by heavenly messengers—followed detailed formulas, which indicated how many candles to light, which prayers to intone, and which feast days to observe. Much like a chemist's formula or chef's recipe, the details needed to be precise. In Spain, a very popular cycle known as the Masses of St. Amador promised to release a soul from purgatory if the following masses were said in the proper order:

> One mass, first Sunday in Advent, seven candles
> One mass, Christmas, seven candles
> One mass, Epiphany, seven candles
> One mass, Ascension of Christ, three candles
> One mass, Pentecost, seven candles

One mass, Assumption of the Virgin Mary, seven candles
Seven Masses of the Holy Spirit, seven candles each
Three masses of the Holy Trinity, three candles each
Five masses of the Five Wounds, five candles each
Three masses of the Holy Archangels, three candles each
One mass of the Holy Apostles, twelve candles
One mass of the Holy Martyrs, twelve candles
One mass of the Holy Confessors, five candles
One mass of the Holy Virgins, five candles
One mass, feast of All Saints, three candles
Three requiem masses, three candles each

But such precise instructions applied only in Valencia and Zaragoza. In another Spanish diocese, where a different missal was used, the formula could be different, even though the cycle still went by the same name. These discrepancies did not seem to bother the faithful very much, if at all, for such mass cycles were immensely popular. In Madrid, for instance, nearly every will and last testament written before 1565 requested the Masses of St. Amador.[4]

Seeking to put an end to such "superstitions" and to local diversity, the Council of Trent had pronounced in its twenty-second session (1562) that all bishops were to "completely banish from the Church the practice of any fixed number of masses and candles" that did not have its origin in "true religion."[5] It was a significant distinction for the council to make, evocative of Erasmian principles, and it was also an admission of guilt on some of the charges Protestants had been making all along about the "superstition" that had crept into Catholic ritual. Dependent on local bishops for its enforcement, this decree against superstitious rituals went into effect piecemeal. In some places, such as the diocese of Toledo in Spain, it was immediately put into effect after the Toledo synod of 1565. And change seems to have occurred immediately. After that date "superstitious" mass cycles such as the Masses of St. Amador instantly vanish from all last wills and testaments in this diocese. Elsewhere, however, beyond this diocese or others like it that acted on the council's decrees, in locales where the secular or ecclesiastical authorities dragged their feet, or resisted the decrees of Trent, such problems remained unsolved.

The answer to all of these problems was the Roman missal, issued by a papal commission in 1570, which would replace every other local *secundum usum* missal, save, again, for those that were more than two hundred years old. Gone were the local variations in the celebration of the Mass. Gone, too, were the mass cycles, except for one: the Masses of St. Gregory, a cycle of thirty masses on thirty consecutive days, also for the release of a soul from purgatory. The tradition linking these masses to Pope Gregory the Great was far too ancient and venerable, and too difficult to dismiss. But even this cycle had to conform to the rubric of the mass as laid out in the Roman missal. The uniformity imposed by this missal was far greater than that of the breviary: the latter applied only to clerics; the former was for all Catholics. The Roman missal was a sea change for the whole Catholic world, on every continent, for one could conceivably step out of the mass on one continent and into it on another without skipping a beat or being the least bit puzzled by differences of any sort. Such an eventuality would require the miracle of mystical transport, that is, an instantaneous zipping of the self from place A to place B—a rare, but "possible" occurrence in Catholic belief—but the point of the hypothetical illustration is not the transport, rare as it is, but the uniformity of worship experienced through it, which became commonplace. The only local variation the Roman missal could not wipe out was inconsequential: the accent with which the priest pronounced the Latin words of the Mass.

The Roman missal would be slightly revised in 1604 and 1634, but it remained firmly fixed as the sole standard for the celebration of the mass of the Roman Rite in the Catholic Church until 1965, when the reforms of the Second Vatican Council did away with it, and its so-called Tridentine Mass. Measuring its effect is akin to measuring the effect of any language on a culture, and just as difficult, for the Roman missal became the lingua franca of Catholic ritual and Catholic devotion, regardless of the accent with which it was spoken. Latin became an integral part of Catholic identity, in a context that was different from that of the Middle Ages. Since the Council of Trent had decreed that all of the Church's ritual was to be in Latin, the Roman missal reified the supremacy not only of the universal over the local, but also of the difference between the clergy (all of whom had to learn Latin) and the laity (only some of whom had Latin lessons), and between Catholics (whose ritual was in Latin) and Protestants (whose ritual was in the local vernacular).

Latin remained a sacred language for Catholics: a link between heaven and earth, past and present, and every location on the globe. It was a universal language, commonly understood by the clergy and the elites, but not by the vast majority of the faithful. As is the case with all ritual, paradox was no obstacle to overcome; rather, it had the potential of deepening the sense of mystery. The Latin tongue bound all Catholics together, as did the predictability of the ritual. It mattered little that the Latin had a local accent: the ritual was understood and appreciated at that deeper level, one where symbol, ritual, metaphor, and poetry trump discursive reason. The fact that Latin could not be understood word for word did not make Catholic ritual necessarily distant from worshipers, or incomprehensible. Worshipers unschooled in Latin could partake of the ritual in alternate ways, as something intimate on some level other than the strictly rational. The power of Latin itself as a mysterious language could lend the mass a transcendent feel and an immediacy unequaled by any vernacular liturgy. Protestants saw it differently. For them, as for some skeptics, the continued use of Latin only deepened their conviction that Catholic ritual was dead wrong, useless, riddled with priestcraft and superstition, and not much different from magic, with all of its hocus-pocus (a reference to the words of consecration spoken by the priest: *hoc est corpus meum*, or "this is my body").

The Latin Mass of Trent was preliterate and literate, opaque and transparent all at once; it was a paradoxical ritual in a tongue common to all and alien to all, an exalted

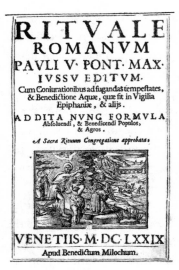

Standardizing ritual. Title page of the 1615 edition of the *Rituale Romanum*, issued during the pontificate of Pius V.

sacred code that unified through its antiquity and its distance from everyday speech. As all roads once led to Rome, now, after Trent, all Masses led to Rome—and ostensibly to God as well—with an exactness and uniformity that the ancient Romans would have envied, and that all Protestants loathed.

Further reforms were streamlined—and guaranteed—by Pope Sixtus V in 1588, when he created fifteen commissions, or congregations, in which cardinals would oversee crucial aspects of church governance. The Congregation for Sacred Rites and Ceremonies handled all questions regarding ritual, as well as the entire canonization process for saints. Among the accomplishments of this body, one of the most significant was the publication in 1614 of the *Rituale romanum*, or Roman Ritual, which ensured even more consistency and universality by standardizing all of the services performed by a priest that were not included in the missal, such as baptism, marriage, extreme unction, and the rite of exorcism.

The ritual reforms of Trent emphasized that worship was not to be slavishly tethered to the Bible alone, or to vernacular tongues, that curse of Babel. Stressing universality and uniformity, they also gave Catholics everywhere a common bond and an instantly recognizable symbolic code. Defending the salvific power of the Mass, and its efficacy in freeing souls from purgatory, Trent also intensified a significant distinction between Catholics and Protestants. Research has proved that throughout the Catholic world, mass requests intensified drastically after Trent and remained at a very high level until the eighteenth century. Ironically, then, an increased interest in purgatory proved to be the ultimate response of the Catholic Church to Luther's ninety-five theses and his assault on purgatory and on suffrages for the dead.

In sum, although certain customary gestures and rites changed, the liturgical reforms effected after Trent strengthened, even amplified, the substance of medieval Catholic ritual. These innovations defended tradition while repudiating excesses deemed superstitious. Their character should not be read as proof that the process of reform in

Catholicism was a downward cascade, flowing irresistibly from on high to a docile laity, and nor should it be interpreted as dividing elites from subalterns, or "official" religion from "popular" religion. On the contrary, the success of liturgical reforms—which seem to have *intensified* popular interest in certain rituals—was due not to the power of the clergy or the docility of the laity, but to the appeal of the reforms themselves as clergy and laity alike lived out their faith within the same matrix of beliefs. That these reforms were not accepted immediately at the same time by all Catholics everywhere does not lessen their significance or indicate some sort of failure. On the contrary, the unevenness of the changes points to that ancient dialectic between the local and the universal, as well as to the many complexities of the Catholic Church, an institution that tends to measure time unhurriedly and to revel in the exceptions it grants to some of its rules.

Saints and Mystics

While Protestants denied freedom of the will and scoffed at the possibility of mystical ecstasy in this life, Catholics did all they could to affirm their convictions in perfectionism ever more stridently. And the loudest affirmations came from men and women engaged in the pursuit of perfection, many of whom came to be regarded as saints. Three developments worked in tandem to produce this living, breathing testimony. First, a genuine spirit of renewal produced a higher number of zealous men and women who lived exemplary lives. Second, the papacy reformed the canonization process, assuming greater control, tightening standards, and exercising its authority to promote certain paradigms, again asserting the superiority of the universal over the local. Third, the printing press made it possible for accounts of these extraordinary individuals to circulate widely and to exert a greater influence on Catholic piety and polemics.

When it comes to canonization—the process through which the Catholic Church officially proclaims a saint by adding that person's name to the list (canon) of recognized saints—numbers are both illuminating and misleading. To go strictly by the numbers is to miss the fact that for every holy man or woman who made it through the elaborate and very expensive process of canonization, there were many others who did not. Canonization required both powerful and persistent patrons, such as religious orders, monarchs, and prominent churchmen, and a multigenerational continuity, that is, patrons who would carry the process through over a span of decades, even centuries.

Keeping in mind that canonized saints are a select minority, yet representative of a larger whole, we see that the statistics do reveal a self-conscious effort on the part of the Catholic Church to recognize its leading reformers and "prove" Protestantism wrong through their achievements. All in all, thirty-two "Counter-Reformation" saints were eventually recognized in the seventeenth and eighteenth centuries. It was nothing new that the list should contain a lopsided imbalance between laity and clergy, with clergy as the overwhelming majority. Of these, nearly half (46 percent) were Italian, and more than one-third (37 percent) were Spanish, representing the two nations most intensely involved in reform of the church. France came in a distant third, with only 8 percent. Of the total number, those who established or led religious orders led the way, followed closely by those who led reform movements within their orders, and then by bishops who reformed their dioceses and missionaries who had gained universal recognition. Surprisingly, only one martyr made the list, even though England had a high number of high-profile candidates and Japan had thousands of lesser renown. Most of these martyrs—European as well as Asian—would be canonized eventually, but not until the nineteenth and twentieth centuries.

This imbalance between reformers and martyrs provides us with an important clue about the priorities of Catholic Church during this time and the values it sought to promote through its official saints. Once again, polarities play an essential role, for the complexion of the list of early modern saints reflects Rome's own preoccupation with the dialectical relationship between lay and clerical, local and universal, and self and other. The characteristics that link all of these extraordinary men and women largely correspond with Rome's take on the balance between each of those polarities. First, the vast majority of these saints embody the superiority of the clerical life and of the role played by clergy in the renewal of Christian life. Second, the accomplishments of these saints tend to cross geographical, national, and political boundaries: even though so many of them were Spanish or Italian, these holy men and women transcend the local very intensely and definitively. Third, the very lives of these saints are models of heroic virtue, of precisely the kind of moral and spiritual perfection that Protestants deemed absolutely impossible, and they also tend to represent the church triumphant and militant. In sum, they were the very embodiment of Catholic identity over and against Protestant error.

Because all standards of proof for historical claims had been altered by Renaissance scholars such as Lorenzo Valla and by Protestant Reformers, it was inevitable that the process of canonization would be subjected to reform and streamlining. The biggest change, by far, was the imposition of new standards of proof for sanctity, and of a new procedure that required the interviewing of witnesses and the collection of data through formal inquests ultimately directed from Rome. The pivotal year for these changes was 1588, when the task of processing all sainthood cases was assigned to the newly created Congregation for Sacred Rites and Ceremonies. Ultimately, the power to confirm anyone's status as a saint rested with the pope, but the rules initiated in 1588 turned the process of confirmation into a bureaucratic procedure involving many individuals in various locations over a long period of time. Along the way, a great deal of authority came to be vested in the senior expert on canon law in the Congregation of Rites, who, in his role as "promoter of the faith," assumed responsibility for ensuring that all rules were observed and that a certain level of empirical skepticism be injected into the procedure. Ironically, this *promotore della fede* (advocate of the faith) came to be known as "the devil's advocate," precisely because it was his job to question all evidence, even if as a mere formality.

The rigor imposed on the process of canonization after 1588 came into full effect swiftly and efficiently, and it confirmed the centrality of Rome and the authority of the pope over all local developments and the supremacy of the universal over the local. But no swiftness could be attributed to the new process itself, which favored thinking in terms of decades and centuries rather than years. The first case to go through the new procedures, that of Teresa of Ávila, took forty years to complete, for it started in 1582 and ended with her canonization in 1622. Yet Teresa of Ávila's case could be said to have sailed through. Her close companion and fellow reformer John of the Cross would not be canonized until 1726, and some cases opened in the same time period are still pending four centuries later.

And while swiftness was not a priority, the centralization of the process in Rome certainly was. In 1622, a paradigm was established for enhancing public knowledge of the pope's role while at the same time allowing for local celebrations that mirrored the central event in Rome. The simultaneous canonization of four major Catholic reformers in March 1622 was a celebration not only of the reform of the Church, but also of the hierarchical link that bound every locality to the papacy. Ceremonies and celebrations were held for each of the four reformers canonized that day in their home country as well as in Rome—save for one whose home was Rome itself: Philip Neri, founder of the Oratory (d. 1595). The other three saints—Ignatius Loyola, the founder of the Jesuit order (d. 1556); Francis Xavier, extraordinary missionary to Asia (d. 1552); and Teresa of Ávila, reformer of the Carmelite order (d. 1582)—all had multiple ceremonies in Spain, some of which included fireworks.

Canonization was essential for saint making, but holy men and women could also earn recognition or serve as exemplars by other means. Even before the reforms of Trent, by 1540, the process of canonization itself depended heavily on the printing press, and more specifically on the writing and publishing of hagiographical texts. The existence of a sacred biography was in effect a requirement for a candidate for canonization to be taken seriously. The practice of commissioning an aspiring saint to write his or her autobiography, or of relying on that prospective saint's confessors and close associates to write a biography became commonplace, lending a distinctly modern air of authenticity to the genre. Ignatius Loyola and Teresa of Ávila both penned or dictated autobiographical accounts. And both had their lives retold by those who knew them intimately or relied on other firsthand narratives.

Saints' lives proved very popular throughout the Catholic world after 1560, as evidenced by the number of hagiographies published and the number of editions and translations. In Spain, an epicenter for the production and consumption of such texts, the numbers are very revealing. Whereas only 23 hagiographies were published between 1500 and 1559, more than 350 came off the presses between 1600 and 1639. In the 1620s alone, more than 120 such titles were published. And then, as now, publishers' decisions depended on sales.

Hagiography eventually gained a distinctly clerical character—which is not surprising considering the top-down model of reform—and also a learned, or "scientific," dimension. The chief goal of this new scholarly type of writing was to provide clergy with lives of the saints that could ostensibly stand up to critical scrutiny, for the hagiographies were written to promote the cult of the saints when skepticism was on the rise; they were at once devotional and polemical. These developments would lead to a massive project, begun in 1607 by a Dutch Jesuit, Heribert Rosweyde (1569–1629), which would take centuries to complete. Rosweyde was soon joined by another Jesuit, Jean Bolland (1569–1665), who outlived him and continued and expanded the project. Eventually, a team of scholars searching diligently for manuscripts and printed texts, and collating narratives, made their work available to the reading public in an ever-growing set of volumes with the title *Acta sanctorum*. Although some prominent reformers such as Carlo Borromeo thought the project was much too ambitious, the Bollandists, as these Jesuit professional hagiographers came to be known, charged ahead, producing a never-ending stream of "scientific" hagiographies in heavy tomes. By 1681, twenty-four volumes had been produced; by 1794—despite the suppression of the Jesuits in 1773—the collection had grown to fifty-three volumes, covering all the saints in the church's liturgical calendar from January to October.

Such statistics suggest that hagiography may well have been one of the most vigorous Catholic responses to Protestantism. This genre served two purposes at once: as devotional texts attuned to popular piety and as narratives that conveyed Catholic beliefs and values. Translated and reprinted numerous times, these hagiographies became best sellers, and arguably the most effective means of inculcating Catholic values among clergy and laity alike. Less exacting and less tedious than catechisms, which called for memorization, these marvel-rich narratives offered pointed lessons on the truth of Catholic teaching through specific examples. That one could and should "aspire to a perfect life," as De Sales put it, was the main lesson. If these men and women did it, so can you. Most hagiographers wasted no time on subtlety. Every event, every gesture in their narratives, was imbued with meaning and purpose. One of the most popular post-Tridentine hagiographers, the Jesuit Pedro de Ribadeneyra, summed up the advantages of hagiography:

> It is the greatest glory for the entire Catholic Church to make known her countless illustrious progeny. For if one distinguished child is all it takes to bring honor to an entire family, what will so many remarkable children do for their Mother? Moreover, they are a mighty shield, and a defense against the unfaithful . . . and a hammer, and a dagger against heretics. Nothing can undermine their error and folly better than the examples of the saints; for teaching through accomplishment is far superior to teaching by mere words, and the deeds of the saints are holy, and totally contrary to all the delusions and falsehoods of the heretics.[6]

And nothing was as contrary to Protestantism in these hagiographies as accounts of miracles and mystical ecstasies. Protestantism was opposed not only to the Catholic paradigm for holiness and the cult of the saints, but also to the very notion that the natural and supernatural realms could converge in the person of the saint, especially in their bodies. Hagiography was all about miracle, and so was the canonization process, which required proof of miracles performed by the holy person in question. Catholic saints were healers, above all: thaumaturges who channeled divine omnipotence through their holy bodies and relics. They tweaked or bypassed the laws of nature, even to the point of being in two places at once (bilocation), floating in the air or flying (levitation), reading other's thoughts (telepathy), or subsisting on no food other than the Eucharist (*inedia*). After death, their bodies sometimes refused to decompose, or exuded wonder-working blood and oil. Most of these phenomena had been part and parcel of Christian belief since the first century, and all of them had been highlighted in medieval hagiographies, but in the face of the Protestant challenge, they were woven more tightly and intensely into saints' lives, with a greater sense of purpose, as proof positive of the metaphysical superiority of Catholicism. At bottom, the process of canonization and the writing of hagiographies rested on a simple, yet immensely cheeky Catholic syllogism that offended every Protestant: humans can indeed reach a high degree of holiness, and these holy men and women (saints) can indeed work miracles; therefore, any Christian church that has no saints or miracles must be a false church.

To top it all off, many of these contemporary saints also claimed to have intimate relations with God, and all sorts of mystical ecstasies. Forget about Luther's and Calvin's inscrutable and transcendent God. The God of these Catholic saints was not far removed from humanity or some unknowable entity: he was eminently accessible in the here and now, not just in the hereafter. And his love could bridge the chasm between creature and creator in a blinding flash, and bring one to ecstasy, momentarily obliterating the curse of original sin. St. John of the Cross could address him as a lover, in poems: "Reveal your presence, / and let your gaze and beauty slay me."[7] St. Veronica Giuliani (1660–1727) addressed Christ in the most intimate terms as he was about to stigmatize her, crying out to him, "Oh Spouse of my heart, my one and only love . . . vouchsafe that I may suffer and be crucified for love of Thee."[8] St. Teresa of Ávila identified about fifteen different types of ecstasy, and she had constant exchanges with angels and Jesus himself. She could also have visions of the Trinity and fully comprehend the mystery through infused knowledge. As she explained in her autobiography: "the soul finds itself wise, suddenly, and the mystery of the most Holy Trinity and other extremely sublime matters are so clearly revealed to it, that there is no theologian in the world with whom it would hesitate to dispute the truth of these great things."[9] And it was not just canonized saints who reported such experiences. In fact, more testimonies of mystical encounters of the divine came from noncanonized mystics than from those officially recognized as saints. Ana de San Bartolomé (1549–1626), St. Teresa's closest companion and a relatively obscure figure who was never canonized, wrote two accounts of her own life that are filled with descriptions of her supernatural encounters. Sister María de Ágreda (1602–1665)— another noncanonized mystic—claimed not only to have constant contact with the

Virgin Mary, but also to have served as her scribe, for the Mother of God supposedly dictated her biography to her.

Miracles

Alongside the upsurge in the number of saints and mystics who communed with God came a corresponding expansion of the miraculous, not just in terms of frequency and quantity, but also in terms of the kind of phenomena reported and accepted. As the sixteenth century gave way to the seventeenth, the boundary between the natural and supernatural seemed to shift in Catholicism. From Teresa of Ávila in Spain, whose corpse refused to decompose, to Joseph of Cupertino in Italy, who flew through the air and read people's minds, to Martín de Porres in far-off Peru, who could be in two places at the same time and also communicate with animals, the Catholic world pulsated with the expectation of everything that the Protestants ridiculed as impossible, and with an eagerness to enshrine and venerate the miraculous with more fervor than ever before, thus intensifying the differences between Protestant and Catholic cultures.

Yet this promotion of the miraculous was no free-for-all, but rather a highly controlled process that always required the approval of the church's hierarchy, or even of

Ecstasy as polemic. In response to the Protestant denial of nonbiblical miracles the Catholic Church reemphasized its intimate connection with the supernatural realm and miraculous events, along with its ability to guide men and women to mystical ecstasy. This 1646 painting by Bartolomé Esteban Murillo depicts the intermingling of the natural and supernatural, the heavenly and the mundane. A friar assigned to kitchen duty has become rapt in ecstasy in the midst of his duties. While he levitates and eyewitnesses stare in surprise, angels carry out the cooking assigned to him. St. Teresa of Ávila summed up the possibility of such an intermingling of heaven and earth by saying, "Even in the kitchen, the Lord can be found among the pots." Though Murillo most probably never encountered a Protestant in the flesh, and was not commissioned by the Franciscans of Seville to refute Protestantism through his painting, what he produced was nonetheless a virtual refutation of the Protestant Reformation.

the pope himself. Miracles were nothing new, but the presence of millions of Protestant skeptics certainly was, and that made it all the more necessary for the church to assume as much control over miracles as possible. That closer control by the clergy, so typical of the Counter-Reformation, can be recognized in the cases of "feigned sanctity" handled by the Inquisition and similar courts. By claiming the power to distinguish between real and fraudulent claims, and to consecrate those that were genuine, the church made clear that all miracles came through it. And miracles had a double edge: they not only confirmed and strengthened the faithful; they also served as polemical weapons in the church's struggle against Protestantism.

This renewed emphasis on the miraculous was not at all about counting ever-higher numbers of miracles, as if a new age had dawned in which the divine was breaking through as never before. The church wanted to reaffirm its commitment to tradition and the continuity of truth within it, so there could be no newfangled miracles; the emphasis was on the unwavering constancy of the miraculous in the Catholic Church.

Healing miracles were the most common, and these occurred in numerous ways: through prayers, vows, the veneration of images and relics, and pilgrimages to shrines. Then there were the miracles associated with holy men and women: their visions, ecstasies, levitation, bilocation, stigmata, and a long list of other phenomena. These were all miracles that could be found in medieval hagiographies, but there was a greater interest in the most extreme of phenomena, and on detailed descriptions. Take the case, for instance, of one of Sister María de Ágreda's levitations, as described by a bishop who knew her and eventually wrote an account of her life:

> The body . . . was raised a little above the ground, and as light as if it had no weight of its own, so much so that like a feather, it could be moved by a puff of breath even from a distance. The face was more beautiful than it normally appeared. . . . The whole attitude was so modest and so devout that she seemed a seraph in human form. She frequently remained in this state of ecstasy for two or even three hours.[10]

Even more remarkable was the claim that this same nun had visited North America many times without ever leaving her convent in Ágreda, Spain, and that she had evangelized the natives of West Texas and New Mexico. As if this were not enough, as we have seen, she wrote a massive autobiography of the Virgin Mary, which she claimed was dictated to her by the Mother of God herself. Such outrageously bold claims were all part of a larger pattern. Holy people were expected to have intimate contact with the divine, through apparitions of Jesus, the Virgin Mary, or other saints in heaven, who sometimes had messages they wanted delivered. St. Margaret Mary Alacoque (1647–1690) claimed to have received a request from Jesus Christ in June 1675 to begin a new devotion to his Sacred Heart and establish a feast on the church calendar, on "the Friday after the Octave of Corpus Christi." The request was accompanied by a pledge: "I promise thee that My Heart shall expand Itself to shed in abundance the influence of Its divine love upon those who shall thus honor It, and cause It to be honored."[11] Devotion to the Sacred Heart of

Jesus caught on, as did many other "revealed" practices, but only after receiving approval from Rome.

Sacred spaces multiplied, too, in expectation of the miraculous. New shrines could be established in places where miracles or apparitions had taken place. In the Americas, especially, creating shrines became an essential part of the Christianization of the natives. Older shrines could be promoted, too, as miracles multiplied. Bishops often seized the opportunity to refurbish miracle-working shrines and turn them into major pilgrimage sites, as did Bishop Mathias Hovius at Sharp Hill in the Spanish Netherlands, at a landscape that had been soaked with the blood of religious conflict. Such developments could transcend local-universal and lay-clerical polarities, for there were many cases of shrines that gained universal renown and were vigorously promoted by the clerical elites. One of these, the Holy House at Loreto, defied logic and the new Renaissance take on history, but nonetheless became one of the best known of all miracle sites, and one of the most emblematic of the Catholic Reformation.

The Holy House of Loreto—located in the north of Italy, near the Adriatic Sea—was supposedly none other than that in which the Virgin Mary had been born and in which Jesus had been reared, which angels had brought to Ancona from Nazareth in the 1290s, when Crusaders lost their grip on the Holy Land and Muslims threatened to destroy it. A local devotion at first, the miraculously transported stone house and its image of the Virgin Mary gained an ever-expanding reputation for healing miracles, especially in the fifteenth century. In 1469, a large basilica was built over the Holy House to accommodate the throngs of pilgrims who came to Loreto, and in 1507 the house itself was enclosed within a marble shrine. Three years later, Pope Leo X raised the shrine to the highest possible level by extending the same indulgence to it as applied to all of the pilgrimage churches in Rome.

Immune to the new empirical historical research pioneered by the likes of Lorenzo Valla in the fifteenth century, the improbable Holy House became an international pilgrimage site, attracting large crowds and some of the greatest leaders of the Catholic Reformation, including St. Ignatius Loyola, St. Francis Xavier, St. Carlo Borromeo, St. Philip Neri, and St. Francis de Sales. Even the skeptical French essayist Michel de Montaigne could not resist its pull. In 1581 he spent three days at the shrine, took communion, listened to pilgrims' tales of miraculous cures, and left behind some silver figurines (ex-votos) representing himself, his wife, and his daughter. He was lucky to find a vacant spot for these avatars. "No other place I have ever visited makes so great a show of religion," he said. "All the residue of the shrine is so thickly covered with rich *ex votos* given by diverse cities and prices that, right down to the ground, there is not an inch of space which is not covered with some device of gold or silver."[12] Devotion to this shrine became so intense that eventually replicas of it were built throughout the Catholic world, universalizing its presence. In some cases, its replication was deemed instrumental in the introduction or reintroduction of Catholicism, as happened in Prague in 1626, soon after the defeat of the Hussites at the Battle of White Mountain, or in Mexico or in the wilds of New France, where Jesuits were quite fond of establishing devotion to the Virgin and the Holy House of Loreto.

Miracles closely associated with the Eucharist also continued a long tradition. Throughout the Middle Ages, the map of Europe became dotted with shrines to miraculous hosts that bled or levitated or survived desecration and fire. These hosts were not just Christ himself, present on earth, but relics that had confirmed his presence in the face of natural disasters or heretics and infidels bent on profaning the sacred. Eucharistic miracles were at once local and universal: they occurred in specific places, but they involved the body of Christ, which was ubiquitous. They also confirmed the Catholic doctrine of transubstantiation and the unique power of the clergy who routinely handled the sacrament to make it possible for bread and wine to become the body and blood of Christ. In the face of the Protestant challenge, eucharistic miracles also served to prove the "others" wrong and more sharply distinguished Catholic identity from heretical error.

Four prominent examples of such miracles highlight how medieval traditions and current concerns were interwoven. In Morrovalle, Italy, in 1560, a consecrated host that had survived a fire intact was not only enshrined, but also declared a "genuine miracle" by Pope Pius IV. Papal involvement did not end there. Pius IV also issued a bull granting a plenary indulgence to anyone who would go to confession and visit the miraculous host on the anniversary of the fire. In 1597 in Alcalá, Spain, twenty-four consecrated hosts were rescued from a Morisco who intended to desecrate them. The hosts were stored away, but as the years passed, they would not decay. In 1619, after close inspection by church authorities and a physician who declared that they had circumvented the laws of nature, the hosts were enshrined. In 1620, King Philip III made a short-distance pilgrimage to the shrine, along with the entire royal family and a large retinue of courtiers. In this case, what stands out is not papal involvement, but that of medical science and the civil authorities.

Philip III's veneration of the miraculous hosts at Alcalá was just one example of a long-standing tradition of eucharistic devotion in the Spanish royal family. His father, Philip II, had been very devoted to the Eucharist, and had often stopped the royal carriage and knelt on the road, bareheaded, whenever he spied a priest taking the viaticum, or consecrated host, to a dying person. In his later years, when gout made it impossible for him to get out of the carriage, he had ordered his son, the future Philip III, to do the venerating for him. Philip II had also rescued thousands of relics from Protestant lands, and one of his favorites was a host that had miraculously bled when stepped on by a Dutch iconoclast in the city of Gorkum. This host, known as the Sagrada Forma, or Sacred Host of Gorkum, which had three reddish spots arranged in the same pattern as nails on a boot heel, was enshrined at the royal palace of the Escorial, where it was regularly venerated by King Philip II and his heirs. His great-grandson Charles II would be especially devoted to the Sagrada Forma, even to the point of building a special sacristy for it at the Escorial and commissioning a painting that depicted him and members of his court venerating the sacred relic.

The Sacred Host of Gorkum was but one of many eucharistic relics that had manifested the real presence of Christ in the face of Protestant violence. But it did not always take a direct attack by heretics to turn such miracles into anti-Protestant polemic. A case in point is the miracle at Faverney, in the Franche-Comté region of eastern France, in 1608. As in Morrovalle, the threat to the consecrated host had come from a fire, but in this instance, the miracle was apparent in the midst of the disaster, not after it, and was ostensibly observed by hundreds of people. The official report, which was signed by many eyewitnesses, told how on Pentecost Sunday, when the abbey church of Notre Dame de Faverney was packed with worshipers, a fire suddenly engulfed the altar at which two consecrated hosts were on display. As the fire raged out of control and the altar broke into pieces, the monstrance containing the hosts remained suspended in the air, beyond reach of the flames, and remained there, levitating, for thirty-three hours. News of the event spread quickly. At Faverney and at Rome, the authorities did their utmost to give this miracle an anti-Protestant spin. The archbishop of Besançon wasted no time in saying that God had performed the miracle

> for his greater glory, the conversion of heretics, the universal well-being of his Church, the defense of truth, and particularly for the good of our diocese, and the peace and joy of all Christian princes . . . and every place in which this great miracle comes to be known, to the consolation and edification of all of His people, and increased grace, virtue, and devotion in each of us.[13]

Rome quickly became involved, too. Pope Paul V sent a special delegate to investigate, and the miracle was swiftly confirmed by the Congregation of Rites, which sealed its findings with the creation of a special feast for the host of Faverney, to be celebrated every 30 October. In a bull proclaiming the authenticity of the miracle, Pope Paul V minced no words. This miracle was a decisive victory over the Huguenots:

> The dazzling truth of Catholic dogma confounded the heretics who at that time were working hard to introduce their errors into that province. Not one among them dared to raise his voice in public to contradict the facts recorded in the official report; and their silence is but one more proof of the authenticity of the miracle.[14]

Such otherworldliness had its worldly uses, then, especially when it came to polemics and the definition of Catholic identity. And for Catholics here was the essence of their religion, most wonderfully reified: the intermingling of the natural and supernatural, the worldly and the otherworldly.

Lay Involvement and Education

For all its otherworldliness, this reinvigorated Catholicism could be exceedingly pragmatic and down to earth, especially when it came to lay devotion. Ever conscious of the need to reform the church "in head and limbs," the Council of Trent gave a great boost to those lay movements that were already an essential part of the church's life.

First and foremost, the council sought to promote lay participation in confraternities, that is, in lay associations that devoted themselves to specific devotions and acts of charity. Confraternities had been around for centuries, and they had played an increasingly important role in religious and civic life in the late Middle Ages. Their functions were as varied as the needs of any community, and as much of an intermingling of material and spiritual concerns as one might expect from a culture that so closely linked the natural and supernatural. Confraternities were deeply involved not just in specific devotions, such as the use of the prayer beads of the rosary, or the adoration of the Eucharist, or the celebration of certain feasts, but also in charitable and philanthropic activities, such as the running of hospitals, almshouses, orphanages, and rehabilitation centers for former prostitutes. Wherever Protestants disbanded confraternities, they did much more than extinguish all sorts of rituals and public celebrations; they also wiped out much of the local charitable infrastructure, which they then redesigned and placed in the hands of civil authorities, to be funded by compulsory taxes rather than by voluntary acts of charity.

The Council of Trent refashioned and renewed confraternity life just as it refashioned and renewed nearly every other aspect of Catholic life and culture. Its approach was twofold, first this ancient component of lay piety was not only sanctioned but also encouraged to grow, especially in those aspects of Catholic life that were distinctly counter-Protestant, such as devotion to Mary, the rosary, the souls in purgatory, and the Eucharist; second, confraternities were brought more directly under clerical control, and integrated more fully into parish life. Sponsored by bishops, local clergy, and especially by religious orders such as the Jesuits and Capuchins, confraternities flourished after Trent. In Venice, for instance, confraternities grew in number from 120 in the early 1500s to 387 in the 1700s. And individual confraternities could have thousands of members: one in Naples counted more than six thousand in 1563, decades before the boom in membership peaked. In Cuenca, Spain, 62 percent of men and 40 percent of women belonged to at least one confraternity in the 1570s, and many belonged to more than one. The impact of the confraternities extended beyond their members, too, for the roles they performed could touch the entire community. By the 1590s, nearly every will in nearby Madrid requested the presence of at least one confraternity at the funeral, and many testators asked to become last-minute members so they could be buried in confraternity garb. In Seville, seventeenth-century confraternities would develop the most elaborate and intense Holy Week processions in all of Europe, events that defined the character of the city, and continue to do so even today.

In places where Protestantism had made inroads, confraternities could play a pivotal role in reestablishing Catholic piety and defining a new Catholic identity. In Bohemia and Poland, for instance, newly minted confraternities helped establish rural devotion to St. Isidore the Farmer, a Spanish saint canonized in 1622 who was promoted as the model peasant: ever pious, ever industrious, ever obedient to landlords. In places where Catholicism was firmly entrenched, confraternities could flex their muscles even against the highest authority in the land. When King Philip II of Spain attempted to turn over some of the philanthropic activities of confraternities to civil authorities, and to fund them through taxes instead, the confraternities rose in protest and made him abandon that plan. Their chief complaint was a ringing affirmation of Tridentine Catholic teaching: if works of mercy were to be taken from the hands of the laity and turned over to government officials, and if all voluntary almsgiving were replaced with mandatory taxes, how were the faithful to earn their salvation?

All in all, by promoting a theology of personal responsibility for charity and devotion, and by encouraging the proliferation of confraternities, the Catholic Church found a creative way to harness lay piety. But the clergy could not dominate the confraternities, even if some of them had wished to do so. Though confraternities had to have at least one chaplain, and though the church hierarchy attempted to enlarge the role of these chaplains, along with episcopal oversight, confraternities remained very much in lay hands, turning Tridentine theology into action.

Another change, parallel to the growth of confraternities, was a gradual increase in the centrality of parish life in towns and cities, which brought the laity together more closely

Summing up the faith. The catechisms written by Peter Canisius proved immensely popular. In these two pages from a 1792 German edition of the version for young children—still being published and used more than two centuries after it was written—we see the question-and-answer format, along with biblical citations. On the left page, from the section on the sacraments, the question asked is "What is marriage?" On the right page we see in a review section of "Main Elements," a woodcut of Moses receiving the ten commandments from God, above the question "What is the third main element of Catholic teaching?" The biblically based answer is "It is the ten commandments of God, about which Christ said: 'If you want to enter life, keep the commandments.' (Matthew 19)."

under a common roof and a common pastor. And along with this shift of attention toward the parish came also an effort to educate the laity, not just through more frequent sermons, but also through direct instruction. In some locations, lay confraternities played a significant role in the religious instruction of children. But the most significant development of all was the production and distribution of catechisms. The two most popular and influential of these were the *Catechism of the Council of Trent* (1566), which neatly summarized the Catholic faith, and which pastors were supposed to use in the instruction of their flocks, and the three versions of the catechism written by St. Peter Canisius, a Jesuit priest. The intermediate version of Canisius's *Summa doctrinae Christianae* (1555), written expressly for adolescents, would be translated and published over and over for two centuries.

Another key component of Tridentine education was the publication of hundreds of devotional treatises aimed specifically at the laity, such as Luis de Granada's *The Sinner's Guide* (1565), Lorenzo Scupoli's *The Spiritual Combat* (1585), Francis de Sales's *Introduction to the Devout Life* (1609), and Jeremias Drexel's *Heliotropium; or, Conformity of the Human Will with the Divine Will* (1627), all of which went through many editions and translations. Some medieval texts were also resurrected in new translations and editions, including the venerable fifteenth-century *Imitation of Christ* by Thomas à Kempis. Most of these texts shared a common trait: they tried to distill monastic piety for lay folk, proclaiming that holiness could be attained outside the cloister walls, within the world, or as De Sales put it, that "a resolute soul can live in the world without being infected by any of its moods."[15] Although aimed at the laity, their ethic was very ascetic and puritanical. Centered on a strong dualism between flesh and spirit, they fostered a contempt for "the world" as fervent as that of a desert hermit. Even at their mildest, as in the case of De Sales's *Introduction to the Devout Life*, these texts could portray the world as a stinking sewer and the body as the soul's worst enemy. The advice De Sales gave on dancing attests to the austere mentality of much of this literature:

> Balls and dances . . . lean very much towards evil and are consequently full of risk and danger. . . . They extinguish the spirit of devotion, weaken its powers, cool the fervor of charity, and arouse countless evil affections in the soul. This is why they must be used only with the greatest caution. . . . I say that after dancing we must turn to consideration of good and holy things to prevent the baneful effects that the empty pleasure taken in dancing might stamp on our minds. What are such considerations?
>
> 1. While you were at the ball many souls were burning in the flames of hell for sins committed at dances or occasioned by their dancing.
> 2. At the very same time many devout, religious persons were in God's presence, singing his praises and contemplating his beauty. How much more useful was their time spent than yours!
> 3. While you were dancing, many souls departed out of this world in great anguish, and thousands of men and women were suffering dreadful pain in their beds, in hospitals, or out on the streets. . . . Do you not know that some day you shall groan like them while others will dance as you did?

4. Our Lord, our Lady, the angels and saints saw you at the ball. Ah, how greatly
   they pitied you when they saw your heart filled with pleasure by so vain an amusement. . . . Alas! While you were there time was passing away and death was
   drawing nearer. See how he mocks at you and invites you to join his dance![16]

The ultimate goal of this devotional literature was a moral and spiritual perfection no
less intense than that of the best monks and nuns. These texts were a call to sainthood,
and their authors assumed that the human will was able not only to avoid sin, but also to
become adept at loving God and leading a mystical life. "Wherever we may be, we can
and should aspire to a perfect life," advised De Sales.[17] This lofty goal—deemed unreachable by Protestants—was considered by De Sales to be not just within the grasp of the
laity, but also the very essence of the ideal Catholic life.

Another component of lay education, alongside catechisms and devotional literature, was the creation of schools for the children of the emerging bourgeois class, which,
in turn, was linked to the establishment of confraternities solely dedicated to religious
instruction—a phenomenon we will encounter when dealing with the history of the new
religious orders, especially the Jesuits and the Piarists.

As far as higher education was concerned, theology retained its place of honor
as queen of the sciences, but this ranking did not necessarily mean that all subjects were
rigidly subjugated to theology. On the contrary, as Catholic universities evolved, many
subjects and disciplines other than theology steadily gained a higher status, not just as
"handmaidens" to it, but as complimentary partners, essential to its broader reach.

As far as theology was concerned, the "queen of the sciences" remained a clerical
specialty, and within this highly specialized field, Catholics reemphasized the very methods that Protestants had so vehemently attacked, giving rise to a new scholasticism. One
medieval theologian in particular who grew in stature during this period was Thomas
Aquinas (1224–1274). Not only was his *Summa theologicae* promoted by the Council
of Trent; in 1567 Pope Pius V proclaimed him a doctor of the Universal Church, and
from 1570 until well into the eighteenth century, numerous editions of his *Opera omnia*
continued to be published.

But there was far more to the scholastic revival than the revival of Aquinas and
medieval scholasticism. A roster of brilliant theologians, most of them Spanish and many
of them Jesuits, took on all subjects, moving Catholic theology into a new age, writing in
Latin, relying not just on the Bible but also on Plato and Aristotle, the church fathers, and
all the medieval scholastics reviled by Protestants. While engaged in theological questions of the most technical nature, especially on subjects related to the relation between
divine grace and human free will, these neo-scholastics also exerted a profound influence on the discussion of very practical questions in political theory, ethics, economics,
and jurisprudence. The most notable of these thinkers were Dominicans and Jesuits:
Francisco de Vitoria, O.P. (1486–1546), Melchior Cano, O.P. (1509–1560), Francisco
Suárez, S.J. (1548–1617), Luis de Molina, S.J. (1535–1600), and Roberto Bellarmino,

S.J. (1542–1621). The practical, social impact of this second scholasticism on subsequent generations of post-Tridentine clergy and on their flocks should never be underestimated. Once it gained a secure and privileged place in the seminary curriculum throughout the Catholic world, this reinvigorated scholasticism also found its way into the pulpit, the confessional, and devotional texts, serving as the lingua franca of Catholic moral theology.

Conclusion

Catholic reform had multiple aims, and its contours were enormously complex. But at the same time, Catholic reform was guided by a single holistic metaphor: healing the Body of Christ, that is, restoring the well-being of the church, in head and limbs.

As we have seen, inherent polarities marked the Catholic approach to the mystical body of the church, making it impossible to single out one factor as the very essence of Catholic reform. The constant tension generated by three polarities in particular—clergy-laity, universal-local, self-other—as well as the constant need to keep them in balance, made the metaphor of the Body of Christ not just useful, but indispensable. Like all metaphors, it allowed for a multiplicity of meanings and for the coincidence of opposites. It transcended the polarities and at the same time made them comprehensible on a symbolic level. It also had an eminently practical dimension, insofar as it allowed for all reforms, no matter how specific, or small, or local, to be pitched as necessary for all Catholics, everywhere. It embraced all changes and modifications, and, at the same time, anchored them in tradition, for just as a human body changes appearance over time and the person continues to be the same, the Body of Christ was the same as always, yet ever evolving. Reforms in ritual, changed emphases in the cult of the saints, or in that of miracles, and improvements in education and lay piety, all seemingly disparate endeavors, found a common point of reference in the Body of Christ. Moreover, as the *Catechism of the Council of Trent* made clear, this ancient metaphor had a solid biblical basis, which could be rubbed in face of the Protestant "other."[18]

In other words, it was a perfect metaphor.

And its usefulness should be kept in mind as we move to examine the reform of the Catholic clergy.

CHAPTER SIXTEEN

Catholic Reform

Fashioning a New Clergy

Reforming the Secular Clergy

Convinced that genuine reform could take place only from the top down, the Council of Trent focused much of its attention on bishops and the parish priests, that is, on the secular clerics. The first step toward reform was the immediate elimination of abuses great and small: penalizing or removing all those who sold and bought appointments to office, held more than one post at a time, never or seldom set foot in their churches, or broke their vows of celibacy. Even more important, the council looked to the future, calling on bishops to be more involved in the education and oversight of the clergy who were under their charge and encouraging the creation of seminaries and the constant monitoring of clerical job performance.

To reform the lower clergy, however, those at the summit of the church hierarchy would have to lead the way. And that is precisely what happened. At the very top, the papacy itself acquired a new dignity and a higher sense of responsibility, with a string of popes committed to reform. Four popes in particular did all they could to give their office the exclusive right to interpret and enforce the council's decrees: Pius IV (1559–1565), Pius V (1565–1572), Gregory XIII (1572–1585), and Sixtus V (1585–1590). Pius IV, the pope who oversaw the final sessions of the council and approved its decrees, wasted no time in creating a new Roman Congregation of the Council in August 1564, which was charged with overseeing all publications that touched on Trent's decrees and granting or denying them papal approval. A few months later, in November 1564, Pius IV also issued the *Tridentine Profession of Faith*, a summary of the council's doctrinal decrees, which included a pledge of obedience to the pope. The work was to serve as the Catholic counterpart to Protestant summaries of doctrine, such as the Augsburg Confession (1530), the Helvetic Confessions (1536, 1564), and the Book of Concord (1580). The profession would also serve a central role in the creation of a new clergy, for all clerics and professors had to swear conformity to it in order to receive degrees or assume any office.

Pius IV's successors would continue this trend toward Roman centralization: Pope Pius V standardized ritual by issuing a new Roman missal; Pope Gregory XIII expanded the role of papal nuncios, or representatives at the secular courts of Europe, creating special nunciatures dedicated solely to the task of clerical reform; Pope Sixtus V reshaped the curia (the papal administration) through the creation of fifteen congregations, or ministries, all directly under papal supervision, six of which concerned themselves with the Papal States, and nine of which oversaw the running of the church as a whole. Some of these congregations already existed, such as that of the Bishops, the Council, and the Inquisition, but Sixtus V created new ones as well, some of which were given authority to oversee the clergy, such as the Congregations for the Regular Clergy and for the Consistory of Cardinals. In addition, Pope Sixtus V created the Congregation for Rites, to ensure uniformity in rituals performed by the clergy, and he established the Vatican Printing Press, also overseen by a congregation, to give the papacy its own voice among the reading public. Sixtus V would also require all bishops to visit Rome regularly for a review of their performance: every three years for Italian bishops, and every ten years for bishops elsewhere. Finally, the post-Trent papacy also began to increase its role in the selection and appointment of bishops, a task that had been handled at the local level traditionally, often by secular rulers.

With such restructuring and reform at the very top in Rome, and so much of it keyed to issues of reform, success was more likely for any reformer, but not necessarily guaranteed. Creating a new well-educated and zealous clerical class proved a very long and difficult task, one unevenly spread out over the Catholic world.

In some dioceses, reforming bishops such as Milan's Carlo Borromeo (1538–1584), or Braga's Bartolomeu Fernandes dos Mártires (1514–1590) implemented Trent's reforms immediately, holding synods, visiting parishes, disciplining wayward clerics, and establishing seminaries. In Portugal, the reforming zeal of Fernandes dos Mártires transformed the diocese of Braga into a model for others to follow. In Milan, Borromeo established three seminaries, including one devoted to rural clergy, while he dodged bullets and personally ministered to the poor and sick. Other dioceses were reformed much more slowly and less thoroughly. The differences could be stark. In Spain, where synods and provincial councils were held immediately after Trent, and where seminaries had been springing up even before the Council of Trent made them mandatory, the enforcement of clerical and liturgical reforms was taken very seriously. In France, where the crown objected to Trent's affirmation of papal supremacy, and where violence and chaos ruled the day, reforms moved much more slowly, and attempts to establish diocesan seminaries routinely failed. Not until the 1630s, when two clerics named Vincent de Paul and Jean-Jacques Olier took up that task as their special mission, would seminaries be established in sufficient numbers throughout France. In the Holy Roman Empire, which lacked an effective central authority, the reform of secular clerics was predictably uneven: some cities, such as Eichstadt, had seminaries as early as 1564, whereas Münster had to wait until 1610, and Prague until 1631.

Resistance came from many quarters. Nearly everywhere, those who caused the most trouble were clerics from privileged families or from religious orders that claimed to be outside of the bishop's jurisdiction. At times, civil authorities also stood in the way for various reasons—social, political, and economic. For a long time, in many places the bishops themselves were a problem, fearful of violence and paralyzed by inertia. One dismayed Catholic's observations about the German bishops in 1567 also applied to the high clergy in many other places:

> Even the more wise and judicious bishops and prelates are today afraid lest if they demand a slight reformation they may suffer repulse at the hands of their canons. They are frightened by the misery of the age and always in terror of new commotions. One man waits for another to break the ice, and if they attempt anything their efforts are deprecated by lay counselors and politicians. So it is that visitation of dioceses has been neglected . . . ; that synods are not held; that the Council of Trent is neither received nor promulgated; that candidates for ordination are not properly examined; and that clerical vice of the most horrible kind can go on with impunity.[1]

Gradually, however, the impasse was broken. By 1650 it would be difficult to find a diocese or parish that had not been touched by the reforms of the Council of Trent, or secular clergy who still fit the old stereotypes. And a great deal of the credit had to be given not just to courageous bishops and secular priests, but also to their professional brethren, the regular clergy.

Renewing the Regular Clergy

One of the most remarkable features of the Catholic Reformation is how the church as a whole was transformed by monasticism, broadly defined, that is, by that clerical class that was subdivided into different orders and guided by rules of a monastic character. And this development seems all the more remarkable in light of the fact that in the early sixteenth century, monasticism as a whole was woefully corrupt and under severe attack. Erasmus's contempt for monks and monasticism in general reflected an attitude that was common among reform-minded humanists. "No vow is more sacred than that of baptism," he argued, taking aim at the monastic assumption that true holiness required vows of poverty, chastity, and obedience.[2] His critique was not only theological, but also based on observation. Most monks fell far short of their ideals, Erasmus constantly argued, because so many of them had no genuine vocation: "as a cowl doesn't make a monk," he quipped, "neither do clothes make a Frenchman."[3] Beginning with Martin Luther, who had come to loathe "monkery" and everything associated with it as the ultimate corruption of Gospel principles and genuine Christianity, Protestants attacked the institution and its members with great virulence, sometimes even with physical violence. Luther filled his writings and sermons with antimonastic invective and even dedicated a long treatise to debunking the "error" of monastic vows.[4] Ulrich Zwingli called monks "fattened pigs in

Image problem. At the beginning of the sixteenth century, laity and clergy alike were all too familiar with the worst failings of monasticism. While Catholic reformers focused on weeding out or rehabilitating corrupt monastics, Protestants launched an all-out assault on monasticism, dismissing it as inherently corrupt and unnecessary. This 1525 woodcut by Erhard Schön relies on late medieval stereotypes, but conveys the new Protestant message: monasticism must be abolished because monks are the tools of the devil. Here, a demon plays a bagpipe that nobody could fail to identify as a monk's head. Part of the message could be missed now, centuries later, but when this woodcut was made the bagpipe was widely recognized as a symbol for lust.

disguise" whose vows were "grounded solely in hypocrisy and idolatry," adding that there were no people on earth "richer than monks and none more avaricious."[5] In Protestant pamphlet literature, monks figure prominently as exemplars of every vice, and as social parasites living comfortably while others toil for them.

Protestant attacks on monasticism derived from the observation of social realities as much as from theology. In many ways, they reflected public sentiment. Even at the summit of the Catholic Church hierarchy, the problem of monastic corruption had to be admitted. In 1537, the papal commission that wrote the brutally honest *Consiliium de emendanda ecclesia* called for the abolition of all conventual (lax) orders and assessed all monastic institutions as "so deformed that they are a great scandal to the laity and do grave harm by their example."[6]

Nonetheless, these men and women who followed a lifestyle that Protestants rejected as unchristian, and who were always reviled by them as the epitome of corruption, managed to infuse new life into the Catholic Church in unexpected ways even as such grave assessments were being made. They also proved true two of the most significant unquestioned assumptions of Catholic reform: first, monastic or semimonastic institutions did have a useful role to play in society at large; and second, the moral and spiritual health of the regular clergy was key to the renewal of the church as a whole.

Long before the Council of Trent first assembled in 1545, a reforming spirit could be found among the regular clergy here and there. Reform was a constant and inescapable necessity among the monks, nuns, friars, and priests who ostensibly left "the world" behind—as inescapable as the corruption that could so easily infect their communities. Since the various rules (in Latin, *regulae*) they ostensibly followed called for constant self-scrutiny and a life of austerity, it stands to reason that the regular clergy would often reform themselves. But they also often sought to improve the church as a whole and even "the world" itself, especially after the establishment of noncloistered orders such as the Franciscans and Dominicans, whose sole purpose was to minister to that very world whose values they shunned.

In established religious orders, the key to reform was always close at hand, in the rules that the members were supposed to observe. One would think, then, that simply enforcing the rules would be simple enough. But nothing could be further from the truth. Rules were always open to interpretation, and over the centuries many modifications had led to no end of trouble, in terms of both the behaviors allowed and the discord caused within communities. Differences in the interpretation of the Rule of St. Francis, for instance, had torn apart the Friars Minor and even the church as a whole in the thirteenth century.

Any would-be reformer who wished to reinterpret an order's rule more strictly faced two major challenges: aside from the immense difficulty of compelling anyone to reform his or her behavior, it was also legally impossible within the Catholic Church to force anyone to submit to an interpretation of a rule different from that to which a vow had been made. In other words, a Conventual Franciscan could never be forced to become an Observant, or to observe any rule he had not vowed to obey. A difference was acknowledged between rules that were corrupted or ignored and rules that had been legally mitigated. Obvious cases of corruption, such as the flagrant breaking of vows of chastity, could always be legally corrected, and on those grounds Cardinal Francisco Jiménez de Cisneros and other properly authorized reformers could expel hundreds of monks and friars from their communities. But mitigated rules that led to subtler forms of corruption, allowing monks and nuns to have personal servants, for example, or to visit freely with friends and family, could not be summarily undone. In such cases, only the pope or some legislative body within the order itself could enforce changes. Instances of this kind of reform were rare. And even then, those who had taken their vows before such a reversal were not bound to observe the stricter rule.

These legal limits placed on the interpretation and reinterpretation of the rules of orders were the reason the reform of the established regular clergy had to come in two different forms: either through a shake-up from within and the expulsion of unworthy men and women who were breaking the vows they had taken, or through the creation of new branches of established orders, in which the original rule would be observed more strictly. In the sixteenth and seventeenth centuries, both of these types of reform proliferated as never before. A few salient examples can help one understand how the process worked.

Benedictines

The Benedictines were the oldest order in Western Christendom, although to call them an "order" can be misleading, since Benedictine monasteries had been in existence for many centuries before *orders* came into existence in the 900s. It was only with the proliferation of orders in the twelfth and thirteenth centuries that Benedictines gained the characteristics of an order and began to reform themselves by establishing congregations, or autonomous associations that bound certain monasteries together through the abbot of one house, and assemblies known as chapters-general that agreed on a common interpretation of the Rule of St. Benedict.

In late medieval Spain, for instance, there were two Benedictine congregations: Tarragona, established in 1336, and Valladolid, which originated in 1417. Backed by the monarchs of Castile, the austere monks of San Benito el Real of Valladolid managed to extend their reform to more than a dozen monasteries by the mid-fifteenth century, and another two dozen or so by 1517. Among the monasteries in this congregation, Our Lady of Montserrat near Barcelona carried this Benedictine reform into Aragon and Catalonia, under the leadership of García Jiménez de Cisneros, a cousin of the famous reforming cardinal Francisco mentioned earlier. In Germany, a similar process began at the monastery of Bursfeld in 1433. By 1446, when the Bursfeld Union was officially recognized, six monasteries were under its reforming leadership. By 1517 the number had swelled to around a hundred. By 1500, the map of Europe was dotted with Benedictine congregations: in Austria, it was Melk Abbey that established a reforming congregation in 1418; in France, it was the Congregation of Chezal-Benoit; in Hungary, Poland, and Dalmatia, similar congregations also engaged in the work of reform.

In Italy, reform and congregation building can be traced back to the monastery of Santa Giustina at Padua, around 1409, which was given to a small band of reforming monks who followed the Rule of Benedict very strictly. By 1421, the reforming spirit had spread from Santa Giustina to several major Italian monasteries, including San Paolo's in Rome, San Giorgio's in Venice, and none other than Monte Cassino itself, the community established by St. Benedict nearly a millennium earlier, in 529. The growth of this congregation was as impressive as its influence. Renamed the "Cassinine Congregation" in 1504, in reference to the mother house at Monte Cassino, this network of reformed monasteries would eventually number more than two hundred in Italy, and also spread into France.

In 1516, the Cassinine Congregation was joined by the Abbey of Lérins in Provence, along with all of its affiliated monasteries. By then, the Cassinine reform was attracting eminent men, such as the scholar Giovanni Andrea Cortese, an exact contemporary of Martin Luther who served as the abbot at Lérins from 1524 to 1527. Cortese (1483–1548), a consummate scholar who corresponded with the leading lights of the humanist movement and established an academy in Lérins, is credited with bringing the new Italian learning to Provence. He also figures prominently in the reforming movement within the Italian church. Serving as abbot in Modena, Perugia, and finally at San Giorgio's in Venice, he attracted like-minded reformers who sought to create a new devout and zealous clerical class. Eventually, Cortese would help pave the way for the Council of Trent. In 1536, he was one of the nine eminent reformers commissioned by Pope Paul III to draw up a plan for church reform, which produced the influential document *Consiliium de Emendanda Ecclesia.* Elevated to the post of cardinal in 1542 and named bishop of Urbino, Cortese would use his influence at the papal court to foster clerical reform in any way possible.

Franciscans

Among other regular clergy, the process of reform in the sixteenth century usually entailed the creation of a separate order in the same family tree, so to speak. The Franciscans, especially, were prone to this kind of branching, which was not at all a fragmentation or diminution, but rather an augmentation of their influence. Most of these reforms placed a heavy emphasis on returning to a life of self-denial, prayer, and contemplation, but in many cases, this mystical turn was also accompanied by a keen dedication to some sort of public ministry, be it preaching, teaching, or caring for the sick and poor.

In Spain, an emphasis on strict adherence to the original Rule of St. Francis led to the development of the discalced, or barefoot movement. Beginning around 1496, in Granada, the discalced reform sputtered for several decades, constantly under attack by other Franciscans, until it finally found a very able leader in of St. Peter of Alcántara (1499–1562), an austere mystic who allegedly slept only two hours a day. Under Peter's leadership, the Discalced Franciscans began to flourish in Spain and throughout Europe, the Americas, and the East Indies. Known as Alcantarines, these barefoot friars acquired a reputation for holiness and dedication to their public ministry, even as their order continued to be embroiled in nearly constant disputes with other Franciscans.

In Italy, a desire to return to the "primitive" Rule of St. Francis among the Observants led to the creation of yet another branch, which came to be known as the Capuchins, because of the peaked hood (*cappuccio*) that distinguished their habit. Led by Matteo da Bascio (1495–1552), the Capuchins received papal approval in 1528. A parallel order for women, the Capuchines, was established ten years later. In essence, their austerity was very similar to that of the Discalced Franciscans: they were committed to absolute poverty and simplicity. Like the Discalced Franciscans, they would spread throughout Europe and also engage in missionary work in the Americas, Asia, and Africa. Barefoot and bearded, the Capuchin friars begged, prayed, and preached, and ministered especially to the ill and downtrodden. Not even the defection of their vicar-general Bernardino Ochino (1487–1564) to Calvinism in 1542 could stifle their growth. By 1574, there were 3,500 Capuchins housed in three hundred different communities. Though suspected of heresy and banned from preaching for several years after the defection of Ochino, the Capuchin Franciscans would earn a reputation for holiness and service to the needy.

Carmelites

Another branching order was that of the Carmelites, who claimed the oldest "primitive" rule of all, supposedly written by the prophet Elijah for a community of holy men on Mt. Carmel eight centuries before the birth of Christ. Founded in the twelfth century, ostensibly as a revival of the strictest and most ancient of monastic rules, the Carmelites had grown as soft as many other orders. The reform of this order would be led by the Spanish nun Teresa de Jesús (1515–1582), who would become better known as St. Teresa of Ávila.

A nun at the lax Convent of the Incarnation in Ávila, Spain, Teresa set her sights on returning to the primitive rule after coming into contact with Peter of Alcántara, the leader of the Franciscan Discalced reform. Despite heavy opposition from civil and church authorities, Teresa managed to establish a new convent in Ávila in 1562, St. Joseph's, which was to subsist entirely by begging, and in which the sisters would devote themselves to silent, interior prayer, rather than to vocal or sung prayer on behalf of

Gloriosos Petrum et Paulum Apostolos sæpius sibi adstantes, opemq; aduersus dæmonis illusiones pollicentes intuetur: nec vana promissio: nam ea fuit diuinitus illustrata gratia, vt facile omnes dæmonis versutias vinceret.

Ad fontes, redux. The desire to refashion Catholic institutions according to ancient models extended to monasticism. Many reformers, such as Teresa of Ávila, sought to reinstate older rules for their orders. This 1613 engraving by Adriaen Collaert clearly seeks to associate Teresa the reformer with an apostolic lineage by showing her as being blessed and invested with power over demonic forces by none other than SS. Peter and Paul.

patrons. By the time of her death in 1582, Teresa had managed to establish seventeen new Discalced convents for women in Spain, and she had spurred a parallel reform among the male Carmelites. Peter of Alcántara's role in all this was crucial, and a prime example of the cross-fertilization that could take place within the monastic world. He and Teresa and had much in common: both were mystics given over to visions and spiritual ecstasies. And it was due to Peter, in his role as confessor, that Teresa began to gain acceptance as a genuine mystic rather than a demonically deceived or insane nun. It was also due to Peter's encouragement and to the inspiration she derived from his return to a "primitive" rule that Teresa was finally able to launch the reform of her own order, against great odds.

After Teresa's death, the female Discalced Carmelites continued growing, expanding into Italy, France, and Flanders. The male Carmelite reformers faced much stiffer opposition from within their own order. Their leading reformer, Juan de Yepes, better known as St. John of the Cross (1542–1591), was a spiritual disciple of St. Teresa, and a mystic and poet as well. His efforts to introduce the Discalced reform caused him no end of trouble. In 1575, the chapter-general of the Carmelites voted to dissolve the three monasteries that the Discalced had established and to return all the friars to their original communities. The Discalced refused to obey this order, however, and responded by holding a defiant chapter meeting of their own some months later, at which they reaffirmed their autonomy. After appeals to Rome had been made by both sides, the Discalced ended up being excommunicated for disobedience. John of the Cross was seized by his own brethren and imprisoned in Toledo, under appalling conditions, as mentioned in an earlier chapter. Eventually, thanks to the intervention of King Philip II, a special province was created for Discalced friars in 1580, under the administration of the Carmelite director general—an arrangement that ensured the continued mistreatment of reformers such as John of the Cross. In late 1593, two years after the death of John of the Cross, the Discalced Carmelite friars would finally obtain total autonomy, under their own director general.

Cistercians

A similar reforming spirit swept through other orders as well. Among the Cistercians, the Feuillants were established as a separate congregation in 1589, thanks to the efforts of Jean de la Barrière (1554–1600). Their austerities were so extreme as to seem a deliberate physical and spiritual refutation of Protestant *sola fide* theology. The Feuillants were strict vegetarians who abstained from eating red meat, poultry, fish, eggs, and butter. In addition to renouncing salt, pepper, and all spices, they gave up wine as well, and ate on the floor, on their knees. Their diet was very similar to that of many prisoners: bread, oatmeal, and boiled greens. As if all this were not severe enough, they renounced shoes too, and slept on the floor, with stones for pillows, for only four hours a day. They also spoke to one another as little as possible, and engaged in constant prayer and physical labor. Lest such a commitment to self-denial be dismissed as marginal extremism, it should be added that the Feuillants attracted enough of a following as to allow them to expand into Italy, and a female branch of this austere order, the Feuillantes, which was established at roughly the same time, attracted a good number of women from the upper echelons of society.

Yet nothing highlights the difficulty of reforming an entire order more clearly than the limitations of the Feuillant branch of the Cistercian order. Despite the decrees of the Council of Trent, and the efforts of reforming individuals and communities, the Cistercians as a whole remained impervious to change for quite some time, especially in France, where the practice of naming commendatory abbots—abbots who received the income attached to a monastery, or monasteries, but did not have to take vows or even live with the monks—remained common for some time after the closing of the Council of Trent.

A prime exemplar of this sort of corruption was a French nobleman who would transform himself into a reformer, Armand-Jean le Bouthillier de Rancé (1626–1700). Born into privilege, De Rancé entered a clerical career with no religious vocation, as many young men of his class used to do, simply to enrich himself and his family. By the age of thirty, he had accumulated five abbeys and several other benefices, including that of first chaplain to the brother of King Louis XIII, Gaston, the Duke of Orleans. By his own account, De Rancé spent more time at the royal court than at any of his five abbeys, one of which was that of La Trappe in Normandy. "In the morning preach like an angel, in the afternoon hunt like a devil," is how he summed up his life at court.[7] In 1657, however, the death of one of his closest friends, the Duchess of Montbazon, led him to a gradual religious conversion. In 1660, upon the death of the Duke of Orleans, which he witnessed firsthand, De Rancé began to divest himself of all of his church posts, one by one, except for the Abbey of La Trappe, to which he retired. At La Trappe, in 1664, the former courtier began a reform much like those that other orders had undertaken. Returning to a "strict observance" of the Rule of St. Benedict, De Rancé turned La Trappe into an austere model community, despite considerable opposition from the monks. Less extreme in their self-denial than the Feuillants, the monks of La Trappe devoted themselves to a life of ceaseless prayer and work, in which silence played a key role. Eventually, as the monks of La Trappe extended their reform to other monasteries in the eighteenth century, they would come to be known informally as Trappists, and formally as Cistercians of the Strict Observance. Their austerity and mystical fervor would make the Trappists silent witnesses to the reforming spirit that guided early modern Catholic monasticism, a spirit at once rooted in ancient traditions and in a very new, self-conscious rejection of Protestantism.

Trappists, Feuillants, Discalced Carmelites, Capuchins, and Discalced Franciscans were but a few of the many new branches that sprung from centuries-old orders in the sixteenth and seventeenth centuries. Ironically, even though this monastic revival was wholly opposed to all the key points of Protestantism, in many ways it nonetheless shared one key characteristic with Protestantism and with humanism: the desire to renew the present by returning *ad fontes*, to a distant past free of corruption. That point, in and of itself, speaks volumes about the complexities of early modern Catholicism, and of the reform of its regular clergy—complexities that manifested even more intensely in new orders that were committed not to renewing ancient paradigms, but to creating a new kind of clergy who could engage directly with new environments.

Creating New Orders

As the world changed in the sixteenth and seventeenth centuries, many Catholics relied on their ancient heritage to meet the challenge, not as retrograde conservatives, but rather as adaptive innovators who drew on past experience with great flexibility. In the sixteenth and seventeenth centuries, this meant adapting to the following changes: the growth of cities and of literate urban populations, along with all of the social ills that accompanied this urbanization; the religious divisions caused by the Protestant Reformation; the expansion of Christendom overseas to Asia, Africa, and the Americas; the rise of the modern nation-state and of empirical science, along with the rise of secularism and skepticism.

The creation of new religious orders as a response to change was a well-established pattern in medieval Catholicism, with an impressive record of success. It stands to reason, then, that men and women concerned with the welfare of the church and society would instinctively rely on what was tried and true, and that they would do so with confidence. The statistics speak for themselves: if one adds up the new branches of older orders together with the wholly new orders created between 1500 and 1699, the total number is greater than that for all religious orders created in the previous fifteen centuries combined.

All in all, more than thirty orders were established in the sixteenth and seventeenth centuries. Their range of activities varied as much as their size, impact and significance: while the Somascans ministered to the poor and the Hospitallers to the sick, the Ursulines focused on the education of girls; and while the Eudists established

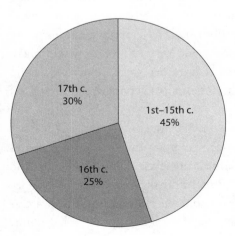

Establishment of new religious orders, 1st–17th centuries

seminaries, the Lazarists devoted themselves to missionary activity among the poor rural folk of Europe. Some orders remained small and localized, such as the Sisters of St. Joseph of Bourg, whereas others, such as the Jesuits, surpassed most others in terms of their numbers and global reach. While it is undeniable that these new orders had much to do with the successful implementation of the Tridentine reforms, it would nonetheless be an error to see the Council of Trent as their point of origin, for the inclination to create new orders had been gathering momentum steadily, decades before the council assembled, and even helped to shape decisions made at Trent. All of those orders established after 1563 were indelibly stamped, however, with the council's reforming spirit.

Like the new branches that sprouted from older orders, the new orders contained a mixture of traits that were distinctly "modern" and at the same time traditional and defiantly anti-Protestant. Shaped as much by the desire to remain faithful to the past as by the desire to meet the challenges of the present, most of these orders sought not only to stamp out corruption, but also to deny Protestants their say on as many levels as possible, both mundane and theological. Covering each and every order is not necessary here. Instead, let us focus on those orders that best exemplified the reformation of the regular clergy in early modern Catholicism.

Barnabites

Among those orders that sprang up before the Council of Trent, we have already encountered the Theatines (chapter 6) and the Capuchins. Another reforming pre-Tridentine order was that of the Barnabites, who established the church of St. Barnabas in Milan in 1530. Committed to the renewal of the clerical state and to ministering to the poor and the sick, the Barnabites did much to pave the way for Carlo Borromeo and to assist him. Borromeo, in turn, would support and encourage their work, and spur them to rewrite their rule in the 1570s to bring it more closely in line with the Tridentine decrees. Two traits distinguished the Barnabites from other orders, and both reflected the modern character of their reforming spirit. First, as indicated by their formal name—Clerics Regular of St. Paul—they returned *ad fontes* by making the epistles of St. Paul the centerpiece of their preaching and teaching. Second, to remain close to their flocks, they took a special vow: to never seek high church offices, and to never accept such offices unless ordered to do so by the pope. Spreading out from Milan to other locations in Italy, Savoy, France, Austria, and Bohemia, the Barnabites dedicated themselves to various ministries, but remained firmly committed to learning and education. A relatively small order, they nonetheless had a profound impact on both the clergy and laity wherever they went.

Ursulines and Visitandines

One of the most salient characteristics of Catholic reform was the role assumed by women. And few other new orders—male or female—were as impressive as the Ursulines and Visitandines, which assumed different roles but shared a common zeal and a spirit of innovation.

Of these two, the Company of St. Ursula, more commonly known as the Ursulines, blazed the most daring trail. Founded in 1535 by St. Angela de Merici (1474–1540) in the Italian city of Brescia, the Ursulines were the very first religious order for women dedicated to teaching, a profession associated with the cult of St. Ursula, an early Christian martyr. Although the Ursulines were loosely organized and plagued by controversies during the first four decades of their existence, they spread quickly throughout Europe after 1584. Eventually, they would also reach some of its overseas colonies. In 1639, for instance, the first convent for women in North America would be established, in New France, by an Ursuline nun, Marie Guyart, better known as Marie de l'Incarnation (1599–1672).[8] In Italy, most Ursulines were uncloistered or semicloistered, some living in communities, and others living at home with their families. Elsewhere, especially in France, they were eventually cloistered. But whether they were cloistered or not did not seem to matter much, as far as their effectiveness was concerned. The Ursulines excelled at their teaching ministry, not only because of their methods and dedication, but also because they fulfilled a very modern need: that of educating the daughters of the rising urban bourgeoisie and of ensuring that they were properly instructed in Christian doctrine and morals. They also fulfilled another role that became the hallmark of many of the new orders, for they ministered to the needy. Their success is revealed by their numbers, even though their loose organization makes it difficult to come up with exact figures: it is estimated that in France alone, by 1750 there were about ten thousand Ursulines living in 350 communities. The Council of Trent had declared it preferable for religious women to be cloistered and given over to a contemplative life, but the Ursulines excelled at the active life amid the harsh realities of the "world," even to the point of surpassing in numbers the most renowned of male teaching orders, the Jesuits. Anyone looking for flexibility and adaptation in early modern Catholicism need look no further than the Company of St. Ursula.

The Ursulines also exhibited a self-confidence that transcended gender and social conventions concerning the role of religious women. Angela de Merici's deathbed farewell, which expressed a deep confidence in the power of the human will to do good and earn salvation "manfully and faithfully," summed up the Catholic ethos of the Ursulines succinctly:

> May the strength and true comfort of the Holy Ghost be with all of you, that you may thereby be enabled to bear and execute manfully and faithfully the task which you have undertaken,—and may also look forward to the great reward which God has prepared for you. . . . Since God has trusted this undertaking to you, so will He give you strength to carry it out, provided only that you fail Him not. Do your duty, therefore, go about your active functions, be full of trust, of courage, of high hope, send up your heart-cry to God in your need; and doubt not but you will see Him do great things for you, while

you will aim at doing all things for the praise and glory of His Infinite Majesty, and for the spiritual welfare of the souls dear to Him.[9]

Women could also bring change to the more traditional monastic model, that of the strictly cloistered contemplative order. One such new reforming order was that of the Sisters of the Visitation of Mary, also known as Visitandines or the Salesian Sisters. Founded in 1610 at Annecy in the Duchy of Savoy by Francis de Sales, bishop of Geneva, and by an aristocratic young widow, Jeanne de Chantal (1572–1641), the Visitandines embodied the ideals of moderation championed by Francis de Sales in his devotional texts and his reforming work.

Though cloistered and devoted to prayer and contemplation, the Visitandines avoided all extremes in self-denial. This departure from tradition led to another innovation: freed from the rigors of fasting, self-mortification, and sleep deprivation, they could open their membership to the elderly, the physically handicapped, the poor, and even the chronically ill. In other words, their moderate approach to penance allowed them to admit a wide range of women who would normally have been banned from monastic life. Their growth was phenomenal: between 1615 and 1622, there were 13 convents established; by 1641, when Jeanne de Chantal died, the number had increased to 86; by 1715, it was up to 147. In the eighteenth century, the order expanded outside of France to other

Reforming saints. When it came to depicting reform, early modern Catholic artists blurred the lines between regular and secular clergy as often as the lines between the heavenly and earthly realms. This eighteenth-century painting by Francisco Bayeu Subias seeks to immortalize the moment when Francis de Sales, bishop of Geneva, presented Jeanne de Chantal with a rule for her new order, the Visitandines.

countries in Europe, and eventually to the New World. And the Visitandines' seclusion behind cloister walls would not prevent them from having an effect on the outside world. An exemption won for them by Francis de Sales was that of allowing lay women to spend time within the cloister, which gave the Visitandines freedom to conduct retreats, and to influence the lives of the laity. It is no accident that one of the most significant and distinctive of all modern Catholic devotions sprang from one of their convents, where one of the sisters, Margaret Mary Alacoque (1647–1690), claimed to receive extraordinary revelations from Jesus Christ himself. The message and the icon relayed to the outside world by Sister Margaret Mary in the late seventeenth century would capture the imagination of Catholics everywhere. Suddenly, devotion to the Sacred Heart of Jesus became immensely popular. The icon of Christ baring his glowing heart, scarred and bleeding, encircled by a crown of thorns, would become so emblematic of Catholic culture that to most modern Catholics it could easily have seemed as ancient as the church itself.

Hospitallers

Ultimately, the renewal of contemplative life exemplified by the Visitandines and others like them would play a significant role in Catholic culture, sharpening its distinctiveness vis-à-vis Protestantism. Nonetheless, the influence of contemplatives was limited, especially when compared to other new orders that ministered to the corporeal needs of the laity as much as to their souls. And some orders specialized precisely in tending to the poor, the sick, and the dying. One of the most impressive of these was the Brothers Hospitallers, founded in Granada, Spain, by João Cidade Duarte, a former soldier, shepherd, laborer, peddler, and bookseller who took on the religious name of Juan de Dios, or John of God (1495–1550).

The trajectory of John's life itself is a product of the religious reforms that swept through Spain in the early sixteenth century, and an example of the way clerical reformers could influence the laity and produce more reformers. Unlike many founders of religious orders, John was not a monastic when he began his ministry; he was a restless wanderer with religious leanings who developed an interest in helping the needy and in distributing devotional texts and pictures. Many of the texts he sold, which obviously had an impact on him, were those that Cardinal Jiménez de Cisneros had brought to light (see chapter 6). Inspired to move to Granada by a vision he had of the child Jesus, he opened a book store near one of the city's gates, at which he sold his texts nearly at cost, with hardly any profit to keep his business afloat. In January 1539, a sermon by none other than John of Ávila (see chapter 6) produced a sudden conversion in him. After selling his business and giving all the proceeds to the poor, the future John of God began to wander through the streets of Granada much like an Old Testament prophet, calling all to repentance and begging God's mercy.

The response to John was not much different from that received by some of the Old Testament prophets he was emulating. Pelted with stones, jeered and mocked, he was quickly judged insane and thrown into the Royal Hospital of Granada, where he encountered the mad, the sick, and the dying, as well as the worst wretchedness in medical care. Vowing to dedicate the rest of his life to the care of the sick, and to improving conditions for them, he convinced the authorities that he had regained his sanity, and after being released, he established a hospital of his own in Granada in 1540, with the help of John of Ávila.

For the following ten years, John, the bookseller-turned-nursemaid, astonished Granada and set new standards for medical care, taking in the sick wherever he found them, nursing them back to health, helping them to die a good death, begging for alms everywhere, with a haunting refrain that preyed upon everyone's selfishness and altruism all at once: "Hermanos, haceos bien a vosotros mismos" (Brethren, be good to yourselves). One could not find a more practical summation of Catholic teaching on charity: love of neighbor is also love of self, for every act of charity brings a reward. Everyone wins in the end with such a formula, the needy as well as the generous. Soon enough, John of God—as he came to be called—began collecting more than alms. Inspired by his example, disciples flocked to his side, and to the aid of the sick of Granada. Nobles, priests, and bishops offered him support and the hospital flourished, along with his ministries to widows, orphans, prostitutes, and the poor and homeless. By the time he died in 1550, he had gathered enough followers and patrons to ensure the survival of his mission and its expansion.

Under the leadership of Antonio Martín, one of John of God's first disciples, the Hospitallers flourished. Having attracted the attention of King Philip II, they began to benefit from his support, first with a new hospital in Madrid, then with a second one in Córdoba, and several others throughout Spain, all funded by the crown. In 1572, the order of Brothers Hospitallers was formally approved by Pope Pius V, and soon thereafter it began to spread beyond Spain, to Europe and its overseas colonies. In 1584, Pope Gregory XIII gave the Hospitallers charge of a hospital in Rome, that of St. John Calybita, which became the mother house of the entire order, shifting its center from Spain to Rome. The work of the Hospitallers in France, which began in 1601, was as impressive, perhaps, as that of the Ursulines. By the 1750s, in France alone they would run forty hospitals and care for more than four thousand patients.

Like the Ursulines, St. John of God and his followers had found a dire need in society and a way of dealing with it. Guided by practical concerns as much as by spiritual values (both of which they saw as inseparable), the Brothers Hospitallers came to embody both clerical and social reform.

In an age when Europeans were revamping medieval approaches to poor relief and medical care, religion played a key role. Protestants and Catholics found different ways of funding poor relief and hospitals, and of improving upon systems and institutions that needed to adjust to the new social and political realities created by increased urbanization and the advent of a money-based rather than a barter economy, but necessity was the mother of invention in this area of human experience as much as in many others. Catholics and Protestant communities in the sixteenth and seventeenth century had similar social problems to solve, and they found different ways to confront them. Catholics, on the whole, tended to rely on the voluntary initiative of individuals, confraternities, and religious orders, and on the salvific power of charity, which spurred them to action. Protestants, in contrast, tended to rely on the state and on taxation. To debate whether one approach was more efficient than the other, or more "modern," would be an unnecessary distraction here, at this point. The issue at hand is how clerical reform and social concerns merged in early modern Catholicism. To focus on what might have been most efficient is to miss the point that religion is shaped by social and political realities as much as it shapes them. St. John of God's response to specific challenges, while thoroughly Catholic, also involved all sorts of pragmatic problem solving.

Some historians have argued that St. John of God is the father of modern hospitals, a medical and social trailblazer of the first rank.[10] A mystic prone to visions, a would-be prophet taken for mad, St. John of God was as much a beneficiary of reform as a reformer. Everything he experienced and accomplished was inseparably linked to the work of other reformers, such as Cardinal Francisco Jiménez de Cisneros, who promoted the translation and publication of the texts that led to John of God's conversion, and St. John of Ávila, whose preaching and teaching gave shape to John of God's commitment to a life of social service. Ultimately, St. John offers us a glimpse of the multiple dimensions of reform in early modern Catholicism and of the ways all improvements can be linked to one another, not just in one's own day, but across generations.

Piarists

Another prime exemplar of the interweaving of religion and social reform was St. Joseph (José) de Calasanz (1556–1648), the founder of the Order of Poor Clerks Regular of the Mother of God of the Pious Schools, an order dedicated to educating disadvantaged children. Mercifully known as Piarists or Scolapians, the priests of this order took an additional vow, committing themselves to a teaching ministry. Their work began in 1597, when Joseph, a Spanish priest who had moved to Rome, opened a free school for poor children in the two rooms lent to him by the pastor of the church of Santa Dorotea. This school—the very first of its kind in Europe—had as its aim the uplifting of an entire social class, child by child, and made no distinctions between its religious and pragmatic aims. Joseph's pupils not only were given religious instruction, as one might expect, but also were taught all the basic academic subjects in their own language, rather than in Latin—as was then assumed necessary—with an emphasis on pragmatic skills that could prepare them for work in commercial enterprises, such as learning about weights and measures and interest rates. In addition, they were provided with free paper, quills, and ink. Hundreds of poor parents rushed to get their children into Joseph's school within a matter of weeks. Thanks to the support of several patrons and members of the high clergy—including popes Clement VII and Paul V—and to the fervor of the other priests who quickly joined

Joseph, the school grew and prospered, and so did the community led by Joseph. In 1621 Pope Gregory XV officially recognized them as a religious order.

Over the following two decades, the Piarists and their free public schools continued to flourish, but not without difficulty or controversy. Their most pressing problem, ironically, was their success. As their reputation increased, so did the demand for Piarist schools. Finding the right men and training them to teach was not only difficult, but also a lengthy process. Joseph de Calasanz was a severely ascetic micromanager, a perfectionist who expected the most from his priests, and subjected all candidates to rigorous scrutiny. His surviving 4,869 letters are full of minute instructions, detailing even what sort of underwear was best for the students in cold climates. But as the demand for his schools increased, the recruitment process became overburdened. Eventually, Joseph found it impossible to deal with the issue of supply and demand. At one point, he boastfully complained, "If I had ten thousand priests now in one month I could send them out to all those places which are desperately begging for us."[11]

In comparison to other difficulties they faced, however, the inability to meet demand was a good problem. Internal struggles for leadership within the order, coupled with opposition from some who disliked the whole notion of educating the poor and from religious orders that feared losing their patrons to the Piarists, caused no end of grief for Joseph de Calasanz. In 1630, charges made by one of his own power-hungry priests, Mario Sozzi, led to Joseph's removal as superior general. Though cleared of all charges and reinstated, Joseph continued to attract criticism from some of his own priests, and also from outside the order. Much of the external opposition came from the Jesuits, that other new order engaged in education. (Never let it be said that religious orders are necessarily free of the stain of original sin, or of the vice of jealousy, or of the need to compete for patrons and donations).

But that was not the worst of it. In addition, the Piarists attracted suspicion for two controversies, one very noble and the other as tawdry as they come. First, the Piarists made many powerful enemies by supporting Galileo Galilei in his struggles against church authorities, and by teaching his radically new heliocentric theory in their schools. Then, in 1646, they sank into the deepest abyss when their superior general was exposed as a sexual predator who not only had abused many children, but also created a network of pederasts within the order itself. The superior in question came from a prominent Roman family rife with papal lawyers, and he had every reason to think he could sin with impunity, at least in this life. His partners in crime rode on his coattails. He was Stefano Cherubini, onetime headmaster of the Piarist school in Naples and former visitor-general of the order. A bon vivant who was the polar opposite of the austere Joseph de Calasanz, the well-connected Cherubini had schemed against his superior for years and finally replaced Joseph as head of the order. Even worse, proof came to light that the sexual abuse had been known about for many years within the Piarist order, even by the holy but hapless Joseph, and that nothing had been done about it, save for shuffling the pederasts from one school to another. The potential scandal was carefully hushed up, and the ironically named Cherubini was removed from office for "administrative inefficiency," but this outrage was the proverbial straw that broke the camel's back. In 1646 the status of the order was reduced to that of a society, which meant that all of its priests were placed under the authority of their local bishops. In essence, the order was disbanded. Shortly afterward, Joseph de Calasanz died at the age of ninety-two, his life's work seemingly undone. But the Piarists and their schools were too useful to discard. Within a few years of Joseph's passing, the order would emerge again full of vigor, ready to conquer new mission fields.

Success, controversy, scandal, and a brush with extinction marked the first few decades of the Piarist order. What can we make of this? That an order of priests dedicated to serving the poor should be disbanded for supporting Galileo and for the sexual abuse of children, and that they should spring back to life in a few years, spiffy clean, as if nothing had happened, tells us a lot about the early modern Catholic Church. Above all, the case of the Piarists reveals how complex and difficult the process of reform could be. In addition, it proves how easily corruption could seep in, and how vigilance against corruption could lead to self-correction. The Piarists were gradually restored to full status as an order in stages, in 1660, 1669, and 1698. Ultimately, Joseph de Calasanz would be beatified in 1748 and canonized in 1767. By that time the Piarists had spread far and wide in Europe and its overseas colonies. One of their greatest successes would be their mission in Poland, where, alongside their Jesuit rivals, they helped to turn back the Protestant tide that had nearly engulfed that large corner of the map. Their greatest achievement, perhaps, was the model they established for free public education and their role in inspiring clerics and others to devote themselves to teaching. Among those who would later look to the Piarists as a model would be St. Jean-Baptiste de La Salle in the eighteenth century, St. John Bosco in the nineteenth, and many secular national public school systems in the twentieth. Among their most illustrious alumni, the Piarists would be able to count Joseph Haydn, Wolfgang Amadeus Mozart, Franz Schubert, Francisco Goya, and Victor Hugo. An enviable list indeed, especially for a religious order that had nearly vanished.

The Oratory of Philip Neri

Another community that blurred the lines between religious and social reform, but in a very different way, was the Congregation of the Oratory, founded by St. Philip Neri (1515–1595). Refusing to claim any single ministry as their specialty, the members of this congregation fulfilled multiple needs, often with a flair as distinctive as Neri's personality. Born in Florence and reared near the Dominican friary of San Marco, the former epicenter of Savonarola's apocalyptic campaign against vice, Filippo Neri moved to Rome in 1533, already affected by his very intense religious experiences. After working as a tutor and studying theology and philosophy for a few years, Philip suddenly sold all of his books, gave the proceeds to the poor, and took on the life of an urban hermit, praying at night inside the churches and catacombs of Rome, having visions and mystical raptures, frequenting hospitals, engaging others in religious conversation, preaching, admonishing, and recruiting them to visit the sick and the dying—a most unusual way of life for a mere layman. Among those he met and befriended was Ignatius Loyola, the founder of the Jesuit order, who would have a profound influence on him. In 1548, after years of engaging in his irregular street ministry, Philip established a lay confraternity that dedicated itself to ministering to the sick and sheltering and feeding the thousands of pilgrims who flocked to Rome every year. Three years later, in 1551, convinced by his confessor that he could accomplish much more as a priest, Philip was ordained, and took up residence at the church of San Girolamo.

Already well known in Rome—but not beloved by all—Philip acquired a higher stature and a more influential circle of friends and patrons. His love for the sacrament of penance, and his dedication to hearing confessions for hours on end quickly earned him a reputation as an extraordinary priest and confessor. Conversions of all sorts began to be attributed to him, along with the miraculous gift of being able to perceive the sins that his penitents were too ashamed to confess. Realizing that confession and absolution could only accomplish so much, and that many of his penitents seemed hungry for a deeper religious life, Philip established regular gatherings at which everyone would listen to readings, discuss spiritual matters, pray, sing, and listen to sacred music. These meetings, which became immensely popular because of their festive, upbeat character, drew more attention to Philip, along with ever larger crowds. Before long, space ran out, and a special room dubbed "the Oratory" had to be built for them—a name that came to be applied to the meetings and to the community gathered at them. Eager to draw even more people to these events, and ever willing to stretch boundaries in order to combat sin and foster virtue and holiness, Philip devised a counterfeast of sorts during Carnival in 1559: an outdoor extravaganza that included a twelve-mile pilgrimage through the seven holiest churches in Rome, and an outdoor picnic and concert at midday.

Censure of Philip was inevitable, given his unique approach, but so was his success. Philip attracted so many eminent clergy to his side—including Carlo Borromeo, Jacopo Sadoleto, and Gian Matteo Giberti—that to go against him one also needed to challenge some of the most respected authorities in Rome. Although he was accused of "introducing novelties" and of setting up "new sects," and very briefly suspended from hearing confessions, nothing came of that censure, or of other similar attempts to derail him. In 1567, Pope Pius V came close to disbanding the Oratory, only to back down after weighing the consequences. Philip's success was as extraordinary as his good humor and his ability to charm Rome. As a community of priests grew around Philip and the Oratory migrated to larger spaces, Pope Gregory XIII confirmed the obvious in 1575 by granting it the official status of a religious congregation. By the time Philip died twenty years later, his congregation had made great strides in places far from Rome, and so had his reputation as a saint. Philip would be canonized in 1622, a mere twenty-seven years after his passing, along with his near contemporaries Teresa of Ávila, Francis Xavier, and Ignatius Loyola. In comparison, it had taken seventy years for Francis Xavier to be recognized as a saint, sixty-six for Ignatius, and forty for Teresa.

As had earlier been the case with the Theatines, the size of this community did not matter as much as its influence. Preaching was one of the hallmarks of the Oratory in Rome, and as the congregation spread to other cities in Italy and beyond—from Portugal to Poland—so did its distinctive commitment to the sermon as a centerpiece of educational and moral reform. But Oratorians were not just good preachers who knew how to address the laity; they were also liturgical virtuosi who knew how to stir the emotions through music. Among those who enlivened worship at the Oratory, none was more influential than the composer Giovanni Pierluigi da Palestrina (1525–1594), the choral director at St. Peter's and the undisputed master of polyphonic sacred music. Recognized as one of the greatest Renaissance musicians, Palestrina participated in the liturgical life of the Oratory and composed music for its services.

Neri's Oratory also changed the course of history, literally, through one of its members, Cesare Baronio, also known as Baronius (1538–1607). Commissioned by Neri to refute the Lutheran version of church history—which sought to prove the falsehood of every Catholic teaching and institution that they rejected—Baronius would dedicate forty-three years of his life (1564–1607) to writing a twelve-volume history of the church, the *Annales ecclesiastici*. Relying heavily on excerpts taken from historical documents, Baronius's *Annales* offered Catholics textual proofs of the historical validity of their faith according to the new empirical standards required by Renaissance historiography (even though Baronius included some texts that had already been declared inauthentic, such as *The Donation of Constantine*). The *Annales* also provided Catholics with a heavyweight rebuttal of the Lutheran *Magdeburg Centuries* (1559), a history of the church written by Matthias Flacius Illyricus and a team of historians at the University of Magdeburg. The *Centuries* had given the Lutherans a polemical advantage simply by being published first: as long as there was no equivalent Catholic version, history was all theirs. Baronius's response, which had been prompted by Neri and was so much a part of the ethos of the Oratory, reclaimed the past for Catholics and offered a serious challenge to the *Magdeburg Centuries* and the Protestant narrative.

Ultimately, Neri's Oratory proved most influential as an exemplar of a new kind of ministry. Living together without vows, involving the laity in the liturgy more intensely and in innovative ways, dedicating themselves to preaching, teaching, and hearing confessions, the Oratorians of Rome provided a template for similar communities elsewhere, not just in Italy, but throughout Catholic Europe. These priestly communities were not religious orders in the strict sense, but they functioned very much like them, insofar as they shared a common identity and sense of purpose. Placing themselves directly under the authority of their local bishop, dedicating themselves to serving the laity, such associations were at once different from the secular clergy, but also, at the same time, very much like them. And this similarity was deliberate, for these oratories were immensely concerned with improving the religious life of those who ministered to the laity most

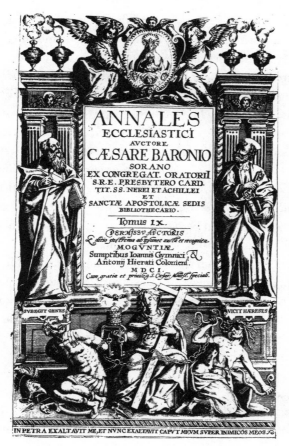

Heavyweight rebuttal. St. Philip Neri's Oratory attracted many talented clergy who devoted themselves to a variety of ministries, proving that clerical reform could have multiple effects. One of Neri's earliest recruits, Cesare Baronio, wrote a massive history of the Catholic Church that challenged Protestant narratives and shaped Catholic identity. This title page from the fourth volume of this work, published in 1601, identifies the author as a member of Neri's Oratory and employs polemical iconography. A prominent sign of Catholic distinction crowns the page: the Virgin Mary flanked by angels. In the center, SS. Peter and Paul flank the descriptive information, aligning it with apostolic authority. Below, a female figure representing Holy Mother Church holds the cross in one hand and a papal tiara in the other, above which the Holy Spirit hovers, and at her feet two bound figures cower in submission, one representing heresy (an old hag) and the other persecution (a Roman soldier).

directly. It is no accident, then, that many of those inspired by Neri and his Oratory were deeply involved in the education of secular clerics.

The Oratory of Jesus and Mary

Gradually, oratories sprung up all over the map. But it was in France, especially, that they came to play a major role in church reform. Their significance there stemmed largely from two factors: the devastation of France by the Wars of Religion, which lasted from 1562 to 1598, and the steadfast resistance the French monarchs mounted against the decrees of the Council of Trent, and especially against the creation of diocesan seminaries. Where bishops dared not tread, and where religious orders held back, Oratorian communities took the lead, zeroing in on the education of the young and the training of secular clerics.

Among those in France who sought to follow in Neri's footsteps and to improve the secular clergy, one of the most successful was Pierre de Bérulle (1575–1629), onetime confessor of King Louis XIII, who founded the Oratory of Jesus and Mary in Paris in 1611. A mystic at heart, yet also a brilliant organizer, the charismatic Bérulle led the expansion of Oratorian communities throughout France at an astonishing pace. By 1630, a year after his death, there were sixty houses with four hundred members, seventeen colleges, and four seminaries. And between 1631 and 1702, twelve houses, 181 members, eleven colleges, and seventeen seminaries were added.

Pierre de Bérulle's approach to reform was comprehensive. Like most of his clerical peers, he was convinced that the health of the church as a whole depended on the health of its clergy: reform the head, and the whole body of the faithful will benefit. But this was only part of the picture for Bérulle, who yearned for a spiritual revival at all levels, including secular and regular clergy, and the laity, too. All the faithful, as he saw it, had a role to play as *dévots*, or devout Christians. Convinced of the value of prayer and contemplation, and driven by a deeply Christocentric piety, Bérulle spearheaded a devotional revival in France that has come to be known as *l'invasion mystique*, or the "mystic invasion." On one level, he worked closely with lay people, especially with a group of *dévots* led by his cousin Barbe Avrillot, better known as Madame Acarie (1566–1618). His Oratorian clerics also devoted themselves to missionary work within France itself, particularly in the countryside, where the influence of the church had always been weakest. On another level, encouraged by Madame Acarie's circle, he also brought about the establishment of Discalced Carmelite and Ursuline nunneries in France. The first Carmelite nunnery, established in 1604, was led by none other than St. Teresa of Ávila's closest associate, Ana de San Bartolomé (1549–1626). Despite many setbacks and controversies, the new plantings flourished, and more than sixty new convents were established between 1604 and 1660. Thanks to Bérulle and Madame Acarie, and those they encouraged, a new mystical fervor swept through France in the seventeenth century—an "invasion" that shifted the spiritual center of gravity of the Catholic world from Spain to France.

Bérulle's legacy cannot be easily summarized or pigeonholed. In addition to effecting the aforementioned reforms, he sided with the skeptical philosopher and mathematician René Descartes (1596–1650). He also remained close to the royal family and to some of the most powerful figures in France, and worked as a diplomat, attracting the ire of others, especially of the mighty Cardinal Richelieu (1585–1642), who opposed his plan to ally France more closely with Spain. In 1627, as his relations with Richelieu reached a low point, Bérulle was raised to the status of cardinal by Pope Urban VIII. Around this same time, as he neared the end of his life, Bérulle authored two devotional texts that distilled his Christocentric piety and made it accessible to many readers: *Discourse on the State and Grandeurs of Jesus Christ* (1623) and *The Elevation to Jesus Christ Concerning His Principal States and Mysteries* (1625).

Lazarists, Eudists, and Sulpicians

After Bérulle's death, his reforming spirit lived on in the work of others who had been deeply influenced by him, especially his successor at the Oratory, Charles de Condren (1588–1641), and a handful of other reformers who founded more seminaries and missionary congregations, such as Vincent de Paul (Lazarists or Vincentians), Jean Eudes (Eudists), and Jean-Jacques Olier (Sulpicians).

Vincent de Paul (1580–1660) met Bérulle in 1609, while working as the queen's almoner, a position he had acquired via a most unusual route. Ordained a priest in 1600, De Paul was captured by Turkish pirates five years later and sold as a slave in North Africa. In 1607, after two years spent in slavery, he managed not only to escape from his Muslim master, but also to convert him to the Christian faith. Then, after returning to France quite by chance, he ended up at the royal court, where Queen Marguerite entrusted him with all her works of charity. Inspired by Bérulle, Vincent de Paul dedicated himself to ministering to the needy. Since he had patrons at court and amongst the high nobility, De Paul was able to mount several projects, including missions to the poor and to peasants. In addition, he took up the cause of ministering to those who had been convicted to serve in the galleys, a relatively common punishment in his day.

Vincent de Paul's missions to the peasants, which began in earnest in 1617, soon led a number of highly dedicated priests to place themselves under his guidance, and by 1625 to the formal establishment of the Congregation of Fathers of the Mission. Vowing to live in a community and to devote themselves to "the salvation of the poor country people" while rendering all services free of charge, the priests of the congregation fanned out throughout France and to other countries, even beyond Europe. Eventually, this congregation would come to be known under two other names: Vincentians (in reference to their founder) and Lazarists (in reference to the large priory of Saint-Lazare, outside of Paris, which became their mother house in 1632). The commitment of the Lazarist fathers to preaching and teaching was intense. For instance, between 1652 and 1660, the last eight years of De Paul's life, they mounted more than seven hundred missions just at the house of Saint-Lazare alone.

Such a high number of missions required a commensurately high number of priests, so Vincent and his Lazarists did their utmost to ensure a steady and ever-growing supply by establishing seminaries, not just for their own congregation, but also for entire dioceses. The first such seminary entrusted to them was that of Cahors in 1643. Soon enough, other bishops began to hand over the education of their clergy to the Lazarists, and their hold over seminary education in France became intense. During the remainder of De Paul's life, six more seminaries would be placed in their hands. By 1660, the year

Formidable patronage, remarkable results. Prominent reformers often had intimate connections at the highest levels of ecclesiastical and civil society. This painting by the Dominican priest and artist Jean André, celebrates the charitable work of SS. Vincent de Paul and Louise de Marillac. While the saint and former duchess of Aiguillon transact business with aristocratic ladies, the Sisters of Charity tend to abandoned infants.

of his death, he had dotted the map of France with eleven seminaries. During the following forty years (1660–1700), twenty-seven more would be added. By 1760 the Lazarists would run one-third of all of the seminaries in France, a sum total of fifty-two. Beyond France, the growth of their influence was also impressive: by 1641 they were active in Rome; by 1687 they could be found elsewhere in Italy, Ireland, Poland, and Spain. By 1718 they had made it into Portugal. In addition, they ran very dangerous missions along the North African coast, targeting the Barbary pirates and their Christian captives.

Vincent de Paul also teamed up with a devout widow, Louise de Marillac (1591–1660), to establish an order for women, the Sisters of Charity (1633). These nuns, also known as Daughters of Charity, devoted themselves to alleviating the misery of the poor in hospitals, orphanages, insane asylums, nursing homes for the aged, and soup kitchens, most of which had been established by De Paul and his missionary priests with financial support from those in high places. By the time of Louise de Marillac's death in 1660—six months before the death of Vincent de Paul—the Sisters of Charity had more than forty houses in France, which ministered to thousands of the needy, day after day.

Another disciple of Bérulle who became a dynamic reformer was Jean Eudes (1601–1680). A native of Normandy, Eudes took a vow of celibacy at age fourteen and joined the Oratory in 1623. Twenty years later, with Bérulle's support, he founded a new community, the Congregation of Jesus and Mary, and established a seminary at Caen. Following the Oratorian paradigm, those who joined this congregation took no vows and remained under the jurisdiction of their bishops. They also devoted themselves to the training of secular priests, and assumed charge of five additional diocesan seminaries between 1643 and 1670, and seven more over the following century. Some of these seminaries concentrated on training poor students for rural ministries.

Committed also to mission work, the Eudists focused on creating a more devout laity, placing great emphasis on the cult of the Sacred Hearts of Jesus and Mary, reaching out to the fallen and downtrodden. An indefatigable preacher, Jean Eudes led the way by conducting more than a hundred preaching missions himself, and publishing several devotional texts. Much like Vincent de Paul, Eudes also played an instrumental role in the founding of other religious communities devoted to serving the needy: the Good Shepherd Sisters, the Sisters of the Sacred Hearts of Jesus and Mary, and the Little Sisters of the Poor. In 1641, he also founded the Congregation of Our Lady of Charity of the Refuge, which sought to rehabilitate former prostitutes through dedication to prayer, penance, and social work.

A third exemplary clerical reformer who followed Bérulle's footsteps was Jean-Jacques Olier (1608–1657). Ordained a priest in 1633, after he had spent some time at Saint-Lazare with Vincent de Paul, the young Olier also established a close relationship with Charles de Condren, Bérulle's successor at the Oratory. In 1641 Olier established a seminary at Vaugirard and began to reform his parish. News of his success at Vaugirard traveled quickly in clerical circles, and the following year Olier was offered the challenge of reforming what was then the most notoriously corrupt and vice-filled parish in all of Paris—and according to some, in all of France, or even all of Europe: Saint-Sulpice, on the Left Bank, which covered the Fauburg Saint-Germain and included the Sorbonne itself. Where others had met with failure, Olier triumphed, beyond what anyone might have expected. Olier brought a squadron of dedicated priests to Saint-Sulpice who transformed the parish by waging war on sin, ignorance, and poverty, dispensing instruction, correction, solace, and material aid of all sorts. Among the wealthy and powerful, Olier also met with success, even though he criticized the king's chief minister Cardinal Mazarin openly and campaigned against dueling, that last recourse of the nobility in honor disputes.

Olier's crowning achievement was the creation of a seminary at Saint-Sulpice, which he designed to attract dedicated men from all over France and quickly became, in essence, a national seminary and a blueprint for others who adopted its rules and methods. The Sulpicians, as Olier's priests came to be known, remained a community of secular priests who took no special vows and subjected themselves to their bishop. Eventually, in addition to the seminary in Paris, four other seminaries of the Society of Saint-Sulpice would be established: at Viviers, Nantes, Le Puy, and Clermont. Although their influence was greatest in France, and in French Canada, the effect of the Sulpicians on the Catholic Church as a whole was also significant, given the prominent role of France itself on the world stage. One statistic alone proves the success and influence of the Sulpicians more convincingly than any other: by the late eighteenth century, on the eve of the French Revolution, more than half of the bishops of France were their alumni.

Preaching in rural areas, ministering to his own flock at Saint-Sulpice, setting up seminaries and offering help to the poor, the tireless Olier also authored several influential devotional texts in his later years, including *The Christian Day* (1655), and *Introduction to the Christian Life and Virtues* (1657). Considering that Olier was born in 1608, a mere half century after the closing of the Council of Trent, the great strides toward reform made within Catholicism fall into perspective. The gulf separating Olier's generation from that of Carlo Borromeo was immense, indeed. Ultimately, the renewal set in motion by Trent owed much to the decrees of the council, but it owed much more to the work of specific individuals and to their zeal and devotion, which drew upon a certain religious mind-set and a range of spiritual experiences that were vastly different from those of Protestants. The first chapter of the *Spiritual Directory of Saint Sulpice*, which encapsulated Olier's vision, summed up this difference in mystical terms: the primary aim of the Lazarists was "to live completely for God in Christ Jesus our Lord so that the interior dispositions of His Son may permeate the deepest recesses of our souls and enable each of us to repeat what St. Paul confidently said of himself, 'It is no longer I who live, but it is Christ who lives in me' [Galatians 2:20]." This Christocentric piety focused intensely on the Eucharist as the prime mover in priestly formation. Convinced that eucharistic devotion could transform the dispositions of every priest into those of Christ, Olier offered a poetic summation of the power of the real presence of Christ in the sacrament, which causes—as he saw it—a sort of transubstantiation in the priest-communicant and transforms him into the very body of Christ for others:

> Each day after Holy Communion I feel Christ diffused all through me, as though I felt his presence in all my members. . . . He leads me, he animates me, as though he were my soul and my life. . . . Leading me, stopping me, opening my lips, closing them, directing and regulating my sight—in a word, doing all for me. . . . He [Christ] is not content thus to come into my heart to consume it in himself, but he dwells in me in order to produce in souls the effect of divine communions and diffuses himself then in them as through a Host and a sacrament.[12]

With such a vision to guide them, the Sulpicians embodied a spirit of reform that was at once a very up-to-date affirmation of ancient Catholic tradition and a conscious rejection of Protestantism. It was a vision formed as much from inner convictions as from a need to distance oneself from the heretical "other."

Of course, the Sulpicians were not the only ones to reify this dialectic. Every new order, and every reformed old order shared in the same ethos, though each did so in its own way.

Conclusion

The holistic metaphor of the church as the Body of Christ, which was at the heart of early modern Catholicism, implicitly suggested that the clergy were the head, but simultaneously intimated that all parts of the body were interdependent. In other words, the reform of the clergy was not an end in itself, but a means to an end.

The reform of the Catholic clergy that had begun before Luther came along in 1517, and had picked up pace before the closing of the Council of Trent in 1563, burst into full flower in the closing decades of the sixteenth century and bore fruit most abundantly in the seventeenth, and the chief beneficiaries of this development—in the long run—were the lay people served by these reformed clerics.

Detailing the full extent of this renewal has not been the aim of this chapter, for such a complete history would be disproportionate in a survey such as this. Delving into such detail is also unnecessary. The few illustrative samples chosen here may not tell the whole story, but they provide us with a clear glimpse of the range of clerical reforms undertaken before and after Trent, so many of which were realized through the initiative of remarkable individuals.

Many of the reformers mentioned in this chapter would eventually be canonized as saints. This is not surprising. Scholars who analyze the statistics of canonization will be the first to point out that the surest way to be recognized as a saint is to establish a religious order, especially after the Council of Trent made the canonization process more involved and more expensive than in centuries past. To be canonized, one needed patrons with extraordinary patience, high motivation, and deep pockets. Religious orders tended to have all three of these, in spades, much more so than anyone else in the Catholic Church. That such men and women would be canonized is not at all surprising. What is truly remarkable is that there were so many of them at this time, and that they and their followers accomplished so much.

And even more remarkable is the fact that all of their efforts combined sometimes seemed to be dwarfed by those of another order, all by itself, an order established by an ex-soldier who had several run-ins with the Spanish Inquisition: the Society of Jesus, better known as the Jesuits, an order so remarkable that it needs a chapter all of its own.

CHAPTER SEVENTEEN

Catholic Reform

The Society of Jesus

Issues of scale or size should not matter most when dealing with the new orders established in the sixteenth and seventeenth centuries: what really counts, ultimately, is the peculiar genius of Catholicism to reinvent the monastic calling in this time of crisis and its ability to mold it in so many different ways to fit particular needs. That adaptive evolutionary trait, clearly evident in the new orders covered in the previous chapter, should never be overlooked, for it was the aggregate impact of so many different efforts at reform that allowed Catholicism to survive and thrive.

Yet there is no denying that one order—the Society of Jesus (the Jesuits)—commands a special place within this narrative as unique and as arguably the most extraordinary, innovative, and influential of all of the new clergy. Regrettably, it is also the order whose history is most distorted by myths and caricatures. Often introduced in Anglo-American books as "the shock troops of the Counter-Reformation" or "the Pope's army," and reduced to the status of militant, soldierlike zealots led by a superior general in Rome called "the black Pope," the Jesuits need to be placed in context, as one of many new and successful orders (and therefore as their rival, to some extent), and as men whose efforts were shaped by much more than blind obedience to directives from Rome, for Jesuits were clerics who uniquely reified the cold, clear reason and pragmatism that had always been an integral part of the Catholic tradition. They also went about their sacred business with consummate zeal and an ardent faith, and—most important—a distinctly modern approach.

The Jesuits were a big surprise to Catholic and Protestant alike. Apostles of the unexpected and improbable, they often surprised themselves too, as they broke mold after mold and invented and reinvented ways of ministering. At the same time, paradoxically, they also remained very faithful to the church and the principles established by their remarkable founder—a most unlikely reformer who found his vocation by accident, although the Jesuits themselves would say that their sudden appearance was no mere fluke, but the work of Divine Providence.

An Unlikely Start

It all began with a cannonball, and one hell of a wound. The injured man was a Basque noble, Íñigo López de Loyola (better known as Ignatius Loyola); the place was Pamplona, the year 1521, in the month of May. The battle was but another skirmish in the interminable conflict now known as the Hapsburg-Valois Wars (1494–1559), which at this stage pitted the French king Francis I against Emperor Charles V. Pamplona was in Navarre, near the Pyrenees mountains and the border with France. Ignatius had been born nearby in 1491, at his family's enclave of Loyola, when Navarre was still an independent state. But he had become a subject of the king of Spain, whose kingdom had swallowed up Navarre in 1512. Like most nobles of his rank, Ignatius was a courtier and a knight, and he lived like one, carousing, fighting, and gambling, quick to lean on his family's prestige in time of trouble. He was also very fond of reading chivalric literature, and much like the fictional Don Quixote later created by Miguel de Cervantes (1547–1616), Ignatius desperately sought to imitate the valiant knights in those books. The war had provided him with the perfect opportunity to live out his fantasies and earn the acclaim deserved by every great knight. Religion was the last thing on his mind as he defended Pamplona from the enemy.

This narrow world of his changed in an instant. Struck on both legs by a cannonball, Ignatius lost his future as a warrior and also nearly his life. During his long and painful convalescence he had plenty of time to rue his fate and to scheme against it. Displeased with the way that his shattered right leg had healed, Ignatius had the bone rebroken, trimmed with a saw, and reset—without anesthesia—thus prolonging his recovery. But the surgery led to more disappointment; one leg remained shorter than the other, and he would have to limp his way through life. As he healed, ever so slowly, he pined for good chivalric novels to read, but the only two books at his disposal were of a very different sort: *The Life of Christ* by Ludolph of Saxony, and the *Golden Legend* by Jacob de Voragine. Both of these books were medieval devotional texts that had been recently translated into Castilian Spanish. The *Life of Christ* was not so much a retelling of the Gospel narratives as a manual for meditation and prayer. Its most distinctive feature was its imaginative technique: it taught the reader to project him- or herself into the biblical story and live out the details. *The Golden Legend* was a collection of saints' lives that stressed their heroic virtues and miraculous gifts.

Gradually, Ignatius was drawn in by these books, so strange to him, and before long, a transformation unfolded. Instead of longing to imitate Amadis of Gaul, he asked himself, "What if I should do what St. Francis did, and what St. Dominic did?"[1] Plunging ever deeper into the meditations suggested in the *Life of Christ*, Ignatius the worldly soldier gradually began to focus on the divine rather than the earthly. He learned how to analyze his thinking, intuitively, and how to discern connections between his thoughts, actions, and feelings. At some point during his convalescence, all this introspection led to a mystical experience and a thorough conversion, after which—by his own account—he "never gave the slightest consent to the things of the flesh."[2]

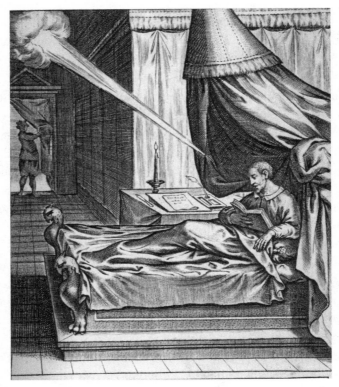

From chivalry to holiness. St. Ignatius Loyola, an avid reader of medieval chivalric novels, underwent a conversion while convalescing from wounds received in battle. This etching by Peter Paul Rubens, part of a set of eighty illustrations commissioned for a biography of Ignatius first published in 1609, depicts the moment when divine inspiration began to affect him as he read devotional texts. This biography, which was written to promote the cause of his canonization, was authored by three Jesuits: Nicholas Lancicius, Filippo Rinaldi, and Peter Pazmany.

Still bent on imitating role models, his mind fixed on saintly rather than chivalric paradigms, Ignatius set off on a pilgrimage to Jerusalem as soon as he could walk again, in February 1522. Before embarking at Barcelona, however, he made a pilgrimage to the nearby shrine of Our Lady of Montserrat, where he pledged his troth to the Virgin Mary after a three-day general confession of all of his sins and an all-night vigil under her image. Leaving his sword and dagger at the altar, he took a back road to Barcelona through the town of Manresa. And instead of heading straight for Jerusalem, he stayed there. Between late March 1522 and mid-February 1523, Ignatius underwent yet another transformation, which he would later describe in his autobiography. Living on alms, dressed in a sackcloth cloak, he went to mass daily and spent most of his time at prayer, often in a nearby cave. Denying himself meat and wine, he fasted excessively, never cut or combed his hair or beard, and let his nails grow long. Swept by strong conflicting emotions, he plunged into the darkest of dark nights of the soul, even toying with suicide, and then rose to the brightest and highest of zeniths. At Manresa, Ignatius experienced dimensions beyond the intellect and the senses, from the worst of demonic temptations to the most exalted of divine ecstasies, visions, and revelations, including one that would give shape to the rest of his life, in which he was able to grasp at a fundamental level through the Holy Trinity how God was linked to all of creation and how he was leading it back to himself through Christ. The Ignatius who emerged from Manresa, his hair and nails trimmed, his eyes fixed again on Jerusalem, was a very different man. And everything this newly transfigured mystic had experienced and learned during those eleven months would be put to use in creating not just a unique religious order, but also a distinctive piety and a dynamic method of replicating his own transformative experiences—a method that could change lives in remarkable ways.

A Manual for Conversions

Eventually, Ignatius would perfect his introspective meditations and turn his method of discerning God's will into a detailed process and into a written manual for those who were to direct other men and women through that process. This text and the meditative plan it described would be called *The Spiritual Exercises*. The text itself makes for tough reading because it is neither a narrative nor a discursive exposition of ideas: it is a technical manual for spiritual directors, and its purpose is to outline how a long retreat should be conducted. Ideally, the retreat master was to lead an individual through the *Exercises*, one-on-one, over a period of thirty days, but the process could also be shortened to a few days. This is not a text to be read and savored. In our day and age, a totally secular equivalent would be a manual for directors of twelve-step addiction rehabilitation seminars.

Ignatius would not begin to write the first rudimentary versions of the *Spiritual Exercises* for several more years after his experiences at Manresa, and he would revise the text several times before it was formally approved by the church in 1548. Although the first and final printed editions belong to a later chapter in his life, it will prove useful to pause the biographical narrative and examine the *Spiritual Exercises* briefly, for Ignatius's later accomplishments cannot be fully understood or appreciated apart from the experiences, strategies, and methods distilled into that text. Ignatius's future contributions would not be those of a theologian and much less those of a philosopher. His peculiar genius was a charismatic gift for leadership, and for organization, not for writing or teaching. All the more reason, then, to use the *Exercises* as a lens for more clearly discerning what made this reformer tick, and what made his impact so formidable.

First and foremost, the *Exercises* are a thorough repudiation of Protestant theology and a practical application of Catholic principles dismissed by Protestants. This is not to say that Ignatius had Luther or Zwingli in mind as he developed the *Exercises*, or that he crafted them in response to Protestantism. On the contrary, one of the most significant characteristics of the *Exercises* is the way in which Ignatius wasted no time on the "other's" errors and relied directly on Catholic tradition, reifying it positively, from within, rather than as some grand polemical strategy. The title says it all: these are exercises, that is, this is a way of training one's will, of strengthening one's relationship with the divine, of straining to earn salvation, of gaining spiritual muscle, of improving and perfecting the self. Forget about a human will that can do nothing to earn its salvation, or about justification by faith alone or grace alone. Forget predestination, implicit or explicit. Forget about sinning boldly. The *Exercises* are all about human initiative and human capacity to analyze and overcome personal weaknesses. God is part of the process, yes, but the *Exercises* are not as much about what God does for humans as about what every Christian can do to reach out and to grow ever closer to God. The *Exercises* teach how to take charge of one's salvation, how to change and improve and aim for perfection. All these points are succinctly summarized in the very first paragraph:

> By the term Spiritual Exercises we mean every method of examination of conscience, meditation, contemplation, vocal or mental prayer, and other spiritual activities. . . . For, just as taking a walk, traveling on foot, and running are physical exercises, so is the name of spiritual exercises given to any means of preparing and disposing our soul to rid itself of all its disordered affections and then, after their removal, of seeking and finding God's will in the ordering of our life for the salvation of our soul.[3]

The *Exercises* take it for granted that God has a specific plan for every person, and that if one puts in the time and effort, God will reveal that plan. Once one knows what God's expects, one can indeed choose the correct path and—with the right kind of effort— receive God's help to stay on it for the rest of one's earthly life. Free will reigns supreme in the *Exercises*. And so does the power of the human mind.

Employing some of the methods he had picked up from *The Life of Christ* during his convalescence and other devotional manuals, along with other methods he intuitively developed during his own spiritual odyssey, Ignatius crafted a process of introspection that relied heavily on the imagination and on a systematic approach to self-awareness and self-correction. Prayer was an essential part of the process, too, as for Ignatius, prayer involved not just the soul but also the mind, and praying was essential for establishing the proper relationship with God, obtaining divine assistance, and ensuring salvation. The key was to "ask God for what one should desire." In other words, one had to ask for the right disposition. Take, for instance, two of the very first prayers to be made at the outset:

> The Preparatory Prayer is to ask God our Lord for the grace that all my intentions, actions, and operations may be ordered purely to the service and praise of his Divine Majesty. . . . In the present meditation I will ask for shame and confusion about myself, when I see how many people have been damned for committing a single mortal sin, and how many times I have deserved eternal damnation for my many sins.[4]

Or consider the prayer for attaining contemplation of the love of God. What should one ask to desire in this crucial step?

> Here it will be to ask for interior knowledge of all the great good I have received, in order that, stirred to profound gratitude, I may become able to love and serve his Divine Majesty in all things.[5]

The core activity in the *Exercises* was that of meditation, à la Ludolph of Saxony's *Life of Christ*: one projected oneself into specific tableaux, using imagination to experience them as fully as possible and then applied the lessons learned through that exercise immediately in the process of self-scrutiny. Many meditations were biblical and focused on events in the life of Jesus, as found in the Gospels, such as the birth of Christ:

> To see the persons; that is, to see Our Lady, Joseph, the maidservant, and the Infant Jesus after his birth. I will make myself a poor, little, and unworthy slave, gazing at them, contemplating them, and serving them in their needs, just as if I were there, with all possible respect and reverence. Then I will reflect upon myself to draw some profit.[6]

Other meditations focused on specific doctrines and teachings of the church, on the Ten Commandments, for instance, or the seven deadly sins. The most famous—or infamous—was the meditation on hell, in which one was asked to use all of one's senses: to see the fire and the souls burning in it; to hear the wailing, shrieking, and blaspheming; to smell the smoke, sulfur, and filth; to taste the bitterness of the tears of the damned; to touch the flames and feel how the souls burn in them.

The hell of the *Exercises* is not metaphorical, and neither is its very active devil. Another key aim of the process was to heighten one's awareness of the reality of the devil and his wiles, and of the many ways he tempts humans to sin and to despair of God's mercy. Learning the "discernment of spirits" is crucial in the *Exercises*, for, as Ignatius saw it, the devil was not just real, but ceaselessly active, and a master of deceit. This dualistic streak in the *Exercises* is tempered by confidence in God's saving plan: the devil may be a powerful foe, but he is definitely nothing but a limp and lame loser when approached the right way, with Christ on one's side. Moreover, his deceit can be identified and thwarted, with the proper training. One of the final meditations of the *Exercises* contrasts Satan and his demons with Christ and his saints, and asks one to ponder the contrast between those who follow the standard of Satan and those who serve under the standard of Christ. Although many a scholar has seized on this image of the two standards as conclusive proof that the Jesuits and their spirituality were militaristic, the standards have nothing to do with armies encamped for war, much less for an apocalyptic cosmic battle. This particular exercise is not about armies gathered for an apocalyptic battle, but about individuals realizing that they can be a "servant and friend" of Christ, being "sent on an expedition" to "aid all persons" in the pursuit of a life of virtue.[7]

The central significance of the *Exercises* for the development of Jesuit spirituality lies not in its tempered dualism, but in its worldly asceticism,[8] which rivaled that of Calvinists, as it stressed the principle that the purpose of human existence is to find God *in* this world, become his "servant and friend" and work *within* the world to magnify God's glory through selfless and humble service to others. In other words, as Jesuits came to see it, the world was a place to redeem rather than to run from, and leading a virtuous life was the best way to magnify God's glory on earth, an insight that became so central to their ethos that it was turned into a motto: *ad maiorem Dei gloriam* (for the

Drastic choice. A key meditation in the *Spiritual Exercises* of St. Ignatius concerns the proposition that one cannot avoid choosing between God and devil, or, as Ignatius puts it, between the battle standard of "Christ, our Commander-in-chief and Lord" and that of "Lucifer, mortal enemy of our human nature." This meditation on the two standards stresses both the freedom of the will and the absolute necessity of prayer, grace, and divine guidance.

greater glory of God). This commitment would provide the Jesuits with great zeal and a flexibility that allowed them to adapt their ministry to many different environments. That willingness to stretch should never be mistaken for license. The Jesuits remained doggedly faithful to the Catholic tradition while being innovative. This commitment to the historical and hierarchical nature of Catholicism was summed up by Ignatius in an appendix to the *Exercises* titled "Rules for Thinking, Judging, and Feeling with the Church." These eighteen rules were a summation of Catholic theology and ethics, a creed of sorts. Behind each rule, as if on its horizon, one can easily make out everything that Protestants have rejected, and the first rule sums up the Jesuit approach succinctly:

> With all judgment of our own put aside, we ought to keep our minds disposed and ready to be obedient in everything to the true Spouse of Christ, Our Lord, which is our Holy Mother, the Hierarchical Church.

The thirteenth rule expands on the first, but in such a pointed way that it would become emblematic of the Jesuit ethos, as controversial as the order itself and the very measure of what made Jesuits so formidable and so frightful to their enemies:

> To keep ourselves right in all things we ought to hold fast to this principle: What I see as white, I will believe to be black if the hierarchical Church thus determines it.[9]

The development of the Jesuit ethos—or as they themselves called it "our way of proceeding" (*noster modo procedendi*)—is inseparable from the *Exercises*, for it was through the *Exercises*, even before they were in written form, that Ignatius recruited and trained his first followers, who in turn, with all who joined them too, would administer the *Exercises* to other potential recruits and to the laity they served. Undergoing the *Exercises* was essential for becoming a Jesuit, and administering them was the Jesuits' unique, incandescent skill: the experience itself was the foundation on which every Jesuit institution would rest, the core of the Jesuits' personal and communal identity, and the infrangible thread that linked them all to one another and to their flocks, not just around the globe, but across generations.

The Winding Path to Rome

The tight orderliness and clear sense of purpose that would later distinguish Ignatius and his men could hardly be found in the clueless pilgrim headed for Jerusalem in 1523 with the vague aim of "helping souls" over there, indefinitely. On his arrival, he discovered that the rulers of the Holy Land would not allow him to remain, so he sailed back to Spain, and began to prepare for the priesthood. Older than most of his fellow students, often ridiculed for his age, garb, and limp, as well as for his begging on the streets, he pursued his studies in Barcelona, Alcalá, and Salamanca.

While a student in Spain, Ignatius ran afoul of the Inquisition more than once. Had he kept to himself at Alcalá, he would have aroused no suspicion, but he openly "engaged in giving spiritual exercises and teaching Christian doctrine" and began to attract followers, so he soon found himself accused of being an Alumbrado, or "enlightened one," a member of a peculiarly vague heretical movement with mystical and antinomian tendencies. Imprisoned and tried, he was freed but ordered "not to speak about matters of faith" until he had four more years of theological training under his belt.[10] Leaving the University of Alcalá and moving to that of Salamanca brought no respite from inquisitorial mistrust. Thrown into prison again on suspicion of heresy, and grilled on the content of the *Exercises*, he was acquitted but reprimanded for his constant attempt to "help souls" as a mere layman without an official church post. Fed up with the stifling spiritual and intellectual climate of Spain, Ignatius packed his books in late 1527 and left for the University of Paris—enemy territory, where it was rumored that Spaniards were roasted on spits.

Paris proved very fruitful ground for Ignatius, and he would remain there for seven years, until 1535. Taking up residence at the much-maligned Collège de Montaigu, the alma mater of Erasmus and Calvin. Ignatius pursued his studies with determination even though he "found himself deficient in fundamentals" and had to sit in introductory courses with much younger students, mere children in his eyes.[11] He also pursued his ministry with equal zeal, "helping souls" and convincing fellow students to undergo his *Exercises*. Before long, Ignatius was attracting disciples as well as controversy. But this time around, he prevailed despite all obstacles thrown his way. As a cluster of fellow students grew exceedingly close to him, and a sense of a common mission developed among them, Ignatius took the first uncertain steps toward the development of what would become the Society of Jesus. These first six Jesuits were a diverse bunch who presaged the international character of the order: Francis Xavier, a fellow Basque from Navarre; Pierre Favre, from Savoy; Simón Rodríguez, from Portugal; and Diego Laynez, Alonso Salmerón, and Nicolás Bobadilla, all from different parts of Spain.

On 15 August 1534, at a chapel on the hill of Montmartre, overlooking Paris, Ignatius and his six companions vowed to go to Jerusalem and spend their lives there "for the good of souls," or, if that proved impossible, to let the pope decide how best to use their talents. The next few years were eventful for these seven men, and crucial in their self-definition. Their first few years together were full of twists and turns. Unable to sail to Jerusalem, because of war there with the Turks, Ignatius and his companions remained in Venice for a while, carrying out various ministries, and picking up a few more recruits. By 1537, they had all been ordained as priests and remained closely bound to one another, but they had yet to seek formal recognition as an order. While in Venice they began to call themselves the Society of Jesus, which recognized that as they lacked any formal status, Christ himself was their sole superior. Realizing that it was futile to aim for Jerusalem, they turned to the second part of their vow, headed for Rome and offered their services to Pope Paul III in 1539.

After some tense waiting, the Society of Jesus was finally approved by Paul III on 27 September 1540. At this point, Ignatius and his companions had very imprecise plans regarding their purpose and mission: Pope Paul III's bull of approval took a scattershot approach, commissioning them to preach, hear confessions, promote spiritual exercises, catechize children and the illiterate, and engage in charitable work. Having set up a home base in Rome and elected Ignatius as their superior general for life, they very quickly grew in number and fanned out, gaining a sense of vision as they engaged with the needs they encountered.

A New and Different Order

As it rapidly expanded, the Society of Jesus acquired its own innovative character. Unlike other orders, the Jesuits had no uniform garb, no fixed prayer times, no communal prayer. They also refused to accept pious bequests that involved saying masses for the dead, and they agreed not to become bishops or cardinals, unless expressly appointed to such posts by the pope. Ignatius also insisted that they not engage in extreme fasts or self-mortification. This relaxation of traditional monastic and clerical obligations had a clear purpose: it allowed Jesuits as much flexibility as possible within the world. Prayer was important, and the early Jesuits had their share of mystics—including Ignatius himself—but undisturbed contemplation driven by asceticism was not their goal. Instead, Jesuits were to be "contemplatives in action," constantly engaged in pastoral mission, wrestling with the world, finding God in it and in the prayers they could squeeze in as they toiled away. Fasts, sleep deprivation, self-flagellation, strict observance of the canonical hours, and the physical toll exacted by such exertions would have been an impediment to their spiritual goals and their ministry. With these traditional obligations reduced, and as their spiritual life was not centered on a monastic community, Jesuits were free to move about swiftly and in small numbers, even singly. The whole world was their cloister. Their sense of community was increased, not lessened, by this flexibility, for their communal identity was interior, and they carried it with them wherever they went. Their propensity to spread out over the map, widely and thinly, gave rise to a compulsion for communication with the superior general in Rome and with one another. Every Jesuit represented his whole community, wherever he found himself, and any town or hamlet or any untamed wilderness with just a Jesuit or two was linked to all Jesuits everywhere.

Jesuits were also characterized by their vow to accept any mission deemed necessary by the pope. This vow strengthened their sense of purpose, and it strengthened the papacy. Eventually, it would be this vow, more than anything else about them, that would lead to those caricatures of the Jesuits mentioned at the beginning of this chapter, which depict them as rabid zealots and "soldiers" or "shock troops" of the pope.

The Ministry of Teaching

Although the Jesuits had engaged in catechizing as one of their ministries from the start, and had assiduously taught their new recruits, it was not until the viceroy of Sicily asked them to open a school for the children of Messina in 1548, that they realized that their approach to education seemed to meet a very special need. The schooling of young men would emerge as the best way to accomplish their goal of "helping souls" and promoting the faith—a realization later immortalized in the maxim "Give me the child for seven years, and I will give you the man." As one prominent Jesuit would put it, just a few years after the opening of the school at Messina: "All the well-being of Christianity and of the whole world depends on the proper education of youth."[12] And so it was that Jesuits stumbled onto their main mission and gained their prominence.

Establishing permanent schools had not been part of the plan. In fact, this commitment imperiled the initial ideal of mobility, of being ever ready to go where they were needed most. But the immediate success of the Collegio di San Nicolò in Messina made evident that mobility would be sacrificed for good reason. At Messina, Ignatius gambled, choosing "to fall short" in some commitments in order to fulfill the viceroy's request for a school. Although he had no men to spare at that time, Ignatius sent twelve to Messina, including some of his ablest. The payoff was spectacular. Just a few months after the Messina school opened, requests began to pour in for the establishment of more schools. Palermo, Naples, and Venice soon got their Jesuit schools, all funded by wealthy patrons. Ignatius himself was quick to grasp the significance of the educational mission, and when one of the first Jesuits sent to Germany asked him in 1554 how the order might best help that nation, Ignatius wrote back, "Colleges" (the preferred Jesuit term for their schools). Jesuit colleges were established in quick succession all over the map of Catholic Europe, in Italy, Germany, Bohemia, Austria, France, Portugal, and Spain, and eventually on other continents as well. By the late 1560s, the Jesuits were running about 150 colleges; in 1606, they had 293 educational institutions throughout the world, 38 of them in Latin America, India, and Japan; by 1615 the number had grown to 370.

The growth of the Jesuit order and the growth in the number of Jesuit schools were related. Because the demand for schools always outstripped the supply of Jesuits, the order needed an ever-growing number of recruits. And their schools were the perfect place to find them, in spades. The numbers speak for themselves: although the order had been established by just a few men in 1540, it numbered around 1,000 in 1556, when Ignatius died, 3,500 a mere decade later, 5,000 by 1580, and 13,000 by 1615.

The Jesuit curriculum adhered to the most advanced educational principles of the day, those of Renaissance humanism. In an age of increasingly complex trade and ever-growing bureaucracies, the Jesuit schools provided a sorely needed service in their training of civic leaders, entrepreneurs, and functionaries. In this respect, their orientation was "worldly," but the Jesuits also kept an eye firmly fixed on spiritual values too, and on egalitarian principles, as summed up in the inscription at the entrance to the Jesuit school established in Rome in 1551: "School of Grammar, Humanities, and Christian Doctrine, Free." And the significance of such a great bargain—free schooling—should never be underestimated; the Jesuits were themselves well aware of its importance to their mission, and their success.

The Jesuit colleges immersed their students in the study of grammar and rhetoric, Latin and Greek—sometimes also Hebrew—and mathematics and science. The teaching was carried out not just by Jesuits who were ordained priests, but also by younger members known as "scholastics" who were on their way to ordination. Becoming a teacher, then, was part of the long training most Jesuits underwent. For Jesuits, distinguishing between "worldly" and "spiritual" subjects was unnecessary, even wrongheaded. To search for truth, goodness, and beauty in any subject was to search for God, and to magnify God's glory. Consequently, all subjects were to be pursued with equal intensity. Reading pagan authors such as Cicero, wrestling with Euclidean geometry, and staging theatrical productions were just as necessary for the creation of virtuous Christians as was catechetical instruction. Through their involvement in their colleges, then, the Jesuits became a very scholarly order, renowned for their erudition. Jesuits therefore gravitated to universities, too, both as students and as faculty.

Eventually, the Jesuit order would have experts in nearly every field, from astronomy and botany to literature and ancient languages. Most of these experts taught at some point in their lives, or all their lives. Many excelled in theology and philosophy, as one might expect, among whom the most significant were Roberto Bellarmino (1542–1621), professor at the University of Louvain and the Roman College; Luis de Molina (1535–1600), professor at the University of Évora, in Portugal; and Francisco Suárez (1548–1617), professor at the Universities of Alcalá and Salamanca. Some became historians, biographers, and political theorists, such as Juan de Mariana (1536–1624), who, in addition to teaching at Rome, Sicily, and Paris, authored a thirty-volume history of Spain and a controversial treatise on kingship, and Pedro de Ribadeneyra (1527–1611), onetime teacher at colleges in Sicily and Germany, biographer of Ignatius Loyola, hagiographer, and author of a history of the persecution of Catholics in England. Juan Eusebio Nieremberg (1595–1658), who taught natural science at the Jesuit college in Madrid, published pioneering scientific texts and at the same time composed very traditional devotional literature, including fire-and-brimstone meditations on hell. The polymath Athanasius Kircher (1601–1680) lately proclaimed "the last man who knew everything" by some admirers, mastered a dozen or more subjects, including hydraulics, and helped the great sculptor Bernini design his Roman fountains.[13] Even their rare renegades could embody the Jesuit pursuit of excellence in all subjects, as well as their flexibility. For instance, Baltasar Gracián, former rector of the Jesuit college in Tarragona and acclaimed preacher, rose to prominence as a writer, earning esteem as one of the great stylists of his day and among the most important literary figures in Spanish baroque literature. His masterpiece, the novel *El criticón*, was published without his superior's permission, but it earned him only censure rather than expulsion from the order.

Given their excellence and their ubiquity, Jesuit schools would contribute to Catholic culture in innumerable ways. They would also become one of the most effective means of combating Protestantism, even though that was not at all their original purpose. As schools sprang up in areas where "heretical" churches were established, the Jesuits

Finding God in a volcano. Members of the Society of Jesus were guided by their motto, *ad maiorem Dei gloriam* (to the greater glory of God), and were encouraged to find and proclaim the divine presence everywhere, including in mathematics and empirical science. One Jesuit with extremely wide-ranging interests was Athanasius Kircher, who plumbed the marvels of music theory, magnetism, mathematics, optics, geology, astronomy, medicine, ancient Babylonian and Chinese history, and Egyptian hieroglyphs. The illustrations in Kircher's books sought to provide readers with visual access to the divinely crafted wonders of creation, and to enlighten both mind and soul. This image from his *Mundus subterraneus* (1665) shows a cutaway view of the volcano Mt. Vesuvius. An ardent empiricist, Kircher had himself lowered into the smoldering crater to measure its temperatures.

made a point of opening their doors to children of all confessions, be they Hussites in Bohemia, Lutherans in Germany, or Calvinists in Poland. The allure of a free top-notch education proved irresistible to many non-Catholic parents, and the result was the conversion to Catholicism of many entire families, even of whole regions. For instance, the reestablishment of Catholic supremacy in Poland can be traced to Jesuit schooling, particularly to the conversion of nobles through their Jesuit-educated children. In Germany and Austria, Jesuit colleges were often the prime wedge against Protestantism. The effect of the colleges in Trier and Mainz was denounced in 1565 by a Protestant: "the progress of the Holy Gospel was greatly hindered there by the Jesuits, men whom the devil has hatched out in these latter times as his final brood for the corruption and ruin of the Church of God."[14] Though laced with vitriol, this assessment was not far off the mark. In Trier in the late 1560s, the 450 students at the Jesuit college were fervently devoted not only to the Virgin Mary, but also to searching for Protestant books and destroying them. Few documents testify as convincingly to the repute that Jesuit colleges earned as bulwarks against Protestantism than a letter written in 1580 by Alexander Farnese, Duke of Parma, commander of the Spanish army in the Netherlands, in which he said to his uncle King Philip II: "Your Majesty desired me to build a citadel at Maastricht. I thought that a college of the Jesuits would be a fortress more likely to protect the inhabitants against the enemies of the Altar and Throne. I have built it."[15]

The Ministry of Souls

Colleges were not the only focus of Jesuit activity. Years before they opened the first school in Messina, Jesuits had already earned a reputation as preachers, confessors, spiritual directors, and ministers to the needy and the sick. None of these ministries were dropped in favor of the schools; they flourished along with them.

As far as preaching was concerned, Jesuits were well trained in rhetoric and used that skill in the pulpit at all levels, from sermons in rural missions to homilies for aristocracy and royalty. At the upper end of society, Jesuits achieved great influence as court preachers: Emond Auger, Pierre Coton, and Louis Bourdaloue in France, for instance; Jeremias Drexel, the devotional writer and polemicist, at the Bavarian court of Prince-Elector Maximilian I; Piotr Skarga, at the Polish court of King Sigismund III (where he converted many a Calvinist noble); António Vieira at the Portuguese court of John IV; Jerónimo de Florencia, at the Spanish court of King Philip III.

Jesuits acquired an even greater popularity in high places as confessors. Some, like Florencia, doubled as court preachers and confessors. But the Jesuits did not limit themselves to courts. Licensed by the pope to administer the sacrament of penance anywhere without episcopal permission, and empowered with the ability to forgive sins usually reserved for bishops, Jesuits provided the laity with additional access to the confessional. They also refused to charge penitents the fee for confessing that was usual in many places. But there was something else, less tangible, that allowed Jesuits to carve out a very special niche for themselves among the faithful, both high and low: their approach to penance. Trained to be sensitive to human weakness, and to emphasize empathy and encouragement over scolding, Jesuits developed not just a style all their own as confessors, but also a subtle and complex theology of sin that would come to be known as casuistry or probabilism. In essence, the Jesuits placed every sin on a sliding scale, its seriousness determined by all of the factors surrounding the act. A poor woman who stole food to feed her family, for instance, might have committed a less serious sin than a comfortable burger who embezzled funds. In other words, circumstances determined the seriousness of the sin. And the circumstances taken into consideration by Jesuit confessors were many indeed, both external, such as family pressures, and internal, such as a penitent's emotional state.

Jesuit elaboration of a medieval principle in the case of one particular sin became emblematic of their approach. The sin was lying and the principle was that of "mental reservations," which concerned cases in which telling the truth might be injurious to oneself or to others. The mental reservation was a compromise solution that, as many Jesuits saw it, allowed justice to prevail; the larger principle at work was that of the end justifying the means, known as "situation ethics." The following example demonstrates the mental reservation at work. A Catholic family in England is hiding a Jesuit priest in their attic; agents of the crown come searching for him, knock on the door, and ask whether the priest is in the house. What should those who are hiding the priest say? If they tell the truth, they will avoid the sin of lying, but the priest will be hung, drawn, and quartered, and they will also suffer heavy penalties. A mental reservation solves the dilemma: they can say, "No, he is not here," and at the very same time reserve a qualifying phrase in their minds, such as, "No, he is not here, *for you.*" A similar example would be that of a Jesuit arrested by Queen Elizabeth's agents who is asked, "Are you a priest?" Is saying no a sin? What if he adds a mental reservation to his answer, such as, "No, *I* am not a priest of Mithras or Osiris"? Though this approach to sin seemed compassionate and sensible to many, both high and low, it also offended Catholics of a more punctilious sort and created quite a stir within the Jesuit community and the church at large. It also earned the Jesuits an unsavory reputation as advocates of deceit and moral laxity. This issue would become one of the most divisive controversies of the seventeenth century.

Opposition to their casuistry did not prevent the Jesuits from becoming the preferred official confessors of Catholic aristocrats and rulers. And they adopted this role quickly, with Ignatius's approval. Once, when Ignatius learned that two Jesuits had refused to serve as confessors of King John III of Portugal, he praised their gumption but ordered them to accept the post, adding, "When the head is healthy, the rest of the body reaps the benefits."[16] Given this directive from the very top, Jesuits could soon be found in this most sensitive and potentially influential of posts throughout the courts of Europe. Though not favored by King Philip II of Spain, they did become confessors to his successors, as well as to Henry IV of France, the dukes of Savoy and Bavaria, several Italian dukes and French nobles, and many bishops, including the elector bishops of Cologne and Mainz. At the Hapsburg court in Vienna they became a permanent fixture in the 1560s, serving as confessors not just to the emperor, but also to his immediate family. This situation became so commonplace, and so disconcerting to some within the order who saw it as full of potential pitfalls, that it had to be discussed at the Fifth General Congregation of 1592–1593. It also led the superior general Claudio Acquaviva to write a definitive manual, *Instructions for Confessors of Princes*, in 1602, a text so much in demand that it was repeatedly reprinted. At the time of the Thirty Years' War (1618–1648), Jesuit confessors played key roles in many Catholic courts, enhancing the political influence of their order, and at the same time tarnishing its reputation in the eyes of many, including some popes. Some Jesuits in high places fell prey to court intrigues, like Nicolas Caussin, onetime confessor to the French king Louis XIII who became involved in theological wrangling over Jesuit moral theology. Others, like Juan Everardo Nithard, confessor to Mariana of Austria, regent of Spain after the death of her husband King Philip IV in

1665, would rise to the very top, becoming the kingdom's unofficial prime minister, as well as its inquisitor general. Ousted from the court of the hapless King Charles II after a palace coup, Nithard was elevated by the pope to the ranks of bishop, archbishop, and cardinal, proving that he, like many Jesuits of his generation, knew how to cling to high places.

The Ministry of Charity

Jesuits clung to low places too, zealously ministering to those who were in need. From their earliest days, even before the order was formally recognized in 1540, Ignatius and his companions had engaged in works of charity or mercy, ministering to the sick, the poor, and the homeless. Once the order was established, all new recruits were required to engage in such service as part of their training. Jesuits sometimes established charitable institutions of their own; more often they worked through those already in existence. In both cases, Jesuits perfected a unique approach, for they involved the laity through the creation or expansion of lay confraternities that would commit themselves to running these charitable institutions.

Hospitals ranked high on the Jesuits' list of priorities, and there they engaged in nearly every kind of ministry: preaching, hearing confessions, consoling the dying, taking care of the physical needs of the sick, even cleaning the floors. Some Jesuits would become physicians, too. In times of plague, Jesuits were often in the front lines, doing the work everyone else was afraid to do. In 1569, when Lisbon was hit hard by a plague, seventeen Jesuits died while tending the sick. Prisons were another Jesuit concern. Visiting prisoners, hearing their confessions, giving spiritual counsel, encouraging conversions, accompanying the condemned to their executions—all of these became part of their collective ministry. They also often helped those imprisoned for debt and obtained pardons or less severe sentences for others convicted of wrongdoing. Ministering to prostitutes was another concern of the Jesuits, from very early on. Their aim was conversion, and a genuine change in life. Toward that end, they established halfway houses for prostitutes to be rehabilitated and choose a new path. For former prostitutes who went into domestic service, the houses provided training and placement; for those who would marry, the Jesuits made arrangements and came up with dowries; for those who wished to enter monastic life, they provided the necessary spiritual guidance and created special convents for *conversae*, that is, reformed prostitutes. The model for all such Jesuit institutions was set by Ignatius himself, who established the Casa Santa Marta halfway house in Rome in 1543, along with a lay confraternity to run it, the Compagnia della Grazia. Orphans, vagrant children, and the sons and daughters of prostitutes also received considerable attention from the Jesuits, with orphanages established and lay confraternities created to run them. In addition, the education of these vulnerable children was a particular concern.

Lay confraternities were essential to Jesuit social work. They were nothing new—medieval charity had depended on them—but Jesuits put their own stamp on these brotherhoods and sisterhoods. The *Spiritual Exercises* was key, for it served as a common formative experience for all men and women who joined Jesuit-sponsored confraternities. Focusing on devotion and social service with equal intensity, the lay-run confraternities were like "tertiaries" of older religious orders, but without the vows or solemn promises. At first the Jesuit-inspired confraternities formed ad hoc, in response to specific local needs. By 1565, however, more order was imposed, with the confraternity created for the younger boys at the Collegio Romano as its model, which focused on developing a life of prayer and of service to the poor under the patronage of the Virgin Mary and the guidance of a Jesuit priest. This Marian confraternity, called the Sodality of Our Lady, quickly turned into a franchise of sorts, with branches in cities all over Europe and its colonies. The number of lay people attracted to these sodalities was as impressive as their geographical reach. For some historians these Jesuit Sodalities of Our Lady are the ultimate accomplishment of the Catholic Reformation.[17]

The Ministry of Print

Jesuits also ministered to a wide audience by writing and publishing at an impressive rate. As one would expect of an order committed to learning and education, Jesuits authored books on many subjects, especially on religion. Devotional manuals in the vernacular were a particularly favored genre, for they were at once an extension of the sermon, the *Exercises*, the catechism, and sometimes of polemics; they could spark conversions, mold souls, foster devotion, ensure doctrinal correctness, and enlighten the laity. The international character of the order ensured that texts that were well received in one tongue would soon be translated into others. A case in point is that of Spanish Jesuit Gaspar Loarte (1498–1578), whose *Exercise of a Christian Life* (1557) went through sixteen different editions by 1600, including an English translation that would even have an impact on English Puritans. The *First Booke of the Christian Exercise* (1582) by English Jesuit Robert Parsons (1546–1610) went through eight editions even though it was illegal in England, and it was translated into German, Italian, French, and Latin; the Italian translation alone went through nine editions. The German Jesuit Jeremias Drexel (1581–1638), author of more than thirty titles in Latin, provides a later example. His *Considerations on Eternity* (1620), *The Guardian Angel's Clock* (1622), and *Heliotropium; or, Conformity of the Human Will with the Divine Will* (1627) enjoyed several translations and editions, and were also best sellers. In Munich alone, by 1642 some 170,700 copies of his works had already passed through booksellers and into the hands of Catholics, both lay and clerical. And Loarte, Parsons, and Drexel are only three examples of hundreds of authors with similar publication histories.

Even though devotional manuals contained plenty of instruction, Jesuits did not neglect catechisms. The first and most successful was that of Peter Canisius (1521–1597), one of the earliest Jesuits, and one of the busiest. His catechism, *Summa doctrinae Christianae* (1555), appeared a decade before that of the Council of Trent, and was intended for advanced students. It was later revised and appeared in two shorter versions, one of intermediate length for less advanced students (*Catechismus minor*), and an even shorter version for young children (*Parvus catechismus*). The intermediate *Catechismus minor* was rapidly translated into every major European vernacular and reprinted constantly for generations, with at least 130 editions by 1685. The instructional value of Canisius's *Summa* was incalculable and his name became synonymous with *catechism* among Catholics; its polemical use earned Canisius the title "Hammer of Heretics." Other catechisms published by Jesuits could not catch up in popularity to that of Canisius, but they made their mark all the same. The catechism by Diego de Ledesma (1519–1575) also went through numerous editions and translations, and the Jesuits brought the version to New France for use among the natives. Written in French, the Jesuit catechism by Emond Auger (1530–1591) appeared in 1563 as a direct point-by-point response to John Calvin's *Formulary for Teaching the Christian Faith to Children* and was translated into Dutch, Spanish, and Italian. With its overt polemical thrust, however, its popularity faded within two decades, totally eclipsed by Canisius's *Summa*.

While polemics might not have been too appropriate for a catechism, counter-Protestant texts certainly had their place in the literary output of the Jesuits. Given the contentious nature of the age, it was inevitable that the lines between theology and polemics or theology and apologetics would be blurred. Jesuits engaged with Protestants at various levels, passively and actively, through theology, philosophy, and history. The greatest Jesuit theologians were therefore often the greatest polemicists and apologists as well. Even if one considers only those texts that were overtly polemical, the list of titles is immensely long. Among the most important of these authors, the first to rise to prominence was Francis Coster (1532–1619), a Dutch Jesuit and prolific writer who took on the Protestants head-on in several heavy Latin tomes, including his *Enchiridion controversiarum* (1585), which went through various editions and translations into vernaculars. And when several Protestant theologians dared to refute his *Enchiridion*, Coster published detailed counter-blasts against each of them.

Another fierce polemicist at the learned level was Gregorio de Valencia (1549–1603), a Spanish professor of theology at the University of Ingolstadt, and director of the Jesuit Roman College. His *De rebus fidei hoc tempore controversis* (1591), reprinted in an expanded edition in 1610, was a collection of essays he had written against Protestants on specific theological issues. This impressive work was overshadowed by Roberto Bellarmino's three-volume polemical compendium, published between 1586 and 1593: *Disputationes de controversiis Christianae fidei adversus hujus temporis haereticos* (Disputations About the Controversies of the Christian Faith Against the Heretics of This Time). In this massive undertaking, Bellarmine—as he is known in the English-speaking world—sought to address the major disagreements between Catholics and Protestants, and to do so without personal invective or vitriol. The success of this deeply learned scholastic tour de force can be measured by the number of Protestant theologians who felt compelled to write against it for generations, from Theodore Bèze to Thomas Hobbes, and by the number of chairs established at Protestant universities to refute it. The work is wide ranging, but two of its most influential sections were those that defended papal authority and denied that the pope was the Antichrist. Less voluminous but equally venomous in Protestant eyes was the polemical work of Martin Becan (1563–1624), confessor to Emperor Ferdinand II, a Flemish theologian and professor at Cologne, Würzburg, and Vienna, who took on Reformed Protestantism in his *Manual of Controversies* (1623), a text that went through numerous editions and earned the nickname "The Little Becan." And these works were just the top layer of frost on the tip of the proverbial iceberg.

The Ministry of Politics

Jesuits did much more than simply write against Protestants; they also grappled with them in daily life, at street level, through their ministries in places where religious allegiances were contested. And they did so not only through their schools and missions, but also through texts, and especially through writings that addressed the rights and duties of Catholics who lived under Protestant rulers. Two countries in particular became political hot spots on the Jesuit map: England and France. In England, after the accession of Elizabeth to the throne in 1558, Catholics faced persecution for refusing to take the Oath of Supremacy, which affirmed the monarch's authority over that of the pope. In 1570 the situation for Catholics worsened when Queen Elizabeth was excommunicated by Pope Pius V, which absolved all her subjects from obeying her and her laws, turning every Catholic into a potential traitor. In France, the political situation was more complex, for it involved a power struggle among the nobility and a very bloody civil war that pitted Catholic against Protestant. In both of these countries, Jesuits played a key role in addressing basic questions regarding civil authority, and more specifically about the rights of subjects threatened by religious violence and persecution.

In England, Jesuits entered the fray as subversives and as foreign agents, since they had all received their training abroad and had to slip into Elizabeth's realm in disguise. Some, like Edmund Campion, were caught and executed as traitors. Others, like Robert Parsons, managed to escape and carry on their mission from the continent, writing tirelessly, and setting up printing presses and colleges and seminaries for English Catholic exiles. Parsons is credited with establishing three such seminaries in Spain, at Valladolid, Seville, and Madrid, and one in France, at Saint-Omer. Though he never returned to England, he wrote continually, encouraging English Catholics to resist compromise with their queen and her church. He also called for foreign intervention and the removal of Elizabeth, and he was instrumental in the inception of the failed invasion of England by the Spanish Armada in 1588, which sought to replace Elizabeth with King Philip II.

Among those who labored for the Catholic cause from exile, none was more significant than William Allen (1532–1594), Parsons's friend and fellow Jesuit, Allen established seminaries too, most notably that of Douai, in Flanders, and the English College at Rome. From the presses of the Douai College, Allen oversaw the publication of numerous Catholic texts that were smuggled into England, including a new translation of the Bible into English. Allen's own writings, like those of Parsons, stressed resistance to compromise and the necessity of returning England to the Catholic fold. One of these texts, *A True, Sincere, and Modest Defense of English Catholics* (1584), subtly argued that Catholics were not treasonous subversives, but rather the best subjects that Queen Elizabeth could hope for, since they alone held on to the true faith in her realm, and could return it to orthodoxy. The implicit argument was not hard to miss: if Elizabeth

Exposing covert Jesuit strategies. This English broadsheet from 1680, "A Jesuit Displaid," pokes fun at the Jesuits and seeks to expose their practice of assuming false identities and pretending to be anything but what they really were. The various objects that make up this composite caricature of a "wandering father ' are all instruments of various trades that the Jesuits in England practiced to disguise their true identity. The text explains what the objects are and how they allow the Jesuits to ply their subversive "Romish" trade secretly among an unsuspecting English populace. As the text puts it, the Jesuit is "Gardner, Groome, Cooke, he's everything to all, so his Laborious Zeale may dam a Soul."

were to abandon Protestantism, she would have the support of Catholics, but if she were to remain in the Protestant fold, these subjects were not bound in any way to accept her authority. It was an argument as potentially seditious as any made by Calvinists such as John Knox, Theodore Bèze, or John Ponet against Catholic "tyrants." Allen was elevated to the post of Cardinal in 1587, in anticipation of the invasion of England in 1588; had the Armada succeeded, he would have become archbishop of Canterbury.

Jesuits would acquire a very negative reputation in English culture, summed up in the adjective *Jesuitical*, which came to connote equivocation, dishonesty, deceit, evasiveness, subtle or overly subtle reasoning, craftiness, slyness, and intrigue. This image was a response to the work carried out by Jesuits like Allen and Parsons on the continent and by their confreres who snuck into England, such as John Gerard, and it was compounded by their practice of casuistry, and their continued involvement in Catholic efforts to recover the throne, such as the failed Gunpowder Plot of 1605.

In France, as in England, Jesuit involvement in politics was both theoretical and practical, and they came to rival their enemies, the Calvinists, when it came to a reputation as seditious agitators. Taking up the very question that had bedeviled Calvinists—what are the duties of a faithful Christian in an unchristian realm?—the Jesuits came up with similar theories of resistance. Although the French Jesuits developed their own political theology, much of their thinking was guided by one of their Spanish confreres, Juan de Mariana (1536–1624), who had been a professor at Rome and Paris. A prolific author, Mariana is best known for his controversial mirror-of-princes manual, *On the King and His Education* (1598), in which he addressed the question of whether it is ever lawful to overthrow a tyrant. His answer, while extremely cautious and complex, was nonetheless in the affirmative: under certain circumstances, any individual citizen can justly assassinate a king who violates the laws of religion, imposes taxes without the consent of the people, seizes the property of individuals and squanders it, or prevents the meeting of a democratic parliament. While this argument had medieval antecedents, its articulation in an age of religious turmoil made it incendiary. Moreover, unlike his scholastic forebears who had acknowledged kings' sole ownership of the power granted them by their people, Mariana argued that any time a king abused his power, the people were entitled to reclaim it.

Mariana's scholastic arguments might have remained obscure had they not been linked with three cases of regicide in France that involved lone assassins. In the case of Henry III in 1589 the linkage stemmed from a passage in the sixth chapter of *On the King*, in which Mariana seemed to praise the assassin, Jacques Clement. In the case of the 1594 attempt on Henry IV, the connections seemed justifiable because the would-be assassin, Jean Châtel, had been taught by the Jesuits at the Collège de Clermont and moreover, sufficient evidence was found to execute one of his Jesuit teachers as a coconspirator. In 1595, fearing more treachery, the crown expelled the Jesuits from France. Returning in 1603 after the Edict of Nantes had brought the Wars of Religion to an uneasy truce, the Jesuits continued to be viewed with suspicion. When Henry IV was stabbed to death by a Catholic zealot in 1610, these suspicions seemed justified and the Parlement of Paris ordered the public burning of Mariana's book *On the King*.

Fifteen years later, the Jesuits earned more distrust for themselves in France and elsewhere thanks to the work of Antonio Santarelli (1569–1649), who argued in his *Treatise on Heretics, Schismatics, and Apostates* (1625) that the pope had the power to depose and punish civil authorities and to absolve their subjects from obedience. Since this book had been approved by the order's superior general, Mutio Vitelleschi (1563–1645), and since the same argument could be found in the writings of other Jesuits, including Suárez and Bellarmino, it seemed clear to many that this was the official position of the entire Jesuit order. In France, the uproar caused by Santarelli's book was especially intense. Condemned by both the Paris Parlement and the theological faculty of the Sorbonne, Santarelli's *Treatise*, too, was consigned to the flames. In addition, all Jesuits in France were asked to sign a denunciation of Santarelli's subversive errors; to fail to comply was to risk a charge of treason.

Conclusion: The Price of Success

No wonder, then, that when a book began to circulate around 1612 claiming to be the Jesuit secret master plan for world domination, there were many eager to believe it was the real thing. Written by a miffed Polish ex-Jesuit who had been expelled from the order in 1611, this book, *Monita secreta*, passed itself off as an instruction manual written by none other than the Jesuit superior general, Claudio Acquaviva (1543–1615). Its contents confirmed the worst suspicions every opponent of the Jesuits had ever harbored. In brief, it "revealed" that the Jesuits sought nothing other than wealth and power, and were well trained to acquire both by any means. Translated and published in many countries, it would enjoy a long publishing history, well into the twentieth century—a testament to the distrust that Jesuits had earned for themselves, and ironically, an oblique measure of their success. No one fears the unsuccessful. The verbal caricature of the Jesuits drawn by a nineteenth-century Protestant historian reveals this fear, transparently:

> Wherever the Jesuits have planted missions, opened seminaries, and established colleges, they have been careful to inculcate these principles in the minds of the youth; thus sowing the seeds of future tumults, revolutions, regicides, and wars. These evil fruits have appeared sometimes sooner, sometimes later, but they have never failed to show themselves, to the grief of nations and the dismay of kings. . . . To what country of Europe shall we turn where we are not able to track the Jesuit by his bloody footprints?[18]

Protestants were not alone in their fear and loathing of Jesuits. In the Catholic Church, Jesuit methods and success aroused stiff opposition in some quarters and bitter rivalries. The most spirited opposition came at first from the Dominicans. Their preeminent theologian, Melchior Cano (1509–1560), went even as far as to malign the Society

A proud legacy. After a century in existence, the Jesuit order developed a sense of itself as uniquely successful, and of St. Ignatius Loyola as a powerful heavenly patron who was central to their identity. In this title page from the second edition of Daniello Bartoli's ten-thousand-page history of the Jesuits, the Flemish artist Cornelis Bloemaert stressed and reinforced both conceits. At the very center of the image, the order's worldwide reach is made clear by a globe and four figures representing the peoples of Africa, Asia, Europe, and the Americas. A divinized St. Ignatius hovers protectively and proudly over the work of his order, in full command of the light being shed on all that transpires below.

of Jesus as a sectarian movement with heretical leanings, as dangerous as the Alumbrados, Lutherans, and Calvinists. As if this were not enough, he also identified them as precursors of the Antichrist. Franciscans would later become bitter rivals of the Jesuits in the mission fields, especially in China. In the seventeenth century, the Jesuits would be at the very center of the worst firestorm within the Catholic Church, that of the Jansenist controversy. And in the eighteenth century, they would become so controversial that they would be suppressed by the papacy, and nearly cease to exist.

Despite all of the controversy they engendered, the Society of Jesus made an undeniably significant contribution to the shaping of early modern Catholicism. Though their story obviously fits most neatly within the subject of clerical reform, it would be shortsighted to see the Jesuits solely in that context. Their ability to involve the laity in reform and their commitment to reforming the laity are among their chief accomplishments. Most definitely clerical, the Jesuits nonetheless blurred the boundaries of reform. It could also be argued that they embraced the metaphor of the church as the Body of Christ uniquely, and somewhat paradoxically, for while they strained to achieve perfection as the head, that is, as clerics, the perfection they sought included the challenge of perfecting the laity too, and of helping the mystical body to grow strong by leaps and bounds.

One of their greatest accomplishments has to do with their commitment to expanding the Body of Christ through missionary activity in Europe and around the globe, on five continents. This part of the Jesuits' role in the Catholic Reformation has yet to be dealt with. It was such a colossal undertaking, and so much a part of a different context of Catholic Reform, that it needs be taken up in a later chapter. The subject of the Jansenist controversy, briefly mentioned, will also have to wait for a later chapter.

For now, the words of an English Jesuit poet can do the summing up. Robert Southwell (1561–1595), was admitted into the order in 1580 and sent as a missionary to England in 1586 at his own request. After ministering in secret to English Catholics for six years, he was imprisoned, tortured, and executed. On the scaffold, as he was about to be hanged, drawn, and quartered he denied the charge of treason against Queen Elizabeth and her government. Of the poems he left behind, one in particular expressed the essence of the Jesuit ethos eloquently in verse. The final two stanzas of "Look Home" read as follows:

> Man's soul of endless beauty image is,
> Drawn by the work of endless skill and might;
> This skillful might gave many sparks of bliss
> And, to discern this bliss, a native light;
> To frame God's image as his worths required
> His might, his skill, his word and will conspired.
>
> All that he had his image should present,
> All that it should present it could afford,
> To that he could afford his will was bent,
> His will was followed with performing word.
> Let this suffice, by this conceive the rest,—
> He should, he could, he would, he did, the best.[19]

CHAPTER EIGHTEEN

Missions to the New World

One of the most distinctive features of the early modern period was the expansion of Europe through trade, exploration, and colonization—and one of the most salient components of this expansion was the development of Catholic overseas missions. This expansion, which began before the advent of Protestantism, not only was affected by the reforms that swept through the Catholic Church; it was also a defining part of that very process, for the missionary enterprise first developed for the conversion of the heathen abroad became linked to missionary efforts on home turf.

For the first century of their existence—more or less—Protestants had no overseas missions to speak of. The reason for this disparity is simple: Protestant states did not get seriously involved in overseas ventures until the seventeenth century, and those early enterprises were much smaller in scale than those of Catholic Spain and Portugal.

It would not be until the eighteenth century, as Protestant nations and colonists expanded their global reach further, that Protestants would begin to earnestly launch missions. And it would not be until the nineteenth that their efforts would begin to rival those of the Catholic Church. There are many reasons for this asymmetry, most of which have to do with differences in patterns of trade and colonization rather than on religious convictions, but those developments are beyond our scope. We are concerned only with the early modern period here, and in that era to be a Christian missionary usually meant one thing: to be a Catholic missionary.

Indies over There, Indies over Here

In December 1511, when Martin Luther was still an Augustinian monk pursuing a doctoral degree and Ignatius Loyola no more than a brawling knight in training, Dominican friars were busy establishing an outpost of the Catholic Church in a wild and strange part of the world thousands of miles away, across the Atlantic Ocean. The tropical island of Hispaniola had been overrun by Spanish adventurers in search of gems and precious metals, and the mission entrusted to these friars by the Spanish crown was to minister to the colonists and to Christianize the Taino natives. Six friars had arrived in August 1510, subsequently joined by fourteen more. By all external appearances, the church seemed to be thriving. When that second band of Dominicans arrived, in 1511, there were already three dioceses in the Indies: two in Hispaniola, one in the nearby island of Puerto Rico.

The friars were shocked by what they found, however: the colonists had enslaved the natives, and also abused and killed them at will, in great numbers. Many of the Spanish settlers simply worked their slaves to death, mostly in the fruitless search for gold. For the Dominicans, ministering to their greedy violent countrymen was difficult, and converting the oppressed natives next to impossible. After months of stunned hopelessness, one of the friars broke the silence as only a member of the Order of Preachers could. On the first Sunday of Advent, 4 December 1511, Antonio de Montesinos (d. 1545) blasted away at a church full of colonists in a fiery sermon they would never forget. "I am the voice of one crying in the wilderness," he thundered. Linking himself to the prophet Isaiah and to John the Baptist, Montesinos threatened his congregation with hell and damnation:

> This voice declares that you are in mortal sin, and live and die therein by reason of the cruelty and tyranny that you practice on these innocent people. Tell me, by what right or justice do you hold these Indians in such cruel and horrible slavery? By what right do you wage such detestable wars on these people who lived mildly and peacefully in their own lands, where you have consumed infinite numbers of them with unheard of murders and desolations? . . . And what care do you take that they receive religious instruction and come to know their God and creator, or that they be baptized, hear Mass, or observe holidays and Sundays? Are they not men? Do they not have rational souls? Are you not bound to love them as you love yourselves? How can you lie in such profound and lethargic slumber? Be sure that in your present state you can no more be saved than the Moors or Turks who do not have and do not want the faith of Jesus Christ.

Thus began a long and never fully resolved confrontation between churchmen and settlers in Spain's American colonies. The Catholic Church was forced to think deeply about its role in the emerging colonial enterprises of Europeans, and to formulate strategies for converting millions of newly discovered pagans.

Not very many years later, Catholic writers would construct a providential balance sheet of sorts, on which the expansion of the church into these alien lands was compensation for the lands and millions of souls lost to Protestantism. "In the place of many thousands of souls that have been led astray in Upper and Lower Germany . . . the almighty good God . . . has chosen another people in another world, who knew hitherto nothing about Christ and his true faith," recorded one German Catholic.[1] That compensation did not come only in the Americas, for the sixteenth and seventeenth centuries proved an unprecedented period of expansion for the Catholic Church.

As Montesinos mounted the pulpit in Hispaniola to rebuke the colonists on that December day, on the other side of the globe Portuguese missionaries were building stone-and-mortar churches on the very civilized west coast of the Indian subcontinent, among a mixed population of Hindus, Muslims, and ancient native Christians who traced their faith back to the apostle Thomas. The Portuguese had captured the city of Goa just a year before, and they were setting up not just a trading post and colony, but also an active missionary enterprise. Within a few years, they would be sailing to Southeast Asia, China, and Japan, spreading their religion along with their wares, factories, and trading incentives.

So it happened that Asia and the Americas, which lay half a globe apart, were colonized and Christianized simultaneously, greatly increasing the reach of the Catholic Church. Both places came to be known as Las Indias, or the Indies, to the Iberians who spearheaded the expansion. Only one of the two Indies was somewhat aptly named, for India at least was part of the Indies in the east. The Indies across the Atlantic Ocean were given the wrong name from the start: here was a whole new world previously unknown to Europeans, not the India promised to the Spanish monarchs by Columbus. But the name stuck.

The establishment of outposts of the Catholic Church in either of the Indies—America or Asia—was its own challenge, and each effort had its unique history. Outposts also sprang up in Africa, in much smaller numbers, and that continent, too, became an "Indies." Despite all the differences among these far-flung missions, they were part of a long-term process viewed by the church itself as a single enterprise. Though mission work in the Indies began before Protestantism changed the religious landscape of Europe, missions came to be a significant component of the Catholic Reformation, for by the mid-sixteenth century Europe itself was viewed as a mission field, full of people who needed converting. And it was not just Protestants who needed to be reached, but also nominal Catholics whose ignorance of their own faith put them in the same category as all of the heathen in faraway lands. Europeans seemed to have discovered "Indies" in their midst, especially in rural and mountainous areas. When, in 1553, the Jesuit Silvestro Landini referred to his missionary turf as "my Indies," he was speaking about the island of Corsica. Appalled by the "thousand superstitions" of the Corsicans and by the corruption of their secular clergy, Landini had no trouble seeing his flock as primitives.[2]

Landini was giving voice to a common sentiment. Others described southern Italy and Sicily as a "new Japan" or "new Brazil,"[3] or as "an ignorant India," in need of spiritual assistance.[4] And similar terms were used to describe certain regions in Spain, such as Asturias, Galicia, and Andalusia. In 1568 Andrés de Prada, a canon from Asturias, wrote to the superior general of the Jesuits describing his region as "an Indies within Spain."[5] Jesuits were not alone in holding this opinion. In 1554, Felipe de Meneses, rector of the Dominican Colegio de San Gregorio in Valladolid complained that there were "Indies within Spain, in the kingdom of Castile" and "mountains of ignorance."[6] Such comparisons served a purpose: by identifying all areas rife with ignorance as "Indies," whether in

"Indies over here." In the sixteenth century many reforming ecclesiastics began to approach the unlettered peasants of Europe as near-pagans who needed missionaries as much as non-Christians in foreign lands. At the same time, these reformers became increasingly uneasy with folk customs and traditional festivals, such as the Feast of Fools, depicted here by Pieter van der Heyden, in a copy of an earlier work by Pieter Breughel the Elder. Consequently, "Christianizing" the rustics of Europe became as much of a priority—and sometimes a higher priority—than sending missionaries overseas.

Europe or abroad, churchmen were not just linking center and periphery, but also calling attention to the need for missionary activity. In Europe itself, there was often no better way to ask for more missionaries to be deployed in a specific area than to compare that area to the Indies. Pragmatic considerations aside, however, such a perception revealed a mentality that had little tolerance for ignorance and a commitment to wiping it out. One might argue that this was a distinctly *modern* mentality—and a clerical one, too—that revealed a new conception of what it meant to be "Christian," a conception narrower and more precise than it had been in previous centuries. It was a mentality keenly aware of the gap between ideals and actual realities and of the need to close that gap. To engage in missionary work, then, was to reform; and it mattered little whether the missionary dealt with Caribbean cannibals or Calabrian peasants. It was all one huge enterprise driven by a common sense of purpose and a vision of the Catholic Church as seamless and truly global.

So it was that within Catholic culture, missionaries could become celebrities and their accounts of their experiences best sellers. Mission work became ever more appealing—not in spite of the difficulties involved, but precisely *because* of them. Mission work required sacrifice and heroic virtue, and it held out the possibility of martyrdom. In other words, being a missionary involved bringing salvation to others, and earning it for oneself, in the fullest Catholic sense: it was all about earning salvation by "works-righteousness" and about personal holiness, those two theological issues rejected by Protestants. For members of religious orders, reports from the mission fields stirred the heart and taught many lessons. In 1550, Peter Canisius explained the usefulness of these reports when he forwarded some missionary letters to his fellow Jesuits in Cologne:

> You will read in these letters about your brothers' most gallant struggles, about their burning zeal, their indefatigable labours, their apostolic faith, and their neighbourly charity, so great as hardly to be believed. . . . I shall be surprised indeed if you can read the story of such wonderful and perfect doings without profit to your souls.

Canisius—one of the busiest of Jesuits, who had an astounding record of accomplishments—then opened up about the effect these reports had on him: "For myself, I was profoundly affected and felt myself quite a changed man, especially when I measured my meanness against the glorious example of my brethren."[7] If Canisius the old warhorse could be made to feel inadequate when reading mission narratives, then it is reasonable to surmise that they probably had an even more profound effect on green novices primed for action.

Missionary work had its own allure, then, and recruits could always be found. Directors of missions had difficult choices to make, however. Despite the steady supply of candidates, there were never enough men to go around. Within the Jesuit order, thousands of letters poured into Rome asking the superior general for more missionaries to be sent here and there. Thousands of letters were also written by Jesuit novices requesting the toughest assignments of all, as far from home as possible. With too many Indies to Christianize, mission directors often turned down such requests. Two of the most prominent spiritual writers of the Catholic Reformation, Luis de Granada (1505–1588), a Dominican, and Juan Eusebio Nieremberg (1595–1658), a Jesuit, were far from alone in having their requests for an overseas ministry declined. The needs of the church in Europe also had to be satisfied.

Those who were assigned to the European Indies faced tasks less monumental than those tackled by their brethren overseas, but the challenges were nonetheless daunting. First, they had to teach a largely illiterate laity the basics of Christian doctrine and ethics; then they had to instruct them on the meaning of symbols and rituals, and expunge whatever local customs seemed aberrant or superstitious. Most often, they also had to take on roles not fulfilled by local diocesan clergy, who were simply nowhere to be found in many areas, or tended to be just as ignorant as their flocks. In many places, these intra-European missionaries simply replaced the local clergy, or were the first to implement the reforms of the Council of Trent. Sometimes strong opposition came from within the church, that is, from the local bishops or parish clergy who resented the missionaries or felt threatened by their presence. In areas that had gone Protestant or had Protestant neighbors, they often faced open hostility and strong resistance from various quarters.

The process of eradicating ignorance, superstition, and corruption in the Indies of Europe had obvious parallels to the mission efforts overseas. The instructions given by José de Acosta to his Jesuit missionary brethren in Peru in the late 1570s applied just as much to peasants in the Cantabrian hinterlands as to the natives of Andean altiplano:

> The utmost care must be taken to ensure that salutary rites are introduced in the place of pernicious ones, erasing certain ceremonies with others. Thus, priests must be convinced that the use of holy water, images, rosaries, beads, candles, palms, and other items of which Holy Church approves and makes frequent use, are extremely profitable for the recently converted.[8]

European rustics could be viewed as "converts," and Protestants most certainly were, but in practice the obstacles faced by missionaries overseas were far greater and more complex. Europeans at least shared a common culture with the missionaries and centuries of exposure to Christianity. Even if only superficially linked to urban and aristocratic Christians by common tongues, rituals, and symbols, the rustics and their betters were nonetheless linked. Similarly, while Protestants most certainly had a different take on religion, at least they were Christians. In contrast, the natives of the overseas Indies had little in common with Europeans in terms of language, culture, and religion, and they were often asked to abandon deeply rooted ancestral customs. And foreign missions were often closely linked to commercial and colonizing enterprises, and all too often enveloped in mutual distrust between Europeans and natives or acts of violence and exploitation. The differences between the "Indies over there" and the "Indies over here" do therefore seem to dwarf the similarities.

Having established that mission efforts "over there" and "over here" were linked, we must turn our attention to the missionary effort "over there," which needs to be understood on its own terms.

The American Indies

The expansion of the Catholic Church in the American Indies was linked to a colonial, imperialistic enterprise that involved wars of conquest and the exploitation of the land and its people. Consequently, much of the history of the American missions is about the ways the European colonists dealt with the native populations they encountered, and how the Catholic Church responded to the challenge of spreading the faith in the midst of an encounter marked by violence, injustice, bigotry, and racism. In other words, the history of the American missions is largely about an encounter in which all of the "pagans" were considered inferiors and treated as such by Europeans. For no matter how marvelous or impressive the achievements of the most sophisticated natives might have appeared to Europeans, those alien cultures always seemed deficient. And they also seemed demonic, no matter how civilized.

The evangelization of the so-called New World began with the second voyage of Christopher Columbus in late 1493, for along with the settlers and livestock he brought from Spain in his seventeen ships, he also brought some clergy. All plans for the church on these strange new lands—which Columbus thought were off the coast of Asia—were tentative at best, and disorganized and feeble at worst. These first clerics were not really missionaries. Although converting the "savages" on Hispaniola and elsewhere was on their minds, their principal function was to minister to the colonists. Violence and chaos plagued their ministry: waging constant war against the natives and enslaving them, the colonists doomed all mission efforts to failure and also created an ever-growing rift between themselves and the clerics. When the first few Franciscans arrived, in 1500, a pattern of abuse was already very much in place. And when the first Dominican friars arrived, in 1510, with the express purpose of reaching out to the natives, the situation they faced was dismal.

The legal claim to these lands and people made by the Spanish monarchs and backed by the pope was religious in nature. According to medieval custom, because of Christ's command "make disciples of all nations" (Matthew 28:19), the pope could claim universal dominion over all lands inhabited by pagans. Fully aware of this papal assertion, and that the Portuguese had already obtained several bulls from Rome that granted them exclusive rights to their outposts in Africa and India, King Ferdinand and Queen Isabella of Spain petitioned Pope Alexander VI—himself a Spaniard—for the exclusive right to colonize all pagan lands at the western end of the Atlantic. In May 1493, Pope Alexander granted their request in his bull *Inter caetera* ("Among Other Things"), which emphasized that the rights of the Spanish monarchs to subjugate these new people were religious in nature and brought with them certain duties. "Among other works well pleasing to the Divine Majesty and cherished of our heart, this assuredly ranks highest," said Alexander VI, "that in our times especially the Catholic faith and the Christian religion be exalted and be everywhere increased and spread, that the health of souls be cared for and that barbarous nations be overthrown and brought to the faith itself." In case this directive was not clear enough, the pope reminded the Spanish monarchs that their chief responsibility was "to lead the peoples dwelling in those islands and countries to embrace the Christian religion," and to appoint "God-fearing, learned, skilled, and experienced men, in order to instruct the aforesaid inhabitants and residents in the Catholic faith and train them in good morals."[9]

What happened during those first few decades in the Caribbean could not have been further from those lofty goals. The tragic events would later be chronicled by a Dominican friar, Bartolomé de Las Casas (1484–1566), in his *Brief Account of the Destruction of the Indies*. First published in 1552, this would become one of the best-selling books of its age, translated into nearly every European language, and continually

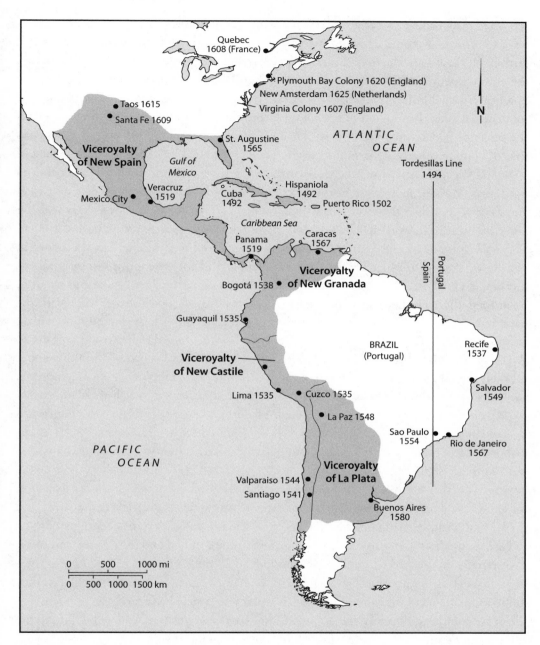

Quebec
1608 (France)

Plymouth Bay Colony 1620 (England)
New Amsterdam 1625 (Netherlands)
Virginia Colony 1607 (England)

Taos 1615
Santa Fe 1609

**Viceroyalty
of New Spain**

St. Augustine
1565

*ATLANTIC
OCEAN*

Tordesillas Line
1494

*Gulf of
Mexico*

Veracruz
1519

Mexico City

Cuba
1492

Hispaniola
1492

Puerto Rico 1502

Caribbean Sea

Panama
1519

Caracas
1567

Bogotá 1538

**Viceroyalty
of New Granada**

Spain | Portugal

Guayaquil 1535

BRAZIL
(Portugal)

Recife
1537

**Viceroyalty
of New Castile**

Lima 1535

Cuzco 1535

La Paz 1548

Salvador
1549

Sao Paulo
1554

Rio de Janeiro
1567

*PACIFIC
OCEAN*

**Viceroyalty
of La Plata**

Valparaiso 1544

Santiago 1541

Buenos Aires
1580

N

0   500   1000 mi
0 500 1000 1500 km

Colonizing and Christianizing. The Spanish and Portuguese monarchs were the first Europeans to lay claim to the Americas, and the first to send missionaries to convert the natives to Christianity. The Iberian empires were eventually challenged successfully in the seventeenth century by France, England, and the Dutch Republic. By the eighteenth century, their respective claims carved up the two continents unevenly. Given the early prominence of Spain and Portugal, and the aggressive mission activity of the French, Catholic efforts dwarfed those of Protestants well into the late eighteenth century.

reprinted. Las Casas, an early settler of Hispaniola, followed in the footsteps of his fellow Dominican Antonio de Montesinos, and he carried the defense of the natives much farther, all the way to the royal court in Spain. Las Casas would become an iconic figure, the embodiment of the Christian conscience that seemed so glaringly absent in the early Spanish colonial enterprise. His *Brief Account* provides a revealing glimpse of the dissonance between the religion of the colonists and their actions, and of the negative effect the violence had on mission efforts. An illustrative case highlighted by Las Casas was that of Hatuey, a native chieftain from Hispaniola who fled by canoe to nearby Cuba in 1511 and warned the natives there about the Spanish and their atrocities. According to Las Casas, Hatuey showed them some gold and gems he had brought along in a basket and said: "See, this is the God of the Christians. . . . This is a God they greatly worship and they want us to worship him too, and that is why they fight to enslave us and kill us."

Captured by the Spanish, Hatuey was sentenced to death, as Las Casas put it, "solely for fleeing from such cruel and evil people and for defending himself and his brethren from those who wanted to oppress and kill them." Tied to a stake and about to be burned alive, Hatuey was approached by a Franciscan friar who tried to explain the basic tenets of the Christian faith, including those concerning heaven, and hell, which, according to Las Casas, "he had never heard of before." Asked if he would convert to avoid hell and go to heaven, Hatuey replied with a question of his own: "Thinking about it briefly, he asked the friar if Christians all went to heaven. The friar said yes. And then the chief said without further thought that he would rather go to hell than to heaven, so he wouldn't have to see such cruel people again or be near them." Las Casas summed up the gross failure of the Spanish enterprise represented by this event: "Such is the dishonorable reputation that God and our faith have earned thanks to the Christians who went to these islands."[10]

Whether events occurred exactly as related by Las Casas is of little consequence, for such anecdotes rang true. The *Brief Account* was written to prick consciences and shame Spain into altering policies that many of the missionaries found contrary not just to Christian ethics, but also to the very purpose of the colonial and missionary enterprise as originally established through Pope Alexander VI's bull *Inter caetera*.

Montesinos and Las Casas spoke in the name of the church as a whole, but they did so as members of the Dominican order, and it was largely because of the pressure that the order could exert back home, in Spain, that some reforms were enacted. Gaining the ear of King Ferdinand (Isabella had died in 1504), the Dominicans convinced him to enact a new set of regulations for the colonists, and he did so rather quickly, in late December 1512. Known as the Laws of Burgos, these thirty-five statutes set strict guidelines for the treatment of the natives of the Indies, seeking to protect them from abuse and ensure their conversion to Christianity. The Laws of Burgos outlawed the direct punishment of natives by anyone other than an appointed official, set limits on the amount of work they could do, required they be provided with adequate food and housing, and ordered that all of them be instructed in the Christian faith. The most important provision, which had long-lasting effects, was the institution of the *encomienda*, a land-grant system that gave colonists the right to exploit a limited number of natives (no fewer than 40 and no more than 150), according to the size of the property allotted to them. In exchange for their labor, the *encomendero* who owned the land was made responsible for their well-being and their catechization. Though very precise and detailed, and very much in favor of protecting the natives, the Laws of Burgos proved nearly impossible to enforce. The abuses continued—and even worsened in many places—and this situation led to further conflict between the colonists and anyone who stood in their way, particularly the clergy who never stopped denouncing them and petitioning the crown for enforcement of the law.

Another reform gone wrong, which had also been spawned by Dominican complaints about the treatment of the natives, was the Requerimiento, a new law issued in 1513 that required the Spanish to give the natives fair warning of what was about to befall them. In blunt terms, the Requerimiento, which was to be read to all newly encountered natives, announced that the pope had made the Spanish monarchs their overlords, and if they refused to accept that fact, then the Spanish had a right to wage war against them. In essence, the text was an assertion of the papal bull *Inter caetera*, and religion was at the heart of it, since along with the sovereignty of the Spanish monarchs, the natives were also asked to "receive and obey the priests whom their Highnesses send to preach to them and to them our Holy Faith." Promising that no one would be compelled to convert, the text simultaneously required that all be subjected to religious instruction in the Christian faith.

Though intended to legitimize Spanish sovereignty and provide a semblance of fairness and magnanimity, the Requerimiento quickly turned into an empty ritual that mocked the natives, along with the very legality of the conquest itself. Read in Spanish to startled locals who could not understand a word, or often to no one at all from shipboard, or from hilltops, or on empty beaches and villages that the inhabitants had fled in fear, the Requerimiento gave the natives no real choice: it simply told them that from that day forward they were going to be ruled by the colonists and their priests. Resistance would not only be futile, they were told, but a fatal error: "If you do not accept this, and maliciously make delay in doing so," warned the text,

> we shall enter into your country with our full force, and with the help of God, make war against you everywhere in any way that we can, and subject you to the yoke and obedience of the Church and of their Highnesses; we shall also take you and your wives and your children, and shall turn you all into slaves, and as such shall sell and dispose of all of you as their Highnesses may command; and we shall take away everything you own, and inflict as much pain and damage on you as we can, as to vassals who do not obey, and refuse to receive their lord, and resist and contradict him; and we protest that the deaths and losses which shall result from all this are your fault, and not that of their Highnesses, or ours, nor of these knights who come with us.[11]

The spirit of the Requerimiento and its usage drew howls of protest from the Dominicans and other missionaries, and from some colonists. Bartolomé de Las Casas condemned the Requerimiento: "it mocks truth and justice," he said, "and is a great insult to our Christian faith and to the mercy and love of Jesus Christ; it is totally lacking in legality." Nonetheless, it would continue to be read at encounters with new natives until 1556.

The missionary enterprise became more complex, and more deeply mired in conflict when the Spanish conquered the Aztec empire in 1521. Whereas up until then the colonists had been dealing with rather thinly settled islands and uncivilized natives, they suddenly found themselves as overlords of millions of heathen subjects whose culture and society had reached a remarkable sophistication. The capital city of this empire, Tenochtitlán, was a marvel such as none of the Spanish conquistadores had ever seen. Built on an island in the center of a lake and surrounded by other inhabited islands, it was linked to the mainland by long causeways. With up to two hundred thousand inhabitants, it was one of the largest cities on earth at that time. It was also full of impressive stone buildings and pyramids, and all the riches that the Spanish had been searching for since 1492. The city seemed awash in gold, silver, and precious gems. One of the men who helped conquer it, Bernal Díaz del Castillo, would later describe his first glimpse of the Aztec capital:

> When we saw so many cities and villages built in the water and other great towns on dry land we were amazed and said that it was like the enchantments they tell of in the legend of Amadis, on account of the great towers and temples and buildings rising from the water, and all built of masonry. And some of our soldiers even asked whether the things that we saw were not a dream. . . . I do not know how to describe it, seeing things as we did that had never been heard of or seen before, not even dreamed about.[12]

Though overawed, and vastly outnumbered by the natives, Díaz and his four hundred fellow conquistadores, led by Hernán Cortés, quickly took over the city, killed its emperor, ransacked its treasures, and leveled it flat. On top of the rubble they built their own city, Mexico City, named after the Mexica people who were native to the area. They also renamed the Aztec empire "New Spain." The total destruction of Tenochtitlán had a sharp religious edge to it. Though its architecture was impressive, it was a place wholly given over to grisly rites of human sacrifice and a religion so bloody that it struck the Spanish as demonic. The accounts written by the conquerors tended to legitimize their actions on religious grounds, as the overthrow of devil worship. Ironically, at the same time as Cortés and his men began the wholesale destruction of Aztec religious art, the first Protestant iconoclasts were beginning their attacks on Catholic religious imagery in Wittenberg. Even more deeply ironic is that the term these two very different groups of Christians employed for the images they destroyed was exactly the same: *idols*. But whereas the iconoclasts at Wittenberg thought all religious imagery was forbidden by the second commandment—even images of Jesus—and removed the Catholic *idols* to have none at all, the Spanish conquistadores replaced the "horrible" and "frightful" Aztec *idols* with "beautiful" Catholic crosses and images.

Dealing with bloodthirsty idols. The Spanish adventurers who first encountered the practice of human sacrifice in Mesoamerica were horrified by it and made its elimination one of their first priorities. In the process of eradicating the native religion, ironically, they embarked on an icono-clastic crusade against "idolatry" that paralleled the one being carried out by Protestants in Europe against the Catholic rituals and symbols held dear by the Spanish themselves.

Abolishing human sacrifice along with the Aztec priesthood and obliterating temples and images was one thing; making the natives give up their religion was quite another. Erecting churches over their ruined temples and installing Christian images would never suffice. Neither would herding these natives into the newly built churches, if they could be built fast enough. The Spanish knew all too well that those who are forcibly converted tend to cling to their old religion, not just because of their experiences in the Caribbean, but also because of the Marranos and Moriscos, those Jews and Muslims back in Spain who had been forced to convert but continued to practice their ancestral religion in secret.

But how were the conquerors to teach the fundamentals of the faith, baptize, and turn millions of demon-crazed pagans into Catholics? Not even if all of the clergy in Old Spain were to be suddenly ferried to New Spain could such a task be easily accomplished. Consequently, the Spanish in New Spain adopted a strategy of gradual, long-term conver-sion, the first step of which was to baptize as many natives as possible, and the second of which was to expose them to the new faith, keep an eye on their behavior, and hope for the best. Part of this strategy involved gathering the natives in close proximity to the conquerors and their clergy. Another part involved bringing clergy to New Spain, to assume the herculean task ahead.

The process of converting the former Aztec empire began in earnest in 1524, with the arrival of twelve Franciscan friars who walked barefoot all the way from the port of Veracruz to the newly renamed Mexico City, a trek of about two hundred miles. Expectations ran high. The twelve men seemed so exemplary, so well prepared for their task, and so much of a contrast with the greedy conquistadores. One of them, Toribio de Benavente, so impressed the natives with his devotion to poverty that he was given the name "Motolinia," which in the local Nahuatl tongue meant "he who is poor" or "he who afflicts himself." Friar Toribio not only adopted the name, but also learned the local language. Among the twelve Franciscans, expectations ran high too. Making obvious comparisons to the twelve apostles of Jesus, they and those around them began to think of the mission to New Spain as a new era in the history of the church, even the history of the world. The Franciscans themselves harbored millenarian hopes, especially those held by the followers of Joachim of Fiore, a thirteenth-century Franciscan who had prophesied the advent of a new egalitarian "age of the Holy Spirit," when the entire human race would give up private property and live as monastics. Their message to the Aztec elite, with whom they met right away, was as soothing as one could hope for, and the epitome of colonial paternalism. They should all convert, argued the friars, because the advent of the Spanish was all part of God's plan—a God who had their best interests at heart and had toppled their demonic religion through the agency of the conquistadores. Their defeat was but the beginning of a new glorious future. The Franciscans presented themselves as selfless agents of a benevolent lord, the pope:

> Fear not . . . we are only messengers sent to you by a great lord called the Holy Father, who is the spiritual head of the world, and who is filled with pain and sadness at the state of your souls. . . . He has sent us to search out and to save your souls. This is why we have come. We do not seek gold, silver, or precious stones; we seek only your health.[13]

Following an ancient missionary custom, the Franciscans began by aiming high at the elites, hoping that their conversion would lead to that of their subalterns. It was, after all, the way much of Europe had been converted centuries before. But they also reached out to the commoners, not just in Mexico City, but also in scattered missions throughout New Spain.

In 1526, the mission to New Spain received a boost with the arrival of the first Dominicans. They were followed by another mendicant order in 1533, the Mercedarians. The Jesuits would not arrive until 1572, but despite the heroic efforts of earlier missionaries, there was still plenty of work left for them to do. Christianizing an area as large as New Spain required patience and a huge number of missionaries, and there never seemed to be enough of them. As they fanned out in all directions from Mexico City, their missions were spread somewhat sparsely over the map. The preferred method of establishing a presence anywhere was to build fortified convents, gather the natives around them in *pueblos* (villages), baptize them, teach them European methods of farming and stock raising along with a new ethical code and a new religion, and protect them as much as possible from abuse and exploitation by the Spanish colonists. Ever searching for new mission fields, ever seeking to approach the natives on their terms, the missionaries studied local tongues and customs. As a result, many of them became explorers, mapmakers, historians, linguists, and ethnographers. Their war against idolatry also made them agents of destruction, for much of native culture was bound to ancestral religion, and the missionaries were intent on consigning all aspects of that heritage to oblivion. Juan de Zumárraga, a Franciscan and the first bishop of Mexico City, who was appointed in 1528, boasted a mere four years later that he had already demolished five hundred temples and twenty thousand idols. Though much of the material culture of the natives was lost, at least some items were preserved, largely through the missionaries' efforts to catalogue and analyze the salient features of the cultures they were transforming. The Franciscans, for instance, wrote texts in twenty-two different Mesoamerican languages.

The growth of the church in New Spain was phenomenal, at least in terms of numbers. Estimates of how many natives were baptized differ: one estimate argues for nine million by 1537, another for ten million by 1550. Some friars baptized as many as four thousand natives in a single day. One of the original twelve Franciscans, Toribio de Benavente, or "Motolinia" was credited with four hundred thousand baptisms in the course of his forty-four years as a missionary, an average of almost ten thousand per year. What these numbers might have meant in terms of genuine conversions or in terms of the depth of understanding involved is anyone's guess, given that whatever instruction was dispensed to these millions was at best rudimentary and at worst negligible. In most cases, Christianization was attempted more through ritual and symbols than by catechetical instruction. With missionaries vastly outnumbered by natives, discursive education on a personal level was simply impossible.

Most natives were given simple lessons in the central tenets of the faith, and taught key prayers such as the Pater Noster and the Ave Maria. They were also taught about the sacraments, including that of penance, and about the Ten Commandments and the seven virtues and seven sins. Much of this instruction could be given in sermons rather than classes or teaching sessions. Such lessons were the skimpy framework on which the missionaries built a firmer religious life for the natives, the substance of which was not theological or discursive, but rather symbolic: a faith centered not so much on doctrines as on devotion to Catholic rituals and symbols. Attendance at Mass and other liturgical functions, such as processions, and devotion to the cult of Christian images was the stuff of faith and of Catholic identity as far as the missionaries were concerned. In its simplest terms, it was a religion that asked the natives to avoid ancestral customs in worship and ethics and take up new devotions and a new moral code.

It was perhaps the most pragmatic strategy they could employ, given the enormity of their task. But it was also a very risky venture, since rituals and symbols convey information inexactly and equivocally, and their meaning is always open to interpretation and slippages as well as misunderstandings. In one case, for example, some natives of New Spain developed a fervent devotion to St. James. Known as Santiago in Spanish, St. James was the patron saint of Spain and the reconquest of the Iberian Peninsula from its Muslim rulers, and he was always depicted as a knight on a steed, trampling Moors, his sword held aloft in his right hand. Sometimes, a Moor or two under the horse would be portrayed as decapitated or maimed. It was a grisly image, but it was favored by the conquistadores, for obvious reasons, as was the cult of the saint it represented. The missionaries were at first delighted by the devotion of their newly Christianized flock, but they soon discovered something beneath the surface of this devotion that they found totally unacceptable: the natives were actually devoted to the figure of the horse rather than to Santiago, given peculiar resonances that the steed had with a native deity. Horrified, the missionaries chastised their flock and put an immediate end to what they had mistaken for genuine devotion. They also had to reeducate the natives, and teach them some of the finer points of Christian worship.[14]

Mistaking a Christian icon for a pagan deity, or willfully transforming a Christian image into a pagan idol, was but one problem caused by the forced introduction of Christianity among the natives. In many cases, as had happened with the Marranos and Moriscos back in Spain, the natives continued to worship in secret as they always had, behind the backs of their new overlords. Discovering that the natives had slipped back into idolatry was common, and the missionaries and the colonists were always on the lookout for hidden idols and secret worship spaces. Sometimes, the consequences for the natives could be awful and unpredictable.

Take, for instance, the case of the Maya in Yucatán, in the early 1560s. Convinced that the Mayans under his charge were turning into good Christians, the Franciscan provincial of Yucatán, Diego de Landa, treated his native flock with paternalistic benevolence. Like most missionaries, Landa had been a passionate advocate for the human rights of the natives and had proved himself their defender against abuse by the colonists. When he discovered in 1562 that some of them had reverted to worshiping their idols and taken to mixing Christian and pagan symbols, and had begun to practice human sacrifice anew, Landa launched a violent inquisition and a persecution of those responsible for this relapse into idolatry. Destroying their previously hidden idols, employing torture to extract information, and even killing about 150 natives in the process, the Franciscan became the aggressor rather than the protector. Ironically, it would be the complaints lodged against him by the colonists that forced the Spanish authorities to bring an end to Landa's extrajudicial inquisition. Though he was brought to trial for overstepping his authority, he was found innocent of wrongdoing, and ten years later was appointed bishop of Yucatán. This case provides us with many lessons about the missions to the American Indies, but three in particular stand out. First, that the Christianization of the natives could be a thin veneer beneath which much of the old pagan religion still thrived. Second, that the missionaries could be so heavily invested in their work as to feel personally betrayed by backsliders and secret idolaters. Third, that the roles played by missionaries and colonists did not always fit predictable patterns, and sometimes the men of God could prove themselves more ferocious than the greedy colonialists.[15]

A prominent feature of the New World missions was the absence of native clergy. And this was a major obstacle to Christianization. By the time of Landa's idolatry case in 1562, the Spanish could have been drawing on the progeny of the conquered natives for additional missionaries. But the Spanish steadfastly refused to accept natives or men of mixed Spanish and native lineage (*mestizos*) to the priesthood, even at the cost of keeping their clerical class thinly spread. Although schools were opened to native children, especially those of the former Aztec aristocracy, and though natives were thoroughly Hispanicized and Christianized in these schools, not even these native elites were considered suitable candidates for the priesthood. This glaring shortcoming in the church of the Indies was part of a much larger issue that stirred debate but was never resolved: the prejudicial and paternalistic attitude that considered the natives to be inferior and incapable of assuming positions of authority. This approach affected the entire colonial enterprise from top to bottom, including the missions.

Debating Human Rights

The crisis of conscience that had first come to the surface in that Advent sermon of Montesinos in 1511, which pitted colonists versus missionaries, was not driven by a simple dialectic of Church versus state, or even of spiritual interests versus worldly interests. Sometimes clerics disagreed vehemently with one another: the Franciscan Toribio de Benavente, the tireless baptizer, wrote to Charles V in 1555 complaining of Bartolomé de Las Casas as "a grievous man, restless, importunate, turbulent, injurious, and prejudicial," and an apostate who should be locked away in a European convent for the rest of his life.[16] Or, sometimes, church and state could join forces to protect the natives from wayward clerics, as in the case of Landa. The main question that emerged out of the constant tension between colonists and missionaries was whether the natives were as fully human as their European conquerors. The natives encountered for the first quarter century of the colonial enterprise seemed so "savage" and "ignorant" to the Spanish that some of the colonists took them to be subhuman, a different species, closer to animals than humans. This rationale fueled much of the excessive abuse heaped on the natives by the conquerors. With no writing, no cities, no masonry buildings, no wheel, no metal weapons or tools, and practically no clothing, the natives seemed not just uncivilized, but wholly lacking in the most essential traits of humanity and incapable of rising any higher than their benighted state. The civilized natives encountered later in Mexico and Peru might have had cities, masonry buildings, and astronomers, but they practiced human sacrifice and were still sorely lacking in other basic markers of full humanity: they too had yet to discover the wheel or devise an alphabet with separate glyphs for individual sounds. For many of the Spanish, these deficiencies were sufficient proof of the inferiority of all natives, no matter what.

Those who condemned the colonists' abuses based their arguments on a different premise, holding that the natives were fully human and therefore equal to their conquerors in nature and fully deserving of the same respect. The natives were "primitive" when compared to Europeans, but were in essence behind only in development, much like children who have not yet fulfilled their adult potential. As the debate unfolded over several decades, positions hardened and clarified. On the side of the natives, Dominicans led the charge, defending their full humanity. They were joined by Franciscans, and later the Jesuits. By far the most vociferous among these human rights activists was none other than Bartolomé de Las Casas, who was backed by some formidable theologians known collectively as "the school of Salamanca" because of their posts at that university. The leading lights of this school were Francisco de Vitoria (1492–1546), and Melchior Cano (1509–1560), both Dominicans. On the side of those colonists who thought the natives were a race apart, jurists, philosophers, and some clerics ransacked the Western classics for texts and arguments that would help prove their point. Their champion would be Juan Ginés de Sepúlveda (1490–1573), a theologian and humanist scholar who had never set foot in the Indies, but just happened to be chaplain to Emperor Charles V. This long-simmering tension between colonists and missionaries came to a head in the late 1540s, as a result of the promulgation in 1542 of the "New Laws of the Indies for the Good Treatment and Preservation of the Indians," which prohibited the outright enslaving of natives, reformed the *encomienda* system, and called for its eventual abolition. The New Laws were a response to all of the abuses that surrounded the observance of the Laws of Burgos of 1512, and were largely based on recommendations made to the court of Charles V by Bartolomé de Las Casas. Needless to say, the New Laws caused an uproar in the colonies and considerable opposition in some influential circles in Spain.

The louder the complaints from the missionaries, the more the colonists lobbied for their position. In 1544 they thought they had found in Juan Ginés de Sepúlveda the man best suited to argue their case. Asked by the archbishop of Seville to write a treatise that would defend the colonial enterprise on the basis of the inferiority of the natives, Sepúlveda penned *Democates secundus*, in which he argued that the natives of the Indies were "natural slaves." This argument was taken straight out of Aristotle's *Politics*, which proposed that there were indeed human beings whose intellect was so limited that they could do "nothing better" than "to use their body." These "lower sorts," argued Aristotle, "are by nature slaves, and it is better for them as for all inferiors that they should be under the rule of a master."[17] When Sepúlveda's book was condemned by both University of Alcalá and University of Salamanca, the ultimate result was the arrangement of a crown-sponsored debate held at Valladolid, Spain, in 1550, in which Sepúlveda and his backers took on Las Casas and the pro-native theology of the school of Salamanca. At stake was no mere philosophical question, but the very legitimacy of the crown's policies in the Indies.

At this debate, Las Casas argued once again for the full humanity of the natives. But the arguments made by his side, favorable though they were to the natives, also defended a paternalistic outlook that stripped that natives of any immediate hope for self-determination. The natives were fully human, yes, argued Las Casas, but their culture was at a far lower stage of development than that of their conquerors. The crown should defend their full human rights, but at the very same time govern them for their own good, for as long as their culture remained inferior, they would not be able to make the right choices for themselves. In the end, no one won this debate, and no new laws issued from it. One issue was settled by it, nonetheless, at least for the time being, with a practical outcome on the missions in the Indies. While defending the full humanity of the natives, Las Casas and his side affirmed their intellectual and cultural immaturity. This conclusion would help close the door on further debate on whether the church should ordain to the priesthood any New World natives, or any equally "immature" people such as Africans and some Asians. If champions of the natives such as Las Casas were not willing to grant them self-autonomy, and if their paternalistic arguments were so well articulated, who, then, would be willing to argue in favor of their ordination to the priesthood? And how could the argument be made? Ultimately, the Valladolid debate affirmed the paternalistic status quo that had guided the colonial enterprise from the start and did nothing to promote the full integration of millions of new Christians and a whole region into the Catholic Church. At the same time, however, it could be argued that the debate on the issue of "natural slavery" sparked by Spanish colonization was a significant step in the development of human rights theories, and in the curbing of the worst injustices that marked the European conquest of the New World.

African Slaves

Because of the high death rate among the natives, who succumbed to European diseases, mistreatment, suicide, and massacres, the Spanish colonists began to buy African slaves at a fast clip in 1501—so many of them that by 1517 about two-thirds of the population of Hispaniola was African. By then, the natives were well on their way to extinction, not just in Hispaniola, but in most of the Caribbean islands. Although the Spanish did not involve themselves in the slave trade's transportation, they eagerly bought human cargo from the Portuguese, who had access to slaves in Africa through their outposts along its western coast. The ambivalence of papal pronouncements on slavery allowed for this trade to develop. Though Pope Eugene IV had condemned the practice in his bull *Sicut dudum* in 1435, Pope Nicholas V had granted King Alfonso V of Portugal the right to "reduce any Saracens and pagans and any other unbelievers" to perpetual slavery, in his bull *Dum diversas* in 1452. In 1462, Pope Pius II once again condemned slavery as a "great crime," in his bull *Magnum scelus*, but his pronouncement had little effect on the business of buying and selling human beings in Africa, where the practice was endemic, and where the Portuguese profited from it. Concern for the natives of the Indies, who were dying off in alarming numbers, made many a churchman eager to pick and choose among such contradictory pronouncements, and to call for the importation of more "sturdy" laborers from Africa. Even the venerable Bartolomé de Las Casas thought it was a good idea to alleviate the suffering of the natives through the importation of African slaves, though he later repented for ever having encouraged such a deal with the devil.

As the New World colonies expanded, so did the importation of slaves. Purchased from African chieftains for two ecus each and sold for two hundred, African slaves were a most profitable venture, even when one factored in the death of nearly half of the cargo on every slave ship bound for the Indies. Cartagena, a port city on the Caribbean coast of present-day Colombia, became the chief market in this trade, and at its peak it processed a thousand or more slaves per month. From there, those who had survived the transatlantic crossing were traded as any other commodity and dispersed throughout the Spanish colonies. Eventually, they would also be imported directly by the Portuguese colonists of Brazil and by the French and British colonists in the Caribbean and North America.

How this African population was ministered to in the colonies remains a relatively understudied subject. The Africans, just like the natives of the Indies whose place they took, were subjected to Christianization, but to far less schooling. Like the natives, they were barred from the priesthood, even if freed or of partially white lineage. They differed from the natives in one important respect, however: while natives tended to stay in one location (if they survived) and could be Christianized over time, across several generations, the African population was continuously replenished by fresh arrivals, year after year, generation after generation. This constant influx of Africans made mission work among them extremely difficult, and prevented the extinction of their beliefs and rituals.

Whereas the enslavement and abuse of natives by the colonists had sparked controversy in the colonies and back in Spain, that of the Africans caused relatively less concern. Individuals who devoted themselves to improving the plight of African slaves were fewer in number, and not as aggressively indignant as the Dominicans in the early days of the conquest. Most prominent is St. Peter (Pedro) Claver (1581–1654), a Jesuit, who swore to be "the slave of the blacks forever" and spent forty-four years ministering to them in Cartagena under appalling conditions. Claver, who enters colonial history in 1610, more than a century after its starting point, was as devoted to compassion as Las Casas had been to making waves. Meeting every slave ship that pulled into Cartagena and ministering to the physical and emotional needs of those who had survived the trip, Claver dispensed as much comfort and advocacy as was possible under the circumstances. In addition to assembling a team of catechists who learned African dialects and instructed the slaves ever so minimally as they passed through the slave market, Claver eventually baptized more than three hundred thousand people, rivaling the records set by the most prolific baptizers of Mexico and Peru. Despised by the slave traders, shunned, ridiculed, and abused by many of the white residents of Cartagena, and often rejected by the understandably angry slaves he constantly approached, Claver persisted in his ministry, proving himself an uncommon missionary and an exceptional human being. In summary, Claver embodied the very best the Catholic Church had to offer the African slaves through his compassion, and the very worst through his inability to put the slightest dent in a loathsome and seemingly interminable holocaust.

Peru and South America

All the issues that affected the missions in the Caribbean and in Mesoamerica traveled south with the Spanish as they continuously conquered more land. In 1533, another vast and highly developed empire became theirs when Francisco Pizarro defeated the Inca emperor Atahualpa. In one fell swoop, the entire northern tier of the Andean highlands became theirs to rule and exploit. After establishing a new capital at Lima in 1535, the Spanish kept marching down the Andes and sailing down the western coast of South America. In 1541, Pedro de Valdivia vanquished the natives of present-day Chile and founded the city of Santiago. The settlement and exploitation of this land, which was not rich in precious metals, would be marked by prolonged warfare against various native peoples. In 1545 the Spanish discovery of the seemingly inexhaustible silver veins at Potosí, in present-day Bolivia, would make Spain the richest nation on earth and exact an enormous toll on the natives forced to work in the mines. Conquering and settling present-day Paraguay, Uruguay, and Argentina was a relatively slow process, drawn out between the 1530s into the 1600s, which proceeded in fits and starts and was marked by constant warfare with the natives. Although the Spanish could not settle or directly rule all of the land they claimed, by 1650 they were the titular rulers of a vast American empire that stretched in an unbroken swath from California and the present-day southwestern United States all the way to the Straits of Magellan, and also included the Caribbean Basin and Florida. And wherever they planted their flag, missionaries followed, natives were baptized, and the agonizingly slow process of turning millions of them into Catholic Christians was set into motion. In some areas, such as California, the establishing of missions would extend well into the eighteenth century.

All the established religious orders would play a major role in the Christianization process within these vast new areas, especially the Franciscans and Dominicans. It did not take the Jesuits long to become involved too. Founded in 1540 with just a handful of members, they were already present in the American Indies by 1549, when they sent five men to the Portuguese colony of Brazil. They began to play a very important role in Spanish colonies by the 1570s, in New Spain as well as the continent of South America. In New Spain, they established a college in Mexico City in the early 1570s, and then fanned out northward, all the way into present-day Texas, New Mexico, Arizona, and California, establishing missions—including the one now known as the Alamo in

San Antonio—gathering natives into *pueblos*, shielding them from exploitation, teaching them European farming and stock raising. In Peru, they arrived in 1568, and after establishing themselves in Lima, they built churches and schools in many towns, focusing much of their energy on the natives. At Juli, in the high Andean plateau, on the shores of Lake Titicaca, they established a training school for missionaries in 1577, where their novices could learn native languages. Their unique contribution was the development of settlements, known as reductions, in areas where the colonists had barely made any inroads, along the borderlands between the Spanish and Portuguese empires, in present-day Bolivia, Argentina, Paraguay, Uruguay, and Brazil.

The Jesuit reductions were a new twist on the *pueblos* that the Spanish had been establishing for natives since early colonial days. In essence, the pattern was the same: a settlement run by missionaries where the natives were educated and Christianized, and sheltered from contact with colonists. But the Jesuits went further, establishing a far greater degree of autonomy for their reductions along lines suggested in 1588 by the Jesuit José de Acosta (1539–1600) in his pioneering treatise *On Securing the Salvation of the Indies*. These reductions were in essence independent fiefdoms within the Spanish and Portuguese colonies where the Jesuits were in complete control, and the natives were protected from slave raids and exempt from the *encomienda* system. Knowing that the crown would naturally want something in return, the Jesuits arranged for the reductions to pay tribute in lieu of forced labor, and payments came from the handicrafts, livestock, and food produced by the natives as a result of the skills taught to them by the Jesuits. Relatively sheltered from gross exploitation, the natives in the reductions received not just religious instruction, but also a classical education and practical training as carpenters, tanners, tailors, silversmiths, hatters, and printers. The Jesuits also fostered art and music, blending aboriginal and European traditions, and the natives became especially adept at making musical instruments. Some of the most impressive reductions were those established among the Guaraní, in which the natives farmed communal lands but had relatively short work days that allowed them to devote time to other pursuits. The Guaraní reductions had a high literacy rate, and developed their own impressive version of baroque architecture. Over 150 years these reductions grew into economically vigorous towns and cultural centers, each of which had communal and personal farms, a church, a college, a hospital, a home for widows, artisans' workshops, and warehouses.

The Jesuit reductions were among the most humane and successful missions in the Americas. But that success ultimately led to their downfall. As they grew in economic influence, their independence and power and that of the Jesuits who controlled them became an increasing worry to the Spanish and Portuguese crowns, and to the papacy. In 1756, the Spanish and Portuguese authorities launched an attack on the reductions, killing many of the inhabitants and leaving the missions in ruins—a tragic event somewhat accurately fictionalized in the 1986 film *The Mission*. The mistreatment and enslavement of the natives followed, and the Jesuits were expelled from the Indies.

Apparitions, Miracles, and Saints

With so much controversy surrounding the Christianizing of the New World natives, it is easy to overlook that Catholicism in the American Indies did take root and flourish. We can get a good sense of how colonial Catholicism developed, and its combinations of the Old World and the New World, by looking at three cases that reified Catholic beliefs in an extreme, yet orthodox manner.

The best-known miracle of the colonial era is that of the apparition of the Virgin Mary in 1531 to a native peasant who went by the Spanish name of Juan Diego, on a hill near Mexico City, at a site where the Spanish had demolished an Aztec temple to the mother-goddess Tonantzin. The narrative of this apparition followed a very traditional medieval European pattern in which the Virgin or some celestial being appears to a humble person and asks that a shrine be built on that very spot. In Spain, many such accounts also involved the discovery of a long-lost icon or the miraculous appearance of an image of celestial origin. Though the map of Spain bristled with such shrines, the most significant and best-known of these miraculously derived image shrines were Our Lady of Guadalupe, in Extremadura, Our Lady of the Pillar, in Zaragoza, and Our Lady of Montserrat, in Catalonia. Guadalupe and Montserrat had "black Madonnas," that is, statues of the Virgin Mary made of dark wood, in which Mary's face and hands had an ebony complexion. Without exception, these apparition accounts were epic narratives in which the visionaries had to struggle to convince church authorities of the legitimacy of their claims. Simultaneously they told of the convergence of the universal and the local and of the sometimes uneasy dialectic between the individual and church, and the laity and clergy. Though these shrines served many purposes, one of their prime functions was the joining of heaven and earth, or, in practical terms, the sacralization of local space.

In the case of the 1531 apparition in Mexico, the existing paradigms were suddenly transferred across the ocean, into a different context. The new twist was not just the sacralization of the Mexican landscape, but also its Christianization: the replacement of a pagan deity with a very Mexican Virgin Mary through the agency of Juan Diego, a recently converted pagan. The narrative had a simple and predictable structure: the Virgin Mary appears to Juan Diego as a light-enshrouded young lady and asks in his native Nahuatl tongue that a shrine be built for her on that very spot; Juan Diego reports his encounter to the bishop of Mexico City, Juan de Zumárraga; the bishop orders Juan Diego to return to that spot and to ask the young lady for a miraculous sign that will confirm her identity as the Virgin Mary; Juan Diego does as ordered, sees the young lady again, and asks for that all-important miraculous sign; the young lady tells Juan Diego to gather some Spanish roses from the top of the hill, even though Mexico has no such flowers and it is December, when it is normally impossible to find any blooming plants; Juan Diego collects the miraculous blossoms and the young lady wraps them up in his native peasant cloak, known as a *tilma*, and sends him back to the bishop; when Juan Diego unfurls the *tilma* to show the bishop the roses—which he thinks are the miraculous sign required of

Avatar of the Catholic New World. The miraculous image that came to be known as Our Lady of Guadalupe reified the hybridization of Spanish and Mexican religion in myriad ways.

the Virgin—a much more impressive miracle is made manifest: where the roses had been wrapped there is now imprinted on the cactus-fiber cloth a beautiful and very colorful image of the dark-skinned young lady. The image itself follows conventional European iconography, but is heavily laden with elements that can be interpreted through an Aztec symbolic prism, or as direct references to Aztec religion and culture: for instance, the traditional aura around the Virgin makes it seem as if she is eclipsing the bloodthirsty sun god Huitzilopochtli; the blue color of her star-studded mantle—a Christian symbol of purity—also happens to be reserved for the Aztec aristocracy; the mantle itself resembles the one worn by Tonantzin, the Aztec goddess of earth, fertility and rain; the Virgin's black sash is the same as those normally worn by pregnant Aztec women. Guadalupe, the name given to the site of the apparition, linked it more closely to Europe, however, than to the Aztec empire. So it was that Our Lady of Guadalupe became a New World iteration of a Spanish avatar and a symbol of the blending of cultures and religions.

According to the traditional narrative, Bishop Zumárraga built a shrine for the image immediately in 1532, and the advent of the Virgin, who combined both cultures so intensely but at the same time proclaimed the vanquishing of the old religion, was credited with the conversion of millions of natives and the end of human sacrifices. Although the first reliable record of the icon's existence dates from 1556—and it reveals a conflict between Dominicans who were fostering devotion to this image and Franciscans who believed it to be man-made fraud—the fog that shrouds the origins of this miracle seems rather inconsequential. By 1648, when the first full account of the apparition was published, the story and the icon had already seized the popular imagination. Pilgrims were visiting the shrine in such large numbers by 1622 that a new and more elaborate church had to be built, and as even more pilgrims were drawn to the site, that church was replaced by an even grander edifice in 1709. In the nineteenth century, Our Lady of Guadalupe would acquire a more intensely nationalistic sort of veneration, and turn into an icon of Mexican identity.

The Virgin of Guadalupe was only one of many such Marian apparitions. Throughout the colonial era, similar apparitions and similar miraculous images would be reported throughout the Indies. Each one was like a reflection in a hall of mirrors: a local image of a Spanish image that was, in turn, an image of a Virgin that was here and there and everywhere, on earth and in heaven, and an image of every miraculous image ever discovered; all these images resembled one another but were nonetheless unique and deeply rooted in both a particular place and in heaven, all at once. And in the nineteenth century, most of these icons and their shrines would take on the role of national avatars as well, and even of the struggle for independence from Spain. These Virgins—the Our Ladies of this or that place—were arguably the most densely coded symbols of the fusion of American, Spanish, and Catholic identity, and of the transformations wrought in the Indies by the missionaries.

Just as images of the Virgin embodied Old World paradigms in New World ways, so did the holy men and women of the Indies. Two saints in particular stand out as prime exemplars of the variety of New World sanctity. The heroic ascetic feats and mystical ecstasies of Isabel Flores, better known as St. Rose of Lima (1586–1617), mirrored those of European saints so closely that she seems the very embodiment of a pure Old World Catholicism, unaffected by the New World. Born in Peru but reared as a transplanted Spaniard, her saintliness was inwardly oriented, and as much a withdrawal from the world writ large as from her own particular world in Lima. Emulating the life of the fourteenth-century saint Catherine of Siena, about whom she had learned while still a child, Rose of Lima committed herself to a life of abstinence and severe penance, and at the age of twenty entered the Dominican convent in Lima. Her fasts were as extreme as those of St. Catherine and so were her acts of self-mortification. Surviving on the smallest possible amount of food and drink, wearing a spiked metal crown on her head and a tight iron chain around her waist, denying herself sleep, she also lined her bed with stones, thorns, and shards of broken glass and pottery, so that even when her body gave in to exhaustion her rest would bring her pain. Sequestered behind convent walls, often rapt in mystical ecstasy, Rose of Lima could have been anywhere on earth. Location seemed not to matter. But there was one aspect of her life that was distinctly American: she offered all of her excruciating penances not just for her sins or the conversion of sinners or the suffrage of souls in purgatory, as all nuns were wont to do, but also, quite specifically, as atonement for all of the idolatry in Peru. So, even behind thick convent walls, or in the sheltered environment of a Spanish enclave such as Lima, the natives and their idols could enter into the most reclusive consciousness. Revered locally as a saint in her own lifetime and as a miracle worker, Rose of Lima would be the first person born in the Americas to be canonized by Rome, in 1671, and therefore also the first to attract universal veneration. A very similar pattern of self-abnegation, prayer, mystical ecstasy, and miracle working was also followed by Mariana de Jesús de Paredes, better known as the Lily of Quito (1618–1645), and many other nuns who exemplified continuity with Old World Catholicism and adherence to the strict cloister reforms of the post–Council of Trent era.

A very different profile of holiness is that of St. Martín de Porres (1579–1639), a contemporary and friend of Rose of Lima. Born out of wedlock to a Spanish soldier of noble lineage and a freed African slave, Martín grew up as a poor outcast in colonial Lima. Reared in a pious environment by his African mother, who was a devout Catholic, Martín dedicated himself to prayer and self-denial from an early age. Barred from full membership in a religious order because of his racially mixed heritage, Martín entered the Dominican Convent of the Holy Rosary in Lima as a servant when he was fifteen, leaving behind an apprenticeship as a barber surgeon. As the Dominicans recognized his talents and his intense devotion, Martín began to assume other roles: first that of almoner, distributing alms to the poor, then that of running the infirmary. And it was in the infirmary that Martín began to catch everyone's attention, for he seemed particularly adept at tending the sick and especially at healing them.

As his reputation spread throughout Lima and beyond, Martín was allowed to become a lay brother in 1603. By that time he was already being revered as a living saint and sought out as a healer. Astonishing miracles were attributed to him: the ability to be in two places at the same time (bilocation), or to instantly go from one place to another (mystical transport), or to float in the air (levitation), to pass through walls and closed doors, and to read minds and communicate with animals. Martín's African lineage barred him from the priesthood, and from becoming a missionary, but he dedicated himself to helping the poor and sick of Lima with extraordinary energy, dispensing alms, establishing an asylum for orphans and the homeless, teaching catechism to the natives and blacks who lived in the worst slums of Lima. When he died, in 1639, relic seekers flocked to his funeral and tore at his habit. Although canonization proceedings were launched shortly thereafter, Martín's case would lag far behind that of Rose of Lima, mostly because of his race, but also because of his lowly status as a colonial and lay brother. He would not be beatified until 1837, and he would have to wait until 1962 to be canonized. Martín exemplified traditional Catholic belief in the power of sanctity over the laws of nature. That he did so against great odds in a rigidly hierarchical society revealed that religion could transcend that stratification and that the process of Christianizing the Indies could indeed reach all the way down to the household of a freed slave. Martín was an extreme wonder worker, at once a mystic and a social worker, an embodiment of the coincidence of opposites, and of the crossing of ostensibly impenetrable boundaries, literally as well as figuratively. Above all, he reminds us centuries later that the Catholic Reformation was not just complex, but also truly global in its reach.

Brazil

The Spanish were not the only Europeans carving out an empire in the American Indies. Early in the race for colonies, in 1500, Portugal claimed the eastern tip of South America after one of its Asian-bound fleets was blown off course onto the shores of present-day Brazil. Since this accidental landfall lay on the Portuguese side of the meridian agreed upon in the Treaty of Tordesillas (1494) between Spain and Portugal—an arbitrary longitude that gave each nation the right to colonize all discoveries on one side of it or the other—the captain of the expedition, Pedro Álvares Cabral, successfully claimed his find for the crown of Portugal. The rest, as they say, is history: from that toehold, the Portuguese would lay successive claims, moving the line ever westward until they carved out the largest single parcel of land in the New World.

Colonization of this claim would not begin for another three decades, but once it did, missions followed inevitably. The area had no advanced civilizations such as those of the Aztecs and Incas, and many of the tribes encountered suffered the same fate as the Caribbean natives had at the hands of the Spanish decades earlier. "Pacification" of Brazil's hundreds of different tribes, some of which aggressively resisted all attempts at domination, became an essential and unfortunate prelude to most missionary enterprises. From very early on, the Portuguese began to import African slaves, especially for the cultivation of sugar, which became the region's most profitable export by the mid-sixteenth century. The Portuguese presence in these colonies was relatively thin compared to that of the Spanish in theirs—and so was the total population. It is estimated that by 1620, the vast coastal area had a total of no more than two hundred thousand inhabitants, including all races. The unexplored and untouched interior, large and wild beyond comprehension, might have had around 2.5 million thinly scattered natives. At that same time the population in the Spanish Indies was about 10 million. And while the Spanish Indies had many dioceses by 1551, Brazil had but one, in Bahia, and another would not be established until 1676—all this despite the fact that between 1580 and 1640 Portugal was subsumed into the Spanish crown and all of its empire was ruled by the Spanish monarchs. In the 1690s the discovery of gold deep in the southeastern interior would transform this colonial economy, and the colony itself, but by then many enduring patterns had been set into place, and chief among them was the institution of slavery, which involved the conscription of natives as well as the importation of Africans. Unlike the Spanish, the Portuguese had no *encomienda* system, which meant that the natives could be subjected to outright slavery.

A handful of Franciscans were the first missionaries in Portuguese America, but they were too few to be able to accomplish much. The first sustained mission effort came from the newly founded Jesuits in the late 1540s. Much like the first Dominicans in Hispaniola more than a generation earlier, these Jesuits were horrified by what they found when they arrived in 1549: a "savage" native population, some of whom practiced cannibalism, and all of whom were being exterminated, abused, and exploited by the settlers. Led by Manuel da Nóbrega (1517–1570), the Jesuits assumed two difficult roles, as protectors of the natives and as educators. Convinced that the only way to convert the natives was to focus on the children, who were not too set in their ways, Nóbrega and the Jesuits began to establish schools in which a new generation would be educated in the Christian faith, and in Portuguese and Latin. Early on, the Jesuits also discovered that music was very useful in keeping their students focused, and as a result, it became part of the curriculum too. As more Jesuits arrived, their reach expanded. By 1554, Nóbrega and his men had established various missions with schools, including one that would eventually become the city of São Paulo. It is estimated that by 1570 about forty thousand natives lived in fourteen Jesuit missions. But by 1585 these outposts were on the verge of collapse given the constant toll of European diseases and the slave raids of the Portuguese colonists.

Convinced that the only way these missions could survive was to move them as far away from the European settlements as possible, the Jesuits pushed inland, and established isolated "reductions," as discussed earlier, especially in the yet-unclaimed borderlands between the Spanish and Portuguese empires. Unencumbered by national ties, the Jesuits carried out their mission work in these reductions while oblivious to the demands of empire building. A further boost to the Jesuit missions came in 1655, when António Vieira (1608–1697), a Jesuit reared and educated in Brazil, obtained a grant from the Portuguese crown that placed additional new reductions with more than two hundred thousand natives directly under the rule of the Society of Jesus. By 1661, however, the economic success of these missions had elicited so much envy and suspicion from colonists and other clergy that the authorities sent him back to Portugal and dismantled his work. It was a sign of worse troubles to come. Eventually, in the eighteenth century, the two Iberian empires would encroach on all of the Jesuit reductions and wipe them out.

As the colony of Brazil grew, other orders joined the missionary effort. The Carmelites arrived in 1580, the Benedictines in 1581, and a sustainable Franciscan effort in 1585. As had happened many times before in the Indies, the Franciscans found it necessary to condemn the "scandalous and un-Christian habits" of the colonists before they could turn their attention to the natives. The same would be true for all subsequent missionaries who arrived throughout the seventeenth century, as more cities, towns, and plantations were established, the Catholic Church grew and the frontier kept being pushed further along the coast and back inland. The constant arrival of African slaves made the missionary challenge all the greater, and in many areas it became impossible to stamp out the influence of African religions. The vast Amazon rain forest remained an impenetrable frontier, too, and its natives far beyond reach. By 1700, save for the isolated and ill-fated reductions in its interior, Brazil remained a relatively thinly settled behemoth of a colony, its slaves and natives—and some of its settlers—only tentatively Christianized. It would be nearly impossible back then to imagine that in the early twenty-first century, Brazil would have the sixth-largest economy in the world and more Catholics than any other country on the earth.

New France

As a result of the Wars of Religion that ravaged their realm, French entry into colonial ventures and missionary work came only at the beginning of the seventeenth century. The French efforts to colonize North America were halting at first, and nowhere near the scale of the Spanish and Portuguese enterprises, but by 1609 the first two missionaries from the Recollect branch of the Franciscan order were sent to the small outposts that the explorer Samuel de Champlain had established on the far northeastern seaboard of North America. In 1611, the first two French Jesuits crossed the Atlantic. And in 1613 another small Jesuit mission was established. Given the tenuousness and vulnerability of the small French outposts, however, all three missions failed. A fourth mission established by four Jesuits on the St. Lawrence River in 1625 also met with disaster when the English attacked four years later.

The first mission to survive was established in 1632 by the Jesuits. For the next eighteen years, between 1632 and 1650, a total of forty-six Jesuits dedicated themselves to converting the natives and ministering to the colonists. Their heroic efforts among the natives, in a harsh land, at the peak of the Little Ice Age, where the winters were long and brutally cold, did not yield many results in terms of numbers of conversions. But they did gain an appreciative audience back in Europe through the reports they sent to their superiors, all of which were published in Paris by a printer with deep connections to the royal court, Sébastien Cramoisy. The *Jesuit Relations*, as these reports were titled, were published annually between 1632 and 1673, and filled with very detailed accounts of life among the "savages" of North America. The Jesuits observed and studied their potential converts with all of the care and detachment of modern-day ethnographers, detailing their beliefs, customs, language, food, hunting methods, and anything else that struck them worthy of recording. The hardships endured by the missionaries, and the exotic tales recorded in the *Relations* were a superb public relations coup not only for the French monarchy's imperialistic endeavors, but also for the Jesuit order and the Catholic Church as a whole. They also convinced many a young man to join the Jesuits and to seek a place in the missions field. There was no glamour involved in such work at all, of course, save that of sheer adventure, or supreme sacrifice.

The 1634 account by Paul Le Jeune (1591–1664), superior of the Jesuits in North America, of "what one must suffer in wintering with the savages," described an unimaginable world—precisely the kind of exotic, adventurous stuff that made the French proud of their colonial and missionary enterprises and made young novices itch for such challenges. His description of life inside a native Montagnais dwelling in the dead of winter was as detailed as it was horrifying and potentially thrilling; its only parallels were meditations on hell written by other Jesuits. And like those infernal meditations, this one, too, was something of a wake-up call, intended to reform the lives of Europeans:

> You cannot stand upright in this house, as much on account of its low roof as the suffo-cating smoke; and consequently you must always lie down, or sit flat upon the ground, the usual posture of the Savages. When you go out, the cold, the snow, and the danger of getting lost in these great woods drive you in again more quickly than the wind, and keep you a prisoner in a dungeon which has neither lock nor key. This prison, in addition to the uncomfortable position that one must occupy on a bed of earth, has four other great discomforts, cold, heat, smoke, and dogs. . . . I will say, however, that both the cold and the heat are endurable, and that some remedy might be found for these two evils. But as to the smoke, I confess to you that it is martyrdom. It almost killed me, and made me weep continually though I had neither grief nor sadness in my heart . . . [and] it caused us to place our mouths against the earth in order to breathe; as it were to eat the earth, so as not to eat the smoke. . . . How bitter is this drink! How strong its odor! How hurtful to the eyes are its fumes! I sometimes thought I was going blind; my eyes burned like fire.

After he was through describing such horrors and many more—including those caused by the dogs—Le Jeune coldly and calmly moved on to the next unpleasant topic: "I have said enough about the inconveniences of the Savages' houses," he wrote. "Let us speak of their food."[18]

Much to the dismay of Le Jeune and his fellow Jesuits, as they made progress with different tribes, they found themselves caught in intertribal rivalries and wars among the Montagnais, Huron, Algonquin, and Iroquois. They also had Dutch and English colonists to their south who did their utmost to stir up trouble. In 1634, the Jesuits carried their mission into Huron territory under the direction of Jean de Brébeuf (1593–1649), who had been one of the earliest missionaries and had the most experience with the natives. This mission of Sainte-Marie was very successful, but it was constantly imperiled by conflict with the Iroquois, who were enemies of the Huron. Beginning in 1642, the Huron and the Jesuits would be subjected to raids, and those captured would be subjected to unspeakably cruel tortures. One Jesuit who managed to escape, Isaac Jogues (1607–1646), not only had been forced to witness the torture and execution of many of his converts, whom he loved as if they were his own children, but also had endured—among many other torments—having his fingers bitten off. After recover-ing, Jogues returned to the mission, only to be captured again and killed in 1646. In 1648–1649, the mission came to a tragic end. Jean Brébeuf, along with his companion Gabriel Lalemant (1610–1649), was subjected to the most horrifying mutilations, includ-ing being lacerated, burnt, flayed, and "baptized" with boiling water, but he would die without pleading for mercy, uttering nothing but words intended to convert his torturers. Brébeuf's stoic endurance so impressed the Iroquois that after they had slowly killed him—inch by blistering inch—they cut out his heart, roasted it, ate it, and washed it down with his blood, hoping they could ingest his courage.[19] In total, eight Jesuits lost their lives between 1642 and 1649. All would be canonized, and together they came to be known as the North American Martyrs.

These setbacks served only to embolden the missionaries, and reports of the suffering of the martyrs emboldened many young recruits to seek out the same fate. By 1654, the Jesuits were establishing missions among the dreaded Iroquois, and by 1670 they were preaching and teaching among all five of their nations. As France poured more of its resources, and more colonists, into New France, the Jesuit missionaries ventured ever farther into the wilderness, as agents of the church and the crown. Gradually, they made their way west and south, along the Great Lakes. By 1667 they had carved out a post in present-day Wisconsin, near Green Bay. In 1673 they sent one of their own, Jacques Marquette (1637–1675), and a lay explorer, Louis Joliet (1645–1700), to discover what lay beyond the lakes. The two went down the Wisconsin River to the Mississippi, and then all the way to its confluence with the Arkansas River. Only the presence of the Spanish further downstream caused them to turn around and head back to Wisconsin, through present-day Illinois. Joliet would keep exploring, but Father Marquette spent the remaining year of his brief life among the Illini natives. During the 1690s, the Jesuits expanded along the middle section of the Mississippi River, and established several missions in the present-day American Midwest.

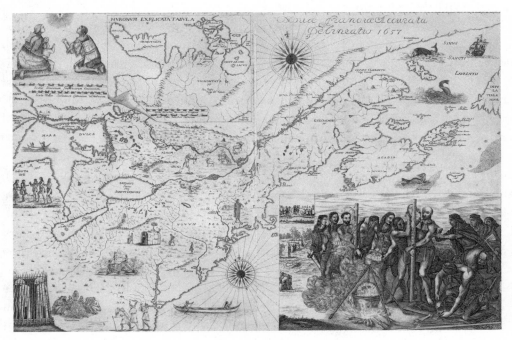

New France. This 1657 map of North America by Francesco Giuseppe Bressani is illustrated with details pertaining to the missions and exploratory voyages of the Jesuits. In the upper left corner, two native converts kneel in prayer. In the lower right corner is a crude depiction of the martyrdom of Jean de Brébeuf and Gabriel Lalemant. (Library and Archives Canada, MIKAN 3805607)

The Jesuit approach in New France was similar to that of their brethren in Spanish America, and as we will see in the following chapter, in Asia: convert the natives by learning their language and culture, becoming "savages" along with them, and accommodating the Christian religion to their way of life rather than try to Europeanize them. Many of the Jesuits in New France became experts in native languages. They, too, established "reductions," keeping the natives as protected as possible from predation by the colonists. They also attempted to open schools for native children within the French settlements, but those ventures failed at first. Though they achieved a great deal of success in converting the natives, the constant encroachment of French settlers, and the ravages of European diseases eventually nullified their efforts to a great extent.

The Jesuits were not the only missionaries in New France. The Recollects had been the pioneers between 1607 and 1629, and worked among the Huron and Montagnais. The first Mass in what is now Montreal was officiated by a Recollect friar, and the first dictionaries of the Huron, Algonquin, and Montagnais tongues were compiled by Joseph Le Caron (1586–1632), a Recollect. Though the Jesuits took their place in 1629, the Recollects returned in 1670 and established several missions. The explorations of one of their order who arrived in 1675, Louis Hennepin (1626–1705), rivaled those of the Jesuit Marquette. Among the marvels "discovered" by Hennepin were Niagara Falls, in what is now the border between Ontario, Canada, and New York State, and St. Anthony Falls, in present-day Minneapolis.

In 1635, nine young nuns from a new order arrived in response to a request made by the Jesuit superior Paul Le Jeune. The mission of these Hospitallers of St. Joseph was to minister to the sick and to educate native girls. By 1639, they had built the Hôtel-Dieu Hospital in Quebec City, which was funded entirely by the largesse of the Duchess of Aiguillon (1604–1675), a niece of the powerful Cardinal de Richelieu. And by 1645, they had opened another Hôtel-Dieu Hospital in Montreal. These nuns also opened and staffed schools for girls, including nursing schools, as well as other charitable institutions.

The Ursulines also made the trek across the Atlantic, arriving in New France in 1639. Led by Marie Guyart, better known as Sister Marie de l'Incarnation (1599–1672), and funded by the noblewoman Marie-Madeleine de Chauvigny (1603–1671), the Ursulines established a convent in Quebec and opened a school for both native and French girls. Eventually, Ursuline communities and schools spread throughout New France, reaching as far south as New Orleans, where a community was established early in the eighteenth century. As they spread their reach, the Ursulines continued to attract young women from both Old and New France and to establish schools for native American girls. A third order of nuns arrived in New France in 1658, the Congrégation de Notre-Dame, led by Marguerite Bourgeoys (1620–1700). Founded specifically as a noncloistered religious order that would dedicate itself to the sick and needy, the order opened a girls' school in Montreal, and eventually many others throughout New France.

The Sulpicians, who arrived in 1657, became the parish priests of Montreal. They also engaged in missionary work among the natives within the city, whom they moved just outside of Montreal, for their protection, in 1676, and farther out again in 1697. The Sulpicians were also assigned to cover all present day Nova Scotia, New Brunswick, Cape Breton, and Prince Edward Island. One of their members, Father François Dollier de Casson (1636–1701), outperformed the busiest of Jesuits, working as a parish priest, missionary, military chaplain, and explorer, claiming what is now southern Ontario for the king of France, proving that the Great Lakes were all connected, mapping what is now western Ontario and the upper Great Lakes region, building a canal, surveying Montreal and laying out its streets, writing a history of the city, and serving as vicar-general of the diocese of Quebec.

A cornerstone of later mission efforts in New France was the Séminaire de Québec, founded in 1663 by François de Laval (1623–1708), the first bishop of New France. In 1665, he linked this enterprise with the Seminary of Foreign Missions of Paris, providing a much-needed connection with resources in the Old World. The role of the seminary was to train priests who would staff parishes and missions as far west as the Mississippi River and as far south as New Orleans. In 1668, under orders from King Louis XIV, the Séminaire began to admit native Americans too.

All in all, the mission effort in New France expanded the horizons of early modern Catholicism and boosted the European colonial enterprise. In this respect, it was much like all the other missions in the New World. Although the missionaries performed unparalleled heroic feats among the natives, their work was constantly undermined by the ever-growing number of colonists and by the tensions with the natives that were caused by this seemingly unstoppable migration. Ultimately, the transfer of New France to the English crown in 1763, and the sale of the Louisiana Territory to the United States in 1803—which placed all the accomplishments of the French missionaries in the hands of governments that had relatively little interest in converting the natives—was the ultimate undoing of much of their legacy, especially in areas beyond Quebec.

The French missions shared much more in common with the Spanish and Portuguese models than with those set up later by the English in their North American colonies, who tended to show as little concern for the salvation of the natives as for their property rights. Yet all these Catholic missions were inseparable from European imperialism, and even at their kindest, they always remained unapologetically condescending to the natives. The treatment of the natives and their ultimate fate means that in our own day and age all of this history tends to be judged as an unmitigated tragedy, but in the seventeenth century it was not only held in the highest esteem by Catholics, but also deemed proof of the authenticity and universality of their church, and of its faithfulness to Christ's command to "go and make disciples of all nations" (Matthew 28:19). For many Catholics, clerical and lay, the missions were proof of the divine guidance enjoyed by their church, and of how wrong the Protestants were. And what Catholic missionaries accomplished in Asia would only further confirm this perspective among their brethren back home in Europe.

CHAPTER NINETEEN

Missions to the East Indies

One factor above all determined that missions to Asia and to the Americans would be different: the European enterprise in Asia was not inextricably tied to territorial conquest or the subjugation and displacement of natives. In the vast majority of cases—the Philippines was the exception—Catholic missionaries went halfway around the globe to convert Asians as agents of the church, not of some European state. Although their missions were deeply tied to merchants and the commercial expansion of Europe, they were not accompanied by soldiers and would-be settlers. Given that lack of armed muscle, and the fact that many of the people they were trying to convert were highly civilized and even disdainful of Europeans, the challenges missionaries in Asia faced were different from those of the American missionaries, and arguably greater. Despite their faith in their providential role, the cold hard truth is that the odds were stacked against them from the start.

First, there was the problem of logistics: how to find enough men, how to train them, how to get them there, and how to negotiate with local authorities. Then there were linguistic and cultural differences to be surmounted, political minefields to be traversed, and prejudices to be overcome on both sides. Distance was a major obstacle, too, as were the hazards of travel. It is estimated that about one-third of all of the Jesuits who set out for China from Lisbon died before reaching their destination. Then there was the issue of scale and proportion. The numbers were ridiculously lopsided: a few hundred men, at most, trying to convert hundreds of millions of so-called pagans on the largest landmass on earth. That these men managed to make only relatively minuscule gains is not surprising. That they tried at all, and managed to make some converts, is what is surprising. Once again, even more so than in the case of the American missions, the significance of the missionaries' efforts lies not in the number of converts made, but the changes they wrought, both on the foreign cultures they encountered and on the church back in Europe.

In the case of the East Indies, as in that of the West Indies, the history of missions in the age of the Reformations is exclusively Catholic, and for the same reasons. The first Protestant nations involved in commerce with the region—the Netherlands and England—were absent from the scene until the seventeenth century, and at that time, they had very different interests and goals from their Catholic European competitors, Spain and Portugal. For this simple reason, as in the previous chapter, the history of missions is part of the Catholic rather than the Protestant Reformation.

Eastward from India

Goa is where it all started, in a very messy way. This port city at the midpoint of the western coastline of India caught the eye of the Portuguese. They had begun to trade with India in 1498, and soon thereafter became embroiled in as much fighting as trading. Having a port they could call their own would help them immensely, so, in 1510, they allied themselves with local Hindu forces who wanted to drive out a Muslim king at Goa, and in a one-day battle they conquered the city and slaughtered about six thousand Muslims. As a reward, they were allowed to establish a colony there. Naturally, they soon brought their church with them, and Franciscan missionaries arrived in 1518. By 1558 Goa would have an archbishop, and by 1600, the archbishop of Goa would serve as Primate of all of Asia.

The Portuguese were not the only Christians in India, however. The "St. Thomas Christians" along the Malabar Coast, farther south, had been there for a long time. These Christians had close ties to the Syriac Church and claimed that the apostle Thomas had founded their church in the first century. The Portuguese immediately established relations with them, and would eventually bring them into communion with the Roman Catholic Church, in 1599. From their bishopric of Cochin, missionaries fanned out to other parts of India. Converting the Hindus and Muslims proved much more difficult for Portuguese missionaries. And, as was the case in the Americas, the greedy, violent, and dissolute behavior of Europeans made it difficult to prove that Christ made much of a difference in anyone's life.

In 1542, a new missionary arrived in Goa who would transform the Asian enterprise. Francis Xavier (1506–1552) was one of the first six Jesuits, a former roommate and close friend of Ignatius Loyola, and a fellow Basque. Xavier would eventually earn renown as a great missionary and "apostle of the Indies," mostly because of his fervor, his ambitious reach, and the number of converts he made, but restlessness distinguished him from the start. He spent his first few years in India evangelizing a region at the very southern tip of India, among the Paravars of the Pearl Fishery Coast. His success there was immense, even though he did not speak their language. By 1544, he had baptized more than ten thousand people. After three years among the Paravars, Xavier set his sights on the islands of the Malay Archipelago, farther to the east, in present-day

Malaysia and Indonesia, where the Portuguese had established trading outposts. While there, he worked mostly in the Moluccas among people even less civilized than the Paravars, including some head-hunting tribes. In 1548 he returned to Goa and began to turn its College of Holy Faith—which had just been handed over to the Jesuits—into a missionary training center. But he did not stay long enough to see the project through to completion. By 1549 he was in Japan, ferried there by Portuguese merchants, along with three fellow Jesuits and a Japanese companion, Anjiro, whom he had met and converted in the Moluccas and brought back to Goa. Though some Portuguese traders had already been to Japan, and had introduced firearms, Xavier and his companions were among the first Europeans to set foot in the country. And they were awed by what they found, and seized by a sense of affinity for the people and their culture. Describing them as "the best people yet discovered," Xavier set about the difficult task of preaching the Gospel to the Japanese through interpreters.

Xavier's time in Japan was relatively brief, but he managed to plant the seeds for a much larger enterprise. Among other key steps, Xavier figured out that the emperor at this time was in a weak position, and strategically he cultivated the support of the local lords, or daimyos. Despite his limited knowledge of Japanese, he also figured out that the translation of certain basic terms, including *God*, was highly problematic, and settled on the use of Latin words, such as *Deus* for "God," in place of Japanese equivalents that might have been misconstrued. Xavier pressed ahead, preaching and teaching, always on the move, winning converts. Yet the ever-perceptive Xavier had also figured out that the Japanese had such great admiration for China, and that to convert the Japanese in great numbers, it would be best first to convert the Chinese. He sailed back to Goa in 1551, to arrange for this enormous effort.

Once again, a brief foray into the unknown had yielded a rich harvest. When Xavier departed from Japan, he left his fellow Jesuits in charge of five Christian communities numbering in total about two thousand souls, and with the promise that he would find more missionaries to join them. His plans for Japan would prove fruitful, but those for China came to naught, at least for Xavier. Forbidden entry to China, he made arrangements to be smuggled in. But as he waited for the smuggler's boat in a makeshift shelter on an island off the coast of China in December 1552, he was overtaken by a high fever and died. His miraculously incorruptible corpse was taken back to Goa, where it is still enshrined and venerated, and one of his arms was sent to Rome, where it is still enshrined near the tomb of St. Ignatius Loyola, in the Church of the Gesù. As early as 1555 his fellow Jesuits began to press for his canonization. Among the converts back in Japan his sainthood was a foregone conclusion. In 1585 three visiting Japanese envoys asked the papal court in Rome to hurry up the process, so that they could "build churches and altars to him, set up images of him, celebrate his feast day, and pray daily for his intercession."[1] Xavier was canonized in 1622, along with Ignatius Loyola, and wherever the Jesuits went, they spread devotion to their own St. Francis, the missionary who had converted thousands in far-off lands. We cannot know for sure how many converts should be attributed to Xavier; estimates have ranged from tens of thousands to hundreds of thousands, or as high as a million. There is something to be learned from the obviously inflated figure of one million: Xavier's success became so legendary that it required such numbers.

But how did Xavier become larger than life, second only to the apostle Paul in renown as a missionary? Xavier reifies not only the mission effort itself and Catholic sainthood, but also the publicity surrounding both of these themes. From the start, while he was still alive, his letters achieved an iconic and didactic value. Published in various languages, they gave the reading public of Europe a glimpse of the man and his work, as well as of the exotic locales where he labored. A 1544 letter from India was published in French and German in 1545; his first letter from Japan, written in 1549, was translated and published in thirty different editions over the following fifty years. These letters established a paradigm closely followed by all Jesuits who came after him: their field reports became an integral part of the mission enterprise. Internally, they served logistical needs; externally, they involved the Catholic laity in the missions and made the missionaries part and parcel of early modern Catholic culture. A present-day publicist might say that they were an excellent means of self-promotion and successful advertising. A historian might say that they were a continual exercise in Catholic self-fashioning and identity formation. The Jesuits and the church were well aware of the value of publicity on different terms. A century later, this successful propaganda medium was still serving its purpose, as we have seen evidenced by the *Jesuit Relations* written from New France. In addition to letters, there were also books. Pedro de Ribadeneyra (1527–1611), author of the first biography of Ignatius Loyola (1572), portrayed Xavier not just as a great missionary, but also as a miracle worker. The first full summary of Xavier's life appeared in 1594, written by the Jesuit Orazio Torsellino (1545–1599), who depended heavily on a manuscript biography written in 1580 by Xavier's coworker in the mission field, Manuel Teixeira. Torsellino's book was translated into many languages and published throughout Catholic Europe first in anticipation of Xavier's canonization, and then in celebration of it. Torsellino also published a collection of Xavier's letters. Several other hagiographies would follow in the seventeenth and eighteenth centuries.

In sum, Xavier became larger than life thanks to the new medium of printing, and because of the way his case was promoted by the Jesuits in Rome and in every church and school of theirs. And his fame also made missions in general and the Asian missions in particular a significant component of Catholic culture. Though he was only one of many who labored to convert those called "the heathen," Xavier managed to capture the Catholic imagination as no other missionary did, and in doing so, he aided in the creation of a global-minded mentality in early modern Catholicism. In other words, he brought the universal reach of the church and its missions to mind wherever he was venerated at the local level.

Japan

The five Christian communities Xavier had left behind in Japan continued to grow rapidly after his departure, and even more rapidly after more Jesuit missionaries arrived in 1552. With the conversion of several local lords (daimyos) in the 1560s and the arrival of even more missionaries, continual growth seemed ensured. By 1570 there were more than twenty thousand converts under the care of thirty Jesuits, served by schools and also seminaries for the training of native Japanese clergy. By 1582 on the island of Kyushu alone, at the southern end of Japan, there were 130,000 Christians and native Japanese Jesuit priests. Had the emperor remained weak and the state decentralized, it is highly likely that this growth would have continued or even increased. But in the 1580s the political situation began to change, as Toyotomi Hideyoshi, a daimyo who became the emperor's regent or chief adviser (*kampaku*), began to reunify Japan and to centralize power once again, at the expense of the daimyos. At exactly the same time, Franciscan, Dominican, and Augustinian missionaries began to arrive, and to promote the Christian faith much less tactfully than the Jesuits, especially among the lower classes. Distrustful of the new religion and its adherents, and especially of the daimyos who supported it and the pushy new missionaries who seemed to be working as rabble-rousers and agents of a foreign power, Hideyoshi ordered all missionaries to leave Japan in 1587. As yet he lacked the power to enforce the degree, but the continuing conversions now took place under a dark cloud.

As Hideyoshi consolidated his power and Jesuits and the missionary newcomers continued to make converts, he was keeping his eye on another place just over the southern horizon, where for the past quarter century Christians had been behaving very badly. The place was the archipelago that the Spanish had named the Philippines, in honor of their monarch Philip II. Ferdinand Magellan had claimed the islands for Spain during his circumnavigation of the globe in 1521, but the Spanish had left them virtually untouched until 1565, when, eager to give the Portuguese a run for their money, they sent a fleet to colonize Manila, New World–style. The Philippines was the only sizable territory in Asia taken over completely by a European power and Christianized through state-sponsored missions. In essence, those islands became much like any of the Spanish colonies in the Americas, with one notable exception: the Spanish made no effort to settle the Philippines and always remained a tiny minority, very unevenly distributed. Some of the islands remained largely untouched. In 1571, the Spanish founded the city of Manila, and ten years later it had a large enough clerical presence to be named a bishopric. In 1595, when Manila became an archbishopric, an estimated 650,000 natives had converted. Administered from the Viceroyalty of New Spain, and reached only from the Pacific port of Acapulco, the Philippines became an odd extension of the American Indies. The so-called Manila galleons that sailed back and forth across the Pacific Ocean but once a year brought gold, silver, supplies, correspondence, and clergy from Mexico; some of the silver and gold was used to purchase Asian goods, mostly from China; and that cargo was taken back to Acapulco, where it sold for a tidy profit. The connection was fragile, but it worked most of the time, and by 1600 Manila was humming with business and also a thriving church.

This Spanish presence to the south worried Hideyoshi, who was well informed. He knew that the Spanish were not at all like the Portuguese, who merely traded. The Spanish were into conquering and ruling, as they had proved in the Philippines. Since all the missionaries on Japanese soil were now subjects of the king of Spain, due to Philip II's takeover of the Portuguese throne in 1580, and since most of the new tactless mendicant missionaries came from Spain, via Mexico and Manila, the normally suspicious Hideyoshi had good reason to fear the worst from Christians. And his fears seemed confirmed in late 1596, when reports reached him of an Acapulco-bound Manila galleon with soldiers, artillery, ammunition, and missionaries aboard that had been blown off course and ended up in Japan. One of its crew had boasted, or joked, about the way in which the Spanish used their missionaries to take over other lands. Hideyoshi's response to the news was as swift as it was brutal, but it was also carefully measured, so as not to frighten away

The price of success. The rapid spread of Christianity in some regions of Japan proved too threatening to the Japanese emperors, who feared European expansionism as well as the presence of an alien religion on their soil. In Europe, Catholic authorities interpreted the fate of the missionaries and their converts as a challenge to redouble their efforts in Asia rather than as an indication of inevitable failure. The twenty-six martyrs of Nagasaki received intense attention, not just because it was a first major setback, but because the method of execution was so profoundly ironic and so clearly linked to the central symbol of the Christian faith. This 1626 engraving by Wolfgang Kilian, printed in Augsburg, was accompanied by a German text that described their suffering in great detail.

all the European merchants. In February 1597 twenty-six Christians were rounded up and crucified in Nagasaki, to send a clear signal to their coreligionists. They were all males, and represented a cross section of the Japanese mission church: six non-Japanese Franciscans, three Japanese Jesuits, and seventeen lay Japanese. Three of the lay martyrs were mere boys, one of the Franciscans had been born in Mexico, and another in India, of a Portuguese father and an Indian convert mother.

Hideyoshi had only one year left to live, however, and after his death, as persecution slackened, the Catholic missions continued to grow. By 1600, well-organized Catholic communities could be found in nearly every Japanese province, along with hundreds of newly built churches. In addition, fifteen daimyos had joined the church. Among the most remarkable features of this Japanese Catholic Church was its appeal across class lines, from daimyos at the top to peasants and artisans at the bottom. It was also a church in which the Japanese played a large role, not just in lay ministries, but also as clerics. Among the Jesuits, for instance, there were seventy Japanese brothers by 1590, fully half of the total number of Jesuits in Japan. Nagasaki was the most Catholic city of all, with ten churches and eight parishes by 1611, two hospitals, and one convent for women. Tokugawa Ieyasu, who had assumed power after Hideyoshi's death, distrusted the Christians as much as his predecessor, but did relatively little to hinder their growth, fearing the loss of his trade with westerners. But his distrust grew more intense with the arrival of Dutch and English merchants, who, as good Protestants, did their best to convince him that conquest was the ultimate plan of the "papist" Iberians, and that he could easily carry on trade with them instead, totally free of the burden and threat posed by European missionaries. If he were to rid himself of the Catholic Church, they promised, they would not try to replace it with any other.

The flourishing of the Catholic Church of Japan came to an abrupt and bitter end in 1614 when Tokugawa Ieyasu issued an edict of persecution and began to hunt down all *Kirishitan*, as Christians were known. In addition to destroying churches and driving missionaries away, Ieyasu's forces began a brutal process of de-Christianization in which thousands were tortured and tens of thousands simply abjured their faith. It is estimated that about one thousand Catholics willingly accepted martyrdom after unspeakable suffering at the hands of torturers. Ieyasu's objective was not to kill, but to force all Christians to abandon their new and dangerous faith. One practice employed in this process was to ask everyone in Japan to trample on images of Christ and the Virgin Mary. Those who refused to dishonor these icons, known as *fumie*, would be identified as Christians and subjected to torture, and eventually to execution if they persisted in their refusal. Many mass executions took place over the next few decades. That at Nagasaki in 1622 offers a glimpse of what the Christians were up against: forty-two Japanese Christians were beheaded first as twenty-five clergy watched, before they themselves were roasted alive, slowly. Women and children were not spared. Similarly horrific events would keep taking place over an entire generation, until the Catholic Church vanished. Resistance proved futile. In 1637–1638, the Shimabara Rebellion, an uprising in Kyushu that combined economic, political, and religious grievances and was led by Catholics, ended in defeat and the execution of thirty-seven thousand of the rebels, along with the final expulsion of all Catholic merchants in 1639 and stricter control of all contacts with Western foreigners. But the Christian faith did not vanish altogether. After the clergy were all gone, Japanese Catholics survived by dissembling, much like their coreligionists in Elizabethan England, or the Jewish conversos in Iberia, becoming "hidden Christians" (*kakure Kirishitan*), passing on their faith at home, disguising their rituals as traditional Japanese ceremonies, restricting marriages within the circle of faith as much as possible. When Japan opened itself to contact with the West once again in 1854 and the official persecution of Christians finally ceased, many of the first Western arrivals were surprised to discover that the *Kirishitans* were still around, and eager to live their ancestral faith openly. Such was the ultimate legacy of the Catholic mission to Japan.

India

While the Catholic Church flourished in Japan, relatively little headway was made in India, even though Goa was the epicenter of all Asian missions. During the sixteenth century, the church had grown only in the Portuguese trading posts and within the walls of Portuguese enclaves. The Muslims on the subcontinent proved as unreachable as those anywhere else; the Hindus were difficult to convert too, mainly because of the caste system, and also of the approach of the missionaries. The progress made by Xavier was typical of the outreach of the sixteenth century: most of his missions were directed at outcasts and the marginalized rather than at the elites—Indians who had much to gain by abandoning their status. Reaching the elites proved difficult because the Portuguese insisted on a thorough Westernization of their converts, forbidding native dress, dietary customs, and names, thereby short-circuiting the caste system and turning all converts into outcasts in the eyes of their fellow Indians. They also insisted on retaining Latin as the liturgical language, and they frowned on the use of native languages within enclaves such as Goa. Even among the native Christians of the Malabar Coast, tensions developed concerning their rites and customs, which the Portuguese tended to see as deviations that needed to be brought in line with Rome. Native perception of the Catholic Church as rigid and intolerant was only deepened by the establishment of the Inquisition in Goa in 1560.

A different attitude toward the Indian missions developed gradually and unevenly. Among the first missionaries to show a genuine appreciation of Indian culture—and of the need to accommodate the Christian message to it—was the English Jesuit Thomas Stephen (1549–1619), who learned the Konkani tongue and compiled a grammar and primer of Christian doctrine. He also learned Sanskrit and Marathi. Stephen's accommodationist work would be surpassed by another Jesuit, Robert de Nobili (1577–1656), who arrived in 1605. Assigned to convert natives beyond the enclave of Goa, De Nobili insisted on distinguishing between native customs and questions of faith and on approaching Indians on their own terms. To prove his point, De Nobili went native: he dressed in saffron-dyed garb; wore wooden clogs rather than leather shoes; abstained from meat, fish, eggs, and wine; marked his brow; and wore a thread across his chest, just like a Brahmin ascetic. In addition, he encouraged his converts to become Christians within their own culture. A quick learner, De Nobili also became fluent in Sanskrit, Telugu, and Tamil and studied the sacred texts of the Vedas, to be able to engage knowledgeably with Indians in religious and philosophical discussions. He would go on to write several treatises on Christian theology for Indians in their own languages, addressing their philosophical concerns. He translated the Psalms and other Christian prayers into Tamil. In addition, he rejected the practice of using Latin words for key theological concepts and became a pioneer in the use of Tamil words to express Christian beliefs. De Nobili met with considerable resistance, not just from Hindus, but also from fellow Catholic missionaries. Supported by his Jesuit superiors in Rome from early on, De Nobili forged ahead and had won sixty Brahmin converts by 1609. Many more followed. But controversy surrounded him constantly, despite the fact that Pope Gregory XV approved of his methods in 1622.

De Nobili's dream was to create a native Indian priesthood and an Indian church that would transcend the caste system and look, sound, and feel Indian rather than Roman. Although De Nobili had converted about forty thousand Indians by the time he died in 1656, few other missionaries followed his lead, the number of conversions shrank, and his dream never came to pass. Opposition to his methods never let up, even increased over time. "Nativization," that is, the accommodation of Christianity to native cultures, was also an issue in China, where, as we shall see, its practice would provoke a major controversy. De Nobili's methods and those of his fellow Jesuits in China who followed the same path were eventually condemned by Pope Benedict XIV in two bulls, *Ex quo singulari* (1742) and *Omnium solicitudinum* (1744). By then, however, the mission effort in India—which had shown some promise under the leadership of De Nobili—had proved itself unable to win over many converts.

China

When Francis Xavier died in 1552, waiting to sneak into China, the prospects for sending missionaries to that vast and powerful empire seemed very dim, and the chances of converting it infinitely remote. Not long after his death, however, the door to China opened slightly. First, as a reward for vanquishing some pirates on the southern Chinese coast, the Portuguese were granted a commercial toehold at that same spot. So, they established the port of Macau in 1557, allowing for the presence of clergy in that enclave and more constant contact between Europe and China. Second, as soon as Jesuits arrived in the 1560s and Dominicans in the 1580s, both orders set up churches and schools for the thousand or so Portuguese who resided in Macau. In 1576 Pope Gregory XIII appointed the colony's first bishop. All along, though the rest of China remained closed to them, plans to send missionaries into China proper were part of the Catholic Church's long-term strategy, and especially of the Jesuits, and of their superior in Asia, Alessandro Valignano (1539–1606), who favored an approach that would tailor Christianity to Asian cultures. And Catholic missionary efforts began to pay off in the 1580s, in fits and starts, first with some Spanish Franciscans and Augustinians from the Philippines, who fumbled in their attempt, and with Jesuits from Macau, who were slightly more successful.

One of the first of these Jesuits was Michele Ruggieri (1543–1607), an Italian who had spent time in India and was in favor of accommodating Christianity to native cultures, especially those of highly civilized people such as the Chinese. Ruggieri himself began to learn the local tongue as soon as he was assigned to China, and he set up a school in Macau where Chinese would be taught to all new arrivals. After a brief and unsuccessful attempt to establish a Jesuit outpost at Zhaoqing, about a hundred miles inland from Macau, Ruggieri returned in 1582 with a like-minded younger Jesuit who had been hand-picked for the mission by Valignano: the Italian Matteo Ricci (1552–1610), who, among other things, was very proficient in mathematics, geography, and astronomy, and would also quickly master classical and colloquial Mandarin Chinese, despite its being— in his opinion—"the most ambiguous spoken and written language ever to be found."[2]

Ricci and Ruggieri aimed high, convinced that if they won over the elites, then the conversion of the masses would eventually follow. They also adopted a subtle approach, seeking to first impress the Chinese with Western advances in science and mathematics, so they might drop their prejudice against all things non-Chinese as worthless. To this end, Ricci brought to his mission Western clocks, musical, mathematical and astronomical instruments, books, and astronomical, geographical, and architectural treatises illustrated with maps and diagrams. He and Ruggieri also strategically decorated their house with works of Christian art, so the natives might inquire about their meaning. Impressed by Ricci's command of nearly every subject, as well as by his prodigious memory and the novelty of his artifacts, Chinese elites quickly flocked to him, especially high-ranking imperial officials known to Europeans as mandarins. Western mechanical clocks impressed the Chinese the most, along with prisms and maps of the entire world that showed regions and continents previously unknown to them.

Obviously uninterested in the mass baptisms that had made Xavier so famous, and fully aware that such a strategy would immediately prompt persecution and expulsion, Ricci and Ruggieri gently and patiently engaged with the mandarins on their own terms, conversing freely about all subjects, occasionally touching on questions of religion. Committed to the creation of a native Catholic church in China, they dressed as Buddhist monks—mistakenly thinking that this would help the Chinese accept them more readily—and plunged into the study of Chinese culture, gradually working out a way to synthesize Christianity with whatever their mandarin audience respected the most. To this end, Ricci looked for ways of convincing the Chinese that their most cherished beliefs were not antithetical to Christianity, but rather highly compatible, even brought to perfection by Christian theology, ethics, and philosophy. This strategy was designed to convince through comparison and synthesis rather than antithesis. For such a strategy to work, those employing it had to immerse themselves in Chinese culture, and to genuinely admire it. This approach required enormous patience, and a total immersion in an ancient foreign culture with a multilayered religious and philosophical tradition that included Taoism, Buddhism, and Confucianism. Such a deliberately slow approach was incompatible with the methods employed by most Catholic missionaries at that time, which were designed to win converts quickly. The glacial pace of Ricci's and Ruggieri's approach could be easily measured: by 1586, three years into the mission, there were but forty converts.

All along, as they engaged in dialogue with local mandarins in Zhaoqing, Ruggieri and Ricci had their sights set much higher. Their long-term strategy was to pave the way for two developments: first, the influx of more missionaries to China; second, an invitation to the imperial capital at Beijing, where they might win converts at the highest possible level. To achieve the first of these goals, Ruggieri and Ricci began to compile a Portuguese-Chinese dictionary and to develop a consistent transcription of Chinese words into the Latin alphabet. With some help from locals, Ricci also translated a Latin catechism and the Ten Commandments into Chinese. To achieve the second goal, Ruggieri took off for Rome in 1588, on orders from Valignano, to convince the pope that an official embassy should be sent to the emperor in Beijing—a diplomatic mission that could potentially turn into a religious one, with Jesuits playing a major role. Although Ruggieri never did convince the pope to send an embassy to the Chinese emperor, and never got to return to China himself, he promoted knowledge about China and the mission effort by translating into Latin the key Confucian text *The Four Books*.

Ricci persevered against great odds. Evicted from Zhaoqing in 1589, he obtained permission to set up residence in Shaozhou, where he resided until 1595 with a few fellow Jesuits, making great strides in his understanding of Chinese culture and converting some notable locals. At Shaozhou Ricci realized that he could make much more progress by dressing and acting like a mandarin rather than as a Buddhist monk. From there, he moved further north to Nanchang, leaving the mission in Shaozhou in the hands of other Jesuits. At Nanchang, he was welcomed not only by the local provincial governor, but also by two imperial princes, and soon he won renown among the Chinese intelligentsia as "the scholar from the West." While at Nanchang (1595–1598), he wrote a number of books that would endear him to the Chinese, with three, in particular, propelling him to stellar heights: first, *On Friendship*, a compilation of one hundred maxims that blended classical Western and Confucian wisdom and quickly gained a wide audience in China; second, a treatise on memory, which summarized Western methods of memorization and helped explain his own astounding ability to remember details; and third, a summary of Christian beliefs, *The True Meaning of the Lord of Heaven*, which would have a long-lasting impact on his Chinese audience but would stir up controversy within the Catholic Church. The last text takes the form of a dialogue between two scholars, one Western and the other Chinese. Its aim is not so much to teach Christian doctrine to the Chinese as to show the Chinese that Christianity was eminently reasonable, on their own terms. The Chinese scholar expounds the principles of traditional Confucianism, Buddhism, and Taoism while the Westerner employs classical Confucian teachings to explain the logic of Christian doctrine. To paraphrase Ricci himself, this treatise sought to prove the conformity of natural reason with the law of the Christian God and with the ancient sages of China. The text also criticized some Chinese rites and beliefs as illogical, especially those that had to do with reincarnation and the worship of idols.

Reprinted at least four times before Ricci's death and credited with many conversions, *True Meaning* would also command respect from many Chinese who read it but were not converted. The text became an essential manual for other missionaries in China. But it planted the seeds of a great controversy by adopting certain Confucian terms to explain Christian doctrines—an issue that we will take up shortly.

In 1598 Ricci traveled to Beijing with a powerful Chinese patron, but he failed to gain an audience with the emperor. Setting up yet another residence, in Nanking in 1599, he attracted many eminent visitors and befriended highly influential Chinese scholars and intellectuals. He also converted some prominent mandarins and wrote several more books in Chinese, all the while pining for the chance to meet with the emperor, who, as he saw it, held the sole key to the ultimate success of the entire Christian mission. Finally, in January 1601 Ricci was invited to meet with Emperor Kangxi in Beijing. Loaded with gifts, he presented the emperor with items thought sure to pique his curiosity: two

Going native. One of the distinctive features of the Jesuit mission to China was the way the missionaries tried to adapt themselves and their message to the native culture, and how intensely they focused on the elite class. This image of Matteo Ricci and Xu Guanggi, a prominent Chinese convert, reveals the extent to which accommodations were made.

mechanical clocks (one of which rang the hours), a painting of Jesus Christ, two paintings of the Virgin Mary, a prayer book, a gem-encrusted cross, an annotated world map, and a harpsichord. These gifts did not open up the emperor for conversation as hoped, but they did win Ricci and his Jesuit companions residence at the imperial court, where they were to maintain the clocks and other instruments and teach the harpsichord. Funded by a royal salary as honorary mandarins, Ricci and his brethren spent nine years hobnob-bing with the most important members of the Chinese intelligentsia, doing their subtle best to win converts, writing books, and passing on Western scientific and mathematical advances to the Chinese.

Although Ricci never did manage to convert the emperor, he at least won his respect and made it possible for Christian missions to be tolerated, something he viewed as a miraculous giant step, given that when he entered China a mere two decades earlier, the country had been closed to missionaries. By the time he died, in Beijing in 1610, Ricci could not be credited with having made hordes of converts, and his critics would view this as something of a failure. The numbers for the entire Catholic missionary enterprise were impressive, however, and speak for themselves. In 1584, a year after Ricci began his mission, there were only three Christians in all of China. A year later there were 20; in another year, 80; by 1596 there were about 100; by 1603, after twenty years on his mission, about 600; by the time of his death in 1610, about 2,500, with 400 in Beijing alone. And the vast majority of these converts were intellectuals and members of the ruling class. By 1670 there would be more than a hundred thousand Chinese Catholics, ministered to by a mere two dozen Europeans and one native Chinese priest. Ricci and his fellow Jesuits were much more interested in beating the odds than in playing the numbers game vis-à-vis missionaries who counted their converts in the tens or hundreds of thousands. They knew that in Christian history the greatest gains had been made through the conversion of rulers and elites, and they were willing to gamble on their ability to pull off a similar feat once again, because the odds of converting China were much more favorable if they were present in the emperor's court. After all, by securing official posts at court for himself and members of his order, Ricci secured the protection of all missionaries in China.

A Jesuit who followed in Ricci's footsteps was Giulio Alenio (1582–1649). Alenio was sent to China in 1610—the year of Ricci's death—and spent his first three years there teaching mathematics in Macau while waiting for an opportunity to go further inland. Eventually, he became the first missionary to enter Kiangsi, and he would go on to es-tablish several churches in Fujian. Like Ricci, he embraced the dress and manners of the Chinese elite, and even came to be known as a "Western Confucian." During his thirty years in the mission field, Alenio wrote several books in Chinese on a wide variety of subjects—some scientific, some devotional, and some polemical. One of his best-known texts was an adaptation of the meditative sections of *The Spiritual Exercises* titled "The Illustrated Life of Our Lord Jesus Christ." Centuries later, Protestant missionaries would also find the book useful. Nonetheless, as much as he tried to blend in, Alenio did not

Iconic subtlety. In this image from Giulio Alenio's *Illustrated Life of Our Lord Jesus Christ*, traditional European iconic forms and content are dominant, but with a subtle twist. As is common in Christian iconography, Christ holds a globe, which symbolizes his cosmic divine rulership. But this globe contains astronomical symbols rather than continents and oceans. While Jesuits in Europe employed globes to boast of how much of the world they were conquering for Christ, those in China preferred to use the globe as a symbol for the central message of they pitched at Chinese elites: the integral connection between scientific and religious truths.

shrink from engaging in controversy. Another of his well-known texts, "The True Origin of All Things," was a detailed refutation of what he considered the principal errors of Chinese philosophy and religion.

After Ricci's death, the history of missions in China becomes more complex and turbulent. Though Jesuits remained a fixture at the imperial court, led from 1630 to 1666 by the German astronomer Johan Adam Schall von Bell, not all Jesuits in China agreed with the patient and subtle elitist strategies of Ricci, and some eager new arrivals began to preach directly to the common people and to win converts among them in greater numbers. Compounding the unease felt by many Chinese elites, a steady flow of even less patient Franciscan and Dominican missionaries began to seep into China from the Philippines in 1633. These newcomers proved themselves a thorn in the side of the Chinese elite and the Jesuits, largely because they were more successful at making converts. Resolutely opposed to compromise and committed to evangelizing China quickly, they gained a greater following among ordinary Chinese people and cast serious doubt on the orthodoxy and efficiency of Ricci's approach. Two issues were especially troubling to them: the use of traditional Chinese terms for Christian concepts, and the acceptance of certain Chinese rites as mere cultural variants of Christian devotion. The clash between these differences in approach, which would become known as the Chinese rites controversy, would eventually tear asunder the fabric of the Chinese mission and ensure its failure.

Among the Chinese terms that most disturbed the Franciscans and Dominicans none seemed worse to them than "Lord of Heaven," which Ricci had accepted as a valid translation of the Christian *God*, or *Deus* in Latin. For the Franciscans and Dominicans, this translation provided only a facile solution to a complex set of problems and was too laden with Confucian meaning. Among the many Chinese rites that the missionary newcomers considered inappropriate, none seemed worse to them than the veneration of ancestors, which Ricci and the Jesuits had interpreted as purely mundane and as parallel to Catholic concern for the souls in purgatory. Many were also disturbed by ceremonies in which all mandarins were required to honor Confucius, which the Jesuits accepted as purely secular. After decades of debate in China and back home in Europe—debates that caused turmoil among missionaries in China and no small measure of acrimony within the church—Rome would side with the newcomers against the Jesuits, adversely affecting not just the missions in China, but also those in India and elsewhere in Asia.

The history of Catholic missions in China is difficult to wedge into the chronology of European history, simply because it does not conveniently undergo a major transition with the Peace of Westphalia in 1648. In many ways, the early modern period—even the age of Reformations—reaches well into the eighteenth century in China, from the perspective of missions history. Consequently, it is necessary to briefly mention the most significant events and developments that took place after 1650.

Imperial distrust of the foreign missionaries increased in the 1640s, despite the presence of highly esteemed Jesuits at court. The first native Chinese priest was ordained only in 1664, and although more such ordinations would follow, the move toward a native priesthood came at a very bad time. At the time of that first native ordination in 1664, most of the foreign clergy in the province of Guangdong were in prison, the result of growing official distrust. A brief reprieve from persecution came in 1671, when thanks to the efforts of Ferdinand Verbiest (1623–1688), a Jesuit at the imperial court, these missionaries were freed from prison. In 1688 a new missionary order of French priests began to arrive, also thanks to efforts by Verbiest, but the rites controversy doomed all of their efforts.

The first great setback came in 1705, when Rome proclaimed all rites concerning ancestors incompatible with the Catholic faith and therefore forbidden. This decision eventually led the Chinese emperor to outlaw Christianity everywhere but Beijing and to ban all Christian missions from the provinces in 1721. In addition, some junior princes of the imperial family who had converted were banished. The death blow to all accommodationist missionary efforts everywhere—and specifically to Ricci's plan of achieving the conversion of China gradually and in a very Chinese way—was dealt by Pope Benedict XIV in the 1740s through his two bulls *Ex quo singulari* and *Omnium solicitudinum*. The Catholic Church in China entered a dark age of repression and persecution in the mid-eighteenth century, and by 1787, the last foreign priest had been driven out. The church founded by Ricci survived nonetheless, but under severe constraints.

Numbers alone are not sufficient to measure the significance of the Catholic Church in China from the 1580s to the 1780s, for, as is also the case with overseas empires, the reciprocal impact of the periphery on the center has to be taken into account. The missions in China shaped the collective identity of European Catholics in numerous ways, especially by increasing awareness of the global reach of the church and of its responsibility to preach the gospel in far-off lands. Moreover, the cultural exchange begun by the missionaries proved invaluable not just in the development of East-West relations, but also in the development of the European consciousness.

Europeans first learned about China and its culture from missionaries. When great Enlightenment skeptics such as Voltaire sought to displace the centrality of the Judeo-Christian tradition they turned east, claiming that the origins of civilization were to be found in China rather than the Near East or Europe. Ironically, such assertions relied on texts written by the missionaries they loathed. The Chinese rites controversy directly concerned a relatively small number of people, in Rome and out in the missions, but its ramifications were considerable. On the positive side, the controversy raised many questions about the nature of the faith and its relationship to culture, questions that would assume ever greater significance in centuries to come. On the negative side, the bickering in Asia and the ultimate decision made in Rome had a catastrophic impact on the growth of the church in China.

Rome and the French Missions

All the Asian missions, as well as those in America, were initiated and controlled for a long time by the two Iberian kingdoms of Spain and Portugal. Moreover, between 1580 and 1640, when Spain swallowed up Portugal, everything related to missions around the globe was in the hands of the Spanish Hapsburg monarchs Philip II (d. 1598), Philip III (d. 1621), and Philip IV (d. 1665). In surveying the complex and often tragic history of missions, it is impossible not to notice this tight interweaving of church and state or of mission and the politics of one peninsula at the western edge of Europe. Even in the case of the Portuguese in Asia, whose empire was largely commercial, the worldly ambitions of the European interlopers caused problems for missionaries and aroused suspicion from Asian rulers. And even in the case of the Jesuits or Franciscans or Dominicans, whose members came from many different countries, there was no escaping the authority of whichever Iberian monarch had jurisdiction over them.

Painfully aware of the problems caused by such incestuous church-state relations, and also worried by the increasingly large role being played in commerce and colonization by the Dutch and the English, both Protestant nations, some in Rome pressed for greater centralized church control of the mission effort. To that end, Pope Gregory XV established the Congregation for the Propagation of the Faith in January 1622. The Propaganda Fide, as the congregation was known in Latin, was in part a response to what had been going on in America and Asia, and in part an outgrowth of the reforms of the Council of Trent. Eventually, in light of the significance of his powers, the cardinal prefect of Propaganda would eventually earn the title "red pope." The first secretary of the Propaganda Fide, Francesco Ingoli (1578–1649), wrote three reports on the state of the missions, in 1625, 1628, and 1644, in which he identified twelve causes of disorder and abuse. The chief problem, Ingoli thought, was the partition of the entire globe into two missionary zones, one for Spain and one for Portugal, which led to rivalry and hostility. Even worse, the privileges granted to the Iberian monarchs by the papacy in the late fifteenth century encroached on the spiritual domain of the church. As a result of such entanglement, complained Ingoli, anyone on earth approached by Spanish or Portuguese missionaries could easily suspect them of being imperial agents rather than ministers, and could easily think of Christianization and Westernization as synonymous, as happened in India, where being baptized came to be known as "turning Portuguese."

One of the steps proposed by the Propaganda Fide was the creation of indigenous clergy, which it sought to achieve through the appointment of apostolic vicars who would report directly to the Propaganda in Rome rather than to any civil colonial authority and would be in charge of establishing seminaries in their missions for the training of native clergy. The Iberian states and their clergy offered stiff resistance. An early clash was caused by the appointment of Matteo de Castro (1594–1677) as apostolic vicar of Bijapur, which was outside of the jurisdiction of Goa. De Castro was a Brahmin from Goa who had converted to Christianity and taken a Portuguese name, as the missionaries required. The opposition mounted by the archbishop and clergy of Goa to his appointment was so intense and lasted for so long, that their constant obstructions and meddling nullified Castro's effectiveness. The war of independence waged by the Portuguese against the Spanish from 1640 to 1688 only made things worse. In 1642, the newly crowned rebel king of Portugal, John IV, banned all non-Portuguese missionaries from India. In 1652 the Portuguese Cortes (parliament) ordered that no papal documents were to be acknowledged or accepted in the missions without their approval. In 1672 another decree by the Cortes banned all missionaries and bishops who did not first pass through Lisbon to offer a vow of fidelity to the Portuguese crown.

The Propaganda Fide was more successful in circumventing Portuguese obstructions in China, where European power was not so strong. The road to success was found in a roundabout way. It began when Alexandre de Rhodes (1591–1660), a French Jesuit who had a mission in the southernmost Chinese province of Annam (present-day Vietnam), petitioned Rome for additional missionaries in 1650, and obtained from Pope Innocent X a promise to send secular clergy and bishops. In 1653, with De Rhodes's help and encouragement, and the support of the Company of the Blessed Sacrament (a confraternity in France with influential and wealthy aristocratic members), the Paris Foreign Missions Society was created, with the express purpose of avoiding entanglements with any colonizing European state and sending secular priests abroad as missionaries who would be directly connected to the Propaganda Fide in Rome. The first three members, François Pallu (1626–1684), Pierre Lambert de la Motte (1624–1679), and Ignace Cotolendi (1630–1662), volunteered to go as missionaries to China. In July 1658, two of these founders of the Paris Foreign Missions Society were consecrated as bishops at Rome: Pallu was named apostolic vicar of Tonkin, a vast area encompassing parts of present-day Vietnam, Laos, and southern China; de la Motte as apostolic vicar of Cochinchina, another large area encompassing five provinces in southeastern China. In 1660 the third founder, Cotolendi, was appointed apostolic vicar of Nanjing, also a large area in eastern China comprising five provinces. At the same time in another region of the globe, a fourth member, François de Laval (1623–1708), was appointed as apostolic vicar of New France, and in 1663, he would establish a seminary in Québec.

Appointing these bishops was one thing; getting them to their new sees was quite another, given the control that Spain and Portugal had over sea routes to Asia, and given that the Dutch and English were not likely to ferry Catholic missionaries. To circumvent this problem, the Company of the Blessed Sacrament set up a trading company of its own in 1660, the Compagnie de Chine, which would later merge with two other trading companies to form the French East India Company. Once again, commercial and missionary efforts were combined, despite the Propaganda's bid for independence from nationalistic interests. Even with numerous setbacks, the three men finally made it to Asia and began to fulfill the commission entrusted to the Paris Foreign Missions Society, which was not just to convert pagans, but to "strive by all means and methods possible to educate young people and to make them fit for the priesthood."[3] At their new seminary in Paris, established in 1663, the Foreign Missions Society trained its own clergy and sent forth a hundred missionaries in its first fifty years of existence, mostly to China and Southeast Asia. In this relatively brief half a century the missionaries of the society established a seminary in Siam, baptized more than forty thousand converts, and trained thirty of them for the priesthood. They also established a convent for native nuns, and trained native catechists. The collapse of the missions in eighteenth-century China would affect them too, and restrict them to Southeast Asia. But at nearly the same time, they expanded by taking over the Jesuit missions in India when that order was dissolved.

Africa

The history of Catholic missions in Africa is inseparable from that of Portuguese exploration and involvement in the slave trade. It also begins much earlier than the history of missions to the Indies. Although a low priority for early modern Catholics, the smaller African missionary field was of enduring significance, given the later history of European involvement in that continent, and the phenomenal growth of Christianity in the late twentieth and early twenty-first centuries. Without a doubt, the African missions are something of a paradox: at once typical in respect to their connection to European exploration and anomalous in respect to their limited size and scope. And for this reason they are a fitting subject with which to close these two chapters on Catholic missions.

Backflow. European missions were much more than religious enterprises that flowed outward or cultural encounters that had an impact in far-off lands. Politics and commerce were inseparably linked to missions. And every mission created its own backflow, with myriad repercussions back in Europe. This engraving shows three envoys from the kingdom of Siam making their entrance to the French court of Louis XIV in 1686. This Siamese embassy was accompanied by the Jesuit missionary Guy Tachard, who stands beside them in this image. Eventually, Europeans would come to appreciate much in Asian culture, and even the harshest critics of Christianity, such as Voltaire—who began his history of civilization in China rather than Babylonia or Egypt—would have the missionaries to thank, in part, for broadening their horizons.

As the Portuguese gradually sailed farther and farther south along the Atlantic African coast in search for a passage to Asia in the late fifteenth century, they encountered diverse African peoples along the Guinea coast, in Equatorial Africa, in Kongo, Angola, Mozambique, Madagascar, and Kenya. The Portuguese set up trading posts wherever they could turn a profit, and in some places they also set up missions. For the most part, these missions were small and yielded relatively few converts. Their greatest success was in the kingdom of Kongo (present-day Gabon, Democratic Republic of the Congo, Republic of the Congo, and Angola). By 1491, the Portuguese had sent missionaries to this kingdom and converted its king, Nzinga a Nkuwu, who sent his son and heir Nzinga Mbembe to be educated in Portugal. When this son returned and assumed the throne, he changed his name to King Alfonso I, and he welcomed Portuguese missionaries, who opened schools and won many converts.

The progress of the Kongo missions was soon compromised in the early sixteenth century by the sudden interest that the Portuguese took in the slave trade. Although they never raided for slaves themselves, nor allowed for any Christians to be enslaved, the Portuguese did encourage the Kongolese to raid and enslave their non-Christian neighbors. Eventually, the raids took a toll on the integrity of the Kongo kingdom itself, principally because it bound them ever more tightly to the Portuguese. The raiding and enslaving also closed off the possibility of expansion for the church, since having a fresh supply of slaves close at hand mattered too much to the Portuguese and their subservient Kongolese partners. Despite the degradation brought by the slave trade, missionaries met with some success in certain locations. The Capuchins and Jesuits, for instance, established churches and won converts in what is present-day Angola.

On the coast of the Indian Ocean, in the colony the Portuguese named Mozambique, the missions were very thinly spread, mostly along the shoreline. The first mission, established in 1500 by Franciscans, made slow and very modest progress in winning converts. Everything changed in 1560, however, when Jesuits arrived. Before long, two local rulers, the king of Inhambane and the emperor of Mutapa were baptized, along with many of their subjects. Dominicans also joined in the effort, as did Carmelites, and by 1614 Mozambique had its own bishop. But many factors prevented great progress from being made. Among the greatest impediments were the weakness of Portuguese control, constant harassment by Muslims, and the behavior of the colonists, which was far from exemplary. In addition, here as elsewhere in Africa, the slave trade proved too disruptive and demoralizing for all involved.

On the island of Zanzibar, and on the coast of present-day Kenya, Augustinians made converts too. On the giant island of Madagascar, small-scale gains were also made by a succession of missionary orders, despite a very slow and troubled start. The first missionaries sent in 1540 were all massacred, but the Dominicans who followed their trail survived and made progress. Jesuits came in the seventeenth century and managed to convert a local ruler, the king of Anosy, and to send his son Ramaka to Goa, to be educated by them. King Ramaka soon turned on the Jesuits, however, and their mission came to naught. They were followed by Lazarists, sent by St. Vincent de Paul, in connection with French attempts to colonize part of the island. The Lazarists labored away and suffered loss after loss until the French pulled out of Madagascar in the 1570s. Ultimately, Madagascar, like the rest of Africa, remained barely affected by the European presence and by the missions, despite the heroic efforts made by those missionaries who dared to go there, to be largely ignored and forgotten by those Catholics in early modern Europe who relished knowing that the whole globe was theirs to convert.

Africa was far too large, its interior too daunting a challenge, and its wild riches too incomprehensible to profit-seeking Europeans, with one lamentable exception. Africa was rich in slaves, a disposable and renewable commodity, and so lucrative a trade it seemed to blind Europeans to all else that the continent had to offer. So Africa and its seemingly endless supply of human cargo remained barely within the field of vision of Catholic Europe, especially when compared to the Indies, East and West, where the empire builders, wealth seekers, and soul savers cooperated edgily to extract the maximum profit for God and king. But Africa was theirs to convert, nonetheless, a potential member of the Body of Christ, no matter how tenuous or painful its incorporation might have seemed. In sum, the struggling missions in Africa proved to Catholics that their Church was truly universal, and therefore the only true church, even if its global reach was largely determined by European states hell-bent on profit making and empire building.

The Legacy

Ironically, even paradoxically, the worldly ambitions of certain European nations drove the expansion of the Catholic Church in the sixteenth and seventeenth centuries. In the New World, empire builders and colonists brought the missionaries. In Asia and Africa, it was the merchants. Hardly anyone in the Catholic world spoke of this arrangement as an unholy alliance. On the contrary, those who ran church and state in the nations involved in this expansion saw it as providential, perhaps even as predestined, or as a divine counterbalancing act, as God's response to the Protestant revolt in Europe.

Christianizing the East Indies and Africa proved so enormous a task that all gains and triumphs could easily seem eclipsed by setbacks and tragic disasters. Measuring the significance of this effort in numbers of souls converted is not only wrongheaded, but also useless. The significance of this chapter in the history of early modern Catholicism is to be found in the effort itself rather than in the outcome. The missions to Africa, small as they were, haunted by the specter of the slave trade, are not easy to assess in terms of their impact on early modern Catholicism. The missions to Asia, in contrast, are an odd combination of hubris and selflessness and an object lesson in the complexities of history. Though the missions to Asia could not be entirely divorced from European greed and self-interest, they were nonetheless a quest more spiritual than those to the New World, where colonization and exploitation were truly inseparable from the missionary enterprise. The effect of these missions on the development of Catholic identity has yet to be systematically plumbed, but few would be rash enough to deny that they had any impact. The effect of the missions on those who converted in Asia, or on those who persecuted the converts was so immediate and obvious it requires hardly any analysis insofar as the Catholic Reformation is concerned. When all is said and done, these missions came to represent universality as nothing else could in early modern Catholicism. Sometimes, the representations could be literal and physical, and their impact unfathomable.

Two works of art can help us fathom the meaning of the Asian missions to the Catholic mentality, not just in the early modern age, but down to the twenty-first century. Both are images of St. Francis Xavier created at more or less the same time: one in Prague, in the Czech Republic; the other just outside of Tucson, Arizona, on a Native American reservation.

The image in Prague is one of thirty baroque religious statues on the Charles Bridge, which spans the Vltava River. The original sculpture by Ferdinand Brokoff erected in 1711 was swept away by a flood in 1890, but the one standing there today is a faithful replica, meticulously crafted in 1913 by Čeněk Vosmík. Installed on the bridge eighty-nine years after Prague was reclaimed from Hussite and Protestant control, while the city was still something of a mission territory, the statue was a gift from the theologians at the university. It depicts a group of Indian and Japanese "pagans" huddled at the saint's feet, being baptized by him. This ensemble, in turn, is held aloft by a cluster

From the "Indies over there" to the "Indies over here." St. Francis Xavier and his converts as immortalized on the Charles Bridge in Prague, a city that was subjected to intense Catholic mission activity in the seventeenth century, after Emperor Frederick II defeated native Protestants at the Battle of White Mountain in 1620.

of exotic figures who struggle with their load, Atlas-like: one Chinese, one Tatar, one Indian, and one Moor—all depicted with caricatured features that in our own day and age might be considered tactless and repugnant.

This statue, along with the other twenty-nine on the bridge, was part of the effort to re-Catholicize Prague after nearly two centuries of Hussite and Lutheran heresy had left it devoid of Catholic identity. That the theological faculty should have commissioned this depiction of St. Francis, in which the heathens command more attention than he does, shows not only how significant the myth of the great Jesuit missionary had become, but also how important those "pagans" were to the Catholic mentality of those who were, in essence, missionaries within Mother Europe itself, in the Indies of the formerly heretic Prague. Curiously, neither the Nazis nor the communists, those totalitarian missionaries who ruled Prague for half of the twentieth century, dared to cast this unseemly idol into the river. And now it puzzles and offends many a tourist, and perhaps not a few Czechs too.

The image in Arizona is at the San Xavier del Bac mission, about nine miles south of downtown Tucson, in a reservation for the Tohono O'odham people. The whitewashed adobe church in which the image is enshrined was built in the eighteenth century. The mission itself, which is named after Francis Xavier, was created in 1692 by Father Eusebio Kino, a Jesuit who wished to be sent to the East Indies, but ended up in the New World instead and went on to establish nearly two dozen missions in the Sonoran Desert. The area Kino evangelized was part of the wild outermost reaches of the Viceroyalty of New Spain, and the natives converted by him needed protection from the Spanish and from the neighboring Apache, their hard-to-convert enemies. In the eighteenth century, the Jesuits who ran this mission installed a wooden life-size replica of the uncorrupted corpse of St. Francis, which still is on display at Goa in India.

That the Jesuits should have linked Goa to this remote desert spot and installed such an image for veneration by their illiterate converts shows how much Xavier meant to the mission effort, and the place that incorruptible corpse in far-off India held in their imagination. That the image should have acquired miracle-working powers adds yet another layer of significance to it. That layer, however, is but one of many, for the effigy is currently dressed in a Franciscan habit and is still an object of veneration, approached reverently by Native Americans, Mexicans, and Arizonan Anglos, who kiss its head and whisper prayers, oblivious to all the tourists who stare at them in disbelief.

This miracle-working effigy is decked with ex-votos that testify to its healing powers, just as if the Middle Ages had never come to an end: images of human limbs, eyes, and inner organs, thank-you notes, photographs—so many of them that they have to be constantly removed and stashed away, a seemingly endless stream of thank-yous that are archived beyond view. The Franciscan habit is hard to detect under the linens, but easy to explain: when the Jesuits order was dissolved in the eighteenth century, Franciscans took over the mission and still run it today, despite many rude interruptions. The mendicants have improbably made the Basque Jesuit one of their own. The miracles attributed to the

Linking Europe, Asia, and the Americas. When Jesuit missionaries established a mission in 1692 in northern New Spain (present-day Arizona), they named it after their own illustrious St. Francis Xavier, and installed a wooden effigy of St. Francis's incorruptible body, which rests in Goa, India. The miracle-working shrine, which links three continents and celebrates the success of missionary work, attracts pilgrims to this day.

effigy and to St. Francis Xavier are much harder to explain, especially in the twenty-first century. But they do speak volumes about the place of the early modern missions in the Catholic mentality, and especially about the convergence of the universal and the local.

This St. Francis in the Sonoran Desert bespeaks of the miraculous, the improbable, and the impossible, just like the one on the bridge in Prague, and all the others set up by Jesuits in their churches around the world, and like every Catholic Francis who proudly inserts a bold *X* between his first and last names. All of them represent more than the legacy of one saint: they reify confidence in the power of the individual human will aided by grace and in the painful yet grand resurgence of Catholicism in the early modern era.

Designed to overawe. The interior of the finished St. Peter's is arguably more impressive than its exterior, intended to overawe the senses as well as the spirit. This detailed eighteenth-century painting by Giovanni Paolo Pannini captures both the sumptuousness of the decorations as well as the colossal scale of the building, which dwarfs everyone who enters it.

PART FOUR

Consequences
Prelude: Rome, 1626

I n August 1626, Christian Europe is at war. Catholic and Protestant armies have been fighting against each other for eight long years, with no end in sight. The most serious fighting has taken place in Lower Saxony, at the Battle of Lutter—a place-name eerily close to Luther's surname—where the Protestant forces of Christian IV of Denmark have been routed by the armies of the Catholic League. This defeat will draw Protestant Sweden into the war. The fighting will go on for another twenty-two years and devastate much of Germany.

By the time this Thirty Years' War ends in 1648, religious differences will mean something else than they did at its beginning. So will religion itself, for many who survive the mayhem.

This very same year of 1626, witch trials begin in the prince bishoprics of Würzburg and Bamberg that will eventually lead to the execution of more than one thousand men, women, and children. These witch hunts are but two of hundreds carried out in this period by both Protestants and Catholics, waging against the devil and his minions.

As witches burn elsewhere, Orazio Grassi, a Jesuit priest and astronomer publishes a reply to Galileo Galilei's book *The Assayer*, which had appeared in 1623. In *The Assayer*, Galileo had argued against Aristotle and the scholastics in favor of mathematical and scientific empiricism, and had sought to prove Grassi wrong on the subject of comets. Pope Urban VIII, a patron of Galileo who had read *The Assayer* with great delight, is unaware in 1626 that the Inquisition will find Galileo guilty of heresy in 1633 for insisting that the earth orbits the sun and for arguing that all biblical references to the sun orbiting the earth should be interpreted metaphorically.

The consequences of what began to unfold in 1517 can be felt but not yet fully fathomed in 1626.

On 18 November, more than 120 years after the first stone was laid for the new St. Peter's and 1,300 years since the original basilica was dedicated by Emperor

Constantine, Pope Urban VIII consecrates this enormous church with all of the pomp required by such an occasion. As every church bell in Rome peals, and as thousands throng the site, Pope Urban officially sanctifies the mammoth structure. Though more work still needs to be done on both interior and exterior, the project first envisioned by Pope Nicholas V has been realized, bit by bit, even as the world changed at an unprecedented pace. The new St. Peter's is larger and more imposing than any other church on earth. It is so immense, in fact, that it could easily accommodate two medieval Gothic cathedrals within itself, and still have room left for a few more shrines. The total expense is estimated at 46.8 million ducats, more or less. This colossal sum does not take into account other incalculable costs, especially that of the fragmentation of Christendom sparked in 1517 by the indulgences linked to its building scheme.

The solid grandeur of this newly consecrated St. Peter's challenges the quaking uncertainties of the age, and the fervid doubt and the devils that keep seeping into Europe from all directions. But it is also an affront to the values most cherished by Protestants everywhere. To them, this basilica is an offensive blot on the surface of the earth, made all the more hideous by its cost. While the building seeks to reify permanence, even eternity itself, to Protestants all it can signify is decay.

The world that used to be called Christendom exists no more, and no one expects its resurrection. This basilica is a monument to the dissolution of that corpse. Yet for the Catholic faithful gathered there, it does more than hint at redemption. The brash Roman bells intone nothing but heavenly defiance of all the wreckage, ruin, bloodshed, and confusion that bedevil the world. Those who hear the optimistic pealing of the bells might be cheered, even enraptured, but few of them can really see or imagine the godlessness that hovers just over the horizon.

No one at this consecration can yet imagine how Gian Lorenzo Bernini's soaring bronze canopy over the main altar, begun in 1623, will elevate to perfection the basilica's interior. Nor can anyone conceive of the grandiose keyhole-shaped colonnade and piazza that Bernini will add out front in 1656–1667, as a crowning touch, to embrace and overawe innumerable multitudes for centuries to come.

And no one who hears those pealing bells in 1626 can have any way of knowing that as craftsmen put the finishing touches on that colonnade forty-one years from then, a gaunt English sage named Isaac Newton will be peering into the night sky with his telescopes, reckoning a clockwork universe in which all Reformations are nothing more than irritating footnotes.

CHAPTER TWENTY

The Age of Religious Wars

W hat makes any violence "religious" in nature? This is a tough question, especially when it comes to the sixteenth and seventeenth centuries: how can religion be isolated as the sole or chief cause of anything when all dimensions of a society—political, social, cultural, and economic—are inextricably tied to religion in myriad ways?

Religion permeated every aspect of life in late medieval and early modern Europe so thoroughly that to isolate it is to misunderstand it. And the same could be said for other reductionist tendencies: seeking to assign causality to any single factor, especially in the distant past, leads to distorted perspectives. Yet to be too cautious in assessing the effect of religious disagreement on behavior is also a mistake. Religion was too *real* in the early modern age, and too multidimensional, and so were religious commitments. As long as one understands this difference between the early modern age and our own, and one is careful enough to take it into account, linking religion to violence is not only correct, but also necessary. Discerning the religious dimension of early modern violence is relatively easy. Several telltale indicators are easy enough to spot, and four of these are the most obvious:

1. Whenever opposing parties square off against one another over religious differences and self-consciously articulate their grievances in religious terms
2. Whenever factions or parties identify themselves by a name that refers to a specific religious allegiance (such as *Catholic* or *evangelical*)
3. Whenever individuals and entire groups are killed in the name of religion and the accounts written employ overtly religious rhetoric
4. Whenever killing acquires ritualistic qualities with references to religion

And what counted as *religious* in the early modern era? A whole lot. Religion was many things: beliefs, rituals, ethics, and, above all, an identity. Whenever religious differences tear apart a society, questions of identity loom large, for as soon as there is some "other" who is wrong, everyone is forced to choose an identity, or at least to pretend that he or she has made a choice: "I am this, not that." And it is this process of identification, for the self as well as for the group the self identifies with, that is most often at the root of all religious conflict.

The phrase "age of religious wars" was once the most common identifying label applied to an entire century, roughly 1550 to 1650, especially in textbooks. As used here, the term *war* carries a metaphorical punch, much as in the Cold War or the culture wars, for it is intended to evoke a real sense of conflict without implying that armies and battles must be involved in the narrative. In the early modern era, the armies and battles were all too real, but so too were riots, persecutions, martyrdoms, and other such forms of conflict caused by religious divisions. Making sense of the various ways violence unfolded requires patience, and an eye for details, along with a willingness to distinguish among the various regional manifestations of carnage.

Germany and Switzerland

From the very start, the Protestant Reformation caused enormous social and political strife and outright bloodshed linked to religion. The first areas affected by this violence were those where Protestantism had arisen: Germany and Switzerland. And the violence that erupted there set a pattern for all subsequent strife. It came in various forms—iconoclasm, persecutions, riots, rebellions, massacres, wars—and it was always so inextricably linked to worldly concerns that distinguishing between the sacred and profane was impossible. Though the unfolding of these Reformations has been covered already, an analysis of the violence engendered by them has been saved for this chapter, where more attention could be paid to it, in greater detail.

At the highest political level, the first epicenter of all contention was Martin Luther, whose defiance of pope and emperor at the Diet of Worms in 1521 turned him and all who aided him into outlaws. Frederick the Wise, Elector of Saxony, who rescued Luther and spirited him to safety at Wartburg castle, instantly created a conflict between himself and his nominal overlord, emperor Charles V, and the same went for any other prince or any city within the Holy Roman Empire that supported Lutheran reforms. To side with Luther was to challenge the emperor. Though Charles V sought to settle this conflict through peaceful means, and above all through a church council, a military response to Luther and his protectors and followers always remained an option and a very real possibility. It would be a quarter of a century before that warfare broke out between the emperor and his disobedient princes, but the threat of war hung like a pall over the Holy Roman Empire for decades.

At the local level, violence erupted almost immediately after Luther's condemnation at Worms. Luther's colleague Andreas Bodenstein von Karlstadt inspired iconoclastic riots in Wittenberg while Luther was hiding at Wartburg castle. Karlstadt's actions, in turn, created a conflict within the Lutheran camp itself, calling Luther's leadership into question, pitting Karlstadt and his followers against those who preferred a more cautious pace for religious reform. Luther quickly gained the upper hand on his return to Wittenberg in 1522, forcing Karlstadt to leave, but the rift created by this controversy never healed.

In Switzerland, iconoclasm began to take place around the same time, at first only sporadically, but it was gaining steady momentum in 1523–1524, and rapidly evolving into the wholesale destruction of images, relics, sacred vessels, and anything else deemed idolatrous. From 1525 until 1536 iconoclasm became the preferred revolutionary strategy of Protestants in the northern Swiss cantons. Though violence against images might seem inconsequential in our own day and age, it was a highly charged issue in the sixteenth century. Iconoclasm was about much more than the destruction of property: it was a challenge to the existence of a particular social and political order, and above all a means to a larger end, the abolition of the Roman Catholic Church at the local level. It is therefore not at all surprising that the arc of destruction that swept through the northern Swiss cantons ultimately led to war.

The Battle of Kappel, in October 1531, was one of the earliest armed conflicts in which Protestants and Catholic killed and maimed each other in the name of religion. This battle, which pitted about seven thousand Catholic warriors from five cantons against a mere two thousand combatants from Zurich, was a disaster for the Protestants. Several pastors were among the five hundred dead Zurichers who littered the battlefield when the fighting ceased, including none other than their chief reformer, Ulrich Zwingli. When Zurich sued for peace, the Catholic cantons responded with a compromise in a treaty known as the Second Peace of Kappel. The treaty was a recognition of the stalemate reached by the Swiss Confederacy, and the first legal recognition of the legitimacy of Protestant churches by Catholic authorities. The treaty allowed any community that had become Protestant to retain its legal privileges, and it stipulated that all thirteen cantons had the right to choose one or the other church, thus establishing two significant precedents: first, the right of communities to choose their religion, and second, the coexistence of two distinct churches within the same nation.

Though the arrangement was a wobbly, ad hoc compromise in the face of an intractable problem, rather than a well-thought-out solution, it would avert more bloodshed for years to come, in spite of constant friction between the two religions. In some communities Catholics and Protestants went as far as to share the use of a common church building. The Swiss, therefore, hold the distinction of being the first Europeans to go to war over the religious divisions caused by Protestantism, and also the first to find a peaceful compromise.

By the time the Swiss went to war with each other, however, religious violence of another sort had already swept through parts of northern Switzerland and much of Germany. The so-called Peasants' War of 1524–1525 was a disjointed series of uprisings driven by an incendiary interweaving of religious rhetoric and economic, political, and social grievances.[1] As we have already seen in chapter 9, many of the demands made by those who rose up against their superiors were couched in biblically based "Gospel" talk and Lutheran-sounding appeals to Christian freedom. The violent acts of the peasant rebels, which they sometimes defended with apocalyptic language, caused the potential targets of their wrath to react with even greater violence. Thomas Müntzer may not have been fully representative of the rebel movement he joined, but his rhetoric reflected a certain mentality that was distinctly religious, and which Catholics and Lutherans alike found alarming. His readiness to embrace violence, and his claim that the kingdom of Christ could be made manifest only through the slaughter of the "ungodly" propertied class by the "godly" peasants, provided a revealing glimpse of the bloodlust that could lurk beneath the surface in religious rhetoric.

It is no coincidence that Ulrich Zwingli, the urbane humanist, and Thomas Müntzer, the monomaniacal preacher-turned-rebel, both died in battle as warriors for a sacred cause. Though they were poles apart when it came to their theological vision, and could have gladly taken the field against each other, Zwingli and Müntzer shared a loathing for compromise and a willingness to encompass bloodshed as a necessary consequence of Gospel-based reforms. The rhetoric of violence could be merely ideological, but often it was a call to arms, and a weapon as deadly as any sword or piece of artillery.

Even as the peasant armies were being slaughtered, another sort of violence with a very long history took hold of the age—the violence of religious persecution and public executions. It all began gradually and unevenly, in various locations. In 1523 two Augustinian monks, Henry Voes and John Esch, had been burned at the stake in Brussels for espousing Lutheran doctrines. In 1524, in Vienna, Caspar Tauber had been beheaded and burnt for denying purgatory and transubstantiation; and in Holstein, Hendrik van Zutphen, another Augustinian monk, had been burnt at the stake as a Lutheran. In 1525, the first Protestant iconoclast was executed in France by Catholic authorities: Jean Leclerc, a wool carder from Meaux, who was tortured with exceptional ferocity before being consigned to the flames. Similar isolated cases did not make for a wave of persecution, but they did reaffirm an ancient paradigm: heretics deserved a painful death and little mercy; and they merited a very public execution, both as an expiatory ritual cleansing of the community they had polluted with their errors and as a warning to others who might have been lured or inspired by them.

It did not take long for Protestants to carry out their own persecutions—not so much against Catholics, relatively few of whom were killed at first, but rather against their own "false brethren." Luther was troubled by heretics within his own camp from early on, but he did not resort to violence directly. By 1525, he had driven Karlstadt, Müntzer, and the Zwickau Prophets out of Wittenberg, and he had refrained from calling for their deaths. Yet when it came to rebellion rather than heresy, Luther was willing to contemplate violence, and to call for the slaughter of the peasant rebels, whom he compared to rabid dogs. Zwingli took a harsher approach. By 1525, under his leadership, the city of Zurich was aggressively harassing those who refused to accept infant baptism. And in 1527, when adult rebaptism was declared a capital crime, the execution of Anabaptist "heretics" became routine. The first of these martyrs, Felix Mantz, was drowned in Lake Zurich, a fitting punishment, according to the Zwinglians, for someone who had abused the waters of baptism. After Mantz, other Anabaptists would bravely endure martyrdom, or flee to safer corners of the map. Ironically, but logically, martyrdom confirmed for them their identity as the true church of Christ, a most painful self-fulfilling prophecy.

Not all Anabaptists were willing to undergo martyrdom. The same violent apocalyptic obsessions that had driven Thomas Müntzer affected other radicals. Convinced that the time had come for the establishment of the New Jerusalem, Melchior Hoffman managed to gain like-minded disciples, first in Strassburg, and later in Münster, in northwestern Germany. The so-called Melchiorites who took over the city of Münster in 1534 knew no moderation, and they held mercy toward the "godless" in contempt. Their violent rule in Münster, where private property was abolished and polygamy and routine executions became the norm, proved beyond a shadow of a doubt for contemporaries that religion could go horribly wrong. The three cages containing the mangled remains of the leaders of the Münsterite kingdom, which hung from the steeple of St. Lambert's church, were intended as a warning sign to all potential heretics. For those perceptive enough to grasp their meaning, the events at Münster presaged more such horrors to come; for those who focused only on the immediate events, Münster was frightful enough all on its own. Unfortunately, those who could see beyond the immediate events would be proved right.

As far as the Holy Roman Empire as a whole was concerned, religious violence remained fairly well contained for decades. But that containment was mostly accidental. Charles V hoped to settle religious divisions through a council, but since it was also clear to him that this option was not really open, he wished to see the enforcement of the 1521 Edict of Worms and the eradication of Protestantism, and if he had only had the relative calm to focus on Germany, he would have gladly waged war against the Lutheran princes who defied him and betrayed the Roman Catholic faith. But his distractions were far too numerous and pressing. His French archrival, Francis I, never gave him a moment's rest, especially in Italy. He managed to capture Francis at the Battle of Pavia in 1525, holding him prisoner in Madrid, and extracted a pledge of nonaggression from him in 1526, but Francis bounced back more fiercely, allying himself with Protestant princes, and even with the Ottoman Turks. And the Turks were a much worse distraction. Their continual advance through the Balkans into the heart of Europe seemed unstoppable and caused no end of grief for Charles V. By 1529, they were at the gates of Vienna, laying siege to the very heart of Charles's ancestral Hapsburg lands. Chasing away the Turks from Vienna offered little relief; they continued to lurk ever so close and were able to annex Hungary in 1541.

Charles also had other formidable distractions: popes who schemed against him; Muslim pirates in the Mediterranean; and the ever-restive conquistadores and natives who were his to rule across the Atlantic Ocean, as king of Spain. The ultimate irony of Charles V's long reign, and the most convincing proof of his inability to control events, was the sack of Rome in 1527 by thirty-four thousand of his soldiers—fourteen thousand of whom were Germans—and the imprisonment of Pope Clement VII by these rioting troops. Had Pope Clement not joined the League of Cognac formed by Francis I, and had Charles not been drawn further into conflict in Italy, he could have easily sent that very same army into Saxony, sacked Wittenberg, and captured Luther.

Just as Charles V had to worry about Francis I and the Turks constantly, so too all Protestant princes in Germany had to worry about Charles. They knew all too well that if his other enemies ever gave him rest, Charles would most likely pounce on the Lutherans. Historical hindsight allows us to take the survival of Lutheranism for granted, but for Protestants in the 1520s and 1530s, disaster seemed just around the corner. Consequently, forming military alliances was an absolute necessity. When Landgrave Philip of Hesse gathered the major Protestant Reformers at Marburg in 1529, his intention was to form a coalition of all who opposed Rome and the emperor. But theological differences proved too large, making it impossible to form a Swiss-German pan-Protestant bund, or alliance. The end result was instead the creation of the Schmalkaldic League, in 1531, a defensive bund of German Lutheran principalities and cities led by Philip of Hesse and John Frederick I of Saxony. In 1538, Lutheran Denmark also joined. Membership in the league guaranteed the support of the other members in case of an attack by Charles V. Although this was a defensive alliance, the league constantly harassed Charles V by expanding the reach of Lutheranism through the addition of new states and the confiscation of church lands.

Fractured Germany was reluctantly granted peace by Charles V for fifteen years after the formation of the Schmalkaldic League. In 1546, however, thanks to the convergence of several factors, Charles was finally free to take on his renegade Lutheran subjects. First, Luther died in February; then Charles reached an accord with Pope Paul III, who gave his blessing and support:

> In the name of God and with the help and assistance of his Papal Holiness, his Imperial Majesty should prepare himself for war, and equip himself with soldiers and everything pertaining to warfare against those who objected to the Council [of Trent], against the Schmalkald League, and against all who were addicted to the false belief and error in Germany, and that he do so with all his power and might, in order to bring them back to the old faith and to the obedience of the Holy See.[2]

Such a blessing was not enough, however. What tipped the scales in 1546 was that Charles found himself in a rare moment of truce with his archrivals Francis I and the Turks, and that he managed to get one of the leading Lutheran princes, Duke Moritz of Saxony, to break ranks and fight against his Lutheran brethren. The defection by Moritz, who remained Lutheran, allowed Charles V to claim that his campaign against the Schmalkaldic League was strictly political—an assertion of his authority over his vassals—rather than some sort of religious war, but all involved knew that Charles's ultimate goal was the religious reunification of the Holy Roman Empire. Charles V descended upon the league with his imperial troops—one-third of them Spanish—in the spring of 1547. In March

1547, King Francis I died; in April, at the Battle of Mühlberg, the Lutherans were defeated. Finally, Charles was on top. Both Luther and Francis I were out of the picture and the two leading Schmalkaldic princes, Landgrave Philip of Hesse and John Frederick I, Elector of Saxony, were imprisoned. Charles V rewarded Duke Moritz for his betrayal of the league by transferring to him the electorship that had been held by the vanquished John Frederick. The annihilation of the Lutheran Church was a very real possibility.

Trouncing the Lutheran princes was not the same thing as doing away with Lutheranism, however. Convinced that he could effect a reconciliation between Rome and Lutheran Germany, Charles V embarked on the ambitious and thankless task of working out a compromise that would allow his Lutheran subjects to return to the Catholic fold without abandoning their religious convictions. This was a difficult enough task, but it was made all the harder by the fact that Charles V still believed that the ultimate resolution lay in the hands of the Council of Trent. In other words, Charles pinned his hopes on something that was ultimately beyond his control, rather than on his military victory. The end result of Charles V's high-minded reconciliation project was a *formula reformationis* titled "Declaration of His Roman Imperial Majesty on the Observance of Religion Within the Holy Empire Until the Decision of the General Council"—a troublesome blueprint for reform better known as the Augsburg Interim. Its basic premise was its chief flaw: the authors of the Augsburg Interim assumed that on most issues, Catholics and Lutherans could reach compromises, and that a union between the two churches could be imposed from above, by law. The document, which was drafted chiefly by a Catholic bishop, Julius von Pflug, with the aid of several other Catholic churchmen and one Lutheran theologian, Johann Agricola, laid out all of the compromises in twenty-six articles. Though the Catholics made some concessions, the Augsburg Interim yielded no ground to the Lutherans on most issues, and it proved a ticking time bomb, theologically and politically.

In essence, the Augsburg Interim required that Lutherans become Catholics again. They were to accept the authority of the pope, to reinstate bishops, to accept seven sacraments, and to return to Catholic rituals and practices. They also had to accept Catholic teachings they had rejected, such as transubstantiation and saintly intercession, and to abandon teachings central to their faith, including those of *sola scriptura* and *sola fide*. The concessions made to the Lutherans were superficial rather than substantial: they were given the right to have married clergy and to receive communion under both species of bread and wine.

Approved at the Diet of Augsburg in 1548, the interim was not well received by either camp. Though it had been authored largely by Catholics and was much more favorable to Catholics than to Lutherans, Pope Paul III viewed the interim as a challenge to his own authority and at first refused to approve it. Catholic princes tended to reject it too, on the grounds that it served only to give the emperor more authority over them. On the Lutheran side, many rulers and pastors rejected the interim outright and refused to obey it. Enforcement proved difficult in areas where Charles V had no troops garrisoned, although in some places, such as Swabia, recalcitrant pastors were exiled or imprisoned, and in a few rare cases, even martyred. In northern Germany, Bremen and Magdeburg went as far as to defy the emperor and take up arms against him, and Magdeburg became a center of resistance, full of recalcitrant refugees. Prominent Reformers were affected: Martin Bucer, for instance, refused to comply and fled from Strassburg to England. The Augsburg Interim also created deep fissures within the Lutheran Church itself and planted seeds of discord that would later yield a bitter harvest.

Had Luther still been alive, this inner conflict might have been avoided, for he would have surely rejected the interim outright. But the man who had begun to assume Luther's mantle, Philip Melanchthon, had always been much more willing to compromise and make peace. Unwittingly, by playing the role of conciliator, Melanchthon sowed greater discord among his own. Dissatisfied with the Augsburg Interim but eager to find a peaceful solution to religious quarreling, Melanchthon produced his own "interim" with the backing of the turncoat Moritz of Saxony. This so-called Leipzig Interim held firm on theological issues, defending core Lutheran beliefs, but allowing for concessions on issues of ritual and practice, arguing that some rites were "indifferent" or nonessential (termed *adiaphora*), that is, insufficiently significant to stand in the way of union between Lutherans and Catholics. As one slogan put it, "In essentials, unity; in nonessentials, liberty; and in all things, charity."

Though some of the items considered *adiaphora* by Melanchthon were indeed small, such as liturgical rubrics, others were not, such as the reinstatement of bishops, or the sacraments of confirmation and extreme unction. Though some Lutherans accepted the line drawn by Melanchthon between essential and nonessential issues, many found his compromises totally or partially unacceptable. Ultimately, all that the Leipzig Interim accomplished was the creation of two opposing camps within the Lutheran Church: those who sided with Melanchthon, who came to be known as Philippists, and those who opposed his crypto-Catholic accommodations, who called themselves Gnesio-Lutherans, or "genuine" Lutherans. The rift created by the controversy over adiaphora only grew wider over time, extending into other more substantial theological issues. Eventually, as we shall see in the next chapter, this doctrinal wrangling would nearly wreck the Lutheran Church from within, proving that inner factionalism could be much more dangerous than any Catholic emperor.

Had Charles V been able to maintain his grip in Germany, there is no telling where the Augsburg and Leipzig interims might have led. But that is not what happened. After a few dissent-filled years of half measures, during which the religious divisions in Germany remained largely unchanged, the ungainly and divisive compromises devised by Charles V and Melanchthon ultimately gave way first to war, and then to the acceptance of a stalemate. In April 1552, the inconstant Moritz of Saxony switched sides again, allied himself with King Henry II of France, secretly assembled a large army, and pounced on Charles V, who was once again busy preparing to fight France. First, Moritz and his fellow Lutheran princes surprised everyone by marching on Augsburg and capturing it, just as the Imperial Diet assembled there. Charles V was not ready to respond. Confident that the victory he had achieved over the Lutheran princes in 1547 was complete, he had left himself exposed in Innsbruck without a substantial army. Moritz then chased down the hapless Charles and nearly captured him. Charles fled across the mountains to Carinthia, where he suddenly found himself disgracefully vanquished and bereft of any army. The victory at Mühlberg had been undone in one fell swoop, and so had all the emperor's plans for the religious reunification of Germany.

War between the Lutherans and imperial forces continued for a few more months, but the outcome of this so-called Rebellion of the Princes was already evident when Charles V made his undignified retreat from Innsbruck. In August 1552, Charles signed away all of his imperial dreams in a truce known as the Peace of Passau. The terms were steep: Philip of Hesse and John Frederick of Saxony were to be freed and restored to their realms, and all provisions of the Augsburg Interim were to be instantly nullified. Though the final capitulation of Charles would not be sealed for another three years, with his signing of the Peace of Augsburg in 1555, the terms agreed on at Passau confirmed the Lutheran victory. Passau also marked the end of religious warfare in Germany, at least for the following sixty years or so, and the beginning of a new order in which the question of religion was left entirely in the hands of local rulers, be they princes, dukes, or city councils. The Latin formula devised to describe the new status quo confirmed by the Peace of Augsburg was simple enough: *cuius regio, eius religio.* Freely rendered into English, it affirmed, "Religion belongs to the ruler." In essence, the settlement at Augsburg in 1555 closely resembled the arrangement that the Swiss had devised for themselves in 1531. Confessional fragmentation had become the order of the day in the Holy Roman Empire, and with it came an uneasy and grudging sort of toleration, rife with friction. Ultimately, the Peace of Augsburg diminished the emperor's power and augmented the independence of each of the three hundred states within the empire's chaotic map, creating an uneasy truce that rested on a political and military stalemate, as well as on a powder keg of unresolved tensions in Germany. In sum, an armistice was reached that gave Germans some sixty years of relative peace, but it would cost them dearly during the Thirty Years' War of 1618–1648.

France

During the first few decades of the Reformation era, while Switzerland and Germany felt the sting of religious violence, France remained relatively quiet. But as early as 1525, when the first execution of a Protestant heretic took place, it seemed evident that bloodshed was inevitable.

Unlike Switzerland, with its loose confederate structure, and unlike the Holy Roman Empire, with its weak emperor, France had a strong centralized monarchy and a vigorous king who could insist on religious uniformity and brook no dissent. *Un roi, une loi, une foi*—"one king, one law, one faith"—was the motto that guided Francis I in his dealings with Protestants in his realm. It mattered little that King Francis made military allegiances with Protestant princes in Germany, or even with the Muslim Turks. Francis viewed these arrangements with foreigners as mere strategic moves, intended to safeguard the well-being and autonomy of his kingdom. When it came to religion, his sole concern was France. French kings had a long tradition of jealously guarding their right to substantial control over the Catholic Church in their realm, and of thinking of the church on local rather than universal terms. They also viewed their royal office as sacred in character and inseparable from the church itself. What heretics did beyond the borders of France was therefore inconsequential for Francis, but what they did within France was of the utmost importance. To challenge the church, as he saw it, was to challenge the legitimacy of his rule.

Throughout the 1520s and early 1530s, the Protestant cause grew steadily in France, in small pockets, quietly, almost invisibly. The constant threat of persecution by the crown led to the emergence of two sorts of Protestants in France during this early period: those who resolutely broke with Rome, who were always relatively few in number, and those who sought to reform the Catholic Church gradually from within even though they agreed in principle with many or all of the tenets of Protestantism, whose numbers could never be counted. The reforming circle of bishop Guillaume Briçonnet and his disciples in Meaux was a prime example of this polarization, for while it produced zealous Protestants like Guillaume Farel, it also cultivated a hidden sort of dissent. The same was true of the court of the king's sister, Renée de France, Duchess of Ferrara, who harbored both types of dissenters. Those who chose to break with Rome openly gravitated toward the Protestantism of the Swiss Reformed rather than toward Lutheranism. Given the king's intolerance of religious dissent, these self-proclaimed "evangelicals" had but two stark choices: to risk life and limb by openly challenging the Catholic Church, or to flee from France. In choosing one path or the other, they necessarily made themselves scarce, through either martyrdom or exile. Those who were less zealous and willing to compromise eventually earned the name Nicodemites—an allusion to the Pharisee Nicodemus, who would visit Jesus only in secret. These men and women believed that what mattered the most was one's unseen interior relationship with the divine rather than any external observances, and that it was therefore permissible to attend Catholic rituals and pretend to be a good Catholic to escape persecution. The exact origin of *Nicodemite* remains a matter of debate, but one thing is beyond dispute: it quickly became a dirty word among those who chose not to follow their path, like John Calvin.

Nicodemites were viewed by zealous Protestants as a serious obstacle to growth, since their willingness to hide and dissemble made the establishment of a Reformed Church unnecessary. Consequently, the leaders of the Reformed cause condemned Nicodemism in the strongest possible terms. In their writings, John Calvin and Pierre Viret made it clear that all who wanted to side with the truth had but two choices: to stand firm against the Catholic Church in France or to seek exile.

Ironically, it was persecution and exile that eventually caused the French Reformed Church to grow. The turning point came in October 1534, with the so-called Affair of the Placards, when stalwart evangelicals hung posters in Paris and other French cities denouncing the Catholic mass, and King Francis reacted with unforgiving violence. Suspects were rounded up throughout the realm, tried, and executed. In addition, Francis tightened up censorship in the nascent printing industry, and established a court dedicated expressly to the prosecution of heresy—a court so fiercely dedicated to its task that it came to be known as the Chambre Ardente, or the "Burning Court." Hundreds fled for their lives. Among them was John Calvin, who not only found refuge in Geneva, but also managed to turn that city-state—beyond the reach of King Francis's authority—into the prime training center for missionaries to send into France. Another later refugee was the lawyer-turned-printer Jean Crespin, who also ended up in Geneva and helped produce hundreds of Protestant texts that would find their way into France, including his own account of the martyrdoms endured by Protestants. Crespin's *Book of Martyrs*, first published in 1554, would go through numerous editions and become one of the most significant texts of the French Reformation. It was not only a compendium of the violence employed in persecution, but also a primer for developing resolve in the face of inhuman cruelty, and perhaps for accepting religious violence as an inescapable fact of life. Some who read Crespin's work perhaps turned it into a wellspring of righteous anger as well.

Not much growth took place in the French Reformed Church during the remainder of Francis I's reign, to 1547. The king's tight and efficient grip included the persecution of heresy. In addition, the evangelicals in exile were powerless: all they could do was to offer assistance to new refugees and train ministers. With the death of Francis the situation changed. King Henry II was in all respects much weaker a ruler than his father, even though he eagerly continued to pursue the war against Charles V. His reign was marked by an increase in the autonomy of the nobility and the appearance of factions at court, and especially by the rise to prominence of three aristocratic families that would eventually play a key role in the unraveling of France: the Guises, the Montmorencys, and the Bourbons. Through intrigue and constant infighting, these three factions did their utmost to weaken the power of the crown and to return France to an earlier medieval model: a feudal realm in which the king was a figurehead and the nobility ran their fiefdoms as they saw fit. This slippage in central authority would prove extremely favorable to the growth of Protestantism, which could gain the support and protection of local nobles. But it proved disastrous for the unity of France.

The political disintegration of France only increased in intensity when King Henry II was killed in a jousting accident in 1559, while celebrating the peace treaty of Cateau-Cambrésis he had just signed with Spain, ending the Hapsburg-Valois Wars. The three young sons of Henry II who followed him on the throne in relatively quick succession were even weaker rulers than their father, and their reigns were marked by the influence of their Italian-born mother, Catherine de' Medici and by a downward spiraling into anarchy and civil war. Fifteen-year-old King Francis II could do nothing during his brief reign (1559–1560) to stop the exponential growth of the Reformed Church throughout his realm, especially in areas that had traditionally asserted their independence: Gascony, Dauphiné, and Languedoc in the south; Normandy in the north; Brittany and Poitou in the west. His younger brother, who was aged ten when he came to the throne, as Charles IX, could do even less. His reign, from 1560 to 1574, coincided with the beginning of the so-called Wars of Religion, and would be chaotic and bloody. His brother and successor, Henry III (1574–1589), could do nothing to stop the bloodshed and would oversee even worse chaos.

The unprecedented growth of the Huguenot churches had begun in the 1550s, under Henry II. By 1560, thanks in large measure to the efforts of John Calvin and the exile community in Geneva, France had been flooded with Protestant texts and with well-trained missionaries who quickly established vigorous, disciplined dissenting churches wherever the local authorities were favorably disposed. Many in the nobility had also been won over, making the Calvinist churches even more secure, and ever bolder in their commitment to convert all of France. By 1561 there were roughly 2,150 Reformed churches throughout France, all worshiping openly, establishing disciplinary consistories at the local level, and holding regional and national synods. These Calvinists, who came to be known as Huguenots, were still a minority—outnumbered about fifteen to one in the total population—but they were very well organized, highly committed, and disproportionately composed of merchant and professional elites and about two-fifths of the nobility. So thickly concentrated in some areas as to be an actual local majority here and there, Huguenot communities formed a virtual archipelago of Calvinist islands scattered throughout France. They could also be found nearly everywhere, in areas in between. And they had powerful patrons among the high nobility, including the Bourbon family.

Emboldened by their rapid growth and their escalating power, some Huguenot communities began to follow the subversive iconoclastic pattern established by the Swiss Reformed back in the 1520s. This new war against idolatry began in Rouen and La Rochelle in 1560, when churches were attacked and images demolished. The iconoclasm soon spread, despite Calvin's strong condemnation of it. "I proclaim far and wide," he said, "that if I were a judge I would punish these furious attacks no less harshly than the King demands in his edicts."[3] Violence will only beget violence, he warned. And he was right. In 1561, the Huguenots' idol smashing spread to more than twenty cities and towns. Unlike the Swiss, who had organized public debates as a response to iconoclasm, the French resorted to sheer violence: in Tours, Carcassonne, Cahors, Sens, and other cities, Catholics carried out bloody reprisals against the Huguenots. In a last-ditch effort to avert disaster, the queen regent, Catherine de' Medici, arranged for a meeting of Catholic and Calvinist theologians at Poissy, in 1561, hoping the two competing churches could iron out some sort of compromise. Like all other such attempts at reconciliation, the Colloquy of Poissy failed miserably, and it was soon made totally irrelevant by circumstances. In March 1562, Francis, Duke of Guise, who was on his way home with two hundred troops, came upon some Huguenots holding worship services in a barn in the town of Vassy, within his territories in northeastern France. By this time the Guise family—one of the three competing noble factions at court—had assumed leadership of the Catholic cause, and was resolutely committed to accomplishing what the king and his mother could not: the annihilation of the Huguenot church in France. Though Catherine de' Medici had issued an edict in January 1562 that granted Huguenots the right to worship privately within towns and cities and publicly outside their precincts, the Duke of Guise chose to interrupt the Huguenot service. Scuffles followed between the Huguenots and the duke's troops. Rocks were hurled, and shots were fired. Before long, the barn had been set ablaze, scores of Huguenots had been slaughtered and hundreds more maimed and wounded. This massacre at Vassy sparked a whirlwind of further religious violence, initiating the conflict known as the French Wars of Religion, which would devastate France over the following thirty-six years.

Historians have imposed much more order upon this bloody civil conflict than it merits by distinguishing nine separate wars between 1562 and 1598, most of them relatively brief and self-contained. In truth, these "wars" should be seen as one long protracted struggle in which religion was the prime factor, and in which much of the violence acquired an aura of sacrality and was not at all limited to soldiers. Yes, other factors played a role too—social, political, economic, cultural, and geographic—but there is no getting around the fact that religious differences were the cause and the driving force of much of the mayhem. And the conflict reached a stalemate in 1598, rather than a resolution, continuing to simmer throughout much of the seventeenth century as well, and lending French culture a singularly peculiar perspective on religion. The intensity and scale of the slaughter, and the ritualization of violence gave the French Wars of Religion a distinctive character. Seldom before had religion led to such carnage and so much deliberate cruelty, especially within one nation: not even the savage Albigensian Crusade of the thirteenth century could match these wars in terms of scale. And the earlier religious wars in Germany and Switzerland were so dwarfed as to seem subdued in comparison.

Once the fighting began, no one was able to stop it. With a succession of weak monarchs on the throne, the polarized nobility seized enough control of the kingdom's resources to wage war on one another unchecked. The populace as a whole was swept up in the violence, sometimes as unwitting victims, sometimes—indeed often—as eager participants. Though soldiers were engaged, and battles between armies punctuated the conflict, noncombatants could also take part and pay or exact a heavy price, depending on which end of the sword they found themselves. Sieges, massacres, assassinations and executions took their toll on the population, as did riots and foraging armies. Vengeance and retribution became the order of the day, and a way of life. Hatred trumped Christian charity, and all the vitriol found its way into print, giving rise to a veritable flood of texts that fueled the killing and gave rise to the printing of more poisonous texts, in a never-ending vicious cycle. In sum, France became hell on earth.

Immediately after the massacre of Vassy, the Huguenots took up arms against the Catholics, even though Calvin was opposed to the use of violence and rebellion against established authorities. The fighting that ensued was sporadic, punctuated by numerous truces and peace treaties that were ignored, and by mob violence on both sides. A simple listing of the ever-shifting leadership of both sides of this civil war reveals four key aspects of the Wars of Religion: brutality; the complex, chaotic, ever-shifting cast of characters; the dominant role of the Bourbon and Guise families; and last, but not least, the fact that so many of its leaders were named Henry.

The Huguenots were first led by Louis I de Bourbon (b. 1530), the first Prince de Condé, until he was killed in battle in 1569. Leadership then passed to a non-Bourbon, Admiral Gaspard de Coligny (b. 1519), until he was assassinated in 1572. From then on, two Bourbons assumed command: Henry, Prince de Condé (b. 1552) and son of the late Louis, and his cousin Henry of Navarre (1553–1610), son of Queen Jeanne d'Albret of Navarre and brother-in-law to the late Louis. After Henry, Prince de Condé, died in 1588, from wounds suffered in battle, his cousin Henry of Navarre assumed sole leadership.

On the Catholic side, the leading role was played not by the Valois kings, but by the Guises. Their first leader, Francis, Duke of Guise (b. 1519), was assassinated in 1563. He was succeeded by his brother Charles, cardinal of Lorraine (b. 1524), a formidable power broker at court, and by his son Henry, Duke of Guise (b. 1550), an able military commander. When Cardinal Charles died in 1574, of natural causes—one of the few leaders to do so—he was succeeded by his nephew, Louis (b. 1555), the brother of Henry. These two Guise brothers, Duke Henry and Cardinal Louis, then led the Catholic faction, which they formally organized into a coalition known as the Catholic League, until they were both assassinated on orders of King Henry III, less than a day apart, on 23 and 24 December 1588. Eight months later, on 1 August 1589, King Henry III himself would be killed in revenge by a Dominican friar. The nobles of the Catholic League founded by the Guises, several of whom were part of the family and equally committed to the annihilation of the Huguenots and the Bourbons, would keep fighting King Henry IV until 1598, even after he became Catholic. The end came through a combination of factors, chief of which were the exhaustion of the nation and King Henry IV's adroitness at restoring authority to the crown.

Leaders of the French Wars of Religion, 1562–1598

Catholics	Huguenots
Francis, Duke of Guise—killed 1563	Louis de Bourbon, Prince de Condé—killed 1569
Charles, Cardinal of Lorraine—died 1579	
Catholic League—established 1576	Admiral Gaspard de Coligny—killed 1572
Henry, Duke of Guise—killed 1588	Henry, Prince de Condé—killed 1588
Louis, Cardinal of Lorraine—killed 1588	Henry of Navarre (King Henry IV)—converts to Catholicism in 1593; killed 1610
Catholic League—allied with Spain 1589–1598	

This agonizing bloodbath can be summed up on the political level as a collapse of central authority in France in which a succession of powerful nobles who financed their armies with tax revenues battled it out against one another, taking control of specific regions and cities, fragmenting the realm and marginalizing the crown. On a social level, the Wars of Religion can be summed up as the extreme polarization of an entire nation in which identities were radically reshuffled and religious and regional allegiances trumped all others, and in which long-held rules of civility were abandoned altogether. At both of these levels, the normal function of religion became reversed: instead of acting as a "social glue"—that term so favored by functionalist social scientists—it acted as a social dynamite, or an acid that dissolved common bonds and caused conflict.

Though historians have identified nine separate wars, it is more instructive to see this conflict in light of four distinct phases. First, during the decade of 1562–1572 the Huguenots stood firm, gained some ground, and forced a stalemate. The second phase was astonishingly brief and brutal, for it comprises the St. Bartholomew's Day Massacre of August 1572. Though short in duration, this event dwarfs all others in the long history of the wars, in terms of both scale and impact. It began in Paris, where all of the leading

Sacred mayhem. The St. Bartholomew's Day massacre in Paris, August 1572, as depicted by François Dubois, a Huguenot painter. Dubois condenses time and space in this horrifying tableau, showing the viewer events that occurred at different times of the day in places that are not near each other. In doing so, Dubois provides a visual narrative of the event. In addition to giving the viewer a sense of the wanton carnage—most evident in the corpse-clogged Seine River—Dubois highlights two key events: at the top, near the center, we see Queen Regent Marie de' Medici gloating over a pile of corpses at the entrance to the Louvre Palace; in the second building to the right of that scene we see the murder of Admiral Coligny, whose body is being hurled from a window.

Huguenots had assembled to celebrate an ostensibly peacemaking wedding between their leader, Henry of Navarre, and the Catholic Margaret de Valois, the sister of King Charles IX. A few days after the wedding, on 24 August, the feast of St. Bartholomew, following orders from the king himself, who had been convinced by his mother, Catherine de' Medici, that the Huguenots were plotting to kill him, a massacre of the Huguenots began. At first, only the Huguenot leaders were slain by the king's men. Gaspard de Coligny, chief among the Huguenot elites, was one of the first to be brutally murdered; he was killed in his chambers and his body then taken outside and mutilated by a mob, dragged through the streets and hung upside down. Reports of his head being sent to Rome circulated, but, in fact, no such grisly parcel ever reached the pope. The other leading Huguenots, Henry of Navarre and his cousin the Prince de Condé, managed to cheat death by feigning a conversion to Catholicism. Few others were as fortunate, or inconstant.

As the Huguenot corpses began to pile up in the streets, Catholic Parisians joined in the slaughter, hunting down and killing as many of their Calvinist neighbors as they could find. Somewhere between two thousand and three thousand men, women, and children of all ranks were stabbed and hacked to death in their homes or out in the open during the following three days; many of the slain were dragged through the streets or piled into carts and dumped into the Seine River, which ran red with their blood. And that was just the beginning, for thousands more were similarly slaughtered by mobs throughout France as soon as the news radiated out from Paris. No one knows exactly how many thousands died altogether, but recent conservative estimates range between totals of seven thousand and ten thousand. At the highest levels of European civil and ecclesiastical power, the reaction was mixed. Emperor Maximilian II was as appalled as all Protestant rulers. In Spain, King Philip II was delighted by the news. In Rome, Pope Gregory XII sent King Charles IX a golden rose, ordered a Te Deum to be sung in thanksgiving, and commissioned Giorgio Vasari to paint three murals in the papal Sala Regia depicting scenes from the massacre. He also issued a medal to commemorate the slaughter. The medal bore his likeness on one side, and an avenging angel on the reverse, sword in hand, hovering over a heap of Huguenot corpses.

After this bloodbath, the surviving Huguenots hardened in their resolve, and shifted their political and theological thinking toward more aggressive arguments for resistance. The intensity of the violence increased, too. A third phase began in 1573 and lasted until 1589, during which indecisive combat led to a further fragmentation of France and the War of the Three Henrys, in which the Huguenot leader Henry of Navarre, Henry of Guise and his Catholic League, and King Henry III battled one another, and the line between religion and politics was blurred more than ever. This phase, which also saw the rise of the *politiques*—those Frenchmen who preferred to put religion aside altogether for the sake of peace—ended with the assassination of the heirless King Henry III, with the next in line to the throne being none other than the Huguenot Henry of Navarre. The fourth and final phase, which brought more political chaos, but was less destructive and less overtly religious in nature, lasted from 1589 to 1598.

Bereft of their assassinated leader Henry of Guise, the nobles of the Catholic League allied themselves with the Spanish King Philip II, battled the newly crowned Huguenot King Henry IV, and managed to maintain control of several areas, including Paris. After a long and unsuccessful siege of the capital city, hoping to neutralize his opposition, King Henry IV abjured his Huguenot faith and joined the Catholic Church in July 1593. "Paris is worth a Mass," he supposedly joked. Sincere or not, the conversion worked in King Henry's favor, for in addition to securing his control of Paris, it knocked the wind out of the Catholic League and won him the allegiance of the *politiques* and many a moderate noble. Over the following five years, through negotiations, financial deals, and a few successes on the battlefield, Henry IV triumphed over his Catholic League rivals, one by one, and solidified his position. In April 1598 he was able to proclaim the Edict of Nantes, which granted legal toleration to the Huguenots. The opposition had melted away by then. When the Spanish sued for peace in May, as King Philip II was close to death, the success of the edict was ensured. Religion had finally been put aside for the time being, and the bloodletting brought to an end. France regained its collective sanity relatively quickly. Freed from a suicidal inner conflict, it also began to reclaim its place on the European stage.

The Edict of Nantes guaranteed the coexistence of Protestants and Catholics in France and restored the civil rights of Huguenots, including the right to establish their own church and worship as they saw fit, and the right to work for the state or in any profession. It also gave them the right to petition the king directly, and ensured royal protection from the Inquisition for any French subject traveling abroad. The edict was a limited compromise, however, not a total acceptance of religious freedom. It reaffirmed the Roman Catholic Church as the official religion of France, and it dealt only with Huguenots and Catholics, making no mention of Anabaptists, or any other religious minorities. It also required everyone in the realm to pay a tithe to the Catholic Church, placed restrictions on Catholic-Protestant intermarriage, and demanded that Huguenots respect Catholic holidays. Its most significant restriction placed absolute geographical boundaries on the Reformed Church, which was to be limited strictly to the cities, towns, and areas where it was already established, thus stifling the expansion of the Huguenot church.

While the edict did bring an end to the bloodshed and the chaos, Catholic-Huguenot animosities continued to simmer. The Wars of Religion had left the French scarred and incapable of full reconciliation, and the Edict of Nantes itself stood in the way of absolute toleration. King Henry IV deserves credit for restoring calm, but, ultimately, no king could erase the lingering aftereffects of the trauma endured by his people, or the hatred that continued to fester. In May 1610, Henry IV was stabbed to death by François Ravaillac, a Catholic fanatic who claimed to receive messages from God that condemned King Henry for his leniency toward the Huguenots. In some ways, Henry's assassination can be viewed as a continuation of the Wars of Religion: it may have been the act of a madman, but it nonetheless revealed the continued existence of deep antagonisms within France, and of the enduring allure of violence to those who took religion to heart. In other words, though Ravaillac acted on his own, his actions clearly mirrored the many massacres carried out by French men and women over the span of an entire generation and of Pope Gregory XII's hearty approval of the St. Bartholomew's Day Massacre.

The ultimate legacy of the Edict of Nantes is not easily assessed. Sporadic fighting continued after Henry IV's death. Three Huguenot rebellions would erupt in the 1620s. Henry IV's successor, King Louis XIII (r. 1610–1643), quelled these uprisings with swift ferocity, sometimes revivifying the old rituals of violence. For instance, in 1622, the Huguenot town of Nègrepelisse was burned to the ground and all its inhabitants massacred; in 1627–1628, the fourteen-month-long siege of the Huguenot port city of La Rochelle reduced its population from twenty-five thousand to five thousand. After these rebellions were crushed, Louis XIII stripped the Huguenots of all the military, territorial, and self-governing rights they had been granted by the Edict of Nantes, debasing even further their already inferior status. His successor, Louis XIV (r. 1643–1715), would go further, revoking the edict in 1685 and renewing persecution. Hundreds of thousands of Huguenots fled France, and full religious liberty was not restored until 1787, a full century later. By that time, the legacy of intolerance and violence in France had become emblematic of all that was wrong with religion for skeptics and atheists such as Voltaire (1694–1778) and the Baron d'Holbach (1723–1789). In the long run, then, religion itself became the ultimate victim of the religious violence created in France by the Reformation.

The Netherlands

At about the same time that France sank into violent mayhem, the neighboring Low Countries entered a similar nightmare. The catalyst, again, was religion, and the growth of Calvinist communities. Unlike in France, however, the violence in the Netherlands was linked to a war of independence. So, although not all Netherlanders shared the same faith and sometimes fought against one another, the larger thrust of the conflict was not a fratricidal war, but a struggle against a despised foreign ruler who sought to enforce religious uniformity along with authoritarian rule. It was a complex and prolonged war, which, like others of its age, involved civilians and blurred the line between religion and all other aspects of life, but in which religion stood out as a major cause of much of the violence.

The Low Countries were one of the most densely populated and urbanized regions of Europe, and they enjoyed the highest per capita income. Much like Switzerland, the Netherlands was a patchwork political entity defined not so much by ethnic, linguistic, or dynastic unity as by a history of interaction, mutual interests, and geography. Three languages were spoken within the Low Countries: Dutch and Flemish in the north (both variants of Low German), and Walloon, a dialect of French in the south. The southern city of Antwerp—one of the most prosperous in all of Europe—was a major commercial center for products from northern and southern Europe. Fishing, farming, cloth manufacturing, and overseas trade made the area self-sufficient and affluent. Politically, the seventeen provinces of the Low Countries were a product of medieval feudal arrangements: bound by complex ties to one another and to more powerful neighboring lords; semi-independent, yet pawns of a kind, ultimately never fully autonomous. In the later Middle Ages, as a result of dynastic marriages, the Netherlands came to be ruled by the Dukes of Burgundy, who allowed them a great degree of local independence. In 1477 the Netherlands became linked to the Hapsburg dynasty when Mary of Burgundy married Maximilian, Archduke of Austria, the future Emperor Maximilian I. Their son Philip the Fair became Duke of Burgundy and ruler of the Netherlands, and after his untimely death in 1506, the titles passed to his six-year-old son Charles. Ten years later, this same Charles, whose maternal grandparents were Ferdinand of Aragon and Isabella of Castille, became king of Spain, and in 1519 Holy Roman Emperor Charles V. Born and reared in Flanders, Charles understood the culture and appreciated its traditions. In addition, his native tongues were Flemish and French. His rulership was uncontroversial in the Netherlands, even though he persecuted early followers of Luther in that realm. Religion aside, he continued to rule his subjects there as his ancestors had done, for the most part, allowing them considerable independence. In 1549, Charles formally severed the ancient feudal ties that had bound the Low Countries to the French king and the Holy Roman Emperor, and he proclaimed its seventeen provinces a single dynastic entity that would pass on to all his Hapsburg heirs. So it was that the Netherlands passed into the hands of the Hapsburg monarchs of Spain, and that the stage was set for future turmoil.

When Charles V abdicated in 1556, he divided his realms into two inheritances, giving the empire and the ancestral Hapsburg lands to his brother Ferdinand, and the remainder to his son Philip, who picked up the lion's share—including the New World, southern Italy, and the Low Countries, realms that were all foreign to him. Reared in Spain, and culturally, linguistically, and temperamentally alienated from the Netherlanders, Philip quickly made himself odious to them. Determined to rule all his possessions as he ruled Spain, he increased taxes and tried to bypass the nobility and the Netherlandish parliament (the States General), by appointing wealthy and powerful men he trusted as governors of each province. Ostensibly, these stadtholders were to do his bidding. In addition, he appointed his half-sister Margaret, Duchess of Parma, as regent, and he created the Council of State to advise her. The council was to be headed by a president, and for this post Philip chose a man very loyal to him, Anthony Perrenot, Lord of Granvelle.

Immediately, both Margaret and Granvelle were viewed with suspicion, as puppets of the Spanish king who were hell-bent on circumventing the will of the States General. Driving a wedge deeper between himself and his subjects, King Philip also decided to redraw the ecclesiastical map of the Netherlands, to create three new archbishoprics and fourteen new bishoprics, and to appoint Granvelle as Primate of the Netherlandish church. Since Philip II held the power of appointment, and all these new bishops would take part in the States General, the plan aroused suspicion and resistance. Even more alarming was the increasingly active role played by the Inquisition in the Netherlands, which gave rise to fears that Philip II intended to duplicate the Spanish model and impose it on his northern subjects. Such fears seemed justified by the execution of 103 heretics in Antwerp between 1557 and 1562, many more than were killed in all of Spain during the same five years. To many, it seemed that Philip was not only hijacking the Netherlandish church, but also creating an autocratic power structure antithetical to traditional autonomy.

Resistance to all these changes grew stiffer with every attempt to implement them. By 1559, Philip's frustration was as great as that of his subjects, and he threatened to never convene the States General again. Tellingly, he never set foot in the Netherlands after 1559, even though the region would demand much of his attention until the day he died in 1598. Philip's authoritarian posture did nothing to calm an already volatile situation. In 1565 bad weather led to a devastatingly poor harvest, and to famine, lending the name the "Hunger Year" to 1566. As far as many Netherlanders were concerned, the ever-intrusive Philip did little or nothing to alleviate the situation. Had no other factors intervened, Philip and the Netherlanders would surely have had an uneasy relationship. But one factor did in fact intervene, which whipped up the political turbulence exponentially, turning it into a devastating cyclone: the growing presence of Calvinists in the Low Countries, especially in the southern provinces.

Calvinism had made great inroads into the southern Netherlands by 1566. In France, the Huguenots were already numerous and eagerly defending themselves by force of arms, and it therefore stands to reason that these southern provinces that bordered France were the entry point for Calvinist missionaries into the Low Countries. The number of converts made by 1566 is unknown, but the impact of Calvinists and their ministers in the Netherlands is beyond doubt. As Calvinist numbers grew and persecution increased, three sympathetic members of the Council of State asked Philip II to abolish the Inquisition, but to no avail. These three aristocrats—William the Silent, Prince of Orange (1533–1584), Lamoral, Count of Egmont (1522–1568), and Philip de Montmorency, Count of Horn (1524–1568)—would figure prominently in the struggle to come. In early April 1566, hundreds of nobles, Catholic and Protestant, presented a list of grievances in person to Philip II's representative, Margaret of Parma. Afraid to face these aristocrats, Margaret at first hesitated to respond. But a common identity was forged among the petitioners and all Netherlanders that day when one of the nobles asked, "What, madam, is your highness afraid of these beggars?" The name stuck: all those who opposed Spanish rule would henceforth be known as Beggars.

While the elites were making these pleas, Calvinist preachers were turning the land into one enormous outdoor church, and the Netherlanders into zealous agents of divine wrath. Preaching to crowds numbering in the thousands, Calvinist ministers stirred up animosity toward the "idols" and rituals of the Catholic Church, just as Swiss preachers had done in the 1520s. Many in these enormous crowds, which were made up of all segments of Netherlandish society, were armed for self-protection, and ready for trouble. As these massive outdoor gatherings increased in frequency and the crowds in numbers—some contemporary reports speak of throngs of five thousand to fourteen thousand—so too did tension grow, along with the potential for violence.

In August 1566, the pent-up frustration broke loose, plunging the Netherlands into chaos: mobs numbering in the thousands began to ransack churches and monasteries, destroying images and sacred objects, and killing or injuring anyone who tried to object. The iconoclastic fury quickly swept like a wildfire throughout the Netherlands, from south to north. The artistic or financial value of the items destroyed mattered not at all to the mobs that destroyed every image, relic, or sacred vessel they could find. By early autumn 1566, hundreds of church interiors lay in ruins, along with many outdoor shrines, monasteries, convents, and clerical residences, as tens of thousands of newly minted Calvinists clamored for the abolition of the Roman Catholic Church and freedom from Spanish rule. The revolt of the Netherlands had begun, and the sacred symbols of the oppressor's religion were its first victims. The so-called Hunger Year (Hongerjaar)

Wonder year. In the summer of 1566, mobs of Protestants inspired by Calvinist preachers swept through the churches of the Netherlands destroying the sacred art that their forebears had donated and venerated. In this engraving by an anonymous artist, Calvinists topple "idols" and their trappings, sweeping the land clean, while the Catholic clergy pray to the papal Antichrist for help. The devil hovers above with an armful of costly ritual objects, saying: "It makes no difference whether you pray or crap in your pants; it's over for us."

had been turned into the "Wonder Year" (Wonderjaar), and the Beggars, as they called themselves, initiated a religiously inspired conflict that would last, on and off, for nearly three generations, claim thousands of lives, and lead to the creation of two distinct states out of the seventeen provinces, one predominantly Calvinist and the other resolutely Catholic.

The Revolt of the Netherlands, also known as the Eighty Years' War, was further proof of the cruelty that early modern Christians could inflict on one another in the name of religion. By the same token, this conflict offered undeniable evidence of the linking of religious, cultural, political, economic, and social factors in the early modern age. One could be tempted to say that this was one revolt that had nearly as many causes as it did participants. Yet the role of religion in this mayhem can be more adequately assessed through metaphor than through quantitative data: as in France, religion was the catalyst that set off the powder keg, the ghost behind the violence, the grammar of disagreement, the straw that broke the camel's back, the elephant in the room, and so on. The conflict played a large role in the development of the Dutch Republic, one of Europe's first tolerant societies, and, simultaneously, in the decline and ultimate demise of Spain, one of its most intolerant ones.

Philip II's immediate response to the iconoclastic fury was to send ten thousand Spanish troops to the Netherlands under the leadership of Fernando Álvarez de Toledo, the third Duke of Alba (1507–1582), with strict orders to annihilate all the rebel heretics. After his arrival in 1567, the Duke of Alba quickly made short work of the Beggars, imposing order on most of the southern provinces, capturing and executing the noble leaders Egmont and Horn—both were Catholics—and twenty other nobles, torturing and killing thousands of suspected Calvinists, and seizing their property. The tribunal for processing all rebels, which Alba named the Council of Troubles, came to be known among the dissidents as the Council of Blood. As Alba gained control of the southern provinces, thousands of Calvinists fled northward, tipping the religious balance. Under the leadership of William, Prince of Orange, the rebel Beggars in the north did their utmost to harass Alba and fend him off. Unable to vanquish the northern provinces but remaining in full control of the provinces in the south, Alba set in motion a process that would result in the partition of the Low Countries, with ten Catholic provinces in the south and seven Calvinist provinces in the north.

As in France, in the Netherlands, too, fighting brought not a resolution of the conflict but rather increased bloodshed and greater atrocities. William of Orange proved himself a very able military leader, and a Calvinist hero too, despite a lackluster performance at first and a somewhat ambivalent approach to religion. In 1576, he al- most managed to reclaim the southern provinces when he convinced the ten Catholic provinces of the south to overlook religious differences and join the seven rebel Calvinist provinces—after Spanish troops in Antwerp mutinied and sacked the city, killing around eight thousand of its inhabitants—with the sole objective of driving the Spanish out and achieving genuine independence. This pact, the Union of Brussels, never materialized, however. In 1578 Philip II replaced the Duke of Alba with his nephew, Alexander Farnese (1545–1592), the future Duke of Parma and son of Margaret of Parma. At about the same time, he also replaced Margaret as regent with his half-brother, John of Austria (1547–1578), another of Charles V's illegitimate offspring. Farnese arrived in the Netherlands with twenty thousand battle-ready troops, and immediately went to work, coaxing the Catholic southerners to break with the northern Calvinist rebels, capturing towns and cities that could not be coaxed. By 1579 he had strong-armed the south into forming the Union of Arras, a coalition committed to battling and subduing the north. In response, William of Orange herded the northern provinces into the opposing Union of Utrecht, which in 1581 deposed Philip II and declared itself fully independent and autonomous. Though no one could know it at the time, the creation of these two Unions sealed the partition of the Netherlands, and the extension of the religious violence well into the following century.

In the early to mid-1580s, Farnese waged war against those in the south who still refused to bow to Philip II and the pope. Although the rebels in the north suffered a crushing blow in July 1584 with the assassination of William of Orange by a Catholic zealot, Farnese unwittingly strengthened their resolve and their numbers by securing the entire south, including the self-proclaimed Calvinist city-state of Antwerp. Farnese's victory caused thousands of Calvinists to flee northward after 1585, swelling the ranks of the rebels in the northern provinces.

Fighting between the Spanish and the northern rebels continued without any reprieve until 1609, including a stint during which England entered the fray. For the Netherlanders, the war was one of attrition rather than victory: the best they could do was to wear down the Spanish, at great cost in human suffering. The deep hatred that the northern Netherlanders developed for the Spanish and their Catholicism poisoned relations between the two nations for centuries. For the Spanish, the war became a bottomless sinkhole into which poured substantial resources, financial as well as human. The Army of Flanders engaged in battle after battle and siege after siege, year after year, only to see victory elude it. Philip II and his son Philip III would both invest much of the wealth extracted from the gold and silver mines of the New World into this venture, believing that these enemies of "altar and throne" had to be vanquished for the sake of the honor of Spain and that of God. The horrors and atrocities of the war deeply affected the soldiers sent to fight, very much like the Vietnam War would do to American soldiers four centuries later. In Spain itself, the returning veterans who had abandoned their civility while fighting the Netherlanders coined a new way of reprimanding anyone who acted boorishly or with no regard for rules: "Where do you think we are, Flanders?"[4]

In April 1609, worn down by the Netherlanders and by the lenders who helped him finance the war, King Philip III signed a truce with the rebels that in effect recognized their republic as an independent sovereign state, ever so tentatively. Truces do not end conflicts, however. In 1619 the fighting resumed, this time as part of the Thirty Years' War, to which we will turn in the next section. Until 1648, the Netherlands would know no lasting peace, and up until the end, religion remained a key component of this protracted conflict, though increasingly less so as time passed. By 1648, the Republic of the Netherlands, then known as the United Provinces, would be the most tolerant place in all of Europe. Though officially Calvinist, it allowed Catholics, Anabaptists, and Jews the right to live there and to worship, under certain restrictions. All in all, however, the scarring occasioned by the Eighty Years' War became a distinguishing feature of the Netherlandish character: a permanent reminder of the pain religion can cause. Not surprisingly, agnostic skepticism would flourish in the Netherlands in the seventeenth century, with that awful scar very much in mind.

The Thirty Years' War

The settlement reached at the Diet of Augsburg in 1555 had ended the fighting over religion in the Holy Roman Empire but not the friction between contending confessions. East of the Rhine River and north of the Danube, all the way to the border with Russia, Europe was a chaotic patchwork of different confessions, each claiming to be the one true church, each eager to defend its toehold on earth. All of Scandinavia and much of northeast Germany were solidly Lutheran, and had state-sponsored churches, but the rest of the map defied precise rendering. Bohemia had its Hussite heritage, and relative religious freedom. Calvinists could be found in pockets here and there, in the Palatinate and Brandenburg; in Hungary, Poland, Lithuania; and as far east as Transylvania. Anabaptists were widely scattered too, and in Poland there were Socinians and spiritualist free thinkers. And this thumbnail sketch does not portray the many intramural quarrels that shook these confessions, or the resurgence of the Catholic Church after the Council of Trent.

Within the Holy Roman Empire, which continued to be ruled by the Catholic Hapsburgs, there was little that the emperors could do to reverse Protestant gains, but in the hereditary Hapsburg lands along the tense frontier with the Ottoman Turks—Carinthia, Carniola, Styria—and in the Tyrol they did succeed in imposing Catholic uniformity through conversions and expulsions between 1598 and 1605. This forced re-Catholicization, though anomalous for its day, was no different from the Empire's *cuius regio, eius religio* principle, which granted rulers the right to choose the religion of their subjects. It also reflected the selectivity with which the principle was applied, for the Hapsburgs could not enforce a similar change elsewhere, no matter how much they may have desired to do so. Forced change hinged on a variety of circumstances, chief of which was the amount of resistance that could be offered to any ruler who dared to enforce religious uniformity. The likelihood of any such forced change, or of reversals on the part of any ruler, or of dynastic change, or of new advances made by any minority or majority, created a constant tension in these multiconfessional areas, and a highly charged atmosphere for potential conflict.

By 1605, the uneasy peace that had held for half a century since Augsburg was on the verge of unraveling. Both the Calvinists and Catholics had taken on a more aggressive

stance, and made territorial gains. The Calvinists, who were not included in the agreement reached at the Peace of Augsburg, had assumed control of the Palatinate and several
other principalities; the Catholics had regained control of several key cities and territories, most notably Cologne, Würzburg, Aachen, Bamberg, Münster, Strassburg, and
Paderborn—and also Donauwörth, which was forcibly re-Catholicized by Maximilian I,
Duke and Elector of Bavaria. And wherever Jesuit schools sprang up, Protestants were
immediately put on the defensive. In 1608, Protestants attending the Imperial Diet decided to boycott it because of increased pressure on them to return confiscated property
to the Catholic Church. Fearing worse to come, as foreshadowed by Duke Maximilian's
takeover of Donauwörth, they formed a military alliance, the Evangelical (or Protestant)
Union, under the leadership of the Calvinist Frederick IV, Prince Elector of the Palatinate
(1574–1610), and his son and successor, Frederick V (1596–1632). In response, the
Catholic states formed their own alliance in 1609, the Catholic Union, led by Maximilian
I, Duke of Bavaria, the "conqueror" of Donauwörth. As had been the case when the
Protestants formed the Schmalkaldic League in 1531, pacts did not lead immediately to
fighting, but drew the blueprints for future conflict.

It did not take long, relatively speaking, for war to erupt. The epicenter was volatile Bohemia, which had broken with Rome a century before Luther did, and which was
ruled by the Catholic Hapsburgs; the year was 1618. The initial cause of conflict was a
local one, involving Bohemia's relation to Hapsburg authority, but the alliances that had
been made—which stretched like viscous webs across the map—turned this local dispute
into one of the longest and most destructive wars of the early modern age. Though the
rapid escalation of the conflict seemed to catch some by surprise, the signs of its inevitable
unfolding had been in place for more than a generation. And it would prove the worst of all
early modern wars, in terms of the violence and the suffering it caused. This war was also
the most complex, especially in terms of the utter mixing of sacred and profane, which, by
the final decade of the war, made it nearly impossible to discern clear continuities between
the bloodshed of the day and the original religious divisions that had led to the fighting.

It all began when two representatives of the Holy Roman Emperor Matthias
(1557–1619) were tossed out of a high castle window in Prague, on 23 May 1618. That
they both landed unhurt in a manure pile mattered little, even though Catholics interpreted their survival as a miracle. The Defenestration of Prague, as the incident came to
be known, was an act of rebellion against the Hapsburg King of Bohemia, Ferdinand
(1578–1637), who had been crowned in 1617. Ferdinand—future Holy Roman
Emperor—had already re-Catholicized Styria and was determined to do the same in
Bohemia. Although his cousin Emperor Rudolph II (1552–1612) had granted religious
toleration in Bohemia, Ferdinand had already begun to whittle away at this right, and
the "defenestration" was intended as a clear sign that Bohemians were not at all inclined
to accept re-Catholicization meekly. As the rebels took control of Prague, an impending
crisis became apparent to the Catholic and Protestant states that had made alliances
some ten years earlier. Their alarm intensified when Emperor Matthias died in March

1619, and his successor had to be chosen. Though the seven electors were divided along confessional lines, with three Protestants on one side, and four Catholics on the other, the electors unanimously chose one of their own, King Ferdinand of Bohemia, as the next Holy Roman Emperor. In Prague, the rebels had already taken their own decisive step by deposing Ferdinand as king of Bohemia, and replacing him with Frederick V, the Calvinist Duke-Elector of the Palatinate and leader of the Evangelical Union, a move that seemed all the more defiant in light of the imperial election. Had the deposed Ferdinand been merely the king of Bohemia, he would have had fewer resources to marshal against the rebels, but as Holy Roman Emperor, he could unleash greater fury against them and their rebel usurper Frederick V of the Palatinate.

With all the wheels now set in motion for war between the Catholic emperor Ferdinand and his nemesis Frederick, the Calvinist at the helm of the Protestant Union, the allied states readied their armies and headed for battle. Ferdinand convinced his cousin King Philip III of Spain to send troops. The immediate result was disaster for the Bohemian rebels, who were crushed by the Catholic Bavarians at the Battle of White Mountain in 1620, and for Frederick, whose Palatinate was conquered by the Spanish and Bavarians in 1622. Vanquished, Frederick lost not just his lands, but also the elector-ship, which was transferred to Duke Maximilian of Bavaria as a reward for his loyalty. Emperor Ferdinand II had trounced the rebels. Henceforward, Bohemia was subjected to an intense re-Catholicization effort, with amazingly successful results, at least on the surface. Bohemia—and Prague especially—would become a showcase of triumpha-list Catholicism, even as ancient Hussite resentment seethed beneath the surface. But Ferdinand's victory, decisive and fateful for Bohemia, proved a provocation for further conflict on an even larger scale.

Duration, geographical reach, number of participants, shifting of allegiances, battles, and atrocities combine to provide a bewildering narrative. The figure here conveys both the scale and complexity of the struggle, purely in terms of its military participants, and in terms of political rather than religious allegiances, with participants listed accord-ing to their position toward the emperor.

While there is no denying that religion was a catalyst and a constant factor in the war, political issues were also immensely significant. And no political concern loomed larger than that of Hapsburg power, with the emperors seeking to maintain and enhance their dominant role, and their opponents—both within and beyond the empire—eager to resist them. With Frederick and the Bohemians defeated and Ferdinand II seemingly unstoppable, the Protestant princes had little trouble rounding up foreign allies. A new Protestant League was formed that linked a number of German states with Denmark, England, and the Netherlands. Led by King Christian IV of Denmark (1577–1648), a Lutheran, and secretly supported by Catholic France, this coalition fought the imperial and Bavarian forces from 1626 to 1629, when Denmark sued for peace.

But just as it seemed that Ferdinand II had won again, and that he was poised to restore the Catholic Church in the empire through the Edict of Restitution, another

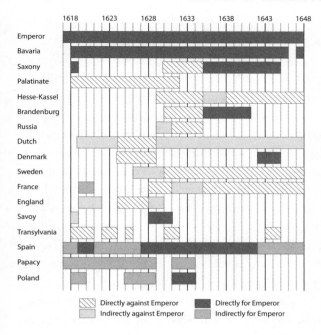

A long and messy war. Whether or not to call the Thirty Years' War a "religious conflict" is a matter of debate. Although most of the fighting occurred between armies with opposing confessional allegiances, religious identity was not always the sole factor behind the violence, and some participants changed sides over the years. This chart lays out the bewildering complexity of the roles played by all the various participants.

foreign Lutheran sovereign came to the rescue of the Protestant cause: King Gustavus Adolphus of Sweden (b. 1594). The Swedes entered the war in 1630 and won some significant battles, but after Gustavus Adolphus was killed in 1632 at the Battle of Lützen, they lost momentum. Once again, as Ferdinand II gained the upper hand, foreign opposition snatched total victory from his hands. This time the rescuer of the Protestant League was none other than a Catholic, Louis XIII of France, who could not abide the thought of a strong Hapsburg Empire to his east. With France openly involved in the fray, the fighting continued, then, until 1648, with no decisive victories for anyone, and no respite for Germany. In addition to Austria and Spain, which took part in the first phase, this war had expanded to include at various stages Denmark, Sweden, Savoy, Poland, Russia, France, England, and the Netherlands, all of whom did most of the fighting on German soil, at great cost to the German people.

The Thirty Years' War was the first modern military conflict to involve so many nations and to affect civilian populations directly, as enormous armies moved across the landscape without sufficient provisions, living off the reserves of the unfortunate natives they encountered. Technological advances in weaponry, especially in firearms and field artillery, made larger armies necessary, logistics more complex, and the casualties higher. By the end of the war, the imperial army consisted of about 40,000 soldiers, who lumbered from one engagement to another with a supporting retinue of nearly 140,000 additional noncombatants: wives, children, prostitutes and pimps, doctors, blacksmiths, farriers, carpenters, cooks, and so on. In essence, they formed a large city, ever on the move, ravaging the countryside like locusts. Sieges and massacres became routine, and both sides committed atrocities. One example alone, which became emblematic in the later stages of the war, conveys a sense of the ultimate cost of all the fighting.

The siege of the Lutheran city of Magdeburg began in November 1630. After five months of relentless shelling by artillery, and the inevitable starvation brought on by every siege, Magdeburg was finally captured by imperial soldiers in May 1631. The Magdeburgers, many of whom took no part in their city's obstinate resistance—but had been trapped within the city's walls—fell prey to the fury of the imperial troops, who went on an orgy of killing, raping, and pillaging, and deliberately set the city on fire. Unable to stop their soldiers, the commanders simply watched as twenty-five thousand of Magdeburg's thirty thousand residents perished. For two weeks corpses were dumped into the Elbe River. By the time the war ended, in 1648, only about 450 souls lived in what was left of once-thriving Magdeburg. The verb *Magdeburgisieren* ("to Magdeburgize") became widely used to describe the indiscriminate slaughter caused by war. And the sarcastic terms *Magdeburg justice* and *Magdeburg mercy* became popular among avenging Protestants who took their frenzied turn at killing Catholics whenever they could.[5]

The effects of the Thirty Years' War on certain parts of the Holy Roman Empire were devastating: in some regions, as many as 50 percent or more of the inhabitants had been wiped out or driven away by 1648. The total population loss is estimated at around 30 percent.

The role played by religion in this war is undeniable, but difficult to assess. On the one hand, religion was closely interwoven into nearly every aspect of the war—so much so that the war can be seen as the ultimate consequence of the Protestant Reformation on Germany. Anyone who visits Luther's grave at Wittenberg will find a poignant reminder of the value placed on this long war by those who endured it, for a ghostly marker indicates where the corpse of King Gustavus Adolphus rested briefly next to Luther's while on its way back to Sweden. Right there, the bold golden Latin script seeks to sacralize the soldier-king who came to rescue Luther's Reformation, and to celebrate his memory as a religious champion, worthy of proximity to Luther himself. Yet on the other hand, this war also became a point of transition, after which religion ceases to be a major source of conflict on the continent, either as a matter of ideological conviction or as a question of identity. Indications of this transition were evident in those participants who chose to switch allegiances, sometimes more than once, such as Saxony, or by Catholics such as King Louis XIII of France who made alliances with Protestants. As far as Continental Europe is concerned, this prolonged bloodletting is a tragic watershed, after which war becomes more mundane, and killing in the name of religion increasingly rare. Across the English Channel, the British Isles still had its own last gasp of religious conflict to deal with, and a similar transition to endure, which we will consider in the next section.

The fighting finally came to an end with the signing of the Peace of Westphalia in 1648. This settlement formally recognized the independence of the Republic of the Netherlands and of Switzerland. It also granted the individual states within the Holy Roman Empire the right to make treaties and alliances of their own, further enhancing the fragmentation of Germany and diminishing the authority of the emperor. As far as religion was concerned, the Peace of Westphalia not only reinforced the *cuius regio, eius religio* settlement of the Peace of Augsburg, sealing the religious division of Germany, but also finally acknowledged the legitimacy of Calvinists, alongside the Catholics and Lutherans. Spain lost the most, having been left bankrupt, exhausted, isolated, and still at war with France, the one nation that would emerge as dominant after the dust from all the fighting settled.

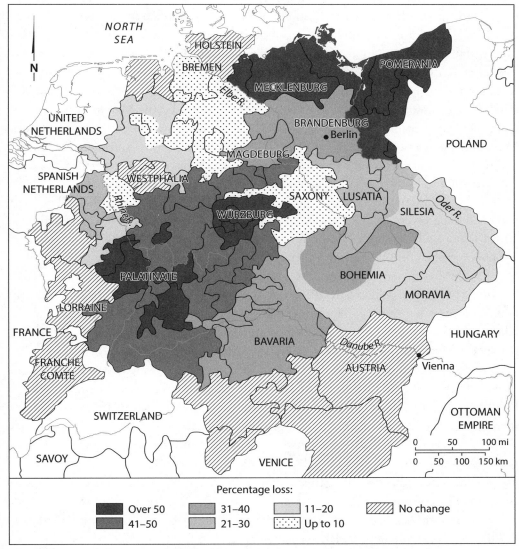

Human toll. The Thirty Years' War had a devastating effect on some areas, especially in Germany, where much of the fighting took place. Whether by sheer slaughter or by emigration, some regions suffered substantial or extreme population losses. This map visualizes the extent of this demographic catastrophe.

England, Scotland, and Ireland

While various nations on the European continent endured religious violence in the latter half of the sixteenth century and the first half of the seventeenth, the British Isles enjoyed a period of relative peace, with the emphasis on "relative." England had never been truly violence-free from 1534 on: Henry VIII and his Tudor progeny had all made martyrs of those who opposed their ecclesiastical policies. Mary Tudor, in particular, earned a reputation for cruelty as "Bloody Mary" by persecuting and killing about three hundred Protestants during her brief reign (1553–1558). Her half-sister Elizabeth was equally ruthless toward Catholics, especially after 1570, but was glorified in her own day and for centuries afterward in English lore—proof positive that history is written by the victors. Her legacy, as promoted by those who glorified her, was the *via media*, the wise compromise between Catholicism and Protestantism that made England unique and superior to other nations in English eyes. The publication of John Foxe's *Acts and Monuments* in 1563, better known as *The Book of Martyrs*, which chronicled the Marian persecution in great detail and became a perennial best seller, did much to permanently demonize Queen Mary and the Catholic Church, and also—like Crespin's French equivalent—to glorify and normalize the horrors of religious violence. In truth, however, Elizabeth's persecution exceeded that of Mary, extending the martyrdoms over an entire generation.

Elizabeth managed to avoid war, especially in 1588, when King Philip II of Spain launched the greatest fleet ever assembled, the Armada, to invade England and claim the crown for himself. Though Elizabeth had little to do with the English victory, some of the honor rubbed off on her, simply because she was on the throne when it happened.

Elizabeth's halfway measures concerning religion, it has been argued, served not just to postpone religious conflict, but also to heighten the intensity of unresolved tensions among her subjects. Her immediate successor James I (1566–1625) and his son Charles I (1600–1649), both of whom fervently defended the *via media* and showed little patience with dissent, only helped to intensify the discontent that seethed beneath the calm surface. Scotland was deceptively calm. After the religious revolution in 1559, strict Calvinism that brooked no dissent had been adopted. Moreover, the chief architect of this Reformation, John Knox, had sown potent seeds of discord by formulating revolutionary theories of resistance against ungodly rulers that were far more radical in their day than those of any Huguenot. Relations between Calvinist Scotland and Anglican *via media* England remained tense, even though after 1603 they shared the same monarch. Ireland had no native religious dissent against Catholicism, but it became a hotbed of resistance against the imposition of the Anglican and Scottish churches on its soil, whether by fiat or by immigration, as the larger island to its east sought to establish dominion over it. For the most part, it enjoyed relative peace, unprepared for the violence that awaited it.

The greatest tension in England was generated by Calvinists who were opposed to any compromise with idolatrous worship and whose community expanded steadily rather than by Catholic Recusants, whose numbers and influence greatly declined during

Elizabeth's reign. Ever intent on cleansing the Anglican Church from all traces of popery, these Puritans, who were intellectual and spiritual heirs of John Calvin, gained considerable momentum throughout the reigns of Elizabeth and James I. Looking northward for inspiration, English Puritans admired the model of the Presbyterian Church of Scotland, even as they vehemently disagreed with one another on the best way of achieving a true complete Reformation in England. King James VI of Scotland, Elizabeth's heir presumptive, had been reared as a good Presbyterian and thus offered the Puritans a ray of hope. But he proved an enormous disappointment. On his way to claim the English throne in 1603, James was presented with the Millenary Petition, a list of requests signed by more than a thousand Puritans who requested genuine change in the Anglican Church, but he met few of the demands. One of those few requests he did fulfill, however, brought more recognition to his name than any other accomplishment of his: the English translation of the Bible he sponsored, known as the King James Version.

Despite his Calvinist upbringing, King James defended the Anglican status quo with a conviction that could pass for fervor. "No bishops, no king," he insisted, in defense of the episcopal polity of the Church of England. An advocate of the divine right of kings, and ever distrustful of Parliament, King James quickly proved himself an unapologetic autocrat. As disgruntlement with his high-handed rule intensified, for numerous reasons other than religion, more and more of his subjects joined the Puritan cause, especially after he removed many Puritan clergy from their posts and these ex-clerics fomented discontent among the laity. Though they could not agree with one another—some at one extreme arguing that the Church of England had to be reformed from within and others at the other extreme claiming that genuine reform required separation from that church—their cause gradually increased in potency, mixing religious and political concerns into a explosive mixture. Some Puritans went into exile to escape persecution, especially to the Netherlands and Calvinist areas of Germany. Others, such as the separatists who sailed across the Atlantic in 1620 to establish a godly republic in New England that would be free of popery and error, were ready for wholesale change, perhaps even for confrontation.

When James I died in 1625, political and religious tensions intensified in England. Even more dismissive of Parliament than his father, and more enamored of the rites that Puritans condemned as "popery," Charles I enraged many of his subjects right from the start, causing his oft-bickering opponents to join forces and form a fairly cohesive dissenting party. Among the worst of his offenses were his incessant clamoring for money, his contempt for Parliament, and his dependence on William Laud (1573–1645), the archbishop of Canterbury, who was committed to imposing a uniformity on English worship that many found uncomfortably close to Catholicism. Archbishop Laud's love of "high" ritual—which included the use of elaborate vestments, incense, bells, and candles—was offensive to many in England, and totally unacceptable in Calvinist Scotland. Had Laud limited his homogenizing zeal to England, there is no telling what might have ensued. But he reached too far, and set off a chain of events that would lead to his beheading as well as that of King Charles.

Their fatal mistake was to try to impose high Anglican worship on the Calvinist Scots in 1638. The Scots rebelled immediately, swearing to uphold their religious and civil liberties, as John Knox had taught them to do. The fighting that ensued in 1639, which came to be known as the First Bishops' War (1639–1640), bankrupted King Charles and further emboldened the Scots, whose Parliament abolished bishops and declared the Scottish Kirk free of royal control. Unable to raise or fund an army, Charles called Parliament to grant him the means of doing so in March 1640, but since many of its members were Puritans or dissenters, it made demands Charles found unacceptable and he dissolved it almost immediately in April. Left without the means to pay for an army, King Charles soon found himself facing a Scottish invasion and occupation of northern England, and the prospect of further rebellion closer to home. Left with no choice after the Second Bishops' War, Charles reluctantly summoned Parliament again, and unwittingly sparked a revolution. The so-called Long Parliament that assembled in 1640 (and would technically remain in session until 1653) immediately set itself to claiming unprecedented powers, removing the king's chief ministers from power, rearranging the councils that ran the government, impeaching Archbishop Laud for treason, and legislating other changes that diminished the king's authority. Ultimately, the disagreements between Parliament and King Charles would lead to civil war. Although Marxist-inspired historians have tried to interpret this Puritan revolution as purely social and economic in nature, such interpretations no longer hold sway. Interpreting religion more broadly than Marxists are wont to do, many historians agree that religious concerns were the prime catalyst of the revolution that began in 1640.

Between 1640 and 1642 Parliament grew increasingly polarized, and the chief issue dividing parliamentarians was religious: whether to dissolve the episcopal polity of the Church of England and do away with the Book of Common Prayer, both items that the Puritans considered "popish." Meanwhile, King Charles and Archbishop Laud could contribute nothing to the discussion, much less do anything to regain control. Gradually, two parties evolved: one committed to radically changing the Anglican Church, and the other devoted to upholding the king's authority and to resisting that radical change. When King Charles ineptly attempted a coup in January 1642 by breaking into Parliament with four hundred armed supporters, only to find that the leaders of his opposition were not there, the parliamentary impasse turned into open war. Driven out of London, King Charles raised an army of loyalists, who would come to be known as Cavaliers. The Puritans raised their own army in response, and would come to be known as the Roundheads, because of their preference for short haircuts, a stern rejection of the high fashion favored by their opponents. The Puritans had several tactical advantages from the start for they controlled London and most of the heavily populated southern half of England, along with Parliament, which could levy taxes to support their cause. The royalists, in contrast, held the more sparsely populated north of England and had no easy access to funds other than those supplied by the landed gentry on their side. Fighting between these two armies began in 1642 and lasted until 1646. Though it never came close to rivaling any of the conflicts on the continent in terms of deaths or devastation, or of impact on the general population, the English Civil War was brutal and destructive. During the first year, King Charles seemed to gain the upper hand, but after the Puritans secured the participation of Scotland, the king and his Cavaliers steadily lost out to the Roundheads.

One of the chief reasons for the eventual triumph of the Roundheads was the rise of a remarkable leader, Oliver Cromwell (1599–1658), who molded the rebel army into a disciplined and highly effective fighting force. An obscure and relatively poor country squire before the fighting began, Cromwell proved himself a genius at war who would be credited with creating the New Model Army and with defeating the king and his Cavaliers. Cromwell's men, who recited the psalms as they went into battle and considered themselves God's elect, learned to outmaneuver and vanquish their enemies with all the conviction that can be expected from soldiers who identify with the ancient Israelites. After trouncing the Cavaliers at the battle of Marston Moor in 1644, Cromwell could boast, "God made them as stubble to our swords."[6] By 1645, after another crushing defeat, at Naseby, the king's men had no chance of winning. In 1646, King Charles himself was captured by Cromwell's Roundheads and imprisoned. The army of the elect had managed to accomplish what no other Protestant force ever had: the utter humiliation of a monarch.

Having defeated the king, the Puritans immediately lost their common sense of purpose and fell into two years of wrangling over how best to reform England. Three major factions developed in the process. The most conservative Puritans were the Presbyterians, who wanted England to have a church like that of Scotland and Geneva, with no bishops. They also favored retaining the monarchy, along with a vigorous Parliament to keep it in check. Of the three factions, the Presbyterians had the highest representation in Parliament. The second faction, the Independents, favored doing away with compulsory membership in a national church. Instead, they preferred to allow the existence of multiple autonomous churches with purely voluntary membership. As far as governing was concerned, they advocated a redefinition of the powers of the monarchy and Parliament so that both would be more responsive to the voice of the people. Oliver Cromwell and most of his army officers were Independents, and this fact alone gave this grouping special clout. The third faction, which was less unified, consisted of an array of radical Puritan dissenters who wanted a thorough transformation of England, both spiritually and politically. Most of these radical sects had sprung up during the civil war, and they often disagreed with one another. Three sects were the most vocal, and most radical: the apocalyptically inclined Fifth Monarchy Men, who were convinced that the Final Judgment was near; the Levellers, who sought to abolish social distinctions and establish an egalitarian and democratic England; and the Diggers, who called for the abolition of private property and the creation of an agrarian communist utopia. These sects were well represented in the rank and file of Cromwell's army, and were therefore a force to be reckoned with. Frustrated by all the wrangling, the Presbyterians and Cavaliers attempted a coup in December 1648, to restore the captive king to power, but Cromwell quickly and decisively trounced them, entered London, and took over Parliament, ejecting all who did not agree with him and the Independents. Since the task of preventing the unwanted from entering Parliament was assigned to one of his colonels, Thomas Pride, this event became known as Pride's Purge. The greatly reduced sixty-member Parliament that assumed control of England as a result earned the name Rump Parliament.

Their opposition vanquished, Cromwell and his Rump Parliament moved quickly to consolidate their power. King Charles I was charged with treason and tried by a High Court of Justice. Though the king insisted that the court had no genuine authority and that no monarch could ever be tried for treason, the High Court found him guilty and had him beheaded on 30 January 1649. A very composed Charles proclaimed himself "a martyr of the people" at his execution, but Cromwell and his Puritans did not give his claim a second thought. As they saw it, Charles I was no martyr, and regicide was a logical and theologically correct necessity in the face of his idolatrous and tyrannical rule. Calvinist resistance theory had defended such a course of action against monarchs since the 1550s, and the time was finally ripe. Convinced that their actions were guided by God and favored by God, Cromwell's faction set up a Puritan republic that would endure until 1660.

Among the first tasks undertaken by Cromwell's Puritan Commonwealth was the invasion of Ireland, where the native nobility had rebelled against English rule in

Holy regicide. Calvinist resistance theories were put to practice by English Puritans in 1649, with the execution of King Charles I. Though King Charles claimed he could not be tried for treason, the Calvinist Puritans asserted their conviction that no monarch could disregard their interpretation of God's law with impunity.

1641, formed a Catholic Confederacy, allied themselves with English Royalists, and engaged in the killing of Protestants on Irish soil. Cromwell's Irish campaign was ostensibly launched to punish the rebels and thwart an invasion of England by a combined Anglo-Irish Royalist army, but his larger aims soon became apparent: Ireland was to be stripped of its papist religion and subjugated to the Puritan Commonwealth. The process of rendering the Irish into obedient subjects and good Puritans was brutal from the very start. It began with the siege of Drogheda in September 1649, a stronghold for English Royalists and Irish Catholic Confederates, where more than three thousand soldiers and civilians were massacred even after the town surrendered. "I am persuaded that this is a righteous judgment of God on these barbarous wretches," said Cromwell of his orders to show no mercy.[7]

Similar massacres followed, with thousands slaughtered in Wexford. Cromwell the military genius had discovered the power of terror: by making resistance seem suicidal and worse than futile, he paralyzed his enemies. By the time the fighting ceased in 1651, tens of thousands of Irish had fled their island, and hundreds of thousands lay in their graves, victims of a fatal combination of wanton killing, famine, and disease. Thousands more had also been sent to the West Indies in chains, as indentured servants. Cromwell's own expert, William Petty, estimated in his Down Survey that the total number of deaths caused in Ireland since 1641 was about 618,000 or more, which, if correct, amounted to nearly 40 percent of the island's population—a toll as heavy as any paid by Germany, and heavier than any paid by France or the Netherlands. And most of those deaths had occurred after Cromwell's 1649 invasion.

Cromwell also confiscated vast tracts of land from the Irish nobility, parceling it out to Adventurers, or those who had helped finance his Irish campaign, thus encouraging the creation of a colonial caste system in which English Puritans would be in charge of Christianizing the papist Irish subjects who toiled as tenant farmers. The results were disastrous for the Irish. Whereas Irish Catholics had owned about 60 percent of the land before Cromwell, only 8 percent was theirs afterward. This low percentage would increase to 20 percent after the monarchy was restored in England in 1660, but the net gain was inconsequential. Even more ruinous for the Irish were the laws put into effect in 1652 through the Act for the Settlement of Ireland, which legalized the land transfers and established discrimination against them on their own soil. As in England, Catholicism was outlawed and a price was put on every priest's head. In addition, Catholics were forbidden to live in towns or hold public office. These laws were slightly amended in 1660 when the Puritan Commonwealth was replaced once again by a monarchy, and they would be tinkered with again after that, but similar restrictions remained in place until the nineteenth century. Reflecting on these so-called Penal Laws, the Irish statesman and political philosopher Edmund Burke (1729–1797) would later say they were "a machine of wise and elaborate contrivance, as well fitted for the oppression, impoverishment and degradation of a people, and the debasement in them of human nature itself, as ever proceeded from the perverted ingenuity of man."[8]

Having subdued Ireland, Cromwell turned to Scotland, which he and his New Model Army invaded and occupied in 1650–1651. As in Ireland, the pretext was the possible treachery of those who backed the monarchy and supported the claims of the dead king's son and heir, Charles II, who was in exile on the Continent. The net result was the subjugation of Scotland to England and the creation of a single political entity in the British Isles. In England itself, Cromwell found nothing but frustration in dealing with Parliament. Accustomed to commanding an army that did all his bidding, he found it difficult to wait for the approval of sixty men who sometimes disagreed with him and with one another. In 1653 he dissolved Parliament and installed himself as sole ruler of England, Scotland, and Ireland under the title of Lord Protector. For the remainder of his reign, during which time he conducted himself much as an absolute monarch, the Puritan Protectorate would be abuzz with religious activity and with the control of behavior and morals. Religious pluralism flourished, since all sects except Anglicans and Catholics were granted full toleration. Discontent flourished too, but with the New Model Army and Cromwell in control, all challenges were quickly snuffed out, as the few highland Scots who dared to rebel in 1653 discovered. Cromwell's grip proved so firm that even after his death in September 1658, the Protectorate sputtered on for another year or so, in disarray, until a full Parliament, then filled with previously banned Anglicans, restored the monarchy. In May 1660, Charles II landed at Dover bringing an end to the Puritan experiment.

King Charles II immediately restored the pre-1642 political status quo but could not turn back the clock on the religious ferment that had swept through his realms or stifle the ill will that many of his subjects had developed toward religion in general and "enthusiasm" in particular. Nor could he quell anti-Catholic sentiments or constant fears of a Catholic resurgence—fears that deepened as his son and heir, James (1633–1701), made clear his admiration of all things Catholic. With the death of Charles II in 1685, England entered another period of instability in which religious and political issues created a volatile mixture. As in 1642, attempts to meddle with the religious status quo cost a king dearly. But this time around, the nation was not bloodied by civil war. The conflict came to a head in June 1688, when James II extended full toleration to Catholics in England, which created an uproar and distrust of James that was compounded by the birth of a male heir, who seemed likely to be raised as a Catholic. Through shrewd maneuvering, the king's opponents staged a successful coup in November 1688, which came to be that is known as the Glorious Revolution. Mary, the oldest daughter of King James, and her Dutch husband, William of Orange—both Protestants—replaced James without any bloodshed, save for the nosebleed suffered by James II when William and Mary landed in England.

James II not only survived his nosebleed; he went on to ally himself with Irish Catholics, and to attempt the overthrow of his usurper, William. In 1690, James and his supporters wrested most of Ireland from English control, as a prelude to a larger war that would allow him to reclaim the throne. But the tide soon turned at the Battle of the

Boyne, fought near Drogheda in July 1690, at which William's Protestant forces won a resounding victory. Defeated, James limped back to exile in France and sheer irrelevance, taking with him the dream of a renewed Catholic monarchy in England, Ireland, and Scotland. The yearly celebration of this key Protestant victory in heavily Protestant Ulster in Northern Ireland, which continues to be observed to this day in a tense atmosphere, offers us a glimpse into the darker side of those Reformations from long ago, the end of which can never be adequately pinned down—at least, not yet.

Conclusion

After a century and a half, religious turmoil and violence largely came to an end in Europe. Looking back with all the advantages of hindsight, we can discern the emergence of a certain impatience with religious fervor in England and all those lands where religious violence had taken a heavy toll. It is not because of mere chance that England, France, the Netherlands, and Germany bred so many secularists, skeptics, rationalists, and empirical scientists in the seventeenth century. Religious instability, often accompanied by violence, made it necessary for conflict-weary Europeans to back off from religion and to find truths that were less divisive and grounded in logic and empirical observation rather than in divine revelation, sacred texts, or ecclesiastical authorities. If one views the rise of secularism as the ultimate unfolding of the Reformation in England and elsewhere, then King Charles I may have been right when he declared himself "a martyr for the people." His violent death still serves as a poignant reminder that zealotry seldom leads to peace, and that, ironically, the toleration we now enjoy and cherish was gained through many sacrificial victims.

CHAPTER TWENTY-ONE

The Age of Orthodoxy

O rthodoxy and heresy have always been intertwined in Christian history as inseparable binary components of a complex process of self-definition. More than that, orthodoxy has most often been arrived at through a very painful process of sifting through opinions and counteropinions. Orthodoxy requires exclusion, even punishment. Orthodox affirmations are negations too, and bound inseparably to anathemas, that is, to decrees that condemn and expel heretics from the body of the faithful. Contention is the mother of orthodoxy, and hairsplitting its midwife. Clarifying, defining, drawing distinctions down to the finest razor-edged point—these are the essential components of the path to orthodoxy. It is a nasty, messy process, for sure, and all too often a bloody one too.

In 1517 the search for orthodoxy made Western Christendom implode. The Christian religion had imploded for similar reasons numerous times before, and distinct churches had come into existence, all claiming to be orthodox: Arian, Donatist, Nestorian, Monophysite, and so on. In 1054, the pope in Rome and the patriarch in Constantinople excommunicated each other and all their followers, creating a schism that pitted "Catholic" against "Orthodox." These various schisms were all occasioned by disagreement on what was "genuine" or "true" in the Christian faith. Politics certainly played a key role in all this fragmenting, as did social, economic, ethnic, and cultural issues. But the idiom of fragmentation was always theological. After 1054, theological contention never ceased in the West, among Catholics, and even intensified as theology became an increasingly sophisticated discipline.

But nothing like the implosion of 1517 had ever shaken Christendom before. Its scale was unprecedented: it was an exponential increase in fragmentation that led to the creation of multiple competing churches all at once, each claiming to be the only genuine custodian of orthodoxy. Even worse, once this exponential increase in splintering was set in motion, a seemingly unstoppable branching pattern emerged, even within each of the churches that claimed to be the "one true church." It is so distinct a pattern, and so obvious, that mathematicians might someday reduce it to fractal equations such as those that have been devised for the branching patterns of trees, rivers, nerves, blood vessels, and snowflakes.

The period that follows immediately after this great implosion could be called the age of disagreements, the age of hairsplitting, the age of doctrinal refinement, or the age of neo-scholasticism, but this era that begins with the death of Luther in 1546 and stretches all the way into the early 1700s came to be known as the age of orthodoxy. This appellation refers to the history of theology, and it was fashioned by Protestant church historians who wanted to defend the correctness of their own particular beliefs. Referring to orthodoxy rather than disagreements, or to hairsplitting, puts a positive spin on what transpired in the realm of theology during this period and reifies the legacy of the victors in these intra- and interconfessional struggles.

To call this period the age of orthodoxy is to emphasize its stability and to assume a very specific and inevitable endpoint. But doctrine was far from stable in this era, and outcomes decidedly uncertain. Arriving at "orthodoxy" was a painful process of self-definition and community formation among contending religious traditions and established churches. In sum, it was a tidying up of the mess left behind by the first generation of Protestant Reformers. The successful challenge to Roman Catholic hegemony by these religious leaders had given rise to fierce rivalries not just with Catholic opponents but also among themselves. Formulating much of their theology in the heat of battle, often in response to very specific challenges from multiple opponents, the first generation of Protestant Reformers had left many loose ends dangling in the fabric of their theology, especially in reference to key issues such as exegesis (how to interpret the Bible), soteriology (how one is saved), sacramentology (the nature and function of rituals), and ecclesiology (the nature and function of the church). Catholics had their loose ends too, though fewer in number, thanks to the definitions of the Council of Trent. But one key issue in particular, that of soteriology, had been defined by Trent in a paradoxical way. And in the overheated polemical climate of the age, the council's paradoxical definition left the door open for competing interpretations and intra-Catholic friction.

All in all, then, contention was inevitable, both internally and externally, as various churches—each of which proclaimed that there could be only one true faith—struggled to guide their flocks and define their own identities in the wake of the religious disintegration of Europe. Social historians have referred to this process as "confessionalization," that is, the development of churches with well-defined identities, precise confessions of faith, and exacting ethical codes. Some even speak of this era as the confessional age. These historians tend to focus on the ways increased doctrinal precision led to the creation of distinct communities, all of which placed great emphasis on uniformity and on certain kinds of behavior. They also often emphasize the process of the control of morals, often referred to as social disciplining, which they link to the formation of the centralized early modern state. In other words, these historians emphasize the practical result of this complex process of self-definition in which church and state worked in tandem and in which theology, politics, and the process of self-definition were often inseparable.[1]

We shall take up that perspective in the next chapter. Even though the issue of confessionalization is really inseparable from that of the creation of creeds and confessions, distinguishing between the process of self-definition and the enforcement of theological and ethical norms required by those definitions is absolutely necessary. One process concerns theology, and the other concerns ethics and politics. For now, our main concern will be the process of self-definition itself rather than its social and political ramifications.

Since the issues that arose within each of the various Reformation traditions have their own distinctive features, the best way to deal with this subject is to take each major confession into account on its own terms, one by one.

Lutherans

The first Reformation church to be riven by questions of theological precision was that of the Lutherans, which, in Melanchthon's own words, succumbed to "theological raging."[2] Two linked events made this reckoning inevitable. The first was Martin Luther's death in 1546. With Luther gone, differences of opinion that had been building up for years among his followers suddenly had a chance to surface. These divisions were sharpened by a second sequence of events: the defeat of the Lutheran princes by Emperor Charles V in 1547, his attempt to impose the Augsburg Interim on their lands in 1548—which many Lutherans viewed as nothing less than a dismantling of their church—and Philip Melanchthon's willingness to compromise. The most pressing issue in 1548 concerned how much accommodation to Catholicism any Lutheran should be willing to make. Melanchthon's response to the Augsburg Interim (a text that came to be known among its critics as the "Leipzig Interim") laid out the core compromise he was willing to make concerning theology and ritual, pledging loyalty to the emperor and appealing to the concept of adiaphora, which he defined as "matters of indifference that may be observed without injury to the divine scriptures."[3]

As this crisis unfolded, two opposing parties took shape: those who were willing to compromise with Catholicism, and those who were adamantly opposed to it. As already seen in the previous chapter, the leader of those who favored compromise was Luther's right-hand man, Philip Melanchthon. Those who agreed with him came to be known as Philippists. Their opponents, who claimed to be upholding the true legacy of Martin Luther, shrewdly dubbed themselves Gnesio-Lutherans, or True Lutherans (from the Greek *gnesios*, or "genuine, authentic"). Led at first by the historian and theologian Matthias Flacius Illyricus, who was later joined by Nikolaus von Amsdorf, the Gnesio-Lutherans would square off against the Philippists on a long list of issues, the most significant and divisive of which concerned the role of the human will in salvation

Luther's troubled successor. After Martin Luther's death in 1546, his right-hand man Philip Melanchthon assumed the leadership of the Lutheran Church, but was immediately challenged from within and assailed from without. A brilliant theologian who was more comfortable with paradox than many of his contemporaries, and more amenable to compromise too, Melanchthon engaged with Catholics, and with fellow Lutherans and Reformed Protestants of various stripes, often in a spirit of conciliation. A lightning rod for controversy, as well as for attempts at conciliation, he looks weary in this 1550 woodcut by Lucas Cranach the Younger.

and how to determine which rituals were genuinely Christian. For the most part, the divisions were of a highly scholarly nature, literally embodied by professors of theology, with the Philippists based at the University of Wittenberg and the Gnesio-Lutherans at the universities in Magdeburg and Jena.

Grappling with all the intricacies of the disagreements between the Philippists and Gnesio-Lutherans—a subject that has enthralled Lutheran historians for centuries—requires patience with fine distinctions. First and foremost, the Philippists were in favor of assigning the human will some role in salvation. Though they upheld Luther's *sola fide* and *sola gratia* principles, emphasizing that salvation was an unmerited gift of God, the Philippists tended to assign a cooperating role to the human will, which, as they saw it, is essential in the redemption of every individual. Melanchthon had laid out their basic premise in his Leipzig Interim, arguing that good works were "so highly necessary that if they are not quickened in the heart there is no reception of divine grace."[4] The Gnesio-Lutherans rejected any such theology as a betrayal of Luther's uncompromising stance against works-righteousness. Accusing the Philippists of synergism, that is, of teaching that salvation depended on some level of human cooperation with divine grace, the Gnesio-Lutherans insisted that the human will could contribute absolutely nothing to the process of salvation.

These were fine points of theology indeed, but they became rallying points for rivalry and identity formation. Most Lutherans might not have fully understood fine soteriological distinctions but they were much clearer on compromise with Catholicism.

These recondite theological questions were just one element in a debate that addressed whether a whole panoply of Catholic rites and beliefs was acceptable. By proposing that much of Catholicism lay in the realm of the "indifferent" or inconsequential (that is, adiaphora), the Philippists painted themselves into a corner, for many Lutherans saw their theological flexibility as a betrayal of Luther.

This willingness to compromise was not all that made the Philippists seem like traitors in the eyes of some of their fellow Lutherans. Their peacemaking tendencies were broad enough to also encompass their Protestant rivals, the Reformed, with whom they sought to form a tighter bond. The burning issue on this front was that of the Eucharist, which had driven the two traditions apart at the Marburg Colloquy in 1529. In opposition to the Reformed, who proposed that Christ could not be physically present in the bread and wine, Luther had adamantly insisted until his dying day on the real presence of Christ, arguing that since Christ was divine he was ubiquitous, that is, capable of being present everywhere simultaneously. To the Gnesio-Lutherans it seemed that Melanchthon and the Philippists were not only willing to fudge on this issue, but actually eager to do so, merely for the sake of concord. In the formulations of Melanchthon and of his followers, including that of his son-in-law Caspar Peucer, the presence of Christ in the Eucharist was phrased ambiguously, through terms such as *exhibited*. Since John Calvin had assumed leadership of the Reformed tradition by the time these irenic efforts of the Philippists came to the fore in the 1550s, the Gnesio-Lutherans dubbed this Philippist position "crypto-Calvinism" (from the Greek *kryptein*, "to hide"). The divisive wrangling over this issue continued after Melanchthon's death in 1560. Peucer, a mathematician and physician, and onetime dean and rector of the University of Wittenberg, would pay a heavy price for his role in this infighting. Formally charged with the "crime" of crypto-Calvinism in 1574 by Lutheran brethren who had gained the upper hand, he spent twelve years imprisoned at the Saxon fortress of Königstein.

That Lutherans were tossing some of their own leading lights into prison over theological disagreements reveals the extent of the rancor among them. Fracturing of this sort weakened Lutheranism from within, making it vulnerable to disintegration, maybe even to extermination. Philippists and Gnesio-Lutherans wrangled for years on end, over the span of three decades. Some among them sought solutions and reconciliation, but disputing parties could not even agree on how to resolve their differences. While the Philippists tended to favor a political solution in which the princes and civil magistrates would impose a settlement on all Lutherans, the Gnesio-Lutherans refused to yield an inch, insisting instead on arriving at a very detailed list of true beliefs and specific condemnations of the "false" teachings of the Philippists.

Though several princes tried to arbitrate, and several colloquia were held, the two sides in this dispute held fast to their positions. Eventually, in the 1570s, a cluster of theologians assembled by Duke Julius of Braunschweig-Wolfenbüttel, began to make headway. On the Philippist side, Martin Chemnitz would lead the way to reconciliation, on the Gnesio-Lutheran side, that role was taken by Jacob Andreae. A key step was the publication in 1573 of Andreae's *Six Sermons on the Divisions Among the Theologians of the Augsburg Confession*, which circulated through both camps and laid the foundation for several subsequent proposals, each of which brought the feuding Lutherans closer to agreeing. By 1576, thanks largely to the efforts of princes such as Duke Ulrich of Württenberg, Elector August of Saxony, and Margrave Karl of Baden, theologians from both sides met at Maulbronn Abbey to compose a formula for reconciliation. Further meetings at Torgau and Bergen Abbey over the following year led to additional refinements in the formula drafted at Maulbronn, and to the issuance of the *Solid Declaration of the Formula of Concord*, which was widely circulated and eventually accepted by fifty-one principalities and thirty-five imperial free cities, in all of which it could be enforced through the principle of *cuius regio, eius religio*. In addition, it was accepted by more than eight thousand pastors. After further minor revisions, this document was published in 1580—the thirtieth anniversary of the Augsburg Confession—within *The Book of Concord*, a compendium of the most significant Lutheran documents. This *Solid Declaration* was initially embraced by two-thirds of the German Lutheran Church. The most notable holdouts were four German principalities (Zweibrücken, Anhalt, Pomerania, and Holstein), the Scandinavian kingdoms (Denmark-Norway and Sweden), and the three cities of Nuremberg, Strassburg, and Magdeburg. The consequences of this dissent will be dealt with presently.

The *Solid Declaration of the Formula of Concord* was not so much a compromise as an absolute surrender by the Philippists, even though a few of their subtle points were taken into account. Its twelve articles were not just a detailed summation of Gnesio-Lutheran theology, but also a thorough condemnation of all of the "errors" of the Philippists. Eight of the twelve articles dealt with soteriology. Two dealt with the Eucharist. One dealt with the issue of adiaphora. The final article dealt with a range of other heresies found mostly among the Radicals. All twelve articles affirmed Gnesio-Lutheran positions as orthodox, in great detail: the total depravity of human nature, salvation by grace alone, the real presence of Christ in the Eucharist, the necessity of shunning certain Catholic rites. In its preface, the victors took control of the narrative, aligning themselves with the Augsburg Confession, and claiming to be the sole defenders of its orthodoxy:

> Now, although the Christian doctrine of the Augsburg Confession has in great part remained unchallenged . . . yet it cannot be denied that some theologians have departed from some great and important articles of the said Confession, and either have not attained to their true meaning, or at any rate have not continued steadfastly therein, and occasionally have even undertaken to attach to it a foreign meaning. . . . Necessity, therefore, requires us to explain these controverted articles according to God's Word and approved writings, so that everyone who has Christian understanding can notice which opinion concerning the matters in controversy accords with God's Word and the Christian Augsburg Confession, and which does not.[5]

Throughout the previous three decades, the chief distinguishing traits of the Philippists had been their flexibility, their fondness for compromise, and their irenic tendencies. In contrast, their adversaries distinguished themselves by their tenacity. It had been an uneven match all along, not in terms of the brilliance of the theologians on either side, but in terms of their core disposition. The Philippists could be more easily worn down.

The *rabies theologorum*, or rage that Melanchthon longed to be freed from, was not easily quelled, however, and even after the *Formula of Concord* was proclaimed, squabbling continued. The largest obstacle to full harmony was formed by the substantial number of Lutherans who refused to accept the compromise. Though many of these pockets of resistance were finally brought around to Gnesio-Lutheran orthodoxy, their unswerving convictions kept some wounds open and prevented some scars from healing. One subject in particular continued to bedevil Lutherans even after 1580: crypto-Calvinism. Fed by the growing presence of Calvinists in Germany, eucharistic controversies remained live, and Lutheran crypto-Calvinists continued to stir up rancor and, in some cases, outright conflict. A prominent activist in this continued turmoil was Nikolaus Krell, chief adviser to Elector Christian I of Saxony, who promoted crypto-Calvinism in the epicenter of Lutheranism, with his ruler's support. Though Krell and his crypto-Calvinists gained the upper hand in Saxony for a few years, as soon as Christian I died, in 1591, their gains quickly evaporated. Frederick William, duke of Saxe-Altenburg, who was appointed regent of Saxony, had little patience for Calvinists, and in 1592–1593 drove them all away or underground. Nikolaus Krell was imprisoned at Königstein—where Caspar Peucer, too, had been locked up—and in 1601, after a much-delayed trial, he was executed.

Orthodoxy thus prevailed in Lutheran Germany after 1580, despite some dissent. Curiously, at the universities, where theology reigned supreme as queen of the sciences, Lutheran scholastics revived some of the approaches that Luther had despised, adding Aristotle to the curriculum, embracing natural theology, and writing enormous and detailed summae in Latin that rivaled those of their medieval predecessors. That Luther had dismissed philosophy as a whore and denounced scholasticism as a betrayal of the Gospel did not trouble these Lutheran neo-scholastics who still defended the principle of *sola scriptura*, for they understood their use of scholastic methodology to be solely exegetical, a means to interpret the Bible. In the most prestigious of the Lutheran universities—Wittenberg, Jena, Leipzig, Rostock, Tübingen, Giesen, and Königsberg—theologians cranked out learned and very orthodox tomes as they trained pastors for the ministry who were simultaneously schooled in Greek, Hebrew, Latin, metaphysics and hermeneutics. Among these scholars, the leading lights were Johann Gerhard (1582–1637), Abraham Calov (1612–1685), and Johan Andreas Quenstedt (1617–1688). Calov produced a twelve-volume summa, titled *Systema locorum theologicorum*; Quenstedt followed with his own ponderous *Theologica didactico-polemica sive systema theologicorum*. But they could not surpass in influence Gerhard's nine-volume magnum opus, his *Loci theologici*, which until well into the twentieth century held a place in Lutheran theological education akin to that of Thomas Aquinas in Catholic universities.

Reformed Protestantism

To speak of "Reformed Protestantism" as a monolithic tradition is justifiable, but also slightly misleading, for it was above all a very adaptable religion: a flexible ideology that adjusted to its environments. Yet the Reformed always tended to adapt without conforming: they held on to core principles and a certain worldview regardless of local circumstances, whether their churches were run by presbyteries or synods, and whether they had consistories or not. Uncompromising zeal was an essential component of their identity and linked them to one another, despite local differences. This is not to say that the Reformed were all of one mind. Not at all. Disagreements were as numerous and as heated among them as in any other religious tradition, and as divisive as those that vexed Lutherans and Catholics.

The most basic division within the Reformed tradition was between the Swiss Reformed and the Calvinists. The Swiss Reformed claimed an older pedigree, holding Ulrich Zwingli and Heinrich Bullinger in the highest esteem. The Calvinists were upstarts of sorts, since John Calvin was a second-generation Reformer who derived his theology from the Swiss Reformed. The two branches of the Reformed family agreed on many substantial points of doctrine, but not all. The Calvinists would end up having a greater influence on Europe as a whole, and the term *Calvinist* came to be synonymous with *Reformed* in many places. Reformed orthodoxy, then, was to a great extent linked to Calvinism.

But the Swiss Reformed never faded away, and continued to remain in dialogue with Calvinists. When it came to theology, Bullinger was the great Swiss systematizer. Unlike Zwingli, who forged his theology in the heat of conflict and died young, Bullinger had the opportunity to develop a consistent and orderly doctrinal legacy. To begin with, Bullinger had the advantage of subscribing to the First Helvetic Confession (1536), along with all of the Swiss Reformed. The confession was a summation of Reformed orthodoxy that he had coauthored with other major reformers, such as Leo Jud of Zurich, Oswald Myconius of Basel, and Martin Bucer of Strassburg. Though never totally free from controversy, this confession did much to clarify contested points of doctrine, such as the meaning of the Eucharist, and to create a modicum of harmony among those who subscribed to it. Bullinger also had the advantage of surviving until the age of seventy-one—rare in his day—and of thus having more time to work through all of the rough spots in Reformed theology. Toward the end of his life, in 1566, he was able to bequeath to his followers the Second Helvetic Confession, a thorough compendium of Reformed theology authored by him that sought to correct and put to rest disagreements that still lingered among the Swiss Reformed. Its influence would be enormous, not just because of its comprehensiveness, but also because of its broad geographical reach. Eventually, it would be consulted by Calvinist theologians in Germany, France, Scotland, Poland, and Hungary, as they sorted out their own definitions of orthodoxy.

Calvinist orthodoxy had two fixed reference points up until Calvin's death in 1564, one geographical, the other textual: Geneva, the city from which Calvin exported the Reformed faith, and Calvin's ever-expanding and ever more detailed editions of the *Institutes of the Christian Religion*, along with his many other treatises and letters. Though he had plenty of opponents and spent much of his time dealing with theological controversies, Calvin was able to impose a degree of uniformity on his followers that surpassed that won by most of his fellow Reformers, largely because of the clarity and thoroughness of his *Institutes*. Yet he was never fully satisfied with that masterful summa, and if he had lived longer, Calvin would have kept rewriting it. Calvin was intensely aware of the many ways in which error and contention could threaten orthodoxy. As he saw it, vigilance and a constant refining of theology to meet the needs of the day were absolute necessities. And so was the constant policing of thought and behavior, along with censoring, correcting, punishing, excommunicating, expelling, or even executing those who strayed from the straight and narrow path. This enforcement of orthodoxy became one of the most salient characteristics of Calvinists everywhere, and one of the reasons for their remarkable success.

After Calvin's death, his successor at Geneva, Théodore de Bèze followed suit for forty years, from 1564 until 1605, maintaining Geneva's status as "the Protestant Rome." His role in the development of Calvinist orthodoxy was pivotal, not just through his writings—including his magisterial *Summa totius Christianismi*, which dealt with the touchy subject of predestination—but also through his constant involvement in controversies and in the spread of the Reformed faith. The fact that Bèze's Genevan Academy continued to train many of the clergy who went on to serve Calvinist communities elsewhere also increased his influence.

Théodore de Bèze was not alone. One of the most significant developments during his tenure in Geneva was the expansion Calvinism, and the creation of new centers of learning where theologizing took place. Among these new centers, the German principality of the Palatinate rose to prominence after 1561, due to its size and power, and to its rulers, the Wittelsbach dynasty, who were committed to the Calvinist cause and the creation of a godly society. The chief contributions of this principality to international Calvinism were its intake of refugees and the swift rise in prominence of the University of Heidelberg, which, along with the University of Leiden in the Netherlands, came to rival the Genevan Academy as a center for Reformed theological study. Another chief contribution was the *Heidelberg Catechism*, which was composed by a team of ministers in 1563, some of whom had spent time in Geneva. Its summary of Reformed Calvinist faith and doctrine would prove immensely influential beyond Germany, and shape international Calvinism for centuries to come.

As Calvinists grew in number and spread over the map, the Swiss Reformed were increasingly eclipsed. But differences between the two camps kept the Swiss from ever being swallowed up by their upstart brethren. Calvinists everywhere tended to oppose three aspects of Swiss Reformed doctrine, and vice versa. This disagreement made it impossible to speak of Reformed orthodoxy as a single theological tradition, but it did not polarize the two communities or turn them into bitter rivals. At best, they maintained fairly good relations with one another, agreeing on many issues, refraining from the "rage" that possessed so many Lutheran theologians. At worst, they bickered and held grudges, and sometimes failed to help one another in times of need. The first of these three points of contention was the Eucharist, that most divisive of subjects. The Swiss insisted on a purely symbolic interpretation, emphasizing its role as a sign of a covenant, rejecting any talk of Christ's presence in the ritual; the Calvinists were inclined to see the ritual as an instrument of grace, rather than a mere sign, and to believe in a spiritual communion between the believer and Christ. The second contested point was that of predestination, and at issue was one of the slimmest theological hairs ever to be split. Whereas the Swiss affirmed single predestination (that God merely predestines those to be saved), the Calvinists insisted on double predestination (that God predestines who will be saved and who will be damned). The third disagreement concerned relations between church and state. The Swiss, faithful to long-standing civic traditions, insisted that the civil magistracy should manage the church; the Calvinists preferred to grant the church more independence, especially when it came to issues of church governance and Christian discipline. One practical question to which the two traditions gave different answers, for instance, was whether the state or the church should be in charge of disciplining and excommunicating.

These disagreements were a far cry from those that tore apart the Lutherans. But soon after Bèze's death, Calvinism fell prey to major discord too, and the subject was one all too familiar to the Lutherans: soteriology, and more specifically, the subject of the human will and its relation to God's grace. Adapting predestination to daily life was always a big challenge to Calvinists, and for some, such as New England puritans, a source of anxiety. "Am I one of the elect or not? Can I play any role in my salvation?" Questions such as these could drive some introspective Calvinists to despair.

Some Calvinists sought to tinker with Calvin's soteriology, offering milder interpretations of predestination that gave the human will some role to play and affirmed that Christ had thus died for all humans, not just for the elect. Jacob Arminius (1560–1609), a Dutch Calvinist, was the chief architect of such an alternative theology, which came to bear his name: Arminianism. In 1610, his followers summarized their beliefs in a document titled *The Remonstrance*, which earned them the name of Remonstrants. Condensing their theological propositions into five succinct points, the Remonstrants emphasized human responsibility as much as divine grace. The fifth article summed up this theology succinctly, stressing the active role humans were expected to play in their own salvation (emphasis in italics):

> Those who are incorporated into Christ by a true faith, and have thereby become partakers of his life-giving Spirit, have thereby full power *to strive* against Satan, sin, the world, and their own flesh, and *to win* the victory, it being well understood that it is ever through the assisting grace of the Holy Ghost; and that Jesus Christ *assists them* through his Spirit in all temptations, extends to them his hand, and if *only they are ready for the conflict*, and *desire his help*, and *are not inactive*, keeps them from falling.[6]

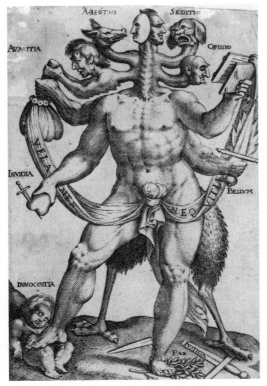

Monstrous error. This engraving from 1618 is a polemical allegory of Arminianism, here portrayed as a five-headed monster, in reference to the Five Articles of Remonstrance of 1610. The accusations leveled against Arminians (or Remonstrants) are as extreme and heavy-handed as the symbolism. The five heads represent avarice, idiocy, duplicity, sedition, and rumor mongering. The monster holds envy in one hand and war in the other, while he crushes innocence with one foot and peace and justice with the other. An extra set of legs—obviously demonic—protrudes from the monster's rear end.

The controversy that ensued was highly divisive, and the theological brawl spilled over into Dutch politics. It also involved Calvinists elsewhere, especially in France and England. No compromise was reached, and ultimately the dispute led to a schism and to a further clarification of certain points of doctrine. In 1619, at the Synod of Dordrecht (known as Dort in English), the Counter-Remonstrants condemned Arminianism and affirmed double predestination. Their five-point summation, which came to be known as Five-Point Calvinism, can be very conveniently memorized in English by means of the acronym TULIP—devised in the nineteenth century—a very appropriate symbol of Dutch identity:

> Total depravity—humans are so corrupted by original sin, sinning is inevitable
> Unconditional election—humans can do nothing to earn salvation: it is all up
>   to God
> Limited atonement—Christ's redemptive act applies only to the elect
> Irresistible grace—those chosen by God cannot refuse his grace
> Perseverance of the saints—the elect cannot lose their salvation

Not all Calvinists accepted the Synod of Dort or its endorsement of the *Heidelberg Catechism*. Condemned by the synod, the Dutch Remonstrants had no choice but to create their own church. Elsewhere, the pronouncements of Dort led to numerous disagreements.

In France, theologians at the Calvinist academy of Saumur, led by Moses Amyraut (1596–1664) began to challenge the doctrines of Dort very subtly in the 1630s, emphasizing what they called hypothetical universalism, that is, the theory that although God wills to save everyone, only those who are favored with his gift of faith can be saved. Saumur quickly fell under a cloud of suspicion, as a wellspring of "novelties." Amyraut was repeatedly charged with heresy, and though cleared by three different synods, he would be declared unorthodox after his death. The definitive condemnation came in 1675, from theologians at Geneva and Basel. This repudiation, known as the *Consensus Helveticus*, reaffirmed the teachings of Dort and a few other points of doctrine, such as the divine inspiration of the Hebrew text of the Bible (some Saumur theologians had denied that the vowel points of the Old Testament were of divine origin). The *Consensus Helveticus* would prove the last such formulation of Calvinist orthodoxy, for by that time the rise of skepticism was already driving theological concerns in other directions, far from minutiae such as vowel points and hypothetical propositions concerning God's will.

In England, the fallout from Dort proved far more intense. Among Puritans, Arminianism was both a despised error and a source of conflict. In addition, both King Charles I and William Laud, archbishop of Canterbury were Arminians, and the crown's determination to impose this Arminianism and high Anglican church uniformity on England, Wales, and Scotland infuriated Puritans. Consequently, resistance to Arminianism can be counted among the many causal factors of the English Civil War. And when Laud and King Charles were executed, their deaths would be justified in large measure on theological grounds, among which their Arminianism could be numbered. As Puritans gained the upper hand in their struggle against King Charles, questions of orthodoxy naturally came to the fore, and this led to the convening of the Westminster Assembly in 1646, to settle all questions concerning religion. The resulting *Westminster Confession*, which upheld Five Point Calvinism, was adopted by the Church of Scotland and Presbyterians and Congregationalists in England and America, as was the *Westminster Catechism* (deeply influenced by that of Heidelberg). But this turn toward the orthodoxy of Dort did not bring an end to disagreements among Calvinists, or stifle Arminianism. Eventually, Arminian theology would be brought to its most dramatic fruition in the eighteenth century by John Wesley (1703–1791), the founder of Methodism.

Attempts to uphold orthodoxy never ceased, but they assumed a different character by the latter part of the seventeenth century, as the hegemony of the established churches began to wane and European culture became increasingly more secularized. Orthodoxy ceased to be a concern for the state, and also for some churches. Geneva, the onetime epicenter of Calvinist orthodoxy, provides us with a revealing example of the eclipse of orthodoxy among the Reformed. In 1675, the leading champion of orthodoxy on the theological faculty of Geneva was François Turrettini (1632–1687), also known by the French version of his surname, Turretin. The grandson of an Italian Calvinist refugee who had arrived in Geneva in 1592, Turrettini was one of the authors of the *Consensus Helveticus*, that definitive text that upheld Dort's five-point Calvinism and condemned all of the novelties of Moses Amyraut and the Saumur theologians. This document was more than a mere opinion piece penned by university professors: it was an instrument of uniformity, with real teeth, for all clergy in Geneva and many other places were obligated to sign it and to swear to uphold its teachings.

Within one generation, however, the *Consensus* would lose those teeth, thanks largely to none other than Jean-Alphonse Turrettini (1671–1737), the son of its author, François. The younger Turrettini, also a professor on the theological faculty, pressed successfully in 1706 for the abolition of the *Consensus* as a required test of faith. After that year, no clergy in Geneva were forced to sign it, or uphold its teachings. In 1725, also thanks to him, no one was forced to uphold the Synod of Dort either. Henceforward, the sole requirement would be "faithfulness" to the Bible and Calvin's catechism. The younger Turrettini embodied a new orthodoxy, quite different from his father's: instead of finding errors in others, he strove to accommodate Calvinism to Enlightenment thought, and champion a smoothing out of religious differences between Lutherans and the Reformed. His goal, so different from that of his heretic-hunting predecessors, was the formation of a unified Protestant Church in which theology had no fine points to be quibbled over, and enlightened behavior was the ultimate measure of orthodoxy.

Catholics

Theological quarrels over orthodoxy were not limited to Protestants in the sixteenth and seventeenth centuries. In the long run, it mattered little that the Council of Trent had provided definitive answers to all of the theological questions raised by the Protestant Reformation. Denying legitimacy to Protestant theology was one thing, fully explaining Catholic theology was quite another, especially since disagreement on certain doctrinal issues had been commonplace in the Middle Ages, and many of these contested issues remained in place in the wake of the Protestant challenge.

An eye-catching pattern runs through the history of Catholicism from the Council of Trent to the early eighteenth century, much like a bright red thread in a white altar cloth. This pattern is the constant presence of the theological question that had triggered the Protestant Reformation: what, exactly, is the relation between the human will and the divine? From the 1550s to well into the 1700s, the Catholic Church had to contend with a string of challenges that, in one way or another, forced its authorities to grapple with the paradoxes affirmed by Trent concerning human nature, divine grace, and predestination.

Soteriology had been left open to further definition by the Council of Trent, even though it was one of the first subjects tackled by it in response to Protestantism. Its decree on justification was a detailed refutation of *sola fide* and *sola gratia* theology, as well of double predestination and other tenets of Protestant soteriology. But its affirmations, like many conciliar pronouncements since those of Nicaea in 325, stressed paradoxes as the very essence of orthodoxy. Concerning salvation, and the subject of the interaction between God's grace and the human will, the council had chosen to affirm that Protestant soteriology was wrong in rejecting paradox, and stressing salvation by grace alone and faith alone. While not denying the absolute necessity of divine grace, or of faith, Trent had affirmed the integrity of the human will, and the role of the individual in choosing or rejecting grace. Its explication of this thorny subject involved a string of intentional incongruities, and raised as many questions as it sought to answer. God's "quickening and assisting grace," it explained, helped sinners to "convert themselves to their own justification, by freely assenting to and co-operating with that said grace." Doubling up on paradox, the text continued:

> While God touches the heart of man by the illumination of the Holy Ghost, neither is man himself utterly without doing anything while he receives that inspiration, forasmuch as he is also able to reject it; yet is he not able, by his own free will, without the grace of God, to move himself unto justice in His sight.[7]

Trent also reaffirmed the doctrine of predestination while warning the faithful not to dwell on the subject: "No one, moreover, so long as he is in this mortal life, ought so far to presume as regards the secret mystery of divine predestination, as to determine for certain that he is assuredly in the number of the predestinate."[8]

Many questions, large and small, could still be asked, and theologians asked them. Questioning was their business, even after Trent, and so was the search for precision, which most of them revered as a virtue. How does grace work exactly, or what role does the human will play, exactly, in a universe where an omnipotent and omniscient God ordains all things? How can predestination and free will be reconciled? What is the difference between prevenient, efficient, and sanctifying grace? Though dealt with in the realm of the abstract, with tools borrowed from philosophy, such questions were not purely theoretical. They had a practical, pastoral dimension as well, for it was the job of all pastors to instruct their flocks on one basic question: how to be saved. And they had a polemical dimension too, as elaborations of orthodoxy over and against the errors of the Protestants.

One of the first controversies to erupt within Catholicism after the Council of Trent dealt with precisely such questions. As was the case with similar disputes, the questions were not being asked to challenge orthodoxy, but rather provide it with greater intellectual rigor. The first theologian to run afoul of church authorities in such a vein was Michel de Bay (1513–1589), a professor at the University of Louvain who had Latinized his name to Baius, in keeping with humanist fashion. A well-respected theologian, he was appointed as one of the Belgian representatives to the final session of the Council of Trent. Seeking to engage Protestant error on its own terms, Baius turned *ad fontes*, to the Bible and the early church fathers, especially St. Augustine of Hippo (354–430) rather than to scholastic theology. Since Protestants focused so much on the questions of free will and predestination, Baius mined Augustine for opinions on both issues. What he came up with, however, proved controversial even before Trent issued its decree on justification. Following Augustine closely, Baius emphasized the corruption of human nature and the effects of original sin, taking aim against any theology that expressed—as he saw it—too much confidence in the power of the free will. His opinions, published in a number of treatises, quickly began to draw complaints that he sounded too much like Luther and Calvin. In 1567, Pope Pius V issued a bull condemning more than six dozen statements made by Baius, but since the Louvain professor had taken great care to ground his arguments in the teachings of St. Augustine, the condemnation was too carefully worded to be effective, and it left many theologians arguing over the meaning of its sentences, and even over the placement of commas. After much hemming and hawing, Baius repented for some of his "errors" publically, but kept insisting privately that he had interpreted Augustine correctly. This controversy had no resolution, then. Instead, it opened a door to more divisive disputes on the subject of grace and free will.

Another theologian who addressed the same issues and kept controversy alive was Luis de Molina (1535–1600), a Spanish Jesuit who was also very interested in proving Luther and Calvin wrong but took an approach diametrically opposed to that of Baius. A professor of theology at the University of Coimbra, Molina tried to reconcile predestination with the freedom of the human will, largely as a result of his engagement with the thirteenth-century *Summa Theologica* of Thomas Aquinas. His treatise on predestination, published in 1588, created a furor in theological circles. Its long title spelled out his argument: *On the Harmony of Free Will with the Gift of Grace, Divine Foreknowledge, Providence, Predestination, and Reprobation*. While this work was a thoroughgoing defense of the integrity of the free will and its role in salvation—a very orthodox proposition—it proved controversial because of its theories concerning the foreknowledge of God and the way it squared predestination with free will. Molina's teachings, which came to be known as Molinism, were as complex and speculative as they came. The gist of his argument was this: God's omniscience allows him to know all possible outcomes, so divine predestination is based on God's foreknowledge of the choices that human beings will, and won't, make. The term coined by Molina for this special kind of divine cognition was *scientia media*, or middle knowledge. And, as Molina saw it, his theory helped affirm the paradox at the heart of Catholic orthodoxy: both grace and free will play a role in salvation. As he put it: "The freedom of the will must be preserved so that in all things the grace of the Giver may stand out."[9]

Opposition to Molina and his *scientia media* was intense, especially from Dominican theologians who considered themselves experts on the theology of Thomas Aquinas. His chief opponent was Domingo Bañez (1528–1604) at the University of Salamanca, who argued that God's predestination must precede all human choices, even those foreseen by God. Charges of heresy were leveled, and disputations between Dominicans and Jesuits were held at various universities, while appeals were made to Rome for a solution. For nine years, between 1598 and 1607, Molinism was intermittently reviewed by a special papal tribunal convened by Clement VIII for the sole purpose of dealing with this issue. This commission, known as the Congregatio Auxiliis, or Congregation on Help (by Divine Grace), considered arguments from both sides, even from the generals of both the Jesuits and Dominicans, but after a grueling eighty-five sessions held in the presence of two successive popes, Clement VIII and Paul V, no decision could be reached. Finally, in 1607, Pope Paul V suspended the proceedings and left the matter up in the air, allowing each of the two sides in the dispute to defend its own position and forbidding each of them from condemning the other, and also forbidding the publication of any books on the controversy. Promising a ruling sometime in the future, Paul V asked both sides to wait patiently for a papal decision.

But that decision never came. And in the uncertain space left open by the papacy, the controversy morphed inevitably into an even larger quarrel, given the significance of the subject. While the Congregatio Auxiliis withheld its judgment and three popes chose not to settle the dispute (Paul V, Gregory XV, and Urban VIII), others far from Salamanca and Rome who were opposed to Molinism took matters into their own hands. One of these well-intentioned meddlers was Cornelius Jansen (1585–1638), a Dutch theologian from the University of Louvain who had turned to the study of St. Augustine and questions regarding grace and free will due to the gravitational pull at Louvain of the controversy surrounding its own Baius. Jansen was more than a mere professor, for in 1636 he was appointed bishop of Ypres, in the war-torn Spanish Netherlands. While teaching at Louvain, and later, while fulfilling his episcopal duties, Jansen was naturally drawn to the unresolved controversies swirling over soteriological issues, and took on the task of writing an immensely detailed refutation of the errors he perceived in Molinism. Since Pope Paul V had forbidden the publication of any books on the Molinist controversy, per se, Jansen had to go about this task obliquely. And just like Baius before him—by whom he was obviously influenced—Jansen did so by drawing on his expertise in the teachings of the great St. Augustine on grace, free will, and predestination. The immense tome written by Jansen over several years, titled *Augustinus*, was published in 1640, after his death, and instantly won him acclaim and a substantial following. Before long, a powerful movement arose within the Catholic Church that bore Jansen's name and occasioned the "Jansenist" controversy, the most serious rift experienced by post-Tridentine Catholicism. So, by taking on the Molinists, Jansen had sparked an even greater crisis. Moreover, he had done so from the grave, through a book that ingeniously circumvented a papal proscription.

Though he could not grapple with the Molinists overtly, Jansen made it clear in his *Augustinus* that he was taking on teachings and practices that his elite readers could easily connect to Molinism and the Jesuit order. Arguing that some in his day had gone too far in their attempt to combat the teachings of Luther and Calvin on divine grace, and that these polemicists had been led by their excessive zeal to ascribe too great a role to the human will in the process of salvation, Jansen went as far as to charge that the Catholic faith was once again being threatened by a resurgence of Pelagianism, that ancient heresy opposed so eloquently by St. Augustine, which taught that human beings can achieve moral perfection and gain salvation without the aid of divine grace. Stressing the damage caused to humanity by original sin, Jansen reiterated Augustine's central principle concerning the human will: *non posse non peccare*. Bereft of grace, humans could not help but sin, always. Following Augustine closely, Jansen also argued, that divine grace was always irresistible and efficacious, and that salvation ultimately depended on God's inscrutable and seemingly arbitrary predestinating will.

Along with such teachings, which held human nature in low esteem, Jansen also put forward a puritanical and rigorist ethic that was diametrically opposed to Jesuit laxity. Life was serious business, and a constant combat with a disordered will: distractions and amusements were therefore obstacles to salvation, and something to be shunned. Constant introspection and self-control were key, and so was an absolute dependence on the church's sacraments, the ultimate means of grace. As Jansen saw it, the sacrament of penance was to be approached with an obsessive scrupulosity, and communion was not something to be approached lightly, or often. Jansen's *Augustinus* took aim against the Jesuit approach to salvation, and in the process, it also displayed several affinities to Puritanism and the Five Point Calvinism of Dort. And that position proved very appealing to some Catholics, especially in France, Italy, and the Netherlands. Though it was too cerebral and austere to gain a broad following, Jansenism did manage to win over some notable figures and to stir up plenty of conflict among Catholics.

The chief opponents of the *Augustinus* were the Jesuits, who charged that Jansen denigrated the integrity of the human will and denied that salvation was accessible to all humans. Ever adept at polemics, the Jesuits also coined the term *Jansenist*, which stressed their opponents' resemblance to Calvinists and Lutherans as followers of an errant newcomer. But just as it drew fire from Jesuits, the *Augustinus* also found many a receptive reader. In a France riven by religious conflict, where Calvinists were living proof of an enviable discipline and moral rigor, Jansenism found fertile soil among reform-minded Catholics. And it also found able leaders, some of whom had been personally connected to Jansen.

Of those who had known Jansen, none assumed a more prominent role than Jean Duvergier de Hauranne (1581–1643), a former schoolmate and patron who had encouraged him to write the *Augustinus* and promoted its teachings long before it was published. Having assumed the abbacy of the monastery of Saint-Cyran in 1620, this friend of Jansen's would become known as the Abbé of Saint-Cyran, or simply Saint-Cyran. Providing Jansenism with a center was one of Saint-Cyran's greatest contributions to the movement. It took shape at the convent of Port-Royal-des-Champs, near Paris, where he served as spiritual director and confessor to its nuns from 1633 to 1636, and at its satellite convent in the city of Paris itself, both of which became hotbeds of Jansenism. Within Port-Royal, a pivotal role would be played by the Arnauld family, principally through its abbess, Mother Marie Angelique Arnauld (1591–1661), and her brother Antoine Arnauld (1612–1694). Mother Marie Angelique instilled the nuns under her charge with Jansenist fervor, and many of the pupils who attended the schools run by them, including, among others, the playwright Jean Racine (1639–1699). Antoine Arnauld, one of the most eloquent of Jansenists, would assume leadership after the death of Saint-Cyran and defend their position tenaciously, principally through two books published in 1643: *The Moral Theology of the Jesuits* and *On Frequent Communion*.

Port-Royal could also count one of the most brilliant men in Europe as one of its own: Blaise Pascal (1623–1662), mathematician, scientist, inventor, and philosopher, who took up residence there, along with his sister Jacqueline, and raised Jansenist polemics to its greatest heights. In addition to inventing the world's first calculating machine, and devising the theory of probability, in 1657 Blaise Pascal published a scathing satire entitled *The Provincial Letters*, which skewered Jesuit theology and pastoral care and arguably did more to publicize the Jansenist cause than any other text. Pascal's most biting sarcasm was reserved for the casuistry of the Jesuits, that is, for their approach to the sacrament of penance, which tended to relativize the seriousness of every sin and to make the act of confession less precise and therefore also less embarrassing or burdensome. Zeroing in on the fact that the Jesuits seemed more interested in helping sinners be comfortable with their sins rather than in effecting genuine remorse and conversion, Pascal made them look devious and ridiculous. In one letter, for instance, he has a Jesuit explain their approach as follows:

> You may judge of the success with which our doctors have labored to discover, in their wisdom, that a great many things formerly regarded as forbidden, are innocent and allowable; but as there are some sins for which one can find no excuse, and for which there is no remedy but confession, it became necessary to alleviate, by [certain] methods . . . the difficulties attending that practice. Thus having shown you . . . how we relieve people from troublesome scruples of conscience by showing them that what they believed to be sinful was indeed quite innocent, I proceed now to illustrate our convenient plan for expiating what is really sinful, which is effected by making confession as easy a process as it was formerly a painful one.[10]

Pascal died young, however, and his leadership remained restricted to the printed page. The Jansenist cause remained largely in the hands of Antoine Arnauld, who faced constant harassment and persecution, and ended his life in exile, in Brussels. After his death in 1694, the Jansenist movement would be led by Pasquier Quesnel, an Oratorian priest whose magnum opus, *Moral Reflections on the New Testament* (1692), not only introduced a new generation to Jansenism, but also eventually eclipsed Jansen's own *Augustinus*.

The Jansenist controversy was as convoluted as it was lengthy. It troubled the Catholic Church for more than a century, and, in the process, morphed into a political issue in France, where Jansenism became linked to two causes: opposition to the absolutist claims of the monarchy and opposition to papal supremacy over the French church (a point of view known as Gallicanism). Political and theological issues became so intertwined as to become inseparable. Within the ecclesiastical realm, their chief enemies were the Jesuits; within the civil realm, their ultimate opponent proved to be the Sun King himself, Louis XIV; and they also had to contend with two figures in France who represented both church and state, the first minister to the king, Armand Jean du Plessis, Cardinal de Richelieu (1585–1642), and his successor, Cardinal Jules Mazarin (1602–1661). Sparks began to fly almost immediately after the publication of *Augustinus*. In 1641, the work was condemned by the Roman Inquisition, and the following year Pope Urban VIII issued a bull, *In eminenti*, that reiterated that condemnation. Despite these censures, *Augustinus* continued to make waves. The Jesuits fought back, and in 1653, thanks largely to their prodding, Pope Innocent X issued a bull, *Cum occasione*, in which he condemned five of Jansen's propositions. This began a long and untidy crisis known as the Formulary Controversy, so-called because the decree of 1653 required all French clergy to agree with a document known as a formulary that summed up the pope's condemnation of Jansenism—a demand some clerics resisted.

The Jansenists took a cautious and clever approach to the formulary, acknowledging that the pope had correctly identified heretical tendencies in the propositions cited in *Cum occasione*, but at the very same time denying that any such propositions could be found in Jansen's *Augustinus*. In addition, they argued that to condemn Jansen's *Augustinus* was to question the orthodoxy of St. Augustine himself. This strategy threw their opponents into disarray, and gave rise to an uneasy, but long truce in theological wrangling. In 1705, however, bowing to pressure from King Louis XIV, finally Pope Clement XI issued the bull *Vineam Domini*, in which he condemned Jansenism outright. Since leadership of the Jansenist movement had passed to Pasquier Quesnel by this time, an even more forceful and detailed condemnation that focused on Quesnel's teachings was needed. Such a censure took several years to prepare, but in 1713, Clement XI issued the bull *Unigenitus*, which cited 101 unorthodox propositions made by Quesnel and condemned them as

> false, captious, evil-sounding, offensive to pious ears, scandalous, pernicious, rash, injurious to the Church and her practice, insulting not only to the Church but also the secular powers seditious, impious, blasphemous, suspected of heresy, and smacking of heresy itself, and, besides, favoring heretics and heresies, and also schisms . . . clearly renewing many heresies respectively and most especially those which are contained in the infamous propositions of Jansenius.[11]

This was the final blow to Jansenism, which had been left severely weakened by the length and intensity of its struggle with both church and state. The eclipse of Jansenism can be detected in the fate of the abbey of Port-Royal, its epicenter. In 1661, in the thick of the Formulary Controversy, the convent was legally prevented from accepting novices. Then, in 1708, Pope Clement XI abolished it. Though its nuns and their supporters valiantly resisted the king's orders, those few who remained were removed against their will in 1709, and most of the buildings of Port-Royal were demolished the following year.

Jansenists as crypto-Calvinists. This 1653 almanac engraving by Abraham Bosse, titled *The Rout and Confusion of the Jansenists*, celebrates the ability of church and state to crush Jansenism and alleges that Jansenists are really Calvinists at heart. In the center, the divinely illumined pope, flanked by allegorical figures representing religion and the power of the church. oversees the defeat of Jansenism. From his throne, the French king drives Jansenists away and into the arms of a welcoming John Calvin. The text boxes at the bottom ascribe expressions to the pope, the king, and the Jansenists. In the Jansenist text box, they exclaim: "Oh, what will become of us miserable Jansenists? Should we finally recognize the error of our ways, or should we go over to the party of the Calvinist doctors?" In 1654, A leading Jansenist from Port-Royal, Isaac-Louis Le Maistre de Sacy, would publish a meticulous point-by-point rejoinder to this cartoon.

To confirm the utter error linked to this abbey, the remains of those buried there were exhumed, too, as Port-Royal was wiped off the map. As far as King Louis XIV and his ministers were concerned, Jansenism had been snuffed out, and the papal bull *Unigenitus* was merely its obituary.

But King Louis and all opponents of Jansenism would be in for a great surprise. At bottom, the Jansenist controversy was a debate over the interpretation of St. Augustine, and the central issue was one of the worst of conundrums: how could the Jansenists be condemned without also proclaiming one of the greatest of church fathers a heretic? Many of the 101 propositions condemned in the bull *Unigenitus*, much like those condemned in 1653 by the bull *Cum occasione*, came straight from St. Augustine himself. *Unigenitus* boldly chose to sweep much of Augustinian theology under the carpet, without actually condemning Augustine, but in doing so it both alienated many in the Catholic Church and gave them firm ground to stand upon as dissidents. In France, resistance was stiff, at least for a while: in 1718, three years after the death of Louis XIV, eighteen bishops, and three thousand clergy appealed the decisions of *Unigenitus* and called for a general council to settle the controversy. Some of these recalcitrant Jansenists even resurrected the old conciliarist theories of the fourteenth and fifteenth centuries that had emerged during the Great Schism, arguing that the authority of councils was superior to that of the pope. But those who questioned *Unigenitus* were outnumbered by four cardinals, a hundred bishops, and about one hundred thousand clergymen who signed on to the pope's side. In 1728, many of the remaining stalwart Jansenists finally admitted defeat, repented, and submitted to the authority of Rome. And in 1730, when agreeing with *Unigenitus* became required by French law, Jansenism began a steep descent into obscurity, though not without further controversy. In 1731, some Jansenists who venerated the relics of one of their own—the extreme ascetic François de Pâris—began to experience odd paroxysms and to utter prophecies. These Convulsionnaires of Saint-Médard, as they came to be known, gave Jansenism a distinctly popular flavor in its dying days, something it had lacked earlier. But these strange events led nowhere. Discredited by church and civil authorities, and by some Jansenists, these Convulsionaries divided the remnant of the Jansenist community and only helped to hasten its demise in France.

Beyond France, Jansenism proved more resilient. In the Netherlands, where religious toleration was observed, Jansenists formed their own church, which continued to exist to this very day and is now known as the Old Catholic Church. In Italy, Jansenism thrived until the late eighteenth century. In 1786, at the Synod of Pistoia, Jansenists managed to affirm the orthodoxy of their doctrines, over and against the condemnations of *Unigenitus*. The ensuing controversy, which involved many in the Italian hierarchy, was decisively resolved by Pope Pius VI in 1794, with his bull of condemnation, *Auctorem fidei*, which drove the final nail into the coffin of Jansenism.

The slow and agonizing demise of Jansenism coincided with another fray that focused on the relation between human and divine nature, though this one was much smaller in scale and impact. This dispute concerned quietism, a mystical movement restricted to a relatively small number of men and women but with central issues that linked it to the other major theological disputes that shook post-Tridentine Catholicism.

Quietists were accused of believing that in the higher reaches of the mystical quest, the perfected human soul was absorbed by God and ceased functioning as an independent self. This was the "quiet" in quietism: a total self surrender in which God took possession of one's mind and will and one no longer needed to talk to God in prayer because God and the soul were now finally united and the praying was really done by God. This mysticism had deep roots in Catholic tradition, but it also echoed previously censured movements, such as the heresy of the Free Spirit (fourteenth to fifteenth century), and Spanish *alumbradismo* (sixteenth century).

Not surprisingly, its chief proponent, Miguel de Molinos (1628–1697), was condemned in 1687 by Pope Innocent XI, in the bull *Coelestis pastor*. Molinos admitted his errors and was imprisoned for the rest of his life. Though his writings attracted a following, they were aimed at the spiritual elite, and never had much of an impact on the church as a whole. In France, quietism took hold of only a few souls, but one remarkable woman kept the movement in the public eye through her writings and her connections at the court of Louis XIV. Jeanne-Marie Bouvier de la Motte-Guyon, a widow better known as Madame Guyon (1648–1717), managed to create a tight circle of followers, including the archbishop François Fénelon (1651–1715), but she and her kindred spirits would be condemned and silenced. Madame Guyon was locked up in the infamous Bastille for seven years. Her greatest influence, ironically, would be among Protestants who picked up her writings, and especially among the Quakers.

The very same set of issues caused no end of trouble among Lutherans and Calvinists during this same era. The raw nerve touched by Luther in 1517—which led to the dissolution of medieval Christendom—not only remained exposed, but actually seemed to assume a dominant role in the intellectual and spiritual lives of Protestants and Catholics alike. What can we make of this five centuries later, when questions concerning free will and divine grace are far from central to public discourse, or even to the training of Christian clergy? At the very least, by focusing on these issues we come much closer to understanding the past on its own terms, for these issues mattered back then. We can also surmise that these questions and all the divisive movements they occasioned made more of a difference in people's daily lives than many of the issues that we twenty-first-century historians have mistakenly elevated to an unwarranted artificial significance.

Conclusion

Christians took theological wrangling to new heights in the sixteenth and seventeenth centuries, in terms of both complexity and intensity. Theologians of all stripes became expert not only at elaborating their own positions in great detail, but also at deconstructing and demolishing those of their opponents, with a surfeit of logic and vigor. If anyone could have gathered all of the competing champions of the various orthodoxies into a single room simultaneously and heard them argue with one another, the resulting din would surely have been loud and unsettling. All would be arguing that there could be but one Truth—with a capital *T*—and each would be claiming sole possession of it. And most of the arguments would have followed some rigorous logic. Agreement was out of the question, and impossible. Moreover, most of the arguments would be about the same limited set of subjects, and very refined in their citation of a common set of texts from the Bible and the church fathers.

Most Western Europeans—including simple folk—were exposed to this arguing in one way or another. And some, surely, were confused and irritated by it all. Might such dissonance have led to skepticism, even to unbelief? And might have all of the deconstructing and demolishing of opposing arguments led some to suspect that all of Christian theology was equally vulnerable and therefore necessarily flawed or too close to nonsense? Might not this relentless bickering have led some to go further and dismiss religion as not just irrational, but actually as dangerous for the well-being of society?

Though many historians have traditionally searched for the roots of skepticism and atheism outside the Christian tradition, some have argued that Christianity itself gave birth to its worst enemies, principally through its fratricidal infighting in the sixteenth and seventeenth centuries.[12] Whether or not theological debates concerning orthodoxy

Theological fatigue. This 1617 engraving, *The Spiritual Brawl*, pokes fun at theological squabbling and offers an easy way to avoid its unpleasantness. The two panels offer a sharp contrast. To the left, as Luther pulls on Calvin's beard and Calvin prepares to hurl a book at Luther, the pope is caught between them, shielding his ears from their shouting. To the right a shepherdess kneels and prays directly to God, without intermediaries. The text above expresses impatience with the bickering of the three competing churches, and adds: "The Word of the Lord abides forever." The text below quotes Psalm 23: "The Lord is my shepherd; I lack nothing." The message is clear: prayer trumps doctrine, and it is best to bypass the established churches and to approach God individually, one-on-one, unencumbered by theological correctness.

provided the rational infrastructure for disbelief and atheism is a question worth posing, but not necessarily worth answering in a definitive way. How could any such causality be convincingly proven? But, by the same token, should it be altogether ignored?

The search for orthodoxy yielded uniformity and disunity simultaneously, binding many together in a shared set of very specific beliefs and a common identity, but at the very same time pitting church against church, and brethren against brethren within the same church. All in all, searching for orthodoxy and squabbling over it—a chief hallmark of the early modern age—was a phenomenon as paradoxical as the doctrines that led to so many disputes. Its positive effects were part of the Christianization of early modern Europe, of the process of confessionalization, which was tied to state formation and social disciplining. At the very same time, however, its negative effects were all too evident, and the arguments produced by it eminently useful for deconstructing the whole edifice of belief. In this respect, the struggle over orthodoxy was also a most significant step in the de-Christianization of Europe.

Jean-Alphonse Turrettini, the aforementioned Genevan cleric who preferred a theology without fine points, might not have seen himself or his fellow tolerant clergy as de-Christianizers, since there were already too many full-blown skeptics and atheists in the eighteenth-century hell-bent on dismantling Christian hegemony in all its various forms. But no matter what crypto-Deists like Turrettini may have thought, we now know that de-Christianization was not solely championed by overt enemies of the Christian establishment. After generations of theological squabbling, it was also carried out from within by Christians weary of conflict who did away with theological orthodoxy and replaced it with codes of behavior, or with a religion that never trespassed the limits of pure reason, as Immanuel Kant (1724–1804) would prefer to say, up in dank Königsberg, that easternmost outpost of German Lutheranism.

Voltaire's enlightened war cry against organized religion, *écrasez l'infâme* (which, roughly translated, means "let's wipe out infamy") was in part based on his abhorrence of religious intolerance and of the social and political enforcement of orthodoxy. By the time he began using the slogan as his signature statement, Voltaire (1694–1778)—who had been educated by the Jesuits—was but one in a vast crowd who had come to distrust and despise all religions, and Christianity in particular. The judgment he passed on Christianity in 1767, in a letter to Frederick the Great of Prussia, echoed the sentiments of many of the leading lights of his generation: "Our religion is without a doubt the most ridiculous, the most absurd, and the most blood-thirsty ever to infect the world."[13] And many of those who nodded in agreement surely had the theological squabbles of the prior century in mind when they did so.

CHAPTER TWENTY-TWO

The Confessional Age

S tarting a Reformation is one thing; turning people into good Christians is quite another. In the sixteenth and seventeenth centuries, genuine reforming required muscle of some sort, most often the kind that only the secular authorities could supply. The need for such support became evident after the first flush of success, and even more so as disputes about orthodoxy heated up. All of the churches of the Reformation era formed a symbiotic relationship with the state, save for those of the Radicals, who sought separation from "the world." Consequently, untangling religion from politics in the age of orthodoxy was impossible. In fact, the two were so tightly intertwined that the body politic was often forced to dismember and mutilate the bodies of some of its citizens in order to preserve that symbiotic status quo.

A case in point is that of Niklaus Krell, chief adviser to Elector Christian I of Saxony (1560–1591), who had introduced Calvinism to the land of Luther, and, among other reforms, had introduced German Bibles with Calvinist footnotes and abolished the exorcism that had traditionally accompanied the rite of baptism. After his prince and patron died and the political and religious winds shifted, Krell was stripped of his chancellorship and imprisoned in 1591. The new elector, the resolutely Lutheran Frederick William I, set about ridding Saxony of Calvinists and making an example of their leader. On 9 October 1601, after enduring a decade of inhumane imprisonment at the fortress of Königstein, a very frail Krell was brought to the New Market in Dresden for execution. His trial had dragged on far too long, as had his appeals, but after innumerable delays, his fate had been sealed. Three Lutheran clergy had been assigned the task of converting Krell to orthodoxy, and had spent the previous few days fruitlessly badgering him. It mattered little that Queen Elizabeth I of England, Henry IV of France, and William of Hesse protested Krell's death sentence. A single blow from the executioner's sword was all it took to deny those pleas. Holding high his victim's head for all to see, the executioner mocked it, asking a question that loosely translates as, "How did you like that Calvinist

Caput Nicolai Crelli
Cancellarii Christiani
Electoris Saxoniæ.

Beware Calvinist! Making one's way through the labyrinth of doctrinal orthodoxy could be perilous for political figures in an age of heightened religious tensions. The reality of that danger is evidenced by this engraving of Niklaus Krell's severed head. Executed for the "crime" of crypto-Calvinism by his Lutheran prince, Krell and his severed head were used as a warning to others who might stray from the fold. This image was a medium of intimidation, perhaps more effective at shaping belief and behavior than the execution itself, since it could reach many who were not present at the event. Curiously, the unknown artist made the gruesome trophy look defiant rather than repentant.

sword stroke, Krell?" The sword itself had been engraved for the occasion with Krell's initials and the Latin inscription "Cave, Calviniane," or "Beware, Calvinist!"[1]

Krell's crime was crypto-Calvinism, a theological offense, but power politics had as much to do with his execution as religion. After all, Krell had been aligning Saxony with states unfriendly to Lutheranism and to Frederick William I. And incredible as it may seem, Krell's beheading was considered a merciful execution. Worse deaths awaited others whose politics mixed with religion the wrong way.

Take the case of the jurist Henning Brabandt, a leading burgomaster in Braunschweig, who challenged his city's patrician oligarchy from 1601 to 1604, alienating the burgermeisters and their local state-run church and turning his political career—unwittingly—into a hellish nightmare. First, he was excommunicated by the Lutheran clergy; then they charged that he was in league with Satan, and that the devil constantly followed him around town in the shape of a raven. Abandoned by most of his followers after this rumor made the rounds, his political movement collapsed, and he fled town. But after being captured and subjected to torture on the rack, Brabandt confessed that he had indeed made a pact with the devil. A few days later, on 17 September 1604, he was savagely executed in public as Lutheran clerics offered him nonstop lessons in orthodoxy. First, two of his fingers were cut off (he had ostensibly used them to seal his demonic contract). Then, his skin was torn off with red-hot pincers, little by little. Still alive, and continually revived with smelling salts so he could feel the utmost pain and listen to the pious entreaties of the clerics, he had to endure castration and disembowelment too, before his heart was finally ripped out of his chest and jammed into his mouth.

This is what some historians have called social disciplining, confessionalism, and confessionalization. Others prefer to call it Christianization.[2] These are relatively new terms for a very old subject, and they signify a change in perspective. In various ways, bureaucrats, chroniclers, and historians have been focusing on the enforcement of beliefs and ethics in the early modern era ever since the sixteenth century itself. At that time, many could not help but notice that something new was occurring. They knew that the changes were part and parcel of their own lives, and of the religious implosion that engulfed their era, and they left behind plenty of material for historians to interpret. But these accounts and records, along with the histories of the Reformation era written well into the twentieth century, did not conceive of these phenomena in a theoretical framework. Some might have viewed their subject as the history of heresy or of persecution, or of toleration, or of the pastoral work of the church, or of superstition and witchcraft, or at least a dozen other such particular subjects. But none would have woven all of these individual components into a grand theory.

Theorizing, then, is what distinguishes the history of the Reformation era written since the 1970s, and especially since the 1980s. Much of the theorizing can be traced to German and French historians, to the ascendancy of social history. For our purposes, we need concern ourselves not with the highly recondite intricacies of this theorizing, but with the phenomena covered by it. Simply put, the issue at hand in this chapter is the effort made jointly by church and state to instill Christian principles into the people of Europe. It was an uneven process, carried out at various levels, and it ranged from something as simple as teaching children the catechism to something as complex as wiping out centuries-old beliefs and superstitions. It was also a lengthy process, with no clear endpoint, but most historians agree that it extended, roughly, from the death of Luther, in 1546, to the end of the Thirty Years' War, in 1648. Sound arguments can also be made for stretching our view of that process all the way to the eighteenth century and the dawn of the Enlightenment.

Concepts such as confessionalization, social disciplining, and confession building have been analyzed, refined, and criticized extensively. These concepts attempt to make sense of a very significant and inescapable issue that will never go away: the increased effort made nearly everywhere by church and state to encourage and regulate a closer adherence to codes of belief and behavior among the populace. Some German historians have argued for a process of state building in which early modern civil authorities employed the church and its teachings to create model, obedient citizens.[3] This approach differs from that of French historian Jean Delumeau, who prefers to see the process of instructing and policing as an effort to close the gap that had always existed between Christian ideals and social realities.[4] Delumeau's Christianization thesis, which assumes that medieval Christians were still far too ignorant of their faith and too attached to ancestral pagan ways, considers a cultural paradigm shift embraced by both church and state as the defining characteristic of the age. Both the German and French theories also link the processes they analyze to "modernization." In this respect, they are similar, though far from identical.

In brief, here is what needs to be known about some of these terms and hypotheses, and their relation to the phenomena covered in this chapter. For the Germans, the terms *confession* and *discipline* are key. *Confessionalization, confessionalism,* and *confession building* refer to processes—covered in the previous chapter—for arriving at orthodoxy, and for safeguarding that orthodoxy as summarized in carefully crafted documents: confessions for Protestants, and conciliar decrees and papal bulls for Catholics. The concepts themselves are somewhat imprecise and in many cases overlap, but they do focus on one well-defined issue: the division of European society into social groups and political entities that subscribed to particular confessions or creeds. In other words, the concepts focus on the process whereby distinct Lutheran, Reformed, Anglican, and Catholic societies came into being and survived. (The Radical churches cannot be considered part of this process because they refused to accept any kind of interrelationship of church and state).

Reformation as state building. In this 1535 painting by Lucas Cranach the Elder, it is evidently clear that Elector John Frederick of Saxony and his Wittenberg Reformers had established a mutually beneficial relationship: while the Elector ensured their survival, they provided him with additional prestige and invested his authority with a divine aura. Some historians stress the political advantage gained by rulers who controlled the church in their domains, arguing that the Protestant Reformation can be best understood as a process of state building and social disciplining.

Orthodoxy tends to be approached in a functionalist or pragmatic perspective rather than theologically. In this perspective, orthodoxy serves two functions: first, it provides every confessional community with self-definition by establishing social and political norms; second, it ensures the survival of every confessional community through the enforcement of those social and political norms. In addition, these theories refer to the ways the competing churches of the Reformation era imposed their will on the people of early modern Europe. Within this conceptual framework, territoriality played a key role, as did civil government, and—that fourth term—social disciplining. In these theories, the main subject is territorial state building, not church building. Religion is viewed as a tool—an efficient instrument wielded principally by the state for its purposes, with the willing and eager collaboration of the church. That means that the "confessions" tend to be seen primarily as efficient means of repression and control. The churches and the clergy are still assigned an essential role, yes, but principally as instruments of the state and agents who enhance secular power and ensure its survival.

The alternative concept of Christianization takes politics into account, but not as the end-all and be-all. Proponents of Christianization see a cooperation between church and state that involves and transcends politics simultaneously. In sum, the theory proposes that the reforming ideals of the Renaissance, which called for a closing of the gap between the ideal and the real, permeated all of Western European society to such an extent that they began to drive many lay and clerical elites into the work of reform. Church and state did not necessarily work for the same objectives, say the proponents of Christianization, but they did join hands in a common effort. While other factors such as the centralization of secular authority and the rise of literacy are taken into account, the main driving force is seen as the early modern quest for ideals, which intensified in the wake of the Protestant Reformation and of all the competition it spawned among Lutherans, Reformed, Anglicans, and Catholics.

These two approaches to the early modern period are not incompatible, and both shed light on significant characteristics of the age. Both have been challenged, and neither has won universal acceptance. But both offer a useful frame of reference, even a conceptual structure around which we can build an understanding of two key facts: first, the Reformations of the early modern era were not some brief event, but rather very prolonged processes of change; and second, all of the "reforming" that took place during this era involved a close cooperation between church and state, and a blurring of the boundaries between religious and mundane concerns.

Instruction

Teaching the faithful became one of the central obsessions of the age, a marked departure from the Middle Ages, when religious instruction was dispensed haphazardly. Though the invention of the printing press, the rise in literacy, and the growth of the bourgeoisie contributed to this new attitude, the increased effort to educate the laity at all levels, which was embraced by elites in church and state, was much more significant. In fact, that effort itself contributed to the rise of literacy and the publication of books.

Confessions and Creeds

First and foremost, each of the major Reformation traditions developed its own detailed list of beliefs, its confession. As we have seen, this process often involved conflicts that could fester for decades. Sometimes schisms would be caused, and new churches would emerge. Regardless of how such documents were produced, however, or what they were called, each competing church had to have one of its own. Such texts distilled the very essence of the communal identity and purpose of each church and have thus come to be viewed as the defining characteristic of religion in the early modern period: hence, the label "confessionalism," or, even more revealing, the use of the label "confession" rather than "church" to refer to each of the competing traditions.

The most significant of these have already been introduced in relation to the development of orthodoxy: the Formula of Concord (Lutheran); the Helvetic and Westminster Confessions, and the Synod of Dort (Reformed); the decrees of the Council of Trent and papal bulls such as *Vineam Domini* and *Unigenitus* (Catholic).

Catechisms

Medieval Catholics had been producing and using catechisms long before Martin Luther produced his first rudimentary catechism in 1520: *A Brief Summary of the Ten Commandments, Beliefs, and the Lord's Prayer.* The concept of the catechism was therefore Catholic, but Protestants chose to keep this one piece of nonbiblical tradition in play because of its proven usefulness, especially in the upbringing of children. As the title of Luther's proto-catechism reveals, catechisms were summaries of the most basic components of the faith: the Apostles' or Nicene Creed, the Ten Commandments, and other doctrines, sacraments, rituals, and prayers. Many, but not all, assumed a question-and-answer or dialogue format.

Ulrich Zwingli was the first Protestant Reformer to issue a full-fledged catechism. *A Brief Christian Introduction* (1523) was intended for the clergy to use in instructing the faithful. Luther's first formal catechism appeared in April 1529, after interviews with clergy and laity revealed the depth of their ignorance on even the most basic of subjects. Originally titled *A German Catechism*, it would come to be known as the *Large Catechism*. One month later, sensing the need for a simplified version, Luther published *The Small Catechism for the Simple Pastor and Preacher*, better known simply as the *Small Catechism*. Nearly free of polemics against the Catholic Church and its teachings, and focused on the fundamental tenets of the faith, this slim volume would play a very important role in shaping Lutheranism. For Luther himself, it became one of his favorite works, of which he was immensely proud. Though many catechisms were written and published by other

Lutheran clerics, Luther's was unsurpassed, and frequently copied. The Gnesio-Lutherans revered it with uncommon fervor, even to the point of claiming that it was inspired by the Holy Spirit, just like the Bible. In 1580, the *Book of Concord* would include both of Luther's catechisms and seal their uniquely definitive authority in Lutheranism.

Not surprisingly, the Reformed produced catechisms of their own, in addition to Zwingli's. Three appeared in in quick succession, not long after 1523, written by Leo Jud, Martin Bucer, and Wolfgang Capito. But all of these would be overshadowed by John Calvin's *Instruction and Confession of Faith*, which first appeared in 1537 and was intended for the teaching of children. Calvin produced an improved version in 1542, *The Catechism of the Church of Geneva*, written in the format of a dialogue between a pastor and a child. It became immensely popular among the Reformed and virtually displaced all other catechisms until 1563, when a group of clerics in the Palatinate produced the *Heidelberg Catechism*, a text that gained an authority equal to that of a formal confession and was proclaimed definitive at the Synod of Dort in 1619.

In England, the various editions of *The Book of Common Prayer* would have catechisms within them, beginning with the 1549 version. The catechism included in the 1559 *Book of Common Prayer* was very succinct, and extremely easy to teach and memorize. Other catechisms were issued too, such as Alexander Nowell's of 1571, but they could never displace the one in the *Book of Common Prayer*, as far as influence on the Anglican faithful was concerned. In 1649, the Westminster Assembly produced two catechisms, the *Shorter* and the *Larger*, which were accepted by Congregationalists, Presbyterians, and Baptists, and would have a profound influence in the English-speaking world for generations.

Catholics had an overabundance of catechisms to choose from, even before the advent of Protestantism. In Spain, for instance, two synods convened by Cardinal Francisco Jiménez de Cisneros in 1497 and 1498 decreed that every pastor was required to provide religious instruction to his flock, and appended a newly crafted catechism to that decree. By the 1540s, so many other catechisms were in circulation in Spain— including one written by St. John of Ávila in rhymed couplets that were to be sung rather than recited—that historians have spoken of a "craze" for catechisms.[5] Nonetheless, many of the Catholic catechisms published after 1530 were written as direct responses to the Protestant challenge. Variety was their chief characteristic: some were written expressly for children, others for adolescents, or even adults, or for clergy. Many were in Latin, but vernacular editions were very common too.

Among the catechisms that proved most influential, few could rival the three question-and-answer catechisms written in quick succession by the Jesuit Peter Canisius, each of which was aimed at a distinct audience: his *Summation of Christian Doctrine* (1554) for young adults, his *Smallest Catechism* (1556) for young children, and his *Small Catechism* (1558) for adolescents. These texts were translated and reissued repeatedly and remained in use for more than a century. Their role in German-speaking lands, in particular, was immense, where they proved very useful in the re-Catholicizing of many regions. Another significant catechism was that of the Council of Trent, first issued in 1566, which came to be known as the *Roman Catechism*. Written by four theologians— three of whom were bishops—and supervised by three cardinals who were guided by the saintly Carlo Borromeo, cardinal archbishop of Milan. Thorough and lengthy, its usefulness in the instruction of the young was limited. Its chief value—and its intended purpose—was in the training of priests, and as an encyclopedic reference of unquestionable authority. Translated into every major vernacular by order of the Council of Trent, and published repeatedly, it held a place of distinction, even if it was not much used for lay instruction. Another catechism that enjoyed a wide circulation was that of the Jesuit Roberto Bellarmino, *A Brief Christian Doctrine* of 1597. Its greatest virtues were its brevity and clarity, and the ease with which it lent itself to memorization. Throughout the seventeenth century, the catechisms of Canisius, Bellarmino, and the Council of Trent would reign supreme among Catholics, each in its own way serving its purpose in its particular niche.

Religious Education

Publishing so many catechisms would have made little sense without a parallel effort to ensure their use, so it is no surprise that all the various confessions promoted the establishment of schools in which doctrine would be taught. While the rise in literacy and the ever-increasing availability of books had much to do with this initiative, the educational goals of Renaissance humanism played a large role too, along with the rise of the modern state, with its expanding bureaucracies and its need for educated functionaries. Even before Luther and Zwingli began to stir up trouble for the Catholic Church, many voices had already called for increased schooling, and especially for better religious instruction. Spain had led the way, thanks to the efforts of reformers such as Francisco Jímenez de Cisneros and St. John of Ávila. To a lesser extent, similar efforts to increase and improve the education of the laity were well under way throughout Europe by 1520.

But there is no denying that the rise of Protestantism speeded up and magnified this existing trend, and that the centrality of the Bible in Protestant life had much to do with that. Protestants were a people of the written word, ostensibly guided by Scripture alone and committed to patterning everything in accordance with Holy Writ. This meant that they not only needed a learned clergy, proficient in the ancient languages of the Bible, but also a literate laity who could encounter the sacred texts directly and become intimate with them. Catholics, in turn, were prompted to boost the educational efforts that were already under way, to counteract the Protestant challenge.

Among Protestants, one pattern became prominent across their confessional boundaries: the role assigned to civil authorities. Nearly everywhere that Protestants gained control, be they Lutherans or Reformed, the task of setting up and overseeing religious instruction and all education became the responsibility of the state. To some extent this arrangement flowed naturally from their political theology, but it was also arrived at out of necessity, since the Catholic clergy who had run most of the schools up until then had been chased away. If Protestants had no political power, this arrangement was impossible, but as soon as they gained sufficient influence anywhere, Protestants normally empowered the state to establish and enforce as thorough a catechizing of the populace as possible. Martin Luther, who championed state-run education, defended it in nearly apocalyptic terms:

> It is the duty of the temporal authority to compel its subjects to keep their children in school. . . . If the government can compel such of its subjects as are fit for military service to carry pike and musket, man the ramparts, and do other kinds of work in time of war, how much more can it and should it compel its subjects to keep their children in school. For here there is a worse war on, a war with the very devil.[6]

In Lutheran Germany, especially after the Peasants' War in 1525, civil governments issued school ordinances that determined all aspects of education, from curriculum development to the hiring and certifying of teachers, to the enforcement of discipline. Normally assigned to state-appointed supervisors, these various responsibilities tended to have religious values at their core, and as their proper end. Religious instruction was not just conducted with the aid of catechisms as a centerpiece of the curriculum, but also seamlessly woven into all subjects and complemented with classroom prayers and hymn singing. In addition, the curriculum itself would devote much attention to *Zucht*, or moral discipline and character formation. Compulsory attendance at frequent worship services rounded out this state-run indoctrination program, along with the requisite penalties for the errant sheep who would not conform to the *Zucht*, which governed all learning. Proponents of the confessionalization thesis, who tend to argue that the Reformation can be best understood as part of the process of modern state building, base their claims largely on this close linkage of church and state in the classroom.

Among the Reformed, a similar arrangement evolved. Ulrich Zwingli had set the tone even before Zurich turned Protestant, writing in his 1523 treatise *On the Education of Youth* that schooling should prepare the young, above all to "serve the Christian community, the common good, the state and individuals." Much of this treatise focused on the practical benefits of a Christian education, and what it could do to shape civic relations, with an emphasis on the values promoted by the Bible, and on the formation of character, especially in molding the thinking, speaking, and behavior of every young person.[7] Responsibility for educating the young was to be shared by the family, the church, and the state, but the practical direction of the schools would be ultimately left to the civil authorities. In a tradition given to creating godly communities, yet open to local variations in the linking of church and state, the particular shape given to public education could differ somewhat, but all Reformed communities were supposed to ensure that their schools were resolutely Christian and closely supervised by the clergy. In France, for instance, where the Huguenots were involved in a life-and-death struggle from 1562 to 1598, schools could not be easily set up, but after toleration was granted to them by the

Edict of Nantes, Huguenot schools were established, maintained, and regulated by the churches and their consistories.

Much of what Zwingli had outlined in his *On the Education of Youth* would be reflected in Reformed communities everywhere. And nearly a century later, the Synod of Dort would reaffirm it, proclaiming that "schools, in which the young shall be properly instructed in the principles of Christian doctrine, shall be instituted, not only in cities but also in towns and country places where heretofore none have existed." Dort also assert that the clergy were to oversee the schools and to visit all of them frequently, both public and private, along with a magistrate "if necessary," in order "to excite the teachers to earnest diligence, to encourage and counsel them in the duty of catechizing, . . . and exciting their pupils to early piety and diligence."[8]

In England, confessionally correct religious instruction was demanded by the state-run Anglican Church. By 1570, all English schoolmasters were required to teach the catechism along with Bible lessons, and to bring their students to sermons and lead them in prayer in the classroom.

Catholics everywhere, even in America and Asia, were similarly exposed to vigorous religious instruction in their schools. The chief difference between Catholics and Protestants was one not of intensity or commitment, but of governance. Whereas Protestants tended to make the state responsible for religious instruction, Catholics built on arrangements that were already in place from medieval times, which in most cases meant leaving the schools in the hands of religious institutions, and especially of those run by regular clergy. In the sixteenth century, new orders such as the Jesuits, Ursulines, and Piarists expanded the teaching mission of the Catholic Church exponentially. But even such growth was insufficient, since Catholics could not rely on the universal reach normally offered by state-run schools. Provisions had to be made, then, for doctrinal instruction outside the schools. Before the Council of Trent, such efforts were haphazard. In Spain, as early as 1497 all pastors were required to set up religious instruction on Sundays and holidays, but enforcement of the rule was difficult. In Italy, by 1536 Sunday schools were established in Milan, a strictly local initiative run by lay confraternities.

By 1560, however, a far-reaching expansion of religious education began to take shape. First, a group of reform-minded clerics and laymen in Rome established a confraternity dedicated to catechizing children and adults not just in churches, but also in homes or even out on the streets. In 1562, Pope Pius IV formally approved their mission, and they soon began to grow in numbers. The priests became a religious order, the Fathers of Christian Doctrine; the laymen organized themselves into the Confraternity of Christian Doctrine. Their cause was substantially furthered by the Council of Trent, which decreed that doctrinal instruction was to be given to all the faithful on Sundays and feast days. By 1571, when Pope Pius V officially recommended to every bishop that this confraternity be established in every parish, it had already spread beyond Italy and its growth seemed unstoppable. In 1607, Pope Paul V confirmed its centrality in Catholic life by making St. Peter's in Rome its very own mother church, and raising it to the level of an archconfraternity, which meant that it now had the authority to affiliate other teaching confraternities to itself and share its privileges and indulgences with them.

All in all, then, Catholics and Protestants found different means to a common end: molding new generations into responsible Christians who were well-versed in the central tenets of their faith and well prepared to live as responsible, productive citizens. It was a lofty goal, indeed. The Synod of Dort hoped to promote "piety and diligence," and so did the Council of Trent, but such virtues were no easier to instill back then than they are now. Much to every Sunday-school teacher's chagrin, impiety and indifference always seemed to lurk in the back of the classroom and on every street that led to its doors. Policing behavior and ferreting out the bad Christians became as much of a necessity as printing up catechisms and opening schools.

Preaching

The age of sermons is one of the many names that could be given to the sixteenth and seventeenth centuries. Never before had so many sermons been delivered, so frequently, and so enthusiastically. As an opponent of Calvin once put it, the Reformation was all about "blasting people's ears with sermons."[9]

Preaching was an ancient and well-established component of church life long before every Protestant Reformer was born. More than that, preaching was enjoying a renaissance as all these reformers came into the world, in regard to not just form and content, but also popularity. An oft-cited example of the growing influence of preaching at this time is Girolamo Savonarola (1452–1498), whose preaching captivated the city-state of Florence and turned it into a "godly" and puritanical republic in 1495–1498. Another example is that of Johan Geiler von Kaiserberg (1445–1510), preacher at the Strassburg cathedral, who attracted huge audiences while advocating reform. Inspired by the ideals of humanism, Geiler composed and delivered sermons that were at once learned and passionate, and above all, accessible to a broad audience. The appeal of his sermons grew to the point that they were rapidly copied and published, reaching audiences far from his pulpit—a pulpit that was especially built for him and under which he was eventually buried. Geiler was far from alone, and the post he filled as designated preacher was but one of many such endowed preacherships. Ulrich Zwingli was invited to Zurich in 1519 to fill a preaching post like Geiler's. Nearly everywhere, good preachers could draw overflow crowds. In Spain, it was not uncommon for people to line up outside of church overnight, waiting for the doors to open, just to hear a popular preacher. At the very same time, complaints about the lack of preaching and the poor quality of sermons also became more frequent among those who favored reform.

The advent of Protestantism increased and transformed the significance of preaching. With their emphasis on the Bible and the preaching of the word of God, Protestants gave the sermon a greater centrality in worship. They also imbued preaching with a new sense of purpose, as a means of fomenting change and of continually educating and motivating the laity. Among Protestants, preaching was a medium that not only conveyed their reforming message, but was itself *the* message. There was a beautiful circularity to the first wave of Protestant sermons preached in any Catholic town, for each sermon aimed at potential converts argued that sermons should be the centerpiece of religious life, and promised a future filled with sermons. More than that, many of the sermons found their way into print, that other medium through which Protestantism spread so quickly and efficiently from place to place. As soon as Protestants gained control anywhere, even if chaos reigned, the sermons would flow; and once they established order, preaching retained a privileged place in their life and culture.

Luther raised sermons to the same significance as the sacraments, insisting that the "pure" preaching of God's word was one of the two earmarks of the true church—the

The power of the pulpit. Lucas Cranach the Younger assigns central significance to preaching in this 1540 depiction of the difference between the "true" church of Luther and that of the pope. We see Luther preaching, a Bible on the pulpit, his right hand pointing to a Lutheran communion service, where the real presence of Christ is correctly understood (signified by the crucifix and the Agnus Dei, or Lamb of God, at the foot of the cross). Directly under the pulpit the ruling family of Saxony is receiving communion. Though they are symbolically central, they are nonetheless beneath Luther. In sharp contrast, to Luther's left, the pope and his clerics are in the jaws of hell, engulfed in flames. Cranach has Luther serve a double function here: he distinguishes between the true and false church, and he assumes the central position usually accorded to Christ in scenes of the Last Judgment, with the pulpit serving as his throne.

other being correct administration of the sacraments. Among Lutherans, then, the sermon became extremely important, not just as a ritual, but as the principal means for constantly bringing the laity face-to-face with the Bible and the demands of Christian life. Hearing the word of God preached was deemed so essential that some Lutheran theologians debated how it was possible for deaf people to be saved. Unsurprisingly, the pulpit became as important for the task of social disciplining as the schools and catechisms, perhaps, one might argue, even more important, for it was the sole constant means of educating and admonishing adults, week after week, during their entire lifetime. The common practice of printing of sermons extended the reach of every pulpit, bringing the sermon into the public squares and the houses of the faithful, even into their workshops, barns, and taverns.

Among the Reformed, preaching acquired an even greater significance for two reasons. First and foremost, since the Reformed de-emphasized the centrality of the Eucharist in worship, the sermon came to assume a much more intense role in their ritual, and also in their culture. Zwingli summed it up when he mounted the pulpit in the Zurich Grossmünster the day after all of its images and altars had been removed, and declared that, finally, Zurichers had a beautiful, luminous, whitewashed space in which to hear the word of God. Preaching was uncoupled from the celebration of the Eucharist, and the Lord's Supper became an infrequent ritual, celebrated only a few Sundays a year. Religious services that consisted solely of sermons became routine, and attending these more than once a week could be required. To emphasize the centrality of the sermon, pulpits were moved from the sides of naves to the center of the sanctuary, upstaging the communion table. Second, from the very start, the Reformed employed sermons as an instrument of change. Unlike Luther, whose first efforts at reform were found in printed texts, Zwingli began his Reformation by preaching. And his sermons were the prime agent of change, the means through which the "idols" and the Mass were toppled in Zurich. The same was true of every other place that eventually became Reformed Protestant: in city after city, and even among rural folk, it was through preachers and their rabidly anti-idolatrous sermons that inroads were made against Catholic hegemony.

The sermon was always at the cutting edge, from Switzerland, to France, to Scotland, the Netherlands, Hungary, and Poland, advancing the Reformed cause. And the cutting edge remained sharp, and very much in motion, even after the idols and the Mass were vanquished. More so than among Lutherans, preaching became a prime teaching tool for the Reformed, and through it all adults could be constantly taught and admonished. Hour-long sermons, delivered several times a week, were offered to captive audiences, whose attendance was carefully monitored. Sleeping or dozing off was not allowed, either, and ushers outfitted with long poles would poke anyone whose attention began to wane. Calvin preached at least five sermons per week: two on Sunday and three on weekdays. Such a grueling preaching load became routine among the Reformed. They were learned sermons, but aimed at the heart and will as much as the intellect. Though biblical exegesis gave structure to the sermon, the content was heavily pragmatic, focused on the living out of one's faith, the practice of virtue, and the necessity of keeping vices at bay.

In England, preaching came to play a similarly central role in social disciplining, though with some fluctuations in intensity. Queen Elizabeth was not too fond of preaching, and did not encourage it, but the Reformed influence on the Church of England was intense enough to override her indifference. During Elizabeth's reign, the bishops took to promoting preaching, and their sponsorship continued after her death. Some nobles even took to endowing so-called lectureships in the larger towns and cities, which allowed some clerics to devote themselves solely to preaching. The Puritans, as one might expect, tried to impose the Reformed model on England during their rule, from 1649 to 1660. More radical groups, especially those with a millenarian bent, brought preaching to new highs and lows, depending on one's perspective, injecting so much "enthusiasm" into public discourse that the Puritan elites felt compelled to muzzle them in 1650 through the Blasphemy Act. The restoration of the monarchy in 1660 brought preaching back to its former status quo, as a steady and moderate means of teaching, admonishing, and setting standards for conduct.

Among Catholics, the upswing in preaching that was already in motion by 1517 intensified as the Protestant challenge grew. Unlike Protestants, however, Catholics did not raise the sermon to a more central place in their worship: they simply expanded its role. Everywhere in the Catholic world, as awareness of the success of Protestant preaching grew, so did support for the training and funding of preachers. Even before the Council of Trent called for a renewal of the pulpit, many leading Catholics were stepping up their efforts to improve the quality of preaching: men such as Tomás de Villanueva in Spain, whose sermons, according to Emperor Charles V, could "stir up even the stones," and Cornelio Musso in Italy, who came to be known as "the Italian Demosthenes" for his brilliant oratorical skills in the pulpit and was chosen to deliver the opening oration at the Council of Trent. Many of these pre-Tridentine preachers took up the tasks of combating Protestantism and addressing moral issues head-on, against the grain of popular opinion. Tomás de Villanueva, for instance, was courageous enough to preach against the popular sport of bullfighting in Spain—a challenge some might have considered riskier than facing a charging bull with nothing but a red cape in one's hands.

After Trent encouraged bishops to promote preaching, and especially after the establishment of seminaries produced a new generation of well-educated clerics, preaching became one of the principal means of instruction and moral reform among Catholics. Moreover, the study of the craft of preaching—known as homiletics—assumed a prominent place in the seminary curriculum. The new religious orders also did much to raise homiletics to new heights and to foster, improve, and expand preaching, especially the Jesuits, Theatines, and Capuchins. By the 1570s, many treatises on the art of preaching were being published, and by 1617 there were at least seven major manuals available to Catholic preachers, including Agostino Valier's *Ecclesiastical Rhetoric* (1576), Luis de Granada's *The Method of Preaching* (1576), Ludovico Carbone's *The Christian Orator*

(1613), and Nicolas Caussin's *On Sacred and Human Eloquence* (1617). Ironically, many of these were inspired by an earlier treatise that had been placed on the 1559 *Index of Forbidden Books*: Erasmus of Rotterdam's *On the Method of Preaching* (1535), which applied the principles of classical rhetoric to preaching.

These manuals in "ecclesiastical rhetorics" transformed the training of Catholic preachers—and improved the quality of sermons—by emphasizing preaching as "persuasion" and as a means for moving people's hearts. Preachers were encouraged to aim for three goals: to delight the senses, instruct the intellect, and bend the will. Detailed instructions were also included on how best to promote virtue and curtail vice, how to increase appreciation for the benefits of God, and how best to ponder the miracles of the saints and the mysteries of the Christian faith. Each in their own way, these manuals imbued Catholic preachers with an awareness that in every sermon they preached, what was at stake was no less than the "salvation of souls" and "the glory of God." While it is impossible to calculate the effect of improved preaching on Catholics with quantitative precision, it is not at all difficult to find accounts that credit it with winning back souls that seemed lost and with transforming the behavior of individuals and communities.

The example of Francis de Sales, titular bishop of Geneva, gives us a glimpse of the new confidence in preaching that was instilled in young Catholic clergy, and of the way this confidence was then folded back into Catholic culture through hagiography. According to the hagiographies published after his death, when St. Francis was appointed provost of the cathedral chapter of Geneva in 1593, he set out to convert the sixty thousand Calvinists who lived in his diocese, convinced that he could do this through preaching. Always unwelcome as he trudged from one Calvinist town to another in Upper Savoy, stung by constant failure, he refused to give up on his mission, or on the power of preaching. So, he began to print up his sermons, and to slip them under the doors of Calvinist households. Persistence paid off: soon enough, he gained his audience, and began to preach to receptive crowds. And eventually he could claim to have converted forty thousand Calvinists. Whether these figures are accurate is besides the point; what matters most in this narrative is the power ascribed to preaching. And we do know he managed to reclaim many lapsed Catholics, and that his spellbinding sermons were, in fact, very well attended, and then published, becoming best sellers for an eager Catholic audience. We also know that by the 1620s, Catholic preachers in the mold of St. Francis de Sales were fanning out in all directions, carrying out urban and rural missions in which, if contemporary accounts are accurate, great strides were made in turning lives around, increasing virtue, and decreasing vice.

Visitations

One of the oldest means of gauging the health of any parish or diocese and of keeping an eye on the faithful could be traced back to the fifth century, and had been sporadically employed throughout the Middle Ages: this method was a review procedure known as a visitation. In essence, a visitation was a commission empowered to inspect, examine, question, evaluate, and—whenever necessary—implement reforms in a specific area. By the late Middle Ages, well-established methods had been set in place for such reviews, but there was no universal policy guiding their content or frequency. In most areas, the authority to launch a visitation was in the hands of the local bishop; in others, however, that right might be exercised by a secular ruler.

The Protestant Reformation revived this ancient way of policing the churches, and raised it to new heights. Blaming the infrequency of visitations for most of the ills and errors that plagued the Catholic Church, Martin Luther began pushing for visitations in the mid-1520s, putting into practice the ecclesiology he had developed in his 1520 treatise *To the Christian Nobility of the German Nation*, in which he had called on secular rulers to take up the reform of the church. Appealing to his own Saxon prince, Elector John the Steadfast, Luther pleaded for a state-run visitation of the churches in his realm, "out of Christian love." In 1528, the first such review was launched, setting the protocols for all subsequent visitations. Teams of visitors empowered by the state—some clerical, some lay—combed Saxony armed with questions for everyone, from pastors and magistrates to aristocrats and peasants. On one level, they were to assess the material and financial state of the church; on another, it was their task to determine how well specific parishes were living up to the spiritual and ethical standards of the Lutheran Reformation. They were empowered also to instruct and correct, as needed, and to set in motion whatever improvements were needed. Since the visitations kept meticulous records, they have left behind a treasure trove of documents, many yet to be tapped, which—like all negative images—provide odd snapshots of religious life in early modern Lutheran Germany. The first Saxon visitation, which lasted from 1528 to 1531, revealed so woeful a state of things, that it prompted many reforms to be instituted, among them the aforementioned establishment of state-run schools. Vice seemed rampant among the laity, and church buildings were in ruins. Some pastors had no income and had taken up tavern keeping. Some were drunkards; many were ignorant and despondent, and leading openly sinful lives. Their flocks were in even worse disarray. Luther complained, "The peasants learn nothing, know nothing, do nothing but abuse their liberty. They do not pray, confess, or take communion, as if they had been freed from religion altogether. As they once used to ignore popery, they now turn us away with contempt."[10]

Such dispiriting reports occasioned a thorough retraining of pastors, however, and the composition of innumerable admonitions and instructions. Numerous other visitations followed in Saxony and elsewhere, including Scandinavia, all prying and poking and searching for defects, each dredging up its own unsightly collection of shortcomings. But for every bit of ugliness uncovered, remedies were often concocted and tried out. Visitors armed with questionnaires, empowered to elicit answers, provided the Lutheran Church with a powerful tool for self-scrutiny and constant reform. They also provided the state with an efficient means of maintaining control of the church.

In England, any sort of continuity was impossible in the state-run church established by King Henry VIII, which went through several very different phases as he and his successors Edward and Mary took it down wildly different paths. It was not until his daughter Elizabeth came to the throne in 1558 that stability could be brought in self-policing to the Church of England. Her policies were similar to those of Lutheran lands: the crown ordered regular visitations for the entire realm, which, if resisted, merited a charge of treason. The English clergy were thus regularly subjected to constant scrutiny, and so were their flocks. In addition, all parsons were required to preach several times a year on the "power, authority, and preeminence" of the English monarch over the Anglican Church as "the highest under God."

Among Reformed Protestants, self-policing took forms other than the visitation, with considerable variations, depending on time and place. Overall, however, beginning with the church established at Zurich, oversight by synods and civil authorities replaced episcopal supervision. Synods worked very much like a parliament within a specific territorial church: they were meetings at which representatives of a closely allied federation of otherwise independent local congregations met to regulate doctrine and discipline. In Zurich, for instance, the synod had jurisdiction only over the churches in the canton of Zurich; the synod in neighboring Bern could not intrude on affairs in Zurich, and vice versa. Occasionally, however, larger territorial synods could be held that brought together the smaller local synods. Given such a loose federal structure—so typically Swiss—the Reformed tradition ended up with a wide array of synodal systems. Insofar as composition, jurisdiction, functions, and relation to civil authorities were concerned, synods varied from region to region. But everywhere the Reformed set up churches—in France, Germany, the Netherlands, Scotland, Hungary, Poland—synods could be found, performing fairly similar regulatory tasks. The church in Calvin's Geneva, curiously enough, remained so fiercely local, despite its international reach, that it never held synods. Embattled as it felt, hemmed in by Catholic France and Savoy on two sides and domineering Reformed Bern on the other, it had no neighbors with whom to federate.

The way most Reformed synods went about the business of self-regulation is best described as a process of upward motion, wherein problems at pew or pulpit level in any individual church could be brought to the attention to the next regional level, and so on. But Reformed churches also had other institutions that helped them deal with disciplinary and doctrinal matters on a local level, which kept such issues from moving up to synods. One of the forms of local control was the practice of home visitation, in which elders and/or pastors would go into individual households and deal with particular problems, much as Lutheran visitors would do with individual churches.

Catholics not only continued to practice visitation, but also enhanced it throughout the post-Trent period. Whether initiated by bishops or secular rulers, all visitations served the same purpose, which was to evaluate, judge, and amend, as much as possible. In 1563, in one of its last sessions, the Council of Trent injected renewed vigor into this ancient Catholic institution, calling on all bishops to launch frequent visitations and to personally engage in them as much as possible. The "principal object" of visitations, according to this decree, was "to lead to sound and orthodox doctrine . . . to maintain good morals and to correct such as are evil . . . to animate the people by exhortations and admonitions to religion, peacefulness, and innocence."[11] As with all directives from Trent, it took some time for this measure to be set into motion, but once it gained momentum, visitations became a hallmark of early modern Catholicism, producing—if the resulting voluminous records left behind are to be taken at face value—a painfully honest and sometimes obsessional assessment of failures of all sorts and of emendations to be made. Above all, much like the Lutheran visitations, the Catholic visitations revealed that admonitions to "peacefulness and innocence" seemed to fall on deaf ears, for the most part, and that clergy felt constantly stymied in their efforts to fully Christianize their flocks.

A large question mark hovers over every visitation document, however, since the sole intent of those who wrote them was to shine a light on everything that was wrong. In many ways, as previously observed, visitations produced negative images. Visitors searched for problems, not for success stories. And they awarded no prizes, only admonitions. Even worse, we have no way of knowing how thorough or impartial visitors were, or how honestly their questions were answered. Historians who have plumbed visitation records have been led to a wide range of conclusions. At one extreme, there are those who see the effort alone as proof of effective social disciplining and confessionalization.[12] At the opposite extreme, some have concluded that the reform efforts of the various churches yielded poor results, at best, or were simply a dismal failure.[13] Questions about success and failure are ultimately unwise and unhelpful, no matter which sources are being analyzed, for measuring the results of something as vast and vague as a Reformation is truly impossible. But we can know one thing for sure: visitation records do give us a glimpse of the kind of social transformation hoped for by the Reformation churches, and of the challenges and disappointments they faced.

Disciplinary Tribunals

"Friendly admonishment" and "fraternal correction" were bywords commonly used by church authorities when dealing with first or second offenses by errant members of their flock. Often, however, mere admonishment proved fruitless. To close the gap between the ideals of reform and worldly corruption, the churches of the Reformation era had to resort to more than finger wagging and scolding; they had to establish a process for judging and punishing offenses. And this practice usually required the participation of the civil authorities, who could bring the strong arm of the law into play, and sometimes imprison or banish offenders, or even burn them alive or chop off their heads.

During the Middle Ages, the Catholic Church had developed a tribunal for dealing with deviance: the Inquisition. Brought into existence in the thirteenth century as a means of dealing with widespread heresies, such as those of the Cathars, Free Spirits, and Waldensians, the Inquisition—much like visitations—was haphazardly employed.

Though it was a church tribunal, it worked hand in hand with civil authorities, especially when it came to the ultimate punishment of death. Unable to execute anyone, church authorities would "relax" or hand over to civil authorities those who were to be killed. Unrepentant heretics, apostates, and sorcerers were those most often executed.

At the onset of the Protestant Reformation, neither Germany nor Switzerland had standing Inquisition tribunals. To a great extent, then, such an institution was foreign to those most immediately responsible for handling the errant followers of Luther and Zwingli. The most vigorous and infamous Inquisition at that time was that of Spain, which very actively pursued Jewish and Muslim converts to Catholicism who were suspected of practicing their ancestral religion in secret. It was also rapidly expanding its reach to cover all heresies and many different kinds of errant behavior. Anyone searching for models of social disciplining in the early modern era need look no further than Spain, which by 1520 had a hyperactive and very independent Inquisition empowered by both church and state. Its chief official, the Grand Inquisitor, was appointed by the crown, and answered only to the monarch and the pope. The Spanish Inquisition received no funding from either church or state and relied exclusively on the property it confiscated from those it arrested and tried. It had its own prisons, and its deliberations were shrouded in secrecy. In other words, it exercised its authority virtually unchecked, and it needed to keep finding deviants in order to remain in existence.

That such a fearsome institution should exist in one location but not in others reveals much about the nature and structure of the early modern Catholic Church. This asymmetry also helps explain why so much of northern Europe could break away from Rome so rapidly and successfully and why Protestantism could not take root in others. Luther and Zwingli were aware of the far-off Inquisition, and feared it to some extent, but only as a remote threat. And each reacted to it differently, for while Luther despised the Inquisition and insisted on *not* duplicating it within his Reformation, Zwingli created very similar tribunals in Zurich, thus bequeathing something of a replica of the Inquisition to the Reformed tradition.

Tribunals for social disciplining in which church and state worked together were naturally abhorrent to Radicals, since their core beliefs included separation of the church from "the world," and abstention from violence. For Radicals, the chief instrument of discipline was the expulsion of offenders, what they called "the Ban." Through their varied arrangements, each Radical community policed its own and enforced prescribed behaviors, usually through the authority vested in the community leaders. Since these communities could expel those who were not living up to their standards, most of them were exceptionally well ordered and disciplined. Even their enemies had to grudgingly admit, sometimes, that the Radicals lived exemplary lives. Yet, in the eyes of some, such as Philip Melanchthon, not even their reputation for good behavior or their heroic martyrdoms could make Radicals tolerable. As he saw it, "the Anabaptist sect" was "wrong, against God, and from the devil," and its apparent virtues nothing but satanic deception:

Christians should keep in mind that the Anabaptist sect is a vain diabolical fraud. . . . All their illuminations from on high are lies, and their much-praised humility is faked, along with their great brotherly love, their sharing of goods, their displays of patience in the face of suffering, and the great audacity and insolence with which they meet their deaths.[14]

So, since the Radicals were closed, self-policing communities that had no interest in changing the behavior of the world, their social disciplining—though exemplary— was severely limited in scope. Attempts to reform the world as a whole belonged to the magisterial churches alone. And each had its own approach.

Among Lutherans, no parallel to the Inquisition would ever exist. True to Luther's two-kingdom theology, which left care of the church and all necessary "worldly" violence in the hands of the state—a teaching clearly expressed as early as 1520—Lutheran churches carried out their disciplining in conjunction with the civil authorities, in various ways and with no uniform protocols. Visitations were a key part of the process, but not the sole means of correcting.

At the local level, pastors and the civil functionary responsible for order shared the responsibility for policing and disciplining the lay folk. As a result, many sins could be treated as crimes. At the territorial level, disciplining was more complex. Since Lutheran churches were ostensibly run by civil rulers, and all pastors were also, in essence, civil servants, the lines between church and state could get awfully blurry. In various parts of Germany, territorial civil authorities ran the church through a council, usually headed by a state functionary and composed of a mixture of clergy and laity. These councils could handle discipline questions, especially in the case of pastors. Different arrangements could be found elsewhere, however. In some territories, all the pastors formed an assembly, and after reaching decisions—including those that concerned discipline—passed them on to civil officials for implementation. In others, such as Württemberg, some sort of morals court was established. In sum, Lutherans tended not to force a thorough improvement of society through special disciplinary courts. Instead, relying on the power of the state and the letter of the civil law, they kept the devil at bay through preaching, teaching, exhorting, and pastoral counseling, treating some sins as crimes in civil courts, and leaving much of the judging to God. And all of these measures were defensive rather than offensive, a means of keeping the world from becoming worse, rather than a means of transforming it into something better.

Among the Reformed, their desire to create truly godly societies led to a different approach, and to the creation of institutions that resembled the Inquisition. In Zurich and throughout Switzerland, the synods were a key instrument for maintaining order, especially among the clergy. In Zurich, for instance, synods could fine pastors for misbehavior, even imprison them briefly, or transfer them to another location. But since the synods had a heavy load of business to handle, they could not handle day-to-day disciplining effectively. The first step toward a more efficient way of enforcing Christian discipline in Zurich was the creation of the marriage court, the Ehegericht, in 1525. Composed of two clerics and two city councilors, this tribunal played a very intrusive role in all marriage disputes, not just arbitrating, but counseling, admonishing, and enforcing the new "godly" laws of Reformed Zurich. In addition, the Ehegericht assumed the power to grant divorces, which had been prohibited by the Catholic Church. The grounds for divorce were few, but reasonable, and emblematic of a pragmatic approach to marriage: adultery, desertion, impotence, madness, and incurable ailments. Zurich's marriage court served as a model for other Swiss cities and cantons that turned Reformed throughout the 1520s and 1530s, and even gave rise in some of these other locations to an all-encompassing tribunal, the Chorgericht, or morals court. These tribunals, normally composed of both clerical and civil judges, had the power to enforce a long list of new laws that regulated behavior much more minutely than ever before. The moral mandates of Bern, issued in March 1529, targeted ungodly behavior with great precision. Bern's list of unacceptable behaviors, which was very much like all the others in Reformed Switzerland, is a daunting snapshot of theocratic utopianism at its most extreme. The Chorgericht punished impiety, unbelief, magic, superstition, gambling, swearing, blaspheming, dancing, drunkenness, licentiousness, child abuse, arguing with one's spouse, and wearing indecent apparel or expensive jewelry.

This tight control of morals became an earmark of the Reformed tradition, so essential to its character that one of its churches—that of Nîmes in France—could reduce it to a formula: "discipline is the sinews of religion."[15] In Geneva, where a morals court was imposed on the city by Calvin in 1541, the tribunal followed the Swiss blueprint. In turn, the Genevan model became the template for international Calvinism, replicated in some fashion, with local variations, wherever Calvinists set up churches. The name given by Calvin to this institution was the *consistory*. It was a branch of the city government, but so tightly bound to the church as to defy distinctions between church and state. Presided over by one of the city's chief magistrates, this court was composed of all the city's pastors and twelve elected lay elders—all of whom were also city councilors. Given the power to summon anyone, for any suspected infraction, the Genevan consistory met once a week, and quickly became a highly intrusive presence, and a constant irritation to Calvin's opponents, whom he dubbed "libertines" because of their opposition to his moral rigor.

The consistory's concern with details reshaped daily life in Geneva: the types of shoes or dresses women could wear; the names parents could choose for their children; how guests should behave at inns; what could or could not be read, and hundreds of other such matters that give life its texture. But the consistory also served as the great arbiter in all sorts of disputes, helping reconcile husbands and wives, parents and children, and feuding neighbors. According to historians who have plumbed its records, this pastoral role of counseling and of mediating disputes often consumed more of the consistory's attention than that of admonishing and punishing, and may have been its greatest accomplishment. Beyond a shadow of a doubt, the Genevan consistory and all other courts modeled after it performed many a positive function. Yet the consistory's commitment to maintaining a godly order was serious indeed, and not driven by Calvin alone, for immediately after his death, in the years 1564–1569, the court reached its peak workload, hauling into its chambers about one out of every eight adult Genevans. The rate of cases handled by other Reformed morals courts was normally lower, but still impressive. At roughly the same time, in two Scottish communities, the rate was about one out of sixty adults. Long-term rates for Valangin, a town near Neuchâtel, reveal a pattern of aggressive vigilance: between 1590 and 1667, an average of one of out every forty adults faced the consistory.

Research in various widely scattered consistory records has revealed certain patterns in the types of offenses prosecuted by Reformed tribunals. For instance, all Reformed morals courts dealt constantly with conflicts and quarrels. Sexual misconduct was a very common preoccupation too. But the types of cases heard by one court could vary significantly from those of another, depending on the local culture. For instance, while Sabbath breaking accounted for 50 percent of the cases heard by one Scottish court between 1605 and 1635, at another Scottish court, such cases amounted to only 28 percent. Some offenses were obviously culture bound: Germanic communities waged campaigns against drinking bouts; Huguenots in the south of France had to deal with Carnival; and only in Scotland was anyone found playing golf during Sunday services. The figures for the Huguenot community of Nîmes, which are among the most complete and thoroughly studied, provide us with a snapshot of Reformed social disciplining between the years 1561 to 1614. And it should be kept in mind that during much of this stretch of time, the Huguenots of Nîmes were caught up in a vicious religious war and had many other issues to worry about, including the likelihood of their extermination.

Discipline required penalties. And here, too, similarities were intertwined with local differences. Penalties were normally lenient for first time offenders, but harsh for stiff-necked reprobates who stood before the consistory time and time again.

Cases handled by the Nîmes Consistory (1561–1614)

Offense	Percentage
Conflicts and quarrels	25
Dogmatic discipline, absence from services	16
Magic, idolatry	15
Dancing	13
Sexual misconduct	9
Betrothal issues	6
Plays, carnivals, unseemly folk customs	6
Family disputes	5
Gambling	4
Drunkenness, gluttony, luxury	3

SOURCE: Philip Benedict, *Christ's Churches Purely Reformed* (Yale University Press, 2002), p. 471.

Sacred shaming. In many locations, the legacy of Reformation-era social disciplining endured well into the modern age. This eighteenth-century print by David Allan, *The Black Stool*, depicts a Presbyterian minister scolding a young man accused of fornication. Though the traditional stool of repentance has been replaced by a grandstand in this church, the ritual remains essentially the same. The sinner hangs his head in shame as the preacher excoriates him, while his partner in sin writhes in the lower foreground, next to her mother. The parents of the young man share the blame too as they sit glumly in the front pew, below him. Such rituals served to punish sinners, educate the community, uphold certain values, and shape behavior.

Excommunication, imprisonment on bread and water, banishment and confiscation of property could await anyone bold or foolish enough to try the consistory's patience in Geneva. Elsewhere, Reformed churches established their own unique penalties. In Scotland, public shaming was a common punishment, and those found guilty of adultery were often forced to sit for several Sundays before the congregation on their church's "stool of repentance." In other locations, adultery would merit execution. And while some consistories imposed fines, others did not.

Did consistories actually manage to reduce the number of drunkards, blasphemers, gluttons, and church-dodging golfers? The records left behind can only allow us to guess, because it never crossed the minds of those involved to track results with statistical precision. As far as they were concerned, bringing the guilty to justice was the only measure of success. And they surely had their hands full, year in, year out, up until the mid-seventeenth century. We do know this: Reformed Protestants dressed austerely and made prostitution illegal. We also know this: rates for illegitimate births dropped in most of these communities, as well as the number of children conceived through premarital sex. But the same pattern can be observed in many Catholic and Lutheran communities too, which leads us to two conclusions: first, we cannot attribute this drop in extramarital sex to Reformed morals courts alone; and second, there must have been other forces at work throughout Europe curbing such behaviors—forces that transcended confessional boundaries, and with which the Reformed morals courts were in step. Whether the Reformed led the way or outperformed their confessional rivals remains a matter of debate.

Well into the late seventeenth century, Reformed Protestants everywhere held fast to this kind of godly policing, meddling, and counseling, acquiring a reputation for sobriety and well-ordered communities where social disciplining was as much of an art as a science. In the process, these communities also left behind records that allow us to peer directly at their obsessions, triumphs, and failures. Too deeply convinced by their own theology of the corruption of human nature to aim for perfection, but equally convinced of the reality of predestination and of the role assigned to the elect, they strained to do God's bidding, believing that the pain they inflicted through their decisions was far less intense or devastating than that which would naturally follow from allowing sin to flourish, unrestrained.

In England, Reformed Protestant influence did not lead to the creation of special tribunals. Instead, as also happened in most Catholic lands at this time, the existing church courts took up the task of social disciplining with considerable fervor. These church courts served various functions, including the handling of wills, defamation cases, and internal church matters, especially those that pertained to the clergy and their performance, but much of their work concerned the morals of the community. These church courts treated many of the same issues as Reformed consistories: heresy, superstition, sorcery, slander, Sabbath breaking, misbehavior in church, neglect of duties, drunkenness, adultery, fornication, bastardy, incest, and all other sexual sins. Their concern with such matters was so intense, that they came to be known as the Courts of Scolds or Bawdy Courts.

All such cases worked their way up from the local level. Normally—but not always—the first courts to deal with offenses were the archdeaconry courts. The next level was that of the courts of the bishops, also known as consistory and commissary courts. The highest level of all was that of the courts of the archbishops, or prerogative courts. During the years of the Puritan Commonwealth, this court system was dismantled, and many of the moral offenses they had previously handled were turned into secular crimes, turned over to the civil courts. Two laws enacted in 1650 reflect this change: first, the Blasphemy Act, which, as previously mentioned, aimed to curtail offenses against God along with the extreme "enthusiasm" of radical nonconformists; second, the Adultery Act, which sought to make fornication and marital infidelity punishable by death. The Puritans also imposed a greater degree of censorship, especially on pamphlets published by the radical fringe. Once the monarchy was restored, the church courts reclaimed their traditional scolding jurisdiction over bawdy offenses.

Catholics were far less uniform than Protestants in their approach to social disciplining, but no less diligent. Their most formidable tribunal, the Inquisition, was confined to the Iberian kingdoms and their empires, and to Italy. Wherever it was established, the Inquisition busied itself on two fronts simultaneously: the extirpation of heresy and the enforcement of morals. Elsewhere, cases of heresy fell under the jurisdiction of local or diocesan ecclesiastical courts, as was the case in England. These church courts were not necessarily less aggressive than the Inquisition, but their zeal for social disciplining could vary, depending on time, place, and circumstances. The enforcement of punishments in areas without an Inquisition became the responsibility of civil authorities, and their aggressiveness could vary, too.

The Spanish Inquisition was by far the largest and most well organized and aggressive of all. In many ways, it set paradigms for all tribunals elsewhere, so it serves as an example through which the work of all Inquisitions can be understood. Established in 1478 by Pope Sixtus IV, who granted the Spanish monarchs Ferdinand of Aragon and Isabella of Castille the right to run it, this Inquisition was initially focused on the problems created by hundreds of thousands of unwilling converts from Judaism who kept practicing their ancestral faith after being baptized. Fairly quickly, this tribunal extended its reach to all heresies, too, and to a great number of moral offenses unconnected to heterodoxy. Headed by the Spanish monarchs and their hand-picked Inquisitor General, rather than the pope or the archbishop of Toledo, the Spanish Inquisition quickly became an efficient and very powerful agent for conformity that was at once ecclesiastical and extraecclesiastical due to its backing from the crown and its independence from the church's hierarchy. Highly centralized, with a supreme tribunal in Madrid and regional tribunals elsewhere, and scrupulously run by well-trained officials according to a detailed set of rules and guidelines, this Inquisition quickly became the most elaborate and well-oiled bureaucracy in the world. Some might argue that it was the first truly modern bureaucracy. Since its record keeping was superb, we have very detailed information about its work. For instance, of the 44,674 trials from the years 1540 to 1700 that are registered in its main archive, the cases can be broken down as the table on page 611 shows.[16]

This list gives us a sense of the kinds of infractions cataloged by Spanish inquisitors, with the small details of its social disciplining excluded. Nowhere on this list appear certain types of cases that were subsumed under a broader category, such as sodomy, cross-dressing, pacts with the devil, witchcraft, irreverence to the church and its rituals, false visions, and feigned sanctity. The list also obscures regional variations. For instance, of the 10,817 cases involving Muslim converts 6,754, or 62.4 percent, came from three out of nineteen tribunals, covering areas where the Morisco population was substantial: Valencia, Zaragoza, and Granada. In contrast, Barcelona had a mere thirty-nine cases and Valladolid but one.

Two other significant aspects of the Inquisition's work not easily discerned in this list are its role in enforcing reform within the church, and its ambidextrous social disciplining of both clergy and laity. Take, for example, solicitation cases, targeted against

Cases processed by all tribunals of the Spanish Inquisition (1540–1700)

Offense	Number of cases	Percentage of total
MAJOR HERESIES		
Islam (Moriscos)	10,817	24.2
Judaism (Conversos)	4,397	9.8
Lutheranism (Protestants)	3,503	7.8
Illuminism (Alumbrados)	143	0.3
Subtotal	**18,860**	**42.2**
MINOR HERESIES AND OTHER CRIMES		
Erroneous propositions	12,117	27.1
Superstition	3,532	7.9
Acts against Inquisition	3,371	7.5
Bigamy	2,645	5.9
Solicitation (seduction)	1,131	2.5
Miscellaneous	3,018	6.7
Subtotal	**25,814**	**57.7**
Total trials	**44,674**	**100**
DEATH SENTENCES		
In person	826	1.8
In effigy	778	1.7

SOURCE: Jaime Contreras and Gustav Henningsen, "Forty-Four Thousand Cases of the Spanish Inquisition, 1540–1700: Analysis of a Data Bank," in *The Inquisition in Early Modern Europe*, ed. John Tedeschi and Gustav Henningsen (Northern Illinois University Press, 1986), p. 114.

clergy who made sexual advances on the laity, especially during the sacrament of confession. Beginning in the 1560s, after the Council of Trent, the Inquisition began a campaign to target this widespread abuse. The Inquisition did not respect rank, or its own former functionaries. In 1559, it imprisoned the head of the Spanish church, Archbishop Bartolomé de Carranza, on suspicion of heresy, and only reluctantly allowed his case to be transferred to Rome, where he was eventually found guilty of several errors. Carranza would spend a total of seventeen years in the prisons of the Inquisition, and die in Rome, just one week after his trial ended. Ironically, earlier in his life, Archbishop Carranza had worked as a theological adviser and censor for the Inquisition.

The Inquisition served other important functions, in addition to trying and punishing offenders. Two were especially significant. First, it was in charge of censorship, and of ferreting out and destroying forbidden books, a job given to learned men such as Carranza. Its reach in this area extended to other nations indirectly, for its agents had the right to inspect every ship that docked in Spanish ports and to seize all forbidden books, and to try as heretics the smugglers who had brought them aboard. Second, in an era of heightened religious fervor, and of a surfeit of mystics, the Inquisition assumed the role of sorting the wheat from the chaff, carefully determining who was genuinely holy and who was an impostor or heretic. Both clergy and laity could be examined on this count, but most such cases pertained to monks and nuns, and the Inquisition's zeal for this task

Ministers of virtue. Tribunals, courts, and inquisitions were not the only agents of social disciplining. The clergy often admonished and instructed individuals in their flocks face-to-face, in their homes or in public places. In this late seventeenth-century engraving by an unknown artist, Rodrigo Niño de Guzmán, a Jesuit priest, convinces some gamblers to burn their playing cards. This Jesuit's ministry in Toledo focused on curbing vice, and he spent much of his time accosting sinners in taverns and brothels.

was so intense that it became routine for subsequently canonized saints to fall under its scrutiny, including Ignatius Loyola, John of Ávila, Joseph of Cupertino, and Teresa of Ávila.

Mere fear of the Inquisition may have done as much to curb offenses as did its trials, for its methods and procedures were unnerving, to say the least, and well known. To begin with, an accusation was all it took for one to be placed under suspicion and investigated. Accusations could come from anyone: a relative, or neighbor, or acquaintance, or one of the many lay spies and informants, known as *familiares*, whom the Inquisition scattered everywhere, strategically. Then, if one was arrested, nothing would be revealed concerning the charges, initially, or who had made the accusations, and one would be presumed guilty unless proven otherwise. One's property could be seized, too, and one could linger in prison for a long time before a verdict was reached. As if all this were not terrifying enough, everyone knew that torture could be introduced into the process at any time if the inquisitors suspected that one was not being truthful or contrite enough.

Even worse, the Inquisition was so proactive, and its power so extensive, that one was always but a step away from it. Inquisitors were required to scour their territory for offenders, and to pay regular visits to its towns and villages. During these *visitas* the Inquisitors would read an "edict of faith" after Sunday Mass at a previously designated church, which all residents were required to attend. This edict was a detailed list of offenses and sins, and, after reading it, the inquisitors would call on everyone to denounce any person they knew to be guilty of any such offense, or to turn oneself in if one was guilty. And they would make it very clear that not coming forward, failing to denouncing any known offender, was itself an offense. It was possible to be brought into a trial as someone who knew of the offence of the accused, but had not tattled. And to complain about any of this, or mock it in any way, that, too, could be deemed an offense.

Inquisitors wielded a big stick, undeniably, but they also had carrots to dangle before the faithful. Anyone who volunteered to work for them as a *familiar*, for instance, would be immune from prosecution in civil or criminal courts. Most of their other incentives were more passive and had to do with penalties. Anyone who repented and confessed during a *visita*, after hearing the edict of faith, would be forgiven, reconciled to the church, and given a lighter penance than those hauled in later by their dragnet. All who cooperated fully in their own trials, showed genuine remorse, and abjured their errors would also receive a lighter penance than those who resisted—as long as their offense was not too serious. First-time offenders always fared better than repeat offenders. Penalties varied according to the four possible verdicts: acquitted, penanced, reconciled, or relaxed (handed over to the civil authorities for execution). Those who were acquitted were set free, but would be marked for life and closely watched thereafter. Those who were not acquitted faced crushing punishments, not physically, but economically and socially. First, they would have all of their assets and property confiscated, and then they would be publically humiliated and ostracized in various ways.

Public shaming was an integral part of the Inquisition's penalty system, and so was deliberate marginalization. To begin with, offenders would have to take part in a ritual known in Spanish as an *auto de fe*, or in Portuguese as an *auto da fé*, in which all who had been found guilty were publicly humiliated. Most *autos* for those who had committed light offenses were held in churches. These secluded events, which never involved large crowds, were known as *autos particulares* or *autillos*, to distinguish them from the more elaborate and well-attended *autos públicos*, which were celebrated outdoors, usually in the central square of a city. All of the offenders in these *autos* were garbed in a humiliating yellow tunic known as a *sanbenito*, and a tall, cone-shaped cap, both of which were encoded with symbols that represented the gravity of their sins. Flames and dragons, for instance, were reserved for grave offenses, and diagonal green crosses for light ones. And this was but the first step in shaming. Once the *auto* was over, the offenders would be required to wear their *sanbenito* in public for a length of time determined by the seriousness of their sin, and once that time expired, their shameful tunics would be hung up in their respective parish churches, with their name clearly displayed on them. Worse still, every *sanbenito* was to remain on display in perpetuity, generation after generation. In a society where honor and reputation were supremely important, this flimsy but permanent monument to one's dishonor dealt a devastating blow not just to the reputation of offenders, but also to all of their kin. Most of those affected knew all too well that they could never recover. So, in many cases, such as that of Teresa of Ávila's grandfather, who was found guilty of Judaizing, the only logical solution was to move somewhere else, and start life anew among strangers. But even if one took the drastic step of running away from one's *sanbenito*, one could not escape one's past entirely, for everyone condemned by the Inquisition was legally forbidden to practice certain professions, own weapons, or wear the types of clothes and jewelry befitting for anyone above the lowest rank in society.

These were the minimum penalties imposed on those who were penanced and reconciled. Depending on the gravity of the sins, other punishments could be added, such as time in prison, or scourging; Archbishop of Toledo Bartolomé de Carranza, for instance, not only was forced to abjure sixteen propositions from his writings before being reconciled to the church, but also was formally stripped of his office and sentenced to five years of imprisonment in a Roman monastery. The ultimate penalty was execution by burning, and it was meted out to those who did not repent. In these cases, the offender would be handed over to the civil authorities, who would carry out the execution at an *auto de fe*. Since some Inquisition prisoners escaped and a few died before they could be brought to the stake for burning, *autos de fe* could often include the burning of effigies. The very nature of the *autos públicos*—which were rites of expiation and cleansing for the community, as well as of intimidation—required the Inquisition to somehow include even those offenders who were absent. The burning mannequins were a grim symbolic reminder, then, of the Inquisition's power over everyone, everywhere, even in foreign lands or the afterlife.

For centuries, thanks largely to sensational Protestant accounts, the Spanish Inquisition had a reputation as a bloodthirsty killing machine, with some estimates assigning tens of thousands of executions to it. Much to everyone's surprise, however, research in the late twentieth century revealed just the opposite to be true, especially of the period that coincides with the so-called confessional age. The figures shocked the scholarly world, turning long-held assumptions on their head: as it turns out, between 1547 and 1700 the Spanish Inquisition executed 826 people, or only 1.8 percent of the total number processed by its tribunals. Equally surprising, it also burned 778 effigies during that same span of time, which means that almost as many people escaped its clutches as were actually killed by it. Moreover, when the methods of the Inquisition began to be compared to those of secular courts throughout Spain and Europe, scholars were equally surprised to discover that the dreaded Inquisition was far kinder to its prisoners than its secular counterparts. Cases were discovered of prisoners under civil jurisdiction who did everything they could to be transferred to the Inquisition, including blaspheming on purpose, or spouting heretical propositions. If nothing else, these discoveries have shown us that long-held assumptions should always be questioned. All the same, however, there is no denying that the Spanish Inquisition, despite its newly discovered relative leniency, was a fearsome agent of social disciplining that few in its day would have seen as kind and merciful.

The Portuguese Inquisition was not only very similar to that of Spain; it also fell under the civil rulership of the Spanish crown in 1580, when King Philip II annexed the kingdom. Portugal and its colonies would remain under Spanish control for the next sixty years, until a successful rebellion against Spain in 1640 gained their independence once again. The most salient difference between the two tribunals was Portugal's more prolonged interest in the pursuit of Jewish conversos. This difference, in turn, had two causes: first, many Spanish conversos had fled to Portugal after 1492, to escape the Inquisition; and second, the Portuguese Inquisition was not established until 1536, which meant that Portugal began to round up conversos for the offense of Judaizing far later than Spain—so much later, in fact, that Spain had almost run out of conversos to prosecute by then. Another difference was the temporary suspension of the Portuguese Inquisition by Pope Innocent XI from 1674 to 1681. In every other respect, the social disciplining undertaken by the Portuguese Inquisition mirrored that of its next-door neighbor.

In Italy, the Inquisition played very much the same role as in Spain and Portugal, and its execution rate was similarly low. Its organization was more complex than that of its Spanish counterpart, with less centralization and more overlapping jurisdictional boundaries and procedures. The chief and ultimate tribunal was Rome; among the many others, the most independent were Venice, Naples, and Sicily. Venice guarded its jurisdiction fiercely; Naples was ruled by the Spanish monarchs, but was not part of the Spanish Inquisition; and Sicily was actually a tribunal of the Spanish Inquisition.

The Roman Inquisition was established in 1542 by Pope Paul III, principally to combat Protestantism. It was originally run by six cardinals, a number that would later be increased to eight by Pius IV and thirteen by Sixtus V. Its focus—much like the number of its members—would shift with the passage of time, to all sorts of heresies, and to offenses of a religious and moral nature, such as blasphemy, superstition, witchcraft, and sexual crimes. As we have seen, in 1588, Pope Sixtus V created fifteen new congregations led by cardinals to aid the pope in running a more centralized church. The first of these was the Inquisition, which was given the imposing formal name of Supreme Sacred Congregation of the Roman and Universal Inquisition. Because of its preeminence, the Roman Inquisition would handle some of the most celebrated cases of the early modern era, such as those of Giordano Bruno, from 1592 to 1600, and Galileo Galilei in 1633.

Outside of Italy, Portugal, and Spain and its territories, in Catholic communities that had no Inquisition, efforts to rout heresy and curb unchristian behavior were no less intense, but far more uneven. For the most part, the task of policing and disciplining was assumed by bishops, especially after the Council of Trent charged them with greater responsibilities and granted them greater authority within their dioceses. Visitations became a key part of their effort, as we have seen. Dealing with heterodoxy and disciplining all offenders fell to the episcopal courts, which, endowed with increased authority over all other local ecclesiastical entities, could now follow up on whatever problems cropped up and all those issues referred to them through the visitations. Many of the same offenses prosecuted by the Inquisition gradually began to be pursued by bishops, in various ways, and always with the close cooperation of civil authorities that seemed equally intent on exercising greater control. And in many cases, the absence of an Inquisition actually allowed bishops and others a greater freedom to exercise their zeal without restraints. So, oddly enough, as we shall see soon when we deal with the way in which the devil was pursued in this age, without the presence of an Inquisition, the disciplining carried out by bishops and civil authorities could be far more thorough, and much harsher.

Conclusion

Catholic social disciplining cannot be easily summarized because it was never neatly packaged. In addition to having various external agents of control and many local variations, the Catholic Church also relied on other means of internal and individual control of its flock: through the sacrament of penance, and the one-on-one exchange between priest and penitent; through its schools, its devotional texts, its preachers, and its lay confraternities.

Protestant social disciplining is also difficult to sum up, especially since several different churches are involved, along with local variations. But its most salient distinguishing feature is easy enough to spot: the way church and state tended to share the task of policing and controlling behavior.

Reforming society itself was a tall order, a challenge greater than that of reforming the church. All of the Reformers of the early modern period knew that the wicked "world" that had been set in opposition to the Kingdom of God in the Gospels by Christ himself could never be fully transformed, much less brought to perfection. Yet most Reformers tried, each in his own way, to make it better, for they knew all too well that the boundary between "the world" and the church was way too permeable, perhaps impossible to discern. Though failure was guaranteed, they hoped for some success, some measure of improvement.

This fervent attempt to improve and Christianize the so-called world may have been overly optimistic, and all too offensive to present-day Western sensibilities, but no one can deny that it is one of the most remarkable features of the early modern age, along with the violence that accompanied it.

Despite all of its obvious connections to early modern state building, social disciplining was much more than an attempt by elites to coerce subalterns into submission. Ultimately, with Catholics, as much as with Protestants, no campaign for moral improvement or orthodoxy could ever succeed without the willing participation of the lay folk. In the case of Catholicism, and also of Protestantism, research in many locations has proved that the laity took charge of their destiny to a considerable extent, and played a key role in improving the world bequeathed to them. Whether it was through lay elders judging cases in Reformed consistories, or of Lutheran princes conducting visitations, or of *familiares* spying on their neighbors for the Inquisition, the "Christianization" of early modern Europe was very much a lay affair, a process of change that took place as much from the bottom up as from the top down.

The disciplinary tribunals of the Reformed churches offer us ample proof of lay involvement. Although most of these tribunals were run by elites of one sort or another, they did not simply impose their authority on passive or grudging subalterns. For such a system to function, denunciations from below were absolutely necessary. And there never seemed to be a shortage of those. In Aberdeen, Scotland, officially appointed "censurers and captors" eagerly scoured the city for foul-mouthed offenders who could be fined on the spot for swearing and blaspheming. And sometimes, lurid details were only too eagerly reported. In Geneva, in 1611, eight witnesses stepped forward to denounce an adulteress, claiming that she and a foreign soldier "were seen kissing in the corner of a window, and she took off her neckband and uncovered her breasts, which he kissed, and he picked her up by the waist, after which nothing more could be seen."[17] Whether the moralistic voyeurs wished they could have seen more is a question not addressed in the court records.

Christianization and confessionalization were never simple processes, much less bloodless, or a resounding triumph. Far from it. In many ways, the early modern effort to turn Europeans into good Christians was one of the messiest and most heartbreaking of all noble causes in Western history. But the participation of the devout laity, as well as their initiative and religious vitality, is something that needs to be taken into account in reckoning its spirit, just as much as all of the top-down efforts of church and state.

CHAPTER TWENTY-THREE

The Age of Devils

Turning people into good Christians was not just a matter of policing their behavior and punishing offenders. For many in the sixteenth and seventeenth century, to reform was to engage in a cosmic war against Satan and his minions. And it was a struggle in which the devil was no metaphor, but rather a real presence, as real as all the innumerable human beings believed to be in league with him or under his grip.

For an unnerving glimpse into such a worldview, let us turn once again to the case of Chancellor Niklaus Krell, that crypto-Calvinist offender mentioned in the previous chapter.

Krell's "crime" of crypto-Calvinism was interpreted by many of his Lutheran contemporaries as much worse than mere heterodoxy. Krell was considered an agent of the devil, and the common people of Saxony were apparently convinced of this through certain signs in nature itself. Among the many odd natural wonders (*Wunder*) seen by his contemporaries as portents and signs that predicted Krell's crypto-Calvinist betrayal of Saxony, and his eventual downfall, the following might seem most bizarre in our day and age: some women were reported to have given birth to toads, and to children with moustaches; an image of Christ had begun to bleed profusely; signs resembling bloody swords had been seen in the sky; anguished cries had been heard in the clouds; and ghosts seven feet tall had walked through the church at Zwickau, interrupting the Sunday service. In addition, many Saxons elsewhere had seen the devil, in various guises; and he had manifested himself with flaming horns in the market place of Elenburg, and produced violent thunderstorms that frightened everyone half to death. And that was not all: Krell, it was said, received frequent visits from the devil. The prison guards at the Königstein fortress testified that Satan himself came to Krell's cell as a black bird and spoke with him in a language that they could not understand. Reports also circulated that an imprisoned crypto-Calvinist friend of Krell's, the court preacher David Steinbach, had been freed from his cell by the devil, and that after being captured, he had confessed

Nearly modern devil. Belief in the reality of the devil was one of the most prominent continuities between the Middle Ages and era of the Reformations. This painting by Michael Pacher, a Tyrolean artist, was completed in 1481, on the eve of the Protestant Reformation, for an altarpiece in an Austrian church. The legend depicted by Pacher is as medieval as they come: a tenth-century bishop, St. Wolfgang, had been tempted by the devil—much as Christ had in the desert according to the gospels—but he managed to outsmart the evil one, and force him into building a church. This Renaissance execution of the encounter between St. Wolfgang and the devil, which includes the geometry of perspective and other details indicative of its modernity, is definitely post-medieval, but also representative of dreadful obsessions that no Renaissance with a capital *R* could displace. The devil's ugliness is otherworldly yet painstakingly detailed, at once medieval and modern. It is also simultaneously Catholic and Protestant, even though Pacher, like everyone in his day, could not imagine the advent of Protestantism.

that the devil had been visiting him for a long time, occasionally using his washbasin and leafing through his books.[1]

Demonizing one's enemies was nothing new. Neither was the inclination to entwine the natural, preternatural, and supernatural. That braiding was one of the chief characteristics of the transition to modernity, and one of its chief problems, too: heaven hung too low and the fires of hell roiled high enough to singe the earth and its atmosphere. Demonizing could be metaphorical at times, certainly, but even in such instances, the imagery reified deeply held beliefs that affirmed the menacing reality of the devil. Moreover, all things diabolical were inseparably linked to a belief system in which pre-Christian, non-Christian, and Christian elements were thoroughly mixed.

By the sixteenth century, elites such as Erasmus of Rotterdam and Guillaume Briçonnet were inveighing against such unholy intermingling, calling for a return to a "pure" Christianity stripped bare of all traces of "superstition" and heathenism. The Protestant goal of restoring the church to ancient pristine forms through scripture alone flowed naturally from this late medieval reformist thrust: *ad fontes* and *sola scriptura* were but two sides of the same coin; or, better yet, two sides of the same scraper with which all of the barnacles that clung to the ship of salvation were to be stripped away. But identifying all the barnacles, so to speak, proved immensely difficult, as the ship's hull had planks made of fossilized barnacles. In other words, many elements of Christian belief and practice were of ancient origin, and thus linked to an extrabiblical matrix. This was especially true of all things demonic, and, to some extent, of "magic" and of the many behaviors that could be deemed superstitions.

A murky haze hung over the devil, clouding all beliefs and rites associated with him. This fog can be attributed to two factors. First, since the Christian devil was an amalgam of ancient Near Eastern and European folklore, and since much of demonological lore was extrabiblical, clear definitions did not begin to emerge until the fifteenth century. And even then, there was much disagreement on the part of experts. Second, many of the rites and beliefs that came to be associated with the devil—and to be rejected by the church as magic and superstition—were deeply embedded in European culture and most often concerned mundane vicissitudes of life (health, fertility, love, finances) rather than spiritual issues. Discerning the difference between what was truly divine or neutral or demonic or between religion and certain ancient problem-solving strategies deemed "magical" was never simple, and required some hermeneutic, that is, some set of guidelines for interpreting phenomena according to specific preconceived assumptions. The same was true when it came to determining where the line should be drawn between magic and religion, or magic and superstition, or religion and superstition. To further complicate matters, sorcery and witchcraft were added to the mix in the fifteenth century, too, and linked to the devil, adding yet more distinctions to be made and more areas of aberrant piety to be eradicated. By the dawn of the sixteenth century, the devil came to be linked to three very murky categories of deviancy: magic, superstition, and witchcraft.

These categories were fuzzy because medieval theologians had never reached consensus on the interpretation of these three deviant forms of belief and ritual. Worse yet, the exact meaning of the concepts and terms remained a contentious issue into the eve of the Reformation era, even as campaigns were mounted to combat magic, superstition, witchcraft, and the devil. And not surprisingly, with the advent of the Protestant Reformation, disagreements became even more intense and numerous.

In the sixteenth century, binary oppositions such as magic-religion, superstition-religion, demonic-heavenly gained intensity and their meaning grew ever more unstable and divisive. Ironically, even though they could not agree on how to combat the devil, magic, and superstition, Catholics and Protestants alike agreed that such combat was absolutely necessary. So, it came to pass that as Catholics launched campaigns against the devil, magic, superstition, and witchcraft, Protestants waged a similar war, at the very same time, in which they railed constantly against much of Catholic ritual as demonic, magical, and superstitious.

Though the primary sources themselves sometimes blur distinctions when dealing with practices condemned by both Catholics and Protestants—making difficult for us to deal with them in isolation from one another—they can nonetheless be separated into four categories, in each of which the devil played some part.

The first and most nebulous deviant category is "superstition." It was an ancient Latin term, which pagan Romans employed in reference to any beliefs or practices that falsely and foolishly placed faith in supernatural causes. Much like the term *pornography* in the twenty-first century, *superstition* was hard to define, but relatively easy to identify. St. Augustine poked fun at a few of the "superstitions" of his late fourth-century Roman world:

> To hold your left thumb in your right hand when you hiccup; . . . to tread upon the threshold when you go out in front of the house; to go back to bed if anyone should sneeze when you are putting on your slippers; to return home if you stumble when going to a place; when your clothes are eaten by mice, to be more frightened at the prospect of coming misfortune than grieved by your present loss.[2]

Augustine did much more than ridicule superstition; he gave it greater definition by linking all of it to demons. At the same time he broadened its meaning too, linking it to magic, idolatry, and devotion to the devil. He was not the first to do so. By his day, Christians had already given superstition an objective, yet still very fuzzy definition, as any false religion or any observance not sanctioned by the church. In fact, by Augustine's day, Christians had already been teaching for a long time that all religions other than their own came from the devil, and that it was through demonic deceit that the human race had been lured away from worship of the one true God.

Augustine, the most revered and oft-cited of the Latin church fathers bequeathed this thinking to the West. In the fifth century, Pope Leo I would affirm it, proposing that the devil gained control of the human race through *superstitiones*. Adopting such a

teaching meant, in practical terms, that whether or not one was aware, all rites and observances not sanctioned by the church put one in league with the devil—or worse, they
were de facto acts of demonic veneration. In the thirteenth century, Thomas Aquinas
would define superstition as "a vice opposed to religion by way of excess; not because in
the worship of God it does more than true religion, but because it offers Divine worship
to beings other than God or offers worship to God in an improper manner."[3]

Superstition, then, was taken to be the root of false religion, and of all idolatry.
In the sixteenth century, *idolatry* would become a fighting word with diverging and
diametrically opposed meanings. For the Catholics who ventured to the Americas and
Asia, all the religions they encountered were nothing but superstition and idolatry; for
the Protestants in Europe, all of Catholic worship was idolatrous and superstitious. In
both cases, the recognition of any idolatry was conjoined with an effort to wipe it out as
something demonic, and with the actual annihilation of sacred art.

The second, closely related category was "magic," or the occult, or hidden arts.
For Augustine, who died in 430 as the Vandals were ravaging the Roman Empire, magic
was all about incantations, signs, divinations, auguries, amulets, cures, and "consulta-
tions and arrangements about signs and leagues with devils." It was all demonically
induced delusion, and "fornication of the soul."[4] For Pope Leo I, merely one generation
after Augustine, the practice of magic was actually the ultimate outcome of superstition, and of commerce with demons. In the seventh century, Isidore of Seville would
further codify magic, providing medieval theologians with a long, detailed list of the
various types of illicit practices "supported by demons."[5] This conception of magic as an
inherently demonic and practically oriented attempt to effect changes on the world or to
gain knowledge of its workings, or foreknowledge of future events would become church
doctrine and guide its policies toward European folk beliefs in the Middle Ages.

By the thirteenth century, the church's duty to combat magic as something
dangerous was widely recognized by elite authorities. Thomas Aquinas summed it up as
follows:

> Man has not been entrusted with power over the demons, to employ them to whatso-
> ever purpose he will; on the contrary, it is appointed that he should wage war against
> the demons. Hence in no way is it lawful for man to make use of the demons' help by
> compacts either tacit or express.[6]

Under this rubric of magic fell a long list of practices, many inseparable from folk customs
or even folk medicine. As anthropologists have revealed, medieval Christians did not
always know how to make even the most fundamental distinctions. In one notorious
case, a thirteenth-century inquisitor found some peasants in southern France who tried to
revive their dead infants by dunking them in a cold stream and invoking the aid of a dog
they called St. Guinefort. The fact that the intercessor was a dog, and that the ritual was
not sanctioned by the church, did not seem to matter to the local folk, who, according to
archeological evidence, stuck to their illicit devotions until the nineteenth century. But

it certainly did matter to the inquisitor who first discovered this peculiar devotion and tried—unsuccessfully—to stamp it out.[7]

In the late Middle Ages, the gap between theology and popular piety widened in the minds of learned elites, and the theological perspective taken by many of them left much of popular piety in the hands of the devil, or cast it into the benighted realm of superstition. By the sixteenth century, Erasmus would be complaining that all pilgrimages and the veneration of relics were not much different from the cult of St. Guinefort, or from the magical arts. And the Protestant Reformers would take one step beyond Erasmus and dismiss nearly all of Catholic ritual as devilish magic.

The third category, narrower than superstition and magic, was "sorcery" or "witchcraft." Although the ultimate definition of witchcraft was not fully developed until the fifteenth century, it had ancient antecedents, older than Christianity itself. In essence, what ended up being known as "witchcraft" was an amalgam of three disparate traditions: first, the ancient, pre-Christian practice of malevolent magic, *maleficium* (literally, "evil making" or "evil doing"), which the Romans had turned into a punishable crime; second, various European folk traditions; and third, learned Christian views on the demonic origins of all unsanctioned rites. This amalgam proved a lethal mix for anyone suspected of the crime of *maleficium* from the fifteenth to the eighteenth century, for the age of devils was, above all, the age of witches, and of their persecution. Catholics and Protestants persecuted *maleficium* with equal ferocity. Estimates for the number of men, women, and children prosecuted as witches for the crime of *maleficium* during this period range between one hundred thousand and two hundred thousand. Few scholars doubt the existence of sorcerers or of the practice of *maleficium*, that is, of the attempted manipulation of natural, preternatural, and supernatural forces by sorcerers who sought to inflict harm on others. What is still a matter of much debate is whether those accused and convicted of witchcraft engaged in the very specific diabolical acts that the various churches of the Reformation era came to link with *maleficium*, a question we shall explore later in this chapter.

The fourth category that was distinct from superstition, magic, and witchcraft, but not altogether divorced from them—was the narrowest of all: "direct personal encounters with the devil." This level of deviance was the ultimate possible outcome of all three demonically centered activities and it involved two distinct sets of phenomena. The first set had to do with all apparitions of the devil and of the exchanges between demons and humans, which led to all sorts of abominable consequences, such as the signing of pacts with the devil. Most such engagements led to charges of witchcraft, but the pact alone was a heinous enough crime, as evidenced in the cases of Niklaus Krell and Henning Brabant.

Catholics and Protestants waged unrelenting war on these encounters, and all diabolical pacts. The second set of phenomena had to do with demonic possessions, that is, with cases of human beings whose bodies had been completely taken over by demons, and also with obsession, or cases of individuals whose minds and wills underwent severe and very focused temptations by demons. Possession was an ancient phenomenon, and a biblical one too, for the Gospel narratives were full of accounts of demon-possessed people who were freed of this affliction by Jesus and his apostles. Catholics and Lutherans believed in possession, but they had radically different approaches to dealing with it; the Reformed were divided on its possibility, and on ways of handling it.

In addition to confronting these four categories of diabolically inclined misbehavior—superstition, magic, witchcraft, and direct encounters with the devil—church elites also had to contend with two "sciences" that had an aura of respectability and enjoyed the support of powerful patrons: astrology and alchemy. Churchmen of all denominations were prone to tie both of these to the devil, too, but they found it hard to prove the connection. Of the two, astrology was attacked more often and more vigorously, principally by theologians, but it remained a highly esteemed profession, and many a royal court had its official astrologer. Alchemists—the precursors of modern chemists—were intent on unlocking the basic structure of the material world and transmuting material elements from lower to higher forms (turning baser metals into gold, for instance). They claimed adherence to an ancient secret tradition and were therefore mistrusted by church authorities, Catholic and Protestant, but nonetheless managed to cling to their exalted profession at the highest places. Some practitioners of astrology and alchemy were also physicians and dabbled in other occult and magical arts. One of these polymaths, Heinrich Cornelius Agrippa von Nettesheim (1486–1535), author of the *Three Books of Occult Philosophy*, was a complex thinker who prospered and eluded persecution in his own day, but would have probably fallen victim to the war against the devil if he had lived a generation or two later. In this nebulous borderland between ancient sciences and the occult arts were not just the furthest reaches of the devil as imagined by any inquisition or church court, but also the lowly origins of modern empirical science.

Established authorities—both Catholic and Protestant—dealt with each of these four demonically linked aberrant behaviors in various ways, according to time and place, but tolerance was never an option. The contours of persecution were determined by the perceived aberrances themselves, as well as by local circumstances, so let us examine each of the four categories of deviance, one by one.

Superstition

For Catholics, any rite or practice unsanctioned by the church that aimed at gaining supernatural favors could be deemed superstitious. Protestant churches followed this guideline too, but they added many of the rites of the Catholic Church to their list of superstitions. The two confessions shared a narrower understanding of superstition firmly limited by two distinguishing traits: passivity and ignorance. This most simple realm of superstition, more mundane than any other, consisted of all attitudes, behaviors, and devotions that were passively and ignorantly accepted and unquestioningly engaged in. This kind of superstition required no special knowledge or training, other than that provided mere exposure to one's culture.

Among Catholics, the campaign against this kind of mundane superstition had begun in the late Middle Ages, but it was conducted at a learned level, by elite reformists, rather than at the parish level. Intellectuals such as Jean Gerson (1363–1429), chancellor of the University of Paris, could decry the many superstitions that existed in his day but lacked the means to put an end to them. Gerson expanded the definition of superstition to include certain practices, attitudes, and expectations that had crept into legitimate rites of the Catholic Church. "There are many things introduced under the appearance of religion among simple Christians," he said, "which it would have been more holy to have omitted." He thus brought the critique of superstition inside the church, so to speak, calling attention to offenses within it. Others, and in particular Guillaume Briçonnet and Erasmus of Rotterdam, followed suit, further developing this internal scrutiny along humanist lines, pushing for an *ad fontes* housecleaning that would bring the church back to its pristine first-century state.

Briçonnet and Erasmus refused to condemn the rites of the church outright, but their critique of superstition took a more radical turn among their followers. When contemporaries of Erasmus blamed him for laying the egg hatched by Luther, most of them had in mind the Erasmian attack on superstition within the Catholic Church. From 1517 on, this critique would be taken in two different directions. paths. Within the Catholic Church, many continued to campaign against superstitious practices and attitudes, but refrained from arguing that any sanctioned rites were superstitious in and of themselves; within the emerging Protestant camp, the critique turned sharply against Catholicism itself, and all its rituals, which also forced Catholics to engage in a much more vigorous housecleaning than ever before. The two paths did link up at some points, especially in regard to obviously non-Christian practices, but they remained opposites.

Protestants all agreed that the Roman Catholic church was thoroughly corrupted by superstition from top to bottom, and much of their war on superstition consisted of their rejection of Catholic piety. Luther retained much more of medieval folk religion than any other major Reformers—especially in regard to all things diabolical—but he nonetheless rejected much of Catholic ritual as useless works-righteousness, especially those rites that gave the impression of guaranteeing a predictable outcome: pilgrimages, the blessing of objects, the use of holy water, the veneration of saints and their relics, the wearing of holy medals, for example. In the Reformed camp, superstition was a much greater concern than the delusion of works-righteousness, and the attack on Catholic piety was more severe.

As Reformed Protestants saw it, the central miracle of the Catholic faith—transubstantiation—was no more than *hocus pocus*, literally, the mumbled *hoc est corpus meum* of eucharistic consecration transformed into a magical incantation, every bit as mystifying as the word *abracadabra*.[8] In 1521, Luther's disregard for the power of rituals was surpassed by that of his colleague Andreas Bodenstein von Karlstadt, who called for the abolition of images and of much of Catholic ritual, including the Mass. Karlstadt's extreme point of view was shared by the Swiss Reformers, all of whom undertook a campaign against Catholic ritual as superstition and idolatry. From Switzerland, this aggressive rejection of Catholic ritual was passed on to all other churches in the Reformed tradition, including that of England. Eventually, in all places where Protestantism took root and flourished, *papistry*, *superstition*, and *idolatry*, became synonymous, and little tolerance would be shown toward anything that smacked of Catholicism. In response to Protestantism, the Catholic Church reaffirmed the absolute legitimacy of its rituals, and, at the very same time, also initiated a campaign to fight superstition on two fronts: internally, in regard to valid rituals, and externally, in regard to practices it deemed un-Christian. Relying on scholastic theology, the Catholic Church took a more methodical approach to the issue of superstition, dividing it into four different types: the improper worship of the true God, idolatry, divination, and vain observances, which include magic and occult arts. Such distinctions were incomprehensible to most of the laity (and some of the clergy too), but they mattered to those who were in charge of enforcing correctness, The fourth category, of "vain observances," was the broadest and involved the greatest number of people, since it covered everything from the trivial, such as remedies for hiccups, to the very worst, such as witchcraft. The Council of Trent did not delve deeply into the problem of superstition, but it did issue call on bishops to "prohibit and abolish all those things . . . which have been introduced by irreverence, which can scarcely be separated from impiety; or by superstition, that false imitation of true piety."[9]

Concerning the one area of Catholic piety where reformists had detected the most intense superstition, the directives of Trent were clear, but not very specific: "in the invocation of saints, the veneration of relics, and the sacred use of images," ordered the council, "every superstition shall be removed."[10] In a similar vein, but with more detailed instructions, Trent also demanded that all the superstitious abuses that surrounded the Mass be done away with:

> That no place may be given to superstition; they shall by edict, and under penalties laid down that priests take care not to celebrate at other than due hours, nor make use of other rites, or other ceremonies and prayers in the celebration of masses, besides those which have been approved by the Church. . . . They shall wholly remove from the Church the observance of a fixed number of certain masses, and of candles, as being invented rather by superstitious worship, than by true religion.[11]

These reforms were quickly implemented in some places, such as Spain, and more gradually in others, such as Germany. By the early 1600s, much of what had offended purists such as Erasmus was still in place, but the more blatant superstitions surrounding Catholic worship had in many places been greatly reduced.

Much harder to combat, and even harder to exterminate, was the vast throng of ancient beings and spirits from local folklore who infested the landscape: fairies, gnomes, trolls, elves, pixies, sprites, gremlins, goblins, nymphs, *duendes*, leprechauns, imps, and others of their ilk. These beings were the stuff of myth, and of the popular imagination. Some were spiritual, others physical. The Catholic Church had long taught that such beings were but demons, and Protestants took the same tack, so their existence was implicitly reaffirmed. Though demonized, and therefore subjected to the same treatment as all things diabolical, these beings stubbornly clung to the collective imagination. Banishing them from folklore, art, and literature was even harder, as proved by William Shakespeare's play *A Midsummer Night's Dream*, written in the 1590s, as the war against superstition and the devil was beginning to peak, and by the works of the Baroness d'Aulnoy (1650–1705), who not only wrote about fairies a century after Shakespeare, but also coined the term *fairy tale* in her book title *Contes des fées* (1697). If the war against the devil had been entirely successful, this genre of literature, which only gained in popularity with the passage of time, would never have come into existence.

Ghosts were even harder to dispel. The interweaving of folk culture and religion was particularly tight on the subject of ghosts, principally because of the Catholic Church's teachings on purgatory. That souls in purgatory could visit the living was an ancient belief sanctioned by the church and reinforced by it in myriad ways. From St. Gregory the Great's *Dialogues* of the sixth century through many medieval texts, and up to the eve of the Reformation, the appearance of souls from purgatory was a common theme in literature, sermons, and especially monastic piety. Most ghostly visits had a common purpose: to ask the living to do more for the soul in purgatory, or to inform the living that their suffrages had worked. But there were also accounts in popular culture that veered from the straight and narrow. In these tales ghosts appeared for all sorts of reasons, some of them most profane, such as to request vengeance. The church taught that many ghostly apparitions were really demonic, and that it was very easy for the devil to fool one into thinking that one was seeing a ghost. Discerning whether an apparition was a genuine revenant (a human visitor from the hereafter) or a demon was tricky, but in most cases, the decision hinged on what the ghost spoke about or requested, for, normally, genuine ghosts should deal only with one subject: purgatory.

The Protestant rejection of purgatory closed off the option of visits from the suffering dead. Protestants believed that the dead went straight to heaven or hell—and that there was no way they could visit the living—and therefore all ghostly visits had to be demonic. Abundant evidence proves that Protestants nonetheless kept believing in ghostly apparitions, despite official denials of human revenants. This dissonance reveals that a gap was created between popular belief and high theology, and that the gap was difficult to bridge. The theologians maintained a firm position, no matter how many ghosts were reported by the laity: as they saw it, all ghosts were demons and had to be treated as such. The most authoritative and influential Protestant treatise on this subject was written by Ludwig Lavater (1527–1586), a theologian at Zurich and son-in-law of Heinrich Bullinger. Lavater's *On Spectres, Apparitions and Great and Unaccustomed Noises*, first published in German (1569) and Latin (1570), was translated into various languages and published repeatedly. Lavater's position was but a reiteration of what had already been taught among Protestants since the 1520s: all ghostly apparitions were demonic. But he addressed the subject with such clarity, and so thoroughly, that his text became definitive.

Such teachings were not necessarily accepted at the popular level, however, and the survival of medieval ghost beliefs shows up in the records of those in charge of social discipline, and in literature. The ghost of Hamlet's father or that of Banquo in *Macbeth* are both ambiguous figures who could be perceived either as human revenants or as demons whose sole intention is to stir up trouble. Shakespeare's Protestant audiences would have understood the brilliant ambiguity of these characters, for living as they did in a world in transition, they were all too familiar with equivocation, and ghostly traces of Catholicism.

Magic

Beyond the vain observances and mundane superstitions that Catholics tried to eliminate, and beyond the Protestant attack on Catholic idolatry and superstition, reformers of both traditions aimed to eradicate a worse sort of commerce with the devil, that of the magical arts. Unlike superstition, magic was not mired in ignorance or passivity: it required some skill and knowledge, and expertise, and involved rites other than those sanctioned by the Catholic Church. At this level, the devil became much more actively involved, even if no evil-doing was involved, or no explicit pacts were made with him and no one was aware of his presence and participation. Though the line between magic and witchcraft could be blurry at times, distinctions were nonetheless made by experts, and a certain range of practices that did not necessarily involve explicit pacts with demons or the inflicting of harm on others came to be identified as magic. This magic tended to fall into two categories: divination and the manufacture and use of special substances.

Divination was the attempt to discern what is hidden, especially in the future, and it was practiced in a vast number of ways, through specialists of various sorts, many of whom claimed special supernatural gifts. These different paths to hidden knowledge were of ancient origin and derived from the assumption that all of nature was encoded with secrets, and that these secrets could be accessed with the right skill or supernatural gift. And there were as many different kinds of divination as there were substances and objects to plumb for secrets. These sundry ways of accessing what was hidden from view were classified by the learned, according to the means through which the knowledge was sought, with the suffix *-manteía* ("prophecy" or "divination"), or *-mancy* in English. Even a partial list of such classifications can seem too long in our day and age, despite the continued presence of these ancient arts in our midst:

> *aeromancy*, "by means of the air and winds"
> *alomancy*, "by salt"
> *anthropomancy*, "by inspection of human viscera"

belomancy, "by the shuffling of arrows"

capnomancy, "by the ascent or motion of smoke"

cartomancy, "by cards"

catroptomancy, "by mirrors"

chiromancy, or *palmistry*, "by the lines of the hand"

geomancy, "by points, lines, or figures traced on the ground"

hydromancy, "by water"

necromancy, "by the evocation of the dead"

oneiromancy, "by the interpretation of dreams"

pyromancy, "by fire"

Catholics and Protestants condemned all such practices as diabolical, and made an effort to wipe them out. Yet the illicit divining survived, as court records prove. The desire to interpret nature as a messenger was so strong, and the struggle against it so complex, that sometimes the oddest twists in divination could actually be deemed orthodox, and completely free of demonic ties. This was especially true among Protestants, and especially German Lutherans, who developed a penchant for reading unusual natural events as divine messages, and turned wonder decoding into one of their most distinctive traits. These "wonders" (*Wunder*) that conveyed divine messages were as numerous and varied as all freakish events: astronomical anomalies, strange lights in the sky, cloud formations, unusual weather, earthquakes, beached whales, deformed animals, shockingly abnormal human births. Such aberrant *Wunder* never predicted the future, but they did convey warnings about worse things to come, and most often they revealed that something was awfully wrong with the moral order of the locale where they were made manifest. Ironically, wonder decoding, something that might have been deemed superstitious, became yet another tool of Christian scolding and social disciplining. In 1578, for instance, when a deformed lamb was born in the village of Stedersdorf, the news was broadcast through Germany in a printed broadsheet. And the author of this vividly illustrated publication decoded the lamb's deformities as a sign of God's impending wrath:

> Perhaps with this four-eared, eight-legged monster with its snake's mouth God is sending us an image of how we prefer to be the devil's serpent and ram rather than righteous sheep and how we are now going backwards like the crab, having attained the crab's walk.[12]

Thanks to the printing press, moralistic interpretations of this sort circulated widely, turning all uncommon events into divine messages. Broadsheets and pamphlets spread the news much as modern newspapers would, and so did books that were entirely dedicated to collecting reports about these missives from heaven, such as Job Fincel's *Wonder Signs* (1566). Fincel's book was more than a catalog of the most noteworthy wonders that had shaken Germany since 1517; it was a prophetic scolding of a "godless" world besotted by its "arid, heathen ways." An instant best seller, it was quickly followed by a second volume in 1569 and a third in 1562. This massive 1,200-page proof-text for the impending Last Judgment—which Fincel warned was very near—would be reprinted numerous times and would have a profound influence on all subsequent wonder books. Caspar Goltwurm's contemporaneous *Book of Wondrous Works and Miraculous Signs* (1557) tried to outdo Fincel by covering all the great wonders that had been recorded since the beginning of history. Questions of orthodoxy seemed not to affect this genre, for Gnesio-Lutherans were as keen on wonders as Philippists. *De Monstris, on Highly Unusual Wondrous Births* (1585), one of several wonder books written by Christoph Irenaeus, a leading light of the Gnesio-Lutherans, focused not on apocalyptic predictions, but on one theme dear to his theological party: corruption of nature by sin. Lutherans would continue publishing wonder books for generations, well into the late seventeenth century. And the devil, curiously, would have absolutely no agency in such events.

The Lutherans were not alone. In 1557, scarcely a year after Fincel's *Wonder Signs* appeared, Conrad Wolffhart—better known by his humanist name Lycosthenes—published his *Chronicle of Omens and Portents* in the Reformed bastion of Basel. Lycosthenes was not only a professor, but also deacon of one of Basel's churches and a nephew of Konrad Pellikan, one of the most distinguished biblical scholars at Zurich. In other words, Lycosthenes could boast of impeccable Reformed credentials. Yet his lavishly illustrated *Chronicle*, published in both Latin and German, was as obsessed with decoding natural phenomena, and with finding the divine messages contained therein as the work of any ancient Roman diviner. Analyzing the epistemology and hermeneutics of divination and dissecting the meaning of technical Latin terms such as *ostentium*, *portentum*, *omen*, and *prodigium*, Lycosthenes, the Reformed grammarian, provided not just a catalog of wonders, but also a definitive field guide for the decoding of all strange signs and events. The *Chronicle* proved immensely popular—in Reformed Switzerland and throughout Europe—and it is known to have influenced the best-known prophet of the age, Nostradamus. In Elizabethan England, much of the *Chronicle* was translated and published in 1581 by Stephen Batman as *Doome Warning All Men to the Judgmente*. This best seller also contained reports of wonders from England that Batman had collected.

In Zurich, the ultimate citadel of Swiss Reformed correctness, Johann Jakob Wick outdid Lycosthenes when it came to collecting *Wunder* reports. A friend of Heinrich Bullinger and an archdeacon of the city's Grossmünster, where Zwingli had once preached, Wick amassed an impressive archive of wonder literature that filled twenty-four thick volumes and contained about 500 pamphlets and 430 broadsheets. Wick also obsessively added written reports sent to him and Bullinger from various places throughout Europe. Much like Fincel, his Lutheran counterpart, Wick was driven by a conviction that the Last Judgment was very near, and that the decoding of God's warnings was an immensely urgent task.

Beyond Switzerland, in Huguenot-flecked France, a scholar with Protestant sympathies made an even farther-reaching contribution to wonder literature. Pierre Boaistuau was a protégé of Protestant-leaning Marguerite de Navarre; he had spent time in England and would present his wonder book to the Protestant Queen Elizabeth. His *Histoires prodigieuses* (1560), which relied heavily on Conrad Lycosthenes, widened the reach of wonder literature and of its moralistic epistemology. The purpose of the book, as he saw it, was to teach the world to perceive "the secret judgment and curse of the wrath of God, conveyed by those things that manifest themselves, which make us sense the violence of his justice." All freakish events, warned Boaistuau, were an encoded call to repentance sent by God "so that we be constrained to enter into ourselves, to knock with the hammer of our conscience, to examine our offences, and be horrified by our misdeeds."[13]

Boaistuau's influence was as vast as the reach of his *Histoires prodigieuses*, which was published numerous times and translated into many languages, including English, under the title *Certaine Secrete Wonders of Nature* (1569). A Spanish translation was published in 1585 with the permission of civil and church authorities, proving that Catholics could be just as interested in wonders as Protestants, and regard their decoding as orthodox. Some Catholics, however, were delighted to turn the tables on Protestants and accuse them of superstition. One such critic was the German priest Johann Oldecopp, who lambasted the "rabbis and Parisees of the Lutheran sect" for reading way too much in "figures of storm winds, thunderclaps, fiery clouds . . . or the form of a small child."[14] Though Oldecopp was casting stones from a glass house, so to speak, he and others felt justified because the interest in wonders never reached the same fever pitch among Catholics as among Protestants.

Though some historians have argued that the Protestant interest in wonders reveals that they never fully abandoned the "magical" mindset of the Middle Ages and were therefore not fully modern, that argument rests on a very narrow definition of "magic." These historians have corrected nineteenth-century Whiggish misconceptions of Protestantism—especially as expressed by Max Weber, who credited Protestants with the disenchantment (*Entzauberung*) of the world—but they nonetheless tend to overlook those many other "magical" rites and beliefs discarded by Protestants. They also fail to distinguish between the passive act of reading natural signs and all the other very active rites such as cartomancy or necromancy, which both Catholics and Protestants attacked as superstitious or demonic magic. When all is said and done, then, wonder decoding falls into a category of its own, which is distinct from active magic and belief in miracles.

Nothing points as convincingly to this distinction as that other misdeed attacked along with active divination: the manufacture and use of potions, elixirs, philters, and other magical substances. This was an ancient practice, as old as the human race, and it had continued to evolve in Christian Europe alongside advances in medicine and science. Concoctions prepared by experts were as innumerable as human needs in a world where empirical science had not yet fully developed. These confections stretched on an ethical spectrum from good to evil. Many of these substances were remedies for illness prepared by healers who had learned their craft from some elder and would pass it on to apprentices. This kind of pharmaceutical practice could be found at various levels, from the illiterate village wise woman to learned scholars who practiced what they called natural magic. All such work was considered good, or "white," magic. Then there were concoctions not intended for healing, but rather for producing certain effects: to make someone fall in love or out of love; to ensnare, enchant, and entrance; and to induce altered states of mind. Among these, love philters were most common. These confections were not necessarily considered injurious, though those on the receiving end might not have always agreed. At the other extreme of the spectrum there were malevolent substances, the sole purpose of which was to inflict harm or suffering, even death. These were regarded as *maleficium*, or literally, evil doing, and were feared and outlawed. Belief in the effectiveness of all of these substances ran deep, at all levels of society, and we have plenty of evidence that such substances were concocted and used.

That was not all. Early modern Europeans also relied on unsanctioned non-Christian rituals to effect good, indifferent, or malevolent changes in the world around them. These rituals were sometimes performed during the preparation of substances, or apart from it. Incantations, hexes, and spells were verbal magic, which could be put to all sorts of uses, both good and evil. They could be spoken, sung, or written. A vast array of practices fell into this category, from spells cast in elaborate arcane rituals to incantations written on parchment and worn as an amulet around the neck. And then there were objects transformed by spells into talismans, which were believed to have some magical agency, usually to ward off evil. But harm could also be caused through hexed objects. The most common form of *maleficium*, which required no expertise, was that of the evil eye, and the most ubiquitous talismans were those that ostensibly deflected it. Christianity had never fully extinguished this ancient belief that simply involved looking at someone and wishing them harm or misfortune, usually out of envy, spite, or resentment.

All of these beliefs and practices existed in a nebulous gray area throughout the middle ages, up until the fifteenth century. The white magic, though formally condemned as diabolical, was not always easily identifiable and thus thrived in the face of illness and disease. The "natural magic" of the learned could blend with herbal therapies, alchemy, and medicine, and it would eventually evolve into empirical science. Both neutral and black magic were outlawed and persecuted in many places, but they survived through apathy, secrecy, and dissimulation, and sometimes through the complicity of clerics who could easily be deemed by us as "superstitious" as their flocks. By the turn of the sixteenth century, however, as the church became much less tolerant of such practices, all magic would turn pitch black and explicitly demonic in the eyes of the church, and all who performed it would be regarded as diabolical sorcerers who had to be hunted down and exterminated. And as this great change was taking place, along came the Protestant Reformation, and, in its wake, the age of the great witch hunts.

Witchcraft: Origins and Antecedents

Sorcery, or witchcraft, was related to magic, but in the later Middle Ages it became quite distinct. Though both magic and sorcery aimed to produce effects beyond natural human powers, and though both were officially believed to do so through the agency of the devil, what came to be known as sorcery, or witchcraft, was identified as a distinct form of *maleficium*, or evil making that required very intimate relations with the devil. The performance of *maleficium* itself had been condemned since time immemorial, long before it acquired the characteristics ascribed to it in the late medieval period. And the punishment had always been extreme. The key biblical text that guided all medieval and early modern thinking on how best to deal with sorcery was Exodus 22:18, which read in Latin, *Maleficos non patieris vivere*. Even after the original Hebrew was consulted, most Protestant translations of this passage tended to agree: "Those who practice sorcery should not be allowed to live." But Luther's German Bible and Calvin's Geneva Bible employed the feminine noun for the sorcery worker: *Zauberinnen* and *sorcière*. The King James English Bible chose a neutral noun: "thou shalt not suffer a *witch* to live."

Witches at work. Belief in witches and in their nefarious rituals was endemic on the eve of the Protestant Reformation, but elite perceptions of witchcraft did not necessarily coincide with those of the common people. This 1510 engraving by Hans Baldung Grien depicts a coven of witches engaged in their demonic craft. Ironically, though Protestants and Catholics could not agree on many issues—and especially on the meaning of ancient Christian rituals—they did tend to agree on the reality of witches and the efficacy of their sorcery.

The witch hunts that unfolded in the late sixteenth century had long and ancient roots. A key development, in the ninth century, which would become part of canon law, was the legal definition of sorcery as apostasy and heresy, a spiritual crime, punishable by the church. *Maleficium* was an offense that straddled church and state: as the act of inflicting harm on others, it was a civil crime; as apostasy and heresy, it was a spiritual crime. This influential legal text, known as the *Canon episcopi*, pronounced "the pernicious art of sorcery and magic" to be "invented by the devil" and called on all bishops to chase away from the church all followers of such "wickedness."[15] The most immediate origins of Reformation witch hunting can be traced to 1320, when Pope John XXII authorized the prosecution of sorcerers by the Inquisition on the grounds that all sorcery was demonic and its practitioners were therefore to be dealt with as heretics. In his day, *maleficium* had already begun to assume certain diabolical characteristics, which he described in his 1326 decretal *Super illius specula*:

> Grievingly we observe . . . that many who are Christians in name only . . . sacrifice to demons, adore them, make or have made images, rings, mirrors, phials, or other things for magic purposes, and bind themselves to demons. They ask and receive responses from them and to fulfill their most depraved lusts ask them for aid. Binding themselves to the most shameful slavery for the most shameful of things, they ally themselves with death and make a pact with hell. By their means a most pestilential disease . . . grievously infests the flock of Christ throughout the world.[16]

Prosecution of sorcerers was sporadic from 1320 on, but as these trials evolved, the notion that sorcerers belonged to an organized satanic cult increased in popularity, especially among the learned. Popular preachers such as Bernardino of Siena (1380–1440) helped spread this belief among the laity too, and sparked many a local persecution along the way. In his own native Siena, in 1427, he called on everyone to turn in these evildoers: "Whether within the city or outside its walls, accuse . . . every witch, every wizard, every sorcerer or sorceress, or worker of charms and spells."[17] In 1435–1437, as Bernardino and others preached against witches, and as tribunals prosecuted them, Johann Nider wrote his *Formicarius*, the first detailed description of witch cult. Shortly thereafter, systematic witch hunts began to take place in the Alpine regions of Switzerland, Savoy, and Dauphiné.

Nider's *Formicarius* could be distributed only in manuscript form and would not be printed until 1479. By then, however, it had stiff competition from about thirty other manuals including one written in 1489, *Of Witches and Women Diviners*, by Ulrich Molitor, which enjoyed a robust printing history during those early days of book publishing. The most important of these newer books, by far, was the *Malleus maleficarum* (Hammer of Witches), attributed to Heinrich Kramer (1430–1505) and Jacob Sprenger (1436–1495), two Dominican inquisitors who had prosecuted witches and were commissioned directly by Pope Innocent VIII in 1484 to write the definitive book on witchcraft. Experts attribute the writing to Kramer (also known by his Latin humanist name

Institoris), who had been chased of out Innsbruck by the local authorities for being too extreme in his witch hunting, and felt compelled to defend his approach. First published in 1486, the *Malleus* was reprinted fourteen times between 1487 and 1520, and sixteen times between 1574 and 1669, and it would teach many an inquisitor and magistrate how to identify, prosecute, and convict witches.

Its very title—which employed the feminine noun *maleficarum*, or *sorceress*—reflected one of the main propositions of the *Malleus*: that most of those involved in satanic *maleficium* were women, and that "all witchcraft came from carnal lust." Assuming that females had a much greater sex drive than males, as was commonly believed in their day, the authors of the *Malleus* argued that the devil could easily lure women to serve him through their "insatiable" lust. It also claimed that having sex with the devil was the first step to becoming a witch, and that those who became witches of the highest rank had to make a pact with the devil, abjure their Christian faith, and seal their devotion to Satan with an oath of homage and a total, eternal surrender of their bodies and souls. Sometimes these pacts were made in private, but more often in solemn ceremonies attended by other witches. The diabolical power granted to witches by this pact was immense:

> These sorceresses . . . stir up hailstorms and harmful winds with lightning; . . . cause sterility in humans and domestic animals; . . . offer to demons or kill the babies whom they do not devour. . . . They also know how to make horses go crazy under their riders; how to move from place to place through the air, either in body or imagination; how to change the attitudes of judges and governmental authorities so that they cannot harm them; how to bring about silence for themselves and others during torture . . . how to reveal hidden things and to foretell certain future events; . . . how to turn human minds to irregular love or hatred; on many occasions, how to kill someone they wish to with lightning, . . . how to take away the force of procreation or the ability to copulate; how to kill infants in the mother's womb with only a touch on the outside; also on occasion how to affect humans and domestic animals with sorcery or inflict death upon them by sight alone without touch; and how to dedicate their own infants to demons.[18]

This was just the tip of the iceberg, so to speak. Any mundane misfortune could be blamed on witches, along with unspeakable crimes such as cannibalism. The factual claims of the *Malleus* concerning the power of witches made it relatively easy to try anyone for witchcraft, which is why so many experts on the history of witchcraft have assigned it such significance. From a legal standpoint—and the *Malleus* was above all a manual for identifying and trying witches in court—this seemingly limitless evil power meant that nearly every misfortune could be attributed to witches and that the evidence needed to convict someone for the crime of *maleficium* tended to be purely circumstantial. Moreover, since curses were commonly used in premodern culture, and since belief in their efficacy ran deep, the potential was always high for any quarrel in which curses had been uttered to turn into a witchcraft accusation. A strained relationship between individuals or any prior verbal threats or insults were all that was needed to establish a likely motive for *maleficium*, and the misfortune itself—be it a lightning strike, or an illness, or an obsessive attraction to someone, or the death of a child or a cow—could easily serve as the ultimate proof.

Almost any accusation could therefore be taken seriously, and in many cases, proving that someone was a witch could be relatively easy, especially if torture was employed to extract a confession from the accused. Even worse, the *Malleus* set up the witch as supernaturally endowed to lie, resist torture, and plant doubts in the minds of judges and civil officials, making it all that much easier for the courts to disregard all denials made by the accused and whatever misgivings might arise from lack of solid evidence.

The publishing success of the *Malleus* and its influence should not be mistaken for wholesale acceptance. Even before it was written, disagreements about witchcraft were common, so as soon as the *Malleus* was published there were dissenting voices. In fact, one of the purposes of the book was to refute skeptics who denied the existence of witchcraft and stood in the way of its prosecution. That the University of Cologne ultimately refused to approve the book—although the authors claimed to have its endorsement—points to the lack of agreement that surrounded witch hunting. While some found the *Malleus* too extreme, others found it lacking, especially when it came to its coverage of the widely held belief that witches worshiped the devil together in wild ceremonies known as Sabbaths, which were an inversion of Christian ritual and in which they danced naked, kissed the devil's rear end, engaged in sexual orgies, sacrificed children, ate human flesh, flew through the air, received in exchange preternatural powers that allowed them to change shapes, and perform other wonders, and were also assigned an "imp" or "familiar spirit," that is, a demonic sidekick who obeyed their commands.

Disagreements over details such as these were never fully resolved, and scholars in our own day disagree on how to best interpret that fact. But experts do tend to agree on two points: first, the *Malleus* figured prominently in all debates over witchcraft for a long time; and second, differences of opinion among those who believed in witchcraft seldom gave them pause or prevented witch hunting.

New Age, New Persecutions

The Protestant Reformation did not cause massive witch hunts, at least not initially. In fact, the advent of Protestantism slowed down the persecution of witches, as Catholics focused their energies on combating Protestants, and the Protestants, in turn, concentrated on surviving and on expanding their reach. However, while the publication of witchcraft texts ceased between 1520 and 1570 and the number of persecutions declined, witch hunting never stopped altogether. Strange as it may seem, one of the few things that Catholics and Protestants agreed on was the need to exterminate witchcraft.

On a purely civil level, in 1532, the Holy Roman Empire adopted a unified criminal code, known as the *Constitutio criminalis Carolina*, in which the practice of *maleficium* through sorcery was designated a capital crime, punishable by death. The *Constitutio* also called for the extraction of confessions through torture. Meanwhile, the nascent Protestant churches began to prosecute witches. In Zurich, under Bullinger's leadership, witchcraft trials began in 1533. Luther, who claimed to have constant confrontations with the devil, praised the execution of four witches in Wittenberg in 1541. Calvin, likewise, called for the "extirpation" of all witches in 1545, when plague broke out in Geneva, and in that year alone forty-three witch trials were held in that relatively small city, which resulted in twenty-nine executions.

These Protestant outbursts against witchcraft were a sign of things to come. By the late 1550s, as the era of orthodoxy, confessionalization and social disciplining dawned, persecutions intensified. In Geneva around ninety people were tried for witchcraft between 1556 and 1570, and thirty of them were executed. The year 1571 was the worst of all in Geneva, when more than one hundred witchcraft trials were held, and thirty-six of them led to executions. Similarly, Lutherans in Weisensteig—with a population of only five thousand—convicted and killed sixty-three witches in 1563, and then broadcast the news in a pamphlet titled *The True and Horrifying Death of Sixty-Three Witches*. For the next century or so, from the 1560s on, the situation only worsened. In the Swiss canton of Neuchâtel, for instance, 360 witchcraft trials would be held between 1588 and 1677, with 243 people executed, a conviction rate of 67.5 percent. In the nearby canton of Luzern, between 1550 and 1675, the conviction rate was nearly 50 percent, with 505 trials and 254 executions.

Devil in the details. This 1555 woodcut depicts the execution of three witches in Dernburg by Lutheran authorities. The artist makes evident the link between the devil and the women being burned through the figure of the demon who hovers over the grisly scene. A long text accompanied this illustration, which detailed all the crimes of *maleficium* committed by these women.

Catholics turned on witches with equal ferocity. In one of the most intense witch hunts of the age, in the lands of the Elector-archbishop of Trier, Germany, 368 people were burned as witches in twenty-two villages in the six years between 1587 and 1593; two of those villages were left with only one female inhabitant apiece. The Trier witch hunt did not target women, however. Its net caught men, women, and children from all classes, even from the governing elite, including burgomasters, councilors and judges, canons of various collegiate churches, and even parish priests. Of those executed, 108 came from the aristocracy. Among the elite victims was Dietrich Flade, chief judge of the electoral court and rector of the university, who had opposed the witch hunt and spoken out against the use of torture. The death of Flade, whose leniency had aroused suspicion, gave even greater license to the witch hunters.

Trier was only a prelude. In Lutheran Quedlinburg, for instance, about 133 witches were executed in a single day in 1589. At Catholic Fulda, about two hundred were burned between 1603 and 1605. Hunts of this sort, as well as many smaller ones, were repeated many times over, in many places throughout Europe, even into the eighteenth century. Experts estimate that one hundred thousand to two hundred thousand witch trials were conducted between the 1560s and 1680s and that these led to somewhere around fifty thousand to sixty thousand executions. The most notorious persecutions were those chain-reaction hunts in which the accused were asked to name their fellow witches under torture. In these massive hunts, accusations would spiral out of control and stereotypes would break down. Instead of focusing on women—as the *Malleus* and other treatises advised—these hunts would drag in anyone who was accused. Such persecutions peaked in the 1620s and 1630s, mostly within the Holy Roman Empire, in areas where local courts had no higher authority to restrain them. The highest tolls were at Bamberg (1623–1633), where six hundred witches were killed, and Würzburg (1626–1631), where among the nine hundred killed were a nephew of the bishop, a score of priests, and a number of small children. In Bonn, which endured a similar persecution at that same time, an eyewitness described the havoc in detail:

> There must be half the city implicated: for already professors, law-students, pastors, canons, vicars, and monks have here been arrested and burned. His Princely Grace [the Elector-archbishop of Cologne] has seventy wards [seminarians] who are to become pastors, one of whom, eminent as a musician, was yesterday arrested; two others were sought for, but have fled. The Chancellor and his wife and the Private Secretary's wife are already executed. . . . A canon of the cathedral, named Rotenhahn, I saw beheaded and burned. Children of three or four years have devils for their paramours. Students and boys of noble birth, of nine, ten, eleven, twelve, thirteen, fourteen years have been burned. In fine, things are in such a pitiful state that one does not know with what people one may talk and associate.[19]

How the process could reach such ferocity was described in heartbreaking detail by Johannes Junius, mayor of the city of Bamberg, who managed to smuggle out a letter to his daughter while he awaited execution in 1628: "Innocent I have come into prison, innocent have I been tortured, innocent must I die. For whosoever comes into the witch prison must become a witch or be tortured until he invents something out of his head. . . . And so I made my confession . . . but it was all a lie."[20]

Trier, Bamberg, Bonn, and Würzburg were extreme cases. And so was Germany as a whole, which racked up about twenty-five thousand executions, or half of the total for all of Europe. The patterns discerned by experts reveal a great unevenness in the

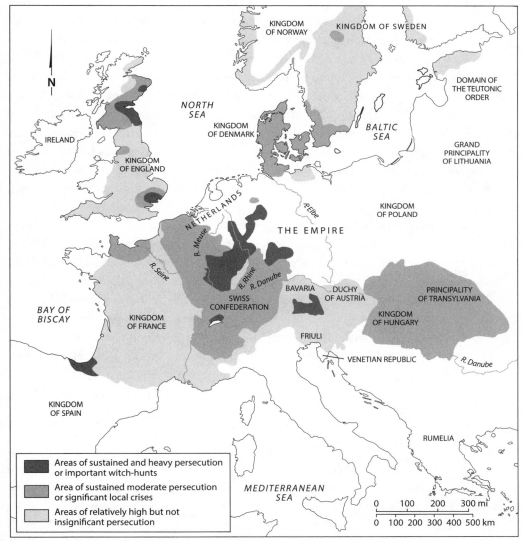

Bewitched landscapes. Witch persecutions flared up very unevenly over the span of a century in the early modern era. Whether or not these witch hunts could be called a panic or craze remains a matter of interpretation, but there is no denying the fact that thousands of women and men—and even some children—were rounded up and executed for serving as agents of the devil.

number of trials held in different regions, and in the execution rates. At the low end of the spectrum, the regions with the least intense witch hunts were Spain, Portugal, Italy, Scandinavia, Hungary, Russia, and northwestern France. At the high end, the areas most deeply scarred by witch hunting were Germany (especially in the south and west), the south of France, the western Swiss cantons, the Duchy of Savoy, and the borderlands between France and Germany: Luxemburg, Alsace, Lorraine, and the Franche-Comté. Execution rates varied immensely too. Spain and its notorious Inquisition, for instance, had not only relatively few witch trials, but also a low execution rates of single-digit percentages. In contrast, some German, French, and Swiss areas killed around 90 percent of those tried for witchcraft. The disparities can be as surprising as they are revealing: Scotland, which had only one-quarter as many people as England, killed more than three times more witches than its southern neighbor.

Then there were differences in the ways the trials were conducted. In some places civil courts were responsible, in others ecclesiastical tribunals or an Inquisition. And in some places—especially those with massive chain-reaction hunts, such as Germany—the process was set in motion from above, by elites who had preconceptions about witchcraft gleaned from the *Malleus* and other such texts. These persecutions tended to erupt in intense bursts and were not so much about *maleficium* as about pacts with the devil, the witches' sabbath, and the inversion of Christian rites. In many ways, these were extermination campaigns, a form of genocide.

In contrast, in other areas, such as England and eastern Europe, the persecution was both steady and prolonged, involving relatively low numbers year after year. These trials tended to be generated from below, by neighbors, and to focus on specific individuals and their alleged acts of *maleficium* rather than on the wholesale extermination of anti-Christian demon-worshiping misfits whose perversions fit the profiles outlined in learned witchcraft manuals. For instance, in Finland, about 1,500 to 2,000 witch accusations during this period involved *maleficium* but made no mention of the Sabbath or of pacts with demons. The fiercest persecutions were those carried out by local authorities who could not be easily reined in by any higher power. Finally, the most salient statistical disparity of all is that, overall, about 75 percent of those executed as witches were women.

The Birth of Demonology

As witch hunts waxed and waned, printers throughout Europe cranked out title after title on demonology and witchcraft for nearly three centuries. Though ancient and medieval Christians had dealt with the devil head-on for well over a millennium, up until the fifteenth century there was no codification, no definitive systematic treatment of the devil and his work on earth though his human minions. And it was not until the sixteenth century that demonology per se—the systematic study of all things diabolical—became a thriving branch of theology, and also of jurisprudence. While at the start of the sixteenth century all the existing books dedicated solely to demonology could easily be contained within a single bookshelf, by 1799 a large room might not be enough, for by then, more than one thousand titles on subjects related to the devil and sorcery had been published. Demonology had come into its own. And these figures apply to western Europe alone, not central or eastern Europe, or the Americas.[21]

Interest in demonology began to grow in the 1530s, a period of relative calm in witch hunting, with the publication of two texts that elaborated further on questions of magic, superstition, and witchcraft. Both were written by Spanish theologians. The first of these, Martín de Castañega's *Treatise on Superstitions and Sorceries* (1529), stressed the reality of the diabolical dimension through a stark duality: "There are two churches in this world," Castañega wrote, "one Catholic, and one demonic . . . and, just as the Catholic Church has sacraments . . . the Diabolical Church has its execraments, which, in everyday speech we call superstitions and sorceries."[22] The second, *A Treatise Reproving All Superstitions and Forms of Witchcraft* (1530), enjoyed a much wider circulation and was reprinted numerous times over the following century. Its author, Pedro Ciruelo, was a biblical scholar and professor of theology at the University of Alcalá. Ciruelo's treatise, a veritable encyclopedia of unsanctioned popular piety, further reinforced the notion that witchcraft was a demonic counterreligion:

> Necromancy is one of the arts taught by the devil to witches, who are men or women that have made a pact with the devil, and who, after rubbing certain ointments on their bodies and saying certain words, they fly through the sky at night and travel to far-off lands to perform their malevolent acts.[23]

Ciruelo emphasized that the devil allowed witches to traverse distances by carrying them physically through the air, but that more often than not, witches simply fell into trances and the devil made them imagine they had gone somewhere and done all sorts of things that seemed so real that they would afterwards be convinced that the illusory events had actually taken place. On this point, as on so many others, Ciruelo said nothing new, but he lent his authority to many of the beliefs that became entrenched among the learned and those who carried out witch hunts.

Though skeptics who rejected such beliefs could be found here and there, the first major challenge to dominant witchcraft theories and to witch hunting came from a Protestant physician, Johann Weyer (1515–1588), a disciple of the learned occultist Heinrich Cornelius Agrippa, mentioned earlier in this chapter. Though he was convinced of the reality of the devil and of his power to deceive human beings, Weyer refused to believe that witchcraft was a demonic counter-religion of the sort described by the *Malleus* or experts such as Ciruelo. Witches were not evil humans endowed with preternatural powers by the devil, he argued, but wretched melancholics who were mentally ill. Most of them, he affirmed, were "stupid, worn-out, unstable old women"[24] who had been seduced by the devil's deceptions, and by the constant use of hallucinogenic drugs. Consequently, he argued, to persecute witches was not only wrong, but unnecessary, illegal, and illogical because their alleged crimes had not actually taken place. Weyer opposed the use of torture, and especially the extraction of confessions. The real solution to the problem of witchcraft, as he saw it, lay in treating the madness of the accused rather than in killing them.

In 1563, Weyer put forward this radically new medical interpretation in a massive book titled *De praestigiis daemonum* ("On the Deceptions of Demons"), which also contained medical advice on how to treat those who thought they were victims of sorcery. This work was followed in 1577 by a condensed version, *De lamiis* ("On Witches"). While Weyer's take on witchcraft as insanity may seem ahead of its time, his thinking was still guided by belief in demons and their power. He also thought that some sorcerers he called *magi infames*—disreputable magicians—really did knowingly deal with the devil, and should be persecuted. In an appendix to *De prestigiis* published in 1577, titled *Pseudomonarchia daemonum* ("The False Kingdom of the Demons"), Weyer provided a catalog of demons, complete with the instructions that "disreputable magicians" used in their approach to them. Weyer's *Pseudomonarchia* was not a manual, but an exposé of what he deemed to be the real threat to society: those occultists who conjured demons while whispering to one another, "The secret of secrets; thou that workst them, be secret in them." To ensure that the *Pseudomonarchia* would not be used to summon demons, Weyer left the incantations incomplete.

Weyer's books enjoyed a fairly wide circulation, but had no discernible effect on witch hunting. Those who agreed with him tended to have little impact too. Among these, Michel de Montaigne (1533–1592), the great French statesman and essayist, was perhaps the best known. But Montaigne wrote no treatise on witchcraft, only an essay, "On Lameness" (1588), in which he echoed Weyer's sentiments, arguing that medical prescriptions were the real solution for the witchcraft problem, not executions. Two followers of Weyer who did seem to have some influence on policy were the jurist Franz Balduin and the mathematician Hermann Witekind, at Heidelberg. Balduin was opposed to witch trials on legal grounds and promoted this position at his university. Witekind, who published an anti-persecution treatise in 1585, under the pen name Augustin Lercheimer, reiterated Weyer's pleas for a more compassionate treatment of deluded old women who confessed their pacts with the devil. As a Calvinist, he also emphasized the supremacy of God's providence, and turned that teaching into an argument against witch hunting: all misfortunes are really nothing other than punishments inflicted by God. And the devil is clever enough, he added, to fool people—including the accused—into thinking that a witch has caused whatever harm is in question.

At the time Balduin and Witekind were writing, witch hunting had already been banned in the Palatinate, so, in fact, they were defending existing local policies. Heidelberg and the Palatinate would remain free of chain-reaction witch hunts and would continue to ban witch hunts for many years. The area around Heidelberg was also the home of another notable Reformed opponent of the persecution and torture of witches, Anton Praetorius, whose condemnation of witch hunting, *A Thorough Report*

About Witchcraft and Witches, first published under a pseudonym in 1598, was reprinted three times under his own name between 1602 and 1629.

In England, Weyer influenced Reginald Scot, who put an anti-Catholic spin on his treatise *The Discoverie of Witchcraft*, first published in 1584. Scot sought to prove, much like Weyer, that most of those prosecuted as witches were "poor, aged, deformed, ignorant people" whose dreary lives had been twisted by illusions. Scot argued that the irrational and unchristian practices of witch hunters—or "witchmoongers," as he called them—stemmed from the superstitious beliefs of the Roman Catholic Church. He bemoaned the fact that while all the "popish charmes, conjurations, exorcismes, benedictions, and curses" had been totally discredited in England, as "ridiculous, and of none effect," "witches, charms, and conjurors," which were just as ludicrous, were "yet thought effectuall" by his fellow Englishmen. And he also made it clear that his purpose was to ensure that "the massemoonger [papist] for his part, as the witchmoonger for his, shall both be ashamed of their professions."[25] His information on witchcraft was gleaned not just from books like Weyer's, but also from his own observations in rural courts, and from his personal experiences with neighbors who believed in witches and leveled accusations against them. Though banned by King James I in 1603, Scot's *Discoverie* was published abroad, in translations, and would later be reprinted numerous times in England.

Skepticism and moderation could not compete with the devil, however—at least not for another century or so. The voices of Montaigne, Weyer, Witekind, Praetorius, and Scot were drowned out by a loud and persistent chorus of experts who never tired of calling for more vigilance and more persecutions. After 1570, a slew of texts on witchcraft poured forth from presses everywhere, the vast majority of which upheld the traditional line. Curiously, this crusade against witchcraft may have been the most intensely ecumenical event of the Reformation era, for Lutheran, Reformed, Anglican, and Catholic pounced on the witches with equal fervor, and also read one another's books.

The Reformed churches led the way in this publishing boom with three books. First, in Zurich, in 1571, Heinrich Bullinger wrote and published *Von Hexen* ("On Witches"), which outlined the Reformed position very carefully. In Geneva, only one year later, theologian Lambert Daneau came out with a dialogue, *Les sorciers*, which was quickly translated into Latin. An English translation, *A Dialogue of Witches*, was published in London in 1575, and a German one in 1576. Daneau, like Bullinger, called for the harshest possible prosecution of witches. In Heidelberg, where witch hunting was banned, Thomas Erastus (1524–1583) attacked Weyer and all lenient skeptics head-on in his *Disputation on Witches*, published in 1572, adding yet another well-respected voice to the Reformed chorus.

Among Lutherans, Nils Hemmingsen published his *Admonishment to Avoid Magical Superstitions* in 1575, in Copenhagen, during an outburst of witch hunting in Denmark. In 1583, Paul Frisius dedicated his highly anecdotal *The Devil's Hoodwink* to Landgrave George I of Hesse-Darmstadt, in support of witch hunting. Arguing that witches were "poor whores of the devil," Frisius insisted that they had no power of their own. Their *maleficium*, which was real enough, came straight from the devil, though they themselves and those around them failed to grasp that. This was the "devil's hoodwink" (*Teuffels Nebelkappen*), which simultaneously blinded the witches to their real powerlessness and cloaked the devil in invisibility. Ultimately, Frisius sought to instill belief in the reality of the devil, who worked his evil in disguise. His devil was a "master conjurer," an "arch-trickster," a "master magician," and an "artist with a thousand skills."[26] The witches, though puppets of the devil, were still blameworthy and more than deserving of death for their intention was evil to the core, and they allowed themselves to become diabolical instruments. All in all, thanks in large measure to Luther's own intense and complex emphasis on the power of the devil Lutherans produced a substantial number of texts on witchcraft and demonology, including "devil books," a genre of literature we will deal with shortly.

In England and Scotland, many treatises on witchcraft were published after 1570, including translations of continental works, but all were eclipsed by *Daemonologie*, written by King James VI of Scotland in 1597, six years before he assumed the English throne as James I. The king's interest in witchcraft stemmed largely from his wedding trip to Denmark in 1590, where he met Nils Hemmingsen, just mentioned above, the author of *Admonishment to Avoid Magical Superstitions*. By coincidence—or by design, as James would come to believe—this voyage was plagued by mishaps, including some ferocious storms at sea on the way back to England. Suspecting sorcery, a witch hunt was launched in Copenhagen, and, as expected, several of the women who were rounded up confessed to having raised the storms with the aid of the devil. A corresponding witch hunt in Scotland, where King James himself did some of the questioning, yielded similar testimony. Touched in such a personal way by *maleficium*, inspired by Hemmingsen's work, and angered by that of the skeptics Johann Weyer and Reginald Scot, who needed to be refuted, King James felt compelled to warn all of his subjects as no monarch had ever done before. And in his preface, he laid all his cards on the table in the opening sentence:

> The fearefull aboundinge at this time in this countrie, of these detestable slaves of the Devill, the Witches or enchanters, hath moved me (beloved reader) to dispatch in post, this following treatise of mine, not in any way (as I protest) to serve for a shew of my learning and ingine, but onely (mooved of conscience) to preasse thereby, so farre as I can, to resolve the doubting harts of many; both that such assaultes of Sathan are most certainly practized, and that the instrumentes thereof, merits most severely to be punished.[27]

The North Berwick witch hunt of 1590, in which more than one hundred suspects were rounded up, including some nobility, was the first of many large-scale witch hunts in Scotland. In the same year that *Daemonologie* was published, from March to October 1597, around four hundred suspected witches were brought to trial in Scotland, and about half of them were executed. Other witch hunts would follow, some of them very intense, especially those of 1628–1631, 1649, 1661–1662, and 1697–1700. The exact number of witch trials and executions is not known, as a result of incomplete records, but it is estimated that the total number of witches killed in Scotland during the Reformation era is about 1,500.

Within the Catholic fold, the learned response to the witchcraft issue was just as severe. One of the most significant texts on the subject appeared in 1580: *Démonomanie des sorciers* ("The demon-mania of sorcerers"). Its author was the French jurist and states-man Jean Bodin (1530–1596). This text was a long and detailed refutation of Johann Weyer and all other skeptics. Convinced of the reality of witches, their pacts with the devil, and of the danger they posed to society, Bodin proposed that normal trial pro-cedures concerning evidence, witnesses, testimony, and torture be relaxed or set aside in witchcraft trials, since, as he saw it, the existing regulations made it hard to convict anyone, and most rumors about witches were true, anyway. His aim was to streamline the trials so that courts could eliminate witches more quickly and efficiently, for, as he said, "anyone accused of being a witch ought never to be fully acquitted and set free unless the calumny of the accuser is clearer than the sun, inasmuch as the proof of such crimes is so obscure and so difficult that not one witch in a million would be accused or punished."[28] Bodin's *Démonomanie* would be reprinted numerous times, just like Weyer's *De Praestigiis*, not just in French, but also in Latin, Italian, and German.

As persecutions intensified, more and more learned treatises were published. Some were written by scholars, others by witch hunters. Peter Binsfeld, episcopal vicar of Trier, the man responsible for one of the largest witch hunts of all, published a treatise in 1589 titled *Of the Confessions of Warlocks and Witches*, which was based on his own experiences with sorcerers. Translated and reissued several times, Binsfeld's *Confessions* served as testimony for the correctness of witch hunting and the use of torture to extract information from sorcerers. It was also an exposé of the deepest and darkest secrets of witches and of the demons with whom they cavorted.

Another expert author was Nicholas Remy, a magistrate and witch hunter in the Duchy of Lorraine, who boasted of having sentenced at least nine hundred sorcerers to death. A highly placed layman, Remy wielded a lot of power as *procureur général* of the Duchy of Lorraine. Remy's sovereign was not the king of France, but Charles III Duke of Lorraine, and none of the verdicts reached in his courts could be appealed anywhere else. Remy's *Daemonolatreiae*, published in 1595—and dedicated to Duke Charles III—was translated into German and reprinted often. It would eventually compete with the *Malleus* for the top spot on the list of definitive witch-hunting textbooks. Since it was based on experience, like Binsfeld's *Confessions*, it had an air of gritty authenticity that was lacking in more scholarly texts. Remy was well aware of this advantage:

> It may be that some will accuse me of being nothing but a retailer of marvelous sto-ries, seeing that I speak of witches raising up clouds and traveling through the air,

penetrating through the narrowest openings, eating, dancing, and lying with Demons, and performing many other such prodigies and portents. But I would have them know first that it was from no scattered rumours, but from the independent and concordant testimony of many witnesses that, as I have said, I have reported these things as certain facts.[29]

Remy's *Daemonolatreiae* earned its renown and longevity by being many things at once: an engaging collection of bizarre, fantastic tales; an encyclopedia of witchcraft; a proof of the devil's existence and power; and a vindication of witch hunting. It was also a clarion call for prosecutors, and an anxious war cry. Remy would brook no compromise, even to the point of arguing that any judge who was lenient toward witches was himself guilty of blasphemy.

A third experienced judge who chose to write about his personal encounters with witchcraft was Pierre de Lancre, who in 1609 conducted a witch hunt in southwestern France among the Basque people. Like Remy, de Lancre also boasted of having executed many witches(around six hundred, he claimed), and of having gained intimate knowledge of their crimes and their infernal rituals. Sent by King Henry IV to the town of Labourd, where residents had complained of being overrun with witches, de Lancre was given plenary authority, which meant that no cases handled by him could be appealed. The result was a chain-reaction panic, similar to those in many other places where a local court handled witch hunting. After he had finished his work at Labourd, de Lancre penned three treatises based on his experiences as a witch hunter. The most influential of these books was his first, *On the Inconstancy of Evil Angels and Demons*, published in 1612. Filled with lurid accounts of the diabolical activities of the Basque witches, including a very detailed description of a witches' sabbath, this sensational book was translated into German in 1630. On the one hand, its attention to the details of the sexual encounters between witches and demons has led some to classify the book as pornography. On the other hand, its vivid descriptions of the landscape and customs of the Basques, which share space with disquisitions on the devil's marks on witches, and on lycanthropy (humans assuming the form of wolves), have led others to see the book as an early attempt at ethnography. De Lancre's two other books, which had less of an impact, expanded on what he had covered in his *Inconstancy*. These two were titled *The Unbelief and False Faith of Sorcery Convicted* (1622) and *On Sorcery* (1627).

The most significant Catholic text—which would eventually eclipse the *Malleus* and Remy's *Daemonolatreiae*—was written not by a prosecutor, but by a learned Jesuit priest, Martín del Rio (1551–1608). Born in Antwerp but of Spanish descent, this polymath who was fluent in at least nine languages and wrote on many different subjects would be called "the wonder of the century" by the Flemish humanist Justus Lipsius (1547–1606). But he is best remembered—and not too fondly—for his *Disquisitionum magicarum* ("Investigations into Magic"), a nearly encyclopedic study of all things diabolical and occult. This work, first published in three parts from 1599 to 1600, was reprinted at least twenty times. And its influence would cross religious boundaries and even oceans, and would eventually be used in 1692 by the Puritan judges of Salem, Massachusetts, in their infamous witch hunt. The last reprint was in 1755, at Cologne. Like many of his fellow Jesuits, Del Rio was always on the move, filling one prestigious post after another. By the time he died, he had held the chairs of philosophy, moral theology, and sacred scriptures at the Universities of Douai, Liège, Louvain, Graz, and Salamanca.

Del Rio dealt with witchcraft and magic as a scholar rather than a jurist, linking the subject to other disciplines such as mathematics, astrology, and alchemy. In doing so, he gave his work an edge that most others lacked, synthesizing theology and law, philosophy, and what was then the cutting edge of science. His explanation for the surge in witches in the sixteenth century was that heresy leads to diabolism, magic, and witchcraft. The thesis itself was not novel, for it had already been proposed by his fellow Jesuit Juan de Maldonado (1533–1583), but his rendering of it struck a deep chord among Catholics, especially those who had to deal with the witchcraft issue. "Magic follows heresy, as plague follows famine," he said. "We have seen heresy flourishing in Belgium and we see swarms of witches laying waste the whole of the North, like locusts. The heretics are strongly opposed by the Jesuits. This book is a weapon in that war."[30]

Unlike Binsfeld, Remy, and Pierre de Lancre, who had prosecuted witches and heard their confessions, Martín del Rio obtained his information secondhand, through research. Ironically, his derivative description of the witches' sabbath became definitive. And it doubtlessly played a role in shaping the assumptions of many a judge and prosecutor. Absurd as the rites described may seem in our day and age, they could seem all too real in their own day:

> There, on most occasions, once a foul, disgusting fire has been lit, an evil spirit sits on a throne as president of the assembly. His appearance is terrifying, almost always that of a male goat or a dog. The witches come forward to worship him in different ways. Sometimes they supplicate him on bended knee; sometimes they stand with their back turned to him. They offer candles made of pitch or a child's umbilical cord, and kiss him on the anal orifice as a sign of homage. Sometimes they imitate the sacrifice of the Mass (the greatest of all their crimes), as well as purifying with water and similar Catholic ceremonies. After the feast, each evil spirit takes by the hand the disciple of whom he has charge, and so that they may do everything with the most absurd kind of ritual, each person bends over backwards, joins hands in a circle, and tosses his head as frenzied fanatics do. Then they begin to dance. They sing very obscene songs in his [Satan's] honour. They behave ridiculously in every way, and in every way contrary to accepted custom. Then their demon-lovers copulate with them in the most repulsive fashion.[31]

What are we to make of all this? Not surprisingly, experts give us conflicting answers to that question, and every approach offers its own theory: economic, social, political, psychological, anthropological, and even biological interpretations compete for attention. Since the number of women killed was three times that of men, many experts have focused on issues of gender. Despite all the disagreement, however, there seems to be some consensus on four points.

The first is that the increase in witch hunting did take place and is no exaggeration, even though the number of trials and executions was lower than previously believed.

The second consensus is that not all witch hunts were alike, and there were competing ideologies and vast regional differences. For instance, we know that some witch hunts were generated from above, by elites, and others from below, by the common people. Another notable difference is that between an older tradition of *maleficium*, or simple harming through magic, and a newer diabolical tradition—developed in the fifteenth century—that focused on the pact, demonic worship, the sabbath, demonic sex, aerial flight, infanticide, cannibalism, shape-shifting, and the use of imps and familiars. We now know that these two traditions existed simultaneously; sometimes they mixed, but often they did not.

The third area of agreement, which is gaining acceptance, is that we must be wary of referring to early modern witch hunts as a "panic" or a "craze," that is, as some irrational blip in Western civilization, or some form of temporary insanity. After all, not every witch was burned in a chain-reaction hunt like those of Trier or Bamberg. A steadier sort of persecution was always there, bubbling up from below alongside the massive witch hunts, and many witch trials were strictly about *maleficium*, not about devil worship. In other words, in many cases witch trials were pragmatic solutions to everyday problems, approached according to an understanding of the world and premises and assumptions that not only made sense, but also were considered rational even by the most learned savants.

A fourth implicit agreement, which is seldom discussed openly, concerns the devil's absence, or, more precisely, his nonbeing. In other words, it is taken for granted— in the same way that inquisitors took for granted that all magic involved *implicit* dealings with the devil—that the devil is not and never has been a "real" being, or, much less a causal agent, and that the most acceptable way to study witchcraft is to share in that assumption. In addition, that shared assumption is most often viewed *not* as a mere conjecture, or a hypothesis, but rather as an incontestable fact. As a result, those who study witchcraft face the challenge of explaining why so many early modern Europeans believed in the devil, and why he was very real to so many of them. This is a thorny problem, for sure: so thorny that most scholars prefer for it to remain as invisible as the devil himself.

The Devil Himself

That the devil was real to many in the early modern world cannot be denied. One may relativize "real" by placing quotation marks around the word, to suggest that, yes, the concept of the devil—rather than the devil himself—played a role in abstract theology and in the lives of early modern men and women. But they themselves would have objected to such a relativist dilution of the devil's reality. Belief is impossible to gauge, for all religious belief encompasses doubt. And belief does not necessarily cancel out a whole range of behaviors, from the cold, insincere, calculated manipulation of others to the manifestation of bizarre, seemingly unexplainable phenomena. In the early modern age, then, the devil could be used to serve certain purposes, but he could also become manifest in many other ways, some predictable and others not at all.

Accounts of personal encounters with the devil and of demonic possessions multiplied in the sixteenth and seventeenth centuries. Naturally, given the differences among the various competing religious camps, the devil's doings could vary in accordance with beliefs, as did the ways he was handled. But no matter how different his profile was in each church, there is no denying that he did show up often, and not only in theological texts and sermons.

On 6 April 1533, at dinner, Martin Luther said:

> The devil seeks me out when I am at home in bed, and I always have one or two devils waiting to pounce on me. They are smart devils. If they can't overwhelm my heart, they grab my head and plague me there, and when that proves useless, I show them my ass, for that's where they belong.[32]

Boasting about his battles with demons was not unusual for Luther. He attributed most of the world's woes to the devil, and often spoke of his encounters with demons. In many ways, he intensified belief in the power of the devil rather than lessened it. His large catechism warned, "The devil rules in the world . . . besides the flesh and the world, you will have the devil about you, whom you will not completely tread underfoot; for Christ our Lord himself could not escape his temptations. . . . The devil is after us; he attacks on all sides"[33]

Luther's diabology was woven from various strands, including German folklore and Christian theology and piety, but the most dominant strand was monastic. Luther was a monk for some twelve years, and it was in the monastery that he came to know the devil firsthand, as he matured spiritually and intellectually. Christian diabology is deeply rooted in the monastic tradition. From its inception, monasticism had been a way of life built out of dualities, its very structures and dimensions devised cosmically, as an extension on earth of the struggle between God and Satan. As monasticism grew in popularity and the monks' struggles with demons became part of Christian lore, evil spirits became an ever-growing preoccupation for the church at large. By the fourth century, the Roman emperor Julian could say of Christians, "These two things are the quintessence of their theology, to hiss at demons and make the sign of the cross on their foreheads."[34]

The devil of the desert fathers still roamed the earth in Luther's time, his ferocity unchecked. But the devil of the monks had acquired other features too. Outside the cloister walls popular beliefs were also shaped by folklore, and at the outer fringes of Christian culture, folklore shaded off into a bewildering array of beliefs in malevolent or mischievous beings, both physical and spiritual, ranging from the Antichrist and witches to monsters, fairies, gnomes, giants, dragons, ghosts, vampires, werewolves, and trolls. At times, the line between the devil and such beings was indistinct. Official theology and popular piety did not always agree, but there was constant two-way traffic between them, most often in a dense typological fog. Like many of his contemporaries, Luther ascribed many functions to the devil that are not explicitly found in the Bible. His devil was a prolific and creative artist, capable of thousands of tricks, each a masterpiece of evil. For instance, Luther thought that the devil could play pranks as a poltergeist. Once, he claimed, the devil had kept him awake at night by throwing nuts at the ceiling.[35] "It is not a unique, unheard-of thing for the devil to bang around and haunt houses," he affirmed. "In our monastery in Wittenberg I heard him for sure. . . . The devil came and knocked three times in the storage chamber as if dragging a bushel away."[36] Similarly, the devil could cause quarrels between people,[37] or fool them into seeing or hearing the most preposterous things.[38] He could trick hunters into thinking he was a hare,[39] or show up as almost any animal—especially an ape.[40] Luther told of a man who was attacked by the devil in the form of a goat, wrestled with the beast, ripped off its horns, and watched it disappear.[41] On another occasion, Luther found a dog in his bed at the Wartburg and flung it out the window, convinced that it was a demon.[42] The devil could also bring on illnesses, either directly or through witches. Luther once complained, "I believe that my illnesses aren't natural but are sheer sorcery."[43] Yet another time, Luther argued that *all* illnesses came from Satan.[44] Sometimes, the devil manipulated the weather too: "There are many demons in the forests, water, swamps, and deserted places. . . . Others are in dense clouds and cause storms, lightning, thunder, and hail and poison the air."[45] The devil haunted the landscape. "Many regions are inhabited by devils," said Luther. "Prussia is full of them."[46]

The best-known story about Luther and the devil—which reveals more about his followers than about Luther—tells of his throwing an inkwell at the devil while he was hiding at the Wartburg in 1521–1522. Though the story is a later invention, never reported by Luther himself, it fits the larger narrative all too well, mostly because Luther's diabolism was bequeathed to his followers in its full complexity. Long after Luther was dead and buried, Lutherans would be wrestling with his devil. In the same way that they reverently scraped off bits from the ink blotch on the wall at the Wartburg castle, believing in its authenticity, Lutherans could also believe that Chancellor Krell and Burgomaster Brabant really deserved execution for being in league with Satan, or that 133 witches should be burnt to death at Quedlinburg on the same day.

This Lutheran preoccupation with the devil gave rise to a new genre of devotional texts in the 1550s: the *Teufelsbuch*, or "devil book." Though the intention of these books was to call for repentance and to warn the faithful about the dangers of specific sins, they also managed to sustain the devil's prominence and to instill fear of him. Closely related to social disciplining and to the attempt to instill the Reformation ethic of "decency, diligence, gravity, modesty, orderliness, prudence, reason, self-control, sobriety, and thrift,"[47] the Lutheran devil books mirrored the Catholic cult of the saints in which each saint had his or her specialty—with specific devils being assigned mastery over certain sins. Some of these texts addressed the central Lutheran issue of faith, such as Andreas Fabricius's *Holy, Clever, and Learned Devil*, Simon Musaeus's *Melancholy Devil*, and Andreas Lange's *The Worry Devil*. Others focused on individual sins that affected everyone: the drunkenness devil, the gluttony devil, the lust devil, and so on. Some introduced highly specialized devils, such as Johann Ellinger's "walk-about devil who loiters on the street," and "frivolous, voluptuous, hopping and skipping dance devil who is an intimate companion of the walk-about devil." Some devil books singled out sins that were specific to one class. Andreas Musculus's *Trousers Devil*, for instance, condemned rich young men who wore sexually suggestive garb. Cyriakus Spangenberg's *Hunt Devil* blasted away at the nobility's obsession with hunting.

The most famous devil book of all, perhaps, is the *Historia von Dr. Johann Fausten*, first published in 1587, which tells the cautionary tale of Faustus, a learned man who allowed his insatiable curiosity to get the best of him and sold his soul to the devil. While these texts portrayed the sinner as responsible for breaking God's law, they nonetheless stressed the power of the devil and the cosmic struggle between humans and the spiritual forces of Satan and his minions. With an estimated 250,000 of these *Teufelsbücher* in circulation by the 1590s, the devil gained much exposure thanks to the Lutheran clergy.

Among the Reformed, no leading light spoke of the devil as frequently, or on such intimate terms as Luther. Nonetheless, the devil played a significant role in Reformed theology. Zwingli believed that the devil was very active in the world and a masterful deceiver, and that he had to be actively opposed. "Ye know well what work the devil has sometimes done in many places," he said, "which if it had not been obstructed would have resulted in great deception and injury of all Christendom."[48] Zwingli also had a tendency to demonize his opponents, and to blame their errors on the devil, especially in the case of Catholics and Anabaptists. In addition, Zwingli was convinced that many of the miracles claimed by the Catholic Church were demonic in origin.

Calvin agreed with Zwingli on all these points, but spoke of the devil much more often, elaborating on his many fiendish roles. Calvin's devil was a liar, a trickster, and a tempter. Above all, the devil was a "constant presence," and "the most daring, the most powerful, the most crafty, the most indefatigable, the most completely equipped" of all enemies, and the best armed, "with all the engines," and, to top it off, "the most expert in the science of war."[49] Fortunately, especially for the elect, this mighty enemy was constantly reined in by God: whatever he did, he could only carry out with God's permission. This meant that the devil acted much like an executioner who fulfilled sentences imposed by God, the supreme judge. As Calvin put it, the devil was the "minister" of the wrath of God.[50] Moreover, Calvin also stressed that without the gift of God's grace, human beings were not much different from devils.

Ever pragmatic, Calvin stressed that being aware of the devil's power was necessary for two reasons: first, it made the elect realize how much grace and protection they needed from God, and second, it made them grateful for being rescued from such a great wicked power. This very providential take on the devil, so closely linked to the doctrine of election, placed all those who were not elect in the devil's camp. By the same token, this view of the devil also made it the responsibility of the elect to wage war against him and his human minions, especially the sorcerers. For the Reformed, then, the devil was very real and very active, constrained by God, but always there to be fought against. Unlike Luther, however, none of the Reformed leaders put much stress on apparitions of the devil, or personal encounters with him. Unlike Lutherans, Calvinists also tended to remove the rite of exorcism that had long been attached to the sacrament of baptism. This practice became controversial and caused much division in some places, such as in Saxony, when the Crypto-Calvinist Chancellor Krell introduced this change in ritual. Given the Reformed influence on England, the devil found in the Anglican Church had Reformed features, but others too that marked him off as distinctly English, unmistakably ambivalent, and as given to puritan restraint as to popish excess.

Among Catholics, all of medieval diabolism remained in place, both among monastics and lay folk. But, as the devil's presence was intensified by the ever-growing number of Protestant heretics, so was the church's vigilance, and its response to all things demonic. Among monastics, the devil seemed to become ever more active and more aggressive, especially as the mystical streak deepened in response to Protestantism. In convents and monasteries all over Catholic Europe, and even in the New World, monks and nuns who claimed extraordinary spiritual experiences were subjected to rigorous questioning, and often processed by the Inquisition. And the monastics themselves grew ever more conscious of the devil and his infinite capacity for deception. For those mystics and would-be mystics who crossed over to the spiritual dimension, and especially for women, becoming a demonologist was essential.

A case in point is Teresa of Ávila, who frequently mentioned the devil and wrote about her encounters with demons as if she were writing about the pots and pans in her convent's kitchen. While many of these passages refer to demonic temptation, a good number of them deal with demonic apparitions. Sometimes the devil appeared in "physical form" and also in "formless" visions. Once, for instance, she claimed she saw two demons wrap themselves around the throat of a priest who was living in a state of mortal sin. On another occasion, at a funeral, she saw the corpse being mauled by demons. Sometimes the demons attacked her. "One night," she said, "I thought they were choking me."[51] Teresa was not alone, or that unusual. By the mid-sixteenth century, convents suddenly seemed full of devils, and of nuns like Teresa, who resisted them, and others who did not.

Teresa herself was subjected to close scrutiny, and her confessors tried to convince her that all her raptures and visions—including those in which she saw Jesus Christ—were straight from the devil. At one point, she was even ordered to respond to her visions of Jesus with obscene gestures. And she also came close to being exorcized of the demons that her superiors suspected had taken control of her body and mind. Cases of nuns who were easily deceived by the devil and of nuns who were possessed by him began to climb rapidly in the 1550s and 1560s, as did Inquisition trials and exorcisms. One such case involving John of the Cross, who was called on to deal with a possessed nun, was typical:

> The exorcisms are accompanied by terrible convulsions in the poor girl: she furiously insults Friar John, foams at the mouth, screams, thrashes about in a frenzy on the floor, and even tries to attack the Friar and his companions. . . . The young exorcist holds a cross before her. . . . The demoniac throws the cross to the ground; but the friar orders her to take it up and kiss, and she obeys, while bellowing.[52]

Exorcisms could turn into titanic struggles that took weeks or months to complete. In most cases, the devil—or devils—would eventually be vanquished. The Catholic Church had well-established rituals to deal with demoniacs, and they involved the use of both verbal and physical components: adjurations, prayers, commands, questions—all in the name of Christ—along with the use of crosses, images, consecrated hosts, and holy water. Distinctions were also made between various degrees of demonic influence: infestation (when devils congregate in a certain location), obsession (when devils assail someone constantly), and possession (when devils take over someone's body and mind).

In the sixteenth century, this rite had yet to be standardized, so there were local as well as personal variations, some of which came to be viewed as corrupt, and too reliant on superstition and magic. In the 1530s Pedro Ciruelo had already warned that the devil himself had corrupted the rite and that many priests employed "gross expressions as well as superstitious formulas" that were mixed with "holy and pious words."[53] To do away with such abuses, the rite of exorcism would be standardized in the *Rituale Romanum*, the definitive liturgical compendium issued by Pope Paul V in 1614. This new rite, which replaced all others, prescribed set firm guidelines concerning the identification of genuine possessions and their treatment. It began solemnly, with this first prayer, in which every dagger symbol indicates that the sign of the cross is to be made over the demoniac:

> I exorcise thee, most vile spirit, the very embodiment of our enemy, the entire specter, the whole legion, in the name of Jesus Christ, to † get out and flee from this creature of God ††.
>
> He Himself commands thee, who has ordered those cast down from the heights of heaven to the depths of the earth. He commands thee, he who commanded the sea, the winds, and the tempests.
>
> Hear therefore and fear, O Satan, enemy of the faith, foe to the human race, producer of death, thief of life, destroyer of justice, root of evils, kindler of vices, seducer of men, betrayer of nations, inciter of envy, origin of avarice, cause of discord, procurer of sorrows. Why dost thou stand and resist, when thou knowest that Christ the Lord will destroy thy strength? Fear him who was immolated in Isaac, sold in Joseph, slain in the lamb, crucified in man, and then was triumphant over hell. †

> Depart therefore in the name of the † Father, and of the † Son, and of the Holy †
> Ghost; give place to the Holy Ghost, by the sign of the † Cross of Jesus Christ our Lord,
> who with the Father and the same Holy Ghost liveth and reigneth one God, for ever
> and ever, world without end.[54]

By 1614, as possession cases continued to proliferate, this codification was more than a reform: it was an affirmation of the power and authority of the rites, sacraments, and sacramentals of the Catholic Church. In other words, by 1614, exorcisms had become one of the strongest proofs the Catholic Church had to offer of its authenticity and its superiority to all Protestant churches.

Exorcism acquired a polemical dimension because possessions were not limited to convents and monasteries, or even to Catholics. As in the case of witchcraft, demonic possession crossed religious boundaries. And some of the most salient differences between the religion of Catholics and Protestants stood in sharpest contrast when it came to possession, for while Catholics had an elaborate rite that was physically grounded in the use of images, sacraments, and the sacramentals of holy water and oil, Protestants employed prayer alone, and the reading of Scripture. These differences also applied to all phenomena involving the devil.

A case in point is that of the difference between Luther's and Teresa of Ávila's approach to diabolical events. Teresa and Luther, both monastics, faced a devil who, above all things, sought to make people despair by reminding them constantly of their sinfulness. But whereas Teresa could boast, "There is nothing which puts devils to flight like holy water . . . and the sign of the cross," Luther, like all Protestants, rejected the Catholic rite of exorcism and the use of images and holy water as nonbiblical superstitions. So, while Teresa praised the power of "everything ordained by the Church," and the difference it could make in the physical realm, Luther's approach was to employ prayer and Bible reading alone, and to taunt the devil, especially with a combination of theological bravado and scatological insults:

> Tonight when I woke up the devil came, wanting to argue with me, objecting and throwing it up to me that I was a sinner. So I said to him: Tell me something new, devil! I already know that very well; as always, I have committed many real and true sins. . . . But all these sins are no longer mine, instead they've been taken by Christ. . . . If this isn't enough for you, devil, I just happened to shit and piss in my pants: wipe your mouth with that and bite hard on it![55]

Many other times, Luther also boasted of chasing the devil away with farts. His followers may not have followed his example, but they nonetheless stuck to prayer and Bible reading as the sole means of dealing with demon possession.

As possessions increased among lay people, Catholics found a distinct advantage in their rite of exorcism, especially in areas where religious allegiance was contested. Successful exorcisms became part of the Catholic polemical arsenal, not just on the local level, but throughout Europe, thanks to the printing press. Among those who capitalized on the polemical dimension of exorcism, one of the earliest—and one of the most impressive—was the Jesuit Peter Canisius (1521–1597), whose successful exorcisms were credited with effecting many conversions back to Catholicism. His exorcism of a young noblewoman, Anna von Bernhausen, in 1570, was among the most dramatic, and most publicly acclaimed.

In France, especially, the polemical use of exorcism acquired an unparalleled intensity. Among the most celebrated, or infamous, is the case of Nicole Obry in 1566, which came to be known as the Miracle of Laon. The demoniac in this case was a married adolescent, about fifteen or sixteen years old, who at first was exorcized by both Huguenots and Catholics. While the Huguenots seemed to be getting nowhere with their prayers, the Catholics gained access to the demons through their rites, and the fallen angels began to speak through Obry. Not surprisingly, the demons openly expressed allegiance to Geneva and the Calvinist cause. The first six demons to be expelled from her body reportedly headed straight for Geneva, and the seventh and most powerful identified himself as "Beelzebub, the Prince of the Huguenots." After a series of public debates with the bishop at the cathedral of Laon, in which the remaining demon inside of Obry constantly boasted of his success among the Huguenots, the bishop finally vanquished the devil by holding up a consecrated host over the girl's body.

The attention paid to this case in print was enormous. On the Catholic side, the Miracle of Laon was promoted as proof positive of the real presence of Christ in the Eucharist and of the divine power inherent in the Catholic Church. Among the Huguenots—who had been unsuccessful with these demons—Obry's possession was portrayed as a fraud, the very embodiment of Catholic superstition and deception, as well as of the diabolical nature of Catholic rituals. Some Huguenots attributed all of these events to witchcraft, too.

The Miracle of Laon was no isolated case: dozens such well-attended spectacles dotted the map of war-torn France. As with the case of would-be mystics, many frauds also attracted attention and caused discord. One of the most extraordinary of such exorcisms was that of Marthe Brossier in 1598–1599, who was publicly exorcized in several different towns and cities. Though Brossier was pronounced a fake in Paris, not all Catholics agreed with the verdict, and she continued to have very public demonic fits outside of France for a few years, and to attract much attention.

Brossier was only one of many such demonically possessed exhibitionists. For the following century, the devil continued to vex religiously divided France, and every public exorcism, genuine or not, elicited polemical responses. In seventeenth-century France, nunneries were hard-hit with a series of mass possessions. Three convents in particular received a great deal of attention because of their communal possessions, in which many nuns were simultaneously possessed and in which the exorcisms became public spectacles as well as polemical causes.

The first such case involved the Ursuline convent at Aix-en-Provence in 1611, where eight nuns became demon possessed, and a priest, Louis Gaufridi, was eventually

Diabolical spectacle. The small details are lost in this panoramic depiction of the public exorcism that came to be known as the Miracle of Laon, which attracted a large audience, not just at the site of the rites, but also far beyond, wherever this print and the accompanying narrative became available. The theatricality of this exorcism, which sought to free a young woman named Nicole Obry from her demons, became a flash point of Catholic-Protestant tensions in France and beyond: while many Catholics interpreted this event as proof of the divine authenticity of their church, Protestants denounced it as nothing more than a grotesque deception, even though their religious tradition continued to profess belief in the devil as real, and as very active in the world.

(The Granger Collection, New York)

convicted of causing this demonic invasion through a pact with the devil. The second and most celebrated diabolical invasion of an entire convent took place at Loudun in 1632–1634. Once again, a priest, Urbain Grandier, was found guilty of unleashing all of these devils on the nuns, and the exorcisms were held in public. The wild gyrations, lewd contortions, and obscene speech of the possessed Ursuline nuns, as well as the exhausting efforts of the exorcists were witnessed by huge crowds, numbering up to seven thousand. An eyewitness described what he saw:

> When the exorcist gave some order to the Devil, the nuns . . . struck their chests and backs with their heads, as if they had their necks broken, and with inconceivable rapidity; they twisted their arms at the joints of the shoulder, the elbow, or the wrist, two or three times around. Lying on their stomachs, they joined the palms of their hands to the soles of their feet; their faces became so frightful one could not bear to look at them; their eyes remained open without winking. Their tongues issued suddenly from their mouths, horribly swollen, black, hard, and covered with pimples, and yet while in this state they spoke distinctly. They threw themselves back till their heads touched their feet, and walked in this position with wonderful rapidity, and for a long time. They uttered cries so horrible and so loud that nothing like it was ever heard before. They made use of expressions so indecent as to shame the most debauched of men, while their acts, both in exposing themselves and inviting lewd behavior from those present would have astonished the inmates of the lowest brothels in the country.[56]

Thousands of others were made aware of all of the bizarre events through printed accounts that expressed conflicting points of view, with Catholics touting their church's power over the demons and Huguenots denouncing the entire spectacle as a hoax.

Catholics had a polemical advantage over the Huguenots. All that the Huguenots could do is argue that the possessions were faked, or the result of madness. Proving their fraudulent nature was difficult, especially in the face of public spectacles such as those at Aix and Loudon. Moreover, to accept the possessions as genuine would be to give credit to Catholic rituals, given that so many of the exorcisms resulted in victories over the devils. Catholics, in contrast, could use the exorcisms as proof of the power of their church and their rituals. Additionally, in those cases where priests were convicted of sending the devil into nuns, Catholics could also boast of the efficacy of their reforms. Few other events could prove that the Catholic Church would not tolerate bad priests better than the public execution of bad priests.

Loudon was not the last spectacular possession event. A third such case arose at Louviers in 1647, where two priests were convicted of causing a diabolical infestation. And one of the largest of all mass possessions, which affected at least fifty nuns, occurred forty years later, in Lyons, between 1687 and 1690. By that time, however, such events attracted much less attention, and this mass possession in Lyons—though larger than the one at Loudon—received much less coverage.

While the French outbursts of mass possession may have attracted more attention than any others in print, they were but part of a larger phenomenon. We have no definitive list, but we do know that mass possession was something rarely seen before the fifteenth century, while there were at least twenty such events in the sixteenth century, in Italy, Germany, Spain, France, and the Netherlands, and twenty or more in the seventeenth century, in the very same lands, and in far-off Peru. We also know of two outbreaks in the eighteenth century: one in Italy in 1721, and one in Germany in 1750. The vast majority of these cases, unlike the three French ones mentioned already, did not involve charges of witchcraft. These mass outbreaks, along with smaller ones, proved divisive, not only in Catholic-Protestant relations, but also within the Catholic community itself. Eventually, all these demonic spectacles would cast too large a shadow over religion in general, especially in certain elite intellectual circles. By the mid-eighteenth century, the devil would come to be viewed by many Enlightenment thinkers as the worst of all superstitions, and the ultimate proof of the absurdity and the danger of all traditional religion.

Conclusion

Political, social, and economic circumstances had a lot to do with each and every diabolical manifestation, and the phenomenon can certainly be better understood when all of these various perspectives are taken into account. But no single approach, all by itself, can explain the phenomenon in its complex totality. Luther referred to the devil as a *Tausendkünstler*, that is, an artist with a thousand skills. If the thousand skills were to be ascribed instead to the men and women who used the devil for their own purposes, then in our day and age Luther might seem even more perceptive. Whether the devil was really there four centuries ago, employing his thousand skills is no easier to prove or disprove now than it was then. The fact remains that whether it was the devil himself or men and women who employed him for their own purposes, the devil played one hell of a role in the birth of modernity during the sixteenth and seventeenth centuries, that era also known as the Age of Reason.

Ironically, the devil continues to cause trouble in our own day and age for anyone who thinks of the ascent from "medieval" to "modern" or from "superstition" to "reason" as one neat upward line on a graph, with no downward dips, or just a few, at most. But the devil is not at fault. The problem is not the devil's presence in the early modern age, which is undeniable. The real problem is that some definitions of *modernity* cannot take him and his thousand tricks into account. Epochal transitions can be slow and messy, and cannot really be charted neatly, especially with single lines that always curve upwards. Protestants put into motion many changes that can easily be identified as modern—changes that ushered in new mentalities and worldviews. But they also prized traits that are difficult to categorize as "modern" or "not modern." In sum, Protestants did not make a clean break with the medieval past. The devil proves this conclusively, and so do some other curious Protestants beliefs and practices.

Protestants continued to believe in a world populated by evil spirits and in divinely crafted natural signs. Consistory and visitation records show that many Protestants did not abandon the "magical" or "superstitious" world of their forebears completely, and had to be constantly reprimanded for their lapses. Some Protestants even ascribed enchanted qualities to their leaders: some Zurichers, for instance, spread a rumor that Zwingli's heart had remained intact when Catholics burned his corpse, and some Lutherans came to believe that pictures of Luther could not be set on fire. These parallel beliefs in incombustibility cannot be pigeonholed. When all is said and done, they are facts to be reckoned with—details that should make everyone acknowledge that the past is as complex as the present, and that the usefulness of concepts such as "modernity" or "postmodernity" can sometimes be very limited.

In brief, when it comes to tracing transitions to modernity, the devil is always in the details.

CHAPTER TWENTY-FOUR

The Age of Reasonable Doubt

The seeker after truth must, once in the course of his life, doubt everything, as far as possible"—so said René Descartes (1596–1650), mathematician and philosopher. This axiom, from his *Principles of Philosophy*, published in 1644, would later be reduced to a simple formula: *de omnibus dubitandum*, everything must be doubted, an expression that summed up a new worldview succinctly. It was a battle cry, the perfect shibboleth for a generation of skeptics. It was also a fitting epitaph for the Reformations that those skeptics' parents, grandparents, and great-grandparents had lived through.

Descartes was no pure skeptic. On the contrary, he was as convinced of the mind's ability to grasp Truth with a capital *T* as any of the Jesuits who had taught him, which is why, in addition to inventing coordinate geometry, he would also offer proofs for the existence of God. His skepticism served a purpose beyond itself: it was a means to certainty. "Indeed," he said, "it will even prove useful, once we have doubted these things, to consider them as false, so that our discovery of what is most certain and easy to know may be all the clearer. This doubt . . . should be . . . employed solely in connection with the contemplation of the truth."[1] Descartes would go as far as to question his own existence, only to affirm it. *Cogito ergo sum* would be his logical conclusion: I think therefore I am. Thought itself was the ultimate proof of his existence. While this pragmatic, goal-oriented skepticism may seem puerile to many twenty-first-century philosophers, it was a giant leap in its day, standing as it did in sharp contrast to the authority-bound faith of previous generations. Unlike the Reformers, Descartes searched for truth in his mind, not in the Bible or in any other text, no matter how ancient or deeply revered.

The very embodiment of certain traits of his era, Descartes did more than straddle boundaries: he scrambled them. Accused of being an atheist, he would claim to be a devout Catholic. Born in France, he would settle in the Netherlands, and live among Calvinists and Jews. Committed to pure empiricism, he would study the pineal gland in the human brain and conclude that it was the principal seat of the soul and the

Doubt everything. A philosopher and mathematician educated by Jesuits, René Descartes raised the logical rigor of skepticism to new levels, stressing the superiority of reason and empirical observation over long-revered authorities. The anonymous seventeenth-century artist responsible for this engraving correctly stressed Descartes's disdain for tradition by placing a heavy tome clearly labeled "Aristotle" on the floor, under Descartes's right foot. But the artist's rendering of Descartes at work was nonetheless wrong on two accounts, for the great skeptic preferred to work in bed and as close to a warm furnace as possible.

connecting point between mind and body. He would also fiercely defend flawed scientific theories, and belittle those who proved him wrong. Called to serve as court philosopher to Queen Christina of Sweden, a Lutheran, he would die without the last rites of the Catholic Church, and be buried in a cemetery for unbaptized infants. After his death, Queen Christina converted to Catholicism and abdicated, and Descartes's remains were transferred to the Abbey of Saint-Germain-des-Prés in Paris, to be interred between two monks. His fellow mathematician, the Jansenist Blaise Pascal, detested him. "I cannot forgive Descartes," said Pascal, "in all his philosophy, he would have been quite willing to dispense with God."[2] Pope Urban VIII agreed, and placed Descartes's writings on the *Index of Forbidden Books* in 1663.

The shift in outlook reflected in Descartes's *de omnibus dubitandum* was immense, and not entirely his to claim. Skepticism had been gathering strength since the fifteenth century, and his near contemporary Francis Bacon (1561–1626) had already promoted such thinking decades ahead of him. But Descartes voiced that skepticism as few others had, giving it the logical rigor of a geometric theorem. In essence, he dispensed with revelation in religion and raised human judgment to an ultimate plane as an autonomous authority. In addition, as far as nature and the material world were concerned, Descartes privileged observation and deduction over all previously revered authorities. Truth was accessible through reason, directly, not encoded in sacred or venerable texts that only certain elite guardians could interpret correctly. Some have argued that this giant step is the basis of modernity, for it shoved God and the churches aside—along with ancient authorities—and claimed a central role for every individual as the ultimate arbiter of truth. And this elevation of the individual human mind above all other authorities is precisely what makes Descartes so emblematic, that is, so great a representative of the amorphous movement to which he belonged. That movement had no name at the time, was far from unified, and can be best envisioned as a series of distinct voices, which steadily joined in harmony, growing louder and louder with the passage of time and eventually merging into a chorus that could drown out the lectures of ancient authorities along with the music of the churches and the howls of those burned alive in the name of religion.

These dissenting voices were not necessarily irreligious—though some of them certainly were—but in the end, their articulation of various strains of skepticism helped secure the collapse of state-enforced religious conformity and of the supremacy of faith over reason. In the process, they also ensured that Christian values would no longer determine the shape of Europe's ethical code, or of personal and communal identity. Though these dissidents did not always agree with one another, they harmonized their voices seamlessly, insofar as the challenge to faith was concerned. Within this chorus of disbelief, at least seven distinct types of nonconformity can be easily identified.

Popular Nonconformism

The broadest and deepest level of nonconformity with church teachings was the indifference and freethinking skepticism of the common folk, of which nearly every clergyman complained. As inquisition and consistory records reveal, a deep-seated resistance to the normative theology and ethics of the churches could be found across a broad spectrum, from sheer apathy and disdain to creative idiosyncrasy to endemic agnosticism. This type of resistance—displays of dogged independence and willful disdain for authority— should not be confused with those traces of superstition and magic that could never be extinguished. Nor is it to be mistaken for organized heresy, that is, for the existence of alternative theologies. These are cases in which lay people insisted on placing their personal judgment above that of their churches, both Catholic and Protestant, even after their "errors" or ignorance were pointed out to them. The Spanish Inquisition, for one, tried numerous offenders who argued with deep conviction that fornication was not a sin, or that the church was not essential for salvation. It also handled full-blown atheists who refused to believe in God, heaven, or hell, even under torture or the threat of execution. Some of these *valentones*, or "tough ones," as they were known, died on a stake for their unbelief, professing their atheism with their last dying breath.

One Inquisition case in northern Italy, that of a literate miller Domenico Scandella, better known as Menocchio, reveals that common folk could mix and match their beliefs as they saw fit, and come up with their own opinion on what was true. Menocchio was tried by the Inquisition more than once, and eventually executed simply because he would not stop expressing his eccentric beliefs in public. Among other things, he was convinced that the universe had come into existence from some preexisting eternal matter, rather than out of nothing, as the church taught. Asked repeatedly by the inquisitors where he had picked up his odd ideas, Menocchio insisted time after time, "My opinions came out of my own head." Or, as he also put it, much to the chagrin of his prosecutors, his beliefs came straight from his "artful mind."[3] Menocchio can be understood as no isolated crank, but rather as representative of an inchoate substrate of independent thinking that stretched across all of Christendom. If one Menocchio was caught by the Inquisition, then there certainly could have been thousands more like him, an assumption proved correct by research carried out in disparate court archives over several decades.

Elite Freethinking

A second type of nonconformism, closely related to the first, was that of elite freethinkers. Clergy in all churches of the Reformation era complained of such types. Sometimes they were mere individuals; sometimes they were lumped together into a loose category, or a well-organized group. John Calvin came up with the epithet *libertine* to describe various sorts of such reprobates. Close to home, in Geneva, the "libertines" were an organized political faction within the city, composed largely of local aristocrats who opposed his puritanical policies. But Calvin also wrote against libertines who, according to him, had a carefully wrought philosophy that ascribed all agency to a single divine spirit that indwelled in all humans and therefore absolved everyone of all responsibility for their actions. "After they have relaxed the reins on each other for each to do what seems best to him under the pretext of being led by God," Calvin charged, "they deduce from this same principle that it is wrong to pass judgment."[4] Calvin referred to these amoral nonconformists as wolves, thieves, sheer poison, mortal pests, ignoramuses, vermin, scum, swine, mad dogs, scoffers, fiends, wild beasts, madmen, rascals, stupid asses, seducers, and serpents. And he was not at all alone in thinking that such people existed. Francis de Sales, the Catholic reformer who would become titular bishop of Geneva, also singled out a type of learned libertine for censure, and warned the faithful to "guard against bad books" and not to read that "infamous Rabelais and certain other writers of our era who make a career out of doubting everything, of despising everything and making fun of the maxims of antiquity."[5] François Rabelais (1494–1553), a humanist Catholic cleric and one of the literary giants of the French Renaissance, would come to be known, among other things, for uttering as his final words, "I go to seek a great Perhaps" and "ring down the curtain, the farce is over."[6]

Ancient Voices

A third type of disbelief, bound closely to the second, was also elitist in nature: that which was linked to the recovery of classical pagan ways of thinking that were intrinsically at odds with Christianity. This is not to say that the Renaissance urge to reclaim and uphold classical culture was necessarily anti-Christian. Quite the contrary, the return *ad fontes* was a key element in the renewal of Christianity in the sixteenth century, and especially of the Protestant Reformation. Nonetheless, there were certain ancient schools of thought, particularly Stoicism and Epicureanism, which could not be fully embraced without abandoning some fundamental Christian principles. Again, this is not to say that every Renaissance humanist who delved into Stoic and Epicurean texts necessarily turned into a skeptic and atheist. John Calvin immersed himself in Stoicism, and Thomas More in Epicureanism. But not everyone reacted to these ancient traditions as did Calvin and More, who embraced what was compatible with Christianity and rejected what was not. Some intellectuals accepted these ancient philosophies with varying degrees of enthusiasm, even to the point of accepting propositions that were incompatible with Christian faith. Given that no one in the sixteenth century could abjure their Christian faith publicly and survive, all who gravitated toward these ancient non-Christian worldviews had to do so as stealthily as possible, and as a result this sort of neo-paganism tended to be subtle rather than overt. But the subtlety of its adherents—among whom there was no uniformity or cohesive agenda—did not lessen their eventual impact on Western culture.

A case in point is that of a single Epicurean text recovered in the fifteenth century: *On the Nature of Things*, a poem by Lucretius, written in the first century, about two generations before the birth of Christ. This text, which had been lost for nearly a millennium, was discovered in a remote monastery and set into circulation by the humanist Poggio Bracciolini (1380–1459). Until then, Lucretius had been known only through descriptions by other ancient writers. In the Christian tradition, he had been dismissed by St. Jerome in the fifth century as a bad poet who had killed himself after being driven insane by a love potion. Once he was brought to light again, however, Lucretius proved Jerome wrong. Those who read him, first in manuscripts and eventually in print, could not help but notice that Lucretius was far from mad, and that he had a lucid and rational understanding of reality that was radically different from that of Christianity, and utterly incompatible with it:

> Everything is made of tiny invisible particles (atoms) that are immutable and indivisible.
> These elementary particles are eternal and infinite in number.
> The particles are in constant motion in an infinite void.
> The universe has no creator or designer, no beginning or end, or purpose.
> Everything comes into being by random chance, from the motion of these atoms.
> Nature is an endless process of trial and error, and a battle for survival.
> Humans are far from unique and as inconsequential as anything else that exists.
> The soul is material and dies with the body; therefore, there is no afterlife.
> All religions are delusions, mere superstitious projections of our fears and desires.
> All religions are cruel and a source of anxiety.

Immaterial spirits do not exist: there are no angels, demons, genii, nymphs, or
ghosts.

The highest goal of life is to enhance pleasure and avoid pain.

Delusion is the worst of all obstacles to pleasure, greater even than pain.[7]

In some ways, this materialistic atheism resembled that of the unscholarly *valentones* later executed by the Spanish Inquisition, but it was more systematically expressed, with greater attention to detail and cogency. Unlike the *valentones*, whose unbelief tended to be inchoate and beyond analysis, Lucretius had a well-developed epistemology that resembled that of modern empirical science and had a curiously religious quality to it, as does the "new atheism" of the early twenty-first century—that very same ethos that led the ancient followers of Epicurus to call him a savior (*soter*). As Lucretius saw it, disciplined observation and the use of reason could lead to a thorough understanding of everything in the universe, and the information gathered by the senses always trumped all other claims to authority, no matter how venerable or muscular. Although it is difficult

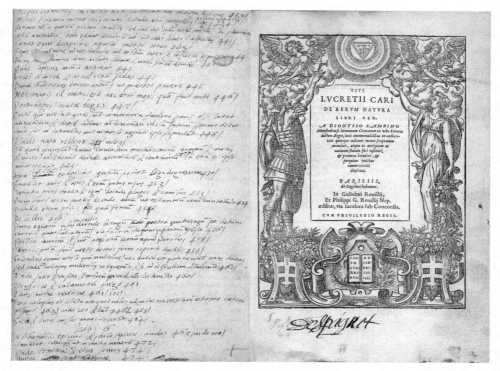

Elite best seller. This heavily annotated copy of Lucretius's *On the Nature of Things* belonged to the French essayist and statesman Michel de Montaigne (1533–1592), one of the main targets of Blaise Pascal's disapproval. The revival of ancient Epicurean philosophy was seen by many traditional Christians, such as Pascal, as a wrong step toward godlessness and the certain doom of the human race. Montaigne obviously paid close attention to several ideas expressed by this ancient pagan proto-atheist.

to assess exactly how much influence this one text had on its age, it is easy to argue that it represented the very unchristian sort of ideology that Renaissance humanists routinely dredged up in their effort to recover as much of antiquity as possible. And this ideology was the heathen chaff that not every intellectual was willing to sort from the wheat of the Christian faith. There is no denying that *On the Nature of Things* and other texts similarly full of unchristian philosophizing were read by many elites who championed independent thinking and promoted ideas opposed to the religious status quo. As manuscripts of Lucretius's text circulated throughout Italy, and talk of him and his ideas increased, the reformist preacher Savonarola poked fun at the studies of "learned men" in Florence who thought the world was made of tiny particles called atoms—a sure sign that the danger of neo-Epicureanism seemed real enough to traditionalists.

Among those in Florence who were reading Lucretius as Savonarola preached, and also copying him down, was none other than Niccolò Machiavelli, the ultimate secularist and political realist whom the church would condemn for his blindness to spiritual Christian values. Another prominent Renaissance man who drank deeply from Epicurean texts was Lorenzo Valla, the scholar who proved that the Donation of Constantine was a hoax and successfully challenged the identity of Dionysius the Areopagite. Valla wrote a dialogue titled *On Pleasure* (1431), in which he gave voice to the most outrageously atheistic and hedonistic propositions. Although Valla could distance himself from those passages by claiming that it was his Epicurean character in the dialogue who held such opinions, not he himself, the views were expressed all the same, and passed on to many readers. By 1516, on the eve of Luther's emergence, editions of *On the Nature of Things* were flowing out of presses in Bologna, Venice, Florence, and Paris.

Voices were raised in the following few decades against the growth of Epicureanism and atheism. In France, to mention but one location where an influx of philosophical rationalism was detected, we have numerous reports of atheism starting from the 1530s. Many of these so-called atheists honed their skepticism on the whetstone of ancient texts, and on the skeptical philosophy taught at the University of Padua in Italy. Among their favored texts, Cicero's *On the Nature of the Gods* and *On Divination* stood high on the list, as did Pliny's *Natural History*, in which he denies divine providence and the immortality of the soul. We have no way of calculating how many such "atheists" existed, since they tended to hide behind a veil of respectability. We also have no way of confirming whether the complaints of those who wrote about them were exaggerated. But in 1564, Pierre Viret, a Reformed pastor at Lausanne and a close associate of Calvin, would warn that "the number of epicureans and atheists is much greater than anyone thinks." He would also complain that these atheists did not believe in "anything at all," and submitted everything to doubt, creating a personal religion for themselves that consisted of nothing more than "opinions that torment human brains."[8]

Though Viret's atheists were invisible, atheistic materialism did make the rounds, and finally, in the 1580s a true disciple finally dared to go public, at full throttle, proposing an infinite universe made of atoms, a material perishable soul, and even the existence of intelligent beings on other planets: Giordano Bruno (1548–1600), a former Dominican monk, was executed at Rome for his many heresies after a lengthy trial. Like many of the Spanish *valentones*, Bruno had to be silenced at the stake for he could not stop spouting his impious errors. Not all disciples of Lucretius were as bold and reckless as Bruno, however. Among the many who were more subtle was the French statesman and essayist Michel de Montaigne (1533–1592) stands out. His rational skepticism was summed up in a signature phrase: "Que sais-je?" (what do I know?). Montaigne not only read *On the Nature of Things*, but also carefully annotated his copy and incorporated much of Lucretius's Epicureanism into his own outlook on life. Considered by many to be a father of modern skepticism, Montaigne stressed the value of his own judgment as the ultimate criterion. Blaise Pascal, the Jansenist mathematician, despised Montaigne even more than he despised Descartes.

In sum, although it is immensely difficult to prove that a single text such as *On the Nature of Things* had a direct and discernible impact on the transition to modernity—regardless of the inflated claims made in a book that won the two most prestigious American literary awards[9]—the circulation of such a text attests to the presence of an elite Renaissance worldview that prized reason over faith and matter over spirit.

Dissembling

A fourth type of nonconformity that gradually ate away at all hegemonic claims for orthodoxy, univocal truth claims, and belief in a single true church was not so much ideological as practical: that of dissembling in the face of persecution. In some places, pretending to belong to a faith one did not believe became necessary a survival technique. In Spain and Portugal, the "new Christians"—Marranos and Moriscos—first brought lying about one's true convictions to new heights, as converts from Judaism and Islam were forced to choose between conversion or permanent expulsion. In France and other Catholic states, the Nicodemites hid their Protestant faith beneath a false veneer. In Protestant areas of the European continent, Catholics who were forced to fake their commitment to Protestantism cannot be numbered precisely, but we do know that they existed and endured. In England, where such Catholics were known as "church papists," they also endured through the reigns of several monarchs, well into the seventeenth century. These dissemblers needed no precise theology to fake their external conformity, but many do seem to have adopted a relativist posture in their predicament—an attitude that privileged inner over outer, spiritual over material, and personal conviction over mere external observance. For some secret dissenters survival was surely a weightier concern than logical arguments about religious convictions.

Church elites everywhere condemned such deception, which amounted to sheer apostasy in their eyes, and church courts everywhere dragged in the fakers they could catch, but there was no surefire way of preventing anyone from dissembling. Because the very nature of this behavior kept it hidden from view, we will never know how many dissemblers were created by the Reformations, or what cumulative effect they might have had, but by the same token, we can safely conjecture that the unremitting condemnation of such behavior by church authorities over several generations is sufficient evidence that its corrosive power was real indeed. Little evidence survives to allow us to determine whether dissembling led to apathy and sheer insincerity, or indeed differed much from apathy and sheer insincerity. But, again, it is not at all unreasonable to assume that—martyrs and exiles aside—those forced to submit to a certain faith against their will day after deadly day might have been more cynical, apathetic, or hostile toward religion than those who were not.

Religious Toleration

A fifth challenge to the traditional place of religion in society and culture was that of religious toleration. Two types of toleration came into being in the sixteenth century as a result of the Reformations: one pragmatic, the other theoretical. Over time, the two forms began to merge and to create a different space for religion in the body politic. Pragmatic toleration required no theory or theology. It was simply a response to an effective stalemate, and it could occur at different levels, from the strictly local to the regional and national.

The free imperial city-state of Strassburg is a good example of locally devised, unplanned toleration. Lutheran influence began to affect the city in 1521, and the Lutheran community grew steadily. At the same time, Reformed influence from Switzerland began to take hold, along with a wide spectrum of radical strains, from pacifist Anabaptists at one extreme to radical millenarians at the other. Erasmus, John Calvin, and the spiritualist Caspar Schwenckfeld all spent time in Strassburg, as did the apocalyptic prophet Melchior Hoffman, who proclaimed it the new Jerusalem. The city even allowed some women's convents to remain in place, and these communities gradually morphed into unique quasi-monastic establishments. In 1548, the Augsburg Interim reintroduced the Catholic Mass too, in the cathedral and other churches. This tolerant pluralism would endure for several generations, but in the late sixteenth century, the Lutherans began to gain the upper hand politically, and in 1598 Strassburg became officially Lutheran.

Augsburg, another free imperial city, offers an even more dramatic example of the ways in which political circumstances could produce de facto toleration with no underlying theological reasoning. In the early 1520s Lutheran and Reformed parties wrestled for control of the city and for the abolition of the Catholic Church; by the late 1520s Anabaptists had carved out their own niche too, thanks to the political stalemate. In the meantime, Catholics retained enough political clout to resist expulsion, even as some of their churches and monastic institutions were given to Protestants by the government. By 1531, the Reformed party had begun to gain more power, and in 1534, the city government restricted the Mass to the eight churches that were directly under the bishop's jurisdiction, including the cathedral. Three years later, when Reformed Protestants gained a decisive majority in the city government, the Mass was outlawed and those eight churches were taken away from the Catholics, and "cleansed" of all of their religious artwork. A small Catholic minority remained in Augsburg, including some aristocratic nuns who refused to vacate their convents but were placed under Protestant superiors and forbidden to have contact with priests. Many other clerics and monastics sought refuge in nearby towns that remained Catholic. For ten years, Augsburg was officially Reformed, with a small oppressed Catholic community and former Lutherans too. In 1547, however, the defeat of the Schmalkaldic League and the subsequent Interim reinstalled the Catholic bishop of Augsburg in his cathedral and returned to him the churches that had been taken over in 1537. In August 1548, Emperor Charles V imposed a new political order on Augsburg, in which Catholics and Protestants were to have equal representation in the city government, although at that time the city was only about 10 percent Catholic. In 1555, the Peace of Augsburg sealed this arrangement by granting equal protection under the law for the beliefs, worship, and property of both Catholics and Protestants. And this applied not just to Augsburg, but to all imperial cities that still had a religiously divided population in 1552. The Peace of Augsburg, however, contained one provision that showed how practical toleration depended on politics: its legal protection of religious freedom applied only to Lutherans and Catholics, not to the Reformed or to Radicals. So, in 1555 all of Augsburg's Protestants were forced by law to become Lutherans, regardless of their prior confessional allegiances. Without much resistance, Augsburg became a biconfessional city, divided between Lutherans and Catholics. The same arrangement also applied in other imperial free cities, including Biberach, Dinkelsbühl, Lindau, and Ravensburg.

Beyond urban environments, at the regional and national level, Catholics and Protestants could live within shouting distance of each other. The Holy Roman Empire itself became something of a confessional patchwork, especially in its western and southern regions. The same was true of Switzerland, with its jigsaw puzzle of a religious map. Geneva, the Protestant Rome, was surrounded by Catholics, and its Catholic bishop resided only twenty-one miles to the south in Annecy. Catholic France was riddled with Calvinist Huguenots, as were many regions of central and eastern Europe, with Calvinists and Anabaptists sprouting up and thriving in the midst of heavily Catholic populations. In Ireland, where England tried to impose its Protestant church on the Catholic natives, the mixing was intense and volatile. Arrangements in divided realms varied, according to time and place: in one city, two congregations might have two separate churches; in another, they might take turns sharing the same worship space; and in yet another, the members of one church might be allowed to travel a few miles beyond the city walls to attend the services they preferred. Tensions abounded, and sometimes conflict too. Arrangements could prove to be fragile, fluid, and tenuous, as in Strassburg, or fairly constant, as in Augsburg.

The United Provinces of the Netherlands were among the most checkered and fractured region of all, with a Catholic minority in the south, a solidly Protestant north, and an untidy mix in between. Cities with multiple confessions were common. Anabaptists, Catholics, Calvinists, Lutherans, and Jews found ways to live cheek by jowl and to coexist in relative harmony, saddled with tensions, for sure, but unburdened by constant strife or acrimony. In the city of Delft, for instance, which was home to the Calvinist painter Jan Vermeer, about a quarter of the population was Catholic, and most of the Catholics lived in one neighborhood known as the Papenhoek, or "Papists' Corner," not by compulsion, but by choice. Although in Delft, as in other Dutch cities, the Reformed Church claimed all church buildings, Catholics went to Mass in "hidden" churches, that is, in residences that had been converted into sacred worship spaces. Delft even had a Jesuit school. De facto toleration in the Dutch Republic was so entrenched by the seventeenth century that being pronounced a heretic by any religious community brought no dire consequences. The philosopher Baruch Spinoza (1632–1677), excommunicated by his Jewish community in Amsterdam and even attacked at one point by a knife-wielding avenger, lived out the rest of his life in peace, philosophizing and making a living as a lens grinder until a fatal illness struck him down. Spinoza, like everyone else in the Netherlands, enjoyed the right to choose his own beliefs, and he would be buried in the churchyard of a Dutch Reformed Church. Even those Netherlanders who belonged to that state-sanctioned Dutch Reformed Church and were subject to its disciplinary measures had nothing worse to fear than expulsion from their church and ostracism by its members. This coexistence, which amounted to toleration, was derived not from any theological or philosophical theories, but rather from the fact that the imposition of draconian uniformity was too costly—socially, politically, and economically—and therefore deemed impossible.

Fragmented societies—grudging though the tolerance and cohabitation might have been—were an unavoidable and an all-too-common reality in the sixteenth and seventeenth centuries. Yes, some regions such as Spain, Portugal, Italy, Scandinavia, England, and Scotland had monolithic churches and little or no toleration. But all other realms were religiously mixed, even if they had certain areas that were solidly Protestant or Catholic. And no matter how repressive the control, nonconformism or heresy could spring up anywhere. In many spots on the map, then, religious fragmentation and de facto toleration became an inescapable fact, on the local as well as the regional level. When trade and travel across political boundaries are brought into the picture, the exchange between people of different confessions becomes even more of a constant, unavoidable reality. The fact that some areas became more tolerant than others by necessity rather than design—as in the contrasting examples of the Dutch Republic and Spain or Italy— does not diminish the significance of the seismic change created by the fragmentation of the map of Christendom. Religion itself acquired a new air of subjectivity, at once puzzling and divisive. And in many places, religion turned into something that had to be overcome, or overlooked, rather than something that bound everyone together. It also became a potential source of confusion, a Babel of the spirit and mind, rather than a source of definitive answers to ultimate questions.

Although toleration often had practical causes, a few freethinkers tried to formulate cogent arguments in its favor. Eventually, many of these individuals would be described as prophets centuries ahead of their time. And they would also influence later thinkers who actually did have an impact on their contemporaries, such as John Locke and Thomas Jefferson. Many present-day national constitutions and the United Nations' Universal Declaration of Human Rights are deeply indebted to these Reformation-era pioneers. In their own day and age, however, their pleas and theories fell on deaf ears.

Among those placed on this very short list, Sebastian Castellio (1515–1563) holds a place of honor. Once a friend of John Calvin and rector of the Collège of Geneva, Castellio came to disagree with Calvin on several issues and left for Basel in 1545, where he drifted even further from Genevan orthodoxy. When the anti-Trinitarian Michael Servetus was burned alive in Geneva in 1553, Castellio was one of the few Protestants to denounce this execution, in a passionate yet coldly logical treatise titled *Whether Heretics Ought to Be Persecuted* (1554). Invoking the Bible and early patristic authorities such as Augustine, Jerome, and John Chrysostom, Castellio argued that the church had no right to kill anyone for his or her beliefs. "To burn a heretic is not to defend a doctrine, but to kill a man," he wrote.[10] Religious disagreements, as he saw it, called for debates, not for executions.

Convinced that Christian love demanded a certain degree of tolerance, and that living a life of compassionate virtue was a far better way to convince others of their errors than to round them up and burn them, Castellio warned that the interpretation of Scripture should never be monopolized by one man, or any civil or ecclesiastical body, much less lead to the killing of fellow human beings. Castellio also argued that consciences should never be coerced and that the state had no right to enforce religious conformity—an argument he would develop further in 1562, in his *Advice to a Desolate France*, which he wrote in response to the horrors of the first few months of the French Wars of Religion. "I find," he said, "that the forcing of consciences is the principal and efficient cause of our ills, that is, of the wars and the sedition that afflict us."[11] The remedy to all of these horrors, he argued, was to stop the bloodshed and to allow everyone to follow their own beliefs. In his last book, *The Art of Doubting*, which he never finished, Castellio went even further, forging a theological defense of the necessity of doubt and the utter folly of insisting on precise doctrinal propositions and arcane rituals. "Reason is a certain eternal word of God," argued Castellio, "far more ancient and certain than writings and ceremonies, according to which God taught his own before there were any ceremonies and writings."[12]

Freethinking spiritualists also argued for a cessation of all confessional rivalries and persecutions. Caspar Schwenckfeld (1489–1561), a Silesian nobleman and early follower of Luther, developed a distinct theology that was derived from Radical principles. A foe of infant baptism, and of the very concept of a state church that enforces religious uniformity, Schwenckfeld not only was opposed to persecution and to killing in the name of religion, but also called on all existing churches to suspend their arguing and their celebration of the Eucharist and to wait for God to settle the religious mess of the age. Although he rejected the establishment of any church, his followers insisted on doing precisely that, and the Schwenckfelder Church—always small, limited in reach, and persecuted—became a soft-spoken advocate of religious toleration.

Another spiritualist who argued for toleration was Dirk Coornhert (1522–1590), a Dutch theologian who also irritated Calvin and was convinced that religion was something personal rather than communal. Believing in an inner connection between every individual and the divine, Coornhert advised individuals to follow their own convictions and not pay undue attention to external observances or formal doctrines. This was a perfect theological argument in favor of the Nicodemism that Calvin attacked with full force and also a formula for toleration. Arguing that the religious divisions of his age could be solved only by God himself through specially inspired prophets, he urged his contemporaries to wait for such an event, and to lay aside all dogma and religious differences in the meantime. Coornhert, like Castellio, also argued forcefully against the killing of heretics.

One did not have to be a spiritualist or an enemy of John Calvin to plead for tolerance. Throughout the sixteenth and seventeenth centuries, arguments for religious pluralism were voiced from various quarters, especially by individuals who lived in religiously fractured societies. Among those who called for tolerance three individuals stand out: Michel de Montaigne, the skeptical French essayist, Baruch Spinoza, the "heretical" Jewish philosopher (both previously mentioned), and a French Protestant scholar, Pierre Bayle (1647–1706). The influence of the English philosopher John Locke (1632–1704) is particularly noteworthy in light of Locke's impact on the founding fathers of the United States. His *Letter Concerning Toleration* (1689) argued that religious liberty was essential to social harmony, for all attempts by the state to force consciences usually led to confrontations and civil unrest. But Locke, an English Protestant, was not willing to extend toleration to Catholics or atheists. Because his exclusion of Catholics was based on the assumption that Catholics were adamantly opposed to toleration, Locke's essay raised the troublesome question, still being debated more than three centuries later: should tolerance can be granted to the intolerant? His exclusion of atheists was similarly based on another common assumption of his day: atheists could not be trusted because all agreements, contracts, covenants, promises, and oaths depended on belief in God.

Rationalism

A sixth challenge to Christian traditions came in various guises: the rise of rationalism. Closely bound to the rise of skepticism, and sometimes indistinguishable from it, rationalism arose from within, as part of Christian culture. Rationalism was nothing new, since Christian theology was intensely logical. Nonetheless, merging reason and faith had not always been easy. Officially, the medieval church had opted for the ultimate superiority of faith, crowned theology as queen of the sciences, and turned philosophy into its handmaiden. The advent of Protestantism heightened the significance of the faith-reason dialectic in many ways, especially because of its emphasis on faith alone and scripture alone, so debates about it intensified as theologians sought to defend the inner logic of their positions over and against those who disagreed with them. At the Marburg Colloquy in 1529, Luther reproached Zwingli for applying too much reason and of being "mathematical" in his approach to the Eucharist, while Zwingli accused Luther of being illogical. Similarly, Catholic polemicists delighted in pointing out inconsistencies and inner contradictions in Protestant theology. As we saw in chapter 21, this constant logical warfare—the sole aim of which was to undercut the faith-based claims of others—was imbued with a self-destructive potential.

One reaction to all of the doctrinal wrangling caused by the Reformations was the search for a reason-based theology that could cut across dogmatic boundaries. Such attempts tended to be made in societies that had been deeply affected by religious conflict. In England, especially, a very robust strain of rationalism began to assert itself in the early seventeenth century. This rationalism was very different from that of the Epicureans, for it sought not to unmask religion as sheer nonsense, but rather to elevate it to logical supremacy. Yet when all is said and done, these rationalistic proposals ended up having as much of a corrosive effect on traditional religion as the challenges made by die-hard skeptics and atheists.

Far from an organized movement, rationalists of various stripes could be found even before the disintegration of Christendom in the 1520s. But throughout the early years of the Reformations, and especially after the mid-sixteenth century, complaints about rationalists become easier to find in the writings of church authorities, both Protestant and Catholic. One of the most detailed descriptions can be found in Pierre Viret's *Christian Instruction* (1563). Viret, who had tried to expose the Epicurean atheists of his age, was also an inveterate opponent of all "libertines," and the first writer to ever make mention of a rationalist strain of libertinism known as "Deism," which to him seemed nothing more than "atheism." He was also careful to distinguish these Deists from run-of-the-mill libertines and Epicureans:

> There are many who confess that they surely believe in some sort of God and some sort of divinity, just like the Turks and the Jews, yet with regard to Jesus Christ and to all that to which the doctrine of the Evangelists and the Apostles testify, they believe that it is all mere fables and daydreams. . . . I have heard that there are some of this ilk who call themselves Deists, an entirely new word, which they want to distinguish from Atheist. For, while the word atheist signifies a person who has no God, they want to make it clear that they are not at all without God, since they certainly believe there is some sort of God, whom they even recognize as creator of heaven and earth, as do the Turks; but as for Jesus Christ, they just know his name, but hold nothing concerning him nor his doctrine.[13]

These Deists, continued Viret, were chameleonlike in their ability to blend in, and quite expert at hypocrisy. On the one hand, they mocked organized religion, but on the other, they pretended to follow the external religious observances of those around them, or of those they wanted to please, or of those whom they feared. In other words, they were clever Nicodemites. They also lacked cohesion and consistency. Some of them, he said, believed in the immortality of the soul, but others denied it, "just like the Epicureans." As far as the role of God was concerned, these Deists preferred to believe that the deity did not concern himself with running the universe. "It horrifies me to think that there are such monsters who call themselves Christians," remarked Viret. And he was even more horrified to think that many of these deists were learned people, scholars, writers, and teachers who were in a position to "poison many people" with their "execrable atheism." Such monsters posed an even greater danger than idolaters and superstitious folk, warned Viret, because of their ability to blend in, earn respect, and affect others. Viret did not shrink back from attributing their growth in numbers, and their influence to the religious divisions of the age. Many grossly abused the freedom of choice in religion that the times had given them, he complained. The mere fact that there was now a choice, said Viret, gave many an opportunity to "live completely without any religion and to corrupt society with their error and atheism."[14]

Among those who first attempted to remove theology from its throne, formally and openly, and to replace it with philosophy, few had more of an impact than the English aristocrat Edward Herbert, Baron of Cherbury (1583–1648). A soldier, diplomat, historian, and poet, as well as a philosopher, Herbert of Cherbury sought to reduce the Christian religion to its most elemental rational components. For this reason, he is known as the father of a tradition that came to be known as Deism, that same name supposedly employed by Viret's "monsters." Cherbury's first treatise on religion, *On Truth* (1624), which argued for the existence of a "natural religion," would be expanded upon and re-published numerous times. The third edition, which was published in 1645, included two brief discourses, "On the Origin of Errors" and "The Religion of the Laity," as well as the "Appendix to the Priests." In 1663, fifteen years after he died, another groundbreaking text of his was published, *On the Religion of the Gentiles*. This was a pioneering effort to compare the major religions of the world that reduced the essence of religion to rationally deduced "self-evident" points that could be arrived at without divine revelation. In it, Herbert of Cherbury proposed a simple five-point creed:

> That there is a supreme Deity
> That this Deity ought to be worshiped
> That true worship and genuine piety consist of virtue
> That men should refrain from wrongdoing and repent for it
> That the goodness and justice of the Deity demand reward and punishment for
>   one's actions, both in this life and after it

In Cherbury's reasonable and natural religion ethics displaced ritual and dogma as "the chief part" of religion. His belief in the essential rationality of these points, and in their commonsense origins in innate ideas possessed by every human being—which he called "common notions"—also led him to propose that these ethically centered five points were the original primitive religion of the human race, which had been corrupted by "the covetous and crafty sacerdotal order."[15] Undercutting the authority of all churches even further, he argued that whatever was contrary to his five points was unreasonable and necessarily false. Therefore, as he saw it, the concept of a divine revelation was a cultural construct, or mere humanly devised tradition, and all truth claims—even those ostensibly revealed—were mere probabilities that had to be judged true or false by the dictates of reason. The clergy, along with their meddlesome interpretations of Sacred Writ, were thus obstacles to overcome rather than guardians of the truth.

Herbert of Cherbury's rationalist take on religion was no isolated challenge, but rather one part of a larger sustained attack on the status quo. Skepticism and rationalism could be found at nearly every turn by those who were eager to maintain tradition. By the 1650s, skeptics, deists, and crypto-deists had become so numerous that French mathematician Blaise Pascal, who had joined the Jansenist cause, would begin to write a thorough defense of traditional Christianity. Although he died in 1662, before he could finish this project, Pascal did leave behind fragmentary notes that would later be published posthumously under the title *Pensées*, or "Thoughts." These fragments contain a detailed deconstruction of pure rationalism and of the inconsistencies of skepticism. "The heart has its reasons, which reason cannot comprehend,"[16] argued Pascal, trying to knock reason off its absolutist throne. Pascal's unfinished defense of the superiority of faith over reason reveals how threatened Christian intellectuals could feel by the attacks of deists, skeptics, cynics, libertines, and rationalists of all stripes. Deists, per se, make no appearance in the *Pensées*, but their way of thinking most certainly does, and so do the two chief villains of the unfinished text, Descartes and Montaigne.

Herbert of Cherbury might have not shown up in Pascal's fragmentary magnum opus, but he was there in spirit, along with numerous others who preferred to make religion thoroughly reasonable. Leaderless and lacking in unity, but far from ineffectual, deists pursued their rational critique of Christianity and organized religion somewhat stealthily for decades, up through the 1670s, when, suddenly, they would coalesce and become much more aggressive and outspoken. One of the first of these new deists was Charles Blount (1654–1693), an English aristocrat, whose unique contribution was his snide critique of Christianity through ancient classical sources. Blount would quickly be overshadowed by two formidable deists, John Locke and John Toland (1670–1722).

At the outermost edge of the Reformation era, John Locke would turn the traditional Christian dialectic between faith and reason on its head by proposing that empirical observation and rational thought were the basis of all truth. Faith could propose truths beyond sensory experience, he argued, but no truth could ever be contradictory to reason.

In his *Essay Concerning Human Understanding* (1690), Locke denied the existence of innate ideas—that centerpiece of Herbert of Cherbury's philosophy—proposing instead that the human mind is a blank slate on which sensation writes its impressions. The mind, in turn, arrives at what is true by processing the data it obtains through the senses. Nothing outside of this tightly closed epistemological loop could ever be considered true, argued Locke. His purpose in this essay was to show that anything that claimed to be "knowledge" or "truth" could be judged by the mind on the basis of its experience. Christianity, therefore, was to be subjected to the same rigorous tests as any empirical scientific proposition.

Locke would expand and deepen his rational critique of religion in *The Reasonableness of Christianity* (1695), in which he argued that the deepest truths of the Christian religion were its ethical precepts, and these could never be contrary to reason. In other words, Locke updated the argument for a natural religion by proposing that every human being was capable of comprehending the ethical duties required for salvation, all of which were reasonable. So, while Locke undid the deism of Herbert of Cherbury by denying the existence of innate ideas, he gave shape to a new sort of deism based on empirical observation and a logical approach to religion as an ethical code that was accessible to all human beings rather than as an esoteric muddle of dogmas, symbols, and rituals.

John Toland, who was nearly forty years younger than Locke, made his chief contribution to deism around the same time. In 1696 Toland came out with his own interpretation of religion, titled *Christianity Not Mysterious*, which was far more radical than Locke's work. Toland's chief argument was as simple as it was revolutionary: he denied the possibility of divine revelation. This meant that there was nothing sacred about the Bible, and that nothing contained in it that was of any worth could be contrary to reason. Christ and his apostles were no miracle-working dogmatists, but enlightened rationalists who aimed to "convince the mind." His twelve apostles, in sum, could be mistaken for deists: "The scope of the Apostles," Toland said, was not to impose "their Authority and Sophistry" upon others. Their goal was to "dispel Ignorance, to eradicate Superstition, to propagate Truth, and Reformation of Manners." Toland also denied the possibility of miracles on the grounds that the laws of nature were inviolable. "Whatever is contrary to Reason can be no Miracle," he argued, "for that contradiction is only another word for Impossible or Nothing." In his conclusion Toland compared himself to the first Protestant Reformers, claiming their revolutionary mantle as his own, absolving himself of any collateral damage he could cause, and admitting that the initial Protestant message was indeed the first step in the unraveling of religion:

> Because several turn'd Libertines and Atheists when Priest-Craft was laid so open at the Reformation, were Luther, Calvin, or Zwinglius to be blam'd for it? Or which should weigh most with them, these few prejudic'd scepticks, or those thousands they converted from the Superstitions of Rome?[17]

Neither a great philosopher nor the best of writers, Toland is significant because of the controversy he caused, which polarized elite society in his own time and magnified the influence of deism. Toland, like Locke, is a transitional figure. Both men are at once heirs of the Protestant Reformation and progenitors of the Enlightenment of the eighteenth century—as unequally responsible for the materialistic atheism of Julien Offray de La Mettrie's *Man the Machine* (1748) as for the optimistic self-evident truths of Thomas Jefferson's Declaration of Independence (1776), and the frigid logical piety of Immanuel Kant's *Religion Within the Limits of Reason Alone* (1793). And their contributions, as well as those of all skeptics, libertines, deists, and atheists covered thus far, cannot be fully understood without taking into account the seventh and most potent challenge to religion in the early modern era: the scientific revolution.

Empirical Science

Nicholas Copernicus, the pioneering astronomer who first proposed that the earth circles the sun, was an exact contemporary of Luther. Both men revolutionized their world, at the same time, in very different ways, a mere 432 miles from each other. Copernicus began his revolution very quietly around 1514, three years before Luther's, by distributing a forty-page manuscript to a few trusted friends. In it he proposed—on the basis of mathematical calculations and astronomical observations—that the sun was stationary and the planets circled it. Unlike Luther, who became one of the best-known figures of his day, Copernicus lived and died in relative obscurity, and only a small number of people would be aware of the revolution he was ushering in. Unlike Luther, who felt compelled to publish his ideas, Copernicus shrank back from going public, and hung on tightly to his manuscript for nearly thirty years. According to legend, the first printed copy of his paradigm-shattering book, *On the Revolutions of the Heavenly Spheres*, was placed in his hands as he lay dying in 1542, and after glancing at it, he passed away. It would be left to others, over the following century, to change the world's perspective on the heavens.

The theory formulated by Copernicus was based on empirical observation, an approach to the study of the material world that would become the very essence of modern science. Empiricism (from Greek *empeiria*, "experience") is a method of investigation that has little or no regard for established authorities. It requires scientists to observe and analyze facts, to formulate a theory or a hypothesis, and to verify the validity of all formulations through rigorous tests. In other words, this empirical research method privileges sensory data, human reason, and individual judgment over all other propositions, including those found in the Bible or the doctrines of the church.

This new way of obtaining knowledge represented by Copernicus would eventually clash with religion and become a rival to it, but in Copernicus's own day, faith and reason were not necessarily incompatible. Nor were religious identities. *On the Revolutions of the Heavenly Spheres*, the work of a Catholic scientist, had been printed in

Nuremberg, a Lutheran city, under the supervision of one of the leading theologians of the Protestant Reformation, Andreas Osiander. The book had ended up in Nuremberg, in Osiander's hands, thanks to a mathematician from Luther's University of Wittenberg, Georg Joachim Rheticus, who had been sent to Poland in 1539 by Philip Melanchthon to study with Copernicus and had become his pupil. Osiander, the theologian, even wrote a preface to *On the Revolutions*, defending its integrity.

Such support, however, was far from universal. Faith and reason had clashed throughout the Middle Ages, and this unresolved tension carried through to the sixteenth and seventeenth centuries. As modern science emerged, the tension increased. One question above all drove the uneasy dialogue: how to reconcile divinely revealed truths with the findings of human reason, especially in cases when the dictates of reason seemed to contradict revelation. Although Copernicus's theory was accepted by Philip Melanchthon, and would later be promoted by scholars at Wittenberg, Luther was not at all taken by it. Here is what Anthony Lauterbach, a frequent dinner guest of Luther's, recorded the great man as saying one evening in June 1539:

> There was mention of a certain new astrologer who wanted to prove that the earth moves and not the sky, the sun, and the moon. This would be as if somebody were riding on a cart or in a ship and imagined that he was standing still while the earth and the trees were moving. [Luther remarked,] "So it goes now. Whoever wants to be clever must agree with nothing that others esteem. He must do something of his own. This is what that fellow does who wishes to turn the whole of astronomy upside down. Even in these things that are thrown into disorder I believe the Holy Scriptures, for Joshua commanded the sun to stand still, and not the earth."[18]

John Calvin was not too keen on Copernicus either, and in one of his sermons he railed against his heliocentric theory: "We shall find some who are so stark raving mad, not only in matters of religion, but showing their monstrous nature in all things, that they will even say that the sun does not budge, and that it is the earth that bestirs itself and that turns around."[19]

So began a complex and sometimes very troubled relationship between religion and the emerging natural sciences. At bottom, it was an epistemic tug of war, with religion pulling for revelation and science pulling for empirical observation and experimentation. The new epistemology represented by Copernicus sought truth in observations, calculations, research, and tests. Venerable authorities were not to be trusted. Not even one's senses could be relied on entirely. This kind of thinking was not intrinsically incompatible with revealed religion, but it was often viewed by clerics as too much of a challenge, for if the teachings of the Bible and the churches could be proved wrong on any one point, then, perhaps, other points could be called into question as well. Fear of the slippery slope of doubt and of its potential consequences kept many elites from embracing the new epistemology with enthusiasm. At bottom, then, the challenge posed by scientific empiricism was that it proposed an alternative access to truth that bypassed the divine revelation guarded by the churches.

Not all new discoveries were threatening, however, and this kept science and religion from clashing constantly. A case in point is that of the physician Andreas Vesalius (1514–1564), an exact contemporary of Calvin who dissected human corpses and published a very thoroughly researched anatomical atlas, *On the Structure of the Human Body*, in 1543, at about the same time as Copernicus's *On the Revolutions* appeared. Vesalius was not the first physician to publish an atlas based on the study of dissected human corpses, but his book had so many detailed and accurate illustrations that it very quickly became the standard authority. Vesalius's discoveries challenged the ancient authority of Galen (second century A.D.), whose information had been based on the dissection of apes rather than humans. Proving Galen wrong on many points posed no threat to the revealed truths of Christianity, even as the proofs themselves increased the acceptability of the empirical method.

New discoveries made throughout the second half of the sixteenth century offered little threat to religious truths, but as the acceptance of empirical research spread among the learned, the theories and teachings of ancient non-Christian authorities such as Aristotle, Ptolemy, and Galen began to be displaced. In astronomy, the dismantling of the classical cosmos continued apace, especially through the work of Tycho Brahe (1546–1601) and his disciple and assistant Johannes Kepler (1571–1630).

Brahe, a Lutheran, improved upon astronomy through the construction of new and more accurate instruments and the gathering of information at observatories he had designed, where he worked with other astronomers. His detailed observations corrected a good number of previously unquestioned assumptions, including calculations of the planetary orbits and of the trajectories of comets that proved—through mathematics—that Ptolemy was wrong about the celestial bodies being fixed in crystalline spheres, and that Aristotle, too, was wrong about the perfection and immutability of the cosmos beyond the moon. Though Brahe would not accept Copernicus's heliocentric theory, he did reject the ancient models, and he proposed his own complex scheme instead, in which the earth remained at the center, with the sun and moon orbiting around it, and the planets orbiting around the sun. Above it all, the fixed stars were centered on the earth. It was an elegant, yet unnecessarily complicated compromise.

Brahe's findings were elaborated upon by his former assistant Johannes Kepler, who made great discoveries of his own. Kepler's life was deeply affected by three of the developments analyzed in previous chapters: disagreements over orthodoxy, the Thirty Years' War, and the witch hunts. Like Brahe, Kepler was a Lutheran, but his rejection of the Formula of Concord caused him to be excommunicated by the Lutheran Church. Since he refused to convert to Catholicism, he lived in a confessional limbo and had to move around quite often to escape persecution, especially after the outbreak of the Thirty Years' War, in 1618. He had a great-aunt who was burned as a witch, and he had to defend his mother against charges of witchcraft. His observations of the planets while working with Brahe led Kepler to formulate several new theories. First and foremost, he agreed with Copernicus and published a defense of his heliocentric theory. He also calculated the planetary orbits so accurately that he was able to prove that they were elliptical (rather than perfectly circular), and as a result, he also discovered the formula for the three laws of planetary motion that still bear his name. In addition, Kepler was the first to propose that the tides on earth are caused by the moon, and that the sun rotates on its own axis. On top of this, he laid the basis for the development of integral calculus. A deeply pious man—though a nonconformist—Kepler saw no conflict at all between religion and science, and claimed he was brought to an ecstatic "sacred madness" by his discoveries.[20] Convinced that astronomy was the surest path to God, Kepler attributed all of his discoveries to divine inspiration.

As Kepler forged ahead with his investigations another mathematician and scientist in Italy was busy making all sorts of new discoveries: Galileo Galilei (1564–1642). Often referred to as the "father of modern astronomy" or the "father of physics" or even the "father of modern science," Galileo embodied the emerging conflict between science and religion. Found guilty of heresy by the Roman Inquisition in 1633 for defending the Copernican heliocentric theory and forced to recant, Galileo also holds a special place in history as a martyr for empiricism. Like Kepler—with whom he corresponded—Galileo employed mathematics and new optical technology in his astronomical observations. In 1609 he built his own improved telescope, and turning it to the heavens, he discovered evidence that proved Aristotle and Ptolemy wrong and called into question fundamental assumptions about the cosmos.

One of his great discoveries was the presence of mountains and craters on the moon. The moon had no smooth surface and was not "purer" than the earth, as the ancient authorities had taught. He also discovered moons orbiting around Jupiter, which proved that the earth was not the absolute center of all motion in the heavens. Turning his telescope to Venus, he discovered that it went through phases, with a large shadow passing over its surface in a steady and predictable rhythm, just like the earth's moon, which proved that Mercury must stand between Venus and the sun, and that the sun was the center of all planetary orbits. In addition, he found spots on the sun, and discovered that the Milky Way was an unimaginably large collection of individual stars. All of these findings, significant as they were by themselves, led Galileo to formulate an even more surprising and novel thesis: that the laws of motion here on earth are the same throughout the entire cosmos. In other words, the heavens were not special at all, or purer, or some vastly different region. The universe was one vast assemblage of material bodies in motion that whirled about according to specific laws discernible to the human mind. This view of the cosmos did away with the seven heavenly spheres, including the highest of all, the empyrean heaven, where, as the church taught, there was no motion, and no time, and God dwelled in eternity—the heaven where Jesus dwelt at the right hand of the Father along with all the saints and where all who were saved would dwell forever. Galileo's cosmos had no locus for God, no place at all for motionlessness and eternity.

No longer the center of the universe, the earth now seemed a mere speck among many, adrift in that boundless expanse of nothingness that was once known as heaven.

The existential *axis mundi* that made human beings the ultimate purpose of creation had not just shifted, but had vanished altogether, along with God's eternal realm. All that was out there was boundless space, flecked with lifeless orbs, all of which gyrated with mathematical precision, much like the innards of a clock. From that time forward, no one who was well educated could envision heaven or eternity itself as part of the visible universe. The poet John Donne (1572–1631) reacted to this paradigm shift:

> And new Philosophy calls all in doubt,
> The Element of fire is quite put out;
> The Sun is lost, and th' earth, and no man's wit
> Can well direct him where to look for it. . . .
> 'Tis all in pieces, all coherence gone.[21]

The gifted mathematician, inventor, and philosopher Blaise Pascal (1623–1662) gave voice to this trauma in starker terms, saying, "The eternal silence of these infinite spaces fills me with dread. . . . I see the terrifying spaces of the universe that surround me. . . . I see nothing but infinities on all sides, surrounding me like an atom and like a shadow that lasts only for an instant and returns no more."[22]

So it was that the heaven of old was displaced, that heaven which was one with the sky above, always visible. The Copernican revolution that Galileo convincingly defended was not only a conceptual paradigm shift, but also a spatial, spiritual, and dimensional one. Many of the most important prayers recited by Christians in church had this heaven in them, as a spatial point of reference. For starters, the new heaven required a wholly new understanding of key prayers—the Gloria, "Glory to God in the *highest*"; the Sanctus, "*heaven* and earth are filled with thine Glory"; the Lord's Prayer, "Our Father who art in heaven"; and the Apostles' Creed, "Jesus Christ . . . who for us men and for our salvation came *down* from heaven. . . . And he *ascended* into heaven, and sits at the right hand of the Father." Before the Copernican revolution in astronomy, heaven was a location, and eternity too; this older heaven shared a boundary with the physical universe and with time. But then, suddenly, anyone who accepted what Copernicus, Kepler, and Galileo proposed had to admit, at least at the rational level, that such a heaven did not exist. As Galileo examined the night sky through his telescope, this old heaven vanished like a puff of smoke. Banished from physics, heaven went into exile in metaphysics, but it would vanish from that location too, in another puff of smoke after being called into question by fiercer skeptics in the eighteenth century.

Galileo started publishing his findings in 1610, with a text titled *The Starry Messenger*, which brought him wide acclaim and condemnation simultaneously. In 1616, even as he was carrying out some of his most daring investigations, he was reprimanded by the church and warned not to defend Copernicus or the heliocentric theory. That same year, Copernicus's *On the Revolutions* was placed on the *Index of Forbidden Books*. This did not deter Galileo, however, especially because he had friends in very high places, including the Jesuit theologian Cardinal Roberto Bellarmino and Cardinal Maffeo

Revolutionary science. This frontispiece to the first edition of Galileo's *Dialogue on the Two Chief World Systems* tried to soften the revolutionary impact of the book's contents by bridging past and present, and pairing ancient authorities with a modern one. The two figures on the left are Aristotle and Ptolemy, arguably the two most revered scientific authorities from antiquity. The figure on the right is Nicholas Copernicus, the sixteenth-century Polish astronomer who proved through mathematical calculations and empirical observation of the night sky that the earth revolved around the sun, rather than vice versa, as had been thought since the dawn of civilization. Unfortunately for Galileo, this frontispiece did not prevent this work from being placed in the *Index of Forbidden Books.*

Barberini, who would go on to become Pope Urban VIII. In 1623 Galileo published *The Assayer*, a sharp-edged attack on a Jesuit astronomer's interpretation of comets. This book, which cost him the support of the Jesuit order, contained a succinct summary of his philosophy, and of the challenge he offered to theologically centered worldviews:

> Philosophy is written in this grand book—I mean the universe—which stands continually open to our gaze, but it cannot be understood unless one first learns to comprehend the language and interpret the characters in which it is written. It is written in the language of mathematics, and its characters are triangles, circles, and other geometrical figures, without which it is humanly impossible to understand a single word of it; without these, one is wandering around in a dark labyrinth.[23]

Galileo's confidence in his intellectual gifts and in his personal connections would cost him dearly. In 1632, he published his *Dialogue Concerning the Two Chief World Systems*, in which he presented arguments for and against the earth- and sun-centered planetary systems—in a dialogue format—but also ably defended Copernican heliocentrism through one of the text's interlocutors. Very quickly, he was hauled before the Inquisition in Rome, which saw right through his thinly veiled ruse. As one of the inquisitors noted:

> Although in the beginning of his book Galileo claims to want to deal with the earth's motion as a hypothesis, in the course of his *Dialogue* he puts the hypothesis aside and proves its motion absolutely, using unconditional arguments. Thus from absolute

premises he draws an absolute conclusion, and sometimes he feels that his reasons are convincing.[24]

Galileo defended himself in two ways. First, he argued that "in disputes about natural phenomena one must begin not with the authority of scriptural passages but with sensory experience and necessary demonstrations." Since both nature and the Bible came "equally from the Godhead," there could be no real contradictions. Besides, the revelation contained in the Bible, inspired by the Holy Spirit, concerned itself with "how one goes to heaven" rather than with "how heaven goes."[25] Second, he argued that the heliocentric theory was not opposed to divine revelation because the Bible should not always be taken literally. His findings did not contradict Scripture, he argued, because the sacred texts were written from a subjective point of view, poetically rather than scientifically. And to prove his point, he repeatedly cited St. Augustine. But he was digging an even deeper hole for himself, for he was a mere layman, with no authority to interpret Holy Writ. Presented with a list of all of his errors and ordered to recant all of them, Galileo signed a confession on 22 June 1633, which read, in part:

> With a sincere heart and unfeigned faith I abjure, curse, and detest the above-mentioned errors and heresies, and in general each and every other error, heresy, and sect contrary to the Holy Church; and I swear that in the future I will never again say or assert, orally or in writing, anything which might cause a similar suspicion about me.[26]

Legend has it that after signing this recantation, Galileo stomped his foot and muttered under his breath, "It still moves," in reference to the orbiting earth. These details may be as much of a fabrication as the inkwell hurled at the devil by Luther, but the expression sums up the scientist's frustration so well that it has nonetheless endured. Galileo spent the last nine years of his life under house arrest in a villa outside of Florence, silenced and humiliated by clerics who found his work too disturbing. The challenge he posed to faith was deemed far too great, even by men who agreed with him silently.

Francis Bacon (1561–1626) was another scientist who posed a threat to traditional faith, but, unlike Galileo, he was never forced to abjure his views by any church. Bacon, an English aristocrat, is often called the father of empiricism and the scientific method. A member of Parliament for thirty-seven years until expelled on charges of corruption in 1621, Bacon spent considerable time philosophizing and writing treatises that contributed to the advancement of the scientific worldview. Bacon's wildly independent mind scoffed at revered authorities from early on. Educated at Trinity College, Cambridge, he would later refer to his education as "degenerate learning" and to his tutors as "men of sharp wits, shut up in their cells of a few authors, chiefly Aristotle, their Dictator."[27] Equally loathsome to him was Christian dogmatism.

Bacon embarked upon the development a new philosophical foundation for science, and through science, for all of society. Conquering and subduing nature, advancing knowledge, shedding divine control and assuming full autonomy were his ultimate goals for the human race. The linchpin of his great project was the inductive method of research, through which empirical experimentation would allow one to verify or deny the truth of any hypothesis or proposition. And the key to this approach, as he saw it, was the absolute separation of rational investigation from religion and adherence to an unconditional skepticism toward all preconceived assumptions about the natural world. In essence, Bacon's outlook was not just intensely materialistic and uncongenial to revealed theology, but also immensely confident in the powers of human reason, and intensely teleological: the purpose of human existence was to decipher the inner workings of nature and to harness it, as much as possible. Moreover, skepticism was the key to knowledge: "If a man will begin with certainties, he shall end in doubts" warned Bacon, "but if he will be content to begin with doubts he shall end in certainties." In *The Advancement of Learning* (1605), Bacon summed up his quest to King James I—to whom he dedicated the book—in one terse, cocky question: "For why should a few received authors stand up like Hercules columns, beyond which there should be no sailing or discovering?"[28]

Bacon's intellectual ambition seemed limitless. His goal was to "penetrate to the more secret and remote parts of nature" with "a more certain, better-grounded way and a more certain and altogether better intellectual procedure."[29] His method—so radically new then and so habitual nowadays—called for experimentation, for the assembly of data and its interpretation, and for the unlocking of all that was hidden in the universe. Observing the regularities of nature was essential, for truth itself was to be found in those regularities, not in any ancient text or any religious symbol or ritual, or in any of the "idols" of the human mind. These incendiary propositions would be developed most clearly in Bacon's *The New Organon* (1620), which was but one part of a much larger work he never completed: *The Great Instauration*. Toward the end of his life, Bacon's assertions grew even bolder. In his posthumously published *New Atlantis* (1627), for instance, he argued that sheer materialism and atheism were much more conducive to the fulfillment of human needs than were Christianity's otherworldly promises.

Bacon turned out to be quite a prophet, though he would not have felt comfortable with such a designation. The epistemology and methodology he championed not only took hold, but also flourished, and with each new discovery, secured their dominance, step by steady step. And each new revelation brought forth by the scientists seemed to raise more questions than it answered, especially when it came to long-held assumptions and established truths. William Harvey (1578–1657) improved upon Vesalius and Michael Servetus by mapping the cardiopulmonary system in the human body and fully explaining its workings. Gradually, empirical research began to define medical science and to make the human body more machinelike and less spiritual or mysterious, and, at the same time, make ancient authorities such as Galen and newcomers such as Paracelsus obsolete.

Robert Boyle (1627–1691), who was convinced of the atomic substructure of reality, applied the empirical method to the study of substances and did much to separate the quasi-occult science of alchemy from what we now know as the science of chemistry. His influential 1661 treatise *The Sceptical Chymist; or, Chymico-Physical Doubts & Paradoxes* summed up in its title the very essence of the scientific revolution it represented, with its reference to both skepticism and doubt.

William Oughtred (1575–1660) made an incalculable contribution to the advance of science by inventing the slide rule in 1622, a mathematical instrument for multiplying and dividing that remained in use until the 1970s, when it was replaced by electronic devices. At a much higher level, Isaac Newton (1642–1727) and Gottfried Wilhelm Leibniz (1646–1716) would both invent calculus, a problem-solving branch of mathematics that undergirded all subsequent advances in physics, engineering, economics, and higher mathematics. Newton also discovered the law of gravity and made great strides in the science of optics and the design of telescopes—before he turned his attention to the Bible and a quest for a scientific law of prophecy.

Just as Newton improved on Galileo when it came to making telescopes and analyzing the workings of the universe and celestial bodies, so did Anton van Leeuwenhoek (1632–1723) improve on Galileo's microscope (*occhialino*) and on the exploration of a whole other universe, smaller than any ever imagined. Achieving greater magnification, Leeuwenhoek was the first to see and describe bacteria and single-cell organisms, spermatozoa, the circulation of blood corpuscles in capillaries, and a host of other startling marvels not mentioned in the Bible. In England, Robert Hooke (1635–1703) got the lion's share of attention through his book *Micrographia* (1665), which achieved three firsts: it was the first book to describe observations made through a microscope, the first scientific best seller, and the first major publication of the Royal Society of London for Improving Natural Knowledge—which was itself the world's first learned society dedicated solely to science.

A century later, during the French Revolution, after the cathedral of Notre Dame in Paris had been transformed into the Temple of Reason, some hardcore atheists would

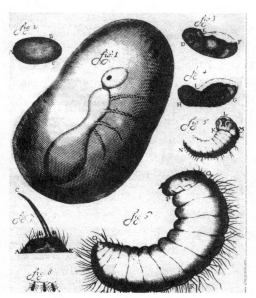

Microscopic bombshells. As the telescope revealed hidden truths about heavenly wonders too distant to see with the naked eye, the microscope opened a window into the previously unseen realm of incredibly small things. It could be argued, then, that the expansion of the universe in two directions made possible by the science of optics—both of seemingly infinite dimensions— forced human beings to reconsider the nature of reality and of their place in the universe in ways no philosophy or religion had ever considered. These illustrations of ant eggs and larvae are from Antoni van Leeuwenhoek's own microscope observations, which he sent to the Royal Society on 9 September 1687.

earnestly suggest that scientists become the new priestly class and that their experiments be revered as sacraments. This most extreme of all of the many trajectories taken by early modern rationalists would be held up by generations of traditional Christian historians as emblematic of the struggle into which Christians were thrown by the rise of rationalism and modern science, and also as the ultimate logical outcome of that movement. The fact that the Temple of Reason and its scientist-priests did not last very long at all mattered little; the mere fact that they came to be at all proved the magnitude of the dichotomies and tensions set into place in the seventeenth century.

Reasonable Faith

By the mid-seventeenth century, at the close of the Thirty Years' War, the splintering of Christendom that had begun in 1517 had reached its peak. This is not to say that the fracturing stopped; for on the contrary, it accelerated. Fundamental social, political, and cultural changes had placed all Christian squabbling in a different frame of reference. After 1650 or so, the Christian religion steadily began to lose its supremacy. The religious pluralism that divided Europe began to include an ever-increasing number of doubters and skeptics who could scoff at tradition with impunity. Among the intellectual elites, especially in those lands that had been most ravaged by religious divisions, an alternative epistemology and a different view of the world began to take hold. As Thomas Sprat, the historian of the Royal Society, stated in 1667, "The universal disposition of this Age is bent upon a rational religion."[30] Ironically, the most intense period of Christianization in the history of the West had led to the advent of a secular de-Christianizing spirit and of a horde of rationalists who strained to purge their benighted cultures of the stain of traditional religion. Consequently, the churches that had labored to narrowly define their creeds, educate the lay folk, discipline the reprobate, and stamp out superstition and the devil, began to be dismissed by many as unreasonable domineering purveyors of the ultimate superstition.

Critiques of religion and of Christianity in particular grew in intensity through-out the seventeenth and eighteenth centuries, gaining ever more ground among educated elites who trusted reason rather than faith, Holy Writ, or ancient authorities. By the eighteenth century, these critics would be referring to their progressive movement as "enlightenment." No single phenomenon had caused this change. It developed much as a rogue wave does on the high seas, when a number of individual waves merge to form a colossal wall of water capable of sinking the largest of ships. In this chapter, we have traced several of the waves of doubt that combined and swept over fractured Christendom in the early modern age. These rationalistic waves flooded the ship of faith, but they did not sink it. Moreover, although many of these self-proclaimed enlightened critics claimed to base their arguments on reason, they often resorted to base ridicule and to less-than-rational rhetoric in their war against faith and established religion. Bombastic attacks full of vitriol—most of which were aimed at like-minded "enlightened" skeptics rather than at believers—could not cripple religion, much less strike a death blow against it at any level of society. At the very same time that Descartes and Bacon were crafting their gospels of doubt, traditional religion continued to thrive, among both the elites and the common folk. Beleaguered, but not crushed, the faithful moved on, adapting to an increasingly materialistic and secular world, learning to cope with its scorn. Though many ignored the rationalists, some heeded their prophetic critiques and found ways of reshaping and deepening their faith, or of incorporating it with rationalism. Others fought back instead.

Among those who took on skeptics like Descartes and Montaigne, Blaise Pascal arguably stands out as the most brilliant and perceptive. Though his genius made him atypical in every respect, Pascal was nonetheless the perfect adversary and perhaps also the most adept at expressing what it was about the life of faith that made it immune to even the most acerbic critiques. After all, he spoke the skeptics' logical tongue and shared their passion for making sense of the natural world as well as their commitment to empirical science: his credentials were unimpeachable. A child prodigy, Pascal had solved all of Euclid's theorems on his own by the age of twelve, and he published an impressive mathematical paper on conic sections by the time he was sixteen. Descartes at first refused at first to believe this paper could be the work of so young a child, and he attributed it to Pascal's father. Blaise Pascal also built the world's first digital calculating machine when he was nineteen, to help his tax-collector father in his work. He experimented with liquids and atmospheric pressure, invented the syringe and the hydraulic press, and proved by means of a mercury-filled tube that a vacuum can indeed exist in nature. Descartes—by now jealous of Pascal's achievements—mocked this experiment, quipping that Pascal had "too much vacuum in his head."[31] Since he was a compulsive gambler, Pascal also took to calculating odds at dice games, and in the process he laid the foundations for the theory of probability. This was not the profile one would ordinarily expect for a Christian apologist, but Pascal was far from ordinary.

On 23 November 1654, Pascal experienced an intense, direct encounter with the divine realm. We know of this mystical experience because he wrote down a brief description of it that was sewn into the lining of his coat and found by chance after his death. This cryptic document, known as "The Memorial" defies analysis. But it is the clearest window we have on to Pascal's mind and soul. In part, it reads as follows:

> From about half past ten in the evening until half past midnight.
> Fire
> God of Abraham, God of Isaac, God of Jacob, not of philosophers and scholars.
> Certainty, certainty, heartfelt, joy, peace.
> God of Jesus Christ.
> God of Jesus Christ.
> My God and your God.
> 'Thy God shall be my God.'
> The world forgotten, and everything except God.

He can only be found by the ways taught in the Gospels.
Greatness of the human soul.
'O righteous Father, the world had not known thee, but I have known thee.'
Joy, joy, joy, tears of joy. . . .
Jesus Christ.
Jesus Christ.
I have cut myself off from him, shunned him, denied him, crucified him.
Let me never be cut off from him! . . .
Sweet and total renunciation
Total submission to Jesus Christ . . .
Everlasting joy in return for one day's effort on earth.
I will not forget thy word. Amen.[32]

Pascal's involvement with the Jansenist movement and his unfinished defense of the supreme value of faith—published as his *Pensées*—can be best understood as extensions of an ineffable yet undeniable awareness of a supernatural dimension that undergirded all material existence but still transcended it. The very structure of the *Pensées*, as well as its patchy contents, testify to this awareness. Pascal, the rationalist genius who devoted most of his life to unlocking the secrets of the material world, wrote the *Pensées* to convince his fellow diehard rationalists that human beings could never be ultimately satisfied by earthly life, or by reason alone. This world, he argued, was much too absurd for rational beings. And the rational beings were far too irrational, driven by impulses and fears they could never conquer, much less understand:

> This is our true state; this is what makes us incapable of certain knowledge and of absolute ignorance. We float on a vast ocean, ever uncertain and adrift, blown this way or that. Whenever we think we have some point to which we can cling and fasten ourselves, it shakes free and leaves us behind. And if we follow it, it eludes our grasp, slides away, and escapes forever. Nothing stays still for us. This is our natural condition and yet the one farthest from our inclination. We burn with desire to find firm ground and an ultimate secure base on which to build a tower reaching up to the infinite. But our whole foundation cracks, and the earth opens up into abysses.[33]

The so-called existentialist philosophers of the twentieth century owed much to Pascal, although not their nihilism. For Pascal no abyss was greater than that of death. It was the most irrational of all insults, the ultimate injustice in the face of which no rational being could ever be fulfilled. Death was the chief source of human misery, a cruel conundrum that no reasoning could explain away. Yet it was also the chief distinction of the human race. "Man's greatness," he argued, "lies in his knowing himself to be wretched."[34] Ultimately, though, human consciousness was superior to the entire material universe:

> Man is but a reed, the most feeble thing in nature, but he is a thinking reed. The entire universe need not arm itself to crush him. A vapor, a drop of water, suffices to kill him. But if the universe were to crush him, man would still be more noble than that which

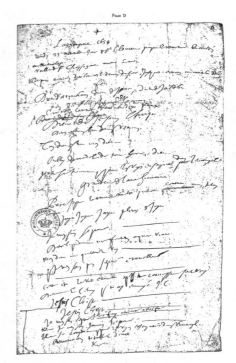

Soul on fire. Blaise Pascal was one of the most brilliant mathematicians and scientists of his day, yet he saw no contradiction between faith and reason and devoted himself to defending the absolute value of his Catholic beliefs, as well as his Jansenism. His description of an intense mystical rapture he experienced in 1654—a document known as "Pascal's Memorial"—was found after his death in the lining of a coat. The text contrasts the biblical "God of Abraham, Isaac and Jacob" with "the God of the philosophers" and equates feeling on "fire" to having "certitude." Here we see the furiously scrawled text of this document, in Pascal's own hand. In his unfinished defense of the Christian faith, published posthumously, Pascal challenged doubters most succinctly by observing: "the heart has its reasons, which reason cannot understand."

killed him, because he knows that he dies and the advantage which the universe has over him; the universe knows nothing of this.[35]

The only way to fulfillment, Pascal argued, was to latch on to the eternal, to God himself, and to lead a virtuous life that would be rewarded with eternal contemplation of the divine. Pascal the gambler, the conjurer of probability, chose a wager as his final argument. Bet on the existence of God, he proposed to his fellow rationalists, for you have nothing to lose, and much to gain if he does exist. If you assume that God exists and commit yourself to the virtuous life demanded by his Ten Commandments, and if it turns out that he does not exist after all, then you will have lived a virtuous life before you are extinguished. That, in and of itself, he said, was a life worth living, a nod by Pascal to the deists and skeptics who wanted to reduce religion to ethics. If God does exist, however, having wagered on his existence and on the necessity of a virtuous life will bring unimaginable rewards. Conversely, having lived as if God did not exist, ignoring his commandments will be disastrous, for if God does exist he shall surely demand justice. There is but one reasonable bet to make.

Pascal's wager was a scientist's response to materialistic rationalism and to the threats it posed for the Christian faithful. This wager—and the *Pensées* as a whole— brings us face-to-face with the enormous changes that had taken place between 1517 and 1654, the year of Pascal's mystical encounter with the God of Abraham, Isaac, and Jacob. By 1654, the Christian religion no longer gave shape and meaning to culture in the West as it had for more than a millennium, and it was being gradually supplanted by an inchoate faith in rationalism, from the top down, and by secularism, from all directions. Undeniable though these changes were, they did not define the age as a whole. Faith and religious devotion were far from dead. Some might argue that religion had never been more lively, or more exuberant, not even in the so-called age of faith that had just ostensibly faded away. Some, however, would prefer to see this undeniable ebullience as no more than nervous blustering in the face of impending doom.

CHAPTER TWENTY-FIVE

The Age of Outcomes

C hanging the world had been the objective of all reformers, both Catholic and Protestant. Some reformers had more grandiose goals than others, but all shared the same conviction: somehow, they hoped, their efforts would lessen the gap between the ideal and the actual. The second half of the sixteenth century and most of the seventeenth century became a time of reckoning, when the ideals and goals of all reforming visions were put into effect, or came to fruition, or were tested by events. In summary, it was an age of outcomes: the endpoint and eventual unfolding of the Reformations. To analyze how these efforts played out, especially in regard to the role religion should play in "the world," is to sum up the legacy of the Reformations.

Dealing with "the World"

In 1589 an instruction manual titled *The Spiritual Combat* was published in Venice, full of advice on how to become absolutely perfect. It was an outrageous goal, yet this text did not consider it at all unrealistic or impossible. Aiming for perfection, it argued, was required by the Christian religion, which promised that one could become "so united to God as to become one Spirit with him." At the very same time, however, the text admitted that reaching such a goal was indeed "the hardest of all struggles." It also let the reader know on its very first page that there were far too many misconceptions about the path to the goal. "If you seriously desire to attain to those high Degrees of Perfection that the Christian Religion calls you to," read the opening lines in an early English translation, "it will be necessary for you in the first place to know wherein true Perfection of a spiritual Life consists." Then the author let loose a tirade against widely accepted external earmarks of holiness:

> Many . . . have thought that perfection consists of leading an austere Life, in great Mortifications of the Body, in much Fasting, Watching, and like rigorous Exercises;

others, especially Women, think this perfection consists in the Repetition and daily Recital of many Prayers, in hearing many Sermons, and frequenting the Church, and the Sacraments, and many also of them, that are accounted good and religious persons, persuade themselves that all they have to do is to be silent and reserved, and to live at home retired, and at quiet in a sober and regular manner . . . but all are far short of their desired Perfection, and are deceived in the right way leading to it.[1]

In some ways, this complaint was old hat by 1589, and what the text proposed was not much different from what Erasmus had advised eight decades earlier: genuine holiness

A new world of meaning. By 1596, when this map was produced by the Dutch Protestant Jodocus Hondius, the meaning of "the world" had taken a new visual turn for many Europeans because of their engagement in exploration, trade, colonization, and missionary enterprises. Here we see the allegorical and literal meaning of "world" combined and set into a new context. Against the backdrop of a fairly accurate map of the continents and oceans of planet earth, Hondius depicts a very traditional set of figures that actually transcend the Catholic-Protestant divide: an allegorical Christian knight guided by the Holy Spirit (*spiritus*, above his head) is engaged in battle with the world (*mundus*), sin (*peccatum*), the flesh (*caro*), the devil (*diabolus*), and death (*mors*). The allegorical figures are as carefully labeled and explained as the world map that dwarfs them.

requires a total inner surrender to the divine rather than faith in externals. Unlike Erasmus, however, the author of this text spent no time ridiculing external devotions or poking fun at superstitions. This unquestionably Catholic book was a manifesto for a new sort of piety, and a new approach to perfection.

Written in Italian rather than Latin, this manual was aimed at lay folk, although its title, *The Spiritual Combat* had a monastic ring to it. Monks and nuns were the real experts in perfection seeking, and engaging in spiritual warfare was an ancient trope in monastic literature. A thousand years earlier, the first lines of the Rule of St. Benedict had sounded a battle cry: "Listen carefully, my son . . . and incline the ear of your heart. To you my words are now addressed, whoever you may be, who are renouncing your own will *to do battle* under the Lord Christ, the true King, and are taking up the strong, bright *weapons* of obedience." Erasmus had invoked martial imagery too, in his elitist and acerbic *Enchiridion; or, Manual of the Christian Soldier*. But this new text of 1589 was imbued with a very different spirit, more egalitarian, more reverent of tradition, and convinced of the transformations that could take place in everyone.

The Spiritual Combat was an instant success, and a phenomenal best seller. Over the following two decades, more than sixty editions would be published in Italian, German, French, English, Spanish, and Latin. Others would follow in Polish, Croatian, Portuguese, Armenian, Greek, Arabic, and even Japanese. In Russia, a nineteenth-century Orthodox monk published a paraphrase titled *The Invisible Fight*. That copycat Russian monk was following a long tradition, too, for *The Spiritual Combat* had a way of multiplying itself through readers who felt compelled to distill its advice for different audiences. One of the readers was none other than the great Catholic reformer St. Francis de Sales, titular bishop of Geneva, who called the text "my Director," "the golden book," "the favorite book," "the dear book," and recommended it to everyone. He carried a copy in his pocket for two decades and read it every day, over and over. In due time Francis wrote his own devotional manual, *Introduction to the Devout Life*, which also became a best seller in many languages, including rare ones, such as Basque. And at no point in the following four hundred years would it ever go out of print. As was the case with *The Spiritual Combat*, De Sales's *Introduction* was even published in Protestant lands, carefully abridged, sometimes under a totally different title.

The author of *The Spiritual Combat* was most likely a Theatine priest, Lorenzo Scupoli (1530–1610), who hid his true identity behind the pen name of Juan de Castañiza. As a member of one of the new orders spawned by the Catholic Reformation, Scupoli embodied the new spirit of his church, and of his age, and was thus obsessed with the issues of improvement and perfection. The Reformations that had begun a generation before Scupoli's birth were all intensely concerned with perfection. Before Luther and Zwingli, Catholic reformers had already been intent on closing the gap between the ideal and the actual, that is, of reaching as much perfection in the here and now as possible, both personally and communally. Reforming the church in head and members also meant reforming the world, through a trickle-down effect. Moreover, Catholic soteriology had focused keenly on the issue of perfection, emphasizing that entry into heaven required a soul totally cleansed of all sin. To live out one's life as a Catholic, therefore, meant to aim for perfection, and sainthood. For those who could not meet that lofty goal on earth, purgatory would give them a second chance in the hereafter, through suffering.

Luther had rejected this soteriology, denying that moral or spiritual perfection could ever be achieved by any human, even with the aid of grace. Consequently, he also rejected purgatory and the institution of monasticism. But he could not dispense with the divine law altogether, and taught that good behavior would flow from the gift of grace. Zwingli and Karlstadt had agreed with Luther on this issue, but both of them were more keen on perfection than Luther, and both expected full adherence to the ten commandments, including the one against graven images. The Radicals, each in their own way, aimed for so much perfection that they chose to flee from "the world" and all its corruption—just like the monks they rejected and ridiculed—and to expel slackers and reprobates from their midst. For Catholics, the Council of Trent and all the reforms it spawned reaffirmed the need for perfection, and for closing the gap between the corrupt actuality of "the world" and the highest ideals of the Christian faith.

Perfection continued to be a burning issue in all major churches throughout the sixteenth century and well into the seventeenth, and it lay at the heart of the major doctrinal squabbles of the era, all of which concerned how much effort could be expected of the human will in the process of salvation. Lutherans and the Reformed wrestled with this question at a great cost to unity. Catholics expected a lot of effort, which made *The Spiritual Combat* so popular among them, and gave rise to the Quietist and Jansenist controversies. But what could have made *The Spiritual Combat* and De Sales's *Introduction to the Devout Life* popular among Protestants? What kernel of truth did Protestants find useful in such treatises, after they had been stripped of references to papal authority, the cult of the saints or transubstantiation?

That kernel had everything to do with the search for a transformation of life on earth—a genuine reform in behavior, both personal and social, which would close or at least shrink the gap between Christian ideals and everyday life. While skeptics and atheists multiplied like locusts, and theologians wrangled, and witches were hunted down, and blood was spilled in the name of religion, the very fabric of "the world" was being rewoven. Social disciplining was part of this effort to change behavior, but far from the sum of it all. Many other profound changes that transcended disciplining resulted from the Reformations, changes that differed among the various confessions and ultimately led to the creation of societies and cultures with significantly distinct traits. So, while it is possible to speak of a general trend of "Christianizing" and of social disciplining, it should never be assumed that all end results were necessarily similar. The ultimate legacy of the Reformations, after all, was the creation of a religiously fragmented Europe, with multiple churches, each of which approached "the world" and life on earth in different ways.

Ethics

Protestants and Catholics developed their ethical codes around the same core values, which were carefully enumerated in the ten commandments, the seven deadly sins, and the seven virtues. While these proscriptive lists assured a certain degree of compatibility between Protestant and Catholic societies—giving them both precise dos and don'ts— there is no denying that substantial differences also came into play. One key factor was hermeneutics (interpretation). For instance, the commandment against graven images was taken literally by Karlstadt, the Reformed, and the Radicals, but not by Lutherans or Catholics. Another key element was theology. For instance, while Catholics viewed the virtue of charity as indispensable for salvation, given their belief in a merit-based soteriology, Protestants sundered the connection between charity and redemption, given their rejection of works-righteousness. The result was the creation of very different public welfare systems in Catholic and Protestant societies. Similarly, Protestant soteriology made monasticism irrelevant and led to its elimination in Protestant societies. A third key factor was metaphysics, especially the way the relations between spiritual and material were conceived. For instance, among Catholics, the clergy were granted a separate social and political status because their consecration as priests and their daily commerce with the divine in the sacraments gave them an elevated ontological status, superior to that of the laity; among Protestants, their tendency to isolate spirit and matter stripped the clerical state of any claim to a superior social and political status. These are but three of the most significant conceptual variants. And social, cultural, political, and economic factors were always constantly informing thinking, for the influence between ideals and concrete realities always flowed in both directions.

The most significant differences between Catholic and Protestant ethical codes stemmed from distinctions between the sacred and the profane. Whereas medieval Catholicism had distinguished between "the world" and the church or between "the world" and Christian values, Protestants tended to redefine that distinction, making it less sharp and more complex. In response to Protestantism, early modern Catholics had to reassess their take on "the world." This basic distinction had never been an absolute dichotomy, but pious speech was riddled with dualistic imagery, such as the expression that spoke of "the world, the flesh, and the devil" as the antithesis of holiness, or that other expression "leaving the world," which referred to those who entered the monastic life. The advent of Protestantism brought new perspectives on the difference between sacred and profane, a distinction that, in turn, caused concrete social and political changes.

Political Life

In 1513, on the eve of the Protestant Reformation, the Florentine statesman Niccolò Machiavelli tackled one of the chief questions facing every Christian magistrate or ruler: is it possible to engage with "the world" in governing, policing, judging, or soldiering without violating Christian morals? Machiavelli's answer earned him the condemnation of both Catholics and Protestants:

> How men live is so different from how they should live that a ruler who does not do what is generally done, but persists in doing what ought to be done, will undermine his power rather than maintain it. If a ruler who wants always to act honorably is surrounded by many unscrupulous men his downfall is inevitable. Therefore, a ruler who wishes to maintain his power must be prepared to act immorally when this becomes necessary.[2]

Machiavelli was writing not a treatise on moral theology, but a guide to political success. Setting aside "fantasies about rulers," and taking into consideration only "what happens in fact" rather than what should happen, Machiavelli offered a coldly logical assessment. In essence, he was accepting and promoting a view of "the world" as wholly profane and incompatible with Christian virtues. The only "virtue" useful to rulers, he argued, was *virtù*, which was the exact opposite of Christian virtue: the ability to assess every situation individually and to act according to circumstances rather than any static values or religious commandments. Machiavelli's *virtù*, therefore, had everything to do with cunning, strength, and virility and nothing to do with a rigid ethical code. The ultimate virtue in "the world" was the ability to disregard virtue.

It was precisely this view of worldly affairs that had dominated Catholic thinking for a millennium, and had led to the exaltation of the monastic life as the surest path to salvation. Although there were some exceptions—kings, queens, and other rulers and lay people who ended up as canonized saints—generally, the terms *religious* and *spiritual* had a very specific meaning, referring to the clergy and those who left "the world" behind. Protestants refused to accept such an assumption, and in various ways they redrew the boundaries between the Christian and "the world," and the church and "the world."

Luther had a very complex and paradoxical approach to "the world" and the sacred and profane, given his conviction that every human was *simul justus et peccattor*, that is, a constant sinner who could nonetheless be redeemed. Yet his core message concerning political life proved very appealing to rulers of all sorts, from princes to urban magistrates.

Luther redefined the place of the clergy in society. And he did so as early as 1520, in his *Address to the Christian Nobility of the German Nation*, in which he rejected the existence of two classes of Christians, one "spiritual" and one "temporal." Arguing that all baptized Christians were "priests" and "spiritual" in God's sight, Luther demolished a basic distinction undergirding the social and political order of his day. He was careful to point out that this equality applied to status only, not to function, and that there would always be a need for specialists who dedicated themselves to ministering to the faithful. So, although he retained the clerical office, Luther's abolition of the old distinctions did have a practical impact, for it erased one of the most significant of all class distinctions, turning clerics into officials who were defined by their function as ministers of the Word rather than by any ontological or legally distinct status.

On the level of the civil rulers Luther also dismissed the traditional distinction between spiritual and temporal, with even more of a practical impact. Arguing that it was the duty of the civil rulers to oversee the church and to reform it when it refused to reform itself, Luther did more than demolish a basic distinction: he redefined the relationship of church and state completely. Though he still insisted on a distinction between body and spirit, Luther nullified such dichotomies, secularizing the church and spiritualizing the state:

> Inasmuch as the temporal power has become a member of the Christian body it is a spiritual estate, even though its work is physical. Therefore, its work should extend without hindrance to all the members of the whole body to punish and use force whenever guilt deserves or necessity demands, without regard to whether the culprit is pope, bishop, or priest.[3]

Luther thus simultaneously affirmed a basic dichotomy and blurred the line between church and state, the "world" and the Christian. The net effect of this third level of theorizing—known as Luther's doctrine of the two kingdoms—was a further secularizing of all things formerly "spiritual," and a further spiritualizing of things formerly "secular." His clearest articulation of the two-kingdom doctrine came in 1523, in the treatise *On Secular Authority: To What Extent It Should Be Obeyed*. Inspired by St. Augustine's distinction between the city of God and the city of Man, Luther proposed in this treatise that every Christian lives in two kingdoms simultaneously, one earthly and one spiritual, and the two are intertwined and inseparable. Ultimately, God governs the world, but he rules the earthly kingdom through secular and churchly authorities jointly, by the sword, that is, by means of laws and sheer compulsion, even violence. The spiritual kingdom is ruled by grace and the gospel, and it needs no compulsion or laws. "God has ordained the two governments: the spiritual, which by the Holy Spirit under Christ makes Christians and pious people; and the secular, which restrains the unchristian and wicked so that they are obliged to keep the peace outwardly." In addition, Luther argued that "all who are not Christians belong to the kingdom of the world and are under the law." Moreover, those who fell into this category were the vast majority of the human race, and this made laws and "the sword" even more necessary, for without these "men would devour one another, seeing that the whole world is evil and that among thousands there is scarcely a single true Christian."

Luther's conviction that original sin had corrupted the human race led him to stress an unavoidable imbalance in society. "The world and the masses are and always will be un-Christian, even if they are all baptized and Christian in name. Christians are few and far between," he proposed, adding that "the wicked always outnumber the good."[4] This imbalance meant that earthly laws, and the use of coercion, were not in any way beneath Christian godliness. On the contrary, because they ensured peace and order, they could be seen as an expression of brotherly love and "divine service." Magistrates, executioners, and soldiers therefore held a Christian office with as much godly dignity as ministers of the Word. In 1528, three years after he called for the slaughter of rebellious peasants, Luther would say:

> When I think of a soldier fulfilling his office by punishing the wicked, killing the wicked, and creating so much misery, it seems an un-Christian work completely contrary to Christian love. But when I think of how it protects the good and keeps and preserves wife and child, house and farm, property, and honor and peace, then I see how precious and godly this work is. . . . For the hand that wields this sword and kills with it is not man's hand, but God's; and it is not man, but God, who hangs, tortures, beheads, kills, and fights. All these are God's works and judgments.[5]

Luther had an ambivalent take on civil rulers, however, which kept him from collapsing the line between spiritual and temporal or between Church and state. On the one hand, he could call on them to reform the Church as "emergency bishops," or see them

Dealing with vice. This seventeenth century Italian engraving portrays the devil as a very busy shopkeeper whose store is always open, full of eager customers, and well stocked with the seven deadly sins. Early modern devotional literature, both Catholic and Protestant, tended to emphasize the dangers posed by temptation. When it came to ethics, at least, and to the omnipresent lure of sin and vice, Catholics and Protestants could agree on many points. But when it came to discerning the line between religion and politics or to deciding how involved the state should become in the enforcement of religious values, or the curbing of vices, disagreement was intense.

as divinely sanctioned avengers. On the other hand, he could disparage them. "You must know," he said, "that since the beginning of the world, a wise prince is a mighty rare bird, and an upright prince even rarer." Calling them "fools" and "scoundrels," he warned that not much good could be expected of them, especially "in divine matters which concern the salvation of souls." In fact, he added, any prince who happened to be a good Christian was "one of the greatest miracles."[6] Luther's paradoxical attitude toward civil rulers, and toward "the world" in general, was bequeathed to his followers. This stance led to the creation of a government-run church that was simultaneously dependent on civil rulers and mistrustful of them. It also led to a pragmatic ethic of civil service that did not privilege any office as holier or more spiritual than any other, at least in theory. In practice, the clergy continued to have a near monopoly on the spiritual life of the faithful. Most significant, the ambiguities and paradoxes of Luther's two-kingdom doctrine allowed for Christians to dirty their hands in the world and become active citizens. No longer was it necessary for a Christian to choose between two realms, or to place one under the other, or to mix the two. This solution to the problem of "the world" also prevented Lutherans from developing theocratic tendencies.

The Reformed, in contrast, had a more optimistic view of political life and a stronger conviction of its ability to mold citizens into good Christians. Unlike Luther, Zwingli had no fondness for paradoxes or dichotomies. As Zwingli saw it, Christians lived in a single sphere, not two kingdoms. He also believed that the magistrates of his own day were the successors of the elders of the New Testament Church, and that civil rulers, therefore, had authority over both church and state as "servants of God in the place of God, under the guidance of Christ."[7] Bullinger, his successor, also shared in this view, and after Zwingli's death in 1531, he further developed this theocratic political theology and put it into practice, enriched with a more direct connection to the Old Testament and the notion of a covenanted people. This political theology, which stressed the continuity of God's covenant, placed great emphasis on obedience to the moral law of God. Here was yet another area of disagreement with Lutherans, who stressed salvation by faith alone and freedom from the law. Obedience was key to salvation, both personally and communally, and therefore the civil law and the moral law had to be one and the same. And godliness—which consisted of pure worship of God and love of neighbor—thus had to be enforced by a single authority: the magistracy. To say that the Swiss Reformed sought to sanctify or sacralize "the world" is to miss the most important point of all: they did not even think of "the world" as some distinct realm that had always encircled the faithful and would always be opposed to them, much less as something alien to the church. In other words, their world had no quotation marks around it: their world was the local community, which all Christians were obligated to transform into a godly society.

This Swiss Reformed vision was perhaps best articulated by Martin Bucer, the Strassburg Reformer, when he was exiled to England. Hoping to instill the right approach to rulership in thirteen-year-old King Edward VI, Bucer penned a manual in 1550 titled *On the Kingdom of Christ*, in which he urged him to become a proper Christian ruler.

Bucer had no time for subtlety, and little patience either, as is often the case with exiles, so this text was as explicit and as thorough a plea for the establishment of a theocracy as had ever been written. Aside from containing numerous specific instructions, Bucer's text also laid out the rationale for the theocratic ethic by raising earthly kings to an exalted position as images of Christ on earth. Like Zwingli—and unlike Luther—Bucer stressed the total intertwining of church and state: "Just as the kingdoms of the world are subordinated to the Kingdom of Christ," he argued, "so also is the Kingdom of Christ in its own way subordinated to the kingdoms of this world." Earthly Christian rulers were thus "perpetually at war both with evil men and evil spirits." In other words, coercion and violence were a sacred duty. Bucer's vision of a "fully restored" kingdom of Christ in England brims over with the earnestness that is so characteristic of the Reformed tradition: King Edward, he said, should aim to lead "all classes of men" in his realm to work "thoughtfully, consistently, carefully, and tenaciously" to ensure that "Christ's Kingdom may as fully as possible be accepted and hold sway" over everyone. Another prominent Reformed trait is the emphasis placed on the earthly benefits of theocracy. The ruler who ensures that his subjects lead sober, purposeful, godly lives and are "purged more fully day by day from sins" will be not only shielding them from well-deserved divine chastisements, but also ensuring that "they live well and happily both here and in the time to come."[8] Three and a half centuries later, the ur-sociologist Max Weber would refer to this attitude as "worldly asceticism."

Bucer had relatively little influence on the short-lived King Edward VI, but, eventually, much of what he proposed would be taken to heart by English Puritans. And the Puritans themselves would also be greatly influenced by other branches of the Reformed tradition, most notably that of Geneva, where John Calvin and Theodore de Bèze gave political theology an even sharper edge. Calvin's take on "the world" was very similar to Zwingli's and Bucer's, though Calvin preferred to give the church more autonomy vis-à-vis the state. Calvin also made a very important distinction between rulers. On the one hand, rulers aligned with God were endowed with great authority:

> When those who bear the office of magistrate are called gods, let no one suppose that there is little weight in that appellation. It is thereby intimated that they have a commission from God, that they are invested with divine authority, and, in fact, represent the person of God, as whose substitutes they in a manner act.[9]

On the other hand, rulers who failed to follow God's will or opposed it placed themselves in a precarious situation. This distinction rested on a definition of civil government that stressed its religious dimension. Calvin's take on the nature and function of the state was succinctly outlined in his address to King Francis I, which was published with his *Institutes* in 1536. Summarizing what was at stake at that time, Calvin distilled the message of the Reformed Protestant cause, and the core of his theology, into a sentence already quoted in chapter 12, but worth repeating here:

It will then be for you, most serene King, not to close your ears . . . especially when a very great question is at stake: how God's glory may be kept safe on earth, how God's truth may retain its place of honor, how Christ's Kingdom may be kept in good repair among us.

Here we find the gist of Calvinism: an uncompromising tradition that was at once theological and political, best summed up in its motto *soli Deo gloria*, "Glory to God alone." Calvin's concept of the glory of God and of the honor due to him was derived, as we have seen, from Zwingli, but Calvin developed it further, for a flock under the constant threat of extinction, devising a political theology that argued that Christians owed their ultimate allegiance to God alone, above all earthly rulers, and especially above earthly rulers who sullied God's glory in any way, whether through laxity or outright affront. Like Zwingli and Bucer before him, Calvin revived the jealous God of the Old Testament. Reward and punishment were essential to God's relationship with his people: Calvin's God demanded his proper glory, along with obedience, rewarding those who gave him his due and punishing those who dared not to. This is why Calvinists became formidable agents of change and social, political, and moral transformation. As Catholics could not help but notice, Calvin's political theology had a seditious edge to it, for he questioned the legitimacy of rulers who did not do God's bidding. So, while trying to convince Francis I that the evangelicals were obedient, virtuous, model citizens, Calvin delivered a mixed message that contained a serious challenge to any ruler's authority:

> That king who in ruling over his realm does not serve God's glory exercises not kingly rule but brigandage. Furthermore, he is deceived who looks for enduring prosperity in his kingdom when it is not ruled by God's scepter, that is, his Holy Word.[10]

This cheeky admonition by the young Calvin, written before he had set foot in Geneva, summed up what would make him and his followers so formidable a challenge to those in power. Everywhere they established communities, Calvinists would be activists, working as agents of the divine, trying to reshape localities and whole nations according to their vision, challenging the authority of anyone who disagreed—no matter how exalted their status—spreading their activism as widely as possible.

The Radical tradition tended to have a very negative attitude toward "the world" and everything associated with it, especially after the disastrous Anabaptist takeover of the city of Münster in 1534–1535. Perfectionists to the core, most Radicals created "gathered" churches composed only of genuine believers who had accepted baptism as adults. These churches were kept pure through the expulsion of members who failed to live up to expectations. Involvement with "the sword"—that is, with any coercive force—tended to be strictly forbidden, and so did mixing with those who did not belong to their pure church. The essence of the political theology of most Radicals was summed up in the Schleitheim Articles:

Concerning separation, we have agreed that a separation should take place from the evil
which the devil has planted in the world. We simply will not have fellowship with evil
people, nor associate with them, nor participate with them in their abominations. . . .
Lastly, it should be pointed out that it is not fitting for a Christian to be a magistrate for
these reasons: the authorities' governance is according to the flesh, but the Christian's
is according to the spirit. . . . Worldly people are armed with spikes and iron but
Christians are armed with the armor of God—with truth, with justice, with peace,
faith, and salvation, and with the word of God.[11]

Such a dualistic approach to political life was abhorrent to all of the magisterial Reformers,
since their Reformations depended closely on civil governments, in various ways.

Aside from the Radicals, then, all Protestants embraced political life and deemed
it absolutely necessary. Although they held different positions on relations between
church and state, the churches of the magisterial Reformation redefined the nature and
function of both spheres, secularizing the church to some extent, and, at the very same
time, sacralizing the state. The net result was a blurring of traditional boundaries and
the creation of communities in which the laity gained a greater voice in the governance
of the church and the clergy gained a greater say in the shaping of society. In practical
terms, Protestants changed the nature and function of the clergy by stripping them of
the higher ontological, social, and political status that the Catholic Church had upheld
for more than a millennium. For all practical purposes, they were laicized; that is, they
became common citizens, just like everyone else, subject to the same laws and law courts.
Free to marry, they became husbands and fathers, mere heads of household. They were
also mere officeholders who could be removed from their posts by the communities they
shepherded. According to some historians, this was not only the greatest appeal of the
Protestant message, especially to urban populations, but also one of the chief distinguishing features of the transition from medieval to modern. But turning the clergy into
common citizens was not necessarily the same as stripping them of authority. The new
Protestant clergy could prove much more meddlesome and overbearing than the Catholic
priests they replaced. A case in point is Geneva, which had more than four hundred
clerics before it turned Protestant, and only a handful afterward. The control exercised by
those few Protestant ministers was far greater than any of those hundreds of priests and
monks had ever dreamed possible.

Among Catholics, no changes took place whatsoever insofar as basic definitions
were concerned: the clergy retained their special status, and the church reaffirmed its immensely complex relation to civil rulers. Few arrangements were simple; few boundaries
were solid or impermeable. The prince-bishops of Germany retained their dual status as
ecclesiastical and civil rulers; the popes retained their state in central Italy; cardinals and
bishops could serve as ministers of state; abbots hung on to their positions as landlords
and local magnates; and kings and local rulers continued to exert immense control over
the church in their lands, including the right to appoint bishops—or, as in the case of the
kings of France, the right to bar the publication of the decrees of the Council of Trent.

At the very same time, civil rulers continued to be installed into their offices through rituals that were conducted by the clergy, and they also humbled themselves to their confessors occasionally, or, in some cases, frequently. In addition, celibacy, priesthood, monasticism, and the contemplative life continued to be upheld as higher callings while the laity were encouraged to strive for holiness within "the world."

While asceticism and withdrawal from "the world" were still revered after Trent, so was engagement in politics and society. Change emerged on two fronts: first among the clergy, with the creation of ministries that engaged "the religious" more deeply and intimately with the world; second among the laity, who were increasingly encouraged to Christianize the world through their own efforts at perfection. As new approaches to life in the world emerged, older values were not necessarily discarded. This layering and overlapping was an essential feature of Catholicism, as old as the church itself, a structural attribute that was not diminished by the challenges of the early modern era, but rather enhanced. New contemplative and active religious orders could come into existence at the same time and flourish side by side, and alongside old orders, and the laity could be encouraged to become more active in the church while the authority of the clergy was increased. To many Protestants, this plurality of approaches and seeming lack of cogency in Catholicism was proof positive its falsehood and error. For Catholics, however, this diversity was proof of the church's universality and its faithfulness to tradition.

That a life of genuine devotion could be led in the world as well as behind cloister walls or in some far-flung mission field was already taken for granted in many Catholic circles by the time that Francis de Sales wrote his *Introduction to the Devout Life* in 1609. The "world" was still considered an opposite pole to all things spiritual, for sure, but it was no longer necessarily viewed as a fatal trap. As De Sales wrote, "A vigorous and constant soul can live in the world without receiving any worldly taint, can find springs of sweet piety in the midst of the briny waters of the world, and can fly among the flames of earthly concupiscences without burning the wings of the holy desires of the devout life."[12] This was a change in emphasis, not something new. But the difference made by this shift in focus should not be underestimated, for just as laity were encouraged to sanctify the world, some clergy were taught to embrace the world too, and to find God in its deepest recesses. This helps explain how those Jesuits wangled their way to the emperor's palace in China with their scientific instruments and to nearly every Catholic European court with their casuistry.

By the mid-seventeenth century, the only churches in fragmented Europe that would have agreed with Machiavelli's assessment of the world as a realm totally alien to genuine virtue would be those of Protestant Radicals. Engagement with "the world" was part and parcel of all major Christian traditions. Protestants tended to sacralize the profane and to secularize the sacred. They also tended to embrace political life as a means of transforming and Christianizing the world, with all of the eagerness of the young and idealistic. Catholics, for the most part, continued to emphasize dualities within a very sacramental worldview, and to approach political life and all transformations from a variety of perspectives, tempered by a millennium and a half of experience in wrestling with the world, the flesh, and the devil.

Social Welfare

Religious fragmentation was but one of several interrelated transformations that shook the West simultaneously at the end of the fifteenth and beginning of the sixteenth centuries. Wide-ranging structural changes in finances, commerce, farming, and the production of goods swept through Europe, all caused by a variety of factors that ranged from climate change to the development of new technologies, to population growth, to increased urbanization, and many others, including the influx of precious metals from the New World. The era of the Reformations—roughly 1450 to 1650—was also that of the so-called price revolution, during which an unprecedented rate of inflation and tremendous price increases were constant.

All of these major economic and social changes not only caused great dislocations and increased the number of poor people, but also changed the nature of poverty itself. By 1500, it is estimated that nearly one-quarter of the population lacked enough food to eat or secure shelter, and that vast numbers of urban and agricultural laborers lived on the margins, always on the edge of ruin or starvation. A crippling injury, a debilitating disease, one flood, or one dismal harvest was often all it took to turn an entire family into paupers. The inescapable presence of beggars, vagrants, orphans, and other luckless people was a constant reminder that Christian Europe was much too far from perfect. Given such dire conditions, and that care of the poor had long been part and parcel of European religious life, it stands to reason that social welfare issues became a focus of attention within the maelstrom of the Reformations. The solutions found became one of the most significant legacies of the age.

Catholics had a long tradition to contend with and build upon. Poverty had been a burning concern throughout the Middle Ages, especially between the twelfth and fourteenth centuries, when it became closely linked to heresy. First the heretical Cathars and Waldensians made poverty a virtue, and then the mendicant orders, especially the Franciscans, some of whom were also pronounced heretical. At issue was whether one needed to be poor and without property to be saved, with the heretics claiming that only the truly poor could gain heaven. Care of the poor, the needy, and the infirm was never at issue, for that practical question was well beyond dispute: the demands of Christian charity made the needy everyone's concern, individually as well as collectively. Almsgiving was a salvific act, which earned one merit. The poor, therefore, had a sacred dimension and served a quasi-sacramental function, as instruments of redemption. Theologians distinguished "corporal" and "spiritual" works of mercy. The list was as dualistic, as numerally fixated, as detailed, and as symmetrical as one might expect from medieval theologians:

Seven Corporal Works of Mercy	**Seven Spiritual Works of Mercy**
To feed the hungry	To instruct the ignorant
To give drink to the thirsty	To counsel the doubtful
To clothe the naked	To admonish sinners
To house the homeless	To bear wrongs patiently
To visit the sick	To forgive offenses willingly
To ransom the captive	To comfort the afflicted
To bury the dead	To pray for the living and the dead

Classifying mercy in this way meant that all of these activities had an overtly religious dimension and were inherently churchly. And this was especially true of the corporal works of mercy—what we nowadays call social welfare—all of which transcended the personal concerns of every individual and involved financial expense or redistribution of resources. Most of the solutions found for such problems were decentralized and connected in some way to church life, and the funding came from various sources: through the bishops, the clergy, or lay confraternities and wealthy donors. Charitable institutions, even when founded by lay people or connected to municipal councils, tended to have a religious character. Begging was commonplace, and most often the only means of survival for those at the very bottom of society, as well as for some religious orders that had chosen voluntary poverty. Most significant, there was no common safety net, no uniformity in care, and no master plan for handling the problems of the poor and needy. Although civil authorities involved themselves to some extent in regulating charity and begging, there were substantial differences in their involvement, according to time and place. In England, for instance, King Edward III issued the Ordinance of Labourers in 1350, which regulated wages and the movement of beggars, vagrants, and laborers. Similar laws were enacted elsewhere, especially after the Black Death devastated Europe (1348–1350). But all public charity, even if administered by the state, depended on private contributions, most of which were funneled through the church. Charitable institutions therefore competed with one another for funding, and quite often their efforts overlapped. Given the proliferation of confraternities in the late medieval period, many of which were dedicated to works of mercy, the decentralization of charity and poor relief became ever more acute, even as the state began to step in.

Although some reform-minded individuals called for greater coherence and stricter controls over beggars and homeless vagrants, improvements in the efficiency of social welfare progressed slowly and unevenly in the early 1500s. The advent of Protestantism acted as a catalyst and speeded up the processes that had already been under way. Martin Luther invoked the needs of the poor in three of his ninety-five theses, but only as a means of critiquing indulgences. The forty-fifth thesis, for instance, says: "Christians should be taught that he who sees a needy person, but passes him by although

Reforming charity. Vagrants and beggars were an unavoidable sight during the early modern period, and as urbanization increased and trade grew, the problem of dealing with the poor and disabled intensified. Although the creation of charitable institutions increased, keeping up with the needs of the less fortunate proved difficult. Protestants and Catholics developed different strategies for dispensing charity, but they did share ambivalence toward poverty and agree that it was necessary to distinguish between the "deserving" and "undeserving" poor. This seventeenth-century engraving by Wenceslas Hollar, *The Beggar's Guild*, portrays various types of indigent men and suggests that begging is a craft or profession.

he gives money for indulgences, gains no benefit from the pope's pardon, but only incurs the wrath of God." Luther also brought up poverty in some of his early tracts, but he did not make social welfare reform a central part of his message. Much to Luther's chagrin, it would be his colleague Karlstadt who first grappled with social welfare reform head-on, in his 1522 pamphlet *On the Abolition of Images and That There Should Be No Beggars Among Christians*. The long title was an accurate reflection of the pamphlet's contents, for Karlstadt linked two seemingly disparate subjects, arguing that idolatry and begging were equally wrong, and that the wealth invested in religious imagery and church decorations should instead go to the needy. Martin Bucer would develop this argument further the following year, in sermons he delivered at Weissenburg that were later summarized and published, and also in 1524, in his *Basis and Reason for the Innovations*, a defense of his reforming policies at Strassburg. In this treatise, Bucer condemned the cult of saints and images, and the promotion of pilgrimages as "unchristian" on two levels: as theologically and morally wrong. "It is both against faith and love," he argued, summing up a new social ethic that was inseparable from the larger theological matrix of the Protestant Reformation.[13]

Karlstadt and Bucer's opposition to begging—they both wanted to eradicate it completely—stemmed from shared theological convictions and also from pragmatic social and political concerns that had already gripped them and their contemporaries even before they became Protestants. On the theological level, they viewed begging as wrong because, as Bucer had so aptly put it, the existence of beggars was a contradiction and a sign of failure: it proved that Christians were not living up to their calling. When viewed against the backdrop of costly images and reliquaries and of the resources spent on pilgrimages and processions, all of which were theologically incorrect to begin with, the presence of beggars and homeless vagrants seemed to them an even worse admission of failure and of a reversal of Christian values. In addition, Bucer and Karlstadt opposed begging because of their theological rejection of works-righteousness. In opposition to Catholic soteriology, which held that acts of mercy were meritorious and helped one to earn salvation, Karlstadt and Bucer insisted that the giving of alms was not at all a salvific gesture. In essence, they argued that the needy were not agents of salvation who presented the faithful with an opportunity to score points with God, but rather a problem that Christians were required to solve.

From a pragmatic perspective, which Bucer and Karlstadt shared with Catholics, begging was not just an inefficient way to deal with poverty, but also a threat to the social order. Beggars and vagrants were sometimes aggressive, even violent. Some turned to crime; many were blamed for spreading disease. Moreover, a beggar in genuine need was impossible to spot, especially when so many of them were strangers who wandered from town to town. Medieval poor laws had tried to deal with this issue by distinguishing between those who were "deserving" and "undeserving" of charity, that is, between those who were fully capable of working but chose to beg instead, and those who were genuinely unable to work. Many of these laws had also tried to limit begging to locals, whose needs were easier to identify. This pragmatic concern would very quickly surface in some early Protestant pamphlets, such as *On Work and Begging: How One Should Deal with Laziness and Make Everyone Work*, written by Wenceslaus Linck in 1523, to promote welfare reform in Altenburg.

While Luther did not agree with Karlstadt or Bucer on the issue of religious imagery, he did agree on that of poor relief, and as early as 1523 proposed the establishment of community chests to handle and properly distribute the sudden windfall of funds from benefices and monastic institutions that had been abolished. These Lutheran community chests, many of which were established in the 1520s, were used to fund clerical salaries and also to help the needy. Lutheran poor relief, much like the Lutheran Church itself, would be left largely in the hands of civil authorities.

Zwingli focused more directly on the subject of welfare reform than Luther, not just for theological or personal reasons, but because in his city of Zurich, the issue had been under review for quite some time. The Zurich city council had passed an ordinance in 1520—four years before the city became Protestant—that sought to take poor relief out of the church's hands and centralize it under municipal guidance. Zwingli's attack on idolatry, a centerpiece of his struggle to undo the Catholic Church in Zurich, did have some points of resemblance with that of Karlstadt and Bucer. Like them, Zwingli thought that the "idols" were lavished with attention and resources that should have gone to the poor. And he developed an interpretation of the poor as the true images of Christ, a trope found in some medieval writers, including Bernard of Clairvaux (in the twelfth century). But Zwingli's great contribution to this issue was practical rather than theological. In 1525, he overhauled the city's poor relief and established a model that many other churches in Switzerland and South Germany would follow: the full centralization of social welfare through state-run agencies that were funded by taxes and tithes. By the time Calvin converted to Protestantism, that pattern was well established, as was the theology that undergirded it. Calvin made one notable modification by placing deacons in charge of the needy.

Despite some differences, then, Protestants tended to follow a common blueprint when it came to social welfare: the establishment of a centralized system that was run by civil authorities rather than by churches, confraternities, or individual donors. Karlstadt's great concern became normative too, for among the controls established by Protestants, those that focused on begging were often among the most prominent. On the whole, the Protestant solution rested on removing the individual citizen or Christian from the process of poor relief, and in sundering all direct connections between donors and the needy. Begging was abolished in most Protestant localities, and as a result, anyone who claimed to need assistance would have to be certified as genuinely needy by the municipal agency that was in charge of poor relief. Charity became strictly local, and also desacralized.

By making social welfare the responsibility of the secular authorities rather than the church or the faithful themselves, Protestant communities streamlined poor relief, but in the process they also narrowed the funnel through which the needy could seek assistance, and at the same time, they helped reduce or strip away its sacred character. Yes, the new process was assigned theological significance by the church elites, as a genuine display of Christian charity that ensured an efficient distribution of aid within the community, much as within a family. Theologians even spoke of the poor as new "images" and as the proper replacement for the idols of Roman Catholicism. But theologians and clerics also tended to insist that as long as only the truly deserving should receive aid, then only those who were truly deserving of membership in the churches should be certified as "deserving." To qualify for the community's charity, then, the deserving poor needed to reflect the community's morals and piety. And while no one begged in public any more, the unlucky still had to go, hat in hand, to beg from a deacon, a civil servant, or a magistrate.

Catholics were driven by the very same pragmatic concerns that were already in place before Protestants came along with their solutions, and they reformed social welfare too, in keeping with tradition and their theology. An observer of this process in the Netherlands, one of the first locations where reforms were initiated, was Juan Luis Vives (1493–1540), a Spanish humanist of converso lineage who was living in exile in Bruges. Inspired by the debates that swirled around him concerning social welfare, and by reforms already undertaken in the Netherlands and elsewhere Vives published a Latin treatise in 1526 titled *On Helping the Poor*, which was reprinted several times and translated into German and Italian. Anyone looking for any distinctive Catholic or Protestant traits in this treatise is bound to be disappointed, for it lacks a theological edge.

Vives's refusal to glorify or sanctify poverty angered the Franciscans but did not deter his treatise from having considerable influence. "It is certainly a shameful and disgraceful thing for Christians . . . to find so many needy persons and beggars in our streets," said Vives.[14] Like so many of his contemporaries, Vives was horrified by beggars, and irked by the high number of able-bodied vagrants and criminals who chose to beg rather than to work. The solutions he proposed were somewhat similar to those of the Protestants: all beggars were to be carefully investigated and regulated, and hospitals were to be run by the civil government. All nonnative beggars were to be banished, and all who remained would be forced to work, as long as they were able to do so. Although he was short on details, Vives did propose that some be trained as tradesmen, and that the rest be assigned to work for the public good, repairing roads, digging ditches, or weaving baskets. Vives was no innovator: his proposals were based on reforms that had already taken place in Catholic Bruges and Ypres, and in Protestant Nuremberg and Strassburg.

As the enactment of poor laws spread throughout Europe, it was at first difficult to differentiate between Catholics and Protestants, insofar as the regulations on begging and on discerning the difference between the deserving and undeserving. In Catholic Spain, a number of local poor laws were influenced by Vives's treatise. In 1540, Charles V and his regent Cardinal Juan Pardo de Tavera, archbishop of Toledo, enacted a poor law for the entire realm that called for establishment of a licensed begging system, just like those of Protestant lands, which was to distinguish natives from vagrants and the deserving from the undeserving. Although this law was hard to enforce, evidence of its partial success, at least in Toledo, can be found in the picaresque novel Lazarillo de Tormes:

> The year's wheat harvest had been bad, so the town authorities decided to get rid of all outsiders who begged in the city. The town crier announced it: all persons foreign to Toledo caught begging would be punished with a taste of the whip. The law was enforced, and four days after the pronouncement went into effect I saw a procession of unfortunates being led down Cuatro Calles being duly flogged. The sight frightened me to such an extent that I no longer dared to go out begging.[15]

The poor laws of 1540 sparked some debate, and they were argued against most vehemently by the Dominican theologian Domingo de Soto at Salamanca, who defended the right of Christians to beg freely. In 1565, King Philip II issued another set of poor laws with even more teeth, which aimed to curb uncontrolled begging. This law, which assigned the task of sorting out the deserving poor to parish officials but tightened enforcement by secular authorities, including "commissioners of vagabonds," was a very Catholic solution, which stood in place until the eighteenth century.

In Spain, as elsewhere in Catholic Europe, especially after the Council of Trent, the reform of social welfare included this sort of cooperation between church and state. While the enactment and enforcement of laws against uncontrolled begging tended to be the work of civil authorities, nearly all other aspects, including the funding and staffing of charitable institutions, were left in the hands of the clergy and lay confraternities. Among the secular clergy, bishops could contribute heavily from their income, and the parish priests could get involved in more mundane tasks, such as certifying the deserving poor. Among the regular clergy, there was a wide range of involvement, depending on which religious order was involved. Some of the new orders created after Trent dedicated themselves totally to charitable work, such as the Brothers Hospitallers, founded by St. John of God in 1572, and the Visitandines, founded by St. Francis de Sales and St. Jane Frances de Chantal in 1610 (though the Visitandines were soon afterward ordered to lead a cloistered life). The lion's share of charitable work fell not to the clergy, however, but to lay confraternities. Continuing with renewed vigor the efforts they had begun in the Middle Ages, confraternities established and ran many different kinds of charitable institutions: poor houses, hospitals, orphanages, asylums, and rehabilitation centers for former prostitutes. They also engaged in personal services, such as visiting the sick, assisting the dying, providing dowries for poor young women, or funerals and burials for the destitute. Throughout Catholic Europe the number of confraternities soared in the sixteenth century, and peaked in the seventeenth. Placed under episcopal control by the Council of Trent, and linked to parishes, or sometimes to religious orders, confraternities offered the laity a chance to engage with "the world" and in a life of devotion simultaneously. Belonging to more than one confraternity was not at all uncommon. Some were exclusively male or female, some mixed. Some tended to attract patricians, others merchants and artisans, and others a wide spectrum of social types. Membership could vary from a mere handful to thousands, as in the case of one confraternity in Naples that boasted of 6,000 members in 1563. Toledo, Florence, and Venice could each boast of having more than a hundred confraternities.

The success of the confraternities can be attributed in great part to the affirmation of a theology of merit by the Council of Trent, which made it clear that salvation hinged not just on the avoidance of sin, but also on the performance of works of charity. In some ways, the complex social welfare system embraced by the Catholic Church—which depended so heavily on the work of lay confraternities—could be considered a deliberate response to the Protestant challenge, at once theological and pragmatic. Such an assertion cannot be proven with statistics or charts and graphs, but it can certainly be backed up with telling examples. One such instance comes from Spain, which had one of the highest concentrations of confraternities in early modern Europe. When King Philip II announced a plan to streamline social welfare in 1581 that would centralize charity and funnel much of it through the crown and its officials, the confraternities offered such stiff resistance that he had to back down. Another plan hatched toward the end of his reign in 1595 also fizzled quickly. Opposition to this plan stemmed largely from one issue: if the king were to take control of charity, then he would imperil everyone's chance of salvation. The existence of poverty was part of God's plan, after all. "God made the poor to aid the rich, rather than the rich to aid the poor," said one Spanish friar.[16] The Spanish writer Mateo Alemán agreed, expressing himself in very un-Protestant terms:

Divine providence has distributed its gifts (for our greater good), scattering them . . . so that all can be saved. God has made some powerful, and some he has made needy. To the rich He gave temporal goods and to the poor He gave spiritual goods, so that the rich can purchase their grace from Him through the distribution of their earthly possessions among the poor.[17]

These arguments may seem impractical, but they were theologically sound. If salvation depends on good works and almsgiving, and the state becomes the sole provider of alms and social welfare, how is anyone to earn the merits needed for entry into heaven?

Much more comparative research still needs to be done on poor relief, so there is yet no consensus on which of the two systems—Protestant or Catholic—might have been more effective. But the question of success often leads down troublesome paths to questionable conclusions, anyway. What matters most is that both Protestants and Catholics engaged in the reform of social welfare with similar goals in mind, and that they came up with different solutions. Protestants tended to secularize charity, to distance donor from recipient, and to fund it through tithes and taxes; Catholics tended to sacralize it, to encourage interaction between donor and recipient, and to fund it through almsgiving. This divergence, in and of itself, speaks volumes about the differences between Catholic and Protestant cultures and about their legacies.

Sex, Marriage, and the Family

Attitudes toward sex and marriage were the source of one of the sharpest differences between Catholics and Protestants. Medieval Catholicism prized virginity and celibacy, and deemed a life without sexual activity superior and more "perfect." So, while the church praised marriage and deemed it a sacrament, and even spoke of sexual intercourse as a duty for every married couple, it made clear that the married were second-class Christians, and that the sole legitimate purpose of sex was procreation. St. Jerome had summed up this view in the fourth century, and passed it on to medieval Christians. Marriage was to be praised solely because it brings potential virgins into the world, and while marriage fills the earth, virginity fills heaven. In summary, any sexual activities, or even any sexual thoughts that were not strictly and purely focused on the begetting of children, were sinful. Sex was a problem, then, and one's sexuality a constant source of temptation and impurity. This attitude stemmed from the fundamental assumption, driven deeply into the Catholic mentality for centuries by celibate clerics, that it was nearly impossible for human beings to separate sex from the sin of lust. This galling curse had been inflicted on the human race by original sin, as St. Augustine had emphasized. *Ecce unde*, he said of the male reproductive organs: "behold the place" where our curse is made manifest most aggressively. Even married folk constantly risked sin. A confessional manual from the late fifteenth century enumerated seven different ways man and wife could sin while fulfilling their "marital duty":

1. Engaging in unnatural acts and positions, contraception, coitus interruptus, sodomy, onanism.
2. Desiring a different partner during intercourse with one's spouse.
3. Desiring a different partner while one is *not* having intercourse with one's spouse.
4. Refusing the "marital duty" to one's spouse without good reason.
5. Having sex during forbidden times (e.g., menstruation, pregnancy, lactation, Sundays, Lent).
6. Having sex with one's spouse when one knows that spouse to be adulterous.
7. Having sex for sheer pleasure.[18]

Other confessional manuals had even longer lists. Hemmed in by such constraints, held in lower esteem than celibates by the church, reminded at every turn that they had chosen a less perfect way of life, married folk had to find their joys and their way to heaven under a dark cloud, with thousands of traps underfoot and the fires of hell or purgatory on the horizon. No wonder, then, that priests, monks, and nuns would often attract new recruits by arguing that the celibate life was not only superior to marriage, but also easier.

Protestants rejected this attitude. And on this subject, there were very few disagreements. Even the Radicals were on the same page on most issues. First and foremost, Protestants spurned the theological claim that abstention from sex or any other act of self-denial was meritorious, for that smacked of works-righteousness. Second, they objected to the superior status given to celibacy by Catholics, arguing that no such teaching could be found in the New Testament. Third, they argued that a celibate life was unnatural and that it created warped personalities and led to all sorts of sexual perversions. Protestants were fond of citing God's observation in Genesis that "it is not good for the man to be alone," and his command to Adam and Eve, "Be fruitful and multiply" (Genesis 1:28, 2:18). And they reveled in citing cases of monks, nuns, and priests who found it impossible to be celibate.

For Martin Luther, the Catholic Church's teaching on sex and marriage was a total inversion of values, and he based much of his criticism on natural rather than theological grounds. Marriage, he argued, was the only way to preserve chastity, the only proper way to handle uncontrollable natural urges. He went as far as to say that "one cannot be unmarried without sin."[19] Luther married a former nun who had escaped from a convent with his help, and he boasted of his experience with sex and marriage, and of how he differed from the celibate theologians of the Catholic Church. When tempted by the devil—which in Luther's case often meant despairing of salvation and focusing on the damning power of specific actions—he sometimes chased the devil away by thinking of sex, that ultimate monastic taboo, or by having sex with his wife. "The best fights that I've had with the devil," he bragged, "have taken place in my bed, side by side with my Kate."[20] All of the magisterial Reformers took the same tack, arguing that celibacy was an impossible goal for most human beings, and therefore "unjust and against

God."[21] Most of the Radicals agreed. Karlstadt lamented that "celibacy often destroys boys."[22] Zwingli, who had broken his vow of celibacy while he was pastor of the village of Glarus, spoke from experience when he said that chastity was a gift given to very few. While still a Catholic priest he had pleaded, "Since we have learned, alas, that we cannot remain continent, and since God has not granted us that,—we desire that marriage be not forbidden us."[23]

Doing away with a celibate clergy and with monasticism, along with all ascetic practices, the Protestant Reformers redefined sexuality, and also the nature and function of marriage and the family. Marriage became as honorable a calling in life as any other, and so did the rearing of children. Having clergy who were married and had children did much to elevate the status of marriage immediately among Protestants, beginning in the 1520s. All of the major Reformers were married, and so were most pastors, even though in some locales for a while flocks continued to call their pastors' wives "priest's whores." Moreover, the human need for love and companionship became as important among Protestants as the need to procreate, and so did the need for a *good* marriage. John Calvin grieved deeply when his wife died, saying, "I have been bereaved of the best companion of my life."[24] Luther recorded: "There is no bond on earth so sweet nor any separation so bitter as that which occurs in a *good* marriage."[25] The absolute necessity of having a good marriage was taken so seriously that Protestants began to allow divorce and remarriage—something that the Catholic Church had forbidden since time immemorial. Marriage courts that handled domestic disputes would try to reconcile couples, but only up to a certain point. When it became apparent that a marriage was an irreparably hellish arrangement, Protestant courts would reluctantly admit that the marriage had "ceased to exist" and allow the couple to divorce. Martin Bucer in Strassburg was one of the earliest pioneers on this unexplored frontier. Eventually, divorce would become a common last-ditch solution to troubled marriages among all Protestants, even in Calvin's puritanical Geneva.

How well Protestant families lived up to ideals is still a matter of dispute. Although court records reveal that some families fell short of the goals prescribed for them in texts and sermons, it is enormously difficult to find evidence of how nondysfunctional families lived out their lives. Whether such data exist is largely irrelevant, anyway. As with so many claims made for the Protestant Reformation, pro or con, the question of success misleads more than enlightens. Protestants promoted the family as the prime incubator for all virtues and social stability, and the ideal of the perfect, celibate, world-denying saint was not just discarded, but also ridiculed. Perfection was deemed impossible, and holiness was to be found in the messiness of wedded commitment, monogamous sex, and child rearing. That acceptance of married life and all its challenges, in and of itself—along with the disappearance of celibate priests, monks, and nuns—was a major change. Protestant clergy stressed familial love, mutual respect, and a very patriarchal authority structure in which the father, or paterfamilias, ruled his household with firm and unquestionable authority. Ideally, every father was to be both lord and pastor of his household. In response to a complaint that invisible demons were running amok in his house at night, hurling pots and dishes at him, and laughing out loud, an advice seeker was told by Luther to embrace his family and invoke his office as paterfamilias:

> Dear Brother, be strong in the Lord and firm in your faith! Don't yield to that robber! . . . Let the devil play with the pots. In the meantime, pray to God with your wife and children [and say,] Be off, Satan! I'm lord of this house, and you aren't. By divine authority I'm head of this household, and I have a call from heaven to be pastor of this church. . . . Who invited you into this house?[26]

As far as wives were concerned, all Protestants agreed with the apostle Paul, insisting that they should be submissive and obedient to their husbands (Colossians 3:18–21). They also called on wives to dedicate their lives to their husbands and households. After Calvin's wife died, he praised her by saying that she had been totally devoted to him and would have gladly shared all hardships with him, including death. More than that, he said: "During her life she was the faithful helper of my ministry. From her I never experienced the slightest hindrance."[27] Although Luther often joked about his wife bossing him around, and praised her for her logical prowess, business acumen, and managerial skills, he also said, "Women have narrow shoulders and wide hips, therefore they ought to be domestic; their very physique is a sign from their Creator that he intended them to limit their activity to the home."[28]

Protestants also changed some of the laws related to marriage that they deemed unscriptural and unjust, especially those that concerned "secret" marriages contracted without a cleric or witnesses, and those that dealt with impediments to marriage, such as relations to cousins and godparents and their families.

Among Catholics, little changed—at least in comparison to Protestants. The Council of Trent reaffirmed the superiority of not only celibacy and virginity, but also monasticism and the celibate priesthood. Nothing at all changed concerning sex either, which continued to be linked to lust, and to extend to the realm of mere thoughts. Marriage was for procreation, first and foremost, and indissoluble, no matter how dysfunctional the union. The body itself continued to be viewed as a constant drag on the spiritual life, weighing down the soul, tempting it with forbidden delights, inexorably. Sexuality was a daily encounter with a spiritual minefield, even for those who were married. But husband and wife could at least find some outlet in fulfilling their marital "duty." For those who were unmarried, the body was a wide gateway to sin, an inescapable vortex with no legitimate outlet. In his *Introduction to the Devout Life*, Francis de Sales advised singles to avoid dancing. For those who could not avoid it, he counseled the utmost caution. On dancing and other nighttime activities he warned that they

> open the pores of the bodies of those that practise them, so they also open the pores of their souls, and expose them to the danger of some serpent, taking advantage therefrom to breathe some loose words or immodest suggestions into the ear, or of some basilisk casting an impure look or glance into the heart, which being thus opened,

Excess personified. Catholics and Protestants disagreed on the value of self-denial, especially when it came to sex and marriage: while Protestants considered celibacy unnatural and unnecessary, Catholics continued to praise celibacy and virginity as a far superior spiritual state. Catholic polemicists often accused Protestants of self-indulgence, and many of them found an easy target in the married Martin Luther, who is here portrayed in a 1580 caricature as a man who cannot control his appetites. Luther not only has trouble carrying around the weight of his own distended belly, but also finds it hard to balance his vocation as a churchman with this duties of a husband and father. Peddling the pope's crown, Luther wheels about his paunch and some books by Protestant theologians, with a cabinet full of other Reformers strapped to his back. Behind him, his wife Katarina von Bora struggles to hold a baby with one hand and a dog with the other while balancing a beer barrel and a large Bible on her back.

is easily seized upon and poisoned. . . . [T]hese idle recreations are ordinarily very dangerous . . . and excite a thousand evil affections in the soul.[29]

For those who were married, he advised that husband and wife "cherish each other with a sacred and divine love."[30] De Sales defined marriage as a "true and holy friendship" and a "communication of life, of industry, of goods, of affections, and of an indissoluble fidelity." And he warned that "communication founded on sensual pleasures is so gross that it does not merit the name of friendship."[31]

Catholic devotional literature tended not to shower husbands with as much advice and admonitions as that of Protestants. The traditional role of paterfamilias was emphasized, but not as in Protestant literature, where the household could become a church and the father its pastor But wives received more attention. And in some cases, in devotional texts, the roles assigned to them paralleled to those of Protestant fathers. One treatise, Luis de León's *The Perfect Wife* (1583), sums up this tendency. The "perfect wife" described by this Augustinian friar was at once totally subject to her husband and a powerful linchpin of society. Though confined to the home and warned not to involve herself in public affairs, the perfect wife was also responsible for "governing the family," making her household financially prosperous, and rearing and socializing the future citizens under her care.[32] In her role as wife, mother, teacher, and chief financial officer of the household, this perfect wife played a key role, then, in the preservation of Christian virtues and the fundamental values of her society. *The Perfect Wife* enjoyed a long life in print, mainly because it acquired a reputation as an instruction manual for young brides, for whom it seemed the perfect wedding gift. Although in our own day it has been denounced as misogynous, especially for its emphasis on childbearing, breast-feeding, and child rearing as supremely important and defining functions of womanhood, and for its insistence that women stay out of the public sphere, in its own day this text was welcomed as a step forward, principally because it asked women to be primarily responsible for the financial well-being of their households, the survival of core values, and the continuity of social order itself.

An undeniable difference between Catholics and Protestants had more to do with dead women than with those who were living and breathing. While Protestants rejected veneration of the Virgin Mary and all saints, Catholics enhanced such devotions in their piety and ritual. Protestant worship was centered strictly on a male deity—Father, Son, and Holy Spirit—whereas Catholic worship became ever more suffused with a feminine presence, for it was not just the Mother of God who was constantly venerated and addressed in prayer, but also that vast and ever-expanding multitude of other holy women who thronged the heavenly court. And although only dead and canonized women could be venerated and addressed in prayer, there were always living women— sometimes within physical reach—and recently dead and not yet canonized women who were considered holy, even perfect, and definitely on their way to heaven: remarkable women who channeled heaven and ennobled the church on earth, such as Teresa of Ávila, Angela de Merici, Jane Frances de Chantal, Rose of Lima, Margaret Mary Alacoque, and untold numbers of others who were never formally canonized, such as María of Ágreda, who became an unofficial adviser and confessor to King Philip IV of Spain. Protestants had no such gender balance when it came to worship, ritual, and everyday adulation.

The impact of the Reformations on women was a much less significant issue in the sixteenth and seventeenth centuries than it is in our own, but it is nonetheless a topic that became a whetstone in the late twentieth century for those with axes to grind. Disagreements abound. While some decry the irredeemable misogyny of both Catholics and Protestants, others assign blame to one camp and praise to the other. What are we to make, for example, of the emptying of the cloisters and the end to female monasticism? On the one hand, some argue—much like the Protestant Reformers themselves—that

BONVM EST PRESTOLARI CVM SILENTIO SALVTARE DEI·

Woman in charge. Were Catholic women better off than Protestant women when it came to autonomy and the availability of roles within their church? Or was it the other way around? On the one hand, Catholic women, such as Sister Jerónima de la Asunción, shown here, had the option of leading missions to Asia and of establishing and running schools, hospitals, and orphanages. On the other hand, Protestant women were emancipated from the rules of convent life and their sexuality, as well as their maternal nurturing were raised to a new level of respect. Sister Jerónima's portrait, painted by Diego Velázquez in 1620, just before she sailed to the Philippines, shows us a determined self-confident woman very much in charge, about to embark on a dangerous mission to an alien land. She has the look of a soldier about to enter battle, her crucifix a sword, her prayer book a shield, her glare a stern reminder that she is a force to be reckoned with.

freeing women from strict enclosure, male clerical supervision, and a life of sexual deprivation was a great step forward, an advance toward modernity. On the other hand, others argue, monastic life offered women a great deal of autonomy and offered an alternative to the drudgery of the patriarchal household and child rearing. To take that sphere of activity away from women, and to give them no choice but to be housewives, they contend, can be seen only as a great setback. Then there are those who prefer to make no judgments one way or another, and to allow the past to be understood on its own terms, free from teleological trajectories or presentist agenda.

Conclusion

The Reformations of the early modern age had various outcomes, insofar as relations with "the world" were concerned. All in all, the end result was a reshaping of that world, and a narrowing of the gap between the ideal and the real. That reshaping and narrowing was not uniform, but it did have one salient effect: the religious fragmentation of Europe. Ultimately, this fragmentation would lead to the emergence of a much different world, one in which the role of religion would be redefined.

The most significant long-term consequence of this redefinition was somewhat ironic, for the religious fervor of the Reformations eventually forced religion to assume a less prominent role in the world it sought to improve. The simple fact that Christendom was no longer unified by a single church and a common set of beliefs and values made it necessary for Europeans to deal with one another on more "worldly" or secular terms. In other words, fragmentation and religious disagreements led to the adoption of common frames of reference outside the realm of religion. This change did not happen overnight. And it did not take place at the same rate everywhere.

Social, political, and ethical issues were addressed on two levels: the local and the universal. At both levels, especially where religious uniformity was the rule, religion shaped distinct societies. This pattern held firm, more or less, until the Thirty Years' War (1618–1648). During that prolonged watershed event, the role of religion was redefined, somewhat unevenly, but undeniably, as the blood flowed and the treasuries were drained. After the war, secular values began to erode the shaping power of religion much more rapidly than ever before.

By 1648 it had become all too clear to far too many Westerners that religion was no longer a social glue binding civilization together, but rather something corrosive and explosive, which in the long run would have to be circumvented, perhaps even ignored. It took nearly a century and a half—from roughly 1500 to 1650—for this realization to gain prominence in the Western world. After 1650, religion did not lose its dynamism or its power to effect real change in individuals and societies. Far from it. But it did definitely begin to play an increasingly diminishing role in shaping "the world" it had so intensely hoped to transform.

CHAPTER TWENTY-SIX

The Spirit of the Age

A s the Reformations changed attitudes toward the world, and life in the world, so did they help create a new zeitgeist, or spirit of the age, and a new culture. The relation between religion and the spirit of any age is always a two-way interaction: as religion is shaped by economic, demographic, social, cultural, and political factors, so does it shape all of these, in ways that are difficult to represent on spreadsheets, charts, and graphs. The effects of religion may not be quantifiable, but they are easy enough to spot, especially when it comes to the way religion is lived out, and in the styles and sensibilities that mark off any age: as easy to spot as the wig on Johann Sebastian Bach's head.

Piety

Did the various Reformations increase fervor, or lessen it? This question is as troublesome and as wrongheaded as that which asks whether the Reformations succeeded or not. Religious fervor is hard to measure. It is also very easy for historians to be misled by certain kinds of evidence. For instance, if one analyzes the records kept by church courts, inquisitions, and visitations, what one will find are aberrations, problems, and failures. Similarly, if one reads the correspondence of churchmen, one is likely to find complaints about the ignorance, sinfulness, and lack of fervor of their flocks, or their hollow attachment to external gestures. In contrast, if one reads nothing but devotional literature and counts the number of such texts published, or if one simply counts the number of sermons preached in a city, or the number of confraternities within it, one could get the impression that the laity must have been very devout indeed. These unavoidable discrepancies have led historians to different conclusions about levels of devotion or of success and failure. To assign grades or points to a revolution as complex as the Reformations of the early modern age as one would to a student's essay is not just difficult, but also wrong. Quantification offers no definitive proof of devotion or of success. After all, some of the most momentous revolutions in the modern age have also been the most horrific and destructive, and the most intent on violently coercing external acts of devotion to their ideals from the greatest possible number of those ruled by them—acts that they tally and use as proof of genuine devotion and of their resounding "success." Fortunately, in the case of the Reformations of the early modern age, questions regarding fervor, success, or failure are rendered moot by the undeniable fact that piety changed dramatically, and that this change not only made a world of difference, but also can be easily discerned and analyzed.

Protestants developed many different kinds of piety, some of which remained closer to traditional Catholicism than others. Overall, Protestants developed pieties that focused on an omnipresent, omniscient male deity who needed no intermediaries and favored no location in particular over another. Their pieties also tended to assume that human nature was far from perfectible, and that the main purpose of prayer was to praise and thank the divinity and to align oneself with his will rather than to ask for alterations in reality. Forgiveness came straight from the divine, not through any human agency. The realm of the sacred and spiritual also tended to be carefully circumscribed in their piety, behind a firm barrier that isolated it from the profane and material. And those who had died were dead and gone; nothing could be done for them by those they left behind.

Catholics, in contrast, retained the piety of their forebears, but they intensified new types of devotions, especially some that were diametrically opposed to Protestant theology and piety. They approached the divine directly, but also through intermediaries, and they sought its presence in myriad specific locations. The sacred was diffused throughout the profane for Catholics, as was the spiritual in the material world. Though the deity was male, there were female beings to address in prayer and worship—fellow human beings—who served as intercessors, advocates, and protectors. Prayer served many functions at once, including that of pleading for miracles that would alter reality. Forgiveness was in the hands of the church and its priests through the sacrament of penance. And the dead were connected to the living, as intercessors in heaven or as souls in purgatory who needed one's help.

Within Protestantism, with its wide array of different churches and of various traditions within individual churches, certain traits were shared by all. First and foremost, Protestants developed a piety that was centered squarely on the Bible, and in which the sermon assumed a central place in worship. The use of Latin in ritual was discarded by all Protestants and replaced by the local vernacular. They also discarded the cult of the saints, the veneration of images and relics, pilgrimages, and processions. Protestants rejected asceticism, and monasticism too (although a few extremely rare quasi-monastic communities of single women survived in some places, such as Strassburg). Purgatory ceased to exist for Protestants, and so did suffrages for the dead. For the most part, Protestants rejected the continued occurrence of miracles, though they certainly believed in those recorded in the Bible and eagerly interpreted natural "wonders" as signs from God. They also tended to reject mystical ecstasies and visions and the supernatural phenomena that normally accompanied them. Ritual and worship changed among them too, in some cases much more than in others, but by and large, most Protestants redefined the meaning of those ancient symbols and rituals that they kept, especially baptism and the Eucharist. As the map was stripped of holy places, so was the calendar wiped clean of special feasts such as Corpus Christi or saint's days, and, in some cases, of special seasons such as Lent or Advent. And when it came to the issue of authority, Protestants rejected the pope, redefined the structure of the church, and also the nature and function of the clergy, stripping them of any special status and turning them into common citizens.

Such essential similarities can be drawn with a broad brush, but Protestant churches were also highly conscious of the numerous ways in which they differed from one another. Painting with a slightly smaller and finer brush, the differences can be made readily apparent.

Of all the Protestant churches, the Church of England retained the highest number of Catholic traits, especially the office of bishop, and liturgies that paralleled those of Catholicism. But even within Anglicanism there was a spectrum of pieties, from "high" (closer to Catholicism) to "low" (closer to Reformed Protestant). One of the most heated controversies in Elizabethan England was all about whether or not the clergy should use certain kinds of liturgical vestments. The retention of religious imagery was also hotly contested. And throughout England, some of the old feasts continued to be observed, with modifications. In Dorchester, for instance, the feast of St. George—patron saint of England—continued to be celebrated without direct reference to the saint himself, and the traditional icon paraded on that day through the streets, which had previously showed him fighting a dragon, was reduced to just a dragon, all by itself.

Lutheranism retained many traditional Catholic elements too, and it was somewhat close to Anglicanism when it came to piety. One distinguishing feature of Lutheranism was its high regard for Luther himself, although this waned with every passing generation. Lutheran piety was sermon centered, but also focused on the Eucharist, through which, Lutherans believed, Christ was made really present in the bread and wine. That some Lutheran churches had bishops—as in Scandinavia—while others did not made little difference to the nature of Lutheran piety. For the most part, Lutherans developed a very Bible-centered piety that was guided by well-educated clergy. Bible reading in the home was encouraged, and so was prayer, with parents playing a key role in the Christian upbringing of their children. Religious imagery that depicted biblical scenes was allowed within the churches, especially images of Christ, but the icons were for instruction and inspiration only, not for veneration. Music and congregational hymn singing played a very large role in the Lutheran liturgy. Finally, Lutherans could be intensely interested in decoding natural "wonders," and the threatening presence of devil remained a concern for them, more so than in other Protestant churches.

The Reformed prided themselves in rejecting "popery" and "idolatry" more thoroughly than the Lutherans. All branches of the Reformed family shared some traits in common, but none was more prominent than their conception of the divine as omniscient, omnipotent, and wholly spiritual. One aphorism of Zwingli's ("Whatever you

Lutheran piety. This 1555 altarpiece by Lucas Cranach the Younger captures much of the essence of Lutheran piety as well as of the political realities that were essential to the survival of Luther's church. Four themes dominate this altarpiece from the church of SS. Peter and Paul at Weimar. First and foremost, this is a Christocentric, Gospel-based icon in which Cranach makes the redemptive sacrificial death of Jesus Christ on the cross most prominent, as required by Lutheran doctrine. Second, Cranach also depicts Jesus Christ triumphing over death and the devil in the lower left of the central panel, another key theme in Lutheran theology. Third, the members of the ruling dynasty of Electoral Saxony included in this altarpiece outnumber the biblical figures. Fourth, Luther figures prominently in the central panel too, holding a Bible and receiving the blood that streams from Christ's side.

invest in matter detracts from the spirit") and one aphorism of Calvin's ("To God alone be the glory") combined to guide their piety, which was centered on stark distinctions between sacred and profane, and spiritual and material. Their desire to create godly communities made the Reformed formidable agents of change and of social disciplining. An intense devotion to a transcendent deity who foreordained everything, including the actions of his chosen people, made them fearsome minorities as well as formidable rulers. It also made worship and prayer a process of praise and thanksgiving and of petitions that focused on the softening and bending of the human will rather than on suspending the laws of nature. Bare, imageless churches expressed Reformed piety as well as Reformed aesthetics. Sobriety, moderation, and restraint guided their way of life. Convinced that they were agents of the divine on earth and that they had a mission to fulfill, the Reformed developed a piety that was as focused on action as on prayer.

The Radicals differed wildly from all other Protestants, and often from one another too. The world-denying piety of the Anabaptists, their pacifism, and their belief in a gathered church and adult baptism set them apart and constantly threatened their survival, but that threat was successfully countered by their steadfastness, rootlessness, and endogamy. Their piety was as community centered as it was Bible centered, for they were a people set apart, a small minority ever surrounded by hostile or suspicious neighbors. Their exemplary adherence to the Ten Commandments and the ethic of the gospels could attract praise even from their harshest critics, including those who persecuted them. Apocalypticism gripped the Radicals, on and off, but, curiously, many Anabaptist communities ended up resembling monastic institutions, as communities set apart from "the world," or, even in some cases, as communes where none of the members claimed private property. Those who were not Anabaptists—the so-called Spiritualists and Anti-Trinitarians—all stressed three points in their piety, despite their individuality and differences of opinion: the inner connection between the individual and the divine, the uselessness of ancient doctrines, and the necessity of toleration. It is impossible to sum up the piety of this most radical and individual grouping as we can for other Protestant traditions. Some of them, it can be argued, resembled the Deists of the eighteenth century more than they did their contemporaries, which has led some historians to label their piety as ahead of its time.

Catholics, on the whole, tended to intensify those elements in their piety that Protestants rejected. Above all, Catholic piety continued to embrace opposite polarities simultaneously: sacred and profane, spiritual and material, immanent and transcendent, temporal and eternal, local and universal. The Catholic deity was just as male, transcendent, and ubiquitous as that of the Protestants, but he was also quite immanent and fond of localization, even in a bread crumb; he was just as omnipotent and omniscient, but also quite ready to alter the course of events and even the laws of nature in response to prayer. The Catholic deity excelled in miracles and irruptions, and in the constant bending of natural laws. He was certainly the only being in the universe deserving of worship, but not the only being in heaven who could be approached for favors. The Catholic deity had revealed himself in the Bible, of course, but unlike the Protestants, Catholics also believed in a historical institution, their church, in which no single individual could ever claim to have the correct interpretation all by him- or herself, and in which all exegesis had to incorporate centuries of divinely inspired tradition. The pope hardly figured in Catholic piety. He was central to the administration of the Catholic Church, for sure, but not necessarily to its worship and ritual. The pope figured much more prominently in early Protestant piety—as the sum of all evil—than he did in Catholic piety, where he tended to be viewed more as a short-lived ruler than as a spiritual leader.

Catholic piety could focus as much on the individual as on the community, as much on the here and now as on the afterlife and eternity, as much on a particular relic or shrine as on the wounds of Christ or the inner relations among the three persons of the Holy Trinity. In response to Protestantism, certain of its ancient paradoxical features became more prominent than ever, especially in the realm of the mystical and miraculous. Catholic piety shouted out loudly that perfection was possible. But that perfection had to be understood paradoxically, for the holy men and women who embodied that perfection tended to remain painfully aware of their sinfulness up until the very end. St. Teresa of Ávila, the very same woman who claimed intimacy with the divine, saw no contradiction in saying, moments before she died, that she was the "worst" sinner in the world.

The seventeenth century would have an overabundance of mystics and visionaries, some of whom were deemed frauds, but many of whom went on to enrich Catholic piety and begin new devotions, each and every one of them based on a divine communication to some holy human being: the Sacred Heart of Jesus, revealed to St. Margaret Mary Alacoque; the Immaculate Heart of Mary, revealed to St. John Eudes; the Blue Scapular of the Immaculate Conception, revealed to Venerable Ursula Benicasa. And as Descartes and Galileo were making their discoveries, St. Joseph of Cupertino was levitating in Italy, and Sister María of Ágreda bilocating in Spain and New Mexico and taking dictation from the Virgin Mary, and serving as an unofficial confessor to King Philip IV, in letter after intimate letter. At a less exalted, but no less significant level, the effervescence of Catholic confraternities, which multiplied as never before, led to an unprecedented wave of civic devotion and social service.

France, in particular, saw an upsurge in mystics who attracted attention and followers. The origins of this phenomenon are usually traced to Cardinal Pierre de Bérulle (1575–1629), onetime confessor to King Henry IV, founder of the Congregation of the French Oratory, and sponsor of the Discalced Carmelite reform in France. Bérulle attracted influential disciples who not only worked for the reform of the French Catholic Church, but also popularized certain devotions among the laity, such as that of the Sacred Heart of Jesus and of the Immaculate Heart of Mary. Others authored influential mystical texts, among whom the most significant were Jean-Jacques Olier, founder of the Sulpician order, Jean Eudes, founder of the Eudists, and Louis de Montfort, a tireless missionary and preacher, and author of the influential *True Devotion to Mary*. Yet if one pays attention to some who were deeply devout, one can easily get the impression that much of what we identify as evidence of a lively religious culture was no more than a hollow shell. Jeanne Marie Bouvier de la Motte Guyon—better known simply as Madame Guyon and a mystic who ended up charged with the heresy of Quietism and spent several years imprisoned in the Bastille—thought that the preachers and pastors of her age only grazed the surface, and that all hearts in her day were still "made of ice." Her advice to those in charge of Christianizing the world revealed a deep dissatisfaction with the results they had obtained:

> If all who worked for the conquest of souls tried to gain them by the heart, initially, introducing them to prayer and interior life, they would make infinite and permanent conversions. In reality, as long as we burden them with a thousand precepts for external exercises, the changes are temporary with very little fruit. Instead we should attract the soul by the occupation of the heart with Jesus Christ.[1]

Among Protestants, at the very tail end of the Reformation era, a wave of devotional fervor known as Pietism captured the hearts and minds of many. Pietism began among some pastors and their congregations as a grassroots response to perceived deficiencies in the seventeenth-century Lutheran Church, particularly its apparent incapacity to inspire intense spiritual awakenings and moral transformations, but this initiative rapidly crossed confessional boundaries. Intensely inward and mystical, but seriously committed to the transformation of society as well as of individuals, Pietism had its roots in the work of some mystically inclined Lutherans who found the state-run church and its theology too cold and hollow.

Among these forerunners, three stand out: Jacob Böhme (1575–1624), an unorthodox Lutheran visionary who authored several controversial texts; Johann Arndt (1555–1621), a Lutheran-turned-Calvinist whose devotional manual *True Christianity* was deeply influenced by late medieval Catholic mysticism and eventually inspired many Protestants; and Heinrich Müller (1631–1675), a Lutheran theologian at the University of Rostock who belittled the baptismal font, the pulpit, the confessional, and the altar as "the four dumb idols of the Lutheran Church."

The acknowledged founder of Pietism was a man influenced by the aforementioned three, Philip Jakob Spener (1635–1705), a philosopher and theologian who studied at Strassburg and developed connections with both Lutheran and Reformed universities, including that of Geneva. Invited to serve as pastor of the Lutheran Church of Frankfurt in 1666, Spener was dismayed by the lack of fervor he encountered. Convinced that "practical" Christianity was far more important that rigid orthodoxy or conformity to any status quo, and that his society needed to be jolted out of its lethargic complacency, Spener began to organize "little-churches-within-the Church," that is, meetings of small numbers of the faithful in which Bible reading and discussion would take place, and all would be encouraged to live out the gospel. Spener began with a small group at his own home, and called it a *collegia pietatis*, or school of piety. The name "pietist" stuck as similar small conventicles began to assemble and to spread far beyond Frankfurt, and beyond the confines of the Lutheran Church, although opponents sought to discredit the movement.

In 1675 Spener published a devotional treatise entitled *Pia desideria*, or *Earnest Desire for a Reform of the True Evangelical Church*. This immensely popular text distilled Spener's vision for an active Christianity that was more squarely centered on love of God and neighbor and on ethics than on rigid orthodoxy. Its aim was to effect personal transformations through spiritual rebirth and renewal, and to gradually transform the church and society one conversion at a time. *Pia Desideria* is a curious blend of late medieval Catholic spirituality, Radical Protestantism and spiritualism, Lutheran and Calvinist theology, and a vigorous anti-Catholicism. Though the text leans toward Arminianism and what Luther called "works-righteousness," and though it also advocates a sympathetic treatment of all who fail to see the light, *Pia Desideria* nonetheless makes it clear that the Church of Rome is still an enemy of the gospel.

Pietism reinvigorated Protestantism as the number of skeptics, Deists, and atheists began to increase, especially among the intellectual elites, and as the established churches were losing their grip, socially and politically. It fostered direct participation by the laity in their own spiritual development within the faltering established churches, but also independently of them. Its individualism, its emphasis on a very intimate personal relation with the divine, and its commitment to a life of ethical striving was a far cry from Luther's theology, and it earned Spener the condemnation of the faculty of the University of Wittenberg in 1695. But by then Spener had moved to Calvinist Brandenburg and beyond confessional purity. The movement he had begun swept through Lutheran as well as Reformed lands, largely untroubled with condemnations from Wittenberg theologians, and it would eventually influence some Radicals and Anglicans too, and infuse the German Enlightenment with a uniquely religious character that was largely absent from the Enlightenment in France, Scotland, and England. In many ways, the ethics and philosophy of religion of Immanuel Kant, the greatest of all German Enlightenment figures, can be seen as an extension of Pietism.

Reared by Pietist parents, Kant would reduce religion to ethics, and ethics to the golden rule of the gospels and the Sermon on the Mount. Though he preferred to call the golden rule the "categorical imperative" and to dissect reason with an obsessive passion for coldly abstract distinctions, Kant's philosophy was, at bottom, a complex rationalist version of the "practical Christianity" dear to Pietists, stripped clean of any metaphysical assumptions. Pietism reached its peak in the eighteenth century and influenced John Wesley (1703–1791), the founder of Methodism. Its emphasis on personal conversion and an intimate experience of the divine was later reflected in Protestant revivalism too.

Baroque Culture

Pietism was no oddity, but a reflection of one of the most salient characteristics of its age: a stirring of devotion as the world began to shift its focus from faith to reason and from biblical proof-texts to scientific experiments and empirical proofs. In this transitional age, currents we now consider antithetical to one other flowed together and intermingled, often changing their composition and character in response. It is characterized by an excess in polarities: the overabundance of competing truth claims and conflicting worldviews; the simultaneous presence of traits that we in our own day consider "medieval" or "modern"; the ice floes of cold reason swirling in the bloody overflow from religious warfare and witchcraft persecutions; the leering presence of the devil alongside that of the Deist watchmaker God.

For those who struggled to steer the world toward the life of the spirit, no excess seemed too excessive. The fierceness of the competition for souls and the spirit of the age in concert created a vortex of exorbitance. When it came to competing for souls, it was not just a case of churches wrestling with one another as in the earlier days of the Reformations, but of "the world" itself and reason, materiality, and sensuality luring away the fold. Some devout elites saw that dreadful countertrinity of the world, the flesh, and the devil gaining the upper hand, besting the Father, Son, and Holy Spirit. All of the arts of the age reflect a love of ostentation, prolixity, complexity, and the bombastic. And as everyone in our day and age knows, the arts—especially those favored by the elite—are the clearest expression of the spirit of the times. Artists and cultural mavens of the late eighteenth and early nineteenth century who found all of this excess extremely distasteful gave the age a pejorative name: *baroque*. The exact origin of the term *baroque* is disputed, but as first used by those who loathed the culture of the seventeenth and early eighteenth century, the term implied something curious, odd, bizarre, grotesque, or freakish. Experts suggest that it was probably derived from a word for a large irregular pearl or a fake jewel. The name has stuck, even though it no longer tends to be employed in a derogatory sense. And certainly the period did exhibit a propensity for elaboration, prolixity, complexity, repetition, and excessive detail that is easy to identify.

The baroque sensibility first developed most fully among Catholics in Italy in the late sixteenth and early seventeenth century, then spread across national boundaries and confessional lines, and endured well into the eighteenth century. Often interpreted as *the* art of the so-called Counter-Reformation, and as an attempt by Catholics to win souls through the overwhelming of the senses, the baroque style is not easily contained in a strictly religious context. Nor should it be seen as a carefully constructed and precise plan to wage war against Protestantism through the arts. The baroque style is also intimately connected to discoveries in science and mathematics, at least insofar as its technical aspects are concerned. Baroque art and music, are, after all, a dazzling display of mastery over the natural order and of exacting precision, closer in essence to the work of Galileo than to the sermons of St. Francis de Sales. And there is no denying that three of the greatest musicians of the baroque age were Protestants who composed numerous masterpieces of religious music for Protestant ears and hearts: Georg Philipp Telemann (1681–1767); George Friedrich Handel (1685–1759); and Johann Sebastian Bach (1685–1750). Yet there is no getting around the fact that the baroque style was intimately connected at first to the Catholic Church, that it flourished under its sponsorship, and that some of its greatest masterpieces were religious in nature.

In architecture, baroque church buildings became theaters in which the awesome power of the liturgy was showcased in grand splendor: solid proofs of the transcendent power of matter itself. The basilica of St. Peter in Rome was not constructed in the Baroque style, but the finishing touches put upon it by Gianlorenzo Bernini elevated an already colossal and impressive structure to an unprecedented overwhelming grandiosity, not just through his sinuous ten-story bronze canopy over the main altar, built between 1624 and 1633—which serves multiple symbolic functions at once and is the only structure within the sacred space that seems to be alive—but also through the piazza he carved out from the urban space in front of the church.

Bernini's vast piazza, which can hold up to a quarter of a million people, served practical and symbolic functions all at once, with a sense of overkill. Shaped like a keyhole, in reference to the keys of the Kingdom held by St. Peter and his successors, bounded by colonnades that contain 284 four-story Doric columns, topped off by 96 statues of saints,

Bernini's piazza at St. Peter's

each fifteen feet high, this space sets apart St. Peter's from everything that surrounds it, marking it off in a most dramatic way as a singularly important structure, and at the same time creating a space in which the pope can interact with the faithful in person. The two arms of the colonnade that extend from the basilica also express, literally and figuratively, the church's embrace of the world.

   Baroque architecture developed differently according to time and place but shared common traits. In Spain, for instance, a style known as Churrigueresque developed in the mid-seventeenth century. It was one of the most extreme forms of the baroque style, with elaborate sculptural ornamentation. Named after the Spanish architect and sculptor José Benito de Churriguera (1665–1725), the Churrigueresque style spread from Europe to the New World, where it became a definitive style in colonial architecture. This overly ornate style became so popular that in the late seventeenth century, the Romanesque exterior of the Cathedral of Santiago de Compostela, one of the prime pilgrimage shrines of Catholic Europe, was enveloped in a protective Churrigueresque shell—a fitting symbolic gesture that reified the superimposition of baroque sensibilities over an ancient medieval core that needed to be preserved and could never be discarded. And a baroque exterior was imposed on an entire nation: Bohemia. After the Hussite and Protestant defeat at the Battle of White Mountain in 1620 ensured the return of Catholicism to the region, the imposition of the baroque style was inseparable from the re-Catholicization effort of its Hapsburg rulers, and in the land of the heretic Jan Hus, the Churrigueresque would be imposed. To this day the capital city of Prague retains the indelible stamp of a faith that seemed identical to a very specific aesthetic sensibility, at once local and universal, beneath which dissent and cold indifference never vanished.

As Copernicus, Kepler, and Galileo reshuffled the heavens, calling the location of God's celestial throne into question, Baroque sensibilities sought to reify that Heaven of old where God and the saints dwelt eternally. Beginning in the sixteenth century, eternity itself would be depicted in churches, usually in such a way as to give the impression that ceilings or domes were opening up to heaven. Employing the painting technique known as trompe l'oeil (French for "trick the eye"), artists such as Antonio da Correggio, Andrea Pozzo, and Franz Joseph Spiegler skillfully created the illusion that the tall vaulted ceilings and massive domes of churches were not really there at all. Every one of these ceiling paintings is filled with bodies, both angelic and human, which are suspended in midair, straining sinuously toward a focal point in the upper reaches of heaven itself. The movement of all the bodies is carefully orchestrated, much like some celestial dance—a spectacle that became a staple of baroque church decoration, as evidenced by two examples.

The illusionist ceilings of the Jesuit artist Andrea Pozzo are numerous, but his *Apotheosis of Saint Ignatius*, in the Jesuit church of Sant'Ignazio in Rome (1685–1694) is arguably the most impressive. It shows St. Ignatius Loyola, the founder of the Jesuit order, ascending into the empyrean heaven, beckoned by the cross-carrying Christ who floats above him, bathed in the golden light of eternity. As in all such paintings, the upward

Apotheosis of St. Ignatius

sweep of the composition is as much an attempt to depict the negation of gravity as of time and space. The church itself, perhaps one of the most impressive displays of baroque excess, seems outdone by this ceiling.

At the far end of the baroque age, the heaven depicted by Dominicus Zimmerman at the abbey church of Wies in Bavaria (1754) is very complex. Zimmerman, a contemporary of aggressive Enlightenment atheists, gave the Final Judgment a very modern turn by bringing all who would enter that church into the picture, and by depicting eternity behind closed doors. Up above, Christ sits on a rainbow, judging the human race. But the blessed and the damned—normally depicted in great detail—are nowhere to be seen. At one end of the ceiling, Zimmerman depicts the empty throne of Jesus, and at the other end, a door, over which is curled none other than the ancient symbol for eternity, the Ouroboros, a serpent devouring its own tail. The message encoded in the ceiling is very clear: those being judged by Jesus Christ are none other than those who are standing

Church ceiling at Wies

beneath the ceiling fresco, for whom time has not yet run out; they still have time to earn either eternal bliss or eternal damnation, concealed behind the closed door. The baroque theatricality of it all is overwhelming. And it is also as modern as the disbelief it seeks to deny.

Baroque art depicted heaven in other ways, most dramatically in its rendition of the mystical ecstasies of saints. When one considers that Protestants rejected not only the Catholic mystical tradition, but also the Catholic understanding of holiness, sainthood, and miracles, and—on top of that—religious art, it is easy to see why Catholics found it both useful and important to revel in the artistic depiction not just of saints, but also of their most intense mystical experiences, and especially those ecstasies that seemed to prove that Protestants were very wrong. Protestants tended to be anti-ecstatic, soberly focused on the spiritual and physical limitations imposed on humans by their ontological status as creatures who, in addition to being vastly inferior to their Creator, also happened to be fallen from their original state and inescapably predisposed to sin and corruption.

St. Teresa of Ávila, who was canonized in 1622, provided the baroque age with a saint as excessive as its sensibilities. Of all of Teresa's many ecstasies, that which became best known, eventually, was the "transverberation," described in chapter 29 of her autobiography. This ecstasy involves an angel who stabs her with a *dardo*, a dart or

Bernini's *Ecstasy of St. Teresa*

thin spear, and drives it into her heart and, farther down, into her entrails. While her wording clearly indicates that this happened more than once, this peculiar ecstasy, so redolent of Cupid and all the eroticism jammed into his quiver, was somehow collapsed into a singular experience, and even a feast day for the Catholic Church (August 26). Gianlorenzo Bernini, the very artist who lent so much theatricality to St. Peter's, had a lot to do with this condensation and propagation of one of the weirdest, and most baroque and anti-Protestant, moments in the interior life of an ecstatic master. Bernini's rendition of this ecstasy in marble, executed for the Coronaro family chapel at the church of Santa Maria della Vittoria, Rome, in 1652, reified the very essence of baroque Catholicism. His swooning St. Teresa, immortalized at the very moment of ultimate ecstasy—at once heavenly and earthly, spiritual and physical—embodies polar opposites in a transcendent fainting that is as much an out-of-body trance as it is the ultimate embodied thrill. More than that, Bernini, the baroque artist, has turned the most intimate and ineffable of experiences into a deliriously expressible state close to death and eternity, and obviously inseparable from love, and physical elation.

Catholic artists were constantly commissioned to represent ecstasies not just for monks and nuns, but for all the faithful, in frescoes, paintings, altarpieces, and illustrations for books. But mystical ecstasy could not be a *novelty*; on the contrary, it had to be part of a long continuum stretching back to Jesus and the apostles, even to Moses and the prophets, and Abraham, and all the way back to the book of Genesis. Ecstasy had to be a historical fact, a trait that linked the communion of saints, and the quick and the dead. One such past ecstasy that gained popularity among baroque artists concerned Bernard of Clairvaux (1090–1153), who, according to legend, had been visited by the Virgin Mary and given milk to drink directly from her breast. This ecstasy, known as the lactation of St. Bernard, was intensely physical, focused on primal human needs, and the boundaries between heaven and earth, and spirit and matter are not just blurred, but erased. Given its metaphorical punch, it stands to reason that this ecstasy would become a baroque favorite. In Claude Mellan's rendition of this event, Bernard's ecstasy is much more than a swoon: it is an ontological implosion, an affront to reason and propriety. At once taboo and totem, Mellan's *Lactation* is an assault on the metaphysical boundaries upheld by Protestants and an affirmation of every belief at the core of Catholicism. His mouth agape, his throat awash in the milk of the Mother of God, St. Bernard—known as the "Mellifluous Doctor" because of the sweetness of his words—is reduced to silence. All he can do is to be his most exceptional, most ecstatic, most Catholic, most baroque self.

Baroque sensibilities eventually captured the Protestant artistic imagination too. Given their theology and their distrust or abhorrence of religious art, those sensibilities found other outlets for expression, especially in architecture. One feature of Protestant churches deeply shaped by the baroque was the pulpit from which the Word was preached. Even the Calvinists got into erecting imposing and ornate pulpits, a prime exemplar of which is the pulpit in the church of St. Bavo in Haarlem, in the Netherlands. Built in

Lactation of St. Bernard

1678, this pulpit, like many others in the Calvinist Netherlands, is at once elaborate and restrained, and free of iconography.

In Lutheran Germany, the baroque style affected the pulpit even more intensely through the creation of the *Kanzelaltar*, a symbolic and practical interweaving of pulpit and altar that often also incorporated the baptismal font and the organ into a single ensemble. Situated at the center of the sanctuary, the *Kanzelaltar* was the visual focal point of the worship space. Functionally and symbolically, it wedded the four key elements of Lutheran ritual: baptism, the preaching of the Word, the celebration of the Eucharist, and the interweaving of Word and sacrament in music. Its gilded simplicity spoke of mediation in baroque terms, through ornament and symbolic excess. Here God was encountered, his presence mediated through scripture reading and exegesis, the two sacraments, and exquisitely crafted hymns and chorales. By the eighteenth century, some Protestant churches could be as ornately decorated as Catholic churches. Protestant fondness for the baroque style reached its apogee, some would argue, in the Frauenkirche of

Baroque Protestant pulpit

Dresden, built between 1726 and 1743, destroyed by firebombing in 1945, and restored with painstaking care to its former glory after the reunification of Germany in 1989. Not to be outdone by Lutherans, the Calvinists of Berlin went on to build their own ornate Oberpfarr- und Domkirche, more commonly known as the Berliner Dom.

Baroque music, like baroque art, is easily identifiable. And it was a style that crossed confessional boundaries much more easily than art, for music was much less likely to be linked to idolatry by Protestants. Among Catholics, the decrees of the Council of Trent had a profound impact on the development of sacred music, as the council had banned the use of popular tunes in the liturgy and any complex polyphony that obscured the words being sung. This ruling forced composers to develop exclusively religious music and to develop new styles. One of the first pioneers in the new Tridentine style was Giovanni di Palestrina (1525–1594), who composed more than 100 Masses and 450 motets. But Palestrina's music was restrained and transitional, and is usually labeled "Renaissance" rather than "baroque." The full flowering of baroque music began around 1600, with Giovanni Gabrieli (1555–1612), organist at St. Mark's Cathedral in Venice, who is the composer normally identified as the first great innovator. Gabrieli pulled out all the stops, figuratively and literally, blending choral and instrumental music and employing as many as five choruses at a time.

Very quickly, the baroque style extended to secular music as well, and developments there were just as dramatic, in every sense of the word, for the new style gave birth to opera, a hybrid art form that told a story set entirely or partially to music, and sometimes included dance, with an emphasis on visual display, elaborate staging, and sumptuous costumes. Even the setting for opera came to require excess. Venice built the first opera house in 1637, and others quickly followed throughout Italy, each ever more ornate. By 1700 opera houses could be found throughout Europe, some full of statuary and trompe l'oeil frescoes, and as much filigree as one might find in any baroque church. Operas, like the theater of that era, often dwelled on purely secular and ancient classical subjects, including pagan mythology. One of the great innovators in opera, Claudio Monteverdi (1567–1643), also from Venice, set several trends at once with his *Orpheus*, first staged in 1610. Monteverdi composed liturgical music too, along with ballets, constantly traversing the line between sacred and profane, a trait that would become routine for baroque composers, whose livelihood depended on commissions from two sources: the church and the aristocracy. When it came to music, political boundaries and confessional lines seemed not to matter. A contemporary of Monteverdi, also considered one of the pioneers of the baroque style, was Heinrich Schütz (1585–1672), a Lutheran who composed liturgical music and staged the first German opera, *Dafne*, in 1627. Fittingly, Schütz's remains would eventually be buried at the Lutheran Frauenkirche in Dresden.

The patterns established by musicians such as Monteverdi and Schütz would be followed by their disciples and admirers throughout Europe, making the seventeenth and early eighteenth centuries a remarkably rich era for musical innovation. Although music did not heal religious divisions, it was one of the few areas of human endeavor—along with trade and commerce—in which boundaries were eagerly crossed. Among both Catholics and Protestants, music served the realm of the sacred as well as that of the profane, bringing both to new aesthetic heights. One of the greatest of Catholic composers, Antonio Vivaldi (1671–1741), was also a priest, and many of his compositions were written for the girls of the Ospedale della Pietà in Venice, an orphanage where he was employed as a music teacher. In 1770, Jean-Jacques Rousseau described what he saw and heard at this orphanage and others in Venice, which still kept alive the musical legacy of Vivaldi:

> I have not an idea of anything so voluptuous and affecting as this music; the richness of the art, the exquisite taste of the vocal part, the excellence of the voices, the justness of the execution, everything in these delightful concerts concurs to produce an impression which certainly is not the mode, but from which I am of opinion no heart is secure.[2]

Rousseau, a native of Geneva, and a renegade who distrusted the cold, pure reason favored by many of his Enlightenment contemporaries, had found the perfect description of the effect that baroque music, both sacred and secular, could have on the emotions. It was art of the highest order that reached the heart and soul and transcended doctrine.

Anyone who has hears Vivaldi's *Requiem* for the first time, or Bach's *St. Matthew Passion*, or Handel's *Messiah*—especially its "Hallelujah" chorus—will have trouble discerning whether that stirring music was composed for Protestants or Catholics.

Fanning the Flames of Hell

It can be argued that the flowering of doubt and skepticism that accompanied the up-heavals of the Reformation era was fertilized by a surfeit of belief and religious zealotry, and that, paradoxically, the excesses of faith were also engendered by an overabundance of doubt. It is an ancient conundrum, as old as the human race: those who cast doubt on belief often deepen faith among those who believe, and those who stridently insist on promoting their beliefs over and against those who deny them often strengthen that unbelief. So, as baroque sensibilities took hold of religious and secular life and as rival churches claimed sole possession of heaven, the flames of hell were aggressively fanned.

This obsession with hell—though obviously connected to all things demonic and ultimately inseparable from them—needs to be distinguished from the preoccupa-tion with the devil manifested by so many Christians during this era. And it is precisely because of this distinction that the two topics are being approached separately in this book. The demonic had to do with life on earth: with the temptation, deceit, mayhem, and suffering the devil brought to the living in the here and now. Hell had to do with the afterlife, and the dead condemned to suffer in it for eternity. It was the abode of Satan and his demonic hosts, surely, but it was a different subject altogether, in which the focus was not the evil angelic beings from hell, but rather the place itself. Ultimately, hell was something to avoid, a very real place—as real as the devil—that could evoke extreme fear and serve manifold interlocking functions, spiritual as well as material.

Protestants and Catholics could seem very similar in their obsession with hell, especially in the seventeenth century, when highly detailed meditations on the subject flourished. Devotional texts that focused on death and the hereafter in which hell fig-ured prominently were a popular best-selling genre. Hellfire sermons rang out in both Protestant and Catholic churches, and their warning cry was always clear: eternity could best be understood in connection to sin and hell. As one Spanish Jesuit put it: "Watch your step. Why do you mock eternity; why don't you fear the eternal death, why do you love this temporal life so much? You are on the wrong track; change your life."[3] If such warnings were not enough, graphic descriptions of hell might do the trick:

> I wish you could open a window through which you would view what happens in hell, and see the torments inflicted on the rich who live in ease and have no compassion for the poor. Oh, if you could see how their flesh is boiled in those cauldrons and how they are baked in those inexorable flames, where every single devil will sear them with firebrands. . . . And it will be very good to imagine how those who can't stand the summer heat outside of their roomy cellars will suffer in the blaze of the eternal fire.[4]

Some historians have seen the proliferation of books, essays, and sermons on hell in this period as evidence of processes of confessionalization, social disciplining, and state building shared by Protestants and Catholics. Scaring the hell out of people, literally, was a strategy of the early modern state: it was a way to create a more fearful and docile citizenry, with the help of the church. Whether or not this reductionist interpretation of the place of hell in early modern culture will stand the test of time remains to be seen, but it is safe to bet that hell itself will not be easily dismissed by those who study this period.

One of the most significant devotional texts of the seventeenth century was Juan Eusebio Nieremberg's *The Difference Between the Temporal and the Eternal*, a treatise that was not only published repeatedly, but also translated into many other languages. Nieremberg's *Difference* was as intensely dualistic and ascetical in tone as the title suggests. "Everything that is precious on earth, everything honored and esteemed, is smoke and shadow," warned Nieremberg, "considering its brief duration and the eternity of that fire of the life to come."[5] He also elaborated on the torments each sense will be subjected to for eternity as retribution for sin, and presses further beyond the "fire-bodies" of Ignatius Loyola's *Spiritual Exercises*, forever engulfed in flames, inside and out, to consider even greater internal suffering and "insufferable sadness."[6] Adding fuel to the flames, Nieremberg goes on to claim that one's own memory will become one of the worst and cruelest torturers in hell. In brief, one will blame oneself for eternity, without rest, without end. Nieremberg drove home the point with prose as overbearing as a baroque altarpiece:

> The miserable wretch in Hell will remember with great regret how many times he could have deserved Heaven, and how he ended up deserving Hell instead, and shall say to himself: "Oh how many times I could have prayed, but wasted the time on playing instead! Now I'm paying for it! How many times I should have fasted, but gave in to my appetite! Now I'm paying for it! How many times I could have given alms, but spent the money on sin! Now I'm paying for it! How many times I was asked to forgive my enemies, but instead I took vengeance on them! Now I'm paying for it! How many times I should have been patient, but suffered grudgingly! Now I'm paying for it! How many times I could have performed acts of charity and humility, but I was cruel to my brothers! Now I'm paying for it! How many times I could have partaken of the sacraments, but instead remained unwilling to avoid occasions of sin! Now I'm paying for it!" You never lacked an opportunity to serve God, but never availed yourself of the chance; and now you're paying for it. See here, you damned wretch, how you lost Heaven by giving in to yourself and fooling around with childish things. . . . It is all your fault, and now you're paying for it.[7]

Despite its florid Churrigueresque excess, so fossilized, this is a very modern hell, for the guilty ego torments itself forever, with no psychotherapists to consult. But this is not all. This realm of everlasting self-inflicted pain is smack in the midst of the fiery pit and the slimy stink hole, where all of damned humanity is crammed together like grapes in a wine press. And Nieremberg makes it clear that there will never, ever, be any relief:

That fire shall never die, as Isaiah says, nor will you ever die, so that your torments can be everlasting. After a hundred years, and after one hundred thousand million years, your torments shall be as alive and strong as on the first day.[8]

Nieremberg was definitely not alone. Many other writers and preachers harped on these themes, ad nauseam. Most of them stoked the fires of Hell in the imagination, through graphic meditations. Drexelius, or Jeremias Drexel (1581–1638), another Jesuit, penned many best sellers, including *Considerations on Eternity*, first published in 1620, and *Death, the Messenger of Eternity*, published in 1627. Drexel's books on eternity were not philosophical or theological explorations of eternity, but rather very pragmatic guides that aimed to improve their readers' attitude and behavior. In our own day, they might be called self-help books. Drexel's *Considerations on Eternity* is filled with the kinds of meditations that Jesuits were famous for, such as the following, which merits being quoted at length, simply because the cadence of its seemingly interminable sentences is inseparable from its message:

Suppose there is a mountain composed of minute grains of sand, as large as the whole world, or in mass and size even greater, and that only a single grain be taken from this mountain by an angel each year. How many thousands of years, and again thousands upon thousands; how many hundred thousands, nay how many thousand millions of years will have passed before the mountain would appear to diminish and decrease? . . . Let us suppose that finally the last gain of this immense mountain has actually been counted; yet eternity exceeds it by an incomparable length (and nothing is more certain), because there is no comparison, no proportion between the finite and the infinite. Eternity admits of no confines, no boundaries; therefore the damned will burn during this long, this incomprehensible term of years in perpetual flames, until a mountain of so great size . . . be transferred to another place. But the measure and limit of their torments will be so far from being ended at that time, that it can then be said: "Now eternity is just beginning; nothing has been subtracted from it, it is still entire. After a thousand years, after a hundred thousand years, there is not yet an end nor middle nor beginning of eternity, but its measure is *always*."[9]

Such meditations had a point, beyond intimidation. Drexel was a Jesuit, after all, and Jesuit core training as found in the *Spiritual Exercises* focused on meditations with a purpose. Drexel himself delivered the message several times, just in case the reader was too slow to catch the drift of such exercises:

"Momentary is that which delights; eternal that which tortures" . . . these words, thus engraved on the heart, must then especially be pondered on and more frequently repeated, when pleasure attracts, when passion incites, when luxury entices, when the flesh is rebellious, when the spirit grows weak, when there is occasion or danger of sin.[10]

Historians who stress "social disciplining" as the main characteristic of this period might say that Drexel was doing his best to create compliant citizens for the rising nation states.

But Drexel would have disagreed with such an assessment. What he had in mind went beyond pragmatism, or indoctrination:

> Think therefore of the ancient days, and have in mind the eternal years. Think on eternity, my friend, think, think on eternal punishments and eternal joys, and never (safely do I promise it) will you complain about any adversity. The following words will never fall from your lips: "This is too severe; this is intolerable; this is too hard." You will say that all things are tolerable and easy, and never will you be more satisfied with yourself than when you are most afflicted.[11]

Here was the payoff: with eternity as one's horizon, life could be tolerable, even good. In an age without anesthesia, vaccines, antibiotics, indoor plumbing, air conditioning, or widespread use of underarm deodorants, this might well have been the soundest practical advice anyone could offer. And readers must have agreed, for it sold consistently well for over a century, in German, Polish, French, Italian, and English.

Much like baroque music, hell crossed confessional boundaries. Protestant texts and sermons on hell are remarkably similar to Catholic ones, save for occasional anti-Catholic references. The following meditation by the Puritan clergyman Robert Bolton (1571–1632) is very typical, and, like that of Drexel, needs to be quoted in full because— as with much of baroque literature—style and substance are indivisible:

> If the severall paines of all the diseases and maladies incident to our nature, as of the stone, gout, colicke, . . . or what other you can name, most afflicting the body: nay, and add besides all the most exquisite and unheard of torments (and if you will, those of the Spanish Inquisition), which ever were or shall be inflicted upon miserable men, by the boudiest executioners of the greatest tyrants . . . and collect them all into one extremest anguish; and yet it were nothing to the torment which shall for ever possesse and pague the least part of a damned body. And as for the soule: let all the griefes, horrours and despaires that ever rent in peeces any heavy heart, and vext conscience. . . . And let them all be heaped together into one extremest horrour, and yet it would come infinitely short of that deperate rage and restlesse anguish, which shall eternally toru-ture the least and lowest faculty of the soule! What do you think will be the torment of the whole body? What will be the terrour of the whole soule? Here both invention of words would faile the ablest Oratour upon earth, or the highest Angell in heaven.

Bolton's long-winded description of the pains of hell was intended to serve the same purpose as Drexel's—although he would have loathed being compared to a papist. When viewed against the backdrop of hell, all temptations, and all misfortunes could seem much easier to overcome. With hell in view, he averred, one could live with "unwearied care and watchfulnesse" and "abstaine from fleshly lusts," seek out good company and engage with them in "all holy conversation and goodnesse." Inserting a heavy dose of Calvinist theology into his meditation, Bolton assured readers that hell could help "thriftily and industriously to husband the poore remainder of our few and evill dayes for the making our Calling and Election sure." Hell, ironically, served to motivate the elect. "In a word," Bolton concluded, thinking of hell could convince the saints "to do or suffer anything for Jesus Christ" with the utmost "resolution and zeale."[12]

As Bolton, Drexel, Nieremberg, and countless others were fanning the flames of hell in order to improve the lives of their flocks and close the gap between Christian ideals and "the world," others were already scoffing at hell and heaven and a deity who could be so cruel as to create beings to punish them for eternity. Such was the unraveling witnessed by the devout in the age of the baroque, a process that had begun in earnest in 1517, when a monk began to question the theology of indulgences and purgatory. The exuberant excess of the baroque can be fully understood only when it is placed in context, with 1517 at one end of the horizon and the Enlightenment at the other. For while Bolton and Drexel would be viewed as "bizarre" or "baroque" by the nineteenth century, the godless taunts of Enlightenment philosophes would become not just "normal," but dominant. By 1750, for many who considered themselves enlightened the world was no longer something to perfect, and neither was anyone's life. A new world had come into existence. As one French essayist put it:

> The new order of things . . . no longer sees anything great in all that is bounded by space and time. The duration of Empires and the succession of ages appear to it but as instants. The widest Kingdoms to its eyes are but as atoms, and it sees the earth reduced to a point where it loses itself in the infinite space that surrounds it. . . . [I]t perceives all the absurdity and the nothingness of that chimerical immortality which had been its idol.[13]

A new war against the idols had begun. These idols were not physical, like those attacked in the sixteenth century, but the war would be just as intense, with far-reaching consequences that still define own day and age. That the war rages still, with no clear victory for the skeptics, is in no small measure due to the contradictory, yet enduring legacies of the Reformations.

Epilogue

Assessing the Reformations

H alf a millennium after the "monkish squabble" ignited by Martin Luther set Western Christendom ablaze, we still strain to understand what happened, exactly, and how that conflagration affects us.

Those who wrote the history of this epochal turn as it was occurring five centuries ago did so in a partisan way, to promote their own confessional agenda. And the same is true of most histories of this era written over the following four centuries. Nowadays, however, relatively few historians take sides or champion one church or tradition over others. This is not to say that the narratives we have are free of bias. Every historian has to choose an approach to the past, some lens through which to analyze it. Choices have to be made. And when it comes to the act of choosing an approach, every historian is influenced by personal preferences and beliefs. Some, too, have axes to grind, both large and small. There are also trends to consider: approaches to the past are always changing, much like fashion: trends in thinking come and go, like the width of men's neckties and the length of women's skirts, and in some measure these trends reflect the zeitgeist, or spirit of a particular age.

The chief problem with any zeitgeist is that it is ephemeral, which means that anything deeply in tune with the spirit of a particular age is stamped with an expiration date. In other words, as soon as any age passes, whatever is in tune with it will seem antiquated, perhaps even stale or wrong. This means that summing up any past age in terms of one's own zeitgeist can lead to disaster.

A case in point is that of the German historian Karl Holl, whose grand summation of the Protestant Reformation—written a century ago—can now seem horribly ludicrous.

In the early 1900s, as Marxism was gaining credibility, some European scholars sought to prove that its dialectical materialism wrong by holding up the Protestant Reformation as a prime example of an epochal change driven by ideas and beliefs rather than by class struggle or purely material concerns. Three of the most influential theorists to take up this cause were German Protestants. Two of them were founders of the social sciences: Ernst Troeltsch (1865–1923) and Max Weber (1864–1920). One was a historian: Karl Holl (1866–1926).

Ernst Troeltsch attempted to prove the significance of Protestantism for the development of modern civilization in his *Protestantism and Progress* (1911), arguing that the first steps toward modernity were taken by the Protestant Reformers, but that modern secularism should be attributed to Enlightenment skepticism instead and to the sociopolitical and economic conditions of the eighteenth century rather than to the Reformers.

Max Weber had attempted to do something similar a few years earlier in *The Protestant Ethic and the Spirit of Capitalism* (1905), which focused mainly on the economic impact of Calvinist predestinarian theology. In the highly influential essay "Science as a Vocation" (1918), Weber would also argue that Protestantism caused the disenchantment (*entzauberung*) of the West, freeing it from the benighted magical thinking of Catholicism.

Karl Holl took a slightly different tack in defending the ultimate legacy of the Protestant Reformation by focusing on culture rather than on society or economics. His efforts, summed up in *The Cultural Significance of the Reformation* (1911), focused on Luther and on the development of what he called a religion of conscience (*Gewissensreligion*). While the grand theories of Troeltsch and Weber still attract attention and foment discussion a century later, those of Holl have been forgotten. And there is good reason for that. Unlike Troeltsch and Weber, who linked social and economic factors to theology on an international plane, Holl remained solely focused on theology, and on Germany—and worse yet, he dared to make sweeping generalizations from his narrow perspective. Some of Holl's assessments stand as a warning to all who attempt definitive grand summations, and especially to anyone who prefers to detach ideas from their historical context.

Holl's central proposition was that "Luther threw two major *ideas* as active *forces* into the stream of culture." The first of these ideas-turned-into-forces was "a new concept of personality." The second was "a new concept of community." Paradoxically, he argued, Luther's doctrine of justification by faith alone had led not to a sense of resignation or moral pessimism, but to the elevation of "the independence of the individual" and the creation of a culture deeply imbued with a "sense of responsibility." In other words, by stressing that the salvation of each individual was a gift directly willed by God on a one-to-one basis—rather than something mediated by priests to vast multitudes—Luther had thereby expanded "the right of the individual personality to a degree unheard of."[1] Holl's generalization assumed, of course, that ideas drove cultural and social change, and that theological concepts as abstract and paradoxical as Luther's did indeed imprint a very specific and easily identifiable character on an entire nation.

Holl's theorizing was in keeping with the many assumptions of the German school of *Geistesgeschichte*, which literally translates as "history of spirit," but is more properly understood as "history of ideas." *Geistesgeschichte* was an approach to the past that focused on qualitative phenomena rather than quantitative data, and on amorphous concepts and generalizations—such as a "sense of responsibility" or the "independence of the individual"—which were as difficult to pin down as to dissect or disprove. Convinced that ideas were the main cause of all significant changes in history, and that this causality was an unquestionable fact, Holl dared to theorize even further, and to sum up the effects of Lutheran theology on the political and economic life of "the German people." And it was here, in this area of theorizing about the pragmatic application of Reformation principles, that Holl took his grand summations to excess. For in straining to prove that Lutheran theology necessarily created a specific, indelible character in individuals, societies, and cultures, Holl fell into the trap of predicting inevitable results, as if he were a scientist who had discovered a law of nature in his laboratory.

His chief prediction concerned the behavior of one of his abstractions—"the German people"—and it turned out to be grossly wrong. Arguing that Luther "lacked all comprehension of politics" and that his two-kingdom theology and stress on the supremacy of the individual conscience made it impossible for German Lutherans to revel in "power politics" or to exalt the state over the individual, Holl was driven to assert, definitively, that "this Lutheran disposition of the German people" made it impossible for them to have "an instinct favorable to expansionist politics," and that "imperialism, in the sense of dominion in the world or even a solitary dominion, could never possess the German people." The spirit of Luther, he declared, was "totally unintelligible for an Englishman." This meant that Germans were incapable of ever seeking an empire, or of abusing other nations.

Holl's ability to ignore certain facts was exceptional. For instance, neither Germany's two African colonies nor its dominion over Catholic, Slavic-speaking Poles in Pomerania and Silesia gave Holl much pause, at least when it came to his grand theories. The existence of vast numbers of Catholics in Bavaria and other regions of Germany was a fact that also seemed to elude him, or not to matter at all. Even worse, the Great War that erupted in 1914, Germany's conquest of Belgium, and its trench-riddled occupation of eastern France did nothing to change Holl's mind. And when Germany was finally defeated in 1918, and cast by the victors in the role of aggressor, Holl defended his thesis with renewed vigor.

Revising his text for a second edition in the 1920s, Holl found a way to explain how his theory had been proved correct by Germany's humiliating loss. As he saw it, the Great War clearly revealed that crucial difference between the English and the Germans, that is, the difference between a theology that fosters imperialism and a theology that hinders it. Germany's defeat was caused not by a lack of nerve or of resources, Holl argued, but by the kaiser's betrayal of the nation's core Lutheran principles. As long as "the German people" were persuaded by their leaders that they were fighting a "defensive war," they held fast against their imperialist enemies, said Holl, but as soon as they were told by the kaiser that their struggle was "a war of conquest," their power vanished: traumatized by the prospect of conquering and subduing others, "the German people" simply gave up the fight.[2]

How Holl might have revised his thesis if he had lived long enough to see the rise of the Third Reich, the outbreak of the Second World War, and the eager embrace of imperialism and systematic genocide by "the German people" remains a matter of speculation. After all, when Holl died in 1926, Adolf Hitler was nothing more than a recently imprisoned rabble-rouser, and the Nazis were a fringe party that attracted a mere 3 percent of the popular vote.

Holl's colossal error is instructive. Assessing the significance of any historical event requires extreme caution, an awareness of one's time-bound horizons, and a high tolerance for complexity and paradox. Moreover, in addition to avoiding abstractions and reductionism, one must also be willing to admit that all assessments might seem insightful or valid only to one's own generation. As Troeltsch wisely observed, the significance of the past can be discerned only through the prism of the present day. Consequently, to aim for absolute, timeless, empirical certainty in the assessment of legacies—as Holl did—is to court disaster and ensure oblivion.

Revolutions and Paradigm Shifts

How can one best sum up the legacy of the Reformations without falling into a trap as ignominious as Holl's?

Given the complexity of the Reformations, and the time-bound nature of all approaches to history, summing up is a gamble. But it is still necessary, and not as hazardous at it may seem. So, fully aware of the contingency of all summations, let us approach the subject with due caution and restrict ourselves to empirically defensible observations. In addition, let us consider an approach that crosses disciplinary boundaries, avoids abstractions, and bundles as many perspectives as possible.

One such approach is to focus squarely on the changes that took place in the sixteenth and seventeenth centuries and to view the Reformations as a *paradigm shift*, that is, as a change in conceptual worldview—a change that is as inseparable from thought as it is from the material factors that led to it. This is a concept widely accepted by historians of science.

Paradigm shifts are those instances in history when thinking changes irreversibly, those transitional moments when basic assumptions are abandoned and replaced by new ones. A paradigm shift realigns all subsequent thinking and has practical implications. A prime example is the so-called Copernican revolution, after which it gradually became impossible for anyone to propose that the sun orbits the earth without being taken for a fool. Paradigm shifts occur not just in science, but also in belief systems and religions, even though when it comes to beliefs and religions, much more so than in empirical science, the older interpretations can survive, or even thrive, alongside the new ones. In the realm of beliefs, then, a paradigm shift does not necessarily kill off older ways of thinking—although that is sometimes possible, as proved by the disappearance of polytheism in Europe—but it does certainly bring about the existence of a rival interpretation of reality.[3]

Another term for paradigm shifts is *revolutions*. This synonymous association goes back to Thomas Kuhn's *The Structure of Scientific Revolutions*, which promoted the concept of paradigm shifts as essential to the development of modern science. In this seminal work, Kuhn employed the term *revolution* metaphorically, arguing that scientific knowledge evolves constantly through discoveries that transform thinking, and, in many

Revolution. Catholics understood the Protestant Reformation as a revolution and its leaders as hell-bent on destroying the Catholic Church. This late sixteenth-century woodcut seeks to align that revolution with the devil himself. From left to right we see Luther (still in a monk's habit), Melanchthon (about to smash a window), Zwingli (pulling down two steeples), Oecolampadius (flat on the ground, holding a snapped chain), Schwenckfeld (on a ladder, axe in hand), Calvin (digging at the foundations), and Carlstadt (pulling on a chain), all aided by demons in their demolition work. The four steeples on the church represent the four great fathers of antiquity: St. Gregory the Great, St. Augustine, St. Jerome, and St. Ambrose, all being yanked at with heavy chains. The title of the print lets the literate viewer know that despite their furious efforts, the revolutionaries will not succeed: "Mirror of the militant, true, steadfast, age-old Catholic Church of God, against which many tyrants, heathens, Jews, and heretics revolt, tear down, burn, and break by storm, but which Church to this day remains steadfast against all storms, and which until the end of the world by God's grace shall endure."

cases, also bring about technological, economic, political, and social change. This notion of epistemic change as revolution—which is now widely accepted—is also apt for any significant change in history, and especially for the Reformations that were initiated in the early sixteenth century.

It is no mere coincidence, then, that a long tradition exists of referring to the Reformations as a revolution, especially in the case of Protestantism. It began in the sixteenth century, among Catholics, who tended to see Protestants as rebels and to speak of their movement as a revolt. By the nineteenth century, scholars had also begun to use the term freely, as Frederic Seebohm did in his survey history *The Era of the Protestant Revolution* (1874). In the twentieth century, especially from the 1960s on, referring to the Protestant Reformation as a revolution became even more common, and less connected to old Catholic polemics. In 1974, for instance, Robert Kingdon proposed that the Protestant Reformation was an anticlerical revolution. At about the same time, Steven Ozment began to eloquently argue that Protestants were revolutionaries.[4] In the second decade of the twenty-first century, Brad Gregory chose to subtitle his book on the legacy of Protestantism "How a Religious *Revolution* Secularized Society."[5]

When viewed as a revolution, the Protestant Reformation easily acquires multiple dimensions that transcend religion itself, in the political, social, economic, and cultural realms. Yet there is no denying that religion is the axis from which these other manifestations of change radiate, much like spokes on a wheel. And on that axis, what we find tightly compressed at the core of the revolutionary paradigm shift is a bundle of new conceptions and redefinitions. At that very core, the Protestant Reformation is above all a metaphysical and epistemic revolution, a new way of interpreting reality and of approaching the ultimate. To put it in the simplest terms, the Protestant Reformation transformed the nature of religion itself, especially of religion as it is lived out. All the changes effected by the Protestant Reformation are inextricably linked to a revolutionary redrawing of the boundaries between heaven and earth, the sacred and the profane, the temporal and the eternal. And this conceptual reconfiguring never took place in some rarefied ether of pure thought: it was inextricably bound to social, political, economic, and cultural change, in two directions, simultaneously, as a *result* of changes in the immediate past and also as a *causal factor* of changes in the present and immediate future.

Epochal paradigm shifts such as that of the Protestant Reformation relate dynamically to worldly realities: they are not only shaped by changes in the everyday world that make it possible to reshuffle the conceptual realm and to think differently and reject the status quo; they also, in turn, necessarily cause even greater changes in the everyday world.

The various Reformations of the sixteenth and seventeenth century can certainly be viewed together as a massive paradigm shift—given the dissolution of religious unity in the West—but it is far more accurate to see the Reformations as a series of intertwined paradigm shifts, some of which caused deeper changes than others. Though any enumeration of the major changes caused by the Reformations is open to challenge, there are three major shifts in worldview—at the very least—that should be beyond dispute.

These three revolutionary shifts involve beliefs, naturally, and stem from metaphysical concepts championed by Protestants—concepts that were philosophical and theological, but that had immense practical ramifications. All three brought forth new approaches to the sacred and to the world itself.

To speak of these new approaches as "desacralizing" is proper, for in all three cases the realm of the sacred shrank as that of the profane was enlarged, but it needs to be kept in mind that in no case was the sacred altogether dismissed. The sacred and supernatural remained "real," most surely, but all three of these paradigm shifts redefined its scope and essence, making it more purely spiritual and therefore less accessible through the material world. Though the sacred may have become more keenly present in a *spiritual* sense for some, or for many, it certainly became much less *material*. And this shift in perspective, which can rightly be called a process of *desacralization*, changed the world more profoundly and irreversibly than any other paradigm shift brought about by scientists at that time, including Copernicus and Galileo, whose theories affected but a few learned men.

Disenchantment, Secularization, or Desacralization?

What is *desacralization*, exactly, and how does it differ from *secularization* or any other term used to describe paradigm shifts in the era of the Reformations?

A century ago Max Weber argued that secularization was the ultimate legacy of the Protestant Reformation, and what he meant by *secularization* was very specific: Weber simply proposed that Protestants had driven magic (*zauber*) from their world. Because there is no exact English equivalent for his German phrasing—*entzauberung der Welt*—translators settled for the nearest equivalent, and his thesis came to be known in English-speaking cultures as "the disenchantment of the world."[6] But Weber was no disinterested objective observer: his agenda was to affirm the superiority of Protestantism, and to align it with the "progress" that had made Western civilization so much more "advanced" than the rest of the world. At issue in all subsequent discussions of this thesis, which attracted much attention, was the very definition of religion, and how it differs from magic (*zauber*).

Weber's thesis stood largely unchallenged until the 1980s, when historian Robert Scribner attempted to deconstruct it and render it useless. Relying on anthropological approaches to ritual, Scribner defined *magic* very broadly and argued that Protestants still retained some "magical" elements in their religion, especially in their core rituals of baptism and the Eucharist—which ostensibly effected specific changes in the fabric of reality, much like any magical incantation. Applying the adjective *thaumaturgic* to all these core Christian rituals that ostensibly changed reality—a term anthropologists employ when speaking of rites that seek to work magic or miracles in any religion—Scribner went on to argue Protestants were still stuck in a "religio-magical space," just like Catholics. The fact that Protestants also continued to believe in the devil and witchcraft, seemed further proof for Scribner that Protestants had failed to "disenchant" their world and that it was a huge mistake to view Protestantism as some giant step toward modernity and secularism.[7]

In one fell swoop, it seemed, Scribner had managed to redefine the very meaning of *magic* and *disenchantment*, as well as of *religion*. And he had accomplished this by blurring or dissolving the line between magic and all ritual, or magic and religion. Ironically, then, much like the magicians he had in mind—who could ostensibly effect change through the incantation of a single word, such as *abracadabra*—Scribner sought to redefine religion and magic through the incantation of the term *thaumaturgy*. In doing so, he thought he had also made it impossible to trace the emergence of secularism and modernity back to Protestantism. When all was said and done, then, Scribner's Protestantism ended up looking a lot like Catholicism, still mired in the same old hocus-pocus.

But what if one were to look beyond the troublesome magic-religion dialectic, so central to Weber and to Scribner? Might it be possible to find some other approach to the paradigm shift that so obviously sets the era of the Reformations apart as a clear rupture in Western history without engendering further disagreement and confusion? Is there some way of acknowledging that the Reformations were more than a murky transitional period between the Middle Ages and modernity while sidestepping the minefields of *disenchantment* and *secularization*? Is it possible to isolate the key change wrought by the Reformations in some other way?

One option is to focus on desacralization. As used here, the term *desacralization* refers strictly to paradigm shifts within the Christian religion itself. More specifically, it refers to the way Protestantism redefined the realm of the sacred and numinous and realigned the relation between creation and the Creator. In other words, the concept of desacralization sidesteps the issue of secularization by focusing solely on the reshaping of Christian beliefs and rituals, rather than on campaigns against magic and superstition, and by referring strictly to theological and spiritual boundary making from within the Christian community itself. To speak of desacralization is to isolate those conceptual factors in Protestantism that created a culture decidedly uneasy with the mixing of heaven and earth or the sacred and the mundane.

In sum, desacralization is a process of subtraction from within, of Christians eagerly reducing the scope of the supernatural on earth, rather than a process of erosion by external factors of any kind, be they political, social, economic, cultural, or intellectual. This is not to say that external factors had no role to play in the evolution of a new Christian viewpoint, but rather to emphasize that Protestants—who were themselves affected by these factors—were aggressive agents of the process of desacralization.

But what were the contours of this desacralization, specifically? Three essential reconfigurations of reality stand out most starkly, each of which concerned some of the most fundamental concepts in the Christian religion: first, how matter relates to spirit; second, how the natural relates to the supernatural; and third, how the living relate to the dead.

Matter and Spirit

Ever since the inception of their religion, Christians had accepted a binary understanding of the cosmos: God was spirit, and God had created a material world, ontologically related to him, but metaphysically different and inferior. Humans were the pinnacle of this creation, part matter and part spirit, composed of a mortal body and an immortal soul. Bridging these two essential realms of existence was the role of religion, or, more specifically, of the church and its clergy, and the bridging was effected in myriad ways through rituals and symbols. Consequently, the medieval Christian world pulsated with accessibility to the divine, replete as it was with material points of contact with the spiritual realm.

Protestants made matter and spirit much less compatible. And their rejection of material access points to the spiritual realm turned Protestants into iconoclasts, literally and figuratively, even those who retained some material aspects of Catholic worship, such as the Lutherans and Anglicans. This ontological and metaphysical reconfiguration varied among Protestants, but it found its most extreme expression in the Reformed tradition, and in two of their guiding principles: *finitum non est capax infiniti* (the finite cannot contain the infinite), and *quantum sensui tribueris tantum spiritui detraxeris* (the physical detracts from the spiritual). *Idolatry* entered the Western vocabulary in a new way, thanks to this worldview. It no longer applied to pagans only, but also to much of Europe's ancestral religion as practiced by Catholics, and to their conception of the sacred. By redefining the meaning of Catholic symbols and rituals, then, Protestants also redefined the nature and function of the clergy, and of the relation between church and state.

Reformed Protestants thought that idolatry threatened the well-being of society as a whole: it was a sin that polluted everyone and invited the wrath of God. Lutherans, Anglicans, and Radicals took a different tack, but still rejected materiality in religion, and any religious behavior that smacked of idolatry or superstition. In addition, the iconoclastic theology shared by all Protestants also argued that the material resources "wasted" on idols were an affront to Christian charity and a reification of wrongful class distinctions. The medieval church had long argued that images were the *libri pauperum*, or books of the poor and illiterate. Protestant iconoclasts rejected this argument because, as they saw it, images kept the laity under the thumb of the Catholic clergy.

The Protestant redefinition of matter and spirit was thus revolutionary on two fronts. First, it was a theological upheaval, and a redefinition of the sacred. Reformation iconoclasm was also revolutionary in a sociopolitical and economic sense, for it was an act of violence against the costly symbolic code of medieval Christianity and its guardians, the Roman Catholic clergy. The young men who led the iconoclastic riot that turned Geneva into a Reformed city knew this, instinctively, for they called the images they destroyed "the gods of the priests."[8] By redefining the meaning of Catholic symbols and rituals, then, Protestants also redefined the nature and function of the clergy (something Luther himself perceived and feared in the extreme iconoclasm of his colleague Karlstadt). So it was, then, that by redefining the relationship between matter and spirit and denying the possibility of physical access to the divine, Protestants changed the social and political order, and the very nature of religion itself.

Religion was no longer a search for the immanence of the divine in this world, an attempt to encounter heaven in sacred spaces or through pilgrimages and the veneration of images and relics. Nor was it a search for the miraculous and otherworldly mediated by priests who enjoyed a higher ontological status and had the power to change bread and wine into the body and blood of Christ the Savior. Religion was something else, something more transcendent, more focused on an unseen spiritual realm and on a code of ethics, something internalized by individuals and communities, something less tactile, but definitely more worldly.

The Natural and Supernatural

As a whole, despite the differences among them, Protestants rejected the commonplace irruptions of the sacred favored in medieval religion. More specifically, Protestants did away with miraculous phenomena and denied the possibility of merging with God in mystical ecstasy.

One of the most distinctive traits of Protestantism was its rejection of miracles, and all of those practically oriented supernatural events that historians now classify as thaumaturgy. God could work miracles, certainly, but as Protestants saw it, the age of miracles had passed, and God's supernatural interventions were a thing of the past, strictly limited to biblical times. As Luther put it:

> Those visible works are simply signs for the ignorant, unbelieving crowd, and for their sakes that are yet to be attracted; but as for us who already know all we do know, and believe the Gospel, what do we want them for? . . .Wherefore it is no wonder that they have now ceased since the Gospel has sounded abroad everywhere, and has been preached to those who had not known of God before, whom he had to attract with outward miracles, just as we throw apples and pears to children.[9]

As if this were not enough, Luther added one crowning objection to all miraculous claims: the devil could manipulate nature and deceive people, and often did, especially in the Catholic Church. This polemically charged Protestant tradition of attributing Catholic miracle claims to the devil was, above all, an affirmation of their conviction in the inviolability of natural laws. Nature could be manipulated by Satan and humans could certainly be fooled by him, Protestants argued, but genuine supernatural miracles were restricted to biblical times.

So, even though some Protestants (especially Lutherans) continued to believe in demonic skulduggery and natural signs and portents that conveyed messages, such as cloud formations, astronomical and meteorological anomalies, and monstrous births— wonders (*mirabilia*) rather than miracles (*miraculi*)—and even though supernatural miracles eventually worked their way back in to Protestant piety in various limited ways

Enlightenment. Long before the eighteenth century, Protestants conceived of themselves as "enlightened." One substantial difference distinguishes them from men of the later Enlightenment, however: their belief in the devil, and the ease with which they tended to ascribe demonic qualities to the Catholic Church. In this 1640 English engraving by Thomas Jenner we see the greatest leaders of the Protestant Reformation gathered around a candle that represents the light of the divine word. At the bottom we see a cardinal, a demon, a pope, and a monk straining to blow out the candle. The words on the tablecloth express the same sentiment as in the previous Catholic illustration, but with the Catholics in the role of frustrated villains: "The candle is lighted; we cannot blow it out." A key dimension of the Protestant "enlightenment"—despite the devil who was still so much a part of it—was the desacralization or "disenchantment" of the world.

during the late seventeenth and eighteenth centuries, Protestantism might have desacralized and disenchanted the world much more through its take on miracles than through any other of its principles.

Even more significant, it could be argued, was the change that Protestants brought to the relationship between human beings and God. Save for a few Radical extremists, Protestants rejected the ultimate goal of medieval Catholic piety and of monasticism in particular: that of mystical union with God.

Purgation, illumination, union—these were the three basic steps in the mystical quest that the Catholic and Eastern Orthodox churches had accepted and elaborated upon since the second century of the Christian era. Becoming ever purer and more God-like, even to the point of experiencing supernatural encounters with God in this life, was the goal of monasticism, ostensibly, and the promise held out to every potential saint. This quest and its attending experiences were discarded by Protestants as utter nonsense or, even worse, as demonically inspired madness.

The Protestant rejection of monasticism, based as it was on a reevaluation of key assumptions about human nature, figures prominently as a social change effected by theology: it not only caused the largest redistribution of property in Western history before the Bolsheviks came along, but also brought about a social and economic revolution. Suddenly, an entire social class was abolished, along with their sizable assets. In addition, on both the material and the conceptual level, a way of life that focused intensely on otherworldliness was extinguished. The desacralizing impact of the extinction of monasticism seems obvious enough, and needs little elaboration. The impact of the rejection of mysticism—the main goal of monasticism—is harder to discern, but no less significant. Those men and women who reached the pinnacle of holiness were considered living proof of the divinization of matter. They not only conversed with Christ and the Virgin Mary, but also had ineffable encounters with the Godhead; they also swooned in rapture, went into trances, levitated, bilocated, read minds, prophesied, manifested the wounds of Christ on their bodies, and healed the sick and lame. Once they died, their corpses could emit a wonderful aroma and remain intact.

All of this was rejected by Protestants, save for a few Radicals who claimed to have direct access to the divine realm. Even Martin Luther, who was influenced by the medieval mystics Tauler and Suso, could not abide the ultimate claims made by all ecstatics, and despised those who claimed direct contact with the divine as *schwärmer*, that is, as unhinged fanatics. John Calvin recoiled in horror at the thought that humans might claim any sort of divinization, for his God was "entirely other" and "as different from flesh as fire is from water."[10] Such a crossing of boundaries was impossible, argued Calvin, for the human soul "is not only burdened with vices, but is utterly devoid of all good."[11] Protestants sometimes used the word *saint* to refer to the elect of God, but they had no *saints* in the Catholic sense; that is, they denied that anyone could ever reach moral and spiritual perfection in this life, work miracles, or intercede for the living in heaven. Protestant *saints* lived out their call on earth without otherworldly encounters or miraculous feats. Moreover, they ceased to be links with the numinous, and were not to be venerated or to be approached as intercessors.

To restrict the supernatural to heaven and the ancient past in this manner was to change the very essence of the Christian religion as it had been lived for the previous 1,500 years. Religion was no longer a conduit of the miraculous and mystical—as in the Gospels and Acts of the Apostles and all the hagiographies of the previous millennium— but rather a conduit of inner and outer conformity to the Word and will of God. Religion was definitely still focused on a supernatural reality, but that reality was manifest on earth in a much less direct or intrusive way. So it was that as the rules of nature became less malleable in the hands of God, religion itself became something much more natural, and more worldly.

The Living and the Dead

A third great reconfiguration involved the relation between the here and now and the hereafter, and of the links between earthly time and eternity, and the living and the dead. This reconfiguration of the *communio sanctorum* led to the creation of a segregated society in which the living and the dead could no longer mingle, physically or spiritually. The dead were truly *dead and gone*: the saints in heaven could no longer be approached for favors, and the souls of the departed needed no prayers from the living, since there was no purgatory from which to be freed. For Protestants, death became the deepest abyss of all, an unbridgeable metaphysical and ontological chasm in time and space. As Luther put it:

> The summons of death comes to us all, and no one can die for another. Every one must fight his own battle with death by himself, alone. We can shout into each other's ears, but everyone must himself be prepared for the time of death: I will not be with you then, nor you with me.[12]

Consequently, Protestant popular literature attacked the Catholic cult of the dead with singular ferocity, singling it out as one of the surest signs of the falsehood of the Roman Catholic Church, and of the exploitation of the laity by the clergy.

The spiritual and cultural consequences of this sea change are qualitative and therefore harder to reckon than the material consequences, which are very easy to observe and quantify. The disappearance of all postmortem rituals was an economic revolution. Suffrages for the dead always involved money: whether it was a single mass or a perpetual chantry, some cost always had to be borne by the living, who constantly saw part of their inheritance consumed by the dead, or, to be more precise, by the clergy who were charged with the duty to say all those masses for the dead. Many postmortem rituals were funded in one way or another through real estate: either through rents or through outright gifts of property to the church. Over the decades and centuries, the transfer of funds and property to the church snowballed into a gargantuan inheritance. And wherever Protestantism gained the upper hand, all the property and funds that the clergy had been consuming in the name of the dead were redistributed, and usually put to pragmatic this-worldly use.

This reconfiguring of the hereafter in the sixteenth century changed the here and now. Once purgatory was extinguished and eternity was dismissed from theological discourse as a distant, unreachable dimension, the social, political, and economic claims that upheld the privileged role of the clergy in the Catholic Church collapsed like a house of cards. If clerics were not the keepers of the keys to eternity, then what was their function? How on earth could they claim a superior status? Luther began this redefinition by speaking of "the priesthood of all believers." At a popular level, dozens of pamphleteers immediately denounced all clerical claims of superiority. As a former monk put it, why should the clergy turn themselves into "sacred cows," promoting the illusion of separateness and special "spiritual right," claiming "all kinds of exemptions and privileges from Heaven"? One of the leaders of the Protestant faction in Strassburg summed up his party's argument by saying that all clergy should be subject to the same civil obligations as the laity, instead of being "treated as gods," and that any claim to the contrary was "against God, against the love of one's neighbor, against all sense of fair play, against human nature and reason, and detrimental to the community at large."[13]

And as the clerics were desacralized, so were all maps and calendars. Gone were shrines and sacred feast days; time and space were desacralized too. And so was the world.

Protestantism stripped religion of mediation and intimacy with the dead. As the living could no longer do anything for the dead in purgatory and the saints in heaven were stripped of their power to intercede with God, the living out of religion changed radically. Religion was no longer about bridging the here and hereafter constantly, nor was it a province of human activity monopolized by priests. Religion was something strictly for the living, something much less hieratic and otherworldly and therefore more pragmatically focused on this world.

Fragmentation Then and Now

The significance of all this radical desacralizing can be best appreciated by contemplating how Catholics responded to it. The most direct impact of Protestantism on Catholics was the creation of a reactionary climate of hypersacralization, in which the Catholic Church emphasized all the beliefs, rituals, and institutional norms rejected by Protestants of every stripe. When it came to links between matter and spirit or the natural and supernatural, or the living and the dead, Catholics intensified them: as Protestants desacralized their world, Catholics infused theirs with a newly energized sacrality.

The sixteenth and seventeenth centuries were a golden age for miracles and mysticism, during which the miraculous physical phenomena associated with mystical ecstasy became more pronounced than ever before among Catholics. And when it came to the here and now and the hereafter, Catholics began to embrace their dead even more tightly than ever before, spending ever larger sums on masses for the dead and funerals, increasing their devotion to the cult of the saints, recording countless apparitions by souls in purgatory who confirmed the efficacy of suffrages for the dead. All in all, then, the paradigm shifts effected by Protestants transformed Catholicism too, enhancing certain of its key traits in unprecedented ways, bringing about among them a fervent hypersacralizing of the world.

The ultimate result of this polarization was the emergence of two very different kinds of Christianity and of two worldviews within Western culture that developed as much from reacting to "others" as from cogently devised theologies. As Protestantism spread throughout Europe, the inevitable clash of cultures wreaked all sorts of havoc, even bloodshed. And as Protestants spread over the map of Europe, their worldview rubbed uncomfortably against that of Catholics, nearly everywhere. Only two areas of what had once been Christendom remained largely untouched by a Protestant presence: the Italian and Iberian Peninsulas and their outlying islands. Everywhere else, in some form or another, in varying degrees, Catholics had to share space with Protestants, and to

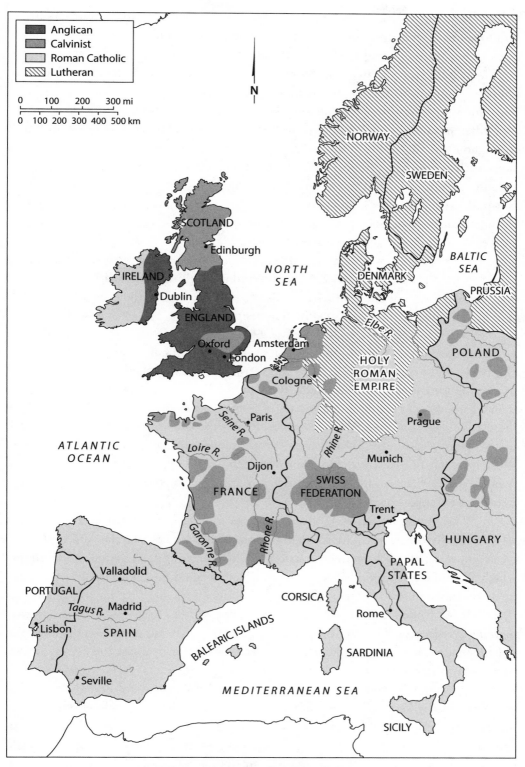

Mapping the legacy of the Reformations

be confronted in various ways by their desacralizing worldview. Conversely, Protestants had to contend with the offense of Catholic hypersacralization.

All of Europe had to contend with these differences, despite the fact that there were large homogeneous areas where everyone belonged to the same church and no other churches could exist, such as in Spain and Italy. Although there were many Catholics and Protestants who never ventured far beyond their respective borders or met anyone of a different faith, encounters between Protestants and Catholics took place constantly throughout Europe, not just because there were many areas with mixed religious populations, such as France, Germany, the Netherlands, Hungary, Ireland, and Poland, but also because of commerce and the constant interaction between cities, states, and nations. Naturally, at the elite level, among rulers, diplomats, artists, scholars, and the merchant class, exchanges were much more common than among peasants, but the significance of such exchanges should never be underestimated. The constant flow of information and of personal encounters among elites of different faiths over the space of several generations would eventually lead to increased toleration, and to a dulling of the sharp edges that had once defined the competing confessions. Relativism, skepticism, and even atheism would thrive in this chaotic vortex created by fragmentation.

Many factors—material as well as intellectual and spiritual—contributed to the secularization of the West. Searching for a single determinant is not only wrong, but also futile. Yet there is also no denying the significant role that the fragmentation caused by the Reformations played in gradually turning religion into a private concern rather than a public one, that is, into a matter of personal conviction rather than something imposed on everyone by established authorities. By the late seventeenth century, the role that religion began to play in much of Europe might seem familiar to us. Religion was still very much alive and thriving, but it was increasingly restricted to smaller social and political spaces, bereft of the power to sway governments, impose itself on vast multitudes by law, and extinguish dissent through violence.

The fragmentation of Christendom was the most immediate and long-lasting effect of the Reformations. This splintering, and the plurality of churches and worldviews created by it, changed Western civilization radically, creating spaces large and small into which all of the other preexisting secularizing forces could flow. Eventually, these other forces increased in strength and volume—their momentum intensified by the fragmentation itself and by desacralization—and they overflowed from these spaces, gradually submerging ever-larger portions of the fragments, turning what had once been the continent of Christendom into a mere archipelago of islands enveloped by a vast and ever-rising tide of secularism and unbelief.

Western Christendom ceased to exist, but Christians thrived nonetheless within the chaos, warily keeping an eye on one another and on the rising tide of unbelief and materialism. Paradoxically, within the whirlwind of conflict and violence, and the desacralizing and hypersacralizing, spiritual and moral greatness were also sometimes brought to new heights on all sides by brave souls, in the most unexpected ways. Meanwhile, among the secularists and materialists, some took comfort—as many still do—in finding their precursors among the reformers and dissidents of the early modern age.

To understand the world we live in, to fully know how the West came to be what it is, one must understand how it was shaped by the Reformations of the early modern age. To ask whether the Reformations changed the world for the better or for the worse is to pose a legitimate question that most historians prefer to avoid. The world is what it is, we historians tend to say, and there is no going back, no changing what transpired. Still, this question that demands a value judgment continues to be asked by many outside the historical profession, even in our own day. Does this persistence prove that the legacy of that era is still with us five centuries later?

Most certainly.

As long as this question is asked—which assumes that improving the world is possible—the legacy of the Reformations endures.

Notes

ABBREVIATIONS IN NOTES

Erasmus

Allen Epistolae: *Opus epistolarum Des. Erasmi Roterodami: Denuo recognitum et auctum*, ed. Percy Stafford Allen, Helen Mary Allen, and Heathcote William Garrod, 12 vols. Clarendon Press, 1906–1958.

AS: *Desiderius Erasmus, Ausgewählte Schriften*, ed. Werner Welzig, 8 vols. Wissenschaftliche Buchgesellschaft, 1967–1980.

Luther

LW: *Luther's Works*, ed. Jaroslav Pelikan et al., 55 vols. Concordia Publishing House, 1955–1986.

WA: *D. Martin Luthers Werke: Kritische Gesamtausgabe*, 73 vols. H. Böhlau, 1883–2009.

WA-BR: *D. Martin Luthers Werke: Kritische Gesamtausgabe, Briefwechsel*, 18 vols. H. Böhlau, 1883–2009.

Walch SS: *Dr. Martin Luthers Sämmtliche Schriften*, ed. Johann Georg Walch. Concordia Publishing House, 1880–1910.

WAT: *D. Martin Luthers Werke: Kritische Gesamtausgabe, Tischreden*, 6 vols. H. Böhlau, 1883–2009.

Zwingli

ZW: *Huldreich Zwinglis Sämtliche Werke*, ed. Emil Egli and Georg Finsler, 17 vols. C. A. Schwetschke und Sohn, 1905–1991.

ZW-Lat: *The Latin Works and the Correspondence of Huldrych Zwingli, Together with Selections from His German Works*, ed. S. M. Jackson, 3 vols. G. P. Putnam's Sons, 1912.

ZW-S: Ulrich Zwingli, *Selected Works*, ed. Samuel Macauley Jackson. University of Pennsylvania Press, 1972.

Calvin

OC: *Ioannis Calvini opera quae supersunt omnia*, ed. G. Baum, E. Cunitz, and E. Reuss, 59 vols. C. A. Schwetschke, 1863–1900.

CHAPTER ONE: *An Age of Breakthroughs*

1. Giannozzo Manetti, *De vita ac gestis Nicolai quinti summi pontificis*, quoted by Ludwig Pastor, *The History of the Popes, from the Close of the Middle Ages*, 2 vols., ed. Frederick Ignatius Antrobus, 3rd ed. (B. Herder, 1906), vol. 2, p. 175.

2. Quoted in Bard Thompson, *Humanists and Reformers* (Eerdmans, 1996), p. 40.

3. Jan de Vries, "Population," in *Handbook of European History, 1400–1600*, ed. Thomas Brady, Heiko Oberman, and James Tracy (Eerdmans, 1994), vol. 1, p. 1.

CHAPTER TWO: *Religion in Late Medieval Christendom*

1. Archivo Municipal de Toledo: CC, Y *leg.* 1611, "Querella Maria Gomez Ana Diaz," cited by Scott Taylor, *Honor and Violence in Golden Age Spain* (Yale University Press, 2008), p. 157.

2. Johan Huizinga, *Autumn of the Middle Ages*; Bernd Moeller, *Imperial Cities and the Reformation*; Steven Ozment, *Protestants*.

3. Eamon Duffy, *Stripping of the Altars*; John Bossy, *Christianity in the West*.

4. William Christian, *Local Religion in Sixteenth Century Spain*.

5. Carlo Ginzburg, *Cheese and the Worms*; Philippe Ariès, *Hour of Our Death*.

6. Jean-Claude Schmitt, *The Holy Greyhound* (Cambridge University Press, 1983).

7. Keith Thomas, *Religion and the Decline of Magic*, p. 49.

8. Jean Delumeau, *Catholicism Between Luther and Voltaire*.

9. Georges Duby, *The Three Orders: Feudal Society Imagined* (Paris, 1978; English trans., 1982).

10. The Latin *clericus* is derived from the Greek *klerikos*, meaning "of or pertaining to an inheritance." In the case of Christians, this is an obvious reference to the authority that their leaders claimed to have directly from Christ and his twelve apostles. By the second century, the term was already being used as a name of the ministerial or priestly order in the church.

11. Matthew 16:18. In this gospel passage Jesus renames the apostle Simon by means of a multilingual pun, giving him the name *Cephas*, in Aramaic, which is the equivalent of *petra* in Greek, from which "Peter" is derived.

12. John Calvin, *Inventory of Relics*, OC 6.452.

13. John Calvin, *On Shunning the Rites of the Ungodly*, OC 5.239.

14. John Calvin, *Quatrieme Sermon*, OC 8.437.

15. Bernal Diaz del Castillo, *History of the Conquest of New Spain*, trans. David Carrasco (University of New Mexico Press, 2009), pp. 170–171, 178–179.

CHAPTER THREE: *Reform and Dissent in the Late Middle Ages*

1. Girolamo Savonarola, "On the Renovation of the Church," in *The Catholic Reformation: Savonarola to Ignatius Loyola*, ed. and trans. John C. Olin (Harper & Row, 1969), pp. 14–15.

2. John C. Olin, ed. and trans., *The Catholic Reformation: Savonarola to Ignatius Loyola* (Harper & Row, 1969), pp. 44–53.

3. Berndt Moeller, "Piety in Germany Around 1500," in *The Reformation in Medieval Perspective*, ed. Steven Ozment (Quadrangle Books, 1971), p. 51.

4. Lucien Febvre, "Une question mal posée: Les origines de la Réforme Française," in *Au couer religieux du XVIᵉ siècle* (Sevpen, 1957), p. 37.

5. Johann Huizinga, *The Waning of the Middle Ages* (Doubleday, 1954), p. 151.

6. John Colet, "Oratio habita ad clerum in convocatione" (1512), in Fredric Seebohm, *The Oxford Reformers*, 2nd ed. (Longmans, Green & Co. 1869), pp. 230–247.

7. Gerald Strauss, *Manifestations of Discontent in Germany on the Eve of the Reformation* (University of Indiana Press, 1971), p. 61.

8. Cited by Sarah Stanbury, "The Vivacity of Images: St. Katherine, Knighton's Lollards, and the Breaking of the Idols," in *Images, Idolatry, and Iconoclasm in Late Medieval England*, ed. Jeremy Dimmick, James Simpson, and Nicolette Zeeman (Oxford University Press, 2002), pp. 131–132.

9. Cited by Steven Ozment, *Age of Reform* (Yale University Press, 1980), p. 163.

10. Though he claimed the papacy under this name, Cossa would never be included in the Catholic Church's list of legitimate popes and the numeral 23 would remain unused until Cardinal Angelo Roncali became pope in 1958 and assumed the name John XXIII.

11. Cited by Gordon Leff, *Heresy in the Later Middle Ages* (Barnes & Noble, 1967), vol. 2, pp. 684–685.

12. J. H. Robinson, *Translations and Reprints from the Original Sources of European history* (Department of History, University of Pennsylvania, 1912), series 1, vol. 3, no. 6, pp. 31–32.

13. Translated by O. J. Thatcher and E. H. McNeal, *A Source Book for Mediaeval History* (Charles Scribner's, 1905), p. 332.

14. See Victor Turner, *From Ritual to Theatre* (Performing Arts Journal Publications, 1982), p. 82; Clifford Geertz, "Religion as a Cultural System," in *Anthropological Approaches to the Study of Religion*, ed. Michael Banton (F. A. Praeger, 1966), p. 28.

CHAPTER FOUR: *Italian Humanism*

1. *Opus epistolarum Des. Erasmi Roterodami: denuo recognitum et auctum*, ed. Percy Stafford Allen, Helen Mary Allen and Heathcote William Garrod (Clarendon Press, 1906–1958), vol. 2, p. 284.

2. Translation from Rodolfo Lanciani, *Pagan and Christian Rome* (Houghton, Mifflin, & Co., 1893), pp. 296–297. For a drawing of the girl, see Leonard Barkan, *Unearthing the Past* (Yale University Press, 1999), pp. 57–62.

3. Allen, *Opus Epistolarum Des. Erasmi* Roterodami, vol. 1, p. 352.

4. Quoted by Eugene F. Rice in "The Humanist Idea of Christian Antiquity: Jacques Lefèvre d'Étaples and His Circle," *Studies in the Renaissance* 9 (1962): 135.

5. J. C. Olin, *Catholic Reformation*, p. 13.

6. Bernd Moeller, "The German Humanists and the Beginnings of the Reformation," ed. and trans. H. C. E. Midelfort and M. U. Edwards, *Imperial Cities and the Reformation* (Fortress Press, 1972), p. 36.

7. W. H. Woodward, *Vittorino da Feltre and Other Humanist Educators* (Bureau of Publications, Teachers College, Columbia University, 1963), p. 177.

8. *De Ingenuis Moribus*, 106, trans. Donald Kelley, in *Renaissance Humanism* (Twayne Publishers, 1991), p. 97.

9. *The Treatise of Lorenzo Valla on the Donation of Constantine*, trans. C. B. Coleman (Yale University Press, 1922), p. 115.

10. Lorenzo Valla, *De Falso Credita et Ementita Constantini Donatione*, in *Wegbereiter der Reformation*, ed. Gustav Benrath (Schünemann, 1967), pp. 478–479.

11. For a summary, see Kristeller's "Humanism," in *The Cambridge History of Renaissance Philosophy*, ed. C. B. Schmitt et al. (Cambridge University Press, 1988), pp. 113–137. See also his *Renaissance Thought: The Classic, Scholastic and Humanistic Strains* (Harper & Brothers, 1961).

12. Hans Baron, *The Crisis of the Early Italian Renaissance: Civic Humanism and Republican Liberty in an Age of Classicism and Tyranny*, 2 vols., 2nd ed. (Princeton University Press, 1966).

13. Niccolò Machiavelli, *The Prince* (Oxford University Press, 2005), chap. 15, p. 54.

14. Ibid., chap. 25, p. 85.

15. "Five Questions Concerning the Mind," in *The Renaissance Philosophy of Man*, ed. E. Cassirer, P. O. Kristeller, and J. H. Randall (University of Chicago Press, 1948), p. 201.

16. *De Doctrina Christiana*, book 2, chap. 40. *Select Library of the Nicene and Post-Nicene Fathers of the Christian Church*, ed. Philip Schaff (Charles Scribner's Sons, 1907), vol. 2, p. 554.

17. *Oration on the Dignity of Man*, in *The Renaissance Philosophy of Man*, p. 232.

18. Ibid., p. 227.

CHAPTER FIVE: *Humanism Beyond Italy*

1. Franz Friedlieb, *Germaniae exegeseos volumina duodecim* (Hagenau, 1518), in *Manifestations of Discontent in Germany on the Eve of the Reformation*, ed. and trans. Gerald Strauss (Indiana University Press, 1971), p. 72.

2. Other significant Protestant Reformers with classical versions of their names: Glareanus / Heinrich Loris; Oswald Myconius / Oswald Geisshüsler; Justus Menius / Joducus Menig; Hieronymus Zanchius / Girolamo Zanchi; Ursinus / Zacharias Baer; Urbanus Rhegius / Urban Rieger; and Peter Melius / Peter Juhász.

3. Quoted by J. H. Hexter, "The Education of the Aristocracy in the Renaissance," in *Reappraisals in History* (Harper and Row, 1963), p. 63.

4. Cited by Lewis W. Spitz, "The Course of German Humanism," in *Itinerarium Italicum*, ed. Heiko A. Oberman, with Thomas A. Brady Jr. (Brill, 1975), p. 409.

5. Complutensian Polyglot Bible (Alcalá, 1514–1517), vol. 1, fol. 3r, "Prologus ad sanctissimum et clementissimum dominum nostrum," trans. John C. Olin, in *Catholic Reform: From Cardinal Ximenes to the Council of Trent, 1495–1563* (Fordham University Press, 1990), pp. 62–63.

6. Marcel Bataillon, *Erasme et l'Espagne* (Paris, 1937), 3rd ed., ed. Daniel Devoto and Charles Amiel, 3 vols. (Droz, 1991).

7. Lu Ann Homza, *Religious Authority in the Spanish Renaissance* (Johns Hopkins University Press, 2000).

8. Complutensian Polyglot Bible, vol. 1, fol. 3v, col. 1, "Prologus ad Lectorem."

9. Recent editions include Pedro Ciruelo, *Reprobación de las supersticiones y hechizerias*, ed. Alva V. Ebersole (Ediciones Albatros Hispanófila 1978), and an English translation, *Pedro Ciruelo's A Treatise Reproving All Superstitions and Forms of Witchcraft*, trans. Eugene A. Maio and D'Orsay W. Pearson (Fairleigh Dickinson University Press, 1977).

10. Quoted by Roland Bainton, *Erasmus of Christendom* (Scribner, 1969), p. 58.

11. Convocation Sermon (1512), trans. John C. Olin, in *The Catholic Reformation: Savonarola to Ignatius Loyola* (Harper and Row, 1969), pp. 32, 37.

12. Eugene Rice, ed., *The Prefatory Epistles of Jacques Lefèvre d'Étaples* (Columbia University Press, 1972), p. 60.

13. Introduction to the *Commentary on the Psalms* (1509), trans. P. L. Nyhus, in *Forerunners of the Reformation*, ed. Heiko Oberman (Holt, Rinehart and Winston, 1966), p. 297.

14. Preface to the *Commentaries on the Four Gospels*, in Rice, *Prefatory Epistles*, p. 436.

15. Rice, *Prefatory Epistles*, p. 469.

16. *Opus Epistolarum Des. Erasmi Roterodami*, ed. P. S. Allen, 12 vols. (Clarendon Press, 1906–1958), vol. 5, letter no. 1496 (hereafter Allen, *Epistolae*).

17. *Imitation of Christ*, chap. 1, pt. 5, trans. Leo Sherley-Price (Penguin Classics, 1952), p. 28.

18. Allen, *Epistolae*, vol. 2, p. 384.

19. Ibid.

20. Desiderius Erasmus, *Enchiridion*, trans. John P. Dolan, in *The Essential Erasmus* (New American Library, 1964), p. 38. Latin text: Desiderius Erasmus, *Ausgewählte Schriften*, ed. Werner Welzig, 8 vols. (Darmstadt: Wissenschaftliche Buchgesellschaft, 1967–1980), vol. 1, pp. 90–91.

21. *Enchiridion*, pp. 61–62.

22. Ibid., pp. 63–64.

23. Ibid., pp. 66–67.

24. *Enchiridion, Ausgewählte Schriften*, vol. 1, 202: "multo religiousius honoranda mentis illius imago, quae spiritus sancti artificio experessa est *litteris* evangelicis."

25. *Enchiridion* (Dolan), p. 67.

26. "The Shipwreck," trans. Craig R. Thompson, in *The Colloquies of Erasmus* (University of Chicago Press, 1965), p. 142.

27. *Enchiridion* (Dolan), p. 67.

28. "De utilitate colloquiorum" (1526), in *The Colloquies of Erasmus*, trans. Craig R. Thompson (University of Chicago Press, 1965), p. 626.

29. Allen, *Epistolae*, vol. 1, p. 178.

30. *Praise of Folly*, trans. Hoyt Hopewell Hudson (Princeton University Press, 1969), p. 66.

31. "Pilgrimage," in *Ten Colloquies of Erasmus*, ed. and trans. Craig R. Thompson (Liberal Arts Press, 1957), p. 295.

32. *Huldreich Zwinglis Sämtliche Werke*, ed. E. Egli et al. (Berlin: C. A. Schwetschke und Sohn, 1905–1990), vol. 2, p. 217.

33. Heinrich Bullinger, *In librum de originie erroris circa invocationem et cultum deorum ac simulachrorum* (Zurich, 1539), p. 153.

34. Erasmus of Rotterdam, letter to Philip Melanchthon (1524), in *Erasmus and His Age: Selected Letters of Desiderius Erasmus*, ed. Hans J. Hillerbrand, trans. Marcus A. Haworth (Harper & Row 1970), p. 183.

CHAPTER SIX: *Forerunners of the Catholic Reformation*

1. See Nelson H. Minnich, *The Fifth Lateran Council (1512–17): Studies on Its Membership, Diplomacy and Proposals for Reform* (Variorum, 1993).

2. Francis X. Martin, *Friar, Reformer, and Renaissance Scholar: Life and Work of Giles of Viterbo, 1469–1532* (Augustinian Press, 1992); John W. O'Malley, *Giles of Viterbo on Church and Reform: A Study in Renaissance Thought* (E. J. Brill, 1968).

3. Egidio da Viterbo, "Address to the Fifth Lateran Council, 1512," in *Catholic Reform from Cardinal Ximenes to the Council of Trent, 1495–1563*, by John C. Olin (Fordham University Press, 1990), p. 58.

4. In Olin, *Catholic Reform*, pp. 58, 54–55.

5. Lauro Martines, *Fire in the City: Savonarola and the Struggle for Renaissance Florence* (Oxford University Press, 2006); Rachel Erlanger, *The Unarmed Prophet: Savonarola in Florence* (McGraw-Hill, 1988).

6. Anne Borelli and Maria C. Pastore Passaro, eds. and trans., *Selected Writings of Girolamo Savonarola: Religion and Politics, 1490–1498* (Yale University Press, 2006), pp. 63, 68, 75.

7. Quoted in U. Baldassarri and A. Saiber, eds., *Images of Quattrocento Florence* (Yale University Press, 2000), pp. 281–282.

8. Erika Rummel, *Jiménez de Cisneros: On the Threshold of Spain's Golden Age* (Arizona Center for Medieval and Renaissance Studies, 1999).

9. John C. Olin, in *Catholic Reformation: Savonarola to St. Ignatius Loyola* (Harper and Row, 1969), p. 94.

10. Ibid., p. 188.

11. Ibid., p. 136.

12. *Obras completas del santo Maestro: Juan de Ávila*, 6 vols., ed. Luis Sala Balust and Francisco Martín Hernández (Editorial Católica, 1970–1971), vol. 1, p. 47.

13. John O'Malley, *Trent and All That* (Harvard University Press, 2000).

CHAPTER SEVEN: *Luther: From Student to Monk*

1. Philip Schaff, *History of the Christian Church*, 2nd ed. (Charles Scribner's Sons, 1916), vol. 6, p. 171.

2. Julian of Norwich, *Showings*, trans. Edmund Colledge (Paulist Press, 1978), pp. 165–166.

3. Thomas Aquinas, *Summa Theologica*, part II-II, questions 180–182.

4. Quoted by Alfonso Maria de' Liguori, *Instructions and Considerations on the Religious State* (Richardson and Son, 1848), p. 96.

5. "A Brief Reply to Duke George" (1533), in *D. Martin Luthers Werke: Kritische Gesamtausgabe* (Weimar: H. Böhlau, 1883–2009), vol. 38, p. 143 (cited hereafter as WA).

6. Luther's *Table Talk*, WA-Tischreden, vol. 1, p. 240, no. 518 (cited hereafter as WAT).

7. Ibid., p. 224, no. 501.

8. Ibid., p. 47, no. 122.

9. *Preface to Luther's Latin Writings*, 1545, WA vol. 54, pp. 185–186.

10. *Commentary on Psalm 117*, WA, vol. 31.1, p. 249.

11. Many examples of this fear are cited by Martin Brecht, *Martin Luther: His Road to Reformation, 1483–1521* (Fortress Press, 1985), pp. 73–78.

12. Otto Scheel, ed., *Dokumente zu Luthers Entwicklung* (J. C. B. Mohr, 1929), document no. 461.

13. Ibid., document no. 86.

14. Ibid., document no. 487.

15. Kurt Aland, ed., *Martin Luther's 95 Theses with the Pertinent Documents from the History of the Reformation* (Concordia Publishing House, 1967), p. 43.

16. *Commentary on Romans* (1516), WA, vol. 56, p. 381.

17. *Preface to Latin Writings*, WA, vol. 54, p. 185.

18. W. Köhler, ed., *Dokumente zum Ablassstreit von 1517* (J. C. B. Mohr, 1902), document no. 31.

19. Paul Kalkoff, *Ablass und Reliquienverehrung an der Schlosskirche zu Wittenberg unter Friedrich dem Weisen* (F. A. Perthes 1907), p. 17.

20. Roland Bainton, *Here I Stand: A Life of Martin Luther* (Abingdon-Cokesbury Press, 1950), p. 78.

21. Letter to Albrecht of Mainz, in *Luther's Works*, ed. Jaroslav Pelikan et al., 55 vols. (Concordia Publishing House, 1955–1986), vol. 48, pp. 43–49 (cited hereafter as LW).

22. Quoted by Martin John Spalding, *The History of the Protestant Reformation* (John Murphy & Co., 1865), vol. 1, p. 78.

23. *Ninety-Five Theses*, LW, vol. 31, p. 30.

24. Ibid., p. 32.

25. All quotes from the ninety-five theses can be found in LW, vol. 31, pp. 25–33.

26. WAT, vol. 3, p. 656, no. 3846.

27. WAT, vol. 2, p. 595, no. 2668a; Bainton, *Here I Stand*, p. 91.

28. Johann Georg Walch, ed., *Dr. Martin Luthers Sämmtliche Schriften* (Concordia Publishing House, 1880–1910), vol. 15, p. 208 (cited hereafter as Walch SS); Bainton, *Here I Stand*, p. 96.

29. WA Briefwechsel BR (cited hereafter as WA-BR), vol. 1, letter 161; Bainton, *Here I Stand*, p. 109.

30. WA-BR, vol. 2, letter 250; Bainton, *Here I Stand*, p. 101.

31. Walch SS, vol. 2, p. 427; Bainton, *Here I Stand*, pp. 116–117.

32. Walch SS, vol. 2, p. 404; Bainton, *Here I Stand*, p. 119.

CHAPTER EIGHT: *Luther: From Rebel to Heretic*

1. *Concerning the Answer of the Goat in Leipzig*, LW, vol. 39, p. 124.

2. The two Wettin lines were created by the Treaty of Leipzig in 1485, which partitioned the family territories between Prince Elector Ernest and his brother Duke Albert. See Karlheinz Blaschke, *Sachsen im Zeitalter der Reformation* (Gütersloher Verlagshaus, 1970).

3. Bernd Moeller, *Imperial Cities and the Reformation*, trans. H. C. E. Midelfort and Mark Edwards (Fortress Press, 1972), p. 41.

4. Ibid., p. 46.

5. Ibid., p. 48.

6. Quoted by Thomas A. Brady, *German Histories in the Age of Reformations, 1400–1650* (Cambridge University Press, 2009), p. 153.

7. *Bulla decimi Leonis, Contra errors Martini Lutheri et sequacium* (Strassburg, 1520).

8. *D. Martini Lutheri Opera latina varii argumenti ad reformationis historiam imprimis pertinentia*, ed. Heinrich Schmidt, 7 vols. (Heyder and Zimmer, 1868), vol. 5, pp. 11–12.

9. WA-BR, vol. 2, letter no. 295.

10. *An Open Letter to the Christian Nobility of the German Nation*, LW, vol. 44, p. 130.

11. LW, vol. 44, p. 178.

12. Ibid., p. 212.

13. Ibid., p. 157.

14. *Babylonian Captivity*, LW, vol. 36, p. 17.

15. LW, vol. 31, p. 344.

16. Ibid., p. 360.

17. Ibid.

18. Ibid., p. 353.

19. Ibid., p. 356.

20. WA, vol. 6, p. 629.

21. Ibid., pp. 598, 603, 604.

22. P. Kalkoff, ed. and trans., *Die Depeschen des Nuntius Aleander vom Wormser Reichstage 1521* (Verein für Reformationsgeschichte, 1886), p. 43.

23. Adolf Wrede, ed., *Deutsche Reichstagsakten, Jüngere Reihe: Reichstagsakten Unter Kaiser Karl V* (Perthes, 1896), vol. 2, pp. 552–553n3.

24. Kalkoff, *Depeschen des Nuntius Aleanders*, p. 140.

25. Wrede, *Deutsche Reichstagsakten*, vol. 2, pp. 575–582.

26. Ibid., vol. 2, p. 595.

27. Steven Ozment, *The Reformation in the Cities* (Yale University Press, 1980), p. 76.

28. Heinrich von Kettenbach, "Ein Sermon von der Christlichen Kirche" (1522), in *Flugschriften aus den ersten Jahren der Reformation*, ed. Otto Clemen, 4 vols. (R. Haupt, 1907–1911), vol. 2, p. 83.

29. *Ein clag und bitt der deutschen nation an der almechtigen got umb erlosung auss dem gefenknis des Antichrist*, in *Satiren und Pasquille aus der Reformationszeit*, ed. Oskar Schade, 3 vols. (C. Rümpler, 1856–1858), vol. 1, p. 1.

30. *Schirmred ains layeschen Burgers zu Constanz* (1525), in Ozment, *Reformation in the Cities*, p. 80.

CHAPTER NINE: *Luther: The Reactionary*

1. WAT, vol. 3, pp. 634–636, no. 3814.

2. WAT, vol. 5, pp. 87–88, no. 5358b. For a list of Luther's demonic encounters, see Jeffrey Burton Russell, *Mephistopheles: The Devil in the Modern World* (Cornell University Press, 1986), p. 39.

3. WAT, vol. 1, pp. 204–205, no. 469.

4. The title chosen by Heiko Oberman for his Luther biography was most apt: *Luther: Mensch zwischen Gott und Teufel* (Berlin, 1982), published in English as *Luther: Man Between God and the Devil* (Yale University Press, 1989).

5. WAT, vol. 6, pp. 219–220, no. 6832.

6. For possession narratives, see WAT, vol. 3. no. 3677 and no. 3739; vol. 4., no. 4776; vol. 5., no. 5207, 5375e, and 6211; vol. 6, no. 6822.

7. WAT, vol. 1, pp. 215–218, no. 491.

8. WA-Br, letter no. 442, vol. 2, p. 407.

9. Albrecht Dürer, "Das Tagebuch der niederlandischen Reise," in *Albrecht Dürers schriftliches Vermächtnis*, ed. Max Osborn (Leonhard Simion, 1905), p. 94.

10. *Von Gewychtem Wasser und Saltz* (Wittenberg, 1520). For a more detailed discussion of Karlstadt's position, see Carlos Eire, *War Against the Idols* (Cambridge University Press, 1986), pp. 56–73.

11. *Von Gelubden Unterrichtung* (Wittenberg, 1521).

12. *Von Beiden Gestaldten der Heylige Messe* (Wittenberg, 1521).

13. *Predig Andresen Bodenstein von Carolstatt zu Wittenberg von Emphahung des heiligen Sacraments* (Wittenberg, 1522), reprinted as *Karlstadt's Battles with Luther: Documents in a Liberal-Radical Debate*, trans. Ronald J. Sider (Fortress Press, 1978), p. 7.

14. "On the Removal of Images," in *A Reformation Debate: Karlstadt, Emser, and Eck on Sacred Images: Three Treatises in Translation*, trans. Bryan Mangrum and Giuseppe Scavizzi, 2nd ed. (University of Toronto, Centre for Reformation and Renaissance Studies, 1998), pp. 41–42.

15. Ibid., pp. 35–36.

16. *Second Invocavit Sermon*, LW, vol. 51, p. 76.

17. *First Invocavit Sermon*, LW, vol. 51, p. 73.

18. *Against the Heavenly Prophets*, LW, vol. 40, pp. 79, 83.

19. Ibid., p. 222.

20. Ibid., p. 116.

21. Ronald Sider, *Karlstadt's Battles with Luther*, p. 52.

22. Ibid., p. 65.

23. Ibid.

24. Ibid., p. 70.

25. Gordon Rupp, *Patterns of Reformation* (Fortress Press, 1969), p. 165.

26. *The Prague Protest*, in *The Radical Reformation*, by Michael Baylor (Cambridge, 1991), pp. 2–4.

27. Ibid., p. 3.

28. Ibid., pp. 7, 10.

29. *Open Letter*, LW, vol. 40, p. 51.

30. *Sermon to the Princes*, in Baylor, *Radical Reformation*, pp. 28, 31.

31. Ibid., p. 32.

32. *Defense*, in Baylor, *Radical Reformation*, p. 93.

33. Ibid., p. 81.

34. Ibid., p. 84.

35. Ibid., p. 90.

36. Ibid., p. 89, 77.

37. Ibid., p. 89.

38. *Prague Protest*, in Baylor, *Radical Reformation*, p. 2.

39. *Defense*, in Baylor, *Radical Reformation*, p. 88.

40. WA, vol. 18, p. 358; *Against the Robbing and Murdering Hordes of Peasants*, in Kyle C. Sessions, *Reformation and Authority: The Meaning of the Peasants' Revolt* (Heath, 1968).

41. Peter Blickle, *The Revolution of 1525*, trans. Thomas Brady and H. C. Erik Midelfort (Johns Hopkins University Press, 1985).

42. Abraham Friesen, *Reformation and Utopia: The Marxist Interpretation of the Reformation* (F. Steiner, 1974).

43. *Memmingen Federal Constitution*, in Baylor, *Radical Reformation*, pp. 240–241.

44. LW, vol. 46, p. 32.

45. Ibid., p. 40.

46. Ibid., p. 17.

47. Ibid., p. 31.

48. Ibid., p. 37.

49. Ibid., p. 68.

50. Ibid., pp. 29–30.

51. Peter Matheson, ed. and trans., *The Collected Works of Thomas Müntzer* (T. & T. Clark, 1988), pp. 140–142.

52. LW, vol. 46, p. 48.

53. Ibid., p. 49.

54. Ibid., p. 84.

55. Ibid., p. 63.

56. Rudolf Endres, "The Peasant War in Franconia," in *The German Peasant War of 1525*, ed. Bob Scribner and Gerhard Benecke (Allen & Unwin, 1979), p. 79.

57. LW, vol. 46, p. 83.

58. Ibid., p. 84

59. WAT, vol. 3, p. 75, no. 2911b.

60. Johannes Poliander, *Ein Urtayl uber das hart Büchlein D. Martinus Luthers wider die auffrurn der Pawern* (1525), in *Flugschriften der Bauernkriegszeit*, ed. Adolf Laube and Hans Werner Seiffert (Akademie-Verlag, 1975), p. 430.

61. Eugene Rice, *The Foundations of Early Modern Europe, 1460–1559* (Norton, 1970), p. 151.

62. Johannes Findling, *Anzeigung swayer falschen Zungen des Luthers wie er mit der ainen die pauern verfüret mit der anders si verdammet hat* (1525), in *Flugschriften der Bauernkriegszeit*.

63. Johannes Janssen, *History of the German People at the Close of the Middle Ages*, trans. A. M. Christie (K. Paul, Trench, Trübner, & Co., 1900), vol. 4, pp. 143–145.

64. Blickle, *Revolution*, pp. 183–184.

65. Samuel P. Huntington, "Modernisierung durch Revolution," in *Empirische Revolutionsforschung*, ed. K. Von Beyme (Westdeutscher Verlag, 1973), p. 94.

66. Manfred Schulze, *Fürsten und Reformation: Geistliche Reformpolitik weltlicher Fürsten vor der Reformation* (J. C. B. Mohr, 1991).

67. Heiko Obermann, *The Two Reformations* (Yale University Press, 2003), p. 110.

68. Walch SS, vol. 15, no. 716.

69. Quoted by Philip Schaff, *History of the Christian Church*, 2nd ed., 8 vols. (Scribner's, 1882–1910), vol. 8, p. 362.

CHAPTER TEN: *The Swiss Reformation*

1. Franz Lau and Ernst Bizer, *Reformationsgeschichte Deutschlands bis 1555* (Vandenhoeck & Ruprecht, 1964), chap. 17.

2. Ulrich Zwingli, *Uslegen und gründ der schlussreden oder Articklen*, in *Huldreich Zwinglis Sämtliche Werke*, ed. Emil Egli and Georg Finsler (C. A. Schwetschke und Sohn, 1905–1990), vol. 2, p. 147 (cited hereafter as ZW).

3. Ulrich Zwingli, *Selected Works*, ed. Samuel Macauley Jackson (University of Pennsylvania Press, 1972), p. xvi n. 7 (cited hereafter as ZW-S).

4. ZW 2.217.

5. *The Latin Works and the Correspondence of Huldrych Zwingli, Together with Selections from His German Works*, ed. S. M. Jackson, 3 vols. (G. P. Putnam's Sons, 1912), vol. 1, p. 219 (cited hereafter as ZW-Lat).

6. Acts of the First Disputation, 29 January 1523, in ZW-S, p. 85.

7. Samuel Macauley Jackson, ed., ZW-S, p. 49.

8. Ibid., p. 65.

9. Oskar Farner, *Huldrych Zwingli*, vol. 3, *Seine Verkündigung und ihre ersten Früchte, 1520–1525* (Zwingli Verlag, 1954), p. 490.

10. *Answer to Valentin Compar*, ZW, 4.88.

11. *Commentary on True and False Religion*, ed. Samuel Macauley Jackson and Clarence Nevin Heller (Labyrinth Press, 1981), pp. 97–98.

12. Letter to Martin Bucer, 3 June 1524, in *Correspondance de Martin Bucer*, ed. Jean Rott (E. J. Brill, 1979), vol. 1, p. 257.

13. Gottfried W. Locher, *Zwingli's Thought: New Perspectives* (E. J. Brill, 1981), p. 34.

14. *Commentary on True and False Religion*, pp. 92–93.

15. Zwingli, *On Providence and Other Essays* (Labyrinth Press, 1983), p. 166.

16. Zwingli, *Commentary on True and False Religion*, p. 341.

17. Zwingli, *On Providence*, pp. 138, 180, 186.

18. Ernst Gagliardi, Hans Müller, and Friz Büsser, eds., *Johannes Stumpfs Schweizer- und Reformationschronik* (Birkhäuser, 1955); Jeanne de Jussie, *Le levain du Calvinisme* (J.-G. Fick, 1865), English translation by Carrie F. Klaus, *The Short Chronicle* (University of Chicago Press, 2006).

19. J. H. Merle D'Aubigné, *History of the Great Reformation of the Sixteenth Century* (Robert Carter, 1846), p. 767.

20. ZW 6/1, pp. 497–498.

21. Letter to Willibald Pirckheimer, July 1529, in *Opus epistolarum Des. Erasmi Roterdami*, ed. P. S. Allen and H. M. Allen (Oxford, 1906–1958), vol. 8, 231.

22. D'Aubigné, *History*, p. 771.

23. LW, vol. 38, p. 32.

24. Ibid., p. 15.

25. Ibid., p. 32.

26. Ibid., p. 56.

27. Ibid., p. 25.

28. Ibid., p. 35.

29. Oswald Myconius, "Original Life of Zwingli," in ZW-Lat, vol. 1, p. 23.

CHAPTER ELEVEN: *The Radical Reformation*

1. J. J. Hottinger and H. H. Vögeli, eds., *Heinrich Bullingers Reformationsgeschichte*, 3 vols. (Bepel, 1838), vol. 1, p. 382.

2. *The Schleitheim Articles*, in *The Radical Reformation*, ed. Michael Baylor (Cambridge University Press, 1991), p. 175.

3. Zwingli, *On Baptism*, in G. W. Bromiley, *Zwingli and Bullinger* (Westminster Press, 1953), p. 140.

4. Ernst Troeltsch, *Protestantism and Progress: A Historical Study of the Relation of Protestantism to the Modern World*, trans. W. Montgomery (Beacon Press, 1958), pp. 48, 95–96, 104, 153, 174.

5. Roland Bainton, *Studies on the Reformation* (Hodder and Stoughton, 1963), vol. 2, p. 199.

6. Franklin Littell, *The Origins of Sectarian Protestantism: A Study of the Anabaptist View of the Church* (Macmillan, 1964).

7. George Hunston Williams, *The Radical Reformation* (Weidenfeld and Nicolson 1962; Sixteenth Century Journal Publishers, 1992).

8. Ibid., p. 1296.

9. James Stayer et al., "From Monogenesis to Polygenesis: The Historical Discussion of Anabaptist Origins," *Mennonite Quarterly Review* (1975): 83–121; Peter Iver Kaufman, "Social History, Psychohistory, and the Prehistory of Swiss Anabaptism," *Journal of Religion* 68, no. 4. (October 1988): 527–544.

10. Peter Matheson, *The Collected Works of Thomas Müntzer* (T. & T. Clark, 1988), pp. 121–129.

11. *Chronicle of the Hutterian Brethren* (Plough Publishing House, 1989), cited by Williams, *Radical Reformation*, p. 217.

12. Ulrich Zwingli, *Contra Catabaptistarum Strophas Elenchus*, ZW 6.1, 22–196, or "Refutation of the Tricks of the Catabaptists" (1527); S. M. Jackson, trans., *Selected Works of Huldrich Zwingli* (University of Pennsylvania Press, 1901).

13. Baylor, *Radical Reformation*, p. 175.

14. Jackson, *Selected Works of Zwingli*, p. 127.

15. Karl Rembert, *Die Wiedertaüfer in der Herzogtum Jülich* (Berlin 1899), p. 564, in Harold Bender, "The Anabaptist Vision," *Church History* 13, no. 1. (March 1944): 3–24.

16. George H. Williams, ed., *Spiritual and Anabaptist Writers* (Westminster Press, 1957), pp. 138–144.

17. The Count of Alzay in the Palatinate, cited by Bender, "Anabaptist Vision," p. 6.

18. Thieleman J. Van Braght, *Het Bloedig tooneel of Martelaers spiegel der doops-gesinde of weereloose Christenen* (1685); English translation: *Martyr's Mirror: The Story of Seventeen Centuries of Christian Martyrdom* (Herald Press, 2001).

19. James Stayer, *The German Peasants' War and Anabaptist Community of Goods* (McGill-Queen's University Press, 1991), p. 4.

20. "Then I heard him call out in a loud voice, 'Bring the guards of the city here, each with a weapon in his hand.' And I saw six men coming from the direction of the upper gate, which faces north, each with a deadly weapon in his hand. With them was a man clothed in linen who had a writing kit at his side. They came in and stood beside the bronze altar. . . . Then the LORD called to the man clothed in linen who had the writing kit at his side and said to him, 'Go throughout the city of Jerusalem and put a mark on the foreheads of those who grieve and lament over all the detestable things that are done in it'" (Ezekiel 9:1–4).

21. Hans Hut, *On the Mystery of Baptism*, in Baylor, *Radical Reformation*, p. 169.

22. Hans Hillerbrand, *The Reformation: A Narrative History Related by Contemporary Observers and Participants* (Harper and Row, 1964), p. 257.

23. Kelens Löffler, ed., *Die Widertäufer zu Münster* (E. Diederichs, 1923), p. 81, in Williams, *Radical Reformation*, p. 567n24.

24. Hillerbrand, *Reformation*, p. 259.

25. *A Restitution of Christian Teaching, Faith, and Life*, in Lowell Zuck, *Christianity and Revolution: Radical Christian Testimonies, 1520–1650* (Temple University Press, 1975), pp. 98–101.

26. Zuck, *Christianity and Revolution*, pp. 102–104.

27. Karl Gottlieb Bretschneider, ed., *Philippi Melanthonis Opera quae Supersunt Omnia*, 28 vols. (C. A. Schwetschke, 1834–1860), vol. 8, p. 742.

28. Quoted in Hans Hillerbrand, *The Division of Christendom* (Westminster/John Knox Press, 2007), p. 132.

29. *Letter to John Campanus*, in Williams, *Spiritual and Anabaptist Writers*, pp. 150–155.

30. Ibid., p. 156.

31. Frank, *Paradoxa*, in *The Reformation in Its Own Words*, ed. Hans Hillerbrand (SCM Press, 1964), pp. 292–294.

CHAPTER TWELVE: *Calvin and Calvinism*

1. G. Baum, E. Cunitz, and E. Reuss, eds., *Ioannis Calvini Opera quae supersunt Omnia*, 59 vols. (C. A. Schwetschke, 1863–1900), vol. 12, pp. 7–10 (cited hereafter as OC).

2. OC, vol. 12, p. 61.

3. Théodore de Bèze, *The Life of John Calvin*, in *Selected Works of John Calvin*, ed. H. Beveridge and J. Bonnet (Grand Rapids: Baker, 1983), vol. 1, p. lxxxiv.

4. *Inventory of Relics*, OC, vol. 6, p. 452.

5. "Les Réformateurs et la superstition," *Actes du Colloque l'Amiral de Coligny et son temps, Paris, 24-28 octobre 1972* (Société de l'Histoire du Protestantisme Français, 1974), p. 471. See also J. Samuel Preus, "Zwingli, Calvin and the Origin of Religion," *Church History* 46, no. 2 (June 1977): 186–202.

6. B. J. Kidd, ed., *Documents Illustrative of the Continental Reformation* (Clarendon Press, 1911), pp. 528–532.

7. Preface to the 1559 edition, *Institutes of the Christian Religion*, ed. John T. McNeill, trans. Ford Lewis Battles, 2 vols. (Philadelphia, 1960), vol. 1, p. 4.

8. Ibid., p. 30.

9. Ibid., p. 31.

10. Ibid., p. 11.

11. Ibid., p. 12.

12. For an overview, see Alan Kors, *Atheism in France, 1650–1729* (Princeton University Press, 1990).

13. *Institutes*, book III, chap. 21.5 (Philadelphia, 1960), p. 926.

14. *Institutes*, book I, chap. 17.11 (Philadelphia, 1960), p. 224.

15. *Preface to the Commentary on Psalms*, in *Calvin: Commentaries*, ed. Joseph Haroutounian (Westminster Press, 1958), p. 35.

16. Ibid., p. 36.

17. Calvin to Farel, 19 May 1539, in *Letters of John Calvin: Compiled from the Original Manuscripts and Edited with Historical Notes*, by Jules Bonnet, 4 vols. (Presbyterian Board of Publication, 1858), vol. 1, p. 141.

18. *Preface to the Commentary on Psalms*, Haroutounian, p. 32.

19. *Draft Ecclesiastical Ordinances*, 1541, in *Calvin: Theological Treatises*, ed. J. K. Reid (Westminster Press, 1954), p. 58.

20. Ibid., p. 62.

21. Ibid., pp. 63-64.

22. OC, vol. 14, p. 432. See W. G. Naphy "Baptisms, Church Riots and Social Unrest in Calvin's Geneva," *Sixteenth Century Journal* 26, no. 1. (Spring 1995): 87–97.

23. Cited by Edith Simon and E. W. C. Wilkins in *The Reformation* (Time Life Books, 1966), p. 60.

24. See Carlo Ginzburg, *Il Nicodemismo* (G. Einaudi, 1970); Carlos Eire, "Calvin and Nicodemism: A Reappraisal," *Sixteenth Century Journal* 10, no. 1 (Spring 1979): 44–69.

25. *Petit Traicté monstrant que c'est que doit faire un homme fidele, cognoissant la verité de l'Evangile quand il est entre les papistes*, OC, vol. 6, p. 580.

26. *De fugiendis impiorum illicitis sacribus*, OC, vol. 5, pp. 310, 312.

27. OC, vol. 11, p. 646.

28. *Troisieme Sermon*, OC, vol. 8, p. 412.

29. Ibid.

30. OC, vol. 13 p. 596.

31. *De Fugiendis*, OC, vol. 5, p. 274.

32. Report of the Venetian Ambassador, in *Documents Illustrative of the Continental Reformation*, ed. B. J. Kidd (Clarendon Press, 1911), pp. 679–681.

33. William Allen, S.J., *A True, Sincere, and Modest Defense of English Catholics* (1584), facsimile ed., *English Recusant Literature* (Scolar Press, 1971), vol. 68, pp. 77–84.

34. August Kluckhohn, ed., *Briefe Friedrichs des Frommen* (C. A. Schwetschke, 1868), vol. 1, p. 271.

35. Anonymous, cited by Donald Kelley, *The Beginning of Ideology* (Cambridge University Press, 1981), p. 89.

36. D. Laing, ed., *The Works of John Knox*, 6 vols. (Woodrow Society, 1846–1864), vol. 4, p. 240.

37. John Bale, *Pageant of Popes* (T. Marshe, 1574), Epistle Dedicatory, fol. 15v.

38. R. C. Winthrop, ed., *Life and Letters of John Winthrop* (Ticknor and Fields, 1867), p. 19.

39. *Defensio orthodoxae fidei de Sacra Trinatate, contra prodigiosos errores Michaelis Serveti Hispani* (1554), OC, vol. 8, p. 498.

40. Sebastian Castellio, *Concerning Heretics, Whether They Are to Be Persecuted*, trans. Roland Bainton (Columbia University Press, 1935), pp. 122–123.

41. *Writings of the Rev. John Knox, Minister of God's Word in Scotland* (W. Clowes, for Religious Tract Society, 1800), pp. 228–229.

42. *Vindiciae contra Tyrannos* (1579), in Julian H. Franklin, *Constitutionalism and Resistance in the Sixteenth Century: Three Treatises* (Pegasus, 1969), p. 149.

43. Letter of 11 April 1823, in *Thomas Jefferson: Letters and Addresses*, ed. William B. Parker and Jonas Viles (Sun Dial Classics, 1902), p. 274.

44. Michael Walzer, *The Revolution of the Saints* (Harvard University Press, 1965); Quentin Skinner, *The Foundations of Modern Political Thought*, vol. 2 (Cambridge University Press, 1978).

45. *Commentary on John's Gospel*, OC, vol. 47, p. 90.

CHAPTER THIRTEEN: *England, Wales, Ireland, and Scotland, 1521–1603*

1. Excerpt from "The Defense of the Seven Sacraments," in *English History in the Making*, ed. William L. Sachse (Xerox College Publications, 1967), vol. 1, pp. 182–183.

2. A. G. Dickens, *The English Reformation*, 2nd ed. (Collins, 1989).

3. Christopher Haigh, *English Reformations* (Oxford University Press, 1993); Haigh, *The Reign of Elizabeth I* (Macmillan, 1984); J. J. Scarisbrick, *The Reformation and the English People* (Blackwell, 1984); Eamon Duffy, *The Stripping of the Altars*, 2nd ed. (Yale University Press, 2005); Duffy, *The Voices of Morebath* (Yale University Press, 2001).

4. A. G. Dickens and Dorothy Carr, eds., *The Reformation in England to the Accession of Elizabeth I* (Edward Arnold, 1967), pp. 26–27.

5. Henry Gee and William John Hardy, eds., *Documents Illustrative of English Church History* (Macmillan, 1914), pp. 243–244.

6. William Roper, *The Life of Sir Thomas More by His Son-in-Law* (Burns & Oates, 1905), p. 101.

7. Eamon Duffy, *The Voices of Morebath* (Yale University Press, 2001), p. 131.

8. S. R. Cattley, ed., *The Acts and Monuments of John Foxe: A New and Complete Edition* (Seeley & Burnside, 1838), vol. 6, p. 658.

9. Gerald Bray, *Documents of the English Reformation* (Fortress Press 1994), pp. 322–323.

10. Brian Cummings, ed., *The Book of Common Prayer: The Texts of 1549, 1559, and 1662* (Oxford University Press, 2013), p. 137.

11. Newton Key and Robert Bucholz, eds., *Sources and Debates in English History, 1485–1714* (Blackwell, 2009), p. 74.

12. Quoted in Alison Weir, *The Life of Elizabeth the First* (Random House, 1998), p. 474.

13. Steven W. May, ed., *Queen Elizabeth I: Selected Works* (Simon and Schuster, 2006), p. 84.

14. W. H. Frere and C. E. Douglas, eds., *Puritan Manifestoes* (Society for Promoting Christian Knowledge, 1907), p. 21.

15. Mark Noll, ed., *Confessions and Catechisms of the Reformation* (Baker Book House, 1991), pp. 214–227.

16. See Duffy, *Voices of Morebath*.

17. Colman Barry, ed., *Readings in Church History 2: The Renaissance and Reformation* (Newman Press, 1965), pp. 70–72.

18. Philip II to the Duke of Alba, 16 December 1569, quoted in Thomas McCoog, *The Society of Jesus in Ireland, Scotland, and England, 1541–1588* (E. J. Brill, 1996), p. 82.

19. G. Baum, E. Cunitz, and E. Reuss, eds., *Ioannis Calvini Opera quae supersunt Omnia*, 59 vols. (C. A. Schwetschke, 1863–1900), vol. 15, pp. 90–91.

20. Marvin Breslow, ed., *The Political Writings of John Knox* (Folger Shakespeare Library, 1985), pp. 42, 50.

21. *The Writings of John Knox* (Presbyterian Board of Publication, 1842), p. 229.

22. John Knox, *History of the Reformation in Scotland*, ed. Cuthbert Lennon (Andrew Melrose, 1905), p. 131.

23. Ibid., p. 323.

CHAPTER FOURTEEN: *Catholic Reform: Facing the Challenge*

1. Frances Andrews, *The Early Humiliati* (Cambridge: Cambridge University Press, 1999), pp. 16–17.

2. Quoted by Henry Kamen, *The Phoenix and the Flame: Catalonia and the Counter Reformation* (Yale University Press, 1993), pp. 207–208.

3. "The Defense of the Seven Sacraments," in *English History in the Making*, ed. William L. Sachse (John Wiley and Sons, 1967), vol. 1, pp. 182–183.

4. Michel Roset, *Les chroniques de Genève*, ed. H. Fazy (Geneva, 1894), p. 198.

5. The books found in the Latin Vulgate text approved by Trent but rejected by Protestants are Tobit, Judith, Wisdom, Sirach, Baruch, and Maccabees 1 and 2, along with some sections of Esther and Daniel.

6. *Canons and Decrees of the Council of Trent*, trans. H. J. Schroeder (TAN Books, 1978), p. 43.

7. Ibid., p. 38.

8. Ibid., p. 182.

9. "Tiempos recios," in *Libro de la vida*, chapter 33.5. E. Allison Peers translates this expression as "bad times," in *The Life of Teresa of Jesus* (Image Books, 2004), p. 288.

10. Quoted in Henry Charles Lea, *A History of the Inquisition in Spain*, 4 vols. (Macmillan, 1906–1908), vol. 3, p. 567.

CHAPTER FIFTEEN: *Catholic Reform: Healing the Body of Christ*

1. On the ninth article of the Apostles' Creed, "I believe in the Holy Catholic Church," see *The Catechism of the Council of Trent*, trans. J. Donovan (reprint; TAN Books, 1982), p. 72.

2. St. Francis de Sales, *The Catholic Controversy*, trans. Benedict Mackey (Burns and Oates; 1886; reprint, TAN Books, 1989), p. 212.

3. Victor Turner, *From Ritual to Theatre* (Performing Arts Journal Publications, 1982), p. 82; Clifford Geertz, "Religion as a Cultural System," in *Anthropological Approaches to the Study of Religion*, ed. Michael Banton (F. A. Praeger, 1966), pp. 28–29.

4. José Luis González Novalín, "Misas supersticiosas y misas votivas en la piedad popular del tiempo de la reforma," in *Míscelanea José Zunzunegui* (Vitoria, 1975), vol. 2, p. 293. For archival evidence, see Carlos Eire, *From Madrid to Purgatory* (Cambridge University Press, 1995), pp. 224–229.

5. *Canons and Decrees of the Council of Trent*, session 22, chap. 9, trans. H. J. Schroeder (TAN Books, 1978), p. 151.

6. Pedro de Ribadeneyra, S.J., *Flos sanctorum de las vidas de los santos* (1599–1601), quoted by José Luis Sanchez Lora, *Mujeres, conventos, y formas de la religiosidad barroca* (Fundación Universitaria Española, 1988), p. 377.

7. Juan de la Cruz, "Cantico espiritual," *Obras completas*, 14th ed. (Biblioteca de Autores Cristianos, 1994), p. 133.

8. Montague Summers, *The Physical Phenomena of Mysticism* (Rider & Company, 1950), p. 152.

9. Teresa de Jesús [St. Teresa of Ávila], *Vida*, chap. 27.9, *Obras completas*, 9th ed. (Biblioteca de Autores Cristianos, 1997), p. 145.

10. Quoted by Herbert Thurston, "Some Physical Phenomena of Mysticism," *The Month* 133 (January–June 1913): 333.

11. *The Autobiography of Saint Margaret Mary Alacoque*, trans. Sisters of the Visitation (reprint, TAN Books, 1986), p. 106.

12. *The Journal of Montaigne's Travels in Italy by Way of Switzerland and Germany in 1580 and 1581*, ed. and trans. W. G. Waters, 3 vols. (John Murray, 1903), vol. 2, pp. 197–198, 202.

13. M. Boivin, *Relation fidelle du miracle du Saint-Sacrement arrivé à Faverney, en 1608* (Chez Prudont, 1838), p. 8.

14. Cited by E. Cobham Brewer, *A Dictionary of Miracles* (J. B. Lippincott, 1894), p. 493.

15. Francis de Sales, *Introduction to the Devout Life*, trans. John K. Ryan (Image Books, 1966), p. 34.

16. Ibid., pp. 210–211.

17. Ibid., p. 45.

18. Romans 12:3–5; Corinthians 12:12–26; Ephesians 1:18–23; Colossians 3:14–16.

CHAPTER SIXTEEN: *Catholic Reform: Fashioning a New Clergy*

1. Letter of Peter Canisius to the bishop of Würzburg, trans. James Brodrick, in *Saint Peter Canisius* (Loyola Press, 1980), p. 654.

2. "A Fish Diet," in *Collected Works of Erasmus: Colloquies*, ed. Craig R. Thompson (University of Toronto, Press, 1997), p. 718.

3. "Patterns of Informal Conversation," *Collected Works of Erasmus: Colloquies*, ed. Craig R. Thompson (University of Toronto Press, 1997), p. 18.

4. "On Monastic Vows," in *Luther's Works*, vol. 44, pp. 251–400.

5. *Huldrych Zwingli Writings*, ed. and trans. H. Wayne Pipkin (Pickwick Publications, 1984), vol. 2, pp. 202–225.

6. *Consilium de Emendanda Ecclesia*, trans. J. C. Olin, *The Catholic Reformation* (Fordham University Press, 1992), p. 193.

7. François-René, Viscount de Chateaubriand, *La vie de Rancé* (Paris, 1844), p. 35.

8. Marie Guyart Martin is not to be confused with another well-known Marie de l'Incarnation: Barbe Avrillot (1566–1618), also known as Madame Acarie, who brought the Discalced Carmelite reform to France.

9. Translated by Bernard O'Reilly, *St. Angela Merici and the Ursulines* (Burns & Oates, 1880), pp. 200–202.

10. Paul Dreyfus, *Saint Jean de Dieu, 1495-1550: Le père de l'hôpital* (Bayard Editions and Centurion, 1995).

11. Quoted by Karen Liebreich, *Fallen Order: Intrigue, Heresy and Scandal in the Rome of Galileo and Caravaggio* (Grove Press, 2004), p. 37.

12. M. Faillon, *Vie de M. Olier, fondateur du Seminaire de Saint-Sulpice* (F. Wattelier, 1873), vol. 2, p. 228.

CHAPTER SEVENTEEN: *Catholic Reform: The Society of Jesus*

1. *Autobiography*, in *Ignatius of Loyola The Spiritual Exercises and Selected Works*, ed. George Ganss, S.J., et al. (Paulist Press, 1991), p. 70.

2. Ibid., p. 71.

3. *Spiritual Exercises*, in *Ignatius of Loyola The Spiritual Exercises and Selected Works*, ed. George Ganss, S.J., et al. (Paulist Press, 1991), p. 121.

4. Ibid., p. 121.

5. Ibid., p. 176.

6. Ibid., p. 150.

7. Ibid., pp. 155–156.

8. The term *worldly asceticism* was coined by the sociologist Max Weber in the early twentieth century, in his influential book *The Protestant Ethic and the Spirit of Capitalism* (1905). Weber used the term to contrast the austere ethic of Calvinists with the "otherworldly" self-denial of Catholics. According to Weber, Calvinist self-denial was focused not on shunning the world to attain heaven, but on being successful on earth, as a means of confirming one's predestined status as God's elect.

9. *Spiritual Exercises*, pp. 211–214.

10. *Autobiography*, pp. 93–95.

11. Ibid., p. 99.

12. Pedro de Ribadeneyra, S.J., *Monumenta paedagogica Societatis Jesu*, 2nd ed., 5 vols. (Institutum Historicum Societatis Iesu, 1985–1986), vol. 1, p. 475.

13. *Athanasius Kircher: The Last Man Who Knew Everything*, ed. Paula Findlen (Routledge, 2004).

14. *Beati Petri Canisii Societatis Iesu Epistulae et Acta*, ed. Otto Braunsberger, 8 vols. (Herder, 1896–1923), vol. 5, p. 182.

15. Quoted by David Mitchell, *The Jesuits: A History* (F. Watts, 1981), pp. 61–62.

16. Quoted by Harro Höpfl, *Jesuit Political Thought: The Society of Jesus and the State, 1540–1630* (Cambridge University Press, 2004), p. 15.

17. Louis Chatellier, *The Europe of the Devout the Catholic Reformation and the Formation of a New Society* (Cambridge University Press, 1989).

18. J. A. Wylie, *The History of Protestantism* (Cassell, Petter & Galpin, 1874), vol. 2, p. 399.

19. *Poetry of the English Renaissance, 1509–1660*, ed. William Hebel and Hoyt H. Hudson (F. S. Crofts & Co., 1941), p. 236.

CHAPTER EIGHTEEN: *Missions to the New World*

1. Quoted in R. Po-Chia Hsia, *A Jesuit in the Forbidden City: Matteo Ricci, 1552–1610* (Oxford University Press, 2010), p. 19.

2. *Monumenta Historica Societatis Iesu, Epistolae Mixtae* (A. Avrial, 1900), vol. 3, p. 116.

3. Quoted in Raimondo Turtas, "Missioni popolari in Sardegna tra '500 e '600," *Rivista di Storia della Chiesa in Italia* 44 (1990): 369.

4. Quoted in Tacchi Venturi, *Storia della Compagnia* (Civiltà Cattolica, 1950) vol. 1, p. 367.

5. Quoted in José Luis González Novalín, *El inquisidor general Fernando de Valdés* (Universidad de Oviedo, 1968), 78.

6. Felipe de Meneses, *Luz del alma christiana* (Valladolid, 1554), p. 23.

7. Quoted in James Brodrick, *Saint Peter Canisius* (Sheed and Ward, 1935; Loyola Press, 1980), p. 140.

8. José de Acosta, *De procuranda indorum salute*, ed. L. Pereña et al. (Consejo Superior de Investigaciones Científicas, 1987), vol. 2, pp. 274, 276.

9. *European Treaties Bearing on the History of the United States and Its Dependencies to 1648*, ed. Frances Gardiner Davenport (Carnegie Institution of Washington, 1917), pp. 75–78.

10. Bartolomé de Las Casas, *Brevísima relación de la destrucción de las Indias* (Linkgua Digital, 2004), pp. 23–24.

11. Translation of *Requerimiento*, in *Religious Intolerance in America*, ed. John Corrigan and Lynn Neal (University of North Carolina Press, 2010), pp. 43–44.

12. Bernal Díaz del Castillo, *The History of the Conquest of New Spain*, ed. David Carrasco (University of New Mexico Press, 2008), p. 156.

13. Quoted in Robert Bireley, *The Refashioning of Catholicism, 1450–1700* (Catholic University of America Press, 1999).

14. See William Taylor, "Santiago's Horse: Christianity and Colonial Indian Resistance in the Heartland of New Spain," in *Violence, Resistance, and Survival in the Americas*, ed. Franklin Pease and William Taylor (Smithsonian Institution Press, 1994).

15. See Inga Clendinnen, *Ambivalent Conquests: Maya and Spaniard in Yucatan, 1517–1570* (Cambridge University Press, 2003).

16. Quoted by Lawrence Clayton, *Bartolomé de Las Casas: A Biography* (Cambridge University Press, 2012), p. 266n100.

17. Aristotle, *Politics*, I.5.

18. *The Jesuit Relations and Allied Documents*, ed. Reuben Gol Thwaites, 71 vols. (Burrows Brothers, 1896–1901), vol. 7, pp. 36–43.

19. Ibid., vol. 34, pp. 23–35.

CHAPTER NINETEEN: *Missions to the East Indies*

1. Quoted by Maria Cristina Osswald, "The Iconography of the Cult of Francis Xavier, 1552–1640," *Archivum Historicum Societatis Iesu* 71 (2002): 259–277, 260.

2. Quoted by Michela Fontana, *Matteo Ricci: A Jesuit in the Ming Court* (Rowman and Littlefield, 2011), p. 36.

3. *Les missions etrangères: Trois siècles et demi d'histoire et d'aventure en Asie*, ed. Marcel Launay and Gérard Moussay (Perrin, 2008), p. 37.

CHAPTER TWENTY: *The Age of Religious Wars*

1. Peter Blickle, *The Revolution of 1525*, trans. T. A. Brady and H. C. E. Midelfort (Baltimore: Johns Hopkins University Press, 1985).

2. Gerhard Friedrich Bente, *Historical Introductions to the Lutheran Confessions*, 2nd ed. (Concordia Publishing House, 2005), p. 219.

3. OC 19: 120–121.

4. "Estamos aquí o en Flandes?" quoted by Geoffrey Parker, "El ejército español y los Países Bajos en los inicios de la Edad Moderna," in *Encuentros en Flandes: Relaciones e intercambios hispanoflamencos a inicios de la Edad Moderna*, ed. Werner Thomas and Robert A. Verdonk (Leuven University Press, 2000), p. 276.

5. Wolfgang Adam and Siegrid Westphal, eds., *Handbuch kultureller Zentren der Frühen Neuzeit: Städte und Residenzen im alten deutschen Sprachraum* (Walter de Gruyter, 2013), p. 1385; C. V. Wedgewood, *The Thirty Years' War* (New York Review of Books Classics, 2005), p. 281.

6. Quoted by Peter Gaunt, *Oliver Cromwell* (New York University Press, 2004), p. 45.

7. Quoted by John Morrill, "The Drogheda Massacre in Cromwellian Context," in *The Age of Atrocity: Violence and Political Conflict in Early Modern Ireland*, ed. David Edwards, Padraig Lenihan, and Clodagh Tait (Four Courts Press, 2007), p. 257.

8. Quoted by Samuel Smiles, *History of Ireland and the Irish People, Under the Government of England* (London: William Strange, 1844), p. vii.

CHAPTER TWENTY-ONE: *The Age of Orthodoxy*

1. For more details and recommended readings, see chapter 22.

2. Melanchthon would thank death for finally freeing him from the "rage of the theologians" (*rabies theologorum*). Quoted by Barbara Sher Tinsley in *Pierre Bayle's Reformation: Conscience and Criticism on the Eve of the Enlightenment* (Susquehanna University Press, 2001), p. 211.

3. Leipzig Interim, *The Encyclopedia of American Religions, Religious Creeds*, ed. J. Gordon Melton (Gale Research Company, 1988), p. 13.

4. Friedrich Bente, *Historical Introduction to the Lutheran Confessions* (Concordia Publishing, 2005), p. 249.

5. *Concordia: The Lutheran Confessions—A Reader's Edition of the Book of Concord*, ed. Paul T. McCain, 2nd ed. (Concordia Publishing House, 2007), pp. 505–506.

6. *Reformed Reader: Classical Beginnings, 1519–1799*, ed. William Stacy Johnson and George W. Stroup (Westminster and John Knox, 1993), p. 290.

7. *Canons and Decrees of the Council of Trent*, ed. H. J. Schroeder (TAN Books, 2009), pp. 31–32.

8. Ibid., p. 38.

9. Luis de Molina, *Concordia liberi arbitrii cum gratia donis*, 14.23, ed. J. Rabeneck (Collegium Maximum, S.J., 1953), p. 149.

10. Blaise Pascal, letter 10, *The Provincial Letters* (Kessinger Publishing, 2004), p. 103.

11. *The Canons and Decrees of the Council of Trent, with a Supplement*, trans. Theodore Alois Buckley (George Routledge and Company, 1851), p. 357.

12. Alan Kors, *Atheism in France, 1650–1729: The Orthodox Sources of Disbelief* (Princeton University Press, 1990).

13. *Oeuvres complètes de Voltaire* (Imprimerie de la Société Littéraire-Typographique, 1785), vol. 65, p. 357.

CHAPTER TWENTY-TWO: *The Confessional Age*

1. Johannes Janssen, *History of the German People at the Close of the Middle Ages*, trans. A. M. Christie, 10 vols. (Kegan Paul, Trench, Trübner & Co, 1906), vol. 9, pp. 230–232.

2. Heinz Schilling, "Confessionalization: Historical and Scholarly Perspectives of a Comparative and Interdisciplinary Paradigm," *Confessionalization in Europe, 1555–1700*, ed. J. M. Headley, H. J. Hillerbrand, and A. J. Papalas (Ashgate, 2004), pp. 21–36; Joel F. Harrington and Helmut Walser Smith, "Confessionalization, Community, and State Building in Germany, 1555–1870," *Journal of Modern History* 69 (March 1997): 77–101; Wolfgang Reinhard, "Reformation, Counter-Reformation, and the Early Modern State: A Reassessment," *Catholic Historical Review* 75, no. 3 (July 1989): 383–404; Jean Delumeau, *Catholicism Between Luther and Voltaire* (Westminster Press, 1977).

3. Ernst Walter Zeeden, *Die Entstehung der Konfessionen: Grundlagen und Formen der Konfessionsbildung im Zeitalter der Glaubenskämpfe* (Oldenbourg, 1965); Heinz Schilling, ed., *Die reformierte Konfessionalisierung in Deutschland* (Gütersloher Verlagshaus, 1986); Hans-Christoph Rublack, ed., *Die lutherische Konfessionalisierung in Deutschland* (Gütersloher Verlagshaus, 1992).

4. Jean Delumeau, *Catholicism Between Luther and Voltaire* (Westminster/John Knox Press, 1977).

5. Robert Bireley, S.J., *The Refashioning of Catholicism, 1450–1700* (Catholic University of America Press, 1999), p. 102.

6. "On Keeping the Children in School," sermon (1530); LW, vol. 46, p. 257.

7. See G. W. Bromiley, *Zwingli and Bullinger* (Westminster Press, 1953), pp. 96–118.

8. *A Digest of Constitutional and Synodical Legislation of the Reformed Church in America*, ed. E. T. Corwin (Board of Publication of the Reformed Church in America, 1906), pp. 104–105.

9. OC, vol. 8, p. 412.

10. Letter to Spalatin of February, 1529, in *Dr. Martin Luthers Briefe, Sendschreiben und Bedenken*, ed. Wilhelm M. L. De Wette (G. Reimer, 1825), vol. 3, p. 424.

11. Council of Trent, Decree on Reformation, chap. 3.

12. Heinz Schilling, "Confessional Europe," in *Handbook of European History, 1400–1600*, ed. Thomas Brady, Heiko Oberman, and James Tracy (Eerdmans, 1995), pp. 641–675.

13. Gerald Strauss, *Luther's House of Learning* (Johns Hopkins University Press, 1978). See also Geoffrey Parker, "Success and Failure During the First Century of the Reformation," *Past and Present* 136 (1992): 43–82.

14. Philip Melanchthon, *Verlegung etlicher unchristlicher Artikel Welche de Widerteuffer furgeben* (Wittenberg, 1535), fols. Aii *v*, Biii *r*, and Eiii *v*.

15. Raymond Mentzer, "Disciplina nervus ecclesiae: The Calvinist Reform of Morals at Nîmes, *Sixteenth Century Journal* 18 (1987): 89–115.

16. Jaime Contreras and Gustav Henningsen, "44,000 Cases of the Spanish Inquisition (1540–1700): Analysis of a Historical Data Bank," in *The Inquisition in Early Modern Europe: Studies in Sources and Methods*, ed. Gustav Henningsen and John Tedeschi (Northern Illinois University Press, 1986), p. 114.

17. Philip Benedict, *Christ's Churches Purely Reformed* (Yale University Press, 2002), p. 464.

CHAPTER TWENTY-THREE: *The Age of Devils*

1. Johannes Janssen, *History of the German People at the Close of the Middle Ages*, trans. A. M. Christie (Kegan Paul, Trench, Trübner & Co. 1905), vol. 9, pp. 158–159. Janssen cites *Gläubliche un Wunderbarliche Berichte von Prodigien und Teufelserschinungen* (1601) Bl. v. 9, v. 12.

2. *De doctrina Christiana*, bk. 2, chap. 20, para. 31. Translation from *Select Library of Nicene and Post-Nicene Fathers of the Christian Church*, 1st ser., ed. Philip Schaff, 14 vols. (Christian Literature Co., 1886–1890), vol. 2, p. 545.

3. *Summa theologica*, II–II:92:1.

4. *De doctrina Christiana*, bk. 2, chap. 20, para. 30, and chap. 23, para. 35.

5. *Etymologies*, bk. 8.

6. *Summa theologica*, II–II:96:2.

7. Jean-Claude Schmidt, *The Holy Greyhound*, trans. Martin Thom (Cambridge University Press, 1983).

8. While some lexicographers dispute this etymology, it has been part and parcel of the Protestant heritage in England since the seventeenth century, or earlier. Archbishop of Canterbury John Tillotson gave voice to such suspicions in one of his anti-Catholic tracts: "in all probability those common juggling words of hocus pocus are nothing else but a corruption of *hoc est corpus* by way of ridiculous imitation of the Priests of the Church of Rome in their trick of Transubstantiation." John Tillotson, *A Discourse Against Transubstantiation* (London, 1684), p. 34.

9. Session XXII: Decree Touching the Things to Be Observed and Avoided in the Celebration of the Mass, in *The Canons and Decrees of the Council of Trent*, trans. Theodore Alois Buckley (George Routledge and Company, 1851), p. 147.

10. Session XXV: On the Invocation, Veneration, and on the Relics of the Saints, and Sacred Images, in ibid., p. 215.

11. Session XXII, in ibid., p. 148.

12. Quoted by Philip Soergel, *Miracles and the Protestant Imagination: The Evangelical Wonder Book in Reformation Germany* (Oxford University Press), p. 23.

13. Pierre Boaiustuau, *Histoires prodigieuses les plus mémorables qui ayent esté observées depuis la nativité de Jésus-Christ jusques à nostre siècle* (Paris, 1560), preface, n.p.

14. *Die Chronik des Johann Oldecopps*, ed. Karl Euling (Literarischen Verein in Stuttgart, 1891), pp. 474–475.

15. Joseph Hansen, *Quellen und Untersuchungen zur Geschichte des Hexenwahns im Mittelalter* (Bonn Universitäts-Buchdruckeri und Verlag, 1901), p. 38.

16. John XXII, *Super illius specula*, trans. Alan Charles Kors and Edward Peters, *Witchcraft in Europe 400–1700: A Documentary History* (University of Pennsylvania Press, 2001), pp. 119–120.

17. Bernardino of Siena, in *Medieval Popular Religion, 1100–1500: A Reader*, ed. John Shinners (Broadview Press, 1997), p. 245.

18. *The Hammer of Witches: A Complete Translation of the Malleus Maleficarum*, by Christopher Mackay (Cambridge University Press, 2009), p. 282.

19. George L. Burr, ed., *The Witch Persecutions*, 6 vols. (University of Pennsylvania History Department, 1898–1912), vol. 3, pp. 18–19.

20. Brian Levack, ed., *The Witchcraft Sourcebook* (Routledge, 2004), p. 201.

21. Stuart Clark, *Thinking with Demons: The Idea of Witchcraft in Early Modern Europe* (Oxford University Press, 1997), pp. 687–726.

22. Martín de Castañega, *Tratado muy sotil y bien fundado de las supersticiones y hechizerías y vanos conjuros y abusiones* (Logroño, 1529), quoted by María Tausiet Carlés, "Religión, ciencia y superstición en Pedro Ciruelo y Martín de Castañega," *Revista de Historia Jerónimo Zurita* 65–66 (1992): 141.

23. Pedro Ciruelo, *Tratado en el qual se repruevan todas las supersticiones y hechizerias* (Barcelona, 1628), p. 45.

24. *On Witchcraft: An Abridged Translation of Johann Weyer's De Praestigiiis Daemonum*, ed. Benjamin Kohl and H. C. Erik Midelfort, trans. John Shea (Pegasus Press, 1998), p. 96.

25. Reginald Scot, *The Discoverie of Witchcraft* (1584) (reprint, Elliot, Stock, 1886), p. xx.

26. Paul Frisius, *Dess Teuffels Nebelkappen: Das ist kurtzer begriff dess gantzen Handels der Zauberey belangend* (Frankfurt am Main, 1583), ff. Bvii, r.–Cii, v., Ciii, r.

27. *The Demonology of King James I*, ed. Donald Tyson (Llewelyn Publications, 2011), p. 221.

28. Jean Bodin, *Démonomanie*, in *Witchcraft in Europe 400-1700: A Documentary History*, ed. Alan Charles Kors and Edward Peters (University of Pennsylvania Press, 2001), p. 302.

29. Nicholas Remy, *Demonolatry*, ed. Montague Summers, trans. E. A. Ashwin (J. Rodker, 1930), p. xii.

30. *Martin del Rio: Investigations into Magic*, ed. and trans. P. G. Maxwell-Stuart (Manchester University Press, 1999), pp. 28–29.

31. Ibid., pp. 92–93.

32. WAT 1, 491.

33. *Luther's Large Catechism*, trans. John N. Lenker (Luther Press, 1908), pp. 70, 150, 186.

34. Julian "the Apostate," Epistolae, 19, in *The Works of the Emperor Julian, with an English translation by Wilmer Cave Wright* (Loeb Classical Library, 1930), vol. 3, p. 52.

35. WAT 6, 6816.

36. WAT 6, 6832.

37. WAT 2, 1429.

38. WAT 3, 3601.

39. WAT 4, 4040.

40. WAT 6, 6814.

41. WAT 6, 6815.

42. WAT 5, 5358b.

43. WAT 3, 2982b.

44. WAT 6, 6813.

45. WAT 3, 2829.

46. WAT 3, 3841.

47. Peter Burke, *Popular Culture in Early Modern Europe*, 3rd ed. (Harper Torchbooks, 2004), p. 213.

48. Samuel Macauley Jackson, ed., *Selected Works of Huldrich Zwingli* (University of Pennsylvania, 1901), chap. 3.

49. *Institutes*, I.15.13.

50. *Institutes*, II.4.3 and I.14.18.

51. "Vida," in *Santa Teresa de Jesus: Obras completas*, ed. Efrén de la Madre de Dios and Otger Steggink (Biblioteca de Autores Cristianos, 1997), p. 167.

52. Cited by Alison Weber, "Saint Teresa, Demonologist," in *Culture and Control in Early Modern Spain*, ed. Anne Cruz and Elizabeth Perry (University of Minnesota Press, 1992), p. 182.

53. Ciruelo, *Treatise Reproving All Superstitions*, p. 266.

54. *Rituale Romanum* (Lecoffre, 1885), pp. 486–487.

55. "Vida," p. 166; Luther, WAT 6, 6827.

56. Quoted in Levack, *Witchcraft Sourcebook*, p. 257.

CHAPTER TWENTY-FOUR: *The Age of Reasonable Doubt*

1. J. Cottingham, R. Stoothoff, and D. Murdoch, eds., *Descartes: Selected Philosophical Writings* (Cambridge University Press, 1988), p. 160.

2. Blaise Pascal, *Pensées*, ed. and trans. W. F. Trotter (Dover Publications, 2003), p. 23.

3. Carlo Ginzburg, *The Cheese and the Worms* (Johns Hopkins University Press, 1992), pp. 27–28.

4. John Calvin, *Treatises Against the Anabaptists and Against the Libertines*, ed. and trans. Benjamin Wirt Farley (Baker Academic, 1982), p. 254.

5. *Oeuvres de Saint François de Sales*, 27 vols. (Niérat, 1892–1932), vol. 15, p. 377.

6. Cited in D. J. Enright, *The Oxford Book of Death* (Oxford University Press, 1987), p. 330.

7. Stephen Greenblatt, *The Swerve: How the World Became Modern* (W. W. Norton, 2011), pp. 182–202.

8. Pierre Viret, *Instruction Chrestienne en la doctrine de la loy et de l'Evangile* (1564), preface to the *Church of Montpelier*, vol. 2, fols. iii–iii verso. Text quoted by Henri Busson in *Le rationalisme dans la littérature française de la Renaissance*, 2nd ed. (Vrin, 1971), p. 518.

9. Greenblatt's *The Swerve* received the National Book Award and the Pulitzer Prize.

10. Quoted by John T. McNeill, *The History and Character of Calvinism* (Oxford University Press, 1967), p. 176.

11. Sebastian Castellio, *Conseil à la France désolée* (1562), p. 6.

12. Quoted in Steven Ozment, *Mysticism and Dissent* (Yale University Press, 1973), p. 196.

13. Viret, *Instruction Chrestienne* (1564), vol. 2, fols. v–vi.

14. Ibid.

15. Edward Herbert of Cherbury, quoted in W. R. Sorley, *A History of English Philosophy* (Cambridge University Press, 1937), pp. 40–41.

16. *Pensées*, p. 216.

17. John Toland, *Christianity Not Mysterious* (London, 1702), pp. 54, 145, 173–174.

18. Martin Luther, *Luther's Works*, vol. 54, *Table Talk*, ed. Helmut T. Lehmann (Fortress Press, 1967), no. 4638, pp. 358–359.

19. John Calvin, Eighth Sermon on 1 Corinthians 10–11, in *Calvini opera* 49: 677, ll. 25–49, trans. Christopher Kaiser, in "Calvin, Copernicus, and Castellio," *Calvin Theological Journal* 21, no. 1 (April 1986): 17.

20. Johannes Kepler, *Harmonies of the World*, trans. Charles Glen Wallis (Forgotten Books, 2008), p. 2.

21. John Donne, "An Anatomy of the World" (1611), in *The Major Works*, ed. John Carey (Oxford University Press, 2000), p. 212.

22. *Pensées*, pp. 64, 218.

23. Galileo Galilei, *The Assayer*, quoted in Peter Morton, ed., *A Historical Introduction to the Philosophy of Mind: Readings, with a Commentary* (Broadview Press, 2010), p. 62.

24. Maurice Finocchiaro, ed., *The Galileo Affair: A Documentary History* (University of California Press, 1989), p. 272.

25. "Letter to the Grand Duchess Christina," in ibid., pp. 93–96.

26. *Galileo Affair*, p. 292.

27. Quoted in Arthur Rowland Skemp, *Francis Bacon, Life and Work* (Dodge Publishing, 1912), p. 63.

28. Francis Bacon, *The Advancement of Learning*, 2nd ed., ed. William Aldis Wright (Clarendon Press, 1876), book 1.5.8 and book 2, "To the King," 1, pp. 41, 76.

29. Francis Bacon, *Novum organum*, ed. Lisa Jardine and Michael Silverthorne (Cambridge University Press, 2000), p. 36.

30. Thomas Sprat, *The History of the Royal Society* (1667), quoted in John Spurr, "Rational Religion in Restoration England," *Journal of the History of Ideas* 49 (1988): 563.

31. Quoted by Keith Devlin, *The Unfinished Game: Pascal, Fermat, and the Seventeenth-Century Letter That Made the World Modern* (Basic Books, 2008), p. 55.

32. *Pensées*, p. 266.

33. Ibid., p. 62.

34. Ibid., p. 32.

35. Ibid., p. 64.

CHAPTER TWENTY-FIVE: *The Age of Outcomes*

1. Juan de Castañiza [Lorenzo Scupoli], *The Spiritual Combat; or, The Christian Pilgrim in His Spiritual Conflict and Conquest* (London, 1698), pp. 1–2.

2. Niccolò Machiavelli, *The Prince*, chap. 15, ed. Quentin Skiner and Russell Price (Cambridge University Press, 1988), pp. 54–55.

3. Martin Luther, "To the Christian Nobility of the German Nation," *Martin Luther, Three Treatises*, trans. Charles Jacobs (Fortress Press, 1970), pp. 16–17; LW 44.

4. Martin Luther, "Temporal Authority," in *Luther Selected Political Writings*, ed. J. M. Porter, (Fortress Press, 1974), pp. 55–56; LW 45.

5. Martin Luther, "Whether Soldiers, Too, Can Be Saved," LW 46, p. 96.

6. Luther, "Temporal Authority," pp. 62–63.

7. *Huldreich Zwinglis sämtliche Werke*, ed. E. Egli et al. (C. A. Schweschtke und Sohn, 1905–1991); "Usslegen und grund der schlussreden," vol. 2, p. 343.

8. *De regno Christi*, in *Melanchthon and Bucer*, ed. Wilhelm Pauck (Westminster/John Knox Press, 1969), pp. 175–176, 185–186, 225.

9. Calvin, *Institutes*, IV.20.4.

10. John Calvin, "Prefatory Address to King Francis I," in *The Institutes of the Christian Religion*, ed. J. T. McNeill, trans. Ford Lewis Battles, 2 vols. (Westminster Press, 1960), vol. 1, p. 12.

11. Michael Sattler, "The Schleitheim Articles," in *The Radical Reformation*, ed. Michael Baylor (Cambridge University Press, 1991), pp. 175–176.

12. Francis de Sales, *Introduction to the Devout Life*, trans. Allan Ross (Burns Oates and Washbourne, 1934), p. xxiv.

13. "Grund und Ursach aus göttlicher Schrift der Neuerung an dem Nachtmahl des Herren zu Strassburg Vorgenommen," in *Martin Bucers Deutsche Schriften*, ed. R. Stupperich (G. Mohn, 1960–), vol. 1, p. 273.

14. *De subventione pauperum*, quoted by Linda Martz, *Poverty and Welfare in Habsburg Spain: The Example of Toledo* (Cambridge University Press, 1983), p. 8.

15. Author unknown, *The Life of Lazarillo de Tormes* (1554), chap. 3, trans. Alfonso García Osuna (McFarland, 2005), p. 54.

16. Tomás de Trujillo, *Tratado de la limosna* (Estella, 1563), p. 225.

17. Mateo Alemán, *Guzmán de Alfarache* (1604), pt. 2, bk. 3 (Madrid 1723), p. 367.

18. "Ain Püchlein von der erkanntnuss der Sünd" (Augsburg, 1494), cited in Steven Ozment, *Protestants: Birth of a Revolution* (New York: Image/Doubleday, 1993), pp. 152–153.

19. Albert Leitzmann and Otto Clemen, eds., *Luthers Werke im Auswahl* (W. de Gruyter, 1930), vol. 8, p. 32, item 244.

20. WAT 1.508.

21. *Grund und ursach auss Göttlichem Rechten* (1526), quoted by S. Ozment, *Reformation in the Cities* (Yale University Press, 1973), p. 89.

22. *De celibatu, monachatu, et viduitate* (Wittenberg, 1521) p. D3b.

23. "A Friendly Request and Exhortation," in Samuel Macauley Jackson, *The Latin Works of Huldreich Zwingli* (Putnam's, 1912), vol. 1, p. 181.

24. Letter to Pierre Viret, 7 April 1549, in *Letters of John Calvin*, ed. and trans. Jules Bonnet (Constable, 1858), vol. 2, p. 202.

25. *Luthers Werke im Auswahl*, vol. 8, p. 35, item 250.

26. WAT 3. 3814.

27. *Letters of John Calvin*, Bonnet, vol. 2, p. 202.

28. *Luthers Werke im Auswahl*, vol. 8, p. 4, item 55.

29. *Introduction to the Devout Life*, chap. 33.

30. Ibid., chap. 38.

31. Ibid., chap. 17.

32. Luis de León, *La perfecta casada* (Madrid, 1786), p. 2, 100–103.

CHAPTER TWENTY-SIX: *The Spirit of the Age*

1. *The Complete Madame Guyon*, ed. and trans. Nancy James (Paraclete Press, 2011), pp. 86, 211.

2. *The Confessions of Jean Jacques Rousseau*, book 6 (FQ Books, 2010), p. 218.

3. Juan Eusebio Nieremberg, *De la diferencia entre lo temporal y lo eterno*, in *Obras escogidas del R.P. Juan Eusebio Nieremberg*, ed. Eduardo Zepeda-Henríquez, 2 vols. (Ediciones Atlas, 1957), vol. 2, p. 223.

4. Diego Murillo, *Discursos predicados sobre todos los evangelios* (Zaragoza, 1611), cited in Ana Martínez Alarcón, *Geografía de la eternidad* (Tecnos, 1987), p. 79.

5. Nieremberg, *De la diferencia*, p. 227.

6. Ibid., p. 218.

7. Ibid., pp. 219–220.

8. Ibid., p. 223.

9. Jeremias Drexel, S.J., *Considerations on Eternity*, trans. Sister Marie José Byrne (Frederick Pustet, 1920), pp. 70–71.

10. Ibid., p. 104.

11. Ibid., p. 193.

12. Robert Bolton, *The Foure Last Things* (London, 1632), pp. 103–104, 110–111.

13. Cited by Robert Palmer, "Posterity and the Hereafter in Eighteenth-Century French Thought," *Journal of Modern History* 9, no. 2. (June 1937): 166.

EPILOGUE: *Assessing the Reformations*

1. Karl Holl, *The Cultural Significance of the Reformation*, trans. Karl Hertz, Barbara Hertz, and John Lichtblau (Meridian Books, 1959), pp. 30–31.

2. Ibid., pp. 61–63.

3. For the classic definition of *paradigm shift*, see Thomas Kuhn, *The Structure of Scientific Revolutions* (University of Chicago Press, 1962).

4. Robert Kingdon, "Was the Protestant Reformation a Revolution? The Case of Geneva," in *Transition and Revolution*, ed. Robert Kingdon (Minneapolis, 1974), p. 57; Steven Ozment, *Protestants: Birth of a Revolution* (Image, 1993).

5. Brad Gregory, *The Unintended Reformation: How a Religious Revolution Secularized Society* (Belknap Press of Harvard University Press, 2012).

6. First expressed in Weber's essay "Wissenschaft als Beruf" (Science as a Vocation), published in 1918. Available in English as Max Weber, *The Vocation Lectures*, ed. David Owen and Tracy B. Strong, trans. Rodney Livingstone (Hackett, 2004).

7. "The Reformation, Popular Magic, and the 'Disenchantment' of the World," *Journal of Interdisciplinary History* 23, no. 3 (1993), reprinted in Scribner's *Religion and Culture in Germany* (E. J. Brill, 2001).

8. Antoine Fromment, *Les actes et gestes merveilleux de la cité de Genève* (G. Fick, 1854), pp. 144–145.

9. *Dr. Martin Luther's sämmtliche Werke*, 2nd ed., ed. Ernst Ludwig Enders, 25 vols. (Heyder and Zimmer, 1862–1885), vol. 12, p. 236, translated in Wilhelm Herrmann, *The Communion of the Christian with God, Described on the Basis of Luther's Statements*, 2nd ed., trans. J. Sandys Stanyon (Putnam's, 1906), p. 231.

10. Commentary on John's Gospel, CO 47.90.

11. *Institutes* II.3.2, McNeill ed., p. 292.

12. "First Invocavit Sermon," LW 51:70.

13. Wenceslaus Link and Wolfgang Capito, in Ozment, *Reformation in the Cities*, p. 87.

Bibliography

CHAPTER ONE

Expanding Horizons

David Abulafia, *The Discovery of Mankind: Atlantic Encounters in the Age of Discovery*. Yale University Press, 2008.

Eric Axelson, *Congo to Cape: Early Portuguese Explorers*. Barnes & Noble, 1973.

C. F. Beckingham, *Between Islam and Christendom: Travelers, Facts and Legends in the Middle Ages and the Renaissance*. Variorum Reprints, 1983.

Jerry H. Bentley, *Old World Encounters: Cross-Cultural Contacts and Exchanges in Pre-Modern Times*. Oxford University Press, 1993.

John Williams Blake, *West Africa: Quest for God and Gold, 1454–1578*. Curzon Press, 1977.

Pierre Chaunu, *European Expansion in the Later Middle Ages*. North Holland Publishing Company, 1979.

Felipe Fernández-Armesto, *Before Columbus: Exploration and Colonisation from the Mediterranean to the Atlantic, 1229–1492*. Macmillan, 1987.

Paul Freedman, *Out of the East: Spices and the Medieval Imagination*. Yale University Press, 2009.

Anthony Grafton, *New Worlds, Ancient Texts: The Power of Tradition and the Shock of Discovery*. Belknap Press, 1995.

J. H. Parry, *The Age of Reconnaissance: Discovery, Exploration and Settlement, 1450 to 1650*. University of California Press, 1981.

M. N. Pearson, ed., *The Portuguese in India*, vol. 1, part 1 of *The New Cambridge History of India*. Cambridge University Press, 1987.

J. R. S. Phillips, *The Medieval Expansion of Europe*, 2nd ed. Oxford University Press, 1998.

David R. Ringrose, *Expansion and Global Interaction, 1200–1700*. Pearson Longman, 2001.

P. E. Russell, *Portugal, Spain and the African Atlantic, 1343–1490*. Variorum, 1995.

James D. Ryan, "European Travelers Before Columbus: The Fourteenth Century's Discovery of India." *Catholic Historical Review* 79 (1993): 648–70.

Geoffrey V. Scammell, *The World Encompassed: The First European Maritime Empires, 800–1650*. University of California Press, 1981.

Ronald Watkins, *Unknown Seas: How Vasco da Gama Opened the East*. John Murray, 2003.

Eviatar Zerubavel, *Terra Cognita: The Mental Discovery of America*. Rutgers University Press, 1992.

The Ottoman Empire

Caroline Finkel, *Osman's Dream: The Story of the Ottoman Empire, 1300–1923*. Basic Books, 2006.

Daniel Goffman, *The Ottoman Empire and Early Modern Europe*. Cambridge University Press, 2002.

Colin Imber, *The Ottoman Empire, 1300–1650: The Structure of Power*. Palgrave Macmillan, 2002.

Halil Inalcik, *The Ottoman Empire: The Classical Age, 1300–1600*. Phoenix Press, 2001.

M. Mehmet Fuad Köprülü, *The Origins of the Ottoman Empire*. State University of New York Press, 1992.

Metin Kunt and Christine Woodhead, eds., *Süleyman the Magnificent and His Age: The Ottoman Empire in the Early Modern World*, Longman, 1995.

V. J. Parry, *A History of the Ottoman Empire to 1730*. Cambridge University Press, 1976.

Stephen Turnbull, *The Ottoman Empire 1326–1699*. Osprey Publishing, 2003.

The Printing Press

Elizabeth Eisenstein, *The Printing Press as an Agent of Change: Communications and Cultural Transformations in Early Modern Europe*. Cambridge University Press, 1979.

Lucien Febvre, *The Coming of the Book: The Impact of Printing 1450–1800*, 3rd ed. Verso, 2010.

Stephan Fussel, *Gutenberg and the Impact of Printing*. Ashgate, 2005.

Sandra Hindman, ed., *Printing the Written Word: The Social History of Books, Circa 1450–1520*. Cornell University Press, 1991.

Rudolf Hirsch, *The Printed Word: Its Impact and Diffusion*. Variorum Reprints, 1978.

Janet Ing, *Johann Gutenberg and His Bible: A Historical Study*. Typophiles, 1988.

Albert Kapr, *Johann Gutenberg: The Man and His Invention*. Brookfield, VT: Scolar Press, 1996.

John Man, *Gutenberg: How One Man Remade the World with Words*. John Wiley, 2002.

Paul Needham and Joseph Michael, *Adventure and Art: The First Hundred Years of Printing*. Rutgers University Press, 1999.

Andrew Petegree, *The Book in the Renaissance*. Yale University Press, 2011.

Sesto Prete, *The Humanists and the Discovery of Printing*. Scherpe Verlag, 1982.

Brian Richardson, *Printing, Writers and Readers in Renaissance Italy*. Cambridge University Press, 1999.

Economic and Social History: Late Middle Ages

John Alberth, *From the Brink of the Apocalypse: Confronting Famine, War, Plague, and Death in the Later Middle Ages*. Routledge, 2010.

C. T. Allmand, ed., *War, Literature, and Politics in the Late Middle Ages*. Liverpool University Press, 1976.

Norman F. Cantor, *In the Wake of the Plague: The Black Death and the World It Made*, Free Press, 2001.

Georges Duby, *The Three Orders: Feudal Society Imagined*. University of Chicago Press, 1980.

Steven A. Epstein, *An Economic and Social History of Later Medieval Europe, 1000–1500*. Cambridge University Press, 2009.

Jean Favier, *Gold and Spices: The Rise of Commerce in the Middle Ages*. Holmes and Meier, 1998.

David Herlihy, *The Black Death and the Transformation of the West*. Harvard University Press, 1997.

Lisa Jardine, *Worldly Goods: A New History of the Renaissance*. W. W. Norton, 1998.

Keith D. Lilley, *Urban Life in the Middle Ages, 1000–1450*. Palgrave, 2002.

Robert Lopez, *The Commercial Revolution of the Middle Ages, 1000–1350*. Prentice Hall, 1971.

Harry Miskimin, *The Economy of Early Renaissance Europe, 1300–1460*. Cambridge University Press, 1975.

David Nicholas, *The Later Medieval City, 1300–1500*. Longman, 1997.

J. R. S. Phillips, *The Medieval Expansion of Europe*. Oxford University Press, 1988.

Henri Pirenne, *Economic and Social History of Medieval Europe*. Routledge and Kegan Paul, 2006.

Michael M. Postan and John H. Habakkuk, eds., *The Cambridge Economic History of Europe*, vols. 1–3. Cambridge University Press, 1963–1987.

Norman J. G. Pounds, *An Economic History of Medieval Europe*, 2nd ed. Longman, 1994.

Political History: Late Middle Ages

Andrew Ayton and J. L. Price, eds., *The Medieval Military Revolution*. Taurus, 1995.

Clifford R. Backman, *The Worlds of Medieval Europe*. Oxford University Press, 2009.

Colette Baeaune, *The Birth of an Ideology: Myth and Symbols of Nation in Late Medieval France*. University of California Press, 1991.

Gene Bruckner, *The Civic World of Early Renaissance Florence*. Princeton University Press, 1977.

F. R. H. Du Boulay, *Germany in the Later Middle Ages*. Athlone, 1983.

Richard W. Kaeuper, *War, Justice, and Public Order: England and France in the Later Middle Ages*. Oxford University Press, 1988.

Ernst H. Kantorowicz, *The King's Two Bodies: A Study in Mediaeval Political Theology*. Princeton University Press, 1957.

M. H. Keen, *England in the Later Middle Ages*. Routledge, 2003.

Joachim Leuschner, *Germany in the Late Middle Ages*. North Holland Publishing Company, 1980.

P. S. Lewis, *The Recovery of France in the Fifteenth Century*. Harper & Row, 1972.

Angus Mackay, *Spain in the Middle Ages*. Macmillan, 1977.

Lauro Martines, *Power and Imagination: City-States in Renaissance Italy*. Johns Hopkins University Press, 1988.

John Najemy, *Italy in the Age of the Renaissance: 1300–1550 (Short Oxford History of Italy)*. Oxford University Press, 2005.

Teofilo Ruiz, *Spain's Centuries of Crisis: 1300–1474*. Wiley-Blackwell, 2011.

Len Scales, *The Shaping of German Identity: Authority and Crisis, 1245–1414*. Cambridge University Press, 2012.

Graeme Small, *Late Medieval France*. Palgrave Macmillan, 2009.

John A. F. Thomson, *The Transformation of Medieval England, 1370–1529*. Longman, 1993.

CHAPTER TWO

Surveys: Medieval Culture and Civilization

Robert Bartlett, *The Making of Europe: Conquest, Colonization, and Cultural Change, 950–1350*. Princeton University Press, 1994.

John Bossy, *Christianity in the West, 1400–1700*. Oxford University Press, 1985.

Robert Fossier, ed., *The Cambridge Illustrated History of the Middle Ages*, 3 vols. New York: Cambridge University Press, 1986–1997.

Johan Huizinga, *The Autumn of the Middle Ages*, trans. Rodney J. Payton. University of Chicago, 1997.

Ernest Fraser Jacob, *The Fifteenth Century, 1399–1485*, vol. 6 of *Oxford History of England*. Clarendon Press, 1993.

Jacques LeGoff, *Medieval Civilization*. Blackwell, 1990.

Edward Peters, *Europe and the Middle Ages*, 3rd ed. Prentice Hall, 1997.

Brian Tierney, *Western Europe in the Middle Ages, 300–1475*, 6th ed. McGraw Hill, 1998.

Surveys: Medieval Church

Adriaan H. Bredero, *Christendom and Christianity in the Middle Ages: The Relations Between Religion, Church and Society*. Eerdmans, 1994.

F. Donald Logan, *A History of the Church in the Middle Ages*. Routledge, 2002.

Francis Oakley, *The Western Church in the Later Middle Ages*. Cornell University Press, 1985.

R. W. Southern, *Western Society and the Church in the Middle Ages*. Penguin Books, 1990.

Piety

Robert Bartlett, *The Natural and the Supernatural in the Middle Ages*. Cambridge University Press, 2008.

Robert Bartlett, *Why Can the Dead Do Such Great Things? Saints and Worshippers From the Martyrs to the Reformation*. Princeton University Press, 2013.

Hein Blommestijn, Charles Caspers, and Rijcklof Hofman, *Spirituality Renewed: Studies on Significant Representatives of the Modern Devotion*. Peeters, 2003.

Daniel E. Bornstein, ed., *Medieval Christianity*, vol. 4 of *A People's History of Christianity*. Fortress Press, 2006.

Euan Cameron, *Enchanted Europe: Superstition, Reason, and Religion, 1250–1750*. Oxford University Press, 2010.

Giles Constable, *The Reformation of the Twelfth Century*. Cambridge University Press, 1998.

Patrick Geary, *Living with the Dead in the Middle Ages*. Cornell University Press, 1994.

Bernard Hamilton, *Religion in the Medieval West*. Oxford University Press, 2003.

Sarah Hamilton, *The Practice of Penance, 900–1500*. Boydell Press, 2001.

Albert Hyma, *Christian Renaissance: A History of the Devotio moderna*. Archon Books, 1965.

David Knowles, *Christian Monasticism*. Oxford University Press, 2002.

C. H. Lawrence, *Medieval Monasticism: Forms of Religious Life in Western Europe in the Middle Ages*. Longman, 2001.

Jean Leclercq, *The Love of Learning and the Desire for God*. Fordham University Press, 1982.

Bernard McGinn, *The Harvest of Mysticism in Medieval Germany*, vol. 4 of *The Presence of God: A History of Christian Mysticism*. Herder/Crossroad, 2005.

Bernard McGinn, *The Varieties of Vernacular Mysticism (1350–1550)*, vol. 5 of *The Presence of God: A History of Christian Mysticism*. Crossroad/Herder & Herder, 2012.

James Obelkevich, ed., *Religion and the People, 1000–1700: Studies in the History of Popular Religious Beliefs and Practices*. University of North Carolina Press, 1979.

Wybren Scheepsma, *Medieval Religious Women in the Low Countries: The 'Modern Devotion,' the Canonesses of Windesheim, and Their Writings*. Boydell Press, 2004.

Godefriedus J. C. Snoek, *Medieval Piety from Relics to the Eucharist*. E. J. Brill, 1995.

Jonathan Sumption, *Pilgrimage: An Image of Medieval Religion*. Faber & Faber, 2001.

John Van Engen, *Sisters and Brothers of the Common Life: The Devotio moderna and the World of the Later Middle Ages*. University of Pennsylvania Press, 2008.

A. Vauchez, *Laity in the Middle Ages: Religious Beliefs and Devotional Practices*, ed. D. J. Bornstein. University of Notre Dame Press, 1997.

Caroline Walker Bynum, *Christian Materiality: An Essay on Religion in Late Medieval Europe*. Zone Books, 2011.

Intellectual History

Marcia L. Colish, *The Medieval Foundations of the Western Intellectual Tradition, 400–1400*, Yale University Press, 1997.

G. R. Evans, *Philosophy and Theology in the Middle Ages*. Routledge, 1994.

Étienne H. Gilson, *The Spirit of Medieval Philosophy*. University of Notre Dame Press, 1991.

Herbert Grundmann, *Religious Movements in the Middle Ages*, trans. Steven Rowan. University of Notre Dame Press, 1996.

David Knowles, *The Evolution of Medieval Thought*, ed. D. E. Luscomb. Longman, 1989.

John Marenbon, *Later Medieval Philosophy (1150–1350)*. Routledge, 1994.

A. S. McGrade, ed., *The Cambridge Companion to Medieval Philosophy*. Cambridge University Press, 2003.

Heiko Oberman, *The Harvest of Medieval Theology: Gabriel Biel and Late Medieval Nominalism*, rev. ed. Baker Book House, 2000.

Steven Ozment, *The Age of Reform, 1250–1550*. Yale University Press, 1980.

Robert Pasnau, ed., *The Cambridge History of Medieval Philosophy*, 2 vols. Cambridge University Press, 2015.

Jaroslav Pelikan, *The Growth of Medieval Theology (600–1300)*, vol. 3 of *The Christian Tradition*. University of Chicago Press, 1980.

Josef Pieper, *Scholasticism Personalities and Problems of Medieval Philosophy*. St. Augustine's Press, 2001.

R. W. Southern, *Scholastic Humanism and the Unification of Europe*, 2 vols. New York: Blackwell, 1995–2000.

CHAPTER THREE

Corruption

Francis A. Burkle-Young and Michael L. Doerrer, *The Life of Cardinal Innocenzo del Monte: A Scandal in Scarlet*. Mellen Press, 1997.

Mary Hollingsworth, *The Cardinal's Hat: Money, Ambition and Housekeeping in a Renaissance Court*. Profile, 2004.

K. J. P. Lowe, *Church and Politics in Renaissance Italy: The Life and Career of Cardinal Francesco Soderini, 1453–1524*. Cambridge University Press, 1993.

G. J. Meyer, *The Borgias: The Hidden History*. Bantam Books, 2013.

Edwin Mullins, *The Popes of Avignon: A Century of Exile*. Bluebridge, 2011.

Gerard Noel, *The Renaissance Popes: Statesmen, Warriors, and the Great Borgia Myth*. Carrol & Graf, 2006.

Yves Renouard, *The Avignon Papacy, 1305–1403*. Faber and Faber, 1970.

Daniel Williman, *The Right of Spoil of the Popes of Avignon, 1316–1415*. American Philosophical Society, 1988.

Schism and Reform

Antony Black, *Council and Commune: The Conciliar Movement and the Fifteenth-Century Heritage*. Burns & Oates, 1979.

Anthony Black, *Monarchy and Community: Political Ideas in the Later Conciliar Controversy, 1430–1450*. Cambridge University Press, 1970.

Renate Blumenfeld-Kosinski, *Poets, Saints, and Visionaries of the Great Schism, 1378–1417*. Pennsylvania State University Press, 2006.

Joseph Canning, *Ideas of Power in the Late Middle Ages, 1296–1417*. Cambridge University Press, 2011.

G. Christianson, T. M. Izbicki, and C. M. Bellitto, eds., *The Church, the Councils, and Reform: The Legacy of the Fifteenth Century*. Catholic University of America Press, 2008.

John Hine Mundy and Kennerly M. Woody, eds., *The Council of Constance: The Unification of the Church*. Columbia University Press, 1961.

Joëlle Rollo-Koster, *Raiding Saint Peter: Empty Sees, Violence, and the Initiation of the Great Western Schism (1378)*. E. J. Brill 2008.

Joëlle Rollo-Koster and Thomas M. Izbicki, *A Companion to the Great Western Schism (1378–1417)*. E. J. Brill, 2009.

John J. Ryan, *The Apostolic Conciliarism of Jean Gerson*. Scholars Press, 1998.

Phillip H. Stump, *The Reforms of the Council of Constance (1414–1418)*. E. J. Brill, 1994.

R. N. Swanson, *Universities, Academics and the Great Schism*. Cambridge University Press, 1979.

Brian Tierney, *Foundations of the Conciliar Theory: The Contribution of the Medieval Canonists from Gratian to the Great Schism*. E. J. Brill, 1998.

Dissent and Heresy: Surveys

Caterina Bruschi and Peter Biller, eds., *Texts and the Repression of Medieval Heresy*. Boydell & Brewer, 2003.

Jeffrey Burton Russell, *Dissent and Order in the Middle Ages: The Search for Legitimate Authority*. Wipf & Stock, 2005.

Michael Frassetto, *The Great Medieval Heretics: Five Centuries of Religious Dissent*. Bluebridge, 2010.

Michael Frassetto, ed., *Heresy and the Persecuting Society in the Middle Ages: Essays on the Work of R. I. Moore*. E. J. Brill, 2006.

Michael Frassetto, *Heretic Lives: Medieval Heresy from Bogomil and the Cathars to Wyclif and Hus*. Profile, 2007.

Herbert Grundmann, *Religious Movements in the Middle Ages: The Historical Links Between Heresy, the Mendicant Orders, and the Women's Religious Movement in the Twelfth and Thirteenth Century*. University of Notre Dame Press, 1995.

Richard Kieckhefer, *The Repression of Heresy in Medieval Germany*. University of Pennsylvania Press, 1979.

Jennifer Kolpacoff Deane, *A History of Medieval Heresy and Inquisition*. Rowman & Littlefield, 2011.

Malcolm Lambert, *Medieval Heresy: Popular Movements from the Gregorian Reform to the Reformation*, 3rd ed. Blackwell, 2002.

Gordon Leff, *Heresy in the Later Middle Ages: The Relation of Heterodoxy to Dissent, 1250–1450*. Manchester University Press, 1999.

Gordon Leff, *Heresy, Philosophy, and Religion in the Medieval West*. Ashgate, 2002.

R. I. Moore, *The Birth of Popular Heresy*. University of Toronto Press, 1995.

R. I. Moore, *The Origins of European Dissent*. University of Toronto Press, 1994.

R. I. Moore, *The War on Heresy*. Belknap Press, 2012.

J. M. M. H. Thijssen, *Censure and Heresy at the University of Paris, 1200–1400*. University of Pennsylvania Press, 1998.

Walter L. Wakefield and Austin P. Evans, *Heresies of the High Middle Ages*. Columbia University Press, 1991.

Scott L. Waugh and Peter D. Diehl, eds., *Christendom and Its Discontents: Exclusion, Persecution, and Rebellion, 1000–1500*. Cambridge University Press, 1996.

Albigensians/Cathars

M. D. Costen, *The Cathars and the Albigensian Crusade*. Manchester University Press, 1997.

Malcolm Lambert, *The Cathars*. Oxford: Blackwell, 1998.

Emmanuel Le Roy Ladurie, *Montaillou, the Promised Land of Error*. Vintage, 1979.

Mark Gregory Pegg, *The Corruption of Angels: The Great Inquisition of 1245–1246*. Princeton University Press, 2001.

Jonathan Sumption, *The Albigensian Crusade*. Faber, 1999.

Waldensians

Gabriel Audisio, *Preachers by Night: The Waldensian Barbes (15th–16th centuries)*. E. J. Brill, 2007.

Gabriel Audisio, *Waldensian Dissent: Persecution and Survival, c. 1170–c. 1570*. Cambridge University Press, 1999.

Euan Cameron, *The Reformation of the Heretics: The Waldenses of the Alps, 1480–1580.* Oxford University Press, 1984.

Free Spirits

Robert E. Lerner, *The Heresy of the Free Spirit in the later Middle Ages.* University of California Press, 1972.

Raoul Vaneigem, *The Movement of the Free Spirit.* Zone Books, 1994.

Lollards

Margaret Aston, *Lollards and Reformers: Images and Literacy in Late Medieval Religion.* Hambledon Press, 1984.

Gillian R. Evans, *John Wyclif: Myth and Reality.* InterVarsity Press Academic, 2005.

Kantik Ghosh, *Wycliffite Heresy: Authority and the Interpretation of Texts.* Cambridge University Press, 2002.

J. Patrick Hornbeck, *What Is a Lollard? Dissent and Belief in Late Medieval England.* Oxford University Press, 2010.

Stephen E. Lahey, *John Wyclif.* Oxford University Press, 2009.

Ian Christopher Levy, *John Wyclif: Scriptural Logic, Real Presence, and the Parameters of Orthodoxy.* Marquette University Press, 2003.

Katherine C. Little, *Confession and Resistance: Defining the Self in Late Medieval England.* University of Notre Dame Press, 2006.

Robert Lutton, *Lollardy and Orthodox Religion in Pre-Reformation England.* Boydell & Brewer, 2006.

James Edward McGoldrick, *Luther's Scottish Connection.* Fairleigh Dickinson University Press, 1989.

Richard Rex, *Lollards.* Palgrave, 2002.

Michael Van Dussen, *From England to Bohemia: Heresy and Communication in the Later Middle Ages.* Cambridge University Press, 2012.

Hussites

Frantisek M. Bartos, *The Hussite Revolution, 1424–1437.* East European Monographs, 1986.

Thomas A. Fudge, *Jan Hus: Religious Reform and Social Revolution in Bohemia.* I. B. Tauris, 2010.

Thomas A. Fudge, *Magnificent Ride: The First Reformation in Hussite Bohemia.* Ashgate, 1998.

Howard Kaminsky, *A History of the Hussite Revolution.* University of California Press, 1967.

Jiri Kejr, *The Hussite Revolution.* Orbis Press Agency, 1988.

John M. Klassen, *The Nobility and the Making of the Hussite Revolution.* East European Monographs, 1978.

John M. Klassen, *Warring Maidens, Captive Wives and Hussite Queens: Women and Men at War and at Peace in Fifteenth Century Bohemia.* East European Monographs, 1999.

Matthew Spinka, *John Hus: A Biography.* Princeton University Press, 1968.

Victor Verney, *Warrior of God: Jan Zizka and the Hussite Revolution.* Frontline Books, 2009.

CHAPTER FOUR

Surveys

Fernand Braudel, *Out of Italy, 1450–1650*. Flammarion, 1991.

Jacob Burckhardt, *The Civilization of the Renaissance in Italy*. 1860. New American Library, 1960.

Paul Johnson, *The Renaissance: A Short History*. Modern Library, 2002.

Lisa Kaborycha, *A Short History of Renaissance Italy*. Prentice Hall, 2011.

Benjamin G. Kohl and Alison Andrews Smith, eds., *Major Problems in the History of the Italian Renaissance*. D. C. Heath, 1995.

Richard Mackenney, *Renaissances: The Cultures of Italy, 1300–1600*. Palgrave Macmillan, 2005.

John Najemy, ed., *Italy in the Age of the Renaissance: 1300–1550*. Oxford University Press, 2004.

Charles G. Nauert Jr., *Humanism and the Culture of Renaissance Europe*, 2nd ed. Cambridge University Press, 2006.

J. H. Plumb, *The Italian Renaissance: A Concise Survey of Its History and Culture*. Harper & Row, 1965.

Albert Rabil Jr., ed., *Renaissance Humanism Foundations, Forms, and Legacy*, 3 vols. University of Pennsylvania Press, 1988.

Ronald G. Witt, *In the Footsteps of the Ancients: The Origins of Humanism from Lovato to Bruni*. E. J. Brill, 2000.

Ronald G. Witt, *Two Latin Cultures and the Foundation of Renaissance Humanism in Medieval Italy*. Cambridge University Press, 2012.

Frances A. Yates, *Renaissance and Reform: The Italian Contribution*. Routledge, 1999.

Scholarship: Education and Historiography

Peter Burke, *The Renaissance Sense of the Past*. Edward Arnold, 1969.

Christopher S. Celenza, *The Lost Italian Renaissance: Humanists, Historians, and Latin's Legacy*. Johns Hopkins University Press, 2004.

D. S. Chambers and F. Quiviger, eds., *Italian Academies of the Sixteenth Century*. Warburg Institute, University of London, 1995.

Paula Findlen, "Historical Thought in the Renaissance," in *A Companion to Western Historical Thought*, ed. Lloyd Kramer and Sarah Maza, 99–122. Blackwell, 2002.

Deno Geanakoplos, *Greek Scholars in Venice: Studies in the Dissemination of Greek Learning from Byzantium to Western Europe*. Harvard University Press, 1962.

Anthony Grafton, *What Was History? The Art of History in Early Modern Europe*. Cambridge University Press, 2007.

Paul F. Grendler, *Books and Schools in the Italian Renaissance*. Variorum, 1995.

Paul F. Grendler, *Universities of the Italian Renaissance*. Johns Hopkins University Press, 2002.

Donald R. Kelley, ed., *History and the Disciplines: The Reclassification of Knowledge in Early Modern Europe*. University of Rochester Press, 1997.

Nancy S. Struever, *The Language of History in the Renaissance: Rhetoric and Historical Consciousness in Florentine Humanism*. Princeton University Press, 1970.

N. G. Wilson, *From Byzantium to Italy: Greek Studies in the Italian Renaissance*. Duckworth, 1992.

Scholarship: Rhetoric, Philology, Philosophy, Theology

Paul Richard Blum, ed., *Philosophers of the Renaissance*. Catholic University of America Press, 2010.

R. R. Bolgar, *The Classical Heritage and Its Beneficiaries*. Cambridge University Press, 1954.

Alison Brown, *The Return of Lucretius to Renaissance Florence*. Harvard University Press, 2010.

Ernst Cassirer, *The Individual and the Cosmos in Renaissance Philosophy*. University of Pennsylvania Press, 1979.

Brian P. Copenhaver and Charles B. Schmitt, *Renaissance Philosophy*. Oxford University Press, 1992.

William Craven, *Giovanni Pico della Mirandola, Symbol of His Age: Modern Interpretations of a Renaissance Philosopher*. Droz, 1981.

Amos Edelheit, *Ficino, Pico and Savonarola: The Evolution of Humanist Theology, 1461–1498*. E. J. Brill, 2008.

Konrad Eisenbichler and Olga Zorzi Pugliese, eds., *Ficino and Renaissance Neoplatonism*. Dovehouse Editions, 1986.

Arthur Field, *Origins of the Platonic Academy of Florence*. Princeton University Press, 1988.

Stephen Greenblatt, *The Swerve: How the World Became Modern*. W. W. Norton, 2011.

James Hankins, ed., *Cambridge Companion to Renaissance Philosophy*. Cambridge University Press, 2007.

James Hankins, *Humanism and Platonism in the Italian Renaissance*. Edizioni di Storia e Letteratura, 2003–2004.

James Hankins and Ada Palmer, *The Recovery of Ancient Philosophy in the Renaissance: A Brief Guide*. L. S. Olschki, 2008.

Paul Oskar Kristeller, *Eight Philosophers of the Italian Renaissance*. Stanford University Press, 1964.

Paul Oskar Kristeller, *The Philosophy of Marsilio Ficino*. Smith, 1964.

Paul Oskar Kristeller, *Renaissance Thought: The Classic, Scholastic and Humanistic Strains*, rev. ed. Harper and Row, 1961.

Alexander Lee, *Petrarch and St. Augustine: Classical Scholarship, Christian Theology, and the Origins of the Renaissance in Italy*. E. J. Brill, 2012.

Edward P. Mahoney, ed., *Philosophy and Humanism: Renaissance Essays in Honor of Paul Oskar Kristeller*. E. J. Brill, 1976.

John Monfasani, *Greeks and Latins in Renaissance Italy: Studies on Humanism and Philosophy in the 15th Century*. Ashgate, 2004.

Lodi Nauta, *In Defense of Common Sense: Lorenzo Valla's Humanist Critique of Scholastic Philosophy*. Harvard University Press, 2009.

Heiko A. Oberman and Thomas A. Brady Jr., eds., *Itinerarium Italicum: The Profile of the Italian Renaissance in the Mirror of Its European Transformations*. E. J. Brill, 1975.

Gerard Passannante, *Lucretian Renaissance: Philology and the Afterlife of Tradition*. University of Chicago Press, 2011.

Nesca A. Robb, *The Neoplatonism of the Italian Renaissance*. Octagon Books, 1968.

Quentin Skinner and Eckhard Kessler, eds., *Cambridge History of Renaissance Philosophy*, general ed. Charles B. Schmitt. Cambridge University Press, 2008.

Charles Trinkaus, *In Our Image and Likeness: Humanity and Divinity in Italian Humanist Thought*. University of Notre Dame Press, 1995.

Charles Trinkaus, *Renaissance Transformations of Late Medieval Thought*. Ashgate, 1999.

Political Thought: Surveys

J. H. Burns and Mark Goldie, eds., *The Cambridge History of Political Thought, 1450–1700*. Cambridge University Press, 1991.

Janet Coleman, *History of Political Thought: From the Middle Ages to the Renaissance*. Blackwell Publishers, 2000.

Anthony R. Pagden, ed., *The Languages of Political Theory in Early-Modern Europe*. Ideas in Context. Cambridge University Press, 1987.

J. G. A. Pocock, *The Machiavellian Moment: Florentine Political Thought and the Atlantic Republican Tradition*. Princeton University Press, 1975.

Quentin Skinner, *The Foundations of Modern Political Thought*, vol. 1. Cambridge University Press, 1978.

Leo Strauss and Joseph Cropsey, eds., *History of Political Philosophy*. University of Chicago Press, 1987.

Political Thought: Civic Humanism

Hans Baron, *The Crisis of the Early Italian Renaissance: Civic Humanism and Republican Liberty in an Age of Classicism and Tyranny*. Princeton University Press, 1966.

Hans Baron, *In Search of Florentine Civic Humanism: Essays on the Transition from Medieval to Modern Thought*. Princeton University Press, 1988.

Eugenio Garin, *Italian Humanism: Philosophy and Civic Life in the Renaissance*. Greenwood Press, 1975.

James Hankins, ed., *Renaissance Civic Humanism: Reappraisals and Reflections*. Cambridge University Press, 2000.

Mark Jurdjevic, *Guardians of Republicanism: The Valori Family in the Florentine Renaissance*. Oxford University Press, 2008.

Political Thought: Machiavelli

Erica Benner, *Machiavelli's Ethics*. Princeton University Press, 2009.

Philip Bobbitt, *Garments of Court and Palace: Machiavelli and the World That He Made*. Grove Press, 2013.

Sebastian de Grazia, *Machiavelli in Hell*. Princeton University Press, 1989.

Felix Gilbert, *Machiavelli and Guicciardini: Politics and History in Sixteenth-Century Florence*. Princeton University Press, 1965.

Paul Oppenheimer. *Machiavelli: A Life Beyond Ideology*. Continuum, 2011.

Quentin Skinner, *Machiavelli: A Very Short Introduction*. Oxford University Press, 2000.

Peter Stacey, *Roman Monarchy and the Renaissance Prince*. Cambridge University Press, 2007.

Miles J. Unger, *Machiavelli: A Biography*. Simon & Schuster, 2011.

Maurizio Viroli, *Machiavelli's God*. Princeton University Press, 2010.

Corrado Vivanti, *Niccolò Machiavelli: An Intellectual Biography*. Princeton University Press, 2013.

CHAPTER FIVE

Surveys

William J. Bouwsma, *The Waning of the Renaissance*. Yale University Press, 2000.

Anthony Goodman and Angus MacKay, eds., *The Impact of Humanism on Western Europe During the Renaissance*. Routledge, 1990.

Lucille Kekewich, ed., *The Impact of Humanism*. Yale University Press, 2000.

Anthony Levi, *Renaissance and Reformation: The Intellectual Genesis*. Yale University Press, 2002.

Charles G. Nauert, *Humanism and the Culture of Renaissance Europe*. Cambridge University Press, 2006.

Lewis W. Spitz, *The Renaissance and Reformation Movements*. Rand McNally, 1971.

Europe in General

F. Akkerman, G. C. Huisman, and A. J. Vanderjagt, eds., *Wessel Gansfort (1419–1489) and Northern Humanism*. E. J. Brill, 1993.

Karl A. E. Enenkel and Jan Papy, eds., *Petrarch and His Readers in the Renaissance*. E. J. Brill, 2006.

Myron P. Gilmore, *Humanists and Jurists: Six Studies in the Renaissance*. Belknap Press, 1963.

Myron P. Gilmore, *The World of Humanism*. Harper 1952.

Franz Posset, *Renaissance Monks: Monastic Humanism in Six Biographical Sketches*. E. J. Brill, 2005.

Erika Rummel, *Biblical Humanism and Scholasticism in the Age of Erasmus*. E. J. Brill, 2008.

Germany

Reinhard P. Becker, ed., *German Humanism and the Reformation*. Continuum, 1982.

Noel L. Brann, *Abbot Trithemius (1462–1516): The Renaissance of Monastic Humanism*. E. J. Brill, 1981.

John F. D'Amico, *Roman and German Humanism, 1450–1550*. Variorum, 1993.

Gerhard Hoffmeister, ed., *The Renaissance and Reformation in Germany*. Ungar, 1977.

Christine R. Johnson, *The German Discovery of the World: Renaissance Encounters with the Strange and Marvelous*. University of Virginia Press, 2008.

James M. Kittelson, "Humanism and the Reformation in Germany," *Central European History* 9, no. 4 (December 1976): 303–322.

Peter Mack, *Renaissance Argument: Valla and Agricola in the Traditions of Rhetoric and Dialectic*. E. J. Brill, 1993.

Bernd Moeller, "The German Humanists and the Beginnings of the Reformation," in *Imperial Cities and the Reformation: Three Essays*, 19–38. Fortress Press, 1972.

Heiko A. Oberman and Thomas A. Brady Jr., eds., *Itinerarium Italicum: The Profile of the Italian Renaissance in the Mirror of Its European transformations*. E. J. Brill, 1975.

James H. Overfield, *Humanism and Scholasticism in Late Medieval Germany*. Princeton University Press, 1984.

David H. Price, *Johannes Reuchlin and the Campaign to Destroy Jewish Books*. Oxford University Press, 2011.

Erika Rummel, *The Case Against Johann Reuchlin: Religious and Social Controversy in Sixteenth-Century Germany*. University of Toronto Press, 2002.

Erika Rummel, *The Confessionalization of Humanism in Reformation Germany*. Oxford University Press, 2000.

Lewis W. Spitz, *Conrad Celtis, the German Arch-Humanist*. Harvard University Press, 1957.

Lewis W. Spitz, *Luther and German Humanism*. Variorum, 1996.

Lewis W. Spitz, *The Religious Renaissance of German Humanists*. Harvard University Press, 1963.

Kurt Stadtwald, *Roman Popes and German Patriots: Antipapalism in the Politics of the German Humanist Movement from Gregor Heimburg to Martin Luther*. Droz, 1996.

James M. Weiss, *Humanist Biography in Renaissance Italy and Reformation Germany: Friendship and Rhetoric*. Ashgate/Variorum, 2010.

France

Mikhail Bakhtin, *Rabelais and His World*. MIT Press, 1968.

Peter G. Bietenholz, *Basle and France in the Sixteenth Century: The Basle Humanists and Printers in Their Contacts with Francophone Culture*. Droz, 1971.

Anne Denieul-Cormier, *Time of Glory: The Renaissance in France, 1488–1559*. Doubleday, 1968.

Philippe Desan, ed., *Humanism in Crisis: The Decline of the French Renaissance*. University of Michigan Press, 1991.

Werner Gundersheimer, ed., *French Humanism, 1470–1600*. Harper & Row, 1969.

Mack P. Holt, ed., *Renaissance and Reformation France, 1500–1648*. Oxford University Press, 2002.

Henry Hornik, *Studies on French Renaissance: Theory and Idealism*. Slatkine, 1985.

Donald R. Kelley, *The Foundations of Modern Historical Scholarship: Language, Law, and History in the French Renaissance*. Columbia University Press, 1970.

A. H. T. Levi, ed., *Humanism in France at the End of the Middle Ages and in the Early Renaissance*. Manchester University Press, 1970.

David O. McNeil, *Guillaume Budé and Humanism in the Reign of Francis I*. Droz, 1971.

Sheila M. Porrer, *Jacques Lefèvre d'Etaples and the Three Maries Debates*. Droz, 2009.

Eugene F. Rice Jr., *The Humanist Idea of Christian Antiquity: Lefevre D'Etaples and His Circle*. Literary Licensing, 2011.

Franco Simone, *The French Renaissance: Medieval Tradition and Italian Influence in the Shaping of the Renaissance in France*. Macmillan, 1969.

James V. Skalnik, *Ramus and Reform: University and Church at the End of the Renaissance*. Truman State University Press, 2002.

Arthur A. Tilley, *The Dawn of the French Renaissance*. New York: Russell & Russell, 1968.

Frances A. Yates, *French Academies of the Sixteenth Century*. Kraus Reprint, 1968.

England and Scotland

Peter Ackroyd, *The Life of Thomas More*. Chatto & Windus, 1998.

Robert P. Adams, *The Better Part of Valor: More, Erasmus, Colet, and Vives, on Humanism, War, and Peace, 1496–1535*. University of Washington Press, 1962.

Jonathan Arnold, *Dean John Colet of St. Paul's: Humanism and Reform in Early Tudor England*. I. B. Tauris, 2007.

William E. Campbell, *Erasmus, Tyndale, and More*. Bruce Publishing, 1950.

A. D. Cousins and Damian Grace, eds., *Companion to Thomas More*. Fairleigh Dickinson University Press, 2009.

Gregory D. Dodds, *Exploiting Erasmus: The Erasmian Legacy and Religious Change in Early Modern England*. University of Toronto Press, 2009.

John B. Gleason, *John Colet*. University of California Press, 1989.

John Guy, *Thomas More*. Oxford University Press, 2000.

Ernest R. Holloway, *Andrew Melville and Humanism in Renaissance Scotland, 1545–1622*. E. J. Brill, 2011.

Sears Reynolds Jayne, *John Colet and Marsilio Ficino*. Oxford University Press, 1963.

Peter Iver Kaufman, *Augustinian Piety and Catholic Reform: Augustine, Colet, and Erasmus*. Mercer University Press, 1982.

Anthony Kenny, *Thomas More*. Oxford University Press, 1983.

George M. Logan, ed., *The Cambridge Companion to Thomas More*. Cambridge University Press, 2011.

Richard Marius, *Thomas More: A Biography*. Knopf, 1984.

Leland Miles, *John Colet and the Platonic Tradition*. Open Court, 1961.

James Monti, *The King's Good Servant but God's First: The Life and Writings of Saint Thomas More*. Ignatius Press, 1997.

E. E. Reynolds, *Thomas More and Erasmus*. Burns & Oates, 1965.

Frederic Seebohm, *The Oxford Reformers: John Colet, Erasmus, and Thomas More*. Longmans, Green, 1913; AMS Press, 1971.

Roger K. Warlick, *John Colet and Renaissance Humanism*. PhD diss., Boston University, 1965.

Roberto Weiss, *Humanism in England During the Fifteenth Century*, 2nd ed. Oxford University Press, 1957.

Hanan Yoran, *Between Utopia and Dystopia: Erasmus, Thomas More, and the Humanist Republic of Letters*. Lexington Books, 2010.

Spain

David Coles, *Humanism and the Bible in Renaissance Spain and Italy: Antonio de Nebrija (1441–1522)*. PhD diss., Yale University, 1983.

Lu Ann Homza, *Religious Authority in the Spanish Renaissance*. Johns Hopkins University Press, 2000.

John E. Longhurst, *Erasmus and the Spanish Inquisition: The Case of Juan de Valdés*. University of New Mexico Press, 1950.

Reginald Merton, *Cardinal Ximenes and the Making of Spain*. Kegan Paul, Trench, Trubner, 1934.

Seamus O'Connell, *From Most Ancient Sources: The Nature and Text-Critical Use of the Greek Old Testament Text of the Complutensian Polyglot Bible*. Vandenhoeck & Ruprecht, 2006.

Erika Rummel, *Jiménez de Cisneros: On the Threshold of Spain's Golden Age*. Arizona Center for Medieval and Renaissance Studies, 1999.

Erasmus of Rotterdam

John W. Aldridge, *The Hermeneutic of Erasmus*. John Knox Press, 1966.

Cornelis Augustijn, *Erasmus, His Life, Works and Influence*. University of Toronto Press, 1991.

Roland H. Bainton, *Erasmus of Christendom*. Scribner, 1969.

Istvan Bejczy, *Erasmus and the Middle Ages: The Historical Consciousness of a Christian Humanist*. E. J. Brill, 2001.

Peter G. Bietenholz, *History and Biography in the Work of Erasmus of Rotterdam*. Droz, 1966.

Louis Bouyer, *Erasmus and His Times*. Newman Press, 1959.

Richard L. DeMolen, *The Spirituality of Erasmus of Rotterdam*. De Graaf, 1987.

A. G. Dickens and Whitney R. D. Jones, *Erasmus the Reformer*. Methuen, 1994.

Wallace K. Ferguson, *Erasmus and Christian Humanism*. University of Saint Thomas, 1963.

Constance M. Furey, *Erasmus, Contarini, and the Religious Republic of Letters*. Cambridge University Press, 2006.

Leon Halkin, *Erasmus: A Critical Biography*. Blackwell, 1993.

Manfred Hoffmann, *Rhetoric and Theology: The Hermeneutic of Erasmus*. University of Toronto Press, 1994.

Johan Huizinga, *Erasmus and the Age of Reformation*. Harper, 1957; Dover Publications, 2011.

Albert Hyma, *The Life of Desiderius Erasmus*. Van Gorcum, 1972.

Jan Krans, *Beyond What Is Written: Erasmus and Beza as Conjectural Critics of the New Testament*. E. J. Brill, 2006.

Margaret Mann Phillips, *Erasmus and the Northern Renaissance*. Rowman & Littlefield, 1981.

Marjorie O'Rourke Boyle, *Christening Pagan Mysteries: Erasmus in Pursuit of Wisdom*. University of Toronto Press, 1981.

Marjorie O'Rourke Boyle, *Erasmus on Language and Method in Theology*. University of Toronto Press, 1977.

Hilmar M. Pabel, *Herculean Labours: Erasmus and the Editing of St. Jerome's Letters in the Renaissance*. E. J. Brill, 2008.

John B. Payne, *Erasmus: His Theology of the Sacraments*. John Knox Press, 1970.

Albert Rabil Jr., *Erasmus and the New Testament: The Mind of a Christian Humanist*. Trinity University Press, 1972.

Erika Rummel, *Erasmus and His Catholic Critics*. De Graaf, 1989.

Erika Rummel, *Erasmus as a Translator of the Classics*. University of Toronto Press, 1985.

R. J. Schoeck, *Erasmus of Europe: The Making of a Humanist*, 2 vols. Edinburgh University Press, 1990–1993.

Douglas H. Shantz, *Crautwald and Erasmus: A Study in Humanism and Radical Reform in Sixteenth Century Silesia*. Editions Valentin Koerner, 1992.

James D. Tracy, *Erasmus of the Low Countries*. University of California Press, 1996.

James D. Tracy, *Erasmus, the Growth of a Mind*. Droz, 1972.

James D. Tracy, *The Low Countries in the Sixteenth Century: Erasmus, Religion and Politics, Trade and Finance.* Ashgate, 2005.

CHAPTER SIX

Surveys

Stephen D. Bowd, *Reform Before the Reformation: Vincenzo Querini and the Religious Renaissance in Italy.* E. J. Brill, 2002.

Abigail Brundin and Matthew Treherne, *Forms of Faith in Sixteenth-Century Italy.* Ashgate, 2009.

D. S. Chambers, *Renaissance Cardinals and Their Worldly Problems.* Variorum, 1997.

David J. Collins, *Reforming Saints: Saints' Lives and Their Authors in Germany, 1470–1530.* Oxford University Press, 2008.

Eric A. Constant, "A Reinterpretation of the Fifth Lateran Council Decree *Apostolici regiminis* (1513)," *Sixteenth Century Journal* 33 (2002): 353–379.

Jan L. de Jong, *Power and the Glorification: Papal Pretensions and the Art of Propaganda in the Fifteenth and Sixteenth Centuries.* Pennsylvania State University Press, 2013.

Jennifer Mara DeSilva, ed., *Episcopal Reform and Politics in Early Modern Europe.* Truman State University Press, 2012.

Richard M. Douglas, *Jacopo Sadoleto, Humanist and Reformer.* Harvard University Press, 1959.

Ryan D. Giles, *Laughter of the Saints: Parodies of Holiness in Late Medieval and Renaissance Spain.* University of Toronto Press, 2009.

Elisabeth G. Gleason, *Gasparo Contarini: Venice, Rome, and Reform.* University of California Press, 1993.

Kenneth Gouwens and Sheryl E. Reiss, *The Pontificate of Clement VII: History, Politics, Culture.* Ashgate, 2005.

Denys Hay, *The Church in Italy in the Fifteenth Century.* Cambridge University Press, 2002.

Paul A. Kunkel, *The Theatines in the History of Catholic Reform Before the Establishment of Lutheranism.* Catholic University of America Press, 1941.

Francis X. Martin, *Friar, Reformer, and Renaissance Scholar: Life and Work of Giles of Viterbo, 1469–1532.* Augustinian Press, 1992.

Peter Matheson, *Cardinal Contarini at Regensburg.* Clarendon Press, 1972.

Nelson H. Minnich, *The Catholic Reformation: Council, Churchmen, Controversies.* Variorum, 1993.

Nelson H. Minnich, *The Fifth Lateran Council (1512–17): Studies on Its Membership, Diplomacy and Proposals for Reform.* Variorum, 1993.

Paul Murphy, *Ruling Peacefully: Cardinal Ercole Gonzaga and Patrician Reform in Sixteenth-Century Italy.* Catholic University of America Press, 2007.

John W. O'Malley, *Giles of Viterbo on Church and Reform: A Study in Renaissance Thought.* E. J. Brill, 1968.

Rady Roldán-Figueroa, *The Ascetic Spirituality of Juan de Avila.* Leiden: Brill, 2010.

Erika Rummel, *Jiménez de Cisneros: On the Threshold of Spain's Golden Age.* Arizona Center for Medieval and Renaissance Studies, 1999.

Jan van Herwaarden, *Between Saint James and Erasmus: Studies in Late-Medieval Religious Life, Devotion and Pilgrimage in the Netherlands.* E. J. Brill, 2003.

Anne Winston-Allen, *Convent Chronicles: Women Writing About Women and Reform in the Late Middle Ages*. Pennsylvania State University Press, 2004.

Giuseppe Maria Zinelli, *The Life of St. Cajetan, Count of Tiene: Founder of the Theatines*. BiblioBazaar, 2010.

Savonarola

Alison Brown, *Medicean and Savonarolan Florence: The Interplay of Politics, Humanism, and Religion*. Brepols, 2011.

Stefano Dall'Aglio, *Savonarola and Savonarolism*. Centre for Reformation and Renaissance Studies, 2010.

Michael de la Bedoyere, *The Meddlesome Friar and the Wayward Pope: The Story of the Conflict Between Savonarola and Alexander VI*. Hanover House, 1957.

Amos Edelheit, *Ficino, Pico and Savonarola: The Evolution of Humanist Theology, 1461/2–1498*. E. J. Brill, 2008.

Rachel Erlanger, *The Unarmed Prophet: Savonarola in Florence*. McGraw-Hill, 1988.

Tamar Herzig, *Savonarola's Women: Visions and Reform in Renaissance Italy*. University of Chicago Press, 2008.

Lauro Martines, *Fire in the City: Savonarola and the Struggle for Renaissance Florence*. Oxford University Press, 2006.

R. Richard Renner, *Savonarola, the First Great Protestant*. Greenwich Book Publishers, 1965.

Desmond Seward, *The Burning of the Vanities: Savonarola and the Borgia Pope*. Sutton, 2006.

Donald Weinstein, *Savonarola: The Rise and Fall of a Renaissance Prophet*. Yale University Press, 2011.

CHAPTER SEVEN

Introductions to Luther

Scott H. Hendrix, *Martin Luther: A Very Short Introduction*. Oxford University Press, 2010.

Denis R. Janz, *The Westminster Handbook to Martin Luther*. Westminster John Knox Press, 2010.

Bernhard Lohse, *Martin Luther, an Introduction to His Life and Work*. Fortress Press, 1986.

Donald K. McKim, ed., *The Cambridge Companion to Martin Luther*. Cambridge University Press, 2003.

Hans Schwarz, *True Faith in the True God: An Introduction to Luther's Life and Thought*. Augsburg Fortress, 1996.

Victor A. Shepherd, *Interpreting Martin Luther: An Introduction to His Life and Thought*. Regent College Publications, 2008.

Biographies of Luther

James Atkinson, *Martin Luther and the Birth of Protestantism*. Marshall Morgan & Scott, 1982.

Roland H. Bainton, *Here I Stand: A Life of Martin Luther*. Penguin, 2002.

Martin Brecht, *Martin Luther: His Road to Reformation, 1483–1521*. Fortress Press, 1985.

A. G. Dickens, *Martin Luther and the Reformation*. English Universities Press, 1967.

Eric W. Gritsch, *Martin, God's Court Jester: Luther in Retrospect*. Fortress Press, 1983.

Hans-Peter Grosshans, *Luther*. Fount, 1997.

H. G. Haile, *Luther: An Experiment in Biography*. Princeton University Press, 1983.

Scott H. Hendrix, *Luther*. Abingdon Press, 2009.

James M. Kittelson, *Luther the Reformer: The Story of the Man and His Career*. Augsburg, 1986.

Richard Marius, *Martin Luther: The Christian Between God and Death*. Belknap Press, 1999.

Martin Marty, *Martin Luther*. Viking Penguin, 2004.

Michael A. Mullett, *Martin Luther*. Routledge, 2004.

James A. Nestingen, *Martin Luther: A Life*. Augsburg, 2003.

Heiko A. Oberman, *Luther: Man Between God and the Devil*. Yale University Press, 2006.

Walther von Loewenich, *Martin Luther: The Man and His Work*. Augsburg, 1986.

Derek Wilson, *Out of the Storm: The Life and Legacy of Martin Luther*. St. Martin's Press, 2008.

The Young Luther: Life and Influences

Erik Erikson, *Young Man Luther: A Study in Psychoanalysis and History*. Norton, 1993.

Maria Grossmann, *Humanism in Wittenberg, 1485–1517*. De Graaf, 1975.

Steven Ozment, *Homo spiritualis: A Comparative Study of the Anthropology of Johannes Tauler, Jean Gerson and Martin Luther (1509–16) in the Context of Their Theological Thought*. E. J. Brill, 1969.

Franz Posset, *Front-Runner of the Catholic Reformation: The Life and Works of Johann von Staupitz*. Ashgate, 2003.

Franz Posset, *The Real Luther: A Friar at Erfurt and Wittenberg*. Concordia Publishing House, 2011.

Lewis W. Spitz, *Luther and German Humanism*. Variorum, 1996.

David C. Steinmetz, *Luther and Staupitz: An Essay in the Intellectual Origins of the Protestant Reformation*. Duke University Press, 1980.

Luther's Thought

Heinrich Bornkamm, *Luther's World of Thought*. Concordia Publishing House, 2005.

Gerhard Ebeling, *Luther: An Introduction to His Thought*. Fortress Press, 1970.

Bengt Hägglund, *The Background of Luther's Doctrine of Justification in Late Medieval Theology*. Fortress Press, 1971.

Marilyn Harran, *Luther on Conversion: The Early Years*. Cornell University Press, 1983.

Denis R. Janz, *Luther and Late Medieval Thomism: A Study in Theological Anthropology*. Wilfrid Laurier University Press, 1983.

Robert Kolb, *Martin Luther: Confessor of the Faith*. Oxford University Press, 2009.

John R. Loeschen, *Wrestling with Luther: An Introduction to the Study of His Thought*. Concordia Publishing House, 1976.

Bernhard Lohse, *Martin Luther's Theology: Its Historical and Systematic Development*. Fortress Press, 1999.

Alister E. McGrath, *Luther's Theology of the Cross: Martin Luther's Theological Breakthrough*. Basil Blackwell, 1985.

Steven Paulson, *Luther for Armchair Theologians*. Westminster John Knox Press, 2004.

David C. Steinmetz, *Luther in Context*. Indiana University Press, 1986.

Jared Wicks, *Man Yearning for Grace: Luther's Early Spiritual Teaching*. Corpus Books, 1968.

Luther's Initial Steps Against Rome

David Bagchi, *Luther's Earliest Opponents: Catholic Controversialists, 1518–1525*. Fortress Press, 1991.

Erwin Iserloh, *The Theses Were Not Posted: Luther Between Reform and Reformation*. Beacon Press, 1968.

Gordon Rupp, *Luther's Progress to the Diet of Worms*. Harper & Row, 1964.

CHAPTER EIGHT
Luther's Life and Thought

James Atkinson, *The Trial of Luther*. Stein and Day, 1971.

David V. N. Bagchi, *Luther's Earliest Opponents: Catholic Controversialists, 1518–1525*. Fortress Press, 1991.

Heinrich Bornkamm, *Luther and the Old Testament*, trans. Eric W. and Ruth C. Gritsch, ed. Victor I. Gruhn. Fortress Press, 1969.

Christopher Boyd Brown, *Singing the Gospel: Lutheran Hymns and the Success of the Reformation*, Harvard University Press, 2005.

Martin Brecht, *Martin Luther 1521–1532: Shaping and Defining the Reformation*. Fortress Press, 1990.

Rosemary Devonshire Jones. *Erasmus and Luther*. Oxford University Press, 1968.

A. G. Dickens, *The German Nation and Martin Luther*. Harper & Row, 1974.

Gert Haendler, *Luther on Ministerial Office and Congregational Function*, trans. Ruth C. Gritsch, ed. Eric W. Gritsch. Fortress Press, 1981.

John M. Headley, *Luther's View of Church History*. Yale University Press, 1963.

Johannes Heckel, *Lex Charitatis: A Juristic Disquisition on Law in the Theology of Martin Luther*. Eerdmans, 2010.

Scott H. Hendrix, *Luther and the Papacy: Stages in a Reformation Conflict*. Fortress Press, 1981.

Erwin Iserloh, *The Theses Were Not Posted: Luther Between Reform and Reformation*, trans. Jared Wicks, introduction by Martin E. Marty. Beacon Press, 1968.

Tuomo Mannermaa, *Christ Present in Faith: Luther's View of Justification*. Fortress Press, 2005.

Jaroslav Pelikan, *Spirit Versus Structure: Luther and the Institutions of the Church*. Harper & Row, 1968.

Franz Posset, *The Real Luther: A Friar at Erfurt and Wittenberg*. Concordia Publishing. House, 2011.

E. Gordon Rupp, *Luther's Progress to the Diet of Worms*. Harper & Row, 1964.

E. Gordon Rupp, *The Righteousness of God: Luther Studies*. Hodder & Stoughton, 1953.

Ralph F. Smith, *Luther, Ministry, and Ordination Rites in the Early Reformation Church*. P. Lang, 1996.

Ian D. K. Siggins, *Luther and His Mother*. Fortress Press, 1981.

David C. Steinmetz, *Luther in Context*, 2nd ed. Baker Book House, 2002.

Walther von Loewenich, *Luther's Theology of the Cross*. Augsburg, 1976.

Randall C. Zachman, *Assurance of Faith: Conscience in the Theology of Martin Luther and John Calvin*. Fortress Press, 1993.

Luther's Germany

Thomas A. Brady Jr., *Turning Swiss: Cities and Empire, 1450–1550*. Cambridge University Press, 1985.

Michael Hughes, *Early Modern Germany, 1477–1806*. Macmillan, 1992.

H. C. Erik Midelfort, *Mad Princes of Renaissance Germany*. University Press of Virginia, 1994.

Bernd Moeller, *Imperial Cities and the Reformation: Three Essays*. Labyrinth Press, 1982.

Joachim Whaley, *Maximilian I to the Peace of Westphalia, 1490–1648*, vol. 1 of *Germany and the Holy Roman Empire*. Oxford University Press, 2012.

Emperor Charles V

Wim Blockmans, *Emperor Charles V, 1500–1558*. Arnold, 2002.

Marc Boone and Marysa Demoor, eds., *Charles V in Context: The Making of a European Identity*. Faculty of Arts and Philosophy, Ghent University, 2003.

Karl Brandi, *The Emperor Charles V*. Jonathan Cape, 1963.

Aurelio Espinosa, *Empire of the Cities: Emperor Charles V, the Comunero Revolt, and the Transformation of the Spanish System*. E. J. Brill, 2009.

Harald Kleinschmidt, *Charles V: The World Emperor*. Sutton, 2004.

William S. Maltby, *The Reign of Charles V*. Palgrave, 2002.

James Reston Jr., *Defenders of the Faith: Charles V, Suleyman the Magnificent, and the Battle for Europe, 1520–1536*. Penguin Press, 2009.

Texts, Images, and Propaganda

Steven Ozment, *Protestants: The Birth of a Revolution*. Doubleday, 1992.

Steven Ozment, *The Reformation in the Cities*. Yale University Press, 1975.

Helga Robinson-Hammerstein, *Pamphlets of the German Reformation: Monsters, Miracles & Martinians*. Four Courts, 2001.

Paul A. Russell, *Lay Theology in the Reformation: Popular Pamphleteers in Southwest Germany, 1521–1525*. Cambridge University Press, 1986.

Robert Scribner, *For the Sake of Simple Folk: Popular Propaganda for the German Reformation*. Oxford University Press, 1994.

Miriam Usher Chrisman, *Conflicting Visions of Reform: German Lay Propaganda Pamphlets, 1519–1530*. Humanities Press, 1996.

Tessa Watt, *Cheap Print and Popular Piety, 1550–1640*. Cambridge University Press, 1991.

CHAPTER NINE

Luther's Life and Work

David Andersen, *Martin Luther, the Problem of Faith and Reason: A Reexamination in Light of the Epistemological and Christological Issues*. Verlag für Kultur und Wissenschaft, 2009.

Charles P. Arand, *That I May Be His Own: An Overview of Luther's Catechisms*: Concordia Publishing House, 2000.

Martin Brecht, *Martin Luther: The Preservation of the Church, 1532–1546*. Fortress Press, 1993.

Heinrich Bornkamm, *Luther in Mid-Career, 1521–1530*. Fortress Press, 1983.

Heinrich Bornkamm, *Luther's Doctrine of the Two Kingdoms in the Context of His Theology*. Fortress Press, 1966.

Mark U. Edwards Jr., *Luther's Last Battles: Politics and Polemics, 1531–1546*. Cornell University Press, 1983.

James M. Estes, *Peace, Order and the Glory of God: Secular Authority and the Church in the Thought of Luther and Melanchthon, 1518–1559*. E. J. Brill, 2005.

Eric W. Gritsch, *A History of Lutheranism*, 2nd ed. Fortress Press, 2010.

Joseph Herl, *Worship Wars in Early Lutheranism: Choir, Congregation, and Three Centuries of Conflict*. Oxford University Press, 2004.

William H. Lazareth, *Christians in Society: Luther, the Bible, and Social Ethics*. Fortress Press, 2001.

Neil R. Leroux, *Luther's Rhetoric: Strategies and Style from the Invocavit Sermons*. Concordia Publishing House, 2002.

Neil R. Leroux, *Martin Luther as Comforter: Writings on Death*. E. J. Brill, 2007.

Tuomo Mannermaa, *Two Kinds of Love: Martin Luther's Religious World*. Fortress Press, 2010.

Marjorie O'Rourke Boyle, *Rhetoric and Reform: Erasmus' Civil Dispute with Luther*. Harvard University Press, 1983.

Christopher J. Probst, *Demonizing the Jews: Luther and the Protestant Church in Nazi Germany*. Indiana University Press, 2012.

Ronald Rittgers, *The Reformation of Suffering: Pastoral Theology and Lay Piety in Late Medieval and Early Modern Germany*. Oxford University Press, 2012.

Ronald Rittgers, *The Reformation of the Keys: Confession, Conscience, and Authority in Sixteenth-Century Germany*. Harvard University Press, 2004.

William R. Russell, *Praying for Reform: Martin Luther, Prayer, and the Christian Life*. Augsburg Fortress, 2005.

Bryan Spinks, *Luther's Liturgical Criteria and His Reform of the Canon of the Mass*. Grove Books, 1982.

Samuel Torvend, *Luther and the Hungry Poor: Gathered Fragments*. Fortress Press, 2008.

Timothy J. Wengert, ed., *Pastoral Luther: Essays on Martin Luther's Practical Theology*. Eerdmans, 2009.

Andreas Bodenstein von Karlstadt

Mark U. Edwards Jr., *Luther and the False Brethren*. Stanford University Press, 1975.

Harry Loewen, *Luther and the Radicals: Another Look at Some Aspects of the Struggle Between Luther and the Radical Reformers*. Wilfred Laurier University Press, 1974.

Amy Nelson Burnett, *Karlstadt and the Origins of the Eucharistic Controversy: A Study in the Circulation of Ideas*. Oxford University Press, 2011.

Augustine Pater, *Karlstadt as the Father of the Baptist Movements: The Emergence of Lay Protestantism*. University of Toronto Press, 1984.

James S. Preus, *Carlstadt's Ordinaciones and Luther's Liberty: A Study of the Wittenberg Movement, 1521–22*. Harvard University Press, 1974.

Gordon Rupp, *Patterns of Reformation*. Fortress Press, 1969.

Ronald J. Sider, *Andreas Bodenstein von Karlstadt: The Development of His Thought, 1517–1525*. E. J. Brill, 1974.

Thomas Müntzer and the Zwickau Prophets

Harold S. Bender, "The Zwickau Prophets, Thomas Müntzer and the Anabaptists." *Mennonite Quarterly Review* 27, no. 1 (January 1953): 3–16.

Abraham Friesen, *Thomas Muentzer, a Destroyer of the Godless: The Making of a Sixteenth-Century Religious Revolutionary*. University of California Press, 1990.

Hans Jürgen Goertz, *Thomas Müntzer: Apocalyptic Mystic and Revolutionary*. T&T Clark, 1993.

Eric W. Gritsch, *Reformer Without a Church: The Life and Thought of Thomas Muentzer*. Fortress Press, 1967.

Eric W. Gritsch, *Thomas Müntzer, a Tragedy of Errors*. Fortress Press, 1989.

[Interdisciplinary group of scholars from the German Democratic Republic Academy of Sciences and various GDR universities], *Theses Concerning Thomas Müntzer, 1489–1989*. Panorama DDR, 1988.

Susan Karant-Nunn, *Zwickau in Transition, 1500–1547: The Reformation as Agent of Change*. Ohio State University Press, 1987.

Olaf Kuhr, "The Zwickau Prophets, The Wittenberg Disturbances, and Polemical Historiography." *Mennonite Quarterly Review* 70, no. 2 (April 1996): 205.

E. Gordon Rupp, *Thomas Müntzer: Prophet of Radical Christianity*. John Rylands Library, 1966.

E. Gordon Rupp, *Thomas Müntzer, Hans Huth and the Gospel of All Creatures*. John Rylands Library, 1961.

Tom Scott, *Thomas Müntzer, Theology and Revolution in the German Reformation*. St. Martin's Press, 1989.

The Peasant Uprising of 1524–1525

Michael G. Baylor, *The German Reformation and the Peasants' War: A Brief History with Documents*. Bedford/St. Martin's, 2012.

Peter Blickle, *From the Communal Reformation to the Revolution of the Common Man*. E. J. Brill, 1998.

Peter Blickle, *The Revolution of 1525: The German Peasants' War from a New Perspective*. Johns Hopkins University Press, 1981.

Gerhard Brendler, *Martin Luther, Theology and Revolution*. Oxford University Press, 1991.

Robert N. Crossley, *Luther and the Peasants' War: Luther's Actions and Reactions*. Exposition Press, 1974.

Friedrich Engels, *The Peasant War in Germany*. Allen & Unwin, 1927.

Hubert Kirchner, *Luther and the Peasants' War*. Fortress Press, 1972.

Harold Ristau, *Understanding Martin Luther's Demonological Rhetoric in His Treatise* Against the Heavenly Prophets *(1525)*. Edwin Mellen, 2010.

Tom Scott, *Town, Country, and Regions in Reformation Germany*. E. J. Brill, 2005.

Kyle C. Sessions, ed., *Reformation and Authority: The Meaning of the Peasants' Revolt*. Heath, 1968.

Lloyd B. Volkmar, *Luther's Response to Violence: Why the Reformer Hurled His Harsh 'No!' Against the Peasants*. Vantage Press, 1974.

CHAPTER TEN

Switzerland

Reginald C. E. Abbot, *The Rise of the Swiss Confederation*. J. H. and J. Parker, 1861.

E. Bonjour, H. S. Offler, and G. R. Potter, *A short History of Switzerland*. Clarendon Press, 1952.

Thomas A. Brady Jr., *Turning Swiss: Cities and Empire, 1450–1550*. Cambridge University Press, 1985.

Amy Nelson Burnett, *Teaching the Reformation: Ministers and Their Message in Basel, 1529–1629*. Oxford University Press, 2006.

Carlos M. N. Eire, *War Against the Idols: The Reformation of Worship from Erasmus to Calvin*. Cambridge University Press, 1986.

Bruce Gordon, *The Swiss Reformation*. Manchester University Press, 2002.

Hans R. Guggisberg, *Basel in the Sixteenth Century: Aspects of the City Republic Before, During, and After the Reformation*. Center for Reformation Research, 1982.

Pamela Johnston and Bob Scribner, *The Reformation in Germany and Switzerland*. Cambridge University Press, 1993.

Douglas Miller, *The Swiss at War, 1300–1500*. Osprey Publishing, 1979.

Helmut Puff, *Sodomy in Reformation Germany and Switzerland, 1400–1600*. University of Chicago Press, 2003.

Jill Raitt, ed., *Shapers of Religious Traditions in Germany, Switzerland, and Poland, 1560–1600*. Yale University Press, 1981.

Mark Taplin, *Italian Reformers and the Zurich Church, 1540–1620*. Ashgate, 2003.

John Martin Vincent, *Switzerland at the Beginning of the Sixteenth Century*. Johns Hopkins University Press, 1904.

Robert C. Walton, *Zwingli's Theocracy*. University of Toronto Press, 1967.

Lee Palmer Wandel, *Always Among Us: Images of the Poor in Zwingli's Zurich*. Cambridge University Press, 1990.

Lee Palmer Wandel, *Voracious Idols and Violent Hands: Iconoclasm in Reformation Zurich, Strasbourg, and Basel*. Cambridge University Press, 1995.

John Howard Yoder, *Anabaptism and Reformation in Switzerland: An Historical and Theological Analysis of the Dialogues Between Anabaptists and Reformers*. Pandora Press, 2004.

Zwingli: Biography

Jean Henri Merle d'Aubigne, *For God and His People: Ulrich Zwingli and the Swiss Reformation*. BJU Press, 2000.

Oskar Farner, *Zwingli the Reformer: His Life and Work*. Archon Books, 1968.

E. J. Furcha and H. Wayne Pipkin, eds., *Prophet, Pastor, Protestant: The Work of Huldrych Zwingli After Five Hundred Years*. Pickwick Publications, 1984.

Ulrich Gäbler, *Huldrych Zwingli, His Life and Work*. Fortress Press, 1986.

Samuel Macauley Jackson, *Huldreich Zwingli, the Reformer of German Switzerland: Together with an Historical Survey of Switzerland Before the Reformation, by John Martin Vincent; and a Chapter on Zwingli's Theology by Frank Hugh Foster*. AMS Press, 1972.

George R. Potter, *Ulrich Zwingli*. London Historical Association, 1977.

Jean Rilliet, *Zwingli: Third Man of the Reformation*. Westminster Press, 1964.

Zwingli: History and Theology

Jacques Courvoisier, *Zwingli, a Reformed Theologian*. John Knox Press, 1963.

Esther Chung-Kim, *Inventing Authority: The Use of the Church Fathers in Reformation Debates over the Eucharist*. Baylor University Press, 2011.

Rupert E. Davies, *The Problem of Authority in the Continental Reformers: A Study in Luther, Zwingli, and Calvin*. Epworth Press, 1946.

Thomas J. Davis, *This Is My Body: The Presence of Christ in Reformation Thought*. Baker Academic, 2008.

Charles Garside, *Zwingli and the Arts*. Yale University Press, 1966.

Cyril Charles Richardson, *Zwingli and Cranmer on the Eucharist*. Evanston: Seabury-Western Theological Seminary, 1949.

W. P. Stephens, *The Theology of Huldrych Zwingli*. Oxford University Press, 1986.

W. P. Stephens, *Zwingli: An Introduction to His Thought*. Oxford University Press, 1992.

Lee Palmer Wandel, *The Eucharist in the Reformation: Incarnation and Liturgy*. Cambridge University Press, 2006.

Jim West, ed., *The Humor of Huldrych Zwingli: The Lighter Side of the Protestant Reformation*. Edwin Mellen Press, 2007.

Bullinger

J. Wayne Baker, *Heinrich Bullinger and the Covenant: The Other Reformed Tradition*. Ohio University Press, 1980.

Pamela Biel, *Doorkeepers at the House of Righteousness: Heinrich Bullinger and the Zurich Clergy, 1535–1575*. P. Lang, 1991.

Aurelio García Archilla, *Theology of History and Apologetic Historiography in Heinrich Bullinger*, Mellen Research University Press, 1992.

Bruce Gordon and Emidio Campi, *Architect of Reformation: An Introduction to Heinrich Bullinger, 1504–1575*. Baker Academic, 2004.

Charles S. McCoy and J. Wayne Baker, *Fountainhead of Federalism: Heinrich Bullinger and the Covenantal Tradition*. Westminster/John Knox Press, 1991.

CHAPTER ELEVEN

Surveys and Introductions

Eberhard Arnold, *The Early Anabaptists*, 2nd ed. Plough Publishing, 1984.

George Huntston Williams, *The Radical Reformation*, 3rd ed. Sixteenth Century Journal Publishers, 1992.

Walter Klaassen, *Anabaptism: Neither Catholic nor Protestant*, 3rd ed. Pandora Press, 2001.

Donald B. Kraybill, *Who Are the Anabaptists? Amish, Brethren, Hutterites, and Mennonites.* Herald Press, 2003.

John D. Roth and James M. Stayer, eds., *A Companion to Anabaptism and Spiritualism, 1521–1700.* E. J. Brill, 2007.

E. Gordon Rupp, *Patterns of Reformation.* Fortress Press, 1969.

J. Denny Weaver, *Becoming Anabaptist: The Origin and Significance of Sixteenth-Century Anabaptism*, 2nd ed. Herald Press, 2005.

Theology and Ethics

Gerald Biesecker-Mast, *Separation and the Sword in Anabaptist Persuasion: Radical Confessional Rhetoric from Schleitheim to Dordrecht.* Herald Press, 2006.

Dennis E. Bollinger, *First-Generation Anabaptist Ecclesiology, 1525–1561: A Study of Swiss, German, and Dutch Sources.* Edwin Mellen Press, 2008.

Kenneth Ronald Davis, *Anabaptism and Asceticism: A Study in Intellectual Origins.* Herald Press, 1974.

Robert Friedmann, *The Theology of Anabaptism: An Interpretation.* Herald Press, 1973.

Karl Kautsky, *Communism in Central Europe in the Time of the Reformation.* Russell & Russell, 1959.

William E. Keeney, *The Development of Dutch Anabaptist Thought and Practice from 1539–1564.* B. de Graaf, 1968.

Walter Klaassen, *Living at the End of the Ages: Apocalyptic Expectation in the Radical Reformation.* Institute for Anabaptist and Mennonite Studies, Conrad Grebel College, 1992.

Peter James Klassen, *The Economics of Anabaptism, 1525–1560.* Mouton, 1964.

Franklin H. Littell, *The Origins of Sectarian Protestantism: A Study of the Anabaptist View of the Church.* Macmillan, 1964.

Steven E. Ozment, *Mysticism and Dissent: Religious Ideology and Social Protest in the Sixteenth Century.* Yale University Press, 1973.

Werner O. Packull, *Hutterite Beginnings: Communitarian Experiments During the Reformation.* Johns Hopkins University Press, 1995.

Werner O. Packull, *Mysticism and the Early South German-Austrian Anabaptist Movement, 1525–1531.* Herald Press, 1977.

John D. Rempel, *The Lord's Supper in Anabaptism: A Study in the Christology of Balthasar Hubmaier, Pilgram Marpeck, and Dirk Philips.* Herald Press, 1993.

James M. Stayer, *Anabaptists and the Sword.* Coronado Press, 1972.

James M. Stayer, *The German Peasants' War and Anabaptist Community of Goods.* McGill-Queen's University Press, 1991.

Peter H. Stephenson, *The Hutterian People: Ritual and Rebirth in the Evolution of Communal Life.* University Press of America, 1991.

Guy E. Swanson, *Religion and Regime: A Sociological Account of the Reformation.* University of Michigan Press, 1967.

Gary K. Waite, *Eradicating the Devil's Minions: Anabaptists and Witches in Reformation Europe, 1525–1600.* University of Toronto Press, 2007.

John Christian Wenger, *Even unto Death: The Heroic Witness of the Sixteenth-Century Anabaptists.* John Knox Press, 1961.

Anabaptist Reformers and Traditions

Myron S. Augsburger, *The Fugitive: Menno Simons, Spiritual Leader in the Free Church Movement.* Herald Press, 2008.

Harold S. Bender, *Conrad Grebel, c. 1498–1526: The Founder of the Swiss Brethren Sometimes Called Anabaptists.* Wipf and Stock, 1998.

Harold S. Bender, Ernst Correll, and Edward Yoder, *The Life and Letters of Conrad Grebel.* Mennonite Historical Society, Goshen College, 1950.

Klaus Deppermann, *Melchior Hoffman: Social Unrest and Apocalyptic Visions in the Age of Reformation.* T. & T. Clark, 1987.

Hans-Jürgen Goertz, ed., *Profiles of Radical Reformers: Biographical Sketches from Thomas Müntzer to Paracelsus.* Herald Press, 1982.

Leonard Gross, *The Golden Years of the Hutterites: The Witness and Thought of the Communal Moravian Anabaptists During the Walpot Era, 1565–1578*, rev. ed. Pandora Press, 1998.

Helmut Isaak, *Menno Simons and the New Jerusalem.* Pandora Press, 2006.

Walter Klaassen and William Klassen, *Marpeck: A Life of Dissent and Conformity.* Herald Press, 2008.

Werner O. Packull, *Peter Riedemann: Shaper of the Hutterite Tradition.* Pandora Press, 2007.

Calvin Augustine Pater, *Karlstadt as the Father of the Baptist Movements: The Emergence of Lay Protestantism.* University of Toronto Press, 1984.

H. Wayne Pipkin, *Scholar, Pastor, Martyr: The Life and Ministry of Balthasar Hubmaier.* International Baptist Theological Seminary, 2008.

E. Gordon Rupp, *Thomas Müntzer, Hans Huth and the "Gospel of All Creatures."* John Rylands Library and Aberdeen University Press, 1961.

John L. Ruth, *Conrad Grebel, Son of Zurich.* Herald Press, 1975.

C. Arnold Snyder, *The Life and Thought of Michael Sattler.* Herald Press, 1984.

Jacobus ten Doornkaat, *Dirk Philips: Friend and Colleague of Menno Simons, 1504–1568*, ed. C. Arnold Snyder. Pandora Press, 1998.

Münster

Willem de Bakker, Michael Driedger, James Stayer, *Bernhard Rothmann and the Reformation in Münster, 1530–35.* Pandora Press, 2009.

Sigrun Haude, *In the Shadow of "Savage Wolves": Anabaptist Münster and the German Reformation During the 1530s.* Humanities Press, 2000.

George B. von der Lippe and Viktoria M. Reck-Malleczewen, eds. and trans., *History of the Münster Anabaptists: A Critical Edition of Friedrich Reck-Malleczewen's Bockelson: A Tale of Mass Insanity.* Palgrave Macmillan, 2008.

Hermann von Kerssenbrock, *Narrative of the Anabaptist Madness: The Overthrow of Münster, the Famous Metropolis of Westphalia*, trans. Christopher S. Mackay. E. J. Brill, 2007.

Relations with Magisterial Reformers

Willem Balke, *Calvin and the Anabaptist Radicals.* Eerdmans, 1981.

Mark U. Edwards, *Luther and the False Brethren.* Stanford University Press, 1975.

Harry Loewen, *Luther and the Radicals: Another Look at Some Aspects of the Struggle Between Luther and the Radical Reformers.* Wilfred Laurier University, 1974.

John S. Oyer, *Lutheran Reformers Against Anabaptists: Luther, Melanchthon, and Menius, and the Anabaptists of Central Germany.* M. Nijhoff, 1964.

Antonio Rotondò, *Calvin and the Italian Anti-Trinitarians.* Foundation for Reformation Research, 1968.

Spiritualists and Anti-Trinitarians

Roland H. Bainton, *Hunted Heretic: The Life and Death of Michael Servetus, 1511–1553.* P. Smith, 1978.

Jerome Friedman, *Michael Servetus: A Case Study in Total Heresy.* Droz, 1978.

Lawrence Goldstone and Nancy Goldstone, *Out of the Flames: The Remarkable Story of a Fearless Scholar, a Fatal Heresy, and One of the Rarest Books in the World.* Broadway Books, 2002.

Ruth Gouldbourne, *Flesh and the Feminine: Gender and Theology in the Writings of Caspar Schwenckfeld.* Paternoster, 2006.

Hans R. Guggisberg, *Sebastian Castellio, 1515–1563: Humanist and Defender of Religious Toleration in a Confessional Age.* Ashgate, 2003.

Patrick Hayden-Roy, *The Inner Word and the outer world: a biography of Sebastian Franck.* P. Lang, 1994.

Paul L. Maier, *Caspar Schwenckfeld on the Person and Work of Christ: A Study of Schwenckfeldian Theology at Its Core.* Van Gorcum, 1959.

R. Emmet McLaughlin, *Caspar Schwenckfeld, Reluctant Radical: His Life to 1540.* Yale University Press, 1986.

R. Emmet McLaughlin, *Freedom of Spirit, Social Privilege, and Religious Dissent: Caspar Schwenckfeld and the Schwenckfelders.* V. Koerner, 1996.

Gerrit Voogt, *Constraint on Trial: Dirk Volckertsz Coornhert and Religious Freedom.* Truman State University Press, 2000.

Collections of Essays

Jeremy M. Bergen, Paul G. Doerksen, and Karl Koop, eds., *Creed and Conscience: Essays in Honour of A. James Reimer.* Pandora Press, 2007.

Gerald R. Brunk, ed., *Menno Simons, a Reappraisal: Essays in Honor of Irvin B. Horst.* Eastern Mennonite College, 1992.

Walter Klaassen, ed., *Anabaptism Revisited: Essays on Anabaptist/Mennonite Studies in Honor of C. J. Dyck.* Herald Press, 1992.

Werner O. Packull and Geoffrey L. Dipple, eds., *Radical Reformation Studies: Essays Presented to James M. Stayer.* Ashgate, 1999.

C. Arnold Snyder, ed., *Commoners and Community: Essays in Honour of Werner O. Packull.* Pandora Press, 2002.

CHAPTER TWELVE
Guides

Donald K. McKim, ed., *Cambridge Companion to John Calvin.* Cambridge University Press, 2004.

Herman J. Selderhuis, ed., *The Calvin Handbook.* Eerdmans, 2009.

Calvin: Biography

William J. Bouwsma, *John Calvin: A Sixteenth Century Portrait*. Oxford University Press, 1988.

Bernard Cottret, *Calvin: A Biography*. Eerdmans, 2000.

Alexandre Ganoczy, *The Young Calvin*. Westminster Press, 1987.

Bruce Gordon, *Calvin*. Yale University Press, 2009.

Alister McGrath, A *Life of John Calvin: A Study in the Shaping of Western Culture*. Blackwell, 1990.

Michael A. Mullett, *John Calvin*. Routledge, 2011.

T. H. L. Parker, *John Calvin: A Biography*. Westminster Press, 1975.

Calvin: Thought and Theology

Irena Backus and Philip Benedict, eds., *Calvin and His Influence, 1509–2009*. Oxford University Press, 2011.

Jon Balserak, *Establishing the Remnant Church in France: Calvin's Lectures on the Minor Prophets, 1556–1559*. E. J. Brill, 2011.

Karl Barth, *The Theology of John Calvin*. Eerdmans, 1995.

Jean-Daniel Benoit, *Calvin in His Letters: A Study of Calvin's Pastoral Counseling*. Sutton Courtenay Press, 1991.

André Biéler, *The Social Humanism of Calvin*. John Knox Press, 1964.

J. Todd Billings, *Calvin, Participation, and the Gift: The Activity of Believers in Union with Christ*. Oxford University Press, 2007.

J. Todd Billings and I. John Hesselink, eds., *Calvin's Theology and Its Reception*. Westminster/John Knox Press, 2012.

Quirinus Breen, *John Calvin: A Study in French Humanism*. Archon Books, 1968.

Julie Canlis, *Calvin's Ladder: A Spiritual Theology of Ascent and Ascension*. Eerdmans, 2010.

James L. Codling, *Calvin: Ethics, Eschatology, and Education*. Cambridge Scholars, 2010.

Edward A. Dowey Jr., *The Knowledge of God in Calvin's Theology*, 3rd ed. Eerdmans, 1994.

William A. Dyrness, *Reformed Theology and Visual Culture: The Protestant Imagination from Calvin to Edwards*. Cambridge University Press, 2004.

Stephen Edmondson, *Calvin's Christology*. Cambridge University Press, 2004.

Brannon Ellis, *Calvin, Classical Trinitarianism, and the Aseity of the Son*. Oxford University Press, 2012.

Christopher Elwood, *The Body Broken: The Calvinist Doctrine of the Eucharist and the Symbolization of Power*. Oxford University Press, 1998.

Timothy George, ed., *John Calvin and the Church: A Prism of Reform*. Westminster/John Knox Press, 1990.

B. A. Gerrish, *Grace and Gratitude: The Eucharistic Theology of John Calvin*. Fortress Press, 1993.

Basil Hall, *John Calvin: Humanist and Theologian*. London Historical Association, 1967.

Ralph C. Hancock, *Calvin and the Foundations of Modern Politics*. Cornell University Press, 1989.

Paul Helm, *Calvin at the Centre*. Oxford University Press, 2010.

Paul Helm, *John Calvin's Ideas*. Oxford University Press, 2005.

R. Ward Holder, *John Calvin and the Grounding of Interpretation: Calvin's First Commentaries*. E. J. Brill, 2006.

Arnold Huijgen, *Divine Accommodation in John Calvin's Theology*. Vandenhoeck & Ruprecht, 2011.

Serene Jones, *Calvin and the Rhetoric of Piety*. Westminster/John Knox Press, 1995.

Anthony N. S. Lane, *John Calvin: Student of the Church Fathers*. T & T Clark, 1999.

Daniel Y. K. Lee, *The Holy Spirit as Bond in Calvin's Thought*. Peter Lang, 2011.

Peter A. Lillback, *The Binding of God: Calvin's Role in the Development of Covenant Theology*. Baker Book House, 2001.

Gerard Mannion and Eduardus Van der Borght, eds., *John Calvin's Ecclesiology: Ecumenical Perspectives*. T & T Clark, 2011.

Kilian McDonnell, *John Calvin, the Church, and the Eucharist*. Princeton University Press, 1967.

Elsie Anne McKee, *John Calvin on the Diaconate and Liturgical Almsgiving*. Droz, 1984.

Donald McKim, ed., *Calvin and the Bible*. Cambridge University Press, 2006.

Richard A. Muller, *After Calvin: Studies in the Development of a Theological Tradition*. Oxford University Press, 2003.

Richard A. Muller, *The Unaccommodated Calvin: Studies in the Foundation of a Theological Tradition*. Oxford University Press, 2000.

Wilhelm Niesel, *The Theology of Calvin*. Westminster Press, 1956.

T. H. L. Parker, *Calvin: An Introduction to His Thought*. Nashville: Westminster/John Knox Press, 1995.

T. H. L. Parker, *The Oracles of God: An Introduction to the Preaching of John Calvin*. T & T Clark, 2002.

Charles Partee, *Calvin and Classical Philosophy*. E. J. Brill, 1977.

Charles Partee, *The Theology of John Calvin*. Westminster/John Knox Press, 2008.

Barbara Pitkin, *What Pure Eyes Could See: Calvin's Doctrine of Faith in Its Exegetical Context*. Oxford University Press, 1999.

Paul Rorem, *Calvin and Bullinger on the Lord's Supper*. Grove Books, 1989.

Antonio Rotondò, *Calvin and the Italian Anti-Trinitarians*. Foundation for Reformation Research, 1968.

David C. Steinmetz, *Calvin in Context*. Oxford University Press, 1995.

George Stroup, *Calvin*. Abingdon Press, 2009.

Thomas F. Torrance, *Calvin's Doctrine of Man*. Lutterworth Press, 1949.

Thomas F. Torrance, *The Hermeneutics of John Calvin*. Edinburgh: Scottish Academic Press, 1988.

Henk van den Belt, ed., *Restoration Through Redemption: John Calvin Revisited*. E. J. Brill, 2013.

Willem van't Spijker, *Calvin: A Brief Guide to His Life and Thought*. Westminster/John Knox Press, 2009.

Jason Van Vliet, *Children of God: The Imago Dei in John Calvin and His Context*. Vandenhoeck & Ruprecht, 2009.

Ronald Wallace, *Calvin's Doctrine of the Word and Sacrament*. Eerdmans, 1957.

François Wendel, *Calvin: Origins and Development of His Religious Thought (1963)*. Labyrinth Press, 1987.

Randall C. Zachman, *Image and Word in the Theology of John Calvin.* University of Notre Dame Press, 2009.

Randall C. Zachman, *John Calvin as Teacher, Pastor, and Theologian.* Baker Academic, 2006.

Randall C. Zachman, *Reconsidering John Calvin.* Cambridge University Press, 2012.

Calvin: Geneva and the World

Willem Balke, *Calvin and the Anabaptist Radicals.* Eerdmans, 1981.

Philip Benedict, *Christ's Churches Purely Reformed: A Social History of Calvinism.* Yale University Press, 2004.

F. D. Blackly, ed., *Calvin and the Libertines of Geneva.* Clarke, Irwin 1968.

Michael W. Bruening, *Calvinism's First Battleground Conflict and Reform in the Pays de Vaud, 1528–1559.* Springer, 2006.

Carlos M. N. Eire, *War Against the Idols: The Reformation of Worship from Erasmus to Calvin.* Cambridge University Press, 1986.

Jill Fehleison, *Boundaries of Faith: Catholics and Protestants in the Diocese of Geneva.* Truman State University Press, 2010.

R. T. Kendall, *Calvin and English Calvinism to 1649.* Oxford University Press, 1979.

Robert M. Kingdon, *Adultery and Divorce in Calvin's Geneva.* Harvard University Press, 1995.

Robert M. Kingdon, *Geneva and the Coming of the Wars of Religion in France, 1555–1563.* Droz, 1956.

Robert M. Kingdon, Thomas A. Lambert, and Isabella M. Watt, eds., *Registers of the Consistory of Geneva in the Time of Calvin.* Eerdmans, 2000.

Scott M. Manetsch, *Calvin's Company of Pastors: Pastoral Care and the Emerging Reformed Church, 1536–1609.* Oxford University Press, 2012.

John T. McNeill, *The History and Character of Calvinism.* Oxford University Press, 1954.

E. William Monter, *Calvin's Geneva.* R. E. Krieger, 1975.

William G. Naphy, *Calvin and the Consolidation of the Genevan Reformation.* Westminster/John Knox Press, 2003.

Heiko A. Oberman, *John Calvin and the Reformation of the Refugees.* Droz, 2009.

Jeannine E. Olson, *Calvin and Social Welfare: Deacons and the* Bourse française. Susquehanna University Press, 1989.

Andrew Pettegree, Alastair Duke, and Gillian Lewis, eds., *Calvinism in Europe, 1540–1620.* Cambridge University Press, 1997.

Keith Randell, *John Calvin and the Later Reformation.* Hodder & Stoughton, 1990.

W. Stanford Reid, *John Calvin: His Influence in the Western World.* Zondervan Publishing, 1982.

John Witte Jr., *Sex, Marriage, and Family Life in John Calvin's Geneva.* Eerdmans, 2005.

Theodore Bèze, Guillaume Farel, Pierre Viret: Life and Work

Irena Backus, *Reformed Roots of the English New Testament: The Influence of Theodore Beza on the English New Testament.* Pickwick Press, 1980.

Henry Martyn Baird, *Theodore Beza: The Counsellor of the French Reformation, 1519–1605.* B. Franklin, 1970.

John S. Bray, *Theodore Beza's Doctrine of Predestination*. De Graaf, 1975.

Henri Heyer, *Guillaume Farel: An Introduction to His Theology*. E. Mellen Press, 1990.

Robert M. Kingdon, *Geneva and the Consolidation of the French Protestant Movement*. University of Wisconsin Press, 1967.

Jan Krans, *Beyond What Is Written: Erasmus and Beza as Conjectural Critics of the New Testament*. E. J. Brill, 2006.

Robert Dean Linder, *The Political Ideas of Pierre Viret*. Droz, 1964.

Jeffrey Mallinson, *Faith, Reason, and Revelation in Theodore Beza*. Oxford University Press, 2003.

Scott M. Manetsch, *Theodore Beza and the Quest for Peace in France, 1562–1598*. E. J. Brill, 2000.

Tadataka Maruyama, *The Ecclesiology of Theodore Beza*. Droz, 1978.

Jill Raitt, *The Eucharistic Theology of Theodore Beza*. American Academy of Religion, 1972.

Shawn D. Wright, *Our Sovereign Refuge: The Pastoral Theology of Theodore Beza*. Paternoster, 2004.

Jason Zuidema and Theodore Van Raalte, *Early French Reform: The Theology and Spirituality of Guillaume Farel*. Ashgate, 2011.

CHAPTER THIRTEEN

Surveys

G. W. Bernard, *The Late Medieval English Church: Vitality and Vulnerability Before the Break with Rome*. Yale University Press, 2012.

Susan Brigden, *New Worlds, Lost Worlds: The Rule of the Tudors, 1485–1603*. Viking, 2000.

Patrick Collinson and Polly Ha, eds., *The Reception of Continental Reformation in Britain*. Oxford University Press, 2010.

Claire Cross, *Church and People, 1450–1660: The Triumph of the Laity in the English Church*. Fontana, 1976.

A. G. Dickens, *The English Reformation*, 2nd ed. Pennsylvania State University Press, 1991.

Eamon Duffy, *Saints, Sacrilege and Sedition: Religion and Conflict in the Tudor Reformations*. Bloomsbury, 2012.

Eamon Duffy, *The Stripping of the Altars: Traditional Religion in England, 1400–1580*. Yale University Press, 1992.

John Guy, *Tudor England*. Oxford University Press, 1988.

Christopher Haigh, *English Reformations: Religion, Politics, and Society Under the Tudors*. Oxford University Press, 1993.

Felicity Heal, *The Reformation in Britain and Ireland*. Oxford University Press, 2003.

Norman L. Jones, *The English Reformation: Religion and Cultural Adaptation*. Blackwell, 2002.

Diarmaid MacCulloch, *The Later Reformation in England, 1547–1603*. St. Martin's, 1990.

Peter Marshall, *Reformation England, 1480–1642*. Oxford University Press, 2003.

Diana Newton, *Papists, Protestants, and Puritans, 1559–1714*. Cambridge University Press, 1998.

J. J. Scarisbrick, *The Reformation and the English People*. Blackwell, 1984.

Ethan H. Shagan, *Popular Politics and the English Reformation*. Cambridge University Press, 2003.

Robert Tittler and Norman Jones, eds., *A Companion to Tudor Britain*. Blackwell, 2004.

Nicholas Tyacke, *England's Long Reformation, 1500–1800*. UCL Press, 1998.

Henry VIII

G. W. Bernard, *The King's Reformation: Henry VIII and the Remaking of the English Church.* Yale University Press, 2005.

J. A. Guy, *Henry VIII: The Quest for Fame.* Allen Lane, 2014.

David Knowles, *Bare Ruined Choirs: The Dissolution of the English Monasteries.* Cambridge University Press, 1976.

D. M. Loades, *Henry VIII Court, Church and Conflict.* National Archives, 2007.

Diarmaid MacCulloch, *The Reign of Henry VIII: Politics, Policy, and Piety.* St. Martin's Press, 1995.

Peter Marshall, *Religious Identities in Henry VIII's England.* Aldershot: Ashgate, 2006.

Peter Marshall and Alec Ryrie, eds., *The Beginnings of English Protestantism.* Cambridge University Press, 2002.

Richard Rex, *Henry VIII and the English Reformation*, 2nd ed. Palgrave Macmillan, 2006.

Alec Ryrie, *The Gospel and Henry VIII: Evangelicals in the Early English Reformation.* Cambridge University Press, 2003.

J. J. Scarisbrick, *Henry VIII.* Yale University Press, 1997.

David Starkey, *Henry: Virtuous Prince.* Harper, 2008.

David Starkey, *Six Wives: The Queens of Henry VIII.* Chatto & Windus, 2003.

Greg Walker, *Persuasive Fictions: Faction, Faith, and Political Culture in the Reign of Henry VIII.* Ashgate, 1996.

L. E. C. Wooding, *Henry VIII.* Routledge, 2009.

Edward VI

Stephen Alford, *Edward VI, the Last Boy King.* Allen Lane, 2014.

Stephen Alford, *Kingship and Politics in the Reign of Edward VI.* Cambridge University Press, 2002.

Barrett L. Beer, *Rebellion and Riot: Popular Disorder in England During the Reign of Edward VI.* Kent State University Press, 2005.

Hester W. Chapman, *The Last Tudor King: A Study of Edward VI.* Jonathan Cape, 1958.

Catharine Davies, *A Religion of the Word: The Defence of the Reformation in the Reign of Edward VI.* Manchester University Press. 2002.

W. K. Jordan, *Edward VI: The Young King.* Allen & Unwin, 1968.

Jennifer Loach, *Edward VI.* Yale University Press, 2002.

Jennifer Loach, *Protector Somerset: A Reassessment.* Headstart History, 1994.

David Loades, *The Reign of King Edward VI.* Headstart History, 1994.

Diarmaid MacCulloch, *The Boy King: Edward VI and the Protestant Reformation.* St. Martin's Press, 1999.

Chris Skidmore, *Edward VI: The Lost King of England.* St. Martin's Press. 2007.

Mary I

Susan Doran and Thomas S. Freeman, eds., *Mary Tudor: Old and New Perspectives.* Palgrave Macmillan, 2011.

Eamon Duffy, *Fires of Faith: Catholic England Under Mary Tudor*. Yale University Press, 2009.

Eamon Duffy and David Loades, eds., *The Church of Mary Tudor*. Burlington: Ashgate, 2005.

John Edwards, *Mary I: England's Catholic Queen*. Yale University Press, 2011.

John Edwards and Ronald Truman, eds., *Reforming Catholicism in the England of Mary Tudor: The Achievement of Friar Bartolomé Carranza*. Ashgate, 2005.

Jennifer Loach, "Mary Tudor and the Re-Catholicisation." *History Today* (November 1994): 16–22.

David Loades, *Mary Tudor: A Life*. Basil Blackwell,1989.

David Loades, *The Reign of Mary Tudor: Politics, Government, and Religion in England, 1553–58*. Longman, 1991.

Rosalind K. Marshall, *Mary I*. HMSO, 1993.

Linda Porter, *The First Queen of England: The Myth of Bloody Mary*. St. Martin's, 2008.

Judith M. Richards, *Mary Tudor*. Routledge, 2008.

Robert Tittler and Judith Richards, *The Reign of Mary I*, 3rd ed. Routledge, 2014.

Elizabeth I

Jessie Childs, *God's Traitors: Terror and Faith in Elizabethan England*. Bodley Head, 2014.

Patrick Collinson, *The Birthpangs of Protestant England*. St. Martin's, 1988.

Claire Cross, *The Elizabethan Religious Settlement*. Headstart History, 1992.

Susan Doran, *Elizabeth I and Religion, 1558–1603*. Routledge, 1994.

Christopher Durston and Jacqueline Eales, eds., *The Culture of English Puritanism, 1560–1700*. St. Martin's, 1996.

Christopher Haigh, *Elizabeth I*. Longman, 2001.

William Haugaard, *Elizabeth and the English Reformation*. Cambridge University Press,1968.

Norman Jones, *The Birth of the Elizabethan Age*. Blackwell, 1993.

K. J. Kesselring, *The Northern Rebellion of 1569*. Palgrave Macmillan, 2007.

Peter Lake, *Moderate Puritans and the Elizabethan Church*. Cambridge University Press, 2004.

Peter Lake and Michael Questier, eds., *Conformity and Orthodoxy in the English Church, 1560–1660*. Boydell Press, 2000.

Carole Levin, *The Reign of Elizabeth I*. Palgrave, 2002.

David Loades, *Elizabeth I*. Hambledon and London, 2003.

Judith Maltby, *Prayer Book and People in Elizabethan and Early Stuart England*. Cambridge University Press, 1998.

D. M. Palliser, *The Age of Elizabeth: England Under the Later Tudors, 1547–1603*, 2nd ed. Longman, 1992.

Benton Rain Patterson, *With the Heart of a King: Elizabeth I of England, Philip II of Spain, and the Fight for a Nation's Soul and Crown*. St. Martin's Press, 2007.

Michael C. Questier, *Conversion, Politics and Religion in England, 1580–1625*. Cambridge University Press, 1996.

Judith M. Richards, *Elizabeth I*. Routledge, 2012.

Susan Ronald, *Heretic Queen: Queen Elizabeth I and the Wars of Religion*. St. Martin's, 2012.

Catholics

John Bossy, *The English Catholic Community, 1570–1850*. Darton, 1979.

Ronald Corthell, *Catholic Culture in Early Modern England*. University of Notre Dame Press, 2007.

Victor Houliston, *Catholic Resistance in Elizabethan England*. Ashgate 2007.

Lisa McClain, *Lest We Be Damned: Practical Innovation and Lived Experience Among Catholics in Protestant England, 1559–1642*. Routledge, 2004.

Arnold Pritchard, *Catholic Loyalism in Elizabethan England*. University of North Carolina Press, 1979.

Michael Questier, *Catholicism and Community in Early Modern England*. Cambridge University Press, 2006.

Ethan Shagan, *Catholics and the "Protestant Nation": Religious Politics and Identity in Early Modern England*. Manchester University Press, 2005.

Alexandra Walsham, *Church Papists: Catholicism, Conformity, and Confessional Polemic in Early Modern England*. Boydell Press, 1993.

Lucy E. C. Wooding, *Rethinking Catholicism in Reformation England*. Clarendon Press, 2000.

Puritans

Francis J. Bremer, *Puritanism: A Very Short Introduction*. Oxford University Press, 2009.

John Coffey and Paul C. H. Lim, eds., *The Cambridge Companion to Puritanism*. Cambridge University Press, 2008.

M. M. Knappen, *Tudor Puritanism: A Chapter in the History of Idealism*. University of Chicago Press, 1966.

John Morgan, *Godly Learning: Puritan Attitudes Towards Reason, Learning, and Education, 1560–1640*. Cambridge University Press, 1986.

H. C. Porter, *Puritanism in Tudor England*. Macmillan, 1970.

John Henry Primus, *The Vestments Controversy: An Historical Study of the Earliest Tensions Within the Church of England in the Reigns of Edward VI and Elizabeth*. J. H. Kok, 1960.

Bernard Verkamp, *The Indifferent Mean: Adiaphorism in the English Reformation to 1554*. Ohio University Press, 1977.

Significant Individuals

Peter Ackroyd, *The Life of Thomas More*. Chatto & Windus, 1998.

J. Patrick Coby, *Thomas Cromwell: Machiavellian Statecraft and the English Reformation*. Lexington Books, 2009.

David Daniell, *William Tyndale: A Biography*. Yale University Press, 1994.

Michael Davies, *Cranmer's Godly Order: The Destruction of Catholicism Through Liturgical Change*. Augustine Publishing, 1976.

Maria Dowling, *Fisher of Men: The Life of John Fisher*. St. Martin's Press, 1999.

Geoffrey Elton, *Thomas Cromwell*. Headstart History, 1991.

Stella Fletcher, *Cardinal Wolsey: A Life in Renaissance Europe*. Continuum, 2009.

John Guy, *Thomas More*. Oxford University Press, 2000.

Peter Gwyn, *The King's Cardinal: The Rise and Fall of Cardinal Wolsey*. Barrie and Jenkins, 1990.

Robert Hutchinson, *Thomas Cromwell: The Rise and Fall of Henry VIII's Most Notorious Minister.* Weidenfeld & Nicolson, 2007.

David Loades, *Thomas Cranmer and the English Reformation.* Headstart History, 1991.

George M. Logan, ed., *The Cambridge Companion to Thomas More.* Cambridge University Press, 2011.

Diarmaid MacCulloch, *Thomas Cranmer.* Yale University Press, 1998.

Richard Marius, *Thomas More: A Biography.* Knopf, 1984.

Brian Moynahan, *God's Bestseller: William Tyndale, Thomas More, and the Writing of the English Bible.* St. Martin's Press, 2003.

Richard Rex, *The Theology of John Fisher.* Cambridge University Press, 1991.

Carol Schaefer, *Mary Queen of Scots.* Crossroad, 2002.

John D. Staines, *The Tragic Histories of Mary Queen of Scots, 1560–1690.* Ashgate, 2009.

Retha M. Warnicke, *Mary Queen of Scots.* Routledge, 2006.

Ralph S. Werrell, *The Roots of William Tyndale's theology.* J. Clarke, 2013.

Hanan Yoran, *Between Utopia and Dystopia: Erasmus, Thomas More, and the Humanist Republic of Letters.* Lexington Books, 2010.

Ireland

Elizabethanne Boran and Crawford Gribben, *Enforcing Reformation in Ireland and Scotland, 1550–1700.* Ashgate, 2006.

Karl Bottigheimer, "The Failure of the Reformation in Ireland: *Une question bien posée,*" *Journal of Ecclesiastical History* 36, no. 2 (1985): 196–207.

Ciaran Brady and R. Gillespie, eds., *Natives and Newcomers: Essays on the Making of Irish Colonial Society, 1534–1641.* Irish Academic Press, 1986.

Nicholas Canny, *Making Ireland British, 1580–1650.* Oxford University Press, 2001.

Nicholas Canny, "Why the Reformation Failed in Ireland: *Une question mal posée.*" *Journal of Ecclesiastical History* 30, no. 4 (1979): 423–450.

Stephen Ellis, *Ireland in the Age of the Tudors, 1447–1603: English Expansion and the End of Gaelic Rule.* Longman, 1998.

Alan Ford, *The Protestant Reformation in Ireland.* Portland: Four Courts Press, 1997.

W. Ian P. Hazlett, *The Reformation in Britain and Ireland: An Introduction.* T & T Clark, 2003.

Colm Lennon, *Sixteenth Century Ireland: The Incomplete Conquest.* Gill & Macmillan, 2005.

John McGurk, *The Elizabethan Conquest of Ireland: The 1590s Crisis.* Manchester University Press, 1997.

T. W. Moody, *A New History of Ireland: Volume III Early Modern Ireland, 1534–1691.* Clarendon Press, 1976.

James Murray, *Enforcing the English Reformation in Ireland: Clerical Resistance and Political Conflict in the Diocese of Dublin, 1534–1590.* Cambridge University Press, 2009.

Wales

Trevor Herbert and Gareth Elwyn Jones, eds., *Tudor Wales.* University of Wales Press, 1988.

Glanmor Williams, *Recovery, Reorientation, and Reformation: Wales, 1415–1642.* Clarendon Press, 1987.

Glanmor Williams, *The Reformation in Wales.* Headstart History, 1991.

Scotland

Ian B. Cowan, *The Scottish Reformation: Church and Society in Sixteenth-Century Scotland.* St. Martin's Press, 1982.

Jane Dawson, *The Politics of Religion in the Age of Mary, Queen of Scots: The Earl of Argyll and the Struggle for Britain and Ireland.* Cambridge University Press, 2002.

Gordon Donaldson, *The Scottish Reformation.* Cambridge University Press, 1960.

Audrey-Beth Fitch, *The Search for Salvation: Lay Faith in Scotland, 1480–1560.* John Donald, 2009.

Michael F. Graham, *The Uses of Reform: "Godly Discipline" and Popular Behavior in Scotland and Beyond, 1560–1610.* E. J. Brill, 1996.

Clare Kellar, *Scotland, England and the Reformation, 1523–1561.* Oxford University Press, 2003.

Alan R. MacDonald, *The Jacobean Kirk, 1567–1625: Sovereignty, Polity and Liturgy.* Ashgate, 1998.

Roger Mason, *John Knox and the British Reformation.* Ashgate, 1998.

Alec Ryrie, *The Origins of the Scottish Reformation.* Manchester University Press, 2006.

Margo Todd, *The Culture of Protestantism in Early Modern Scotland.* Yale University Press, 2002.

Popular Piety

Eamon Duffy, *Marking the Hours: English People and Their Prayers, 1240–1570.* Yale University Press, 2006.

Eamon Duffy, *The Voices of Morebath: Reformation and Rebellion in an English Village.* Yale University Press, 2001.

Elizabeth Evenden and Thomas S. Freeman, *Religion and the Book in Early Modern England: The Making of Foxe's "Book of Martyrs."* Cambridge University Press, 2011.

Ian Green, *Print and Protestantism in Early Modern England.* Oxford University Press, 2000.

John N. King, *Foxe's "Book of Martyrs" and Early Modern Print Culture.* Cambridge University Press, 2006.

Robert Lutton and Elisabeth Salter, eds., *Pieties in Transition: Religious Practices and Experiences, 1400–1640.* Ashgate, 2007.

Christopher Marsh, *Popular Religion in Sixteenth-Century England: Holding Their Peace.* St. Martin's Press, 1998.

Peter Marshall, *Beliefs and the Dead in Reformation England.* Oxford University Press, 2002.

Christine Peters, *Patterns of Piety: Women, Gender, and Religion in Late Medieval and Reformation England.* Cambridge University Press, 2003.

Doreen Rosman, *From Catholic to Protestant: Religion and the People in Tudor England.* UCL Press, 1996.

Keith Thomas, *Religion and the Decline of Magic.* Scribner, 1971.

Alexandra Walsham, *The Reformation of the Landscape: Religion, Identity, and Memory in Early Modern Britain and Ireland.* Oxford University Press, 2011.

Tessa Watt, *Cheap Print and Popular Piety, 1550–1640.* Cambridge University Press, 1996.

Robert Whiting, *The Blind Devotion of the People: Popular Religion and the English Reformation.* Cambridge University Press, 1989.

CHAPTER FOURTEEN
Surveys and Guides

Alexandra Bamji, Geert H. Janssen, and Mary Laven, eds., *The Ashgate Research Companion to the Counter-Reformation*. Ashgate, 2013.

Guy Bedouelle, *The Reform of Catholicism, 1480–1620*. Pontifical Institute of Mediaeval Studies, 2008.

Robert Bireley, *The Refashioning of Catholicism, 1450–1700: A Reassessment of the Counter Reformation*. Catholic University of America Press, 1999.

A. G. Dickens, *The Counter Reformation*. Harcourt, Brace & World, 1969.

H. Outram Evennett, *The Spirit of the Counter-Reformation*. University of Notre Dame Press, 1970.

Ronnie Po-chia Hsia, *The World of Catholic Renewal, 1540–1770*. Cambridge University Press, 1999.

Erwin Iserloh, Joseph Glazik, and Hubert Jedin, *Reformation and Counter Reformation*. Seabury Press, 1986.

Martin D. W. Jones, *The Counter Reformation: Religion and Society in Early Modern Europe*. Cambridge University Press, 1995.

Henry Kamen, *The Phoenix and the flame: Catalonia and the Counter Reformation*. Yale University Press, 1993.

Michael A. Mullett, *The Catholic Reformation*. Routledge, 1999.

John O'Malley, ed., *Catholicism in Early Modern History: A Guide to Research*. Center for Reformation Research, 1988.

John O'Malley, *Trent and All That: Renaming Catholicism in the Early Modern Era*. Harvard University Press, 2000.

Keith Randell, *The Catholic and Counter Reformations*. Hodder & Stoughton, 2000.

A. D. Wright, *Counter-Reformation: Catholic Europe and the Non-Christian World*. Ashgate, 2005.

Reforming Efforts

David Bagchi, *Luther's Earliest Opponents: Catholic Controversialists, 1518–1525*. Fortress Press, 1991.

Jennifer Mara DeSilva, ed., *Episcopal Reform and Politics in Early Modern Europe*. Truman State University Press, 2012.

Elisabeth G. Gleason, ed., *Reform Thought in Sixteenth-Century Italy*. Scholars Press, 1981.

Emily Michelson, *The Pulpit and the Press in Reformation Italy*. Harvard University Press, 2013.

Paul V. Murphy, *Ruling Peacefully: Cardinal Ercole Gonzaga and Patrician Reform in Sixteenth-Century Italy*. Catholic University of America Press, 2007.

Bert Roest, *Franciscan Literature of Religious Instruction Before the Council of Trent*. E. J. Brill, 2004.

Council of Trent

Giuseppe Alberigo, "The Council of Trent," in *Catholicism in Early Modern History: A Guide to Research*, ed. John O'Malley. Center for Reformation Research, 1988.

Erwin Iserloh, Josef Glazik, and Hubert Jedin, *History of the Church*. Vol. 5, *Reformation and Counter Reformation*. Seabury, 1980–1982.

Hubert Jedin, *History of the Council of Trent*. T. Nelson, 1957–1961. [This English translation covers two of the five volumes of the German original and is limited to the years 1545–1547.]

Hubert Jedin, *Papal legate at the Council of Trent, Cardinal Seripando*. B. Herder, 1947.

John O'Malley, *The Council of Trent: Myths, Misunderstandings, and Unintended Consequences*. Gregorian & Biblical Press, 2013.

John O'Malley, *Trent: What Happened at the Council*. Belknap Press, 2013.

Nelson H. Minnich, *Councils of the Catholic Reformation: Pisa I (1409) to Trent (1545–63)*. Ashgate Variorum, 2008.

Miles Pattenden, *Pius IV and the Fall of the Carafa: Nepotism and Papal Authority in Counter-Reformation Rome*. Oxford University Press, 2013.

Adam Patrick Robinson, *The Career of Cardinal Giovanni Morone (1509–1580): Between Council and Inquisition*. Ashgate, 2012.

Anthony David Wright, *The Early Modern Papacy: From the Council of Trent to the French Revolution, 1564–1789 A.D.* Longman, 2000.

Inquisition and Dissent

Salvatore Caponetto, *The Protestant Reformation in Sixteenth-Century Italy*. Thomas Jefferson University Press, 1999.

Elisabeth G. Gleason, ed., *Reform Thought in Sixteenth-Century Italy*. Scholars Press, 1981.

Paul F. Grendler, *The Roman Inquisition and the Venetian press, 1540–1605*. Princeton University Press, 1977.

Clive Griffen, *Journeymen-Printers, Heresy, and the Inquisition in Sixteenth-Century Spain*. Oxford University Press, 2005.

Alastair Hamilton, *Heresy and Mysticism in Sixteenth-Century Spain: The Alumbrados*. J. Clark, 1992.

Paul J. Hauben, *Three Spanish Heretics and the Reformation: Antonio del Corro, Cassiodoro de Reina, Cypriano de Valera*. Droz, 1967.

Gustav Henningsen, John Tedeschi, and Charles Amiel, *The Inquisition in Early Modern Europe: Studies on Sources and Methods*. Northern Illinois University Press, 1986.

Henry Kamen, *The Spanish Inquisition: A Historical Revision*, 4th ed. Yale University Press, 2014.

John Edward Longhurst, *Luther's Ghost in Spain, 1517–1546*. Coronado Press, 1969.

Kimberly Lynn, *Between Court and Confessional: The Politics of Spanish Inquisitors*. Cambridge University Press, 2013.

E. William Monter, *Frontiers of Heresy: The Spanish Inquisition from the Basque lands to Sicily*. Cambridge University Press, 2002.

Cullen Murphy, *God's Jury: The Inquisition and the Making of the Modern World*. Houghton Mifflin Harcourt, 2012.

Joseph Perez, *The Spanish Inquisition: A History*. Yale University Press, 2005.

Edward Peters, *Inquisition*. Free Press, 1988.

Ryan Prendergast, *Reading, Writing, and Errant Subjects in Inquisitorial Spain*. Ashgate, 2011.

Helen Rawlings, *The Spanish Inquisition.* Blackwell, 2006.

Lisa Vollendorf, *The Lives of Women: A New History of Inquisitional Spain.* Vanderbilt University Press, 2005.

CHAPTER FIFTEEN
Ritual

Simon Ditchfield, *Liturgy, Sanctity, and History in Tridentine Italy: Pietro Maria Campi and the Preservation of the Particular.* Cambridge University Press, 1995.

Susan C. Karant-Nunn, ed., *Varieties of Devotion in the Middle Ages and Renaissance.* Brepols, 2003.

Karin Maag and John D. Witvliet, eds., *Worship in Medieval and Early Modern Europe: Change and Continuity in Religious Practice.* University of Notre Dame Press, 2004.

Reinold Theisen, *Mass Liturgy and the Council of Trent.* St. John's University Press, 1965.

Miracles, Saints, and Mysticism

Gillian T. W. Ahlgren, *Teresa of Avila and the Politics of Sanctity.* Cornell University Press, 1996.

Jodi Bilinkoff, "The Many 'Lives' of Pedro de Ribadeneyra," *Renaissance Quarterly* 52, no. 1 (1999): 180–196.

Peter Burke, "How to Become a Counter-Reformation Saint," in *The Counter-Reformation: The Essential Readings*, ed. David Luebke, 129–142. Wiley-Blackwell, 1999.

Simon Ditchfield, "How Not to Be a Counter-Reformation Saint: The Attempted Canonization of Pope Gregory X, 1622–45," *Papers of the British School at Rome* 60 (1992): 379–422.

Thomas Dubay, *Fire Within: St. Teresa of Avila, St. John of the Cross, and the Gospel, on Prayer.* Ignatius Press, 1989.

Carlos M. N. Eire, "Early Modern Catholic Piety in Translation," in *Cultural Translation in Early Modern Europe*, ed. Peter Burke and R. Po-chia Hsia, 83–100. Cambridge University Press, 2007.

H. Outram Evennett, "Counter-Reformation Spirituality," in *The Counter-Reformation: The Essential Readings*, ed. David Luebke, 47–64. Wiley-Blackwell, 1999.

Craig Harline, *Miracles at the Jesus Oak: Histories of the Supernatural in Reformation Europe.* Yale University Press, 2011.

John M. Headley and John B. Tomaro, eds., *San Carlo Borromeo: Catholic Reform and Ecclesiastical Politics in the Second Half of the Sixteenth Century.* Folger Shakespeare Library, 1988.

Edward Howells, *John of the Cross and Teresa of Avila: Mystical Knowing and Selfhood.* Crossroad Publishing, 2002.

José C. Nieto, *Mystic, Rebel, Saint: A Study of St. John of the Cross.* Droz, 1979.

Terence O'Reilly, *From Ignatius Loyola to John of the Cross: Spirituality and Literature in Sixteenth-Century Spain.* Variorum, 1995.

Paolo Parigi, *The Rationalization of Miracles.* Cambridge University Press, 2012.

Godfrey E. Philips, *Loreto and the Holy House: Its History Drawn from Authentic Sources.* 1917; reprint, Kessinger Publishing, 2010.

Rady Roldán-Figueroa, *The Ascetic Spirituality of Juan de Avila.* E. J. Brill, 2010.

Carole Slade, *Teresa of Avila, Author of a Heroic Life.* University of California Press, 1995.

Philip M. Soergel, *Wondrous in His Saints: Counter-Reformation Propaganda in Bavaria.* University of California Press, 1993.

Peter M. Tyler, *St. John of the Cross.* Continuum, 2010.

Donald Weinstein and Rudolph M. Bell, *Saints and Society: The Two Worlds of Western Christendom, 1000–1700.* University of Chicago Press, 1982.

Confraternities

Christopher Black, *Italian Confraternities in the Sixteenth Century.* Cambridge University Press, 1989.

Christopher Black and Pamela Gravestock, eds., *Early Modern Confraternities in Europe and the Americas: International and Interdisciplinary Perspectives.* Ashgate, 2006.

Louis Chatêllier, *The Europe of the Devout: The Catholic Reformation and the Formation of a New Society.* Cambridge University Press, 1989.

David M. D'Andrea, *Civic Christianity in Renaissance Italy: The Hospital of Treviso, 1400–1530.* University of Rochester Press, 2007.

John Patrick Donnelly and Michael W. Maher, eds., *Confraternities and Catholic reform in Italy, France, and Spain.* Thomas Jefferson University Press, 1999.

Maureen Flynn, *Sacred Charity: Confraternities and Social Welfare in Spain, 1400–1700.* Cornell University Press, 1989.

Lance Gabriel Lazar, *Working in the Vineyard of the Lord: Jesuit Confraternities in Early Modern Italy.* University of Toronto Press, 2005.

Lorenzo Polizzotto, *Children of the Promise: The Confraternity of the Purification and the Socialization of Youths in Florence, 1427–1785.* Oxford University Press, 2004.

Nicholas Terpstra, ed., *The Politics of Ritual Kinship: Confraternities and Social Order in Early Modern Italy.* Cambridge University Press, 2000.

Nicholas Terpstra, Adriano Prosperi, and Stefania Pastore, eds., *Faith's Boundaries: Laity and Clergy in Early Modern Confraternities.* Brepols, 2012.

Susan Verdi Webster, *Art and Ritual in Golden Age Spain: Sevillian Confraternities and the Processional Sculpture of Holy Week.* Princeton University Press, 1998.

Barbara Wisch and Diane Cole Ahl, eds., *Confraternities and the Visual Arts in Renaissance Italy: Ritual, Spectacle, Image.* Cambridge University Press, 2000.

CHAPTER SIXTEEN

Secular Clergy

Joseph Bergin, *Cardinal de La Rochefoucauld, Leadership and Reform in the French Church.* Yale University Press, 1987.

Kathleen M. Comerford, *Ordaining the Catholic Reformation: Priests and Seminary Pedagogy in Fiesole, 1575–1675.* L. S. Olschki, 2001.

Kathleen M. Comerford, *Reforming Priests and Parishes: Tuscan Dioceses in the First Century of Seminary Education.* E. J. Brill, 2006.

John M. Headley and John B. Tomaro, eds., *San Carlo Borromeo: Catholic Reform and Ecclesiastical Politics in the Second Half of the Sixteenth Century.* Folger Shakespeare Library, 1988.

Regular Clergy

Louis Abelly, *The Life of the Venerable Servant of God Vincent de Paul: Founder and First Superior General of the Congregation of the Mission.* New City Press, 1993.

Jodi Bilinkoff, *The Avila of Saint Teresa.* Cornell University Press, 1989.

Philip Caraman, *Saint Angela: The Life of Angela Merici, Foundress of the Ursulines.* Farrar, Straus, 1964.

Maria Craciun and Elaine Fulton, eds., *Communities of Devotion: Religious Orders and Society in East Central Europe, 1450–1800.* Ashgate, 2011.

Leon Cristiani, *Saint Vincent de Paul, 1581–1660.* St. Paul Editions, 1977.

Father Cuthbert, O.S.F.C., *Capuchins: A Contribution to the History of the Counter-Reformation.* Longmans, Green, 1929.

Olier de Condren, *Priesthood in the Writings of the French School: Bérulle.* Catholic University of America Press, 1949.

Antonio Gallonio, *The Life of Saint Philip Neri.* Ignatius Press, 2005.

Paul Hanbridge, Melchior Pobladuta, and Gabe Lomas, *The Capuchin Reform a Franciscan Renaissance: A Portrait of Sixteenth Century Capuchin Life.* Media House, 2003.

Lady Amabel Kerr, *The Life of Cesare Cardinal Baronius of the Roman Oratory.* Art and Book, 1898.

Karen Liebreich, *Fallen Order: Intrigue, Heresy, and Scandal in the Rome of Galileo and Caravaggio.* Grove Press, 2004.

The Lives of St. Joseph Calasanctius, Founder of the Pious Schools, and of the Blessed Ippolito Galantini, Founder of the Congregation of Christian Doctrine. T. Richardson, 1850.

Thaddeus MacVicar, *Franciscan Spirituals and the Capuchin Reform.* Franciscan Institute, St. Bonaventure University, 1986.

Querciolo Mazzonis, *Spirituality, Gender, and the Self in Renaissance Italy: Angela Merici and the Company of St. Ursula.* Catholic University of America Press, 2007.

Charles de Montzey, *The Life of the Venerable John Eudes.* Thomas Richardson and Son, 1883.

Louis Ponnelle and Louis Bordet, *St. Philip Neri and the Roman Society of His Times.* Sheed & Ward, 1932.

Bernard Pujo, *Vincent de Paul, the Trailblazer.* University of Notre Dame Press, 2003.

Cyriac K. Pullapilly, *Caesar Baronius, Counter-Reformation Historian.* University of Notre Dame Press, 1975.

Mary Purcell, *The World of Monsieur Vincent.* Loyola University Press, 1989.

Peter-Thomas Rohrbach, *Journey to Carith: The Sources and Story of the Discalced Carmelites.* Institute of Carmelite Studies, 1966.

Paul Türks, *Philip Neri: The Fire of Joy.* T&T Clark, 1995.

Erik Varden, *Redeeming Freedom: The Principle of Servitude in Bérulle.* Pontificio Ateneo S. Anselmo, 2011.

Charles E. Williams, *French Oratorians and Absolutism, 1611–1641.* P. Lang, 1989.

A. D. Wright, *Federico Borromeo and Baronius: A Turning-Point in the Development of the Counter-Reformation Church.* Department of Italian Studies, University of Reading, 1974.

Wendy M. Wright, *Bond of Perfection: Jeanne de Chantal & François de Sales.* Paulist Press, 1985.

CHAPTER SEVENTEEN

Surveys

J. C. H. Aveling, *The Jesuits*. Stein & Day, 1982.

William V. Bangert, *A History of the Society of Jesus*. Institute of Jesuit Sources, 1986.

Manfred Barthel, *Jesuits: History & Legend of the Society of Jesus*. W. Morrow, 1984.

Heinrich Boehmer, *Jesuits: An Historical Study*. Gordon Press, 1975.

James Brodrick, *The Origin of the Jesuits*. 1940; reprint, Loyola University Press 1986.

James Brodrick, *The Progress of the Jesuits*. 1946; reprint, Loyola University Press, 1986.

Michael Foss, *The Founding of the Jesuits, 1540*. Wey Bright & Talley, 1966.

Christopher Hollis, *The History of the Jesuits*. Weidenfeld & Nicolson, 1968.

Jean Lacouture, *Jesuits: A Multibiography*. Basic Books, 1997.

David Mitchell, *The Jesuits: A History*. MacDonald, 1981.

John W. O'Malley, *The First Jesuits*. Harvard University Press, 1993.

John W. O'Malley, *Saints or Devils Incarnate? Studies in Jesuit History*. E. J. Brill, 2014.

Alain Woodrow, *The Jesuits: A Story of Power*. Geoffrey Chapman, 1995.

Thomas Worcester, ed., *The Cambridge Companion to the Jesuits*. Cambridge University Press, 2008.

Jonathan Wright, *God's Soldiers: Adventure, Politics, Intrigue, and Power: A History of the Jesuits*. Doubleday, 2004.

Jonathan Wright, *The Jesuits: Missions, Myths, and Histories*. Harper Perennial, 2005.

Education

John Atteberry and John Russell, eds., *Ratio Studiorum: Jesuit Education, 1540–1773*. John J. Burns Library, Boston College, 1999.

John J. Callahan, *Discovering a Sacred World: Ignatius Loyola's Spiritual Exercises and Its Influence on Education*. Regis University, 1997.

Christopher Chapple, ed., *The Jesuit Tradition in Education and Missions: A 450-Year Perspective*. University of Scranton Press, 1993.

Jean Dietz Moss, "The Rhetoric Course at the Collegio Romano in the Latter Half of the Sixteenth Century," *Rhetorica* 4 (Spring 1986): 137–151.

John W. Donohue, *Jesuit Education, an Essay on the Foundations of Its Idea*. Fordham University Press, 1963.

Vincent Duminuco, ed., *The Jesuit Ratio Studiorum*. Fordham University Press, 2000.

Allan P. Farrell, *The Jesuit Code of Liberal Education: Development and Scope of the Ratio Studiorum*. Bruce, 1938.

George Ganss, *Saint Ignatius' Idea of a Jesuit University*. Marquette University Press, 1956.

Oskar Garstein, *Rome and the Counter-Reformation in Scandinavia: Jesuit Educational Strategy, 1553–1622*. E. J. Brill, 1992.

Ladislaus Lukacs, *Church, Culture and Curriculum: Theology and Mathematics in the Jesuit Ratio Studiorum*. Saint Joseph's University Press, 1999.

Robert A. Maryks, *Saint Cicero and the Jesuits: The Influence of the Liberal Arts on the Adoption of Moral Probabalism*. Ashgate, 2008.

William J. O'Brien, ed., *Jesuit Education and the Cultivation of Virtue.* Georgetown University Press, 1990.

Clade Nicholas Pavur, *The Ratio Studiorum: The Official Plan for Jesuit Education.* Institute of Jesuit Sources, 2005.

Culture, Thought, Arts, and Sciences

Mordechai Feingold, *Jesuit Science and the Republic of Letters.* MIT Press, 2003.

Evonne Levy, *Propaganda and the Jesuit Baroque.* University of California Press, 2004.

Thomas M. McCoog, *The Mercurian Project: Forming Jesuit Culture, 1573–1580.* Institute of Jesuit Sources, 2004.

J. Michelle Molina, *To Overcome Oneself: The Jesuit Ethic and Spirit of Global Expansion, 1520–1767.* University of California Press, 2013.

John W. O'Malley and Gauvin Alexander Bailey, *The Jesuits and the Arts, 1540–1773.* St. Joseph's University Press, 2005.

John W. O'Malley, Gauvin Alexander Bailey, Steven Harris, and T. Frank Kennedy, eds., *The Jesuits: Cultures, Sciences, and the Arts, 1540–1773.* University of Toronto Press, 1999.

John W. O'Malley, Johann Bernhard Staudt, Gauvin Alexander Bailey, and Steven J. Harris, eds., *The Jesuits II: Cultures, Sciences, and the Arts, 1540–1773.* University of Toronto Press, 2006.

Ignatius Loyola

Philip Caraman, *Ignatius Loyola: A Biography of the Founder of the Jesuits.* Harper & Row, 1990.

Harvey D. Egan, *Ignatius Loyola the Mystic.* Michael Glazier, 1987.

Michael Ivens, *An Approach to Saint Ignatius of Loyola.* Way Books, Campion Hall, 2008.

John M. McManamon, *Text and Contexts of Ignatius Loyola's "Autobiography."* Fordham University Press, 2013.

W. W. Meissner, *Ignatius of Loyola: The Psychology of a Saint.* Yale University Press, 1992.

Mary Purcell, *The First Jesuit, St. Ignatius Loyola.* Newman Press, 1957.

André Ravier, *Ignatius of Loyola and the Founding of the Society of Jesus.* Ignatius Press, 1987.

J. Ignacio Tellechea Idígoras, *Ignatius of Loyola the Pilgrim Saint.* Loyola University Press, 1994.

The Spiritual Exercises

Frédéric Conrod, *Loyola's Greater Narrative: The Architecture of the Spiritual Exercises in Golden Age and Enlightenment Literature.* Peter Lang, 2008.

Robert E. McNally, *The Council of Trent, the Spiritual Exercises, and the Catholic Reform.* Fortress Press, 1970.

Prominent Jesuits

William V. Bangert, *Jerome Nadal, S.J., 1507–1580: Tracking the First Generation of Jesuits.* Loyola University Press, 1992.

Richard J. Blackwell, *Galileo, Bellarmine, and the Bible.* University of Notre Dame Press, 1991.

James Brodrick, *Robert Bellarmine, Saint and Scholar.* Burns & Oates, 1961.

James Brodrick, *Saint Peter Canisius.* Loyola University Press, 1962.

Cándido de Dalmases, *Francis Borgia: Grandee of Spain, Jesuit, Saint.* Institute of Jesuit Sources, 1991.

John P. Doyle and Victor M. Salas, eds., *Collected Studies on Francisco Suárez, S.J.* Leuven University Press, 2010.

Peter Godman, *The Saint as Censor: Robert Bellarmine Between Inquisition and Index.* Brill, 2000.

D. Scott Hendrickson, *Jesuit Polymath of Madrid: The Literary Enterprise of Juan Eusebio Nieremberg.* E. J. Brill, 2015.

Benjamin Hill and Henrik Lagerlund, eds., *The Philosophy of Francisco Suárez.* Oxford University Press, 2012.

José Pereira, *Suárez: Between Scholasticism and Modernity.* Marquette University Press, 2007.

Daniel Schwartz, ed., *Interpreting Suárez: Critical Essays.* Cambridge University Press, 2012.

Politics

Dauril Alden, *The Making of an Enterprise: The Society of Jesus in Portugal, Its Empire, and Beyond, 1540–1750.* Stanford University Press, 1996.

Robert Bireley, *Religion and Politics in the Age of the Counterreformation: Emperor Ferdinand II, William Lamormaini, S.J., and the Formation of Imperial Policy.* University of North Carolina Press, 1981.

Luke Clossey, *Salvation and Globalization in the Early Jesuit Missions.* Cambridge University Press, 2008.

Mordechai Feingold, ed., *The New Science and Jesuit Science: Seventeenth Century Perspectives.* Kluwer Academic Publishing, 2003.

Róisín Healy, *The Jesuit Specter in Imperial Germany.* Brill, 2003.

Harro Höpfl, *Jesuit Political Thought: The Society of Jesus and the State, 1540–1640.* Cambridge University Press, 2004.

Thomas M. McCoog, *The Society of Jesus in Ireland, Scotland, and England 1541–1588: "Our Way of Proceeding?"* E. J. Brill, 1996.

Honorio Muñoz, *Vitoria and War: A Study on the Second Reading On the Indians or On the Right of War "De juri belli."* Santo Tomas University Press, 1937.

Eric Nelson, *The Jesuits and the Monarchy: Catholic Reform and Political Authority in France 1590–1615.* Ashgate, 2005.

Robert E. Scully, *Into the Lion's Den: The Jesuit Mission in Elizabethan England and Wales, 1580–1603.* Institute of Jesuit Sources, 2011.

Stefania Tutino, *Empire of Souls: Robert Bellarmine and the Christian Commonwealth.* Oxford University Press, 2010.

Reijo Wilenius, *The Social and Political Theory of Francisco Suárez.* Suomalaisen Kirjallisuuden Kirjapaino, 1963.

CHAPTER EIGHTEEN

Surveys

Santa Arias and Raul Marrero-Fente, eds., *Coloniality, Religion, and the Law in the Early Iberian World.* Vanderbilt University Press, 2014.

C. R. Boxer, *The Church Militant and Iberian Expansion, 1440–1770*. Johns Hopkins University Press, 1978.

Jorge Cañizares-Esguerra, *Puritan Conquistadors: Iberianizing the Atlantic, 1550–1700*. Stanford University Press, 2006.

Daniel T. Reff, *Plagues, Priests, and Demons: Sacred Narratives and the Rise of Christianity in the Old World and the New*. Cambridge University Press, 2005.

Christianizing the Natives

Louise M. Burkhart, *The Slippery Earth: Nahua-Christian Moral Dialogue in Sixteenth-Century Mexico*. University of Arizona Press, 1989.

Fernando Cervantes, *The Devil in the New World: The Impact of Diabolism in New Spain*. Yale University Press, 1994.

Fernando Cervantes and Andrew Redden, eds., *Angels, Demons and the New World*. Cambridge University Press, 2013.

John Charles, *Allies at Odds: The Andean Church and Its Indigenous Agents, 1583–1671*. University of New Mexico Press, 2010.

Mark Z. Christensen, *Nahua and Maya Catholicisms: Texts and Religion in Colonial Central Mexico and Yucatan*. Stanford University Press, 2013.

Inga Clendinnen, *Ambivalent Conquests: Maya and Spaniard in Yucatan, 1517–1570*. Cambridge University Press, 2003.

Viviana Díaz Balsera, *The Pyramid Under the Cross: Franciscan Discourses of Evangelization and the Nahua Christian Subject in Sixteenth-Century Mexico*. University of Arizona Press, 2005.

John D. Early, *Maya and Catholic Cultures in Crisis*. University Press of Florida, 2012.

John D. Early, *Maya and Catholicism: An Encounter of Worldviews*. University Press of Florida, 2006.

Nicholas Griffiths and Fernando Cervantes, eds., *Spiritual Encounters: Interactions Between Christianity and Native Religions in Colonial America*. University of Birmingham Press, 1999.

Serge Gruzinski, *Man-Gods in the Mexican Highlands: Indian Power and Colonial Society, 1550–1800*. Stanford University Press, 1989.

Susanne Klaus, *Uprooted Christianity: The Preaching of the Christian Doctrine in Mexico Based on Franciscan Sermons of the 16th Century Written in Nahuatl*. A. Saurwein, 1999.

J. Jorge Klor de Alva, "Spiritual Conflict and Accommodation in New Spain: Toward a Typology of Aztec Responses to Christianity," in *The Inca and Aztec States, 1400–1800: Anthropology and History*, ed. George A. Collier, Renato I. Rosaldo, and John D. Wirth, 345–366. Academic Press, 1982.

Jaime Lara, *Christian Texts for Aztecs: Art and Liturgy in Colonial Mexico*. University of Notre Dame Press, 2008.

Jaime Lara, *City, Temple, Stage: Eschatological Architecture and Liturgical Theatrics in New Spain*. University of Notre Dame Press, 2004.

Sabine MacCormack, *Religion in the Andes: Vision and Imagination in Early Colonial Peru*. Princeton University Press, 1991.

Kenneth Mills, *Evil Lost to View? An Investigation of Post-Evangelisation Andean Religion in Mid-Colonial Peru*. Institute of Latin American Studies, University of Liverpool, 1994.

Kenneth Mills, *Idolatry and Its Enemies: Colonial Andean Religion and Extirpation, 1640–1750.* Princeton University Press, 1997.

David Tavárez, *Invisible War: Indigenous Devotions, Discipline, and Dissent in Colonial Mexico.* Stanford University Press, 2011.

Franciscan Missions

Robert H. Jackson and Edward Castillo, *Indians, Franciscans, and Spanish Colonization: The Impact of the Mission System on California Indians.* University of New Mexico Press, 1995.

John Leddy Phelan, *The Millennial Kingdom of the Franciscans in the New World.* Cambridge University Press, 2013.

Kent G. Lightfoot, *Indians, Missionaries, and Merchants: The Legacy of Colonial Encounters on the California Frontiers.* University of California Press, 2005.

John J. O'Hagan, *Lands Never Trodden: The Franciscans and the California Missions.* Caxton Press, 2013.

Gregory Orfalea, *Journey to the Sun: Junipero Serra's Dream and the Founding of California.* Scribner, 2014.

Craig H. Russell, *From Serra to Sancho: Music and Pageantry in the California Missions.* Oxford University Press, 2009.

James A. Sandos, *Converting California Indians and Franciscans in the Missions.* Yale University Press, 2004.

Antonine Severin Tibesar, Victor Andres Belaunde, and Alexander Wyse, *Franciscan Beginnings in Colonial Peru.* Academy of American Franciscan History, 1953.

Ursuline Missions

Anya Mali, *Mystic in the New World: Marie de l'Incarnation.* Brill, 1996.

Denis Mahoney, *Marie of the Incarnation: Mystic and Missionary.* Doubleday & Co., 1964.

Natalie Zemon Davis, *Women on the Margins: Three Seventeenth-Century Lives.* Harvard University Press, 1995.

Jesuit Missions

Takao Abé, *The Jesuit Mission to New France: A New Interpretation in the Light of the Earlier Jesuit Experience in Japan.* E. J. Brill, 2011.

Carole Blackburn, *Harvest of Souls: The Jesuit Missions and Colonialism in North America, 1632–1650.* McGill-Queen's University Press, 2000.

Liam Brockey, *Journey to the East: The Jesuit Mission to China, 1579–1724.* Belknap Press of Harvard University Press, 2008.

Lucien Campeau, *Gannentaha: First Jesuit Mission to the Iroquois, 1653–1665.* William Lonc, 2005.

Lucien Campeau, *The Jesuit Missions in Acadia and New France, 1616–1634.* Steve Catlin, 2005.

Philip Caraman, *The Jesuit Republic of Paraguay.* Incorporated Catholic Truth Society, 1986.

Philip Caraman, *Lost Paradise: An Account of the Jesuits in Paraguay, 1607–1768.* Sidgwick and Jackson, 1975.

Nicholas P. Cushner, *Why Have You Come Here? The Jesuits and the First Evangelization of Native America.* Oxford University Press, 2006.

Joseph A. Gagliano and Charles E. Ronan, eds., *Jesuit Encounters in the New World: Jesuit Chroniclers, Geographers, Educators, and Missionaries in the Americas, 1549–1767.* Institutum Historicum S.I., 1997.

Barbara Ganson, *The Guaraní Under Spanish Rule in the Río de la Plata.* Stanford University Press, 2003.

Allan Greer, *Mohawk Saint: Catherine Tekakwitha and the Jesuits.* Oxford University Press, 2005.

Ana Carolina Hosne, *Jesuit Missions to China and Peru, 1570–1610: Expectations and Appraisals of Expansionism.* Routledge, 2013.

William F. Jaenike, *Black Robes in Paraguay.* Kirk House, 2008.

Tracy Neal Leavelle, *Catholic Calumet: Colonial Conversions in French and Indian North America.* University of Pennsylvania Press, 2012.

Luis Martín, *The Intellectual Conquest of Peru: The Jesuit College of San Pablo, 1568–1767.* Fordham University Press, 1968.

Bronwen Catherine McShea, "Cultivating Empire Through Print: The Jesuit Strategy for New France and the Parisian 'Relations' of 1632 to 1673," PhD diss. Yale University, 2011.

Andrés I. Prieto, *Missionary Scientists: Jesuit Science in Spanish South America, 1570–1810.* Vanderbilt University Press, 2011.

Frederick J. Reiter, *They Built Utopia: The Jesuit Missions in Paraguay, 1610–1768.* Scripta Humanistica, 1994.

Brazil

John Hemming, *Red Gold: The Conquest of the Brazilian Indians.* Harvard University Press, 1978.

William T. Reinhard, *The Evangelization of Brazil Under the Jesuits (1549–1568): An Evaluation.* Pontifical Gregorian University, 1969.

Eduardo Viveiros de Castro, *Inconstancy of the Indian Soul: The Encounter of Catholics and Cannibals in 16th-Century Brazil.* Prickly Paradigm Press, 2011.

Slavery

Massimo Livi Bacci, *El Dorado in the Marshes: God, Slaves and Souls Between the Andes and the Amazon.* Polity, 2010.

Arnold Lunn, *A Saint in the Slave Trade: Peter Claver, 1581–1654.* Sheed & Ward, 1947.

Margaret M. Olsen, *Slavery and Salvation in Colonial Cartagena de Indias.* University Press of Florida, 2004.

H. Henrietta Stockel, *Salvation Through Slavery: Chiricahua Apaches and Priests on the Spanish Colonial Frontier.* University of New Mexico Press, 2008.

John Thornton, *Africa and Africans in the Making of the Atlantic World,* 2nd ed. Cambridge University Press, 1998.

Angel Valtierra, *Peter Claver, Saint of the Slaves.* Newman Press, 1960.

Natives and Human Rights

Rolena Adorno, *The Intellectual Life of Bartolomé de Las Casas.* Graduate School of Tulane University, 1991.

Daniel Castro, *Another Face of Empire: Bartolomé de Las Casas, Indigenous Rights, and Ecclesiastical Imperialism.* Duke University Press, 2007.

Lawrence A. Clayton, *Bartolomé de Las Casas: A Biography.* Cambridge University Press, 2012.

Lawrence A. Clayton, *Bartolomé de Las Casas and the Conquest of the Americas.* Wiley-Blackwell, 2011.

Lewis Hanke, *Aristotle and the American Indians: A Study in Race Prejudice in the Modern World.* Indiana University Press, 1970.

Anthony Pagden, *The Fall of Natural Man: The American Indian and the Origins of Comparative Ethnology.* Cambridge University Press, 1982.

Elias Sevilla-Casas, ed., *Western Expansion and Indigenous Peoples: The Heritage of Las Casas.* Mouton, 1977.

David M. Traboulay, *Columbus and Las Casas: The Conquest and Christianization of America, 1492–1566.* University Press of America, 1994.

Paul S. Vickery, *Bartolomé de Las Casas: Great Prophet of the Americas.* Paulist Press, 2006.

Saints and Colonial Catholicism

Giuliana Cavallini, *St. Martín de Porres, Apostle of Charity.* B. Herder, 1963.

Alex García-Rivera, *St. Martín de Porres: The "Little Stories" and the Semiotics of Culture.* Orbis Books, 1995.

Frank Graziano, *Cultures of Devotion: Folk Saints of Spanish America.* Oxford University Press, 2007.

Frank Graziano, *Wounds of Love: The Mystical Marriage of Saint Rose of Lima.* Oxford University Press, 2004.

Allan Greer and Jodi Bilinkoff, *Colonial Saints: Discovering the Holy in the Americas, 1500–1800.* Routledge, 2003.

Francis Johnston, *The Wonder of Guadalupe: The Origin and Cult of the Miraculous Image of the Blessed Virgin in Mexico.* Augustine Publishing, 1981.

John F. Moffitt, *Our Lady of Guadalupe: The Painting, the Legend and the Reality.* McFarland & Co., 2006.

Martin Austin Nesvig, *Ideology and Inquisition: The World of the Censors in Early Mexico.* Yale University Press, 2009.

Martin Austin Nesvig, ed., *Local Religion in Colonial Mexico.* University of New Mexico Press, 2006.

Frances Parkinson Keyes, *The Rose and the Lily: The Lives and Times of two South American Saints.* Hawthorn Books, 1961.

Stafford Poole, *Our Lady of Guadalupe: The Origins and Sources of a Mexican National Symbol, 1531–1797.* University of Arizona Press, 1995.

William B. Taylor, *Marvels & Miracles in Late Colonial Mexico.* University of New Mexico Press, 2011.

William B. Taylor, *Shrines and Miraculous Images: Religious Life in Mexico Before the Reforma.* University of New Mexico Press, 2010.

CHAPTER NINETEEN

Surveys

Liam Brockey, *Journey to the East: The Jesuit Mission to China, 1579–1724*. Belknap Press of Harvard University Press, 2007.

Charles E. Ronan and Bonnie B. C. Oh, eds., *East Meets West: The Jesuits in China, 1582–1773*. Loyola University Press, 1988.

Andrew C. Ross, *A Vision Betrayed: The Jesuits in Japan and China, 1542–1742*. Edinburgh University Press, 1994.

Francis Xavier

Kala Acharya, Carlos Mata, et al., eds., *St. Francis Xavier, His Times and Legacy*. Somaiya Publications, 2007.

James Brodrick, *Saint Francis Xavier, 1506–1552*. Image Books, 1957.

Franco Mormando and Jill G. Thomas, eds., *Francis Xavier and the Jesuit Missions in the Far East*. Jesuit Institute of Boston College, 2006.

Georg Schurhammer, *Francis Xavier, His Life, His Times*. Jesuit Historical Institute, 1973–1982.

India

C. Joe Arun, ed., *The Interculturation of Religion: Critical Perspectives on Robert de Nobili's Mission in India*. Asian Trading Corporation, 2007.

Vincent Cronin, *Pearl to India: The Life of Roberto de Nobili*. Dutton, 1959.

Ines G. Zupanov, *Missionary Tropics: The Catholic Frontier in India, 16th–17th Centuries*. University of Michigan Press, 2005.

China and Southeast Asia

Gianni Criveller, *Preaching Christ in Late Ming China: The Jesuits' Presentation of Christ from Matteo Ricci to Giulio Aleni*. Taipei Ricci Institute and Fondazione Civiltà Bresciana, 1997.

J. S. Cummins, *A Question of Rites: Friar Domingo Navarrete and the Jesuits in China*. Ashgate, 1993.

George H. Dunne, *Generation of Giants: The Story of the Jesuits in China in the Last Decades of the Ming Dynasty*. University of Notre Dame Press, 1962.

Michela Fontana, *Matteo Ricci: A Jesuit in the Ming Court*. Rowman & Littlefield, 2011.

Jacques Gernet, *China and the Christian Impact: A Conflict of Cultures*. Cambridge University Press, 1985.

Florence C. Hsia, *Sojourners in a Strange Land Jesuits and Their Scientific Missions in Late Imperial China*. University of Chicago Press, 2009.

Ronnie Po-chia Hsia, *A Jesuit in the Forbidden City: Matteo Ricci, 1552–1610*. Oxford University Press, 2010.

Sangkeun Kim, *Strange Names of God: The Missionary Translation of the Divine Name and the Chinese Responses to Matteo Ricci's "Shangti" in Late Ming China, 1583–1644*. Peter Lang, 2004.

Mary Laven, *Mission to China: Matteo Ricci and the Jesuit Encounter with the East*. Faber and Faber, 2011.

Tiziana Lippiello and Roman Malek, eds., *Scholar from the West: Giulio Aleni S.J. (1582–1649) and the Dialogue Between Christianity and China.* Fondazione Civiltà Bresciana, Monumenta Serica Institute, 1997.

George Minamiki, *The Chinese Rites Controversy.* Loyola University Press, 1985.

David E. Mungello, *Curious Land: Jesuit Accommodation and the Origins of Sinology.* University of Hawaii Press, 1989.

David E. Mungello, *The Forgotten Christians of Hangzhou.* University of Hawaii Press, 1994.

John Parker, *Windows into China: The Jesuits and Their Books, 1580–1730.* Trustees of the Public Library of the City of Boston, 1978.

Peter C. Phan, *Mission and Catechesis: Alexandre de Rhodes and Inculturation in Seventeenth-Century Vietnam.* Orbis Books, 1998.

Arnold H. Rowbotham, *Missionary and Mandarin: The Jesuits at the Court of China.* University of California Press, 1942.

Christopher Shelke and Mariella Demichele, eds., *Matteo Ricci in China: Inculturation Through Friendship and Faith.* Gregorian & Biblical Press, 2010.

Jonathan D. Spence, *The Memory Palace of Matteo Ricci.* Viking, 1984.

Nicolas Standaert, *Chinese Voices in the Rites Controversy: Travelling Books, Community Networks, Intercultural Arguments.* Institutum Historicum Societatis Iesu, 2012.

Nicolas Standaert, *Yang Tingyun, Confucian and Christian in Late Ming China: His Life and Thought.* Brill, 1988.

John D. Young, *East-West Synthesis: Matteo Ricci and Confucianism.* Centre of Asian Studies, University of Hong Kong, 1980.

Japan

Charles R. Boxer, *The Christian Century in Japan, 1549–1650.* University of California Press, 1951.

John Dougill, *In Search of Japan's Hidden Christians: A Story of Suppression, Secrecy and Survival.* Tuttle Publications., 2012.

George Elison, *Deus Destroyed: The Image of Christianity in Early Modern Japan.* Harvard University Press, 1973.

Fidel Villarroel, *Lorenzo de Manila: The Protomartyr of the Philippines and His Companions.* University of Santo Tomas Press, 1988.

Victoria Weston, ed., *Portugal, Jesuits and Japan: Spiritual Beliefs and Earthly Goods.* University of Chicago Press, 2013.

Tibet

Philip Caraman, *Tibet: The Jesuit Century.* Institute of Jesuit Sources, 1997.

Enzo Gualtiero Bargiacchi, *Bridge Across Two Cultures: Ippolito Desideri S.J. (1684–1733), a Brief Biography.* Istituto Geografico Militare, 2008.

Trent Pomplun, *Jesuit on the Roof of the World: Ippolito Desideri's Mission to Eighteenth-Century Tibet.* Oxford University Press, 2010.

Philippines

H. de la Costa, *The Jesuits in the Philippines, 1581–1768.* Harvard University Press, 1967.

John Leddy Phelan, *The Hispanization of the Philippines: Spanish Aims and Filipino Responses, 1565–1700.* University of Wisconsin Press, 1959.

Vicente L. Rafael, *Contracting Colonialism: Translation and Christian Conversion in Tagalog Society Under Early Spanish Rule.* Cornell University Press, 1988.

CHAPTER TWENTY

Surveys

Richard S. Dunn, *The Age of Religious Wars, 1559–1715.* W. W. Norton, 1979.

Benjamin J. Kaplan, *Divided by Faith: Religious Conflict and the Practice of Toleration in Early Modern Europe.* Belknap Press of Harvard University Press, 2007.

David Maland, *Europe at War, 1600–1650.* Macmillan, 1980.

Julius R. Ruff, *Violence in Early Modern Europe, 1500–1800.* Cambridge University Press, 2001.

Judy Sproxton, *Violence and Religion: Attitudes Towards Militancy in the French Civil Wars and the English Revolution.* Routledge, 1995.

Holy Roman Empire and Germany

Wim Blockmans, *Emperor Charles V, 1500–1558.* Arnold, 2002.

Karl Brandi, *Emperor Charles V: The Growth and Destiny of a Man and of a World-Empire.* Jonathan Cape, 1954.

Richard A. Cahill, *Philipp of Hesse and the Reformation.* P. von Zabern, 2001.

William S. Maltby, *The Reign of Charles V.* Palgrave, 2002.

Rory McEntegart, *Henry VIII, the League of Schmalkalden, and the English Reformation.* Boydell Press, 2002.

Bernd Moeller, *Imperial Cities and the Reformation: Three Essays.* Labyrinth Press, 1982.

Nathan Rein, *The Chancery of God: Protestant Propaganda Against the Empire, Magdeburg, 1546–1551.* Ashgate, 2008.

James Reston Jr., *Defenders of the Faith: Charles V, Suleyman the Magnificent, and the Battle for Europe, 1520–1536.* Penguin Press, 2009.

William J. Wright, *Capitalism, the State, and the Lutheran Reformation: Sixteenth-Century Hesse.* Ohio University Press, 1988.

France

Megan C. Armstrong, *The Politics of Piety: Franciscan Preachers During the Wars of Religion, 1560–1600.* University of Rochester Press, 2004.

Frederic J. Baumgartner, *Change and Continuity in the French Episcopate: The Bishops and the Wars of Religion, 1547–1610.* Duke University Press, 1986.

William Beik, *Urban Protest in Seventeenth-Century France: The Culture of Retribution.* Cambridge University Press, 1997.

Philip Benedict, *Graphic History: The Wars, Massacres and Troubles of Tortorel and Perrissin.* Droz, 2007.

Philip Benedict, *Rouen During the Wars of Religion.* Cambridge University Press, 1981.

Stuart Carroll, *Noble Power During the Wars of Religion: The Guise Affinity and the Catholic Cause in Normandy.* Cambridge University Press, 1998.

Philip Conner, *Huguenot Heartland: Montauban and Southern French Calvinism During the Wars of Religion.* Ashgate, 2002.

Barbara B. Diefendorf, *Beneath the Cross: Catholics and Huguenots in Sixteenth-Century Paris.* Oxford University Press, 1991.

Barbara B. Diefendorf, *The Saint Bartholomew's Day Massacre: A Brief History with Documents.* Bedford/St. Martin's, 2009.

Christopher Elwood, *The Body Broken: The Calvinist Doctrine of the Eucharist and the Symbolization of Power in Sixteenth-Century France.* Oxford University Press, 1999.

Mack P. Holt, *The Duke of Anjou and the Politique Struggle During the Wars of Religion.* Cambridge University Press, 1986.

Mack P. Holt, *The French Wars of Religion, 1562–1629.* Cambridge University Press, 2005.

Donald Kelley, *The Beginning of Ideology: Consciousness and Society in the French Reformation.* Cambridge University Press, 1981.

Robert M. Kingdon, *Geneva and the Coming of the Wars of Religion in France, 1555–1563.* 1956; reprint, Droz, 2007.

Robert M. Kingdon, *Myths About the St. Bartholomew's Day Massacres, 1572–1576.* Harvard University Press, 1988.

Robert J. Knecht, *The French Wars of Religion, 1559–1598.* Longman, 2010.

Mark W. Konnert, *Local Politics in the French Wars of Religion: The Towns of Champagne, the Duc de Guise, and the Catholic League, 1560–95.* Ashgate, 2006.

Scott M. Manetsch, *Theodore Beza and the Quest for Peace in France, 1562–1598.* Brill, 2000.

Kathleen A. Parrow, *From Defense to Resistance: Justification of Violence During the French Wars of Religion.* American Philosophical Society, 1993.

Luc Racaut, *Hatred in Print: Catholic Propaganda and Protestant Identity During the French Wars of Religion.* Ashgate, 2002.

Ann W. Ramsey, *Liturgy, Politics, and Salvation: The Catholic League in Paris and the Nature of Catholic Reform, 1540–1630.* University of Rochester Press, 1999.

Penny Roberts, *City in Conflict: Troyes During the French Wars of Religion.* Manchester University Press and St. Martin's Press, 1996.

Nancy Lyman Roelker, *One King, One Faith: The Parlement of Paris and the Religious Reformations of the Sixteenth Century.* University of California Press, 1996.

Elizabeth C. Tingle, *Authority and Society in Nantes During the French Wars of Religion, 1558–98.* Manchester University Press, 2006.

James B. Wood, *The King's Army: Warfare, Soldiers, and Society During the Wars of Religion in France, 1562–1576.* Cambridge University Press, 1996.

Natalie Zemon Davis, "The Rites of Violence: Religious Riot in Sixteenth-Century France," *Past & Present*, no. 59 (May 1973): 51–91.

Netherlands

Graham Darby, ed., *Origins and Development of the Dutch Revolt.* Routledge, 2001.

Alastair Duke, *Reformation and Revolt in the Low Countries.* Hambledon Press, 1990.

David Freedberg, *Iconoclasm and Painting in the Revolt of the Netherlands, 1566–1609.* Garland, 1988.

Arie-Jan Gelderblom, Jan L. de Jong, and Marc van Vaeck, eds., *The Low Countries as a Crossroads of Religious Beliefs*. Brill, 2004.

Pieter Geyl, *The Revolt of the Netherlands, 1555–1609*. E. Benn, 1966.

Craig Harline and Eddy Put, *A Bishop's Tale: Mathias Hovius Among His Flock in Seventeenth-Century Flanders*. Yale University Press, 2000.

Jonathan Israel, *The Dutch Republic: Its Rise, Greatness and Fall, 1477–1806*. Clarendon Press, 1998.

Benjamin J. Kaplan, *Calvinists and Libertines: Confession and Community in Utrecht, 1578–1620*. Oxford University Press, 1995.

Christine Kooi, *Calvinists and Catholics During Holland's Golden Age: Heretics and Idolaters*. Cambridge University Press, 2012.

Phyllis Mack Crew, *Calvinist Preaching and Iconoclasm in the Netherlands, 1544–1569*. Cambridge University Press, 1978.

Guido Marnef, *Antwerp in the Age of Reformation: Underground Protestantism in a Commercial Metropolis, 1550–1577*. Johns Hopkins University Press, 1996.

Geoffrey Parker, *The Dutch Revolt*. Penguin, 2002.

Andrew Pettegree, *Emden and the Dutch Revolt: Exile and the Development of Reformed Protestantism*. Oxford University Press, 1992.

Judith Pollmann, *Religious Choice in the Dutch Republic: The Reformation of Arnoldus Buchelius, 1565–1641*. St. Martin's Press, 1999.

Simon Schama, *The Embarrassment of Riches: An Interpretation of Dutch Culture in the Golden Age*. Vintage, 1997.

Els Stronks, *Negotiating Differences: Word, Image, and Religion in the Dutch Republic*. Brill, 2011.

K. W. Swart, *William of Orange and the Revolt of the Netherlands, 1572–84*. Ashgate, 2003.

James Tanis and Daniel Horst, *Images of Discord: A Graphic Interpretation of the Opening Decades of the Eighty Years' War*. W. B. Eerdmans, 1993.

James D. Tracy, *The Founding of the Dutch Republic: War, Finance, and Politics in Holland, 1572–1588*. Oxford University Press, 2008.

Henk van Nierop, *Treason in the Northern Quarter: War, Terror, and the Rule of Law in the Dutch Revolt*. Princeton University Press, 2009.

England

Martyn Bennett, *The Civil Wars in Britain and Ireland, 1638–1651*. Blackwell, 1997.

Michael Braddick, *God's Fury, England's Fire: A New History of the English Civil Wars*. Allen Lane, 2008.

Andrew Bradstock, *Radical Religion in Cromwell's England*. I. B. Tauris, 2011.

Bernard Capp, *A Door of Hope Re-opened: The Fifth Monarchy, King Charles and King Jesus*. University of Warwick, 2008.

Christopher Durston, *Cromwell's Major-Generals: Godly Government During the English Revolution*. Manchester University Press, 2001.

Graham Edwards, *The Last Days of Charles I*. Sutton Publishing, 1999.

Wilfrid Emberton, *The English Civil War Day by Day*. Sutton Publishing, 1995.

Christopher Hill, *The World Turned Upside Down: Radical Ideas During the English Revolution*. Peregrine Books 1984.

David Hoile, *The Levellers: Libertarian Radicalism and the English Civil War*. Libertarian Alliance, 1992.

Ronald Hutton, *The British Republic, 1649–1660*, 2nd ed. Palgrave MacMillan, 2000.

Ronald Hutton, *The Restoration, a Political and Religious History of England and Wales, 1658–1667*. Oxford University Press, 1985.

Padraig Lenihan, *Confederate Catholics at War, 1641–49*. Cork University Press, 2001.

John Morrill, ed., *Revolution and Restoration: England in the 1650s*. Collins & Brown, 1992.

Jane H. Ohlmeyer, ed., *Ireland from Independence to Occupation, 1641–1660*. Cambridge University Press, 1995.

Steven Pincus, *1688: The First Modern Revolution*. Yale University Press, 2009.

Charles W. A. Prior and Glenn Burgess, eds., *England's Wars of Religion, Revisited*. Ashgate, 2011.

Keith Roberts, *Cromwell's War Machine: The New Model Army, 1645–60*. Pen and Sword, 2005.

Trevor Royle, *The British Civil War: The Wars of the Three Kingdoms, 1638–1660*. Little, Brown, 2004.

Kevin Sharpe, *Rebranding Rule: The Restoration and Revolution Monarchy, 1660–1714*. Yale University Press, 2013.

David Stevenson, *The Scottish Revolution, 1637–1644: The Triumph of the Covenanters*. John Donald, 2003.

C. V. Wedgwood, *The King's Peace, 1637–1641*. Collins, 1955.

C. V. Wedgwood, *The King's War, 1641–1647*. Collins, 1958.

C. V. Wedgwood, *The Trial of Charles I*. Collins Fontana, 1967.

James Scott Wheeler, *Cromwell in Ireland*. St. Martin's Press, 1999.

Austin Woolrych, *Commonwealth to Protectorate*. Phoenix Press, 2000.

Martyrdom

Thomas P. Anderson and Ryan Netzley, eds., *Acts of reading: Interpretation, Reading Practices, and the Idea of the Book in John Foxe's* Actes and Monuments. University of Delaware Press, 2010.

Elizabeth Evenden and Thomas S. Freeman, *Religion and the Book in Early Modern England: The Making of Foxe's "Book of Martyrs."* Cambridge University Press, 2011.

Brad S. Gregory, *Salvation at Stake: Christian Martyrdom in Early Modern Europe*. Harvard University Press, 1999.

Megan L. Hickerson, *Making Women Martyrs in Tudor England*. Palgrave Macmillan, 2005.

John N. King, *Foxe's "Book of Martyrs" and Early Modern Print Culture*. Cambridge University Press, 2006.

David Loades, ed., *John Foxe at Home and Abroad*. Ashgate, 2004.

Catharine Randall Coats, *Embodying the Word: Textual Resurrections in the Martyrological Narratives of Foxe, Crespin, de Bèze and d'Aubigné*. P. Lang, 1992.

Thirty Years' War

Robert Bireley, *The Jesuits and the Thirty Years War: Kings, Courts, and Confessors*. Cambridge University Press, 2003.

Derek Croxton, *Westphalia: The Last Christian Peace.* Palgrave Macmillan, 2013.

Herbert Langer, *The Thirty Years' War.* Blandford Press, 1980.

Geoffrey Parker, ed., *The Thirty Years' War.* Routledge & Kegan Paul, 1987.

Theodore K. Rabb, ed., *The Thirty Years' War.* Heath, 1972.

C. V. Wedgewood, *The Thirty Years' War.* Yale University Press, 1939; reprint, with foreword by Anthony Grafton, New York Review Books, 2005.

Peter H. Wilson, *The Thirty Years' War: Europe's Tragedy.* Belknap Press of Harvard University Press, 2009.

CHAPTER TWENTY-ONE
Lutherans

Charles P. Arand, James A. Nestingen, and Robert Kolb, *Lutheran Confessions: History And Theology of The Book of Concord.* Fortress Press, 2012.

Irene Dingel, Robert Kolb, Nicole Kuropka, and Timothy J. Wengert, *Philip Melanchthon: Theologian in Classroom, Confession, and Controversy.* Vandenhoeck & Ruprecht, 2012.

Gregory B. Graybill, *Evangelical Free Will: Phillipp Melanchthon's Doctrinal Journey on the Origins of Faith.* Oxford University Press, 2010.

Michael J. Halvorson, *Heinrich Heshusius and Confessional Polemic in Early Lutheran Orthodoxy.* Ashgate, 2010.

Randolph C. Head and Daniel E. Christensen, eds., *Orthodoxies and Heterodoxies in Early Modern German Culture: Order and Creativity, 1500–1750.* E. J. Brill, 2007.

Scott H. Hendrix and Timothy J. Wengert, eds., *Philip Melanchthon—Then and Now (1497–1997): Essays Celebrating the 500th Anniversary of His Birth.* Lutheran Seminaries, 1999.

Theodore R. Jungkuntz, *Formulators of the Formula of Concord: Four Architects of Lutheran Unity.* Concordia Publishing, 1977.

Robert Kolb, *Bound Choice, Election, and Wittenberg Theological Method: From Martin Luther to the Formula of Concord.* Eerdmans, 2005.

Robert Kolb, ed., *Lutheran ecclesiastical culture, 1550–1675.* E. J. Brill, 2008.

Robert Kolb, *Luther's Heirs Define His Legacy: Studies on Lutheran Confessionalization.* Variorum, 1996.

Robert Kolb, *Nikolaus von Amsdorf (1483–1565): Popular Polemics in the Preservation of Luther's Legacy.* De Graaf, 1978.

Karin Maag, ed., *Melanchthon in Europe: His Work and Influence Beyond Wittenberg.* Baker Books, 1999.

E. P. Meijering, *Melanchthon and Patristic Thought: The Doctrines of Christ and Grace, the Trinity, and the Creation.* E. J. Brill, 1983.

James A. Nestingen and Robert Kolb, eds., *Sources and Contexts of the Book of Concord.* Fortress Press, 2001.

Oliver K. Olson, *Matthias Flacius and the Survival of Luther's Reform.* Harrassowitz Verlag, 2002.

Jacob A. O. Preus, *The Second Martin: The Life and Theology of Martin Chemnitz.* Concordia Publishing House, 1994.

John Schofield, *Philip Melanchthon and the English Reformation.* Ashgate, 2006.

Lewis W. Spitz and Wenzel Lohff, eds., *Discord, Dialogue, and Concord: Studies in the Lutheran Reformation's Formula of Concord*. Fortress Press, 1977.

Robert Stupperich, *Melanchthon: The Enigma of the Reformation*. 1965; reprint, James Clarke, 2006.

Timothy J. Wengert, *Defending Faith: Lutheran Responses to Andreas Osiander's Doctrine of Justification, 1551–1559*. Mohr Siebeck, 2012.

Timothy J. Wengert, *Law and Gospel: Philip Melanchthon's Debate with John Agricola of Eisleben over Poenitentia*. Baker Books, 1997.

Timothy J. Wengert, *Philip Melanchthon, Speaker of the Reformation: Wittenberg's Other Reformer*. Ashgate Variorum, 2010.

Reformed

Brian G. Armstrong, *Calvinism and the Amyraut Heresy: Protestant Scholasticism and Humanism in Seventeenth-Century France*. University of Wisconsin Press, 1969.

J. Wayne Baker, *Heinrich Bullinger and the Covenant: The Other Reformed Tradition*. Ohio University Press, 1980.

Peter Y. De Jong, ed., *Crisis in the Reformed Churches: Essays in Commemoration of the Great Synod of Dort, 1618–1619*. Reformed Fellowship, 1968.

Andrew C. Fix, *Prophecy and Reason: The Dutch Collegiants in the Early Enlightenment*. Princeton University Press, 1991.

W. J. Torrance Kirby, *The Zurich Connection and Tudor Political Theology*. E. J. Brill, 2007.

Martin I. Klauber, *Between Reformed Scholasticism and Pan-Protestantism: Jean-Alphonse Turretin (1671–1737) and Enlightened Orthodoxy at the Academy of Geneva*. Susquehanna University Press, 1994.

Jeffrey Mallinson, *Faith, Reason, and Revelation in Theodore Beza, 1519–1605*. Oxford University Press, 2003.

Bodo Nischan, *Prince, People, and Confession: The Second Reformation in Brandenburg*. University of Pennsylvania Press, 1994.

Alan P. F. Sell, *The Great Debate: Calvinism, Arminianism, and Salvation*. Walter, 1982.

Keith L. Sprunger, *Dutch Puritanism: A History of English and Scottish Churches of the Netherlands in the Sixteenth and Seventeenth Centuries*. E. J. Brill, 1982.

Keith D. Stanglin and Thomas H. McCall, *Jacob Arminius: Theologian of Grace*. Oxford University Press, 2012.

David N. Steele, Curtis C. Thomas, and S. Lance Quinn, *The Five Points of Calvinism: Defined, Defended, Documented*. P & R Publishing, 2004.

Thomas Marius Van Leeuwen, Keith D. Stanglin, and Marijke Tolsma, eds., *Arminius, Arminianism, and Europe: Jacobus Arminius, 1559–1609*. E. J. Brill, 2009.

Cornelis P. Venema, *Heinrich Bullinger and the Doctrine of Predestination: Author of "the Other Reformed Tradition"?* Baker Academic, 2002.

Derk Visser, ed., *Controversy and Conciliation: the Reformation and the Palatinate, 1559–1583*. Pickwick Publications, 1986.

Benjamin B. Warfield, *The Westminster Assembly and Its Work*. Oxford University Press, 1931.

Michiel Wielema, *March of the Libertines: Spinozists and the Dutch Reformed Church, 1660–1750*. Verloren, 2004.

Catholics

Nigel Abercrombie, *The Origins of Jansenism.* Clarendon Press, 1936.

John J. Conley, *Adoration and Annihilation: The Convent Philosophy of Port-Royal.* University of Notre Dame Press, 2009.

J. D. Crichton, *Saints or Sinners? Jansenists and Jansenisers in Seventeenth-Century France.* Veritas, 1996.

Michael De la Bedoyere, *The Archbishop and the Lady: The Story of Fénelon and Madame Guyon.* Pantheon, 1956.

Marc Escholier, *Port-Royal: The Drama of the Jansenists.* Hawthorn Books, 1968.

Thomas P. Flint, *Divine Providence: The Molinist Account.* Cornell University Press, 1998.

Nancy C. James, *The Conflict over the Heresy of Pure Love in Seventeenth-Century France: The Tumult over the Mysticism of Madame Guyon.* Edwin Mellen Press, 2008.

Nancy C. James, *Pure Love of Madame Guyon: The Great Conflict in King Louis XIV's Court.* University Press of America, 2007.

Matthias Kaufmann and Alexander Aichele, eds., *A Companion to Luis de Molina.* E. J. Brill, 2014.

Leszek Kolakowski, *God Owes Us Nothing: A Brief Remark on Pascal's Religion and on the Spirit of Jansenism.* University of Chicago Press, 1995.

Charles H. Parker, *Faith on the Margins: Catholics and Catholicism in the Dutch Golden Age.* Harvard University Press, 2008.

William Wood, *Blaise Pascal on Duplicity, Sin and the Fall: The Secret Instinct.* Oxford University Press, 2013.

Anthony Wright, *The Divisions of French Catholicism, 1629–1645.* Ashgate, 2011.

CHAPTER TWENTY-TWO

Summary Introductions

Joel F. Harrington and Helmut Walser Smith, "Confessionalization, Community, and State Building in Germany, 1555–1870," *Journal of Modern History* 69 (March 1997): 77–101.

Wolfgang Reinhard, "Reformation, Counter-Reformation, and the Early Modern State: A Reassessment," *Catholic Historical Review* 75, no. 3 (July 1989): 383–404.

Introductory Essay Collections

J. M. Headley, H. J. Hillerbrand, and A. J. Papalas, eds., *Confessionalization in Europe, 1555–1700.* Ashgate, 2004.

Heiko Oberman, ed., *Religion, Political Culture and the Emergence of Early Modern Society.* E. J. Brill, 1992.

Ronnie Po-chia Hsia, ed., *Social Discipline in the Reformation: Central Europe, 1550–1750.* Routledge, 1992.

Confessionalizing

Philip Benedict, *Christ's Churches Purely Reformed: A Social History of Calvinism.* Yale University Press, 2002.

Robin Briggs, *Communities of Belief: Cultural and Social Tension in Early Modern France.* Oxford University Press, 1989.

Jean Delumeau, *Catholicism Between Luther and Voltaire: A New View of the Counter-Reformation*. Westminster Press, 1977.

Jennifer Mara DeSilva, ed., *Episcopal Reform and Politics in Early Modern Europe*. Truman State University Press, 2012.

John M. Frymire, *Primacy of the Postils: Catholics, Protestants, and the Dissemination of Ideas in Early Modern Germany*. E. J. Brill, 2010.

W. Fred Graham, ed., *Later Calvinism: International Perspectives*. Sixteenth Century Journal Publishers, 1994.

Charles D. Gunnoe Jr., *Thomas Erastus and the Palatinate: A Renaissance Physician in the Second Reformation*. E. J. Brill, 2011.

Mack P. Holt, *Adaptations of Calvinism in Reformation Europe: Essays in Honour of Brian G. Armstrong*. Ashgate, 2007.

R. Po-chia Hsia, ed., *The Cambridge History of Christianity, Vol. 6: Reform and Expansion, 1500–1660*. Cambridge University Press, 2007.

Ábrahám Kovács and Béla Levente Baráth, eds., *Calvinism on the Peripheries: Religion and Civil Society in Europe*. Harmattan, 2009.

Thomas F. Mayer, *Reforming Reformation: Catholic Christendom, 1300–1700*. Ashgate, 2012.

John McCallum, *Scotland's Long Reformation: New Perspectives on Scottish Religion, 1500–1660*. Ashgate, 2013.

Graeme Murdock, *Beyond Calvin: The Intellectual, Political and Cultural World of Europe's Reformed Churches, c. 1540–1620*. Palgrave Macmillan, 2004.

Bodo Nischan, *Prince, People, and Confession: The Second Reformation in Brandenburg*. University of Pennsylvania Press, 1994.

Charles H. Parker, *The Reformation of Community: Social Welfare and Calvinist Charity in Holland, 1572–1620*. Cambridge University Press, 1998.

Menna Prestwich, ed., *International Calvinism, 1541–1715*. Oxford University Press, 1985.

Diana Robin, *Publishing Women: Salons, the Presses, and the Counter-Reformation in Sixteenth-Century Italy*. University of Chicago Press, 2007.

Erika Rummel, *The Confessionalization of Humanism in Reformation Germany*. Oxford University Press, 2000.

Heinz Schilling, *Civic Calvinism in Northwestern Germany and the Netherlands: Sixteenth to Nineteenth Centuries*. Sixteenth Century Journal Publishers, 1991.

Robert Scribner, Roy Porter, and Mikulás Teich, eds., *The Reformation in National Context*. Cambridge University Press, 1994.

John Spurr, *The Post-Reformation, 1603–1714*. Pearson Longman, 2006.

Nicholas Tyacke, ed., *England's Long Reformation, 1500–1800*. Routledge, 2003.

Mary Noll Venables, "In the Shadow of War: The Reign of Ernst the Pious in Seventeenth-Century Saxony," PhD diss., Yale University, 2004.

Peter Wallace, *The Long European Reformation: Religion, Political Conflict, and the Search for Conformity, 1350–1750*. Palgrave Macmillan, 2012.

Jeffrey Watt, *The Long Reformation*. Houghton Mifflin Harcourt, 2004.

Catechizing

Lyle D. Bierma, *The Doctrine of the Sacraments in the Heidelberg Catechism: Melanchthonian, Calvinist, or Zwinglian*. Princeton Theological Seminary, 1999.

Lyle D. Bierma, *The Theology of the Heidelberg Catechism: A Reformation Synthesis.* Westminster John Knox Press, 2013.

Lyle D. Bierma, with Charles D. Gunnoe, Karin Maag, and Paul W. Fields, *Introduction to the Heidelberg Catechism: Sources, History, and Theology.* Baker Academic, 2005.

Denis Janz, *Three Reformation Catechisms: Catholic, Anabaptist, Lutheran.* Edwin Mellen Press, 1982.

Alexander F. Mitchell, *Catechisms of the Second Reformation.* James Nesbit, 1860.

Timothy J. Wengert., ed., *Pastoral Luther: Essays on Martin Luther's Practical Theology.* Eerdmans, 2009.

Educating

Amy Nelson Burnett, *Teaching the Reformation: Ministers and Their Message in Basel, 1529–1629.* Oxford University Press, 2006.

Miriam Usher Chrisman, *Lay Culture, Learned Culture: Books and Social Change in Strasbourg, 1480–1599.* Yale University Press, 1982.

David Cressy, *Literacy and the Social Order: Reading and Writing in Tudor and Stuart England.* Cambridge University Press, 1980.

Brian Cummings, *Literary Culture of the Reformation: Grammar and Grace.* Oxford University Press, 2002.

Mark U. Edwards Jr., *Printing, Propaganda, and Martin Luther.* University of California Press, 1994.

Jean-François Gilmont, ed., *The Reformation and the Book.* Ashgate, 1998.

I. Green, "For Children in Yeeres and Children in Understanding: The Emergence of the English Catechism Under Elizabeth and the Early Stuarts." *Journal of Ecclesiastical History* 37 (1986): 397–425.

Carmen Luke, *Pedagogy, Printing, and Protestantism: The Discourse on Childhood.* State University of New York Press, 1989.

Geoffrey Parker, "An Educational Revolution? The Growth of Literacy and Schooling in Early Modern Europe," *Tijdschrift voor Geschiednis* 93 (1980): 210–222.

Geoffrey Parker, "Success and Failure During the First Century of the Reformation," *Past and Present* 136 (1992): 43–82.

John S. Pendergast, *Religion, Allegory, and Literacy in Early Modern England, 1560–1640.* Ashgate, 2006.

Rebecca C. Peterson, *Early Educational Reform in North Germany and Its Effects on Post-Reformation German Intellectuals.* Edwin Mellen Press, 2001.

Cyriac K. Pullapilly, *Caesar Baronius, Counter-Reformation Historian.* University of Notre Dame Press, 1975.

Gerald Strauss, *Luther's House of Learning: Indoctrination of the Young in the German Reformation.* Johns Hopkins University Press, 1978.

Maarten Wisse, Marcel Sarot, and Willemien Otten, eds., *Scholasticism Reformed: Essays in Honour of Willem J. Van Asselt.* E. J. Brill, 2010.

Preaching

Scott Hendrix, ed., *Preaching the Reformation: The Homiletical Handbook of Urbanus Rhegius.* Marquette University Press, 2003.

Peter McCullough, Hugh Adlington, and Emma Rhatigan, *The Oxford Handbook of the Early Modern Sermon*. Oxford University Press, 2011.

Frederick J. McGinness, *Right Thinking and Sacred Oratory in Counter-Reformation Rome*. Princeton University Press, 1995.

John W. O'Malley, *Religious Culture in the Sixteenth Century: Preaching, Rhetoric, Spirituality, and Reform*. Variorum, 1993.

Hilary Dansey Smith, *Preaching in the Spanish Golden Age: A Study of Some Preachers of the Reign of Philip III*. Oxford University Press, 1978.

Larissa Taylor, ed., *Preachers and People in the Reformations and Early Modern Period*. E. J. Brill, 2003.

Susan Wabuda, *Preaching During the English Reformation*. Cambridge University Press, 2002.

Disciplining

Philip Benedict, *Faith and Fortunes of France's Huguenots, 1600–85*. Ashgate, 2001.

Amy Nelson Burnett, *The Yoke of Christ: Martin Bucer and Christian Discipline*. Northeast Missouri State University, 1994.

Anne J. Cruz and Mary Elizabeth Perry, eds., *Culture and Control in Counter-Reformation Spain*. University of Minnesota Press, 1992.

Carlo Ginzburg, *The Cheese and the Worms: The Cosmos of a Sixteenth-Century Miller*. Johns Hopkins University Press, 1980.

Bruce Gordon, *Clerical Discipline and the Rural Reformation: The Synod in Zurich, 1532–1580*. P. Lang, 1992.

Philip S. Gorski, *The Disciplinary Revolution: Calvinism and the Rise of the State in Early Modern Europe*. University of Chicago Press, 2003.

Clive Griffin, *Journeymen-Printers, Heresy, and the Inquisition in Sixteenth-Century Spain*. Oxford University Press, 2005.

Stephen Haliczer, ed., *Inquisition and Society in Early Modern Europe*. Croom Helm, 1987.

Stephen Haliczer, *Sexuality in the Confessional: A Sacrament Profaned*. Oxford University Press, 1996.

Henry Heller, *The Conquest of Poverty: The Calvinist Revolt in Sixteenth Century France*. E. J. Brill, 1986.

R. Po-chia Hsia, *Social Discipline in the Reformation: Central Europe, 1550–1750*. Routledge, 1989.

Richard L. Kagan, *Lucrecia's Dreams: Politics and Prophecy in Sixteenth-Century Spain*. University of California Press, 1990.

Henry Kamen, *The Spanish Inquisition: A Historical Revision*, 4th ed. Yale University Press, 2014.

Andrew W. Keitt, *Inventing the Sacred: Imposture, Inquisition, and the Boundaries of the Supernatural in Golden Age Spain*. E. J. Brill, 2005.

Robert M. Kingdon, *Adultery and Divorce in Calvin's Geneva*. Harvard University Press, 1995.

Kimberly Lynn, *Between Court and Confessional: The Politics of Spanish Inquisitors*. Cambridge University Press, 2013.

Patricia Manning, *Voicing Dissent in Seventeenth-Century Spain: Inquisition, Social Criticism and Theology in the Case of El Criticón*. E. J. Brill, 2009.

Thomas F. Mayer, *The Roman Inquisition on the Stage of Italy, 1590–1640.* University of Pennsylvania Press, 2014.

Raymond A. Mentzer, ed., *Sin and the Calvinists: Morals Control and the Consistory in the Reformed Tradition.* Sixteenth Century Journal Publishing, 1994.

Raymond A. Mentzer, ed., *Society and Culture in the Huguenot World, 1559–1685.* Cambridge University Press, 2002.

Raymond A. Mentzer, Françoise Moreil, and Philippe Chareyre, eds., *Dire l'interdit: The Vocabulary of Censure and Exclusion in the Early Modern Reformed Tradition.* E. J. Brill, 2010.

E. William Monter, *Enforcing Morality in Early Modern Europe.* Variorum Reprints, 1987.

Sara T. Nalle, *Mad for God: Bartolomé Sánchez, the Secret Messiah of Cardenete.* University Press of Virginia, 2001.

William G. Naphy, *Calvin and the Consolidation of the Genevan Reformation.* Westminster John Knox Press, 2003.

Helen Rawlings, *The Spanish Inquisition.* Blackwell, 2006.

Philip F. Riley, *Lust for Virtue: Louis XIV's Attack on Sin in Seventeenth-Century France.* Greenwood Press, 2001.

Glenn S. Sunshine, *Reforming French Protestantism: The Development of Huguenot Ecclesiastical Institutions, 1557–1572.* Truman State University Press, 2003.

Lisa Vollendorf, *The Lives of Women: A New History of Inquisitional Spain.* Vanderbilt University Press, 2005.

John Witte Jr. and Robert M. Kingdon, *Sex, Marriage, and Family in John Calvin's Geneva.* W. B. Eerdmans, 2005.

CHAPTER TWENTY-THREE

Witchcraft and Witch Hunts

Bengt Ankarloo, Stuart Clark, and William Monter, eds., *The Period of the Witch Trials.* University of Pennsylvania Press, 2002.

Lara Apps and Andrew Gow, *Male Witches in Early Modern Europe.* Manchester University Press, 2003.

Jonathan Barry, Marianne Hester, and Gareth Roberts eds., *Witchcraft in Early Modern Europe: Studies in Culture and Belief.* Cambridge University Press, 1996.

Wolfgang Behringer, *Witches and Witch-Hunts: A Global History.* Polity Press, 2004.

Edward Bever, *Realities of Witchcraft and Popular Magic in Early Modern Europe: Culture, Cognition, and Everyday Life.* Palgrave Macmillan, 2008.

Sigrid Brauner, *Fearless Wives and Frightened Shrews: The Construction of the Witch in Early Modern Germany.* University of Massachusetts Press, 1995.

Robin Briggs, *Witches and Neighbours: The Social and Cultural Context of European Witchcraft.* HarperCollins, 1996.

Robin Briggs, *The Witches of Lorraine.* Oxford University Press, 2007.

Hans Peter Broedel, *The* Malleus maleficarum *and the Construction of Witchcraft: Theology and Popular Belief.* Manchester University Press, 2003.

Stuart Clark, *Thinking with Demons: The Idea of Witchcraft in Early Modern Europe.* Clarendon Press, 1997.

Jane P. Davidson, *The Witch in Northern European Art, 1470–1750*. Luca Verlag, 1987.

Rainer Decker, *Witchcraft and the Papacy: An Account Drawing on the Formerly Secret Records of the Roman Inquisition*. University of Virginia Press, 2008.

Erik Durschmied, *Whores of the Devil: Witch-Hunts and Witch-Trials*. Sutton, 2005.

Jeanne Favret-Saada, *Deadly Words: Witchcraft in the Bocage*. Cambridge University Press, 1980.

Carlo Ginzburg, *The Night Battles: Witchcraft and Agrarian Cults in the Sixteenth and Seventeenth Centuries*. Johns Hopkins University Press, 1983.

Linda C. Hults, *The Witch as Muse: Art, Gender, and Power in Early Modern Europe*. University of Pennsylvania Press, 2005.

Brian P. Levack, ed., *The Oxford Handbook of Witchcraft in Early Modern Europe and Colonial America*. Oxford University Press, 2013.

Brian P. Levack, ed., *Witchcraft in England*. Garland, 1992.

Brian P. Levack, *The Witch-Hunt in Early Modern Europe*. Pearson Longman, 2006.

Brian P. Levack, ed., *Witch-Hunting in Continental Europe: Local and Regional*. Garland, 1992.

P. G. Maxwell-Stuart, *Witchcraft in Europe and the New World, 1400–1800*. Palgrave, 2001.

H. C. Erik Midelfort, *Witch Hunting in Southwestern Germany, 1562–1684: The Social and Intellectual Foundations*. Stanford University Press, 1972.

E. William Monter, *European Witchcraft*. Wiley, 1969.

E. William Monter, *Witchcraft in France and Switzerland: The Borderlands During the Reformation*. Cornell University Press, 1976.

Jon Oplinger, *The Politics of Demonology: The European Witchcraze and the Mass Production of Deviance*. Susquehanna University Press, 1990.

Éva Pócs, *Between the Living and the Dead: A Perspective on Witches and Seers in the Early Modern Age*. Central European University Press, 1999.

Thomas Robisheaux, *The Last Witch of Langenburg: Murder in a German Village*. W. W. Norton, 2009.

Lyndal Roper, *Oedipus and the Devil: Witchcraft, Sexuality, and Religion in Early Modern Europe*. Routledge, 1994.

Lyndal Roper, *Witch Craze: Terror and Fantasy in Baroque Germany*. Yale University Press, 2004.

Geoffrey Scarre, *Witchcraft and Magic in Sixteenth and Seventeenth Century Europe*. Humanities Press International, 1987.

H. Sidky, *Witchcraft, Lycanthropy, Drugs, and Disease: An Anthropological Study of the European Witch-Hunts*. Peter Lang, 1997.

Robert W. Thurston, *Witch Hunts: A History of the Witch Persecutions in Europe and North America*. Pearson Longman, 2007.

Gary K. Waite, *Eradicating the Devil's Minions: Anabaptists and Witches in Reformation Europe, 1525–1600*. University of Toronto Press, 2007.

Gary K. Waite, *Heresy, Magic, and Witchcraft in Early Modern Europe*. Palgrave Macmillan, 2003.

Gerhild Scholz Willimas, *Defining Dominion: The Discourses of Magic and Witchcraft in Early Modern France and Germany*. University of Michigan Press, 1995.

Charles Zika, *The Appearance of Witchcraft: Print and Visual Culture in Sixteenth-Century Europe.* Routledge, 2008.

Charles Zika, *Exorcising Our Demons: Magic, Witchcraft, and Visual Culture in Early Modern Europe.* Brill, 2002.

Magic and Superstition

Michael D. Bailey, *Fearful Spirits, Reasoned Follies: The Boundaries of Superstition in Late Medieval Europe.* Cornell University Press, 2013.

Michael D. Bailey, *Magic and Superstition in Europe: A Concise History from Antiquity to the Present.* Rowman & Littlefield, 2007.

Euan Cameron, *Enchanted Europe: Superstition, Reason, and Religion, 1250–1750.* Oxford University Press, 2010.

Kathryn A. Edwards, ed., *Werewolves, Witches, and Wandering spirits: Traditional Belief and Folklore in Early Modern Europe.* Truman State University Press, 2002.

R. Po-chia Hsia, *The Myth of Ritual Murder: Jews and Magic in Reformation Germany.* Yale University Press, 1988.

Frank Klaassen, *The Transformations of Magic: Illicit Learned Magic in the Later Middle Ages and Renaissance.* Pennsylvania State University Press, 2013.

Gunnar W. Knutsen, *Servants of Satan and Masters of Demons: The Spanish Inquisition's Trials of Superstition, Valencia and Barcelona, 1478–1700.* Brepols, 2009.

Helen Parish and William G. Naphy, eds., *Religion and Superstition in Reformation Europe.* Manchester University Press, 2002.

Alec Ryrie, *The Sorcerer's Tale: Faith and Fraud in Tudor England.* Oxford University Press, 2008.

Geoffrey Scarre and John Callow, *Witchcraft and Magic in Sixteenth- and Seventeenth-Century Europe.* Palgrave, 2001.

Verena Theile and Andrew D. McCarthy, *Staging the Superstitions of Early Modern Europe.* Ashgate, 2013.

Keith Thomas, *Religion and the Decline of Magic: Studies in Popular Beliefs in Sixteenth- and Seventeenth-Century England.* Penguin, 2003.

Frances Timbers, *Magic and Masculinity: Ritual Magic and Gender in the Early Modern Era.* Palgrave Macmillan, 2009.

Frederick Valletta, *Witchcraft, Magic and Superstition in England, 1640–70.* Ashgate, 2000.

Stephen Wilson, *Magical Universe: Everyday Ritual and Magic in Pre-Modern Europe.* Hambledon and London, 2000.

The Devil, Possessions, and Exorcisms

Norman Cohn, *Europe's Inner Demons: The Demonization of Christians in Medieval Christendom.* Pimlico, 1993.

Michel de Certeau, *The Possession at Loudun.* University of Chicago Press, 2000.

Erin Glunt Dolias, *The Marvelous Tale of Alis de Tesieux: Revenants, Reformation, Reform, and Revolving Meaning in a Sixteenth-Century Ghost Story.* PhD diss., Yale University, 2013.

Sarah Ferber, *Demonic Possession and Exorcism in Early Modern France.* Routledge, 2004.

Alberto Ferreiro, ed., *The Devil, Heresy, and Witchcraft in the Middle Ages: Essays in Honor of Jeffrey B. Russell.* E. J. Brill, 1998.

H. C. Erik Midelfort, *Exorcism and Enlightenment: Johann Joseph Gassner and the Demons of Eighteenth-Century Germany.* Yale University Press, 2005.

Robert Muchembled, *A History of the Devil: From the Middle Ages to the Present.* Polity Press, 2003.

Jonathan L. Pearl, *The Crime of Crimes: Demonology and Politics in France, 1560–1620.* Wilfrid Laurier University Press, 1999.

Robert Rapley, *A Case of Witchcraft: The Trial of Urbain Grandier.* McGill-Queen's University Press, 1998.

Jeffrey Burton Russell, *Lucifer, the Devil in the Middle Ages.* Cornell University Press, 1984.

Jeffrey Burton Russell, *Mephistopheles: The Devil in the Modern World.* Cornell University Press, 1986.

Moshe Sluhovsky, *Believe Not Every Spirit: Possession, Mysticism, & Discernment in Early Modern Catholicism.* University of Chicago Press, 2007.

D. P. Walker, *Unclean Spirits Possession and Exorcism in France and England in the Late Sixteenth and Early Seventeenth Centuries.* University of Pennsylvania Press, 1981.

Natural and Supernatural

Lorraine Daston and Katharine Park, *Wonders and the Order of Nature, 1150–1750.* Zone Books, 1998.

Philip M. Soergel, *Miracles and the Protestant Imagination: The Evangelical Wonder Book in Reformation Germany.* Oxford University Press, 2012.

Occult Philosophy and Learned Magic

Philip Ball, *The Devil's Doctor: Paracelsus and the World of Renaissance Magic and Science.* Farrar, Straus and Giroux, 2006.

Nicholas H. Clulee, *John Dee's Natural Philosophy: Between Science and Religion.* Routledge, 1988.

Deborah E. Harkness, *John Dee's Conversations with Angels: Cabala, Alchemy, and the End of Nature.* Cambridge University Press, 1999.

Glyn Parry, *Arch-Conjuror of England: John Dee.* Yale University Press, 2013.

Ryan J. Stark, *Rhetoric, Science, and Magic in Seventeenth-Century England.* Catholic University of America Press, 2009.

Benjamin Woolley, *The Queen's Conjuror: The Science and Magic of Dr. Dee.* HarperCollins, 2001.

Frances A. Yates, *Occult Philosophy in the Elizabethan Age.* Routledge & Kegan Paul, 1979.

CHAPTER TWENTY-FOUR

Introductions to Early Modern Thought

Desmond M. Clarke and Catherine Wilson, eds., *The Oxford Handbook of Philosophy in Early Modern Europe.* Oxford University Press, 2011.

Michael Funk Deckard and Peter Losonczi, eds., *Philosophy Begins in Wonder: An Introduction to Early Modern Philosophy, Theology, and Science.* Pickwick Publications, 2010.

Daniel Garber, Michael Ayers, Roger Ariew, and Alan Gabbey, *The Cambridge History of Seventeenth-Century Philosophy.* Cambridge University Press, 1998.

James Hankins, ed., *The Cambridge Companion to Renaissance Philosophy.* Cambridge University Press, 2007.

Donald Rutherford, ed., *The Cambridge Companion to Early Modern Philosophy.* Cambridge University Press, 2006.

Jeffrey Tlumak, *Classical Modern Philosophy: A Contemporary Introduction.* Routledge, 2006.

Toleration

Roland Bainton, *The Travail of Religious Liberty: Nine Biographical Studies.* Westminster Press, 1951.

Henk Bonger, *The Life and Work of Dirck Volkertszoon Coornhert.* Rodopi, 2004.

Hans R. Guggisberg, *Sebastian Castellio, 1515–1563: Humanist and Defender of Religious Toleration in a Confessional Age.* Ashgate, 2003.

Jonathan Israel, *Locke, Spinoza and the Philosophical Debate Concerning Toleration in the Early Enlightenment.* Koninklijke Nederlandse Akademie van Wetenschappen, 1999.

Benjamin J. Kaplan, *Divided by Faith: Religious Conflict and the Practice of Toleration in Early Modern Europe.* Belknap Press of Harvard University Press, 2007.

John Christian Laursen and Cary J. Nederman, eds., *Beyond the Persecuting Society: Religious Toleration Before the Enlightenment.* University of Pennsylvania Press, 1997.

John Christian Laursen and María José Villaverde, eds., *Paradoxes of Religious Toleration in Early Modern Political Thought.* Lexington Books, 2012.

Alan Levine, *Early Modern Skepticism and the Origins of Toleration.* Lexington Books, 1999.

John Marshall, *John Locke, Toleration and Early Enlightenment Culture.* Cambridge University Press, 2006.

Stuart B. Schwartz, *All Can Be Saved: Religious Tolerance and Salvation in the Iberian Atlantic World.* Yale University Press, 2008.

Gerrit Voogt, *Constraint on Trial: Dirk Volckertsz Coornhert and Religious Freedom.* Truman State University Press, 2000.

Rationalism

Carl Becker, *The Heavenly City of the Eighteenth Century Philosophers*, 2nd ed. Yale University Press, 2003.

C. J. Betts, *Early Deism in France: from the So-Called "Déistes" of Lyon, 1564, to Voltaire's "Lettres philosophiques," 1734.* Martinus Nijhoff, 1984.

Peter Byrne, *Natural Religion and the Nature of Religion: The Legacy of Deism.* Routledge, 1989.

Ernst Cassirer, *The Individual and the Cosmos in Renaissance Philosophy.* Barnes & Noble, 1964.

J. A. I. Champion, *The Pillars of Priestcraft Shaken: The Church of England and Its Enemies.* Cambridge University Press, 1992.

Gerald R. Cragg, *The Church and the Age of Reason, 1648–1789.* Atheneum, 1961; reprint, Penguin Books, 1990.

Michael F. Deckard and Peter Losonczi, eds., *Philosophy Begins in Wonder: An Introduction to Early Modern Philosophy, Theology, and Science.* Pickwick Publications, 2010.

Louis Dupré, *Passage to Modernity: An Essay in the Hermeneutics of Nature and Culture*. Yale University Press, 1993.

Peter A. French, Howard K. Wettstein, and Bruce Silver, eds., *Renaissance and Early Modern Philosophy*. Blackwell, 2002.

Stephen Greenblatt, *The Swerve: How the World Became Modern*. W. W. Norton, 2011.

James A. Herrick, *The Radical Rhetoric of the English Deists: The Discourse of Skepticism, 1680–1750*. University of South Carolina Press, 1997.

Anthony Kenny, *The Rise of Modern Philosophy*. Oxford University Press, 2006.

Roger D. Lund, ed., *The Margins of Orthodoxy: Heterodox Writing and Cultural Response, 1660–1750*. Cambridge University Press, 1995.

Stephen A. McKnight, *Sacralizing the Secular: The Renaissance Origins of Modernity*. Louisiana State University Press, 1989.

Christia Mercer and Eileen O'Neill, eds., *Early Modern Philosophy: Mind, Matter, and Metaphysics*. Oxford University Press, 2005.

Michael Moriarty, *Early Modern French Thought: The Age of Suspicion*. Oxford University Press, 2003.

Steven Nadler, *The Best of All Possible Worlds: A Story of Philosophers, God, and Evil*. Farrar, Straus and Giroux, 2008.

G. H. R. Parkinson, ed., *Renaissance and Seventeenth Century Rationalism*. Routledge, 1993.

Roy Porter, *The Creation of the Modern World: The Untold Story of the British Enlightenment*. W. W. Norton, 2000.

Susan E. Schreiner, *Are You Alone Wise? The Search for Certainty in the Early Modern Era*. Oxford University Press, 2011.

Kurt Smith, *Matter Matters: Metaphysics and Methodology in the Early Modern Period*. Oxford University Press, 2010.

Leo Weinstein, ed., *The Age of Reason: The Culture of the Seventeenth Century*. G. Braziller, 1965.

Catherine Wilson, *The Invisible World: Early Modern Philosophy and the Invention of the Microscope*. Princeton University Press, 1995.

John W. Yolton, ed., *Philosophy, Religion and Science in the Seventeenth and Eighteenth Centuries*. University of Rochester Press, 1990.

Significant Rationalists

Susanna Akerman, *Queen Christina of Sweden and Her Circle: The Transformation of a Seventeenth-Century Philosophical Libertine*. E. J. Brill, 1991.

R. D. Bedford, *The Defence of Truth: Herbert of Cherbury and the Seventeenth Century*. Manchester University Press, 1979.

Janet Broughton, *Descartes's Method of Doubt*. Princeton University Press, 2003.

Justin Champion, *Republican Learning: John Toland and the Crisis of Christian Culture, 1696–1722*. Manchester University Press, 2003.

Stephen H. Daniel, *John Toland, His Methods, Manners, and Mind*. McGill-Queen's University Press, 1984.

Edward H. Davidson and William J. Scheick, *Paine, Scripture, and Authority: The Age of Reason as Religious and Political Idea*. Lehigh University Press, 1994.

K. Joanna S. Forstrom, *John Locke and Personal Identity: Immortality and Bodily Resurrection in 17th-Century Philosophy.* Continuum, 2010.

Glenn A. Hartz, *Leibniz's Final System: Monads, Matter and Animals.* Routledge, 2007.

James Hill, *Descartes and the Doubting Mind.* Continuum, 2012.

Matthew L. Jones, *The Good Life in the Scientific Revolution: Descartes, Pascal, Leibniz, and the Cultivation of Virtue.* University of Chicago Press, 2006.

John Marshall, *John Locke: Resistance, Religion and Responsibility.* Cambridge University Press, 1994.

Christia Mercer, *Leibniz's Metaphysics: Its Origins and Development.* Cambridge University Press, 2001.

Murray Miles, *Insight and Inference: Descartes's Founding Principle and Modern Philosophy.* University of Toronto Press, 1999.

Steven Nadler, *The Philosopher, the Priest, and the Painter: A Portrait of Descartes.* Princeton University Press, 2013.

Pauline Phemister, *The Rationalists: Descartes, Spinoza and Leibniz.* Polity, 2006.

Russell Shorto, *Descartes' Bones: A Skeletal History of the Conflict Between Faith and Reason.* Doubleday, 2008.

Robert Sullivan, *John Toland and the Deist Controversy: A Study in Adaptations.* Harvard University Press, 1982.

Catherine Wilson, *Leibniz's Metaphysics: A Historical and Comparative Study.* Princeton University Press, 1989.

R. S. Woolhouse, *Descartes, Spinoza, Leibniz: The Concept of Substance in Seventeenth-Century Metaphysics.* Routledge, 2002.

Blaise Pascal

Donald Adamson, *Blaise Pascal: Mathematician, Physicist, and Thinker About God.* St. Martin's, 1995.

James A. Connor, *Pascal's Wager: The Man Who Played Dice with God.* Harper, 2006.

Nicholas Hammond, *The Cambridge Companion to Pascal.* Cambridge University Press, 2003.

Graeme Hunter, *Pascal the Philosopher: An Introduction.* University of Toronto Press, 2013.

Dawn M. Ludwin, *Blaise Pascal's Quest for the Ineffable.* P. Lang, 2001.

Robert J. Nelson, *Pascal, Adversary and Advocate.* Harvard University Press, 1981.

Marvin R. O'Connell, *Blaise Pascal: Reasons of the Heart.* Eerdmans, 1997.

Skepticism

Franklin L. Baumer, *Religion and the Rise of Scepticism.* Harcourt Brace, 1960.

Brendan Dooley, *The Social History of Skepticism: Experience and Doubt in Early Modern Culture.* Johns Hopkins University Press, 1999.

Timothy Dykstal, *The Luxury of Skepticism: Politics, Philosophy, and Dialogue in the English Public Sphere, 1660–1740.* University Press of Virginia, 2001.

Alan Kors, *Atheism in France, 1650–1729.* Princeton University Press, 1990.

Henrik Lagerlund, ed., *Rethinking the History of Skepticism: The Missing Medieval Background.* E. J. Brill, 2010.

Gianni Paganini and José R. M. Neto, eds., *Renaissance Scepticisms.* Springer, 2009.

Richard Popkin, *The History of Scepticism: from Savonarola to Bayle.* Oxford University Press, 2003.

Ellen Spolsky, *Satisfying Skepticism: Embodied Knowledge in the Early Modern World.* Ashgate, 2001.

Michelle Zerba, *Doubt and Skepticism in Antiquity and the Renaissance.* Cambridge University Press, 2012.

Empirical Science: Surveys

Denise Albanese, *New Science, New World.* Duke University Press, 1996.

James J. Bono, *The Word of God and the Languages of Man: Interpreting Nature in Early Modern Science and Medicine.* University of Wisconsin Press, 1995.

Robin Briggs, *The Scientific Revolution of the Seventeenth Century.* Longman, 1969.

Peter Dear, *Revolutionizing the Sciences: European Knowledge and Its Ambitions, 1500–1700.* Princeton University Press, 2001.

Amos Funkenstein, *Theology and the Scientific Imagination from the Middle Ages to the Seventeenth Century.* Princeton University Press, 1986.

Ofer Gal and Raz Chen-Morris, *Baroque Science.* University of Chicago Press, 2013.

Richard C. Gamble, ed., *Calvin and Science.* Garland, 1992.

A. Rupert Hall, *The Revolution in Science, 1500–1750.* Longman, 1983.

Lawrence M. Principe, *The Scientific Revolution: A Very Short Introduction.* Oxford University Press, 2011.

Steven Shapin, *The Scientific Revolution.* University of Chicago Press, 1996.

Daniel Stolzenberg, ed., *The Great Art of Knowing: The Baroque Encyclopedia of Athanasius Kircher.* Stanford University Press, 2001.

Claus Zittel, Romano Nanni, and Nicole C. Karafyllis, eds., *Philosophies of Technology: Francis Bacon and His Contemporaries.* E. J. Brill, 2008.

Empirical Science: Copernicus and Galileo

Richard J. Blackwell, *Science, Religion and Authority: Lessons from the Galileo Affair.* Marquette University Press, 1998.

Jean Dietz Moss, *Novelties in the Heavens: Rhetoric and Science in the Copernican Controversy.* University of Chicago Press, 1993.

Annibale Fantoli, *Galileo: For Copernicanism and for the Church.* Vatican Observatory Publications/University of Notre Dame Press, 2003.

Peter Machamer, *The Cambridge Companion to Galileo.* Cambridge University Press, 1998.

Ernan McMullin, ed., *The Church and Galileo.* University of Notre Dame Press, 2005.

Pietro Redondi, *Galileo Heretic.* Princeton University Press, 1987.

Jürgen Renn, ed., *Galileo in Context.* Cambridge University Press, 2001.

Jack Repcheck, *Copernicus' Secret: How the Scientific Revolution Began.* Simon & Schuster, 2007.

Dava Sobel, *A More Perfect Heaven: How Copernicus Revolutionised the Cosmos.* Bloomsbury, 2011.

William A. Wallace, *Domingo de Soto and the Early Galileo: Essays on Intellectual History.* Ashgate, 2004.

Richard S. Westfall, *Essays on the Trial of Galileo.* Vatican Observatory Publications and University of Notre Dame Press, 1989.

Robert S. Westman, *The Copernican Question: Prognostication, Skepticism, and Celestial Order.* University of California Press, 2011.

David Wootton, *Galileo: Watcher of the Skies.* Yale University Press, 2010.

CHAPTER TWENTY-FIVE

Economics

Philip S. Gorski, *The Protestant Ethic Revisited.* Temple University Press, 2011.

Hartmut Lehmann and Guenther Roth, eds., *Weber's "Protestant Ethic": Origins, Evidence, Contexts.* Cambridge University Press, 1993.

Gordon Marshall, *Presbyteries and Profits: Calvinism and the Development of Capitalism in Scotland, 1560–1707.* Oxford University Press, 1980.

William H. Swatos Jr. and Lutz Kaelber, eds., *The Protestant Ethic Turns 100: Essays on the Centenary of the Weber Thesis.* Paradigm Publishers, 2005.

Max Weber, *The Protestant Ethic and the Spirit of Capitalism.* Routledge, 2001.

Politics

Lorna Jane Abray, *The People's Reformation: Magistrates, Clergy, and Commons in Strasbourg, 1500–1598.* Cornell University Press, 1985.

Robert Bireley, *Religion and Politics in the Age of the Counterreformation: Emperor Ferdinand II, William Lamormaini, S.J., and the Formation of Imperial Policy.* University of North Carolina Press, 1981.

Peter Blickle, *Communal Reformation: The Quest for Salvation in Sixteenth-Century Germany.* Atlantic Highlands: Humanities Press, 1992.

Peter Blickle, Hans-Christoph Rublack, Winfried Schulze, and Kaspar von Greyerz, eds., *Religion, Politics, and Social Protest: Three Studies on Early Modern Germany.* Allen & Unwin, 1984.

Thomas A. Brady Jr., *Communities, Politics, and Reformation in Early Modern Europe.* E. J. Brill, 1998.

Thomas A. Brady Jr., *Politics of the Reformation in Germany: Jacob Sturm (1489–1553) of Strasbourg.* Humanities Press, 1997.

Thomas A. Brady Jr., *Ruling Class, Regime and Reformation at Strasbourg, 1520–1555.* E. J. Brill, 1978.

Thomas A. Brady Jr., *Turning Swiss: Cities and Empire, 1450–1550.* Cambridge University Press, 1985.

Miriam U. Chrisman, *Strasbourg and the Reform: A Study in the Process of Change.* Yale University Press, 1967.

Thomas H. Clancy, *Papist Pamphleteers: The Allen-Persons Party and the Political Thought of the Counter-Reformation in England, 1572–1615.* Loyola University Press, 1964.

Marc Forster, *The Counter-Reformation in the Villages: Religion and Reform in the Bishopric of Speyer, 1560–1720.* Cornell University Press, 1992.

Kevin Gould, *Catholic Activism in South-West France, 1540–1570.* Ashgate, 2006.

Tadhg Ó Hannracháin, *Catholic Reformation in Ireland: The Mission of Rinuccini, 1645–1649.* Oxford University Press, 2002.

Harro Höpfl, *The Christian Polity of John Calvin.* Cambridge University Press, 1985.

Steven Ozment, *Protestants: The Birth of a Revolution.* Doubleday, 1992.

Kaspar von Greyerz, *The Late City Reformation in Germany: The Case of Colmar, 1522–1628.* Steiner, 1980.

Thomas Rist, *Shakespeare's Romances and the Politics of Counter-Reformation.* Edwin Mellen, 1999.

Heinz Schilling, *Religion, Political Culture and the Emergence of Early Modern Society: Essays in German and Dutch History.* E. J. Brill, 1992.

Quentin Skinner and Martin van Gelderen, eds., *Freedom and the Construction of Europe: Religious and Constitutional Liberties.* Cambridge University Press, 2013.

Robert C. Walton, *Zwingli's Theocracy.* University of Toronto Press, 1967.

Political and Social Thought

Robert Bireley, *The Counter-Reformation Prince: Anti-Machiavellianism or Catholic Statecraft in Early Modern Europe.* University of North Carolina Press, 1990.

Roland Boer, *Political Grace: The Revolutionary Theology of John Calvin.* Westminster/John Knox Press, 2009.

Bonnie Lee Brummel, *Luther on Poverty and the Poor: A Study of Luther's Exegetical Understanding and Use of the Biblical Language of Poverty and the Poor, 1513–1525.* PhD diss., Columbia University, 1979.

W. D. J. Cargill Thompson, *The Political Thought of Martin Luther.* Barnes & Noble, 1984.

F. Edward Cranz, *An Essay on the Development of Luther's Thought on Justice, Law, and Society.* Harvard University Press, 1959.

Per Frostin, *Luther's Two Kingdoms Doctrine: A Critical Study.* Lund University Press, 1994.

John H. Leith, *John Calvin's Doctrine of the Christian Life.* Westminster/John Knox Press, 1989.

Quentin Skinner, *The Foundations of Modern Political Thought*, 2 vols. Cambridge University Press, 1978.

W. M. Spellman, *European Political Thought, 1600–1700.* St. Martin's Press, 1998.

William R. Stevenson Jr., *Sovereign Grace: The Place and Significance of Christian Freedom in John Calvin's Political Thought.* Oxford University Press, 1999.

Charity and Poor Relief

John Patrick Donnelly and Michael W. Maher, eds., *Confraternities and Catholic Reform in Italy, France, & Spain.* Thomas Jefferson University Press, 1999.

Timothy G. Fehler, *Poor Relief and Protestantism: The Evolution of Social Welfare in Sixteenth-Century Emden.* Ashgate, 1999.

Maureen Flynn, *Sacred Charity: Confraternities and Social Welfare in Spain, 1400–1700.* Cornell University Press, 1989.

Ole Peter Grell and Andrew Cunningham, eds., *Health Care and Poor Relief in Protestant Europe, 1500–1700.* Routledge, 1997.

Ole Peter Grell, Andrew Cunningham, and Jon Arrizabalaga, eds., *Health Care and Poor Relief in Counter-Reformation Europe.* Routledge, 1999.

Lance Gabriel Lazar, *Working in the Vineyard of the Lord: Jesuit Confraternities in Early Modern Italy.* University of Toronto Press, 2005.

Carter Lindberg, *Beyond Charity: Reformation Initiatives for the Poor.* Fortress Press, 1993.

Brian Pullan, *Rich and Poor in Renaissance Venice: The Social Institutions of a Catholic State, to 1620.* Harvard University Press, 1971.

Thomas Max Safley, ed., *The Reformation of Charity: The Secular and the Religious in Early Modern Poor Relief.* E. J. Brill, 2003.

Lee Palmer Wandel, *Always Among Us: Images of the Poor in Zwingli's Zurich.* Cambridge University Press, 1990.

Keith Wrightson and David Levine, *Poverty and Piety in an English Village: Terling, 1525–1700.* Oxford University Press, 1995.

Marriage and Family

Marc R. Forster and Benjamin J. Kaplan, eds., *Piety and Family in Early Modern Europe: Essays in Honour of Steven Ozment.* Ashgate, 2005.

Bridget Heal and Ole Peter Grell, *The Impact of the European Reformation: Princes, Clergy and People.* Ashgate, 2008.

Steven Ozment, *Flesh and Spirit: Private Life in Early Modern Germany.* Viking, 1999.

Steven Ozment, *Magdalena and Balthasar: An Intimate Portrait of Life in Sixteenth-Century Europe.* Yale University Press, 1989.

Steven Ozment, *When Fathers Ruled: Family Life in Reformation Europe.* Harvard University Press, 1983.

Helen Parish, *Clerical Celibacy in the West, 1100–1700.* Ashgate, 2009.

Helen Parish, *Clerical Marriage and the English Reformation: Precedent Policy and Practice.* Ashgate, 2000.

Mary Hampson Patterson, *Domesticating the Reformation: Protestant Best Sellers, Private Devotion, and the Revolution of English Piety.* Fairleigh Dickinson University Press, 2007.

Marjorie Elizabeth Plummer, *From Priest's Whore to Pastor's Wife: Clerical Marriage and the Process of Reform in the Early German Reformation.* Ashgate, 2012.

Darren Provost, *Martin Bucer and the Reformation of Marriage and Divorce in Early Sixteenth-Century Ulm.* PhD diss., Yale University, 2005.

Lyndal Roper, *The Holy Household: Women and Morals in Reformation Augsburg.* Oxford University Press, 1989.

CHAPTER TWENTY-SIX

Protestant Piety

Dale W. Brown, *Understanding Pietism.* Evangel Publishing House, 1997.

Frederick Herzog, *European Pietism Reviewed.* Pickwick Publications, 2003.

Robert Kolb, *Nikolaus von Amsdorf (1483–1565): Popular Polemics in the Preservation of Luther's Legacy.* De Graaf, 1978.

Carter Lindberg, ed., *Pietist Theologians: An Introduction to Theology in the Seventeenth and Eighteenth Centuries.* Blackwell, 2005.

Eric Lund, *Johann Arndt and the Development of a Lutheran Spiritual Tradition.* PhD diss., Yale University, 1979.

Mary Hampson Patterson, *Domesticating the Reformation: Protestant Best Sellers, Private Devotion, and the Revolution of English Piety.* Fairleigh Dickinson University Press, 2007.

Jill Raitt, ed., *Shapers of Religious Traditions in Germany, Switzerland, and Poland, 1560–1600.* Yale University Press, 1981.

Simon Schama, *The Embarrassment of Riches: An Interpretation of Dutch Culture in the Golden Age.* Vintage Books, 1987.

K. James Stein, *Philipp Jakob Spener: Pietist Patriarch.* Covenant Press, 1986.

F. Ernest Stoeffler, *The Rise of Evangelical Pietism.* E. J. Brill, 1965.

David Walsh, *The Mysticism of Innerworldly Fulfillment: A Study of Jacob Boehme.* University Presses of Florida, 1983.

Andrew Weeks, *Boehme: An Intellectual Biography of the Seventeenth-Century Philosopher and Mystic.* State University of New York Press, 1991.

Harry Yeide Jr., *Studies in Classical Pietism: The Flowering of the Ecclesiola.* Peter Lang, 1997.

Catholic Piety

Marie-Florine Bruneau, *Women Mystics Confront the Modern World: Marie de l'Incarnation and Madame Guyon.* State University of New York Press, 1998.

Thomas M. Carr Jr., *The Cloister and the World: Early Modern Convent Voices.* Rookwood Press, 2007.

Louis Châtellier, *The Europe of the Devout: The Catholic Reformation and the Formation of a New Society.* Cambridge University Press, 1989.

Michel de Certeau, *The Mystic Fable: The Sixteenth and Seventeenth Centuries.* University of Chicago Press, 1995.

Jill Fehleison, *Boundaries of Faith: Catholics and Protestants in the Diocese of Geneva.* Truman State University Press, 2010.

Alexander J. Fisher, *Music, Piety, and Propaganda: The Soundscapes of Counter-Reformation Bavaria.* Oxford University Press, 2014.

Harold J. Heagney, *Behold This Heart: The Story of St. Margaret Mary Alacoque.* P. J. Kenedy, 1947.

Nancy C. James, *Conflict Over the Heresy of Pure Love in Seventeenth-Century France: The Tumult over the Mysticism of Madame Guyon.* Edwin Mellen Press, 2008.

Raymond Jonas, *France and the Cult of the Sacred Heart: An Epic Tale for Modern Times.* University of California Press, 2000.

Amy Leonard, *Nails in the Wall: Catholic Nuns in Reformation Germany.* University of Chicago Press, 2005.

Denis Mahoney, *Marie of the Incarnation: Mystic and Missionary.* Doubleday & Co., 1964.

Anya Mali, *Mystic in the New World: Marie de l'Incarnation, 1599–1672.* E. J. Brill, 1996.

André Ravier, *Francis de Sales, Sage and Saint.* Ignatius Press, 1988.

André Ravier, *Saint Jeanne de Chantal: Noble Lady, Holy Woman.* Ignatius Press, 1989.

Joseph Raja Rao Thelagathoti, *The Mystical Experience and Doctrine of St. Louis-Marie Grignion de Montfort.* Editrice Pontificia Università Gregoriana, 2005.

Ping-Yuan Wang, *Writing Lives and Defining Community: Cloistered Women in the Catholic Reformation.* PhD diss., Yale University, 2009.

Wendy M. Wright, *Bond of Perfection: Jeanne de Chantal & François de Sales.* Paulist Press, 1985.

Baroque Culture

Morton C. Abromson, *Painting in Rome During the Papacy of Clement VIII (1592–1605): A Documented Study.* Garland, 1981.

Christopher Braider, *The Matter of Mind: Reason and Experience in the Age of Descartes.* Oxford University Press, 2002.

Xavier Bray, Alfonso Rodríguez G. de Ceballos, Daphne Barbour, and Judy Ozone, eds., *The Sacred Made Real: Spanish Painting and Sculpture, 1600–1700.* Yale University Press, 2009.

David R. Castillo and Massimo Lollini, eds., *Reason and Its Others: Italy, Spain, and the New World.* Vanderbilt University Press, 2006.

Massimo Ciavolella and Patrick Coleman, eds., *Culture and Authority in the Baroque.* University of Toronto Press, 2005.

James A. Connor, *The Last Judgment: Michelangelo and the Death of the Renaissance.* Palgrave Macmillan, 2009.

Joseph Connors, *Borromini and the Roman Oratory: Style and Society.* MIT Press, 1980.

Peter Davidson, *The Universal Baroque.* Manchester University Press, 2007.

Xander van Eck, *Clandestine Splendor: Paintings for the Catholic Church in the Dutch Republic.* Waanders, 2008.

Raymond Erickson, ed., *The Worlds of Johann Sebastian Bach.* Amadeus Press, 2009.

John Eliot Gardiner, *Bach: Music in the Castle of Heaven.* Knopf, 2013.

Christine Göttler, *Last Things: Art and the Religious Imagination in the Age of Reform.* Brepols, 2010.

Robert Harbison, *Reflections on Baroque.* Reaktion Books, 2000.

Karsten Harries, *The Bavarian Rococo Church: Between Faith and Aestheticism.* Yale University Press, 1983.

Karl Heller, *Antonio Vivaldi: The Red Priest of Venice.* Amadeus Press, 1997.

Helen Hills, *Invisible City: The Architecture of Devotion in Seventeenth-Century Neapolitan Convents.* Oxford University Press, 2004.

Judith Hook, *The Baroque Age in England.* Thames and Hudson, 1976.

Ronda Kasl, ed., *Sacred Spain: Art and Belief in the Spanish World.* Yale University Press, 2009.

Irving Lavin, *Bernini and the Unity of the Visual Arts.* Oxford University Press, 1980.

Irving Lavin, *Visible Spirit: The Art of Gianlorenzo Bernini.* Pindar, 2007.

Evonne Levy and Kenneth Mills, eds., *Lexikon of the Hispanic Baroque: Transatlantic Exchange and Transformation.* University of Texas Press, 2013.

Andreas Loewe, *Johann Sebastian Bach's St John Passion: A Theological Commentary.* E. J. Brill, 2014.

Torgil Magnuson, *Rome in the Age of Bernini.* Humanities Press, 1982.

Giancarlo Maiorino, *The Cornucopian Mind and the Baroque Unity of the Arts*. Pennsylvania State University Press, 1990.

José Antonio Maravall, *The Culture of the Baroque: Analysis of a Historical Structure*. University of Minnesota Press, 1986.

Sergiusz Michalski, *The Reformation and the Visual Arts: The Protestant Image Question in Western and Eastern Europe*. Routledge, 1993.

Mia M. Mochizuki, *The Netherlandish Image After Iconoclasm, 1566–1672: Material Religion in the Dutch Golden Age*. Ashgate, 2008.

Franco Mormando, *Bernini: His Life and His Rome*. University of Chicago Press, 2011.

Jake Morrissey, *Genius in the Design: Bernini, Borromini, and the Rivalry That Transformed Rome*. William Morrow, 2005.

Steven Ozment, *The Serpent & the Lamb: Cranach, Luther, and the Making of the Reformation*. Yale University Press, 2011.

Robert T. Petersson, *The Art of Ecstasy: Teresa, Bernini, and Crashaw*. Atheneum, 1970.

Virginia Chieffo Raguin, ed., *Art, Piety and Destruction in the Christian West, 1500–1700*. Ashgate, 2010.

Jeremy Roe and Marta Bustillo, eds., *Imagery, Spirituality and Ideology in Baroque Spain and Latin America*. Cambridge Scholars, 2010.

Peter N. Skrine, *The Baroque: Literature and Culture in Seventeenth-Century Europe*. Methuen, 1978.

Susan Verdi Webster, *Art and Ritual in Golden-Age Spain: Sevillian Confraternities and the Processional Sculpture of Holy Week*. Princeton University Press, 1998.

Rosario Villari, ed., *Baroque Personae*. University of Chicago Press, 1995.

Peter Williams, ed., *Bach, Handel, Scarlatti, Tercentenary Essays*. Cambridge University Press, 1985.

Daniel Zager, ed., *Music and Theology: Essays in Honor of Robin A. Leaver*. Scarecrow Press, 2007.

Hell

Piero Camporesi, *The Fear of Hell: Images of Damnation and Salvation in Early Modern Europe*. Pennsylvania State University Press, 1991.

Carlos Eire, "The Good Side of Hell: Infernal Meditations in Early Modern Spain," *Historical Reflections/Réflexions historiques* 26, no. 2 (Summer 2000): 285–310.

Carlos Eire, *A Very Brief History of Eternity*. Princeton University Press, 2010.

Isabel Moreira and Margaret Toscano, eds., *Hell and Its Afterlife: Historical and Contemporary Perspectives*. Ashgate, 2010.

D. P. Walker, *The Decline of Hell: Seventeenth-Century Discussions of Eternal Torment*. University of Chicago Press, 1964.

Illustration Credits

Page xx: Italy, The loggia of benedictions at Saint Peter in Rome (folio 53, recto), drawing by Maarten van Heemskerck (1498–1574). De Agostini Picture Library / Bridgeman Images.

Page 6: Map by Bill Nelson.

Page 9: Dance macabre skeletal figures in the room. Image taken from *La great danse macabre des heomes et des feemes hystoriee eaugmentee de beaulx dis en latin.* [With woodcuts.] G.L. Originally published / produced in [Mathias Husse] lyon le .xviii. iour de feurier 1499. © British Library Board / Robana / Art Resource, NY.

Page 11: Map by Bill Nelson.

Page 13: Hartmann Schedel (1440–1514) "Nvremberga," *Liber chronicarum Nuremberg.* Nuremberg: Anton Koberger, July 12, 1493. General Collection, Beinecke Rare Book and Manuscript Library, Yale University.

Page 15: Hans Leonhard Schäufelein (1480–1540). Illustration from *Theuerdank* (allegorical work commissioned by Emperor Maximilian I), 15th–16th century, Woodcut, 15.8 × 13.9 cm (image); 30.5 × 20.2 cm (sheet). Detail. Gift of Aldis Browne, 1988.1.119, © Fine Arts Museums of San Francisco.

Page 20: The Seven Sacraments Altarpiece, detail of baptism, confirmation and confession, from the left wing, c.1445 (oil on panel), Weyden, Rogier van der (1399–1464). Koninklijk Museum voor Schone Kunsten, Antwerp, Belgium / Bridgeman Images.

Page 26: St. Catherine of Siena Dictating Her Dialogues, c.1447–61 (tempera on panel), Giovanni di Paolo di Grazia (1403–82). Detroit Institute of Arts, Founders Society Purchase / Bridgeman Images.

Page 29: Adriaen Ysenbrandt (Netherlandish, active 1510–1551). The Mass of Saint Gregory the Great, about 1510–1550, Oil on panel, Unframed: 36.2 × 29.2 cm (14 1/4 × 11 1/2 in.), Framed: 47.3 × 38.4 × 4 cm (18 5/8 × 15 1/8 × 1 9/16 in.), The J. Paul Getty Museum, Los Angeles. Digital image courtesy of the Getty's Open Content Program.

Page 32: Michael Ostendorfer (1490–1559), Die Pilgerfahrt zur Kirche der "Schönen Maria" in Regensburg, 1523, with autograph of Albrecht Dürer, 1523. Kunstsammlungen der Veste Coburg, Germany. www.kunstsammlungen-coburg.de.

Page 33: Map by Bill Nelson.

Page 38: Master E.S., Ars Moriendi, as found in The Master E. S. and the "Ars moriendi"; a chapter in the history of engraving during the XVth century, with facsimile reproductions of engravings in the University Galleries at Oxford and in the British Museum, by Lionel Cust,

4a. Oxford, Clarendon Press, 1898. Digitized by Internet Archive from The Getty Research Institute. Courtesy of HathiTrust. http://hdl.handle.net/2027/gri.ark:/13960/t5gb4ph0g.

Page 45: Raphael (Raffaello Sanzio) (1483–1520) Pope Leo X, 1475–1521, Giovanni de' Medici, with Cardinal Giulio de' Medici, 1478–1534, later to become Pope Clement VII and Luigi de Rossi, c. 1517. Alfredo Dagli Orti / The Art Archive at Art Resource, NY.

Page 46: Gautier de Coinci (1177/8–1236), Miracles de Nostre Dame (Paris, 1327). Courtesy of The Hague, National Library, 71 A 24.

Page 48: Berruguete, Pedro (1450–1504). Santo Domingo y los albigenses (Saint Dominic or Domingo Guzman of Castile, 1170–1221 founded Dominican order, and Albigensians) painted 1493–99. Gianni Dagli Orti / The Art Archive at Art Resource, NY.

Page 54: Map by Bill Nelson.

Page 58: Jena Codex Antithesis Christi et Antichristi (signature IV B 24)—Pope, cardinal and bishop in the embrace of an apocalyptic beast, fol. 69r. Detail. Collection of the National Museum, Prague, Czech Republic.

Page 67: Raphael (Raffaello Sanzio) (1483–1520). The School of Athens, ca. 1510–1512. Fresco. Detail. Scala / Art Resource, NY.

Page 73: Johann Theodor de Bry, Portrait of Lorenzo Valla, c. 1597–1599. Paper, h 140mm × w 100mm. Courtesy of Rijksmuseum, Amsterdam.

Page 79: Antonio Maria Crespi detto il Bustino (attributed), Portrait of Niccolò Machiavelli, oil on canvas, 60 × 51 cm. Milano, Veneranda Biblioteca Ambrosiana, Pinacoteca, inv. n. 1382, © Veneranda Biblioteca Ambrosiana, Milan / De Agostini Picture Library.

Page 82: *Platonis opera a Marsillo Ficano traducta* (1518). General Collection, Beinecke Rare Book and Manuscript Library, Yale University.

Page 88: Epitaph of Conrad Celtis. Harris Brisbane Dick Fund, 1927, The Metropolitan Museum of Art. www.metmuseum.org.

Page 93: Elenherii Byzeni, "Triumphus Doctoris Reuchlin," 1518. Woodcut. In *Nagy képes világtörténet*—Volume 3, ed. Henrik Marczali. Franklin-társulat, 1899. National Széchényi Library—Hungarian Electronic Library.

Page 97: Polyglot Bible (*Biblia polyglotta*) [1514–1517]. General Collection, Beinecke Rare Book and Manuscript Library, Yale University.

Page 101: Holbein, Hans the Younger (1497–1543). The Family of Saint Thomas More. Snark / Art Resource, NY.

Page 106: Erasmus of Rotterdam, by Albrecht Dürer. Fletcher Fund, 1919, The Metropolitan Museum of Art. www.metmuseum.org.

Page 112: Sebastian Munster, *La cosmographie universelle* (Basle: Heinrich Petri, 1550), p. 130. Biblioteca Nacional de España (R/33638).

Page 117: Woodcut of Giralomo Savonarola preaching, from Villari, P & Casanova, E 1898, *Scelta di prediche e scritti di Fra Girolamo Savonarola con nuovi documenti intorno alla sua vita* GC Sansoni Editore, Firenze, p. [30]. Digitized by Google. Original from University of Wisconsin. Courtesy of HathiTrust. http://catalog.hathitrust.org/Record/001932318.

Page 118: Artist Unknown. Francisco Jimenez de Cisneros, 1436–1517. Spanish Franciscan, cardinal and Primate of Spain, 15th century fresco. Detail. Catedral Toledo. Gianni Dagli Orti / The Art Archive at Art Resource, NY.

Page 121: Bartolomeo Giuseppe Tasnière, engraving of Catherine of Genoa after Domenico Piola's artwork. Rome, National Institute for Graphics, with kind permission of the Ministry of Heritage and Culture and Tourism.

Page 183: Johannes Cochlaeus consuming the feces of a devil. Woodcut (16th century), detail. 36 × 28.3 cm. Inv.: 286-10. bpk, Berlin / Kupferstichkabinett, Staatliche Museen, Berlin / Jörg P. Anders / Art Resource, NY.

Page 189: Portrait of Andreas Bodenstein von Karlstadt, 16th century engraving. From *Andreas Bodenstein von Karlstadt* by Hermann Barge. Leipzig: Friedrich Brandstetter, 1905. Digitized by Google, original from University of Minnesota. Courtesy of HathiTrust. http://hdl.handle.net/2027/umn.31951002044169d.

Page 192: Luther as "Junker Jorg" by Lucas Cranach the Elder. Gift of Felix M. Warburg and his family, 1941, The Metropolitan Museum of Art. www.metmuseum.org.

Page 198: 5 Mark—DDR (1975)—obverse. Courtesy of Deutsche Bundesbank.

Page 204: Otto Henne am Rhyn (1828–1914), *Kulturgeschichte des deutschen Volkes*, v. 2. Berlin, Baumgärtel, 1897. Digitized by Google. Original from University of California. Courtesy of HathiTrust. http://hdl.handle.net/2027/uc1.c2800822.

Page 207: Peasants' war 1525, plundering of Weissenau monastery, pen drawing, from chronicle of abbot Jakob Murer, 1525. INTERFOTO / Alamy.

Page 211: From Albrecht Dürer, *Vnderweysung der Messung*. Gedruckt zü Nuremberg : [s.n.], 1525. Digitized by Internet Archive. Original from The Getty Research Institute. Courtesy of HathiTrust. http://catalog.hathitrust.org/Record/100237681.

Page 215: Clouet, Jean (1475/85–1540). Francois I, King of France (1494–1547). Erich Lessing / Art Resource, NY.

Page 220: Hendrick Hondius, Portrait of Ulrich Zwingli, States General, 1599. Paper, h 167mm × w 121mm. Courtesy of Rijksmuseum, Amsterdam.

Page 222: Map by Bill Nelson.

Page 225: Urs Graf, Schrecken des Kriegs, 1521. Wikimedia Commons.

Page 233: Helmet and Sword of Ulrich Zwingly. Swiss National Museum KZ-5633 and KZ-5634. Photo: Swiss National Museum, DIG-1734.

Page 237: The Iconoclasts. Woodcut, c. 1530. Photo: akg-images.

Page 243: Ludwig Rabus (1524–1592) *Historien der Heyligen Außerwoelten Gottes Zeugen, Bekennern und Martyrern* (Strassburg: Der Sybend Theyl, 1557). Courtesy of University Library of Vienna.

Page 249: Felix Manz wird am 5. Januar 1527 als Täufer in der Limmat ertränkt [1605–1606]. Central Library Zurich, MS.B316, f.284v.

Page 261: Schleitheim Confession title page, ca. 1560. Courtesy of Mennonite Church USA Archives-Goshen X-31.1, Box 18-3.

Page 263: Map by Bill Nelson.

Page 265: Hutterite family as illustrated in Erhard's 1588 *Historia*. Courtesy of Mennonite Church USA Archives-Goshen X-31.1, Box 17-30.

Page 270: Melchior Hoffman, Anabaptist prophet. © Juulijs / Fotolia.

Page 273: Christoffel van Sichem, Portrait of Bernardus Knipperdolling, ca. 1608. Paper, h 184 mm × w 139 mm. Courtesy of Rijskmuseum, Amsterdam.

Page 275: Münster Rebellion, Germany: Execution of leaders of the rebellion. Universal History Archive / UIG / Bridgeman Images.

Page 287: John Calvin (1509?–1564). Engraving. Album / Art Resource, NY.

Page 291: Jean Calvin, *The Institution of Christian Religion*, trans. Thomas Norton. London: Richarde Harrison, 1562. Bridwell Library Special Collections, Perkins School of Theology, Southern Methodist University.

Page 297: Geneva, Switzerland, 1642 engraving by Mérian. Bibliothèque Universitaire Geneva. Gianni Dagli Orti / The Art Archive at Art Resource, NY.

Page 306: Perrissin, Jean (1536–1611). Lyon Temple, or Paradise, audience listening to preacher, c.1565. University Library Geneva. Gianni Dagli Orti / The Art Archive at Art Resource, NY.

Page 311: Photo by author.

Page 324: Anonymous. The Family of Henry VIII of England. Detail. Visual Arts Library / Art Resource, NY.

Page 330: NPG 4165, King Edward VI and the Pope (includes John Russell, 1st Earl of Bedford; Thomas Cranmer; King Edward VI; King Henry VIII; John Dudley, Duke of Northumberland; Edward Seymour, 1st Duke of Somerset) by Unknown artist, oil on panel, circa 1575, Credit line: © National Portrait Gallery, London.

Page 333: Iohn Foxe, *Actes and monuments of these latter and perillous dayes* . . . p. 1503. London: John Day, 1563. General Collection, Beinecke Rare Book and Manuscript Library, Yale University.

Page 338: Attributed to Crispyn de Passe the Elder, ca. 1565–1637. Portrait of Queen Elizabeth I. 1596. Engraving, 16 × 12 1/8 in. Yale Center for British Art, Paul Mellon Collection.

Page 349: Giovanni Battista Cavalieri, *Ecclesiae Anglicanae Trophaea sive Sanctor Martyrum*. Rome: Ex officina Bartholomæi Grassi, [1584]. Digitized by Internet Archive, Original from The Getty Research Institute. Courtesy of HathiTrust. http://hdl.handle.net/2027/gri .ark:/13960/t7mp61k9v.

Page 359: From *An oration against the unlawfull insurrections of the protestantes of our time, under pretence to refourme religion* by Peter Frarin of Andwerp, trans. into English by John Fowler. Antwerp, 1565. As found in *The Reformation in England* by S. R. Maitland. J. Lane, 1906. Digitized by Google. Original from University of California Press. Courtesy of HathiTrust. http://hdl.handle.net/2027/uc1.$b245547?urlappend=%3Bseq=136.

Page 366: *Speculum Romanae Magnificentiae*, 1567. Engraving and etching. © The Trustees of the British Museum. All rights reserved.

Page 370: Harvard Art Museums / Fogg Museum, Gift of Belinda L. Randall from the collection of John Witt Randall, R3320.

Page 374: Thomas Murner, *Von dem grossen Lutherischen narren*. Strassburg, K. J. Trübner, 1918. Digitized by Google. Original from University of Michigan. Courtesy of HathiTrust. http://hdl.handle.net/2027/mdp.39015046821941.

Page 375: Martin Luther and Lucifer, woodcut ca. 1520. Detail. © Everett Collection Historical / Alamy.

Page 381: The Council of Trent, 1588–89 (fresco), Cati, Pasquale (1550–1620) / Santa Maria in Trastevere, Rome, Italy / Bridgeman Images.

Page 385: *Index librorvm prohibitorvm*. Romae, Apud Impressores Camerales, 1596–1624 [i.e. 1629?]. Call number *64-518, Houghton Library, Harvard University.

Page 392: Ignatius of Loyola in St Peters Basilica. Photo: Alma Pater (own work) [CC BY-SA 3.0 (http://creativecommons.org/licenses/by-sa/3.0)], via Wikimedia Commons.

Page 398: Iglesia Católica. *Rituale Romanum Pauli V. Pont. Max Iussu Editum*, 1679. Digitized by Google, original from Universidad Complutense de Madrid. Courtesy of HathiTrust. http://hdl.handle.net/2027/ucm.5326787101.

Page 404: Murillo, Bartolomé Esteban (1618–1682). The Angels' Kitchen. Erich Lessing / Art Resource, NY.

Page 410: Petrus Canisius, *Kleiner Katechismus in Fragen und Antworten für Kinder*. Zug, [Switzerland]: Johann Michael Aloys Blunschi, 1792. Bridwell Library Special Collections, Perkins School of Theology, Southern Methodist University.

Page 417: Schoen, Erhard (c.1491–1542). Devil playing the bagpipes; perched on the shoulders of a monk whose head forms the bagpipe. Ca. 1530. Hand-coloured woodcut with eyes and markings added in black ink. PD 1972, U.1097. British Museum, London, Great Britain. © The Trustees of the British Museum / Art Resource, NY.

Page 421: Adriaen Collaert (1555–1623) and Theodoor Galle (1571–1633), De H. Petrus en Paulus staan Theresa vaak ter zijde bij het overwinnen van demonen, 1613. Engraving, h 186 mm × w 215 mm. Courtesy of Rijksmuseum, Amsterdam.

Page 424: Pie chart of new religious orders. Bill Nelson.

Page 427: Bayeu Y Subias, Francisco (1734–95) Saint Francis de Sales giving the constitution of the Order of the Visitation to Jeanne Francoise Chantal. Gianni Dagli Orti / The Art Archive at Art Resource, NY.

Page 435: Caesare Baronio, *Annales ecclesiastici*, Tomus IX. Moguntiae : sumptibus Ioannis Gymnici [et] Antonij Hierati . . . , 1601. Digitized by Google. Original from Universidad Complutense de Madrid. Courtesy of HathiTrust. http://hdl.handle.net/2027/ucm.5325025252.

Page 438: St. Vincent de Paul and the Sisters of Charity, c.1729 (oil on canvas), Andre, Jean (Frere) (1662–1753) (attr.to), Detail. Musée de l'Assistance publique, Hôpitaux de Paris, France / Bridgeman Images.

Page 444: Peter Paul Rubens (1577–1640), Plate 4 in *The Life of St Ignatius Loyola* by Nicholas Lancicius, S.J., Filippo Rinaldi, S.J. and Peter Pazmany, S.J., 1609. Courtesy of Boston College.

Page 448: Ignatius of Loyola, *Les Exercices Spritvels de S. Ignace de Loyola*. Anvers: Cnobbaert, 1673. Department of Archives and Special Collections, William H. Hannon Library, Loyola Marymount University.

Page 454: Athanasius Kircher, *Mundus subterraneus in XII libros digestus* . . . , Volume 1. apud Joannem Janssonium à Waesberge & filios, 1678. General Collection, Beinecke Rare Book and Manuscript Library, Yale University.

Page 461: Arthur Tooker. c.1682–85. Etching. © The Trustees of the British Museum. All rights reserved.

Page 464: Bartoli, Daniello, *Della vita e dell'istituto di S. Ignatio* . . . (Rome: Nella stamparia d'Ignatio de' Lazari, 1659). Courtesy of Saint Louis University Libraries Special Collections.

Page 469: The Festival of Fools after Pieter Bruegel the Elder by Pieter van der Heyden. The Elisha Whittelsey Collection, the Elisha Whittelsey Fund, 1969, The Metropolitan Museum of Art. www.metmuseum.org.

Page 473: Map by Bill Nelson.

Page 477: *Codex Magliabechiano* CL. XIII.3. Courtesy of Library of Congress, Prints and Photographs Division, Washington, DC.

Page 488: Virgen De Guadalupe. Location: Colegio Retamar, Madrid, Spain. Album / Art Resource, NY.

Page 495: Francesco Giuseppe Bressani (1612–1672), *Novae Franciae accurata delineatio*, 1657. Library and Archives Canada, MIKAN 3805607.

Page 503: Wolfgang Kilian (1581–1663), *Drey Seelige Martyrer der Societet Jesu*, 1628. Engraving. Bayerische Staatsbibliothek München, Einbl. VII, 24 l.

Page 509: Athanasii Kircheri, *China monumentis : qua sacris quà profanis nec non variis naturae [et] artis spectaculis aliarumque rerum memorabilium argumentis illustrata.* Amstelodami : Apud Jacobum à Meurs, 1667. Digitized by Google from Universidad Complutense de Madrid. Courtesy of HathiTrust. http://hdl.handle.net/2027/ucm.5325300989.

Page 511: Alenio, Giulio, *Life and Passion of Christ.* China ca. 1640. Call Number: 52-1049, Houghton Library, Harvard University.

Page 516: Louis XIV giving an audience to the King of Siam's Ambassadors at Versailles September 1 1686. 1687. Engraving, 82 × 52 cm. Inv.: 26985LR. Photo: Jean-Gilles Berizzi. Louvre, Paris. © RMN-Grand Palais / Art Resource, NY.

Page 519: St. Francis Xavier, Charles Bridge, Prague. Photo: Elinor Teele.

Page 521: Exterior of the Mission Xavier del Bac. Photo: Frank Kovalchek [CC BY 2.0 (http://creativecommons.org/licenses/by/2.0)], via Wikimedia Commons.

Page 522: Giovanni Paolo Panini Piacenza (1691–1765). Interior of St. Peter's, Rome, 1756–1757. Oil on canvas, 64 5/8 × 92 3/4 in. Athenaeum purchase, 1834. Boston Athenaeum.

Page 539: Dubois, Francois (1529–1584). Massacre of St. Bartholomew's Day, Aug. 23, 1572. Scala / White Images / Art Resource, NY.

Page 545: Anonymous, De beeldenstorm door de geuzen, 1566. Paper, h 177mm × w 220mm. Detail. Courtesy of Rijksmuseum, Amsterdam.

Page 551: Chart of participants in 30 Years' War. Bill Nelson.

Page 553: Map of population losses 30 Years' War. Bill Nelson.

Page 558: Beheading of King Charles I of England, 1649. Woodcut. In Mason Jackson, *The Pictorial Press: Its Origin and Progress.* London: Hurst and Blackett, 1885. Digitized by Google. Original from University of California. Courtesy of HathiTrust. http://hdl.handle.net/2027/uc1.b4703133.

Page 565: Lucas Cranach the Younger (1515–1586), "Philip Melanchthon, Bust to the Right," Woodcut; third state of three (Hollstein), Sheet: 13 1/4 × 8 7/16 in. (33.7 × 21.5 cm). Harris Brisbane Dick Fund, 1927, The Metropolitan Museum of Art. www.metmuseum.org.

Page 572: Anonymous, Allegorical five headed monster, 1575–1618. Paper, h 245mm × w 150mm. Detail. Courtesy of Rijksmuseum, Amsterdam.

Page 581: The Rout and Confusion of the Jansenists (engraving) (b/w photo), French School, (17th century). Bibliothèque des Arts Decoratifs, Paris / Bridgeman Images.

Page 584: Clerical Barter. Contemporary pamphlet about the dispute between Martin Luther and Johannes Calvin: "Clerical Barter." Copper engraving, c. 1598. Photo: akg-images.

Page 587: Anonymous, German. Caput Nicolai Grellii. Gift of Dr. Leon Kolb, 1955.45.359, © Fine Arts Museums of San Francisco.

Page 589: Lucas Cranach the Younger (German, 1515–1586), *Martin Luther and the Wittenberg Reformers,* about 1543, oil on panel, 27 5/8 × 15 5/8 in. (72.8 × 39.7 cm). Toledo Museum of Art (Toledo, Ohio). Gift of Edward Drummond Libbey, 1926.55. Photo credit: Photography Incorporated, Toledo.

Page 597: Lucas Cranach the Younger (1515–1586). Comparison: Right and Wrong Church. Martin Luther Preaching. Woodcut, 1546. Inv.: A 6628. bpk, Berlin / Kupferstichkabinett, Staatliche Kunstsammlungen, Dresden / Herbert Boswank / Art Resource, NY.

Page 608: David Allan, The Black Stool (The Stool of Repentance). Scottish National Gallery.

Page 612: Saint Louis University Libraries Special Collections. [Gift of Dorothy Carpenter Moore; in the Moore Carpenter Recusant History Collection.]

Page 619: St Wolfgang and the Devil, Life of St Wolfgang, 1471–1475, by Michael Pacher (ca 1435–1498), oil on canvas, 103 × 91 cm. De Agostini Picture Library / Bridgeman Images.

Page 633: Baldung Grien, Hans (1484–1545). Witches' Sabbath, 1510. Color woodcut printed from two blocks. 37.5 × 25.4 cm. British Museum, London, Great Britain. © The Trustees of the British Museum / Art Resource, NY.

Page 637: Burning of witches at the stake at Derneburg Harz, Germany, from broadside newsletter, October 1555. Detail. The Art Archive at Art Resource, NY.

Page 639: Map by Bill Nelson.

Page 656: Exorcism, 1566. The exorcism of Nicole Aubry by a bishop at the cathedral of Notre-Dame of Laon, France, c. 1566. Copy of an engraving by Jean Boulaese, 1575. The Granger Collection, New York.

Page 661: Descartes, Rene (La Haye, Touraine, France, 1596–Stockholm, 1650). French philosopher, mathematician, physicist, and writer. Engraving. Album / Art Resource, NY.

Page 665: *Titi Lucretii Cari De rerum natura libri sex* (On the Nature of Things). Reproduced by kind permission of the Syndics of Cambridge University Library, classmark: Montaigne.1.4.4.

Page 682: Galileo Galilei (1564–1642) *Systema cosmicvm*. Avgvstæ Treboc[corum] [Strasburg] : impensis Elzeviriorvm, typis Davidis Havtti, 1635. General Collection, Beinecke Rare Book and Manuscript Library, Yale University.

Page 685: Antoni Van Leeuwenhoek's illustration of the evolution of an ant, 18th c. Engraving. INTERFOTO / Alamy.

Page 689 (left): Pascal, Blaise (1623–1662). French mathematician, physicist and philosopher. Engraving. Iberfoto / Superstock.

Page 689 (right): Manuscript of Pascal's Memorial reprinted by permission of the Bibliothèque nationale de France.

Page 692: © the British Library Board. The 'Christian Knight' world map, c.1596. Taken from *Typus totius Orbis Terrarum in quo & Christiani militis certanem super terram* by Jodocus Hondius, 1596. Maps.188.k.1.(5).

Page 698: Botteghino che fa sempre facende, 1687. Etching. © The Trustees of the British Museum. All rights reserved.

Page 706: Seven beggars, Plate number P2024. 9 × 27 cm. Detail. The Thomas Fisher Rare Book Library, University of Toronto.

Page 715: Eduard Fuchs, *Die karikatur der europäischen völker vom altertum bis zur neuzeit*, p. 73. Berlin : A. Hofmann & comp., 1904. Digitized by Google. Original from Cornell University. Courtesy of HathiTrust. http://hdl.handle.net/2027/coo.31924020567321.

Page 717: Velazquez, Diego (1599–1660). Sister Jerónima de la Fuente. Museo del Prado Madrid. The Art Archive at Art Resource, NY.

Page 722: Christ on the Cross, 1552–55 (oil on 3 panels), Cranach, Lucas, the Elder (1472–1553). Weimar altarpiece, Evangelisch-Lutherischen Kirchengemeinde Weimar.

Page 728: Piranesi, Giovanni Battista (1720–1778). Saint Peter's Basilica and Square with Colonnades. Ca. 1750. Engraving. bpk, Berlin / Kunstbibliothek, Staatliche Museen, Berlin / Knud Petersen / Art Resource, NY.

Page 729: Pozzo, Andrea (1642–1709) Entrance of St. Ignatius to Paradise, Roma, Chiesa S. Ignazio. Scala / Art Resource, NY.

Page 730: Zimmerman, Johann Baptist (1680–1758). Center fresco of the Wies church, Bavaria. Erich Lessing / Art Resource, NY.

Page 731: Photo by author.

Page 733: Claude Mellan (1598–1688) after Jacques Stella (1596–1657), Saint Bernard Kneeling before the Virgin and Child, 1640. Print, Engraving; first state of two, 14 1/8 × 9 5/16 in. (35.9 × 23.6 cm). Harris Brisbane Dick Fund, 1953, The Metropolitan Museum of Art. www.metmuseum.org.

Page 734: Henk Tobbe, St. Bavo Church Haarlem, Pulpit. Photography courtesy of Henk Tobbe.

Page 745: *Mirror of the militant, true, steadfast, age-old Catholic Church of God, against which many tyrants, heathens, Jews, and heretics revolt, tear down, burn, and break by storm.* [Germany?, c. 1570?] Bridwell Library Special Collections, Perkins School of Theology, Southern Methodist University.

Page 751: Thomas Jenner, The candle is lighted, we cannot blow out, c.1640. Etching. © The Trustees of the British Museum. All rights reserved.

Page 755: Map by Bill Nelson.

Index

Note: Page numbers in *italics* refer to illustrations, captions, and tables; those followed by "n" indicate endnotes.